Philip Kotler
Northwestern University

Gary Armstrong
University of North Carolina

Peggy H. Cunningham
Queen's University

Principles of
Marketing

Sixth
Canadian
Edition

PEARSON
Prentice
Hall

Toronto

National Library of Canada Cataloguing in Publication

Kotler, Philip
   Principles of marketing / Philip Kotler, Gary Armstrong, Peggy H. Cunningham. — 6th Canadian ed.

Includes index.
ISBN 0-13-121619-8

   1. Marketing—Textbooks. I. Armstrong, Gary II. Cunningham, Margaret H. III. Title.

HF5415.K636 2005   658.8   C2004-900398-4

0-13-121619-8

Vice-President, Editorial Director: Michael J. Young
Acquisitions Editor: Laura Paterson Forbes
Marketing Manager: Steve McGill
Developmental Editor: Pam Voves
Production Editor: Cheryl Jackson
Substantive and Copy Editor: Lesley Mann
Proofreader: Valerie Adams
Production Coordinator: Deborah Starks
Page Layout: Debbie Kumpf
Permissions Manager: Susan Wallace-Cox
Permissions Research: Alene McNeill
Art Director: Julia Hall
Cover and Interior Design: David Cheung
Cover Image: Getty Images

3 4 5   09 08 07 06 05

Printed and bound in the United States of America.

Statistics Canada information is used with the permission of the Minister of Industry, as Minister responsible for Statistics Canada. Information on the availability of the wide range of data from Statistics Canada can be obtained from Statistics Canada's Regional Offices, its World Wide Web site at http://www.statcan.ca, and its toll-free access number 1-800-263-1136.

About the Authors

As a team, Philip Kotler, Gary Armstrong, and Peggy Cunningham provide a blend of skills uniquely suited to writing an introductory marketing text. Professor Kotler is one of the world's leading authorities on marketing. Professors Armstrong and Cunningham are award-winning teachers of undergraduate business students. Together they make the complex world of marketing practical, approachable, and enjoyable.

Philip Kotler is the S. C. Johnson & Johnson Distinguished Professor of International Marketing at the Kellogg Graduate School of Management, Northwestern University. He received his master's degree at the University of Chicago and his Ph.D. at M.I.T., both in economics. Dr. Kotler is author of *Marketing Management: Analysis, Planning, Implementation, and Control* (Prentice Hall), now in its eleventh edition and the most widely used marketing textbook in graduate schools of business. He has authored several successful books and has written over 100 articles for leading journals. He is the only three-time winner of the coveted Alpha Kappa Psi award for the best annual article in the Journal of Marketing. Dr. Kotler's numerous major honours include the Paul D. Converse Award given by the American Marketing Association to honour "outstanding contributions to science in marketing" and the Stuart Henderson Britt Award as Marketer of the Year. He was named the first recipient of two major awards: the Distinguished Marketing Educator of the Year Award given by the American Marketing Association and the Philip Kotler Award for Excellence in Health Care Marketing presented by the Academy for Health Care Services Marketing. He has also received the Charles Coolidge Parlin Award which each year honors an outstanding leader in the field of marketing. In 1995, he received the Marketing Educator of the Year Award from Sales and Marketing Executives International. Dr. Kotler has served as chairman of the College on Marketing of the Institute of Management Sciences (TIMS) and a director of the American Marketing Association. He has received honorary doctorate degrees from DePaul University, the University of Zurich, and the Athens University of Economics and Business. He has consulted with many major U.S. and foreign companies on marketing strategy.

Gary Armstrong is Crist W. Blackwell Distinguished Professor of Undergraduate Education in the Kenan–Flagler Business School at the University of North Carolina at Chapel Hill. He holds undergraduate and masters degrees in business from Wayne State University in Detroit, and he received his Ph.D. in marketing from Northwestern University. Dr. Armstrong has contributed numerous articles to leading business journals. As a consultant and researcher, he has worked with many companies on marketing research, sales management, and marketing strategy. But Professor Armstrong's first love is teaching. His Blackwell Distinguished Professorship is the only permanent endowed professorship for distinguished undergraduate teaching at the University of North Carolina at Chapel Hill. He has been very active in the teaching and administration of Kenan–Flagler's undergraduate program. His recent administrative posts include Chair of the Marketing Faculty, Associate Director of the Undergraduate Business Program, Director of the Business Honors Program, and others. He works closely with business student groups and has received several campus-wide and Business School teaching awards. He is the only repeat recipient of the school's highly regarded Award for Excellence in Undergraduate Teaching, which he won three times.

Peggy Cunningham is Associate Professor of Marketing at Queen's University School of Business. She received her undergraduate degree from Queen's University, completed her MBA at the University of Calgary, and earned her Ph.D. in marketing from Texas A&M University. She is the Director of Queen's new MBA program for students with undergraduate business degrees. She has considerable international experience and has been a visiting professor at universities and government training programs in France, Germany, China, the U.K., and the U.S. Her prior industry experience and current consulting practice help her to bring the perspective of the practitioner to the study of marketing. She conducts research in the fields of ecommerce, marketing ethics, strategic alliances, and cause-related marketing. Her work is published in a number of journals, including the *Journal of the* Academy *of Marketing* Science. She is also the Canadian co-author with Philip Kotler of *Marketing Management*, Canadian Eleventh Edition. She is a devoted teacher who tries to inspire her students to realize their full and unique potential. In recognition of these efforts, she has received several teaching and service awards, including the Frank Knox award for teaching excellence, a Queen's campus-wide award granted by undergraduate students. She was named as the Academy of Marketing Science Outstanding Teacher in 2001. She has applied her love of teaching to a wide range of courses, including marketing management and strategy, principles of marketing, services marketing, international marketing, marketing ethics, and customer relationship management.

Brief Contents

Contents

Preface to the Sixth Canadian Edition

The Power of Marketing

The goal of *Principles of Marketing,* Sixth Canadian Edition, is to introduce new marketing students to the fascinating world of modern marketing in an enjoyable and practical way. Many people see marketing only as advertising or selling. But real marketing does not involve the art of selling what you make, so much as knowing *what* to make! Organizations gain market leadership by understanding consumer needs and finding solutions that delight customers. If customer value and satisfaction are absent, no amount of advertising or selling can compensate.

Simply put, the aim of marketing is to **build and manage profitable customer relationships.** Marketers study consumer needs and wants, select target markets they can serve best, and design products, services, and programs to serve these markets. They attract new customers by promising superior value, and keep and grow current customers by delivering superior satisfaction.

Marketing is much more than just an isolated business function—it is a philosophy that guides the entire organization toward sensing, serving, and satisfying consumer needs. The marketing department cannot accomplish the company's customer relationship-building goals by itself. It must partner closely with other departments in the company and with other organizations throughout its entire value-delivery network to provide superior customer value and satisfaction. Thus, marketing calls upon everyone in the organization to "think customer" and to do all they can to help build and manage profitable customer relationships.

Marketing is all around us, and we all need to know something about it. Marketing is used not only by manufacturing companies, wholesalers, and retailers, but also by all kinds of individuals and organizations. Lawyers, accountants, and doctors use marketing to manage demand for their services. No politician can get

the needed votes, and no resort the needed tourists, without developing and carrying out marketing plans.

People throughout these organizations need to know how to define and segment markets, develop attractive value propositions, and build strongly positioned brands. They must know how to price their offerings to make them attractive and affordable, and how to choose and manage intermediaries to make their products available to customers. They need to know how to advertise and promote products so that customers will know about and want them. Moreover, they must know how to adapt their marketing strategies and management to a host of new technological and global realities. Clearly, marketers need a broad range of skills in order to build profitable relationships with customers.

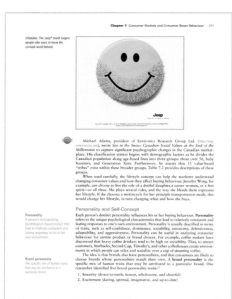

More Powerful Content

Welcome to the Sixth Canadian Edition of *Principles of Marketing!*

Principles of Marketing, Sixth Canadian Edition, provides an authoritative, comprehensive, innovative, managerial, and practical introduction to marketing. It is designed to help students learn about and apply the basic concepts and practices of modern marketing as they are used in a wide variety of settings.

Major Themes in *Principles of Marketing*

Technological advances, rapid globalization, economic shifts, and cultural and environmental developments are causing profound changes in the marketplace. As the marketplace changes, so must the marketers who serve it. These new developments signify a brand new world of opportunities for forward-thinking marketers.

In light of these new developments, *Principles of Marketing*, Sixth Canadian Edition, builds on four key themes that go to the heart of modern marketing theory and practice.

1. *Building and managing profitable customer relationships.* Today's marketers must be good at *managing customer relationships*. They must attract customers with strong value propositions, then keep and grow customers by delivering superior customer value and satisfaction and effectively managing the company-customer interface. Today's outstanding marketing companies are connecting more selectively, directly, and deeply with customers to form profitable customer relationships and build customer equity.

   Marketers must also execute *partner relationship management*. They must work closely with partners inside and outside the company to jointly build profitable customer relationships. Successful marketers are now connecting effectively with other company departments to build strong company value chains, and with outside partners to build effective demand and supply chains and effective customer-focused alliances.

2. *Building and managing strong brands.* Well-positioned brands with strong brand equity provide the basis upon which to build profitable customer relationships. Today's marketers must be good at positioning their brands vigorously and managing them well.

3. *Harnessing new marketing technologies in this digital age.* New digital and other high-tech marketing developments, including the explosion of the Internet, are having a dramatic impact on both buyers and the marketers who serve them. Today's marketers must know how to leverage new computer,

information, communication, and transportation technologies to connect more effectively with customers and marketing partners in this new digital age.

4. *Marketing in a socially responsible way around the globe.* As technological developments make the world an increasingly smaller place, marketers must market their brands globally and in socially responsible ways.

New and Updated *Real Marketing* Applications

Principles of Marketing, Sixth Canadian Edition, tells the stories that reveal the drama of modern marketing. While the majority of vignettes and *Real Marketing* exhibits are brand-new to this edition, we also retain some of the popular classics from previous editions. We think it's important to show how strategies at best-practice and up-and-coming organizations change and continuously evolve. Some real marketing examples from the this edition include the following:

- VanCity Credit Union's ability to craft strong relationships by offering genuine customer value

- Tim Hortons' savvy in bringing its brand to life in a way that has captured the Canadian imagination.

- Canadian Tire's strategic melding of its online and bricks-and-mortar worlds to create a robust, two-tiered system for consumers.

- Mountain Equipment Co-op's success in building customer relationships by promoting social responsibility while shunning traditional marketing tactics.

- Magna International's legendary product and process development expertise that make it a world leader in B2B marketing.

- The Forzani Group's unique, multi-banner concept that allows it to tailor its mix of quality products to meet the specific needs and preferences of a broad base of consumers.

- The passion of Canada's largest engineering firm, SNC-Lavalin, for delivering projects on time and within budget while strictly adhering to its code of ethics no matter where in the world it operates.

- Queen's Marketing Association's student-led initiatives to involve people from across the country in marketing's best practices.
- MTV's phenomenal success in international markets.
- Google's survival amid the dot-com meltdown.
- Home Depot's penchant for taking care of those who take care of customers.
- Dell Inc.'s stunning direct selling formula.
- Coca-Cola's international marketing prowess.

What's New...What's Changed

1. *A solid new "customer relationships" framework.* This new edition is organized around a powerful *managing profitable customer relationships* framework for teaching and learning marketing.

   - A retitled and heavily revised Chapter 1, "Marketing: Managing Profitable Customer Relationships," establishes this *customer relationships* theme at the start of the text. A new Chapter 1 section, *Managing Customer Relationships,* pulls together the latest thinking on creating superior customer value and satisfaction in order to attract, retain, and grow customers and maximize customer equity. The closing section of Chapter 1 presents a final relationships theme—*connecting*—that summarizes how changes in technology have impacted how companies connect with customers, marketing partners, and the world around them.

   - A retitled and streamlined Chapter 6, "Managing Marketing Information," includes a major new section on customer relationship management (CRM), and software and analytical techniques for organizing and applying customer information from all customer touchpoints to build stronger customer relationships.

   - The customer and marketing partner relationships theme is carried forward into later chapters. In all, from the first chapter to the last, *Principles of Marketing* is organized around a powerfully enhanced theme: *developing and managing profitable customer and marketing partner relationships.*

2. *A new chapter: "Marketing in the Digital Age."* The new Chapter 3 addresses the impact of the Internet and other developments in today's high-tech marketing environment on marketing strategy and customer relationship building. The new digital age is having a dramatic impact on both buyers and the marketers who serve them. To succeed—even to survive—marketers must rethink their strategies and practices. The new chapter explores the major forces shaping the digital age; major Internet marketing developments in B2C, B2B, C2C, and C2B domains; and strategies and tactics for setting up a successful ecommerce presence. Unlike most other texts, which treat this material as an end-of-book afterthought, *Principles of Marketing* presents it up front, where it becomes an important part of the underlying fabric of marketing. This early coverage sets a platform for countless examples of digital developments integrated throughout the remainder of the text.

3. *Building strong brands and brand equity.* Chapter 10, "Product, Services, and Branding Strategies," now includes a separate and expanded section: *Building Strong Brands.* The section includes new material on brand equity, brand positioning, managing brands, and rebranding. Chapter 9, "Segmentation, Targeting, and Positioning: Building the Right Relationships with the Right Customers," presents a new discussion on developing brand positioning statements.

4. *Socially responsible marketing around the globe.* The sixth Canadian edition of *Principles of Marketing* continues its strong coverage of socially responsible marketing and global marketing.

   - *Marketing ethics, environmentalism, and social responsibility.* A repositioned Chapter 4, "Marketing and Society: Social Responsibility and Marketing Ethics," moves coverage of this important topic to the forefront. Students are thus given a framework for more effective understanding of the additional coverage that appears in almost every chapter.

   - *Global marketing.* This important topic is integrated chapter-by-chapter plus featured in a full chapter focusing on global marketing considerations.

5. *Canadian perspective.* Marketing in Canada presents unique challenges: regional and language differences, multiculturalism, population dispersion, distinct regulatory policies and philosophies, the small domestic marketplace and resulting mandate for global sales, a highly concentrated retail environment, and unique

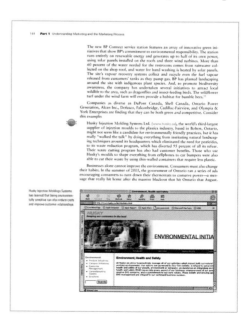

cultural and ethical norms. Despite the fact that over 85 percent of our exports go to the United States, there is a growing divide between the cultures of the two countries. Sensitivity to these differences must be aligned with the fact that many Canadian firms are operating units of large, multinational firms; thus, marketing in Canada often necessitates integrating Canadian strategies with the global programs of the parent firm. To highlight this uniqueness, Canadian issues and examples are presented in detail throughout the text. For example, excerpts from the Canadian Marketing Association's Code of Ethics and Standards of Practice are presented for the first time in Chapter 4, "Social Responsibility and Marketing Ethics." The latest releases from the 2001 Census illuminate discussion of Canadian demographics in Chapter 5, "The Marketing Environment," and key provisions of the *Personal Information Protection and Electronic Documents Act* are detailed in Chapter 17, "Personal Selling and Direct Marketing."

6. *Other additions and enhancements.* The sixth Canadian edition contains new material on a wide range of subjects, including customer relationship management and partner relationship management; the digital age and Internet marketing; customer lifetime value and customer equity; brand equity, brand building, brand management, and rebranding; value propositions, positioning, and positioning statements; demand chain and supply chain management; the new direct marketing model and database marketing; customized marketing; online marketing research; value pricing and dynamic pricing; integrated marketing communications and buzz marketing; Web selling and online sales training; marketing and diversity; environmental sustainability; global marketing strategy; and much more.

A New Look and Feel

- Many new chapter-opening examples and *Real Marketing* exhibits have been added to illustrate important concepts using real business applications.
- A brand-new design and redrawn figures give this edition a fresh, new feel. All tables, figures, examples, and references throughout the text have been thoroughly updated.
- Vivid new photos and advertisements have been added.
- All of the real-life Company Cases are new or revised, as are the videos that accompany the text. These cases and videos help to bring the real world directly to the student and into the classroom.

More Powerful Learning Aids

- *Looking Ahead: Previewing the Concepts.* A section at the beginning of each chapter briefly previews chapter concepts, links them to concepts in previous chapters, presents chapter learning objectives, and introduces the chapter-opening marketing story.
- *Chapter-opening marketing stories.* Each chapter starts with a dramatic marketing story that introduces the chapter material and sparks student interest.
- *Real Marketing highlights.* Go behind the scenes for an in-depth look at real marketing practices at large and small companies.
- *Visuals.* Marketing is a visual subject matter, so throughout each chapter we feature plenty of colourful figures, photographs, advertisements, and illustrations to help reinforce key concepts and applications.
- *Looking Back: Reviewing the Concepts.* A summary at the end of each chapter reviews major chapter concepts and chapter objectives.

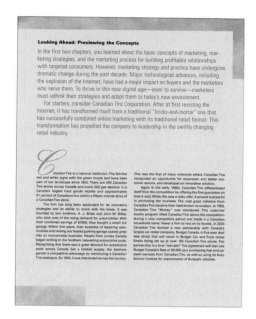

- *Reviewing the Key Terms.* Key terms are highlighted within the text, clearly defined in the margins of the pages in which they appear, and listed at the end of each chapter.

- *Discussing the Concepts* and *Applying the Concepts.* Each chapter contains a set of discussion questions and application exercises covering major chapter concepts.

- *Company Cases.* Company cases are provided at the end of each chapter. These cases challenge students to apply marketing principles to real companies in real situations.

- *Appendix.* "Marketing Arithmetic" appears at the end of the text, providing additional, practical information for students. An additional resource, "Measuring and Forecasting Demand," appears on the Companion Website at www.pearsoned.ca/kotler.

- *Indexes.* At the end of the book, name and subject indexes reference all information and examples in the book.

More Powerful Supplements: In Your Class, Everywhere, Anywhere

For the Instructor

NEW

Instructor's Resource CD-ROM with TestGen, Instructor's Resource Manual, and PowerPoint Presentations

This CD provides one source for many of your supplement needs and allows you to print only the chapters or materials that you wish to use or search for resources by topic.

Pearson TestGen is a special computerized test item file that enables instructors to view and edit the existing questions, add questions, generate tests, and print the tests in a variety of formats. Powerful search and sort functions make it easy to locate questions and arrange them in any order desired. TestGen also enables instructors to administer tests on a local area network, have the tests graded electronically, and have the results prepared in electronic or printed reports. The Pearson TestGen is compatible with IBM or Macintosh systems.

The *Instructor's Resource Manual* contains chapter outlines, learning objectives, chapter overview, lecture suggestions, in-class exercises, and suggestions on how to use the text effectively. The manual also provides answers to the end-of-chapter questions, cases, Video Short exercises, and CBC case questions.

PowerPoint Express and Extendit! Slides. Two sets of PowerPoint slides are available with this edition. PowerPoint Extendit! presentations include up to 25 slides per chapter with Weblinks and images and figures used in the text. They are also available for downloading from the Companion Website. PowerPoint Express slideshows are shorter and more basic, aimed at instructors who like to customize more. Both sets of PowerPoint files can also be accessed on the Companion Website.

CBC Pearson Education Canada/CBC Video Library

Pearson Education Canada and the CBC have worked together to bring you 18 segments from such notable CBC programs as *Venture, Marketplace,* and *Undercurrents.* Designed specifically to complement the text, this case collection is an excellent tool for bringing students into contact with the world outside the classroom. These programs have extremely high production quality, present substantial content, and have been chosen to relate directly to chapter topics. (Please contact your Pearson Education Canada sales representative for details. These videos are subject to availability and terms negotiated upon adoption of the text.)

Video Shorts

At the end of each chapter, students are directed to the Video Shorts located on the Companion Website, and are asked to watch a four-minute video featuring an entrepreneurial company and then answer three or four related questions.

Colour Overhead Transparencies

This supplement includes key figures from the text, key concepts, and various print advertisements and photos.

Innovative Online Courses and Teaching/Learning Support

Online course content is available with text adoption for Blackboard, WebCT, and CourseCompass platforms. You need no technical expertise. Teach a complete online course or a Web-enhanced course. Add your own materials, take advantage of online testing and Gradebook features, and use innovative bulletin board and discussion-thread functions. All course content and access is free upon adoption of this text.

Companion Website (www.pearsoned.ca/kotler)

Go beyond the text. Our acclaimed Web resource provides professors and students with a customized course website that features a complete array of teaching and learning material. Instructors have password-protected access to the instructor resources listed above. Download the Instructor's Resource Manual, PowerPoint slides, video cases, and additional resources. Or, try the Syllabus Builder to plan your own course! Contact your Prentice Hall representative about securing a password. Additionally, two appendices from the fourth edition—Measuring and Forecasting Demand and Careers in Marketing—have been updated and posted to the site.

Pearson Custom Publishing (www.prenhall.com/custombusiness)

Pearson Custom Publishing can provide you and your students with texts, cases, and articles to enhance your course. Choose material from Darden, Ivey, Harvard Business School Publishing, NACRA, and Thunderbird to create your own custom casebook. Contact your Pearson sales representative for details.

Online Learning Solutions

Pearson Education Canada supports instructors interested in using online course management systems. We provide text-related content in WebCT, Blackboard, and Course Compass. To find out more about creating an online course using Pearson content in one of these platforms, contact your Pearson sales representative.

New! Instructor's ASSET

Pearson Education is proud to introduce Instructor's ASSET, the Academic Support and Service for Educational Technologies. ASSET is the first integrated Canadian service program committed to meeting the customization, training, and support needs for your course. Ask your Pearson sales representative for details!

Your Pearson Sales Representative

Your Pearson sales rep is always available to ensure you have everything you need to teach a winning course. Armed with experience, training, and product knowledge, your Pearson rep will support your assessment and adoption of any of the products, services, and technology outlined here to ensure our offerings are tailored to suit your individual needs and the needs of your students. Whether it's getting instructions on TestGen software or specific content files for your new online course, your Pearson sales representative is there to help. (Also available for your students. Ask your Pearson sales rep for details!)

For the Student
Study Guide

The Study Guide includes chapter overviews, objectives, key terms and definitions, and detailed outlines for note-taking and review. Short essay questions centre on a case that is designed to illustrate and apply topics in marketing. Each case in the section either is a synopsis of a recent article in marketing or has been drawn from the author's experiences in the field. To reinforce students' understanding of the chapter material, the guide includes a section of multiple-choice and true/false questions. Suggested answers for all short essay, multiple choice and true/false questions are provided for students' self-checking.

Companion Website

The Companion Website includes a variety of resources for students. The site acts as an online study guide, with multiple choice, true/false, matching questions and short essay questions that can be submitted for grading. Internet application exercises, live Weblinks, and a search function encourages students to explore the Web to find information relevant to their course and business interests. Browse the Virtual Library for additional introductory marketing resources. Take the Case Pilot Challenge and use this free interactive case analysis tool to develop your skills in case study analysis. View all the video resources that accompany this text.

The online study guide includes:

- Chapter Objectives
- PowerPoint Express
- Flashcard Glossary
- Chapter Quiz
    - Concept Check
    - Concept Challenge
- Internet Exercises

- Digital Connections
- Destinations
- Animated Figures
- CBC Videos and Cases
- Video Shorts and Exercises
- Case Pilot
- Comprehensive Cases
- Virtual Library
- Measuring and Forecasting Demand
- Careers in Marketing

The Marketing Plan: A Handbook by Marian Burk Wood

Concise and user-friendly, this new text guides students through the process of developing a realistic, customized marketing plan by applying concepts learned in the classroom. It includes Marketing PlanPro, an award-winning commercial software package that leads students through the entire marketing plan process. The Marketing PlanPro CD-ROM features various sample marketing plans, step-by-step guides, help wizards, and customizable charts. Ask your Prentice Hall representative how this new handbook can be value-packaged with this textbook at a deep discount.

Navigating WebCT or Navigating BlackBoard— A Student's Guide

Beginning with a brief introduction to the Internet and the World Wide Web, these lively guides help students understand and master the basic navigation path through a WebCT or BlackBoard Online Course. The guides cover WebCT 3.7 or BlackBoard 5.0+. It's the definitive offline tool for the online student! These guides are available as a value-package option.

Acknowledgments for the Sixth Canadian Edition

No book is the work only of its authors. We owe much to the pioneers of marketing who first identified its major issues and developed its concepts and techniques. Our thanks also go to our colleagues at the School of Business, Queen's University, J. L. Kellogg Graduate School of Management, Northwestern University, and at the Kenan-Flagler Business School, University of North Carolina at Chapel Hill, for ideas and suggestions. We owe special thanks to Lew Brown and Martha McEnally, both of the University of North Carolina at Greensboro, for their valuable work in preparing high-quality company cases. We also thank Andrea Meyer of WorkingKnowledge for her fine contributions.

Many reviewers at other colleges provided valuable comments and suggestions. We are indebted to the following colleagues:

Bryan Barbieri, *Concordia University*

Lilly Buchwitz, *Wilfrid Laurier University*

Rachelle Dupuis, *University of New Brunswick, Saint John*

Webb Dussome, *University of Alberta*

Gordon Fullerton, *St. Mary's University*

Lee Ann Keple, *Athabasca University*

Robert Krider, *Simon Fraser University*

Shirley Lichti, *Wilfrid Laurier University*

Bob MacKalski, *McGill University*

Marianne Marando, *Seneca College*

Jean-Paul Olivier, *Red River College of Applied Arts, Science, and Technology*

Lynne Ricker, *University of Calgary*

Dr. Shelley M. Rinehart, *University of New Brunswick, Saint John*

John Russell, *Lethbridge Community College*

Kirby Shannahan, *University of New Brunswick*

Donald Shiner, *Mount Saint Vincent University*

Dr. T. Rick Whiteley, *The University of Western Ontario*

Maxwell Winchester, *University College of the Fraser Valley*

Finally, we thank Lesley Mann for her patience, friendship, high quality editorial and developmental assistance, and her dedication to making this book Canada's best over a series of editions.

We also owe a great deal to the people at Pearson Education Canada who helped develop this book. Acquisition Editors Kelly Torrance and Laura Forbes provided energetic support and ably managed the many facets of this complex revision project. Developmental Editor Pam Voves provided timely and detailed feedback and necessary nudging. We also owe thanks to Cheryl Jackson, Production Editor, who helped shepherd the project smoothly through production. Additional thanks go to Marketing Manager Steve McGill for his initiative and creative eye, and Michael Young, Vice-President and Editorial Director, for his enthusiasm and support.

Finally, we owe many thanks to our families. We thank the Armstrong family (Kathy, KC, Keri, Mandy, and Matt) and the Kotler family (Nancy, Amy, Melissa, and Jessica) for their constant support and encouragement.

Philip Kotler
Gary Armstrong

Special thanks go to the Cunningham family: my best marketing critic—my daughter Krista; my ever-patient husband, Paul; and my parents, who have always believed in me—George and Joan Milne. To them, we dedicate this book.

Peggy Cunningham

A Great Way to Learn and Instruct Online

The Pearson Education Canada Companion Website is easy to navigate and is organized to correspond to the chapters in this textbook. Whether you are a student in the classroom or a distance learner you will discover helpful resources for in-depth study and research that empower you in your quest for greater knowledge and maximize your potential for success in the course.

Companion Website

[**www.pearsoned.ca/kotler**] Enter

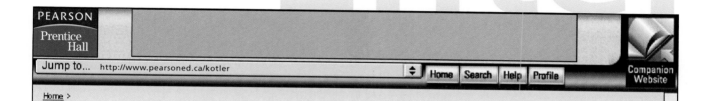

PEARSON
Prentice Hall

Jump to... | http://www.pearsoned.ca/kotler | Home | Search | Help | Profile

Companion Website

Home >

PH Companion Website

Principles of Marketing, Sixth Canadian Edition, by Kotler/Armstrong/Cunningham

Student Resources

The modules in this section provide students with tools for learning course material. These modules include:

- Chapter Objectives
- PowerPoint Express
- Glossary
- Chapter Quiz
  - Concept Check
  - Concept Challenge
- Internet Exercises
- Digital Connections
- Destinations

- Animated Figures
- CBC Video Cases
- Video Shorts Exercises
- Case Pilot
- Comprehensive Cases
- Virtual Library
- Measuring and Forecasting Demand
- Careers in Marketing

In the quiz modules students can send answers to the grader and receive instant feedback on their progress through the Results Reporter. Coaching comments and references to the textbook may be available to ensure that students take advantage of all available resources to enhance their learning experience.

Instructor Resources

A link to the protected Instructor's Central site provides instructors with additional teaching tools. Downloadable PowerPoint Presentations, Electronic Transparencies, and an Instructor's Manual are just some of the materials that may be available in this section. Where appropriate, this section will be password protected. To get a password, simply contact your Pearson Education Canada Representative or call Faculty Sales and Services at 1-800-850-5813.

Part I
Understanding
Marketing and the
Marketing Process

Chapter 1

Marketing: Managing Profitable Customer Relationships

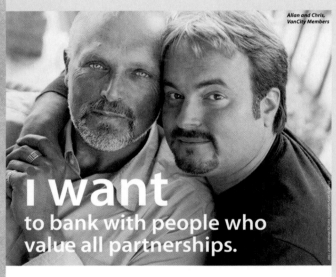

Allan and Chris,
VanCity Members

i want
to bank with people who
value all partnerships.

At VanCity, we do.

In fact, from the day we first opened our doors at VanCity, we've always strived to do what we believe is the right thing. Especially in our commitment to community support, equality and social justice. So it should come as no surprise that we support the lesbian and gay community.

And why wouldn't we? After all, we were the first financial institution in Canada to offer loans to women without requiring a man to co-sign, because it was the right thing to do. We were among the first to implement industry-leading workplace policies that respect *all* families by including same-sex employee benefits, because it was the right thing to do. And we publicly acknowledge lesbians, gays and their families as full and equal partners in our society, because it too, is the right thing to do.

At VanCity, we will always value the rights and the dignity that all people deserve. And isn't that the kind of partnership you want with the people you bank with?

To find out more, call us, go to our web site or visit a VanCity branch near you.

604-877-7000 · 1-888-VanCity · vancity.com

VanCity
It's right here.™

After studying this chapter you should be able to

1. define what marketing is and discuss its core concepts

2. define marketing management and compare the five marketing management orientations

3. discuss customer relationship management and strategies for building lasting customer relationships

4. analyze the major challenges facing marketers in the new "connected" millennium

Looking Ahead: Previewing the Concepts

Welcome to the exciting world of marketing! In this chapter, to start you off, we will introduce you to the basic concepts of marketing. We'll first define marketing and its key concepts. Next, we'll examine perhaps the most important concept of modern marketing—customer relationship management. Above all else, marketing seeks to create and manage profitable customer relationships by delivering superior value to customers. Three additional themes support the ability of organizations to build strong relationships. First is their sense of ethics and social responsibility. Without these, organizations would never be able to instil trust among important stakeholders. Second is their ability to build strong brands. Brands help define what products and services mean in the context of consumers' lives. The final theme is the international acumen of organizations, whether in terms of being able to meet new competitors entering Canadian markets from overseas or being able to market beyond our national borders. We will build on these themes throughout the book.

In this chapter we'll also outline the challenges marketing faces as we move through the twenty-first century. Understanding these basic concepts and forming your own ideas about what they really mean to you will give you a solid foundation for all that follows.

To set the stage, let's first look at VanCity Credit Union. VanCity is an exemplar of an organization that has grown and prospered because it has crafted strong relationships based on creating genuine customer value for its customers and key stakeholders. It has won ground against Canada's large banks by distinguishing itself on its record of social responsibility and ethics. VanCity has built a strong brand and has been able to withstand the attacks of many overseas financial institutions.

W hile credit unions are relatively unknown in eastern Canada, they are major financial institutions in western Canada and in Quebec. One of the best-known and most respected credit unions is VanCity Credit Union, Canada's largest credit union. Not only is VanCity a respect-ed financial institution, it is a master marketer and relation-ship builder.

The Vancouver City Credit and Savings Union was founded and incorporated in 1946 to provide financial advice and assistance for residents of British Columbia. In

2003 VanCity boasted 286 000 members, with 39 branches located throughout Greater Vancouver, the Fraser Valley, and Victoria. VanCity also owns Citizens Bank of Canada, which serves members across the country by telephone, ATM, and the Internet. Both VanCity and Citizens Bank are guided by a commitment to corporate social responsibility. They have adopted strict ethical guidelines to guide their business practices and take pride in offering services to people "from all walks of life."

Currently, there are approximately 750 credit unions in Canada. Credit unions have a membership of over 10 million people (including people who are members of *caisses populaire*—the Quebec version of a credit union). Like banks, credit unions offer many financial services—everything from savings and chequing accounts to investment advice. However, unlike banks, credit unions are co-operatives that are owned by their customers or "members," as credit unions call them. Profits are returned to members in the form of patronage dividends or better services and prices. Furthermore, credit unions have a strong sense of their social and environmental responsibility as well as their financial responsibility. VanCity believes its attention to this "triple bottom line" sets it apart from other financial institutions.

VanCity describes itself as a democratic, ethical, and innovative provider of financial services to its members. It prides itself on being values-driven and is committed to doing business in a way that not only strengthens its own long-term success, but also contributes to the social, economic, and environmental well-being of the communities in which it operates. VanCity's marketing prowess and customer relationship focus have long contributed to its success. Its mission—to achieve results that allow its key stakeholders to thrive and prosper—is realized by building strong relationships with the stakeholders: its members, employees, and communities.

VanCity achieves extremely high levels of customer satisfaction. Results of a 2002 independent national customer service survey granted VanCity a first-place finish for customer satisfaction among British Columbia's major financial institutions, far surpassing every major Canadian bank. Moreover, the year 2002 was VanCity's best year ever financially. It grew by over 60 percent and welcomed 18 000 new members.

VanCity measures success not just by profits, but also by its community impact, the level of involvement of its members, its environmental sustainability, and the number of new members it attracts. In 2002 alone VanCity gave back $11.9 million in membership and patronage dividends and grants. It donated $1 million to the community projects selected by its members for support. And its employees raised $86 000 for Family Services of Greater Vancouver.[1] In

recognition of such achievements, VanCity has received numerous awards to recognize its accomplishments. It's been named the best financial institution in both Vancouver and Burnaby. It recently won the Mayor's Environmental Achievement Award and the Spirit of Vancouver Award.

VanCity uses both traditional and non-traditional marketing tools. It uses advertising to promote awareness of its ethics-led culture. It is renowned for its ability to innovate and successfully launch new products and services valued by its membership. For example, it was VanCity that first developed ethical investment funds. VanCity also follows an aggressive pricing policy that ensures members are always getting some of the best rates available. Finally, it has also grown and prospered as a result of its excellent service culture.

VanCity takes pride in understanding and serving all members of its communities, whether they be Aboriginal Canadians, people from visible minorities, or people following alternative lifestyles. One recent print and outdoor campaign featured two gay men in an obviously affectionate pose and the tag-line, "I want to bank with people who value all partnerships." Unlike other organizations that pay only lip service to the gay and lesbian community and hide gay-targeted advertisements in specialized publications, VanCity used mainstream media as a means of demonstrating its real commitment to this community. As a VanCity marketing manager noted, "It's a bold move, but we feel it's the right one from a business perspective and from a values-alignment perspective.... it's not just about an advertising strategy, it has to be how we serve the members."

To truly build relationships with this community, VanCity can't just rely on advertising. It has done other things to make gays and lesbians feel welcome. It hired a business development manager just for the gay and lesbian segment. It opened a branch in Vancouver's West End, home to a huge gay population. When Aaron Webster, a gay man, was murdered in Stanley Park, VanCity took up a collection and gathered donations on behalf of several community groups to find those responsible for his death.

As you can see, VanCity's strength is its ability to build and sustain relationships with multiple constituencies. To accomplish this, VanCity has learned that it must first understand the perspectives and needs of its key stakeholders. Thus, it listens to its members, its staff, and its communities. It conducts focus groups, comprehensive member surveys, and employee surveys. Moreover, it asks its members to vote on key issues. In this way, it involves its stakeholders and encourages them to partner in all it does. Today, the ability to build superior relationships is a major marketing capability.[2]

What Is Marketing?

To create value and satisfaction, marketing, more than any other business function, deals with customers. Although we will explore more detailed definitions of marketing later in this chapter, perhaps the simplest definition is: *Marketing is the managing of profitable relationships.* The two-fold goal of marketing is to attract new customers by promising superior value, and to keep and grow current customers by delivering satisfaction.

Wal-Mart has become the world's largest retailer by delivering on its promise, "We sell for less—always." Ritz-Carlton promises—and delivers—truly "memorable experiences" for its hotel guests. AT&T says, "It's all within your reach—one connection: across town, across the country, across the world." At Disney theme parks, "imaginers" work wonders in their quest to create fantasies and "make a dream come true today." Dell leads the personal computer industry by consistently making good on its promise to "be direct," making it easy for customers to custom-design their own computers and have them delivered quickly to their doorsteps. These and other highly successful companies know that if they take care of their customers, market share and profits will follow.

Sound marketing is critical to the success of every organization—large or small, for-profit or non-profit, domestic or global. Large for-profit firms such as Bell, Canadian Tire, Cognos, IBM, Nortel, Zellers, and Fairmont Hotels use marketing. But so do non-profit organizations such as Halifax's St. Mary's University, Toronto's Hospital for Sick Children, and the Vancouver Public Aquarium.

Marketing is practised throughout the world. It provides both domestic and international firms with insights about what drives customer satisfaction. For example, Wal-Mart has been highly successful when expanding outside North America because it has tailored its mix of products and services, the width of its aisles, its shelf capacity, and the look and feel of its stores to meet consumer tastes in the nine different countries in which it operates.

Wal-Mart offers more food products in stores outside North America. In fact, food accounts for 50 percent of its sales in its Latin American stores. It has built smaller stores that are similar to neighbourhood markets in some countries. Wal-Mart also had to differentiate itself from a different set of competitors. The French global retailer Carrefour fought to retain its market share in Brazil and engaged in an aggressive price war against Wal-Mart. In the United Kingdom, Marks & Spencer was the leading children's clothing retailer and the leading department store—but with the launch of its private-label line of clothing in 2001, Wal-Mart overcame this rival. Although Wal-Mart initially struggled in Germany, it became profitable with the launch of new Supercentres and the inclusion of its private-label clothing line.

Despite these successes, Wal-Mart stumbled in some markets. It initially entered China in 1994 but withdrew due to management differences with its Chinese partners and disputes with the Chinese government over the number of stores it could open. It later went back into this market. Its first entry into Japan also failed, but it now hopes to achieve success and a better understanding of Japanese consumers through its partnership with Seiyu Ltd., Japan's fifth largest supermarket chain.[3]

You already know a lot about marketing—it's all around you. You see the results of marketing in the abundance of products that line the store shelves in your nearby shopping mall. You see marketing in the advertisements that fill your TV screen, spice up your magazines, add animation to Internet sites, stuff your mailbox, or enliven your webpages. At home, at school, where you work, where you play—you are exposed to marketing in almost everything you do. Yet, there is much more to marketing than meets the consumer's casual eye. Behind it all is a massive network of people and activities competing for your attention and purchasing dollars.

This book will give you a more complete and formal introduction to the basic concepts and practices of today's marketing. In this chapter, we begin by defining marketing and its core concepts.

Marketing Defined

What does the term *marketing* mean? Many people think of marketing only as selling and advertising. And no wonder—every day we are bombarded with television commercials, newspaper ads, direct mail, Internet pitches, and sales calls. However, selling and advertising are only the tip of the marketing iceberg. Although they are important, they are only two of many marketing functions and are often not the most important ones.

Today, marketing must be understood not in the old sense of making a sale—telling and selling—but in the new sense of *satisfying customer needs*. If the marketer does a good job of understanding consumer needs, develops products that provide superior value, and prices, distributes, and promotes them effectively, these products will sell very easily. Thus, selling and advertising are only part of a larger "marketing mix"—a set of marketing tools that work together to affect the marketplace.

Marketing
A social and managerial process by which individuals and groups obtain what they need and want through creating and exchanging products and value with others.

We define **marketing** as a social and managerial process by which individuals and groups obtain what they need and want through creating and exchanging products and value with others.[4] To explain this definition, we examine these important terms: *needs, wants, and demands; products, services and expenses; value, satisfaction, and quality; exchange, transactions, and relationships*; and *markets*. Figure 1.1 shows that these core marketing concepts are linked, with each concept building on the one before it.

Needs, Wants, and Demands

Needs
States of felt deprivation.

The most basic concept underlying marketing is that of human needs. Human **needs** are states of felt deprivation. Humans have many complex needs. These include basic *physical* needs for food, clothing, warmth, and safety; *social* needs for belonging and affection; and *individual* needs for knowledge and self-expression. These needs are not invented by marketers; they are a basic part of the human composition.

Figure 1.1 Core marketing concepts

Wants
The form taken by human needs as they are shaped by culture and individual personality.

Demands
Human wants that are backed by buying power.

Wants are the form taken by human needs as they are shaped by culture and individual personality. A hungry person in Canada may want a hamburger, french fries, and a pop. A hungry person in Bali may want mangoes, suckling pig, and beans. Wants are shaped by one's society and described in terms of objects that will satisfy needs. When backed by buying power, wants become **demands.** Given their wants and resources, people demand products with benefits that add up to the most value and satisfaction.

Outstanding marketing companies go to great lengths to learn about and understand their customers' needs, wants, and demands. They conduct consumer research and analyze mountains of customer sales, warranty, and service data. Their people at all levels—including top management—stay close to customers. For example, top executives from Wal-Mart spend two days each week visiting stores and mingling with customers. At Disney World, at least once in his or her career, each manager spends a day touring the park in a Mickey, Minnie, Goofy, or other character costume. At consumer products giant Procter & Gamble, top executives even visit with ordinary consumers in their homes and on shopping trips. "We read the data and look at the charts," says one P&G executive, "but to shop [with consumers] and see how the woman is changing retailers to save 10 cents on a loaf of bread [so she can] spend it on things that are more important—that's important to us to keep front and center."[5]

Marketing Offers—Products, Services, and Experiences

Marketing offer
Some combination of products, services, information, or experiences offered to a market to satisfy a need or want.

Companies address needs by putting forth a *value proposition,* a set of benefits that they promise to consumers to satisfy their needs. The value proposition is fulfilled through a **marketing offer**—some combination of products, services, information, or experiences offered to a market to satisfy a need or want. Marketing offers are not limited to physical *products.* In addition to tangible products, marketing offers include *services,* activities or benefits offered for sale that are essentially intangible and do not result in the ownership of anything. Examples include banking, airline, hotel, tax preparation, and home repair services. More broadly, marketing offers also include other entities, such as *persons, places, organizations, information,* and *ideas.*

Many sellers make the mistake of paying more attention to the specific products they offer than to the benefits and experiences produced by these products. They see themselves as selling a product rather than providing a solution to a need. A manufacturer of quarter-inch drill bits may think that the customer needs a drill bit. But what the customer *really* needs is a quarter-inch hole. These sellers may suffer from "marketing myopia"—the short-sightedness that arises when marketers are so taken with their products that they focus only on existing wants and lose sight of underlying customer needs.[6] They forget that a product is only a tool to solve a consumer problem. These sellers will have trouble if a new product comes along that serves the customer's need better or less expensively. The customer with the same *need* will *want* the new product.

Thus, smart marketers look beyond the attributes of the products and services they sell. They create brand *meaning* and brand *experiences* for consumers. For example, Coca-Cola means much more to consumers than just something to drink—it has become an icon with a rich tradition and meaning. And Nike is more than just shoes, it's what the shoes do for you and where they take you. The familiar Nike swoosh stands for high sports performance, famous athletes, and a "Just Do It!" attitude (see Real Marketing 1.1). By orchestrating several services and products, companies can create, stage, and market brand experiences. Disney World is an experience; so is a ride on a Harley-Davidson motorcycle. You experience a visit to Indigo or Chapters or surfing Sony's PlayStation website. In fact, as products and

1.1   Nike: It's Not So Much the Shoes but Where They Take You!

The "swoosh"—it's everywhere! Just for fun, try counting the swooshes whenever you pick up the sports pages or watch a pickup basketball game or tune in to a televised golf match. Nike has built the ubiquitous swoosh into one of the best-known brand symbols on the planet. And the swoosh has come to stand for all of the things that Nike means to those who wear it all around the world.

The power of its brand and logo speaks loudly of Nike's superb marketing skills. The company's strategy of building superior products around popular athletes and its classic "Just Do It!" ad campaign have forever changed the face of sports marketing. Nike spends hundreds of millions of dollars each year on big-name endorsements, such as its partnership with the Toronto Raptors. It also uses splashy promotional events, and lots of attention-getting ads. Over the years, Nike has associated itself with some of the biggest names in sports, from Michael Jordan, Tiger Woods, Pete Sampras, and Mike Schmidt to Mia Hamm, Lance

The ever-present Nike swoosh has come to stand for all that Nike means to those who wear it all around the world. "It's not so much the shoes but where they take you."

Armstrong, and Ronaldo. No matter what your sport, chances are good that one of your favourite athletes wears the Nike swoosh.

Nike knows, however, that good marketing is more than promotional hype and promises—it means consistently building strong relationships with customers based on real value. Nike's initial success resulted from the technical superiority of its running and basketball shoes, pitched to serious athletes who were frustrated by the lack of innovation in athletic equipment. To this day, Nike leads the industry in research-and-development spending.

But Nike gives its customers more than just good athletic gear. Customers don't just wear their Nikes, they *experience* them. As the company states on its webpage (www.nike.com/canada), "Nike has always known the truth—it's not so much the shoes but where they take you." Beyond shoes, apparel, and equipment, Nike markets a way of life, a sports culture, a "just do it" attitude. That's the real meaning of Nike to its customers. Says Phil Knight, Nike's founder and chief executive, "Basically, our culture and our style is to be a rebel." The company was built on a genuine passion for sports, a maverick disregard for convention, and a belief in hard work and serious sports performance. Notes the webpage: "Just Do It" is "both universal and intensely personal. It speaks of sports. It invites dreams. It is a call to action, a refusal to hear excuses, and a license to be eccentric, courageous, and exceptional. It is Nike."

The strong relationships between customers and its brand paid off handsomely for Nike. Over the decade ending in 1997, Nike's revenues grew at an incredible annual rate of 21 percent; annual return to investors averaged 47 percent. In the mid-1990s, Nike levered its brand strength, moving aggressively into new product categories, sports, and regions of the world. Its sports apparel business grew explosively. The company slapped its familiar swoosh logo on everything from sunglasses and soccer balls to batting gloves and hockey sticks. Nike invaded a dozen new sports, including baseball, golf, ice and street hockey, in-line skating, wall climbing, and hiking.

In the late 1990s, however, Nike stumbled and its sales slipped. Many factors contributed to the company's sales woes. The whole industry suffered a setback, as a "brown shoe" craze for hiking and outdoor shoe styles ate into the athletic sneaker business. Competition improved: a revitalized Adidas saw its U.S. sales surge as Nike's sales declined. To make matters worse, college students on many campuses protested against Nike for its alleged exploitation of child labour in Asia and its commercialization of sports.

But Nike's biggest obstacle may be its own incredible success—it may have over-swooshed North America. The brand appeared to suffer from big-brand backlash, and the swoosh may have become too common to be cool. According to one analyst, "When Tiger Woods made his debut in Nike gear, there were so many logos on him that he looked as if he'd got caught in an embroidering machine." A Nike executive admits, "There has been a little bit of backlash about the number of swooshes that are out there." Moreover, with sales of more than $14 billion, Nike has moved from maverick to mainstream. Today, rooting for Nike is like rooting for Microsoft.

To address these problems, Nike has returned to the basics—focusing on innovation, developing new product lines, creating subbrands, and focusing once again on product performance. And despite its recent ups and downs, Nike still flat-out dominates the athletic shoe market.

Competitors can hope that Nike's slump will continue, but few are counting on it. Most can only sit back and marvel at Nike's marketing prowess. One market analyst comments, "Nike remains one of the great American brands, as well known around the world as Coke or McDonald's." The sports giant also appears to be returning to its creative, rebellious roots. According to another analyst, recent advertising is bringing Nike's image back to hip:

> Remember when Nike was unhip? It didn't last long... maybe three years at the end of the '90s, but the conquistadors of cool undoubtedly had a little swoon. But spot by spot, campaign by campaign...good things began to happen. [The comeback culminated in Nike's stunning "Freestyle" ad, which featured five NBA stars performing remarkable moves, stunts, and dribbles, the sounds of which were mixed into an original song that served as the ad's soundtrack. The ad won last year's *Advertising Age* Ad of the Year award and restored] the sports apparel marketer to its previous place at the creative summit.

Still, to stay on top, Nike will have to find new ways to deliver the kind of innovation and value that built the brand so powerfully in the past. No longer the rebellious, anti-establishment upstart, huge Nike must continually reassess and rekindle its meaning to customers. Says Knight, "Now that we've [grown so large], there's a fine line between being a rebel and being a bully. [To our customers,] we have to be beautiful as well as big."

Sources: Quotes from Bill Saporito, "Can Nike Get Unstuck?" *Time,* March 30, 1998, pp. 48–53; Jolie Solomon, "When Cool Goes Cold," *Newsweek,* March 30, 1998, pp. 36–37; Jerry Edgerton, "Can Nike Still Play Above the Rim?" *Money,* May 1999, p. 48; Louise Lee, "Can Nike Still Do It?" *Business Week,* February 21, 2000, pp. 121–128; and Bob Garfield, "Best of Show; and Apparel/Accessories: Nike." *Advertising Age,* May 6, 2002, p. S2. Also see Douglas Robson, "Just Do...Something," *Business Week,* July 2, 2001, pp. 70–71; and Maureen Tkacik, "Nike Net Rises 30% on Corrected Glitch to Its Supply Chain," *Wall Street Journal,* March 22, 2002, p. B2.

services increasingly become commodities, experiences have emerged for many firms as the next step in differentiating the company's offer. Consider, for example, a restaurant that doesn't even serve food:

> [One] entrepreneur in Israel has entered the experience economy with the opening of Cafe Ke'ilu, which roughly translates as "Cafe Make Believe." Manager Nir Caspi told a reporter that people come to cafes to be seen and to meet people, not for the food; Cafe Ke'ilu pursues that observation to its logical conclusion. The establishment serves its customers empty plates and mugs and charges guests $4 during the week and $8 on weekends for the social experience.[7]

"What consumers really want is [offers] that dazzle their senses, touch their hearts, and stimulate their minds," declares one expert. "They want [offers] that deliver an experience."[8]

Value and Satisfaction

Consumers usually face a broad array of products and services that might satisfy a given need. How do they choose among these many products and services?

Consumers make buying choices based on their perceptions of the value that various products and services deliver.

Customer value is the difference between the benefits the customer gains from owning and using a product and the costs of obtaining the product. Customers form expectations about the value of various marketing offers and buy accordingly. How do buyers form their expectations? Customer expectations are based on past buying experiences, the opinions of friends, and marketer and competitor information and promises.

Customer satisfaction with a purchase depends on how well the product's performance lives up to the customer's expectations. Customer satisfaction is a key influence on future buying behaviour. Satisfied customers buy again and tell others about their good experiences. Dissatisfied customers often switch to competitors and disparage the product to others.

Marketers must be careful to set the right level of expectations. If they set expectations too low, they may satisfy those who buy but fail to attract enough buyers. If they raise expectations too high, buyers will be disappointed. Customer value and customer satisfaction are key building blocks for developing and managing customer relationships. We will revisit these core concepts later in the chapter.

Exchange, Transactions, and Relationships

Exchange
The act of obtaining a desired object from someone by offering something in return.

Marketing occurs when people decide to satisfy needs and wants through exchange. **Exchange** is the act of obtaining a desired object from someone by offering something in return. Whereas exchange is the core concept of marketing, a transaction is marketing's unit of measurement. A **transaction** consists of a trade of values between two parties. In a transaction, we must be able to say that one party gives *X* to another party and gets *Y* in return. For example, you pay Sears $350 for a television set.

Transaction
A trade between two parties that involves at least two things of value, agreed-upon conditions, a time of agreement, and a place of agreement.

In the broadest sense, the marketer tries to bring about a response to some marketing offer. The response may be more than simply buying or trading products and services. A political candidate, for instance, wants votes, a church wants membership, and a social-action group wants idea acceptance.

Marketing consists of actions taken to build and maintain desirable *exchange relationships* with target audiences involving a product, service, idea, or other object. Beyond simply attracting new customers and creating transactions, the goal is to retain customers and grow their business with the company. Marketers want to build strong economic and social connections by promising and consistently delivering superior value. We will discuss the important concept of customer relationship management in more detail later in the chapter.

Markets

Market
The set of all actual and potential buyers of a product or service.

The concept of exchange leads to the concept of a market. A **market** is the set of actual and potential buyers of a product. These buyers share a particular need or want that can be satisfied through exchange. The size of a market depends on the number of people who exhibit the need, have resources to engage in exchange, and are willing to offer these resources in exchange for what they want.

Originally, the term *market* stood for the place where buyers and sellers gathered to exchange their goods, such as a village square. Economists use the term *market* to refer to a collection of buyers and sellers who transact in a particular product class, as in the housing market or the grain market. Marketers, however, see the sellers as constituting an industry and the buyers as constituting a market.

Marketers are keenly interested in markets. Each nation's economy and the whole world economy consist of complex, interacting sets of markets that are linked through exchange processes. Marketers work to understand the needs and wants of specific markets and to select the markets that they can serve best. In turn, they can develop products and services that will create value and satisfaction for customers in these markets, resulting in sales and profits for the company.

Marketing

The concept of markets brings us full circle to the concept of marketing. Marketing means managing markets to bring about exchanges for the purpose of satisfying human needs and wants. Thus, we return to our definition of marketing as a process by which individuals and groups obtain what they need and want by creating and exchanging products and value with others.

Creating exchange processes involves work. Sellers must search for buyers, identify their needs, design good products and services, set prices for them, promote them, and store and deliver them. Activities such as product development, research, communication, distribution, pricing, and service are core marketing activities. Although we normally think of marketing as being carried on by sellers, buyers also carry on marketing activities. Consumers do "marketing" when they search for the goods they need at prices they can afford. Company purchasing agents do "marketing" when they track down sellers and bargain for good terms.

Figure 1.2 shows the main elements in a modern marketing system. In the usual situation, marketing involves serving a market of end users in the face of competitors. The company and the competitors send their respective products and messages directly to consumers or through marketing intermediaries to the end users. All of the actors in the system are affected by major environmental forces—demographic, economic, physical, technological, political/legal, and social/cultural.

Each party in the system adds value for the next level. Thus, a company's success depends not only on its own actions, but also on how well the entire value chain serves the needs of final consumers. Zellers cannot fulfill its promise "The lowest price is the law!" unless its suppliers provide merchandise at low costs. And Ford cannot deliver high quality to car buyers unless its dealers provide outstanding service.

Marketing Management

Marketing management
The art and science of choosing target markets and building profitable relationships with them.

We define **marketing management** as the art and science of choosing target markets and building profitable relationships with them. This involves getting, keeping, and growing customers through creating, delivering, and communicating superior customer value. Thus, marketing management involves managing demand, which in turn involves managing customer relationships.

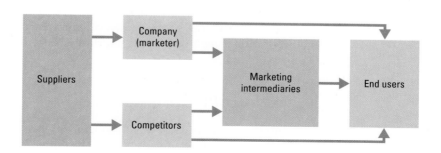

Figure 1.2 Elements of a modern marketing system

Customer and Demand Management

Some people think of marketing management as finding enough customers for the company's current output, but this is too limited a view. Marketing management is not concerned with serving all customers in every way. Instead, marketers want to serve selected customers that they can serve well and profitably. The organization has a desired level of demand for its products. At any point in time, there may be no demand, adequate demand, irregular demand, or too much demand. Marketing management must find ways to deal with these different demand states. It may be concerned not only with finding and increasing demand, but also with changing or even reducing it.

Demarketing

Marketing to reduce demand temporarily or permanently—the aim is not to destroy demand, but only to reduce or shift it.

For example, Banff National Park is badly overcrowded in the summer. And power companies sometimes have trouble meeting demand during peak usage periods. In these and other cases of excess demand, **demarketing** is needed to reduce demand temporarily or permanently; the aim is not to destroy demand, but only to reduce the number of customers or to shift their demand temporarily or permanently.[9] For example, to reduce demand for hydroelectric power and to encourage both consumers and businesses to use power more efficiently, Ontario Power Generation has set up a website encouraging conservation. The site provides examples that demonstrate how customers have reduced costs by conserving power or using it more efficiently. Thus, marketing management seeks to affect the level, timing, and nature of demand in a way that helps the organization achieve its objectives. Simply put, marketing management is *customer management* and *demand management*.

Marketing Management Orientations

We describe marketing management as carrying out tasks to build profitable relationships with target consumers. What *philosophy* should guide these marketing efforts? What weight should be given to the interests of the organization, customers, and society? Very often these interests conflict. There are five alternative concepts under which organizations conduct their marketing activities: the *production, product, selling, marketing,* and *societal marketing* philosophies.

The Production Concept

Production concept

The idea that consumers will favour products that are available and highly affordable.

The **production concept** holds that consumers will favour products that are available and highly affordable. Therefore, management should focus on improving production and distribution efficiency. This concept is one of the oldest philosophies that guide sellers.

The production concept is still a useful philosophy in two types of situations. The first occurs when the demand for a product exceeds the supply. Here, management should look for ways to increase production. The second situation occurs when the product's cost is too high and improved productivity is needed to bring it down.

Although useful in some situations, the production concept can lead to marketing myopia. Companies adopting this orientation run a major risk of focusing too narrowly on their own operations and losing sight of the real objective—satisfying customers' needs.

The Product Concept

Product concept

The idea that consumers will favour products that offer the most quality, performance, and features and that the organization should therefore devote its energy to making continuous product improvements.

The **product concept** holds that consumers will favour products that offer the most in quality, performance, and innovative features. Thus, an organization should devote energy to making continuous product improvements. Some manufacturers believe that if they can build a better mousetrap, the world will beat a path to their door.[10] But they are often rudely shocked. Buyers may well be looking for a better solution to a mouse problem but not necessarily for a better mousetrap. The solution might be a chemical spray, an exterminating service, or something that works better than a mousetrap. Furthermore, a better mousetrap will not sell unless the manufacturer designs, packages, and prices it attractively, places it in convenient distribution channels, brings it to the attention of people who need it, and convinces buyers that it is a better product.

Thus, the product concept also can lead to "marketing myopia." For instance, many universities have assumed that high-school graduates want a liberal arts education and have thus overlooked the increasing challenge of vocational colleges, private training schools, and online education services. Kodak assumed that consumers wanted photographic film rather than a way to capture and share memories and at first overlooked the challenge of digital cameras. Although it now leads the digital camera market in sales, it has yet to make significant profits from this business.

The Selling Concept

Selling concept
The idea that consumers will not buy enough of the organization's products unless the organization undertakes a large-scale selling and promotion effort.

Many organizations follow the **selling concept**, which holds that consumers will not buy enough of the organization's products unless it undertakes a large-scale selling and promotion effort. The concept is typically practised with *unsought goods*—those that buyers do not normally think of buying, such as encyclopedias or insurance. These industries must be good at tracking down prospects and selling them on product benefits.

Most firms practise the selling concept when they face overcapacity. Their aim is to sell what they make rather than make what the market wants. Such marketing carries high risks. It focuses on creating sales transactions rather than on building long-term, profitable customer relationships. It assumes that customers who are coaxed into buying the product will like it. Or, if they don't like it, they will possibly forget their disappointment and buy it again later. These are usually poor assumptions. Most studies show that dissatisfied customers do not buy again. Worse yet, while the average satisfied customer tells three others about good experiences, the average dissatisfied customer tells ten others his or her bad experiences.[11]

The Marketing Concept

Marketing concept
The marketing management philosophy that holds that achieving organizational goals depends on determining the needs and wants of target markets and delivering the desired satisfactions more effectively and efficiently than competitors do.

The **marketing concept** holds that achieving organizational goals depends on determining the needs and wants of target markets and delivering the desired satisfactions more effectively and efficiently than competitors do. Under the marketing concept, customer focus and value are the *paths* to sales and profits.

Instead of a product-centred "make and sell" philosophy, the marketing concept is a customer-centred "sense and respond" philosophy. It views marketing not as "hunting," but as "gardening." The job is not to find the right customers for your product, but the right products for your customers. As stated by famed direct marketer Lester Wunderman, "The chant of the Industrial Revolution was that of the manufacturer who said, 'This is what I make, won't you please buy it.' The call of the Information Age is the consumer asking, 'This is what I want, won't you please make it.'"[12]

Figure 1.3 contrasts the selling concept and the marketing concept. The selling concept takes an *inside-out* perspective. It starts with the factory, focuses on the company's existing products, and calls for heavy selling and promotion to obtain profitable sales. It focuses heavily on customer conquest—getting short-term sales with little concern about who buys or why.

Figure 1.3 The selling and marketing concepts contrasted

In contrast, the marketing concept takes an *outside-in* perspective. As Herb Kelleher, Southwest Airlines's colourful CEO, puts it, "We don't have a Marketing Department; we have a Customer Department." And in the words of one Ford executive, "If we're not customer driven, our cars won't be either." The marketing concept starts with a well-defined market, focuses on customer needs, and integrates all the marketing activities affecting customers. In turn, it yields profits by creating long-term customer relationships based on customer value and satisfaction.

Many successful and well-known companies have adopted the marketing concept. Kraft Canada, Procter & Gamble, RBC Financial, Disney, Bombardier, and Mountain Equipment Co-op follow it faithfully. The goal is to build customer satisfaction into the very fabric of the firm. L.L. Bean, the highly successful catalogue retailer, was founded on the marketing concept. In 1912, in his first circulars, L.L. Bean included the following notice: *"I do not consider a sale complete until goods are worn out and the customer still is satisfied. We will thank anyone to return goods that are not perfectly satisfactory.... Above all things we wish to avoid having a dissatisfied customer."* To this day, L.L. Bean dedicates itself to giving perfect satisfaction in every way. For example, it recently revised its catalogues to make it easier for Canadian customers to place their orders.

In contrast, many companies claim to practise the marketing concept but do not. Implementing the marketing concept often means more than simply responding to customers' stated desires and obvious needs. *Customer-driven companies* research current customers to learn about their desires, gather new product and service ideas, and test proposed product improvements. Such customer-driven marketing usually works well when a clear need exists and when customers know what they want.

In many cases, however, customers don't know what they want or even what is possible. For example, 20 years ago, how many consumers would have thought to ask for cell phones, fax machines, home copiers, 24-hour Internet brokerage accounts, DVD players, handheld global satellite positioning systems, or wearable PCs? Such situations call for *customer-driving* marketing—understanding customer needs even better than customers themselves do and creating products and services that will meet existing and latent needs, now and in the future.

"Customers should not be trusted to come up with solutions," says the CEO of an innovation management firm, "they aren't expert enough for that.... Rather, customers should be asked only [about] what they want a new product or service to do for them." As Sony's visionary leader, Akio Morita, puts it: "Our plan is to lead the public with new products rather than ask them what kinds of products they want. The public does not know what is possible, but we do." And according to an executive at 3M, "Our goal is to lead customers where they want to go before *they* know where they want to go."[13]

Customer-driving marketing: In many cases, however, customers don't know what they want or even what is possible. How many of us would have thought to ask for a "wearable PC."

The Societal Marketing Concept

Societal marketing concept
The idea that the organization should determine the needs, wants, and interests of target markets and deliver the desired satisfactions more effectively and efficiently than competitors in a way that maintains or improves the consumer's and society's well-being.

The **societal marketing concept** holds that the organization should determine the needs, wants, and interests of target markets. It should then deliver superior value to customers in a way that maintains or improves the consumer's and the society's well-being. The societal marketing concept is the newest of the five marketing management philosophies. It questions whether the pure marketing concept overlooks possible conflicts between consumer *short-run wants* and consumer *long-run welfare*. Is a firm that senses, serves, and satisfies individual short-term wants always doing what's best for consumers and society in the long run?

Consider the fast-food industry. Most people view today's giant fast-food chains as offering tasty and convenient food at reasonable prices. Yet many consumer and environmental groups have voiced concerns. Critics point out that hamburgers, fried chicken, french fries, and most other fast foods are high in fat and salt. The convenient packaging leads to waste and pollution. Thus, in satisfying consumer wants, the highly successful fast-food chains may be harming consumer health and causing environmental problems.

Subway is an example of a company that has successfully differentiated itself by being conscious of health and packaging concerns. Subway spokesperson Jared Fogle, who lost 110 kg (245 pounds) by eating at the sandwich chain every day for almost a year, helps Subway draw attention to its freshly made, low-fat sandwiches. Subway's healthy menu items and environmentally friendly packaging (sandwiches are wrapped in wax paper instead of Styrofoam containers) have gone down well with customers. In 2001 Subway surpassed McDonald's to become North America's largest fast-food chain.[14]

As Figure 1.4 shows, the societal marketing concept calls upon marketers to balance three considerations in setting their marketing policies: company profits, consumer wants, *and* society's interests. Originally most companies based their

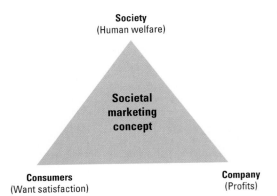

Figure 1.4   Three considerations underlying the societal marketing concept

marketing decisions largely on short-run company profit. Eventually they began to recognize the long-run importance of satisfying consumer wants, and the marketing concept emerged. Now, many companies are beginning to consider society's interests when making their marketing decisions.

One such company is SNC-Lavalin Group Inc., the parent company of one of the leading groups of engineering and construction companies in the world. The SNC-Lavalin companies currently have offices across Canada and in 30 other countries around the world and are currently working in some 100 countries. In 2003 Canadian Business magazine ranked SNC-Lavalin's CEO, Jacques Lemarre, the "Top CEO" in the country. SNC-Lavalin is committed to delivering projects on budget and on schedule to the complete satisfaction of its clients. In addition to its concern for exceptionally high standards for quality, health and safety, and environmental protection, it is known for its strict adherence to its Code of Ethics no matter where in the world it operates. To see SNC-Lavalin Group Inc.'s complete Code of Ethics, view its website at www.snc-lavalin.com/e~/6_016_31.aspx.

Customer Relationship Management

No matter what its orientation, marketing management's crucial task is to create profitable relationships with customers. Until recently, *customer relationship management (CRM)* has been defined narrowly as a customer database management activity. By this definition, it involves managing detailed information about individual customers and carefully managing customer "touchpoints" in order to maximize customer loyalty. We will discuss this narrower CRM activity in Chapter 6, Managing Marketing Information.

More recently, however, customer relationship management has taken on a broader meaning. In this broader sense, **customer relationship management** is the overall process of building and maintaining profitable customer relationships by delivering superior customer value and satisfaction. Thus, today's companies are going beyond designing strategies to *attract* new customers and create *transactions* with them. They are using customer relationship management to retain current customers and build profitable, long-term *relationships* with them. The new view is that marketing is the science and art of finding, retaining, *and* growing profitable customers.

Why the new emphasis on retaining and growing customers? In the past, many companies took their customers for granted. Facing an expanding economy and rapidly growing markets, companies could practise a "leaky bucket" approach to marketing. Growing markets meant a plentiful supply of new customers. Companies could keep filling the marketing bucket with new customers without worrying about losing old customers through holes in the bottom of the bucket.

However, companies today face some new marketing realities. Changing demographics, more sophisticated competitors, and overcapacity in many industries—all

Customer relationship management

The overall process of building and maintaining profitable customer relationships by delivering superior customer value and satisfaction.

Johnson & Johnson's concern for society is summarized in its credo and in the company's actions over the years.

Our Credo

We believe our first responsibility is to the doctors, nurses and patients, to mothers and fathers and all others who use our products and services. In meeting their needs everything we do must be of high quality. We must constantly strive to reduce our costs in order to maintain reasonable prices. Customers' orders must be serviced promptly and accurately. Our suppliers and distributors must have an opportunity to make a fair profit.

We are responsible to our employees, the men and women who work with us throughout the world. Everyone must be considered as an individual. We must respect their dignity and recognize their merit. They must have a sense of security in their jobs. Compensation must be fair and adequate, and working conditions clean, orderly and safe. We must be mindful of ways to help our employees fulfill their family responsibilities. Employees must feel free to make suggestions and complaints. There must be equal opportunity for employment, development and advancement for those qualified. We must provide competent management, and their actions must be just and ethical.

We are responsible to the communities in which we live and work and to the world community as well. We must be good citizens — support good works and charities and bear our fair share of taxes. We must encourage civic improvements and better health and education. We must maintain in good order the property we are privileged to use, protecting the environment and natural resources.

Our final responsibility is to our stockholders. Business must make a sound profit. We must experiment with new ideas. Research must be carried on, innovative programs developed and mistakes paid for. New equipment must be purchased, new facilities provided and new products launched. Reserves must be created to provide for adverse times. When we operate according to these principles, the stockholders should realize a fair return.

Johnson & Johnson

of these factors mean that there are fewer customers to go around. Many companies are now fighting for shares of flat or fading markets. Thus, the costs of attracting new consumers are rising. In fact, on average, it costs five to ten times as much to attract a new customer as it does to keep a current customer satisfied. Sears found that it costs twelve times more to attract a customer than to keep an existing one.[15]

Companies are also realizing that losing a customer means losing more than a single sale. It means losing the entire stream of purchases that the customer would make over a lifetime of patronage. For example, here is a dramatic illustration of **customer lifetime value:**

Customer lifetime value
The value of the entire stream of purchases that the customer would make over a lifetime of patronage.

Stew Leonard, who operates a highly profitable three-store supermarket, says that he sees $98 000 flying out of his store every time he sees a sulking customer. Why? Because his average customer spends about $196 a week, shops 50 weeks a year, and remains in the area for about 10 years. If this customer has an unhappy experience and switches to another supermarket, Stew Leonard's has lost $98 000 in revenue. The loss can be much greater if the disappointed customer shares the bad experience with other customers and causes them to defect. To keep customers coming back, Stew Leonard's has created what the *New York Times* has dubbed the "Disneyland of Dairy Stores," complete with costumed characters, scheduled entertainment, a petting zoo, and animatronics throughout the store. From its humble beginnings as a small dairy store in 1969, Stew Leonard's has grown at an amazing pace. It has built 29 additions onto the original store, which now serves more than 250 000 customers each week. This legion of loyal shoppers is largely a result of the store's passionate approach to customer service. Rule #1 at Stew Leonard's—The customer is always right. Rule #2—If the customer is ever wrong, reread rule #1![16]

Similarly, the customer lifetime value of a Taco Bell customer exceeds $20 000. Lexus estimates that a single satisfied and loyal customer is worth $1 170 000 in lifetime sales.[17] Thus, working to retain and grow customers makes good economic sense. In fact, a company can lose money on a specific transaction but still benefit greatly from a long-term relationship.

Customer lifetime value: To keep customers coming back, Stew Leonard's has created the "Disneyland of dairy stores." Rule #1—the customer is always right. Rule #2—if the customer is ever wrong, reread rule #1!

Attracting, Retaining, and Growing Customers

The key to building lasting customer relationships is to create superior customer value and satisfaction. Satisfied customers are more likely to be loyal customers, and loyal customers are more likely to give the company a larger share of their business. We now look more closely at the concepts of customer value and satisfaction, loyalty and retention, and share of customer.

Relationship Building Blocks: Customer Value and Satisfaction

Attracting and retaining customers can be a difficult task. Customers often face a bewildering array of products and services from which to choose. To attract and keep customers, a company must constantly seek ways to deliver superior customer value and satisfaction.

Customer perceived value
The difference between total customer value and total customer cost.

Customer Value　A customer buys from the firm that offers the highest **customer perceived value**—the customer's evaluation of the difference between all the benefits and all the costs of a marketing offer relative to those of competing offers. For example, Purolator customers gain a number of benefits. The most obvious are fast and reliable package delivery. However, when using Purolator (www.purolator.com), customers may also receive some status and image values. Using Purolator usually makes both the package sender and the receiver feel more important. When deciding whether to send a package via Purolator, customers will weigh these and other values against the money, effort, and psychic costs of using the service. Moreover, they will compare the value of using Purolator against the value of using other shippers—UPS, Federal Express, Canada Post—and select the one that gives them the greatest delivered value.

Customers often do not judge product values and costs accurately or objectively. They act on *perceived* value. For example, does Purolator really provide faster, more reliable delivery? If so, is this better service worth the higher prices that Purolator charges? Canada Post argues that its express service is comparable and its prices are much lower. However, judging by the increasing number of people using courier services and fax machines, many consumers doubt these claims. The challenge faced by Canada Post, therefore, is to change these customer value perceptions.

Customer satisfaction

The extent to which a product's perceived performance matches a buyer's expectations.

Customer Satisfaction   **Customer satisfaction** depends on a product's perceived performance in delivering value relative to a buyer's expectations. If the product's performance falls short of the customer's expectations, the buyer is dissatisfied. If performance matches expectations, the buyer is satisfied. If performance exceeds expectations, the buyer is delighted. Outstanding marketing companies go out of their way to keep their customers satisfied. Satisfied customers make repeat purchases, and they tell others about their good experiences with the product. The key is to match customer expectations with company performance. Smart companies aim to *delight* customers by promising only what they can deliver, then delivering *more* than they promise.[18] (See Real Marketing 1.2.) Recent studies have shown that customer satisfaction, especially with services, has been declining slightly in recent years.[19] It is unclear whether this has resulted from a decrease in product and service quality or from an increase in customer expectations. In either case, it presents an opportunity for companies that can consistently deliver superior customer value and satisfaction.

However, although the customer-centred firm seeks to deliver high customer satisfaction relative to competitors, it does not attempt to *maximize* customer satisfaction. A company can always increase customer satisfaction by lowering its price or increasing its services. But this may result in lower profits. Thus, the purpose of marketing is to generate customer value profitably. This requires a very delicate balance: the marketer must continue to generate more customer value and satisfaction but not "give away the house."

Customer Loyalty and Retention

Highly satisfied customers produce several benefits for the company. Satisfied customers are less price sensitive. They talk favourably to others about the company and its products and remain loyal for a longer period. However, the relationship between customer satisfaction and loyalty varies greatly across industries and competitive situations.

Figure 1.5 on page 21 shows the relationship between customer satisfaction and loyalty in five different markets.[20] In all cases, as satisfaction increases, so does loyalty. Highly competitive markets, such as those for automobiles and personal computers, show surprisingly little difference between the loyalty of less satisfied customers and those who are somewhat satisfied. However, they show a tremendous difference between the loyalty of satisfied customers and *completely* satisfied customers.

Even a slight drop from complete satisfaction can create an enormous drop in loyalty. For example, one study showed that completely satisfied customers are nearly 42 percent more likely to be loyal than merely satisfied customers. Another study, by AT&T, showed that 70 percent of customers who say they are satisfied with a product or service are still willing to switch to a competitor—but customers who are *highly* satisfied are much more loyal. Xerox found that its totally satisfied customers are six times more likely to repurchase Xerox products than are its satisfied customers.[21]

This means that companies must aim high if they want to hold on to their customers. Customer *delight* creates an emotional relationship with a product or service, not just a rational preference. This, in turn, creates high customer loyalty. Hanging on to customers is "so basic, it's scary," claims one marketing executive. "We find out what our customers' needs and wants are, and then we overdeliver."[22]

Figure 1.5 also shows that in non-competitive markets, such as those served by regulated monopolies or dominated by powerful or patent-protected brands, customers tend to remain loyal no matter how dissatisfied. This might seem like an

1.2 Customer Relationships: Delighting Customers

op-notch marketing companies know that delighting customers involves more than simply opening a complaint department, smiling a lot, and being nice. These companies set very high standards for customer satisfaction and often make seemingly outlandish efforts to achieve them. Some companies pay a lot of lip service to satisfying customers, but fail to execute on their promise. Others manage to delight customers. Consider the following examples:

Toronto-based marketing practitioner Jem Ma purchased the car of his dreams recently: a BMW 328Ci. The only hitch? It came without winter tires. He quickly set up an appointment with a downtown BMW dealership near his office. When he arrived, the BMW customer representative confirmed that Ma was booked for a snow tire appointment, but no snow tires were in stock. Upset, Ma went to the owner, who couldn't solve the problem either, but promised to call him back. While the manager did return the call, he told Ma there was nothing they could

Delighting customers: Top-notch marketing companies set very high standards for customer satisfaction and often make seemingly outlandish efforts to achieve them.

do. Frustrated, Ma called BMW Canada's customer service department, only to learn that he would have to wait until January to get the tires. The whole experience infuriated Ma. "I felt like a really small consumer. Customer service is part of the brand and there's a certain level of expectation," he says. He immediately cancelled his subscription to BMW's monthly magazine and he has told almost everyone he talks to about his frustrating experience. "The arrogance and the way it was handled wasn't what I'd expected.... It was actually the worst car service I've received at any dealership." When Kelly Lam, relationship marketing manager with BMW Canada, was asked to explain Ma's experience, she noted that BMW acted to solve the problem as quickly as possible and called Mr. Ma's situation an isolated incident. She also noted that BMW Canada is an industry leader in customer satisfaction.

Compare Jem Ma's experience with that of a recent Lexus buyer. A man bought his first new Lexus—an $87 000 piece of machinery. He could afford a Mercedes, a Jaguar, or a Cadillac, but he bought the Lexus. Taking delivery of his new prize, he luxuriated in the smell of the leather interior and the glorious handling. He tried all the car's toys—the lights, the windshield washer, the gizmo cup holder, the seat heater. Each was designed so well that he felt mounting pleasure. On a whim, he turned on the radio. His favourite classical music station came on in splendid quadraphonic sound that ricocheted around the interior. He pushed the second button; it was his favourite news station. The third button brought his favourite talk station that kept him awake on long trips. The fourth button was set to his daughter's favourite rock station. In fact, every button was set to his specific tastes. The customer knew the car was smart, but was it psychic? No. The mechanic at Lexus had noted the radio settings on his trade-in and duplicated them on the new Lexus. The customer was delighted. This was his car now—through and through! No one told the mechanic to do it. It's just part of the Lexus philosophy: delight a customer and continue to delight that customer, and you will have a customer for life. What the mechanic did cost Lexus nothing. Not one red cent. Yet it solidified the relationship that could be worth high six figures to Lexus in customer lifetime value.

Studies show that going to extremes to keep customers happy, although sometimes costly, goes hand in hand with good financial performance. Satisfied customers come back again and again. Thus, in today's highly competitive marketplace, companies can well afford to lose money on one transaction if it helps to cement a profitable long-term customer relationship.

For companies interested in delighting customers, exceptional value and service are more than a set of policies or actions—they are a company-wide attitude, an important part of the overall company culture. American Express loves to tell stories about how its people have rescued customers from disasters ranging from civil wars to earthquakes, no matter what the cost. The company gives cash rewards of up to $1300 to "Great Performers," within the firm who move mountains to help customers when they have their travellers cheques stolen.

Four Seasons Hotels, long known for its outstanding service, tells its employees the story of Ron Dyment, a doorman in Toronto, who forgot to load a departing guest's briefcase into his taxi. The doorman called the guest, a lawyer in Washington, D.C., and learned that he desperately needed the briefcase for a meeting the following morning. Without first asking for approval from management, Dyment hopped on a plane and returned the briefcase. The company named Dyment Employee of the Year.

There's no simple formula for taking care of customers, but neither is it a mystery. According to the president of L.L. Bean, "A lot of people have fancy things to say about customer service...but it's just a day-in, day-out, ongoing, never-ending, unremitting, persevering, compassionate type of activity." For the companies that do it well, it's also very rewarding.

Sources: See Astrid Van Den Broek, "The Front-line: Marketers Are at Last Doing Something About Ensuring that Their Customer Service Lives Up to Their Brands' Advertising Promises," *Marketing Magazine*, May 21, 2001, www.marketingmag.ca/magazine/current/feature/article.jsp?content= 20010521_17693; Bill Kelley, "Five Companies That Do It Right—and Make It Pay," *Sales & Marketing Management*, April 1988, pp. 57–64; Patricia Sellers, "Companies That Serve You Best," Fortune, May 31, 1993, pp. 74–88; and Len Ellis, "Customer Loyalty," *Executive Excellence*, July 2001, pp. 13–14. The Lexus example was adapted from Denny Hatch and Ernie Schell, "Delight Your Customers," *Target Marketing*, April 2002, pp. 32–39.

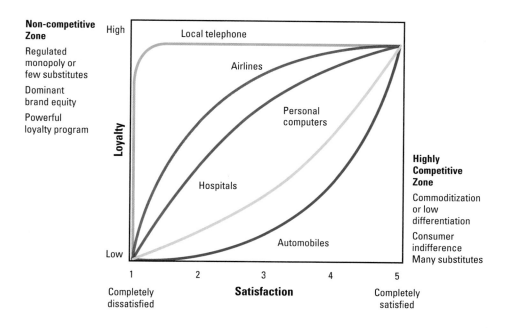

Figure 1.5   The relationship between customer satisfaction and customer loyalty

Source: Thomas O. Jones and W. Earl Sasser Jr., "Why Satisfied Customers Defect," *Harvard Business Review*, November–December 1995, p. 91. Copyright © 1997 by the President and Fellows of Harvard College; all rights reserved. Reprinted by permission of *Harvard Business Review*.

ideal situation for the protected or dominant firm. However, such firms may pay a high price for customer dissatisfaction in the long run. If a firm loses its monopoly, disaster can result. For example, when the telecommunications industry was deregulated in the 1990s, dissatisfied customers gleefully defected to the new competitors. Bell had to work hard to win some of them back. Thus, even highly successful companies must pay close attention to customer satisfaction and its relationship to customer loyalty.

Growing "Share of Customer"

Beyond simply retaining good customers, marketers want to constantly increase their *share of customer*—the share they get of the customer's purchasing in their product categories. They may do this by becoming the sole supplier of products the customer is currently buying. Or they may persuade the customer to purchase additional company products. Thus, banks want a greater "share of wallet." Supermarkets want to increase their "share of stomach." Car companies want a greater "share of garage" and airlines want a greater "share of travel."

One of the best ways to increase share of customer is through cross-selling. Cross-selling means getting more business from current customers of one product by selling them additional offerings. For example, *Reader's Digest,* a Canadian institution for more than 50 years, is Canada's most widely read monthly magazine, serving almost nine million readers per month. *Reader's Digest* sells a lot more than just magazines. Once it builds a connection with the consumer by delivering trusted content that has both a rational and emotional appeal, it sells them a host of products, ranging from books to life insurance.[23]

Building Customer Relationships and Customer Equity

We can now see the importance of not just finding customers, but of keeping and growing them as well. Customer relationship management is oriented toward the long term. Today's smart companies not only want to create customers, they want to "own" them for life, capture their customer lifetime value, and build overall customer equity.

Customer Equity

Customer equity

The total combined customer lifetime values of all of the company's customers.

The aim of customer relationship management is to produce high customer equity.[24] **Customer equity** is the total combined customer lifetime values of all of the company's customers. Clearly, the more loyal the firm's customers, the higher the firm's customer equity. Customer equity may be a better measure of a firm's performance than current sales or market share. Whereas sales and market share reflect the past, customer equity suggests the future. Consider Cadillac:[25]

> In the 1970s and 1980s, Cadillac had some of the most loyal customers in the industry. To an entire generation of car buyers, the name "Cadillac" defined North American luxury. Cadillac's share of the luxury car market reached a whopping 51 percent in 1976. Based on market share and sales, the brand's future looked rosy. However, measures of customer equity would have painted a bleaker picture. Cadillac customers were getting older (average age 60) and average customer lifetime value was falling. Many Cadillac buyers were on their last car. Thus, although Cadillac's market share was good, its customer equity was not. Compare this with BMW. Its more youthful and vigorous image didn't win BMW the early market share war. However, it did win BMW younger customers with higher customer lifetime values. The result: Cadillac now captures only about a 15 percent market share, lower than BMW's. And BMW's customer equity remains much higher—it has more customers with a higher

average customer lifetime value. Thus, market share is not the answer. We should care not just about current sales but also about future sales. Customer lifetime value and customer equity are the name of the game.

Customer Relationship Levels and Tools

Companies can build customer relationships at many levels, depending on the nature of the target market. At one extreme, a company with many low-margin customers may seek to develop *basic relationships* with them. For example, Procter & Gamble does not phone all of its Tide customers to get to know them personally. Instead, P&G creates relationships through brand-building advertising, sales promotions, a 1-800 customer response number, and its Tide FabricCare Network website (www.Tide.com).

At the other extreme, in markets with few customers and high margins, sellers want to create *full partnerships* with key customers. For example, P&G customer teams work closely with Wal-Mart, Safeway, and other large retailers. And Boeing partners with American Airlines, Delta, and other airlines in designing its airplanes that fully satisfy their requirements. In between these two extreme situations, other levels of customer relationships are appropriate. Today, most leading companies are developing customer loyalty and retention programs. Beyond offering consistently high value and satisfaction, marketers can use specific marketing tools to develop stronger bonds with consumers.[26] First, a company might build value and satisfaction by adding *financial benefits* to the customer relationship. For example, many companies now offer *frequency marketing programs* that reward customers who buy frequently or in large amounts. Airlines offer frequent-flier programs, hotels give room upgrades to their frequent guests, and supermarkets give patronage discounts.

A second approach is to add *social benefits* as well as financial benefits. For example, many companies sponsor *club marketing programs* that offer members special discounts and create member communities. For example:[27]

> Swiss watchmaker Swatch uses its club to cater to collectors, who on average buy nine of the company's quirky watches every year. "Swatch: The Club" members get additional chances to buy limited-edition Swatch specials. They also receive the *Swatch World Journal,* a magazine filled with Swatch-centric news from the four corners of the globe. And the club's website is the ultimate meeting place for Swatch enthusiasts. Swatch counts on enthusiastic word of mouth from club members as a boost to business. "Our members are like walking billboards," says the manager of Swatch's club, Trish O'Callaghan. "They love, live, and breathe our product. They are ambassadors for Swatch."

> Harley-Davidson sponsors the Harley Owners Group (H.O.G.), which gives Harley riders "an organized way to share their passion and show their pride." H.O.G. membership benefits include two magazines *(Hog Tales* and *Enthusiast*), a *H.O.G. Touring Handbook,* a roadside assistance program, a specially designed insurance program, theft reward service, a travel centre, and a "Fly & Ride" program enabling members to rent Harleys while on vacation. The company also maintains an extensive H.O.G. website, which offers information on H.O.G. chapters, rallies, events, and benefits. The worldwide club now numbers more than 1300 local chapters and 700 000 members.

A third approach to building customer relationships is to add *structural ties* as well as financial and social benefits. For example, a business marketer might supply customers with special equipment or computer linkages that help them manage their orders, payroll, or inventory. McKesson Corporation, a leading pharmaceutical wholesaler, has invested millions of dollars to set up direct computer links with drug manufacturers and an online system to help small pharmacies manage their inventories, their order entry, and their shelf space. FedEx offers weblinks to its customers to keep them from defecting to competitors such as UPS. Customers can use the website to arrange shipments and track the status of their FedEx packages anywhere in the world.

Building customer relationships: Harley-Davidson sponsors the Harley Owners Group (H.O.G.), which gives Harley owners "an organized way to share their passion and show their pride." The worldwide club now numbers more than 1300 local chapters and 700 000 members.

Customer relationship management means that marketers must focus on managing their customers as well as their products. At the same time, they don't want relationships with every customer. In fact, there are undesirable customers for every company. Ultimately, marketing involves attracting, keeping, and growing *profitable* customers.

Marketing Challenges in the New, "Connected" Millennium

As the world spins through the first decade of the twenty-first century, dramatic changes are occurring in the marketing arena. Richard Love of Hewlett-Packard observes: "The pace of change is so rapid that the ability to change has now become a competitive advantage." Yogi Berra summed it up more simply when he said, "The future ain't what it used to be." Technological advances, rapid globalization, and continuing social and economic shifts—all are causing profound changes in the marketplace. As the marketplace changes, so must those who serve it.

The major marketing developments today can be summed up in a single theme: *connecting*. Now, more than ever before, we are all connected to each other and to things near and far in the world around us. Moreover, we are connecting in new and different ways. Where it once took months to travel across Canada, we can now travel around the globe in only hours. Where it once took weeks to receive news about important world events, we now see them live on satellite broadcasts. Where it once took days for a letter to reach its destination, it now takes only moments to correspond by email.

In this section, we examine the major trends and forces that are changing the marketing landscape and challenging marketing strategy in this new, connected millennium. As shown in Figure 1.6 and discussed in the following pages, sweeping changes in connecting technologies are causing marketers to redefine how they connect with the marketplace. Marketers are rethinking their relationships with their customers, with marketing partners inside and outside the company, and with the world around them. We first look at the dramatic changes that are occurring in the connecting technologies. Then, we examine how these changes are affecting marketing connections.

Technologies for Connecting

The major force behind the new connectedness is explosive advances in computer, telecommunications, information, transportation, and other connecting technologies. The technology boom has created exciting new ways to learn about and track customers, and create products and services tailored to meet customer needs. Technology is helping companies to distribute products more efficiently and effectively, and communicate with customers in large groups or one-to-one. For example, through video conferencing, marketing researchers at a company's headquarters in Vancouver can look in on focus groups in Halifax or Paris without ever stepping onto a plane. With only a few clicks of a mouse button, a direct marketer can tap into online data services to learn anything from what car you drive to what you read to what flavour of ice cream you prefer.

Using today's powerful computers, marketers create detailed databases and use them to target individual consumers with offers designed to meet their specific needs and buying patterns. With a new wave of communication and advertising tools—

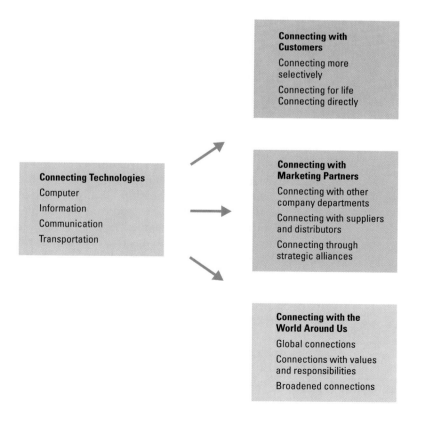

Figure 1.6 Today's marketing connections

Explosive advances in connecting technologies have created exciting new ways to learn about customers and to create tailored products, distribute them more effectively, and communicate with customers in large groups or one-to-one.

ranging from cell phones, fax machines, CD-ROMs, and interactive TV to video kiosks at airports and shopping malls—marketers can zero in on selected customers with carefully targeted messages. Through electronic commerce, customers can design, order, and pay for products and services without ever leaving home, and can receive their purchases in under twenty-four hours. From virtual reality displays that test new products to online virtual stores that sell them, the technology boom is affecting every aspect of marketing.

The Internet

Internet

The vast and burgeoning global web of computer networks with no central management or ownership

Perhaps the most dramatic new technology driving the connected age is the *Internet*. The **Internet** is a vast and burgeoning global web of computer networks with no central management or ownership. Today, the Internet links individuals and businesses of all types to each other and to information around the world.

The Internet has been hailed as the technology behind a New Economy. It allows anytime, anywhere connections to information, entertainment, and communication. Companies are using the Internet to build closer relationships with customers and marketing partners and to sell and distribute their products more efficiently and effectively. Beyond competing in traditional marketplaces, they now have access to exciting new marketspaces.

Internet usage surged in the early 1990s with the development of the user-friendly World Wide Web. In North America alone, it is projected that 60 million households will be connected by the year 2003. Canada continues to lead North America in connectivity. More than 60 percent of Canadians are now online. By comparison, only 52 percent of the U.S. population is online. Despite this lead in connectivity, Canada's consumers continue to purchase online much less readily than their counterparts across the border. According to Internet consulting firm IDC, only 17 percent of the Canadian population purchased online, far less than the 27 percent of the U.S. population that purchased online in 2001. Nonetheless, ecommerce in Canada continues to grow. Canada had almost $40 billion worth of ecommerce in 2001—an increase of 69 percent over 2000. However, large firms dominate the ecommerce sphere and Canada's small- and medium-sized enterprises continue to lag behind their U.S. counterparts in ebusiness adoption.[28]

The Internet is truly a worldwide phenomenon—the number of Internet users worldwide is expected to approach 1 billion by 2004.[29] This growing and diverse Internet population means that all kinds of people are now going to the Web for information and to buy products and services. Notes one analyst: "In just [a few short years], the Net has gone from a playground for nerds into a vast communications and trading centre where…people swap information and do deals around the world.... More than 400 000 companies have hung www.shingle.com atop their digital doorways with the notion that being anywhere on the Net means selling virtually everywhere."[30]

Companies of all types are now attempting to snare new customers on the Web. Many traditional "bricks-and-mortar" companies have now become "click-and-mortar" companies. They are venturing online in an effort to attract new customers and build stronger customer relationships. The Internet has also spawned an entirely new breed of "click-only" companies—the so-called "dot-coms." (For example, justwhiteshirts.com operates a successful online men's clothing store.) During the Web frenzy of the late 1990s, dot-coms popped up everywhere, selling everything from books, toys, and CDs to furniture, home mortgages, and 50 kg bags of dog food via the Internet. The frenzy cooled during the "dot-com meltdown" of 2000, when many poorly conceived etailers and other Web start-ups went out of business. Today, despite its turbulent start, online consumer buying is growing at a healthy rate, and many of the dot-com survivors face promising futures.[31]

If consumer ecommerce looks promising, business-to-business ecommerce is just plain booming. Business-to-business transactions online are expected to reach $5.6 trillion in 2005, compared with only $139 billion in consumer purchases. By 2005, more than 500 000 businesses will engage in ecommerce as buyers, sellers, or both. It seems that almost every business—from garage-based start-ups to established giants such as IBM, Nortel, The Bay, Air Canada, and many others—has moved quickly to exploit the power of the Internet.[32]

Thus, changes in connecting technologies are providing exciting new opportunities for marketers. We will explore the impact of the new Internet age in more detail in Chapter 3. Here, we look at the ways these changes are affecting how companies connect with their consumers, customers, marketing partners, and the world around us (see Figure 1.6 on page 25).

Connecting with Customers

We've already discussed the critical importance of customer relationship management. The most profound new developments in marketing involve the ways in which today's companies are connecting with their consumers and customers. Yesterday's companies focused on mass marketing to all comers at arm's length. Today's companies are building more lasting and more direct relationships with these carefully targeted customers.

Connecting with More Carefully Selected Customers

Few firms today still practise true *mass marketing*—selling in a standardized way to any customer who comes along. Today, most marketers realize that they don't want to connect with just any customers. Instead, most are targeting fewer, potentially more profitable customers.

The world is a "salad bowl" of diverse ethnic, cultural, social, and locational groups. The greater diversity has meant greater market fragmentation. In response, most firms have moved from mass marketing to segmented marketing, in which they target carefully chosen submarkets or even individual buyers. "One-to-one marketing" has become the order of the day for some marketers. They build huge customer databases containing rich information on individual customer preferences and purchases. Then they mine these databases to gain insights by which they can "mass-customize" their offerings to deliver greater value to individual buyers.

At the same time that companies are finding imaginative new ways to deliver more value to customers, they are also beginning to assess carefully the value *of* customers to the firm. They want to connect only with customers that they can serve profitably. In a process called *selective relationship management,* many companies now use customer profitability analysis to weed out losing customers and target the winning ones for pampering. Once they identify profitable customers, firms can create attractive offers and special handling to capture them and earn their loyalty.

But what should the company do with unprofitable customers? If it can't turn them into profitable ones, it may even want to "fire" customers that are too unreasonable or that cost more to serve than they are worth. Firing customers can be a dangerous tactic, however, especially in a country like Canada where markets are relatively small. Thus, some companies are working to improve customer profitability:

> RBC prides itself on having a relationship management strategy for each and every one of its customers. Tracking such facets of customers as their life cycle stage, their likelihood of switching to another financial institution, their channel preference, and their profitability, RBC has been able to improve the average profitability of its customers. Some of its programs are very sophisticated; others deceivingly simple. RBC was highly successful in increasing its mortgage business just by sending targeted mailings to young adults who had an apartment number in their mailing address. An apartment number indicated that these individuals would soon be in the market for their first home. RBC not only offered these young people competitive mortgage rates, it also provided them with useful information about how to buy a first home.

Connecting for a Customer's Lifetime

Just as companies are being more selective about which customers they choose to serve, they are serving those they choose in a deeper, more lasting way. As we discussed earlier, the goal is shifting from making a profit on each sale to making long-term profits by managing the lifetime value of a customer and the firm's total customer equity. Marketers now spend less time figuring out how to increase "share of market" and more time trying to grow "share of customer." They offer greater variety to current customers and train employees to cross-sell and up-sell to market more products and services to existing customers. For example, Chapters.ca began as an online bookseller to complement Chapters' bricks-and-mortar retail operations. Now, after its merger with Indigo Books, Chapters.Indigo.ca also offers music, videos, and gifts. In addition, based on each customer's purchase history, the company recommends related books, CDs, or videos that might be of interest. In this way, Chapters.Indigo.ca captures a greater share of each customer's leisure and entertainment budget.

Connecting Directly

Beyond connecting more deeply with their customers, many companies are also taking advantage of new technologies that let them connect more *directly*. In fact, direct marketing is booming. Customers can now buy virtually all products without even stepping into a store—by telephone, mail-order catalogues, kiosks, and ecommerce. Business purchasing agents routinely shop on the Web for items ranging from standard office supplies to high-priced, high-tech computer equipment.

Complete your GoalMap and you could WIN $10,000 towards an investment·!

. . . and towards your future!

Winning $10,000 can help you kick start your future goals. Use it to:
- Invest it short-term for things like a car, home down payment or travel plans
- Invest it long-term in an RRSP for your retirement
- The choice is yours!

RBC Royal Bank®. **Tell us what you want, and we'll help you get it.**

Relationship management: RBC's GoalMap helps track the plans and dreams of its customers. Using a PIN code, customers register their goals, indicate a time horizon, and identify the investment strategy they are most comfortable with. The result: RBC offers effective, targeted service for each customer.

Some companies sell *only* via direct channels—firms such as Dell Computer, Expedia, Lands' End (www.landsend.com), 1-800-Flowers, and Amazon, to name a few. Other companies use direct connections as a supplement to their other communications and distribution channels. For example, Procter & Gamble sells Pampers disposable diapers through retailers, supported by millions of dollars of mass-media advertising. However, P&G uses its www.pampers.com website to build relationships with young parents by providing information and advice on everything from diapering to baby care and child development. Similarly, you can't buy crayons from the Crayola website (www.crayola.com). However, you can find out how to remove crayon marks from your prized carpeting or freshly painted walls.

Some marketers have hailed direct marketing as the "marketing model of the new millennium." They envision a day when all buying and selling will involve direct connections between companies and their customers. Others, although agreeing that direct marketing will play a growing and important role, see it as just one more way to approach the marketplace. We will take a closer look at the world of direct marketing in more detail in Chapter 8.

Connections with Marketing Partners

In addition to *customer relationship management*, marketers must also be good at **partner relationship management**. In these increasingly connected times, major changes are occurring in how marketers connect with important partners both inside and outside the company jointly to bring greater value to customers.

Connecting Inside the Company

Partner relationship management
Working closely with partners in other company departments and outside the company to jointly bring greater value to customers.

Traditionally, marketers have been charged with understanding customers and representing customer needs to different company departments, which then acted upon these needs. The old thinking was that marketing is done only by marketing, sales, and customer support people. However, in today's connected world, marketing no longer has sole ownership of customer interactions. Every functional area can interact with customers, especially electronically. The new thinking is that every employee must be customer focused. David Packard, co-founder of Hewlett-Packard, wisely said: "Marketing is far too important to be left only to the marketing department."[33]

Today, rather than letting each department go its own way, firms are linking all departments in the cause of creating customer value. Rather than assigning only sales and marketing people to customers, they are forming cross-functional customer teams. For example, Procter & Gamble assigns "customer development teams" to each of its major retailer accounts. These teams—consisting of sales and marketing people, operations and logistics specialists, market and financial analysts, and others—coordinate the efforts of many P&G departments toward serving the retailer and helping it to be more successful.

Connecting with Outside Partners

Rapid changes are also occurring in how marketers connect with their external partners—suppliers, channel partners, and even competitors. Most companies today are networked, relying heavily on partnerships with other firms.

Supply Chain Management   Marketing channels consist of distributors, retailers, and others who connect the company to its buyers. The *supply chain* describes a longer channel, stretching from raw materials to components to final products that are carried to final buyers. For example, the supply chain for personal computers consists of suppliers of computer chips and other components, the computer manufacturer, and the distributors, retailers, and others who sell the computers to businesses and final customers. Each member of the supply chain creates and captures only a portion of the total value it generates.

Through *supply chain management*, many companies today are strengthening their connections with partners all along the supply chain. They know that their fortunes rest not only on how well they perform. Success also rests on how well their entire supply chain performs against competitors' supply chains. They don't just treat suppliers as vendors and distributors as customers. They treat both as partners in delivering customer value. For example, Wal-Mart works with such suppliers as Procter & Gamble, Rubbermaid, and Black & Decker to streamline logistics and reduce joint distribution costs, resulting in lower prices to consumers.

New customer connections: P&G uses its www.pampers.com website to build relationships with young parents by providing information and advice on diapering, baby care, and even child development.

Strategic Alliances   Beyond managing the supply chain, today's companies are also discovering that they need strategic partners to be effective. In the new, more competitive global environment, going it alone is going out of style. *Strategic alliances* are booming across the entire spectrum of industries and services. For example, Dell Computer recently ran advertisements telling how it partners with Microsoft and Intel to provide customized ebusiness solutions. The ads ask: "Why do many corporations choose Windows running on Dell PowerEdge servers with Intel Pentium processors to power their ebusiness solutions?" The answer: "At Dell, Microsoft and Intel, we specialize in solving the impossible."

Companies need to give careful thought to finding partners who might complement their strengths and offset their weaknesses. Well-managed alliances can have a huge impact on sales and profits. A recent study found that one in every four dollars earned by the top 1000 North American companies flows from alliances, double the rate in the early 1990s. As Jim Kelly, CEO at UPS, puts it: "The old adage 'If you can't beat 'em, join 'em' is being replaced by 'Join 'em and you can't be beat.'"[34]

Connecting with the World Around Us

As they are redefining their relationships with customers and partners, marketers are taking a fresh look at the ways in which they connect with the broader world around them. Here we look at trends toward increasing globalization, more concern for social environmental responsibility, and greater use of marketing by non-profit and public sector organizations.

Strategic alliances: Dell recently ran ads telling how it partners with Microsoft and Intel to provide customized ebusiness solutions. "At Dell, Microsoft and Intel, we specialize in solving the impossible."

Global Connections

In an increasingly smaller world, many marketers are now connected *globally* with their customers and marketing partners. The world economy has undergone radical change over the past two decades. Geographical and cultural distances have shrunk with the advent of jet planes, fax machines, world television satellite broadcasts, global Internet hookups, and other technical advances. This has allowed companies to greatly expand their geographical market coverage, purchasing, and manufacturing. The result is a vastly more complex marketing environment for both companies and consumers.

Today, almost every company, large or small, is touched in some way by global competition. While a neighbourhood florist buys its flowers from Mexican nurseries, a Vancouver electronics manufacturer competes in its home markets with giant Japanese and American rivals. A fledgling Internet retailer finds itself receiving orders from all over the world, while a Canadian consumer-goods producer introduces new products into emerging markets abroad.

Both Canadian and American firms have been challenged in their home markets by the skilful marketing of European and Asian multinationals. Companies such as Toyota, Nokia, Airbus, Siemens, Nestlé, Sony, and Samsung have often outperformed their North American rivals. However, Canadian companies in a wide range of industries have found new opportunities abroad. RBC, Nortel, SNC-Lavalin, Labatt, BCE, Imperial Oil, Alcan, and Bombardier have developed truly global operations, making and selling their products worldwide. The North American Free Trade Agreement, signed in 1994, provided a boost to Canadian exporters, and even though the U.S. is still our largest trading partner, Canadian firms market their products throughout the globe.

Similarly, U.S. companies in a wide range of industries have found new opportunities abroad. Coca-Cola, General Motors, ExxonMobil, IBM, General Electric, DuPont, Motorola, and dozens of other American companies have developed truly global operations, making and selling their products worldwide. Even MTV has joined the elite of global brands, delivering localized versions of its pulse-thumping fare to teens in 140 countries around the globe (see Real Marketing 1.3).

Today, companies are not only trying to sell more of their locally produced goods in international markets, but are also buying more components and supplies abroad. For example, Alfred Sung, one of Canada's top fashion designers, may choose cloth woven from Australian wool with designs printed in Italy. He will design a dress and fax the drawing to a Hong Kong agent, who will place the order with a Chinese factory. Finished dresses will be air-freighted to Montreal and New York, where they will be redistributed to department and specialty stores across North America.

Thus, managers in countries around the world are increasingly taking a global, not just local, view of the company's industry, competitors, and opportunities. They are asking: What is global marketing? How does it differ from domestic marketing? How do global competitors and forces affect our business? To what extent should we "go global"? Many companies are forming strategic alliances with foreign companies, even competitors, who serve as suppliers or marketing partners. Winning companies in the future may well be those that have built the best global networks.

Connections with Our Values and Social Responsibilities

Marketers are re-examining their connections with social values and responsibilities and with the very Earth that sustains us. As the worldwide consumerism and environmentalism movements mature, today's marketers are being called upon to take greater responsibility for the social and environmental impact of their actions.

REAL MARKETING

1.3   MTV Global: Music Is the Universal Language

Some say love is the universal language. But for MTV, the universal language is *music*. In 1981, MTV began offering its unique brand of programming for young music lovers across the United States. The channel's quirky but pulse-thumping line-up of shows soon attracted a large audience in its targeted 12-to-34 age group. MTV quickly established itself as America's youth-culture network, offering up "everything young people care about." With success in the United States secured, MTV went global in 1986, selling a few hours of programming to Japan's Asahi network. A short time later, in 1987, it launched MTV Europe, and the network has experienced phenomenal global growth ever since.

MTV now offers programming in 140 countries, including Canada, Brazil, China, France, Germany, Holland, India, Italy, Japan, Korea, Latin America, Poland, Russia, Southeast Asia, Spain, Taiwan, Hong Kong, the United Kingdom, and Germany. The result of this global expansion? Today, MTV reaches twice as many people around the world as CNN, and eight out of ten MTV viewers live outside of the United States. All together, MTV reaches into an astounding 384 million households in 19 different languages on 33 different channels and 17 websites.

What is the secret to MTV's roaring international success? Of course, it offers viewers around the globe plenty of what made it so popular in the United States. Tune in to the network in Paris, or Beijing, or Moscow, or Tierra del Fuego, or anywhere else and you'll see all of the elements that make it uniquely MTV anywhere in the world—the global MTV brand symbols, fast-paced format, vee-jays, rockumentaries, and music, music, music. But rather than just offering a carbon copy of its U.S. programming to international viewers, MTV carefully localizes its fare. Each channel serves up a mix that includes 70 percent local programming tailored to the specific tastes on viewers in local markets. (To see the Canadian site go to www.MTVCanada.com.) A *Business Week* analyst notes:

[MTV is] shrewd enough to realize that while the world's teens want American music, they really want the local stuff, too. So, MTV's producers and veejays scour their local markets for the top talent. The result is an endless stream of overnight sensations that keep MTV's global offerings fresh. Just over a year ago, for example, Avril Lavigne was just another teenager from Napanee,

Ontario. Today, partly due to MTV exposure, she is an international sensation.

[MTV's] policy of 70 percent local content has resulted in some of the network's most creative shows, such as MTV Brazil's month-long *Rockgol*, a soccer championship that pits Brazilian musicians against record industry executives. In Russia, the locally produced *Twelve Angry Viewers* was voted one of Russia's top three talk programs. In a colourful studio amid bright blue steps and large green cushions, a dozen teens watch and discuss the latest videos. Periodically, they break into spontaneous dance or pop one another over the head with inflatable lollipops. Okay, it's not Chekhov. But Russian groups beg to be featured on it.

Ceding so much control to local channels does result in the occasional misstep. While watching MTV in Taiwan, [MTV executives were] aghast to see nude wrestling. That was one time [they] had to intervene.

MTV's unique blend of international and local programming is not only popular, it's also highly profitable. The network's hold on a young, increasingly wealthy population makes its programming especially popular with advertisers. Altogether, its mix of local and international content, combined with early entry in international markets, makes it tough to beat. "MTV Networks International makes buckets of money year after year from a potent combination of cable subscriber fees, advertising, and, increasingly, new media," concludes the analyst. "Revenues at MTV Networks International increased 19 percent [last year]...while operating profits grew a hefty 50 percent. They are expected to more than double by 2004." Meanwhile, the competition struggles just to break even. VIVA, MTV's strongest competitor in Europe, has yet to turn a profit.

Thus, in only two decades, MTV has joined the ranks of the global brand elite, alongside such icons as Coke, Levi's, and Sony. Concludes the analyst: "MTV's version of globalization rocks."

Sources: Excerpts from Kerry Capell, "MTV's World: Mando-Pop. Mexican Hip Hop. Russian Rap. It's All Fueling the Biggest Global Channel," *Business Week*, February 18, 2002, pp. 81–84. Also see Lynn Elber, "US TV Networks Expand Interests Overseas," *Marketing News*, November 7, 1994, p. 7; Alkman, Granitsas, "MTV Is Launching a 24-Hour Network in Indonesian Cities," *Wall Street Journal*, March 13, 2002, p. B7; the MTV Worldwide website, www.mtv.com/mtvinternational; and the Viacom corporate website, www.viacom.com.

Corporate ethics and social responsibility have become hot topics for almost every business arena. And few companies can ignore the renewed and very demanding environmental movement.

The social responsibility and environmental movements will place even stricter demands on companies in the future. Some companies resist these movements, budging only when forced by legislation or consumer outcries. More forward-looking companies, however, readily accept their responsibilities to the world around them. They view socially responsible actions as an opportunity to do well by doing good. They seek ways to profit by serving the best long-run interests of their customers and communities. Some companies—such as Mountain Equipment Co-op, the Royal Bank, Saturn, and The Body Shop—are practising "caring capitalism" and distinguishing themselves by being more civic-minded and caring. They are building social responsibility and action into their company value and mission statements. For example, Ben & Jerry's mission statement challenges all employees, from top management to ice cream scoopers in each store, to include concern for individual and community welfare in their day-to-day decisions.[35]

Broadening Connections

Many different kinds of organizations are using marketing to connect with customers and other important constituencies. In the past, marketing has been most widely applied in the for-profit business sector. In recent years, however, marketing also has become a major component in the strategies of many non-profit organizations.

According to the Canadian Centre for Philanthropy, Canada has over 80 000 registered charities and non-profit organizations. These range from small community-based organizations like the Brockville Volunteer Firefighters Association to large national charities like the United Way and the Heart and Stroke Foundation. They also include churches, hospitals, museums, symphony orchestras, and universities. With cutbacks in government funding, competition for donors is intensifying and non-profit organizations are adapting more and more marketing practices. The Canadian Landmine Foundation, for example, used a hard-hitting TV campaign and developed events such as the "Night of a Thousand Dinners." They designate one night each year where individuals host dinner parties to raise funds for the Adopt-a-Minefield program. The program has been so successful that over 30 countries now participate in this Canadian initiative. Rethink Breast Cancer, which was formed in 2001 to raise awareness among a younger audience while raising funds for research and programs, created an innovative public service announcement to get the important message about breast health across in a new way. Realizing that competition for young people's attention is fierce, Rethink knew they had to have a high-impact spot that would break through the clutter. By creating a PSA that was groundbreaking and funny, the exposure of the campaign would go beyond the donated television ad space and reach people through the media and person-to-person conversations. The resulting campaign featured the message, "If men had breasts, they'd really appreciate them. Take care of yours."[36]

The Arthritis Society, Care Canada, and other charities are turning to the datamining techniques and donor lifetime value analysis used by for-profit firms. Kelly Ducharme, database manager at Care Canada's Ottawa headquarters, notes that datamining helps non-profits target their fundraising efforts while providing donors with more accountability.

Keeping donors active is as important for non-profits as it is for firms to retain their customers. Experts note that it costs about $13 a name to acquire a new donor, so many non-profits are starting to realize that it's cheaper to get incremental revenue out of an existing donor than to try to find a new one.[37]

Even government agencies have shown an increased interest in marketing. The Canadian Army has a marketing plan to attract recruits, Transport Canada has a

Rethink Breast Cancer uses its webpage and a powerful new TV campaign to create new attitudes about this disease.

program to discourage drunk driving, and Health and Welfare Canada has long-standing social marketing campaigns to discourage smoking, excessive drinking, and drug use. Even once-stodgy Canada Post has developed innovative marketing programs to increase use of its priority mail services.

Thus, it seems that every type of organization can connect through marketing. The continued growth of non-profit and public-sector marketing presents new and exciting challenges for marketing managers.

The New, Connected World of Marketing

So, today, smart marketers of all kinds are taking advantage of new opportunities for connecting with their customers, their marketing partners, and the world around them. Table 1.1 compares the old marketing thinking to the new. The old marketing thinking saw marketing as little more than selling or advertising. It viewed marketing as customer acquisition rather than customer care. It emphasized trying to make a profit on each sale rather than trying to profit by managing customer lifetime value. It also concerned itself with trying to sell products rather than to understand, create, communicate, and deliver real value to customers.

Fortunately, this old marketing thinking is now giving way to newer ways of thinking. Modern marketing companies are improving their customer knowledge and customer connections. They are targeting profitable customers, then finding innovative ways to capture and keep these customers. They are forming more direct connections with customers and building lasting customer relationships. (See Real Marketing 1.4 to discover how two commerce students used relationship marketing in their role as co-chairs of the Queen's Marketing Association Conference.)

Using more targeted media and integrating their marketing communications, they are delivering meaningful and consistent messages through every customer contact. They are employing more technologies, such as video conferencing, sales automation software, and the Internet, intranets, and extranets. They see their suppliers and distributors as partners, not adversaries. In sum, they are forming new kinds of connections for delivering superior value to their customers.

We will explore all of these developments in more detail in later chapters. For now, we must recognize that marketing will continue to change dramatically as we progress through the early years of the twenty-first century. The new millennium offers many exciting opportunities for forward-thinking marketers.

Table 1.1   Marketing Connections in Transition

Old Marketing Thinking	New Marketing Thinking
Connections with Customers	
Be sales and product centred	Be market and customer centred
Practise mass marketing	Target selected market segments or individuals
Focus on products and sales	Focus on customer satisfaction and value
Make sales to customers	Develop customer relationships
Get new customers	Keep old customers
Grow share of market	Grow share of customer
Serve any customer	Serve profitable customers, "fire" losing ones
Communicate through mass media	Connect with customers directly
Make standardized products	Develop customized products
Connections with Marketing Partners	
Leave customer satisfaction and value to sales and marketing	Enlist all departments in the cause of customer satisfaction and value
Go it alone	Partner with other firms
Connections with the World Around Us	
Market locally	Market locally *and* globally
Assume profit responsibility	Assume social and environmental responsibility
Marketing only for corporations	Market for non-profits
Conduct commerce in marketplaces	Conduct ecommerce in marketspaces

REAL MARKETING

1.4   Daniel Alter and William Forbes— Queen's Marketing Association Conference (QMAC)

Daniel Alter and William Forbes graduated from Queen's University in 2003 from the Bachelor of Commerce program. While at Queen's they worked together as co-chairs of the 2003 Queen's Marketing Association Conference (QMAC). Their association with the conference not only taught them a lot about marketing, it also allowed them to practise marketing. As you will read below, they came to understand the significance of relationship marketing, the importance of maintaining brand consistency and quality while undertaking a change initiative, and the necessity of treating sponsors with integrity and fairness.

QMAC has established itself as the premier student-run marketing conference in Canada over its 18-year history. Each January the conference brings 150 enthusiastic young marketers from 20 universities across Canada together with 13 distinguished speakers and over 20 corporate partner firms.

Daniel Alter and William Forbes.

Daniel was a member of the QMAC executive for all four years of his university career, progressively taking on more responsibility. William joined the executive in 2002 and quickly demonstrated his desire to lead. As co-chairs for QMAC 2003, Daniel and William were responsible for leading a team of ten students in the organization, planning, and execution of the conference.

In planning for the conference, Daniel and William faced a difficult decision: to make incremental improvements on the recent three-day event or to take on the challenge of expanding the conference to four days. After evaluating the impact of each option on the conference's student delegates and corporate partners, QMAC's key stakeholder groups, the decision was made to expand the conference to a four-day event.

Having made this decision, QMAC needed a marketing plan that would facilitate the expansion of the conference. Daniel and William recognized the key differences in the communication strategies that would be required to market the event to the two different stakeholder groups, as well as the importance of maintaining the level of quality that both groups have come to expect.

QMAC's most significant source of funding is from its corporate partners. Therefore, the first task in facilitating the expansion was to communicate to existing partners the value that would be created by expanding the conference. Existing partners were offered first rights on each new event that was created as a result of the expansion. This demonstrated QMAC's commitment to the relationships it had established with sponsor firms. In evaluating new partnerships, QMAC segmented potential firms into two distinct categories: companies that participate in the conference to gain exposure to students who they wish to recruit as future employees, and firms whose aim is to turn conference delegates into consumers of their products.

Daniel and William recognized an opportunity for growth in the recruiting segment. In order to effectively target companies within this segment, QMAC needed to offer customized and interactive events that suited the needs of each company. One example of this customization strategy was QMAC's approach to prospective partner Frito Lay Canada. QMAC's sponsorship team researched the snack food company and designed the Frito Lay Snack Break, a new event that created synergies between the conference's mission and the company's objectives, which included interacting with top marketing students.

In order to attract high-quality student delegates, QMAC needed to deliver on its mission "to create an enjoyable and educational experience for its delegates, while providing them with recruiting opportunities through a high level of interaction with its valued corporate guests." To further differentiate itself from other student conferences, QMAC created the QMAC Challenge.

The QMAC Challenge is a national marketing competition in which QMAC delegates from across Canada submit marketing plans for a specified product. QMAC 2003 featured the first annual challenge, which was to create a launch plan for a new Molson beer. From the submitted plans, four finalists were chosen to present at the conference and be judged by Dan O'Neill, President and CEO of Molson Inc. This new event exemplifies QMAC's ability to create a venue for student delegates to showcase themselves to potential employers.

One last major concern Daniel and William held about the expansion was maintaining the high quality of service provided by the conference. Through careful planning, the QMAC Executive was able to ensure that the conference's equity was not diluted by the additional demands on the executive's resources. To ensure that the quality was kept to a high standard, Daniel and William constantly challenged themselves and their team to achieve a high level of consistency and detail in all of their work. Over the twelve-month planning period, the executive united in the pursuit of QMAC's vision that drove them to produce an event of incomparable quality. The commitment of the executive created an environment where all ideas were challenged and only the strongest survived through to implementation.

Through their efforts the QMAC executive was able to increase their overall funding by $15 000 and build on the already high quality of the conference. The conference, held in January 2003, was a great success. The immense planning process completed by the student organizers did not go unnoticed. Walt Macnee, President of MasterCard Canada, spoke at the event and had this comment: "I was very impressed with the level of organization, especially the fact that it is fully managed by students." Another speaker, brand coach Ted Matthews, stated, "I have been to many, many conferences in my career and never at one that was better run."

Through their experience as co-chairs, Daniel and William took away two very important lessons: that an organization should innovate when it can and not when it has to, and that any innovation needs to be carefully planned and thoroughly analyzed before it can be set in motion. If one couples these two principles with commitment and passion, great success can be achieved.

Looking Back: Reviewing the Concepts

Today's successful companies—whether large or small, for-profit or non-profit, domestic or global—share a strong customer focus and a heavy commitment to marketing. Many people think of marketing as only selling or advertising. But marketing combines many activities—marketing research, product development, distribution, pricing, advertising, personal selling, and others—designed to sense, serve, and satisfy consumer needs while meeting the organization's goals. The goal of marketing is to build and manage enough profitable customers for the company's current output. Marketing seeks to attract new customers by promising superior value and to keep current customers by delivering satisfaction.

Marketing operates within a dynamic global environment. Rapid changes can quickly make yesterday's winning strategies obsolete. In the twenty-first century, marketers will face many new challenges and opportunities. To be successful, companies will have to be strongly market focused.

1. **Define what marketing is and discuss its core concepts.**

   Marketing is a social and managerial process by which individuals and groups obtain what they need and want through creating and exchanging products and value with others. The core concepts of marketing are *needs, wants,* and *demands; marketing offers (products, services,* and *experiences); value* and *satisfaction; exchange, transactions,* and *relationships;* and *markets. Wants* are the form assumed by human needs when shaped by culture and individual personality. When backed by buying power, wants become *demands.*

   Companies address needs by putting forth a *value proposition,* a set of benefits that they promise to consumers to satisfy their needs. The value proposition is fulfilled through a *marketing offer*—some combination of products, services, information, or experiences offered to a market to satisfy a need or want.

2. **Define marketing management and compare the five marketing management orientations.**

   Marketing management is the art and science of choosing target markets and building profitable relationships with them. This involves getting, keeping, and growing customers through creating, delivering, and communicating superior customer value. Marketing management involves more than simply finding enough customers for the company's current output. Marketing is at times also concerned with changing or even reducing demand. Simply put, marketing management is *customer management* and *demand management.*

   Marketing management can adopt one of five competing market orientations. The *production concept* holds that consumers will favour products that are available and highly affordable. The *product concept* holds that consumers favour products that offer the most in quality, performance, and innovative features; thus, little promotional effort is required. The *selling concept* holds that consumers will not buy enough of the organization's products unless it undertakes a large-scale selling and promotion effort. The *marketing concept* holds that achieving organizational goals depends on determining the needs and wants of target markets and delivering the desired satisfactions more effectively and efficiently than competitors do. The *societal marketing concept* holds that generating customer satisfaction *and* long-run societal well-being are the keys to achieving both the company's goals and its responsibilities.

3. **Discuss customer relationship management and strategies for building lasting customer relationships.**

   Narrowly defined, *customer relationship management (CRM)* involves managing detailed information about individual customers and carefully managing customer "touchpoints" in order to maximize customer loyalty.

More broadly, however, customer relationship management is the overall process of building and maintaining profitable customer relationships by delivering superior customer value and satisfaction. The aim of customer relationship management is to produce high *customer equity,* the total combined customer lifetime values of all of the company's customers.

The key to building lasting relationships is the creation of superior *customer value* and *satisfaction,* and companies need to understand the determinants of these important elements. Faced with a growing range of choices of products and services, consumers base their buying decisions on their perceptions of *value. Customer perceived value* is the difference between total customer value and total customer cost. Customers will usually choose the offer that maximizes their perceived value. *Customer satisfaction* results when a company's performance has fulfilled a buyer's expectations. Customers are dissatisfied if performance is below expectations, satisfied if performance equals expectations, and delighted if performance exceeds expectations.

Satisfied customers buy more, are less price sensitive, talk favourably about the company, and remain loyal longer. Companies not only strive to gain customers but, perhaps more importantly, to retain and grow "share of customer." Companies must decide the level at which they want to build relationships with different market segments and individual customers, ranging from basic relationships to full partnerships. Which is best depends on a customer's lifetime value relative to the costs required to attract and keep that customer.

Today's marketers use a number of specific marketing tools to develop stronger bonds with customers by adding *financial* and *social benefits* or *structural ties.*

4. **Analyze the major challenges facing marketers heading into the new, "connected" millennium.**

Dramatic changes in the marketplace are creating many marketing opportunities and challenges. Major marketing developments can be summed up in a single theme: connecting. The explosive growth in connecting technologies—computer, information, telecommunications, and transportation technologies—has created an exciting New Economy, filled with new ways for marketers to learn about and serve consumers, in large groups or one-to-one. Marketers are rapidly redefining how they connect with their customers, with their marketing partners, and with the world around them. They are choosing their customers more carefully and developing closer, more lasting, and more direct connections with them. Realizing that going it alone is going out of style, they are connecting more closely with other company departments and with other firms in an integrated effort to bring more value to customers. They are taking a fresh look at the ways in which they connect with the broader world, resulting in increased globalization, growing attention to social and environmental responsibilities, and greater use of marketing by non-profit and public-sector organizations. The new, connected millennium offers exciting possibilities for forward-thinking marketers.

Reviewing the Key Terms

Customer equity   22
Customer lifetime value   17
Customer perceived value   18
Customer relationship
   management   16
Customer satisfaction   19
Demands   7
Demarketing   12
Exchange   10

Internet   26
Market   10
Marketing   6
Marketing concept   13
Marketing offer   7
Marketing management   11
Needs   6
Partnership relationship
   management   29

Product concept   12
Production concept   12
Selling concept   13
Societal marketing concept   15
Transaction   10
Wants   7

Discussing the Concepts

1. In your own words, what does the term *marketing* mean?

2. Marketing is managing profitable customer relationships. Discuss the concept of customer value and how it relates to successful marketing.

3. The value proposition is fulfilled through a marketing offer. Pick a company whose product you've recently purchased. Describe the company's value proposition and a marketing offer.

4. Explain the relationships between customer value, satisfaction, and quality.

5. Briefly discuss the differences between the marketing concept and the production, product, and selling concepts. Which concepts are easier to adopt in the short run? Which concept offers the best chance of long-run success? Why?

6. Highly satisfied customers produce several benefits for a company. List some of these benefits. How do companies *delight* customers? How do companies grow their *share of customer*?

7. Today, most leading companies are developing customer-loyalty-and-retention programs. List and describe three ways marketers can use marketing tools to develop stronger bonds with consumers.

8. The major marketing trends today can be summed up in a single theme: *connecting*. List and discuss three important connections made possible by technology. Give specific examples of companies taking advantage of such connections.

Applying the Concepts

1. Few companies have done as much to apply the societal marketing concept as Mountain Equipment Co-op (MEC) (www.mec.ca). The company's founders made a strong and sincere commitment to a wide range of ecological and social causes.

   - Visit the MEC website. What impresses you most? What marketing efforts are evident?

   - What social and ecological causes does the company support?

   - What values does the company communicate? Do these values appear to help or hinder its marketing efforts? What does it mean to MEC to operate as a non-profit?

   - How does this company seem to balance profits, consumer wants, and society's interests?

   - Give an example of how MEC uses the relationship building blocks (customer value and satisfaction) to attract and retain customers.

   - How does the company build relationships or "connections" with customers? Which of the three connecting technologies described in Figure 1.6 (page 25) are compatible with these strategies?

2. More than 50 million people are hooked on eBay, the merchandising giant that began in 1995. The electronic

marketplace created by eBay (and its competitors) is the latest trend in ecommerce. Hoards of people dig through their attics and junk drawers looking for things to sell through eBay's virtual yard sales.

As a result, more than half a million items are sold daily on eBay. It's no wonder that the company's business model has critics taking note. As buyers outbid one another to get the goods, the trash-to-treasure approach to retailing has never been so successful. And eBay is cashing in on the auctioning euphoria. Last year alone, the company's profits totalled more than $117 million.

   - Visit the eBay website at www.ebay.com or www.ebay.ca. What is eBay's *value proposition*? How does this value proposition translate into a *marketing offer*?

   - Users conduct an estimated 170 million transactions a year on eBay. How are markets identified and formed on eBay?

   - How have those markets generated demand? Is this demand different from that found in traditional marketplaces?

   - How does eBay build "connections" with its customers? How could eBay grow its "share of customer"?

Video Short

View the video short for this chapter at **www.pearsoned.ca/kotler** and then answer the questions provided in the case description.

Company Case

Botox: *Almost* Trouble-Free New Faces

In the movie *Face/Off,* John Travolta got a new look by exchanging faces with Nicolas Cage. Unfortunately, he got a lot of trouble along with it. Today, John could receive a much less troublesome new look by using Botox, a treatment discovered by Vancouver's Dr. Jean Carruthers, who came upon the cosmetic potential of Botox in 1982 while treating a woman with eye spasms. Not only has Botox smoothed the visages of aging actors, it has also come to the rescue of countless comedians and late-night talk-show hosts. Beyond doing wonders for their appearance, it's also given them a slew of new jokes as the "next Viagra."

Botox is marketed by Allergan, a specialty pharmaceutical firm. In 1990, Allergan was just a small firm selling little-known eye and skin drugs and over-the-counter contact lens cleaners. The introduction of Botox wasn't such a big deal initially. After all, typical of Allergan specialty products, it was just another specialty drug aimed at a small market (treatment of cross-eye) and supported by little marketing effort.

That was before doctors discovered that injecting Botox around eyes not only eliminated ocular problems, it erased frown lines as well. Once that happened, the buzz was on between doctors and patients. Before long, plastic surgeons across Canada were giving face-saving injections. Demand also grew for the drug from American doctors, but they initially had to give it to patients as an "off-label" treatment since Botox was not approved by the FDA for cosmetic use until the spring of 2002. Even though Allergan could not initially openly market the product for cosmetic purposes in the United States, by 2001 sales of Botox rocketed to $585 million and were growing between 25 percent and 35 percent per year. That translates into over 1.6 million Botox cosmetic procedures performed on roughly 850 000 patients.

The good news for Allergan does not end with wiping out frown lines. Botox also effectively treats migraine headaches, chronic neck and back pain, excessive sweating, and possibly spastic disorders. With all those target markets, Botox could become a blockbuster drug—with more than a billion dollars in sales—bringing Allergan out of the backwaters of the pharmaceutical business.

Botox Cosmetic is botulinum toxin A, a heavily diluted version of the feared botulinum toxin found in spoiled canned soups and vegetables. It contains only 20 units of the toxin, compared to the thousands of units found in spoiled food, but it works in the same way—by paralysing facial muscles to the point where they can no longer contract.

Frown lines are definitely a sign of age, use, and wear. They occur when facial muscles contract, drawing the skin up. When the muscles relax, the lines disappear. As we get older, it becomes more difficult to relax, so that we seldom fully relax our facial muscles.

Although eliminating frown lines sounds great, there is at least one small problem. Totally relaxed forehead muscles leave you incapable of rendering any expression at or above the eyes. For the celebrities and stars that were among the first to use Botox, this resulted in "performance" problems. One TV star commented that when the director kept telling her to show anger, she replied, "I am, I am." Unfortunately, nothing was moving on the upper half of her face. As a consequence, she stopped using Botox except for Emmy awards night!

For others, however, the loss of expression might be a positive. Business people seeking a softer look might want to eliminate frown lines that make them look irritated or impatient. Trial lawyers attempting to establish rapport with juries might want to eliminate expressions of annoyance and anger. And sales representatives might want to appear unperturbed by what their clients and customers are saying. But while some observers think Botox could give us a kinder, gentler-looking population, others think it could turn us into a world of zombies.

Besides loss of expression, Botox produces additional side effects. When used on the forehead and around the eyes, Botox can cause drooping eyelids (you won't be able to close or open them completely—this could be either a sexy or a dopey look). Used around the mouth, Botox may cause slurred speech, a droopy mouth, and constant drooling. Other possible side effects include nausea, allergic reactions, headaches, respiratory infections, flu symptoms, and redness and swelling around the injections. The redness and swelling usually go away in a couple of days.

Because a Botox cosmetic treatment lasts only three to six months, all side effects are temporary. This also means, however, that Botox treatments must be repeated when the effects wear off. While that is bad news for consumers, it's good news for doctors and marketers of the drug. The margins on Botox are quite high—around 80 percent. A vial of Botox Cosmetic costs about $780 and can be used for four treatments. Depending on the doctor's pricing scheme, each treatment can be $975 to $1900. That's quite a nifty profit for a treatment that usually takes less than 15 minutes, and it's quite a bill for the patient, because insurance companies don't pay for Botox Cosmetic treatments.

Botox has become so lucrative and the demand so great that the treatments are sometimes offered in a party atmosphere—like a home Tupperware party where doctors woo partygoers with chocolates, Brie, and champagne before whisking them off to have Botox injections in private. If you don't want to go to a house party for an injection, why not attend Toronto's annual New You Cosmetic Enhancement, Anti-Aging Show at the Metro Convention Centre? The show is the only one of its kind in North America. Twenty thousand people are expected to attend, 75 percent of them female. In addition to getting a Botox injection, attendees can visit more than 250 doctors, as well as drug and skincare booths. Speakers and live demonstrations of laser therapies will also be featured.

Once allowed to advertise Botox for cosmetic purposes, Allergan wanted to capitalize on its popularity. It identified the primary market as the approximately 29 million women between the ages of 30 and 64 with household incomes over $95 000. Within that market, the company believed that 7 million women greatly concerned about their appearance were likely to be heavy users. While women constitute the bulk of the market, there are also plenty of guys who want a smoother forehead. Middle-aged men made up 13.8 percent of the market for Botox in 2001, up from 6.1 percent the year before, making males the fastest-growing user segment.

To reach these markets, Allergan began spending $98 million on marketing in 2002. The backbone of this consumer-oriented campaign was advertisements on TV and in twenty-four magazines such as *People,* the *New Yorker, Vogue,* and *InStyle.* Allergan estimated that 90 percent of the audience would see ads at least ten times a year. Most of the ads featured models in everyday clothing and wearing wedding bands—a look that communicated the message that Botox is for everyone.

In addition to the consumer campaign, Allergan began an industry outreach campaign directed at doctors and pharmacists. Beginning with the company website, health professionals could obtain information about Botox and its use. The company also beefed up its sales force and armed salespeople with promotional materials for distribution to health professionals. Finally, it conducted clinics demonstrating the appropriate use of Botox in treating patients for cosmetic purposes.

All of this was part of CEO David Pyott's plan to move Allergan into position as a major player in the pharmaceuticals industry. When he took office in 1998, he found that Allergan had not changed its strategy in decades. Among his first moves were closing plants, slashing jobs, and cutting overhead. To refocus the company, he selected target industries for growth and started making the moves necessary to achieve that growth. The company increased R&D expenditures by 26 percent and expanded the sales force by 28 percent. As a result, Allergan actually employed more people by the end of 2002 than it had two years earlier. The expanded sales force allowed Allergan to establish relationships with many more doctors and pharmacists, relationships that Pyott believes are the basis for sales growth. After all, patients don't buy treatments directly; doctors buy Botox and use it on patients.

Allergan's major growth opportunity is the ophthalmologic market, where rival Alcon is number one. Allergan believes that it can capture the number one position there within three years. The second growth target will be dermatology, where Botox gives the company a major advantage and where it can grow by acquiring new formulas or purchasing a licence from a foreign producer. Doing that is more cost-effective than developing new products in the R&D laboratory from scratch.

Sales of Botox fuel much of this growth, as Allergan's margins on Botox are about 60 percent. To prevent the competition from developing their own Botox, the formula for making it is one of the most closely held secrets in the world. With the dollars from Botox, Allergan can increase its marketing efforts, add products to its line, and attack competitors. The best news of all is that sales of Botox are not likely to decline unless consumers and movie stars suddenly face up to their age—wrinkles and all.

Questions for Discussion

1. What are the needs, wants, and demands of consumers of Botox products in the different treatment markets? What value does Botox deliver in each market? How does value affect price for Botox?

2. When Allergan sold Botox as a specialty drug for ocular problems, what marketing management orientation was it employing? When it sells Botox as a cosmetic treatment, is it employing the same or a different orientation?

3. When doctors treat patients with Botox in their office, is that an example of a selling concept or a marketing concept? Which concept applies when they hold parties for patients in private homes?

4. Apply the concepts of customer lifetime value and customer equity to Botox. How do doctors and Allergan improve the way they manage customer relationships?

5. How does Allergan connect with its customers (doctors)? How does it connect with final consumers? How does it connect with the world around it? What could it do to improve these connections?

6. Does the marketing of Botox raise any ethical concerns?

Sources: Tralee Pearce, "Cosmetic Canada," *Globe and Mail*, March 22, 2003, p. L1; Richard Corliss, "Smile—You're on Botox," *Time*, February 18, 2002, p. 7; Rafer Guzman, "Takeoffs & Landings," *Wall Street Journal*, November 23, 2001, p. 11C; Michael Lemonick, "The Pros and Cons of Botox," *Time*, April 29, 2002, p. 77; David Noonan and Jerry Adler, "The Botox Boom," *Newsweek*, May 13, 2002, pp. 50–58; Brian O'Reilly, "Facelift in a Bottle," *Fortune*, June 24, 2002, pp. 101–104; Tara Parker-Pope, "Wrinkle-Fighter Botox Is Being Used to Treat a Variety of Ailments," *Wall Street Journal*, February 22, 2002, p. B1; Rhonda Rundle, "FDA Clears Botox for Cosmetic Use," *Wall Street Journal*, April 16, 2002, p. D6; Justin Schack, "Eyes on the Prize," *Institutional Investor*, September 2000, pp. 30–32; and Rachel Zimmerman, "Botox Gives a Special Lift to These Soirees," *Wall Street Journal*, April 16, 2002, p. B1.

CBC Video Case

CBC Log on to your Companion Website at **www.pearsoned.ca/kotler** to view a CBC video segment and case for this chapter.

Chapter 2

Company and Marketing Strategy: Partnering to Build Customer Relationships

After studying this chapter you should be able to

1. explain company-wide strategic planning and its four steps

2. discuss how to design business portfolios and develop strategies for growth and downsizing

3. assess marketing's role in strategic planning and explain how marketers partner with others inside and outside the firm to build profitable customer relationships

4. describe the marketing process and the forces that influence it

5. list the marketing management functions, including the elements of a marketing plan

Looking Ahead: Previewing the Concepts

In the first chapter, you learned the core concepts and philosophies of marketing. In this chapter, we'll dig more deeply into marketing's role in the broader organization and into the specifics of the marketing process. First, marketing urges a whole-company philosophy that puts customer relationship at the centre. Then, marketers partner with other company departments and with others in the marketing system to design strategies for delivering value to carefully targeted customers. Marketers next develop "marketing mixes"—consisting of product, price, distribution, and promotion tactics—to carry out these strategies profitably. These first two chapters will give you a full introduction to the basics of marketing, the decisions marketing managers make, and where marketing fits into an organization. After that, we'll take a look at the environments in which marketing operates.

Let's look first at the Walt Disney Company. Disney is the world's second-largest media and entertainment conglomerate, trailing only Time Warner. The company employs 120 000 workers worldwide. When you hear the name Disney, you probably think of wholesome family entertainment. Most people do. With its theme parks and family films, Disney long ago mastered the concepts of customer relationship building and customer delight that we examined in Chapter 1. For generations, it has woven its special "Disney magic" to create and fulfill fantasies for people around the world. It tailors its website to serve people speaking different languages (for example, see www.Disney.ca). But what you may not know is that the Walt Disney Company has now grown to include much, much more than just theme parks and family films. As you read on, think about the all-strategic planning challenges facing Disney's modern-day Magic Kingdom.

When you think of the Walt Disney Company, you probably think first of theme parks and animated films. And no wonder. Since the release of its first Mickey Mouse cartoon 75 years ago, Disney has grown to become the undisputed master of family entertainment. It perfected the art of movie animation. From pioneering films such as *Snow White and the Seven Dwarfs, Fantasia,* and *Pinocchio* to more recent features such as *The Lion King, Toy Story,* and *Monsters, Inc.,* Disney has brought pure magic to the theatres, living rooms, and hearts and minds of audiences around the world.

But perhaps nowhere is the Disney magic more apparent than at the company's premier theme parks. The resort's four major North American theme parks—Magic Kingdom, Epcot, Disney–MGM Studios, and Disney's Animal Kingdom—brim with such attractions as Cinderella's Castle, Space Mountain, the Tower of Terror, Body Wars, the Kilimanjaro Safari, Big Thunder Mountain Railroad, Typhoon Lagoon, Buzz Lightyear's Space Ranger Spin, and Honey I Shrunk the Audience. In addition to its American locations, Disney has parks in Europe, Japan, and Latin America. Since it faces increasing competition in the United States, Disney plans to almost double the proportion of its international revenue to 30 percent of its total revenue by 2007 from the current level of 18 percent.

The Disney magic initially fizzled when it entered Europe. Many people in France saw the park as a poor cousin to the American offerings, while others saw it as an affront to French culture. Disney worked hard to win over European consumers and they now flock to the original Euro Disney park, as well as a newer site in Paris.

Each year, nearly 40 million people flock to the Disney World Resort alone—15 times more than visit Yellowstone National Park—making it the world's number one tourist attraction. What brings so many people to Walt Disney World? Part of the answer lies in its many attractions. But these attractions reveal only part of the Disney World value proposition. In fact, what visitors like even more, they say, is the park's sparkling cleanliness and the friendliness of Disney employees. In an increasingly rude, dirty, and mismanaged world, Disney offers warmth, cleanliness, and order.

Thus, the real "Disney Magic" lies in the company's obsessive dedication to its mission to "make people happy" and to "make a dream come true." The company orients all of its people—from the executive in the corner office, to the monorail driver, to the ticket seller at the gate—around the customer's experience. On their first day, all new Disney World employees report for a three-day motivational course, where they learn about the hard work of making fantasies come true. They learn that they are in the entertainment business—"cast members" in the Disney "show." The job of each cast member is to enthusiastically serve Disney's "guests."

Before they receive their "theme costumes" and go "on stage," employees take courses titled Traditions I and Traditions II, in which they learn the Disney language, history, and culture. They are taught to be enthusiastic, helpful, and *always* friendly. They learn to do good deeds, such as volunteering to take pictures of guests, so that the whole family can be in the picture. Rumour has it that Disney is so confident that its cast members will charm guests that it forces contact with them. For example, many items in the park's gift shops bear no price tags, requiring shoppers to ask the price.

Cast members are taught never to say, "It's not my job." When a guest asks a question—whether it's "Where's the nearest restroom?" or "What are the names of Snow White's seven dwarves?"—they need to know the answer. If cast members see a piece of trash on the ground, they pick it up. They go to extremes to fulfill guests' expectations and dreams. For example, to keep the Magic Kingdom feeling fresh and clean, five times a year the Main Street painters strip every painted rail in the park down to bare metal and apply a new coat of paint.

Disney's customer-delight mission and marketing have become legendary. Its theme parks are so highly regarded for outstanding customer service that many of North America's leading corporations send managers to Disney University to find out how Disney does it. However, as it turns out, theme parks are only a small part of a much bigger Disney story. These units make up only a small part of today's Walt Disney Company empire. In recent years, Disney has become a real study in strategic planning. Throughout the 1990s, seeking growth, Disney diversified rapidly, transforming itself into a $32 billion international media and entertainment conglomerate. You might be surprised to learn that, beyond its theme parks, the Walt Disney Company now owns or has a major stake in all of the following:

- A major television and radio network (ABC), along with 10 company-owned television stations, 29 radio stations, and 13 international broadcast channels
- Sixteen cable networks (including the Disney Channel, Toon Disney, SoapNet, ESPN, A&E, the (U.S.) History Channel, Lifetime Television, E! Entertainment, and the ABC Family Channel)
- Four television production companies and eight movie production and distribution companies (including Walt Disney Pictures, Touchstone Pictures, Hollywood Pictures, and Miramax Films)
- Five magazine publishing groups (including Hyperion Books and Miramax Books)
- Five music labels (including Hollywood Records and Mammoth Records)
- Nineteen Internet groups (including Disney Online, Disney's Daily Blast, ABC.com, ESPN Sportzone, Family.com, Toysmart.com, NASCAR.com, NBA.com, and NFL.com)
- Disney Interactive (which develops and markets computer software, video games, and CD-ROM)
- Disney Cruise Lines
- Two sports franchises (the Mighty Ducks of Anaheim hockey team and the Anaheim Angels baseball team)

It's an impressive list. However, for Disney, managing this diverse portfolio of businesses has become a real *Monsters, Inc.* Whereas Disney's theme park and family movie operations have been wonderfully successful over the years, the new and more complex Disney has struggled for growth and profitability. For example, during the last half of the 1980s, the smaller, more focused Disney experienced soaring sales and profits—revenues grew at an average rate of 23 percent annually; net income grew at 50 percent a year. In contrast, during the most recent five years, the more diversified Disney's sales have grown at an average rate of only 3 percent annually; net income has *fallen* 23 percent a year.

Thus, for Disney, bigger isn't necessarily better. Many critics assert that Disney has grown too large, too diverse,

and too distant from the core strengths that made it so successful over the years. Others, however, believe that such diversification is essential for profitable long-term growth. One thing seems certain—creating just the right blend of businesses to make up the new Magic Kingdom won't be easy. It will take masterful strategic planning—along with some big doses of the famed "Disney magic"—to give the modern Disney story a happily-ever-after ending.[1]

Like Disney, all companies must look ahead and develop long-term strategies to meet the changing conditions in their industries. The hard task of selecting an overall company strategy for long-run survival and growth is called *strategic planning*.

In this chapter, we look first at the organization's overall strategic planning. Next, we discuss how marketers, guided by the strategy plan, work closely with others inside and outside the firm to serve customers. Finally, we examine the marketing management process—how marketers go about choosing target markets and building profitable customer relationships.

Strategic Planning

Strategic planning

The process of developing and maintaining a strategic fit between the organization's goals and capabilities and its changing marketing opportunities. It involves defining a clear company mission, setting supporting objectives, designing a sound business portfolio, and coordinating functional strategies.

Each company must find the game plan that makes the most sense given its specific situation, opportunities, objectives, and resources. This is the focus of **strategic planning**—the process of developing and maintaining a strategic fit between the organization's goals and capabilities and its changing marketing opportunities.

Strategic planning sets the stage for the rest of the planning in the firm. Companies usually prepare annual plans, long-range plans, and strategic plans. The annual and long-range plans deal with the company's current businesses and how to keep them going. In contrast, the strategic plan involves adapting the firm to take advantage of opportunities in its constantly changing environment.

At the corporate level, the company starts the strategic planning process by defining its overall purpose and mission (see Figure 2.1).

This mission then is turned into detailed supporting objectives that guide the whole company. Next, headquarters decides what portfolio of businesses and products is best for the company and how much support to give each. In turn, each business and product unit must develop detailed marketing and other departmental plans that support the company-wide plan. Thus, marketing planning occurs at the business unit, product, and market levels, supporting company strategic planning with more detailed planning for specific marketing opportunities.[2]

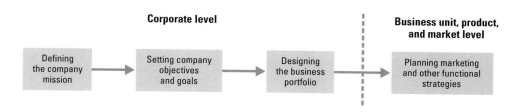

Figure 2.1 Steps in strategic planning

Corporate level

Business unit, product, and market level

Defining the company mission → Setting company objectives and goals → Designing the business portfolio → Planning marketing and other functional strategies

Defining a Market-Oriented Mission

An organization exists to accomplish something. At first, it has a clear purpose or mission, but over time, its mission may become unclear as the organization grows, adds new products and markets, or faces new conditions in the environment. When management senses that the organization is drifting, it must renew its search for purpose. It is time to ask: What is our business? Who is the customer? What do consumers value? What will our business be? What should our business be? These simple-sounding questions are among the most difficult the company will ever have to answer. Successful companies continuously raise these questions and answer them carefully and completely. Many organizations develop formal mission statements that answer these questions. A **mission statement** is a statement of the organization's purpose—what it wants to accomplish in the larger environment. A clear mission statement acts as an "invisible hand" that guides people in the organization.

Mission statement
A statement of the organization's purpose—what it wants to accomplish in the larger environment.

Some companies have defined their businesses in product terms ("We make and sell furniture" or "We are a chemical-processing firm"). But mission statements should be *market-oriented* (see Real Marketing 2.1). Products and technologies eventually become outdated, but basic market needs may last forever.

A market-oriented mission statement defines the business in terms of satisfying basic customer needs. Thus, Rogers is in the communications business, not the cable TV business. Chapters.Indigo.ca sees itself not as a book company, but as a Canadian ecommerce company that serves as a *destination* for online shoppers. By building relationships with its customers, it can serve a variety of their online shopping needs—everything from books to gardening items—in a secure, high-service environment. Likewise, eBay's mission isn't simply to hold online auctions. Instead, it connects individual buyers and sellers in "the world's online marketplace." Its mission is to be a unique Web community in which people can shop around, have fun, and get to know each other, for example, by chatting at the eBay Café.[3] Table 2.1 on page 51 provides several other examples of product-oriented versus market-oriented business definitions.

Hill's Pet Nutrition does more than sell pet food. Its mission is "to help enrich and lengthen the special relationships between people and their pets."

2.1   IBM: Big Blue Dinosaur or Ebusiness Animal?

*O*nly a decade ago, if you'd asked top managers at IBM what business they were in, they might well have answered, "We sell computer hardware and software." Labouring under a bad case of marketing myopia, a heavily product-focused IBM lost sight of its customers' needs. As a result, as customer needs changed, IBM didn't, and its fortunes slipped accordingly. By the early 1990s, "Big Blue's" market share and stock price were falling rapidly.

Since those sadly blue days, however, IBM has undergone a remarkable transformation. The turnaround started in 1993, when new CEO Lou Gerstner brought a renewed customer focus to IBM. As one of his first acts, Gerstner asked all top IBM managers to

IBM defines its business as delivering solutions to customers' ebusiness problems. It asks, "Who do you need?" The answer: "People who get it. People who get it done."

meet face-to-face with important customers—what he called "bear-hugging customers"—and report back concerning their problems and priorities. Gerstner learned that corporate computing is getting more and more confusing for customers. In this new high-tech, connected age, companies must master a dizzying array of information technologies to serve not only their customers but also their suppliers, distributors, and employees. The computer world is more complex, and customers are buying much more from IBM than just computer hardware and software. They are buying solutions to ever-more bewildering information technology (IT) problems. This realization led to a fundamental redefinition of IBM's business. Now, if you ask almost any IBM manager to define the business, they will tell you, "We deliver *solutions* to customers' information technology problems."

The fact is that most customers don't really care whose hardware or software they buy. For example, Pat Zilvitis, chief information officer at Gillette in Boston and a big IBM customer, claims that it's not IBM's PCs, servers, mainframes, or software that attracts him. "I often don't know if I need hardware or software or services, and I don't care," he says. What draws him to IBM is that Big Blue employs an unmatched breadth of products, people, and services to deliver an IT system that works. "I don't view IBM as a hardware vendor anymore," he says. "I think of them as an information technology [partner] that can help me in a number of different ways."

The new customer-solutions focus has greatly promoted the role of services relative to hardware and software in the IBM mix. The company now offers an expanded set of IT consulting, total systems management, strategic outsourcing, and ebusiness services. It helps customers with everything from assessing, planning, designing, implementing, and running their IT systems to bringing them up to speed on ecommerce. Some companies, such as AT&T, Eastman Kodak, and Hertz, have outsourced their entire IT systems to IBM. In such deals, IBM runs the whole IT show—the customer's IT employees work for IBM, and IBM owns the customer's computers, which it then manages.

Services are now IBM's hottest growth area. Its mammoth Global Services division accounts for

40 percent of the company's more than $112 billion in sales and 50 percent of its profits. As one analyst comments, "IBM—International Business Machines—is becoming IBS, where 'S' is for services, software, and solutions." In fact, IBM has now become the world's largest supplier of IT services.

To announce its transformation and to counter the out-of-date notion that IBM provides only computer hardware, IBM launched a $98 million global services ad campaign. The campaign profiled specific IBM people—featured in current ads as "People who get it. People who get it done." One ad showcased Nick Simicich, an IBM ethical hacker (unofficial title: "paid professional paranoid") who purposely invaded customers' critical information systems to see if they were safe from more-hostile hackers. Another featured Patrick McMahon, who helped Prudential re-engineer its sales processes, doubling the number of policies sold and raising commissions 153 percent in the pilot program.

In the latest phase of its customer-solutions makeover, IBM has positioned itself as the "ebusiness solutions company." (It coined *ebusiness* as a catch-all term for Internet, intranet, and ecommerce applications.) As more and more companies use the Internet as their primary connecting technology, ebusiness is growing explosively. IBM wants to be *the* company others turn to for ebusiness strategies and solutions. During the past few years, the company has introduced dozens of new ebusiness services, including customer relationship management, business intelligence, supply chain management, and business process management services. For example, the Canadian Intellectual Property Office selected IBM Global Services to help it move from a traditional paper-based process to one that is Web-enabled. Today, Canadians can access patent documents online. This not only reduces processing time, but it also gives the public better access to information it needs.

Ebusiness appears to be an ideal setting for IBM's soup-to-nuts menu of IT solutions. Big Blue claims to have 10 000 ebusiness customers. For some, this means little more than having IBM host their websites on one of its servers. For others, however, it means having IBM create and implement a totally new business-customer connection. In its latest initiative, IBM now offers what it calls "ebusiness on demand," which allows companies to tap into IBM software and supercomputing power via the Web. "Instead of having to constantly buy, maintain, and upgrade the latest technology," says an analyst, "IBM envisions a simpler world in which companies would buy computing power and programs on an as-needed basis, just as they do electricity from power companies." In fact, recent IBM ads promise "introducing ebusiness on demand—the next utility."

Thus, in a remarkably short time, IBM has transformed itself from a company that "sells computer hardware and software" to one that "delivers customer IT solutions." The marketplace has responded strongly. By the time Gerstner retired in 2002, IBM's market capitalization had grown sixfold; its stock price had soared sevenfold. By defining itself in terms of the customer needs it serves rather than the products it sells, IBM has been transformed from a big blue has-been to a tech-services powerhouse. As one knowledgeable IBM watcher concludes, IBM is now "fantastically positioned for the future."

Sources: See David Kirkpatrick, "IBM: From Big Blue Dinosaur to E-Business Animal," *Fortune*, April 26, 1999, pp. 116–125; Laura Loro, "IBM Touts Position as No. 1 in IT Services," *Advertising Age's Business Marketing*, April 1999, p. 41; Gary Hamel, "Waking Up IBM," *Harvard Business Review*, July–August 2000, pp. 137–146; Spencer E. Ante, "Big Blues Tech on Tap," *Business Week*, August 27, 2001, pp. 66–69; Spencer E. Ante and Ira Sager, "IBM's New Boss," *Business Week*, February 11, 2002, pp. 66–69; and Spencer E. Ante and David Henry, "Can IBM Keep Earnings Hot?" *Business Week*, April 15, 2002, pp. 58–60.

Management should avoid making its mission too narrow or too broad. A pencil manufacturer that says it is in the communication equipment business is stating its mission too broadly. Missions should be *realistic*—Singapore Airlines would be deluding itself if it adopted the mission to become the world's largest airline. Missions should also be *specific*. Many mission statements are written for public relations purposes and lack specific, workable guidelines. Too often, companies develop mission statements that look much like this tongue-in-cheek version:

We are committed to serving the quality of life of cultures and communities everywhere, regardless of sex, age, sexual preference, religion, or disability, whether they be customers, suppliers, employees, or shareholders—we serve the planet—to the highest ethical standards of integrity, best practice, and sustainability, through policies of openness and transparency vetted by our participation

Table 2.1   Market-Oriented Business Definitions

Company	Product-oriented definition	Market-oriented definition
M·A·C Cosmetics	We make cosmetics.	We sell lifestyle and self-expression; tolerance of diversity, and a platform for the outrageous.
Zellers	We run discount stores.	We offer products and services that deliver superior style and value to Canadians.
Canadian Tire	We sell tools and home-improvement items.	We provide advice and solutions that transform ham-handed people into Mr. and Ms. Fixits.
Amazon.com	We sell books, videos, CDs, toys, consumer electronics, hardware, housewares, and other products.	We make the Internet buying experience fast, easy, and enjoyable—we're the place where you can find and discover anything you want to buy online.
Disney	We run theme parks.	We create fantasies—a place where families can dream together.
eBay	We hold online auctions.	We connect individual buyers and sellers in the world's online marketplace, a unique Web community in which they can shop around, have fun, and get to know each other.
Nike	We sell shoes.	We help people experience the emotion of competition, winning, and crushing competitors.

in the International Quality Business Global Audit forum, to ensure measurable outcomes worldwide....[4]

Such generic statements sound good but provide little real guidance or inspiration. In contrast, Celestial Seasonings' mission statement is very specific: *"Our mission is to grow and dominate the specialty tea market by exceeding consumer expectations with: The best-tasting, 100 percent natural hot and iced teas, packaged with Celestial art and philosophy, creating the most valued tea experience."*[5] Missions should fit the market environment. The organization should base its mission on its *distinctive competencies*. McDonald's could probably enter the solar energy business, but that would not take advantage of its core competence— providing low-cost food and fast service to large groups of customers.

Finally, mission statements should be *motivating*. A company's mission should not be stated as making more sales or profits—profits are only a reward for undertaking a useful activity. A company's employees need to feel that their work is significant and that it contributes to people's lives, as Hummingbird's example shows:[6]

Hummingbird, founded in Kingston, Ontario as a small consulting firm, quickly evolved into the dominant player in the connectivity market (www.hummingbird. com/). Today it holds close to an 80 percent share. Its five million users around the world rely on Hummingbird to connect, manage, access, publish, collaborate on, and search their enterprise content. Hummingbird expresses its mission as "empowering organizations to leverage the full range of enterprise information in the creation of shareholder value."

One study found that "visionary companies" set a purpose beyond making money. For example, Walt Disney Company's aim is to "make people happy." But even though profits may not be part of these companies' mission statements, they are the inevitable result. The study showed that eighteen visionary companies outperformed other companies in the stock market by more than six to one over the period from 1926 to 1990.[7]

Setting Company Objectives and Goals

The company's mission needs to be turned into detailed supporting objectives for each level of management. Each manager should have objectives and be responsible for reaching them. For example, Monsanto operates in many businesses, including agriculture, pharmaceuticals, and food products. The company defines its mission as creating "abundant food and a healthy environment." It seeks to help feed the world's exploding population while at the same time sustaining the environment.

This mission leads to a hierarchy of objectives, including business objectives and marketing objectives. Monsanto's overall objective, for example, is to create environmentally better products and get them to market faster at lower costs. For its part, the agricultural division's objective is to increase agricultural productivity and reduce chemical pollution by researching new pest- and disease-resistant crops that produce higher yields without chemical spraying. But research is expensive and requires improved profits to plow back into research programs. So improving profits becomes another major Monsanto objective. Profits can be improved by increasing sales or reducing costs. Sales can be increased by improving the company's share of the North American market, by entering new foreign markets, or both. These goals then become the company's current marketing objectives.

Marketing strategies must be developed to support these marketing objectives. To increase its market share, Monsanto might increase its products' availability and promotion. To enter new foreign markets, the company may cut prices and target large farms abroad. These are its broad marketing strategies. Each broad marketing strategy must then be defined in greater detail. For example, increasing the product's promotion may require more salespeople and more advertising; if so, both requirements will have to be spelled out. In this way, the firm's mission is translated into a set of objectives for the current period.

Designing the Business Portfolio

Business portfolio
The collection of businesses and products that make up the company.

Guided by the company's mission statement and objectives, corporate strategic planners must plan the **business portfolio**—the collection of businesses and products that make up the company. Business portfolio planning involves two steps. First, the company must analyze its *current* business portfolio and decide which businesses should receive more, less, or no investment. Second, it must shape the *future* portfolio by developing strategies for growth and downsizing.

Analyzing the Current Business Portfolio

Portfolio analysis
A tool that management uses to identify and evaluate the various businesses that make up the company.

The major activity in strategic planning is business **portfolio analysis,** whereby management evaluates the businesses that make up the company. The company will want to put strong resources into its more profitable businesses and phase down or drop its weaker ones. Management's first step is to identify the key businesses making up the company. These can be called the strategic business units. A **strategic business unit (SBU)** is a unit of the company that has a separate mission and objectives and that can be planned independently from other company businesses. An SBU can be a company division, a product line within a division, or sometimes a single product or brand.

Strategic business unit (SBU)
A unit of the company that has a separate mission and objectives and that can be planned independently from other company businesses. An SBU can be a company division, a product line within a division, or sometimes a single product or brand.

The next step in business portfolio analysis calls for management to assess the attractiveness of its various SBUs and decide how much support each deserves. Most companies are well advised to "stick to their knitting" when designing their business portfolios. It's usually a good idea to focus on adding products and businesses that fit closely with the firm's core philosophy and competencies. However, some companies have excelled with broad, widely diversified portfolios. An excellent example is General Electric (www.ge.com/). Through skilful management of its portfolio of

The business portfolio: Through skilful management of its portfolio of businesses, General Electric has grown to be one of the world's largest and most profitable companies.

businesses, General Electric has grown to be one of the world's largest and most profitable companies. It is also highly regarded for its integrity. Since it operates worldwide and faces many ethical challenges, GE places a lot of emphasis on abiding by its code of ethics.

Over the past two decades, GE has shed many low-performing businesses, such as air-conditioning and housewares. It kept only those businesses that could be number one or number two in their industries. At the same time, it has acquired other profitable businesses. GE now operates 49 business units, selling an incredible variety of products and services—from consumer electronics, financial services, and television broadcasting to aircraft engines, plastics, and a global Internet trading network. Superb management of this diverse portfolio has earned GE shareholders a 29 percent average annual return over the past ten years. It's also put GE at the top of *Fortune's* Most Admired Companies for five straight years.[8]

Similarly, John Labatt Ltd. (www.labatt.ca) strengthened its portfolio by selling off its less attractive businesses, including food products (Ault Foods, Catelli-Primo Ltd., Johanna Dairies, and Everfresh Juice Co.) and its profitable Sports Network, to invest more heavily in products and technologies for its brewing business.

The purpose of strategic planning is to identify ways in which the company can best use its strengths to take advantage of attractive opportunities in the environment. Thus, most standard portfolio-analysis methods evaluate SBUs on two important dimensions—the attractiveness of the SBU's market or industry and the strength of the SBU's position in that market or industry. The best-known portfolio-planning method was developed by the Boston Consulting Group, a leading management consulting firm.

The Boston Consulting Group Approach   Using the Boston Consulting Group (BCG) approach, a company classifies all of its SBUs or products according to the **growth–share matrix** shown in Figure 2.2. On the vertical axis, *market growth rate* provides a measure of market attractiveness.

Growth–share matrix
A portfolio-planning method that evaluates a company's strategic business units in terms of their market growth rate and relative market share. SBUs are classified as stars, cash cows, question marks, or dogs.

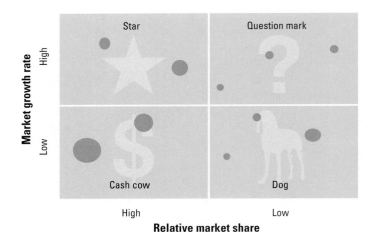

Figure 2.2 BCG growth–share matrix

On the horizontal axis, *relative market share* serves as a measure of company strength in the market. The growth–share matrix defines four types of SBUs:

- *Stars.* Stars are high-growth, high-share businesses or products. They often need heavy investment to finance their rapid growth. Eventually their growth will slow down, and they will turn into cash cows.
- *Cash cows.* Cash cows are low-growth, high-share businesses or products. These established and successful SBUs need less investment to hold their market share. Thus, they produce a lot of cash that the company uses to pay its bills and to support other SBUs that need investment.
- *Question marks.* Question marks are low-share business units in high-growth markets. They require a lot of cash to hold their share, let alone increase it. Management has to think hard about which question marks it should try to build into stars and which should be phased out.
- *Dogs.* Dogs are low-growth, low-share businesses and products. They may generate enough cash to maintain themselves, but do not promise to be large sources of cash.

The ten circles in the growth–share matrix represent a company's ten current SBUs. The company has two stars, two cash cows, three question marks, and three dogs. The areas of the circles are proportional to the SBU's dollar sales. This company is in fair shape, although not in good shape. It wants to invest in the more promising question marks to make them stars, and to maintain the stars so that they will become cash cows as their markets mature. Fortunately, it has two good-sized cash cows whose income helps finance the company's question marks, stars, and dogs. The company should take decisive action concerning its dogs and its question marks. The picture would be worse if the company had no stars, if it had too many dogs, or if it had only one weak cash cow.

Once it has classified its SBUs, the company must determine what role each will play in the future. It can pursue one of four strategies for each SBU. The company can invest more in the business unit to *build* its share. It can invest just enough to *hold* the SBU's share at the current level. It can *harvest* the SBU, milking its short-term cash flow regardless of the long-term effect. Finally, the company can *divest* the SBU by selling it or phasing it out and using the resources elsewhere.

As time passes, SBUs change their positions in the growth–share matrix. Each SBU has a life cycle. Many SBUs start out as question marks and move into the star category if they succeed. They later become cash cows, as market growth falls, then finally die off or turn into dogs toward the end of their life cycle. The company needs to add new products and units continuously so that some will become stars and, eventually, cash cows that will help finance other SBUs.

Problems with Matrix Approaches   The BCG and other formal methods revolutionized strategic planning. However, such approaches have limitations. They can be difficult, time consuming, and costly to implement. Management may find it difficult to define SBUs and measure market share and growth. In addition, these approaches focus on classifying current businesses but provide little advice for future planning.

Formal planning approaches can also place too much emphasis on market-share growth or growth through entry into attractive new markets. Using these approaches, many companies plunged into unrelated and new high-growth businesses that they did not know how to manage—with very bad results. At the same time, these companies were often too quick to abandon, sell, or milk to death their healthy mature businesses. As a result, many companies that diversified too broadly in the past are now narrowing their focus and getting back to the basics of serving one or a few industries that they know best.

Because of such problems, many companies have dropped formal matrix methods in favour of more customized approaches that are better suited to their specific situations. Unlike former strategic-planning efforts, which rested mostly in the hands of senior managers, today's strategic planning has been decentralized. Increasingly, companies are placing responsibility for strategic planning in the hands of cross-functional teams of managers who are close to their markets. Some teams even include customers and suppliers in their strategic-planning processes.[9]

Industry Structure and Competitive Position Determine Strategy and Profitability

The competitive strategy a business adopts and the success of that strategy depends on the structure of the marketplace and the firm's position within that marketplace. Firms competing in a given industry or target market will, at any point in time, differ in their objectives and resources. Some firms will be large and powerful and they will lead the industry. Others will be small and have more limited resources. They will either follow the leaders or will target niche markets ignored by the more powerful players. Some firms will strive for rapid market-share growth, others for long-term profits.

Before selecting a strategy to help the business unit achieve competitive advantage, strategists must understand the forces that drive the profitability of an industry. Michael Porter, a renowned strategist from the Harvard Business School, believes that five forces largely determine the profitability of an industry.[10] The first of these forces is barriers to entry. Barriers to entry protect incumbent firms from the entry of newcomers. For example, patents in the pharmaceutical industry limit the entry of new firms or products. The second force is the power of the customer relative to the focal firm. If a firm acts as a supplier to a powerful customer, that customer will have the ability to demand low prices or products tailored to its needs. For example, in Canada, grocery retailers like Loblaws are very large and powerful relative to their suppliers. Loblaws can thus demand that suppliers meet its conditions and price points. The third force is the power of suppliers relative to the focal firm. If the supplier is more powerful than its customer, it can demand high prices for the goods or services it supplies and the weaker customer will be forced to meet these demands. The fourth force is the presence of substitutes. If there are lots of substitutes for the products or services the focal firm offers, buyers can easily switch if they are unhappy with the prices or the quality of the focal firm's offerings.

The fifth and final force is the degree of competitive rivalry within the industry. In some industries, a "live and let live" attitude prevails among competitors. In other industries, competitors fight each other tooth and nail. Thus, designing competitive business strategies for the SBUs that make up the organization's portfolio of businesses often begins with thorough competitor analysis. The company constantly compares the value and customer satisfaction delivered by its products, prices, channels, and promotion with that of its close competitors. In this way it can discern areas of potential advantage and disadvantage. The company must formally or informally monitor the competitive environment to answer these and other important questions: Who are our competitors? What are their objectives and strategies? What are their strengths and weaknesses? And how will they react to different competitive strategies we might use? Competitive intelligence gathering will be discussed further in Chapter 5.

An SBU's position within the industry is another factor that influences its profitability. For example, the large firms that lead the industry have considerable buying power and clout with suppliers, so they can often negotiate the best prices for supplies and services. This superior buying power will improve their profitability. Market followers may not have to incur the costs of developing a market and educating consumers about the features and benefits of a new product, so they can sometimes have lower costs than leading-edge firms.

Strategies for Strategic Business Units

Once the corporation has designed the mix of businesses that make up the entire operation, it must select a strategy that each business unit will follow to achieve competitive advantage over its rivals in the marketplace. Marketers within the business unit must understand the overall strategy of the business unit so that they design marketing strategies that enable the SBU to achieve its overall strategy.

Almost two decades ago, Michael Porter suggested three winning strategies that businesses competing within a given industry could follow to achieve competitive advantage. As noted in the previous section, Porter believed that SBU profitability was determined by both industry structure and by the strategies pursued by the different businesses in the industry.[11] The three winning strategies include:

Overall Cost Leadership   Here the SBU works hard to achieve the lowest costs of production and distribution so that it can price lower than its competitors and win a large market share. Texas Instruments and Wal-Mart are leading practitioners of this strategy. Marketers in firms following cost leadership strategies work to identify target markets that are large enough to support the high volume sales essential to achieving this strategy. They position their products and prices as representing the best value in the marketplace. They look for markets where buyers are content with standardized goods and services that can be produced inexpensively. They work to keep costs down by using efficient channels of distribution. They communicate with customers using the lowest-cost media available.

Differentiation   Here the company concentrates on creating a highly differentiated product line and marketing program so that it comes across as the quality leader in the industry. Most customers would prefer to own this brand if its price is not too high. IBM and Caterpillar follow this strategy in computers and heavy construction equipment, respectively. Marketers working in business units that stress differentiation work to identify target markets that have the most intense need for the specialized offerings of the firm. Members with intense needs are more willing to pay the premium prices essential to support this strategy. They position the product or service offering as being of the highest quality. They may stress to the customer that they provide a total solution to their problem. They use high-quality distribution outlets or may use specialized outlets to distribute their products since these support the aura of exclusivity that may be associated with this product or service. When designing their communication tactics, they use messages that stress why the customer "deserves the best" and why their product or service is superior to that of its competitors.

Focus   Here the company focuses its effort on serving a few market segments well rather than going after the whole market. Thus, Mountain Equipment Co-op offers products to outdoor enthusiasts who favour non-motorized sports such as rock climbing or kayaking rather than to a broader mix of people who enjoy outdoor recreational activities such as power boating or the use of all-terrain vehicles. They also attract people who share their values with regard to operating in an environmentally and socially responsible manner. The role of marketers in these firms is to find niche markets that will not be attacked by larger, more powerful competitors. Markets work hard to align the offerings of the firm to the precise needs of the target market.

Companies that pursue a clear strategy—one of the above—are likely to perform well. The firm that carries out that strategy best will make the most profits. But firms that do not pursue a clear strategy—middle-of-the-roaders—do the worst. Sears, Chrysler, and International Harvester all encountered difficult times because they did not stand out as the lowest in cost, highest in perceived value, or best in serving some market segment. Middle-of-the-roaders try to be good on all strategic counts, but end up being not very good at anything.

More recently, two marketing consultants, Michael Treacy and Fred Wiersema, offered a new classification of competitive marketing strategies.[12] They suggest that companies gain leadership positions by delivering superior value to their customers. Companies can pursue any of three strategies—called value disciplines—for delivering superior customer value. These are:

- *Operational excellence.* The company provides superior value by leading its industry in price and convenience. It works to reduce costs and to create a lean and efficient value delivery system. It serves customers who want reliable, good-quality products or services, but who want them cheaply and easily. Examples include Dell and IKEA. If a business unit follows this strategy, the marketer's role is similar to that of a marketer working in a firm following a cost leadership strategy.

- *Product leadership.* The company provides superior value by offering a continuous stream of leading-edge products or services that make their own and competing products obsolete. It is open to new ideas, relentlessly pursues new solutions, and works to reduce cycle times so that it can get new products to market quickly. It serves customers who want state-of-the-art products and services, regardless of the costs in terms of price or inconvenience. Examples include Cognos and PeopleSoft, providers of leading-edge software and business intelligence solutions. Marketers working in business units following this strategy work hard to always be abreast of emerging needs and trends that will affect their customers and their needs.

- *Customer intimacy.* The company provides superior value by precisely segmenting its markets and then tailoring its products or services to match exactly the needs of targeted customers. It builds detailed customer databases for segmenting and targeting, and empowers its marketing people to respond quickly to customer needs. It serves customers who are willing to pay a premium to get precisely what they want, and it will do almost anything to build long-term customer loyalty and to capture customer lifetime value. Examples include Quarry Integrated Communications (located in Kitchener–Waterloo) and McKinsey Management Consultants. Business units following a customer intimacy strategy need marketers who are skilled in gleaning customer insight and who are focused on building lasting relationships with customers.

Some companies successfully pursue more than one value discipline at the same time. For example, Federal Express (www.fedex.com/) excels at both operational excellence and customer intimacy. However, such companies are rare—few firms can be the best at more than one of these disciplines. By trying to be good at all of the value disciplines, a company usually ends up being best at none.

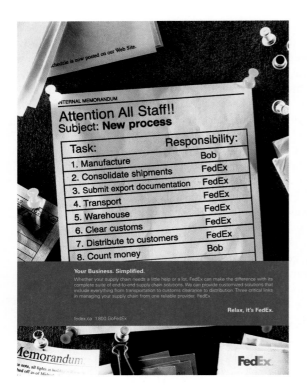

Federal Express uses technology to simultaneously build customer intimacy and achieve operation excellence.

Product–market expansion grid

A portfolio-planning tool for identifying company growth opportunities through market penetration, market development, product development, or diversification.

Market penetration

A strategy for company growth by increasing sales of current products to current market segments without changing the product in any way.

Treacy and Wiersema have found that leading companies focus on and excel at a single value discipline, while meeting industry standards on the other two. They design their entire value delivery system to single-mindedly support the chosen discipline. For example, Wal-Mart focuses obsessively on operational excellence—on reducing costs and streamlining its order-to-delivery process to make it convenient for customers to buy just the right products at the lowest prices.

Classifying competitive strategies as value disciplines is appealing. It defines marketing strategy in terms of the single-minded pursuit of delivering value to customers. It recognizes that management must align every aspect of the company with the chosen value discipline—from its culture, to its organization structure, to its operating and management systems and processes. This customer value focus has motivated firms to go one step further and form long-term relationships with their key customers.

Developing Strategies for Growth and Downsizing

Beyond evaluating current businesses, designing the business portfolio involves finding businesses and products that the company should consider in the future. Companies need growth if they are to compete more effectively, satisfy their stakeholders, and attract top talent. "Growth is pure oxygen," states one executive. "It creates a vital, enthusiastic corporation where people see genuine opportunity." At the same time, a firm must be careful not to make growth itself an objective. The company's objective must be "profitable growth." Marketing has the main responsibility for achieving profitable growth for the company. Marketing must identify, evaluate, and select market opportunities and lay down strategies for capturing them. One useful device for identifying growth opportunities is the **product–market expansion grid**,[13] shown in Figure 2.3. We apply it here to Tim Hortons (www.timhortons.com), one of Canada's dominant food service retailers (see Real Marketing 2.2).

Tim Hortons' strategy is deceptively simple and has long been founded on **market penetration**. It works to open a critical mass of outlets in a predefined geographic region and then it supports them with advertising. Increased awareness and the building of strong brand equity in turn builds requests for new franchises—which is how Tim Hortons plans to continue expansion in both Quebec and western Canada. It also works to train people who come into Tim Hortons first thing in the morning for coffee and breakfast to return several times during the rest of the day. To that end, Hortons routinely upgrades and refurbishes its outlets, adding double drive-throughs and establishing satellite outlets in settings like hospitals and retail stores—bringing the restaurant to the consumer instead of the other way around. "Wherever you are," says one top manager, "there's a coffee and a donut waiting for you."

	Existing products	**New products**
Existing markets	Market penetration	Product development
New markets	Market development	Diversification

Figure 2.3 Product–market expansion grid

2.2 Tim Hortons: Where Things Are Really Perking

Canadians, it appears, *always have time for Tim Hortons*. Generations of competitors have come and gone, but none have managed to defeat "Hortons," headquartered in Oakville, Ontario. In fact, it has become a Canadian icon. Over its 38-year history, Hortons' marketing savvy has turned this once simple doughnut shop into a $2 billion-a-year enterprise. Today, Tim Hortons rivals McDonald's Canada for the number-one spot in terms of fast-food sales. In recognition of its marketing prowess, *Strategy* magazine named it "Marketer of the Year" in 2002. The dominance of the chain can be seen in these facts: one of every three cups of coffee sold in Canada comes from Tim Hortons, and each and every day Canadians dunk over three million doughnuts. Tim Hortons is one of Canada's largest employers, with over 55 000 people working in its headquarters, one of its 2049 franchise outlets in Canada, or one of its 145 franchise outlets in the northern United States.

Tim Hortons works relentlessly to build its brand, which has become an idealized image of the Canadian national character: friendly, neighbourly, unpretentious, gently playful, frugal, trustworthy, and, yes, clean. It

Tim Hortons doesn't advertise until it has enough outlets in a region to justify the expense. It knows advertising has more impact when people can see its outlets in their daily travels.

brings this brand image to life by featuring real people in its ads—both customers and employees. "Tim Hortons never fakes it," notes Philippe Garneau, a partner at Toronto's Garneau Würstlin Philp Brand Engineering. Tim Hortons communicates its brand image through its "True Stories" television vignettes, which are based on the best of hundreds of suggestions the company receives from its customers every year. Each story exemplifies the emotional relationship the customer has with Tim Hortons and portrays how Hortons fits into their daily lives.

The doughnut chain's long-running "Roll up the Rim to Win" promotion has become a beloved part of Canadian slang, and scenes at Hortons are shown weekly on comedy news show *Air Farce*. Some of the approximately $3 million a year that Hortons spends on advertising is also focused on its new products— bagels, sandwiches, and soup—to get consumers to see Tim Hortons as more than a doughnut shop. New products have also increased revenues for both the corporation and its franchisees.

As impressive as these figures are, one has to wonder what else Tim Hortons has done to achieve this success—after all, it really offers fairly standard products such as coffee and baked goods. Hortons' strategy is deceptively simple. First, it has followed one consistent product and positioning strategy throughout its history. Its promise of "Always Fresh" is never broken. Next, it builds outlets in focal areas until there are enough outlets in the area to justify advertising. As Patti Jameson, director of corporate communications, notes, "Advertising is a lot more relevant to people when they actually see the stores on the street." Having the physical presence of a retail outlet made brand messages more relevant and meaningful.

Given Tim Hortons' track record, it's hard to imagine how it could expand any further (if your town is anything like mine). There seems to be an outlet on the corner of every major intersection. Yet even an institution needs to be willing to change and grow. And change is exactly what Hortons has done in recent years. In a bid to broaden its appeal and attract more women and young people, the chain has recently branched out into new product lines, such as iced cappuccino. It also retooled its lunchtime offerings, offering Tim's Own brand of soups and sandwiches.

The firm isn't about to stop there. Since Hortons believes that the breakfast category is underdeveloped in the U.S. and that Americans are poorly served by current "morning destinations," it sees tremendous opportunity south of the border. "In the U.S., they don't have high expectations for morning destinations.... People will grab a coffee from a gas station in the morning, [but] we're promising that consistent experience. No one else is really doing everyday morning coffee and baked goods very well." Two television spots and a series of radio ads each portray Tim Hortons as the real reason morning people are so chipper. The tag line is: "Morning people. Where do

they come from?" While success in the highly competitive U.S. market is far from guaranteed, if the history of professional hockey offers any indication, then Americans may also soon be claiming this Canadian institution as their own.

Sources: Terry Poulton, Special Report: Top Clients 2002, "Long Live the Double Double," *Strategy,* July 29, 2002, p. 19; Natalie Bahadur, "Tim Hortons Plans Aggressive Roll-Out," *Strategy,* March 29, 1999, p. 7; Lesley Daw, "More Than Just a Doughnut Shop," *Marketing Magazine,* December 20/27, 1999, www.marketingmag.ca/; Scott Gardiner, "In Praise of Saint Timmy," *Marketing Magazine,* August 21, 2000, www.marketingmag.ca/; Laura Pratt, "Roll Up the Rim Major Player for Tim Hortons," *Strategy,* May 22, 2000, p. 22; Craig Saunders, "Tim Hortons Issues Wakeup Call," *Strategy,* February 14, 2000, p. 25; Sinclair Stewart, "Top Client, Retail–Restaurants: Tim Hortons Brews Up Fresh Ideas," *Strategy,* August 2, 1999, p. 7; Sinclair Stewart, "Tim Hortons Brews New U.S. Campaign," *Strategy,* September 27, 1999, p. 3.

Market development

A strategy for company growth by identifying and developing new market segments for current company products.

Product development

A strategy for company growth by offering modified or new products to current market segments.

Diversification

A strategy for company growth by starting up or acquiring businesses outside the company's current products and markets.

Downsizing

Reducing the business portfolio by eliminating products of business units that are not profitable or that no longer fit the company's overall strategy.

Second, the firm explores possibilities for **market development**—identifying and developing new markets for its current products. For instance, managers could review new *demographic markets.* Perhaps new groups—such as senior consumers or ethnic groups—could be encouraged to visit Tim Hortons coffee shops for the first time or to buy more from them. Managers also could review new *geographical markets.* Tim Hortons has recently moved south of the border, opening 145 outlets in the northern United States.

Third, Tim Hortons' management focuses on **product development**—offering modified or new products to current markets. Hortons introduced cappuccino, bagels, sandwiches, and soup to get consumers to see it as more than a doughnut shop.

Fourth, Hortons might consider **diversification**. It could start up or buy businesses outside of its current products and markets. For example, like Loblaws, it could begin offering financial services. It could leverage its strong brand name onto products like sportswear that fit with its friendly, relaxed image. However, it must take care: Companies that diversify too broadly into unfamiliar products or industries can lose their market focus.

Companies must not only develop strategies for *growing* their business portfolios but also strategies for **downsizing** them. There are many reasons why a firm might want to abandon products or markets. The market environment might change, making some of the company's products or markets less profitable. This might happen during an economic recession or when a strong competitor opens next door. The firm may have grown too fast or entered areas where it lacks experience. This can occur when a firm enters too many foreign markets without proper research or when a company introduces new products that do not offer superior customer value. Finally, some products or business units just age and die.

When a firm finds products or businesses that no longer fit its overall strategy, it must carefully prune, harvest, or divest them. Weak businesses usually require a disproportionate amount of management attention. Managers should focus on promising growth opportunities, not fritter away energy trying to salvage fading ones.

Strategic Planning and Small Business

Many discussions of strategic planning focus on large corporations with many divisions and products. However, small businesses also can benefit greatly from sound strategic planning. Whereas most small ventures start out with extensive business and marketing plans to attract potential investors, strategic planning often falls by the wayside once the business gets going. Entrepreneurs and presidents of small companies are more likely to spend their time "putting out fires" than planning. But what does a small firm do when it finds that it has taken on too much debt, when its growth is exceeding production capacity, or when it is losing market share to a competitor with lower prices? Strategic planning can help small business managers anticipate such situations and determine how to prevent or handle them.

Each year, the Business Development Bank of Canada hands out awards to the country's top entrepreneurs under 29 years of age. Winners in 2002 included T. J. Brar, founder of Evergreen Herbs Ltd. (Surrey, British Columbia); Neil Cooke, owner of I4C Consulting Inc. (Kanata, Ontario); and Carla MacQuarrie, the entrepreneur who founded Future Aqua Farms Ltd. (West Chezzetcook, Nova Scotia). Strategic planning is the key to the rapid growth and high profit margins of such small comapnies.[14]

Strategic planning for small firms hinges on an objective assessment of the company, its place in the market, and its goals. It includes the following steps:[15]

1. Identify the major elements of the business environment in which the organization has operated over the past few years.

2. Describe the mission of the organization in terms of its nature and function for the next two years.

3. Explain the internal and external forces that will have an impact on the mission of the organization.

4. Identify the basic driving force that will direct the organization in the future.

5. Develop a set of long-term objectives that will identify what the organization will become in the future.

6. Outline a general plan of action that defines the logistical, financial, and personnel factors needed to integrate the long-term objectives into the total organization.

Planning Marketing: Partnering to Build Customer Relationships

The company's strategic plan establishes what kinds of businesses the company will be in and its objectives for each business. Then, within each business unit, more detailed planning takes place. The major functional departments in each unit—marketing, finance, accounting, purchasing, operations, information systems, human resources, and others—must work together to accomplish strategic objectives.

Marketing plays a key role in the company's strategic planning in several ways. First, marketing provides a guiding *philosophy*—the marketing concept—that suggests that company strategy should revolve around building profitable relationships with important consumer groups. Second, marketing provides *inputs* to strategic planners by helping to identify attractive market opportunities and by assessing the firm's potential to take advantage of them. Finally, within individual business units, marketing designs *strategies* for reaching the unit's objectives. Once the unit's objectives are set, marketing's task is to carry them out profitably.

Customer value and satisfaction are important ingredients in the marketer's formula for success. However, as we noted in Chapter 1, marketers alone cannot produce superior value for customers. Although it plays a leading role, marketing

Partner relationship management
Working closely with partners in other company departments and outside the company to jointly bring greater value to customers.

Value chain
The series of departments that carry out value-creating activities to design, produce, market, deliver, and support a firm's products.

can be only a partner in attracting, keeping, and growing customers. In addition to *customer relationship management*, marketers must also practise **partner relationship management**. They must work closely with partners in other company departments to form an effective *value chain* that serves the customer. Moreover, they must partner effectively with other companies in the marketing system to form a competitively superior *value-delivery network*. We now take a closer look at the concepts of a company value chain and value-delivery network.

Partnering with Others in the Company

Each company department can be thought of as a link in the company's **value chain**.[16] That is, each department carries out value-creating activities to design, produce, market, deliver, and support the firm's products. The firm's success depends not only on how well each department performs its work but also on how well the activities of various departments are coordinated.

For example, Wal-Mart's goal is to create customer value and satisfaction by providing shoppers with the products they want at the lowest possible prices. Marketers at Wal-Mart play an important role. They learn what customers need and want and aid Wal-Mart merchants as they endeavour to stock the store's shelves with the desired products at unbeatable low prices. Marketers prepare advertising and merchandising programs and assist shoppers with customer service. Through these and other activities, Wal-Mart's marketers help deliver value to customers. However, the marketing department needs help from the company's other departments. Wal-Mart's ability to offer the right products at low prices depends on the purchasing department's skill in tracking down the needed suppliers and buying from them at low cost. Similarly, Wal-Mart's information technology department must provide fast and accurate information about which products are selling in each store. And its operations people must provide effective, low-cost merchandise handling.

A company's value chain is only as strong as its weakest link. Success depends on how well each department performs its work of adding value for customers and on how well the activities of various departments are coordinated. At Wal-Mart, if purchasing can't wring the lowest prices from suppliers or if operations can't distribute merchandise at the lowest costs, then marketing can't deliver on its promise of the lowest prices.

Ideally, then, a company's different functions should work in harmony to produce value for consumers. But, in practice, departmental relations are full of conflicts and misunderstandings. The marketing department takes the consumer's point of view. But when marketing tries to develop customer satisfaction, it can cause other departments to do a poorer job *in their terms*. Marketing department actions can increase purchasing costs, disrupt production schedules, increase inventories, and create budget headaches. Thus, the other departments may resist the marketing department's efforts. Yet marketers must get all departments to "think consumer" and to develop a smoothly functioning value chain.

> Creating value for buyers is much more than a "marketing function"; rather, [it's] analogous to a symphony orchestra in which the contribution of each subgroup is tailored and integrated by a conductor—with a synergistic effect. A seller must draw upon and integrate effectively...its entire human and other capital resources.... [Creating superior value for buyers] is the proper focus of the entire business and not merely of a single department in it.[17]

Marketing management can best gain support for its goal of customer satisfaction by working to understand the company's other departments. Marketing managers need to work closely with managers of other functions to develop a system of functional plans under which the different departments can work together to accomplish the company's overall strategic objectives.

The value chain: Wal-Mart's ability to offer the right products at low prices depends on the contributions from people in all of the company's departments—marketing, purchasing, information systems, and operations.

Jack Welch, General Electric's highly regarded former CEO, told his employees, "Companies can't give job security. Only customers can!" He emphasized that all General Electric people, regardless of their department, have an impact on customer satisfaction and retention. His message: "If you are not thinking customer, you are not thinking."[18]

Partnering with Others in the Marketing System

In its quest to create customer value, the firm needs to look beyond its own value chain and into the value chains of its suppliers, distributors, and, ultimately, customers. Consider McDonald's. McDonald's 30 000 restaurants worldwide serve more than 46 million customers daily, capturing a 43 percent share of the burger market.[19] People do not swarm to McDonald's only because they love the chain's hamburgers. In fact, consumers typically rank McDonald's behind Burger King and Wendy's in taste. Consumers flock to the McDonald's *system,* not just to its food products. Throughout the world, McDonald's finely tuned system delivers a high standard of what the company calls QSCV—quality, service, cleanliness, and value. McDonald's is effective only to the extent that it successfully partners with its franchisees, suppliers, and others to jointly deliver exceptionally high customer value.

Value-delivery network
The network made up of the company, suppliers, distributors, and ultimately customers who "partner" with each other to improve the performance of the entire system.

More companies today are partnering with the other members of the supply chain to improve the performance of the customer **value-delivery network.** For example, Honda has designed a program for working closely with its suppliers to help them reduce their costs and improve quality. When Honda chose Donnelly Corporation to supply all of the mirrors for its cars, it sent engineers swarming over Donnelly's plants, looking for ways to improve its products and operations. This helped Donnelly reduce its costs by 2 percent in the first year. As a result of its improved performance, Donnelly's sales to Honda grew from $7.5 million annually to more than $90 million in less than 10 years. In turn, Honda gained an efficient, low-cost supplier of quality components. And Honda customers received greater value in the form of lower-cost, higher-quality cars.[20]

Increasingly in today's marketplace, competition no longer takes place between individual competitors. Rather, it takes place between the entire value-delivery networks created by these competitors. Thus, Honda's performance against Toyota depends on the quality of Honda's overall value-delivery network versus Toyota's. Even if Honda makes the best cars, it might lose in the marketplace if Toyota's dealer network provides more customer-satisfying sales and service.

The Marketing Process

Marketing process
The process of (1) analyzing marketing opportunities; (2) selecting target markets; (3) developing the marketing mix; and (4) managing the marketing effort.

The strategic plan defines the company's overall mission and objectives. Marketing's role and activities in the organization are shown in Figure 2.4, which summarizes the entire **marketing process** and the forces influencing company marketing strategy.

Consumers stand in the centre. The goal is to build strong and profitable relationships with customers. As a first step, through market segmentation, targeting, and positioning, the company decides which customers it will serve and how. The company identifies the total market, divides it into smaller segments, selects the most promising segments, and focuses on serving and satisfying these segments. Next, the company designs a marketing mix made up of factors under its control—product, price, place, and promotion. To find the best marketing mix and put it into action, the company engages in marketing analysis, planning, implementation, and control. Through these activities, the company watches and adapts to the marketing environment. We will now look briefly at each element in the marketing process. In later chapters, we will discuss each element in more depth.

Relationships with Consumers

To succeed in today's competitive marketplace, companies must be customer centred—winning customers from competitors, then keeping and growing them by delivering greater value. But before it can satisfy consumers, a company must first understand their needs and wants. Thus, sound marketing requires a careful customer analysis.

Companies know that they cannot satisfy all consumers in a given market—at least not all consumers in the same way. There are too many different kinds of consumers with too many different kinds of needs. And some companies are in a better position to serve certain segments of the market. Thus, each company must divide up the total market, choose the best segments, and design strategies for profitably serving chosen segments better than its competitors do. This process involves three steps: *market segmentation, market targeting,* and *market positioning.*

Market Segmentation

The market consists of many types of customers, products, and needs. The marketer has to determine which segments offer the best opportunity for achieving company

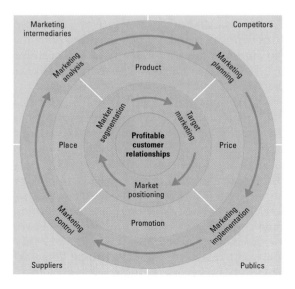

Figure 2.4 Factors influencing company marketing strategy

objectives. Consumers can be grouped and served in various ways, based on geographic, demographic, psychographic, and behavioural factors. The process of dividing a market into distinct groups of buyers with different needs, characteristics, or behaviour, who might require separate products or marketing mixes, is called **market segmentation.**

Every market has market segments, but not all ways of segmenting a market are equally useful. For example, Tylenol would gain little by distinguishing between male and female users of pain relievers if both respond the same way to marketing efforts. A **market segment** consists of consumers who respond in a similar way to a given set of marketing efforts. In the car market, for example, consumers who choose the biggest, most comfortable car regardless of price compose one market segment. Customers who care mainly about price and operating economy make up another segment. It would be difficult to make one model of car that was the first choice of every consumer. Companies are wise to focus their efforts on meeting the distinct needs of one or more market segments.

Target Marketing

After a company has defined market segments, it can enter one or many segments of a given market. **Target marketing** involves evaluating each market segment's attractiveness and selecting one or more segments to enter. A company should target segments in which it can generate the greatest customer value and sustain it over time. A company with limited resources might decide to serve only one or a few special segments. This strategy limits sales, but it can be very profitable. A company might choose to serve several related segments, perhaps those with different kinds of customers but with the same basic wants. Or a large company might decide to offer a complete range of products to serve all market segments.

Most companies enter a new market by serving a single segment; if this proves successful, they add segments. Large companies eventually seek full market coverage. They want to be the General Motors of their industry. GM says that it makes a car for every "person, purse, and personality." The leading company normally has different products designed to meet the special needs of each segment.

Market Positioning

After a company has decided which market segments to enter, it must decide what "positions" it wants to occupy in those segments. A product's *position* is the place the product occupies in consumers' minds relative to the competitors' products. Marketers want to develop unique market positions for their products. If a product is perceived to be exactly like others on the market, consumers would have no reason to buy it.

Market positioning is arranging for a product to occupy a clear, distinctive, and desirable place in the minds of target consumers relative to competing products. Thus, marketers plan positions that distinguish their products from competing brands and give them the greatest strategic advantage in their target markets. For example, the Ford Taurus is "built to last," Chevy Blazer is "like a rock," Toyota's economical Echo states "It's not you. It's the car," and Saturn is "a different kind of company, a different kind of car." Lexus avows "the passionate pursuit of excellence," Jaguar is positioned as "the art of performance," and Mercedes says, "In a perfect world, everyone would drive a Mercedes." The luxurious Bentley promises "eighteen handcrafted feet of shameless luxury." Such deceptively simple statements form the backbone of a product's marketing strategy.

In positioning its product, the company first identifies possible competitive advantages on which to build the position. To gain competitive advantage, the company must offer greater value to target consumers. It can do this either by charging lower prices than competitors do or by offering more benefits to justify higher

---

Market segmentation
Dividing a market into distinct groups of buyers with different needs, characteristics, or behaviour, who might require separate products or marketing mixes.

Market segment
A group of consumers who respond in a similar way to a given set of marketing efforts.

Target marketing
The process of evaluating each market segment's attractiveness and selecting one or more segments to enter.

Market positioning
Arranging for a product to occupy a clear, distinctive, and desirable place relative to competing products in the minds of target consumers.

Positioning: Bentley promises "eighteen handcrafted feet of shameless luxury." In contrast, Toyota promises, "At 41 miles per gallon…it's not you. It's the car." Such deceptively simple statements form the backbone of a product's marketing strategy.

prices. But if the company positions the product as *offering* greater value, it must then *deliver* that greater value. Thus, effective positioning begins with actually *differentiating* the company's marketing offer so that it gives consumers more value.

Once the company has chosen a desired position, it must take strong steps to deliver and communicate that position to target consumers. The company's entire marketing program should support the chosen positioning strategy.

Marketing Strategies for Competitive Advantage

To be successful, the company must do a *better job than competitors* of satisfying target consumers. Thus, marketing strategies must be geared to the needs of consumers but also to the strategies of competitors.

Designing competitive marketing strategies begins with thorough competitor analysis. The company constantly compares the value and customer satisfaction delivered by its products, prices, channels, and promotion with those of close competitors. In this way it can discern areas of potential advantage and disadvantage. The company asks: Who are our competitors? What are their objectives and strategies? What are their strengths and weaknesses? And how will they react to different competitive strategies we might use?

The competitive marketing strategy a company adopts depends on its industry position. A firm that dominates a market can adopt one or more of several *market leader* strategies. Well-known leaders include Coca-Cola (soft drinks), Microsoft (computer software), Caterpillar (large construction equipment), IBM (computers and information technology services), Wal-Mart (retailing), Boeing (aircraft), and AOL (Internet and online services). *Market challengers* are runner-up companies that aggressively attack competitors to get more market share. For example, Pepsi challenges Coke, Komatsu challenges Caterpillar, and MSN challenges AOL. The challenger might attack the market leader, other firms its own size, or smaller local and regional competitors.

Some runner-up firms will choose to follow rather than challenge the market leader. *Market followers* seek stable market shares and profits by following competitors' product offers, prices, and marketing programs. Smaller firms in a market, or even larger firms that lack established positions, often adopt *market nicher* strategies. They specialize in serving market niches that major competitors overlook or ignore. For example, Arm & Hammer has a lock on the baking soda corner of most consumer goods categories, including toothpaste, deodorizers, and others. Oshkosh Truck has found its niche as the world's largest producer of airport rescue trucks and front-loading concrete mixers. And Veterinary Pet Insurance provides 82 percent of all health insurance policies for our furry—or feathery—friends (see Real Marketing 2.3). "Nichers" avoid direct confrontations with the majors by specializing along market, customer, product, or marketing-mix lines. Through smart niching, smaller firms in an industry can be as profitable as their larger competitors.

Developing the Marketing Mix

Marketing mix
The set of controllable, tactical marketing tools—product, price, place, and promotion—that the firm blends to produce the response it wants in the target market.

Once the company has decided on its overall competitive marketing strategy, it is ready to begin planning the details of the marketing mix. The **marketing mix** is the set of controllable, tactical marketing tools that the firm blends to produce the response it wants in the target market. The marketing mix consists of everything the firm can do to influence the demand for its product. The many possibilities can be collected into four groups of variables known as the "four Ps": *product, price, place,* and *promotion*.[21] Figure 2.5 shows the particular marketing tools under each P.

Product is the "goods-and-service" combination the company offers to the target market. Thus, a Ford Taurus "product" consists of nuts and bolts, spark plugs, pistons, headlights, and thousands of other parts. Ford offers several Taurus styles and dozens of optional features. The car comes fully serviced and with a comprehensive warranty that is as much a part of the product as the tailpipe.

Price is the amount of money customers have to pay to obtain the product. Ford calculates suggested retail prices that its dealers might charge for each Taurus. But Ford dealers rarely charge the full sticker price. Instead, they negotiate the price with each customer, offering discounts, trade-in allowances, and credit terms to adjust for the current competitive situation and to bring the price into line with the buyer's perception of the car's value.

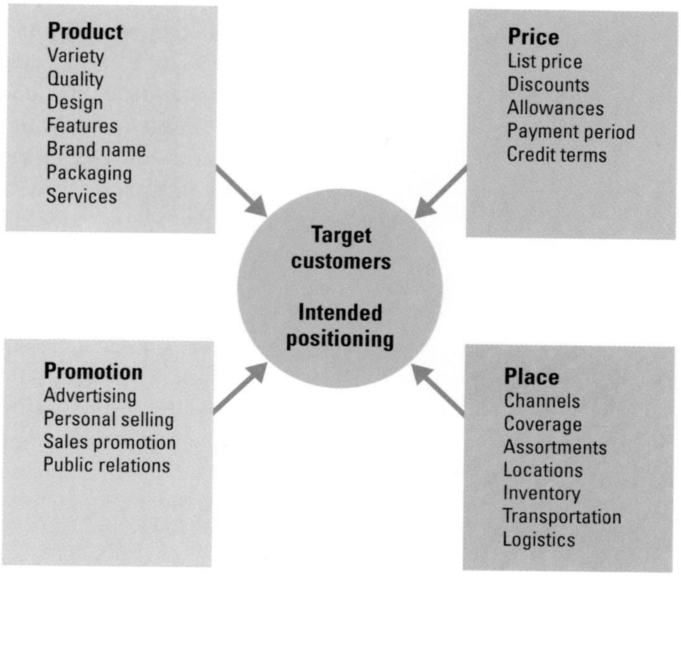

Product
Variety
Quality
Design
Features
Brand name
Packaging
Services

Price
List price
Discounts
Allowances
Payment period
Credit terms

Target customers

Intended positioning

Promotion
Advertising
Personal selling
Sales promotion
Public relations

Place
Channels
Coverage
Assortments
Locations
Inventory
Transportation
Logistics

Figure 2.5 The four *P*s of the marketing mix

2.3 Niching: Health Insurance for Our Furry—or Feathery—Friends

ealth insurance for pets? Clarica, London Life, Prudential, and most other large insurance companies haven't paid much attention to it. But that leaves plenty of room for more focused nichers, for whom pet health insurance has become a lucrative business. The largest of the small competitors is Veterinary Pet Insurance (VPI). VPI's mission is to "make the miracles of veterinary medicine affordable to all pet owners."

VPI was founded in 1980 by veterinarian Jack Stephens. He never intended to leave his practice, but

You promised to take care of me.

I don't understand the "if I can afford it" part.

A wagging tail. A purr of delight. In return for those moments of love, you've promised to take care of your dog or cat.

And whether it's an ear infection, injury or a serious illness, there will come a time when your pet needs medical attention. When that day comes, Veterinary Pet Insurance will help you keep your promise to care.

Besides coverage for accidents and illness, we offer routine care coverage to help pay for an annual veterinary exam, vaccinations—even prescription flea control. And, you can use any veterinarian worldwide. In fact, 9 out of 10 veterinarians who recommend pet insurance recommend VPI. No wonder more and more pet owners depend on Veterinary Pet Insurance, the nation's oldest, largest and number one pet insurance plan.

Veterinary Pet Insurance: We'll help you keep your promise to protect your pet.

Avian and exotic pet coverage available; call for details.

Underwritten by: Veterinary Pet Insurance Co. (CA), Brea, CA; National Casualty Co. (Nat'l), Madison, WI. ©2002 Veterinary Pet Services Inc.

Protect your best friend.

It's easy, affordable and the benefits can start with your next veterinary visit.

Call 800-USA-PETS
(800-872-7387)
Or go to **petinsurance.com**

VETERINARY
PET INSURANCE
Making the miracles of veterinary medicine affordable

Nichers: Market nicher VPI is growing faster than a newborn puppy. Its mission is to "make the miracles of veterinary medicine affordable to all pet owners."

his life took a dramatic turn when he visited a local grocery store and was identified by a client's daughter as "the man who killed Buffy." Stephens had euthanized the family dog two weeks earlier. He immediately began researching the possibility of creating medical pet insurance. "There is nothing more frustrating for a veterinarian than knowing that you can heal a sick patient, but the owner lacks the financial resources and instructs you to put the pet down," says Stephens. "I wanted to change that."

Pet insurance is a still-small but fast-growing segment of the insurance business. Insiders think the industry offers huge potential. Currently, 53 percent of Canadian households own a pet: 30 percent own dogs, 28 percent are cat lovers, and 10 percent have another type of animal such as a reptile. Many people treat their pets as family members—and they buy accordingly. In fact, North Americans now spend a whopping $47 billion a year on their pets. The average dog owner spends almost $300 a year on pet medical care alone.

Unlike in Sweden and Britain, where more than half of all pet owners carry pet health insurance, only 1 percent of pet owners in the United States carry such coverage. However, a recent study of pet owners found that nearly 75 percent are willing to go into debt to pay for veterinary care for their furry—or feathery—companions. And for many pet medical procedures, they'd have to! If not diagnosed quickly, even a mundane ear infection in a dog can result in $1000 worth of medical treatment. A more complicated feline kidney transplant can run as much as $6500. Cancer treatments, including radiation and chemotherapy, could cost a pet owner more than $10 000. All of this adds up to a lot of potential growth for pet health insurers.

VPI's plans cover more than 6400 medical problems and conditions of pets. The insurance helps pay for office calls, prescriptions, treatments, lab fees, X-rays, surgery, and hospitalization. Like its handful of competitors, VPI issues health insurance policies for dogs and cats. Unlike its competitors, VPI recently expanded its coverage to a menagerie of exotic pets as well. Among other critters, the new Avian and Exotic Pet Plan covers birds, rabbits, ferrets, rats, guinea pigs, snakes (except extra-large ones) and other reptiles, iguanas, possums, turtles, hedgehogs, and pot belly pigs. "There's such a vast array" of pets, says a VPI executive, "and people love them. We have to respect that."

How's VPI doing in its niche? It's growing like a newborn puppy. VPI is by far the largest of the handful of companies that offer pet insurance, providing more than 82 percent of all U.S. pet insurance policies. Since its inception, VPI has issued more than 1 million policies, and it now serves more than 250 000 policyholders. Sales have grown 40 percent in each of the past five years, reaching nearly $68 million last year.

That might not amount to much for the large companies that insure people and property, but it's profitable business for nichers like VPI. As importantly, it's a real godsend for the company's policyholders.

"Veterinarians and pet owners want to provide their pets with the best medical care possible," says VPI founder Stephens. "But with advances in veterinary medicine keeping pace with those in human medicine, cost often becomes the deciding factor in the level of care owners can provide. We [always will] strive to make the miracles of modern medicine affordable."

Sources: "Canadians and Their Pets," *Leger Marketing Report*, June 17, 2002, www.legermarketing.com/documents/spclm/020617eng.pdf; Michelle Desai, "VPI—Twenty Years and Still Going Strong" (press release), January 13, 2002; Mary Christine Convey, "Insurers Find Niche in Pet Health Insurance," *National Underwriter*, May 21, 2001, pp. 28–29; Michelle Leder, "How Much Is That $100 Deductible in the Window?" *New York Times*, July 22, 2001, pp. 3, 10; Jane Bennett Clark, "Cover Your Tail," *Kiplinger's Personal Finance*, January 2002, pp. 108–112; and information from the Veterinary Health Insurance website at www.petinsurance.com (June 2002).

Place includes company activities that make the product available to target consumers. Ford maintains a large body of independent dealerships that sell the company's many different models. Ford selects its dealers carefully and supports them strongly. The dealers keep an inventory of Ford automobiles, demonstrate them to potential buyers, negotiate prices, close sales, and service the cars after the sale.

Promotion means activities that communicate the merits of the product and persuade target customers to buy it. Ford spends more than $3 billion worldwide each year on advertising to tell consumers about the company and its products.[22] Dealership salespeople assist potential buyers and persuade them that Ford offers the best car for them. Ford and its dealers offer special promotions—sales, cash rebates, low financing rates—as added purchase incentives.

An effective marketing program blends all of the marketing mix elements into a coordinated program designed to achieve the company's marketing objectives by delivering value to consumers. The marketing mix constitutes the company's tactical tool kit for establishing strong positioning in target markets.

Some critics feel that the four Ps may omit or underemphasize certain important activities. For example, they ask, "Where are services? Just because they don't start with a P doesn't justify omitting them." The answer is that services, such as banking, airline, and retailing services, are products too. We might call them *service products.* "Where is packaging?" the critics might ask. Marketers would answer that they include packaging as just one of many product decisions. All said, as Figure 2.5 suggests, many marketing activities that might appear to be left out of the marketing mix are subsumed under one of the four Ps. The issue is not whether there should be four, six, or ten Ps so much as what framework is most helpful in designing marketing programs.

There is another concern, however, that is valid. It holds that the four Ps concept takes the seller's view of the market, not the buyer's view. From the buyer's viewpoint, in this age of customer relationships, the four Ps might be better described as the four Cs:[23]

Four *Ps*	Four *Cs*
Product	Customer solution
Price	Customer cost
Place	Convenience
Promotion	Communication

Thus while marketers see themselves as selling a product, customers see themselves as buying value or a solution to their problem. And customers are interested in more than the price; they are interested in the total costs of obtaining, using, and disposing of a product. Customers want the product and service to be as conveniently available as possible. Finally, they want two-way communication. Marketers would do well to first think through the four Cs and then build the four Ps on that platform.

Managing the Marketing Effort

The company wants to design and put into action the marketing mix that will best achieve its objectives in its target markets. Figure 2.6 shows the relationship between the four marketing management functions—*analysis, planning, implementation,* and *control.* The company first develops company-wide strategic plans, then translates them into marketing and other plans for each division, product, and brand. Through implementation, the company turns the plans into actions. Control consists of measuring and evaluating the results of marketing activities and taking corrective action where needed. Finally, marketing analysis provides information and evaluations needed for all of the other marketing activities.

Marketing Analysis

Managing the marketing function begins with a complete analysis of the company's situation. The company must analyze its markets and marketing environment to identify attractive opportunities and avoid environmental threats. It must analyze company strengths and weaknesses, as well as current and possible marketing actions, to determine which opportunities it can best pursue. Marketing provides input to each of the other marketing management functions. We discuss marketing analysis more fully in Chapter 5.

Marketing Planning

Through strategic planning, the company decides what it wants to do with each business unit. Marketing planning involves deciding on marketing strategies that will help the company attain its overall strategic objectives. A detailed marketing plan is needed for each business, product, or brand. What does a marketing plan look like? Our discussion focuses on product or brand plans.

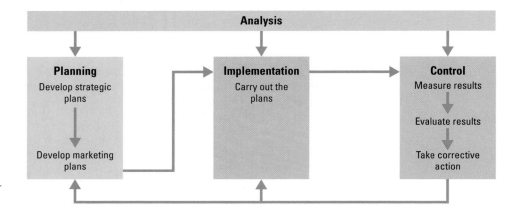

Figure 2.6   The relationship between analysis, planning, implementation, and control

Table 2.2 outlines the major sections of a typical product or brand plan. The plan begins with an executive summary that quickly overviews major assessments, goals, and recommendations. The main section of the plan presents a detailed analysis of the current marketing situation and of potential threats and opportunities. It next states major objectives for the brand and outlines the specifics of a marketing strategy for achieving them.

Marketing strategy

The marketing logic by which the business unit hopes to achieve its marketing objectives.

A **marketing strategy** is the marketing logic by which the company hopes to achieve its marketing objectives. It consists of specific strategies for target markets, positioning, the marketing mix, and marketing expenditure levels. In this section, the planner explains how each strategy responds to threats, opportunities, and critical issues outlined earlier in the plan. Additional sections of the marketing plan lay out an action program for implementing the marketing strategy, along with the details of a supporting *marketing budget*. The last section outlines the controls that will be used to monitor progress and take corrective action.

Table 2.2   Contents of a Marketing Plan

Section	Purpose
Executive summary	Presents a brief summary of the main goals and recommendations of the plan for management review, helping top management to find the plan's major points quickly. A table of contents should follow the executive summary.
Current marketing situation	Describes the target market and the company's position in it, including information about the market, product performance, competition, and distribution. This section includes: • A *market description* that defines the market and major segments, then reviews customer needs and factors in the marketing environment that may affect customer purchasing. • A *product review* that shows sales, prices, and gross margins of the major products in the product line. • A review of *competition* that identifies major competitors and assesses their market positions and strategies for product quality, pricing, distribution, and promotion. • A review of *distribution* that evaluates recent sales trends and other developments in major distribution channels.
Threat and opportunity analysis	Assesses major threats and opportunities that the product may face, helping management to anticipate important positive or negative developments that may have an impact on the firm and its strategies.
Objectives and issues	States the marketing objectives that the company would like to attain during the plan's term and discusses key issues that will affect their attainment. For example, if the goal is to achieve a 15 percent market share, this section looks at how this goal might be achieved.
Marketing strategy	Outlines the broad marketing logic by which the business unit hopes to achieve its marketing objectives and the specifics of target markets, positioning, and marketing expenditure levels. It outlines specific strategies for each marketing mix element and explains how each responds to the threats, opportunities, and critical issues spelled out earlier in the plan.
Action program	Spells out how marketing strategies will be turned into specific action programs that answer the following questions: *What* will be done? *When* will it be done? *Who* is responsible for doing it? *How* much will it cost?
Budget	Details a supporting marketing budget that is essentially a projected profit-and-loss statement. It shows expected revenues (forecast number of units sold and the average net price) and expected costs (of production, distribution, and marketing). The difference is the projected profit. Once approved by higher management, the budget is the basis for materials buying, production scheduling, personnel planning, and marketing operations.
Controls	Outlines the control that will be used to monitor progress and allow higher management to review implementation results and spot products that are not meeting their goals.

Marketers must continually plan their analysis, implementation, and control activities.

Marketing Implementation

Marketing implementation

The process that turns marketing strategies and plans into marketing actions to accomplish strategic marketing objectives.

Planning good strategies is only a first step in successful marketing. A brilliant marketing strategy counts for little if the company fails to implement it properly. **Marketing implementation** is the process that turns marketing *plans* into marketing *actions* to accomplish strategic marketing objectives. Implementation involves day-to-day, month-to-month activities that effectively put the marketing plan to work. Whereas marketing planning addresses the *what* and *why* of marketing activities, implementation addresses the *who, where, when,* and *how.*

Many managers think that "doing things right"—implementation—is as important as, or even more important than, "doing the right things"—strategy. The fact is both are critical to success.[24] However, companies can gain competitive advantages through effective implementation. One firm can have essentially the same strategy as another, yet win in the marketplace through faster or better execution. Still, implementation is difficult: It is often easier to develop good marketing strategies than it is to execute them.

In an increasingly connected world, people at all levels of the marketing system must work together to implement marketing plans and strategies. At Black & Decker, for example, marketing implementation for the company's power tool products requires day-to-day decisions and actions by thousands of people both inside and outside the organization. Marketing managers make decisions about target segments, branding, packaging, pricing, promoting, and distributing. They connect with people elsewhere in the company to get support for their products and programs. They talk with engineering about product design, with manufacturing about production and inventory levels, and with finance about funding and cash flows. They also connect with outside people, such as advertising agencies to plan ad campaigns and the media to obtain publicity support. The sales force urges Home Depot, Wal-Mart, and other retailers to advertise Black & Decker products, provide ample shelf space, and use company displays.

Successful implementation depends on how well the company blends its people, organization structure, decision and reward systems, and company culture into a cohesive action program that supports its strategies. At all levels, the company must be staffed by people who have the needed skills, motivation, and personal characteristics. The company's formal organization structure plays an important role in implementing marketing strategy. So do its decision and reward systems. For example, if a company's compensation system rewards managers for short-run profit results, they will have little incentive to work toward long-run market-building objectives.

Finally, to be successfully implemented, the firm's marketing strategies must fit with its company culture, the system of values and beliefs shared by people in the organization. A study of North America's most successful companies found that these companies have almost cult-like cultures built around strong, market-oriented missions. At such companies as Mountain Equipment Co-op (MEC), VanCity Credit Union, Wal-Mart, Microsoft, Procter & Gamble, and Walt Disney, "employees share such a strong vision that they know in their hearts what's right for their company."[25]

Marketing Department Organization

The company must design a marketing department that can carry out marketing analysis, planning, implementation, and control. If the company is very small, one person might do all of the marketing work, including research, selling, advertising, and customer service. As the company expands, a marketing department organization emerges to plan and carry out marketing activities. In large companies, this department contains many specialists. Thus, Black & Decker has product managers, salespeople and sales managers, market researchers, advertising experts, and other specialists.

Modern marketing departments can be arranged in several ways. The most common form of marketing organization is the *functional organization,* in which different marketing activities are headed by a functional specialist—a sales manager, advertising manager, marketing research manager, customer service manager, or new product manager. A company that sells across the country or internationally often uses a *geographic organization,* in which its sales and marketing people are assigned to specific countries, regions, and districts. Geographic organization allows salespeople to settle into a territory, get to know their customers, and work with a minimum of travel time and cost.

Companies with many, very different products or brands often create a *product management organization.* Using this approach, a product manager develops and implements a complete strategy and marketing program for a specific product or brand. Product management first appeared at Procter & Gamble in 1929. A new company soap, Camay, was not doing well, and a young P&G executive was assigned to give his exclusive attention to developing and promoting this product. He was successful, and the company soon added other product managers.[26] Since then, many firms, especially in consumer product companies, have set up product management organizations. However, recent dramatic changes in the marketing environment have caused many companies to rethink the role of the product manager. Many companies are finding that today's marketing environment calls for less brand focus and more customer focus. They are shifting toward *customer equity management*—moving away from managing just product profitability and toward managing *customer* profitability.[27]

For companies that sell one product line to many different types of markets and customers that have different needs and preferences, a *market* or *customer management organization* might be best. A market management organization is similar to the product management organization. Market managers are responsible for developing marketing strategies and plans for their specific markets or customers. This system's main advantage is that the company is organized around the needs of specific customer segments.

Large companies that produce many different products flowing into many different geographic and customer markets use some *combination* of the functional, geographic, product, and market organization forms. This ensures that each function, product, and market receives its share of management attention. However, it can also add costly layers of management and reduce organizational flexibility. Still, the benefits of organizational specialization usually outweigh the drawbacks.

Marketing Control

Marketing control

The process of measuring and evaluating the results of marketing strategies and plans, and taking corrective action to ensure that marketing objectives are attained.

Because many surprises occur during the implementation of marketing plans, the marketing department must practise constant marketing control. **Marketing control** involves evaluating the results of marketing strategies and plans and taking corrective action to ensure that objectives are attained. It involves the four steps shown in Figure 2.7. Management first sets specific marketing goals. It then measures its performance in the marketplace and evaluates the causes of any differences between expected and actual performance. Finally, management takes corrective action to close the gaps between its goals and its performance. This may require changing the action programs or even changing the goals.

Operating control involves checking ongoing performance against the annual plan and taking corrective action when necessary. Its purpose is to ensure that the company achieves the sales, profits, and other goals set out in its annual plan. It also involves determining the profitability of different products, territories, markets, and channels. *Strategic control* involves considering whether the company's basic strategies are well matched to its opportunities. Marketing strategies and programs can quickly become outdated, and each company should periodically reassess its overall approach to the marketplace. A major tool for such strategic control is a **marketing audit**. The marketing audit is a comprehensive, systematic, independent, and periodic examination of a company's environment, objectives, strategies, and activities to determine problem areas and opportunities. The audit provides good input for a plan of action to improve the company's marketing performance.[28]

Marketing audit

A comprehensive, systematic, independent, and periodic examination of a company's environment, objectives, strategies, and activities to determine problem areas and opportunities and to recommend a plan of action to improve the company's marketing performance.

The marketing audit covers all major marketing areas of a business, not just a few trouble spots. It assesses the marketing environment, marketing strategy, marketing organization, marketing systems, marketing mix, and marketing productivity and profitability. The audit is normally conducted by an objective and experienced outside party who is independent of the marketing department. Table 2.3 shows the kinds of questions the marketing auditor might ask. The findings may come as a surprise—and sometimes as a shock—to management. Management then decides which actions make sense and how and when to implement them.

The Marketing Environment

Managing the marketing function would be hard enough if the marketer had to deal only with the controllable marketing mix variables. But the company operates in a complex marketing environment, consisting of uncontrollable forces to which the company must adapt. The environment produces both threats and opportunities. The company must carefully analyze its environment so that it can avoid the threats and take advantage of the opportunities. The company's marketing environment includes forces close to the company that affect its ability to serve its consumers, such as other company departments, channel members, suppliers, competitors, and

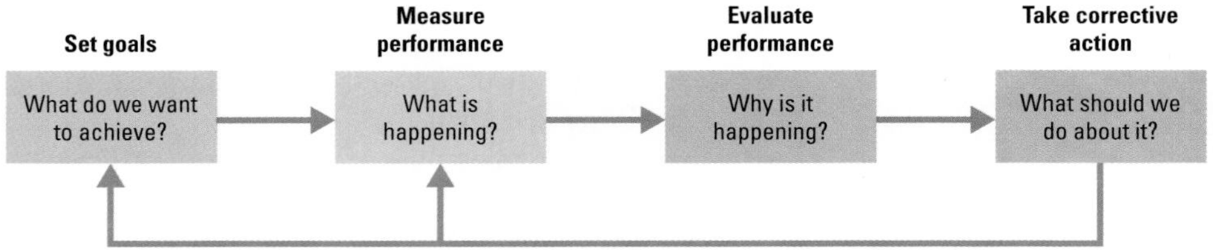

Set goals	Measure performance	Evaluate performance	Take corrective action
What do we want to achieve?	What is happening?	Why is it happening?	What should we do about it?

Figure 2.7 The control process

Table 2.3   Marketing Audit Questions

Marketing Environment Audit

1. The *macroenvironment*: What major *demographic, economic, natural, technological, political,* and *cultural* trends pose threats and opportunities for this company?
2. The *task environment*:
   - *Markets and customers:* What is happening to marketing size, growth, geographic distribution, and profits? What are the major market segments? How do customers make their buying decisions? How do they rate the company on product quality, value, and service?
   - *Other factors in the marketing system:* Who are the company's major *competitors* and what are their strategies, strengths, and weaknesses? How are the company's *channels* performing? What trends are affecting *suppliers*? What key *publics* provide problems or opportunities?

Marketing Strategy Audit

1. *Business mission and marketing objectives:* Is the mission clearly defined and market-oriented? Has the company set clear objectives to guide marketing planning and performance?
2. *Marketing strategy:* Does the company have a strong marketing strategy for achieving its objectives?
3. *Budgets:* Has the company budgeted sufficient resources to segments, products, territories, and marketing-mix elements?

Marketing Organization Audit

1. *Formal structure:* Are marketing activities optimally structured along functional, product, market, and territory lines?
2. *Functional efficiency:* Do marketing and sales communicate effectively? Is marketing staff well-trained, supervised, motivated, and evaluated?
3. *Cross-functional efficiency:* Do marketing people work well with people in operations, R&D, purchasing, human resources, information technology, and other non-marketing areas?

Marketing Systems Audit

1. *Marketing information system:* Is the marketing intelligence system providing accurate and timely information? Is the company using marketing research effectively?
2. *Marketing planning system:* Does the company prepare annual, long-term, and strategic plans? Are they used?
3. *Marketing control system:* Are annual plan objectives being achieved? Does management periodically analyze product, market, and channel sales and profitability?
4. *New product development:* Does the company have an effective new product development process? Has the company succeeded with new products?

Marketing Productivity Audit

1. *Profitability analysis:* How profitable are the company's different products, markets, territories, and channels? Should the company enter, expand, or withdraw from any business segments?
2. *Cost-effectiveness analysis:* Do any marketing activities have excessive costs? How can costs be reduced?

Marketing Function Audit

1. *Products:* What are the company's product line objectives? Should some current products be phased out or new products be added? Would some products benefit from changes in quality, features, or style?
2. *Price:* Are the company's pricing policies and procedures appropriate? Are prices in line with customers' perceived value?
3. *Place:* What are the company's distribution objectives and strategies? Should existing channels be changed or new ones added?
4. *Promotion:* Does the company have well-developed *advertising, sales promotion,* and *public relations* programs? Is the *sales* force large enough and well-trained, supervised, and motivated?

---

publics. It also includes broader demographic and economic forces, political and legal forces, technological and ecological forces, and social and cultural forces. In order to connect effectively with consumers, others in the company, external partners, and the world around them, marketers need to consider all of these forces when developing and positioning an offer to the target market. We discuss the marketing environment more fully in Chapter 4.

Looking Back: Reviewing the Concepts

All companies must look ahead and find the long-term game plan that makes the most sense given its specific situation, opportunities, objectives, and resources. The hard task of selecting an overall company strategy for long-run survival and growth is called *strategic planning*. Strategic planning sets the stage for the rest of the company's planning, including marketing planning.

Guided by the strategic plan, marketers work with others inside and outside the company to design and implement strategies for building profitable relationships with targeted customers.

1. Explain company-wide strategic planning and its four steps.

Strategic planning involves developing a strategy for long-run survival and growth. It consists of four steps: defining the company's mission, setting objectives, designing a business portfolio, formulating strategies for the various business units, and developing functional plans. *Defining a clear company mission* begins with drafting a formal mission statement, which should be market oriented, realistic, specific, motivating, and consistent with the market environment. The mission is then transformed into detailed *supporting goals and objectives* to guide the entire company. Based on those goals and objectives, headquarters *designs a business portfolio*, deciding which businesses and products should receive more or fewer resources. In turn, each business and product unit must develop *detailed marketing plans* in line with the company-wide plan. Comprehensive and sound marketing plans support business strategic planning by identifying specific opportunities.

2. Discuss how to design business portfolios, and the strategies business units use to create advantage in their industries.

Guided by the company's mission statement and objectives, management plans its *business portfolio,* or the collection of businesses and products that make up the company. To produce a business portfolio that best fits the company's strengths and weaknesses to opportunities in the environment, the company must analyze and adjust its *current* business portfolio and develop growth and downsizing strategies for adjusting the *future* portfolio. The company might use a formal portfolio-planning method like the *BCG growth–share matrix.* But many companies are now designing more customized portfolio-planning approaches that better suit their unique situations. Companies select strategies for each business unit that help them deal successfully with the forces dominating their industry. They select one of the following strategies: *cost leadership, differentiation,* or *focus* and/or *operational excellence, product leadership,* or *customer intimacy.* Once the business unit strategy has been determined, the *product–market expansion grid* suggests four possible growth paths: market penetration, market development, product development, and diversification.

3. Assess marketing's role in strategic planning and explain how marketers partner with others inside and outside the firm to build profitable customer relationships.

The company's strategic plan establishes what kinds of businesses the company will be in and its objectives for each. Then, within each business unit the major functional departments—marketing, finance, accounting, purchasing, operations, information systems, human resources, and others—must work together to accomplish strategic objectives. Marketing plays a key role in the company's strategic planning by providing a marketing-concept *philosophy* and *inputs* regarding attractive market opportunities. Within individual business units, marketing designs *strategies* for reaching the unit's objectives and helps to carry them out profitably.

Marketers alone cannot produce superior value for customers—they can be only a partner in attracting, keeping, and growing customers. A company's success depends on how well each department performs its customer value-adding activities and how well the departments work together to serve the customer. Thus, marketers must practise *partner relationship management.* They must work closely with partners in other company departments to form an effective *value chain* that serves the customer. And they must partner effectively with other companies in the marketing system to form a competitively superior *value-delivery network.*

4. Describe the marketing process and the forces that influence it.

The *marketing process* matches consumer needs with the company's capabilities and objectives. Consumers are at the centre of the marketing process. Through market segmentation, target marketing, and market positioning, the company divides the total market into smaller segments, selects segments it can best serve, and decides how it wants to bring value to target consumers. It then designs a *marketing mix* to produce the response it wants in the target market. The marketing mix consists of product, price, place, and promotion decisions.

5. List the marketing management functions, including the elements of a marketing plan.

To find the best strategy and mix and put them into action, the company engages in marketing analysis, planning, implementation, and control. The main components of a *marketing plan* are the executive summary, current marketing situation, threats and opportunities, objectives and issues, marketing strategies, action programs, budgets, and controls. To plan good strategies is often easier than to carry them out. To be successful, companies must also be effective at *implementation*—turning marketing strategies into marketing actions.

Much of the responsibility for implementation goes to the company's marketing department. Modern marketing departments can be organized one or a combination of ways: *functional marketing organization, geographic organization, product management organization,* or *market management organization.* Marketing organizations carry out *marketing control,* both operating control and strategic control. They use *marketing audits* to determine marketing opportunities and problems and to recommend short-run and long-run actions to improve overall marketing performance. Through these activities, the company watches and adapts to the marketing environment.

Reviewing the Key Terms

Business portfolio   52
Diversification   60
Downsizing   60
Growth–share matrix   53
Market development   60
Market penetration   58
Market positioning   65
Market segment   65
Market segmentation   65

Marketing audit   74
Marketing control   74
Marketing implementation   72
Marketing mix   67
Marketing process   64
Marketing strategy   71
Mission statement   48
Partner relationship
    management   62

Portfolio analysis   52
Product development   60
Product–market expansion grid   58
Strategic business unit (SBU)   52
Strategic planning   47
Target marketing   65
Value chain   62
Value-delivery network   63

Discussing the Concepts

1. Define *strategic planning*. List and briefly review the four steps that lead managers through the strategic planning process.

2. What is a mission statement? List and briefly discuss the four characteristics of effective mission statements.

3. Examine the Boston Consulting Group's growth–share matrix. Which one of the cells provides the primary revenues for the organization's SBUs? How can an organization use the BCG growth–share matrix to plan its future?

4. Beyond evaluating current businesses, designing the business portfolio involves finding future businesses and products the company should consider. Using the product–market expansion grid, prepare a list of new business and product ideas for one of the following companies: (a) Sony Canada's consumer products division, (b) Fuji film division, (c) Levi Strauss Docker's division,

(d) TD Canada Trust's senior citizens investment program, or (e) BMW. Be sure to cover all the cells in the grid.

5. Marketing plays a key role in the company's strategic planning by providing a guiding philosophy. What is this philosophy and what impact does it have on the strategic planning process?

6. Partner relationship management (PRM) is increasingly important in meeting the competitive challenges of the twenty-first century. How does PRM use value chains and value-delivery networks to create effective partnerships?

7. Companies must be customer-centred to succeed. What are the three steps in building customer relationships? How does each aid in relationship building?

8. In this age of customer relationships, the four *P*s might be better described as the four *C*s. Comment.

Applying the Concepts

1. Sony has found the right approach for surrounding its customers with electronic wizardry and entertainment. From PlayStation to online games, from movies to TV, DVD, and music, Sony is tops in entertainment. But rivals are on the horizon. With hungry competitors such as Disney, Microsoft, Panasonic, and a host of others, Sony must constantly adjust its strategic plans and look for new opportunities. For more general information on Sony and its offerings, see www.sony.com.

   - After considering Sony's approach to the world of electronics and entertainment, identify new and promising product opportunities for Sony.
   - Choose one of the product opportunities you identified. What makes it distinctive and promising?
   - What target market would you pursue for this product opportunity?
   - What marketing mix would be appropriate?
   - Write a brief marketing plan for this opportunity (see Table 2.2 on page 71).
   - Critique your plan. What are its strengths and weaknesses?

2. For more than a decade, several firms have been waging the Sneaker Wars. Notable companies such as Nike, Reebok, Adidas, New Balance, Puma, and Converse have been battling with no holds barred, and the dust is yet to settle! In fact, tough new competitors such as Vans and Skechers have arrived on the scene. Visit these firms at their websites: www.nike.com, www.reebok.com, www.adidas.com, www.newbalance.com, www.puma.com, www.converseshoes.com, www.vans.com, and www.skechers.com. As a future marketing strategist, answer the following questions:

   - Which firm is the market leader? Which firms are market challengers, market followers, and market nichers?
   - Critique the various websites. Are the websites consistent with your assessments of the companies' industry positions? Why or why not?
   - Assume the position of one of the market challengers. Design a strategy for overtaking the market leader.
   - Assume the position of a market nicher and design a strategy for expanding your business without drawing attacks from your stronger rivals.
   - Select a market nicher. How might this nicher improve its website?

Video Short

View the video short for this chapter at **www.pearsoned.ca/kotler** and then answer the questions provided in the case description.

Company Case

Trap-Ease: The Big Cheese of Mousetraps

One April morning, Martha House, president of Trap-Ease, entered her office in Moncton, New Brunswick. She paused for a moment to contemplate the Ralph Waldo Emerson quotation that she had framed and hung near her desk: "If a man [can]...make a better mousetrap than his neighbour...the world will make a beaten path to his door." Perhaps, she mused, Emerson knew something that she didn't. She *had* the better mousetrap—Trap-Ease—but the world didn't seem all that excited about it.

Martha had just returned from the National Hardware Show in Toronto. Standing in the trade show display booth for long hours and answering the same questions hundreds of times had been tiring. Yet, this show had excited her. Each year, National Hardware Show officials held a contest to select the best new product introduced at the show. The Trap-Ease had won the contest this year, beating out over 300 new products.

Such notoriety was not new for the Trap-Ease mousetrap. *Canadian Business* magazine had written an article about the mousetrap, and the television show *Marketplace* and trade publications had featured it.

Despite all of this attention, however, the expected demand for the trap had not materialized. Martha hoped that this award might stimulate increased interest and sales.

A group of investors had formed Trap-Ease in January after it had obtained worldwide rights to market the innovative mousetrap. In return for marketing rights, the group agreed to pay the inventor and patent holder, a retired rancher, a royalty fee for each trap sold. The group then hired Martha to serve as president and to develop and manage the Trap-Ease organization.

Trap-Ease contracted with a plastics-manufacturing firm to produce the traps. The trap consists of a square, plastic tube measuring about 15 cm long and 4 cm square. The tube bends in the middle at a 30-degree angle, so that when the front part of the tube rests on a flat surface, the other end is elevated. The elevated ends holds a removable cap into which the user places bait (cheese, dog food, or some other tidbit). A hinged door is attached to the front end of the tube. When the trap is "open," this door rests on two narrow "stilts" attached to the two bottom corners of the door. (See Exhibit 1.)

The simple trap works very efficiently. A mouse, smelling the bait, enters the tube through the open end. As it walks up the angled bottom toward the bait, its weight makes the elevated end of the trap drop downward. This elevates the open end, allowing the hinged door to swing closed, trapping the mouse. Small teeth on the ends of the stilts catch in a groove on the bottom of the trap, locking the door closed. The user could then dispose of the mouse while it was still alive, or the user could leave it alone for a few hours to suffocate in the trap.

Martha believed that the trap had many advantages for the consumer when compared with traditional spring-loaded traps or poisons. Consumers could use it safely and easily with no risk of catching their fingers while loading it. It posed no injury or poisoning threat to children or pets. Furthermore, with Trap-Ease, consumers could avoid the unpleasant mess they encounter with the violent spring-loaded traps—it creates no clean-up problem. Finally, the consumer can re-use the trap or simply throw it away.

Martha's early research suggested that women are the best target market for the Trap-Ease. Men, it seems, are more willing to buy and use the traditional, spring-loaded trap. The targeted women, however, do not like the traditional trap. They often stay at home and take

Exhibit 1

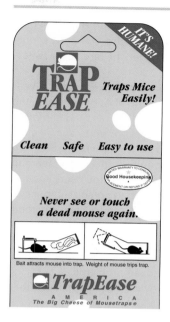

care of their children. Thus, they want a means of dealing with the mouse problem that avoids the unpleasantness and risks that the standard trap creates in the home.

To reach this target market, Martha decided to distribute Trap-Ease through national grocery, hardware, and drug chains such as Safeway, Zellers, Canadian Tire, and Shoppers Drug Mart. She sold the trap directly to these large retailers, avoiding any wholesalers or other intermediaries.

The traps sold in packages of two, with a suggested retail price of $2.49. Although this price made the Trap-Ease about five times more expensive than smaller, standard traps, consumers appeared to offer little initial price resistance. The manufacturing cost for the Trap-Ease, including freight and packaging costs, was about 31 cents per unit. The company paid an additional 8.2 cents per unit in royalty fees. Martha priced the traps to retailers at 99 cents per unit and estimated that, after sales and volume discounts, Trap-Ease would realize net revenues from retailers of 75 cents per unit.

To promote the product, Martha had budgeted approximately $60 000 for the first year. She planned to use $50 000 of this amount for travel costs to visit trade shows and to make sales calls on retailers. She would use the remaining $10 000 for advertising. So far, however, because the mousetrap had generated so much publicity, she had not felt the need to do much advertising. Still, she had placed advertising in *Chatelaine* and in other "home and shelter" magazines (after all, the trap had earned the Good Housekeeping Seal of Approval). Martha was the company's only "salesperson," but she intended to hire more salespeople soon.

Martha had initially forecast Trap-Ease's first-year sales at 500 000 units. By the end of April, however, the company had sold only several thousand units. Martha wondered if most new products got off to such a slow start, or if she was doing something wrong. She had detected some problems, although none seemed overly serious. For one, there had not been enough repeat buying. For another, she had noted that many of the retailers kept their sample mousetraps on their desks as conversation pieces—she wanted the traps to be used and demonstrated. Martha wondered if consumers were also buying the traps as novelties rather than as solutions to their mouse problems.

Martha knew that the investor group believed that Trap-Ease had a "once-in-a-lifetime chance" with its innovative mousetrap, and she sensed the group's impatience. She had budgeted approximately $150 000 in administrative and fixed costs for the first year (not including marketing costs). To keep the investors happy, the company needed to sell enough traps to cover those costs and make a reasonable profit.

Back to the Drawing Board

In these first few months, Martha had learned that marketing a new product is not an easy task. For example, one national retailer had placed a large order with instructions that the order was to be delivered to the loading dock at one of its warehouses between 1:00 and 3:00 p.m. on a specified day. When the truck

delivering the order had arrived late, the retailer had refused to accept the shipment. The retailer had told Martha it would be a year before she got another chance.

As Martha sat down at her desk, she realized she needed to rethink her marketing strategy. Perhaps she had missed something or made some mistake that was causing sales to be so slow. Glancing at the quotation again, she thought that perhaps she should send the picky retailer and other customers a copy of Emerson's famous quotation.

Questions for Discussion

1. Martha and the Trap-Ease investors believe they face a "once-in-a-lifetime" opportunity. What information do they need to evaluate this opportunity? How do you think the group would write its mission statement? How would *you* write it?

2. Has Martha identified the best target market for Trap-Ease? What other market segments might the firm target?

3. How has the company positioned the Trap-Ease relative to the chosen target market? Could it position the product in other ways?

4. Describe the current marketing mix for Trap-Ease. Do you see any problems with this mix?

5. Who is Trap-Ease's competition?

6. How would you change Trap-Ease's marketing strategy? What kinds of control procedures would you establish for this strategy?

7. Develop a budget based on the numbers in the case. Is it realistic? Would you make changes?

CBC Video Case

CBC Log on to your Companion Website at **www.pearsoned.ca/kotler** to view a CBC video segment and case for this chapter.

Chapter 3

Marketing in the Digital Age: Making New Customer Connections

After studying this chapter you should be able to

1. identify the major forces shaping the new digital age

2. explain how companies have responded to the Internet and other powerful new technologies with ebusiness strategies, and how these strategies have resulted in benefits to both buyers and sellers

3. describe the four major ecommerce domains

4. discuss how companies go about conducting ecommerce to profitably deliver more value to customers

5. overview the promise and challenges that ecommerce presents for the future

Looking Ahead: Previewing the Concepts

In the first two chapters, you learned about the basic concepts of marketing, marketing strategies, and the marketing process for building profitable relationships with targeted consumers. However, marketing strategy and practice have undergone dramatic change during the past decade. Major technological advances, including the explosion of the Internet, have had a major impact on buyers and the marketers who serve them. To thrive in this new digital age—even to survive—marketers must rethink their strategies and adapt them to today's new environment.

For starters, consider Canadian Tire Corporation. After at first resisting the Internet, it has transformed itself from a traditional "bricks-and-mortar" one that has successfully combined online marketing with its traditional retail format. This transformation has propelled the company to leadership in the swiftly changing retail industry.

Canadian Tire is a national institution. The familiar red and white signs with the green maple leaf have been part of our landscape since 1922. There are 443 Canadian Tire stores across Canada and some 200 gas stations. It is Canada's largest hard goods retailer and approximately 91 percent of Canadians live within a fifteen-minute drive of a Canadian Tire store.

The firm has long been applauded for its innovative strategies and its ability to move with the times. It was founded by two brothers, A. J. Billes and John W. Billes, who took note of the rising demand for automobiles. With their combined savings of $1800, they bought a small tire garage. Within five years, their business of repairing automobiles and renting out heated parking-garage spaces grew into an incorporated business. People from across Canada began writing to the brothers requesting automotive parts. Recognizing that there was a great demand for automotive parts across Canada but a limited supply, the brothers gained a competitive advantage by introducing a Canadian Tire catalogue. By 1928, it was distributed across the country.

This was the first of many instances where Canadian Tire recognized an opportunity for expansion and better customer service, and developed an innovative solution.

Again in the early 1930s, Canadian Tire differentiated itself from the competition by offering the first guarantee on tires it sold. While this was a risky offer, it proved successful in promoting the business. The next great initiative from Canadian Tire became their best-known innovation. In 1958, Canadian Tire "Money" was introduced. This customer loyalty program lifted Canadian Tire above the competition during a very competitive period and made it a Canadian household name. Never a firm to rest on its laurels, in 2003 Canadian Tire formed a new partnership with Canada's largest car rental company, Budget Canada. A five-year deal was struck that will result in Budget Car and Truck rental kiosks being set up at over 100 Canadian Tire stores. The partnership is a true "win-win." The agreement will also see Budget Canada's fleet of 26 000 cars purchasing fuel and car wash services from Canadian Tire, as well as using its Auto Service Centres for maintenance of Budget's vehicles.

Throughout its history, Canadian Tire has striven to be the number one retailer in Canada. When powerful American competitors Wal-Mart and Home Depot entered the market during the 1990s, Canadian Tire had to take a step back from normal day-to-day activities to understand what customers value about the business. It was becoming increasingly important for Canadian Tire to show Canadians that it wasn't just the closest store in which to shop, but the best store in which to shop. To accomplish this aim, many stores were renovated, new outlets were built, and all operations began to focus on delivering superior customer service. Canadian Tire's renewal is captured in its Statement of Purpose:

> To be the best at what our customers value most. To be the first choice for Canadians in Automotive, Sports and Leisure, and Home Products, providing total customer value through customer-driven service, focused assortments and competitive operations.

Given its history of innovation, it is surprising that Canadian Tire waited until 2002 to launch Canadian Tire Online, its first venture into etailing (www.canadiantire.ca). Some thought Canadian Tire had lost its appetite for modernization and the company was criticized for its reluctance to enter cyberspace. However, the company took a "wait and see" approach so that it could learn from others' mistakes. As a result, Canadian Tire was able to avoid many of the problems other retailers experienced when they rushed online without a workable online strategy. For example, Canadian Tire knew that its website had to be bilingual. While companies operating in the off-line environment can choose to serve people in Quebec or not, retailers operating in the online world must offer services in both official languages. Just one year after its launch, Canadian Tire's website recorded 2 million visits and more than one million unique visitors. The site has enabled all Canadians, whether they live in Halifax or Nunavut, to have access to Canadian products.

To ensure that the ecommerce initiatives continue to meet consumer needs, Canadian Tire Online is working to further develop the webstore's capabilities and service features. In 2001, a line of "Available Only Online" products was introduced. This line includes more than a thousand items and features higher-end appliances and new categories of electronic products such as digital cameras and MP3 players, as well as licensed apparel, luggage, and an extended assortment of power tools.

Most recently, Canadiantire.ca was completely redesigned to make shopping faster, better, and easier for customers. Major enhancements include:

- information about the "Item of the Week" and "Hot Deals of the Week" right on the home page
- a new delivery cost calculator enabling customers to determine delivery costs before beginning the checkout process (delivery costs can be calculated as soon as an item is added to the shopping cart and as additional items are selected)
- a more comprehensive list of product categories within each department in "Around the House," "Workshop," "Sports & Recreation," "Garden & Patio," and "Automotive"—making it faster and easier to browse and shop
- a product assortment that has more than doubled during the last year and now features more than 14 000 items, including 1000 "Available Only Online" items.

In addition, Canadian Tire's unique eFLYER is now fully integrated into the webstore, meaning eFLYER subscribers can shop directly from their eFLYER for the first time ever. Users can also sign up to receive weekly emails featuring information about weekly specials and promotions on the site. And there's a quick link to eFLYER Weekly Specials from the home page.

In melding its online and traditional retail worlds, Canadian Tire has created a powerful new model of retailing—a robust two-tiered system where consumers have the choice of shopping by the method they value most. The model recognizes that, most of the time, customers can visit a local store, but occasionally they will like the convenience and different selection afforded by the Web.[1]

In Chapter 1 we discussed sweeping changes in the marketing landscape that are affecting marketing thinking and practice. Recent technological advances, including the widespread use of the Internet, have created what some call a New Economy. Although there has been widespread debate in recent years about the nature of— even the existence of—such a New Economy, few would disagree that the Internet and other powerful telecommunication technologies have enhanced companies' abilities to compile vast databases that can be analyzed to better understand the needs and preferences of consumers. Marketers will have to develop new strategies and practices better suited to today's new environment. While they will still use such standard marketing strategies and practices as mass marketing, product standardization, mass media advertising, and store retailing, they will also employ customized marketing techniques to address the needs of individual buyers.

In this chapter, we first describe the key forces shaping the new digital age. Then we examine how marketing strategy and practice are changing to meet the requirements of this new age.

Major Forces Shaping the Digital Age

Intranet
A network that connects people within a company to each other and to the company network.

Extranet
A proprietary network that connects a company with its suppliers and distributors.

Internet
A vast public web of computer networks, which connects users of all types all around the world to each other and to an amazingly large "information repository." The Internet makes up one big "information highway" that can dispatch bits at incredible speeds from one location to another.

Many forces are playing a major role in reshaping the world economy, including technology, globalization, environmentalism, and others. Here we discuss four specific forces that underlie the new digital age (see Figure 3.1): digitalization and connectivity, the explosion of the Internet, new types of intermediaries, and customization.

Connectivity

Telecommunication networks enable businesses to share digitized information. Much of the world's business today is carried out over networks that connect people and companies. **Intranets** are networks that connect people within a company to each other and to the company network. **Extranets** connect a company with its suppliers, distributors, and other outside partners. They are closed systems that are password-protected so that only approved organizations should be able to access them. And the **Internet**, a vast public web of computer networks, connects users of all types all around the world. Consumers and businesses alike can connect to each other almost instantaneously, and they can use the Internet to search for data relevant to their needs and interests.

The Internet Explosion

With the creation of Web browsers in the 1990s that allowed non-technical people to access the World Wide Web with ease, the Internet was transformed from a mere communication tool into a certifiably revolutionary technology. During the final decade of the twentieth century, the number of Internet users worldwide grew to

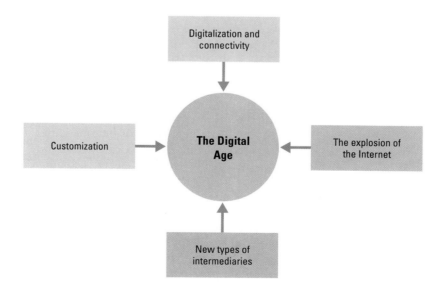

Figure 3.1 Forces shaping the Internet age

almost 400 million. The number of Web surfers worldwide reached 533 million in 2002 and is expected to approach 1.5 billion by 2007.[2]

By early 2002, Internet penetration in Canada reached 75 percent (compared to the United States at 66 percent). Seventy-six percent of Canadian firms use the Internet and nearly one-third of Canada's businesses have a website. Although the dot-com crash in 2000 led to cutbacks in technology spending, online sales in Canada continued to grow. There was a 27.2 percent increase in online sales between 2001 to 2002, when sales totalled $13.7 billion.[3]

The Internet has empowered consumers and businesses alike. The Internet enables consumers and companies to access and share huge amounts of information with just a few mouse clicks. Recent studies have shown that consumers are accessing information on the Internet before making major life decisions. One in three consumers relies heavily on the Internet to gather information about choosing a school, buying a car, finding a job, dealing with a major illness, or making investment decisions. As a result, to be competitive in today's new marketplace, companies must learn to use the Internet to market their products and services or risk being left behind.[4]

Internet marketing
All the Internet-based marketing activities that take place to enable an exchange with a consumer.

More and more companies are using Internet marketing. Internet marketing includes all the online marketing activities that take place to enable an exchange with a consumer. Such activities may include online customer service, online advertising and promotion, email marketing, the provision of product information online, online negotiation of prices, and even online delivery.

Some firms only provide information online. Others actually sell products or services or allow consumers to complete business transactions. When companies follow the latter path, they are said to be utilizing *ecommerce*. Banks, for example, have ecommerce sites that allow users to pay bills, access their accounts, or negotiate loans.

New Types of Intermediaries

New technologies have led thousands of entrepreneurs to launch Internet companies—the so-called dot-coms—in hopes of striking gold. The amazing success of early Internet-only companies, such as AOL, Amazon.com, Yahoo, eBay, and E*TRADE, and dozens of others, struck terror in the hearts of many established manufacturers and retailers. Other companies transformed themselves by being early adopters of Internet marketing and ecommerce. Justwhiteshirts.com, for example, is a Canadian firm that successfully transformed itself in 1997 from a catalogue company to an ecommerce company. ING Direct, a Netherlands-based online bank, threatened traditional Canadian banks and credit unions with its online services. Air Canada was another pioneer that started selling airline tickets online in 1998.

Established store-based retailers of all kinds—from bookstores, music stores, and florists to travel agents, stockbrokers, and car dealers—began to doubt their futures as competitors sprung up selling their products and services via the Internet. They feared, and rightly, being *disintermediated* by the new etailers—being cut out by this new type of intermediary.

The formation of new types of intermediaries and new forms of channel relationships caused existing firms to re-examine how they served their markets. At first, established firms—such as Sears, Canadian Tire, The Bay, Chapters, and Roots—dragged their feet. Many Canadian firms realized that launching a website was just the beginning. To be successful as an ecommerce company, they knew they would have to surmount delivery problems caused by Canada's vast distances, manage warehouses and stock inventory, and provide a level of customer service in both French and English that would match or surpass the quality of their offerings in the offline world. However, when they did begin online operations, many became stronger than the *pure play* ecommerce competitors that pushed them reluctantly onto the Internet. TD Canada Trust is a good example. In fact, although some pure ecommerce competitors are surviving and even prospering in today's marketplace, many once-formidable dot-coms—such as eToys, Pets.com, Garden.com, Webvan, and Mothernature.com—have failed in the face of poor profitability and plunging stock values.

Customization

The Old Economy revolved around *manufacturing companies* that mainly focused on standardizing their production, products, and business processes. They invested large sums in brand building to tout the advantages of their standardized market offerings. Through standardization and branding, manufacturers hoped to grow demand and take advantage of economies of scale. As a key to managing their assets, they set up command-and-control systems that would run their businesses like machines.

In contrast, the New Economy revolves around *information businesses*. Information has the advantages of being easy to differentiate, customize, personalize, and send at incredible speeds over networks. With rapid advances in Internet and other connecting technologies, companies have grown skilled in gathering information about individual customers and business partners (suppliers, distributors, retailers). In turn, they have become more adept at individualizing their products and services, messages, and media.

Dell Computer, for example, lets customers specify exactly what they want in their computers and delivers customer-designed units in only a few days. On its Reflect.com website, Procter & Gamble allows people to reflect their needs for, say, a shampoo by answering a set of questions. It then formulates a unique shampoo for each person. Nike ID (see http://nikeid.nike.com) allows sports enthusiasts to custom-design shoes to meet their specific needs.

At Reflect.com, people formulate their own beauty products—it offers "one of a kind products for a one of a kind you." More than 650 000 people visit the site each month.

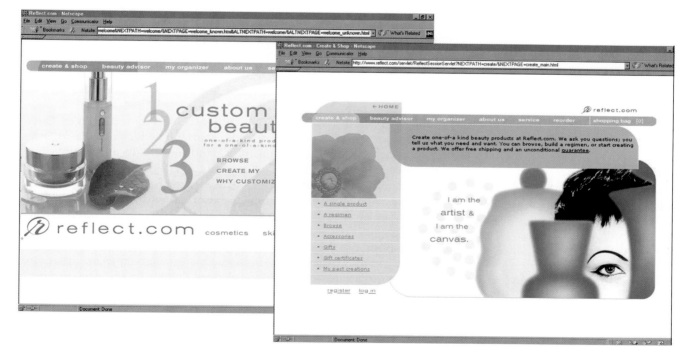

Marketing Strategy in the Digital Age

Conducting business in the digital age will call for a new model for marketing strategy and practice. According to one strategist: "Sparked by new technologies, particularly the Internet, the corporation is undergoing a radical transformation that is nothing less than a new industrial revolution....To survive and thrive in this century, managers will need to hard-wire a new set of rules into their brains. The 21st century corporation must adapt itself to management via the Web."[5] Suggests another, the Internet is "revolutionizing the way we think about...how to construct relationships with suppliers and customers, how to create value for them, and how to make money in the process; in other words, [it's] revolutionizing marketing."[6]

The use of the Internet for marketing is predicted to fundamentally change customers' notions of convenience, speed, price, product information, and service, just as other technological revolutions of the past—the telegraph, telephone, radio, television—transformed marketing practice. Some strategists envision a day when all buying and selling will involve direct electronic connections between companies and their customers. This is already becoming a reality in the business-to-business (B2B) arena where one business sells to another business. According to Statistics Canada, approximately 32 percent of firms bought goods or services over the Internet in 2002, up from 22 percent in 2001 and 18 percent in 2000. Forrester Research predicts that by 2005, 18 percent of all B2B trade in Canada will be done online. Says Forrester vice president Stuart Woodring, "Transacting business online will feel as natural as picking up the phone to call a supplier or hopping into a cab to visit a customer."[7]

The fact is that today's economy requires a mixture of Old Economy and New Economy thinking and action. Companies need to retain most of the skills and practices that have worked in the past. But they will also need to add major new competencies and practices if they hope to grow and prosper in the new environment. Marketing should play the *lead role* in shaping new company strategy.

Ebusiness, Ecommerce, and Internet Marketing in the Digital Age

Ebusiness
The use of electronic platforms—intranets, extranets, and the Internet—to conduct a company's business.

Ecommerce
Buying and selling processes supported by electronic means, primarily the Internet.

Internet marketing
The marketing side of ecommerce—company efforts to communicate about, promote, and sell products and services over the Internet.

Ebusiness involves the use of Internet technology—intranets, extranets, and the Internet—to conduct a company's business. The Internet and advanced telecommunication technologies now help companies carry on their business faster, more accurately, and over a wider range of time and space. Companies such as Cisco, Microsoft, and Oracle run almost entirely as ebusinesses, in which memos, invoices, engineering drawings, sales and marketing information—virtually everything—happens over the Internet instead of on paper.[8]

Electronic or ebusiness includes all electronics-based information exchanges within or between companies and customers. Electronic business isn't new. Bank machines, for example, are tools to enable ebusiness. In contrast, **ecommerce** is more specific than ebusiness. It involves buying and selling processes supported by electronic means, primarily the Internet.

Emarkets are "market*spaces*," rather than physical market*places*. Sellers use emarkets to offer their products and services online. Buyers use them to search for information, identify what they want, and place orders using credit or other means of electronic payment.

Ecommerce includes **Internet marketing** (or online marketing) and *epurchasing (eprocurement)*. Internet marketing consists of company efforts to communicate about, promote, and sell products and services over the Internet. Companies like Amazon and Dell use their Canadian websites (www.amazon.ca, and www.dell.ca) to conduct Internet marketing in Canada. The flip side of Internet marketing is epurchasing, the buying side of ecommerce. It consists of companies purchasing goods, services, and information from online suppliers.

In business-to-business buying, Internet marketers and epurchasers use both public and private ecommerce networks called *exchanges*. These B2B exchanges may be private, linking one company with its suppliers and customers. For example, GE Global eXchange Services (GXS) operates one of the world's largest business-to-business ecommerce networks (www.gxs.com). More than 100 000 trading partners in 58 countries—including giants such as 3M, DaimlerChrysler, Target, J.C. Penney, Sara Lee, and Kodak—use the GXS network to complete some 1 billion transactions each year, accounting for $1.5 trillion worth of goods and services.[9]

Ecommerce and the Internet bring many benefits to both buyers and sellers. Let's review some of these major benefits.

Benefits to Buyers

Internet buying benefits both final buyers and business buyers in many ways. It can be *convenient:* Customers don't have to battle traffic, find parking spaces, and trek through stores and aisles to find and examine products. They can do comparative shopping by browsing through mail catalogues or surfing websites. Direct marketers never close their doors. Buying is *easy* and *private:* Customers encounter fewer buying hassles and don't have to face salespeople or open themselves up to persuasion and emotional pitches. Business buyers can learn about and buy products and services without waiting for and tying up time with salespeople.

In addition, the Internet often provides buyers with greater *product access and selection.* Unrestrained by physical boundaries, online sellers can offer an almost unlimited selection. Compare the incredible selections offered by Web merchants such as Chapters.Indigo (www.chapters.indigo.ca) to the more meagre assortments of their counterparts in the bricks-and-mortar world. For example, while there are approximately three million book titles available in print, most physical bookstores hold approximately 125 000 titles. By selling books online, Indigo can make all three million titles available to its customers.

Beyond a broader selection of sellers and products, ecommerce channels also give buyers access to a wealth of comparative *information* about companies, products, and competitors. Good sites often provide more information in more useful forms than even the most solicitous salesperson. For example, HMV.com offers

Internet buying is easy and private: Final consumers can shop the world from home with few hassles; business buyers can learn about and obtain products and information without tying up time with salespeople.

music and movie bestseller lists, extensive product descriptions, expert and customer reviews, and it even lets you listen to clips of songs so you can try before you buy.

Finally, online buying is *interactive* and *immediate*. Buyers often can interact with the seller's site to create exactly the configuration of information, products, or services they desire, then order or download them on the spot. Moreover, the Internet gives consumers a greater measure of control. Like nothing else before it, the Internet has empowered consumers. For example, 27 percent of car buyers go online before showing up at a dealership, arming themselves with car and cost information. This is the new reality of consumer control.[10]

So that online marketing continues to create value for customers instead of annoying them and intruding on their private lives, **permission-based marketing** will become more important than ever before. Permission-based marketing means getting the consumer's consent before the marketer communicates with them or offers them customized products or services. Moreover, by 2004, Canada's new privacy legislation will require that firms obtain consent before they use a customer's personal information as a basis of continuing dialogue with the customer. When permission-based marketing is used, it can produce outstanding results. Consider a recent joint campaign by TD Waterhouse and the Toronto Raptors:

> TD Waterhouse wanted to let people in Toronto know that it was a new sponsor of the Raptors. They chose a permission-based, interactive email contest to accomplish their aim. Participants had a chance to win a grand prize of a trip for two to Orlando, Fla. for a Raptors/Magic NBA game. Upon entering the contest, people were given the option of clicking on boxes entitling them to receive emails containing biweekly contest updates and notification of special offers. The contest drew 10 000 entrants in the first two weeks: 78 percent requested contest updates, 55 percent agreed to receive announcements from TD Waterhouse, and 27 percent signed up for the Raptors newsletter. It was undoubtedly a slam-dunk for both the Raptors and TD.[11]

Permission-based marketing
Getting the consumer's consent before the marketer communicates with them or offers them customized products or services.

Benefits to Sellers

Ecommerce also yields many benefits to sellers. First, the seller is able to reach a wider audience—an international one, in fact—with its products. The next benefit is that the seller can utilize direct distribution and may in fact eliminate intermediaries, thereby reducing costs, increasing profits, and getting the product into the hands of the consumer faster. The Internet is also a powerful tool for *customer relationship building* because of its one-to-one, interactive nature. Such online interaction allows the firm to learn more about specific needs and wants of its customers. Moreover, online customers can ask questions and volunteer feedback. In fact, the number one reason why consumers visit any website is to find information. This is a big bonus for marketers who normally have to push information about their products and services onto consumers. In the online world, they have the opportunity to present detailed information about their firms, products, and services to a willing and receptive audience. Furthermore, consumers will often "reward" the company that provides them with the best, or most comprehensive, or most useful, information—by buying their products instead of those of their competitors.

Based on this ongoing interaction, companies can increase customer value and satisfaction through product and service refinements. One expert concludes: "Contrary to the common view that Web customers are fickle by nature and will flock to the next new idea, the Web is actually a very sticky space in both business-to-consumer and business-to-business spheres. Most of today's online customers exhibit a clear [tendency] toward loyalty."[12]

The Internet and other electronic channels yield additional advantages, such as *reducing costs* and *increasing speed and efficiency*. Internet marketers avoid the expense of maintaining a store and the related costs of rent, insurance, and utilities. Etailers reap the advantage of a negative operating cycle—for example, Justwhiteshirts.com receives cash from credit card companies just one day after customers place an order, and then can hold on to the money for 46 days until it pays its suppliers.

By using the Internet to link directly to suppliers, factories, distributors, and customers, businesses such as Dell Computer and General Electric are cutting costs and passing savings on to customers. Because customers deal directly with sellers, Internet marketing often results in lower costs and improved efficiencies for channel and logistics functions such as order processing, inventory handling, delivery, and trade promotion. Finally, communicating electronically often costs less than communicating on paper through the mail. For instance, a company can produce digital catalogues for much less than the cost of printing and mailing paper ones.

Internet marketing also offers greater *flexibility*, allowing the marketer to make ongoing adjustments to its offers and programs. For example, once a paper catalogue is mailed to final consumers or business customers, the products, prices, and other catalogue features are fixed until the next catalogue is sent. However, an online catalogue like Canadian Tire's can be adjusted daily or even hourly, adapting product assortments, prices, and promotions to match changing market conditions.

Finally, the Internet is a truly *global* medium that allows buyers and sellers to click from one country to another in seconds. GE's GXS network provides business buyers with immediate access to suppliers in 58 countries, ranging from the United States and the United Kingdom to Hong Kong and the Philippines. A Web surfer from Paris or Istanbul can access an online Tilley Endurables catalogue as easily as someone living in Toronto, the direct retailer's hometown. Thus, even small Internet marketers find that they have ready access to global markets.

Ecommerce Domains

The four major Internet domains are shown in Figure 3.2 and discussed below. They include B2C (business to consumer), B2B (business to business), C2C (consumer to consumer), and C2B (consumer to business). Although we don't feature a detailed discussion here, it should not be forgotten that most Canadian government organizations, from federal to municipal, are now online, making it easier for both businesses and consumers to interact with them.

B2C (Business to Consumer)

B2C (business-to-consumer) ecommerce

The online selling of goods and services to final consumers.

The popular press has paid the most attention to **B2C (business-to-consumer) ecommerce**—the online selling of goods and services to final consumers. Canadian firms have been pioneers in this arena. Canada Trust, for example, was one of the first banks in the world to allow its customers to conduct transactions online. Since Canadians are among the most "wired" people in the world, we have adapted to online banking much more quickly than our American counterparts. Air Canada was another leader, launching its ecommerce site in 1998. Customers can purchase tickets online with their credit cards or Aeroplan points. Air Canada also uses the

	Targeted to consumers	Targeted to businesses
Initiated by business	B2C (business to consumer)	B2B (business to business)
Initiated by consumer	C2C (consumer to consumer)	C2B (consumer to business)

Figure 3.2 Internet marketing domains

Internet extensively for marketing activities—its "Websaver" email announces special last-minute fares every Wednesday to anyone who registers to receive it.

Despite some gloomy predictions, online consumer buying continues to grow at a healthy rate. End consumers accounted for only 27 percent of the almost $14 billion in online sales in Canada in 2002. More than 5.8 million Canadian households (or 49 percent of all 12 million households) had at least one member that regularly used the Internet from home in 2001, up by 1.1 million from 23 percent of households in 2000. Households that use the Internet average almost three hours online per week.[13] Canadian Internet purchasers order items online over six times per year, spending an average of $125 per order. The top product categories for Internet purchases are books, software, clothing, travel, and music.[14]

Online Consumers

When people envision the typical Internet user, some still mistakenly picture a pasty-faced computer nerd or a young, techie, upscale male professional. Such stereotypes are sadly outdated. As more and more people find their way onto the Internet, the cyberspace population is becoming more mainstream and diverse. "The Internet was, at first, an elitist country club reserved only for individuals with select financial abilities and technical skills," says an ecommerce analyst. "Now, nearly every socioeconomic group is aggressively adopting the Web."[15] (See Real Marketing 3.1.)

Growing Internet diversity continues to open new ecommerce targeting opportunities for marketers. For example, "Net kids" and teen segments have attracted a host of Internet marketers. To help online marketers to better target their customers, Internet research companies now segment the increasingly diverse Web population by needs and interests. Internet research companies also stress that Internet consumers differ from traditional offline consumers in their approaches to buying and in their responses to marketing. The exchange process via the Internet has become more customer initiated and customer controlled. People who use the Internet place greater value on information and tend to respond negatively to messages aimed only at selling. Traditional marketing targets a somewhat passive audience. In contrast, Internet marketing targets people who actively select which websites they will visit and what marketing information they will receive about which products and under what conditions. Online consumers are often more demanding than "offline" consumers—sometimes to an unreasonable degree. For example, when Chapters first started selling books online, customers would place an order late at night, then immediately send an email asking what time the next morning they would receive their book. Thus, the new world of ecommerce requires new marketing approaches.

B2C Websites

Consumers can find a website for buying almost anything. For example, National Cheese, a Canadian company that offers Tre Stelle branded cheese products, has an interesting website (www.nationalcheese.com) that features contests, recipes, and a "cheese finder." It also features nutritional information on its cheeses, their qualities and taste. The site even describes the occasions for which each cheese would be appropriate. Clearwater Seafood Company (www.clearwater.ca) of Lunenburg, Nova Scotia, sells live lobsters through its website and ships them anywhere in North America. The site is informative and fun. By scanning "Lobster University" you can learn everything you need to know about lobsters.

The Internet is most useful for products and services when the shopper seeks greater ordering convenience or lower costs. People now go online to order a wide range of goods—clothing from Gap or Roots, books or electronics from Amazon, groceries from Grocery Gateway, furniture from Ethan Allen, or major appliances from Sears Canada. Today more and more Canadian options are available for online shoppers. In fact, $4 of every $7 in online purchases are now made from

REAL MARKETING

3.1   Today's Online Consumers

Just a few years ago, when Forrester Research first began classifying North Americans into "techno-graphic" types according to their affinity for technology, the vast majority of Internet users were overwhelmingly male, young, university educated, and high-techie. How times have changed. Today, Internet users are found in all of Forrester's segments, even those with downscale, late-adopting, technology-challenged families.

For marketers, the Internet now presents a multitude of different kinds of people seeking different types of online experiences. While online consumers still tend to be younger, more affluent, and better educated than the general population, the Internet population is becoming increasingly representative of the Canadian population as a whole. The age group with the highest proportion of Internet users is the 18-to-24-year-old demographic. Eighty-two percent of people in this group report themselves as Internet users. They are heavy users of ICQ, a chat program that allows consumers to chat with one another. However, 75 percent of the 25-to-34-year-old group are also online, followed by 69 percent of people aged 35 to 49. Fifty-six percent of people aged 50 to 64 are online, but only 17 percent of people over 65 use the Internet. Men still make up a slightly larger portion of Internet users, but the percentages are evening out (56 percent of men use the Internet, compared with 50 percent of Canada's women). More and more children are using the Internet and are drawn to sites such as TVO Kids and CBC Kids that are both entertaining and educational.

As more people find their way onto the Internet, the online population is becoming more mainstream and, paradoxically, more diverse at the same time. For example, while English-speaking users still dominate the Web, more and more people from other language groups, such as French Canadians, are going online as sites become available in their language. Younger users are more likely to use the Internet for entertainment and socializing. Yet 45 percent of users are 40 or older and use the Internet for investment and more serious matters.

For marketers, the Internet now presents a multitude of different kinds of people seeking different kinds of online experiences.

As with other things Canadian, regional differences also exist with regard to Internet usage and spending patterns. Ontario still accounts for almost one-half of the national Internet usage and spending, followed by Alberta and British Columbia. There are also marked differences between Canadian and American Internet users. While more Americans shop online (77 percent compared with 68 percent in Canada), more Canadians bank online (61 percent compared with 29 percent in the U.S.), and more have high-speed connections.

This mixed portrait is a far cry from the old image of Net users as geeky white guys (GWGs), technophiles who enjoyed hacking their way through chat rooms and bulletin boards. Since those early days, the Web community has exploded. A detailed analysis of wired North America reveals an audience of Netizens nearly as diverse—and quirky—as consumers offline. Men and women, rich and poor, old and young—all go their separate ways on the Web.

Of course, spending more time on the Web doesn't necessarily equate with spending more money there. A kind of "e-havioural" divide is emerging in how different kinds of people use the Internet. The time-pressed consumers tend to view the Web as a transactional arena—a place to gather information or buy big-ticket items. They visit news, travel, and financial sites, such as americanexpress.com. To them, the Internet is just one more tool to help them get information or buy things.

By contrast, people at the lower end of the socio-economic ladder are more likely to view the Internet as a kind of home entertainment centre for fun and games. They are attracted to portal sites like Yahoo! Canada for its games section with popular card and board games, and Sympatico, which offers crosswords and other entertainment activities. They are more likely to view a variety of entertainment and sweepstakes sites, including icq.com, youwinit.com, and gamesville.com, and they are more likely to view the Internet as a replacement for television.

Along with the socioeconomic differences, many researchers report a growing gender gap on the Internet. Although men and women engage in many activities at roughly equal rates—such as banking and downloading music—the sexes then part company. Men are more likely to go online to buy stocks, get news, compare and buy products, bid at auctions, and visit government websites. Women are more likely to send email, play games, score coupons, and get information on health, jobs, and religion.

This online gender gap forms early. A study of teenagers by Jupiter Media Metrix found that boys are much more likely to download software and play games online. Girls, by contrast, are more interested in reading online magazines, doing homework, and staying in touch with their ebuddies.

Women's Web behaviour shifts with age. For example, women in their twenties and thirties patronize sites offering relationship and parenting information relevant to that life stage. In their forties, they shift to hobby and leisure sites featuring gardening and cooking content. Women in their fifties, meanwhile, turn to websites offering advice on financial investments and health care. "It's like holding a mirror to a woman's life," says a measurement analyst. "At every stage, her online preferences provide a readable map of her offline interests."

Internet researchers differ in their predictions on how long it will take for the Internet audience to mirror the Canadian population. However, they're in remarkable agreement on one point: Say farewell to the geeky white guys. The latest generation of connected Canadians looks a lot more like the folks who cruise your local mall.

Sources: "Top 10 Web Properties: Week of September 02, 2001, Canada," *Nielsen//NetRatings,* http://reports.metratings.com/ca/web/NRpublicreports.toppropertiesweekly (viewed April 29, 2002); "Average Web Usage, Month of March 2002, Canada," *Nielsen//NetRatings,* http://reports.metratings.com/ca/web/NRpublicreports.usagemonthly (viewed April 29, 2002); "The Internet: Who's Connected—Who's Shopping?" *Focus on Culture,* Statistics Canada Catalogue no. 87-004, pp. 10–12; Mark W. Vigoroso, "Report: Canada Closes E-Biz Gap with U.S.," *E-Commerce Times,* March 25, 2002, www.ecommercetimes.com/5perl/story/16928.html; Statistics Canada, "E-commerce: Household Shopping on the Internet 2000," *The Daily,* October 23, 2001, www.statcan.ca/Daily/English/011023/d011023b.htm; Michael J. Weiss, "Online America," *American Demographics,* March 2001, pp. 53–60; "A Nation Online: How Americans Are Expanding Their Use of the Internet," Department of Commerce, February 2002; and Robyn Greenspan, "The Web as a Way of Life," May 21, 2002, accessed online at http://cyberatlas.internet.com/.

Canadian sites.[16] Sites such as Black's Cameras, La Vie en Rose (lingerie), HMV (music and movies), Canadian Tire, and The Body Shop offer their products to Canadians. Hundreds of small, specialty vendors such as Added Touch and Belen Gift and Basket have also gone online. Many of these smaller retailers partner with Yahoo! Canada to build their Web stores, avoiding the trouble and expense of maintaining their own websites.

However, consumers find the Internet less useful when buying products that must be touched or examined in advance. Still, even here there are exceptions. For example, who would have thought that people would order expensive computers from Dell or Gateway without seeing and trying them first? Similarly, Danier Leather (www.danier.com) successfully sells expensive coats and leather clothing using its website in addition to its retail stores. The Internet also provides great value to buyers looking for information about differences in product features and values. Thus, while Birks Jewellers (www.birks.com) and Spence Diamonds (spencediamonds.com) don't sell diamonds online, their websites are full of information about how to choose a diamond and where to find a retail outlet.

B2B (Business to Business)

B2B (business-to-business) ecommerce

Using B2B trading networks, auction sites, spot exchanges, online product catalogues, barter sites, and other online resources to reach new customers, serve current customers more effectively, and obtain buying efficiencies and better prices.

Although the popular press has given the most attention to business-to-consumer (B2C) websites, consumer goods sales via the Web are dwarfed by **B2B (business-to-business) ecommerce**. One study estimates that B2B ecommerce will reach $6.5 trillion in 2005, compared with just $423 billion in 2000. Another estimates that by 2005, more than 500 000 enterprises will use ecommerce as buyers, sellers, or both.[17] These firms are using B2B trading networks, auction sites, spot exchanges, online product catalogues, barter sites, and other online resources to reach new customers, serve current customers more effectively, and obtain buying efficiencies and better prices.

Most major business-to-business marketers now offer product information, customer purchasing, and customer support services online. For example, corporate

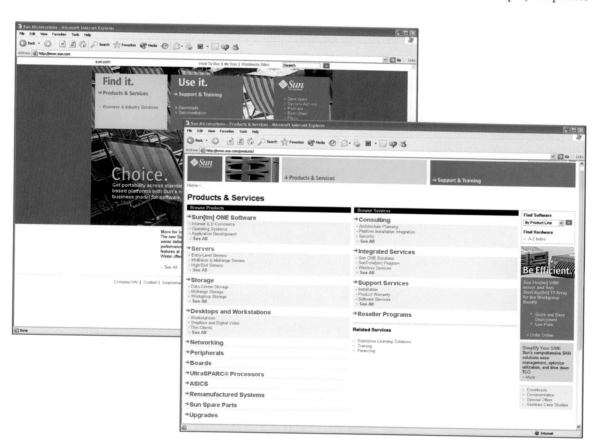

B2B ecommerce: Corporate buyers can visit Sun Microsystems' website, learn in detail about Sun's products, request sales and service information, and interact with staff members.

Open trading networks
Huge emarketspaces in which B2B buyers and sellers find each other online, share information, and complete transactions efficiently.

buyers can visit Sun Microsystems' website (www.sun.com), select detailed descriptions of Sun's products and solutions, request sales and service information, and interact with staff members. Some major companies conduct almost all of their business on the Web. For example, networking equipment and software maker Cisco Systems takes more than 80 percent of its orders over the Internet.

Much B2B ecommerce takes place in **open trading networks**—huge emarketspaces in which buyers and sellers find each other online, share information, and complete transactions efficiently. Here are examples of B2B trading network sites:

> PlasticsNet.com is an Internet marketplace for the plastic products industry, connecting more than 90 000 monthly visitors with more than 200 suppliers. In addition to facilitating online transactions, the site provides a supplier directory, material data sheets, an industry publication, a list of educational programs, and books and seminars relevant to the plastics industry.

> Covisint is the auto industry's public exchange. Created jointly by the Big Three auto makers—DaimlerChrysler, Ford, and General Motors—the site now connects a total of 11 auto makers with some 5000 suppliers worldwide. Auto maker purchasing managers submit parts orders to Covisint's auction engineers, who in turn set up special auctions. In its biggest single auction ever, Covisint conducted a four-day auction in which DaimlerChrysler purchased about US$3.9 billion in auto parts. Compare that with eBay, the top consumer auction website, which recently reported gross merchandise sales of some US$3 billion for the entire fourth quarter.[18]

Private trading networks (PTNs)
B2B trading networks that link a particular seller with its own trading partners.

Despite the increasing popularity of such emarketspaces, one Internet research firm estimates that 93 percent of all B2B ecommerce is conducted through private sites. Increasingly, online sellers are setting up their own **private trading networks (PTNs)**. Open trading networks such as PlasticsNet facilitate transactions between a wide range of online buyers and sellers. In contrast, private trading networks link a particular seller with its own trading partners.

Rather than simply completing transactions, PTNs give sellers greater control over product presentation and allow them to build deeper relationships with buyers and sellers by providing value-added services. As an example, consider what Ontario hospitals are doing:

> There probably isn't a Canadian alive who hasn't heard about the rising costs of healthcare, but you may not have thought about how more efficient marketing and supply chain management could help. A 2001 report found that Ontario hospitals spend more than $1.65-billion a year on supplies and pharmaceuticals. Costs associated with doing this purchasing exceeded $250-million. Now hospitals are starting to fight rising costs by revamping the way they buy supplies. For example, Sunnybrook Hospital and Women's College Health Sciences Centre in Toronto recently joined together to standardize their purchasing processes. To further boost these savings, Sunnybrook also adopted an electronic purchasing system. The system allows the hospital's employees to order from an online catalogue using electronic requisitions that are relayed directly to suppliers. The new technology has not only reduced errors and eliminated paperwork, it has also freed up time. This, in turn, has enabled purchasing staff to hunt for better deals and given doctors and nurses more time to spend with patients.[19]

C2C (consumer-to-consumer) ecommerce
Online exchanges of goods and information between final consumers.

C2C (Consumer to Consumer)

Much **C2C (consumer-to-consumer) ecommerce** and communication occurs on the Web between interested parties over a wide range of products and subjects. In some cases, the Internet provides an excellent means by which consumers can buy or exchange goods or information directly with one another. Services such as Auto Trader (www.trader.ca) let consumers post ads to sell their cars. The *Toronto Star* lets you submit your classified ad online for either its print edition or for posting on its website. And consider the example of eBay:

> eBay offers a popular marketspace for displaying and selling almost anything, from art and antiques, coins and stamps, and jewellery to computers and consumer electronics. Its C2C online trading community of more than 42 million registered users worldwide transacted more than $13.5 billion in trades last year. The company's website (www.ebay.com) hosts more than 2 million auctions each month for items in more than 18 000 categories. eBay Canada (www.ebay.ca) is just one of the firm's auction sites. There are sites tailored to the needs of buyers in over twenty different countries around the world.[20]

C2C means that online visitors don't just consume product information—increasingly, they create it. They join Internet forums, newsgroups, and interest groups such as *Chatelaine*'s online book club or NHL.com to share information, with the result that "word of Web" is joining "word of mouth" as an important buying influence. Word about good companies and products travels fast. Word about bad companies and products travels even faster. For example, AOL alone boasts some 14 000 chat rooms, which account for a third of its members' online time. It also provides "buddy lists," which alert members when friends are online, allowing them to exchange instant messages.

C2B (Consumer to Business)

The final domain is **C2B (consumer-to-business) ecommerce**. While most consumers don't sell things to businesses, they are finding it much easier to communicate with companies thanks to the Internet. Most companies now invite prospects and customers to send in suggestions and questions via company websites. Beyond this,

C2B (consumer-to-business) ecommerce
Online exchanges in which consumers search out sellers, learn about their offers, and initiate purchases, sometimes even driving transaction terms.

eBay's Canadian site features products from a wide range of categories as diverse as fashion items to power tools.

rather than waiting for an invitation, consumers can search out sellers on the Web, learn about their offers, initiate purchases, and give feedback. Using the Web, consumers can even drive transactions with businesses, rather than the other way around. For example, using online auction sites, would-be buyers bid for airline tickets, antiques, hotel rooms, rental cars, and even home mortgages, leaving the sellers to decide whether to accept their offers.

Consumers can also use websites such as www.PlanetFeedback.com to ask questions, offer suggestions, lodge complaints, or deliver compliments to companies. The site provides letter templates for consumers to use based on their moods and reasons for contacting the company. The site then forwards the letters to the customer service manager at each company and helps to obtain a response. Last year, Planet Feedback.com forwarded more than 330 000 consumer letters composed on their site. Not all of the letters were complaints. One-quarter of them offered compliments, while another one-fifth made suggestions for product or service improvements.[21]

Conducting Ecommerce

Companies of all types are now engaged in online marketing and ecommerce. In this section, we first discuss different types of Internet marketers shown in Figure 3.3. Then, we examine how companies go about conducting marketing online.

Pure Play versus Companies Combining Traditional with Online Activities

The Internet gave birth to a new species of Internet marketers—the pure play ("click only") dot-coms—that operate only online without any bricks-and-mortar market presence. In addition, most traditional bricks-and-mortar companies have now added Internet marketing operations, transforming themselves into multi-channel companies who can meet consumers' preferences in both the online and offline environments ("click-and-mortar companies").

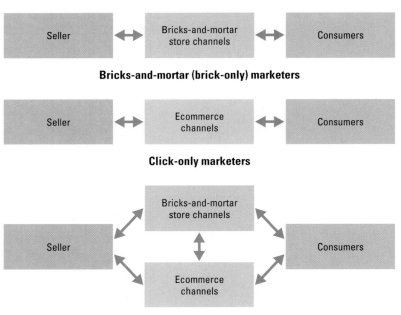

Figure 3.3 Types of Internet marketers

Pure Play Companies

Pure play companies, those that transact only online, come in many shapes and sizes. They include *etailers,* dot-coms that sell products and services directly to final buyers via the Internet. This is how Justwhiteshirts.com started. Today they also operate two Toronto retail outlets in addition to their online operations. Other familiar etailers include Amazon, ING Direct, and Expedia. The pure play group also includes *search engines* and *portals* such as Yahoo! Canada, Sympatico, and Canada.com. Google and AltaVista began as search engines and later added services such as news, weather, stock reports, entertainment, and storefronts, hoping to become the first port of entry to the Internet.

Internet service providers (ISPs), such as Bell's Sympatico and Rogers's cable Internet, are the companies that provide Internet access to consumers in their homes for a fee. There are hundreds of small ISPs serving local regions across Canada, such as Golden.net, which serves the Kitchener/Waterloo/Cambridge area of Ontario. Transaction sites, such as auction site eBay, take commissions for transactions conducted on their sites. Various content sites, such as the *Globe and Mail* (www.globeandmail.com), Canada.com, CBC.ca, TSN.ca, and Yahoo! Canada, provide news, sports, financial, research, and other information. These sites are also referred to as "portals" because they contain a wide variety of consumer information and activities, and usually are partnered with a search engine to become launching points for the consumer's exploration of the Web.

The hype surrounding such pure play Web businesses reached astronomical levels during the "dot-com gold rush" of the late 1990s. However, in the year 2000 many high-flying, overvalued dot-coms came crashing back to Earth and a significant number filed for bankruptcy. Dot-coms failed for many reasons. Many relied too heavily on spin and hype instead of developing sound marketing strategies. Flush with investors' cash, many companies, such as Chapters, spent lavishly offline on mass marketing in an effort to establish brand identities and attract customers to their sites. For example, during the fourth quarter of 1999, the average etailer spent an astounding 109 percent of sales on marketing and advertising.[22]

As one industry watcher concluded, dot-coms failed because they "had dumb-as-dirt business models, not because the Internet lacks the power to enchant and delight customers in ways hitherto unimaginable."[23] They devoted too much effort to acquiring new customers, instead of building loyalty and purchase frequency among current customers. In their rush to cash in, many dot-coms went to market with poorly designed websites that were complex, hard to navigate, and unreliable. When orders did arrive, some dot-coms found that they lacked the well-designed distribution systems needed to ship products on time and handle customer inquiries and problems. Finally, the ease with which competitors could enter the Web, and the ease with which customers could switch to websites offering better prices, forced many dot-coms to sell at margin-killing low prices.

Pets.com, the now defunct online pet store, provides a good example of how many dot-coms failed to understand their marketplaces.

From the start, Pets.com tried to force its way to online success with unbeatable low prices and heavy marketing hype. In the end, however, neither worked. During its first year of operation, Pets.com lost huge sums of money paying US$20 million for the goods it sold for approximately US$9 million. Thus, for every dollar that Pets.com paid suppliers such as Ralston Purina for dog food and United Parcel Service for shipping, it collected only 43 cents from its customers. Moreover, by early spring of 1999, Pets.com had burned more than US$30 million on marketing and advertising to create an identity and entice pet owners to its site. Its branding campaign centred on the wildly popular Sock Puppet character, a white dog with black patches. The singing mascot was also featured in Super Bowl ads that cost Pets.com more than US$3 million. At first, investors bought into Pet.com's "landgrab" strategy—investing heavily to stake

Like many other dot-coms, Pets.com never did figure out how to make money on the Web. Following the "dot-com meltdown," the once-bold etailer retired its popular Sock Puppet spokesdog and quietly closed its cyberdoors.

out an early share, then finding ways later to make a profit. However, even though it attracted 570 000 customers, Pets.com never did figure out how to make money in a low-margin business with high shipping costs. In early 2001, the once-bold etailer retired Sock Puppet and quietly closed its cyberdoors.[24]

At the same time, many pure play dot-coms are surviving and even prospering in today's marketspace. Consider Sympatico.ca:

Owned by Bell Canada, this popular Internet service provider was launched when Bell first saw the Internet as part of its road to the future. Bell Sympatico also owns and operates a network of national and local Canadian Internet media properties, including several city sites: www.calgaryplus.ca, www.edmontonplus.ca, www.montrealplus.ca, www.quebecplus.ca, and www.vancouverplus.ca. Always seeking to increase its value to customers, it recently added a user-friendly way for members to file their tax returns. "It's always an onerous task, doing your taxes," says Leslie Andrachuk, Sympatico.ca's director of national marketing communications. "What we're trying to say is that getting online is a really preferable method—it's easy, it's convenient, and it's affordable." Such value-added services have built relationships with Canadian users who keep coming back to the site again and again.

Thus, for many dot-coms, the Web is still not a moneymaking proposition. Companies engaging in ecommerce need to describe to their investors how they will eventually make profits. They need to define a *revenue and profit model*. Table 3.1 shows that a dot-com's revenues may come from any of several sources.

Companies Combining Traditional with Online Activities

Many established companies moved quickly to open websites providing information about their companies and products. However, most resisted adding ecommerce to their sites. They felt that this would produce *channel conflict*—competition with their offline retailers and agents. These companies struggled with the question of how to conduct online sales without cannibalizing the sales of their own stores, resellers, or agents. However, they soon realized that the risks of losing business to online competitors were even greater than the risks of angering channel partners. If they didn't cannibalize these sales, online competitors soon would. Thus, many

Table 3.1   Sources of Ecommerce Revenue

Product and service sales income	Many ecommerce companies draw a good portion of their revenues from markups on goods and services they sell online.
Advertising income	Sales of online ad space can provide a major source of revenue. Just as magazines and newspapers sell advertising, so do content-focused websites such as Canada.com, Sympatico.ca, Chatelaine.com, and Yahoo! Canada.
Sponsorship income	Similar to sponsorship in traditional media, an online sponsorship is a form of advertising that is semi-permanent. For example, the TTC (Toronto Transit Commission) is a sponsor of Toronto.com, always appearing on its home page.
Alliance income	Online companies can invite business partners to share costs in setting up a website and offer them free advertising on the site.
Membership and subscription income	Web marketers can charge subscription fees for use of their site. Many online magazines (*Marketing, Strategy*) require subscription fees for their online services. Auto-By-Tel receives income from selling subscriptions to auto dealers who want to receive hot car buyer leads.
Profile income	Websites that have built databases containing the profiles of particular target groups may be able to sell these profiles if they get permission first. However, ethical and legal codes govern the use and sale of such customer information.
Transaction commissions and fees	Some dot-coms charge commission fees on transactions between other parties who exchange goods on their websites. For example, eBay puts buyers in touch with sellers and takes from a 1.25 percent to a 5 percent commission on each transaction.
Market research and information fees	Companies can charge for special market information or intelligence. For example, NewsLibrary charges a dollar or two to download copies of archived news stories. Statistics Canada charges for many of its reports. Fees vary by report type.
Referral income	Companies can collect revenue by referring customers to others. Edmunds receives a "finder's fee" every time a customer fills out an Auto-By-Tel form at its Edmunds.com website, regardless of whether a deal is completed.

established bricks-and-mortar companies are now prospering through the use of multiple channels.

Consider Staples, the $16 billion office-supply retailer. After just two years on the Net, Staples captured annual online sales of $768 million in 2002. However, it's not robbing from store sales in the process. The average yearly spending of small-business customers jumps from $900 when they shop in stores to $4200 when they shop online. As a result, although Staples slowed new store openings to a trickle in 2001, it planned to spend $75 million on expanding its Net presence. "We're still going whole hog," says CEO Thomas Stemberg. "The payoffs are just very high."[25]

Most companies that have combined their traditional and online activities have found ways to resolve the resulting channel conflicts.[26] For example, Gibson Guitars found that although its dealers were outraged when it tried to sell guitars directly to consumers, the dealers didn't object to direct sales of accessories such as guitar strings and parts. Avon worried that direct online sales might cannibalize the business of its Avon ladies, who had developed close relationships with their customers. Fortunately, Avon's research showed little overlap between existing customers and potential Web customers. Avon shared this finding with the reps and then moved into Internet marketing. As an added bonus for the reps, Avon also offered to help them set up their own websites.

Despite potential channel-conflict issues, many companies that have combined their traditional and online activities are now having more online success than their pure play competitors. In fact, in a recent study of the top 50 retail sites, ranked by

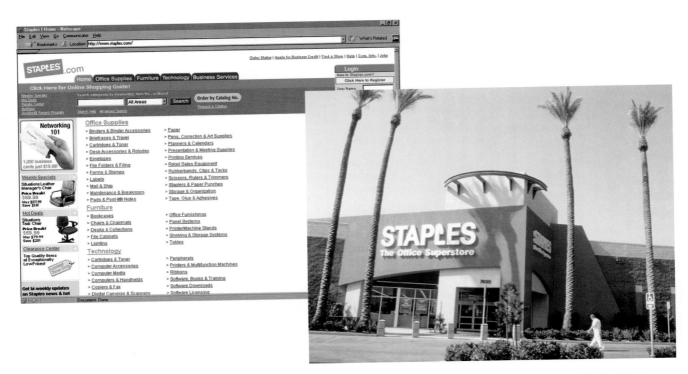

Staples' website now supplements its bricks-and-mortar operations. After two years on the Net, Staples captured online sales of more than $500 million.

the number of unique visitors, 56 percent combined traditional with online activities, whereas 44 percent were Internet-only retailers.[27]

What gives traditional retail companies an advantage? Established companies such as Canadian Tire, Home Depot, Sears, Staples, and Gap have known and trusted brand names and greater financial resources. They have large customer bases, deeper industry knowledge and experience, and good relationships with key suppliers. By combining Internet marketing and established bricks-and-mortar operations, they can offer customers more options. For example, consumers can choose the convenience and assortment of 24-hour-a-day online shopping, the more personal and hands-on experience of in-store shopping, or both. Customers can buy merchandise online, then easily return unwanted goods to a nearby store.

Setting Up an Online Presence

Clearly all companies need to consider *including the Internet as part of their marketing strategy*. Companies can conduct online marketing in any of the four ways shown in Figure 3.4: creating a website, placing ads online, setting up or participating in Web communities, or using email marketing.

Creating a Website

For most companies, the first step in conducting online marketing is to create a website. However, beyond simply creating a website, marketers must design useful information sites and find ways to get consumers to visit the site, stay around, and come back often.

Types of Websites   Websites vary greatly in purpose and content. The most basic type is a **corporate website**. These sites are designed to build customer goodwill and to supplement other sales channels, rather than to sell the company's

Corporate website

A website designed to build goodwill among key stakeholders such as investors, the press, and employees, and to supplement other sales channels, rather than to sell the company's products directly.

Figure 3.4 Setting up for Internet marketing

products directly. For example, Bombardier's website (www.bombardier.com) is bilingual, of course, and includes an investor relations section and a recruiting site, as well as giving other information about the company. The audience for a corporate website is typically investors, employees and potential employees, and other stakeholders. It is not a site meant for consumers, and its marketing activities are minimal.

Corporate websites typically offer a rich variety of information and other features in an effort to answer customer questions, build closer customer relationships, and generate excitement about the company.

Other companies create a **marketing website**. These sites engage consumers in an interaction that will move them closer to a direct purchase or other marketing outcome. Such sites might include a catalogue, shopping tips, and promotional features such as coupons, sales events, or contests. For example, you can't buy diamonds on the Birks website (www.birks.com), but you can learn about cut, clarity, and colour, find the Birks Jewellers nearest you, create a shopping list, get advice about gift giving, and collect desired items in "My Blue Box." For many companies like Birks, it is never likely to make good business sense to sell their products online, but that doesn't mean that these companies can't make good use of the Internet as part of their marketing strategy:

Toyota operates a marketing website at www.toyota.ca. Once a potential customer clicks in and indicates whether they want to use an English or French page, the carmaker wastes no time trying to turn the inquiry into a sale. The site offers plenty of useful information and a garage full of interactive selling features, such as detailed descriptions of current Toyota models and information on dealer locations and services, complete with maps and dealer Web links. Visitors can select equipment and price it, then contact a dealer and even apply for credit. Toyota's website has now replaced its 800 number as the number one source of customer leads.

B2B marketers also make good use of marketing websites. For example, customers visiting GE Plastics' website can draw on more than 1500 pages of information to get answers about the company's products anytime and from anywhere in the world. FedEx's website (www.fedex.com) allows customers to schedule their own shipments, request package pickup, and track their packages in transit.

Designing Effective Websites   Creating a website is one thing; getting people to *visit* the site and keep coming back is another. The key is to create enough value to get consumers to come to the site, stick around, and come back again. Consumers and prospective business customers are not interested in how pretty a company's website is—they're interested in how useful and informative it is, in particular, whether the site will answer their questions about the company and its products. Information must also be easy to find and tasks must be easy to complete.

A recent survey of fervent online surfers shows that people's online expectations have skyrocketed over the last few years. Today's Web users are quick to abandon any website that doesn't measure up. "Whether people are online for work reasons or for personal reasons," says the chairman of the firm that ran the survey, "if a

Marketing website

A website that engages consumers in interactions that will move them closer to a direct purchase or other marketing outcome.

website doesn't meet their expectations, two-thirds say they don't return—now or ever. They'll visit you and leave and you'll never know. We call it the Internet death penalty."[28]

This means that companies must constantly update their sites to keep them current, fresh, and exciting. Doing so involves time and expense, but the expense is necessary if the Internet marketer wishes to cut through the increasing online clutter. In addition, many online marketers spend heavily on good old-fashioned advertising and other offline marketing avenues to attract visitors to their sites. Says one analyst, "The reality today is you can't build a brand simply on the Internet. You have to go offline."[29]

For some types of products, attracting visitors is easy. Consumers buying new cars, computers, or financial services will be open to information and marketing initiatives from sellers.

Marketers of lower-involvement products, however, may face a difficult challenge in attracting website visitors. As one veteran notes, "If you're shopping for a computer and you see a banner that says, 'We've ranked the top 12 computers to purchase,' you're going to click on the banner. [But] what kind of banner could encourage any consumer to visit dentalfloss.com?"[30]

For such low-interest products, the company can create a corporate website to answer customer questions, build goodwill and excitement, supplement selling efforts through other channels, and collect customer feedback. For example, although Kraft Food's LifeSavers Candystand website (www.candystand.com) doesn't sell candy, it does generate a great deal of consumer excitement and sales support:

> The highly entertaining LifeSavers Candystand.com website, teeming with free videogames, endless sweepstakes, and sampling offers, has cast a fresh face on a brand that kid consumers once perceived as a stodgy adult confection. Visitors to the site—mostly children and teenagers—are not just passing through. They're clicking the mouse for an average 27-minute stay, playing Foul Shot Shootout, Waterpark Pinball, and dozens of other arcade-style games. All the while, they're soaking in a LifeSavers aura swirling with information about products. "Our philosophy is to create an exciting online experience that reflects the fun and quality associated with the LifeSavers brands," says the company's manager of new media. "For the production cost of about two television spots, we have a marketing vehicle that lives 24 hours a day, seven days a week, 365 days a year." While Candystand.com has not directly sold a single roll of candy, the buzz generated by the site makes it an ideal vehicle for offering consumers their first glimpse of a new product, usually with an offer to get free samples by mail. In addition, LifeSavers reps use the site as sales leverage to help seal distribution deals when they talk with retailers. And the site offers LifeSavers an efficient channel for gathering customer feedback. Its "What Do You Think?" feature has generated hundreds of thousands of responses since the site launched five years ago. "It's instant communication that we pass along directly to our brand people," says the manager. Comments collected from the website have resulted in improved packaging of one LifeSavers product and the resurrection of the abandoned flavour of another. Candystand is now the number one consumer packaged-goods website, attracting 2.3 million unique visitors a month, more than twice the traffic of the number two site.[31]

A key challenge is designing a website that is attractive on first view and interesting enough to encourage repeat visits. The early text-based websites have largely been replaced in recent years by graphically sophisticated websites that provide text, sound, and animation (for examples, see www.sonystyle.com, www.candyland.com, or www.nike.com). To attract new visitors and to encourage revisits, suggests one expert, Internet marketers should pay close attention to the seven Cs of effective website design:[32]

- *Context:* the site's layout and design
- *Content:* the text, pictures, sound, and video that the website contains
- *Community:* the ways that the site enables user-to-user communication
- *Customization:* the site's ability to tailor itself to different users or to allow users to personalize the site
- *Communication:* the ways the site enables site-to-user, user-to-site, or two-way communication
- *Connection:* the degree to which the site is linked to other sites
- *Commerce:* the site's capabilities to enable commercial transactions

At the very least, a website should be easy to use and physically attractive. Beyond this, however, websites must also be interesting, useful, and challenging. Ultimately, it's the value of the site's *content* that will attract visitors, get them to stay longer, and bring them back for more.

Effective websites contain deep and useful information, interactive tools that help buyers find and evaluate products of interest, links to other related sites, changing promotional offers, and entertaining features that lend relevant excitement.

One of Canada's oldest firms is the McKenzie Seed Company, founded in Brandon, Manitoba, in 1896. It has two divisions: retail consumer products and direct mail. Canada's leading supplier of packaged seeds and related gardening products, McKenzie Seeds prides itself on its unsurpassed quality and a deep commitment to the customer. You can see the famous McKenzie seed racks in over 8000 retailers across Canada every spring. Its website (www.mckenzieseeds.com) offers avid gardeners a wealth of advice and can be used to find local retailers, order anything from their selection of over 1000 flowering or vegetable plants, or as a forum to interact with other passionate gardeners.

From time to time, a company needs to reassess its website's attractiveness and usefulness. One way is to invite the opinion of site-design experts. But a better way

One of Canada's oldest firms has entered the Internet era with an effective website that is chock full of useful information and gardening tips.

is to have users themselves evaluate what they like and dislike about the site. For example, Otis Elevator Company, whose website serves 20 000 registered customers around the world, among them architects, general contractors, and building managers, asks these experts for advice by regularly surveying them. Such customer satisfaction tracking has resulted in many site improvements. For example, Otis found that customers in other countries were having trouble linking to the page that would let them buy an elevator online. Now, the link is easier to find. Some customers were finding it hard to locate a local Otis office, so the company added an Office Locator feature.[33]

Online Ads and Promotions

Online advertising

Paid placement of a company's message on a website other than the company's own website. Online advertising can take the form of paid placement on a search engine, clickable or interactive banners and buttons, text links, static logos, sponsorships, pop-ups or pop-unders, and interstitial pages or microsites.

Marketers can use **online advertising** to build their Internet brands and attract visitors to their websites.

There are many diverse forms of online advertising. Banner advertising is a general term for any graphic display advertisement that a consumer can either click on to be directed to the advertiser's site, or interact with in some way. For example, a company called e-Diets runs banner ads on Yahoo! that allow you to select your height and weight, then be directed to a page that tells you how much weight you need to lose.

Search engines such as Google, AltaVista, and Yahoo! offer many forms of advertising. Paid inclusion lets a business pay a fee to be included in the listings. Paid placement lets the company place its message above the search engine's keyword-generated listings. Keyword banners let the advertiser's banner appear in response to the user's keyword search—for example, rental car companies such as Avis buy keywords and phrases such as "car rental." When a search engine user types that word or phrase into the search field, the advertiser's banner appears on the search results page.

Viral marketing

The Internet version of word-of-mouth marketing—email messages or other marketing events that are so infectious that customers will want to pass them along to friends.

Finally, Internet marketers can use **viral marketing**, the Internet version of word-of-mouth marketing. Viral marketing involves creating an email message or other marketing event that is so infectious, customers will want to pass it along to their friends. Because customers do the work, viral marketing can be very inexpensive. And when the information comes from a friend, the recipient is much more likely to open and read it. "The idea is to get your customers to do your marketing for you," notes a viral marketing expert. Consider this example:

> Gillette used viral marketing to introduce the three-bladed Venus razor for women. To reach college students, Gillette designed a truck that travelled around the Florida spring-break circuit, parking daily near a beach. Women were invited to come in and get some aromatherapy, learn about Venus, enter a "Celebrate the Goddess in You" sweepstakes, and make a digital greeting card with a picture of themselves enjoying the beach. The viral part came when they emailed the digital cards to friends. The emailed messages automatically included a chance for friends to enter the sweepstakes themselves. If email recipients entered the contest, they saw a pitch for the Venus razor. Some 20 percent of the entries came from the viral-marketing cards, greatly expanding the audience reached by the beach-site promotions.[34]

Viral marketing can also work well for B2B marketers:

> To improve customer relationships, Hewlett-Packard sent tailored email newsletters to customers who registered online. The newsletters contained information about optimizing the performance of HP products and services. The newsletters also featured a button that let customers forward the newsletters to friends or colleagues. New recipients were then asked if they'd like to receive future H-P newsletters themselves. In this textbook case of viral marketing, Hewlett-Packard inexpensively met its goal of driving consumers to its

Gillette used viral marketing to introduce the three-bladed Venus razor for women, greatly expanding the audience reached by its "Celebrate the Goddess in You" truck tour and beach-site promotions.

website and ultimately increasing sales. "For those on our original email list, the click-through rate was 10 to 15 percent," says an H-P executive. "For those who received it from a friend or colleague, it was between 25 and 40 percent."[35]

The Future of Online Advertising   A debate has been raging for years among Internet marketing professionals about the relative merits of the Internet as an effective advertising medium. The argument centres on the diametrically opposed "branding vs. clickthrough" points of view. In the early days of Internet advertising only companies that sold merchandise online would invest in online advertising. The only goal of their advertising was to drive traffic to their ecommerce websites. Therefore, all they cared about was clickthrough—the number of times their ad was clicked on. Many advertisers, in fact, demanded that they be permitted to pay only for clicks, rather than per impression. They claimed that ad impressions that didn't result in clickthroughs were "wasted impressions." The other camp believed, and attempted to prove, that ad impressions are not wasted. Instead, it was claimed that they have a branding effect similar to television and print advertising. In other words, it was suggested that it's not whether a consumer clicks on the ad that is important. It is whether they remember seeing it, and whether the ad helps develop a favourable impression of the brand.

Online advertising can be an effective supplement to other marketing efforts such as television and print media advertising. While costs are reasonable compared with those of other advertising media, people using the Internet can easily ignore such advertising and often do. Thus, while many firms are experimenting with Web advertising, it plays only a minor role in most promotion mixes.

As a result, online advertising expenditures still represent only a small fraction of overall advertising media expenditures. In 2002, online advertising spending in the United States amounted to just US$7.2 billion, a mere 3.1 percent of the total spent offline. Moreover, in spite of its early promise, the growth of online advertising spending has slowed recently.

Despite the recent setbacks, some industry insiders remain optimistic about the future of online advertising.[36] And some websites, such as Google, have been successful in creating effective online advertising processes and environments (see Real Marketing 3.2). Whatever its future, companies are now seeking more effective forms and uses for Internet advertising and marketing.

Creating or Participating in Web Communities

Web communities
Websites upon which members can congregate online and exchange views on issues of common interest.

The popularity of forums and newsgroups has resulted in a rash of commercially sponsored websites called **Web communities**, which take advantage of the C2C properties of the Internet. Such sites allow members to congregate online and exchange views on issues of common interest. They are the cyberspace equivalent to a Starbucks coffeehouse, a place where everybody knows your email address.

For example, Today's Parent (www.todaysparent.com) is an online community for parents, while Chatelaine.com gathers people interested in women's health issues, food, fashion, and family, and even offers an online book club. For men there is NHL.com. In addition to getting all the latest news and statistics on your favourite hockey team, you can play fantasy games, chat with other fans, post messages on a bulletin board, and buy tickets to games.

Visitors to these Internet neighbourhoods develop a strong sense of community. Such communities are attractive to advertisers because they draw consumers with common interests and well-defined demographics. People who use these services visit frequently and stay online longer, increasing the chance of meaningful exposure to the advertiser's message:

> *Chatelaine* provides an ideal environment for the Web ads of companies such as Royale bathroom tissue, L'Oréal cosmetics, Crest Whitestrips, and other brands that target women consumers. Midas Muffler recently ran a comprehensive online campaign on *Chatelaine*'s website, which included a microsite with car maintenance tips for women. Many of *Chatelaine*'s advertisers choose this type of powerful, targeted advertising—for example, see the current microsite for Royal Tissue at http://royaletissue.chatelaine.com.

Chatelaine's website, www. chatelaine.com, offers an online community for women, including information on a wide range of topics, recipes, promotions, and talk forums.

3.2 "We Love You, Google Users"— and Advertisers, Too!

When you think back to the early dot-com boom, you probably think of brash, fast-growing startups led by offbeat, young entrepreneurs offering unique work environments to attract creative and talented employees. Google, the Web search services provider, is no different. Founded in September 1998 by Sergey Brin and Larry Page, then 25 and 29 years old, Google got its start in a rented garage, complete with a washer, dryer, and hot tub. Since then, it has grown from three employees to nearly 300. And like many dot-coms, Google offers a relaxed and friendly environment to woo and keep the best employees.

There's no official starting time at Google—or ending time for that matter. It's not about rules here. Far from it. No, workers... "set their own hours, get backrubs from a company masseuse, even bake bread from scratch if the mood strikes them." When he does arrive, [co-founder] Brin skates into the Googleplex, as headquarters is called—past the undulating red, blue, and yellow lava lamps, the crimson couch, and the self-playing ebony grand piano with Muppet-theme sheet music.... At any moment, Yoshka, a 100-plus pound Leonberger dog (think small Saint Bernard), might come trotting around the corner with his owner.

Although this start-up story mirrors that of previous dot-coms, for Google there is one big difference. Whereas other dot-coms have struggled, Google is growing at a phenomenal rate: some 20 percent a *month*. More than 365 million unique visitors use Google's search engine each month to search 2 billion Web pages. They spend nearly 13 million hours a month searching on Google; second-place Yahoo! logs less than half that figure. Google users make more than 150 million queries each day—2000 per second during peak hours. Google is becoming a global player and offers search services in 28 different languages. Even more amazing, most of these searches are answered within half a second.

Perhaps more surprising, unlike most other dotcoms, Google turns a profit. In fact, Google is three times more profitable than eBay was at the same stage in its development. What's behind this incredible success? Google's technology is an important part of the equation. Page and Brin started the company to promote their PageRank search technology, which has revolutionized Internet searching. The Google search engine returns results that are usually more reliable and more useful than those of other search engines.

Beyond this revolutionary technology, Google has triumphed because it has focused heavily on helping users search. Unlike Yahoo! and other competitors, Google opted not to offer email, shopping, and other services. Its website promises "a laser-like focus on

With the world's largest online search audience, Google has become a very attractive advertising medium. It's highly targeted ads reach users when they are already searching for related information.

finding the right answer for each and every inquiry." In fact, the name of the company is a play on the word *googol,* a mathematical term for a 1 followed by 100 zeros. It's a very large number. Google chose the name to reflect its mission to organize and make accessible the immense amount of information available on the Web. By focusing only on Internet searching, Google positions itself as "the World's Best Search Engine— accurate and easy to use." Users rave about Google's simple, search-only home page, uncluttered with news reports or banner ads.

The best part is that Google's extraordinary services are free to users. But how, then, does Google make money? About half of Google's revenues come from contracts with corporate partners to provide search services for their own Internet and intranet sites. Today, more than 130 companies in 30 different countries rely on Google's WebSearch and SiteSearch technologies to power the search services on their websites. These partners include companies such as Yahoo!, Cisco, Palm, Nextel, Virgin, Netscape, Sony, and Cingular Wireless.

The other half of Google's revenues come from advertising sales. By attracting the largest online search audience in the world, Google has made itself a very attractive advertising medium. Here's how it works. Through constant datamining, Google determines which search terms are most popular. It then approaches companies who sell in those categories and offers them space for sponsored ad messages and links for a fee. Then, when someone searches Google for a topic related to the sponsor's product or service, a tasteful ad box appears at the top or side of the Google results page, containing a short ad message and links to the sponsor's website.

Try it yourself. Go to the Google site (www. google.com), type in a search word or phrase, and see what advertiser messages and links appear. For example, if you search "Disneyland," you'll see ads and links at the top of the search list for online travel services Expedia and Orbitz. The ads promise "Save up to 70% on Disneyland Hotels with Expedia!" and "Incredible deals on Disneyland at Orbitz!"

Whereas other forms of online advertising may produce questionable results, advertising on Google delivers. Google's highly targeted ads reach relevant users when they are already searching for information. Moreover, Google's matching process allows advertisers to tailor their ad messages or sites closely to users' search inquiries. As a result, "click-through" rates for the typical ad on Google are four to five times those of traditional banner ads.

Google works hard to make advertising on its site effective. Google's marketers assess each potential advertiser, pinpointing those they think will benefit from advertising on the site and those who won't. It proactively monitors ads to ensure their success. "Especially in a recession, people are looking for results," says a Google marketer. "When you spend money with us, you can actually measure what the return is on investment by measuring the response on our site." Google even lets advertisers know when their ads *aren't* working. One small business owner was shocked when he received an email from Google suggesting that he pull his ads. This unique approach to selling advertising space has resulted in loyalty and satisfaction among the Google clients who do stay. Online advertisers, such as Acura, Expedia, Eddie Bauer, Ernst & Young, and REI, regularly rank Google as their top online advertising choice. This, in turn, has fuelled the company's financial success.

Within three months of starting up, Google was picked as one of *PC Magazine*'s top 100 websites. Its success stems from its fervent passion to bring value to both the users who flock to its site and the advertisers wanting to reach them.

Sources: Quotes and other information from Betsy Cummings, "Beating the Odds," *Sales and Marketing Management,* March 2002, pp. 24–28; Fred Vogelstein, "Looking for a Dot-Com Winner? Search No Further," *Fortune,* May 27, 2002, pp. 65–68; and information gathered from the Google website, www.google.com (July 2002).

 Web communities can be either social or work-related community is Canadagriculture Online (www.agcanada.com). The site includes agricultural discussion groups organized into topics such as "Canadian Cattleman" and "Grain News."

Using Email

Email marketing has been exploding. To compete effectively in this ever more cluttered email environment, marketers are designing "enriched" email messages— animated, interactive, and personalized messages full of streaming audio and video. Then they are targeting these attention-grabbers more carefully to those who want them and will act upon them. (See Real Marketing 3.3.)

3.3 The New World of Email Marketing

*I*n ever-larger numbers, email ads are popping onto our computer screens and filling up our email-boxes. What's more, they're no longer just the quiet, plain-text messages of old. The new breed of email ad is designed to command your attention—loaded with glitzy features such as animation, interactive links, colour photos, streaming video, and personalized audio messages.

But if you think that you're already getting too much email, hang on to your mouse. Jupiter Media Metrix predicts that the number of commercial email messages sent per year will increase by 900 percent between 2000 and 2005. And no wonder. Email allows marketers to send tailored messages to targeted consumers who actually want to receive them, at a cost of only a few cents per contact. Even better, they can target audiences in any country and get responses within 24 hours.

Another advantage of email ads is that companies can track customer responses—how many people open the message, who clicks through to the website, and what they do when they get there. And well-designed email ads really do command attention and get customers to act. ITM Strategies, a sales and marketing research firm, estimates that permission email campaigns typically achieve 10 percent to 15 percent click-through rates. That's pretty good when compared with the 0.5 percent to 2 percent average response rates for traditional direct mail.

Email success stories abound. *Business Week* offers this example:

> Zomba Recording, corporate parent of teen band 'N Sync's label Jive Records, cooked up an ecampaign that made other marketers drool. In March, 200 000 fans received a video message about the album *No Strings Attached* that allowed them to hear band members speak and to listen to a snippet of the song "Bye Bye Bye." Fans went wild: 34 percent of the email recipients, whose names had been collected from the 'N Sync website, downloaded the video. Of those, 88 percent clicked on one of the links. Thousands forwarded the email to friends. In the world of direct marketing, where a 1 percent response rate is considered acceptable, the numbers were extraordinary. *No Strings Attached* had its debut in April and sold 2.4 million copies in its first week—the biggest opening since SoundScan started tracking sales in 1991. "Email is

A new breed of email ads is popping onto our computer screens and filling up our emailboxes. They're designed to command your attention—loaded with glitzy features such as animation, interactive links, colour photos, streaming video, and personalized audio messages.

a technology that kids are really into, so it was a great direct-hit way to get to them," says Jeff Dodes, vice-president for new media and Internet operations at Zomba.

As in any other direct-marketing effort, email success depends on a good customer database. Companies can obtain email addresses from outside list brokers. However, the best way to build an email database easily is simply to ask customers for their email addresses at every point of contact. Marketers must be careful, however, that they respect consumers' right to personal privacy when making these requests. "Already 67 percent of Canadians are refusing to provide their email address to retailers and websites in an effort to avoid SPAM," said Marcie Sayiner, Senior Research Manager at Ipsos-Reid. "While email marketing may be considered the electronic equivalent to junk mail, Canadian Internet Users seem to have less patience with this medium." Even permission-based email can be very annoying. There's a fine line between legitimate marketing and spam, and if marketers cross this line, they can expect a severe customer backlash. Smart marketers are taking action today to prevent this from happening:

Petopia.com, which mails monthly enewsletters and personalized pet birthday messages, has set its computer system to automatically limit the number of emails any one customer receives in a month. Handheld-computer maker Palm Inc. has been experimenting with the length of its e-ads, and recently found that a 150-word message produced a better click-through rate than 300 words did.

Ipsos-Reid reports that Canadians today both love and hate their email. Eighty-eight percent access their email multiple times weekly. Interestingly, 79 percent of Canadian Internet users opt-in to receive the email marketing messages, which is the same percentage who report having received unsolicited mail or spam. Moreover, even though 62 percent prefer to communicate via email than through other methods, 62 percent also note that they receive too much irrelevant email, and 39 percent complain that they can hardly keep up with all the email. Canadian Internet users can also be fickle when it comes to email marketing loyalty. Of those who have opted in to receive email marketing messages, 77 percent have de-registered for a variety of reasons, including the fact that information received was not of interest or the email was sent too often.

Email marketing is thus a double-edged sword. It can be used with great success to build better customer relationships or, if abused, it can end relationships and anger recipients.

Sources: Ipsos-Reid, "Canadian Internet Users Know What They Want When It Comes To Email Marketing" (press release), March 27, 2002, www.ipsos-reid.com/media/dsp_displaypr_cdn.cfm?id_to_view=1466; and Arlene Weintraub, "When E-Mail Ads Aren't Spam," *Business Week,* October 16, 2000, pp. 112–114. Also see Chad Kaydo, "As Good As It Gets," *Sales & Marketing Management,* March 2000, pp. 55–60; Eileen P. Gunn, Marketers Are Keen on Enriched E-Mail," *Advertising Age,* October 16, 2000, p. S12; Amy Harmon, "You've Got Mail. Lots of It, and It's Mostly Junk," *New York Times,* December 24, 2001, p. A1; and Christopher Saunders, "Spam, Saturation Plague E-Mail Marketing," *CyberAtlas,* May 16, 2002, accessed online at http://cyberatlas.internet.com/

Email is becoming a mainstay for both B2C and B2B marketers. 3Com Corporation, a B2B marketer of high-tech computer hardware, made good use of email to generate and qualify customer leads for its network interface cards. The company used targeted email and banner ads on 18 different computer-related websites to attract potential buyers to its own website, featuring a "3Com Classic" sweepstakes where by filling out the entry form, visitors could register to win a 1959 Corvette. The campaign generated 22 000 leads, which were further qualified using email and tel-Internet marketing. "Hot" leads were passed along to 3Com's inside sales force. "[Sales reps] were very skeptical," says a 3Com marketing manager, "but they were blown away by how well the contest did." Of the 482 leads given to reps, 71 turned into actual sales that totalled $2.5 million. What's more, states the manager, "Now I've got 22 000 names in my email database that I can go back and market to."[37]

Companies can also sign on with any of a number of online services, which automatically download customized information to recipients' PCs. The *Globe and Mail,* for example, offers morning news headlines delivered to your email box each morning (see www.theglobeandmail.com/newsletter/). It also offers a host of other online subscriptions—daily, weekly, and monthly news about politics, sports, or whatever you are interested in. And when the email message is delivered to you, it will identify the sender, encourage you to sign up for other services, and explain to you how to unsubscribe. It will also undoubtedly contain sponsorships or advertising.

As with other types of online marketing, companies must be careful that they don't cause resentment among Internet users who are already overloaded with "junk email." Email marketers walk a fine line between adding value for consumers and being intrusive. To avoid being confused with "spammers," reputable marketers should follow several important rules: (1) never send email without first requesting permission, (2) always clearly identify the marketer as the sender of the message, and remind the recipient why they are receiving the message (because they subscribed at such-and-such a site); and (3) always include an unsubscribe link or instructions for unsubscribing with each message sent.

The Promise and Challenges of Ecommerce

Ecommerce continues to offer both great promise and many challenges for the future. We now look at both the promises of ecommerce and the "darker side" of the Web.

The Continuing Promise of Ecommerce

"Dot-com fever" has cooled recently, and a more realistic view has emerged. To be sure, online marketing will become a successful business model for some companies. Banks have been especially successful with their online efforts, The Royal Bank and TD Canada Trust are listed as the two top sites. ING Direct has been successful at building a virtual bank. Other firms, notably Dell Computer, believe in the power of Internet marketing. Michael Dell's goal is one day "to have *all* customers conduct *all* transactions on the Internet, globally." And ebusiness will continue to boom for many B2B marketers, companies such as Cisco Systems, General Electric, and IBM.

However, for most companies, online marketing will remain just one important approach to the marketplace that works alongside other approaches in a fully integrated marketing mix. Eventually, as companies become more adept at integrating ecommerce with their everyday strategy and tactics, the "e" will fall away from ebusiness or emarketing. "The key question is not whether to deploy Internet technology—companies have no choice if they want to stay competitive—but how to deploy it," says business strategist Michael Porter. He continues: "We need to move away from the rhetoric about 'Internet industries,' 'ebusiness strategies,' and a 'new economy,' and see the Internet for what it is:...a powerful set of tools that can be used, wisely or unwisely, in almost any industry and as part of almost any strategy."[38]

The Web's Darker Side

Along with its considerable promise, there is a "darker side" to Internet marketing. Here we examine two major sets of concerns: Internet profitability and legal and ethical issues.

Internet Profitability

One major concern is profitability, especially for B2C dot-coms. Surprisingly few B2C Internet companies are profitable. Of the 456 Internet companies that went public since 1994, only 11 percent are still in business and profitable. Of those still in business and not acquired by another company, only 25 percent are profitable. One analyst calls this "the Web's pretty little secret."[39]

Although the Web audience is becoming more mainstream, online users still tend to be somewhat more upscale and better educated than the general population. This makes the Internet ideal for marketing financial services, travel services, computer hardware and software, and certain other classes of products. However, it makes Internet marketing less effective for selling mainstream products. Moreover, in most product categories, users still do more window browsing and product research than actual buying.

Finally, the Internet offers millions of websites and a staggering volume of information. Thus, navigating the Internet can be frustrating, confusing, and time consuming for consumers. In this chaotic and cluttered environment, many Web ads and sites go unnoticed or unopened. Even when noticed, marketers will find it difficult to hold consumer attention. One study found that a site must capture Web surfers' attention within eight seconds or lose them to another site. That leaves very little time for marketers to promote and sell their goods.

Legal and Ethical Issues

From a broader societal viewpoint, Internet marketing practices have raised a number of ethical and legal questions. In previous sections, we've touched on some of the negatives associated with the Internet, such as unwanted email and the annoyance of pop-up ads. Here we examine concerns about consumer online privacy and security and other legal and ethical issues.

Online Privacy and Security   *Online privacy* is perhaps the number-one ecommerce concern. Most Internet marketers have become skilled at collecting and analyzing detailed consumer information. Marketers can easily track website visitors, and many consumers who participate in website activities provide extensive personal information. This may leave consumers open to information abuse if companies make unauthorized use of the information in marketing their products or exchanging databases with other companies. Many consumers and policy makers worry that marketers have stepped over the line and are violating consumers' right

The Privacy Commissioner of Canada is responsible for ensuring that Canadians' personal privacy rights are maintained.

to privacy.[40] A recent survey found that seven out of ten consumers are concerned about online privacy. In response to these concerns, the Canadian government passed the *Personal Information Protection and Electronic Documents act* in 2001. The act is based on four key principles:

- *Consumer knowledge and consent.* Consumers must know that information about them is being gathered and they must provide consent before firms can collect, use, or disclose consumers' personal information.

- *Limitations.* Firms can only collect and use information appropriate to the transaction being undertaken. For example, if a firm needs to mail you something, it can ask for your home address, but it may not request additional information unrelated to this task.

- *Accuracy.* Firms must be sure that the information they gather is recorded accurately. Firms must appoint a privacy officer to be responsible for this task. For example, to comply with this portion of the legislation, Peter Cullen was recently designated as the new corporate privacy officer at the Royal Bank of Canada.

- *Right to access.* Finally, individuals have the right to know what information is being held about them. They can also demand that errors in their personal information be corrected, and they may request that their personal information be withdrawn from a firm's database.

Many consumers also worry about *online security.* They fear that unscrupulous snoopers will eavesdrop on their online transactions or intercept their credit card numbers and make unauthorized purchases. In turn, companies doing business online fear that others will use the Internet to invade their computer systems for the purposes of commercial espionage or even sabotage. There appears to be an ongoing competition between the technology of Internet security systems and the sophistication of those seeking to break them.

Many companies have responded to consumer privacy and security concerns with actions of their own. Companies such as Expedia and E-Loan have conducted voluntary audits of their privacy and security policies. Other companies are going even further.

Royal Bank of Canada (RBC) has developed a progressive privacy policy to differentiate itself from competitors. For the past two years, the company has used some 15 different programs to show consumers that it strives to exceed government-mandated privacy regulations. For instance, the company is preparing to give away so-called personal firewall software to its online banking customers. RBC also delayed the rollout of wireless banking until it found a Nokia phone with a chip that allowed customers to encrypt passwords and other information. RBC has tried to quantify the effects of its privacy policies, relying on research suggesting that 7 percent of a customer's buying decision relates to privacy issues. Using that and other assumptions, RBC's privacy policies were responsible for $700 million worth of consumer banking business.[41]

Other Legal and Ethical Issues   Beyond issues of online privacy and security, consumers are also concerned about *Internet fraud,* including identity theft, investment fraud, and financial scams. There are also concerns about *segmentation and discrimination* on the Internet. Some social critics and policy makers worry about the so-called *Digital Divide*—the gap between those who have access to the latest Internet and information technologies and those who don't. They are concerned that in this information age, not having equal access to information can be an economic and social handicap. The Internet currently serves upscale consumers well. However, poorer consumers still have less access to the Internet, leaving them increasingly less informed about products, services, and prices.

A final Internet marketing concern is that of *access by vulnerable or unauthorized groups*. For example, marketers of adult-oriented materials have found it difficult to restrict access by minors. In a more specific example, sellers using eBay.com, the online auction website, recently found themselves the victims of a 13-year-old boy who had bid on and purchased more than $3 million worth of high-priced antiques and rare artworks on the site. eBay has a strict policy against bidding by anyone under age 18 but works largely on the honour system. Unfortunately, this honour system did little to prevent the teenager from taking a cyberspace joyride.[42]

Despite these challenges, companies large and small are quickly integrating online marketing into their marketing strategies and mixes. As it continues to grow, online marketing will prove to be a powerful tool for building customer relationships, improving sales, communicating company and product information, and delivering products and services more efficiently and effectively.

Looking Back: Reviewing the Concepts

Recent technological advances have created a new digital age. To thrive in this new environment, marketers will have to add some Internet thinking to their strategies and tactics. This chapter introduces the forces shaping the new Internet environment and discusses the ways in which marketers are adapting. In the next chapter, we'll take a look at other forces and actors affecting the complex and changing marketing environment.

1. Identify the major forces shaping the new digital age.

Four major forces underlie the digital age: digitalization and connectivity, the explosion of the Internet, new types of intermediaries, and customization. Much of today's business operates on digital information, which flows through connected networks. Intranets, extranets, and the Internet now connect people and companies with each other and with important information. The Internet has grown explosively to become *the* revolutionary technology of the new millennium, empowering consumers and businesses alike with the blessings of connectivity.

The Internet and other new technologies have changed the ways that companies serve their markets. New Internet marketers and channel relationships have arisen to replace some types of traditional marketers. The new technologies are also helping marketers to tailor their offers effectively to targeted customers or even to help customers customize their own marketing offers. Finally, the New Economy technologies are blurring the boundaries between industries, allowing companies to pursue opportunities that lie at the convergence of two or more industries.

2. Explain how companies have responded to the new Internet and other powerful new technologies with ebusiness strategies, and how these strategies have resulted in benefits to both buyers and sellers.

Conducting business in the New Economy will call for a new model of marketing strategy and practice. Companies need to retain most of the skills and practices that have worked in the past. However, they must also add major new competencies and practices if they hope to grow and prosper in the New Economy. Ebusiness is the use of electronic platforms to conduct a company's business. Ecommerce involves buying and selling processes supported by electronic means, primarily the Internet. It includes Internet marketing (the selling side of ecommerce) and epurchasing (the buying side of ecommerce).

Ecommerce benefits both buyers and sellers. For buyers, ecommerce makes buying convenient and private, provides greater product access and selection, and makes available a wealth of product and buying information. It is interactive and immediate and gives the consumer a greater measure of control over the buying process. For sellers, ecommerce is a powerful tool for building customer relationships. It also increases the sellers' speed and efficiency, helping to reduce selling costs. Ecommerce also offers great flexibility and better access to global markets.

3. Describe the four major ecommerce domains.

Companies can practise ecommerce in any or all of four domains. B2C (business-to-consumer) ecommerce is initiated by businesses and targets final consumers. Despite recent setbacks following the "dot-com gold rush" of the late 1990s, B2C ecommerce continues to grow at a healthy rate. Although online consumers are still somewhat higher in income and more technology oriented than traditional buyers, the cyberspace population is becoming much more mainstream and diverse. This growing diversity opens up new ecommerce targeting opportunities for marketers. Today, consumers can buy almost anything on the Web.

B2B (business-to-business) ecommerce dwarfs B2C ecommerce. Most businesses today operate websites or use B2B trading networks, auction sites, spot exchanges, online product catalogues, barter sites, or other online resources to reach new customers, serve current customers more effectively, and obtain buying efficiencies and better prices. Business buyers and sellers meet in huge marketspaces—or open trading networks—to share information and complete transactions efficiently. Or they set up private trading networks that link them with their own trading partners.

Through C2C (consumer-to-consumer) ecommerce, consumers can buy or exchange goods and information directly from or with one another. Examples include online auction sites, forums, and Internet newsgroups. Finally, through C2B (consumer-to-business) ecommerce, consumers are now finding it easier to search out sellers on the Web, learn about their products and services, and initiate purchases. Using the Web, customers can even drive transactions with business, rather than the other way around.

4. Discuss how companies can go about conducting ecommerce to profitably deliver more value to customers.

Companies of all types are now engaged in ecommerce. The Internet gave birth to the *pure play* dot-coms, which operate only online. In addition, many traditional bricks-and-mortar companies have now added Internet marketing operations, transforming themselves into "click-and-mortar" competitors. Many companies that combine traditional with online activities are now having more online success than their pure play competitors.

Companies can conduct Internet marketing in any of four ways: creating a website, placing ads and promotions online, setting up or participating in Web communities, or using online email. The first step typically is to set up a website. Corporate websites are designed to build customer goodwill and to supplement other sales channels, rather than to sell the company's products directly. Marketing websites engage consumers in an interaction that will move them closer to a direct purchase or other marketing outcome. Beyond simply setting up a site, companies must make their sites engaging, easy to use, and useful in order to attract visitors, hold them, and bring them back again.

Internet marketers can use various forms of online advertising to build their Internet brands or to attract visitors to their websites. Beyond online advertising, other forms of online marketing include content sponsorships, microsites, and viral marketing, the Internet version of word-of-mouth marketing. Online marketers can also participate in Web communities, which take advantage of the C2C properties of the Web. Finally, email marketing has become a hot new Internet marketing tool for both B2C and B2B marketers.

5. Overview the promise and challenges that ecommerce presents for the future.

Ecommerce continues to offer great promise for the future. For most companies, online marketing will become an important part of a fully integrated marketing mix. For others, it will be the major means by which they serve the market. Eventually, the "e" will fall away from ecommerce and ebusiness as companies become more adept at integrating ecommerce with their everyday strategy and tactics. However, ecommerce also faces many challenges. One challenge is Web profitability—surprisingly few companies are using the Web profitably. The other challenge concerns legal and ethical issues—issues of online privacy and security, Internet fraud, and the Digital Divide. Despite these challenges, companies large and small are quickly integrating online marketing into their marketing strategies and mixes.

Reviewing the Key Terms

Discussing the Concepts

1. List and briefly discuss the four major forces that are shaping the Internet age.

2. Assume that you are a newly appointed information services manager for a company that develops customized tours for senior citizens interested in visiting exotic locations. Explain how you could use intranets, extranets, and the Internet to increase your company's contact with its target market and expand its business.

3. Discuss how a traditional retailer or wholesaler can be disintermediated by the new etailer. Give an example to illustrate.

4. In New Age marketing, ecommerce and the Internet bring many benefits to both buyers and sellers. Describe these benefits.

5. List and describe each of the four major Internet domains. Which domain is growing fastest? Which domain has the brightest future? Explain.

6. The growth of the Internet has spawned two primary types of etailers, pure play and those that combine traditional with online activities. Which type of Internet marketer do you think will be most successful in the future? Explain.

7. Pick a favourite website and write a brief analysis of how the site rates on the seven *C*s of effective website design. What forms of online advertising and promotion does the website employ? How can the site be improved? Be specific.

Applying the Concepts

1. One of the oldest forms of marketing and promotion is word of mouth. On the Internet, word of mouth has become known as viral marketing. To create "buzz," the viral marketer targets a group of carefully chosen trend leaders in a community who can effectively spread the word about the product, event, or service. Viral marketing has worked successfully for a variety of products, including the Doom video game, *The Blair Witch Project,* Harry Potter books, Razor scooters, and Chrysler's PT Cruiser. In addition, viral marketing has revived failing brands such as Lucky Strike cigarettes, Lee jeans, and Vespa scooters.

 a. List three products that you learned about from friends. How did the information offered affect your impression of the product? Did you act based on your friends' recommendations? Why or why not?

 b. Assume you are the marketing manager for a new product to be sold primarily to consumers in their late teens and early twenties. How would you use viral marketing to promote the product? Be specific in describing your plan.

 c. Consider the ethics of viral marketing. What problems might arise with this method? What precautions should an Internet marketer consider to prevent such problems?

2. The purchasing department of the future will likely look much different from today's. The New Era purchasing department will most certainly use open and private trading networks and electronic exchanges. These new purchasing methods will result in sizable cost savings. For example, Best Buy saves US$16 million annually on purchases of US$100 billion of goods and services via electronic exchanges and trading networks. In addition, the huge consumer-electronics retailer can receive as many as 100 bids per hour via electronic networks and receive real-time feedback about potential purchases. In the future, B2B purchasing managers will need to be increasingly "Web smart" to stay even with competitors.

 a. List the advantages and disadvantages of using open and private trading networks and electronic exchanges for purchasing goods and services.

 b. One place that Best Buy "shops" is the Worldwide Retail Exchange (see www.worldwideretailexchange. com). What type of companies found on this site might want to sell to Best Buy? Explain.

 c. Among the first items that firms purchase through trading networks and electronic exchanges are operational supplies and services. Why?

d. Would open networks be a good place to buy goods that are critical to a company's competitive differentiation? Explain.

e. When would a handshake with a long-time vendor be more important than an electronic exchange or open trading network?

Video Short

View the video short for this chapter at **www.pearsoned.ca/kotler** and then answer the questions provided in the case description.

Company Case

eBay: Connecting in China

A Rare Success

Legend has it that Pierre Omidyar, a young engineer, concocted the idea for eBay in 1995 so that his girlfriend would have an easy way to meet and trade with fellow Pez dispenser collectors. Omidyar envisioned eBay's Internet site as becoming a place where a network of buyers and sellers could connect, forming a community. Bill Cobb, the company's global marketing director, calls eBay a step toward "the first worldwide economic democracy."

eBay is just a step in one sense. The company pales in comparison to, for example, Wal-Mart. Wal-Mart raked in about US$220 billion in sales in 2001 from its network of 3000 stores, 1.3 million workers, and countless warehouses. By comparison, eBay generated only US$749 million in revenue from sales fees and advertising on the US$9.3 billion in goods sold through 170 million transactions using its system—less than 4 percent of Wal-Mart's sales. However, eBay has no stores or warehouses or inventory and accomplished its results with fewer than 3000 employees. Further, unlike most of the dot-coms that sprouted in the late 1990s, eBay is profitable, having produced a net profit of US$138 million in 2001.

eBay, however, is no flash-in-the-pan. Analysts predict that its revenues will double to about US$1.5 billion by the end of 2003 and profits will more than double to about US$318 million. Investors seemed to believe the predictions, as eBay's stock was trading at an astounding 113 times earnings at the end of 2001, despite the stock market's depressed condition.

How eBay Works

The idea for eBay's business model is simple—and old. Residents in rural and urban communities have for centuries gathered in town squares and marketplaces to buy, sell, and exchange goods and services. The modern-day flea market is a throwback to these markets.

eBay simply took this old idea and removed the need for a physical meeting between buyer and seller. The Internet provided the cyberspace where the marketing exchange could take place. eBay simply created the software programs to enable the transactions. The eBay system, however, improves on the old market system in that the seller can "display" his or her items to a huge number of potential customers at the same time. Given that there may be more than one person interested in the item, the seller can hold a virtual auction, hoping that demand for the item will produce a higher price than a typical market where the number of potential buyers would be more limited or even nonexistent. Obviously, the process also depends on modern transportation and payment systems that allow the buyers and sellers to arrange for the product's physical delivery, as eBay plays no role in closing the transaction.

eBay charges the sellers insertion fees for listing an item, final-value fees upon a sale, and listing-upgrade fees. Exhibit 1 presents the impact of the final value fee structure at various closing values.

In 2001, eBay's transaction fees accounted for all but US$84 million of its revenues, with this remainder coming from third-party advertising charges.

Exhibit 1 Impact of Final Value Fee Structure

Auction's Gross Closing Value	Final Value Fee	Final Value Fee as a Percent of Gross Closing Value
$25	$1.31	5.25%
$50	$2.00	4.00%
$100	$3.38	3.38%
$1 000	$28.13	2.81%
$10 000	$163.13	1.63%

Source: eBay website, www.ebay.com; and Merrill Lynch analysis.

Because eBay does not take title to anything sold over its system, it has a gross margin of 82 percent. In 2001, eBay's operating expenses totalled 57.8 percent of revenues, with sales and marketing accounting for 33.8 percent; product development, 10 percent; and general and administrative expenses, 14 percent. Even with eBay's projected growth, analysts predicted that its sales and marketing expense would hold at 30 percent of revenues.

eBay's average auction lasted 6.55 days as of the first quarter of 2002, and the average gross value per auction was US$22.50. As of early 2002, the average seller sponsored three auctions and produced $1.72 in net revenue for eBay per auction. eBay classified its offerings into 18 000 categories, with high-priced merchandise, like cars and computers, continuing to grow as a percent of total sales value. In fact, eBay Motors was the company's fastest-growing category in early 2002. Collectibles, like the Pez dispensers, accounted for only about one-third of eBay's items.

eBay's members, or users (never called customers), would tell you that one reason the system has been successful is that they feel like "winners" whenever they are successful at an auction. The members police themselves, providing feedback points to each other so that disreputable buyers and sellers are quickly identified. Members also communicate directly with eBay's staff to point out problems and suggest solutions. In addition, it is very easy for members to use eBay's system.

A New CEO

In 1997, eBay recruited Meg Whitman to become the company's CEO. Whitman had worked at Disney and Hasbro, but was not an Internet junkie. She had degrees from Princeton and Harvard and brought with her a marketing background built on a commitment to customer satisfaction. When Whitman took over, the company had only $49 million in merchandise sales. She helped the company go public in 1998.

Whitman has led eBay through many changes. Recently, the company instituted a "buy-it-now" pricing system that lets a seller set a fixed price at which a buyer can purchase the item without going through the traditional auction process. Whitman estimates that this type of purchase will increase from 20 percent to 33 percent of eBay's sales.

Although the company began as a way for individuals to buy and sell, many people have realized that it is a perfect vehicle for their own businesses. As a result, analysts estimate that there are over 200 000 businesses that exist only on eBay.

New Frontiers

eBay has announced that its goal is to achieve sales of US$3 billion by 2005. To reach this lofty target, Whitman realizes that eBay must develop international markets—especially in light of analysts' suggestions that the company's core U.S. market growth rate is slowing and advertising revenues are down due to the economic slowdown.

eBay has already ventured into international markets. It has operations in Canada (www.ebay.ca), Australia, Austria, France, Germany, Ireland, Italy, New Zealand, Switzerland, and the United Kingdom. In the first quarter of 2002, international revenues accounted for 21 percent of eBay's revenues, up from 18 percent in the last quarter of 2001; and its 2001 international revenue reached US$115 million, up from US$34 million a year earlier.

Despite eBay's progress in international markets, all has not gone well. Yahoo! Japan beat eBay to the punch by offering online auctions in Japan in September 1999. eBay entered Japan five months later, but those five months were critical. eBay charged a fee for each transaction, which Yahoo! did not, and required users to provide a credit card number. Many young Japanese do not use credit cards, preferring to pay by cash or bank draft. Further, although many observers thought online auctions would not work in Japan due to Japanese reluctance to buy used goods from strangers, its economic recession and the emergence of environmental awareness helped to overcome this reluctance. Plus, Yahoo! users could adopt Internet nicknames for their transactions, removing some of the stigma. Then, observers suggested, eBay was slow to adopt local touches, like horoscopes and newsletters, which it needed to attract users. eBay compounded all this by taking a low-key approach to promotion, while Yahoo! bought billboards and opened an Internet café with Starbucks.

All these missteps, analysts argue, resulted in the "network effect." Sellers want to go where there are buyers, and buyers want to go where there is a large selection, i.e., sellers. Once this network reaches critical mass, it becomes very difficult for a competitor to succeed. Sellers and buyers flocked to Yahoo!, and by mid-2001, Yahoo! had captured 95 percent of the US$1.6 billion online market—eBay had only 3 percent. By early 2002, eBay threw in the towel and announced its withdrawal from Japan.

Within weeks, however, eBay announced it had purchased 33 percent of a China Internet auction site, EachNet, for US$30 million. Two young entrepreneurs who met at Harvard Business School started EachNet in 1999. Shao Yibo and Tan Haiyin studied Internet businesses as part of a class project and decided that the eBay model was the only one that would work in Asia. With support from Asian venture capitalists, they launched their site, which by 2002 had 3.5 million registered users and 50 000 items listed for sale.

Although eBay executives argue that the eBay model has universal application, the company's experience in Japan and China highlight key differences as companies move from one national market to another. In China, for example, EachNet's customers hurried to the site to trade practical items like apparel or cellular phones, not the collectibles that fuelled growth in the U.S. market. Rather than use the postal or courier systems to make payment, as one might do in the United States, Chinese traders mostly sell within their own cities. Although transportation systems are improving, they are still creaky by U.S. standards, so shipping items is not easy or reliable. Many Chinese still don't feel comfortable doing business online, especially when they are dealing with other individuals rather than companies. Moreover, ecommerce companies have also been concerned about regulation by the Chinese government. In early 2002, the government

blocked access to foreign-based news and information sites.

China represents the world's fifth largest online economy, with 27 million Internet users. Of these, some 32 percent indicate they made purchases online in the past year. Yet 30 percent of users say they rarely visit an ecommerce site. With a population of over 1 billion people, however, there certainly is plenty of room for growth.

Meg Whitman and eBay's other executives know that to meet their sales and revenue targets, they must be successful in international markets—especially in China. eBay is the world's largest person-to-person trading community. Whitman hopes that China, with the world's largest population, will be a perfect fit for eBay's business model.

Questions for Discussion

1. What are the forces shaping the development of Internet businesses like eBay in the United States? How are these forces similar or different in other countries, such as Japan or China?

2. How does the text's term "customization" apply to eBay's marketing strategy?

3. How does eBay create value for the members of its community?

4. What marketing recommendations would you make to eBay to help it be successful as it enters the Chinese market?

Sources: Jerry Adler, "The eBay Way of Life," *Newsweek,* June 17, 2002, pp. 51–59; Brad Stone, "Meg Gets on the Line," *Newsweek,* June 17, 2002, p. 56; J. Baldauf, "eBay, Inc.," Merrill Lynch Capital Markets, June 6, 2002; H. B. Becker, "eBay, Inc.," Lehman Brothers, Inc., April 24, 2002; "eBay in China," *China E-Business,* April 1, 2002, p. 4; Nick Wingfield and Connie Ling, "Unbowed by Its Failure in Japan, eBay Will Try Its Hand in China," *Wall Street Journal,* March 18, 2002, p. B1; Ina Steiner, "eBay Regroups in Asia: Goodbye Japan, Hello China," www.auctionbytes.com, NewsFlash Number 266, February 27, 2002; Ken Belson, Rob Hoff, and Ben Elgin, "How Yahoo! Japan Beat eBay at Its Own Game, *BusinessWeek Online,* June 4, 2001; Bruce Einhorn, "Can EachNet Become an eBay in China's Image," *BusinessWeek Online,* March 27, 2000; and eBay website, www.ebay.com.

CBC Video Case

CBC Log on to your Companion Website at **www.pearsoned.ca/kotler** to view a CBC video segment and case for this chapter.

Chapter 4

Marketing and Society: Social Responsibility and Marketing Ethics

After studying this chapter you should be able to

1. understand marketing's multiple responsibilities, and identify the major social and ethical criticisms of marketing

2. define *consumerism* and *environmentalism* and explain how they affect marketing strategies

3. describe the principles of socially responsible marketing

4. explain the role of ethics in marketing

Looking Ahead: Previewing the Concepts

In this chapter, we'll focus on marketing as a social institution. First, we'll look at some common criticisms of marketing as it impacts individual consumers, other businesses, and society as a whole. Then, we'll examine consumerism and consumer-based legislation, environmentalism, and other citizen and public actions to keep marketing in check. Finally, we'll see how companies themselves can benefit from proactively pursuing socially responsible and ethical practices. You'll see that social responsibility and ethical actions are more than just the right thing to do; they're also good for business.

Before moving on, let's visit the concept of social responsibility in business. There is a lot of debate about what the duties and obligations of businesses should be. Should business organizations and the marketing people working within them just serve the shareholders or owners of the firm by maximizing profits, obeying the law, and using resources wisely? Or do they have a wider set of responsibilities that includes serving the interests of all primary stakeholders—groups that are affected by corporate actions such as customers, employees, suppliers, distributors, and members of the community at large?

More and more marketers today are taking a stakeholder perspective of social responsibility. While marketers see themselves first and foremost as customer advocates, they also know that marketing is pervasive in today's society. Thus, they are responsible for the impact their actions and marketing programs have on a wide group of stakeholders. Over the last 25 years, companies such as Ben & Jerry's and The Body Shop have reflected their sensitivity to ethics and social responsibility by using pioneering ideas like "values-led business" or "caring capitalism"—putting "principles ahead of profits." But *can* a company dedicated to doing good still do well? *Can* it successfully serve a "triple bottom line"—simultaneously being economically, socially, and environmentally responsible? Organizations like Mountain Equipment Co-op have demonstrated that aligning these goals is not only possible, it is an inspirational business model.

Corporate social revolutionaries—people like Ben Cohen and Jerry Greenfield, who founded Ben & Jerry's Homemade Ice Cream, or Anita Roddick, who gave birth to The Body Shop International—pioneered the concept of "values-led business" or "caring capitalism." Their mission: Use business to make the world a better place. Ben & Jerry's Homemade was born in 1978 as a company that cared deeply about its social and environmental responsibilities. It bought only hormone-free milk and cream and used only organic fruits and nuts to make its ice cream, which it sold in environmentally friendly containers. It went to great lengths to buy from minority and disadvantaged suppliers. From its early Rainforest Crunch to its most recent One Sweet Whirled flavours, Ben & Jerry's has championed a host of social and environmental causes. From the start, Ben & Jerry's donated a whopping 7.5 percent of pre-tax profits to support projects that exhibited "creative problem solving and hopefulness...relating to children and families, disadvantaged groups, and the environment."

Anita Roddick opened The Body Shop in the same decade (1976) with a similar mission: "To dedicate our business to the pursuit of social and environmental change." The company manufactured and retailed natural-ingredient-based cosmetics in simple and appealing recyclable packaging. All products were formulated without any animal testing, and supplies were often sourced from developing countries. Roddick became a vocal advocate for putting "passion before profits," and The Body Shop, which now operates nearly 1850 stores in 47 countries, donates a percentage of profits each year to animal-rights groups, women's causes, homeless shelters, Amnesty International, Save the Rain Forest, and other social causes.

While both companies grew furiously through the 1980s and early 1990s, they have struggled in recent years. In 2000, Ben & Jerry's was acquired by giant food producer Unilever. And Anita Roddick recently handed over The Body Shop's reins to a more business-savvy turnaround team. What happened to the founders' lofty ideals of caring capitalism? Looking back, both companies may have focused on social issues at the expense of sound business management. Neither Ben Cohen nor Anita Roddick really wanted to be businesspeople. Cohen once commented, "There came a time [when I had to admit] 'I'm a businessman.' And I had a hard time mouthing those words."

The experiences of the 1980s revolutionaries taught the socially responsible business movement some hard lessons. The result is a new generation of activist entrepreneurs—not social activists with big hearts who hate capitalism, but well-trained business managers and company builders with a passion for a cause.

Mountain Equipment Co-op (MEC) is one such organization. Its logo has become a Canadian national icon despite the fact that it has shunned traditional marketing tactics like mass media advertising. MEC was born in Vancouver in 1971 to fill a set of unmet needs for quality outdoor equipment at affordable prices. But just filling a need alone didn't make MEC what is has become today. It filled this need in a distinct and unique fashion. As the company's website notes, "MEC's operations are driven by our member's needs and values rather than the financial drive to maximize profit.... Our core purpose has always been to support people in achieving the benefit of self-propelled, wilderness-oriented recreation." Furthermore, its vision for itself as it pictures the future is to provide "leadership for a just world, and action for a healthy planet."

Unlike traditional retailers, MEC is a member-owned co-operative. Throughout its history, MEC consistently offered only a narrow set of products and never let the quality of its products or services slip. While recognizing that it is a retailer that survives by promoting "consumption," it works to do so in an environmentally responsible manner, trying to be "green" in all it does. MEC prides itself on building ecologically friendly stores: it reduces energy consumption, recuperates on-site groundwater, uses recycled building materials whenever possible, and even cultivates small rooftop gardens designed to filter smoggy air and reduce the building's heating and cooling costs.

Another of MEC's initiatives is its Ecological Footprint Calculator. This educational tool was developed to encourage members to think more about the sustainability of their day-to-day life choices and provoke discussion about social values and thoughtful consumption. MEC also encourages its members to use their gear to the full extent of its life. To help them do this, MEC has member education programs on the use and care of its products. It has a product repair program and a gear re-use program in addition to its recycling and donation programs for used equipment. It is also working to expand its rental programs for those who only need gear occasionally.

While MEC certainly focused on customer needs, quality products, and high service, it also grew into the realization that many stakeholder groups were critically connected to its long-term success. It is a values-led organization that knows the power of having a motivated network of top-quality suppliers. It is energized by its employees and it is committed to people and their communities. This orientation is exemplified in its statement of values:

- We conduct ourselves ethically and with integrity.
- We show respect for others in our words and actions.

- We act in the spirit of community and co-operation.
- We respect and protect our natural environment.
- We strive for personal growth and continual learning, and adventure.

MEC also knows that simply working to make a one-time sale to a customer isn't enough. Developing lifetime relationships with its members has been another touchstone of the co-operative. As part of its vision, MEC sets the goal of having MEC members purchase most of their needs for outdoor activities from MEC. It sends members catalogues twice yearly. Each is filled with high-quality information as well as products. It also sends out newsletters and is beginning to rely more and more on its website (www.mec.ca) and ecommerce capabilities to maintain the link with people who have paid $5 for their lifetime membership.

Such relationships are critical since MEC has no doubt that its best marketers are the members themselves. Member-generated word-of-mouth communication has long worked to help the company grow. And grow it has. It boasts over 1.8 million members and its 2002 sales were in excess of $162 million. MEC currently operates stores in Vancouver, Calgary, Edmonton, Winnipeg, Toronto, Ottawa, Montreal, and Halifax. But no matter what it does today or in the future, it hopes to always climb the high road and be an exemplar of ethics, integrity, and environmental responsibility in all it undertakes.[1]

Canadians wish more companies shared MEC's perspective. *Maclean's* 2002 survey of Canadian attitudes revealed that 45 percent of Canadians have a more negative view of the business community than in previous surveys and expressed a general concern about the ethics, morality, and social responsibility of business leaders. In the light of recent business scandals in the United States and Canada, Canadians today are demanding more of business and marketing. Consider the results of a recent poll:[2]

- 88 percent of Canadians believe that business should do more than simply make a profit, create jobs, and obey laws.
- 53 percent of Canadians think that a key differentiator for a company is social responsibility, far ahead of either brand reputation or financial success.
- 52 percent of Canadians have punished a specific company they viewed as not behaving responsibly.
- Slightly over 50 percent of recent North American MBA grads said they would accept a lower salary to work for a socially responsible company.
- The Jantzi Social Index of 60 socially responsible companies showed a 5 percent higher return on investment than the TSE 300 in 2000.

Such trends are important to responsible marketers, who constantly strive to discover what consumers want and respond with marketing offers that give satisfaction and value to buyers and profit to the producer. They adhere to the *marketing concept*, which is a philosophy of creating customer value while making a profit. It is a win–win philosophy of mutual gain.

Suncor, a Calgary-based integrated energy company employing over 3400, is a good example of a company that remains profitable while fulfilling a values-led mission. Its website proclaims,

Today, we see social responsibility as encompassing every area of our business. It's reflected in the kind of workplace opportunities we provide and in how healthy and safe we make that workplace for our employees, our contractors and all others who may be affected by our operations. It comes to life in the way we communicate and interact with stakeholders and in our recognition of the economic and special needs of neighbouring communities. It is made visible by the encouragement we provide to community growth and involvement—whether that means supporting an employee in volunteer efforts, or providing financial help to a community project through the Suncor Energy Foundation.[3]

Sometimes quietly adhering to the marketing concept is not enough—some companies, like Shell Canada, have to let consumers know that they've changed their ways.[4]

Shell got hammered in the press after the Brent Spar decision [Shell's controversial decision in 1995 to sink a disused oil platform off Canada's east coast] and Nigeria [where anti-Shell activist Ken Saro-Wiwa was executed in 1995]. In both cases they were blindsided by the public's reaction and their sales dropped dramatically. It wasn't just customers that reacted. Shell had trouble with recruiting and employee retention. Recognizing that their brand was in trouble, Shell mended their ways working towards better stakeholder and sustainability practices.

To get its message out, Shell Canada also turned to advertising. Beginning in 1995 with a full-page print ad in the *Globe and Mail* that expressed regrets on the Saro-Wiwa case and asked for "clear thinking" on the issue, it began a series of confrontational ads, including its most recent consumer campaign, dubbed "Action Today with Tomorrow in Mind." The campaign included print ads in Canadian magazines and newspapers and two international television commercials. One ad posed the question, "Cloud the issue or clear the air?" to launch into an announcement of Shell's commitment to renewable energy and social responsibility. Another print ad read, "Not all the experts we listen to are employed by Shell," along with a photo of a First Nations Albertan woman who is sharing "traditional environmental knowledge" with Shell.

Shell's stake in Nigeria's oil industry made the company the target of worldwide protests (left) when Nigerian activist Ken Saro-Wiwa was executed. To address public concern, it wasn't enough for Shell Canada to take a new perspective on stakeholder and sustainability issues—it also had to tell Canadians about its new direction. New CEO Linda Cook (below) is leading the charge.

Table 4.1 Lessons for Socially Responsible Companies

A recent *Inc.* article outlined some key lessons for social entrepreneurs:

- *What you sell is important:* The product or service, not just the mission, must be socially responsible.
- *Be proud to be in business:* Unlike the 1980s revolutionaries, the social entrepreneurs are businesspeople—and proud of it—and all appreciate solid business training.
- *Make a solid commitment to change:* Ben & Jerry's Cohen and Greenfield stumbled into making ice cream to make ends meet; The Body Shop's Roddick owned a small hotel in England before opening her first store. In contrast, the new social entrepreneurs' companies, like MEC, are a natural outgrowth of their long-held values.
- *Focus on two bottom lines:* Today's social entrepreneurs are just as dedicated to building a viable, profitable business as to shaping a mission. The CEO of WorldWise, another firm built around the concept of environmentally responsible products, also illustrates such double-bottom-line thinking. "Our whole concept was that our products had to work as well as or better than others, look as good or finer, cost the same or less, and be better for the environment."
- *Forget the hype:* For these socially responsible companies, it's not about marketing and image. They go about doing their good deeds quietly. In 2002 alone, with little fanfare, MEC gave more than $650 000 in grants and contributions back to various communities. It supported environmental education and advocacy projects, land acquisitions, research and studentships such as a land acquisition of Davis Creek in Quebec to protect the Mount Sutton Corridor, support of Toronto's Community Bicycling Network, and Winnipeg's Save the Seine project.

Source: Thea Singer, "Can Business Still Save the World?" *Inc.*, April 30, 2001, pp. 58–71; and MEC website, www.mec.ca.

Not all marketers follow the marketing concept, however. In fact, some companies use questionable marketing practices, and some marketing actions that seem innocent in themselves strongly affect society. Consider the sale of cigarettes. Theoretically, since cigarettes are legal products, companies should be free to sell them and smokers should be free to buy them. But this transaction affects the public interest. First, smokers may be shortening their own lives. Second, smoking places a financial burden on the smoker's family and on society at large. Third, people around smokers may suffer discomfort and harm from second-hand smoke. Thus, the marketing of tobacco products has sparked substantial debate and government has stepped in to restrict how cigarettes can be marketed.[5] This example shows that private transactions may involve larger questions of public policy.

This chapter examines the social effects of companies' marketing practices. We examine several questions: What are the most frequent social criticisms of marketing? What steps have private citizens taken to curb marketing ills? What steps have legislators and government agencies taken to curb marketing ills? What steps have enlightened companies taken to carry out socially responsible and ethical marketing? We examine how marketing affects and is affected by each of these issues. (See Table 4.1 for lessons that socially responsible companies have put into practice.)

Social and Ethical Criticisms of Marketing

Marketing is often criticized. Some of the criticism is justified; much is not. It cannot be denied, however, that marketers must understand the ethical and social issues associated with their profession and work to resolve these issues. There are ethical issues associated with each and every aspect of marketing practice.

Ethicists use two sets of criteria to determine if an action is ethical or unethical: (1) principles and duties (such as the duty to avoid harm), and (2) whether the consequences of an action are beneficial or harmful to individuals and society. Social critics claim that certain marketing practices hurt individual consumers, society as a whole, and other business firms. These topics are explored in the next sections.

Marketing's Impact on Individual Consumers

Consumers have many concerns about how well the marketing system serves their interests. Surveys usually show that consumers hold mixed or even slightly unfavourable attitudes toward marketing practices. Consumers, consumer advocates, government agencies, and other critics have accused marketing of harming consumers through high prices, deceptive practices, high-pressure selling, shoddy or unsafe products, planned obsolescence, and poor service to disadvantaged consumers.

High Prices

Many critics charge that the marketing system causes prices to be higher than they would be under more "sensible" systems. They point to three factors—*high costs of distribution, high advertising and promotion costs,* and *excessive markups.*

High Costs of Distribution   A long-standing charge is that greedy intermediaries mark up prices beyond the value of their services. Critics charge either that there are too many intermediaries, that intermediaries are inefficient and poorly run, or that they provide unnecessary or duplicate services As a result, distribution costs too much, and consumers pay for these excessive costs in the form of higher prices.

How do retailers answer these charges? They argue intermediaries do work that would otherwise have to be done by manufacturers or consumers. Markups reflect services that consumers themselves want—more convenience, larger stores and assortment, longer store hours, return privileges, and others. Moreover, the costs of operating stores keep rising, forcing retailers to raise their prices. In fact, they argue, retail competition is so intense that margins are actually quite low. For example, after taxes, supermarket chains are typically left with anywhere from a bare 1 percent to 10 percent profit on their sales, depending on what product category is examined. If some resellers try to charge too much relative to the value they add, other resellers will step in with lower prices. Low-price stores such as the Dollar Store, Zellers, Wal-Mart, Best Buy, and other discounters pressure their competitors to operate efficiently and keep their prices down.

High Advertising and Promotion Costs   Modern marketing is accused of pushing up prices because of heavy advertising and sales promotion. For example,

A heavily promoted brand of antacid sells for much more than a virtually identical generic or store-branded product. Critics charge that promotion adds only psychological value to the product rather than functional value.

a dozen tablets of a heavily promoted brand of pain reliever sell for the same price as 100 tablets of less promoted brands. Differentiated products—cosmetics, detergents, toiletries—include promotion and packaging costs that can amount to 40 percent or more of the manufacturer's price to the retailer. Critics charge that much of the packaging and promotion adds only psychological value to the product rather than functional value. Retailers use additional promotions—advertising, displays, and sweepstakes—that add several cents to retail prices.

Marketers respond that consumers can usually buy functional versions of products at lower prices. However, they *want* and are willing to pay more for products that also provide psychological benefits—that make them feel wealthy, attractive, or special. Brand name products may cost more, but branding gives buyers assurances of consistent quality. Heavy advertising adds to product costs but adds value by informing millions of potential buyers of the availability and merits of a brand. If consumers want to know what is available on the market, they must expect manufacturers to spend large sums of money on advertising. Also, heavy advertising and promotion may be necessary for a firm to match competitors' efforts. The business would lose "share of mind" if it did not match competitive spending. At the same time, companies are cost-conscious about promotion and try to spend their money wisely.

Excessive Markups   Critics charge that some companies mark up goods excessively. They point to the drug industry, where a pill costing five cents to make may cost the consumer $1 to buy. They point to the pricing tactics of funeral homes that prey on the emotions of bereaved relatives and to the high charges for television and auto repair.

Marketers respond that most businesses try to deal fairly with consumers because they want repeat business. When shady marketers take advantage of consumers, they should be reported to the police, Better Business Bureau (www.bbb.org), and the provincial ministry of consumer and commercial relations. Marketers also respond that consumers often don't understand the reason for high markups. For example, pharmaceutical markups must cover the costs of purchasing, promoting, and distributing existing medicines plus the high research and development costs of finding new medicines.

Deceptive Practices

Marketers are sometimes accused of deceptive practices that lead consumers to believe that they will get more value than they actually do. Deceptive practices fall into three groups: deceptive pricing, promotion, and packaging.

Deceptive pricing includes such practices as falsely advertising "factory" or "wholesale" prices or a large price reduction from a phoney high retail list price. The Competition Bureau has taken action against merchants who advertise false values, sell old merchandise as new, or charge too much for credit. For example, in 2003 the Competition Bureau fined Suzy Shier Ltd., which operates 178 stores across Canada, $1 million for misleading consumers about the ordinary selling price of goods on sale. The company marked clothing with "sale" and "regular" pricetags but had not sold the items at the regular price for a reasonable period of time or in significant quantity. Suzy Shier had been fined $300 000 for similar practices in 1995. Within hours of the announcement La Senza Corp., the owner of Suzy Shier, announced it was selling the company to Toronto-based YM Inc.[6]

Deceptive promotion includes such practices as overstating the product's features or performance, luring the customer to the store for a bargain that is out of stock, or running rigged contests.

Deceptive packaging includes exaggerating package contents through subtle design, not filling the package to the top, using misleading labelling, or describing size in misleading terms. To be sure, questionable marketing practices do occur. For

Telemarketing fraud hurts consumers and the marketing profession. Members of the Deceptive Telemarketing Prevention Forum developed a campaign to educate consumers about phone scams.

example, at one time or another, we've all gotten an envelope in the mail screaming something like "You have won $10 000 000!" or a pop-up Web screen promising free goods or discounted prices. In recent years, sweepstakes companies have come under the gun for their deceptive communication practices. Sweepstakes promoter Publishers Clearing House recently paid heavily to settle claims that its high-pressure tactics had misled consumers into believing that they had won prizes when they hadn't.[7]

Phone fraud has become a significant deceptive practice. According to PhoneBusters, the national reporting centre for telemarketing fraud, deceptive telemarketing and lottery schemes bilked Canadians out of more than $1 million in 2002 alone.[8] Criminals use telecommunications to prey on innocent victims, especially those most vulnerable, such as senior citizens.

The Canadian Marketing Association (CMA) has partnered with government to develop initiatives aimed at preventing and combating this crime. Bill C-20 has equipped enforcement agencies with stronger investigative tools and imposed more restrictions on telemarketers. (Information on Bill C-20 is available on the CMA website at www.the-cma.org/members.html.) The CMA joined the Deceptive

Telemarketing Prevention Forum to launch a public education campaign designed to help consumers avoid becoming victims of telephone fraud. The campaign, "Stop Phone Fraud, It's a Trap!" consists of posters, pamphlets, public service announcements, an upgraded website for PhoneBusters (www.phonebusters.com), and educational materials to help consumers learn how to tell the difference between an honest telemarketer and a scam artist. Training videos are also made available to volunteer groups that work with seniors.[9]

Since deceptive practices hurt the reputation of all marketers, the CMA works to develop codes of ethics and standards of good practice so that industry can regulate itself better. It works with policy makers to strengthen the *Competition Act*. Deceptive practices have led to industry self-regulation standards as well as legislation and other consumer protection actions. The *Competition Act* forbids many of the practices. Advertising Standards Canada has published several guidelines listing deceptive practices. The toughest problem is defining what is "deceptive."

Marketers argue that most companies avoid deceptive practices because such practices harm their business in the long run. If consumers do not get what they expect, they will switch to more reliable products. In addition, consumers usually protect themselves from deception. Most consumers recognize a marketer's selling intent and are careful when they buy, sometimes to the point of not believing completely true product claims.

One noted marketing thinker, Theodore Levitt, claims that some advertising puffery is bound to occur—and that it may even be desirable: "There is hardly a company that would not go down in ruin if it refused to provide fluff, because nobody will buy pure functionality.... Worse, it denies...people's honest needs and values. Without distortion, embellishment, and elaboration, life would be drab, dull, anguished, and at its existential worst."[10]

High-Pressure Selling

Salespeople are sometimes accused of high-pressure selling that persuades people to buy goods they had no intention of buying. It is often said that encyclopedias, insurance, real estate, cars, and jewellery are *sold*, not *bought*. Salespeople are trained to deliver smooth, canned talks to entice purchase. They sell hard because sales contests promise big prizes to those who sell the most.

Marketers know that buyers often can be talked in to buying unwanted or unneeded things. Laws require door-to-door salespeople to announce that they are selling a product. Buyers in most provinces also have a "three-day cooling-off period" in which they can cancel a contract after rethinking it. In addition, when they feel that undue selling pressure has been applied, consumers can complain to the Better Business Bureau or to their provincial ministry regulating commerce.

But in most cases, marketers have little to gain from high-pressure selling. Such tactics may work in one-time selling situations for short-term gain. However, most selling involves building long-term relationships with valued customers. High-pressure or deceptive selling can do serious damage to such relationships. For example, imagine a Procter & Gamble account manager trying to pressure a Wal-Mart buyer, or an IBM salesperson trying to browbeat a General Electric information technology manager. It simply wouldn't work.

Shoddy or Unsafe Products

Another criticism is that products lack the quality they should have. One complaint is that many products are not made well and that many services are not performed well.

A second complaint is that many products deliver little benefit. For example, some consumers are surprised to learn that many of the "healthy" foods being marketed today—from cholesterol-free salad dressings and low-fat frozen dinners to high-fibre bran cereals—may have little nutritional value. In fact, they may even be harmful. The fast-food industry and manufacturers of fatty snacks are also coming under increasing scrutiny as claims are made about the addictive nature of these foods and their effect on the waistlines of Canadian consumers. It has even been suggested that a tax be placed on such items. The argument goes that if fast food is as harmful to our health as tobacco products, why shouldn't it be taxed in a similar way? Companies like Kraft Foods Canada are taking this issue seriously. It is cutting down on portion sizes, developing more nutritious products, and halting in-school marketing to children.[11]

A third complaint concerns product safety. Product safety has been a problem for several reasons, involving issues such as manufacturer indifference, increased production complexity, poorly trained labour, and poor quality control. For years, Consumers Union—the non-profit testing and information organization that publishes the *Consumer Reports* magazine and website (www.consumer.org)—has reported various hazards in tested products: electrical dangers in appliances, carbon-monoxide poisoning from room heaters, injury risks from lawn mowers, and faulty automobile design, among many others. The organization's testing and other activities have helped consumers make better buying decisions and encouraged businesses to eliminate product flaws (see Real Marketing 4.1).

However, most manufacturers *want* to produce quality goods. The way a company deals with product quality and safety problems can damage or help its reputation. Companies selling poor-quality or unsafe products risk damaging conflicts with consumer groups and regulators. More fundamentally, unsafe products can result in product liability suits and large awards for damages. Moreover, consumers who are unhappy with a firm's products may avoid future purchases and talk other consumers into doing the same. Consider what happened to Bridgestone/Firestone following its recent recall of 6.5 million flawed Firestone tires (400 000 tires were recalled in Canada). Product liability and safety concerns have driven the company to the edge of backruptcy:

> Profits have disappeared, and both customers and tire dealers alike are fleeing the Firestone make. Ford, the tire maker's biggest customer, recently announced plans to replace another 13 million Firestone tires that it believes are unsafe. "You have a serious risk of the Firestone brand imploding," warns an industry analyst. How bad will the financial hit get? Cutting ties with Ford will cost the company 4 percent of its US$7.5 billion in revenues—about 40 percent of its sales to car companies. Mounting damages awards from rollover suits and legal bills could easily top the company's US$463 million legal reserve.[12]

Thus, quality missteps can have severe consequences. Today's marketers know that customer-driven quality results in customer satisfaction, which in turn creates profitable customer relationships.

Product safety: Following its recall of 6.5 million flawed Firestone tires, product liability and safety concerns have driven Bridgestone/Firestone to the brink of bankruptcy.

4.1 When *Consumer Reports* Talks, Buyers Listen

For more than 65 years, *Consumer Reports* has given buyers the lowdown on everything from sports cars to luggage to lawn sprinklers. Published by Consumers Union, a non-profit product-testing organization, the magazine's mission can be summed up by CU's motto: "Test, Inform, Protect." With more than four million subscribers and several times that many borrowers, as dog-eared library copies will attest, *Consumer Reports* is one of North America's most read magazines. Its companion website, Consumer Reports Online (www.consumerreports.org), established in 1997, is the Web's largest paid-subscriber site, with 350 000 users.

Beyond being one of the most read publications, *Consumer Reports* is also one of the most influential. In 1988, when its car-testers rated Suzuki's topple-prone Samurai as "not acceptable"—meaning don't even take one as a gift—sales plunged by 70 percent the following month. More recently, when it raved about Saucony's Jazz 3000 sneakers, sales doubled, leading to nationwide shortages.

Although some may view *Consumer Reports* as a deadly dull shoppers' guide to major household appliances, the magazine does a lot more than rate cars and refrigerators. It has looked at almost anything consumable—from mutual funds, home mortgages, and public health policies to retirement communities and prostate surgery. When a recent Consumers Union study found that that less than one-third of consumers trust ecommerce websites, the organization launched Consumer WebWatch (www.consumerwebwatch.org). The project's mission is "to investigate, inform, and improve the credibility of information published on the World Wide Web." The site gives ratings on everything from the disclosure of transaction fees and business partnerships to the publication of privacy policies and the labelling of pop-up ads.

Yet the magazine is rarely harsh or loud. Instead, it's usually understated, and it can even be funny. The very first issue, in 1936, noted that Lifebuoy soap was itself so smelly that it simply overwhelmed your BO with LO. And what reader didn't delight to find in a 1990 survey of soaps that the most expensive bar, Eau de Gucci, at 31 cents per hand-washing, wound up dead last in a blind test?

To avoid even the appearance of bias, CU has a strict no-ads, no-freebies policy. It buys all of its product samples on the open market, and anonymously. CU's steadfast editorial independence has made *Consumer Reports* the bible of consumerism. "We're very single-minded about who we serve," says Rhoda Karpatkin, CU's recently retired president. "We serve the consumer."

A visit to CU's maze of labs confirms the thoroughness with which CU's testers carry out their mission. A chemist performs a cholesterol extraction test on a small white blob in a beaker; a ground-up piece of turkey enchilada, you are told. Elsewhere you find the remains of a piston-driven machine called Fingers that added 1 + 1 on pocket calculators hundreds of thousands of times or

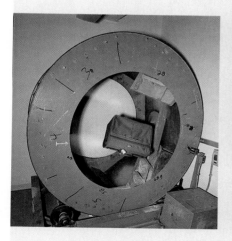

Consumers Union carries out its testing mission: suitcases bang into one another inside the huge "Mechanical Gorilla," and a staffer coats the interior of self-cleaning ovens with a crusty concoction called "Monster Mash."

until the calculators failed, whichever came first. You watch suitcases bang into one another inside a huge contraption—affectionately dubbed the "Mechanical Gorilla"—that looks like a three-metre-wide clothes dryer.

Next door, self-cleaning ovens are being tested, their interiors coated with a crusty substance—called "Monster Mash" by staffers—which suggests month-old chili sauce. The recipe includes tapioca, cheese, lard, grape jelly, tomato sauce, and cherry pie filling—mixed well and baked one hour at 425 degrees. If an oven's self-cleaning cycle doesn't render the resulting residue into harmless-looking ash, five million readers will be so informed.

From the start, Consumers Union has generated controversy. The second issue dismissed the Good Housekeeping Seal of Approval as nothing more than a fraudulent ploy by publisher William Randolph

Hearst to reward loyal advertisers. Good House-keeping responded by accusing CU of prolonging the Depression. To the business community, *Consumer Reports* was at first viewed as a clear threat to business. However, the controversy has more often helped than hurt subscriptions. Through the years, only 13 makers of panned products have filed suit against CU challenging findings unfavourable to their products. To this day Consumers Union has never lost or settled a libel suit.

Sources: Portions adapted from Doug Stewart, "To Buy or Not to Buy, That Is the Question at Consumer Reports," *Smithsonian*, September 1993, pp. 34–43. Other quotes and information from Robin Finn, "Still Top Dog, Consumers' Pitt Bull to Retire," *New York Times*, October 5, 2000, p. B2; Barbara Quint, "Consumers Union Launches Consumer WebWatch," *Information Today*, June 2002, p. 48; and the Consumers Union website, www.consumersunion.org, and the *Consumer Reports* website at www.consumerreports.org (accessed August 2002).

Planned Obsolescence

Critics have charged that some producers follow a program of planned obsolescence, causing their products to become obsolete before they actually should need replacement. For example, critics charge that some producers continually change consumer concepts of acceptable styles to encourage more and earlier buying: One example is constantly changing clothing fashions. Another is the constant re-design of mobile phones. Consumers who decide to upgrade their phone may be dismayed to find that they must replace their in-car kits to make them compatible with their new phone.

Other producers are accused of holding back attractive functional features, then introducing them later to make older models obsolete: Critics claim that this occurs in the consumer electronics and computer industries. For example, Intel and Microsoft have been accused in recent years of holding back their next-generation computer chips and software until demand is exhausted for the current generation. Still other producers are accused of using materials and components that will break, wear, rust, or rot sooner than they should. One writer put it this way: "The marvels of modern technology include the development of a soda can which, when discarded, will last forever—and a…car, which, when properly cared for, will rust out in two or three years."[13]

Marketers respond that consumers *like* style changes. They get tired of the old goods and want a new look in fashion or a new design in cars. No one has to buy the new look and if too few people like it, it will simply fail. Companies that withhold new features run the risk that a competitor will introduce the new feature and steal the market.

For example, consider personal computers. Some consumers grumble that the consumer electronics industry's constant push to produce "faster, smaller, cheaper" models means that they must continually buy new machines just to keep up. Their old computers then enter landfills and present a major disposal problem. Others, however, can hardly wait for the latest model to arrive.

There was a time not so long ago when planned obsolescence was a troubling ghost in the machine. That was then. In today's topsy-turvy world of personal computers, obsolescence is not only planned, it is extolled by marketers as a principal virtue. Moreover, there has been hardly a peep from consumers, who dutifully line up to buy each new generation of faster, more powerful machines, eager to embrace the promise of simpler, happier, and more productive lives. Today's computer chips are no longer designed to wear out; in fact, they will last for decades or longer. Even so, hapless consumers now rush back to the store ever more quickly, not to replace broken parts but to purchase new computers that will allow them to talk longer, see more vivid colours, or play cooler games.[14]

Thus, companies do not design their products to break down earlier, because they do not want to lose customers to other brands. Instead, they seek constant improvement to ensure that products will consistently meet or exceed customer expectations. Much of so-called planned obsolescence is the working of the competitive and technological forces in a free society—forces that lead to ever-improving goods and services.

Poor Service to Disadvantaged Consumers

Finally, the marketing system has been accused of poorly serving disadvantaged consumers. Critics claim that the urban poor often have to shop in smaller stores that carry inferior goods and charge higher prices. A Consumers Union study compared the food shopping habits of low-income consumers and the prices they pay relative to middle-income consumers in the same city. The study found that the poor do pay more for inferior goods. The results suggested that the presence of large national chain stores in low-income neighbourhoods made a big difference in keeping prices down. However, the study also found evidence of "redlining"—a type of economic discrimination in which major chain retailers avoid placing stores in disadvantaged neighbourhoods.[15]

Similar redlining charges have been levelled at the home insurance, consumer lending, and banking industries. Most recently, home and auto insurers have been accused of assigning higher premiums to people with poor credit ratings. The insurers claim that individuals with bad credit tend to make more insurance claims, and that this justifies charging them higher premiums. However, critics and consumer advocates have accused the insurers of a new form of redlining. Says one writer, "This is a new excuse for denying coverage to the poor, elderly, and minorities."[16]

More recently, lenders and other businesses have been accused of "Weblining," the Internet-age version of redlining:

> As never before, the Internet lets companies identify (or "profile") high- and low-value customers, so firms can decide which product deals, prices, and services it will offer. For the most valued customers, this can mean better information and discounts. Low-value customers may pay the most for the least and sometimes get left behind. In lending, old-style redlining is unacceptable because it is based on geographic stereotypes, not concrete evidence that specific individuals are poor credit risks. Webliners may claim to have more evidence against the people they snub. But their classifications could also be based on irrelevant profiling data that marketing companies and others collect on the Web. How important to your mortgage status, say, is your taste in paperbacks, political discussion groups, or clothing? Yet all these far-flung threads are getting sewn into online profiles, where they are increasingly intertwined with data on your health, your education loans, and your credit history.[17]

Clearly, better marketing systems must be built to service disadvantaged consumers. Moreover, low-income people and other vulnerable groups clearly need consumer protection. Industry Canada's Consumer Connection webpage (http://strategis.ic.gc.ca/epic/internet/inoca-bc.nsf/vwGeneratedInterE/Home) provides advice to Canadian consumers on everything from how to manage their money more effectively to how to avoid fraud.

Marketing's Impact on Society as a Whole

The marketing system has been accused of adding to several "evils" in society at large. Advertising has been a special target.

False Wants and Too Much Materialism

Critics, led by Professor Rick Pollay of the University of British Columbia, and organizations like AdBusters have charged that the marketing system in general, and advertising in particular, urges too much interest in material possessions. While Pollay recognized that many of the consequences of advertising were unintended, he damned advertising for undermining family values, reinforcing negative stereotypes, and creating a class of perpetually dissatisfied consumers.[18] Advertising encourages people to judge themselves and others by what they *own* rather than by who they *are*. To be considered successful, some people believe they must own a large home, two cars, and the latest high-tech gadgets.

Today, even though many social scientists have noted a reaction against the opulence and waste of the previous decades and a return to more basic values and social commitment, our infatuation with material things continues. While the Professional Marketing Research Association of Canada has done studies that indicate that Canadians are less materialistic than our American neighbours, it's hard to escape the notion that what all North Americans really value is stuff. We build more shopping malls than high schools. We save less and spend more. Nearly two-thirds of adults agree that wearing "only the best designer clothing" conveys status. Even more feel this way about owning expensive jewellery. Big homes are back in vogue, which means North Americans have more space to fulfill their acquisitive fantasies, from master bathrooms doubling as spas and gyms to fully wired home entertainment centres.[19]

Marketing critics do not view this interest in material things as a natural state of mind but rather as a matter of false wants created by marketing. Businesses hire advertisers to stimulate people's desires for goods, and advertisers use the mass media to create materialistic models of the good life. People work harder to earn the necessary money. Their purchases increase the output of North American industry,

Too much materialism: Our infatuation with material things continues. It's hard to escape the notion that North Americans put too much value on material stuff.

and industry in turn uses advertisers to stimulate more desire for the industrial output. Thus, marketing is seen as creating false wants that benefit industry more than they benefit consumers.

These criticisms overstate the power of business to create needs, however. People have strong defences against advertising and other marketing tools. Marketers are most effective when they appeal to existing wants rather than when they attempt to create new ones. Furthermore, people seek information when making important purchases and often do not rely on single sources. Even minor purchases that can be affected by advertising messages lead to repeat purchases only if the product performs as promised. Finally, the high failure rate of new products shows that companies are not able to control demand.

On a deeper level, our wants and values are influenced not only by marketers, but also by family, peer groups, religion, ethnic background, and education. If North Americans are highly materialistic, these values arose out of basic socialization processes that go much deeper than business and mass media alone could produce. Moreover, some social critics even see materialism as a positive and rewarding force:

> When we purchase an object, what we really buy is meaning. Commercialism is the water we swim in, the air we breathe, our sunlight and our shade.... Materialism is a vital source of meaning and happiness in the modern world.... We have not just asked to go this way, we have demanded. Now most of the world is lining up, pushing and shoving, eager to elbow into the mall. Getting and spending has become the most passionate, and often the most imaginative, endeavour of modern life. While this is dreary and depressing to some, as doubtless it should be, it is liberating and democratic to many more.[20]

Too Few Social Goods

Business has been accused of overselling private goods at the expense of public goods. As private goods increase, they require more public services that are usually not forthcoming. For example, an increase in automobile ownership (private good) requires more highways, traffic controls, parking spaces, and police services (public goods). The overselling of private goods results in "social costs." For cars, the social costs include traffic congestion, air pollution, and deaths and injuries from car accidents.

A way must be found to restore a balance between private and public goods. One option is to make producers bear the full social costs of their operations. The government could require automobile manufacturers to build cars with more safety features and better pollution-control systems. Automakers would then raise their prices to cover extra costs. If buyers found the price of some cars too high, however, the producers of these cars would disappear, and demand would move to those producers that could support the sum of the private and social costs.

A second option is to make consumers pay the social costs. Some Canadians have demanded that people who get lost in backcountry areas while pursuing extreme sports experiences should pay the cost of rescues, or that smokers pay a premium for health care. A number of highway authorities around the world are starting to charge "congestion tolls" in an effort to reduce traffic congestion:

> Singapore, Norway, the United Kingdom, and France are managing traffic with varying tolls; peak surcharges are being studied for roads around [the United States]. [Economists] point out that traffic jams are caused when drivers are not charged the costs they impose on others, such as delays. The solution: Make 'em pay.[21]

Cultural Pollution

Critics charge the marketing system with creating *cultural pollution*. Our senses are being assaulted constantly by advertising. Commercials interrupt serious programs;

Cultural pollution: Our senses are sometimes assaulted by commercial messages.

pop-up ad boxes interfere with our Internet searches, pages of ads obscure printed matter; billboards mar beautiful scenery. These interruptions continuously pollute people's minds with messages of materialism, sex, power, or status. Although most people do not find advertising overly annoying (some even think it is the best part of television programming), critics call for sweeping changes.

Marketers answer the charges of "commercial noise" with these arguments. First, they hope that their ads reach primarily the target audience. But because of mass-communication channels, some ads are bound to reach people who have no interest in the product and are therefore bored and annoyed. People who buy magazines addressed to their interests—such as *Harrowsmith* or *Canadian Business*—rarely complain about the ads because the magazines advertise products of interest. Second, ads make it possible for consumers to receive commercial television and radio free of charge and keep down the costs of magazines and newspapers. Many people think commercials are a small price to pay for these benefits. Finally, today's consumers have alternatives. For example, they can zip and zap TV commercials or avoid them altogether on many cable or satellite channels. Thus, to hold consumer attention, advertisers are making their ads more entertaining and informative.

Too Much Political Power

Another criticism is that business wields too much political power. Oil, tobacco, auto, and pharmaceutical firms lobby governments to promote their interests against the public interest. Advertisers are accused of holding too much power over the mass media, limiting their freedom to report independently and objectively. One critic has asked: "How can [most magazines] afford to tell the truth about the scandalously low nutritional value of most packaged foods...when these magazines are being subsidized by such advertisers as General Foods, Kellogg's, Nabisco, and General Mills?...The answer is *they cannot and do not.*"[22]

North American industries promote and protect their interests. They have a right to representation in Parliament and the mass media, although their influence can become too great. Fortunately, many powerful business interests once thought to be untouchable have been tamed in the public interest. For example, Petro-Canada was formed to give Canadians greater control over the oil industry. Ralph

Nader caused legislation that forced the automobile industry to build more safety into its cars. Amendments to the *Tobacco Products Control Act* made it necessary for cigarette manufacturers to place stronger warnings on their packages about the dangers of smoking.

Marketing's Impact on Other Businesses

Critics charge that a company's marketing practices can harm other companies and reduce competition. Three problems are involved: acquisitions of competitors, marketing practices that create barriers to entry, and unfair competitive marketing practices.

Critics claim that firms are harmed and competition reduced when companies expand by acquiring competitors rather than by developing their own new products. The large number of acquisitions and rapid pace of industry consolidation over the past several decades have caused concern that vigorous young competitors will be absorbed and that competition will be reduced. In virtually every major industry—retailing, entertainment, financial services, utilities, transportation, automobiles, telecommunications—the number of major competitors is shrinking. Consider the glut of acquisitions in the food industry during just the past two years: "The consolidation frenzy led to Unilever's buying Bestfoods, Philip Morris's snatching Nabisco, General Mills' swallowing Pillsbury, Kellogg's taking over Keebler, and PepsiCo's seizing of Quaker Oats."[23]

Acquisition is a complex subject. Acquisitions can sometimes be good for society. The acquiring company may gain economies of scale that lead to lower costs and lower prices. A well-managed company may take over a poorly managed company and improve its efficiency. An industry that was not very competitive may become more competitive after the acquisition. But acquisitions also can be harmful and, therefore, are regulated by the government.

Critics have charged that marketing practices bar new companies from entering an industry. Large companies can use patents and heavy promotional spending, and can tie up suppliers or dealers to keep out or drive out competitors. However, even people opposed to mergers among Canada's banks recognize that there are economic advantages of doing global business on a large scale. Some barriers that limit competition could be challenged by existing and new laws. For example, some critics have proposed a progressive tax on advertising spending to reduce the role of selling costs as a major barrier to entry.

Nowhere are these issues more apparent than in Canada's pharmaceutical industry. In 1993, Canada revised the regulations dealing with patent protection for drugs. Patent protection was brought in line with international standards and extended from 17 to 20 years. In exchange, the pharmaceutical industry made a commitment to increase investments in medical research and development. Increased patent protection was needed, it was claimed, because it takes an average of 10 to 12 years and costs up to $750 million to develop a new drug.

The new law was hotly disputed, however. The generic manufacturers wanted patent protection reduced to 10 years. Furthermore, they claimed that branded drug firms had actually cut jobs since being granted extended protection. In 1998 the federal government implemented changes to the *Patented Medicines Regulations* to ensure that pharmaceutical patents were respected without delaying market entry of generic drugs. Recent evidence suggests the legislation has accomplished its purpose and that pharmaceutical research and development spending in Canada has increased faster than in any other industrialized country—up by 700 percent in a little more than a decade.[24]

Finally, some firms have used unfair competitive marketing practices with the intention of hurting or destroying other firms. They may set their prices below costs, threaten to cut off business with suppliers, or discourage the buying of a competitor's products. Various laws work to prevent such predatory competition. It is difficult, however, to prove that the intent or action was really predatory. In recent years, Wal-Mart, Intel, and Microsoft have all been accused of predatory practices. Since 2000, Air Canada has faced a number of charges of predatory pricing as it has attempted to halt the erosion of its market share by discount airlines such as WestJet, JetsGo, and CanJet.[25]

Citizen and Public Actions to Regulate Marketing

Because some people view business as the cause of many economic and social ills, grassroots movements have arisen from time to time to keep business in line. The two major movements are *consumerism* and *environmentalism*.

Consumerism

The first consumer movements took place in the early 1900s and in the mid-1930s. Both were sparked by an upturn in consumer prices. Another movement began in the 1960s. Consumers had become better educated; products had become more complex and hazardous; and people were questioning the status quo. Many accused big business of wasteful and unethical practices. Since then, many consumer groups have been organized, and several consumer laws have been passed. The consumer movement has spread beyond North America and has become global in nature. Protestors, fearing negative outcomes on consumers and manufacturers alike, have disrupted conferences held by the World Trade Organization (WTO). While the demonstrations were peaceful at the 2002 talks held in Kananaskis outside of Calgary, they have degraded to violence in other areas.[26]

Consumerism

An organized movement of citizens and government agencies to improve the rights and power of buyers in relation to sellers.

But what is the consumer movement? **Consumerism** is an organized movement of citizens and government agencies to improve the rights and power of buyers in relation to sellers. It must be remembered that both parties have rights. Traditional *sellers' rights* include:

- The right to introduce any product in any size and style, provided it is not hazardous to personal health or safety; or, if it is, to include proper warnings and controls.
- The right to charge any price for the product, provided no discrimination exists among similar kinds of buyers.
- The right to spend any amount to promote the product, provided it is not defined as unfair competition.
- The right to use any product message, provided it is not misleading or dishonest in content or execution.
- The right to use any buying incentive schemes, provided they are not unfair or misleading.

The Consumers' Association of Canada (CAC; www.consumer.ca/) has acted as a consumer advocate and has provided information to Canadian consumers for over 50 years. This volunteer-based, non-governmental organization was founded in 1947. With offices in every province, the association lobbies government to secure consumer rights in areas of food, health care, environment, consumer products and services, regulated industries (phone, electricity, telecommunications, cable), financial institutions, taxation, trade, and any other issue of concern to Canadians facing complex buying decisions. The association establishes annual priorities. Recent issues include health-care reform; privacy protection, electrical utilities deregulation, consumer education, and purchasing literacy; GST reform; price visibility; package downsizing; and environmental rights and responsibilities. The association has also outlined the following as fundamental consumer rights:[27]

- *The right to safety.* Consumers have the right to be protected against the marketing of goods that are hazardous to health or life.
- *The right to be informed.* Consumers must be protected against fraudulent, deceitful, or grossly misleading information, advertising, labelling, or other practices. They are to be given the facts needed to make an informed choice.
- *The right to choose.* Consumers have the right to choose, wherever possible, among a variety of products and services at competitive prices. In industries where competition is not workable and government regulation is substituted, consumers must be assured of satisfactory quality and service at fair prices.
- *The right to be heard.* It is important that consumers' voices be heard. Thus, they must receive full and sympathetic consideration in the formulation of government policy, and fair and expeditious treatment in its administrative tribunals.
- *The right to redress against damage.* Consumers have the right to seek redress from a supplier of goods and services for any loss or damage suffered because of bad information, or faulty products or performance, and shall have easy and inexpensive access to settlement of small claims.
- *The right to consumer education.* Canadian consumers have the right to be educated as school children so that they will be able to act as informed consumers through their lives. Adults also have the right to consumer education.

Each proposed right has led to more specific proposals by consumerists. The right to be informed, for example, includes the right to know the true interest on a loan (truth in lending), the true cost per unit of a brand (unit pricing), the ingredients in a product (ingredient labelling), the nutrition in foods (nutritional labelling), product freshness (open dating), and the true benefits of a product (truth in advertising).

In addition to the CAC, some better business bureaus offer tips to consumers to protect themselves from fraud or shady business practices. Consumers have not only the *right* but also the *responsibility* to protect themselves instead of leaving this function to someone else. Consumers who believe they got a bad deal have several remedies available, including writing to the company president or to the media; contacting federal, provincial, or local agencies; and going to small claims court.

Environmentalism

Environmentalism

An organized movement of concerned citizens and government agencies to protect and improve people's living environment.

Whereas consumerists consider whether the marketing system is efficiently serving consumer wants, environmentalists are concerned with marketing's effects on the environment and with the costs of serving consumer needs and wants. **Environmentalism** is an organized movement of concerned citizens, businesses, and government agencies to protect and improve people's living environment. Environmentalists are not against marketing and consumption; they simply want people and organizations to operate with more care for the environment. The marketing system's goal, they assert, should not be to maximize consumption, consumer choice, or consumer satisfaction, but rather to maximize life quality. And "life quality" means not only the quantity and quality of consumer goods and services, but also the quality of the environment. Environmentalists want environmental costs included in both producer and consumer decision making.

In response to these concerns, the Canadian government has undertaken a number of initiatives to improve the environment. It froze production levels of chlorofluorocarbons (CFCs), the major cause of ozone layer depletion, and Canada's environment ministers established a voluntary program intended to reduce excessive packaging. Despite a heated debate, the Kyoto Accord was endorsed in 2002. (To be aligned with the protocol, industrialized countries must cut their greenhouse gas emissions to below 1990 levels within 10 years.)[28]

Marketers cannot ignore the urgency of environmental issues or be blind to the fact that governments are increasingly willing to take action and pass regulations restricting marketing practices. All parts of the marketing mix are affected. Advertisers are accused of adding to the solid waste problem when they use direct mail or newspaper inserts. Manufacturers are criticized for making products that incorporate materials that increase pollution or cannot be recycled.[29] Distribution systems have been cited for adding to air pollution as trucks move products from the factory to the store. Critics claim that even when environmentally friendly products are available, they are priced too high for many consumers to afford.

Buying behaviour has changed as sensitivity to this issue has grown. The late 1980s saw the birth of a new product attribute—environmentally friendly. A recent survey conducted by the Grocery Product Manufacturers of Canada found that 80 percent of respondents said they would be willing to pay more for "green" products. Companies began to respond to these changes in demand. Retailers in both Canada and the United States are demanding more environmentally sensitive products: Wal-Mart has asked its suppliers to provide more of these products, while Loblaw has developed an entire line of products under its "green" President's Choice label. Some people claim that "green marketing" is dead. If you think that is true, just consider some of the initiatives by the Canadian packaging industry:[30]

Canada's packaging industry has been working diligently to meet the goals established by the National Packaging Protocol, a voluntary agreement formulated to reduce the amount of packaging sent to landfills by 50 percent relative to what was sent to the trash in 1988. Thus, in the early 1990s, when Canada's major laundry detergent manufacturers introduced concentrated powders to the market, they not only reduced the amount of detergent that people used, they also resulted in a 40 percent reduction in packaging materials. This is only part of the commitment of the packaging industry, which has invested more than $2 billion in infrastructure to reduce, reuse, and recycle its packaging. Compared to a decade ago, there is almost no packaging produced in Canada that hasn't been improved from an environmental perspective. For example, the

Members of the Packaging Association of Canada (PAC) have worked to reduce the amount of packaging going into landfills and have gained international marketing opportunities in return.

average glass container has a 34 percent recycled content. Weights of containers have been reduced by at least 10 percent, saving fuel and shipping costs. Because the Canadian packaging industry had a jump on almost every other country in the world in designing better environmental packaging, there is strong export demand for Canadian packaging, especially in the US. It's a good initiative when you can sell more by using less.

The first wave of modern environmentalism in North America was driven by environmental groups and concerned consumers in the 1960s and 1970s. They were concerned with damage to the ecosystem and loss of natural areas caused by strip-mining, forest depletion, acid rain, loss of the atmosphere's ozone layer, toxic wastes, and litter. The second environmentalism wave was driven by government, which passed laws and regulations during the 1970s and 1980s governing industrial practices impacting the environment. This wave hit some industries hard. Steel companies and utilities, for example, had to invest billions of dollars in pollution control equipment and costlier fuels.

Environmental sustainability
A management approach that involves developing strategies that both sustain the environment and produce profits for the company.

The first two environmentalism waves are now merging into a third and stronger wave in which companies are accepting responsibility for doing no harm to the environment. They are shifting from protest to prevention, and from regulation to responsibility. More and more companies are adopting policies of **environmental sustainability**—developing strategies that both sustain the environment and produce profits for the company. According to one strategist, "The challenge is to develop a *sustainable global economy:* an economy that the planet is capable of supporting indefinitely.... [It's] an enormous challenge—and an enormous opportunity."[31]

Sustainability is a crucial but difficult goal. John Browne, chairman of giant oil company BP, recently asked this question: "Is genuine progress still possible? Is development sustainable? Or is one strand of progress—industrialization—now doing such damage to the environment that the next generation won't have a world worth living in?"[32] Browne sees the situation as an opportunity. Five years ago, BP broke ranks with the oil industry on environmental issues. "There are good commercial reasons to do right by the environment," says Browne. Under his leadership, BP has become active in public forums on global climate issues and has worked to reduce emissions in exploration and production. It has begun marketing cleaner fuels and invested significantly in exploring alternative energy sources, such as photovoltaic power and hydrogen. At the local level, BP recently opened "the world's most environmentally friendly service station" near London:

Environmental sustainability: BP recently opened "the world's most environmentally friendly service station" near London, featuring an array of innovative green initiatives.

The new BP Connect service station features an array of innovative green initiatives that show BP's commitment to environmental responsibility. The station runs entirely on renewable energy and generates up to half of its own power, using solar panels installed on the roofs and three wind turbines. More than 60 percent of the water needed for the restrooms comes from rainwater collected on the shop roof, and water for hand washing is heated by solar panels. The site's vapour recovery systems collect and recycle even the fuel vapour released from customers' tanks as they pump gas. BP has planted landscaping around the site with indigenous plant species. And, to promote biodiversity awareness, the company has undertaken several initiatives to attract local wildlife to the area, such as dragonflies and insect-feeding birds. The wildflower turf under the wind farm will even provide a habitat for bumble bees.[33]

Companies as diverse as DuPont Canada, Shell Canada, Ontario Power Generation, Alcan Inc., Dofasco, Falconbridge, Cadillac-Fairview, and Olympia & York Enterprises are finding that they can be both green *and* competitive. Consider this example:

Husky Injection Molding Systems Ltd. (www.husky.ca), the world's third-largest supplier of injection moulds to the plastics industry, based in Bolton, Ontario, might not seem like a candidate for environmentally friendly practices, but it has really "walked the talk" by doing everything from instituting natural landscaping techniques around its headquarters which eliminated the need for pesticides, to its waste reduction program, which has diverted 95 percent of all its refuse. Their waste cutting program has also had customer benefits. Those who use Husky's moulds to shape everything from cellphones to car bumpers were also able to cut their waste by using thin-walled containers that require less plastic.

Businesses alone cannot improve the environment. Consumers must also change their habits. In the summer of 2003, the government of Ontario ran a series of ads encouraging consumers to turn down their thermostats to conserve power—a message that really hit home after the massive blackout that hit Ontario that August.

Husky Injection Molding Systems has learned that being environmentally sensitive can also reduce costs and improve customer relationships.

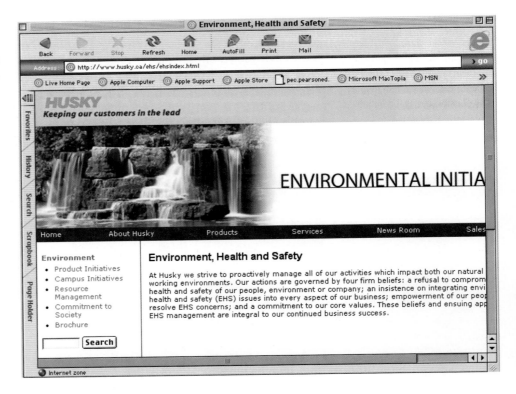

Similarly, the city of Toronto ran a series of ads encouraging consumers to use fewer chemicals and pesticides on their lawns.

Environmentalism creates some special challenges for global marketers. As international trade barriers come down and global markets expand, environmental issues are having a growing impact on international trade. Countries in North America, Western Europe, and other developed regions are developing stringent environmental standards. A side accord to the North American Free Trade Agreement (NAFTA) set up a commission for resolving environmental matters.

However, environmental policies vary widely from country to country, and uniform worldwide standards are not expected for many years. Although countries such as Canada, Denmark, Germany, Japan, and the United States have fully developed environmental policies and high public expectations, other major countries such as China, India, Brazil, and Russia are only in the early stages of developing such policies. Moreover, environmental factors that motivate consumers in one country may have no impact on consumers in another. For example, PVC soft-drink bottles cannot be used in Switzerland or Germany. However, they are preferred in France, which has an extensive recycling process for them. Thus, international companies are finding it difficult to develop standard environmental practices that work around the world. Instead, they are creating general policies and then translating these into tailored programs to meet local regulations and expectations.

Public Actions to Regulate Marketing

Citizen concerns about marketing practices usually will lead to public attention and legislative proposals. New bills will be debated—many will be defeated, others will be modified, and a few will become workable laws. Canada's new privacy law—the *Personal Information Protection and Electronic Documents Act*—is one example.

Many of the laws that affect marketing are listed in Chapter 5. The task is to translate these laws into the language that marketing executives understand as they make decisions about competitive relations, products, price, promotion, and channels of distribution.

Business Actions toward Socially Responsible Marketing

Enlightened marketing
A marketing philosophy holding that a company's marketing should support the best long-run performance of the marketing system; its five principles are consumer-oriented marketing, innovative marketing, value marketing, sense-of-mission marketing, and societal marketing.

Consumer-oriented marketing
A philosophy of enlightened marketing that holds that the company should view and organize its marketing activities from the consumer's point of view.

Today, most companies have grown to accept the new consumer rights, at least in principle. They may oppose certain pieces of legislation as inappropriate ways to solve certain consumer problems, but they recognize the consumer's right to information and protection. Many of these companies have responded positively to consumerism and environmentalism in order to serve consumer needs better.

Enlightened Marketing

The philosophy of **enlightened marketing** holds that a company's marketing should support the best long-run performance of the marketing system. Enlightened marketing consists of five principles: *consumer-oriented marketing, innovative marketing, value marketing, sense-of-mission marketing,* and *societal marketing.*

Consumer-Oriented Marketing

Consumer-oriented marketing means that the company should view and organize its marketing activities from the consumer's point of view. It should work hard to

The City of Toronto encourages consumers to change habits, such as pesticide use, that harm the environment.

sense, serve, and satisfy the needs of a defined group of customers. Consider this example:

> Montreal-based Walsh Integrated Environmental Systems Inc. was founded by David Walsh, right after he graduated from business school. After conducting a 12-week waste audit at Montreal's Royal Victoria Hospital, he realized what a huge waste management problem hospitals faced. Disposing of biohazardous waste costs 20 times as much as getting rid of regular waste and can result in bills of over $450 000 per year. Yet Walsh also saw that other materials, from pop cans to newspapers, were thrown in the biohazardous containers the hospital was using. In fact, about 65 percent of the material in the garbage could go into the regular waste stream. Walsh's new business developed a system called the Waste Tracker that allows hospital staff to track the waste from each department, identify how much is biohazardous, and uncover who is misusing the system. Today his company serves over 300 Canadian and U.S. hospitals and he has expanded his services to include a quality support system that helps hospitals monitor the cleanliness of their rooms and labs as well as control their waste.[34]

Every successful company that we've discussed in this text has had this in common: an all-consuming passion for delivering superior value to carefully chosen customers. Only by seeing the world through its customers' eyes can the company build lasting and profitable customer relationships.

Innovative Marketing

Innovative marketing
A principle of enlightened marketing that requires that a company seek real product and marketing improvements.

The principle of **innovative marketing** requires that the company continuously seek real product and marketing improvements. The company that overlooks new and better ways to do things will eventually lose customers to another company that has found a better way. An excellent example of an innovative marketer is Colgate-Palmolive:

Colgate has become somewhat of a new-product machine in recent years. Worldwide, new products contribute 35 percent of Colgate's revenues, up from 26 percent five years earlier. The American Marketing Association (AMA) recently named Colgate-Palmolive its new-product marketer of the year. Colgate took the honours by launching an abundance of innovative and highly successful new consumer products, including Colgate Total toothpaste, which now captures a 35 percent market share versus Procter & Gamble's 25 percent.

Innovation didn't stop here, however. In 2002, it launched a related product, its battery-powered full-motion toothbrush. In its creative marketing campaign, Colgate held free dental clinics at Toronto's Union Station during rush-hour periods, offering advice from a George Brown College dental hygiene student. Participants were given a coupon for $2 off a brush and all transit passengers were offered a Colgate Total toothpaste sample in exchange for a donation to the United Way. As James Masterson, the senior product manager noted, "The grassroots initiatives provide an opportunity to interact directly with consumers to effectively communicate the benefits of proper oral hygiene in a fun and engaging way."[35]

Value Marketing

Value marketing
A principle of enlightened marketing that holds that a company should put most of its resources into value-building marketing investments.

According to the principle of **value marketing**, the company should put most of its resources into value-building marketing investments. Many things marketers do— one-shot sales promotions, minor packaging changes, advertising puffery—may raise sales in the short run but add less *value* than would actual improvements in the product's quality, features, or convenience. Enlightened marketing calls for building long-run consumer loyalty by continually improving the value consumers receive from the firm's marketing offer.

Sense-of-Mission Marketing

Sense-of-mission marketing
A principle of enlightened marketing that holds that a company should define its mission in broad social terms rather than narrow product terms.

Sense-of-mission marketing means that the company should define its mission in broad *social* terms rather than narrow *product* terms. When a company defines a social mission, employees feel better about their work and have a clearer sense of direction. For example, defined in narrow product terms, Mountain Equipment Co-op sells high-quality outdoor gear. However, the organization states its mission more broadly as one of "social and environmental leadership."[36] Reshaping the basic task of selling consumer products into the larger mission of serving the interests of consumers, employees, the environment, and others in the organization's various "communities" gives MEC a vital sense of purpose. Like MEC, many companies today are undertaking socially responsible actions or even building social responsibility into their underlying missions (see Real Marketing 4.2).

Societal Marketing

Societal marketing
A principle of enlightened marketing that holds that a company should make marketing decisions by considering consumers' wants, the company's requirements, consumers' long-run interests, and society's long-run interests.

Following the principle of **societal marketing**, an enlightened company makes marketing decisions by considering consumers' wants and interests, the company's requirements, and society's long-run interests. The company is aware that neglecting consumer and societal long-run interests is a disservice to consumers and society. Alert companies and organizations view societal problems as opportunities. This is just what Hockey Canada did.

Canadians have a reputation for being polite, reserved and well mannered— unless of course they are watching their children wobbling around a hockey rink. In towns and cities across Canada, parents seem to have gone mad. They scream at their kids, hurl insults at rival teams, and beat refs to within an inch of their lives. For many kids, such behaviour was destroying Canada's best-loved game, so Hockey Canada decided to call a penalty shot. In a series of funny but provocative ads, it reverses the roles of parent and kid. One spot

REAL MARKETING

4.2   Mission: Social Responsibility

In a recent poll, 88 percent of Canadians agreed that business should do more than simply make a profit, create jobs, and obey laws. This sentiment is particularly strong in British Columbia, where nine out of ten people believe B.C. companies should do more to address social, environmental, and community issues. Four in ten Canadians can readily name a good corporate citizen. A poll conducted in the United States suggested that more than three-quarters of the respondents would switch brands and retailers when price and quality are equal for a product associated with a good cause. The research is clear: customers vote with their wallets and their feet, choosing products and services from companies they perceive to be doing well by doing good. It's not surprising, therefore, that cause-related marketing by companies has increased more than 500 percent during the past decade.

Today, acts of good corporate citizenship abound. For example, Tim Hortons Children's Foundation, which was founded in 1975 in memory of Tim Horton and his love for children, has given thousands of children from

Alcan's efforts with regard to sustainability helped it win the top spot in the *Corporate Knights* 2003 ranking of Canada's most socially responsible companies.

across Canada and parts of the United States a camping adventure they'll never forget. The Foundation's largest single fundraiser is Camp Day, when Tim Hortons store owners donate coffee sales and collect public donations. In 2002 alone $4.8 million was raised. Maxwell House, a division of Kraft Foods, created a partnership with Habitat for Humanity to build one hundred homes in as many days, while working to raise awareness for the organization. Post Cereal celebrated its one hundredth anniversary by donating to Second Harvest—one of the largest networks of hunger-relief charities—enough cereal to feed more than one million people. Bell Canada is the long-time sponsor of the Kids Help Phone, which receives over 4000 calls a day from young people who need to talk over problems or are crying out for help.

It seems that almost every company has a pet cause. Alarm company ADT gives away personal security systems to battered women. Avon helps to build awareness about the importance of early detection and breast cancer screening—since 1993, it has raised more than US$165 million for this cause. CIBC, Ford Canada, and Kitchen Aid join forces in the annual "Run for the Cure" as their contribution to the fight against breast cancer. Coca-Cola sponsors local Boys and Girls Clubs, Molson and its co-sponsors have raised millions of dollars for AIDS research, McDonald's Restaurants of Canada is well known for its long-standing Ronald McDonald House program, and Nissan Canada partners with Meals on Wheels to deliver hot lunches to the elderly and shut-ins.

Beyond aligning with good causes, socially responsible companies care about and serve the communities in which they operate. Take Saturn Canada, for example:

As its slogan states, Saturn is "A different kind of company. A different kind of car." The company claims to focus more on its employees, customers, and communities than on revenues and bottom lines. Saturn's CEO notes that "a part of Saturn's business philosophy is to meet the needs of our neighbours."

An example of this philosophy in action is Saturn Playgrounds, a company program for employee involvement and community betterment. The goal is to provide young children with a safe, fun environment during nonschool hours as an alternative to gangs, drugs, and crime. Backed by Saturn retailers, local Saturn employees and customers join with community members to build a community playground in a single day. So far, Saturn and its customers have built over 223 playgrounds in towns across Canada. When Saturn dedicated the new playground built on the grounds of the Toronto Zoo, 6700 owners and their families participated.

But playgrounds aren't the only things needed by communities. Saturn retailers are the eyes and ears of the company, and when a community need arises, Saturn tries to respond. Saturn planted trees in areas hard hit by the 1997 ice storm. In North Bay, it provided funds for a new heart-monitoring unit.

Each year, *Corporate Knights* magazine selects the 50 Most Responsible Companies in Canada, while *Business Ethics* magazine selects its 100 Best Corporate Citizens in the United States. Companies making the rankings are those that excel not only at making the workplace a great place to be, they also work at being environmentally friendly, and they serve their various local, national, and global communities as well as shareholders and customers. The top ten spots on the Canadian list were given to Alcan Inc., the Royal Bank of Canada, Suncor Engery Inc., Nexen Inc., CIBC, Domtar Inc., MTS Inc., Nova Chemicals Corp., and BMO Financial Group. (You can see the full list at www.corporateknights.ca.)

Here are some details about the companies ranked at the top of the Canadian and American lists for corporate citizenship:

Alcan Inc. The company that tops the Canadian list is a multinational firm that prides itself in being market-driven. It employs 52 000 people in 38 different countries, generating US$12.6 billion in revenues from its mining, manufacturing, and chemical operations. In its Sustainability Report, Alcan stresses the need to increase the social and economic benefits arising from its activities while reducing the environmental impact of its operations. As Travis Engen, President and CEO of Alcan, notes, "By including *sustainability* in our title we are stating first and foremost that we believe our success as a global company is directly linked to our actions both inside and outside our operations." He recognizes that issues of sustainability are complex and that there are many unanswered questions. However, in the near term, Alcan is moving toward sustainability by using resources more efficiently, making its workplaces safer, enhancing the skills of its employees, and working more effectively with its partners and host communities. It integrates economic, environmental, and social considerations into its business planning processes. Finally, its philosophy of sustainability is grounded in its corporate values—integrity, accountability, trust and transparency, and teamwork.

IBM. The top U.S. company for 2002, IBM received high praise for its diversity policies and for its community giving programs. This technology giant—with 330 000 employees in 164 countries—gives more than just money. Of the over US$126 million donated last year, less than one-third was in cash. The remainder consisted of technology and technical services, the core of what IBM knows best. Moreover, in 2002 IBM employees contributed 4 million hours of time in a wide range of community projects. Says IBM's vice president of corporate community relations, "With chequebook philanthropy, you could contribute a lot of money and accomplish very little. I think that in the new model, being generous is incredibly important, but the most important aspect of this new model is using our many resources to achieve something of lasting value in the communities where we live, work, and do business."

As these two examples show, social responsibility is no longer viewed as the enemy of good business. Instead, it's at the forefront of sound business practice. "The term 'corporate citizenship' is coming into broader use these days," says the editor of *Business Ethics*, "as awareness grows that business has responsibilities beyond profits." Moreover, doing what's good for a company's communities can also be good for the company. A recent study shows that, on average, companies that make the list of best corporate citizens score 10 percent higher on *Business Week's* rankings of financial performance than the remaining companies in the S&P 500. These good corporate citizens also rank higher on *Fortune* magazine's list of most admired companies. The differences were "strikingly large," says the researcher overseeing the study. "This may be the most concrete evidence now available that good citizenship really does pay off on the bottom line."

Sources: The Tim Horton's website, www.timhortons.com/; Alcan Inc., Corporate Sustainability Report 2002, "Alcan's Journey Towards Sustainability," www.alcan.ca/corporate/alcancom.nsf/ graphics/reports/$file/csr_preamb_e.pdf (accessed July 17, 2003); Paul Welsh, "From trademarks to trustmarks," *Strategy*, February 24, 2003, p. 17; "Saturn Dealers Build Six New Playgrounds in One Weekend," *PR Newswire*, June 4, 1997; and Saturn Corporation, "Community: Saturn Playgrounds," www.saturnbp. com/mysaturn/mycommunity (accessed September 2002). Information also provided by Chuck Novak, Brand Manager Saturn Canada, in an interview with Peggy Cunningham on July 21, 1999. Also see David Bosworth, "GM attracts Site Seers," *Strategy*, June 22, 1998, p. D1; Sinclair Steward, "Putting the Customer First," *Strategy*, November 9, 1998, p. 21; Tom Klusmann, "The 100 Best Corporate Citizens in 2000," *Business Ethics*, March–April 2000; Philip Johansson, "The 100 Best Corporate Citizens for 2001," *Business Ethics*, March–April 2001; Cynthia Wagner, "Economics: Evaluating Good Corporate Citizenship," *The Futurist*, July–August 2001, p. 16; "The 100 Best Corporate Citizens for 2002," *Business Ethics*, April 2002; and information accessed online at the Avon website, www.avoncompany.com/women/ avoncrusade (August 2002). For more information and examples, see the *Corporate Knights* website, "Best 50 Corporate Citizens," www.corporate knights.ca/best50/index.asp, and the *Business Ethics* website, "The 100 Best Corporate Citizens for 2003," www.business-ethics.com/100best.htm.

Hockey Canada saw the bad behaviour of hockey parents as an opportunity to take action to improve the hockey experience for kids. Their irreverent campaign made parents everywhere re-examine their behaviour.

Relax, it's just a game.

HOCKEY CANADA

shows a man pulled over for a traffic violation. As the officer is writing up the ticket, the man's ten-year-old son is losing it in the back seat, furious because his spineless dad won't stand up to the cop. In another, a girl berates her father in front of his golf buddies as he tries to sink a putt. The breakthrough campaign has made us all aware of the problem and caused us to take a fresh look at our behaviour.[37]

A societally oriented marketer wants to design products that are not only pleasing but also beneficial. Examples of products that create immediate consumer satisfaction as well as long-term social benefits abound. Philips Lighting's Earth Light compact fluorescent lightbulb provides good lighting at the same time that it gives long life and energy savings. Toyota's gas-electric hybrid Prius gives both a quiet ride and fuel efficiency. Maytag's front-loading Neptune washer provides superior cleaning along with water savings and energy efficiency. President's Choice "Too Good to Be True" soup mixes, developed for people with special dietary needs, have been welcomed by consumers who want good-tasting, high-fibre, low-fat, easy-to-prepare, healthful food. Another example of a desirable product is Herman Miller's Avian office chair, which is not just attractive and functional but also environmentally responsible:[38]

Herman Miller, one of the world's largest office furniture makers, has received numerous awards for environmentally responsible products and business practices. In 1994, the company formed an Earth-Friendly Design Task Force responsible for infusing the company's design process with its environmental values. The task force carries out life-cycle analyses on the company's products, including everything from how much of a product can be made from recycled materials to how much of the product itself can be recycled at the end of its useful life. For example, the company's Avian chair is designed for the lowest possible ecological impact and 100 percent recyclability. Herman Miller reduced material used in the chair by using gas-assist injection moulding for the frame, which resulted in hollow frame members (like the bones of birds, hence the chair's name). The frame needs no paint or other finish. All materials are recyclable. No ozone-depleting materials are used. The chair is shipped partially assembled, thus reducing the packaging and energy needed to ship it. Finally, a materials schematic is embedded in the bottom of the seat to help recycle the chair at the end of its life. This is truly a desirable product—it's won awards for design and function *and* for environmental responsibility.

Herman Miller's Earth-Friendly Design Task Force infuses the company's design process with environmental values. For example, the Avian chair is designed for the lowest possible ecological impact and 100 percent recyclability.

Companies should try to turn all of their products into such desirable products. They should avoid the temptation to market pleasing products that may sell very well but may end up hurting the consumer and the environment. The product opportunity, therefore, is to add long-run benefits without reducing the product's pleasing qualities.

Marketing Ethics

Conscientious marketers face many moral dilemmas. Each area of marketing practice has ethical issues associated with it. Table 4.2 outlines just a few of the ethical issues marketers may face when fulfilling their roles. When facing these dilemmas, the best thing to do is often unclear. Because not all managers have fine moral sensitivity, companies need to develop *corporate marketing ethics policies*—broad guidelines that everyone in the organization must follow. These policies should cover distributor relations, advertising standards, customer service, pricing, and product development, as well as general ethical standards.

The finest guidelines cannot resolve all the difficult ethical situations the marketer faces. Table 4.3 lists some difficult ethical situations that marketers could face during their careers. If marketers choose immediate sales-producing actions in all these cases, their marketing behaviour may well be described as immoral or even amoral. If they refuse to go along with *any* of the actions, they may be ineffective as marketing managers and unhappy because of the constant moral tension. Managers need a set of principles that will help them to determine the moral importance of each situation and decide how far they can go in good conscience.

But *what* principle should guide companies and marketing managers on issues of ethics and social responsibility? One philosophy is that such issues are decided by the free market and legal system. Under this principle, companies and their managers are not responsible for making moral judgments. Companies can in good conscience do whatever the system legally allows.

A second philosophy puts responsibility not in the system but in the hands of individual companies and managers. This more enlightened philosophy suggests that a company should have a "social conscience." Companies and managers should

Table 4.2   Ethical Issues Associated with Marketing Practice

Marketing Element	Examples of Ethical Issues
Marketing Research	Invalid and/or unreliable research studies (agencies conducting research studies using inappropriate methods or measures)
	Invasion of consumer's privacy
	Disguising sales as research
	Failure to ensure voluntary and informed participation (pressuring consumers to comply through high-pressure tactics or high-value incentives)
	Failure to respect the confidentiality of respondents' (revealing respondents' individual identities)
	Competitive intelligence gathering using unethical tactics (hiring competitors' employees, dumpster diving, spying)
Segmentation and Target Marketing	Redlining: discriminating against poor or disadvantaged consumers
	Targeting inappropriate products to vulnerable audiences (diet pills to anorexic women, violent video games to children)
Positioning	Making socially undesirable products desirable (promoting use of disposable cleaning devices that add to landfill crisis versus re-useable ones)
	Positioning on questionable benefits (relating increased sexual attractiveness to alcohol consumption)
Product	Failure to market products that are safe for the intended use (lead in childrens' toys)
	Product testing (animal testing, failure to test sufficiently to reveal safety concerns)
	Marketing socially controversial products (cigarettes, firearms)
Packaging and Labelling	Actual size vs. apparent size (using design elements to make packages look larger than they are)
	Inadequate efforts with regard to product recalls
	Nutritional information (is information displayed in a fashion that can and will be processed?)
	Unclear or misleading labelling (terms such as "lite," "healthy," etc. are ambiguous and may imply benefits not actually associated with the product)
	Excess or environmentally unfriendly packaging (use of double and triple packaging that does little to protect the product but adds to waste stream, use of harmful dyes, failure to use recycled materials)
Pricing	Price collusion: the illegal practice of forming price agreements with competitors
	Negative option billing: sending unrequested goods and billing consumers for them
	Prejudice in negotiated prices: research has demonstrated that women and racial minorities pay more in negotiated price situations such as car buying
	Price discrimination: charging different segments different prices that are not based on cost (e.g., charging high prices in low-income neighbourhoods)
Advertising	Sex-role stereotyping in advertising (always showing women in domestic roles, not using women's voices in voice-overs in advertising)
	Dehumanizing images and portraying people as products: showing body parts versus the whole human being
	Bait-and-switch advertising: enticing consumers into retail establishments with offers of low-priced goods and then switching them to higher-priced alternatives
Sales and Channel Management	High-pressure sales tactics
	Unfairly disparaging competitors' goods
	Channel loading: pressuring channel members to take unneeded inventory at the end of a sales period to make the firm's sales numbers look better for reporting purposes

apply high standards of ethics and morality when making corporate decisions, regardless of "what the system allows." History provides an endless list of examples of company actions that were legal and allowed but were highly irresponsible.

Table 4.3 Some Morally Difficult Situations in Marketing

1. You work for a cigarette company and up until now have not been convinced that cigarettes cause cancer. However, recent public policy debates now leave no doubt in your mind about the link between smoking and cancer. What do you do?

2. Your R&D department has changed one of your products slightly. It is not really "new and improved," but you know that putting this statement on the package and in advertising will increase sales. What do you do?

3. You have been asked to add a stripped-down model to your line that could be advertised to attract customers to the store. The product won't be very good, but salespeople will be able to switch buyers up to higher-priced units. You are asked to give the green light for this stripped-down version. What do you do?

4. You are considering hiring a product manager who just left a competitor's company. She would be more than happy to tell you all the competitor's plans for the coming year. What do you do?

5. One of your top dealers in an important territory has recently had family troubles, and his sales have slipped. It looks like it will take him some time to straighten out his family trouble. Meanwhile, you are losing many sales. Legally, you can terminate the dealer's franchise and replace him. What do you do?

6. You have a chance to win a big account that will mean a lot to you and your company. The purchasing agent hints that a "gift" would influence the decision. Your assistant recommends sending a fine colour television set to the buyer's home. What do you do?

7. You have heard that a competitor has a new product feature that will make a big difference in sales. The competitor will demonstrate the feature in a private dealer meeting at the annual trade show. You can easily send a snooper to this meeting to learn about the new feature. What do you do?

8. You have to choose between three ad campaigns outlined by your agency. "A" is a soft-sell, honest information campaign. "B" uses sex-loaded emotional appeals and exaggerates the product's benefits. "C" involves a noisy, irritating commercial that is sure to gain audience attention. Pretests show that the campaigns are effective in the following order: C, B, and A. What do you do?

9. You are interviewing a capable woman applicant for a job as a salesperson. She is better qualified than the men just interviewed. Nevertheless, you know that some of your important customers prefer dealing with men, and you will lose some sales if you hire her. What do you do?

10. You are a sales manager in an encyclopedia company. Your competitor's salespeople are getting into homes by pretending to take a research survey. After they finish the survey, they switch to their sales pitch. This technique seems to be very effective. What do you do?

Consider this example:

> Prior to the [United States] *Pure Food and Drug Act,* the advertising for a diet pill promised that a person taking this pill could eat virtually anything at any time and still lose weight. Too good to be true? Actually the claim was quite true; the product lived up to its billing with frightening efficiency. It seems that the primary active ingredient in this "diet pill" was tapeworm larvae. These larvae would develop in the intestinal tract and, of course, be well fed; the pill taker would in time, quite literally, starve to death.[39]

Each company and marketing manager must work out a philosophy of socially responsible and ethical behaviour. Under the social marketing concept, companies and managers must look beyond what is legal and allowed and develop standards based on personal integrity, corporate conscience, and long-run consumer welfare. A clear and responsible philosophy will help the company deal with knotty issues such as the one faced recently by 3M:

> In late 1997, a powerful new research technique for scanning blood kept turning up the same odd result: Tiny amounts of a chemical 3M had made for nearly 40 years were showing up in blood drawn from people living all across North America. If the results held up, it meant that virtually all North Americans may be carrying some minuscule amount of the chemical, called perfluorooctane sulfonate (PFOS), in their systems.
> Even though they had yet to come up with definitive answers—and they insisted that there was no evidence of danger to humans—the company reached

a drastic decision. In mid-2000, although under no mandate to act, 3M decided to phase out products containing PFOS and related chemicals, including its popular Scotchgard fabric protector. This was no easy decision. Since there was as yet no replacement chemical, it meant a potential loss of US$500 million in annual sales.

3M's voluntary actions drew praise from regulators. "3M deserves great credit for identifying the problem and coming forward," says an Environmental Protection Agency administrator. "It took guts," comments another government scientist. "The fact is that most companies...go into anger, denial, and the rest of that stuff. [We're used to seeing] decades-long arguments about whether a chemical is really toxic." For 3M, however, it shouldn't have been all that difficult a decision—it was simply the right thing to do.[40]

As with environmentalism, the issue of ethics provides special challenges for international marketers. Business standards and laws vary widely from one country to the next. For example, whereas bribes and kickbacks are illegal for North American firms, they are standard business practice in many South American countries. One recent study found that companies from some nations were much more likely to use bribes when seeking contracts in emerging-market nations. The most flagrant bribe-paying firms were from Russia and China, with Taiwan and South Korea close behind. The least corrupt were companies from Australia, Sweden, Switzerland, Austria, and Canada.[41] The question arises as to whether a company must lower its ethical standards to compete effectively in countries with lower standards. In one study, two researchers posed this question to chief executives of large international companies and got a unanimous response: No.[42]

When firms give a covert payment to a government official to obtain a concession, they are no longer just committing an unethical act, they are committing an illegal one, violating the Canada's *Corruption of Foreign Public Officials Act* (1998).

For the sake of all of the company's stakeholders—customers, suppliers, employees, shareholders, and the public—it is important to make a commitment to a common set of shared standards worldwide. For example, John Hancock Mutual Life Insurance Company operates successfully in Southeast Asia, an area that by Western standards has widespread questionable business and government practices. Despite warnings from locals that Hancock would have to bend its rules to succeed, the company set out strict guidelines. "We told our people that we had the same ethical standards, same procedures, same policies in these countries that we have in the United States, and we do," says Hancock Chairman Stephen Brown. "We just felt that things like payoffs were wrong—and if we had to do business that way, we'd rather not do business." Hancock employees feel good about the consistent levels of ethics. "There may be countries where you have to do that kind of thing," says Brown. "We haven't found that country yet, and if we do, we won't do business there."[43]

Many professional associations and firms have developed codes of ethics to better manage ethical issues related to marketing. For example, the Canadian Direct Marketing Association has a code to regulate practices of its members; excerpts are given in Table 4.4 on page 156. Companies are also developing programs to teach managers about important ethics issues and help them find the proper responses. They hold ethics workshops and seminars and set up ethics committees. Further, most major North American companies have appointed high-level ethics officers to champion ethics issues and to help resolve ethics problems and concerns facing employees. Under the new Canadian privacy laws, companies must also appoint Privacy Officers to keep an eye on this important issue within their organizations.

PricewaterhouseCoopers (PwC) is a good example. In 1996, PwC established an ethics office and comprehensive ethics program, headed by a high-level chief ethics officer. The ethics program begins with a code of conduct, called "The Way We Do

Ethics programs: PricewaterhouseCoopers established a comprehensive ethics program, which begins with a code of conduct, called "The Way We Do Business." Says PwC's CEO, "Ethics is in everything we say and do."

Business." PwC employees learn about the code of conduct and about how to handle thorny ethics issues in a comprehensive ethics training program, called "Navigating the Grey." The program also includes an ethics help line and continuous communications at all levels. "Ethics is in everything we say and do," says PwC's CEO, Samuel DiPiazza. Last year alone, the PwC training program involved 40 000 employees, and the help line received over 1000 calls from people asking for guidance in working through difficult ethics dilemmas.[44]

Many companies have developed innovative ways to educate employees about ethics:

Ontario Power Generation Inc. and Imperial Oil have appointed high-level ethics officers to champion ethics issues and to help resolve ethics problems and concerns facing employees. Nynex created a new position of vice-president of

Table 4.4   Excerpts from the Canadian Marketing Association's Code of Ethics & Standards of Practice

A1. Purpose of Code of Ethics and Standards of Practice

Preamble: Marketers acknowledge that the establishment and maintenance of high standards of practice are a fundamental responsibility to the public, essential to winning and holding public confidence, and the foundation of a successful and independent information-based marketing industry in Canada.

A2. Application and Governing Legislation

A2.2 Members of the Canadian Marketing Association recognize an obligation—to the public, to the integrity of the discipline in which they operate and to each other—to practice to the highest standards of honesty, truth, accuracy and fairness.

A2.4 No marketer shall participate in any campaign involving the disparagement of any person or group on the grounds of race, colour, religion, national origin, gender, sexual orientation, marital status.

B. Accuracy of Representation

B1 *Accuracy:* Offers must be clear and truthful and shall not misrepresent a product, service, solicitation or program and shall not mislead by statement, or technique of demonstration or comparison.

B4 *Identity:* Every offer and shipment shall identify the marketer and provide the consumer with sufficient information to be able to contact the marketer.

B5 *Disguise:* No person shall make offers or solicitations in the guise of research or a survey when the real intent is to sell products, services, or to raise funds.

B6 *Disparagement:* No offer shall attack or discredit, or disparage products, services, advertisements or companies using inaccurate information.

B7 *Representation:* Photography, artwork or audio-visual representation must accurately and fairly illustrate the product offered.

C. Constituent Elements and Characteristics of the Offer

C1 *Disclosure:* The offer shall contain clear and conspicuous disclosure of the following terms:

- The exact nature of what is offered;
- The price;
- The terms of payment, including any additional charges, such as shipping and handling; and
- The consumer's commitment and any ongoing obligation in placing an order.

C2 *Comparisons:* Comparisons included in offers must be factual, verifiable and not misleading.

C10 *Guarantees and Warranties:* Where an offer includes a guarantee or warranty, the terms and conditions shall be set forth in full with the offer, or made available to the consumer upon request.

D. Fulfilment Practices

D1 *Shipment:* Goods offered shall be shipped within 30 days of the receipt of a properly completed order, or within the time limit stated in the original offer.

D2 *Delay:* The customer shall be advised within 30 days of the receipt of the order, or within the time limit stated in the original offer, if delivery will be late.

D4 *Substitution:* Any substitution of goods to those originally offered and ordered shall be disclosed to the consumer and shall be of the same or better quality, or be approved by the customer before shipment.

E. Media-Specific Standards of Practice

E1.2 *Misrepresentation:* Marketers shall not employ presentations likely to mislead reasonable consumers that the presentation is news, information, public service or entertainment programming.

E2.2 *Printed Media—Description:* All printed materials shall accurately and fairly describe the product or service offered. Type size, colour, contrast, style, placement or other treatment shall not be used to reduce the legibility or clarity of the offer, exceptions to the offer, or terms and conditions.

E3.3 *Telephone—Identification:* Marketers shall identify themselves and the business or organization represented promptly at the beginning of each outbound telemarketing call.

E3.3 *Telephone—Privacy:* No marketer shall knowingly call any person who has an unlisted or unpublished telephone number, except where the telephone number was furnished by the customer to that marketer. In addition:

- Marketers will promptly remove from their lists the telephone numbers of consumers who request them to do so, or non-customers who have registered with the CMA's Do Not Call Service.

E4.2 *Internet and Other Electronic Media—Consent:* Marketers shall not transmit marketing email without the consent of the recipient or unless the marketer has an existing relationship with the recipient.

E4.5 *Internet and Other Electronic Media—Disclosure:* When gathering data from individual consumers that could identify the consumer, and which will be linked with "clickstream" data, marketers shall advise consumers: a) what information is being collected; and b) how the information will be used. The marketer shall provide access to this advisory before consumers submit data that could identify them.

Marketers shall also provide a meaningful opportunity for consumers to decline to have information that identifies them collected, or transferred, for marketing purposes. In addition, access to this advisory shall be provided in every location, site or page from which the marketer is collecting such data.

F. Product Safety

F1 *Introduction:* Products offered by marketers shall be safe in normal use and, where applicable, shall conform to product safety regulations established by Health and Welfare Canada and by the Canadian Standards Association and/or other recognized Canadian authorities.

G. Special Considerations in Marketing to Children

G1 *Age:* For purposes of this Code of Ethics and Standards of Practice, the term *child* refers to someone who has not reached his or her 13th birthday.

In addition:

Marketers are expected to use discretion and sensitivity in marketing to persons between 13 years and the age of majority, to address the age, knowledge, sophistication and maturity of this audience.

G2 *Responsibility:* Marketing to children imposes a special responsibility on marketers. Marketers shall recognize that children are not adults and that not all marketing techniques are appropriate for children.

G3 *Consent:* Except as provided below under G4 Contests, Games or Sweepstakes, all marketing interactions directed to children including collection, transfer and requests for personal information require the express consent of the child's parent or guardian.

H. Protection of the Environment

H1 *Environmental Responsibility:* Marketers recognize and acknowledge a continuing responsibility to manage their businesses to minimize environmental impact.

H2 *Three* R*s:* Marketers shall incorporate the "Three *R*s" of environmental responsibility in the operation of their businesses. More specifically, to:

- Reduce material use;
- Reuse materials; and,
- Recycle materials.

I. Protection of Personal Privacy

Privacy: All marketers shall recognize and abide by the six principles of personal privacy adopted by the Canadian Marketing Association:

PRINCIPLE #1: GIVING CONSUMERS CONTROL OF HOW INFORMATION ABOUT THEM IS USED

1.1 Consumers must be provided with a meaningful opportunity to decline to have their name or other information used for any further marketing purposes by a third party.

PRINCIPLE #2: PROVIDING CONSUMERS WITH THE STAGE OF ACCESS TO INFORMATION

2.1 The industry endorses the stage of the consumer to know the source of his/her name used in any information-based marketing program. Marketers must make all reasonable efforts to provide this information to the consumer on request.

PRINCIPLE #3: ENABLING CONSUMERS TO REDUCE THE AMOUNT OF MAIL THEY RECEIVE

All CMA members must use the Do Not Mail/Do Not Call service of the Association when conducting a campaign in order to delete the name of any consumer, other than a current customer, who has requested that he or she be removed from mail and telemarketing lists. A "current customer" is defined as any consumer who has made a purchase from the marketer within the last six months or during a normal buying cycle.

PRINCIPLE #4: CONTROLLING THE USE OF INFORMATION BY THIRD PARTIES

The purposes for which information is collected shall be identified by the organization at or before the time the information is collected.

PRINCIPLE #5: SAFELY STORING INFORMATION ABOUT CONSUMERS

All those involved in the transfer, rental, sale or exchange of mailing lists must be responsible for the protection of list data and should take appropriate measures to ensure against unauthorized access, alteration or dissemination of list data. Those who have access to such data should agree in advance to use data only in an authorized manner.

PRINCIPLE #6: RESPECTING CONFIDENTIAL AND SENSITIVE INFORMATION

All list owners and users must be protective of the consumer's stage to privacy and sensitive to the information collected on lists and subsequently considered for use, transfer, rental or sale.

J. Enforcement Procedures for the Standards of Practice

J1 Upon receipt of information that would indicate a violation of the criminal laws of Canada, the Association will promptly forward such information to the appropriate authorities and the organization concerned.

J2 Upon receipt of a customer complaint regarding violation of this Code, whether regarding a member or a non-member, the Association will contact the company and use its mediation procedures to attempt to resolve the consumer complaint.

Source: Canadian Marketing Association, "Code of Ethics & Standards of Practice," www.the-cma.org/consumer/ethics.cfm.

ethics, supported by a dozen full-time staff and a million-dollar budget. Since 1991, the ethics department has trained some 95 000 employees. This training includes sending 22 000 managers to full-day workshops that include case studies on ethical actions in marketing, finance, and other business functions.[45]

Citicorp has developed an ethics board game, which teams of employees use to solve hypothetical quandaries. General Electric employees can tap into specially designed software on their personal computers to get answers to ethical questions. At Texas Instruments, employees are treated to a weekly column on ethics over an electronic news service. One popular feature: a kind of "Dear Abby" mailbag, answers provided by the company's ethics officer,...that deals with the troublesome issues employees face most often.[46]

Still, written codes and ethics programs do not ensure ethical behaviour. Ethics and social responsibility require a total corporate commitment. They must be a component of the overall corporate culture. According to PwC's DiPiazza, "I see ethics as a mission-critical issue...deeply imbedded in who we are and what we do. It's just as important as our product development cycle or our distribution system.... It's about creating a culture based on integrity and respect, not a culture based on dealing with the crisis of the day....We ask ourselves every day, 'Are we doing the right things?'"[47]

Canada's 74 000 charities and non-profit organizations are not immune to questions of ethics. While few question the importance of these worthy causes, there has been growing criticism about some of the fundraising methods they use. Two major concerns have surfaced. More charities are using lotteries to raise funds. These not only add to the pressures on people to gamble, they may often jeopardize the welfare of the non-profit. Use of professional telemarketers is another source of ethical concern. They raise funds on the part of non-profit organizations, but the charity may only see a small portion of the money raised. In the face of growing public scrutiny, non-profits have to be as ethically aware and socially responsible as their for-profit counterparts.

The future holds many challenges and opportunities for marketing managers as they move into the new millennium. Technological advances in every area, from telecommunications, information technology, and the Internet to health care and entertainment, provide abundant marketing opportunities. However, forces in the socioeconomic, cultural, and natural environments increase the limits under which marketing can be carried out. Companies that are able to create new values in a socially responsible way will have a world to conquer.

Looking Back: Reviewing the Concepts

In this chapter, we've closed with many important concepts involving marketing's sweeping impact on individual consumers, other businesses, and society as a whole. You learned that responsible marketers discover what consumers want and respond with the right products, priced to give good value to buyers and profit to the producer. A marketing system should sense, serve, and satisfy consumer needs and improve the quality of consumers' lives. In working to meet consumer needs, marketers may take some actions that are not to everyone's liking or benefit. Marketing managers should be aware of the main *criticisms of marketing*.

1. **Understand marketing's multiple responsibilities, and identify the major social and ethical criticisms of marketing.**

   Marketing's *impact on individual consumer welfare* has been criticized for its high prices, deceptive practices, high-pressure selling, shoddy or unsafe products, planned obsolescence, and poor service to disadvantaged consumers. Marketing's *impact on society* has been criticized for creating false wants and too much materialism, too few social goods, cultural pollution, and too much political power. Critics have also criticized marketing's *impact on other businesses* for harming competitors and reducing competition through acquisitions, practices that create barriers to entry, and unfair competitive marketing practices.

2. **Define *consumerism* and *environmentalism* and explain how they affect marketing strategies.**

   Concerns about the marketing system have led to *citizen action movements*. *Consumerism* is an organized social movement intended to strengthen the rights and power of consumers relative to sellers. Alert marketers view it as an opportunity to serve consumers better by providing more consumer information, education, and protection. *Environmentalism* is an organized social movement seeking to minimize the harm done to the environment and quality of life by marketing practices. The first wave of modern environmentalism was driven by environmental groups and concerned consumers; the second wave was driven by government, which passed laws and regulations governing industrial practices affecting the environment. Now, in the twenty-first century, the first two environmentalism waves are merging into a third and stronger wave in which companies are accepting responsibility for doing no environmental harm. Companies now are adopting policies of *environmental sustainability*—developing strategies that both sustain the environment and produce profits for the company.

3. **Describe the principles of socially responsible marketing.**

   Many companies originally opposed these social movements and laws, but most of them now recognize a need for positive consumer information, education, and protection. Some companies have followed a policy of *enlightened marketing*, which holds that a company's marketing should support the best long-run performance of the marketing system. Enlightened marketing consists of five principles: *consumer-oriented marketing*, *innovative marketing*, *value marketing*, *sense-of-mission marketing*, and *societal marketing*.

4. **Explain the role of ethics in marketing.**

   Increasingly, companies are responding to the need to provide company policies and guidelines to help their managers deal with questions of *marketing ethics*. Of course, even the best guidelines cannot resolve all of the difficult ethical decisions that individuals and firms must make. But there are some principles that marketers can choose among. One principle states that such issues should be decided by the free market and legal system. A second and more enlightened principle puts responsibility not in the system but in the hands of individual companies and managers. Each firm and marketing manager must develop a philosophy of socially responsible and ethical behaviour. Under the societal marketing concept, managers must look beyond what is legal and allowable and develop standards based on personal integrity, corporate conscience, and long-term consumer welfare.

   Because business standards and practices vary among countries, the issue of ethics poses special challenges for international marketers. The growing consensus among today's marketers is that it is important to make a commitment to a common set of shared standards worldwide.

Reviewing the Key Terms

Discussing the Concepts

1. Many firms, like Molson, Canada Trust, Procter & Gamble, Bell Canada, and Imperial Oil, have been practising cause-related marketing as a means of fulfilling their social responsibilities. Cause-related marketing is the practice of associating a for-profit firm's products or services with a non-profit cause. While the primary purpose of the program is the accomplishment of marketing objectives, the non-profit also achieves significant benefits from these campaigns. Describe some of the cause-related campaigns you have seen. Do you think they are a legitimate means for firms to fulfill part of their social responsibility?

2. Marketing receives much criticism, some justified and much not. Which of the major criticisms of marketing discussed in the chapter do you think are most justified? Which are least justified?

3. You have been invited to appear along with an economist on a panel assessing marketing practices in the soft-drink industry. You are surprised when the economist opens the discussion with a long list of criticisms of marketing, focusing on the unnecessarily high marketing costs and deceptive promotional practices. Abandoning your prepared comments, you set out to defend marketing, in general, and the soft-drink industry, in particular. How would you respond to the economist's attack?

4. Comment on the state of consumers' rights on the Internet and in ecommerce. Design a "Bill of Rights" that would protect consumers while they shop for products and services on the Internet. Consider such issues as government regulation, ease and convenience of use, warranties, guarantees and return policies, privacy, security, and cost-efficient commerce.

5. What is the basic philosophy supporting enlightened marketing? List and briefly describe each of the five principles of enlightened marketing. Cite several examples of firms that practise enlightened marketing.

6. Compare the marketing concept, discussed in Chapter 1, with the principle of societal marketing. Should all marketers adopt the societal marketing concept? Why or why not?

7. You are the marketing manager for a small firm that makes kitchen appliances. While conducting field tests, you discover a design flaw in one of your most popular models that could potentially cause harm to a small number of consumers. However, a product recall would likely bankrupt your company, leaving all of the employees (including you) jobless. What would you do?

Applying the Concepts

1. The "greening of North America" has much more to do with lifestyles than forestry management. Adopting a "green" lifestyle means that consumers demand products and services that are environmentally responsible. As consumers turn to the green lifestyle, companies respond with environmentally responsible products and programs. McDonald's, Wal-Mart, Loblaw, and Procter & Gamble are a few of the companies that have now adopted a more green way of thinking and acting. Visit the Corporate/Social Responsibility/Environment section of the McDonald's website (www.mcdonalds.com) and the Internet Green Marketplace website (www.envirolink.org) for more information.

a. Assume that you are a marketing manager for Crayola Crayons (www.crayola.com) and formulate a "green policy" that will make your product both competitive and environmentally responsible. As you formulate this policy, consider the product itself, packaging, distribution, promotion, and merchandising with distributors.

b. Visit the McDonald's website. What is the company's green policy? Comment on the appropriateness of this policy.

c. One organization that has been at the centre of promoting an environmentally responsible green policy to corporations is Greenpeace (www.greenpeace.org). Do you find Greenpeace's proposals to be radical? Explain. How might Greenpeace react to the policies you devised for Crayola?

d. Develop a set of rules that would guide organizations toward being environmentally responsible.

2. As business and marketing become more complicated, judging what is fair and honest becomes more difficult for consumer and marketer alike. In some industries and areas of business practice, rules and regulations governing marketing are reasonably well established and understood. However, in the expanding world of Internet marketing, established regulations are few and far between. The wide-open spaces of the Internet have been characterized as the "Old West" of the twenty-first century, where self-rule abounds. While it is certain that the state of regulation will change, it is unclear when and to what extent. For example, the Canadian Radio-television and Telecommunications Commission (CRTC) looked at regulating the Internet but decided against this action (see www.crtc.gc.ca/ENG/NEWS/RELEASES/1999/R990517.htm). Use your favourite search engine to try to answer the following questions:

a. How easy is it to find information about Canadian laws and regulations relating to marketing on the Internet? What problems did you encounter in your search? As an entrepreneur wishing to build a marketing website, where could you go to research the laws that govern the site's content?

b. The Internet offers consumers great opportunities but also potential difficulties, frustrations, and dangers. Offsetting its wonders, the Web is flooded with less-desirable elements such as spam mail, pornography, and unscrupulous offers and schemes. As a marketing manager of a firm that sells via the Internet, you want to interact with your consumers in a positive and uncluttered environment. What organizations should be involved in regulating Internet usage and commerce? What regulations would you propose? What difficulties do you see in implementing those regulations?

Video Short

View the video short for this chapter at **www.pearsoned.ca/kotler** and then answer the questions provided in the case description.

Company Case

Vitango: Fighting Malnutrition

Imagine teaching an elementary school class in which students are constantly inattentive and falling asleep—not because they are bored but because they are malnourished. In many countries, this is not an unusual problem. Two billion people around the globe suffer from anemia—an iron deficiency. Iron deficiency leads to reduced resistance to disease, lowers learning ability in children, and contributes to the death of one out of five pregnant mothers. Two hundred million children do not get enough vitamin A. As a result, 250 000 of them go blind each year; vitamin A deficiency is also a contributing factor in the deaths of 2.2 million children under five each year from diarrhea. Many malnourished children suffer from zinc deficiency, which leads to growth failure and infections. Close to 2 billion people do not get enough iodine, and iodine deficiency is the leading cause of preventable mental retardation in the world. If they only used the ordinary table salt found in homes and restaurants all across North America, this wouldn't happen.

What can businesses do about this deplorable situation? Quite a bit. Companies such as Coca-Cola and Procter & Gamble have invested millions of dollars in research on micronutrients. They are learning how to fortify everyday food and beverages with additional minerals and vitamins to wipe out deficiencies and keep schoolchildren around the world alert and mentally prepared for school.

Fortified foods are common in North America. Iodine has been added to ordinary table salt for decades, milk contains vitamin D and calcium, and cornflakes list all the micronutrients found in them on the box. A quick check of your pantry reveals that many drinks and other foods have vitamins and minerals added to them. Thus, adding micronutrients to foods is not new or unusual in this country.

What are new are the efforts of companies to identify specific deficiencies and to develop new technologies for adding micronutrients to foodstuffs in order to eliminate or reduce the deficiencies in specific countries. A good example is a Coca-Cola beverage product called Vitango in Botswana.

Coca-Cola spent years developing a powdered beverage that, when mixed with water, looks and tastes like a sweeter version of Hi-C. The beverage is fortified with 12 vitamins and with minerals that are chronically lacking in the diets of people in developing countries. Coke tested this product in Botswana in Project Mission. Every day for eight weeks, nurses visited schools where they mixed the beverage and passed out paper cups of the "new Hi-C." At the end of the test period, levels of iron and zinc in the children's blood levels had grown. Some parents noted that their children had become more attentive at school. After the Botswana tests, Coca-Cola also ran tests in Peru to determine how well the nutrients are absorbed into the bloodstream.

Coca-Cola, however, is not yet ready to launch Vitango. One issue is the powdered product form. Given the impurities of much of the water in Africa, Coca-Cola wants to package Vitango in a ready-to-drink formula, not in the powdered version now available. That will require reformulation that could actually drive down the price.

P&G has also developed micronutrient-enriched drinks for distribution in developing countries. In the 1990s, P&G developed its own proprietary technology for iron, vitamin A, and iodine fortification, which it called GrowthPlus. GrowthPlus was the basic ingredient in a product called Nutridelight that P&G launched in the Philippines. Unfortunately, it didn't sell well—primarily because it was priced at 50 percent above the market price of other powdered drinks.

More recently, P&G has launched another product, Nutristar, in Venezuela. Sold at most food stores, it contains eight vitamins and five minerals, comes in flavours such as mango and passion fruit, and promises to produce "taller, stronger, and smarter kids." To date, Nutristar is doing quite well. One reason is that it's available at McDonald's, where it is chosen by consumers with about half of all Happy Meals sold. P&G is also offering free samples in schools.

The major problem with both Coca-Cola's and P&G's nutritional products is price. These products were expensive to develop because of long lead times, the need to enlist the help of nutritional experts around the world, and the need to develop products that appeal to the local population's tastes. If offered at "reasonable" prices, they would be out of the reach of the world's desperately poor, the group that needs them most. Consider P&G's Vitango. The poor people in other countries are *not* eating at McDonald's. In countries such as Botswana, they are barely existing on cornmeal and rice. They simply cannot afford to buy fortified sweetened drinks or, for that matter, any sweetened drinks.

How can P&G and Coca-Cola market such products without pricing them too high for the intended market? Learning its lesson in the Philippines, P&G priced Nutristar about 25 percent higher than other powdered drinks and 30 percent below carbonated soft drinks. Even so, that's still too high for the poverty-stricken. Coca-Cola originally planned to sell Vitango for about 20 cents for an eight-ounce liquid serving but then realized that this price was too high. That's part of the reason for continuing developmental work on the product.

One solution to the pricing problem is to work with governments, but many of them are too poor to be able to afford the products. Or they lack the resources to educate their people on the merits of fortified foods. Enter GAIN—the Global Alliance for Improved Nutrition—an international consortium set up by the Bill and Melissa Gates charitable foundation. GAIN offers companies assistance in lobbying for favourable tariffs and tax rates and for speedier regulatory review of new products in targeted countries. It also gives local governments money to increase the demand for fortified foods, including large-scale public relations campaigns or a government "seal of approval." This program is receiving $70 million over five years beginning in May 2002. Such actions should help Coca-Cola and P&G by educating target populations about the value of fortified foods and beverages so that they will buy such products.

Of course, Coca-Cola and P&G can work with governments on their own, but their actions may be distrusted. After all, these are "for-profit" organizations whose motives may be suspect. GAIN has the advantage that it's a not-for-profit.

While GAIN seems like a wonderful resource for helping malnourished people, it does have its critics. They point out that selling or giving away fortified foods does not solve the underlying problem of poverty. Nor does it teach people good nutritional habits. Moreover, in addition to their vitamins and minerals, many of the "fortified" foods also contain overly large amounts of fat, sugar, and salt. So, for example, whereas the foods might help reduce iron deficiency, they could also lead to obesity. Some observers claim that it would be better to teach people how to grow fruits and vegetables. The problem is that people will die from malnutrition before poverty is eliminated or trees bear fruit.

Other issues must also be addressed. A fortified beverage such as Vitango will help in dealing with malnutrition but can't eliminate it. People will still need to eat a variety of other foods, which makes education very important. Remember that these products contain no juice. They are intended as supplements, not as substitutes for a proper diet. Lack of understanding about how to use products has landed other companies, such as Nestlé with its infant formula, in trouble when they were used inappropriately.

Given all these problems, why would Coca-Cola and P&G develop these products in the first place? One answer is future sales and profits. Products such as Nutristar and Vitango could create a basis from which to launch other Coca-Cola or P&G products, such as snack foods or juice drinks. As sales of carbonated beverages around the world have slowed, these fortified drinks pose a growth opportunity for the companies. Another answer is goodwill, and not just goodwill for the companies involved. By helping other nations of the world, North American corporations can help to lower the disparities between rich and poor countries.

Questions for Discussion

1. Which of the textbook's criticisms of marketing's impact on individual consumers, if any, are found in the cases of Vitango and Nutristar?

2. Which of the criticisms of marketing's impact on society as a whole are found in the Vitango and Nutristar case?

3. Could Vitango and Nutristar be considered enlightened marketing? Why or why not?

4. Are the development and marketing of such products as fortified foods and beverages ethical and socially responsible?

5. How should Coca-Cola proceed with the marketing of Vitango?

Sources: Jill Bruss, "Reaching the World," *Beverage Industry,* December 2001, p. 281; Rance Crain, "U.S. Marketers Must Develop Products to Help Third World," *Advertising Age,* December 3, 2001, p. 20; Betsy McKay, "Drinks for Developing Countries," *Wall Street Journal,* November 27, 2001, pp. B1, B6; and Rachel Zimmerman, "Gates Fights Malnutrition with Cheese, Ketchup Incentives," *Wall Street Journal,* May 9, 2002, p. B1.

CBC Video Case

Log on to your Companion Website at **www.pearsoned.ca/kotler** to view a CBC video segment and case for this chapter.

Case Pilot

Log on to your Companion Website at **www.pearsoned.ca/kotler** to access the case project provided for this part of the text. Take the Case Pilot Challenge!

Chapter 5

The Marketing Environment

After studying this chapter you should be able to

1. describe the environmental forces that affect the company's ability to serve its customers

2. explain how changes in the demographic and economic environments affect marketing decisions

3. identify the major trends in the firm's natural and technological environments

4. explain the key changes in the political and cultural environments

5. discuss how companies can react to the marketing environment

Looking Ahead: Previewing the Concepts

Now that you've seen how the new Internet age has affected marketing, let's look into other areas of the marketing environment. In this chapter, you'll discover that marketing does not operate in a vacuum, but rather in a complex and changing environment. Other *actors* in this environment—suppliers, intermediaries, customers, competitors, publics, and others—may work with or against the company. Major environmental *forces*—demographic, economic, natural, technological, political, and cultural—shape marketing opportunities, pose threats, and affect the company's ability to serve customers and develop lasting relationships with them. To understand marketing, and to develop effective marketing strategies, you must first understand the context in which marketing operates.

First, we'll check out a major development in the marketing environment—millennial fever—and the nostalgia boom that it has produced. Volkswagen responded with the introduction of a born-again New Beetle. As you read on, ask yourself: What has made this little car so right for the times?

As we move further into the twenty-first century, social experts are busy assessing the impact of numerous environmental forces on consumers and the marketers who serve them. Change and uncertainty have marked this era, affecting all groups—but notably the baby boomers, the most commercially influential demographic group in history. The oldest boomers, now in their fifties, are resisting the aging process with the vigour they once reserved for antiwar protests. Other factors are also at work. Today, people of all ages seem to feel a bit over-worked, overstimulated, overloaded, and technostressed. People "are overwhelmed...by the breathtaking onrush of the Information Age, with its high-speed modems, cell phones, and pagers," suggests one expert. "While we hail the benefits of these wired [times], at the same time we are buffeted by the rapid pace of change."

The result of this "millennial fever" is a yearning to turn back the clock, to return to simpler times. This yearning has in turn produced a massive nostalgia wave. Marketers of all kinds have responded to these nostalgia pangs by recreating products and images that help take consumers back to "the good old days." Examples are plentiful: Kellogg has revived old Corn Flakes packaging, Brick microbrewery reintroduced the stubby beer bottle, and car makers have created retro roadsters such as the Porsche Boxster and Chrysler's PT Cruiser. A Pepsi commercial rocks to the Rolling Stones' "Brown Sugar," James Brown's "I Feel Good" helps sell Senokot laxatives, and Janis Joplin's raspy voice crows, "Oh Lord, won't you buy me a Mercedes-Benz?" Heinz reintroduced its classic glass ketchup bottle, supported by nostalgic "Heinz was there" ads showing two 1950s-era boys eating hot dogs at a ballpark. And the television networks launched what one analyst calls a "retro feeding frenzy" of reunion programs "that revisit the good (*M*A*S*H, L.A. Law, The Cosby Show, The Mary Tyler Moore Show, The Beachcombers*), the bad (*That's Incredible!, Laverne & Shirley*), and the truly ancient (*American Bandstand, The Honeymooners*).

Perhaps no company has more riding on the nostalgia wave than Volkswagen. The original Volkswagen Beetle, "the peoples' car," first sputtered into North America in 1949. With its simple, bug-like design, no-frills engineering, and economical operation, the Beetle was the antithesis of the Big 3 automakers' chrome-laden gas-guzzlers. Although most owners would readily admit that their Beetles were underpowered, noisy, cramped, and freezing in the winter, they saw these as endearing qualities. Overriding these minor inconveniences, the Beetle was cheap to buy and own, dependable, easy to fix, fun to drive, and anything but flashy.

During the 1960s, as young baby boomers by the thousands were buying their first cars, demand exploded, and the Beetle blossomed into an unlikely icon. Bursting with personality, the understated Bug came to personify an era of rebellion against convention. By the late 1970s, however, the boomers had moved on, Bug mania had faded, and Volkswagen had dropped Beetle production for the North American market. Still, more than 20 years later, the mere mention of these chugging oddities evokes smiles and strong emotions. Almost everyone over the age of thirty, it seems, has a "feel-good" Beetle story to tell.

In an attempt to surf the nostalgia wave, Volkswagen introduced a New Beetle (www.vw.com/newbeetle) in 1998. Outwardly, the reborn Beetle resembles the original, tapping the strong emotions and memories of times gone by. Beneath the skin, however, the New Beetle is packed with modern features. According to an industry expert, "The Beetle comeback is...based on a combination of romance and reason—wrapping up modern conveniences in an old-style package. Built into the dashboard is a bud vase perfect for a daisy plucked straight from the 1960s. But right next to it is a high-tech, multi-speaker stereo—and options like power windows, cruise control, and a power sunroof make it a very different car than the rattly old Bug. The new version...comes with all the modern features car buyers demand, such as four air bags and power outlets for cell phones. But that's not why folks buy it. With a familiar bubble shape that still makes people smile as it skitters by, the new Beetle offers a pull that is purely emotional."

Advertising for the New Beetle played strongly on the nostalgia theme, while at the same time refreshing the old Beetle heritage. "If you sold your soul in the '80s," tweaks one ad, "here's your chance to buy it back." Other ads read, "Less flower, more power," and "Comes with wonderful new features. Like heat." Still another ad declares "0 to 60? Yes."

Volkswagen invested over $800 million to bring the New Beetle to market. However, this investment appears to be paying big dividends. Demand quickly outstripped supply. Even before the first cars reached VW showrooms, dealers across North America had long waiting lists of people who'd paid for the car without ever seeing it, let alone driving it. One dealer claimed that the New Beetle was such a traffic magnet that he had to remove it from his showroom floor every afternoon at 2 p.m. to discourage gawkers and let his salespeople work with serious prospects.

The New Beetle turned out to be a cross-generational hit, appealing to more than just Woodstock-nostalgic baby boomers. Even kids too young to remember the original Bug loved this new one. One customer confirms the car's broad appeal. "In 1967, my Dad got me a VW. I loved it. I'm sure the new one will take me back," says the customer. "I'm getting the New Beetle as a surprise for my daughter, but I'm sure I'm going to be stealing it from her all the time."

Volkswagen's first-year sales projections of 50 000 New Beetles in North American proved pessimistic. After only nine months, the company had sold more than 64 000 of the new Bugs in the United States and Canada. The smart little car also garnered numerous distinguished awards, including *Motor Trend*'s 1999 Import Car of the Year, *Time* magazine's The Best of 1998 Design, *Business Week*'s Best New Products, and 1999 North American Car of the Year, awarded by an independent panel of top journalists who cover the auto industry. The car was also selected as *Money Magazine*'s Best Car of 2001.

Since its launch, Volkswagen has sold over half a million New Beetles worldwide—not bad at all for a so-called "niche" car. Sales have recently slumped, however. In 2002, Volkswagen hoped to overcome this downturn by adding to its Beetle family. It launched an iconic convertible model, which recalls the classic drop-top Bugs, complete with its thick, folded-top bustle and what *Motor Trend Magazine* calls its huggable personality. To follow up, Volkswagen planned to introduce a reincarnation of its old cult-classic flower-power Microbus in 2005. Although most younger buyers won't remember much about the original Microbus unless they encountered one at a Grateful Dead concert, test models have received rave reviews at auto shows in Japan and Europe.

Most trend analysts believe that the nostalgia craze will only grow as the baby boomers continue to age. If so, the New Beetle, so full of the past, has a very bright future. "The Beetle is not just empty nostalgia," says Gerald Celente, publisher of *Trend Journal*. "It is a practical car that is also tied closely to the emotions of a generation." According to another trend analyst, the New Beetle "is our romantic past, reinvented for our hectic here-and-now. Different, yet deeply familiar—a car for the times."[1]

As Chapter 1 noted, marketers operate in an increasingly connected world. They must be good at *customer relationship management* and *partner relationship management* in order to connect effectively with customers, others in the company, and external partners. However, to do this effectively, marketers must understand the major environmental forces that surround all of these relationships. A company's **marketing environment** comprises the actors and forces outside marketing that affect marketing management's ability to develop and maintain successful relationships with its target customers. As the Volkswagen example shows, the marketing environment offers both opportunities and threats. Successful companies know the vital importance of constantly watching and adapting to the changing environment.

Marketing environment
The factors and forces outside marketing's direct control that affect marketing management's ability to develop and maintain successful transactions with its target customers.

As we enter the twenty-first century, both consumers and marketers wonder what the future will bring. The environment continues to change at a rapid pace. For example, think about how you buy groceries today. How will your grocery buying change over the next few decades? What challenges will these changes present for marketers? Here's what one leading futurist envisions for the year 2025:[2]

> We won't be shopping in 21-aisle supermarkets in 2025, predicts Gary Wright, corporate demographer for Procter & Gamble. The growth of ecommerce and the rapid speed of the Internet will lead to online ordering of lower priced, non-perishable products—everything from peanut butter to coffee filters. Retailers will become "bundlers," combining these orders into large packages of goods for each household and delivering them efficiently to their doorsteps. As a result, we'll see mergers between retailing and home-delivery giants—think Wal-Mart Express, a powerful combo of Wal-Mart and Federal Express. Consumers won't waste precious time searching for the best-priced bundle. Online information agents will do it for them, comparing prices among competitors.

Such pictures of the future give marketers plenty to think about. More than any other group in the company, marketers must be the trend trackers and opportunity seekers. Although every manager in an organization needs to observe the outside environment, marketers have two special aptitudes. They have disciplined methods—marketing intelligence and marketing research—for collecting information about the marketing environment. They also spend more time in the customer and competitor environment. By carefully studying the environment, marketers can adapt marketing strategies to meet new marketplace challenges and opportunities.

Microenvironment
The forces close to the company that affect its ability to serve its customers—the company, market channel firms, customer markets, competitors, and publics.

Macroenvironment
The larger societal forces that affect the whole microenvironment—demographic, economic, natural, technological, political, and cultural forces.

The marketing environment is composed of a *microenvironment* and a *macroenvironment*. The **microenvironment** consists of the actors close to the company that affect its ability to serve its customers—the company, suppliers, marketing intermediaries, customer markets, competitors, and publics. The **macroenvironment** consists of the larger societal forces that affect the whole microenvironment—demographic, economic, natural, technological, political, and cultural forces. We look first at the company's microenvironment.

The Company's Microenvironment

Marketing management's job is to build relationships with customers by creating customer value and satisfaction. However, marketing managers cannot accomplish this task alone. Figure 5.1 shows the major actors in the marketer's microenvironment. Marketing success will require working closely with other company departments, suppliers, marketing intermediaries, customers, competitors, and various publics, which combine to make up the company's value delivery network.

Figure 5.1 The company's
internal environment

The Company

In designing marketing plans, marketing management takes other company groups into account—groups such as top management, finance, research and development (R&D), purchasing, manufacturing, and accounting. All these interrelated groups form the internal environment. Top management sets the company's mission, objectives, broad strategies, and policies. Marketing managers must make decisions within the plans made by top management.

Marketing managers also must work closely with other company departments. Finance is concerned with finding and using funds to carry out the marketing plan. R&D focuses on designing safe and attractive products. Purchasing worries about getting supplies and materials, whereas operations is responsible for producing and distributing the desired quality and quantity of products. Accounting has to measure revenues and costs to help marketing know how well it is achieving its objectives. Together, all of these departments have an impact on the marketing department's plans and actions. Under the marketing concept, all of these functions must "think consumer." They should work in harmony to provide superior customer value and satisfaction.

Suppliers

Suppliers are an important link in the company's overall customer value delivery system. They provide the resources needed by the company to produce its goods and services. Supplier developments can seriously affect marketing. Marketing managers must be aware of supply availability—supply shortages or delays, labour strikes, and other events that can cost sales in the short run and damage customer satisfaction in the long run. Marketing managers also monitor the price trends of their key inputs. Rising supply costs may force price increases that can harm the company's sales volume. Most marketers today treat their suppliers as partners in creating and delivering customer value.

Marketing Intermediaries

Marketing intermediaries
Firms that help the company promote, sell, and distribute its goods to final buyers; they include resellers, physical distribution firms, marketing services agencies, and financial intermediaries.

Marketing intermediaries help the company promote, sell, and distribute its goods to final buyers. They include *resellers, physical distribution firms, marketing services agencies,* and *financial intermediaries. Resellers* are distribution channel firms that help the company find customers or make sales to them. These include wholesalers and retailers, who buy and resell merchandise. Selecting and partnering with resellers is not easy. No longer do manufacturers have many small, independent resellers from which to choose. They now face large and growing reseller organizations, such as

Loblaws, Wal-Mart, and Home Depot. These organizations frequently have enough power to dictate terms or even shut the manufacturer out of large markets.

Physical distribution firms help the company stock and move goods from their points of origin to their destinations. Working with warehouse and transportation firms, a company must determine the best ways to store and ship goods, balancing such factors as cost, delivery, speed, and safety. *Marketing services agencies* are the marketing research firms, advertising agencies, media firms, and marketing consulting firms that help the company target and promote its products to the right markets. When the company decides to use one of these agencies, it must choose carefully, because these firms vary in creativity, quality, service, and price. *Financial intermediaries* include banks, credit companies, insurance companies, and other businesses that help finance transactions or insure against the risks associated with the buying and selling of goods. Most firms and customers depend on financial intermediaries to finance their transactions.

Like suppliers, marketing intermediaries form an important component of the company's overall value delivery system. In its quest to create satisfying customer relationships, the company must do more than just optimize its own performance. It must partner effectively with suppliers and marketing intermediaries to optimize the performance of the entire system.

Thus, today's marketers recognize the importance of working with their intermediaries as partners rather than simply as channels through which they sell their products. For example, Coca-Cola has a ten-year deal with Wendy's (www.wendys. com) that will make Coke the fast-food chain's exclusive soft drink provider. In the deal, Coca-Cola promised Wendy's much more than just soft drinks. It also pledged powerful marketing support:

Along with the soft drinks, Wendy's gets a cross-functional team of 50 Coke employees who are dedicated to understanding the finer points of Wendy's business. It also benefits from Coke dollars in joint marketing campaigns. Bigger still is the staggering amount of consumer research that Coca-Cola provides its

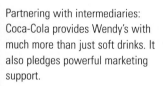

Partnering with intermediaries: Coca-Cola provides Wendy's with much more than just soft drinks. It also pledges powerful marketing support.

partners. Coke provides both analysis of syndicated information and access to Coke's own internal research on consumers' eating-out habits. It goes to great lengths to understand beverage drinkers—and to make sure its partners can use those insights. The company also has analyzed the demographics of every zip code in the United States and used the information to create a software program called Solver. By answering questions about their target audience, Wendy's franchise owners can determine which Coke brands are preferred by customers in their area. Coca-Cola also has been studying the design of drive-through menu boards to better understand which layouts, fonts, letter sizes, colours, and visuals induce consumers to order more food and drink.[3]

Customers

The company needs to study its customer markets closely. *Consumer markets* consist of individuals and households that buy goods and services for personal consumption. *Business markets* buy goods and services for further processing or for use in their production process, whereas *reseller markets* buy goods and services to resell at a profit. *Government markets* are composed of government agencies that buy goods and services to produce public services or transfer the goods and services to others who need them. Finally, *international markets* consist of these buyers in other countries, including consumers, producers, resellers, and governments. Each market type has special characteristics that call for careful study by the seller.

Competitors

The marketing concept states that to be successful, a company must provide greater customer value and satisfaction than its competitors do. Thus, marketers must do more than just adapt to the needs of target consumers. They also must gain strategic advantage by positioning their offerings strongly against those of competitors in the minds of consumers.

No single competitive marketing strategy is best for all companies. Each firm should consider its own size and industry position compared to those of its competitors. Large firms with dominant positions in an industry can use certain strategies that smaller firms cannot afford. But being large is not enough. There are winning strategies for large firms, but there are also losing ones. And small firms can develop strategies that give them better rates of return than large firms enjoy.

Publics

Public

Any group that has an actual or potential interest in or impact on an organization's ability to achieve its objectives.

The company's marketing environment also includes various publics. A **public** is any group that has an actual or potential interest in or impact on an organization's ability to achieve its objectives. We can identify seven types of publics:

- *Financial publics.* These publics influence the company's ability to obtain funds. Banks, investment houses, and shareholders are the major financial publics.
- *Media publics.* These include newspapers, magazines, radio and television stations, and websites that carry news, features, and editorial opinion.
- *Government publics.* Management must take government developments into account. Marketers must often consult the company's lawyers on issues of product safety, truth in advertising, and other matters.
- *Citizen-action publics.* A company's marketing decisions may be questioned by consumer organizations, environmental groups, minority groups, and others. Its public relations department can help it stay in touch with consumer and citizen groups.

- *Local publics.* These include neighbourhood residents and community organizations. Large companies usually appoint a community relations officer to deal with the community, attend meetings, answer questions, and contribute to worthwhile causes.

- *General public.* A company needs to be concerned with the general public's attitude toward its products and activities. The public's image of the company affects its buying.

- *Internal publics.* These include its workers, managers, volunteers, and the board of directors. Large companies use newsletters and other means to inform and motivate their internal publics. When employees feel good about their company, their positive attitude spills over into external publics.

A company can prepare marketing plans for these major publics as well as for its customer markets. Suppose the company wants a specific response from a particular public, such as goodwill, favourable word of mouth, or donations of time or money. The company would have to design an offer to this public that is attractive enough to produce the desired response.

The Company's Macroenvironment

The company and all of the other actors operate in a larger macroenvironment of forces that shape opportunities and pose threats to it. Figure 5.2 shows the six major forces in the company's macroenvironment. In the remaining sections of this chapter, we examine these forces and show how they affect marketing plans.

Demographic Environment

Demography
The study of human populations in terms of size, density, location, age, sex, race, occupation, and other statistics.

Demography is the study of human populations in terms of size, density, location, age, sex, race, occupation, and other statistics. The demographic environment is of major interest to marketers because it involves people, and people make up markets.

The world population is growing at an explosive rate. It now totals over 6.2 billion and will exceed 7.9 billion by the year 2025.[4] The world's large and highly diverse population poses both opportunities and challenges. Think for a few minutes about the world and your place in it. If we reduced the world to a village of 1000 people representative of the world's population, this would be our reality:[5]

- Our village would have 520 females and 480 males, including 330 children and 60 people over age 65, 10 college graduates, and 335 illiterate adults.

- We'd have 52 North Americans, 55 Russians, 84 Latin Americans, 95 Europeans, 124 Africans, and 584 Asians.

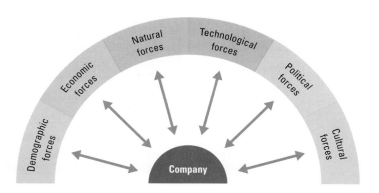

Figure 5.2   Major forces in the company's macroenvironment

- Communication would be difficult: 165 of us would speak Mandarin, 85 English, 83 Hindi, 64 Spanish, 58 Russian, and 37 Arabic. The other half of us would speak one of more than 5000 other languages.

- Among us we'd have 329 Christians, 178 Moslems, 132 Hindus, 60 Buddhists, 3 Jews, 167 non-religious, 45 atheists, and 86 others.

- About one-third of our people would have access to clean, safe drinking water. About half of our children would be immunized against infections.

- The woodlands in our village would be decreasing rapidly, and wasteland would be growing. Forty percent of the village's cropland, nourished by 83 percent of our fertilizer, would produce 72 percent of the food to feed its 270 well-fed owners. The remaining 60 percent of the land and 17 percent of the fertilizer would produce 28 percent of the food to feed the other 730 people. Five hundred people in the village would suffer from malnutrition.

- Only 200 of the 1000 people would control 75 percent of our village's wealth. Another 200 would receive only 2 percent of the wealth. Seventy people would own cars. One would have a computer, and that computer probably would not be connected to the Internet.

The explosive world population growth has major implications for business. A growing population means growing human needs to satisfy. Depending on purchasing power, it may also mean growing market opportunities. For example, to curb its skyrocketing population, the Chinese government passed regulations limiting families to one child each. As a result, Chinese children are spoiled and fussed over as never before. Known in China as "little emperors," Chinese children are being showered with everything from candy to computers as a result of what's known as the "six-pocket syndrome." As many as six adults—including parents, grandparents, great-grandparents, and aunts and uncles—may be indulging the whims of each child. Parents in the average Beijing household now spend about 40 percent of their income on their cherished only child. This trend has encouraged toy companies

The exploding world population presents both opportunities and challenges. The United Nations Population Fund website documents these issues.

such as Japan's Bandai Company (known for its Mighty Morphin Power Rangers), Denmark's Lego Group, and Mattel to enter the Chinese market. And McDonald's has triumphed in China in part because it has catered successfully to this pampered generation.[6]

Thus, marketers must keep close track of demographic trends and developments in their markets, both at home and abroad. They trace changing age and family structures, geographic population shifts, educational characteristics, and population diversity. Statistics Canada (www.statcan.ca) offers a wealth of information for marketers interested in demographic trends. Here, we discuss the most important demographic trends in Canada.

Changing Age Structure of the Canadian Population

According to Statistics Canada, the population of Canada is expected to exceed 32 million by 2006. However, the growth rate of Canada's population has slowed. The single most important demographic trend in Canada is the changing age structure of the population: The Canadian population is getting *older*. As revealed by 2001 census data, the median age rose to 37.6 years as a result of the aging of the largest demographic segment, the baby boomers, and a very low number of births during the 1990s. The combination of these two trends may mean future labour shortages. To better understand this, there is a 1:4 ratio for the number of people aged 15 to 24 entering the workforce for every one person aged 55 to 64. Figure 5.3 shows the changing age distribution of the Canadian population as of 2002. Here, we discuss the three largest age groups—the baby boomers, Generation X, and Generation Y—and their impact on today's marketing strategies.

The Baby Boomers   The post–World War II baby boom, which began in 1947 and ran through 1966, produced 9.8 million **baby boomers** in Canada. Although there was a baby boom in both Canada and the U.S., Canadian marketers have to recognize that our baby boom was unique. It started later than the American version (1947 versus 1946) and lasted longer (the American boom ended in 1964; the Canadian boom continued until 1966). While the American baby boom resulted in 3.5 children per family, the Canadian boom produced an average of four children. Furthermore, the baby boom was not a worldwide phenomenon. Among the other developed countries, only Australia and New Zealand experienced the same expansion in the birth rate. In Europe, there was no baby boom, and in Japan, the birth rate declined during our baby boom years, which explains why these countries have a higher proportion of older people in their societies.[7]

In Canada, the baby boomers have become one of the largest forces shaping the marketing environment. The fact that Linda Cook was recently named CEO of Shell Canada Ltd. at age 44 is important not only because she is one of the few women

Baby boomers
The 9.8 million Canadians born during the baby boom, following World War II and lasting until the mid-1960s.

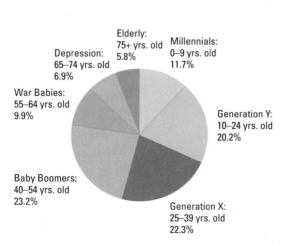

Figure 5.3   Seven Canadian generations

Source: Adapted from Statistics Canada, "Population by Sex and Age Group, 2002," www.statcan.ca/english/Pgdb/demo10a.htm (extracted May 14, 2003).

to attain such a position, but also because it is an indication of the power that baby boomers, in general, are now wielding in Canadian business. The boomers have presented a moving target, creating new markets as they grew through infancy to preadolescent, teenage, young adult, and now middle age. The baby boomers account for a third of the population but make up 40 percent of the workforce and earn over half of all personal income.

Baby boomers cut across all walks of life. But marketers have typically paid the most attention to the small upper crust of the boomer generation—its more educated, mobile, and wealthy segments. These segments have gone by many names. In the 1980s, they were called "yuppies" (young urban professionals); "yummies" (young upwardly mobile mommies), and "DINKs" (dual-income, no-kids couples). In the 1990s, however, yuppies and DINKs gave way to a new breed, with such names as "DEWKs" (dual earners with kids) and "MOBYs" (mother older, baby younger). Now, to the chagrin of many in this generation, they are acquiring such titles as "WOOFs" (well-off older folks), "ZOOMERS" (extremely busy and active older couples), or even "GRUMPIES" (just what the name suggests).

The youngest boomers are now in their late-thirties; the oldest are in their late-fifties. The maturing boomers are experiencing the pangs of midlife and rethinking the purpose and value of their work, responsibilities, and relationships. They are approaching life with a new stability and reasonableness in the way they live, think, eat, and spend. As they continue to age, they will create a large and important seniors market.[8]

Boomers are also reaching their peak earning and spending years. Thus, they constitute a lucrative market for new housing and home remodelling, financial services, travel and entertainment, eating out, health and fitness products, and high-priced cars and other luxuries. It would be a mistake to think of the boomers as aging and staid. Many boomers are rediscovering the excitement of life and have the means to play it out. For example, the median age of a Harley-Davidson buyer is 44.6 years old, squarely in the middle of the boomer age range.[9]

Generation X   The baby boom was followed by a "birth dearth," creating another generation of those born between 1967 and 1976. Seven million strong in Canada, this group represents an extremely important market. Canadian author

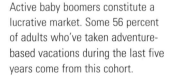

Active baby boomers constitute a lucrative market. Some 56 percent of adults who've taken adventure-based vacations during the last five years come from this cohort.

Generation X
The 7 million Canadians born between 1967 and 1976 in the "birth dearth" following the baby boom.

Douglas Coupland calls them "**Generation X.**" Others call them "baby busters," "the Nexus generation," or "yiffies"—young, individualistic, freedom-minded, few.

The Generation Xers are defined as much by their shared experiences as by their age. Increasing divorce rates and higher employment for their mothers made them the first generation of latchkey kids. Whereas the boomers created a sexual revolution, the Gen-Xers have lived in the age of AIDS. Having grown up during times of recession and corporate downsizing, they have developed a more cautious economic outlook. As a result, the Gen-Xers are a more skeptical bunch, cynical of frivolous marketing pitches that promise easy success.

They buy lots of products, such as sweaters, boots, cosmetics, electronics, cars, fast food, beer, computers, and mountain bikes. However, their cynicism makes them savvy shoppers. They like lower prices and a more functional look. The Gen-Xers respond to honesty in advertising, and they like irreverence and sass and ads that mock the traditional advertising approach. For example, Diet Pepsi Canada and its agency BBDO Canada won the top prize in the Canadian Advertising Success Stories (CASSIES) for the revitalization of the brand in English Canada. The audience was just starting to switch from regular cola to a diet product. Pepsi's insight was that as Gen-Xers started to age, they faced new responsibilities, yet feared leaving their youth behind. The "Forever Young" campaign tapped into this emotion to drive product sales.[10]

Gen-Xers share new cultural concerns. They care about the environment and respond favourably to socially responsible companies. Although they seek success, they are less materialistic; they prize experience, not acquisition. They are cautious romantics who want a better quality of life and are more interested in job satisfaction than in sacrificing personal happiness and growth for promotion.

Once labelled as "the MTV generation" the Gen-Xers have now grown up and are beginning to take over. They do surf the Internet more than other groups, but with serious intent. The Gen-Xers are poised to displace the lifestyles, culture, and materialistic values of the baby boomers. By the year 2010, they will have overtaken the baby boomers as a primary market for almost every product category.[11]

Generation Y
The 6.9 million children of the Canadian baby boomers, born between 1977 and 1994.

Diet Pepsi's award-winning campaign tapped into the changing needs of Generation X.

Generation Y   Also called the "echo boom," **Generation Y**, the children of the baby boomers, now represents approximately 20 percent of the Canadian population. Ranging in age from preteens to mid-twenties, the echo boomer generation is still forming its buying preferences and behaviours.

This group represents a large portion of the teen markets (see Real Marketing 5.1).[12] After years of bust, markets for teens' fashions, music, games, furniture, and food have enjoyed a rebirth. Designers and retailers have created new lines, new products, and even new stores devoted to teens—Clara's, Tommy Hilfiger, DKNY, Gap, Toys "R" Us, Guess, Talbots, Pottery Barn, and Eddie Bauer, to name just a few. New media appeared that cater specifically to this market: *Time, Sports Illustrated,* and *People* have all started new editions for kids and teens. Banks have offered banking and investment services for kids, including investment camps.

Generation Y oldsters are now graduating from college and beginning careers. Like the trailing edge of Generation X ahead of them, one distinguishing characteristic of Generation Y is their utter fluency and comfort with computer, digital, and Internet technology. For this reason, one analyst has christened them the Net-Gens (or N-Gens). He observes:

> What makes this generation different...is not just its demographic muscle, but it is the first to grow up surrounded by digital media. Computers and other digital technologies, such as digital cameras, are commonplace to N-Gen members. They work with them at home, in school, and they use them for entertainment. [They] are so bathed in bits that they are no more intimidated by digital technology than a VCR or a toaster. And it is through their use of the digital media that N-Gen will develop and superimpose its culture on the rest of society. Boomers stand back. Already these kids are learning, playing, communicating, working, and creating communities very differently than did their parents. They are a force for social transformation.[13]

Generation Y represents a complex target for marketers. On average, Gen-Ys have access to 62 TV channels, not to mention mobile phones, personal digital assistants (PDAs), and the Internet, offering broad media access. Studies have shown that Gen-Y consumers are smart, aware, and fair-minded. They like to be entertained in ads directed at them but don't like ads that make fun of people. They love things that are "green" and they relate well to causes. Making connections now with Gen-Ys will pay dividends to marketers beyond capturing their current spending. In future years, as they begin working and their buying power increases, this segment will more than rival the baby boomers in spending and market influence.[14]

Generational Marketing   Do marketers have to create separate products and marketing programs for each generation? Some experts caution that each generation spans decades of time and many socioeconomic levels. For example, marketers often split the baby boomers into three smaller groups—leading boomers, core boomers, and trailing boomers—each with its own beliefs and behaviours. Similarly, they split Generation Y into Gen-Y adults, Gen-Y teens, and Gen-Y kids. Thus, marketers need to form more precise age-specific segments within each group. More important, defining people by their birth date may be less effective than segmenting them by their lifestyle or life stage.

Others warn that marketers have to be careful about turning off one generation each time they craft a product or message that appeals effectively to another. "The idea is to try to be broadly inclusive and at the same time offer each generation something specifically designed for it," notes one expert. "Tommy Hilfiger has big brand logos on his clothes for teenagers and little pocket polo logos on his shirts for baby boomers. It's a brand that has a more inclusive than exclusive strategy."[15]

Changing Canadian Households

When one uses the term *household*, a stereotype of the typical family living in the suburbs with its two children may leap to mind. However, this stereotype is far from accurate. The 2001 census suggests that "Canada is a place of loners and shrinking families, where lovers have increasingly lost interest in a walk down the aisle, the

5.1   The Teen Market: Youth Will Be Served

*G*one are the days when kids saved up their pennies for candy and ice cream at the corner soda fountain. Today's teens are big spenders. According to Canada's *Marketing Magazine*, the average disposable income of a Canadian teenage girl is $131 a week. What's more, "Shopping is their number one hobby." Teens make 54 mall visits a year and they intend to buy something about 50 percent of the time. With so much cash to spend, teens represent a lucrative market for companies willing to cater to their often fickle, trend-driven tastes. To tap into this vast market of potential new customers, all kinds of companies are targeting teens with new or modified products. Some of these products are naturals for the teen market, such as action movies, acne creams, teen magazines, cell phones, and *NSYNC. Since teens are heavy users of

Marketing to teens: Based on focus group research, Wildseed developed cell phones with "smart skins"—replaceable faceplates with computer chips that let teens individualize the phone's functions and appearance to match their personalities.

text messaging and wireless phones, advertisers are itching to forge agreements with wireless phone companies like Bell Mobility, TELUS Mobility, Microcell, and Rogers AT&T Wireless. Roman Bodnarchuk, founder of N5R, a Toronto-based consulting firm that specializes in loyalty marketing, explains why teens and young adults have been attracted to this technology. "BlackBerries are cool, but very expensive. And wireless laptops are not that portable. And besides, email is too slow for these kids, they want instant response. Text messaging (SMS) is portable, it's silent—making communication possible during science class—and cheap." He also notes that marketers have to be teen savvy if they are going to be successful. Teens have come up with a language to fit the space limitations of the tiny phone screens. For example, POS means parents over shoulder; TOY is Thinking of you.

Canadian teen cosmetic manufacturer Caboodles has been hugely successful in reaching the teen segment not only in Canada, but also internationally. Its sales were just shy of $52 million in North America, though the Canadian market makes up just 9 percent of the overall business. The company also markets its popular line to teens in countries as diverse as Italy, Australia, Germany, China, Greece, Dubai, and Guam. Here a few more examples of companies attempting to cash in on the hot teen market:

Wildseed. Software Company Wildseed has spent years conducting research to develop cell phones and intelligent faceplates for teens. For the last two years, the company has regularly summoned teenagers to focus groups, where it pays them $20 to lounge around, eat pizza, play Xbox video games, and give their thumbs-up or thumbs-down on various proposals. What teens want from a cell phone ranges from the concrete (music, messaging, and games) to the abstract (style, personality, and individuality). As a result, Wildseed-inspired phones will have "Smart Skins™"—replaceable intelligent faceplates with computer chips that allow teens to individualize the phone's functions and appearance to match their personalities. For example, skateboarders can choose graffiti-splattered intelligent faceplates that come with edgy urban ringer tones, gritty icons, screen savers, and games.

Fuel. Who says boys don't read? Not the publishers of new *Fuel* magazine! It is distributed through 2500 Canadian schools and has a circulation of 100 000. While lifestyle magazines such as *Seventeen* have long been aimed at teenage girls, similar publications for boys have been startlingly absent. Research revealed, however, that the interests and tastes of the two genders were very different. "Boys were complaining about how they hated seeing tampon ads in the magazine. The more we tested, the more we found that what boys and girls liked and didn't like were at odds with each other." *Fuel* is taking advantage of this insight to break new ground.

Avon. In 2003 Avon rolled out a Teen Business unit to target teenage buyers. The new department will employ teens as sales associates who sell to other teens through catalogues, direct selling, and the Internet. Says Avon's chief executive, Andrea Jung, "Marketing to teens is [part] of our stated strategy to extend Avon's brand equity into new customer segments, new distribution channels, and new product categories."

Ford Motor Company. One study estimates that 4 million U.S. teens will reach driving age every year until 2010. With numbers like those, it's easy to see why car manufacturers market to teens who currently ride bicycles, mount skateboards, or lace up inline skates. For example, the Ford Focus's marketing campaign includes interactive TV commercials, cinema advertising, and lots of promotional alliances targeting tomorrow's drivers. Most Focus marketing takes place at venues like the "Hoop It Up" street basketball tour. The car's campaign is really an example of what every automaker is trying to do to reach teenagers.

Sources: Susan Henrich, "R u redi 4 Text Marketing?" *National Post*, March 17, 2003, www.nationalpost.com; Eve Lazarus, "Caboodles Rules," *Marketing Magazine*, January 20, 2003, www.marketingmag.ca; Kathleen Martin, "Boys Read," *Marketing Magazine*, January 20, 2003, www.marketingmag.ca; Frand Washington, "Aim Young; No, Younger," *Advertising Age*, April 9, 2001; Nancy Keates, "Family Travel: Catering to Kids," *Wall Street Journal*, May 3, 2002, p. W-1; Jennifer Lee, "Youth Will Be Served, Wirelessly," *New York Times*, May 30, 2002, p. G1; "Automakers Agree, Winning Youth Early Key to Future," *Advertising Age*, April 1, 2002, p. S16; and Brian Steinberg, "Pop-In Pasta Aims to Lure Teenagers to Drop the Chips," *Wall Street Journal*, April 8, 2002, p. A.21.

young adults like to shack up with mom and dad, and the eldest citizens are more often living the solitary life." In other words, the 2001 census suggests a number of new paradoxes. On one hand, there is a growing "crowded nest" syndrome. About 41 per cent of young Canadians aged 20 to 29 now live with their parents. There are 8.3 million families in Canada, but fewer have children. Married or common-law couples with children now represent only 44 percent of all families, compared to 49 percent just ten years earlier. While married couples still constitute the majority of Canadian parents, their numbers continue to drop. Thirty percent of parents now live in common-law arrangements. Another trend is seen in the fact that one in five of Canada's children lives in a single-parent household. As a result of these trends, the average Canadian household shrank to 2.6 people in 2001 from 2.9 people in 1981.[16]

Responsibility for household tasks and the care of children is also changing. There are now more dual income families as more and more women enter the workforce. Today, women account for over 48 percent of the workforce. The employment rate of women with children has grown particularly sharply in the past two decades, especially for those with preschool-aged children. Over 60 percent of women with children under age three were employed, more than double the figure in 1976. Human Resources Development Canada, however, reports that women earn an average annual salary of $45 820, 79.3 percent of men's average salary of $58 250.[17]

Geographic Shifts in Population

The population of Canada is expected to grow by approximately 4 percent between 2001 and 2006. As Table 5.1 shows, however, growth rates across all provinces are not uniform. The populations of Newfoundland and Labrador, Saskatchewan, and

Maxwell House and other brands are targeting smaller households with single-serve portions.

the Yukon decreased during the 1998–2002 period, while the populations of the other provinces grew.[18]

Canadians are a mobile people with itchy feet. For more than a century, Canadians have been moving from rural to urban areas. The urban areas show a faster pace of living, more commuting, higher incomes, and greater variety of goods

Table 5.1 Canada's Population

	1998 (thousands)	2002 (thousands)	Change (%)
Canada	30 248.4	31 414.0	3.9
Newfoundland and Labrador	545.3	531.6	−2.5
Prince Edward Island	136.9	139.9	2
Nova Scotia	936.1	944.8	0.8
New Brunswick	753.3	756.7	0.5
Quebec	7 323.6	7 455.2	2
Ontario	11 387.4	12 068.3	5.9
Manitoba	1 137.9	1 150.8	1
Saskatchewan	1 024.9	1 011.8	−1
Alberta	2 906.8	3 113.6	7.1
British Columbia	3 997.1	4 141.3	3.6
Yukon	31.5	29.9	−5
Northwest Territories	41.1	41.4	0
Nunavut	26.4	28.7	8.7

Source: Adapted from Statistics Canada, "Population, Provinces and Territories," www.statcan.ca/english/Pgdb/demo02.htm (extracted May 14, 2003).

and services than can be found in the small towns and rural areas that dot Canada. Moreover, each year about 12 in 1000 swap provinces. For the last few years, Alberta and Ontario have been the top two choices when it came to interprovincial moves. Recent research has shown that interprovincial moves and income are correlated. People who moved from one province to another tended to increase their earnings, especially if they moved away from a "have not" province. The effects were especially strong for men and younger people.[19]

Canada's cities are changing as well. Canadian cities are often surrounded by large suburban areas. Statistics Canada calls these combinations of urban and suburban populations "Census Metropolitan Areas" (CMAs). About 50 percent of Canada's population lives in the top 25 CMAs. Marketers also track the relative growth of these markets to see which areas are expanding and which ones are contracting. Table 5.2 shows Canada's top 20 CMAs and how their population has changed.

Population shifts interest marketers because people in different regions buy differently. For example, 46 percent of people classified as "serious technology users" reside in Ontario, compared with 18 percent that live in British Columbia and the 6 percent that live in Atlantic Canada.[20]

The shift in where people live has also caused a shift in where they work. For example, the migration toward metropolitan and suburban areas has resulted in a rapid increase in the number of people who "telecommute"—work at home or in a remote office and conduct their business by phone, fax, modem, or the Internet.

Table 5.2 Canada's Top 20 Census Metropolitan Areas

	1998 (thousands)	2002 (thousands)
Toronto (Ontario)	4586.7	5029.9
Montreal (Quebec)	3423.9	3548.8
Vancouver (British Columbia)	1998.4	2122.7
Ottawa–Hull (Ontario–Quebec)	1055.6	1128.9
Calgary (Alberta)	903.1	993.2
Edmonton (Alberta)	914.4	967.2
Quebec (Quebec)	686.6	697.8
Winnipeg (Manitoba)	677.8	685.5
Hamilton (Ontario)	657.8	686.9
London (Ontario)	416.0	427.3
Kitchener (Ontario)	408.5	438.0
St. Catharines–Niagara (Ontario)	387.5	392.3
Halifax (Nova Scotia)	348.9	363.2
Victoria (British Columbia)	316.8	318.9
Windsor (Ontario)	295.9	319.9
Oshawa (Ontario)	287.5	310.0
Saskatoon (Saskatchewan)	229.5	231.8
Regina (Saskatchewan)	199.2	197.0
St. John's (Newfoundland and Labrador)	175.2	177.2
Chicoutimi–Jonquière (Quebec)	162.6	156.9

Source: Adapted from Statistics Canada, "Population of Census Metropolitan Areas," www.statcan.ca/english/Pgdb/demo05.htm (extracted May 2, 2003).

This trend, in turn, has created a booming SOHO (small office/home office) market. Fifteen percent of Canadian households report that they have a home office. In addition to commuters, it estimated that there were 618 000 home-based businesses in Canada. Typically, home-based business operators are male (60.3 percent) and between the ages of 25 to 54 (76.4 percent). Many (31 percent) are highly educated. The top five industries for home-based businesses are professional, scientific, and technical services (17.8 percent); agriculture (12.1 percent); trade (10.2 percent); health care and social assistance (9.2 percent); and construction (8.3 percent).[21]

Many marketers are actively courting the home office segment. One example is Kinko's Copy Centers:

> Founded in the 1970s as a campus photocopying business, Kinko's is now re-inventing itself as the well-appointed office outside the home. Where once there were copy machines, Kinko's now features a uniform mixture of fax machines, ultrafast colour printers, and networks of computers equipped with popular software programs and high-speed Internet connections. People can come to a Kinko's store to do all their office jobs: They can copy, send and receive faxes, send out packages by FedEx, use various programs on the computer, go on the Internet, order stationery and other printed supplies, and even teleconference. As more and more people join the work-at-home trend, Kinko's offers an escape from the isolation of the home office. Besides adding state-of-the-art equipment, the company is talking to Starbucks about opening up coffee shops adjacent to some Kinko's stores. The lettering on the Kinko's door sums up the new business model: "Your branch office/Open 24 hours."[22]

A Better-Educated and More White-Collar Population

Figure 5.4 shows how the Canadian population is becoming better educated. The proportion of Canadians aged 25 and over with university degrees increased from 15 percent to 20 percent between 1991 and 2001. Canadians with college diplomas also increased, going from 12 percent to 16 percent in the same period. People with higher educations tend to have higher incomes, thus the demand for higher-quality products ranging from books to computers to cars is also increasing.[23]

Increasing Diversity

Countries vary in their ethnic and racial composition. At one extreme are homogeneous countries like Japan where almost everyone is of Japanese descent. At the

Kinko's has transformed itself to serve the booming home office market.

Figure 5.4 Education profile of Canadians

Source: "Canadian Consumer Demographics," http://retailinteractive.ca, from Ipsos-Reid, Canadian IT Review, Third Quarter, 2000, Industry Canada website, http://strategis.ic.gc.ca/SSG/ ri00150e.html (viewed May 14, 2003).

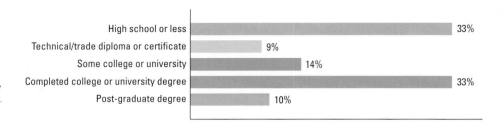

other extreme are such countries as Canada and the United States whose populations are "salad bowls" of mixed races. Anyone who has walked the streets of Vancouver, Montreal, Calgary, or Toronto will immediately understand that visible minorities in Canada are a force to be reckoned with. The United Nations reported that Toronto is the world's most multicultural city, and the Canadian Advertising Foundation recently predicted that the combined purchasing power of ethnic markets will soon exceed $300 billion. Many ethnic markets are growing in size. For example, the Italian and German markets in Canada each have populations of over 400 000. There are almost 4 million people living in Canada who report that they are members of visible minorities. Over 1 million people with Chinese background now live in Canada, along with another 900 000 people with South Asian origins. There are 662 000 black Canadians, almost 200 000 of Arabic descent, and 100 000 with Korean ancestors.[24]

As the ethnic population continues to grow in Canada, large companies, from Sears, Wal-Mart, and Air Canada to Levi Strauss, Procter & Gamble, and General Mills, feature people from different backgrounds in their ads and can now target specially designed products and promotions to one or more of these groups. They can use a variety of media vehicles introduced to serve ethnic marketplaces. There are 18 television networks, 49 radio stations, and 190 newspapers and magazines available to reach different ethnic populations. Since the largest foreign language groups in Canada are Chinese, Italian, and Portuguese, there are more alternatives in these languages, but there are also media available to target smaller populations such as Aboriginal Canadians.[25]

More and more Canadian firms, such as Communications Gratte-Ciel Ltée, are featuring people from different ethnic backgrounds.

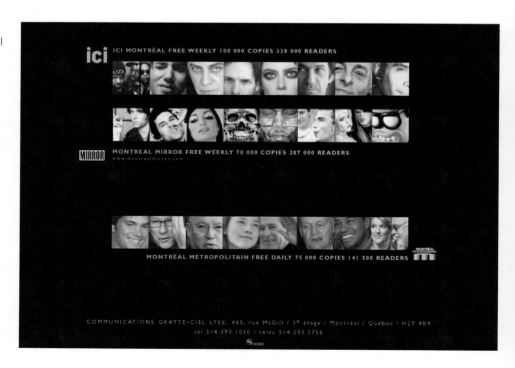

Marketers must avoid negative stereotypes when it comes to serving ethnic markets. Seventeen percent of immigrants hold university degrees, compared with 11 percent of people born in Canada. Immigrants are also more likely to hold managerial or professional jobs and have more stable family lives than people born in Canada.

Targeting ethnic consumers involves far more than mere tokenism, as many ethnic marketing specialists warn. Merely placing a person from a visible minority in an advertisement is not sufficient evidence that one is an ethnic marketer. Communicating in the consumer's native language is often mandatory, but marketers must also face the challenge of not alienating sophisticated second-generation individuals. The TD Bank recently demonstrated the power of providing information in potential customers' native language. The bank launched a Chinese Green Info Line to target potential Chinese investors. Over 300 callers per month take advantage of the service, which has generated considerable investments.

The diversity in the Canadian marketplace isn't restricted to ethnic markets. People's sexual orientation is another point of diversity, and there is growing tolerance of alternative lifestyles in Canada. Over 1 million people attended Lesbian and Gay Pride events in Toronto in 2002 alone. For the first time, the 2001 Census collected data on gay and lesbian couples. It counted a total of 34 200 same-sex common-law couples, representing 0.5 percent of all couples.[26] Since homosexual consumers tend to be cosmopolitan and professional with high incomes, they are desirable target markets for everything from technology products, to health and beauty products, to travel, fashion, entertainment, and financial services. It is not surprising that in 2001 Toronto ran a campaign aimed at attracting more gay and lesbian tourists. Nonetheless, until recently, few national advertisers, with the exception of the large breweries, created advertisements explicitly directed at this audience. One reason is the lack of research on this market. Another reason is the dearth of middle-of-the-road media directed at these consumers. Finally, some marketers feared that advertising in gay media or at gay events would cause a backlash from heterosexual consumers.

These things are changing. Several research firms, including Environics, have started gathering information on the market. A growing body of media is directed at the gay community, including electronic media such as PrideNet (www.pridenet. com). People who have experience advertising to the gay community, such as Tom Blackmore, a partner in the Toronto-based advertising agency Robins Blackmore, say that clients who have used creative materials that are relevant to this audience have experienced remarkable successes from their campaigns. The one mistake that marketers can make with respect to this audience is doing nothing. "It is a market that people have ignored for way too long," Blackmore explains.[27]

Companies in several industries are now waking up to the needs and potential of the gay and lesbian segment. For example, ad spending to reach gay and lesbian consumers is booming. Gay.com, a website that attracts more than 2 million unique visitors each month, has also attracted a diverse set of well-known advertisers, including IBM, eBay, Quicken Mortgage, Saturn, and AT&T. Here is one example of a gay and lesbian marketing effort:

The British Tourist Authority teamed up with British Airways and the London Tourist Board to target the U.S. gay and lesbian travel market. As the campaign designer noted, "We wanted something that was gay-specific (and) fun, but also extremely tasteful. These are educated, savvy consumers." One recent magazine ad shows five young to early-middle-aged men—the target age group is 35 to 50—posing in and around several of London's distinctive red phone booths. The headline reads: "One Call. A rainbow of choices." The campaign has been successful. "The magazine ads got the word out that Britain is gay- and lesbian-friendly and also generated a database of 40 000 names across the country. Now, it's time for a more targeted direct-mail and email campaign to people we know are interested in our offer." Since BTA launched the campaign, both

United Airlines and Virgin Airways have signed on to the program, as have the tourist boards of Manchester, Brighton, and Glasgow.[28]

Diversity goes beyond ethnicity or sexual preferences. For example, almost 18 percent of the Canadian population has some form of disability. This group has considerable spending power as well as great need for tailored products and services. Not only do they value services that make daily life easier, like online grocery shopping from sites like www.GroceryGateway.com, but they are also a growing market for travel, sports, and other leisure-oriented products. The Canadian Abilities Foundation provides a wealth of information ranging from products and services to housing and travel advice on its EnableLink website. Consider another example:

Volkswagen targets people with disabilities who want to travel. For example, it recently launched a special marketing campaign for its EuroVan. The campaign touted the EuroVan's extra-wide doors, high ceilings, and overall roominess as features that accommodate most wheelchair lifts and make driving more fun for those traditionally ignored by mainstream automakers. To make the EuroVan even more accessible, Volkswagen offers its Mobility Access Program. Drivers

People with disabilities present a large and growing market. The Canadian Abilities Foundation provides a website (EnableLink) and magazine (*Abilities*) targeting this segment.

with disabilities who purchase or lease any VW can take advantage of purchase assistance for modifications such as hand controls and wheelchair lifts. Volkswagen even modified its catchy tag line "Drivers Wanted" to appeal to motorists with disabilities, coining the new slogan "All Drivers Wanted." The VW website sums up, "We build cars for people who love to drive. Some just happen to use wheelchairs."[29]

Economic Environment

Economic environment
Factors that affect consumer buying power and spending patterns.

Markets require buying power as well as people. The **economic environment** consists of factors that affect consumer purchasing power and spending patterns. Nations vary greatly in their levels and distribution of income. Some countries have *subsistence economies*—they consume most of their own agricultural and industrial output. These countries offer few market opportunities. At the other extreme are *industrial economies,* which are rich markets for many different kinds of goods. Marketers must pay close attention to major economic trends and consumer spending patterns, both across and within their world markets. Following are some of the major economic trends in Canada.

Changes in Income

In the 1980s, the economy entered its longest peacetime boom. Consumers fell into a consumption frenzy, fuelled by income growth, federal tax reductions, rapid increases in housing values, and a boom in borrowing. They bought and bought, seemingly without caution, amassing record levels of debt. "It was fashionable to describe yourself as 'born to shop.' When the going gets tough, it was said, the tough go shopping. In the 1980s, many...became literally addicted to personal consumption."[30]

During the 1990s, the baby boom generation moved into its prime wage-earning years, and the number of small families headed by dual-career couples continued to increase. Thus, many consumers continued to demand quality products and better service, and they were able to pay for them. However, the free spending and high expectations of the 1980s were dashed by a recession in the early 1990s. In fact, the 1990s become the decade of the "squeezed consumer." Along with rising incomes in some segments came increased financial burdens. Consumers faced repaying debts acquired during earlier spending splurges, increased household and family expenses, and saving ahead for college tuition payments and retirement. These financially squeezed consumers sobered up, pulled back, and adjusted to their changing financial situations. They spent more carefully and sought greater value in the products and services they bought. *Value marketing* became the watchword for many marketers.

The late 1990s and early 2000s saw a turnaround in the economy. Despite a downturn in the U.S. economy and growing uncertainty arising from the September 11, 2001, World Trade Center attack and the 2003 War on Iraq, Canada's economy continued to grow. For example, in the first quarter of 2003, the unemployment rate continued to drop and real personal disposable income increased by more than 2 percent to reach an average per capita that was 13 percent higher than the low reached in 1996. Consumer expenditures continued to grow by more than 4 percent, but savings rates fell. Despite continued spending, consumer confidence has declined slightly.[31] Thus, marketers may need to look for ways to offer today's more financially cautious buyers greater value—just the right combination of product quality and good service at a fair price.

Marketers should pay attention to *income distribution* as well as average income. Income distribution in Canada is still very skewed. At the top are *upper-class* consumers, whose spending patterns are not affected by current economic events and who are a major market for luxury goods. You might see some of these people frequenting the Second Cup coffee shop in upscale Rockcliffe Park, nestled close to the Ottawa River. There is also a comfortable *middle class,* which is somewhat careful about its spending but can still afford the good life some of the time. The *working class* must stick close to the basics of food, clothing, and shelter, and must try hard to save. Finally, the *underclass* (persons on welfare and many retirees) must count their pennies even when making the most basic purchases. People with Canada's lowest incomes are often found on Native reserves. Of the 4400 communities ranked by income by Statistics Canada, the bottom 200 are almost all Native. Education rates are low, unemployment is high, and individual incomes may be as low as $4000 per year. One observer noted, "Reserves, especially in Western Canada, are somewhere between Mexico and Somalia in terms of standard of living. The disparity between the reserves and the rest of Canada is immense. It should be a major embarrassment."[32]

This distribution of income has created a two-tiered market. Many companies are aggressively targeting the affluent. Other companies are now tailoring their marketing offers to two different markets—the affluent and the less affluent. For example, Walt Disney Company (www.disney.com) markets two distinct Winnie-the-Pooh bears:

> The original line-drawn figure appears on fine china, pewter spoons, and pricey kids' stationery found in upscale specialty and department stores such as Nordstrom and Bloomingdale's. The plump, cartoon-like Pooh, clad in a red shirt and a goofy smile, adorns plastic key chains, polyester bed sheets, and animated videos. It sells in Wal-Mart stores and five-and-dime shops. Except at Disney's own stores, the two Poohs do not share the same retail shelf. [Thus, Disney offers both] upstairs and downstairs Poohs, hoping to land customers on both sides of the [income] divide.[33]

Changing Consumer Spending Patterns

Table 5.3 shows the proportion of total expenditures made by the average Canadian household in 2001 for major categories of goods and services. Food, housing, and transportation use up most household income (43 percent). This compares with 48 percent in 1998. Consumer spending patterns have changed considerably in the last 50 years. In 1947, spending on the basics (food, clothing, housing, fuel) accounted for 69 cents out of every dollar. What expenditures account for the other

Income distribution: Walt Disney markets two distinct Pooh bears to match its two-tiered market.

Table 5.3 2001 Average Canadian Household Expenditures

Household characteristics	Canada 2001	
Estimated number of households	11 552 010	
	Average Expenditure per Household $	Households Reporting Expenditures %
Total expenditures	57 742	100.0
Total current consumption	41 140	100.0
Food	6 438	100.0
Shelter	10 984	99.8
Household operation	2 619	99.9
Household furnishings and equipment	1 655	93.1
Clothing	2 398	99.4
Transportation	7 596	97.8
Health care	1 420	97.0
Personal care	960	99.8
Recreation	3 453	97.7
Reading materials and other printed matter	276	85.7
Education	898	44.7
Tobacco products and alcoholic beverages	1 313	83.9
Games of chance (net amount)	267	71.9
Miscellaneous	865	89.7
Personal income taxes	12 218	92.0
Personal insurance payments and pension contributions	3 125	81.1
Gifts of money and contributions	1 259	73.5

Source: Statistics Canada, "Average Household Expenses, Provinces and Territories," www.statcan.ca/english/Pgdb/famil16g.htm (extracted May 6, 2003).

21 cents no longer spent on the basics? Canadians are spending more on two categories—what Statistics Canada refers to as personal goods and services; and recreation, entertainment, education, and cultural services.[34]

However, consumers at different income levels have different spending patterns. Some of these differences were noted over a century ago by Ernst Engel, who studied how people shifted their spending as their income rose. He found that as family income rises, the percentage spent on food declines, the percentage spent on housing remains constant (except for utilities such as gas, electricity, and public services, which decrease), and both the percentage spent on other categories and that devoted to savings increase. **Engel's laws** generally have been supported by later studies.

Changes in such major economic variables as income, cost of living, interest rates, and savings and borrowing patterns have a large impact on the marketplace. Companies watch these variables by using economic forecasting. Businesses do not have to be wiped out by an economic downturn or caught short in a boom. With adequate warning, they can take advantage of changes in the economic environment.

Engel's laws
Differences noted over a century ago by Ernst Engel in how people shift their spending across food, housing, transportation, health care, and other goods and services categories as family income rises.

Natural environment
Natural resources that are needed as inputs by marketers or that are affected by marketing activities.

Natural Environment

The **natural environment** is the natural resources that are needed as inputs by marketers or that are affected by marketing activities. Environmental concerns have grown steadily over the past two decades. Some trend analysts have labelled the 1990s as the "Earth Decade," claiming that the natural environment is the major worldwide issue facing business and the public. The Earth Day movement turned thirty in the year 2000, yet in many cities around the world, air and water pollution have reached dangerous levels. World concern continues to mount over the depletion of the Earth's ozone layer and the resulting "greenhouse effect," a dangerous warming of the earth. And many environmentalists fear that we soon will be buried in our own trash.

Marketers should be aware of trends in the natural environment. The first involves growing *shortages of raw materials*. Air and water may seem to be infinite resources, but some groups see long-run dangers. Air pollution chokes many of the world's large cities. Great Lakes water levels are low, causing problems in many Canadian interior port cities, and water shortages are already a big problem in some parts of the United States and the world. Renewable resources, such as forests and food, also have to be used wisely. Non-renewable resources, such as oil, coal, and various minerals, pose a serious problem. Firms making products that require these scarce resources face large cost increases, even if the materials do remain available.

A second environmental trend is *increased pollution*. Industry will almost always damage the quality of the natural environment. Consider the disposal of chemical and nuclear wastes, the dangerous mercury levels in the ocean, the quantity of chemical pollutants in the soil and food supply, and the littering of the environment with non-biodegradable bottles, plastics, and other packaging materials.

A third trend is *increased government intervention* in natural resource management. The governments of different countries vary in their concern and efforts to promote a clean environment. Some, like the German government, vigorously pursue environmental quality. Others, especially many poorer nations, do little about pollution, largely because they lack the needed funds or political will. Even the richer nations lack the vast funds and political accord needed to mount a worldwide environmental effort. The general hope is that companies around the world will accept more social responsibility, and that less expensive devices can be found to control and reduce pollution.

The Canadian government passed the *Environmental Protection Act* in 1989. This Act established stringent pollution-control measures as well as the means for their enforcement, including fines as high as $1 million if regulations are violated. In the United States, the Environmental Protection Agency (EPA) was created in 1970 to set and enforce pollution standards and to conduct pollution research. Thus, companies doing business in Canada and the U.S. can expect strong controls from government and pressure groups. Instead of opposing regulation, marketers should help develop solutions to the material and energy problems facing the world.

Concern for the natural environment has spawned the "green movement." Today, enlightened companies go beyond what government regulations dictate. They are developing *environmentally sustainable strategies* and practices in an effort to create a world economy that the planet can support indefinitely. They are responding to consumer demands with ecologically safer products, recyclable or biodegradable packaging, better pollution controls, and more energy-efficient operations. AT&T uses a special software package to choose the least harmful materials, cut hazardous waste, reduce energy use, and improve product recycling in its operations. McDonald's eliminated polystyrene cartons and now uses smaller, recyclable paper wrappings and napkins. Beyond this, the company has a long-standing rainforest policy and a commitment to purchasing recycled products and energy-efficient restaurant construction techniques. Loblaw (www.Loblaw.com) began its G.R.E.E.N. program in 1989; today, it is one of the most successful environmental businesses in the world. Over 100 new products have been launched since the program's inception, while manufacturing changes have helped make dozens of other products environmentally friendly. More and more, companies are recognizing the link between a healthy economy and a healthy ecology.[35]

Environmental responsibility: McDonald's has made a substantial commitment to the so-called "green movement."

Technological Environment

Technological environment
Forces that create new technologies, creating new product and market opportunities.

The **technological environment** is perhaps the most dramatic force now shaping our destiny. Technology has released such wonders as antibiotics, organ transplants, and notebook computers. It has also released such horrors as nuclear missiles, nerve gas, and assault rifles. It has released such mixed blessings as the automobile, television, and credit cards. Our attitude toward technology depends on whether we are more impressed with its wonders or its blunders.

The technological environment changes rapidly. Many of today's common products were not available even a hundred years ago. John A. Macdonald did not know about automobiles, airplanes, or the electric light. William Lyon Mackenzie King did not know about xerography, synthetic detergents, or Earth satellites. And John Diefenbaker did not know about personal computers, compact disk players, or fax machines.

New technologies create new markets and opportunities. However, every new technology replaces an older technology. For example, compact disks hurt phonograph records; DVDs are eating away the sales of videos. When old industries fought or ignored new technologies, their businesses declined. Thus, marketers should watch the technological environment closely. Companies that do not keep up with technological change soon will find their products outdated. And they will miss new product and market opportunities.

The United States leads the world in research and development (R&D) spending. Total U.S. R&D spending reached an estimated US$285 billion in 2002. The U.S. federal government was the largest R&D spender, at US$76 billion.[36] Until recently, Canada hasn't had a sterling record when it comes to R&D expenditures. Canada ranks fifteenth in the world in research and development spending as a percentage of all products and services, and the Canadian government would like to see that rise to fifth.

To accomplish this aim, Industry Canada and the National Research Council are funding new efforts to foster increased research. Other government-backed initiatives include the Canada Foundation for Innovation, which awards funds to help post-secondary educational institutions, research hospitals, and non-profit institutions modernize their research infrastructure and equip themselves for state-of-the-art research.

Technological environment: Technology is perhaps the most dramatic force shaping the marketing environment. Here, a herder makes a call on his cell phone.

A recent survey by Inforsource found that spending by Canadian companies on research and development rose by 3.3 percent in 2001 despite the nearly $1 billion cut by the country's leading R&D spender, Nortel Networks Corp. Strong growth in other sectors, particularly the research-intensive biotech industry, offset this cutback. Spending at all other firms, excluding Nortel, rose an average of 23.3 percent. Altogether, Canadian companies spent $11.9 billion on research and development, up from $11.5 billion in 2000. The telecommunication sector is still the biggest investor in R&D, followed by the pharmaceutical and biotechnology sector. Computer software and services represent the next most research-intensive sector.[37]

Some companies spend huge amounts on R&D. Twenty-three Canadian firms spent more than $100 million each; the top five spenders were Nortel ($5 billion), JDS Uniphase Corp. ($505 million), aircraft engine maker Pratt & Whitney Canada Corp. ($440 million), auto parts manufacturer Magna International Inc. ($359 million), and mobile phone maker Ericsson Canada Inc. ($270 million). Marketers in these and other firms need to understand the changing technological environment and the ways that new technologies can serve human needs. They need to work closely with R&D people to encourage more market-oriented research. They also must be alert to the possible negative aspects of any innovation that might harm users or arouse opposition.[38]

It has long been believed that Canadian private sector R&D expenditures have been relatively low because many of the firms operating in Canada are branches of multinational firms that conduct R&D in their home markets. A recent study proved this assumption to be a myth. It revealed that foreign-owned firms in Canada pursue research and development and innovation strategies more actively than do Canadian-owned firms.[39]

Scientists today are researching a wide range of promising new products and services, ranging from practical solar energy, electric cars, and cancer cures to voice-controlled computers and genetically engineered food crops. Today's research usually is carried out by research teams rather than by lone inventors. Many companies are adding marketing people to R&D teams to try to obtain a stronger marketing orientation so that breakthroughs are not only technically feasible but also commercially viable.

As products and technology become more complex, the public needs to know that these are safe. Canada has a complex web of departments and regulations devoted to issues associated with product safety. For example, Agriculture Canada and the Canadian Food Inspection Agency monitor the safety of food products. The Department of Justice oversees the *Consumer Packaging and Labelling Act,* the *Food and Drug Act,* and the *Hazardous Products Act.* Health and Welfare Canada also has a food safety and product safety division. The Department of Transport governs vehicle recalls.

Marketers must be aware of these regulations when applying new technologies and developing new products.

Political Environment

Political environment

Laws, government agencies, and pressure groups that influence and limit various organizations and individuals in a given society.

Marketing decisions are strongly affected by developments in the political environment. The **political environment** consists of laws, government agencies, and pressure groups that influence and limit various organizations and individuals in a given society.

Legislation Regulating Business

Even the most liberal advocates of free-market economies agree that the system works best with at least some regulation. Well-conceived regulation can encourage competition and ensure fair markets for goods and services. Thus, governments develop *public policy* to guide commerce, by enacting laws and regulations that limit business for the good of society as a whole. Almost every marketing activity is subject to a wide range of laws and regulations.

Increasing Legislation   Legislation affecting business around the world has increased steadily over the years. Canada has many laws covering such issues as competition, fair trade practices, environmental protection, product safety, truth in advertising, packaging and labelling, pricing, and other important areas (see Table 5.4).

Table 5.4   Major Federal Legislation Affecting Marketing

The *Competition Act* is a major legislative act affecting the marketing activities of companies in Canada. Specific sections and the relevant areas are:

- Section 34: Pricing—Forbids suppliers from charging different prices to competitors purchasing like quantities of goods (price discrimination). Forbids price-cutting that lessens competition (predatory pricing).
- Section 36: Pricing and Advertising—Forbids advertising prices that misrepresent the "usual" selling price (misleading price advertising).
- Section 38: Pricing—Forbids suppliers from requiring subsequent resellers to offer products at a stipulated price (resale price maintenance).
- Section 33: Mergers—Forbids mergers by which competition is, or is likely to be, lessened to the detriment of the interests of the public.

Other selected acts that have an impact on marketing activities are:

- *National Trade Mark and True Labelling Act*—Established the term *Canada Standard,* or *CS,* as a national trademark; requires certain commodities to be properly labelled or described in advertising for the purpose of indicating material content or quality.
- *Consumer Packaging and Labelling Act*—Provides a set of rules to ensure that full information is disclosed by the manufacturer, packer, or distributor. Requires that all prepackaged products bear the quantity in French and English in metric as well as traditional Canadian standard units of weight, volume, or measure.
- *Motor Vehicle Safety Act*—Establishes mandatory safety standards for motor vehicles.
- *Food and Drug Act*—Prohibits the advertisement and sale of adulterated or misbranded foods, cosmetics, and drugs.
- *Personal Information Protection and Electronic Documents Act*—Establishes rules to govern the collection, use, and disclosure of personal information that recognize the right of privacy of individuals. The law recognizes the needs of organizations to collect, use, or disclose personal information for appropriate purposes. (For full details of the act, see www.privcom.gc.ca/english/02_06_01_e.htm.)

The European Commission has been active in establishing a new framework of laws covering competitive behaviour, product standards, product liability, and commercial transactions for the nations of the European Union. Some countries have especially strong consumerism legislation. For example, Norway bans several forms of sales promotion—trading stamps, contests, premiums—as being inappropriate or unfair ways of promoting products. Thailand requires food processors selling national brands to market low-price brands also, so that low-income consumers can find economy brands on the shelves. In India, food companies must obtain special approval to launch brands that duplicate those already existing on the market, such as additional soft drinks or new brands of rice.

Understanding the public-policy implications of a particular marketing activity is not a simple matter. For example, in Canada, many laws are created at the federal, provincial, and municipal levels, and these regulations often overlap. Moreover, regulations are constantly changing—what was allowed last year may now be prohibited, and what was prohibited may now be allowed.

The North American Free Trade Agreement (NAFTA) replaced the Free Trade Agreement (FTA) in August 1992. It governs free trade between Canada, the United States, and Mexico. NAFTA is an historic document since it is the first trade agreement between two developed nations and a developing country.[40] It is also the cornerstone for creating conditions that will help North American businesses compete worldwide. Access to low-cost inputs from the Mexican market helps U.S. and Canadian firms respond to offshore price competition. These firms can better match strategies of Asian competitors such as the Japanese, who have access to low-cost inputs of material and labour in countries such as China. As trade between the three countries expands, the provisions of NAFTA will continue to be updated and amended. Marketers must work hard to keep up with changes in regulations and their interpretations.

Business legislation has been enacted for various reasons. The first is to *protect companies* from each other. Although business executives may praise competition, they sometimes try to neutralize it when it threatens them. So laws are passed to define and prevent unfair competition.

The second purpose of government regulation is to *protect consumers* from unfair business practices. Some firms, if left alone, would make shoddy products, tell lies in their advertising, and deceive consumers through their packaging and pricing. Various agencies have defined unfair business practices and enforce their regulation.

The third purpose of government regulation is to *protect the interests of society* against unrestrained business behaviour. Profitable business activity does not always create a better quality of life. Regulation arises to ensure that firms take responsibility for the social costs of their production or products.

New laws and their enforcement will continue to increase both nationally and internationally. Business executives must watch these developments of new laws and their enforcement when planning their products and marketing programs. Marketers need to know about the major laws protecting competition, consumers, and society, at the municipal, provincial, federal, and international levels.

Increased Emphasis on Ethics and Socially Responsible Actions   Written regulations cannot possibly cover all potential marketing abuses, and existing laws are often difficult to enforce. However, beyond written laws and regulations, business is also governed by social codes and rules of professional ethics. Enlightened companies encourage their managers to look beyond what the regulatory system allows and to simply "do the right thing." These socially responsible firms actively seek out ways to protect the long-run interests of their customers and the environment. More companies are linking themselves to worthwhile causes and using public relations to build more positive images (see Real Marketing 5.2).[41]

The recent rash of business scandals and increased concerns about the environment have created fresh interest in ethics and social responsibility. Almost every

REAL MARKETING

5.2 Cause-Related Marketing: Doing Well by Doing Good

These days, every product seems to be tied to some cause. Buy Purina pet food products and the company contributes a portion of its sales to its Pets for People Program and to Humane Societies. Shop at Zellers knowing that they have helped millions of Canadians fight cystic fibrosis. A Toyota dealership in Vancouver donated $50 for each car it sold to the Make-a-Wish Foundation. Imperial Oil has one of the longest histories of giving in Canada—since 1936, it has been supporting children's programs, especially kids hockey in communities across Canada. More than 80 percent of Canadian companies are actively pursuing goodwill-inspired marketing initiatives, according to Toronto-based marketing communications consulting agency Harbinger.

Why this sudden interest in partnerships between business and charities? First, there are roughly 80 000 registered charities in Canada (compared to 22 500 that were registered in 1967). The number of charities has grown as government funding of social programs has decreased. However, as social needs increase, non-profits have proliferated to address social issues. Non-profits can no longer just rely on donations to fund their programs but must increasingly rely on corporate support. Thus, cause-related marketing has become an important tactic that increases non-profits' revenues and adds punch to marketing campaigns.

Second, marketers see increasing value in these associations as a means of overcoming diminished brand loyalty or adding a richer layer of meaning to a brand. Causes represent relevant and emotionally involving means of connecting with consumers. This is obviously not a new story for organizations like McDonald's (Ronald McDonald Children's Charities), Tim Hortons (Tim Horton Children's Foundation), or CIBC (Run for the Cure), which have long recognized the power of cause-related marketing campaigns.

Third, consumers are demanding more from business than just the provision of products and services. As many as 88 percent of Canadians believe that businesses should do more than simply make a profit, create jobs, and obey laws, according to the millennium poll on corporate social responsibility, conducted by Toronto-based Environics International.

Cause-related marketing has become a primary form of corporate giving. It lets companies "do well by doing good" by linking purchases of the company's products or services with fund-raising for worthwhile causes or charitable organizations. Cause-related marketing has grown rapidly since the early 1980s, when American Express offered to donate one cent to the restoration of the Statue of Liberty for each use of its charge card. American Express ended up having to contribute US$1.7 million, but the cause-related campaign produced a 28 percent increase in card usage.

Companies now sponsor dozens of cause-related marketing campaigns each year. Many are backed by large budgets and a full complement of marketing activities. Here are other examples:

CP Rail's annual Holiday Train makes an annual run from Montreal to Vancouver, collecting food for the Canadian Food Bank. The train is decorated with 8000 lights and stops at more than 50 towns and cities. It also sent two trains south of the border making a special stop in New York City to honour the victims and heroes of September 11.

Cause-related marketing: The General Mills Box Tops for Education program offers schools a chance to earn cash to pay for everything from field trips, to computers, to playground equipment

CPR promotes this initiative using radio and print ads run in local newspapers where the train stops.

In 1996, General Mills launched its Box Tops for Education program. The program offers schools a chance to earn cash to pay for everything from field trips to computers to playground equipment. Box Tops for Education has really caught on. To participate, students and parents clip box tops and labels from any of more than 330 eligible products, including brands like Yoplait, Big G, Lloyd's, and Betty Crocker. General Mills then pays the school 10 cents for every box top redeemed. To date, the company has given more than $75 million to schools.

Avon, the world's largest direct seller of cosmetics and beauty items, has for years sponsored programs aimed at raising awareness of breast cancer in North America and around the world. The program has raised millions of dollars. Breast cancer is a very relevant issue for its target audience—women. Avon's Breast Cancer Awareness Crusade raises money for programs that provide women—especially low-income, minority, and older women—with education and early cancer screening services. The company sells products featuring a pink ribbon (the international symbol of breast cancer) through its 450 000 sales representatives, then donates proceeds to non-profit and university-based programs. Avon publicizes these efforts in its bimonthly sales brochures and on its website. In addition, the company's famous in-person sales force is fully briefed on the company's efforts, putting a familiar face on the campaign. "We're looking to position Avon as the company for women, whether that's the place to buy a product, to start your own business, where your health needs are addressed, [or] to function as an advocate on behalf of women's health," says Joanne Mazurki, Avon's former director of global cause-related marketing.

Cause-related marketing has stirred some controversy. Critics are concerned that cause-related marketing might eventually undercut traditional "no-strings" corporate giving, as more and more companies grow to expect marketing benefits from their contributions. Critics also worry that cause-related marketing will cause a shift in corporate charitable support toward more visible, popular, and low-risk charities—those with more certain and substantial marketing appeal. For example, MasterCard's "Choose to Make a Difference" campaign raises money for six charities, each selected in part because of its popularity in a consumer poll. Finally, critics worry that cause-related marketing is more a strategy for selling than a strategy for giving—that "cause-related" marketing is really "cause-exploitative" marketing. Thus, companies using cause-related marketing might find themselves walking a fine line between an improved image and charges of exploitation.

However, if handled well, cause-related marketing can greatly benefit both the company and the cause. The company gains an effective marketing tool while building a more positive public image. According to one recent study, 83 percent of consumers have a more positive image of a company that supports a cause they care about. Two-thirds say that if price and quality are equal, they are likely to switch to a civic-minded brand or retailer. Moreover, surveys show that these cause-related contributions usually add to, rather than undercut, direct company contributions. Thus, when cause-related marketing works, everyone wins.

Sources: Mike Lang, "Getting It Right," *Strategy*, September 9, 2002, p. 24; Lucy Saddleton, "Cause-related Marketing on the Rise," *Strategy*, December 1, 2001, www.strategymag.com; Minette E. Drumwright, "Company Advertising with a Social Dimension: The Role of Noneconomic Criteria," *Journal of Marketing*, October 1996, pp. 71–87; Jerry C. Welsh, "Good Cause, Good Business," *Harvard Business Review*, September–October 1999, pp. 21–24; Alison Fass, "A Campaign by Avon on Breast Cancer," *New York Times*, August 17, 2001, p. C3; Michael Jay Polonsky and Greg Wood, "Can the Overcommercialization of Cause-Related Marketing Harm Society?" *Journal of Macromarketing*, June 2001, pp. 8, 15; Sankar Sen and C. B. Bhattacharya, "Does Doing Good Always Lead to Doing Better? Consumer Reactions to Corporate Social," *Harvard Business Review*, May 2001, pp. 225–243; information from Avon, www.avon company.com/women (June 2002); and information from General Mills, www.boxtops4education.com (June 2002).

aspect of marketing involves such issues. Unfortunately, because they usually involve conflicting interests, well-meaning people can disagree honestly about the right course of action in a particular situation. Thus, many industrial and professional trade associations have suggested codes of ethics, and many companies now are developing policies and guidelines to deal with complex social responsibility issues.

The boom in ecommerce and Internet marketing has created a new set of social and ethical issues. Privacy issues are the primary concern. For example, website visitors often provide extensive personal information that might leave them open to abuse by unscrupulous marketers. Moreover, both Intel and Microsoft have been accused of covert, high-tech computer chip and software invasions of customers' personal computers to obtain information for marketing purposes.

Throughout this text, we present Real Marketing exhibits that summarize the main public policy and social responsibility issues surrounding major marketing decisions. These exhibits discuss the legal issues that marketers should understand and the common ethical and societal concerns that marketers face. A broad range of societal marketing issues are discussed in greater depth in Chapter 4.

Cultural Environment

Cultural environment
Institutions and other forces that affect society's basic values, perceptions, preferences, and behaviours.

The **cultural environment** is composed of institutions and other forces that affect a society's basic values, perceptions, preferences, and behaviours. People grow up in a particular society that shapes their basic beliefs and values. They absorb a world view that defines their relationships with others. The following cultural characteristics can affect marketing decision making.

Persistence of Cultural Values

People in a society hold many beliefs and values. Their core beliefs and values have a high degree of persistence. For example, most Canadians believe in working, getting married, giving to charity, and being honest. While such values have been described as dull, reserved, and modest, Canadians view themselves as hard-working, generous, and sophisticated. Our self-confidence is growing and we are acting with increased independence with regard to everything from our financial investment decisions to our views on politics. These beliefs shape more specific attitudes and behaviours found in everyday life. *Core* beliefs and values are passed from parents to children and are reinforced by schools, churches, business, and government.

Secondary beliefs and values are more open to change. Believing in marriage is a core belief; believing that people should get married early in life is a secondary belief. Marketers have some chance of changing secondary values, but little chance of changing core values. For example, family-planning marketers could argue more effectively that people should get married later than that they should not get married at all.

Shifts in Secondary Cultural Values

Although core values are fairly persistent, cultural swings do occur. Consider the impact of popular music groups, movie personalities, and other celebrities on young people's hair styling, clothing, and sexual norms. Marketers want to predict cultural shifts to identify new opportunities or threats. Several firms offer "futures" forecasts in this connection, such as Environics (founded by Toronto-based Michael Adams), Yankelovich Monitor, Market Facts' BrainWaves Group, and the Trends Research Institute. For example, the Environics marketing research firm tracks such regional values as "anti-bigness," "mysticism," "living for today," "away from possessions," and "sensuousness." Such information helps marketers cater to trends with appropriate products and communication appeals.

The Yankelovich Monitor has tracked consumer value trends for years. At the dawn of the twenty-first century, it looked back to capture lessons from the past decade that might offer insight into the 2000s. It identified the following eight major consumer themes:[42]

1. *Paradox.* People agree that "life is getting better and worse at the same time."
2. *Trust not.* Confidence in doctors, public schools, TV news, newspapers, federal government, and corporations drops sharply.
3. *Go it alone.* More people agree with the statement "I rely more on my own instincts than on experts."

4. *Smarts really count.* For example, fewer people agree with "It's risky to buy a brand you are not familiar with."

5. *No sacrifices.* For example, many people claim that looks are important but not at any price, that keeping house for show instead of comfort is over, and that giving up taste for nutrition is no longer acceptable.

6. *Stress is hard to beat.* For example, more people claim that they are "concerned about getting enough rest."

7. *Reciprocity is the way to go.* More people agree that "everybody should feel free to do his or her own thing."

8. *Me.2.* For example, people express the need to live in a world that is built by "me," not by you.

Yankelovich maintains that the decade drivers for the 2000s will primarily come from the baby boomers and Generation Xers. The major cultural values of a society are expressed in people's views of themselves and others, as well as in their views of organizations, society, nature, and the universe.

People's Views of Themselves   People vary in their emphasis on serving themselves versus serving others. Some people seek personal pleasure, wanting fun, change, and escape. Others seek self-realization through religion, recreation, or the avid pursuit of careers or other life goals. People use products, brands, and services as a means of self-expression, and they buy products and services that match their views of themselves.

In the new millennium, consumption is becoming less conspicuous. Of course, some of us are still out to impress the neighbours, but the trend is toward making personally meaningful purchases rather than flashy ones. Canadians want the shopping experience to be quick and convenient. When we do take time to slow down, we look for sensually rich experiences and we like to indulge ourselves. Canadians are increasingly putting their money where their consciences lie, and we are choosing businesses that exhibit humane and ethical values.[43]

The region where we are born or grow up also affects our values, the way we view ourselves, and the products we use. While it does not surprise most Canadians that Quebecers are fiercely independent, they might be surprised at the extent to which they live for today and place a high value on enjoying life. Quebecers are also more security conscious than other Canadians. They put greater importance on family and on the cultivation of friendships. Unlike the rest of Canada, they demonstrate a respect for authority. Picturing themselves as *au courant*, they stress fashion and being up to date on current events. Quebecers place less importance on earning a lot of money than do people from English Canada, and they pride themselves on being more emotional than English Canadians.

Regional differences are not just limited to those between French and English Canadians: Newfoundlanders think that they are the hardest-working segment of the Canadian population, while people from British Columbia express the greatest love of reading. These regional values often translate into different patterns of product usage. Fredericton is the capital of white bread consumption. Montrealers eat more deep brown beans than other Canadians. Consumers in Halifax drink more Diet Coke per capita than other Canadians, and people from Manitoba and Saskatchewan have the highest per capita consumption of Kellogg's Corn Flakes. While marketers are often at a loss when it comes to explaining how regional values translate into different product usage patterns, marketers must still be highly sensitive to these regional differences.

Managing regional differences takes a deft touch as the brewers of Labatt's 50 found. While 50 sales have gone flat in Ontario, they are soaring in Quebec. When talking to Quebec 50 consumers, Labatt found that consumers believed 50 was a Quebec-only brand. Part of the reason was the way 50 was originally launched in

Quebec. It was one of the first products where Quebecers truly found themselves, their values, and lifestyle reflected in advertising. The series of ads run in 1965 starring Olivier Guimond, an extremely popular Quebec comedian, featured the slogan "*Lui y connait ça*," which roughly translates as "This guy knows." Viewed paradoxically as an ordinary, blue-collar guy and a "a real connoisseur of everything," Guimond resonated with Quebec beer lovers and initiated a love affair between the brand and its target.[44]

People's Views of Others   Recently, observers have noted a shift from a "me-society" to a "we-society" in which more people want to be with and serve others. Notes one trend tracker, "People want to get out, especially those...people working out of their home and feeling a little cooped up [and] all those shut-ins who feel unfulfilled by the cyberstuff that was supposed to make them feel like never leaving home." This trend suggests a greater demand for "social support" products and services that improve direct communication between people, such as health clubs and family vacations.[45]

People's Views of Organizations   People have differing attitudes toward corporations, government agencies, trade unions, universities, and other organizations. By and large, people are willing to work for major organizations, and they expect them, in turn, to carry out society's work. Canadians increasingly desire greater autonomy and personal freedom in the workplace, however. If they can't control their work, many are turning to self-employment as a means of achieving the autonomy desired.[46] Starting in the late 1980s, there has been a sharp decrease in confidence in and loyalty toward business and political organizations and institutions. Waves of company downsizings in the 1990s bred further cynicism and distrust. These trends suggest that organizations need to find new ways to win consumer and employee confidence.

People's Views of Society   People differ in their attitudes toward their society: nationalists defend it, reformers want to change it, and malcontents want to leave it. Canadians increasingly want to have intense and energetic lives lived in a more ethical world.[47] People's orientation to their society influences their consumption patterns, levels of savings, and attitudes toward the marketplace. For example, more and more Canadians have a sense of national pride. Some companies, such as Zellers, responded with "made-in-Canada" themes and promotions. Others, such as Clearly Canadian, Molson Canadian, and Upper Canada Brewing Company, made national identity part of their branding strategy.

People's Views of Nature   People have differing attitudes toward the natural world: some feel ruled by it, others feel in harmony with it, and still others seek to master it. A long-term trend has been people's growing mastery over nature through technology and the belief that nature is bountiful. More recently, however, people have recognized that nature is finite and fragile—that it can be destroyed or spoiled by human activities.

Love of nature is leading to more camping, hiking, boating, fishing, and other outdoor activities. Business has responded by offering more products and services catering to these interests. Tour operators are offering more wilderness adventures and retailers are offering more fitness gear and apparel. Marketing communicators are using appealing natural backgrounds in advertising their products. And food producers have found growing markets for natural and organic foods. Canadian organic retail sales growth is expected to increase 20 percent a year to $3.1 billion in 2005. Approximately one in twenty fruit and vegetable farms in Canada considers itself to be an organic producer, and Canada is among the top five world producers of organic grains and oilseeds. Most of Canada's organically grown products are exported to the United States, Europe, and Japan. The worldwide market is huge and sales of organic products are estimated at $20 billion.[48]

People's Views of the Universe   People vary in their beliefs about the origin of the universe and their place in it. Although many Canadians have religious beliefs, attendance at religious services has been dropping off gradually through the years. A recent Statistics Canada survey shows Canadians' continuing slide out the doors of the country's churches, temples, and synagogues. In 1946, 67 percent of adult Canadians regularly attended religious services, but by 2001, the figure had dropped to 20 percent. Yann Martel, Canadian author of the acclaimed *Life of Pi*, noted in an interview that Canadians and Americans are going in opposite directions with regard to religion. "America is a very religious, almost puritanical country. In Canada, secularism is triumphant, and to talk noncynically, nonironically about religion is strange," he says. Only 30 percent of Canadians report religion is very important to them, compared with 59 percent of Americans. The statistics would be even more skewed if it were not for the growing number of devout Muslim, Sikh, and Hindu immigrants now living in Canada. Canadian marketers have to use caution when picking up lifestyle ads from the United States. While showing people in religious settings may draw attention from American consumers, they may strike Canadians as inappropriate.[49]

Responding to the Marketing Environment

Someone once observed, "There are three kinds of companies: those who make things happen; those who watch things happen; and those who wonder what's happened."[50] Many companies view the marketing environment as an "uncontrollable" element to which they must adapt. They passively accept the marketing environment and do not try to change it. They analyze the environmental forces and design strategies that will help the company avoid the threats and take advantage of the opportunities the environment provides.

Environmental management perspective

Firms that adopt this perspective take aggressive action to affect the publics and forces in their marketing environment.

Other companies take an **environmental management perspective**.[51] Rather than simply watching and reacting, these firms take aggressive action to affect the publics and forces in their marketing environment. Such companies hire lobbyists to influence legislation affecting their industries and stage media events to gain favourable press coverage. They run advertorials (ads expressing editorial points of view) to shape public opinion. They press lawsuits and file complaints with regulators to keep competitors in line, and they form contractual agreements to better control their distribution channels.

Often, companies find positive ways to overcome seemingly uncontrollable environmental constraints. Some forestry firms, including Noranda, have joined the Round Table on the Environment, a government-sponsored discussion group, to help all stakeholders affected by forestry policies better understand environmental concerns about forestry management. Tourism marketers in Toronto worked hard to draw crowds back to the city after the SARS scare in early 2003.[52] Marketing management cannot always affect environmental forces. In many cases, it must settle for simply watching and reacting to the environment. For example, a company would have little success trying to influence geographic population shifts, the economic environment, or major cultural values. But whenever possible, smart marketing managers will take a *proactive* rather than a *reactive* approach to the marketing environment (see Real Marketing 5.3).

5.3 Your Companysucks.com

You might think that Crappy Tire was a derogatory name, but this wouldn't be true according to Canadian Tire. While Canadians frequently use the nickname, it is almost a term of endearment, claims the company. At least that is the reasoning the company used when it took Mick Mcfadden to the World Intellectual Property Organization (WIPO) over his website www.crappytire.com. Mike, an Ontario-based automobile salvager, first posted the site to illustrate the price differences between Canadian Tire and its competitors. The suit caused a bit of a sensation and was even picked up by *Business 2.0*. Before taking Mike to the WIPO, Canadian Tire tried twice to buy the URL, first for $3000, then upping the offer to $5000. Mike refused to sell and got the last laugh when the WIPO upheld his right to keep the domain name.

Richard Hatch is another angry consumer who got revenge by using the Web. He is one of the few people in this world with a passion for both Harley-Davidson

Environmental management: The best strategy for dealing with consumer hate sites is to address complaints, such as those of Wal-Mart nemesis Richard Hatch, directly. "If a company solves my problems, why would I keep up the website?"

motorcycles and collecting dolls and cute little toys. One day in 1997, the tattooed, 95 kg Hatch got into a shouting match with an employee in his local Wal-Mart and was banned from the store. Hatch claims that his actions didn't warrant his ousting. He says he'd complained to store managers for months that employees were snapping up the best Hot Wheels and NASCAR collectible toy cars before they hit the shelves.

Wal-Mart didn't budge, and the angry Hatch retaliated. He hired a Web designer and created the Wal-Mart Sucks website (www.walmartsucks.com). In just a few years, according to one account, the website "sprouted beyond Hatch's wildest dreams. [Thousands of] customers have written in to attack rude store managers, complain about alleged insects in the aisles, offer shoplifting tips, and, from time to time, write romantic odes to cashiers."

Extreme events? Not anymore. As more and more well-intentioned grassroots organizations, consumer watchdog groups, or just plain angry consumers take their gripes to the Web, such "sucks.com" sites are becoming almost commonplace. A recent Yahoo! search yielded 140 such sites. According to one source, more than half of the Fortune 1000 companies have encountered some type of website critical of their businesses. The sites target some highly respected companies with some highly disrespectful labels: Microsucks, Gapsucks.org, NonAmazon, Starbucked, BestBuysucks, The I Hate McDonald's Page, Just Do Not Do It (Nike), America Offline, The Most Unfriendly Skies, The Unofficial BMW Lemon Site, AllState Insurancesucks ("Their hands in your pockets"), and Dunkindonuts.org (featuring "unhappy tales about coffee, crullers, and cinnamon buns"), to name only a few.

Some of these attack sites are little more than a nuisance. Others, however, can draw serious attention and create real headaches. "The same people who used to stand on [the] corner and rail against things to 20 people now can put up a website and rail in front of 2 million people," says William Comcowich, whose firm helps companies monitor what's said about them on the Internet.

How should companies react to these attack sites? The real quandary for targeted companies is figuring out how far they can go to protect their image without fuelling the fire already raging at the sites. Some companies have tried to silence the critics through lawsuits, but few have succeeded. For example, McDonald's sued one such site for libel; it spent US$16 million on the case and won the suit but received only US$94 000 in damages. Wal-Mart's attorneys threatened Hatch with legal action but Wal-Mart eventually backed down.

As it turns out, a company has legal recourse only when the unauthorized use of its trademarks, brand names, or other intellectual property is apt to be confusing to the public. And no reasonable person is likely to be confused that Wal-Mart maintains and supports a site named Walmartsucks.com. Given the difficulties of trying to sue consumer hate sites out of existence, some companies have tried other strategies. For example, most big companies now routinely buy up Web addresses for their firm names preceded by the words "I hate" or followed by "sucks.com." In general, however, attempts to block, counterattack, or shut down consumer hate sites may be shortsighted. Such sites are often based on real consumer concerns. Hence, the best strategy might be to proactively monitor these sites and respond positively to the concerns they express.

Some targeted companies actively listen to concerns posted on hate sites and develop Web presentations to tell their own side of the story. For example, Nike is the target of at least eight different attack sites, mostly criticizing it for alleged unfair labour practices in Southeast Asia. In response, Nike commissioned an independent investigation of labour practices in its Indonesian factories and presented the results on its own website (www.Nikebiz.com/social/labour). Monitoring consumer hate sites can yield additional benefits. For example, some sites can actually provide the targeted company with useful information. Walmartsucks.com posts customers' ratings of local stores for cleanliness, prices, and customer service, information that would be costly for Wal-Mart to develop on its own.

According to James Alexander, president of eWatch, an Internet monitoring service, the best strategy for dealing with consumer hate sites is to address their complaints directly. "If a company solves my problem," he says, "why would I keep up the website?" Take Dunkin' Donuts, for example:

> After a disgruntled customer established dunkindonuts.org, an attack site that appeared on many Internet search engines ahead of the company's own Web page, the company contacted about 25 people who had written in with complaints and offered them coupons for free doughnuts. "If this was where customers were going to post their comments, we thought it was important for us to go ahead and address them," says spokesperson Jennifer Rosenberg. Now, the company is in negotiations to buy the site from its founder, 25-year-old David Felton, who says he'll sell because "they have been taking complaints and responding."

By proactively responding to a seemingly uncontrollable event in its environment, Dunkin' Donuts has been able to turn a negative into a positive. At Dunkin' Donuts, sucks.com is now allsmiles.com.

Sources: Quotes and excerpts from Leslie Goff, "<YourCompanyNameHere>sucks.com," *Computerworld*, July 20, 1998, pp. 57–58; and Mike France, "A Site for Soreheads," *Business Week*, April 12, 1999, pp. 86–90. Also see Kieren McCarthy, "Canadian Tire Fights For Right To Be Called 'Crap'," *The Register*, April 18, 2001, www.theregister.co.uk/content/6/18358.html; Matt Callaway, "Some Domain-Name Cases Just Aren't Worth Fighting Over," *Business 2.0*, April 16, 2001, www.business2.com; Jane Langdon, "Web Impacting Corporate Reputation: Companies Want To Know What's Being Said About Them Online—And By Whom," *Strategy*, April 10, 2000, p. B8; Oscar S. Cisneros, "Legal Tips for Your 'Sucks' Site," *Wired*, www.wired.com, August 14, 2000; Hilary Appelman, "I Scream, You Scream: Consumers Vent Over the Net," *New York Times*, March 4, 2001, p. 3.13; and Ronald F. Lopez, "Corporate Strategies for Addressing Internet 'Complaint' Sites," Construction WebLinks, www.constructionweblinks.com (accessed June 2002).

Looking Back: Reviewing the Concepts

Companies must constantly watch and adapt to the *marketing environment* to seek opportunities and ward off threats. The marketing environment comprises all the actors and forces influencing the company's ability to transact business effectively with its target market.

1. Describe the environmental forces that affect the company's ability to serve its customers.

The company's *microenvironment* consists of other actors close to the company that combine to form the company's value delivery system or that affect its ability to serve its customers. It includes the company's *internal environment*—its several departments and management levels—as it influences marketing decision making. *Marketing channel firms*—the suppliers and marketing intermediaries, including resellers, physical distribution firms, marketing services agencies, and financial intermediaries—cooperate to create customer value. Five types of customer *markets* include consumer, business, reseller, government, and international markets. *Competitors* vie with the company in an effort to serve customers better. Finally, various *publics* have an actual or potential interest in or impact on the company's ability to meet its objectives.

The *macroenvironment* consists of larger societal forces that affect the entire microenvironment. The six forces making up the company's macroenvironment include demographic, economic, natural, technological, political, and cultural forces. These six forces shape opportunities and pose threats to the company.

2. Explain how changes in the demographic and economic environments affect marketing decisions.

Demography is the study of the characteristics of human populations. Today's *demographic environment* shows a changing age structure, shifting profiles of Canadian households, geographic population shifts, a better-educated and more white-collar population, and increasing diversity. The *economic environment* consists of factors that affect buying power and patterns. The economic environment is characterized by more consumer concern for value and shifting consumer spending patterns. Today's squeezed consumers are seeking greater value—just the right combination of good quality and service at a fair price. The distribution of income is also shifting, leading to a two-tiered market. Many companies now tailor their marketing offers to two different markets—the affluent and the less affluent.

3. Identify the major trends in the firm's natural and technological environments.

The *natural environment* shows four major trends: shortages of raw materials, higher pollution levels, and more government intervention in natural resource management. Environmental concerns create marketing opportunities for alert companies. The marketer should watch for four major trends in the *technological environment:* the rapid pace of technological change, high R&D budgets, the concentration by companies on minor product improvements, and increased government regulation. Companies that fail to keep up with technological change will miss out on new product and marketing opportunities.

4. Explain the key changes in the political and cultural environments.

The *political environment* consists of laws, government agencies, and groups that influence or limit marketing actions. The political environment has undergone three changes that affect marketing worldwide: increasing legislation regulating business, strong government agency enforcement, and greater emphasis on ethics and socially responsible actions. The *cultural environment* is made up of institutions and forces that affect a society's values, perceptions, preferences, and behaviours. The environment shows long-term trends toward a "we-society," a lessening of trust in institutions, increasing patriotism, greater appreciation for nature, a new spiritualism, and search for more meaningful and enduring values.

5. Discuss how companies can react to the marketing environment.

Companies can passively accept the marketing environment as an uncontrollable element to which they must adapt, avoiding threats and taking advantage of opportunities as they arise. Or they can take an *environmental management perspective,* proactively working to change the environment rather than simply reacting to it. Whenever possible, companies should try to be proactive rather than reactive.

Reviewing the Key Terms

Baby boomers   173
Cultural environment   195
Demography   171
Economic environment   185
Engel's laws   187
Environmental management
    perspective   198

Generation X   175
Generation Y   175
Macroenvironment   167
Marketing environment   167
Marketing intermediaries   168
Microenvironment   167
Natural environment   187

Political environment   191
Public   170
Technological environment   189

Discussing the Concepts

1. What is a company's marketing environment? Describe the factors that affect the marketing environment.

2. Identify the seven publics that impact an organization's ability to achieve its objectives. Which of these publics would likely have the greatest impact on the introduction of a new product designed to reduce signs of aging around the eyes? Explain.

3. The single most important demographic trend in Canada may be the changing age structure of the population. Characterize the differences among baby boomers, Generation X, and Generation Y. How might a marketer selling computers target a person in each of these groups? Let's call the next generation Generation D (the *d*igital generation). What preferences and buying patterns might emerge for this group?

4. Canadians are becoming more concerned about the natural environment. Explain how this trend might affect a company that markets packaging for (a) candy bars, (b) tires, (c) gas-powered lawn mowers, and (d) electrical power. Suggest some effective responses to the concerns that consumers might have about these products.

5. Some assert that corporate scandals, the questionable behaviour of national accounting firms, and accusations of senior-executive greed are creating an ethical crisis in business. Assume you are on a task force

asked to address this crisis. What penalties should exist for unethical behaviour? How should the business community respond to this crisis and ensure ethical and social responsibility?

6. The cultural environment is comprised of the values, perceptions, and preferences of the institutions and people in a society. Select a society whose predominant cultural values differ from those of Canada. Compare and contrast the cultural characteristics of the two societies. How might the differing values affect marketing decisions?

7. Companies with an environmental management perspective take aggressive actions to affect the publics and forces in their marketing environments. As a marketing manager, what are some ways that you might proactively influence your marketing environment?

8. Statistics Canada is posting tables on its website (www.statcan.ca) that outline some of its findings from the 2001 census. These include tables on population projects by age group and sex, the population of Census Metropolitan Areas (CMAs), and recent immigrants by last country of residence. Go to their website. Print one of these tables, analyze it, and describe how this information would help you design a marketing plan for a particular target audience.

Applying the Concepts

1. With all the attention paid to youth in our society, it may be easy to forget that populations are aging in all western industrialized countries. In Sweden, for example, seniors (those people aged 65 and older) comprise 18 percent of the population, while in Canada they form 12.7 percent of the population. Seniors are important consumers in Canadian society. Households headed by seniors represent 21 percent of all Canadian households and account for 13 percent of all expendi-

tures. In certain categories these percentages are even higher: 21 percent of all consumer expenditures on health care and 4 percent on personal care. Don't be fooled into thinking they are ill, poor, or sedentary. About three-quarters of seniors aged 65 to 74 rate their health as good, very good, or excellent. Moreover, approximately one-half of seniors are physically active, ranking walking, gardening, home exercise, swimming, and dancing among their favourite activities. Thus, seniors account for 13 percent of all transportation expenditures and 11 percent of expenditures on recreation. Seniors also play an important role in the voluntary sector, accounting for 17 percent of all charitable giving and time volunteered in Canada.[53]

The Canadian Association of Retired Persons (CARP) acts as a strong voice for people over fifty years of age. It has 400 000 members. The organization raises awareness about the issues, challenges, and stereotypes that plague older Canadians. CARP uses its publication (*50Plus* magazine) and its lobbying efforts to demonstrate and promote travel, physical fitness, mental alertness, active lifestyles, and self-pride.

The association has also secured major partnerships with airlines, hotels, resorts, insurance companies, retailers, entertainment organizations (such as movie theatres), and automobile firms. To what end? CARP and its members are spending their dollars on businesses that design their activities and products with seniors in mind. Watch for fashions, entertainment, and even the Internet to tap into the significant buying power of this growing segment.

a. Construct a brief profile of seniors in Canada. It may be helpful to examine Health Canada's webpage "Canada's Seniors at a Glance" (www. hc-sc.gc.ca/seniors-aines/pubs/poster/seniors/ page1e.htm).

b. Does a retailer such as the Gap have to choose between youth and seniors? How could the Gap appeal to both?

c. Have a look at CARP's webpage (www.50plus. com/). Click through some pages like the travel section. Now, think of a specific consumer goods company. How could the company partner with CARP to build relationships with seniors?

d. CARP, like any business organization, is interested in expanding its membership and influence. Give three suggestions for how the organization might accomplish this.

2. The Look-Look company studies youth culture. Traditionally, market research has been viewed as a straightforward, somewhat boring field. But research at Look-Look is anything but boring! Co-founders Sharon Lee and DeeDee Gordon have assembled a research team to study the habits and desires of today's youth around the globe. Look-Look (www.look-look.com/ dynamic/looklook/html/index_html) studies the whole youth culture by focusing on fashion, entertainment, technology, activities, eating and drinking, and health and beauty.

Look-Look specializes in analyzing the youth mind-set. Look-Look representatives talk to young people in shopping malls, on the Internet, in clothing stores, eating lunch, or walking down the street. Look-Look researchers take pictures of hairstyles, tattoos, body piercings, makeup, and even T-shirts bought in thrift stores. Look-Look has sources of information beyond just photographs. The company has an active database of over 10 000 trendsetting young people (14–30 years old). The company compiles these photographs, analyzes research results, and projects trends. As a result, Look-Look is on the cutting edge of youth culture. Retailers such as the Limited and Calvin Klein turn to Look-Look as a strong and reliable bridge to youth culture.

a. What is unique about Look-Look's approach to marketing research? Do you think that approach makes the company more or less effective in tracking youth culture?

b. What are some of the current trends for young people? What were some of the predominant trends when you were younger?

c. How could Look-Look's analysis help you successfully open a teen fashion-jewellery store in a local mall?

d. What would be the advantages and disadvantages of doing research on the youth market via (1) the Internet and (2) personal interviews in shopping malls?

Video Short

View the video short for this chapter at **www.pearsoned.ca/kotler** and then answer the questions provided in the case description.

Company Case

The Prius: Leading a Wave of Hybrids

There are lots of reasons why North Americans might buy a high-tech auto that gives high gas mileage and emits fewer air pollutants. We love our cars and we readily accept change—especially if it is related to material comfort or our physical well-being. It seems that many people in our culture worship scientific and technological advances and want the latest gizmos. North Americans also complain bitterly about gasoline price increases, even though gasoline is much cheaper in North America than in many other parts of the world. Finally, surveys consistently show that Canadians are "concerned about the environment."

Hoping that all of the above was true, and looking to grab a technological advantage over North American automakers, Toyota introduced the hybrid auto, the Prius, to the North American market in 2000. The name means "to go before," which may be very prophetic. The Prius and its companion hybrid from Honda, the Insight, are the first in a wave of hybrids coming out ahead of similar vehicles from the Big Three automakers.

At first glance, the Prius seems to have a lot going for it. It combines a 1.5-litre, four-cylinder gas engine and a 33-kilowatt electric motor to deliver 114 horsepower. It comfortably seats five, if the three in the back aren't too tall or too big, and has 12 cubic feet (0.3 cubic metres) of trunk space. The electric motor starts the car and operates at low speeds, using a nickel metal-hydride battery. At higher speeds, the Prius automatically switches to the gasoline engine. Under normal highway driving conditions, it should get 106 km per gallon.

Given the benefits associated with the Prius and similar cars produced by Honda (the Insight and the Civic Hybrid), one would expect sales to soar. However, despite the fact that the three cars are cited by Environmental Defence Canada as the "greenest" vehicles available, they are among the poorest selling. To date, Toyota Canada Inc. has sold just 863 of its Prius cars, and Honda has sold just 344 Insight and 225 Civic Hybrid models since the cars were introduced. Compare these numbers with the more than 69 000 gasoline-only Civics, the best-selling passenger car in the country, that Canadians bought in 2002 alone.

The automakers claim that high prices are hindering the sales of the cars. The Prius costs $29 900, approximately $3000 more than the Echo, although they are nearly the same car. Of course, getting twice as many kilometres per litre of gasoline will help to off-set the price differential, but an owner would have to drive hundreds of thousands of kilometres to benefit. Another downside is that the Prius is no muscle machine. On the brighter side, Toyota and its competitors believe that costs will decrease once production of hybrids begins to yield economies of scale. The benefits of scale would not stop with the producer. For example, a major part of the cost of the car is the nickel metal-hydride batteries. A company such as Panasonic could reduce the cost of producing batteries through research and development if the market merited such an investment, and could further reduce the price of batteries through its own economies of scale.

However, realizing that cost reductions are yet to come and that gasoline savings aren't going to be the key to convincing North Americans to purchase the Prius, automakers have asked for tax incentives to stimulate purchase of clean-fuel and high-mileage autos. They've been successful in the United States. In May 2002, the IRS ruled that owners of hybrid gas-and-electric vehicles could claim a federal income-tax deduction of as much as US$2000 for buying a Prius. While Canadian Environment Minister David Anderson accepts the fact that people won't pay a premium for the environment, he has not implemented federal rebates on purchases of the Honda and Toyota hybrid cars. He has yet to see any proof that such rebates spur purchases of eco-friendly vehicles.

Critics deny that price is the problem and claim that the automakers need to spend more money on advertising and marketing. For example, the message still hasn't gotten across to Canadians that drivers of these types of cars do not plug in the vehicles to recharge their batteries. The batteries recharge as the vehicles are driven. They also look toward the Big Three automakers to be more proactive in their production and marketing of environmentally friendly vehicles. In particular, critics have attacked General Motors of Canada Ltd. "Environmental Defence Canada placed six General Motors SUVs and trucks on the list of least environmentally friendly vehicles, and just one, the compact Pontiac Vibe SUV, on the friendly list. GM should lead the way with cleaner, more fuel-efficient vehicles, not drag behind Toyota and Honda."

Toyota, in fact, has been acknowledged for some clever marketing with regard to its Prius. Two years before introduction, Toyota began educating consumers about the Prius. The company established a website to distribute information and also sent ebrochures to 40 000 likely North American buyers just before the introduction. Within two weeks, Toyota sold 1800 cars in North America, thanks to the email message.

In all, Toyota spent US$15 million in 2002 touting the Prius. There were print ads in magazines such as *Newsweek* and *Vanity Fair*, but the bulk of the campaign was in television advertising on channels such as Discovery, the History Channel, the Learning Channel, and MSNBC. Ads running before the actual introduction used the tag line "A car that sometimes runs on gas power and sometimes runs on electric power, from a company that always runs on brain power." These ads helped to position Toyota as an "environmentally concerned" company and more subtly stressed the technology aspect of the car.

After introduction, the ads appealed more to emotion with tag lines such as "When it sees red, it charges"—a reference to the auto's recharging at stoplights. The headline captured the consumer's attention through ambiguity. Only through focusing on the ad could the consumer learn why the headline was accurate. Again, the appeal is based on the technology of the car. Finally, Toyota took advantage of Earth Day to send out green seed cards shaped like Toyota's logo to prospective buyers, wrapped some Priuses in green, and gave away cars at Earth Day events.

In addition to media advertising, Toyota Canada Inc. undertook a number of sponsorships to raise awareness of the Prius. For example, it donated the hybrid vehicle to Ability Rally Racing for the 2003 Canadian Rally Championship—a demanding series of performance rallies across Canada. As Ken Tomikawa, President of Toyota Canada, notes, "Toyota is honoured to make a contribution to this very worthy cause which serves two important goals—to help motor-disabled children, and to draw attention to the importance of using all the technology at our command to reduce pollution and fuel consumption."

Of course, US$15 million is just a drop in the bucket relative to Toyota's overall marketing budget of US$190 million for cars and trucks in 2002, but Toyota was satisfied with the effectiveness of the campaign, given the "newness" of the car and the need to explain its technology.

As expected, the first hybrid auto buyers are "techies" and early adopters (people who are highly likely to buy something new). Many Prius owners are immersed in the technology. They flood chat rooms with discussion of the car. The www.priusenvy.com

website urges owners to "Kick some gas." Such owners immediately began tinkering with the car's computer system. One owner in Philadelphia was able to add cruise control (an option not offered by Toyota) by wiring in a few switches in the car's computer system. The founder of the Priusenvy website figured out how to use the car's dashboard display screen to show files from his laptop, play video games, and view rear-view images from a video camera pointed out the back of the car. One Austrian consumer plans to install a sniffer—a device on the car's computer network that monitors electronic messages. With the sniffer, he will be able to hook up add-ons such as a MiniDisc Player, an MP3 player, a laptop computer, and a TV tuner. Want to know more? Go to www.PriusMod.com. In the past, owners using mechanical skills customized cars with paint, lowered bodies, and souped-up engines. In the future, customization may rely on being computer savvy.

Even though the Internet was a major part of the Prius launch, Toyota does not sell the car from its website. Buyers can use the www.toyota.ca website to price their car and find a dealer. However, since it takes specially trained salespeople to explain and promote the Prius, only 75 percent of Toyota dealers actually handle the car. Many of them are not happy about the need to train salespeople. And why should they be? Margins are higher on gas-guzzlers, which are also easier to sell.

Given dealer reluctance and consumer resistance from all those SUV and truck owners, you have to wonder why Toyota and Honda have spent so much putting their hybrids on the market. While part of the answer is government regulations, a bigger part of the answer is competition. All automakers concede that they will eventually have to move to hybrids to raise gas mileage and lower emissions, and all of them have plans to do so. Ford, for example, plans to introduce an Escape SUV in 2003 that will get 64 km per gallon. DaimlerChrysler says that by 2003, 15 percent of its Durangos (about 33 000 SUVs) will be hybrids that will get 20 percent better fuel efficiency than a conventional Durango. General Motors is betting on hybrid buses and trucks. Toyota hopes, however, that its early entry will be the basis for a system of hybrids from ultracompact "minicars" to luxury sedans, sport-utility vehicles, and even commercial trucks.

All the automakers still have one key question to answer: Are consumers ready for hybrids? Do improved gas usage and emissions standards affect their buying decision? A glance at auto sales in the last ten years would suggest not. The biggest sales growth was in

SUVs and trucks, both of which get much poorer gas mileage than standard compacts. After all, we rarely saw Range Rovers ten years ago; now they're a fairly common sight. North Americans, it seems, think it's a good idea for their neighbours to drive "green machines," not themselves. Many vehicle buyers still seem to place more importance on space, comfort, and power.

Undaunted, Toyota is forging ahead and is taking aim at the mainstream consumer mindset. "When the 2004 Prius arrives in dealerships this fall, it will exceed all expectations," said Ken Tomikawa, President, Toyota Canada Inc. They think that they have a winning combination. The new Prius will feature increased interior space, moving from the compact to midsize class. Its new Hybrid Synergy Drive system will supply significantly better performance, best-in-class fuel economy, and best-in-market emissions performance. Only time will tell if Canadians will drive their way toward a greener world.

Questions for Discussion

1. What microenvironmental factors affect the introduction and sale of the Toyota Prius? How well has Toyota dealt with these factors?

2. Outline the major macroenvironmental factors—demographic, economic, natural, technological, political, and cultural—that have affected the introduction and sale of the Toyota Prius. How has Toyota dealt with each of these factors?

3. Evaluate Toyota's marketing strategy so far. What has Toyota done well? How might it improve its strategy?

4. In your opinion, what are the advantages of Toyota's early entry into the hybrid market? What are the disadvantages? Should Toyota have waited—like Ford, GM, and DaimlerChrysler?

Sources: Steven Chase and Greg Keenan, "Low-Pollution Cars Proving a Tough Sell to Canadians," *Globe and Mail*, February 21, 2003, p. A3; "Toyota Unveils All New Pirus," Toyota website, www.toyota.ca (accessed May 7, 2003); "Hit the Road, Tech," *Fortune,* Winter 2001, pp. 37–38; Jeffrey Ball, "Hybrid Gas-Electric Car Owners Can Get Income-Tax Deductions," *Wall Street Journal*, May 22, 2002, p. D8; Jeff Green, "Attention Techies and Assorted Geniuses: Toyota Prius Wants You," *Brandweek*, May 15, 2000, p. 113; Karl Greenberg, "A Wildflower Grows in Torrance as Toyota Gets Environmentally Aware," *Brandweek*, May 20, 2002, p. 42; Margaret Littman, "Hybrid Engine Cars Do Better with Hybrid Marketing Tactics," *Marketing News,* September 25, 2000, p. 6; John McElroy, "A Long Time Coming," *Ward's Auto World,* July 2001, p. 21; Margot Roosevelt, "Hybrid Power," *Time,* December 11, 2000, pp. 94–95; Norihiko Shirouzu, "Ford Aims to Sell a Gas-Electric SUV That Will Offer Sizable Fuel Efficiency," *Wall Street Journal*, March 7, 2000, p. A2; Sherri Singer, "Toyota Prius," *Machine Design,* January 28, 1989, pp. S52–S53; Emily Thornton, "Enviro-Car: The Race Is On," *Business Week,* February 8, 1999, p. 74; Thomas Weber, "Hacking Your Car: How Auto Buffs Use the Net to Reprogram Vehicles," *Wall Street Journal*, July 2, 2001, p. B1; and David Welch, "46 Miles Per Gallon...47...48," *Business Week,* August 14, 2000, p. 68.

CBC Video Case

CBC 🔘 Log on to your Companion Website at **www.pearsoned.ca/kotler** to view a CBC video segment and case for this chapter.

Chapter 6

Managing Marketing Information

After studying this chapter you should be able to

1. explain the importance of information to the company

2. define the marketing information system and discuss its parts

3. outline the four steps in the marketing research process

4. explain how companies analyze and distribute marketing information

5. discuss the special issues some marketing researchers face, including public policy and ethics issues

Looking Ahead: Previewing the Concepts

In the last chapter, you learned about the complex and changing marketing environment. In this chapter, we'll look at how companies develop and manage information about important elements of the environment—about their customers, competitors, products, and marketing programs. We'll examine marketing information systems designed to give managers the right information, in the right form, at the right time to help them make better marketing decisions. We'll also take a close look at the marketing research process and at some special marketing research considerations. To succeed in today's marketplace, companies must know how to manage mountains of marketing information effectively.

We'll start by looking at a classic marketing blunder—Coca-Cola's ill-considered decision some years ago to introduce New Coke. The company based its decision on substantial marketing research, yet the new product fizzled badly. As you read on, ask yourself how a large and resourceful marketing company such as Coca-Cola could make such a huge research mistake. The moral: if it can happen to Coca-Cola, it can happen to any company.

*I*n 1985, in what has now become an all-time classic marketing tale, the Coca-Cola Company made a major marketing blunder. After 99 successful years, it set aside its long-standing rule—"Don't mess with Mother Coke"—and dropped its original-formula Coke. In its place came *New* Coke, with a sweeter, smoother taste.

At first, amid the introductory flurry of advertising and publicity, New Coke sold well. But sales soon went flat as a stunned public reacted. Coke began receiving sacks of mail and more than 1500 phone calls each day from angry consumers. A group called "Old Cola Drinkers" staged protests, handed out T-shirts, and threatened a class-action suit unless Coca-Cola brought back the old formula. After only three months, the Coca-Cola Company brought old Coke back. Now called "Coke Classic," it sold side-by-side with New Coke on supermarket shelves. The company said that New Coke would remain its flagship brand, but consumers had a different idea. By the end of that year, Classic was outselling New Coke in supermarkets by two to one.

Quick reaction saved the company from potential disaster. It stepped up efforts for Coke Classic and slotted New Coke into a supporting role. Coke Classic again became the company's main brand and the country's leading soft drink. New Coke became the company's "attack brand"—its Pepsi stopper—and ads boldly compared New Coke's taste with Pepsi's. Still, New Coke managed only a 2 percent market share. In the spring of 1990, the company repackaged New Coke and relaunched it as a brand extension with a new name, Coke II. Today, Coke Classic captures almost 17 percent of the soft drink market; Coke II has quietly disappeared.

Why was New Coke introduced in the first place? What went wrong? Many analysts blame the blunder on poor marketing research.

In the early 1980s, although Coke was still the leading soft drink, it was slowly losing market share to Pepsi. For years, Pepsi had successfully mounted the "Pepsi Challenge," a series of televised taste tests showing that consumers preferred the sweeter taste of Pepsi. By early 1985, although Coke led in the overall market, Pepsi led in share of supermarket sales by 2 percent. (That doesn't sound like much, but 2 percent of today's huge soft drink market amounts to almost $2 billion in retail sales!) Coca-Cola had to do something to stop the loss of its market share, and the solution appeared to be a change in Coke's taste.

Coca-Cola began the largest new-product research project in the company's history. It spent more than two years and $7.8 million on research before settling on a new formula. It conducted some 200 000 taste tests—30 000 on the final formula alone. In blind tests, 60 percent of consumers chose the new Coke over the old, and 52 percent chose it over Pepsi. Research showed that New Coke would be a winner, and the company introduced it with confidence. So what happened?

Looking back, we can see that Coke defined its marketing research problem too narrowly. The research looked only at taste; it did not explore consumers' feelings about dropping the old Coke and replacing it with a new version. It took no account of the *intangibles*—Coke's name, history, packaging, cultural heritage, and image. However, to many people, Coke stands alongside baseball, hot dogs, and apple pie as an American institution; it represents the very fabric of America. Coke's symbolic meaning turned out to be more important to many consumers than its taste. Research addressing a broader set of issues would have detected these strong emotions.

Coke's managers may also have used poor judgment in interpreting the research and planning strategies around it. For example, they took the finding that 60 percent of consumers preferred New Coke's taste to mean that the new product would win in the marketplace, as when a political candidate wins with 60 percent of the vote. But it also meant that 40 percent still liked the original formula. By dropping the old Coke, the company trampled the taste buds of the large core of loyal Coke drinkers who didn't want a change. The company might have been wiser to leave the old Coke alone and introduce New Coke as a brand extension, as it later did successfully with Cherry Coke.

The Coca-Cola Company has one of the largest, best-managed, and most advanced marketing research operations in North America. Good marketing research has kept the company atop the rough-and-tumble soft drink market for decades. For example, Coke's research has revealed that Canadians drink about 30 to 35 percent less pop than Americans. About 25 percent of Coke's beverage sales in Canada are non-carbonated teas and juices that appeal to the large population of Asian and European immigrants—hence Coke Canada's introduction of Nestea green tea. In contrast, only 12 percent of Coke's sales in the United States are non-carbonated drinks.

Still, marketing research is far from an exact science. Consumers are full of surprises, and figuring them out can be awfully tough. Coke keeps trying. In 2002, after research revealed Canadian consumers loved the retro taste of old-fashioned fountain drinks, it launched Vanilla Coke in Toronto. This was its first flavour extension in almost 16 years. Only time will tell if the product will be a hit and whether its marketing research has really been able to decipher Canadian tastes and brand preferences, but the early results are promising—by July 2002 Vanilla Coke was the third-best-selling soft drink in the country.[1]

In order to produce superior value and satisfaction for customers, companies need information at almost every turn. As the New Coke story highlights, good products and marketing programs begin with a thorough understanding of consumer needs and wants. Companies also need an abundance of information on competitors, resellers, and other actors and forces in the marketplace.

Technologically driven changes—like datamining and online surveying—are profoundly changing Canada's $650 million market research industry. Technological advances have allowed marketers to take much of their data gathering efforts in-house. Loyalty programs have made it possible to build huge internal databases that allow marketers to track their customers' every purchase. Technology has also upped the flow of raw data, creating a huge demand for talented market researchers who can analyze that data and figure out what it all means. Mining internal databases can't answer all the questions marketers have, however. They also need to conduct specialized studies. As Janet Hawkins of TD Canada Trust notes, analysis of internal data alone can't tell you why consumers behave in a certain way and "it can't tell you about the competition."[2]

Increasingly, marketers are viewing information not only as an input for making better decisions but also as an important strategic asset and marketing tool. A company's information may prove to be its chief competitive advantage. Competitors can copy each other's equipment, products, and procedures, but they cannot duplicate the company's information and intellectual capital. Several companies have recently recognized this by appointing vice presidents of knowledge, learning, or intellectual capital.[3]

Canada's Professional Marketing Research Society (PMRS) cautions international marketers to do their homework before entering Canada, noting that Canadian consumer preferences and attitudes are unique. Says Cam Davis, president of the PMRS, "If they don't understand the distinct attributes of this market, they are going to miss opportunities or make costly mistakes." To make his point, Davis points out some research findings that indicate how different Canadians are from Americans:[4]

> Canadians buy smaller, less expensive vehicles than Americans. Why? Because we place less social importance on owning luxury cars. This insight helped Honda redesign its Acura model for the Canadian marketplace. Even though it had been selling well in the United States, it languished here. However, the redesigned Acura EL—a smaller, less expensive version strictly for the Canadian market—was an immediate success.

> Surprise of surprises, Americans consume more table syrup than we do, while on a per capita basis, we drink more wine, consume more Worcestershire sauce, and read more newspapers than Americans. Surprisingly, Canadians are more safety and security conscious, and we purchase and use more burglar alarms than Americans. U.S. consumers, in contrast, drink more bottled water and root beer than do individual Canadians. They consume more peanut butter, go to more movies, and take more headache medications.

> Canadians also lead the world in moving to become a cashless society. Our use of debit cards far exceeds any other country—54 percent, compared to 44 percent in the Netherlands, 41 percent in France, and 27 percent in the U.S. While we have a love/hate relationship with the banks, we are more confident than Americans that these institutions will protect the security and privacy of our account information. According to Scotiabank, that's why about 60 percent of Canadian Internet users have conducted online financial transactions, compared to less than 30 percent in the U.S.

In today's more rapidly changing environments, managers need up-to-date information to make timely, high-quality decisions. In turn, with the recent explosion of information technologies, companies can now generate information in great quantities. In fact, today's managers often receive too much information. One study found that with all the companies offering data, and with all the information now available through supermarket scanners, a packaged-goods brand manager is bombarded with 1 million to 1 *billion* new numbers each week. Another study found that, on average, North American office workers spend 60 percent of their time processing information; a typical manager reads about a million words a week. Thus, running out of information is not a problem, but seeing through the "data smog" is. "In this oh-so-overwhelming Information age," comments one observer, "it's all too easy to be buried, burdened, and burned out by data overload.[5]

Despite this data glut, marketers frequently complain that they lack enough information of the *right* kind. One recent study found that managers lose as much as three hours a day looking for the right information. Another study found that although half of the managers surveyed said they couldn't cope with the volume of information coming at them, two-thirds wanted even more. The researcher concluded that, "despite the volume, they're still not getting what they want."[6] Thus,

Information overload: "In this oh-so-overwhelming Information age, it's all too easy to be buried, burdened, and burned out by data overload."

Marketing information system (MIS)
People, equipment, and procedures to gather, sort, analyze, evaluate, and distribute needed, timely, and accurate information to marketing decision makers.

most marketing managers don't need *more* information, they need *better* information. Companies must design effective marketing information systems that give managers the right information, in the right form, at the right time to help them make better marketing decisions.

A **marketing information system (MIS)** consists of people, equipment, and procedures to gather, sort, analyze, evaluate, and distribute needed, timely, and accurate information to marketing decision makers. Figure 6.1 shows that the MIS begins and

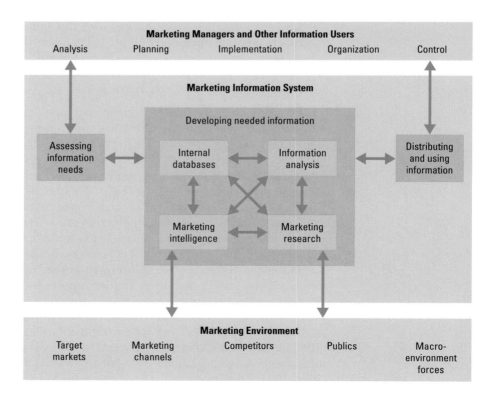

Figure 6.1   The marketing information system

ends with information users—marketing managers, internal and external partners, and others who need marketing information. First, it interacts with these managers to *assess information needs*. Next, it *develops needed information* from internal company databases, marketing intelligence activities, and marketing research. Then it helps users to analyze information to put it in the right form for making marketing decisions and managing customer relationships. Finally, the MIS *distributes* the marketing information and helps managers *use* it in their decision making.

Assessing Information Needs

The marketing information system primarily serves the company's marketing and other managers. However, it may also provide information to external partners, such as suppliers or marketing services agencies. For example, Wal-Mart might give Procter & Gamble and other key suppliers access to information on customer buying patterns and inventory levels. In addition, important customers may be given limited access to the information system. Dell Computer creates tailored Premium Pages for large customers, giving them access to product design, order status, and product support and service information. FedEx lets customers into its information system to schedule and track shipments. In designing an information system, the company must consider the needs of all of these users.

A good marketing information system balances the information managers would *like* to have against what they really *need* and what is *feasible* to offer. The company begins by interviewing managers to find out what information they would like. Some managers will ask for whatever information they can get without thinking carefully about what they really need. Too much information can be as harmful as too little. Other managers may omit things they ought to know, or may not know to ask for some types of information they should have. For example, managers might need to know that a competitor plans to introduce a new product in the coming year. Because they do not know about the new product, they do not think to ask about it. The MIS must watch the marketing environment to provide decision makers with information they need to make key marketing decisions.

Sometimes the company cannot provide the needed information, either because it is not available or because of MIS limitations. For example, a brand manager might want to know how competitors will change their advertising budgets next year and how these changes will affect industry market shares. The information on planned budgets probably is not available. Even if it is, the company's MIS may not be advanced enough to forecast resulting changes in market shares.

Finally, the costs of obtaining, processing, storing, and delivering information can mount quickly. The company must decide whether the benefits of having an item of information are worth the costs of providing it, and both value and cost are often hard to assess. By itself, information has no worth; its value comes from its *use*. In many cases, additional information will do little to change or improve a manager's decision, or the costs of the information may exceed the returns from the improved decision. Marketers should not assume that additional information will always be worth obtaining. Rather, they should carefully weigh the costs of additional information against the benefits resulting from it.

Developing Information

Marketers can obtain needed information from *internal data, marketing intelligence,* and *marketing research*.

Internal Data

Internal databases
Electronic collections of information obtained from data sources within the company.

Many companies build extensive **internal databases**, electronic collections of information obtained from data sources within the company. Marketing managers can readily access and work with information in the database to identify marketing opportunities and problems, plan programs, and evaluate performance.

Information in the database can come from many sources. The accounting department prepares financial statements and keeps detailed records of sales, costs, and cash flows. Operations reports on production schedules, shipments, and inventories. The sales force reports on reseller reactions and competitor activities. The marketing department furnishes information on customer demographics, psychographics, and buying behaviour, and the customer service department keeps records of customer-satisfaction or service problems. Research studies done for one department may provide useful information for several others.

Here are two examples of how Canadian organizations use internal records to make better marketing decisions:

The Canadian Automobile Association (CAA) has an extensive database developed through serving its highly loyal membership of over 4.2 million people or almost three million Canadian households. Members value its services, so if they receive an envelope with the CAA logo on the front, people will open it. The organization is using its database to build better relationships with its customers. It is also working hard to know its members better and better understand their needs. Many members only use the CAA's roadside protection services, yet the organization offers products as varied as insurance and travel-booking facilities.[7]

Financial services provider USAA uses its extensive database to tailor marketing offers to the specific needs of individual customers, resulting in greater than 96 percent customer retention.

TELUS analyzes its internal databases with the aim of creating a win-win situation for both the firm and its customers. The customer wins because interactions with TELUS are timely and relevant. This, in turn, helps TELUS increase its customer retention rates while maximizing its return on customer investment. Using its internal records, TELUS gets to know its customers so well that this telecommunication giant comes close to resembling a small neighbourhood store. It can greet customers by name, it knows their service history, and it can foresee emerging needs for new products and services.[8]

Internal databases can usually be accessed more quickly and cheaply than other information sources, but they also present some problems. Because internal information was collected for other purposes, it may be incomplete or in the wrong form for making marketing decisions. For example, sales and cost data used by the accounting department for preparing financial statements must be adapted for use in evaluating product, sales force, or channel performance. Data ages quickly; keeping the database current requires a major effort. In addition, a large company produces mountains of information, and keeping track of it all is difficult. The database information must be well-integrated and readily accessible through user-friendly interfaces so that managers can find it easily and use it effectively.

Marketing Intelligence

Marketing intelligence
The systematic collection and analysis of publicly available information about competitors and developments in the marketing environment.

Marketing intelligence is the systematic collection and analysis of publicly available information about competitors and developments in the marketing environment. The goal of marketing intelligence is to improve strategic decision making, assess and track competitors' actions, and provide early warning of opportunities and threats.

Competitive intelligence gathering has grown dramatically as more and more companies are now busily snooping on their competitors. Techniques range from quizzing the company's own employees and benchmarking competitors' products to researching on the Internet, lurking around industry trade shows, and rooting through rivals' trash bins. More and more of Canada's large, leading-edge firms, such as CAE Electronics, BCE, Teleglobe Canada, Labatt, and Alcan, have sophisticated CI systems in place. Furthermore, most companies work to ensure that they follow ethical and legal means of gathering competitive intelligence. Others, however, have wandered across the line. For example, much intelligence can be collected from people inside the rival companies—executives, engineers and scientists, purchasing agents, and the sales force. Consider the following examples:[9]

> While talking with a Kodak copier salesperson, a Xerox technician learned that the salesperson was being trained to service Xerox products. The Xerox employee reported back to his boss, who in turn passed the news to Xerox's intelligence unit. Using such clues as a classified ad Kodak placed seeking new people with Xerox product experience, Xerox verified Kodak's plan—code-named Ulysses—to service Xerox copiers. To protect its profitable service business, Xerox designed a Total Satisfaction Guarantee that allowed copier returns for any reason as long as *Xerox* did the servicing. By the time Kodak launched Ulysses, Xerox had been promoting its new program for three months.

> Spies don't always enter a rival's lair through the back door. Sometimes they stride in, and are even welcomed by their hosts. Bob Ayling, ex–chief executive of British Airways, accomplished such a mission when he visited the offices of the recently launched EasyJet.... Ayling approached the company's founder, Stelios Haji-Ioannou, to ask whether he could visit, claiming to be fascinated as to how the Greek entrepreneur had made the budget airline formula work. Haji-Ioannou not only agreed, but allegedly showed Ayling his business plan. [A

year later, British Air] announced the launch of Go. "It was a carbon copy of EasyJet," says...EasyGroup's director of corporate affairs. "Same planes, same direct ticket sales, same use of a secondary airport, and same idea to sell on-board refreshments. They succeeded in stealing our business model—it was a highly effective spying job."

The company can also obtain important intelligence information from suppliers, resellers, and key customers. Or it can get good information by observing competitors. It can buy and analyze competitors' products, monitor their sales, check for new patents, and examine various types of physical evidence. For example, one company regularly checks out competitors' parking lots—full lots might indicate plenty of work and prosperity; half-full lots might suggest hard times.[10]

Some companies have even rifled their competitors' garbage, which is legally considered abandoned property once it leaves the premises. In one garbage-snatching incident, Avon hired private detectives to paw through the dumpster of rival Mary Kay Cosmetics to search for revealing documents. An outraged Mary Kay sued to get its garbage back, but the dumpster had been located in a public parking lot and Avon had videotapes to prove it. In another case, Procter & Gamble admitted to "dumpster diving" at rival Unilever's Helene Curtis headquarters. The target was Unilever's hair-care products—including Salon Selectives, Finesse, and ThermaSilk—which competed with P&G's own Pantene, Head & Shoulders, and Pert brands. "Apparently, the operation was a big success," notes an analyst. "P&G got its mitts on just about every iota of info there was to be had about Unilever's brands." However, when news of the questionable tactics reached top P&G managers, they were shocked. They immediately stopped the project, voluntarily informed Unilever, and set up negotiations to right whatever competitive wrongs had been done. Although P&G claims it broke no laws, the company reported that the dumpster raids "violated our strict guidelines regarding our business policies."[11]

Competitors themselves may reveal information through their annual reports, business publications, trade show exhibits, press releases, advertisements, and web-pages. The Internet is proving to be a vast new source of competitor-supplied information. Most companies now place volumes of information on their websites, providing details to attract customers, partners, suppliers, or franchisees.

Marketing intelligence: Procter & Gamble admitted to "dumpster diving" at rival Unilever's Helene Curtis headquarters. When P&G's top management learned of the questionable practice, it stopped the project, voluntarily informed Unilever, and set up talks to right whatever competitive wrongs had been done.

"In today's information age, companies are leaving a paper trail of information online," says an online intelligence expert. Today's managers "don't have to simply rely on old news or intuition when making investment and business decisions."[12] Using Internet search engines, marketers can search specific competitor names, events, or trends and see what turns up. Intelligence seekers also pore through thousands of online databases. Some are free. For example, AltaVista Canada and CanoeMoney partner to provide a huge stockpile of financial and other information on public companies. For a fee, companies can subscribe to any of more than 3000 online databases and information search services, such as Dialog, DataStar, LEXIS-NEXIS, Dow Jones News Retrieval, UMI ProQuest, and Dun & Bradstreet's Online Access.

 Facing determined marketing intelligence efforts by competitors, most companies are now taking countermeasures. For example, Unilever (www.unilever.com/) has begun widespread competitive intelligence training. According to a former Unilever staffer, "We were told how to protect information, as well as how to get it from competitors. We were warned to always keep our mouths shut when travelling....We were even warned that spies from competitors could be posing as drivers at the mini-cab company we used." Unilever even performs random checks on internal security. Says the former staffer, "At one [internal marketing] conference, we were set up when an actor was employed to infiltrate the group. The idea was to see who spoke to him, how much they told him, and how long it took to realize that no one knew him. He ended up being there for a long time."[13]

The growing use of marketing intelligence raises a number of ethical issues. Although most of the preceding techniques are legal, and some are considered to be shrewdly competitive, many involve questionable ethics. Clearly, companies should take advantage of publicly available information. However, they should not stoop to snoop. With all the legitimate intelligence sources now available, a company does not have to break the law or accepted codes of ethics to get good intelligence.[14]

Marketing Research

In addition to information about competitor and environmental happenings, marketers often need formal studies of specific situations. For example, Sears wants to know what appeals will be most effective in its corporate advertising campaign. Before launching its new Accelerated MBA program, Queen's School of Business wanted to know how many people who had already earned an undergraduate business degree would be interested in taking an MBA. In such situations, marketing intelligence will not provide the detailed information needed. Managers will need marketing research.

Marketing research
The systematic design, collection, analysis, and reporting of data relevant to a specific marketing situation facing an organization.

Marketing research is the systematic design, collection, analysis, and reporting of data relevant to a specific marketing situation facing an organization. Companies use marketing research in a wide variety of situations. For example, marketing research can help marketers assess market potential and market share; understand customer satisfaction and purchase behaviour; and measure the effectiveness of pricing, product, distribution, and promotion activities.

Some large companies have their own research departments that work with marketing managers on marketing research projects. This is how Kraft, Citigroup, and many other corporate giants handle marketing research. In addition, these companies—like their smaller counterparts—frequently hire outside research specialists to consult with management on specific marketing problems and conduct marketing research studies. Sometimes firms simply purchase data collected by outside firms to aid in their decision making.

The marketing research process (see Figure 6.2) consists of four steps: *defining the problem and research objectives, developing the research plan, implementing the research plan,* and *interpreting and reporting the findings.*

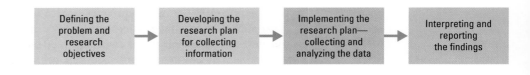

Figure 6.2 The marketing research process

Defining the problem and research objectives → Developing the research plan for collecting information → Implementing the research plan— collecting and analyzing the data → Interpreting and reporting the findings

Defining the Problem and Research Objectives

Marketing managers and researchers must work closely to define the problem and agree on the research objectives. The manager best understands the decision for which information is needed; the researcher best understands marketing research and how to obtain the information.

Defining the problem and research objectives is often the hardest step in the research process. The manager may know that something is wrong, without knowing the specific causes. For example, in the New Coke case, the Coca-Cola Company defined its research problem too narrowly, with disastrous results. In another example, managers of a large discount retail store chain hastily decided that falling sales were caused by poor advertising. As a result, they ordered research to test the company's advertising. When this research showed that current advertising was reaching the right people with the right message, the managers were puzzled. It turned out that the real problem was that the chain was not delivering the prices, products, and service promised in the advertising. Careful problem definition would have avoided the cost and delay of doing advertising research.

After the problem has been defined carefully, the manager and researcher must set research objectives. A marketing research project can have one of three types of objectives. The objective of **exploratory research** is to gather preliminary information that will help define the problem and suggest hypotheses. The objective of **descriptive research** is to describe things, such as the market potential for a product or the demographics and attitudes of consumers who buy the product. The objective of **causal research** is to test hypotheses about cause-and-effect relationships. For example, would a 10 percent decrease in tuition at a private school result in an enrolment increase sufficient to offset the reduced tuition? Managers often start with exploratory research and later follow with descriptive or causal research.

The statement of the problem and research objectives guides the entire research process. The manager and researcher should put the statement in writing to ensure that they agree on the purpose and expected results of the research.

Developing the Research Plan

Once the research problems and objectives have been defined, researchers must determine the exact information needed, develop a plan for gathering it efficiently, and present the plan to management. The research plan outlines sources of existing data and spells out the specific research approaches, contact methods, sampling plans, and instruments that researchers will use to gather new data.

Research objectives must be translated into specific information needs. For example, suppose Campbell decides to research how consumers would react to the introduction of new bowl-shaped plastic containers that it has used successfully for some of its other products. The containers would cost more, but would allow consumers to heat the soup in a microwave without adding water or milk and to eat it without using dishes. This research might call for the following specific information:

- The demographic, economic, and lifestyle characteristics of current soup users. (Busy working couples might find the convenience of the new packaging worth the price; families with children might want to pay less and wash the pot and bowls.)

Exploratory research
Marketing research to gather preliminary information that will help to better define problems and suggest hypotheses.

Descriptive research
Marketing research to better describe marketing problems, situations, or markets, such as the market potential for a product or the demographics and attitudes of consumers.

Causal research
Marketing research to test hypotheses about cause-and-effect relationships.

- Consumer-usage patterns for soup: how much soup they eat, where, and when. (The new packaging might be ideal for adults eating lunch on the go, but less convenient for parents feeding lunch to several children.)
- Retailer reactions to the new packaging. (Failure to get retailer support could hurt sales of the new package.)
- Consumer attitudes toward the new packaging. (The red and white Campbell soup can has become an institution. Will consumers accept the new packaging?)
- Forecasts of sales of both new and current packages. (Will the new packaging increase Campbell's profits?)

Campbell managers will need these and many other types of information to decide whether to introduce the new packaging.

The research plan should be presented in a *written proposal*. A written proposal is especially important when the research project is large and complex or when an outside firm carries it out. The proposal should cover the management problems addressed and the research objectives, the information to be obtained, and the way the results will help management decision making. The proposal also should include research costs.

To meet the manager's information needs, the researcher can gather secondary data, primary data, or both. **Secondary data** consist of information that already exists somewhere, having been collected for another purpose. **Primary data** is information gathered during a research project to answer a specific research question.

Gathering Secondary Data

Researchers usually start by gathering secondary data. The company's internal database provides a good starting point. However, the company can also tap a wide assortment of external information sources, including commercial data services and government sources (see Table 6.1).

Companies can buy data reports from outside suppliers.[15] For example, Information Resources, Inc., sells supermarket scanner purchase data which measure trial and repeat purchasing, brand loyalty, and buyer demographics. The

Secondary data
Information that already exists somewhere, having been collected for another purpose.

Primary data
Information collected for the specific purpose.

The NPD Group offers Canadian companies a wide range of research services to meet their information needs.

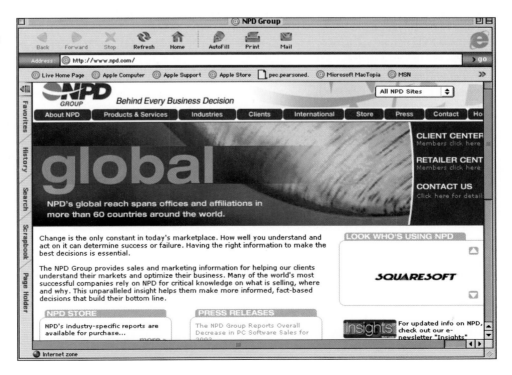

Table 6.1   Selected External Information Sources

For business data:

Scott's Directories lists, on an annual basis, manufacturers, their products, and their North American Industry Classification (NAICS) codes, alphabetically as well as by city and region. The directory also provides the names and telephone and fax numbers of chief executives, as well as corporate information such as annual sales. Directories come in four volumes: Ontario, Quebec, Atlantic Canada, and Western Canada.

Canadian Trade Index and Fraser's Canadian Trade Directory provide information on manufacturers of different product categories, manufacturing equipment, and supplies.

AC Nielsen (www.acnielsen.com) provides supermarket scanner data on sales, market share, and retail prices; data on household purchasing; and data on television audiences.

Information Resources, Inc. (www.infores.com) provides supermarket scanner data for tracking grocery product movement and new product purchasing data.

Arbitron (www.arbitron.com) provides local-market and Internet radio audience and advertising expenditure information, among other media and ad spending data.

Simmons Market Research Bureau (www.smrb.com) provides detailed analysis of consumer patterns in 400 product categories in selected markets.

Dun & Bradstreet (www.dnb.com) maintains a database containing information on more than 50 million individual companies around the globe.

Dialog (http://library.dialog.com) offers access to ABI/INFORM, a database of articles from 8001 publications, and to reports, newsletters, and directories covering dozens of industries.

LEXIS-NEXIS (www.lexis-nexis.com) features articles from business, consumer, and marketing publications plus tracking of firms, industries, trends, and promotion techniques.

Securities and Exchange CompuServe (www.compuserve.com) provides access to databases of business and consumer demographics, government reports, and patent records, plus articles from newspapers, newsletters, and research reports.

Dow Jones Interactive (http://bis.dowjones.com) specializes in in-depth financial, historical, and operational information on public and private companies.

Hoovers Online (www.hoovers.com) provides business descriptions, financial overviews, and news about major companies around the world.

CNN (www.cnn.com) reports U.S. and global news and covers the markets and news-making companies in detail.

Canoe (www.canoe.ca) (Canadian Online Explorer) bills itself as Canada's leading news and information site.

American Demographics (www.americandemographics.com) reports on demographic trends and their significance for businesses.

Marketing journals include the *Canadian Journal of Marketing Research, Journal of Marketing, Journal of Marketing Research, Journal of Consumer Research*, and *Journal of the Academy of Marketing Science.*

Useful trade magazines include *Strategy* (www.strategymag.com), *Marketing Magazine* (www.marketingmag.ca), *Advertising Age, Chain Store Age, Progressive Grocer, Sales & Marketing Management*, and *Stores.*

Useful general business magazines include *Canadian Business, The Globe and Mail Report on Business, Business Week, Fortune, Forbes*, and *Harvard Business Review.*

For government data:

Statistics Canada (www.statcan.ca) provides summary data on demographic, economic, social, and other aspects of the Canadian economy and society.

Industry Canada's Strategis website (www.strategis.ic.gc.ca) provides resources for Canadian businesses.

SEDAR (www.sedar.com) provides financial filings of Canadian public companies.

Securities and Exchange Commission Edgar database (www.sec.gov) provides financial data on U.S. public corporations.

Small Business: many provincial governments post sites aimed at helping small business (for example, see www.ontariobusinesscentral.ca/ and www.smallbusinessbc.ca/). There are also a number of commercial sites tailored to small business owners (for example, see http://sbinfocanada.about.com). *Small Business Canada Magazine* (www.sbcmag.com/) is another useful resource.

Stat-USA (www.stat.usa.gov), a U.S. Department of Commerce site, highlights statistics on U.S. business and international trade.

U.S. Census (www.census.gov) provides detailed statistics and trends about the U.S. population.

For Internet data:

CyberAtlas (http://cyberatlas.internet.com) brings together a wealth of information about the Internet and its users, from consumers to ecommerce.

Internet Advertising Bureau (www.iab.net) covers statistics about advertising on the Internet.

Jupiter Media Metrix (www.jmm.com) provides audience measurement and geodemographic analysis of Internet and digital media users around the world.

Monitor service by Yankelovich and Partners sells information on important social and lifestyle trends. NPD Canada maintains the country's longest-running national diary panel, the *Consumer Panel of Canada.* It also has an *OnLine Panel* that companies can use to get insights about Canada's Web-savvy population as well as specialized reports such as the *Canadian Apparel Market Monitor* and *National Eating Trends,* which reports on in-home and out-of-home consumption behaviour.

Using commercial **online databases,** marketing researchers can conduct their own searches of secondary data sources. General database services such as CompuServe, Dialog, and LEXIS-NEXIS put an incredible wealth of information at the keyboards of marketing decision makers. Beyond commercial websites offering information for a fee, almost every industry association, government agency, business publication, and news medium offers free information to those tenacious enough to find their websites. There are so many websites offering data that finding the right ones can almost become an overwhelming task.

Secondary data can usually be obtained more quickly and at a lower cost than primary data. For example, an Internet or online database search might provide all the information that Campbell needs on soup, quickly and at low cost. A study to collect primary information might take weeks or months to complete and cost thousands of dollars. Also, secondary sources sometimes can provide data that an individual company cannot collect on its own—information that either is not directly available or would be too expensive to collect. For example, it would be too expensive for Campbell to conduct a continuing retail store audit to find out about the market shares, prices, and displays of competitors' brands. But it can buy the InfoScan service from Information Resources, Inc., which provides this information from thousands of scanner-equipped supermarkets in dozens of markets.

Online databases
Computerized collections of information available from online commercial sources or via the Internet.

Online database services such as Dialog put an incredible wealth of information at the keyboards of marketing decision makers. Dialog puts "information to change the world, or your corner of it" at your fingertips.

Secondary data can also present problems. The needed information may not exist—researchers can rarely obtain all the data they need from secondary sources. For example, Campbell will not find existing information about consumer reactions to new packaging that it has not yet placed on the market. Even when data can be found, they might not be very usable. The researcher must evaluate secondary information carefully to ensure that it is *relevant* (fits research project needs), *accurate* (reliably collected and reported), *current* (up-to-date enough for current decisions), and *impartial* (objectively collected and reported).

Primary Data Collection

Secondary data provide a good starting point for research and often help to define problems and research objectives. In most cases, however, the company must also collect primary data. Just as researchers must carefully evaluate the quality of secondary information, they must also take care when collecting primary data to ensure that it will be relevant, accurate, current, and unbiased. Table 6.2 shows that designing a plan for primary data collection calls for a number of decisions on *research approaches, contact methods, sampling plan*, and *research instruments*.

Research Approaches   Research approaches for gathering primary data include observation, surveys, and experiments.

Observational research is gathering primary data by observing relevant people, actions, and situations. For example, B2B office furniture manufacturer Steelcase observed how people work together in teams before designing its new line of furniture specifically for work teams. A consumer packaged-goods marketer might visit supermarkets and observe shoppers as they browse the store, pick up products and examine packages, and make actual buying decisions. Or a bank might evaluate possible new branch locations by checking traffic patterns, neighbourhood conditions, and the location of competing branches. Calgary-based Sunoco Energy Inc. went one step further when testing new retailing concepts for its gas bars. It set up brightly lit, fully stocked, totally refurbished—and fake—convenience stores. It tested everything from different combinations of bold colours to placement of the lottery terminals to the placement of healthy snacks. With margins razor thin, Sunoco knew that if it didn't have attractive convenience stores as well as gas pumps, it would lose out on sales in a highly competitive market.[16]

A wide range of companies now use *ethnographic research*—which combines intensive observation with customer interviews—to gain deep insights into how customers buy and live with their products (see Real Marketing 6.1 on page 224).

Many companies collect data through *mechanical* observation via machine or computer. Other companies use *checkout scanners* to record shoppers' purchases so that manufacturers and retailers can assess product sales and store performance. And DoubleClick, among other Internet companies, places a *cookie*—a bit of information—on consumers' hard drives to monitor their Web-surfing patterns. Similarly, MediaMetrix places special software on consumers' PCs to monitor Web-surfing patterns and produce ratings for top websites.

Observational research

The gathering of primary data by observing relevant people, actions, and situations.

Table 6.2 Planning Primary Data Collection

Research Approaches	Contact Methods	Sampling Plan	Research Instruments
Observation	Mail	Sampling unit	Questionnaire
Survey	Telephone	Sample size	Mechanical instruments
Experiment	Personal	Sampling procedure	Online

Sunoco set up "dummy" convenience stores so that it could test different retail concepts that would help it maximize the profits new store formats would generate.

Observational research can be used to obtain information that people are unwilling or unable to provide. In some cases, observation may be the only way to obtain the needed information. In contrast, some things simply cannot be observed, such as feelings, attitudes and motives, or private behaviour. Long-term or infrequent behaviour is also difficult to observe. Because of these limitations, researchers often use observation along with other data collection methods.

Survey research, the most widely used method for primary data collection, is the approach best suited for gathering *descriptive* information. A company that wants to know about people's knowledge, attitudes, preferences, or buying behaviour often can find out by asking individuals directly.

Some firms provide marketers with a more comprehensive look at buying patterns through **single-source data systems**. These systems start with surveys of huge consumer panels—carefully selected groups of consumers who agree to participate in ongoing research. Then they electronically monitor survey respondents' purchases and exposure to various marketing activities. Combining the survey and monitoring information gives a better understanding of the link between consumer characteristics, attitudes, and purchase behaviour.

The major advantage of survey research is its flexibility. It can be used to obtain many different kinds of information in many different situations. However, survey research also presents some problems. Sometimes people are unable to answer survey questions because they cannot remember or have never thought about what they do and why. David Rider had just this problem. At first, he thought he had hit gold when he qualified to participate in a research study that allowed him to sample free beer. But when he noticed other testers flipping through their pages faster than he did, he was in a sweat. Confronted by 32 multiple-choice questions about each beer he sampled, he faced questions he had never thought of—"How strong is the alcohol taste? Does it have a real beer taste? Does it taste malty, yeasty, nutty, crisp?" His head swirling, feeling as if he'd sampled too much brew, he confessed,

Survey research
The gathering of primary data by asking people questions about their knowledge, attitudes, preferences, and buying behaviour.

Single-source data systems
Electronic monitoring systems that link consumers' exposure to television advertising and promotion (measured using television meters) with what they buy in stores (measured using store checkout scanners).

REAL MARKETING

6.1   Ethnographic Research: Keeping a Close Eye on Consumers

What do customers *really* think about your product and what do they say about it to their friends? How do they *really* use it? Will they tell you? *Can* they tell you? These are difficult questions for most marketers. And too often, traditional research simply can't provide accurate answers. To get better insights, many companies are now turning to an increasingly popular research approach—ethnographic research.

Ethnographic research involves sending trained observers to watch consumers in their "natural environment"—to observe up close the subtleties of how consumers use and feel about products and services.

The 60-ish woman caught on the grainy videotape is sitting on her hotel bed, addressing her husband after a long day spent on the road. "Good job!" she exults. "We beat the s*** out of the front desk and got a terrific room." No, this wasn't an FBI sting operation. Instead, the couple was part of [an ethnographic study in which Best Western

Observing consumers in their "natural environment": Ethnographic researchers videotaped consumers pondering "the dreaded sea of red meat" at their local super markets. The conclusion? Confusion. As a result, many grocers now display beef by cooking method rather than by cuts of meat.

International] paid 25 over-55 couples to tape themselves on cross-country journeys. The effort convinced the hotel chain that it didn't need to boost its standard 10 percent senior citizen discount. The tapes showed that seniors who talked the hotel clerk into a better deal didn't need the lower price to afford the room; they were after the thrill of the deal. Instead of attracting new customers, bigger discounts would simply allow the old customers to trade up to a fancier dinner down the street somewhere, doing absolutely nothing for Best Western....Best Western captured such a wealth of customer behaviour on tape that it has delayed its marketing plan in order to weave the insights into its core strategy. Unfortunately for seniors, that means the rooms won't be getting any cheaper.

In today's intensely competitive marketplace, holding on to customers requires more than a superficial understanding of customers' interactions with a product. Companies must have a deep understanding of how customers feel about and interact with products, then adjust their marketing offers and programs accordingly. Ethnographic research helps provide such an understanding. It combines intense observation with customer interviews to get an up-close and personal view of how people actually live with products. Here's another example:

A woman is shopping for her family's meals for the week. She cruises past the poultry section, stopping only momentarily to drop a couple of packages of boneless chicken breasts into her cart. Then, the dreaded sea of red meat looms before her. Tentatively, she picks up a package of beef. "This cut looks good, not too fatty," she says, juggling her two-year-old on her hip. "But I don't know what it is. And I don't know how to cook it," she confesses. She trades it for a small package of sirloin and her regular order of ground beef. Scenes like this play out daily in supermarkets across the country. But this time, it's being captured on videotape, part of a recent ethnographic study of beef consumers for the U.S. National Cattlemen's Beef Association (NCBA) and major grocery retailers.

Knowing what consumers actually do with beef is vital

to the NCBA. Even though sales of ground beef have risen in recent years, other beef products have lost ground. To get a firsthand understanding of what really goes on in consumers' minds as they shop the meat case, NCBA researchers videotaped not only consumers' store behaviour but also their preparation habits at home. And they interviewed consumers at each step, asking what they thought about beef, why they did or didn't select particular cuts, their thoughts on meat department layouts, how they prepared the family meal, and the availability of recipes.

The conclusion? Confusion. Although the typical shopper would initially say that she wasn't confused about buying beef, "when we went deeper, we found that she wasn't confused because she always buys the same cuts—ground beef, boneless chicken breast, maybe one steak," says Kevin Yost, NCBA's director of consumer marketing. "When you start to broaden the range [of meat selections], she has no idea what you're talking about." The result? Many grocers' meat cases are now being rearranged to display beef by cooking method, rather than by cuts of meat. Simple, three-step cooking instructions will soon be printed on the packages.

Ethnographic research often yields the kinds of intimate details that just don't emerge from traditional focus groups. For example, focus groups told Best Western that it's the men who decide when to stop for the night and where to stay. The videotapes showed it was usually the women. And by videotaping consumers in the shower, plumbing fixture maker Moen uncovered safety risks that consumers didn't recognize—such as the habit some women had of holding on to one unit's temperature-control while shaving their legs. Moen would find it almost impossible to discover such design flaws simply by asking questions.

Procter & Gamble uses ethnographic snooping to try to come up with products that solve problems shoppers didn't even know they had:

Now this is reality TV. But the only one watching is Procter & Gamble. The giant consumer goods marketer now sends ethnographers and video crews into households around the world to capture, on tape, life's daily routines in all their boring glory. P&G thinks such voyeurism will yield a mountain of priceless insights into consumer behaviour that more traditional methods might miss. People, it seems, tend to have selective memories when talking to a market researcher. They might say, for example, that they brush their teeth every morning or indulge in just a few potato chips, when in fact they often forget to brush and eat the whole bag. After a subject family agrees to participate, video crews arrive at the home when the alarm clock rings in the morning and stay until bedtime, usually for a four-day stretch.

In a recent case, P&G marketers huddled around a laptop computer in a Cincinnati conference room to watch a mother make breakfast for her baby in a tidy kitchen in Thailand. She rests her baby on a hip with one arm and stirs a pot of noodles with her other hand. Then she brings baby and bowl to a table, sits the baby on her lap, and feeds him while he grabs for the spoon. Occasionally, she looks at a television set droning the morning news. The P&G managers note several things. She has only one hand to cook with. She isn't using a high chair. There aren't any toys strewn across the floor. "Notice how she glances at the TV while she's feeding the baby," says a P&G director of consumer and marketing knowledge. "You might not have caught some of these things if you had asked her." The behaviours that consumers don't talk about—such as multitasking while feeding a baby—could inspire product and package design in ways that give the company a real edge over rivals.

So, more and more, marketers are keeping a close eye on consumers. "Knowing the individual consumer on an intimate basis has become a necessity," says a research industry consultant, "and ethnography is the intimate connection to the consumer."

Sources: Excerpts adapted from Kendra Parker, "How Do You Like Your Beef?" *American Demographics,* January 2000, pp. 35–37; Gerry Khermouch, "Consumers in the Mist," *Business Week,* February 26, 2001, pp. 92–94; and Emily Nelson, "P&G Checks Out Real Life," *Wall Street Journal,* May 17, 2001, p. B1. For other examples, see Kitty McKinsey, "She Wants to Watch You," *Far Eastern Economic Review,* September 6, 2001, pp. 46–47; and Lawrence Osborne, "Consuming Rights of the Suburban Tribe," *New York Times,* January 13, 2002, p. 6.29.

"I'm honestly answering some questions but, for others, if the answer doesn't immediately pop into my head, I pick one at random and hurry on."[17]

People may also be unwilling to respond to unknown interviewers or talk about things they consider private. Respondents may answer survey questions even when they do not know the answer just to appear smarter or more informed. Or they may try to help the interviewer by giving pleasing answers. Finally, busy people may not take the time, or they might resent the intrusion into their privacy.

Experimental research
The gathering of primary data by selecting matched groups of subjects, giving them different treatments, controlling unrelated factors, and checking for differences in group responses.

Whereas observation is best suited for exploratory research and surveys for descriptive research, **experimental research** is best suited for gathering *causal* information. Experiments involve selecting matched groups of subjects, giving them different treatments, controlling unrelated factors, and checking for differences in group responses. Thus, experimental research tries to explain cause-and-effect relationships. Observation and surveys may be used to collect information in experimental research.

For example, before adding a new sandwich to the menu, McDonald's might use experiments to test the effects on sales of two different prices. It could introduce the new sandwich at one price in its restaurants in one city and at another price in restaurants in another city. If the cities are similar, and if all other marketing efforts for the burger are the same, then differences in sales in the two cities could be related to the price charged.

Contact Methods   Information can be collected by mail, by telephone, via personal interview, or online. Table 6.3 shows the strengths and weaknesses of each contact method.

Mail questionnaires can be used to collect large amounts of information at a low cost per respondent. Respondents may give more honest answers to more personal questions on a mail questionnaire than to an unknown interviewer in person or over the phone. However, mail questionnaires are not flexible—all respondents answer the same questions in a fixed order. Mail surveys usually take longer to complete, and the response rate—the number of people returning completed questionnaires—is often very low. Finally, the researcher often has little control over the mail questionnaire sample. Even with a good mailing list, it is hard to control *who* at the mailing address fills out the questionnaire.

Telephone interviewing is one of the best methods for gathering information quickly, and it provides greater flexibility than mail questionnaires. Interviewers can explain difficult questions, and, depending on the answers they receive, skip some questions or probe on others. Response rates tend to be higher than with mail questionnaires, and interviewers can ask to speak to respondents with the desired characteristics, or even by name.

However, with telephone interviewing, the cost per respondent is higher than with mail questionnaires. Also, people may not want to discuss personal questions with an interviewer. The method also introduces interviewer bias—the way interviewers talk, how they ask questions, and other differences may affect respondents'

Table 6.3   Strengths and Weaknesses of Contact Methods

	Mail	Telephone	Personal	Online
1. Flexibility	Poor	Good	Excellent	Good
2. Quantity of data that can be collected	Good	Fair	Excellent	Good
3. Control of interviewer effect	Excellent	Fair	Poor	Fair
4. Control of sample	Fair	Excellent	Fair	Poor
5. Speed of data collection	Poor	Excellent	Good	Excellent
6. Response rate	Poor	Good	Good	Good
7. Cost	Good	Fair	Poor	Excellent

Source: Adapted with permission from *Marketing Research: Measurement and Method,* 7th ed., by Donald S. Tull and Del I. Hawkins. Copyright 1993 by Macmillan Publishing Company.

answers. Finally, different interviewers may interpret and record responses differently and, under time pressures, some interviewers might even cheat by recording answers without asking questions.

Personal interviewing takes two forms—individual and group interviewing. *Individual interviewing* involves talking with people in their homes or offices, on the street, or in shopping malls. Such interviewing is flexible. Trained interviewers can guide interviews, explain difficult questions, and explore issues. They can show subjects actual products, advertisements, or packages and observe reactions and behaviour. In most cases, personal interviews can be conducted fairly quickly. However, individual personal interviews can cost three to four times as much as telephone interviews.

Group interviewing consists of inviting six to ten people to talk with a trained moderator about a product, service, or organization. Participants typically are paid a small sum for attending. The moderator encourages free and easy discussion, hoping that group interactions will bring out actual feelings and thoughts. At the same time, the moderator "focuses" the discussion—hence the name **focus group interviewing**. The comments are recorded in writing or on videotape for study later.

Focus group interviewing has become one of the major marketing research tools for gaining insight into consumer thoughts and feelings. However, focus group studies usually employ small sample sizes to keep time and costs down, and it may be hard to generalize from the results. Because interviewers have more freedom in personal interviews, the problem of interviewer bias is greater.

Today, modern communications technology is changing the way that focus groups are conducted:

> Video-conferencing links, television monitors, remote-control cameras, and digital transmission are boosting the amount of focus group research done over long-distance lines. In a typical video-conferencing system, two cameras focused on the group are controlled by clients who hold a remote keypad. Executives in a far-off boardroom can zoom in on faces and pan the focus group at will. A two-way sound system connects remote viewers to the backroom, focus group room, and directly to the monitor's earpiece. Recently, while testing new product names in one focus group, the [client's] creative director had an idea and contacted the moderator, who tested the new name on the spot.[18]

Focus group interviewing
Personal interviewing that involves inviting six to ten people to gather for a few hours with a trained interviewer to talk about a product, service, or organization. The interviewer "focuses" the group discussion on important issues.

Video-conferencing allows executives in far-off boardrooms to "sit in" on focus group sessions.

Another form of interviewing is *computer-assisted interviewing*, a contact method in which respondents sit at computers, read questions on the screen, and type in their own answers while an interviewer is present. The computers might be located at a research centre, trade show, shopping mall, or retail location.

The latest technology to hit marketing research is the Internet. Increasingly, marketing researchers are collecting primary data through **online (Internet) marketing research**—*Internet surveys, experiments,* and *online focus groups*. Online focus groups offer advantages over traditional methods:

> Janice Gjersten, director of marketing for an online entertainment company, wanted to gauge reaction to a new website. [She] contacted Cyber Dialogue, which provided focus group respondents drawn from its 10 000-person database. The focus group was held in an online chat room, which Gjersten "looked in on" from her office computer. Gjersten could interrupt the moderator at any time with flash emails unseen by the respondents. Although the online focus group lacked voice and body cues, Gjersten says she will never conduct a traditional focus group again. Not only were respondents more honest, but the cost for the online group was one-third that of a traditional focus group, and a full report came to her in one day, compared to four weeks.[19]

Although online research offers much promise, and some analysts predict that the Internet will soon be the primary marketing research tool, others are more cautious. Real Marketing 6.2 summarizes the advantages, drawbacks, and prospects for conducting marketing research on the Internet.

Sampling Plan   Marketing researchers usually draw conclusions about large groups of consumers by studying a small sample of the total consumer population. A **sample** is a segment of the population selected to represent the population as a whole. Ideally, the sample should be representative so that the researcher can make accurate estimates of the thoughts and behaviours of the larger population.

Designing the sample requires three decisions. First, *who* is to be surveyed (what *sampling unit*)? The answer to this question is not always obvious. For example, to study the decision-making process for a family automobile purchase, should the researcher interview the husband, wife, other family members, dealership salespeople, or all of these? The researcher must determine what information is needed and who is most likely to have it.

Second, *how many* people should be surveyed (what *sample size*)? Large samples give more reliable results than small samples. However, it is not necessary to sample the entire target market or even a large portion to get reliable results. If well chosen, samples of less than 1 percent of a population can often give good reliability.

Third, *how* should the people in the sample be *chosen* (what *sampling procedure*)? Table 6.4 on page 231 describes different kinds of samples. Using *probability samples*, each member of the population has a known chance of being included in the sample, and researchers can calculate confidence limits for sampling error. But when probability sampling costs too much or takes too much time, marketing researchers often take *non-probability samples*, even though their sampling error cannot be measured. These varied ways of drawing samples have different costs and time limitations, as well as different accuracy and statistical properties. Which method is best depends on the needs of the research project.

Research Instruments   In collecting primary data, marketing researchers have a choice of two main research instruments—the *questionnaire* and *mechanical devices*. The questionnaire is by far the most common instrument, whether administered in person, by phone, or online.

Questionnaires are very flexible—there are many ways to ask questions. *Closed-ended questions* include all the possible answers, and subjects make choices among them. Examples include multiple-choice questions and scale questions. *Open-ended questions* allow respondents to answer in their own words. In a survey of airline

Online (Internet) marketing research
Collecting primary data through Internet surveys, experiments, and online focus groups.

Sample
A segment of the population selected for marketing research to represent the population as a whole.

REAL MARKETING

6.2   Online Marketing Research

As more and more consumers connect with the Internet, an increasing number of marketers are moving their research onto the Web. Although online research currently makes up less than 5 percent of all marketing research spending, some industry insiders predict substantial growth. In as little as five years, some say, it could account for 50 percent of all research spending.

Web research offers some real advantages over traditional surveys and focus groups. The most obvious advantages are speed and low costs. Online focus groups require some advance scheduling, but results are practically instantaneous. Survey researchers routinely complete their online studies in only a matter of days. For example, consider a recent online survey by a soft drink company to test teenager opinions of new packaging ideas. The ten- to fifteen-minute Internet survey included dozens of questions along with 765 different images of labels, bottle shapes, and such. Some 600 teenagers participated over a three- to four-day

period. Detailed analysis from the survey was available just five days after all the responses had come in— lightning quick compared to offline efforts.

Internet research is also relatively low in cost. Participants can dial in for a focus group from anywhere in the world, eliminating travel, lodging, and facility costs. For surveys, the Internet eliminates most of the postage, phone, labour, and printing costs associated with other approaches. "The cost [of Web research] can be anywhere from 10 percent to 80 percent less," says Tod Johnson, head of NPD Group, a firm that conducts online research. Moreover, sample size has little influence on costs. "There's not a huge difference between 10 and 10 000 on the Web," says Johnson.

Online surveys and focus groups are also excellent for reaching the hard-to-reach—the often-elusive teen, single, affluent, and well-educated audiences. "It's very solid for reaching...doctors, lawyers, professionals—people you might have difficulty reaching because they are not interested in taking part in surveys," says Paul Jacobson, an executive of Greenfield Online. "It's also a good medium for reaching working mothers and others who lead busy lives. They can do it in their own space and at their own convenience." The Internet also works well for bringing together people from different parts of the country, especially those in higher-income groups who can't spare the time to travel to a central site.

However, using the Internet to conduct marketing research does have some drawbacks. For one, many consumers still don't have access to the Internet. That makes it difficult to construct research samples that represent a broad cross-section of the Canadian population. Still, as Internet usage broadens, many mainstream marketers are now using Web research. General Mills, for example, conducts 60 percent of its consumer research online, reducing costs by 50 percent. And UPS uses online research extensively. "Between 40 percent and 50 percent of our customers are online, so it makes sense," says John Gilbert, UPS marketing research manager. He finds little difference

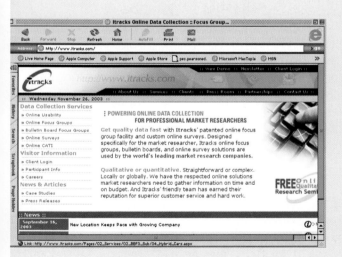

Saskatoon-based itracks offers data collection solutions that enable market researchers to gather rich and reliable data quickly and efficiently.

in the results of traditional and online studies, and the online studies are much cheaper and faster.

Another major problem of online research is controlling who's in the sample. Tom Greenbaum, president of Groups Plus, recalls a cartoon in the *New Yorker* in which two dogs are seated at a computer: "'On the Internet, nobody knows you're a dog,' one says to the other. If you can't see a person with whom you are communicating, how do know who they really are?" he says. To overcome such sample and response problems, many online research firms use opt-in communities and respondent panels. For example, Greenfield Online maintains a 1.3-million-member Internet-based respondent panel, recruited through cooperative marketing arrangements with other sites. Because such respondents opt in and can answer questions whenever they are ready, these online surveys yield high response rates. Whereas response rates for telephone surveys have plummeted to less

than 14 percent in recent years, online response rates typically reach 40 percent or higher.

Even when you reach the right respondents, online surveys and focus groups can lack the dynamics of more personal approaches. "You're missing all of the key things that make a focus group a viable method," says Greenbaum. "You may get people online to talk to each other and play off each other, but it's very different to watch people get excited about a concept." The online world is devoid of the eye contact, body language, and direct personal interactions found in traditional focus group research. And the Internet format—running, typed commentary and online "emoticons" (punctuation marks that express emotion, such as :-) to signify happiness)—greatly restricts respondent expressiveness.

Increasingly, however, advances in technology—such as the integration of animation, streaming audio and video, and virtual environments—will help to overcome these limitations. "In the online survey of the not-so-distant-future," notes an online researcher, "respondents will be able to rotate, zoom in on, and manipulate (like change the colour or size of) three-dimensional products. They'll be able to peruse virtual stores, take items off shelves, and see how they function."

Just as the impersonal nature of the Web hinders two-way interactions, it can also provide anonymity. This often yields less guarded, more honest responses, especially when participants discuss topics such as income, medical conditions, lifestyle, or other sensitive issues. "People hiding behind a keyboard get pretty brave," says one researcher. Adds another:

> From those questions that may simply make you squirm a little ("How much money did you lose in the stock market last month?"), to those you most probably don't want to answer to another human being, even if you don't know the person on the other end of the line ("How often do you have sex each week?"), Internet-based surveys tend to draw more honest responses. I once conducted the same survey in a mall and via the Internet. The question was, "How often do you bathe or shower each week?" The average answer, via the mall interview, was 6.2 times per week. The average via the Internet interview was 4.8 times per week, probably a more logical—and honest—response.

Perhaps the most explosive issue facing online researchers concerns consumer privacy. Critics worry that online researchers will spam our email boxes with unsolicited emails to recruit respondents. They fear that unethical researchers will use the email addresses

More and more companies are moving their research onto the Web. According to this Greenfield Online ad, in many ways, it "beats the old-fashioned kind."

and confidential responses gathered through surveys to sell products after the research is completed. They are concerned about the use of electronic agents (called Spambots or Spiders) that collect personal information without the respondents' consent. Failure to address such privacy issues could result in angry, less cooperative consumers and increased government intervention.

Although most researchers agree that online research will never completely replace traditional research, some are wildly optimistic about its prospects. Others, however, are more cautious. "Ten years from now, national telephone surveys will be the subject of research methodology folklore," proclaims one expert. "That's a little too soon," cautions another. "But in 20 years, yes."

Sources: Ian P. Murphy, "Interactive Research," *Marketing News,* January 20, 1997, pp. 1, 17; "NFO Executive Sees Most Research Going to Internet," *Advertising Age,* May 19, 1997, p. 50; Kate Maddox, "Virtual Panels Add Real Insight for Marketers," *Advertising Age,* June 29, 1998, pp. 34, 40; Jon Rubin, "Online Marketing Research Comes of Age," *Brandweek,* October 30, 2000, pp. 26–28; "Web Smart," *Business Week,* May 14, 2001, p. EB56; Noah Shachtman, "Web Enhanced Market Research," *Advertising Age,* June 18, 2001, p. T18; Thomas W. Miller, "Make the Call: Online Results Are a Mixed Bag," *Marketing News,* September 24, 2001, pp. 30–35; David Jamieson, "Online Research Gets Fewer Euro Votes," *Marketing News,* January 21, 2002, p. 15; Deborah Szynal, "Gaining Steam: Big Bytes," *Marketing News,* March 18, 2002, p. 3; and Mariam Mesbah, "Special Report: Research: Internet Research Holds Potential," *Strategy,* April 14, 1997, p. 40.

users, Air Canada might simply ask, "What is your opinion of Air Canada?" Or it might ask people to complete a sentence: "When I choose an airline, the most important consideration is..." These and other kinds of open-ended questions often reveal more than closed-ended questions because respondents are not limited in their answers. Open-ended questions are especially useful in exploratory research, when the researcher is trying to determine *what* people think but not measuring *how many* people think in a certain way. Closed-ended questions, on the other hand, provide answers that are easier to interpret and tabulate. (See Table 6.5 on page 232.)

Researchers should also use care in *wording* and *ordering* questions. They should use simple, direct, unbiased wording. Questions should be arranged in a logical order. The first question should create interest if possible, and difficult or personal questions should be asked last so that respondents do not become defensive. A carelessly prepared questionnaire usually contains many errors (see Table 6.6 on page 233).

Table 6.4   Types of Samples

Probability Sample	
Simple random sample	Every member of the population has a known and equal chance of selection.
Stratified random sample	The population is divided into mutually exclusive groups (such as age groups), and random samples are drawn from each group.
Cluster (area) sample	The population is divided into mutually exclusive groups (such as blocks), and the researcher draws a sample of the groups to interview.
Non-probability Sample	
Convenience sample	The researcher selects the easiest population members from which to obtain information.
Judgment sample	The researcher uses his or her judgment to select population members who are good prospects for accurate information.
Judgment sample	The researcher finds and interviews a prescribed number of people in each of several categories.

Table 6.5 Types of Questions

A. Closed-ended Questions

Name	Description	Example
Dichotomous	A question offering two answer choices.	"In arranging this trip, did you personally phone Air Canada?" Yes ☐ No ☐
Multiple choice	A question offering three or more answer choices.	"With whom are you travelling on this fight?" No one ☐ Children only ☐ Spouse ☐ Business associates/friends/relatives ☐ Spouse and children ☐ An organized tour group ☐
Likert scale	A statement with which the respondent shows the amount of agreement or disagreement.	"Small airlines generally give better service than large ones." Strongly disagree / Disagree / Neither agree nor disagree / Agree / Strongly agree 1 ☐ 2 ☐ 3 ☐ 4 ☐ 5 ☐
Semantic differential	A scale is inscribed between two bipolar words, and the respondent selects the point that represents the direction and intensity of his or her feelings.	*Air Canada* Large __X__ : ____ : ____ : ____ : ____ : ____ : Small Experienced ____ : ____ : ____ : ____ : __X__ : ____ : Inexperienced Modern ____ : ____ : ____ : __X__ : ____ : ____ : Old-fashioned
Importance scale	A scale that rates the importance of some attribute from "not at all important" to "extremely important."	"Airline food service to me is" Exremely important 1 ____ / Very important 2 ____ / Somewhat important 3 ____ / Not very important 4 ____ / Not at all important 5 ____
Rating scale	A scale that rates some attribute from "poor" to "excellent."	"Air Canada's food service is" Excellent 1 ____ / Very good 2 ____ / Good 3 ____ / Fair 4 ____ / Poor 5 ____
Intention-to-buy scale	A scale that describes the respondent's intentions to buy.	"If in-flight telephone service were available on a long flight, I would" Definitely buy 1 ____ / Probably buy 2 ____ / Not certain 3 ____ / Probably not buy 4 ____ / Definitely not buy 5 ____

B. Open-ended Questions

Name	Description	Example
Completely unstructured	A question that respondents can answer in an almost unlimited number of ways.	"What is your opinion of Air Canada?"
Word association	Words are presented, one at a time, and respondents mention the first word that comes to mind.	"What is the first word that comes to mind when you hear the following?" Airline _____ Canada _____ Travel _____
Sentence completion	Incomplete sentences are presented, one at a time, and respondents complete the sentence.	"When I choose an airline, the most important consideration in my decision is _____ "
Story completion	An incomplete story is presented, and respondents are asked to complete it.	"I flew Air Canada a few days ago. I noticed that the exterior and interior of the plane had very soft colours. This aroused in me the following thoughts and feelings." *Now complete the story.*
Picture completion	A picture of two characters is presented, with one making a statement. Respondents are asked to identify with the other and fill in the empty balloon.	Fill in the empty balloon.
Thematic Apperception Tests (TAT)	A picture is presented, and respondents are asked to make up a story about what they think is happening or may happen in the picture.	Make up a story about what you see.

Table 6.6 A "Questionable Questionnaire"

Suppose that a summer camp director had prepared the following questionnaire to use in interviewing the parents of prospective campers. How would you assess each question?

1. What is your income to the nearest hundred dollars?

People don't usually know their income to the nearest hundred dollars, nor do they want to reveal their income that closely. Moreover, a researcher should never open a questionnaire with such a personal question.

2. Are you a strong or a weak supporter of overnight summer camping for your children?

What do "strong" and "weak" mean?

3. Do your children behave themselves well at a summer camp? Yes ( ) No ( )

"Behave" is a relative term. Furthermore, are "yes" and "no" the best response options for this question? Besides, will people want to answer this? Why ask the question in the first place?

4. How many camps mailed literature to you last April? this April?

Who can remember this?

5. What are the most salient and determinant attributes in your evaluation of summer camps?

What are "salient" and "determinant" attributes? Don't use big words on me!

6. Do you think it is right to deprive your child of the opportunity to grow into a mature person through the experience of summer camping?

A loaded question. Given the bias, how can any parent answer "yes"?

Although questionnaires are the most common research instrument, *mechanical instruments* also are used to monitor consumer behaviour, such as supermarket cameras and people meters. Other mechanical devices measure subjects' physical responses. For example, a galvanometer detects the minute degree of sweating that accompanies emotional arousal. It can be used to measure the strength of interest or emotions aroused by a subject's exposure to marketing stimuli such as an ad or product. Eye cameras are used to study respondents' eye movements to determine at what points their eyes focus first and how long they linger on a given item. Here are examples of new technologies that capture information on consumers' emotional and physical responses:[20]

Mechanical measures of consumer response: devices are in the works that will allow marketers to measure facial expressions and adjust their offers or communications accordingly.

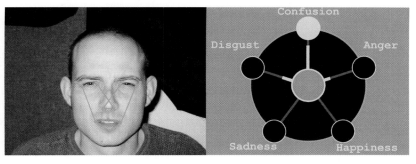

Machine response to facial expressions that indicate emotions will soon be a commercial reality. The technology discovers underlying emotions by capturing an image of a user's facial features and movements—especially around the eyes and mouth—and comparing the image against facial feature templates in a database. Hence, an elderly man squints at an ATM screen and the font size doubles almost instantly. A woman at a shopping centre kiosk smiles at a travel ad, prompting the device to print out a travel discount coupon. Several users at another kiosk frown at a racy ad, leading a store to pull it.

IBM is perfecting an "emotion mouse" that will figure out users' emotional states by measuring pulse, temperature, movement, and galvanic skin response. The company has mapped those measurements for anger, fear, sadness, disgust, happiness, and surprise. The idea is to create a style that fits a user's personality. An Internet marketer, for example, might offer to present a different kind of display if it senses that the user is frustrated.

Implementing the Research Plan

The researcher next puts the marketing research plan into action. This involves collecting, processing, and analyzing the information. The data collection phase of the marketing research process is generally the most expensive and the most subject to error. Researchers should watch fieldwork closely to ensure that the plan is implemented correctly and to guard against problems with contacting respondents, with respondents who refuse to cooperate or who give biased answers, and with interviewers who make mistakes or take shortcuts.

Researchers must process and analyze the collected data to isolate important information and findings. They need to check data for accuracy and completeness and code it for computer analysis. The researchers then tabulate the results and compute averages and other statistical measures.

Interpreting and Reporting the Findings

The marketing researcher must now interpret the findings, draw conclusions, and report them to management. The researcher should try not to overwhelm managers with numbers and fancy statistical techniques. Rather, the researcher should present important findings that are useful in the major decisions faced by management.

However, interpretation should not be left only to the researchers. They are often experts in research design and statistics, but the marketing manager knows more about the problem and the decisions that must be made. The best research is meaningless if the manager blindly accepts faulty interpretations from the researcher. Similarly, managers may be biased—they might accept research results that show what they expected and reject those that they did not expect or hope for. In many cases, findings can be interpreted in different ways, and discussions between researchers and managers will point to the best interpretations. Thus, managers and researchers must work closely when interpreting research results, and both must share responsibility for the research process and resulting decisions.

Analyzing Marketing Information

Information gathered in internal databases and through marketing intelligence and marketing research usually requires more analysis. And managers may need help in applying the information to their marketing problems and decisions. This help may include advanced statistical analysis to learn more about both the relationships within a set of data and their statistical reliability. Such analysis allows managers to go beyond means and standard deviations in the data and to answer questions about markets, marketing activities, and outcomes.

Information analysis might also involve a collection of analytical models that will help marketers make better decisions. Each model represents some real system, process, or outcome. These models can help answer the questions of *what if* and *which is best*. Marketing scientists have developed numerous models to help marketing managers make better marketing mix decisions, design sales territories and sales call plans, select sites for retail outlets, develop optimal advertising mixes, and forecast new-product sales.

Customer Relationship Management (CRM)

The question of how best to analyze and use individual customer data presents special problems. Most companies are awash in information about their customers. In fact, smart companies capture information at every possible customer *touch point*. These touch points include customer purchases, sales force contacts, service and support calls, website visits, satisfaction surveys, credit and payment interactions, market research studies—every contact between the customer and the company.

The trouble is that this information is usually scattered widely across the organization. It is buried deep in the separate databases, plans, and records of many different company functions and departments. To overcome such problems, many companies are now turning to **customer relationship management (CRM)** to manage detailed information about individual customers and carefully manage customer touch points in order to maximize customer loyalty. In recent years, there has been an explosion in the number of companies using CRM. In fact, the Canadian Marketing Association reports that expenditures for CRM-related systems will top $800 million in 2003 and will grow at a rate of 15 percent per year. It adds that 86 percent of Canadian companies now practise CRM in some form. The retail sector is the largest adopter, followed closely by the financial services and technology sectors.[21]

CRM consists of sophisticated software and analytical tools that integrate customer information from all sources, analyze it in depth, and apply the results to build stronger customer relationships. CRM integrates everything that a company's sales, service, and marketing teams know about individual customers to provide a 360-degree view of the customer relationship. It pulls together, analyzes, and provides easy access to customer information from all of the various touch points. Companies use CRM analysis to assess the value of individual customers, identify the best ones to target, and customize the company's products and interactions to each customer.

CRM analysts develop *data warehouses* and use sophisticated *datamining* techniques to unearth the riches hidden in customer data. A data warehouse is a company-wide electronic storehouse of customer information—a centralized database of finely detailed customer data that needs to be sifted through for gems. The purpose of a data warehouse is not to gather information—many companies have already amassed endless stores of information about their customers. Rather, the purpose is to allow managers to integrate the information the company already has. Then, once the data warehouse brings the data together for analysis, the company uses high-powered datamining techniques to sift through the mounds of data and dig out interesting relationships and findings about customers.

Companies can gain many benefits from customer relationship management. By understanding customers better, they can provide higher levels of customer service and develop deeper customer relationships. They can use CRM to pinpoint high-value customers, target them more effectively, cross-sell the company's products, and create offers tailored to specific customer requirements. Consider the following example:[22]

Customer relationship management (CRM)

Managing detailed information about individual customers and carefully managing customer touch points in order to maximize customer loyalty.

Siebel's CRM software integrates individual customer data from every touch point to help build customer relationships. Using CRM, the Siebel customer shown in this ad increased customer satisfaction by 86 percent and revenues per customer by 20 percent.

Our average revenue per customer has increased by 20%.

—Pierre Danon, CEO, BT Retail

Pierre Danon knows the importance of time. His 21 million customers expect a quick response. By using Siebel CRM software to streamline BT's Homemover program, call-handler satisfaction rose 34%. Customer satisfaction reached 86%. Revenues per customer rose 20%. And in just one 12-week period, 5,000 new accounts were identified. Timely improvements even the busiest CEO can appreciate.

SIEBEL

Good service is good business.

To learn more, call 1-800-307-2181 or visit siebel.com/casestudies.

Ping, the golf equipment manufacturer, has used CRM successfully for about two years. Its data warehouse contains customer-specific data about every golf club it has manufactured and sold for the past 15 years. The database, which includes grip size and special assembly instructions, helps Ping design and build golf clubs specifically for each of its customers and allows for easy replacement. If a golfer needs a new nine iron, for example, he [or she] can call in the serial number and Ping will ship an exact club to him [or her] within two days of receiving the order—a process that used to take two to three weeks....This faster processing of data has given Ping a competitive edge in a market saturated with new products. "We've been up; the golf market has been down," says Steve Bostwick, Ping's marketing manager. Bostwick estimates the golf market to be down about 15 percent, but he says Ping has experienced double-digit growth.

Most experts believe that good customer data, by itself, can give companies a substantial competitive advantage. Just ask American Express. At a secret location in Phoenix, security guards watch over American Express's 500 billion bytes of data on how customers have used its 35 million green, gold, and platinum charge cards. Amex uses the database to design carefully targeted offers in its monthly mailing of millions of customer bills.

CRM benefits don't come without cost or risk, not only in collecting the original customer data but also in maintaining and mining it. As noted earlier, Canadian firms are spending huge sums on CRM software. Yet more than half of all CRM efforts fail to meet their objectives. The most common cause of CRM failures is that companies mistakenly view CRM only as a technology and software solution.[23] But technology alone cannot build profitable customer relationships. "CRM is not a technology solution—you can't achieve...improved customer relationships by simply slapping in some software," says a CRM expert. Instead, CRM is just one part of an effective overall *customer relationship strategy*. "Focus on the *R*," advises the expert. "Remember, a relationship is what CRM is all about."[24]

When it works, the benefits of CRM can far outweigh the costs and risks. Based on regular polls of its customers, Siebel Systems claims that customers using its CRM software report an average 16 percent increase in revenues and 21 percent increase in customer loyalty and staff efficiency. "No question that companies are getting tremendous value out of this," says a CRM consultant. "Companies [are] looking for ways to bring disparate sources of customer information together, then get it to all the customer touch points." The powerful new CRM techniques can unearth "a wealth of information to target that customer, to hit their hot button."[25]

Distributing and Using Marketing Information

Marketing information has no value until it is used to make better marketing decisions. Thus, the marketing information system must make the information available to the managers and others who make marketing decisions or deal with customers on a day-to-day basis. In some cases, this means providing managers with regular performance reports, intelligence updates, and reports on the results of research studies.

But marketing managers may also need non-routine information for special situations and on-the-spot decisions. For example, a sales manager having trouble with a large customer may want a summary of the account's sales and profitability over the past year. Or a retail store manager who has run out of a best-selling product may want to know the current inventory levels in the chain's other stores. Increasingly, therefore, information distribution involves entering information into databases and making these available in a user-friendly and timely way.

Many firms use a company *intranet* to facilitate this process. The intranet provides ready access to research information, stored reports, shared work documents, contact information for employees and other stakeholders, and more. For example, iGo, a catalogue and Web retailer, integrates incoming customer service calls with up-to-date database information about customers' Web purchases and email inquiries. By accessing this information on the intranet while speaking with the customer, iGo's service representatives can get a well-rounded picture of each customer's purchasing history and previous contacts with the company.

In addition, companies are increasingly allowing key customers and value-network members to access account and product information and other data on demand on *extranets*. Suppliers, customers, and select other network members may access a company's extranet to update their accounts, arrange purchases, and check orders against inventories to improve customer service. For example, one insurance firm allows its 200 independent agents access to a Web-based database of claim information covering 1 million customers. This allows the agents to avoid high-risk customers and to compare claim data with their own customer databases.[26]

Thanks to modern technology, today's marketing managers can gain direct access to the information system at any time and from virtually any location. They can tap into the system while working at a home office, in a hotel room, at an airport—anyplace where they can turn on a laptop computer and link up. Such systems allow managers to get the information they need directly and quickly and to tailor it to their own needs. From just about anywhere, they can obtain information from company or outside databases, analyze it using statistical software, prepare reports and presentations, and communicate electronically with others in the network.

Other Marketing Research Considerations

This section discusses marketing research in two special contexts: marketing research by small businesses and non-profit organizations, and international marketing research. Finally, we look at public policy and ethical issues in marketing research.

Marketing Research in Small Businesses and Non-profit Organizations

Just like larger firms, small organizations need market information. Start-up businesses need information about their industries, competitors, potential customers, and reactions to new market offers. Existing small businesses must track changes in customer needs and wants, reactions to new products, and changes in the competitive environment.

Managers of small businesses and non-profit organizations often believe that marketing research can be done only by experts in large companies with big research budgets. True, large-scale research studies are beyond the budgets of most small businesses. However, many of the marketing research techniques discussed in this chapter also can be used by smaller organizations in a less formal manner and at little or no expense.

Managers of small businesses and non-profit organizations can obtain good marketing information simply by *observing* things around them. For example, retailers can evaluate new locations by observing vehicle and pedestrian traffic. They can monitor competitor advertising by collecting ads from local media. They can evaluate their customer mix by recording how many and what kinds of customers shop in the store at different times. They can monitor competitor advertising by collecting advertisements from local media. In addition, many small-business managers routinely

Small business owners can get a wealth of information and advice on websites such as the one posted by the British Columbia government.

visit their rivals and socialize with competitors to gain insights. Tom Coohill, a chef who owns two Atlanta restaurants, gives managers a food allowance to dine out and bring back ideas. Atlanta jeweller Frank Maier Jr., who often visits out-of-town rivals, spotted and copied a dramatic way of lighting displays.[27]

Small organizations can obtain most of the secondary data available to large businesses. In addition, many associations, local media, chambers of commerce, and government agencies provide special help to small organizations. The Conference Board of Canada, federal government, and provincial governments offer dozens of free publications that give advice on topics ranging from preparing a business plan to ordering business signs. Local newspapers often provide information on local shoppers and their buying patterns. Many business schools will conduct marketing research for no charge as part of class projects.

In summary, secondary data collection, observation, surveys, and experiments can all be used effectively by small organizations with small budgets. Although these informal research methods are less complex and less costly, they must still be conducted carefully. And with surveys, managers must think carefully about the objectives of the research, formulate questions in advance, recognize the biases introduced by smaller samples and less skilled researchers, and conduct the research systematically.[28]

International Marketing Research

International marketing researchers follow the same steps as domestic researchers, from defining the research problem and developing a research plan to interpreting and reporting the results. However, these researchers often face more and different problems. Whereas domestic researchers deal with fairly homogeneous markets within a single country, international researchers deal with differing markets in many different countries. These markets often vary greatly in their levels of economic development, cultures and customs, and buying patterns.

In many foreign markets, the international researcher sometimes has a difficult time finding good secondary data. Whereas North American marketing researchers can obtain reliable secondary data from dozens of domestic research services, many countries have almost no research services at all. Some of the largest international research services do operate in many countries. For example, Ipsos-Reid (www.ipsos-reid.com/) annually collects information on corporate and brand images, product usage and awareness, and values attitudes from 25 000 consumers living in 50 countries. ACNielsen Corporation (www.acnielsen.com/), the world's largest marketing research company, has offices in more than 100 countries. And 49 percent of the revenues of the world's 25 largest marketing research firms come from outside their home countries.[29] However, most research firms operate in only a relative handful of countries. Thus, even when secondary information is available, it usually must be obtained from many different sources on a country-by-country basis, making the information difficult to combine or compare.

Because of the scarcity of good secondary data, international researchers often must collect their own primary data. Here again, researchers face problems not found domestically. For example, they may find it difficult simply to develop good samples. North American researchers can use current telephone directories, census tract data, and any of several sources of socioeconomic data to construct samples. However, such information is largely lacking in many countries.

To expand their ability to meet the research needs of their international clients, many Canadian research firms are forming alliances with other research firms throughout the world. Such partnerships allow Canadian firms to gather information in numerous markets since their partners speak the language and are familiar with the nuances of the local culture. It helps them find *secondary data* for that market and assess the reliability of that data. Millward Brown's Canadian unit, for example, achieved its global profile after conducting a 36-country brand development study for Levi Strauss. As Michael Adams, president of Toronto-based Environics, noted, "Multinational companies don't care if you're from Hamburg, Chicago or Toronto—they just want you to be able to deliver the goods."[30] (See Real Marketing 6.3 for a profile of a young Canadian marketer at P&G Canada.)

International marketing research can pose some unique challenges. For example, it may be difficult to develop good samples. Whereas North American researchers can use current telephone directories, census tract data, and several other sources of socioeconomic data to construct samples, such information is largely lacking in many countries.

Once the sample is drawn, the North American researcher can usually reach most respondents easily by telephone, by mail, on the Internet, or in person. Reaching respondents is often not as easy in other parts of the world. Researchers in Mexico cannot rely on telephone and mail data collection—most data collection is conducted door-to-door and concentrated in three or four of the largest cities. In some countries, few people have phones—there are only 32 phones per thousand people in Argentina. In other countries, the postal system is notoriously unreliable. In Brazil, for instance, an estimated 30 percent of the mail is never delivered. In many developing countries, poor roads and transportation systems make certain areas hard to reach, making personal interviews difficult and expensive. Finally, few people in developing countries are connected to the Internet.[31]

Some of the largest research services operate in many countries. Roper Starch Worldwide provides companies with information resources "from Brazil to Eastern Europe; from Cape Town to Beijing—if you are there, Roper Starch Worldwide is there."

REAL MARKETING

6.3   Vanessa Vachon, Consumer & Market Knowledge, Procter & Gamble Canada

Vanessa Vachon began her career as an associate manager in the Consumer & Market Knowledge department at Procter & Gamble Canada. She was recently transferred to Switzerland. Procter & Gamble is truly a global organization, with operations in 70 countries throughout the Americas, Africa, Asia, Europe, and the Middle East. It sells over 300 products to five billion consumers in 150 countries around the world.

P&G's aim is to improve the lives of the world's consumers. The company's success has been driven by two main factors: first, its ability to identify and understand consumers' needs all around the globe, and, second, to satisfy those needs currently and over time by using both creative and technical skills. P&G is recognized in the industry for being on the leading edge of consumer knowledge.

The Consumer & Market Knowledge department plays an important role in the company's success. The purpose of the department is to obtain a high level of consumer intelligence, insight, and innovation, as well as leverage research tools to effectively help initiatives

Vanessa Vachon.

progress from the idea generation stage, to successful marketplace introduction and sustained superior performance over time. The department is also instrumental in the development of new research techniques and analysis to enhance superior consumer understanding.

Vanessa graduated from Queen's University with a Bachelor in Commerce (Honours) in April of 2000. At school, she always had a broad range of interests in both her classes and extracurricular activities. For this reason, she did not specialize in a particular area and continued taking courses in marketing, finance, international business, industrial relations, accounting, and business policy. In addition, she also did extensive work with the Association of Collegiate Entrepreneurs, working on business ventures, and leading a conference for the club.

Although Vanessa hadn't planned to become a market researcher, her analysis of her skills and interests, which ranged from psychology to mathematics and advanced analysis, as well as her interest in international business and marketing led her to join the Consumer & Market Knowledge (market research) department at Procter & Gamble. She found a good fit, having a personality that is challenge-seeking, creative, motivated, and enthusiastic, with a passion for winning.

Vanessa thinks Procter & Gamble is a great company that gives its employees the option to specialize in a discipline or develop broader skills across functions. It has excellent training programs and truly values every individual employee. It offers people many personal growth opportunities and challenges. P&G strongly believes that whenever you get too comfortable in a position, it's time to disturb the status quo.

As an associate manager in Consumer & Market Knowledge for Beauty Care, Vanessa's primary role is to be the expert in consumer understanding for her business teams. In her role, she must assess the need to conduct research, and then design, field, and analyze research that will fill knowledge gaps and answer business questions. She provides perspective and recommendations on the viability and success potential of initiatives in the Canadian market. She identifies creative and more efficient ways to target consumers. And, finally, she experiments with new research approaches and techniques.

Day to day, she participates in business team discussions and collaborates on a one-on-one basis with colleagues from other functions in both strategic and tactical discussions. She talks to her counterparts in different P&G sites around the world to share information on consumers. She collaborates with suppliers to design research that will best answer her teams' questions. Finally, she taps into the vast pool of data at P&G to broaden her understanding of Canadian consumers.

Vanessa's biggest hurdle when first joining P&G was learning to make timely decisions and recommendations with limited information. Unlike her experiences at school, she had no case studies with organized information to help her in her task. Vanessa found it challenging to clearly identify underlying issues and business questions and then translate those into appropriate objectives and research designs. In addition, when analyzing the research, it is sometimes difficult to read between the lines and truly capture what consumers are telling you. Moreover, she had to translate her insights into actionable recommendations to business teams. Accomplishing this task meant Vanessa had to tap all the knowledge she acquired in school and during on-the-job training.

Vanessa is extremely motivated, positive, and enthusiastic. She can hardly believe all the skills she has learned, and all the projects she has worked on in only a short period of time with the company. Since day one, she has been given a large amount of responsibility and was treated as a full contributor by her business teams. She feels empowered by this amount of trust, and she truly feels privileged to have the opportunity to work with a team of brilliant individuals, all working toward constantly improving the lives of the world's consumers.

Cultural differences from country to country cause additional problems for international researchers. Language is the most obvious obstacle. For example, questionnaires must be prepared in one language and then translated into the languages of each country researched. Responses then must be translated back into the original language for analysis and interpretation. This adds to research costs and increases the risk of error.

Translating a questionnaire from one language to another is anything but easy. Many idioms, phrases, and statements mean different things in different cultures. For example, a Danish executive noted: "Check this out by having a different translator put back into English what you've translated from English. You'll get the shock of your life. I remember [an example in which] 'out of sight, out of mind' had become 'invisible things are insane.'"[32]

Consumers in different countries also vary in their attitudes toward marketing research. People in one country may be very willing to respond; in other countries, non-response can be a major problem. In some cultures, research questions often are considered too personal—for example, in many Latin American countries people may feel embarrassed to talk with researchers about their choices of shampoo, deodorant, or other personal care products. In most Muslim countries, mixed-gender focus groups are taboo, as is videotaping female-only focus groups.[33]

Even when respondents are *willing* to respond, they may not be *able* to because of high functional illiteracy rates. And middle-class people in developing countries often make false claims in order to appear well-off. For example, in a study of tea consumption in India, over 70 percent of middle-income respondents claimed that they used one of several national brands. However, the researchers had good reason to doubt these results—more than 60 percent of the tea sold in India is unbranded generic tea.

Despite these problems, the recent growth of international marketing has resulted in a rapid increase in the use of international marketing research. Global companies have little choice but to conduct such research. Although the costs and problems associated with international research may be high, the costs of not doing it—in terms of missed opportunities and mistakes—might be even higher. Once recognized, many of the problems associated with international marketing research can be overcome or avoided.

Public Policy and Ethics in Marketing Research

Most marketing research benefits both the sponsoring company and its consumers. Through marketing research, companies learn more about consumers' needs, resulting in more satisfying products and services. More than 7 million Canadians take part in surveys each year and more than two thirds of Canadians have participated at some time in a research study and found it a pleasant experience. In fact, 83 percent believe that participation in survey research gives them an opportunity to provide useful feedback to organizations. However, a growing number of Canadians (57 percent) find survey questions too personal. Clearly, the misuse of marketing research can harm or annoy consumers. Two major public policy and ethics issues in marketing research are intrusions on consumer privacy and the misuse of research findings.[34]

Intrusions on Consumer Privacy

While many consumers feel positively about marketing research, others strongly resent or even mistrust it. A few consumers fear that researchers might use sophisticated techniques to probe their deepest feelings and then use this knowledge to manipulate their buying. Some fear the person at the other end of the phone and wonder about the character of the person to whom they are giving their information. Some Canadians had a right to worry. It wasn't until 2003 that Correctional Service Canada terminated its controversial call centre program, based in three federal penitentiaries. The program offered market research and telemarketing services to private sector clients, but the Solicitor General ended it after it was found that a number of security breaches had occurred.[35]

Many consumers worry about the privacy of their personal information and fear that marketers are building huge databases without their knowledge or permission. For example, DoubleClick has profiles on 100 million Web users. Privacy groups have worried that such huge profiling databases could be merged with offline databases and threaten individual privacy. In fact, DoubleClick did integrate its online data with that collected by a consumer panel firm to construct frighteningly accurate consumer profiles. It stirred up much controversy in both the U.S. and Canada when it announced that it would sell about 100 000 of these Web-user profiles to businesses, complete with names and contact information. David Jones, president of Electronic Frontier Canada in Kitchener, Ontario, says that what made DoubleClick's practice especially dubious is that it went on without the consumer being aware of it." Fearing government investigation and class-action suits, DoubleClick adopted sweeping privacy standards.[36]

Fifty-two percent of Canadians state they have been taken in by previous "research surveys" that actually turned out to be attempts to sell them something. Still other consumers confuse legitimate marketing research studies with telemarketing efforts and say "no" before the interviewer can even begin. Most, however, simply resent the intrusion. They dislike mail or telephone surveys that are too long or too personal or that interrupt them at inconvenient times.[37]

Increasing consumer resentment has become a major problem for the research industry. Response rates are falling throughout North America.[38] The research industry is considering several options for responding to this problem. One is to expand its "Your Opinion Counts" program to educate consumers about the benefits of marketing research and to distinguish it from telephone selling and database building. Another option is to provide a toll-free number that people can call to verify that a survey is legitimate.

Canada's new *Personal Information Protection and Electronic Documents Act*, which came into full force in 2004, helped resolve many of the concerns about personal privacy. Under its provisions, organizations must state the reasons why they are collecting the information. They must obtain consumers' consent before they can collect, use, or transfer information about an individual, and they must limit the information collected to the purpose they state at the beginning of the collection process. Moreover, every organization has to appoint a privacy officer to ensure compliance with the legislation and to field consumer inquiries and complaints. Organizations also have to ensure that the personal information they store is accurate and, upon request, they must inform an individual about the information they have on that individual and give him or her access to that information.[39] (See www.privcom.gc.ca/legislation for details.) In addition to the federal legislation, the Internet Advertising and Marketing Bureau of Canada (IAMBC) scrutinizes the practices of Internet marketers.

Some companies, like American Express, have taken privacy seriously long before there was legislation forcing them to take notice. According to Sally Cowan, who runs the privacy operations of American Express, "Privacy is not the new hot issue at American Express." The company developed a set of formal privacy principles in 1991, and in 1998 it became one of the first companies to post privacy policies on its website. This penchant for customer privacy led American Express to introduce new services that protect consumers' privacy when they use an American Express card to buy items online. American Express views privacy as a way to gain competitive advantage—as something that leads consumers to choose one company over another.[40]

In the end, if researchers provide value in exchange for information, customers will gladly supply it. For example, Amazon's customers do not mind if the firm builds a database of products they buy in order to make personalized future product recommendations. This saves time and provides value. Similarly, Bizrate users gladly complete surveys rating etail sites because they can view the overall ratings of others when making purchase decisions.

Misuse of Research Findings

Research studies can be powerful persuasion tools—companies often use study results as claims in their advertising and promotion. Today, however, many research studies appear to be little more than vehicles for pitching the sponsor's products. In fact, in some cases, the research surveys appear to have been designed just to produce the intended effect. Few advertisers openly rig their research designs or blatantly misrepresent the findings—most abuses tend to be subtle "stretches." Consider these examples:[41]

> A study by Chrysler contended that North Americans overwhelmingly prefer Chrysler to Toyota after test-driving both. However, the study included only 100 people in each of two tests. More importantly, none of the people surveyed owned a foreign car, so they appear to be favourably predisposed to North American produced cars.

> A Black Flag survey asked: "A roach disk...poisons a roach slowly. The dying roach returns to the nest and after it dies is eaten by other roaches. In turn these roaches become poisoned and die. How effective do you think this type of product would be in killing roaches?" Not surprisingly, 79 percent said "effective."

> A poll sponsored by the disposable diaper industry asked: "It is estimated that disposable diapers account for less than two percent of the garbage in today's landfills. In contrast, beverage containers, third-class mail, and yard waste are estimated to account for about 21 percent of the garbage in landfills. Given this, in your opinion, would it be fair to ban disposable diapers?" Not surprisingly, 84 percent said "no."

Thus, subtle manipulations of the study's sample, or the choice or wording of questions, can greatly affect the conclusions reached.

In other cases, so-called independent research studies are paid for by companies with an interest in the outcome. Small changes in study assumptions or in how results are interpreted can subtly affect the direction of the results. For example, at least four widely quoted studies compare the environmental effects of using disposable diapers to those of using cloth diapers. The two studies sponsored by the cloth diaper industry conclude that cloth diapers are more environmentally friendly. Not surprisingly, the other two studies, sponsored by the paper diaper industry, conclude just the opposite. Yet both appear to be correct *given* the underlying assumptions used.

Recognizing that surveys can be abused, several associations—including the Canadian Marketing Association, the Professional Marketing Research Society (PMRS), and the American Marketing Association—have developed codes of research ethics and standards of conduct. You can read the full codes on their websites (www.the-cma.org, www.pmrs-aprm.com, and www.marketingpower.com).[42] In the end, however, unethical or inappropriate actions cannot simply be regulated away. Each company must accept responsibility for policing the conduct and reporting of its own marketing research to protect consumers' best interests and its own.

Looking Back: Reviewing the Concepts

In today's complex and rapidly changing environment, marketing managers need more and better information to make effective and timely decisions. This greater need for information has been matched by the explosion of information technologies for supplying it. Using today's new technologies, companies can now handle great quantities of information—sometimes even too much. Yet marketers often complain that they lack enough of the *right* kind of information or have an excess of the wrong kind. In response, many companies are now studying their managers' information needs and designing information systems to help managers develop and manage market and customer information.

1. Explain the importance of information to the company.

Good products and marketing programs start with a thorough understanding of consumer needs and wants. Thus, the company needs sound information to produce superior value and satisfaction for customers. The company also requires information on competitors, resellers, and other actors and forces in the marketplace. Increasingly, marketers are viewing information not only as an input for making better decisions but also as an important strategic asset and marketing tool.

2. Define the marketing information system and discuss its parts.

The *marketing information system* (MIS) consists of people, equipment, and procedures to gather, sort, analyze, evaluate, and distribute needed, timely, and accurate information to marketing decision makers. A well-designed information system begins and ends with the user. The MIS first *assesses information needs*. The marketing information system primarily serves the company's marketing and other managers. However, it may also provide information to external partners, such as suppliers or marketing services agencies. Then, the MIS *develops information* from internal databases, marketing intelligence activities, and marketing research. *Internal databases* provide information on the company's own sales, costs, inventories, cash flows, and accounts receivable and payable. Such data can be obtained quickly and cheaply but often need to be adapted for marketing decisions. *Marketing intelligence* activities supply marketing executives with publicly available information about developments in the external marketing environment. *Marketing research* consists of collecting information relevant to a specific marketing problem faced by the company. Lastly, the MIS *distributes information* gathered from these many sources to the right managers in the right form and at the right time to help them make better marketing decisions.

3. Outline the four steps in the marketing research process.

The first step in the marketing research process involves *defining the problem and setting the research objectives,* which may be exploratory, descriptive, or causal. The second step consists of *developing a research plan* for collecting data from primary and secondary sources. The third step calls for *implementing the marketing research plan* by gathering, processing, and analyzing the information. The fourth step consists of *interpreting and reporting the findings.* Additional information analysis helps marketing managers apply the information and provides them with sophisticated statistical procedures and models from which to develop more rigorous findings. Both *internal* and *external* secondary data sources often provide information more quickly and at a lower cost than primary data sources, and they can sometimes yield information that a company cannot collect by itself. However, needed information might not exist in secondary sources, and, even if data can be found, they might be largely unusable. Researchers must also evaluate secondary information to ensure that it is *relevant, accurate, current,* and *impartial.* Primary research must also be evaluated for relevancy, accuracy, currency, and impartiality. Each primary data collection method—*observational, survey,* and *experimental*—has its own advantages and disadvantages.

4. Explain how companies analyze and distribute marketing information.

Information gathered in internal databases and through marketing intelligence and marketing research usually requires more analysis. This may include advanced statistical analysis or the application of analytical models that will help marketers make better decisions. In recent years, marketers have paid special attention to the analysis of individual customer data. Many companies have now acquired or developed special software and analysis techniques—called *customer relationship management (CRM)*—that integrate, analyze, and apply the mountains of individual customer data contained in their databases.

Marketing information has no value until it is used to make better marketing decisions. Thus, the marketing information system must make the information available to the managers and others who make marketing decisions or deal with customers. In some cases, this means providing regular reports and updates; in other cases it means making non-routine information available for special situations and on-the-spot decisions. Many firms use company intranets and extranets to facilitate this process. Thanks to modern technology, today's marketing managers can gain direct access to the information system at any time and from virtually any location.

5. Discuss the special issues some market researchers face, including public policy and ethics issues.

Some marketers face special situations, such as in conducting marketing research for small businesses, non-profit organizations, or international situations. Marketing research can be conducted effectively by small businesses and non-profit organizations with limited budgets. International marketing researchers follow the same steps as domestic researchers but often face more and different problems. All organizations need to respond responsibly to major public policy and ethical issues surrounding marketing research, including issues of intrusions on consumer privacy and misuse of research findings.

Reviewing the Key Terms

Discussing the Concepts

1. Many companies build extensive internal databases so that marketing managers can use them to identify marketing opportunities and problems, plan programs, and evaluate performance. If you were the marketing manager for a large motorcycle manufacturer, what types of information would you like to have available in your company's internal database? Explain.

2. Marketing intelligence has become increasingly important to marketing managers for formulating strategy. What other benefits are derived from the marketing intelligence function? Assume that you have been hired as a consultant to a company that is developing a new video/cell phone. What types of intelligence tips would you offer the firm?

3. Imagine that you are the marketing research manager for a small electronics firm that has recently changed management. You are concerned when you receive a memo stating that "marketing research is not really necessary as long as you have a good marketing information system." Write a brief response that outlines the role of marketing research and clarifies how it differs from MIS.

4. Research objectives must be translated into specific information needs. Assume that you are the marketing research director for Apple Computer. What specific information might you need to pick two new colours for the popular iMac line of personal computers? List and briefly justify your choices.

5. Name the type of research that would be appropriate in each of the following situations and explain why.

   a. Kellogg wants to investigate the impact of young children on their parents' decisions to buy breakfast foods.

   b. Your university bookstore wants to know how students would feel about adding a Starbucks coffee facility to the store's existing services.

   c. Swiss Chalet is considering where to locate a new outlet in a fast-growing suburb.

   d. Gillette wants to determine whether a new line of deodorant for teenagers will be profitable.

6. Focus group interviewing is both a widely used and widely criticized research technique in marketing. List the advantages and disadvantages of focus groups. Some experts suggest that the next frontier for focus group research will be the Internet. What are the advantages and disadvantages of using the Internet to conduct focus groups?

7. Assume that your local grocery store has implemented a store service card. The card allows customers to receive special discounts and cash personal cheques. Beginning with the registration process for the card and continuing through its use at the checkout stand, discuss all the types of data that could be collected and how the data could be used to build customer relationships without offending consumers or invading their privacy.

8. As marketing manager for an emerging cosmetics company, you believe it is time to expand into the global marketplace. The board of directors requests an outline of research required to prepare for such an expansion. Prepare a brief report comparing domestic and international marketing research. How might the company change its research approach to gather international data?

Applying the Concepts

1. Companies often conduct marketing research to examine changes in the marketing environment that may affect product design and marketing decisions. Consider the evolution of Barbie, Mattel's most popular doll. Throughout the decades, Barbie has transformed to reflect the changing values and lifestyles of North American women. In the 1950s, in keeping with women's predominant roles in society, Barbie was cast as a homemaker. But in the twenty-first century, Barbie reflects the diversity and individuality valued by today's girls. Mattel now offers NASCAR Barbie and veterinarian Barbie. Barbie even has her own website where girls can play games, create fashion makeovers, and read interactive books. By reinventing Barbie's image, Mattel has maintained the doll's popularity for more than 40 years and built Barbie into a $1.9 billion brand.

   a. Make a list of the ways Barbie has changed to meet the needs of the contemporary young woman. How do these changes affect female image, self-confidence, and prestige? What kind of research might Mattel conduct to examine these changes? Give examples.

b. The Barbie website (www.barbie.com) allows a young girl to custom-design her own Barbie doll. Go to the Fashion Star section and try it. What type of information has Mattel just collected about your demographics and preferences? How could this information be used to build "connections" with young women?

c. You are the marketing manager for a proposed new lifestyle doll for Mattel. Write a brief report outlining the types of research you would conduct to determine the attributes of the new doll. Include which markets and preferences you would collect information on and how you might use the Internet as a research tool.

2. The Internet provides a unique means for targeting minority market segments and gathering information about their preferences. Statistics Canada publishes a number of reports that can help marketers learn more about ethnic markets. Go to www.statcan.ca/english/ Pgdb/popula.htm#ori or www12.statcan.ca/english/census01/release/release4.cfm. The federal government's Canadian Heritage site on Multiculturalism (www.pch.gc.ca/progs/multi) has services of interest to both businesses and minorities. The Toronto-based Black Business and Professional Association (www.bbpa.org) draws consumers and advertisers interested in targeting this community.

a. What unique features of the above sites might assist marketers wishing to reach minority markets?

b. Using the Statistics Canada website (www.statcan.ca), determine the potential size of the Japanese Canadian, Chinese Canadian, and Black Canadian markets. What other information about these significant minorities can you find readily?

c. How might conducting marketing research on minority markets via the Internet differ from more traditional means of conducting research?

Video Short

View the video short for this chapter at **www.pearsoned.ca/kotler** and then answer the questions provided in the case description.

Company Case

Enterprise Rent-A-Car: Measuring Service Quality

Kevin Kirkman wheeled his shiny, blue BMW coupe into his driveway, parked the car, and stepped out to check his mailbox as he did every day when he arrived home. As he flipped through the deluge of catalogues and credit-card offers, he noticed a letter from Enterprise Rent-A-Car. He wondered why Enterprise would be writing to him.

The Wreck

Then he remembered. Earlier that month, Kevin had been involved in a car accident. As he was driving to work one rainy morning, another car had been unable to stop on the slick pavement and had plowed into his car as he waited at a stoplight. Thankfully, neither Kevin nor the other driver had been hurt, but both cars had sustained considerable damage. In fact, Kevin was not able to drive his car.

Kevin had used his cell phone to call the police; and while waiting for the officers to come he had called his auto insurance agent. The agent had assured Kevin that his policy included coverage to pay for a rental car while he was having his car repaired. He told Kevin to have the car towed to a nearby auto repair shop and gave him the telephone number for the Enterprise Rent-A-Car office that served his area. The agent noted that his company recommended using Enterprise for replacement rentals and that Kevin's policy would cover up to $25 per day of the rental fee.

Once Kevin had checked his car in at the body shop and made the necessary arrangements, he had called the Enterprise office. Within ten minutes, an Enterprise employee had arrived at the repair shop to pick him up. They drove back to the Enterprise office, where Kevin had completed the paperwork to rent a Ford Taurus. He drove the rental car for twelve days before the repair shop completed work on his car.

"Don't know why Enterprise would be writing me now," Kevin thought. "The insurance company paid the $25 per day, and I paid the extra because the Taurus cost a little more than that. Wonder what the problem could be?"

Tracking Customer Satisfaction

Kevin tossed the mail on the passenger's seat and drove up the driveway. Once inside his house, he opened the Enterprise letter to find that it was a survey to determine how satisfied he was with his rental experience. The survey itself was only one page long and consisted of thirteen questions (see Exhibit 1).

Enterprise's executives believed that the company had become the largest car rental company in North America (in terms of number of cars, rental locations, and revenue) because of its laser-like focus on customer satisfaction, and because of its concentration on serving the home-city replacement market. It aimed to serve customers like Kevin who were involved in car accidents and suddenly find themselves without a car. While the better-known companies such as Hertz and Avis battled for business in the cutthroat airport market, Enterprise quietly built its business by cultivating insurance agents and body-shop managers as referral agents, so that when one of their clients or customers needed a replacement vehicle, the agents would recommend Enterprise. Although such replacement rentals account for about 80 percent of Enterprise's business, the company also served the discretionary market (leisure/vacation rentals) and the business market (renting cars to businesses for their short-term needs). It had also begun to provide on-site and off-site service at some airports.

Throughout its history, Enterprise has followed the advice of its founder, Jack Taylor, who believed that if the company took care of its customers first and its employees second, profits would follow. As a result, the company was careful to track customer satisfaction.

About one in twenty customers receive a letter like Kevin's. An independent company mailed the letter and a postage-paid return envelope to the selected customers. Customers who completed the survey used the envelope to return it to the independent company. That company compiled the results and provided them to Enterprise.

Continuous Improvement

Meanwhile, back at Enterprise's headquarters, the company's top managers were interested in taking the next steps in their customer satisfaction program. Enterprise had used the percentage of customers who were completely satisfied to develop its Enterprise Service Quality index (ESQi). It used the survey results to calculate an overall average ESQi score for the company and a score for each individual branch. The company's branch managers believed in and supported the process.

However, top management believed that to really "walk the walk" on customer satisfaction, it needed to make the ESQi a key factor in the promotion process. The company wanted to take the ESQi for the branch or branches a manager supervised into consideration when it evaluated that manager for a promotion. Top management believed that such a process would ensure that its managers and all its employees would focus on satisfying Enterprise's customers.

However, the top managers realized they had two problems in taking the next step. First, they wanted a better survey response rate. Although the company got a 25 percent response rate, which was good for this type of survey, it was concerned that it might still be missing important information. Second, it could take up to two months to get results back, and Enterprise believed it needed a process that would get the customer satisfaction information more quickly, at least on a monthly basis, so its branch managers could identify and take action on customer service problems quickly and efficiently.

Enterprise's managers wondered how they could improve the customer-satisfaction-tracking process.

Questions for Discussion

1. Analyze Enterprise's Service Quality Survey. What information is it trying to gather? What are its research objectives?

2. What decisions has Enterprise made with regard to primary data collection—research approach, contact methods, sampling plan, and research instruments?

3. In addition to or instead of the mail survey, what other means could Enterprise use to gather customer satisfaction information?

Exhibit 1   Service Quality Survey

Please mark the box that best reflects your response to each question.

	Completely Satisfied	Somewhat Satisfied	Neither Satisfied Nor Dissatisfied	Somewhat Dissatisfied	Completely Dissatisfied
1. Overall, how satisfied were you with your recent car rental from Enterprise on January 1, 2003?	☐	☐	☐	☐	☐

2. What, if anything, could Enterprise have done better? (*Please be specific*) _____

_____

3a. Did you experience any problems during the rental process?	Yes ☐ No ☐	3b. If you mentioned any problems to Enterprise, did they resolve them to your satisfaction?	Yes ☐ No ☐ Did not mention ☐

	Excellent	Good	Fair	Poor	N/A
4. If you personally called Enterprise to reserve a vehicle, how would you rate the telephone reservation process?	☐	☐	☐	☐	☐

	Both at start and end of rental	Just at start of rental	Just at end of rental	Neither time
5. Did you go to the Enterprise office. . .	☐	☐	☐	☐

	Both at start and end of rental	Just at start of rental	Just at end of rental	Neither time
6. Did an Enterprise employee give you a ride to help with your transportation needs. . .	☐	☐	☐	☐

7. After you arrived at the Enterprise office, how long did it take you to:	Less than 5 minutes	5–10 minutes	11–15 minutes	16–20 minutes	21–30 minutes	More than 30 minutes	N/A
♦ pick up your rental car?	☐	☐	☐	☐	☐	☐	☐
♦ return your rental car?	☐	☐	☐	☐	☐	☐	☐

8. How would you rate the. . .	Excellent	Good	Fair	Poor	N/A
♦ timeliness with which you were either picked up at the start of the rental or dropped off afterwards?	☐	☐	☐	☐	☐
♦ timeliness with which the rental car was either brought to your location and left with you or picked up from your location afterwards?	☐	☐	☐	☐	☐
♦ Enterprise employee who handled your paperwork. . . at the START of the rental?	☐	☐	☐	☐	☐
at the END of the rental?	☐	☐	☐	☐	☐
♦ mechanical condition of the car?	☐	☐	☐	☐	☐
♦ cleanliness of the car interior/exterior?	☐	☐	☐	☐	☐

	Yes	No	N/A
9. If you asked for a specific type or size of vehicle, was Enterprise able to meet your needs?	☐	☐	☐

	Car repairs due to accident	All other car repairs/ maintenance	Car was stolen	Business	Leisure/ vacation	Some other reason
10. For what reason did you rent this car?	☐	☐	☐	☐	☐	☐

	Definitely will call	Probably will call	Might or might not call	Probably will not call	Definitely will not call
11. The next time you need to pick up a rental car in the city or area in which you live, how likely are you to call Enterprise?	☐	☐	☐	☐	☐

	Once—this was first time	2 times	3–5 times	6–10 times	11 or more times
12. Approximately how many times in total have you rented from Enterprise (including this rental)?	☐	☐	☐	☐	☐

	0 times	1 time	2 times	3–5 times	6–10 times	11 or more times
13. Considering *all rental companies,* approximately how many times *within the past year* have you rented a car in the city or area in which you live (including this rental)?	☐	☐	☐	☐	☐	☐

4. What specific recommendations would you make to Enterprise to improve the response rate and the timeliness of feedback from the process?

Sources: Officials at Enterprise Rent-A-Car contributed to and supported development of this case. See also Simon London, "Driving Home the Service Ethic," *Financial Times*, June 2, 2003, www.ft.com.

CBC Video Case

Log on to your Companion Website at **www.pearsoned.ca/kotler** to view a CBC video segment and case for this chapter.

Chapter 7

Consumer Markets and Consumer Buyer Behaviour

After studying this chapter you should be able to

1. define the consumer market and construct a simple model of consumer buyer behaviour

2. name the four major factors that influence consumer buyer behaviour

3. list and understand the major types of buying-decision behaviour and the stages in the buyer decision process

4. describe the adoption and diffusion process for new products

Looking Ahead: Previewing the Concepts

In the previous chapter, you studied how marketers obtain, analyze, and use information to identify marketing opportunities and to assess marketing programs. In this and the next chapter, we'll continue with a closer look at the most important element of the marketing environment—customers. The aim of marketing is to somehow affect how customers think about and behave toward the organization and its marketing offers. To affect the whats, whens, and hows of buying behaviour, marketers must first understand the *whys.* In this chapter, we look at *final consumer* buying influences and processes. In the next chapter, we'll study the buying behaviour of *business customers.* You'll see that understanding buying behaviour is an essential but very difficult task.

To get a better sense of the importance of understanding consumer behaviour, let's look first at Harley-Davidson, maker of North America's top-selling heavyweight motorcycles. Who rides these big Harley "Hogs"? What moves them to tattoo their bodies with the Harley emblem, abandon home and hearth for the open road, and flock to Harley rallies by the hundreds of thousands? You might be surprised, but Harley-Davidson knows very well.

Few brands engender such intense loyalty as that found in the hearts of Harley-Davidson owners. "The Harley audience is granite-like" in its devotion, laments the vice-president of sales for competitor Yamaha. Observes the publisher of *American Iron,* an industry publication, "You don't see people tattooing Yamaha on their bodies." In September 2002, the Harley-Davidson 100th Anniversary Open Road Tour thundered into Barrie, Ontario's Molson Park, the only Canadian stop on the ten-city tour. This was an event unlike any other in terms of its size and scope. Canadian bikers and their families had a once-in-a-lifetime chance to see The Doors and other international rock legends, plus Canadian favourites like Kim Mitchell and April Wine. They could wander through the exhibit "Art of the

Motorcycle" and get up close and personal with Elvis's and Jon Bon Jovi's Harleys. They could join other fans in the 1000-seat theatre showcasing Harley-Davidson's portrayal in the movies, while their kids could take demo rides on Fisher-Price Harley-Davidson ride-on motorcycle toys. And they could just feel good about the event: it helped raise funds to find a cure for muscular dystrophy and provide services for children and adults with neuromuscular diseases.

Harley-Davidson has rumbled its way to the top of the fast-growing heavyweight motorcycle market. Harley's "Hogs" capture more than one-fifth of all North American bike sales and more than half of the heavyweight segment. While you may think of Harley as the quintessential

American brand, it has a long history in Canada. Fred Deeley established the first Canadian dealership in 1917, making it the second-oldest Harley-Davidson dealership in the world. Today the firm acts as the sole distributor for all of Canada, and it is the only Harley distribution system not completely owned and controlled by the American parent. The firm's mission is to see the Harley-Davidson lifestyle as an increasing and permanent part of Canadian society. It works to accomplish this goal by being honest and keeping its promises while trusting and respecting others. The firm has been able to realize many of its dreams, and in recognition of its efforts has twice been placed on the prestigious list of Canada's 50 Best-Managed Companies.

Harley's sales are growing rapidly. In fact, for several consecutive years, sales have far outstripped supply, with customer waiting lists of up to three years for popular models and street prices running well above suggested list prices. "We've seen people buy a new Harley and then sell it in the parking lot for $5000 to $6500 more," says one dealer. Since its initial 1986 public stock offering, Harley-Davidson shares had split four times and were up more than 7100 percent. By 2003, the company had experienced 17 straight years of record sales and income.

Harley-Davidson's marketers spend a great deal of time thinking about customers and their buying behaviour. They want to know who their customers are, what they think and how they feel, and why they buy a Harley rather than a Yamaha, or a Suzuki, or a big Honda American Classic. What is it that makes Harley buyers so fiercely loyal? These are difficult questions—even Harley owners themselves don't know exactly what motivates their buying. But Harley management puts top priority on understanding customers and what makes them tick.

Who rides a Harley? You might be surprised. It's certainly not the Hell's Angels crowd—the burly, black-leather-jacketed rebels that once composed Harley's core clientele. Motorcycles are attracting a new breed of riders—older, more affluent, and better educated. Harley now appeals more to "rubbies" (rich urban bikers) than to rebels. The average Harley customer is a 46-year-old husband with a median household income of $101 700. Harley's big, comfortable cruisers give these new consumers the easy ride, prestige, and twist-of-the-wrist power they want and can afford.

Harley-Davidson makes good bikes, and, to keep up with its shifting market, the company has upgraded its showrooms and sales approaches. But Harley customers are buying a lot more than just a quality bike and a smooth sales pitch. To gain a better understanding of customers' deeper motivations, Harley-Davidson conducted focus groups in which it invited bikers to make cut-and-paste collages of pictures that expressed their feelings about Harley-Davidsons. (Can't you just see a bunch of hard-core bikers doing this?) The company then mailed out 16 000 surveys containing a typical battery of psychological, sociological, and demographic questions, as well as subjective questions such as, "Is Harley more typified by a brown bear or a lion?"

The research revealed seven core customer types: adventure-loving traditionalists, sensitive pragmatists, stylish status seekers, laid-back campers, classy capitalists, cool-headed loners, and cocky misfits. However, all owners appreciated their Harleys for the same basic reasons. "It didn't matter if you were the guy who swept the floors of the factory or if you were the CEO at that factory, the attraction to Harley was very similar," explains a Harley executive. "Independence, freedom, and power were the universal Harley appeals."

These studies confirm that Harley customers are doing more than just buying motorcycles. They're making a lifestyle statement and displaying an attitude. As one analyst suggests: "Never mind that [you're] a dentist or an accountant. You [feel] wicked astride all that power." Your Harley renews your spirits and announces your independence. As the Harley home page announces (www.harley-davidson.com), "Thumbing the starter of a Harley-Davidson does a lot more than fire the engine. It fires the imagination." Adds a Harley dealer: "We sell a dream here. Our customers lead hardworking professional or computer-oriented lives. Owning a Harley removes barriers to meeting people on a casual basis, and it gives you maximum self-expression in your own space." The classic look, the throaty sound, the very idea of a Harley—all contribute to its mystique. Owning this "North American legend" makes you a part of something bigger—a member of the Harley family. The fact that you have to wait to get a Harley makes it all that much more satisfying to have one. In fact, the company deliberately restricts its output. "Our goal is to eventually run production at a level that's always one motorcycle short of demand," says Harley-Davidson's chief executive.

Such strong emotions and motivations are captured in a classic Harley-Davidson advertisement. It shows a close-up of an arm, the biceps adorned with a Harley-Davidson tattoo. The headline asks, "When was the last time you felt this strongly about anything?" The ad copy outlines the problem and suggests a solution:

> Wake up in the morning and life picks up where it left off. You do what has to be done. Use what it takes to get there. And what once seemed exciting has now become part of the numbing routine. It all begins to feel the same. Except when you've got a Harley-Davidson. Something strikes a nerve. The heartfelt thunder rises up, refusing to become part of the background. Suddenly things are different. Clearer. More real. As they should have been all along. The feeling is personal. For some, owning a Harley is a statement of individuality. To the uninitiated, a Harley-Davidson motorcycle is associated with a certain look, a certain sound. Anyone who owns one will tell you it's much more than that. Riding a Harley changes you from within. The effect is permanent. Maybe it's time you started feeling this strongly. Things are different on a Harley.

While no one can question the passion Harley engenders in its buyers, the firm can't take a successful future for granted. As its core customers continue to age, Harley has to take better aim at young people. It needs to know what excites them about a brand. It already understands that young people want to ride anything but their Dad's hog. North American sales of light sport bikes targeted at 25- to 35-year-old men, for example, increased 90 percent from 1998 to 2001, but Harley's competitors (Suzuki, Honda, Yamaha, and Kawasaki) have gobbled up over 90 percent of this market. Harley is fighting back. It recently debuted a $25 000 Harley V-Rod, a low-slung, high-powered sports performance bike. However, the trick for Harley will be to appeal to this younger market without alienating its current fanatical customer base.[1]

The Harley-Davidson example shows that many factors affect consumer buying behaviour. Buying behaviour is never simple, yet understanding it is the essential task of marketing management.

This chapter explores the dynamics of consumer behaviour and the consumer market. **Consumer buying behaviour** refers to the buying behaviour of final consumers—individuals and households who buy goods and services for personal consumption. All of these final consumers together form the **consumer market**. The Canadian consumer market consists of about 31.4 million people who consume many billions of dollars worth of goods and services each year, making it one of the most attractive consumer markets in the world. The world consumer market consists of more than 6.2 *billion* people.[2]

Consumers around the world vary tremendously in age, income, education level, and tastes. They also buy an incredible variety of goods and services. How these diverse consumers connect with each other and with other elements of the world around them has an impact on their choices among various products, services, and companies. Here we examine the fascinating array of factors that affect consumer behaviour.

Consumer buying behaviour
The buying behaviour of final consumers—individuals and households who buy goods and services for personal consumption.

Consumer market
All the individuals and households who buy or acquire goods and services for personal consumption.

Model of Consumer Behaviour

Consumers make many buying decisions every day. Most large companies research consumer buying decisions in great detail to answer questions about what consumers buy, where they buy, how and how much they buy, when they buy, and why they buy. Marketers can study actual consumer purchases to find out the what, where, and how much. But learning about the *why* of consumer buying behaviour is not so easy—the answers are often locked deep in the consumer's head.

The central question for marketers is: How do consumers respond to various marketing efforts the company might use? The starting point is the stimulus–response model of buyer behaviour shown in Figure 7.1. This figure shows that marketing and other stimuli enter the consumer's "black box" and produce certain responses. Marketers must determine what is in the buyer's black box.

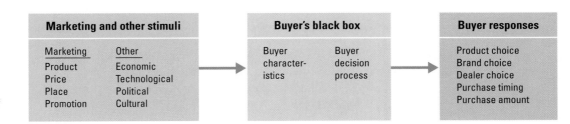

Figure 7.1 Model of buyer behaviour

Marketing and other stimuli		Buyer's black box		Buyer responses
Marketing	**Other**	Buyer character-	Buyer decision	Product choice
Product	Economic	istics	process	Brand choice
Price	Technological			Dealer choice
Place	Political			Purchase timing
Promotion	Cultural			Purchase amount

Marketing stimuli consist of the four *P*s: product, price, place, and promotion. Other stimuli include major forces and events in the buyer's environment: economic, technological, political, and cultural. All of these inputs enter the buyer's black box, where they are turned into a set of observable buyer responses: product choice, brand choice, dealer choice, purchase timing, and purchase amount.

The marketer wants to understand how the stimuli are changed into responses inside the consumer's black box, which has two parts. First, the buyer's characteristics influence how he or she perceives and reacts to the stimuli. Second, the buyer's decision process affects his or her behaviour. We look first at buyer characteristics as they affect buying behaviour and then discuss the buyer decision process.

Characteristics Affecting Consumer Behaviour

Consumer purchases are influenced strongly by cultural, social, personal, and psychological characteristics, as shown in Figure 7.2. For the most part, marketers cannot control such factors, but they must take them into account. To help you understand these concepts, we apply them to the case of a hypothetical consumer— Jennifer Wong, a 26-year-old brand manager working for a multinational packaged-goods company in Toronto. Jennifer was born in Vancouver, but her grandparents came from Hong Kong. She's been in a relationship for two years, but isn't married. She has decided that she wants to buy a vehicle but isn't sure she can afford a car. She rode a motor scooter while attending university and is now considering buying a motorcycle—maybe even a Harley.

Cultural Factors

Cultural factors exert the broadest and deepest influence on consumer behaviour. The marketer needs to understand the role played by the buyer's *culture*, *subculture*, and *social class*.

Culture

Culture

The set of basic values, perceptions, wants, and behaviours learned by a member of society from family and other important institutions.

Culture is the most basic determinant of a person's wants and behaviour. Human behaviour is largely learned. Growing up in a society, a child learns basic values, perceptions, wants, and behaviours from the family and other important institutions. *Maclean's* magazine has conducted 19 annual polls of Canadian values and attitudes. They show some core consistencies but some notable changes. For example, the majority of Canadians noted that our freedom, the beauty of our natural

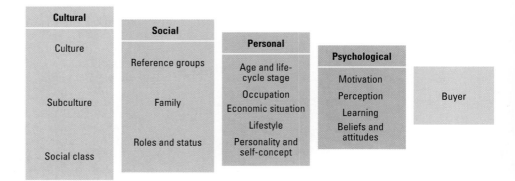

Figure 7.2 Factors influencing consumer behaviour

landscape, our beliefs in respect, equality, and fair treatment, our flag, the achievements of prominent Canadians such as artists and scientists, our social safety net, our international role, and our multicultural and multiracial makeup are symbols of our uniqueness. However, the 2002 poll revealed that some factors are changing dramatically. In particular, Canadians are expressing a growing desire to chart a distinct, independent path from our neighbours to the south. The number of Canadians who now describe the United States as "family" or "best friends" has shrunk by a third—to only one in five—and 57 percent of Canadians believe we are "mainly" or "essentially" different from Americans. This growing sense of independence may also be related to the fact that for the first time in two decades a majority of the electorate supported increased military spending. Canadians are also becoming more pessimistic about the economy as they see more complex global as well as domestic problems with fewer simple solutions.[3]

Every group or society has a culture, and cultural influences on buying behaviour may vary greatly from neighbourhood to neighbourhood, region to region, and country to country. International differences are most pronounced. Whether or not a company adjusts to such difference can spell the difference between success and failure. For example, different cultures assign different meanings to colours. White is usually associated with purity and cleanliness in Western countries. However, it can signify death in Asian countries. When General Motors was competing for the right to build its cars in China, GM executives gave Chinese officials gifts from Tiffany's jewellers. However, the Americans replaced Tiffany's signature white ribbons with red ones, since red is considered a lucky colour in China. GM ultimately won approval of its proposal.[4]

In contrast, business representatives of a community trying to market itself in Taiwan learned a hard cultural lesson. Seeking more foreign trade, they arrived in Taiwan bearing gifts of green baseball caps. It turned out that the trip was scheduled a month before Taiwan elections, and that green was the colour of the political opposition party. Worse yet, the visitors learned after the fact that according to Taiwanese culture, a man wears green to signify that his wife has been unfaithful. The head of the community delegation later noted: "I don't know whatever happened to those green hats, but the trip gave us an understanding of the extreme differences in our cultures." International marketers must understand the culture in each international market and adapt their marketing strategies accordingly.

Jennifer Wong's cultural background will affect her motorcycle-buying decision. Jennifer's desire to own a Harley may result from her being raised in a modern society that has developed motorcycle technology and a whole set of consumer learnings and values.

Marketers are always trying to identify *cultural shifts* to discover new products that might be wanted. For example, the cultural shift toward greater concern about health and fitness has created a huge industry for health and fitness services, exercise equipment and clothing, and low-fat and more natural foods. The shift toward informality has resulted in more demand for casual clothing and simpler home furnishings.

Subculture

Subculture

A group of people with shared value systems based on common life experiences and situations.

Each culture contains smaller **subcultures**, or groups of people with shared value systems based on common life experiences and situations. Subcultures may be based on differences in nationalities and mother tongues, religions, racial groups, and geographic regions. Many subcultures make up important market segments, and marketers often design products and marketing programs tailored to their needs.

Canada had two founding nations and the unique history and language of each of these nations has driven many of the cultural differences that result in different buying behaviours across Canada. The 2001 Canadian census reported that people noting their English language roots (anglophones) accounted for approximately

59 percent of the population, while people whose mother tongue is French (francophones) made up approximately 23 percent of the population. Culture, language, and regional location are important considerations for marketers. Canadian law, for example, makes it mandatory that nutritional information on food labels be bilingual. British Columbia wine growers lament the fact that French Canadians have an affinity for French wine and avoid even high-quality domestic products. Media habits also vary among the two founding cultures. Statistics Canada reports that 48.7 percent of all households in Canada contained at least one regular Internet user in 2001, while the penetration in Quebec was only 42.7 percent. (See Real Marketing 7.1 for more insight on marketing to French-Canadian consumers.)

Canada is increasingly becoming a multilingual society. Statistics Canada reports that one out of every six Canadians reported having a mother tongue other than English or French—in fact, more than 100 languages were reported in the 2001 Census. Allophones, people who report a mother tongue other than English or French, exceed 5.3 million or 18 percent of the population (up from 16.6 percent in the 1996 census). Chinese is the third most common mother tongue in Canada, followed by Italian, German, Punjabi, and Spanish. Among Canada's Aboriginal population, Cree is reported as the most common mother tongue. Examples of these subculture groups are provided next. As we discuss them, it is important to note that each subculture is, in turn, made of many smaller subcultures, each with its own preferences and behaviours.

Native Canadians   Aboriginal Canadians are making their voices heard both in the political arena and in the marketplace. There are just over 983 000 Aboriginal Canadians, including Métis and Inuit. Not only do these Native Canadians have distinct cultures that influence their values and purchasing behaviour, but they also have profoundly influenced the rest of Canada through their art, love of nature, and concern for the environment.

Banks have been particularly responsive to the unique needs of Aboriginal Canadians.[5] Scotiabank, for example, has maintained its relationship with First Nations people through its three on-reserve branches and 24 Aboriginal banking centres. It also uses a lot of grassroots marketing and public relations efforts, including its sponsorship of the Aboriginal Achievement Awards and ten annual scholarships of $2500 for young Aboriginal entrepreneurs. CIBC found that cultural symbols can better link a firm with its Native customers. On its website at www.cibc.com/aboriginal, CIBC features a medicine wheel to symbolize CIBC's holistic and integrated approach to achieving "balance and harmony in (its) relationship with Aboriginal people." The symbol was selected as an indication of CIBC's respect for the cultural integrity and diversity of Aboriginal people in Canada.

Canada's Ethnic Consumers   Consumers from ethnic groups represent some of the fastest-growing markets in Canada. In Toronto, for example, the number of Spanish-speaking people has doubled to 250 000 in just five years. In Canada today, there are 100 different ethnic groups and they account for billions in consumer spending. Many of these groups are large and represent a significant proportion of the population: consider the 4.1 million people with Scottish ancestry, the 3.8 million with Irish backgrounds, the 2.7 million with German roots, and the over 1 million people each reporting Italian, Ukrainian, or Chinese ancestry.[6]

Just take the case of Chinese Canadians. They constitute 3.5 percent of the population as a whole, but they make up a significant percent of the population in our major cities. They constitute 47 percent of Vancouver's population, approximately 31 percent of the populations of Montreal, Calgary, and Edmonton, and 24 percent of Toronto residents.[7]

In the past, most members of this ethnic group came from Hong Kong. Today they are arriving from Taiwan and mainland China. Why should marketers be concerned where Chinese immigrants come from? Primarily for language reasons. While the

REAL MARKETING

7.1   Marketing to Quebec and French-Canadian Consumers

Quebec has long prided itself as being a "distinct society." Marketers must be aware of its uniqueness if they are to be successful in the province. Quebec is characterized by unique laws, a different set of businesses and industries, and distinct attitudes and values when compared with the rest of Canada.

Canadians whose mother tongue is French number 6.2 million or 23 percent of the population. They constitute 82 percent of the population in Quebec, 34 percent in New Brunswick, and lesser percentages in Ontario and Manitoba. Known for their *joie de vivre,* their Latin roots may make French Canadians more emotional and impulsive. Other demographic and socioeconomic differences also influence attitudes and buying behaviours: education and income, for example, are both lower in Quebec than in Ontario.

The majority of Quebec's population (52 percent or 3.7 million people) lives in the Montreal area. Montreal is a vibrant city with a lot of high-tech industries and a busy port. A huge student population keeps the city rocking. Together, the Université de Montréal, Université du Québec à Montréal, McGill University, and Concordia University enrol almost 150 000 students per year. This gives Montreal more university students per capita than any other North American city. Not surprisingly, young Montrealers aged 18 to 35 are the most highly educated in Canada, and Montreal is known as one of the "hippest" centres in the world.

Montreal is the second-largest metropolitan area in Canada (behind Toronto and leading Vancouver) and is the second-largest French-speaking city in the world. However, one must not assume that the population of the Montreal region is homogeneous and made up only of French Canadians. Bilingualism is very common, and as with other large Canadian cities, the population is diverse. The city is home to over 80 ethnic groups, including 165 000 Italians, 100 000 Jewish Canadians, and Canada's largest concentration of Muslims (80 000), along with 50 000 Greeks and 35 000 Chinese.

Marketers who want to appeal to Quebec consumers need to do more than communicate in French. They must understand the values, attitudes, and behaviours that are unique to the Quebec population. French Canadians value their European roots, their distinct music and theatre, their gourmet food and fine wines. French-Canadian women are more fashion conscious and family oriented than women in the rest of Canada, and they spend more on their children than other Canadians. For example, while the average Canadian family spends $271 per child for back-to-school items, residents of Quebec spend $304. Given these differences, it is not surprising that many marketers tailor their campaigns to meet Quebec preferences. McDonald's Restaurants of Canada, for example, dropped the "We love to see you smile" tag line used everywhere else in North America for the visual pun "J'M" (pronounced as "J'aime," meaning "I like") in Quebec.

Even attitudes about housework vary. Research conducted by SC Johnson revealed that while English Canadians just want to get the job done and see house cleaning as a necessary evil, people in Quebec get a sense of pride and accomplishment from the task. Applying these insights to the distinctly Quebec custom of the July 1 Moving Day (when tenants whose leases have expired move from one apartment to

National marketers like the Bank of Montreal tailor their ads to meet the unique perceptions of Quebec consumers.

another), SC Johnson designed a highly successful campaign for its cleaning products. Some companies entering Quebec for the first time treat it in the same way they would entering a foreign market. The Seattle-based coffee giant Starbucks did just that as it made plans to open 50 to 75 outlets in the province. So they could better understand the Quebec culture, they partnered with a Quebec-based firm to avoid making costly cultural blunders.

Marketers must also be aware that Quebec has its own icons and unique media personalities. For example, Bell Canada's long-running *Monsieur B* campaign, which originated in 1992, is almost unknown in the rest of Canada. However, it has approached legendary status in the province, the way other advertising icons like the Green Giant, Aunt Jemima, and the lonely Maytag repairman have done in the rest of Canada. Ford Motor Co. of Canada also found it needed Quebec stars if it was to have an impact on the marketplace. During its summer sell-down, it used the Tina Turner song "Simply the Best" for its campaign in English-speaking Canada. However, the song didn't resonate in Quebec, so instead Ford used two very prominent Quebec actors—Guy A. Lepage and Sylvie Leonard—from the CBC radio show *Un Gar et Une Fille*.

While many of the differences in buying behaviour are influenced by culture, marketers have to know that the legal environment is also different in Quebec. Besides strict language laws, there are stronger restrictions on advertising to children.

Quebec also has a distinct business and retail climate. Lavo Group, for example, is a Quebec packaged goods manufacturer whose products rival those of Procter & Gamble and Colgate in the province. Many Quebecers buy la Parisienne laundry detergent and fabric softener instead of Tide and Downy, Hertel liquid cleanser instead of Mr. Clean, and Old Dutch powder cleanser instead of Comet. When Home Depot entered Quebec in 2000, it was faced with a set of competitors different from those in the rest of Canada. Réno-Depot and RONA have a loyal set of customers in Quebec. To help Home Depot gain acceptance, Montreal-based Cossette Communications developed an advertising campaign that appealed to Quebecers' unique sense of humour. Rather than creating ads with rational appeals that proclaimed Home Depot's high-quality service, Cossette conducted qualitative research to uncover examples of realistic and believable bad shopping experiences of Quebec consumers. The resulting campaign featured one commercial that showed a clerk literally running away from a client, while in a second ad, a group of clerks chanted "It is not my department" despite clients' looks of dismay. The campaign not only created awareness of Home Depot, it was listed among Montrealers' favourites in a recent survey.

For a long time, Quebec lagged behind the rest of Canada in terms of Internet adoption and usage. Today, however, more than 60 percent of Quebec adults are online. There are a growing number of French sites and online services such as La Toiles de Québec, InfinIT, and Le Petit Monde, as well as the French versions of popular portals like Sympatico, Yahoo!, and MSN. Marketers have been quick to leverage this new interconnectivity. Volkswagen, Avon, L'Oréal, and La Senza are some of the Quebec-based companies that have jumped on the bandwagon. Not only are they building French versions of their company websites, they have intensified their email marketing campaigns in the province. The race is on to build databases to further this effort. Sympatico, for example, has an opt-in email database of 700 000 French Canadians, comprising adults aged 25 to 49, most with families.

If marketers respect Quebec's unique laws with regards to contests and sweepstakes, they can utilize these tools to help build their databases. Sympatico experienced phenomenal results when it ran a contest to meet Bryan Adams in Scotland. People had to register online and Sympatico amassed 20 000 new Quebec subscribers as a result. As their marketing manager noted, "French-speaking people love to play. And because they love to play, they tend to give their personal information freely—and by that I mean their postal code, age, and gender." Marketers have to tread softly, however. Quebecers still like to be wooed, especially when it comes to developing a one-to-one relationship. Marketers who understand that people from Quebec prefer more face-to-face interactions and personal contact than do people from the rest of the country can continue to be successful in this dynamic but unique marketplace.

Sources: Bernadette Johnson "E-mail Marketing Begins To Flourish in La Belle Province," *Strategy,* May 20, 2002, p. D 10; Sara Minoque, "Sunny Economy Predicted To Grow Spending," *Strategy Magazine,* January 13, 2003, p. 10; Nancy Carr, "Does a Distinct Society Need Distinct Creative?" *Strategy,* April 9, 2001, p. 13; Canada Online, "2001 Census Statistics on Languages in Canada," http://canadaonline.about.com/cs/statistics/a/statslang.htm#b (accessed June 12, 2003); Helena Katz, "Johnson Sharpens Its Quebec Strategy," *Marketing Magazine,* October 12, 1998, p. 3; Danny Kucharsky, "Starbucks to Open Quebec Cafes," *Marketing Magazine,* March 26, 2001, www.marketingmag.ca; Retail Council of Canada, "Kids Rule For Back-to-School This Year" (press release), August 30, 2001; Shawna Steinberg, "Only in English Canada, you say?" *Marketing Magazine,* November 12, 1998, p. 10; Danny Kucharsky, "Monsieur's Family," *Marketing Magazine,* June 11, 2001, www.marketingmag.ca; Nathalie Fortier, "Building Success: How Cossette Poked Fun at Bad Customer Service to give Home Depot a Firm Foundation in Quebec," *Marketing Magazine,* September 24, 2001, www.marketingmag.ca; Tracey Arial, "Taking Aim at the Giants," *Marketing Magazine,* June 11, 2001, www.marketingmag.ca; and Government of Quebec website, www.gouv.qc.ca/ (accessed June 5, 2002).

Native bands capitalize on their distinct culture to market themselves internationally.

Chinese who come from Hong Kong speak Cantonese, people from Taiwan and mainland China often speak Mandarin. Marketers must also be aware of the differences between new immigrants and those who are "integrated immigrants"—people who are second-, third-, fourth-, fifth-, and even sixth-generation Chinese Canadians. Although marketing information often must be translated into the language of new immigrants, integrated immigrants communicate mainly in English. While Chinese Canadians are influenced by many of the values of their adopted country, they may also share some values rooted in their ethnic history. Since they come from families who have experienced great political and social turmoil, Chinese Canadians cling to "life-raft" values: trust family, work hard, be thrifty, save, and have liquid and tangible goods. Air Canada used its knowledge of these values in a campaign that linked Chinese Canadians' need for security and the desire to keep connected to their homeland with Air Canada's services.

Marketers need to tailor their efforts to meet the needs and preferences of these groups. Cleve Lu, CEO of multicultural marketing communications firm Era Integrated Marketing Communications, provides some tips. Chinese customers feel uncomfortable talking to strangers about personal or financial matters until a solid trust has been built between them and the service provider. Let the customer get to know you first. Chinese Canadians value personal direct mail with product information if they believe it demonstrates that they are cared for by the marketer and they are treated as important, respected clients. A personal phone call after a sale or mailing a greeting card to express appreciation is a good way to solidify relationships and demonstrate cultural understanding.[8]

The Toronto Symphony Orchestra (TSO) is one organization that has been very successful in building relationships with Chinese patrons. It knew that Chinese families had a higher musical literacy than the average population in North America. Almost seven out of ten Chinese children take music lessons, and Chinese parents

The Toronto Symphony Orchestra has built a strong base of Chinese patrons through culturally sensitive marketing and targeted offerings.

believe music is important for brain development. Using a multimedia campaign, the TSO is now producing season brochures in Chinese. It has added a Chinese portion to its website (www.tso.ca/chinese/), and it is a regular advertiser in Chinese newspapers and on Chinese radio programs. Furthermore, the TSO provides customer service in both Cantonese and Mandarin through a Chinese hotline. The TSO also quickly learned to push Chinese consumers' hot buttons, including their love of incentives and giveaways. For example, people calling the Chinese hotline are entered in a lucky draw for a Petrof grand piano.[9]

Many ethnic groups, however, believe that they have been neglected or misrepresented by marketers. A Canadian Advertising Foundation study revealed that 80 percent of people belonging to visible minorities believed that advertising has been targeted almost exclusively at "white" people. Yet 46 percent of this group stated that they would be more likely to buy a product if its advertising featured models from visible-minority populations.[10]

Let's consider our hypothetical consumer. How will Jennifer Wong's cultural background influence her decision about whether to buy a motorcycle? Jennifer's parents certainly won't approve of her choice. Tied strongly to the values of thrift and conservatism, they believe that she should continue taking the subway instead of purchasing a vehicle. However, Jennifer identifies with her Canadian friends and colleagues as much as she does with her family. She views herself as a modern woman in a society that accepts women in a wide range of roles, both conventional and unconventional. She has female friends who play hockey and rugby. And women riding motorcycles are becoming a more common sight in Canada's urban centres.

How does being part of the Internet generation affect Jennifer Wong and her purchase decision? Jennifer is highly computer literate. She uses a computer daily at work, carries a laptop when attending meetings outside Toronto, and has a computer in her apartment. One of the first things she did when considering a motorcycle purchase was to log on to the Internet. She learned a great deal simply by browsing the sites of such manufacturers as Honda, Yamaha, and Harley-Davidson. She especially liked the Harley site and the annual events listed for Harley owners.

Cultural factors: Marketers targeting the Internet generation realize that computer-savvy consumers like Jennifer Wong will automatically check online for information about major purchases.

She was concerned that most of these events took place in the United States, however. Using Harley's response button, she requested information on dealers in her area and information about specific models. Jennifer also found several chat groups and posted questions to members of these groups, especially women riders.

Social Class

Social classes

Relatively permanent and ordered divisions in a society whose members share similar values, interests, and behaviours.

Almost every society has some form of social class structure. **Social classes** are society's relatively permanent and ordered divisions whose members share similar values, interests, and behaviours. Social scientists have identified seven North American social classes (see Table 7.1 for the Canadian perspective).

The cost of entering the upper classes is going up. If the Barenaked Ladies wrote their famous song "If I Had a Million Dollars" today, they would need $10 million dollars to be rich. There are approximately 180 000 Canadians, or 7600 Canadian families, who have socked away this cool sum. Marketers from organizations as diverse as financial institutions to luxury vacation providers scramble to serve this elite market. The gap between rich and poor is growing. The annual income of the top 1 percent of Canadian wage earners was $469 656 in 2000 (compared to $359 143 in 1990), while the annual income for the bottom 10 percent of working Canadians was $10 341 (compared with $10 260 in 1990).[11]

Social class is not determined by a single factor, such as income, but is measured as a combination of occupation, income, education, wealth, and other variables. In some social systems, members of different classes are reared for certain roles and cannot change their social positions. In Canada, however, the lines between social classes are not fixed and rigid: people can move to a higher social class or drop into a lower one. Marketers are interested in social class because people within a given social class tend to exhibit similar buying behaviour.[12]

Social classes show distinct product and brand preferences in areas such as clothing, home furnishings, leisure activity, and automobiles. Jennifer Wong's social class may affect her motorcycle decision. As a member of the Asian Heights group, Jennifer finds herself frequently buying brand-name products that are fashionable and popular with her friends and extended family.

Social Factors

A consumer's behaviour is also influenced by social factors, such as membership in small *groups* and *family*, and social *roles and status*.

Table 7.1   Characteristics of Seven Major Canadian Social Classes

The Upper Class (3 to 5 percent)

Upper uppers (less than 1 percent)

Upper uppers are the social elite who live on inherited wealth and have well-established family backgrounds. They give large sums to charity, own more than one home, and send their children to the finest schools. They are accustomed to wealth and often buy and dress conservatively rather than showing off their wealth.

Lower uppers (about 2 to 4 percent)

Lower uppers have earned high income or wealth through exceptional ability in the professions or business. They usually begin in the middle class. They tend to be active in social and civic affairs and buy for themselves and their children the symbols of status, such as expensive homes, educations, and automobiles. They want to be accepted in the upper-upper stratum, a status more likely to be achieved by their children than by themselves.

The Middle Class (40 to 50 percent)

Upper middles

Upper middles possess neither family status nor unusual wealth. They have attained positions as professionals, independent businesspersons, and corporate managers. They have a keen interest in attaining the "better things in life." They believe in education and want their children to develop professional or administrative skills. They are joiners and highly civic-minded.

Average middles

The middle class is made up of average-pay white- and blue-collar workers who live on the "better side of town" and try to "do the proper things." To keep up with the trends, they often buy products that are popular. Most are concerned with fashion, seeking the better brand names. Better living means owning a nice home in a nice neighbourhood with good schools.

The Working Class (about 33 percent)

The working class consists of those who lead a "working-class lifestyle," whatever their income, school background, or job. They depend heavily on relatives for economic and emotional support, for advice on purchases, and for assistance in times of trouble.

The Lower Class (about 20 percent)

Upper lowers

Upper lowers are working (are not on welfare), although their living standard is just above poverty. Although they strive toward a higher class, they often lack education and perform unskilled work for poor pay.

Lower lowers

Lower lowers are visibly poor. They are often poorly educated and work as unskilled labourers. However, they are often out of work and some depend on public assistance. They tend to live a day-to-day existence.

Sources: See Richard P. Coleman, "The Continuing Significance of Social Class to Marketing," *Journal of Consumer Research,* December 1983, pp. 265–280. © Journal of Consumer Research, Inc., 1983. Also see Leon G. Shiffman and Leslie Lazar Kanuk, *Consumer Behavior,* 6th ed. (Upper Saddle River, N.J.: Prentice Hall, 1997), p. 388; Linda P. Morton, "Segmenting Publics by Social Class," *Public Relations Quarterly,* Summer 1999, pp. 45–46; and John Macionis and Linda Gerber, *Sociology,* 4th Canadian ed. (Toronto: Pearson Education Canada, 2002), pp. 276–280.

Groups

Group

Two or more people who interact to accomplish individual or mutual goals.

A person's behaviour is influenced by many small **groups**. Groups that have a direct influence and to which a person belongs are called *membership groups*. In contrast, *reference groups* serve as direct (face-to-face) or indirect points of comparison or reference in forming a person's attitudes or behaviour. People often are influenced by reference groups to which they do not belong. For example, an *aspirational group* is one to which the individual wishes to belong, as when a teenage hockey player hopes to play someday for the Montreal Canadiens. Marketers try to identify the reference groups of their target markets. Reference groups expose a person to new behaviours and lifestyles, influence the person's attitudes and self-concept, and create pressures to conform that may affect the person's product and brand choices.

The importance of group influence varies across products and brands. It tends to be strongest when the product is visible to others whom the buyer respects. Manufacturers of products and brands subjected to strong group influence must

Opinion leader

Person within a reference group who, because of special skills, knowledge, personality, or other characteristics, exerts influence on others.

figure out how to reach **opinion leaders**—people within a reference group who, because of special skills, knowledge, personality, or other characteristics, exert influence on others.

Many marketers try to identify opinion leaders for their products, so that they can direct marketing efforts toward them. For example, the hottest trends in teenage music, language, and fashion often start in Canada in major cities, then quickly spread to more mainstream youth in the suburbs. Thus, clothing companies who hope to appeal to these fickle and fashion-conscious youth often make a concerted effort to monitor urban opinion leaders' style and behaviour. In other cases, marketers like L'Oréal Canada may use *buzz marketing,* which not only targets opinion leaders, but also gets them talking about the product to their friends:

> How do you launch a new product to a traditionally hard-to-reach audience unfamiliar with the product category? This was the situation L'Oréal Canada faced when launching its new line, Open: Vibrantly Natural Colour Gel. Its market research indicated that young women 16 to 25 wanted noticeable but completely natural-looking colour results. The technology behind the new product, Open, offered all these features, but L'Oréal still had to get the message out, not just to generate product awareness, but also to convey user-friendly product know-how. L'Oréal used a three-step plan. First, they secured distribution of the product in traditional retail outlets. Next, they used some traditional media to build awareness (TV, cinema ads, magazine and transit advertising). But to create buzz and the word-of-mouth so essential to product trial, it added an Internet element (www.lorealparis.ca/en/haircolor), along with a contest run in *Verve* magazine. These two elements gave life to the campaign—50 percent of participants sent multiple e-cards focused on the new product to their network of friends. They received samples, giving them confidence in the product. To create even a bigger stir in the marketplace, L'Oréal used street marketing. A brightly painted semi-trailer travelled to hot spots in Montreal, Toronto, and Vancouver. Each stop drew crowds of young women who not only sampled the product but also passed along the news to their friends. The success of the campaign was measured by the demographics of the audience reached: 72 percent of the visitors were in the target age group and most were new to the L'Oréal brand.[13]

The importance of group influence varies across products and brands. It tends to be strongest when the product is visible to others whom the buyer respects. Purchases of products that are bought and used privately are not much affected by group influences, because neither the product nor the brand will be noticed by others. If Jennifer Wong buys a motorcycle, both the product and the brand will be visible to others she respects, and her decision to buy the motorcycle and her brand choice may be influenced strongly by some of her groups, such as friends who belong to a weekend motorcycle club. Jennifer often feels left out when these friends leave for weekend road trips.

Family

Family members can strongly influence buyer behaviour. The family is the most important consumer buying organization in society, and it has been researched extensively. Marketers are interested in the roles and influence of the husband, wife, and children on the purchase of different products and services.

Husband–wife involvement depends on product category and on stage in the buying process. Buying roles change with evolving consumer lifestyles. In Canada and the United States, the wife has traditionally been the main purchasing agent for the family, especially for food, household products, and clothing. But with 70 percent of women holding jobs outside the home and the willingness of husbands to do more of the family's purchasing, this is changing. For example, women now make or influence up to 80 percent of car-buying decisions and men account for about 40 percent of food-shopping dollars.[14]

Family buying influences: Children can exert a strong influence on family buying decisions. Chevrolet actively woos these "back-seat consumers" with carefully targeted advertising and a Chevy Venture Warner Bros. Edition, complete with DVD player.

Such changes in family buying behaviour suggest that marketers who've typically sold their products to only women or only men are now courting the opposite sex. For example, with research revealing that women now account for nearly half of all hardware store purchases, home improvement retailers such as Home Depot have turned what once were intimidating warehouses into female-friendly retail outlets that even offer bridal registries. In fact, the Canadian president of Home depot is a woman (Annette Verschuren).[15]

Children can also have a strong influence on family buying decisions. For example, children as young as age six may influence the family car purchase decision. "By six, they know the names of cars," says an industry analyst. "They see them on TV." Chevrolet recognizes these influences in marketing its Chevy Venture minivan. For example, it runs ads to woo these "back-seat consumers" in *Sports Illustrated for Kids,* which attracts mostly 8- to 14-year-old boys. "We're kidding ourselves when we think kids aren't aware of brands," says Venture's brand manager, adding that even she was surprised at how often parents told her that kids played a tie-breaking role in deciding which car to buy.[16]

Roles and Status

A person belongs to many groups—family, clubs, organizations. The person's position in each group can be defined in terms of both role and status. With her parents, Jennifer Wong plays the role of daughter; in her company, she plays the role of brand manager. A *role* consists of the activities that others expect from the person. Each of Jennifer's roles will influence some of her buying behaviour. Each role carries a *status* reflecting the general esteem society gives it. People often choose products that show their status in society. For example, the role of brand manager has more status in our society than does the role of daughter. As a brand manager, Jennifer will buy the kind of clothing that reflects her role and status.

Personal Factors

A buyer's decisions are also influenced by such personal characteristics as *age and life-cycle stage, occupation, economic situation, lifestyle,* and *personality and self-concept.*

Age and Life-Cycle Stage

People change in the kinds of goods and services they buy over their lifetimes. Tastes in food, clothes, furniture, and recreation are often related to age. Buying is also shaped by the stage of the *family life cycle*—the stages through which families might pass as they mature. Marketers often define their target markets in terms of life-cycle stage and develop appropriate products and marketing plans for each stage.

Traditional family life-cycle stages include young singles and married couples with children. Today, however, marketers are increasingly catering to a growing number of alternative, non-traditional stages such as unmarried couples, singles marrying later in life, childless couples, same-sex couples, single parents, extended parents (those with young adult children returning home), and others. For example, more and more companies are now reaching out to serve the fast-growing numbers of the recently divorced (see Real Marketing 7.2).

Sony recently overhauled its marketing approach in order to target products and services to consumers based on their life stages. It created a new unit called the Consumer Segment Marketing Division, which has identified seven life-stage segments. They include, among others, Gen Y (under 25), Young Professionals/DINKs (double income no kids, 25 to 34), Families (35 to 54), and Zoomers (55 and over). Sony's goal is to create brand loyalty early on and to develop long-term relationships. "The goal is to get closer to consumers," says a Sony marketing executive.[17]

Occupation

A person's occupation may determine the goods and services that he or she buys. Blue-collar workers tend to buy more rugged work clothes, whereas executives buy more business suits. Marketers try to identify the occupational groups that have an above-average interest in their products and services. A company can even specialize in making products needed by an occupational group. Thus, computer software companies design different products for brand managers, accountants, engineers, lawyers, and doctors.

Economic Situation

A person's economic situation affects product choice. Jennifer Wong can consider buying an expensive motorcycle if she has enough spendable income, savings, or borrowing power. Marketers of income-sensitive goods watch trends in personal income, savings, and interest rates. If economic indicators point to a recession, marketers can take steps to redesign, reposition, and reprice their products.

Lifestyle

Lifestyle
A person's pattern of living as expressed in his or her activities, interests, and opinions.

People coming from the same subculture, social class, and occupation may have quite different lifestyles. **Lifestyle** is a person's pattern of living as expressed in his or her psychographics. It involves measuring consumers' major *AIO dimensions*—*activities* (work, hobbies, shopping, sports, social events), *interests* (food, fashion, family, recreation), and *opinions* (about themselves, social issues, business, products). Lifestyle captures something more than the person's social class or personality. It profiles a person's whole pattern of acting and interacting in the world. Publishers have long used lifestyle segmentation to shape the content of their magazines. For example, *Verve* magazine is aimed at teenage girls, while *Fuel* is designed to capture the lifestyle of Canadian teen males. Becel margarine targets those who want a healthier lifestyle, while beer marketers target those who value the party scene.

Several research firms have developed lifestyle classifications. The most widely used is the SRI *Values and Lifestyles (VALS)* typology (see Figure 7.3 on page 270; also see www.sric-bi.com/VALS). VALS classifies people according to how they spend

REAL MARKETING

7.2   Targeting Non-traditional Life Stages: Just Divorced, Gone Shopping

*D*ivorcees used to be off limits for marketers. Not anymore. Almost 40 percent (37.7 percent) of all marriages in Canada now end in divorce, down from a peak of 50.6 percent in 1987, shortly after our divorce laws were amended. With more than 70 000 couples splitting up every year and the divorce rate growing at close to 3 percent a year, there are over 1.4 million divorcees in Canada. They represent a distinct market segment in a not-really-so-non-traditional life-cycle stage. Consider these examples:

> When [Leila Mesghali] walked out of her marriage of three years, she took only her clothes and some heirloom dishes...A few months after she separated from her husband, however, the decorating urge kicked in. Even on a limited budget, she spent US$6000 on a dark teak armoire, sofa, and bedroom set. "I had a lot of motivation to fill my apartment up quickly," she said. "It was an opportunity to do my own thing."

Life-stage marketing: Marketers are discovering that when couples split, someone goes shopping. Divorcees, much like newly-weds, restock their homes with everything from pots and pans to televisions.

Kim Lombard, a television producer in Toronto, also refurnished from scratch—though not of his own will—after splitting two years ago. "When my wife left me, she took everything," Mr. Lombard said.... [He] quickly spent about $25 000 on a sofa, a good mattress, and a 50-inch television.

A suddenly single banker spent $4000 in an afternoon to outfit a bedroom for his 17-month-old twins, just like the one they already knew.

Marketers are discovering that when couples split, someone goes shopping. Divorcees, much like newly-weds, restock their homes with everything from towels to televisions. Notes one consultant, "The divorce rate is keeping the furniture business alive. There's no doubt that life stages are driving consumers. They buy when they get married; they buy when they get divorced." Says Dan Couvrette, publisher of *Divorce Magazine,* "Next year, at least half of the 2.4 million people who will get divorced in the United States and Canada are going to buy new beds. That's over a million people. You can't find a bigger niche."

Divorcees don't just buy out of necessity; the shopping cure can ease the pain. People going through a divorce, Couvrette says, "represent a tremendous market potential because they'll spend money to get stuff that makes them feel better." Couvrette adds that "even those who suffer financial setbacks—often the case with women leaving long-term marriages—try to treat themselves to the best they can afford.... [Some] 78 percent of the men bought new entertainment systems, while 69 percent of the women opted for new bedroom furniture."

Retail stores, such as Crate & Barrel, Sears, and IKEA, are learning to recognize and accommodate the shopper who may be dazed and alone, trailing a long list of household needs. "Our salespeople say they sometimes feel like therapists," says Joe Dance, a Crate & Barrel spokesman. "They know they can't be all bubbly around someone who might be upset. It's clearly a situation that demands their most sensitive approach."

National retailers are not alone. One furniture maker has trained its salespeople to keep an eye out for customers with such special needs. "We teach our sales associates to look out for that man wandering around. He may have just been kicked out of the house," says one company's owner.

One IKEA spokeswoman, who spent more than five years as a design consultant, estimates that more than 30 percent of the customers she worked with were divorced men. As a result, saleswomen often play the role of surrogate wives. Sharon Klein, a home furnishings consultant with IKEA, regularly assists "gentlemen who want help from someone with a woman's touch in buying just about everything. They come right up to you and say, 'Help!'" And when it comes to their children, she says, "they always want a lot of extras to make their kid's new bedroom more exciting than the one at the other parent's house."

In response to the growing market, advertisers are testing the waters. Sears launched a television featuring a once-loving couple. After separating their washer and dryer in the settlement, they pass each other in the aisles at Sears, smiling awkwardly while shopping for new appliances. "It was a humorous look at a real-life situation," says a Sears marketer. Here's another example:

Some years ago, IKEA ran a television ad that put a positive spin on shopping one's way to a fresh start. It showed a woman driving at night with her daughter asleep in the back seat. She muses aloud about her divorce and embarking on a new life. Flashbacks show her shopping up a storm in the aisles of IKEA.

Many marketers have shunned the divorcee segment as too downbeat. "Divorce is still a niche market with negative connotations," says one analyst. "Historically, advertisers go with more positive images. But that's going to change in keeping with the whole trend to go after more targeted groups." Consider this example:

Montauk Sofas was among the first to run an upbeat breakup ad. A smiling woman cozies up in the embrace of a $2400 extra-plush armchair. The text begins in bold type: "He left me. Good Riddance." and ends: "Who cares...I kept the sofa." The ad has generated such good feelings for Montauk, a Montreal-based furniture manufacturer with seven stores in the United States and Canada, that it has kept running it for five years. "We've gotten an excellent reaction from all walks of life and ages," said Tim Zyto, the owner of Montauk. "Women especially like it. They find it empowering."

Couvrette of *Divorce Magazine* thinks that it's only a matter of time before the once-taboo D-word comes to stand for "divorce registry." "It's not going to be *called* a divorce registry," he predicts, "but everyone's going to know that's what it's for."

Sources: Excerpts and quotes from Julie V. Iovine, "Just Divorced, Gone Shopping," *New York Times,* July 12, 2001, p. F1. Also see Pamela Sebastian Ridge, "Tool Sellers Tap Their Feminine Side," *Wall Street Journal,* March 29, 2002, p. B1; Family Facts Canada, "More Canadians Divorcing—StatCan" (news release), December 4–5, 2002, www.fotf.ca/familyfacts/tfn/2002/120402.html; Statistics Canada, "Divorces, 1999 and 2000," *The Daily,* December 2, 2002, www.statcan.ca/Daily/English/021202/td021202.htm; and DivorceMagazine.com, "Canadian Divorce Statistics (1998)," www.divorcemag.com/statistics/statsCAN.shtml (accessed June 20, 2003).

their time and money. It divides consumers into eight groups based on two major dimensions: self-orientation and resources. *Self-orientation* groups include *principle-oriented* consumers who buy based on their views of the world; *status-oriented* buyers who base their purchases on the actions and opinions of others; and *action-oriented* buyers who are driven by their desire for activity, variety, and risk taking.

Consumers within each orientation are further classified into those with *abundant resources* and those with *minimal resources,* depending on whether they have high or low levels of income, education, health, self-confidence, energy, and other factors. Consumers with either very high or very low levels of resources are classified without regard to their self-orientation (actualizers, strugglers). *Actualizers* are people with so many resources that they can indulge in any or all self-orientations. In contrast, *strugglers* are people with too few resources to be included in any consumer orientation.[18]

Lifestyle segmentation can also be used to understand Internet behaviour. Forrester developed its "Technographics" scheme, which segments consumers according to motivation, desire, and ability to invest in technology.[19] The framework splits people into ten categories, such as:

- *Fast Forwards:* the biggest spenders on computer technology; early adopters of new technology for home, office, and personal use.

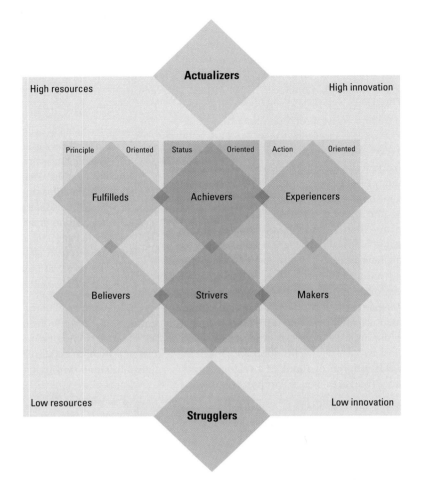

Figure 7.3 VALS lifestyle classifications

Source: Reprinted with permission of SRI International, Menlo Park, CA. VALS is a registered trademark of SRI International.

- *New Age Nurturers:* also big spenders but focused on technology for home uses, such as a family PC.
- *Mouse Potatoes:* consumers who are dedicated to interactive entertainment and willing to spend for the latest in "technotainment."
- *Techno-Strivers:* consumers who use technology primarily to gain a career edge.
- *Handshakers:* older consumers, typically managers, who don't touch computers at work and leave that to younger assistants.

Delta Airlines used Technographics to better target online ticket sales. It created marketing campaigns for time-strapped Fast Forwards and New Age Nurturers, and eliminated "Technology Pessimists" from its list of targets.

Lifestyle classifications are by no means universal—they can vary significantly between countries. For example:[20]

Advertising agency McCann-Erickson London found the following British lifestyles: Avant Guardians (interested in change); Pontificators (traditionalists, very British); Chameleons (follow the crowd); and Sleepwalkers (contented underachievers).

The D'Arcy, Masius, Benton, & Bowles agency identified five categories of Russian consumers: Kuptsi (merchants), Cossacks (characterized as ambitious, independent, and status seeking), Students, Business Executives, and Russian Souls (passive, fearful of choices, and hopeful). Thus, a typical Cossack might drive a BMW, smoke Dunhill cigarettes, and drink Remy Martin liquor, whereas a Russian Soul would drive a Lada, smoke Marlboros, and drink Smirnoff vodka.

Lifestyles: The Jeep® brand targets people who want to leave the civilized world behind.

 Michael Adams, president of Environics Research Group Ltd. (http://erg. environics.net), wrote *Sex in the Snow: Canadian Social Values at the End of the Millennium* to capture significant psychographic changes in the Canadian market-place. His classification system begins with demographic factors as he divides the Canadian population along age-based lines into three groups: those over 50, baby boomers, and Generation Xers. Furthermore, he asserts that 11 value-based "tribes" exist within these broader groups. Table 7.2 provides descriptions of these groups.

When used carefully, the lifestyle concept can help the marketer understand changing consumer values and how they affect buying behaviour. Jennifer Wong, for example, can choose to live the role of a dutiful daughter, a career woman, or a free spirit—or all three. She plays several roles, and the way she blends them expresses her lifestyle. If she chooses a motorcycle for her principle transportation mode, this would change her lifestyle, in turn changing what and how she buys.

Personality and Self-Concept

Personality

A person's distinguishing psychological characteristics that lead to relatively consistent and lasting responses to his or her own environment.

Each person's distinct personality influences his or her buying behaviour. **Personality** refers to the unique psychological characteristics that lead to relatively consistent and lasting responses to one's own environment. Personality is usually described in terms of traits, such as self-confidence, dominance, sociability, autonomy, defensiveness, adaptability, and aggressiveness. Personality can be useful in analyzing consumer behaviour for certain product or brand choices. For example, coffee makers have discovered that heavy coffee drinkers tend to be high on sociability. Thus, to attract customers, Starbucks, Second Cup, Timothy's, and other coffeehouses create environments in which people can relax and socialize over a cup of steaming coffee.

Brand personality

The specific mix of human traits that may be attributed to a particular brand.

The idea is that brands also have personalities, and that consumers are likely to choose brands whose personalities match their own. A **brand personality** is the specific mix of human traits that may be attributed to a particular brand. One researcher identified five brand personality traits:[21]

1. Sincerity (down-to-earth, honest, wholesome, and cheerful)
2. Excitement (daring, spirited, imaginative, and up-to-date)

Table 7.2   The Social Value "Tribes" of Canada

Groups	% Pop. & Size	Motivators	Values	Exemplar
The Elders:				
Rational Traditionalists	15% 3.5M	Financial independence, stability, and security.	Value safety, reason, tradition, and authority. Religious.	Winston Churchill
Extroverted Traditionalists	7% 1.7M	Traditional communities and institutions.	Value tradition, duty, family, and institutions. Religious.	Jean Chrétien
Cosmopolitan Modernists	6% 1.4M	Traditional institutions. Nomadic, experience-seeking.	Education, affluence, innovation, progress, self-confidence, world perspective.	Pierre Trudeau
The Boomers:				
Disengaged Darwinists	18% 4.3M	Financial independence, stability, and security.	Self-preservation, nostalgia for the past.	Ralph Klein
Autonomous Rebels	10% 2.4M	Personal autonomy, self-fulfillment, and new experiences.	Egalitarian; abhor corruption; personal fulfillment; education. Suspicion of authority and big government.	Michael Moore (*Bowling for Columbine*)
Connected Enthusiasts	6% 1.4M	Traditional and new communities; experience-seeking.	Family, community, hedonism, immediate gratification.	Madonna
Anxious Communitarians	9% 2.1M	Traditional communities, big government, and social status.	Family, community, generosity, duty. Needs self-respect. Fearful.	Oprah Winfrey
The Gen-Xers:				
Aimless Dependents	8% 1.9M	Financial independence, stability, security.	Desire for independence. Disengagement. Fearful.	Eminem, Courtney Love, the Osbournes
Thrill-Seeking Materialists	7% 1.7M	Traditional communities, social status, experience-seeking.	Money, material possessions. recognition, living dangerously.	Richard Branson (Virgin Inc.), *Survivor* participants
Autonomous Postmaterialists	6% 1.4M	Personal autonomy and self-fulfillment.	Freedom, human rights, egalitarian, quality of life.	Naomi Klein (author of *No Logo*), Bono of U2
Social Hedonists	4% 9M	Experience-seeking, new communities.	Esthetics, hedonism, sexual freedom, instant gratification.	Samantha (Kim Cattrall's character on *Sex and the City*)
New Aquarians	4% 9M	Experience-seeking, new communities.	Ecologism, hedonism.	Phoebe (from *Friends*), Sarah McLachlan

Sources: Adapted from Michael Adams, *Sex in the Snow: Canadian Social Values at the End of the Millennium* (Toronto: Viking, 1997), pp. 203–217. See also Michael Adams, "The Demise of Demography," *Globe and Mail*, January 8, 1997, p. D5; and Ann Walmsley, "Canadian Specific," *Report on Business*, March 1997, pp. 15–16.

Heavy coffee drinkers tend to be high on sociability, so to attract customers, Second Cup, Starbucks, Timothy's, and other coffeehouses create environments in which people can relax and socialize over a cup of steaming coffee.

3. Competence (reliable, intelligent, and successful)
4. Sophistication (upper class and charming)
5. Ruggedness (outdoorsy and tough)

The researcher found that a number of well-known brands tended to be strongly associated with one particular trait: Levi's with "ruggedness," MTV with "excitement," CNN with "competence," and Campbell's with "sincerity." Hence, these brands will attract persons who are high on the same personality traits.

Many marketers use a concept related to personality—a person's *self-concept* (also called *self-image*). The basic self-concept premise is that people's possessions contribute to and reflect their identities; that is, "we are what we have." Therefore, to understand consumer behaviour, the marketer must first understand the relationship between consumer self-concept and possessions. For example, the founder and chief executive of Barnes & Noble, one of the largest booksellers in the United States, notes that people buy books to support their self-images:

> People have the mistaken notion that the thing you do with books is read them. Wrong.... People buy books for what the purchase says about them—their taste, their cultivation, their trendiness. Their aim...is to connect themselves, or those to whom they give the books as gifts, with all the other refined owners of Edgar Allen Poe collections or sensitive owners of Virginia Woolf collections.... [The result is that] you can sell books as consumer products, with seductive displays, flashy posters, an emphasis on the glamour of the book, and the fashionableness of the bestseller and the trendy author.[22]

Psychological Factors

A person's buying choices are further influenced by four major psychological factors: *motivation, perception, learning,* and *beliefs and attitudes.*

Motivation

We know that Jennifer Wong became interested in buying a motorcycle. Why? What is she *really* seeking? What *needs* is she trying to satisfy?

A person has many needs at any one time. Some are *biological,* arising from states of tension such as hunger, thirst, or discomfort. Others are *psychological,* arising from the need for recognition, esteem, or belonging. A need becomes a *motive*

Motive (drive)
A need that is sufficiently pressing to direct the person to seek satisfaction of the need.

when it is aroused to a sufficient level of intensity. A **motive**, or *drive*, is a need that is sufficiently pressing to direct the person to seek satisfaction. Psychologists have developed theories of human motivation. Two of the most popular—the theories of Sigmund Freud and Abraham Maslow—have quite different meanings for consumer analysis and marketing.

Sigmund Freud assumed that people are largely unconscious of the real psychological forces shaping their behaviour. He saw the person as growing up and repressing many urges. These urges are never eliminated or under perfect control; they emerge in dreams, in slips of the tongue, in neurotic and obsessive behaviour, or ultimately in psychoses. Thus, Freud suggested that a person does not fully understand his or her motivation. Jennifer Wong, for example, may claim that her motive for buying a motorcycle is to satisfy her need for more convenient transportation. At a deeper level, however, she may be purchasing the motorcycle to impress others with her daring and her desire to be a free spirit who doesn't follow convention.

Motivation researchers collect in-depth information from small samples of consumers to uncover the deeper motives for their product choices. The techniques range from sentence completion, word association, and inkblot or cartoon interpretation tests, to having consumers describe typical brand users or form daydreams and fantasies about brands or buying situations (see Real Marketing 7.3).

Many companies employ teams of psychologists, anthropologists, and other social scientists to carry out motivation research. One agency routinely conducts one-on-one, therapy-like interviews to delve into the inner workings of consumers. Another agency asks consumers to describe their favourite brands as animals or cars (say, Cadillacs versus Chevrolets) in order to assess the prestige associated with various brands. Still another agency has consumers draw figures of typical brand users. In one case, the agency asked 50 participants to sketch likely buyers of two different brands of cake mixes. Consistently, the group portrayed Pillsbury customers as apron-clad, grandmotherly types, whereas they pictured Duncan Hines purchasers as svelte, contemporary women.

Abraham Maslow sought to explain why people are driven by particular needs at particular times. Why does one person spend much time and energy on personal safety and another on gaining the esteem of others? Maslow's answer is that human needs are arranged in a hierarchy, as shown in Figure 7.4 (page 276), from the most pressing at the bottom to the least pressing at the top. They include *physiological* needs, *safety* needs, *social* needs, *esteem* needs, and *self-actualization* needs. A person tries to satisfy the most important need first. When that need is satisfied, it will stop being a motivator and the person will then try to satisfy the next most important need. For example, starving people (physiological needs) will not take an interest in the latest happenings in the art world (self-actualization needs), nor in how they are perceived or esteemed by others (social or esteem needs), nor even in whether they are breathing clean air (safety needs). But as each important need is satisfied, the next most important need will come into play.

Motivation research: When asked to sketch typical cake mix users, subjects portrayed Pillsbury customers as grandmotherly types and Duncan Hines users as svelte and contemporary.

7.3 "Touchy-Feely" Research: Psyching Out Consumers

Consumers often don't know or can't describe just why they act as they do. Thus, motivation researchers use a variety of probing techniques to uncover underlying emotions and attitudes toward brands and buying situations. These sometimes bizarre techniques range from free association and inkblot interpretation tests to having consumers form daydreams and fantasies about brands or buying situations.

Such projective techniques may seem pretty goofy. But more and more, marketers are turning to these touchy-feely approaches to probe consumer psyches and develop better marketing strategies. For example, Shell Oil used motivation research in an attempt to uncover the real reasons behind a decade-long sales slump:

The manager of corporate advertising for Shell Oil, Sixtus Oeschle, was at his wits' end. For months, he and his team of researchers had pumped the consumer psyche and they'd come up empty.

The PT Cruiser: The phenomenally successful retro style car that's "part 1920s gangster car, part 1950s hot rod, and part London taxicab"—an actual chrome-and-sheet-metal incarnation of the popular will.

It was time, Oeschle decided, to try something radical. To craft a more potent appeal for its brand of gasoline, Shell would have to go deeper—much deeper. Oeschle called in a consumer researcher who specializes in focus groups conducted under hypnosis. The results, Oeschle says, wowed even the skeptics. After dimming the lights, the researcher took respondents back, back—back all the way to their infancy. "He just kept saying, 'Tell me about your first experience in a gas station.' And people were actually having memory flashbacks.... They were saying, 'I was three and a half years old. I was in the back of my dad's brand new Chevy.' It was like it was yesterday to them. I was stunned."

The real breakthrough, however, came after the respondents awoke out of their trance. "When he brought them all back out, he asked them who'd they prefer as a gasoline purveyor," Oeschle says. "What staggered me was that, to a person, it was always linked to that experience in their youth." One woman volunteered that she always made a point of filling up at Texaco. "We asked her why," Oeschle recalls. "And she said, 'I don't know, I guess I just feel good about Texaco.' Well, this was the little three-and-a-half-year-old in the back of her daddy's car speaking."

Shell is now designing new marketing approaches based on the insights gleaned from the groups of mesmerized motorists. Where Shell had gone wrong, it seems, was in reasoning that, since people don't start buying gas until at least age 16, there was no need to target the tiniest consumers. "They weren't even on Shell's radar," Oeschle laments. "It dawned on us...that we'd better figure out how to favourably impact people from an early age."

Similarly, DaimlerChrysler used a dose of deep motivation research to create a successful new concept car:

A few years back, DaimlerChrysler set out to find the next "wow car," the "segment buster" that would reach across age and income lines, into the subconscious. That meant doing more than the usual focus group research. So DaimlerChrysler hired psychologist Clothaire Rapaille to probe consumers' innermost feelings. The underlying premise: The products we buy mean something; they form part of a greater whole.

Rather than convening traditional focus groups, Rapaille used a method known as "archetype research." He had participants lie on soft mats, listen to mood music, and free-associate in the dark. According to Bostwick, this re-creates the same brain activity you have when you first wake up from a dream. "It's a very special brain activity," he says. "It allows us to actually access some of those unconscious thoughts."

When the lights came back up, Rapaille had learned that Americans are entrepreneurial, individualistic, freedom loving, and inventive—but also juvenile and self-indulgent. More important, he discovered that many suffered nostalgia pangs. In these complex and often unsettling times, car buyers yearned for the good old days—for a time when things seemed simpler and more secure, and when people felt good about themselves. "What that said to us is that people are looking for something that offers protection on the outside, and comfort on the inside," says Bostwick. "We communicated that to our design team."

The result: the PT Cruiser, DaimlerChrysler's phenomenally successful retro-style car. Described by the *Wall Street Journal* as "part 1920s gangster car, part 1950s hot rod, and part London taxicab," the PT Cruiser is what one analyst calls "a focus group on wheels—an actual chrome-and-sheet-metal incarnation of the popular will." Its nostalgic look and protective exterior, combined with a well-appointed and highly functional interior, inspires an emotional reaction from almost everyone. In just two years following its introduction, North American consumers snapped up more than 225 000 PT Cruisers. "We didn't set out to create a market," Bostwick says earnestly. "We just tapped into what people had in their heads in the first place.... The vehicle takes you back, but not to a particular time in the century. It just takes you back to a time you felt cool."

Some marketers dismiss such motivation research as mumbo jumbo. However, like Shell and Daimler-Chrysler, many companies are now delving into the murky depths of the consumer unconscious. "Such tactics have been worshipfully embraced by even the no-nonsense, jut-jawed captains of industry," claims an analyst. "At companies like Kraft, Coca-Cola, Procter & Gamble, and DaimlerChrysler, the most sought-after consultants hail not from [traditional consulting firms like McKinsey. They come] from brand consultancies with names like Archetype Discoveries, PsychoLogics and Semiotic Solutions."

Sources: Examples adapted from Ruth Shalit, "The Return of the Hidden Persuaders," *Salon Media,* September 27, 1999, www.salon.com. Also see Annetta Miller and Dody Tsiantar, "Psyching Out Consumers," *Newsweek,* February 27, 1989, pp. 46–47; Gerry Khermouch, "Consumers in the Mist," *Business Week,* February 26, 2001, pp. 92–94; Alison Stein Wellner, "Research on a Shoestring," *American Demographics,* April 2001, pp. 38–39; Phil Patton, "Car Shrinks," *Fortune,* March 18, 2002, pp. 187–190; and "PT Cruiser," *Journal of Business and Design,* accessed at the Corporate Design Foundation website, www.cdf.org (June 2002).

What light does Maslow's theory throw on Jennifer Wong's interest in buying a motorcycle? We can guess that Jennifer has satisfied her physiological, safety, and social needs; they do not motivate her interest in motorcycles. Her motorcycle interest may come from a strong need for more esteem. Or it may come from a need for self-actualization—she may want to be a daring person and express herself through product ownership.

Figure 7.4 Maslow's hierarchy of needs

Source: From *Motivation and Personality* by Abraham H. Maslow. Copyright © 1970 by Abraham H. Maslow. Copyright 1954, 1987 by Harper & Row Publishers, Inc. Reprinted by permission of Addison-Wesley Educational Publishers Inc. Also see Barbara Marx Hubbard, "Seeking Our Future Potentials," *The Futurist,* May 1998, pp. 29–32.

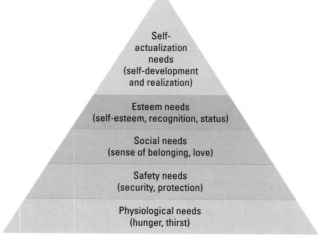

Perception

Perception
The process by which people select, organize, and interpret information to form a meaningful picture of the world.

A motivated person is ready to act. How the person acts is influenced by his or her perception of the situation. All of us learn by the flow of information through our five senses: sight, hearing, smell, touch, and taste. However, each of us receives, organizes, and interprets this sensory information in an individual way. **Perception** is the process by which people select, organize, and interpret information to form a meaningful picture of the world.

People form different perceptions of the same stimulus due to three perceptual processes: selective attention, selective distortion, and selective retention. People are exposed to a great number of stimuli every day. For example, the average person may be exposed to about 5000 ads in a single day.[23] It is impossible for a person to pay attention to all these stimuli. *Selective attention*—the tendency for people to screen out most of the information to which they are exposed—means that marketers must work especially hard to attract the consumer's attention. Their message will be lost on most people who are not in the market for the product. Moreover, even people who are in the market may not notice the message unless it stands out from the surrounding sea of other ads.

Even noted stimuli do not always come across in the intended way. Each person fits incoming information into an existing mindset. *Selective distortion* is the tendency of people to interpret information in a way that will support what they already believe. Jennifer Wong may hear the salesperson mention some good and bad points about a competing motorcycle. Because she already has a strong leaning toward Harley, she is likely to distort those points to conclude that Harley is the better motorcycle. Selective distortion means that marketers must try to understand consumers' perspectives and how these will affect interpretations of advertising and sales information.

People also forget much that they learn. They tend to retain information that supports their attitudes and beliefs. Because of *selective retention,* Jennifer is likely to remember good points made about Harley and to forget good points made about competing motorcycles. Because of selective exposure, distortion, and retention, marketers have to work hard to get their messages through. This fact explains why marketers use so much drama and repetition in sending messages to their market.

Interestingly, although most marketers worry about whether their offers will be perceived at all, some consumers worry that they will be affected by marketing messages without even knowing it—through *subliminal advertising.* In 1957, a researcher announced that he had flashed the phrases "Eat popcorn" and "Drink Coca-Cola" on a screen in a New Jersey movie theatre every five seconds for 1/300th of a second. He reported that although viewers did not consciously recognize these messages, they absorbed them subconsciously and bought 58 percent more popcorn and 18 percent more Coke. Suddenly advertisers and consumer-protection groups became intensely interested in subliminal perception. People voiced fears of being brainwashed, and Canada and California declared the practice illegal. Although the researcher later admitted to making up the data, the issue has not died. Some consumers still fear that they are being manipulated by subliminal messages.

Numerous studies by psychologists and consumer researchers have found no link between subliminal messages and consumer behaviour. It appears that subliminal advertising simply doesn't have the power attributed to it by its critics. Most advertisers scoff at the notion of an industry conspiracy to manipulate consumers through "invisible" messages.

Learning

Learning
Changes in an individual's behaviour arising from experience.

When people act, they learn. **Learning** describes changes in an individual's behaviour arising from experience. Learning theorists say that most human behaviour is learned. Learning occurs through the interplay of *drives, stimuli, cues, responses,* and *reinforcement.*

We saw that Jennifer Wong has a drive for self-actualization. A *drive* is a strong internal stimulus that calls for action. Her drive becomes a motive when it is directed toward a particular *stimulus object,* in this case a motorcycle. Jennifer's response to the idea of buying a motorcycle is conditioned by the surrounding cues. *Cues* are minor stimuli that determine when, where, and how the person responds. Seeing motorcycles roaring down the streets, hearing of a special sale price, and receiving her boyfriend's support are all *cues* that can influence Jennifer's *response* to her interest in buying a motorcycle.

Suppose Jennifer buys a Harley. If the experience is rewarding, she will probably use the motorcycle more and more. Her response to motorcycles will be *reinforced.* If she decides to upgrade from her first bike to a more upscale model, the probability is greater that she will buy another Harley. The practical significance of learning theory for marketers is that they can build up demand for a product by associating it with strong drives, using motivating cues, and providing positive reinforcement.

Beliefs and Attitudes

Belief

A descriptive thought that a person holds about something.

Through doing and learning, people acquire beliefs and attitudes. These, in turn, influence their buying behaviour. A **belief** is a descriptive thought that a person has about something. Jennifer Wong may believe that a Harley motorcycle is a classic bike, that it has more power than its rivals, and that it stands up well to urban driving conditions. These beliefs may be based on real knowledge, opinion, or faith, and may or may not carry an emotional charge.

Marketers are interested in the beliefs that people formulate about specific products and services, because these beliefs compose product and brand images that affect buying behaviour. If some of the beliefs are wrong and prevent purchase, the marketer will want to launch a campaign to correct them.

Attitude

A person's consistently favourable or unfavourable evaluations, feelings, and tendencies toward an object or idea.

People have attitudes about religion, politics, clothes, music, food, and almost everything else. **Attitude** describes a person's relatively consistent evaluations, feelings, and tendencies toward an object or idea. Attitudes put people into a frame of mind of liking or disliking things, of moving toward or away from them. Thus, Jennifer may hold such attitudes as "Buy the best." "Adventurousness and self-expression are among the most important things in life." If so, the Harley motorcycle would fit well into Jennifer's existing attitudes.

Attitudes are difficult to change. A person's attitudes fit into a pattern, and to change one attitude may require difficult adjustments in many others. Thus, a company should usually try to fit its products into existing attitudes rather than attempt to change attitudes. However, there are exceptions in which the great cost of trying to change attitudes may pay off handsomely:

An unspoken rule in food marketing is to avoid using newspaper ads. "Given the general standard of newsprint reproduction, that tempting plate of pasta is likely to wind up with all the appetite appeal of a used muffler." But breaking the rules helped the Quebec Milk Producers (La Fédération des Producteurs de Lait du Québec) change the attitude of adults over 30 and get them back into the habit of drinking milk. And non-traditional newspaper advertising proved to be the best way to reach this older target audience on a daily basis.

In contrast to other newspaper advertising that tends to be visually clamorous and overloaded with information, the Quebec Milk Producers kept their ads relatively clean and uncluttered, and thus, they gave themselves a better shot at standing out. Since adults already knew the health benefits of milk, creators of the campaign decided to take a different tack and decided to play upon the consumer's emotional connection with the product. Each ad showed milk in a simple, highly recognized receptacle—a glass, jug, carton, plastic container, and a baby bottle—on a white background. Each photo was overlaid by a catchy phrase. It was these headlines—"What your inner child is thirsting for," "Remember, you used to cry for it," "The mother of all beverages"—that made an emotional connection between these adult consumers and the product. Was the campaign a success? Not only did it win five Coq d'Or awards, it was "the first time in 25 years of working in advertising that I've ever gotten so many calls and letters from people saying they love our campaign," says Nicole Dubé, director of advertising and promotions for the milk marketers at La Fédération des Producteurs de Lait du Québec.[24]

We can now appreciate the many forces acting on consumer behaviour. The consumer's choice is a result of the complex interplay of cultural, social, personal, and psychological factors.

Types of Buying Decision Behaviour

Buying behaviour differs greatly for a tube of toothpaste, a tennis racket, an expensive motorcycle, or a new car. More complex decisions usually involve more buying participants and more buyer deliberation. Figure 7.5 shows types of consumer buying behaviour based on the degree of buyer involvement and the degree of differences between brands.[25]

Complex Buying Behaviour

Complex buying behaviour
Consumer buying behaviour in situations characterized by high consumer involvement in a purchase and significant perceived differences between brands.

Consumers undertake **complex buying behaviour** when they are highly involved in a purchase and perceive significant differences between brands. Consumers may be highly involved when the product is expensive, risky, purchased infrequently, and highly self-expressive. Typically, the consumer has much to learn about the product category. For example, a personal computer buyer may not know what attributes to consider. Many product features carry no real meaning: a "Pentium III chip," "super VGA resolution," or "64 megs of RAM."

This buyer will pass through a learning process, first developing beliefs about the product, then attitudes, and then making a thoughtful purchase choice. Marketers of high-involvement products must understand the information-gathering and evaluation behaviour of high-involvement consumers. They need to help buyers learn about product-class attributes and their relative importance, and about what the company's brand offers on the important attributes. They need to differentiate their brand's features, perhaps by describing the brand's benefits using print media with long copy. They must motivate store salespeople and the buyer's acquaintances to influence the final brand choice.

Dissonance-Reducing Buying Behaviour

Dissonance-reducing buying behaviour
Consumer buying behaviour in situations characterized by high involvement but few perceived differences between brands.

Dissonance-reducing buying behaviour occurs when consumers are highly involved with an expensive, infrequent, or risky purchase, but see little difference between

Figure 7.5 Four types of buying behaviour

Source: Adapted from Henry Assael, *Consumer Behavior and Marketing Action* (Boston: Kent Publishing Company, 1987), p. 87. © Wadsworth, Inc. 1987. Printed by permission of Kent Publishing Company, a division of Wadsworth, Inc.

	High involvement	Low involvement
Significant differences between brands	Complex buying behaviour	Variety-seeking buying behaviour
Few differences between brands	Dissonance-reducing buying behaviour	Habitual buying behaviour

brands. For example, consumers buying carpeting may face a high-involvement decision because carpeting is expensive and self-expressive. Yet buyers may consider most carpet brands in a given price range to be the same. In this case, because perceived brand differences are not large, buyers may shop around to learn what is available, but buy relatively quickly. They may respond primarily to a good price or for convenience.

After the purchase, consumers might experience *postpurchase dissonance,* or after-sale discomfort, when they notice certain disadvantages of the purchased carpet brand or hear favourable things about brands not purchased. To counter such dissonance, the marketer's after-sale communications should provide evidence and support to help consumers feel good about their brand choices.

Habitual Buying Behaviour

Habitual buying behaviour
Consumer buying behaviour in situations characterized by low consumer involvement and few significant perceived brand differences.

Habitual buying behaviour occurs under conditions of low consumer involvement and little significant brand difference. Consider salt, for example. Consumers have little involvement in this product category—they simply go to the store and reach for a brand. If they keep reaching for the same brand, it is out of habit rather than strong brand loyalty. Consumers appear to have low involvement with most low-cost, frequently purchased products.

In such cases, consumer behaviour does not pass through the usual belief–attitude–behaviour sequence. Consumers do not search extensively for information about the brand, evaluate brand characteristics, and make weighty decisions about which brand to buy. Instead, they passively receive information as they watch television or read magazines. Ad repetition creates *brand familiarity* rather than *brand conviction.* Consumers do not form strong attitudes toward a brand; they select the brand because it is familiar. Because they are not highly involved with the product, consumers may not evaluate the choice even after purchase. Thus, the buying process involves brand beliefs formed by passive learning, followed by purchase behaviour, which may or may not be followed by evaluation.

Because buyers are not highly committed to any brands, marketers of low-involvement products with few brand differences often use price and sales promotions to stimulate product trial. In advertising for a low-involvement product, ad copy should stress a few key points. Visual symbols and imagery are important because they can be remembered easily and associated with the brand. Ad campaigns should include high repetition of short-duration messages. Television is usually more effective than print media because it is a low-involvement medium suitable for passive learning. Advertising planning should be based on classical conditioning theory, in which buyers learn to identify a certain product by a symbol repeatedly attached to it.

Variety-Seeking Buying Behaviour

Variety-seeking buying behaviour
Consumer buying behaviour in situations characterized by low consumer involvement but significant perceived brand differences.

Consumers undertake **variety-seeking buying behaviour** in situations characterized by low consumer involvement but significant perceived brand differences. In such cases, consumers often do a lot of brand switching. For example, when buying cookies, a consumer may hold some beliefs, choose a cookie brand without much evaluation, and then evaluate that brand during consumption. But the next time, the consumer may choose another brand out of boredom or simply to try something different. Brand switching occurs for the sake of variety rather than due to dissatisfaction.

In such product categories, the marketing strategy may differ for the market leader and minor brands. The market leader will try to encourage habitual buying behaviour by dominating shelf space, keeping shelves fully stocked, and running frequent reminder advertising. Challenger firms will encourage variety seeking by offering lower prices, special deals, coupons, free samples, and advertising that presents reasons for trying something new.

Figure 7.6 Buyer decision process

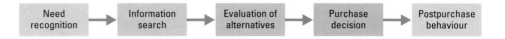

| Need recognition | → | Information search | → | Evaluation of alternatives | → | Purchase decision | → | Postpurchase behaviour |

The Buyer Decision Process

Now that we have looked at the influences that affect buyers, we are ready to look at how consumers make buying decisions. Figure 7.6 shows how the consumer passes through five stages: *need recognition, information search, evaluation of alternatives, purchase decision,* and *postpurchase behaviour.* Clearly, the buying process starts long before the actual purchase and continues long after. Marketers need to focus on the entire buying process rather than just on the purchase decision.

The figure implies that consumers pass through all five stages with every purchase. But in more routine purchases, consumers often skip or reverse some of these stages. A woman buying her regular brand of toothpaste would recognize the need and go right to the purchase decision, skipping information search and evaluation. However, we use the model in Figure 7.6 because it shows all the considerations that arise when a consumer faces a new and complex purchase situation.

Need Recognition

Need recognition
The first stage of the buyer decision process in which the consumer recognizes a problem or need.

The buying process starts with **need recognition**—the buyer recognizes a problem or need. The need can be triggered by *internal stimuli* when one of the person's normal needs—hunger, thirst, sex—rises to a level high enough to become a drive. A need can also be triggered by *external stimuli.* A person passes a bakery and the smell of freshly baked bread stimulates his or her hunger. At this stage, the marketer should research consumers to determine what kinds of needs or problems arise, what brought them about, and how they led the consumer to this particular product.

Jennifer Wong might answer that she felt the need for more convenience when it came to transportation. Her office recently relocated and is no longer near a subway station. She first considered buying a car, but soon realized that parking in downtown Toronto would pose a problem. The rising cost of gas also concerned

Need recognition can be triggered by advertising. This ad asks an arresting question that alerts parents to the need for a high-quality bike helmet.

her. Thus, her focus turned to another option—a motorcycle. By gathering such information, the marketer can identify the factors that most often trigger interest in the product and can develop marketing programs that involve these factors.

Information Search

Information search

The stage of the buyer decision process in which the consumer is aroused to search for more information; the consumer may simply have heightened attention or may go into active information search.

An interested consumer may or may not search for more information. If the consumer's drive is strong and a satisfying product is near at hand, the consumer is likely to buy it. If not, the consumer may store the need in memory or undertake an **information search** related to the need. At the least, Jennifer Wong will probably pay more attention to motorcycle ads, bikes used by friends, and conversations about motorcycles. Or Jennifer may actively look for reading material, phone friends, and gather information in other ways. The amount of searching she does will depend on the strength of her drive, the amount of information she starts with, the ease of obtaining more information, the value she places on additional information, and the satisfaction she gets from searching.

The consumer can obtain information from any of several sources. These include *personal sources* (family, friends, neighbours, acquaintances), *commercial sources* (advertising, salespeople, dealers, packaging, displays), *public sources* (mass media, consumer-rating organizations), and *experiential sources* (handling, examining, using the product). The relative influence of these information sources varies with the product and the buyer. Generally, the consumer receives the most information about a product from commercial sources—those controlled by the marketer. The most effective sources, however, tend to be personal. Commercial sources normally *inform* the buyer, but personal sources *legitimize* or *evaluate* products for the buyer.

People often ask others—friends, relatives, acquaintances, professionals—for recommendations concerning a product or service. Thus, companies have a strong interest in building such *word-of-mouth* sources. These sources have two chief advantages. First, they are convincing: word of mouth is the only promotion method that is *of* consumers, *by* consumers, and *for* consumers. Having loyal, satisfied customers that brag about doing business with you is the dream of every business owner. Not only are satisfied customers repeat buyers, but they are also walking, talking billboards for your business. Second, the costs are low. Keeping in touch with satisfied customers and turning them into word-of-mouth advocates costs the business relatively little.[26]

As more information is obtained, the consumer's awareness and knowledge of the available brands and features increase. In her information search, Jennifer Wong learned about the many motorcycle brands available. The information also helped her drop certain brands from consideration. A company must design its marketing mix to make prospects aware of and knowledgeable about its brand. It should carefully identify consumers' sources of information and the importance of each source.

Evaluation of Alternatives

Alternative evaluation

The stage of the buyer decision process in which the consumer uses information to evaluate alternative brands in the choice set.

We have seen how the consumer uses information to arrive at a set of final brand choices. How does the consumer choose between the alternative brands? The marketer needs to know about **alternative evaluation**—that is, how the consumer processes information to arrive at brand choices. Unfortunately, consumers do not use a simple and single evaluation process in all buying situations. Instead, several evaluation processes are at work.

The consumer arrives at attitudes toward different brands through some evaluation procedure. How consumers evaluate purchase alternatives depends on the individual consumer and the specific buying situation. In some cases, consumers use careful calculations and logical thinking. At other times, the same consumers do little or no evaluating, instead buying on impulse and relying on intuition. Sometimes consumers make buying decisions on their own; sometimes they turn to friends, consumer guides, or salespeople for buying advice.

Suppose Jennifer has narrowed her choices to four motorcycles. And suppose that she is primarily interested in four attributes—quality, ease of handling, ergonomic design, and price. Jennifer has formed beliefs about how each brand rates on each attribute. Clearly, if one motorcycle rated best on all the attributes, we could predict that Jennifer would choose it. But the brands vary in appeal. Jennifer might base her buying decision on only one attribute, and her choice would be easy to predict. If Jennifer wants ease of handling above everything, she will buy the motorcycle that rates highest on this attribute. But most buyers consider several attributes, each with different importance. If we knew the importance weights that Jennifer assigns to each of the four attributes, we could predict her motorcycle choice more reliably.

Marketers should study buyers to determine how they actually evaluate brand alternatives. If they know what evaluative processes go on, marketers can take steps to influence the buyer's decision.

Purchase Decision

Purchase decision

The buyer's decision about which brand to purchase.

In the evaluation stage, the consumer ranks brands and forms purchase intentions. Generally, the consumer's **purchase decision** will be to buy the most preferred brand, but two factors can come between the purchase *intention* and the purchase *decision*. The first factor is the *attitudes of others*. If Jennifer Wong's boyfriend or family feel strongly that Jennifer should buy the lowest-priced motorcycle, then the chances of her buying a more expensive motorcycle will be reduced.

The second factor is *unexpected situational factors*. The consumer may form a purchase intention based on such factors as expected income, expected price, and expected product benefits. However, unexpected events can change the purchase intention. Jennifer may lose her job, some other purchase may become more urgent, or a close friend may report being disappointed in her preferred motorcycle. Or a competitor may drop its price. Thus, preferences and even purchase intentions do not always result in actual purchase choice.

Postpurchase Behaviour

Postpurchase behaviour

The stage of the buyer decision process in which consumers take further action after purchase based on their satisfaction or dissatisfaction.

The marketer's job does not end when the product is bought. After purchasing the product, the consumer will be satisfied or dissatisfied and will engage in **postpurchase behaviour** of interest to the marketer. What determines whether the buyer is satisfied or dissatisfied with a purchase? The answer lies in the relationship between the *consumer's expectations* and the product's *perceived performance*. If the product falls short of expectations, the consumer is disappointed; if it meets expectations, the consumer is satisfied; if it exceeds expectations, the consumer is delighted.

The larger the gap between expectations and performance, the greater the consumer's dissatisfaction. This suggests that sellers should make product claims that accurately represent the product's performance, so that buyers are satisfied. For example, Boeing's salespeople tend to be conservative when they estimate the potential benefits of their aircraft. They almost always underestimate fuel efficiency—they promise a 5 percent savings that turns out to be 8 percent. Customers are delighted with better-than-expected performance; they buy again and tell other potential customers that Boeing lives up to its promises.

Cognitive dissonance

Buyer discomfort caused by postpurchase conflict.

Almost all major purchases result in **cognitive dissonance**, or discomfort caused by postpurchase conflict. After the purchase, consumers are satisfied with the benefits of the chosen brand and are glad to avoid the drawbacks of the brands not bought. However, every purchase involves compromise. Consumers feel uneasy about acquiring the drawbacks of the chosen brand and about losing the benefits of the brands not purchased. Thus, consumers feel at least some postpurchase dissonance for every purchase.[27]

Why is it so important to satisfy the customer? Such satisfaction is important because a company's sales come from two basic groups—*new customers* and *retained customers*. It usually costs more to attract new customers than to retain current ones. And the best way to retain current customers is to keep them satisfied. Customer satisfaction is a key to building lasting relationships with consumers—to keeping and growing consumers and reaping their customer lifetime value. Satisfied customers buy a product again, talk favourably to others about the product, pay less attention to competing brands and advertising, and buy other products from the company. Many marketers go beyond merely *meeting* the expectations of customers—they aim to *delight* the customer.

A dissatisfied consumer responds differently. Whereas, on average, a satisfied customer tells three people about a good product experience, a dissatisfied customer gripes to eleven people. In fact, one study showed that 13 percent of the people who had a problem with an organization complained about the company to more than twenty people.[28] Clearly, bad word of mouth travels farther and faster than good word of mouth and can quickly damage consumer attitudes about a company and its products.

Therefore, a company would be wise to measure customer satisfaction regularly. It cannot simply rely on dissatisfied customers to volunteer their complaints when they are dissatisfied. Some 96 percent of unhappy customers never tell the company about their problem. Companies should set up systems that *encourage* customers to complain (see Real Marketing 7.4). In this way, the company can learn how well it is doing and how it can improve. The 3M Company claims that over two-thirds of its new product ideas come from listening to customer complaints. But listening is not enough—the company also must respond constructively to the complaints it receives.

By studying the overall buyer decision, marketers may be able to find ways to help consumers move through it. For example, if consumers are not buying a new product because they do not perceive a need for it, marketing might launch advertising messages that trigger the need and show how the product solves customers' problems. If customers know about the product but are not buying because they hold unfavourable attitudes toward it, the marketer must find ways to either change the product or change consumer perceptions.

The Buyer Decision Process for New Products

We have looked at the stages buyers go through in trying to satisfy a need. Buyers may pass quickly or slowly through these stages, and some of the stages may even be reversed. Much depends on the nature of the buyer, the product, and the buying situation.

We now look at how buyers approach the purchase of new products. A **new product** is a good, service, or idea that is perceived by some potential customers as new. It may have been around for a while, but our interest is in how consumers learn about products for the first time and make decisions on whether to adopt them. We define the **adoption process** as "the mental process through which an individual passes from first learning about an innovation to final adoption,"[29] and *adoption* as the decision by an individual to become a regular user of the product.

New product
A good, service, or idea that is perceived by some potential customers as new.

Adoption process
The mental process through which an individual passes from first hearing about an innovation to final adoption.

7.4   Got a Problem? Just Phone, Fax, Email, or Web Chat with Us!

What should companies do with dissatisfied customers? Everything they can! Unhappy customers not only stop buying but also can quickly damage the company's image. Some 68 percent of consumers who defect do so because of bad service. Enlightened companies don't try to hide from dissatisfied customers; they go out of their way to encourage customers to complain, and then bend over backward to make disgruntled buyers happy again.

At a minimum, most companies offer toll-free numbers to handle complaints, inquiries, and orders. For example, over the past two decades, the Gerber help line (1-800-4-GERBER) received more than five million calls. Help line staffers, most of them mothers or grandmothers themselves, handle customer concerns and provide baby care advice 24 hours a day, 365 days a year, to more than 2400 callers a day. The help line is staffed by English-, French-, and Spanish-speaking operators, and interpreters are available for most other languages. Callers include new parents, daycare providers, and even health professionals. They ask a wide variety of questions, from when to feed a baby specific foods to how to babyproof a home. One in five of all calls to the help line comes from men.

General Electric's Answer Center may be one of the most extensive 800-number systems. It handles more than three million calls a year, only 5 percent of them complaints. At the heart of the system is a giant database that provides the centre's service reps with instant access to more than a million answers about 8500 models in 120 product lines. The centre receives some unusual calls, such as when a submarine off the Connecticut coast requested help fixing a motor. Still, according to GE, its people resolve 90 percent of complaints or inquiries on the first call, and complainers often become even more loyal customers. GE has now set up two answer centres online (www.ge.oac and www.geappliances.com/geac/) that help customers obtain product and service information, troubleshoot product problems, locate dealers, and even schedule service appointments.

As Susan Leigh, marketing and communications manager for Bell Canada's Contact Centre Solutions Team, notes, call centres themselves have evolved dramatically. Most call centres today are much more than just a bank of phones that receives complaints. They are high-tech, Web-enabled contact centres that employ a sophisticated mix of phone, email, fax, and interactive voice and data technologies. Kraft Canada uses its contact centre to cement relationships with its customers, whether they call for advice on how to prepare simple meals with ingredients they have in their cupboards or how to enrol in classes at the Kraft Kitchens Cooking School. Consider another example:

It's February 14, and you've just remembered that it's Valentine's Day. There's no time for florist shops, so you jump online to www.1800FLOWERS.com. Then you pause. Red roses? Boxed or in a vase? One dozen or two? Just as your head starts to pound, you notice a button on the website. Click on it, and you're connected to a customer service rep at the call centre who can help sniff out your options. A chat page opens on your screen, allowing a

Web-enabled customer contact centres: Customers can initiate a chat session with a 1-800-Flowers service representative who answers questions and "pushes" pages to their browsers. In the future, interactive voice and image technology will even let customers see and talk with reps on their computer screens.

real-time dialogue with the agent. The service rep even "pushes" pages to your browser so you can see different floral arrangements and how much they cost. In minutes, you have placed your order online, with a little hand-holding. Fiction? Not really. Several emarketers, including 1-800-Flowers, are testing or already offer live interaction with service reps. Some feature real-time chat sessions, others voice-over-Web capabilities. In the future, a "call cam" may even let consumers see an agent on their computer screen.

The idea is to make customers' interactions with companies seamless and uniform, no matter which form of communication they choose. Integrate the telephone with Web technology and you have an extremely powerful means of handling customer questions and concerns. This technology lets a customer browse a website on a PC at the same time that a customer service agent browses the site. The two can talk over a separate telephone line or an Internet connection to discuss problems or compare products.

Bell Canada helps its business clients develop and improve their customer contact centres. Experience has shown that building a contact centre can spearhead enormous changes in the way a firm delivers its services and relates to its customers. With Bell's help, a firm's contact centre can anticipate and respond to shifts in customer needs and preferences while reducing costs and increasing revenues. Leigh notes that contact centres have become critical to customer-focused business strategies and are often the differentiating factor that allows a company to gain a

significant competitive advantage. "For instance, a sudden spike in calls to a customer service number often suggests breakdowns elsewhere in the organization, perhaps in quality control, marketing, or shipping," Leigh suggests.

Of course, the best way to keep customers happy is to provide good products and services in the first place. Short of that, however, a company must develop a good system for ferreting out problems and connecting with customers. Such a system is much more than just a necessary evil—customer happiness usually shows up on the company's bottom line. One recent study found that dollars invested in complaint-handling and customer contact systems yield an average return of between 100 and 200 percent. Maryanne Rasmussen, vice-president of worldwide quality at American Express, offers this formula: "Better complaint handling equals higher customer satisfaction equals higher brand loyalty equals higher performance."

Sources: Quotes from Susan Leigh, "Customer Contact Centres a Tool for Growth," *Strategy*, June 7, 1999, p. D14; "On Mother's Day, Advice Goes a Long Way," PR Newswire, Ziff Communications, May 2, 1995; Alessandra Bianchi, "Lines of Fire," *Inc. Technology*, 1998, pp. 36–48; Matt Hamblen, "Call Centers and Web Sites Cozy Up," *Computerworld*, March 2, 1998, p. 1; Ellen Jovin and Jennifer Lach, "Online with the Operator," *American Demographics*, February 1999, pp. 36–39; Bob Wallace and George V. Hulme, "The Modern Call Center," *Informationweek*, April 9, 2001, pp. 38–46; Alice Dragoon, "Put Your Money Where Your Mouthpiece Is," *Darwin*, February 2002, pp. 60–65; and David L. Margulius, "Smarter Call Centers: At Your Service?" *New York Times*, March 14, 2002, p. G1.

Stages in the Adoption Process

Consumers pass through five stages in the process of adopting a new product:

- *Awareness.* The consumer becomes aware of the new product, but lacks information about it.
- *Interest.* The consumer seeks information about the new product.
- *Evaluation.* The consumer considers whether trying the new product makes sense.
- *Trial.* The consumer tries the new product on a small scale to improve his or her estimate of its value.
- *Adoption.* The consumer decides to make full and regular use of the new product.

This model suggests that the new product marketer should consider how to help consumers move through these stages. A manufacturer of large-screen televisions may discover that many consumers in the interest stage do not move to the trial stage because of uncertainty and the large investment. If these same consumers would be willing to use a large-screen television on a trial basis for a small fee, the manufacturer should consider offering a trial-use plan with an option to buy.

Individual Differences in Innovativeness

People differ greatly in their readiness to try new products. In each product area, there are "consumption pioneers" and early adopters. Other individuals adopt new products much later. People can be classified into the adopter categories shown in Figure 7.7. After a slow start, an increasing number of people adopt the new product. The number of adopters reaches a peak and then drops off as fewer non-adopters remain. Innovators are defined as the first 2.5 percent of the buyers to adopt a new idea (those beyond two standard deviations from mean adoption time); the early adopters are the next 13.5 percent (between one and two standard deviations); and so forth.

The five adopter groups have differing values. *Innovators* are venturesome—they try new ideas at some risk. *Early adopters* are guided by respect—they are opinion leaders in their communities and adopt new ideas early but carefully. The *early majority* are deliberate—although they rarely are leaders, they adopt new ideas before the average person. The *late majority* are skeptical—they adopt an innovation only after most people have tried it. Finally, *laggards* are tradition bound—they are suspicious of changes and adopt the innovation only when it has become something of a tradition itself.

This adopter classification suggests that an innovating firm should research the characteristics of innovators and early adopters and should direct marketing efforts at them. In general, innovators tend to be relatively younger, better educated, and higher in income than later adopters and non-adopters. They are more receptive to unfamiliar things, rely more on their own values and judgment, and are more willing to take risks. They are less brand loyal and more likely to take advantage of special promotions such as discounts, coupons, and samples.

Influence of Product Characteristics on Rate of Adoption

The characteristics of the new product affect its rate of adoption. Some products catch on almost overnight (Beanie Babies), whereas others take a long time to gain acceptance, such as high-density television (HDTV). Five characteristics are especially important in influencing an innovation's rate of adoption. For example, consider the characteristics of HDTV in relation to the rate of adoption:

- *Relative advantage* is the degree to which the innovation appears superior to existing products. The greater the perceived relative advantage of using HDTV—say, in picture quality and ease of viewing—the sooner HDTVs will be adopted.

Figure 7.7 Adopter categories based on relative time of adoption

Source: Everett M. Rogers, *Diffusion of Innovations*, 4th ed. (New York: Free Press, 1995). Copyright © 1995 by Everett M. Rogers. Copyright © 1962, 1971, 1983 by The Free Press. Reprinted with the permission of The Free Press, a Division of Simon & Schuster.

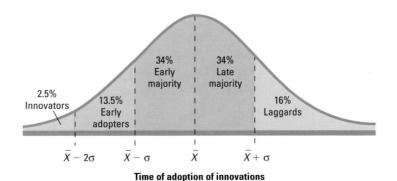

New-product adoption rate: Some products catch on almost overnight. Others, such as HDTV, take a long time to gain acceptance.

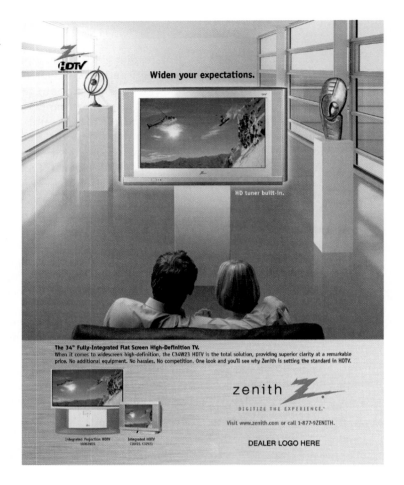

- *Compatibility* is the degree to which the innovation fits the values and experiences of potential consumers. HDTV, for example, is highly compatible with the lifestyles found in upper-middle-class homes. However, it is not very compatible with the programming and broadcasting systems currently available to consumers.
- *Complexity* is the degree to which the innovation is difficult to understand or use. HDTV is not very complex and therefore, once programming is available and prices come down, it will take less time to penetrate homes than more complex innovations.
- *Divisibility* is the degree to which the innovation may be tried on a limited basis. HDTVs are still very expensive. To the extent that people can lease them with an option to buy, their rate of adoption will increase.
- *Communicability* is the degree to which the results of using the innovation can be observed or described to others. Because HDTV lends itself to demonstration and description, its use will spread faster among consumers.

Other characteristics that influence the rate of adoption are initial and ongoing costs, risk and uncertainty, and social approval. The new product marketer must research all these factors when developing the new product and its marketing program.

Consumer Behaviour across International Borders

Understanding consumer behaviour is difficult enough for companies marketing within the borders of a single country. For companies operating in many countries, however, understanding and serving the needs of consumers can be daunting. Although consumers in different countries may have some things in common, their values, attitudes, and behaviours often vary greatly. International marketers must understand such differences and adjust their products and marketing programs accordingly.

Sometimes the differences are obvious. For example, in Canada and the United States, where most people eat cereal regularly for breakfast, Kellogg focuses its marketing on persuading consumers to select a Kellogg brand rather than a competitor's brand. In France, however, where most people prefer croissants and coffee or no breakfast at all, Kellogg's advertising simply attempts to convince people that they should eat cereal for breakfast. Its packaging includes step-by-step instructions on how to prepare cereal. In India, where many consumers eat heavy, fried breakfasts and some consumers skip the meal altogether, Kellogg's advertising attempts to convince buyers to switch to a lighter, more nutritious breakfast diet.

Often differences across international markets are more subtle. They may result from physical differences in consumers and their environments. For example, Remington makes smaller electric shavers to fit the smaller hands of Japanese consumers and battery-powered shavers for the British market, where few bathrooms have electrical outlets. Other differences result from varying customs. In Japan, for example, where humility and deference are considered great virtues, pushy, hard-hitting sales approaches are considered offensive. Failing to understand such differences in customs and behaviours between countries can mean disaster for a marketer's international products and programs.

Marketers must decide on the degree to which they will adapt their products and marketing programs to meet the unique cultures and needs of consumers in various markets. On the one hand, they want to standardize their offerings to simplify operations and take advantage of cost economies. On the other hand, adapting marketing efforts within each country results in products and programs that better satisfy the needs of local consumers. The question of whether to adapt or standardize the marketing mix across international markets has created a lively debate in recent years.

Looking Back: Reviewing the Concepts

The Canadian consumer market consists of about 31.4 people who consume many billions of dollars worth of goods and services each year, making it one of the most attractive consumer markets in the world. The world consumer market consists of more than 6.2 billion people. Consumers around the world vary greatly in age, income, education level, and tastes. Understanding how these differences affect *consumer buying behaviour* is one of the biggest challenges marketers face.

1. Define the consumer market and construct a simple model of consumer buyer behaviour.

The *consumer market* consists of all the individuals and households who buy or acquire goods and services for personal consumption. The simplest model of consumer buyer behaviour is the stimulus–response model. According to this model, marketing stimuli (the four *P*s) and other major forces (economic, technological, political, cultural) enter the consumer's "black box," and produce certain responses. Once in the black box, these inputs produce observable buyer responses, such as product choice, brand choice, dealer choice, purchase timing, and purchase amount.

2. Name the four major factors that influence consumer buyer behaviour.

Consumer buyer behaviour is influenced by four key sets of buyer characteristics: cultural, social, personal, and psychological. Although many of these factors cannot be influenced by the marketer, they can be useful in identifying interested buyers and in shaping products and appeals to serve consumer needs better. *Culture* is the most basic determinant of a person's wants and behaviour. It includes the basic values, perceptions, wants, and behaviours that a person learns from family and other important institutions. *Subcultures* are "cultures within cultures" that have distinct values and lifestyles, and can be based on anything from age to ethnicity. People with different cultural and subcultural characteristics have different product and brand preferences. As a result, marketers may want to focus their marketing programs on the special needs of certain groups.

Social factors also influence a buyer's behaviour. A person's *reference groups*—family, friends, social organizations, professional associations—strongly affect product and brand choices. The buyer's age, life-cycle stage, occupation, economic circumstances, lifestyle, personality, and other *personal characteristics* influence his or her buying decisions. Consumer *lifestyles*—the whole pattern of acting and interacting in the world—are also an important influence on purchase decisions. Finally, consumer buying behaviour is influenced by four major *psychological factors*—motivation, perception, learning, and beliefs and attitudes. Each of these factors provides a different perspective for understanding the workings of the buyer's black box.

3. List and understand the major types of buying-decision behaviour and stages in the buyer decision process.

Buying behaviour may vary greatly across different types of products and buying decisions. Consumers undertake *complex buying behaviour* when they are highly involved in a purchase and perceive significant differences among brands. *Dissonance-reducing buying behaviour* occurs when consumers are highly involved but see little difference among brands. *Habitual buying behaviour* occurs under conditions of low involvement and little significant brand difference. In situations characterized by low involvement but significant perceived brand differences, consumers engage in *variety-seeking buying behaviour*.

When making a purchase, the buyer goes through a decision process consisting of *need recognition, information search, evaluation of alternatives, purchase decision,* and *postpurchase behaviour.* The marketer's job is to understand the buyer's behaviour at each stage and the influences that are operating. During *need recognition,* the consumer recognizes a problem or need that could be satisfied by a product or service in the market. Once the need is recognized, the consumer is aroused to seek more information and moves into the *information search* stage. With information in hand, the consumer proceeds to *alternative evaluation,* when the information is used to evaluate brands in the choice set. From there, the consumer makes a *purchase decision* and actually buys the product. In the final stage of the buyer decision process, *postpurchase behaviour,* the consumer takes action based on satisfaction or dissatisfaction.

4. Describe the adoption and diffusion process for new products.

The product adoption process is composed of five stages: awareness, interest, evaluation, trial, and adoption. Initially, the consumer must become aware of the new product. *Awareness* leads to *interest,* and the consumer seeks information about the new product. Once information has been gathered, the consumer enters the *evaluation* stage and considers buying the new product. Next, in the *trial* stage, the consumer tries the product on a small scale to improve his or her estimate of its value. If the consumer is satisfied with the product, he or she enters the *adoption* stage, deciding to use the new product fully and regularly.

With respect to the diffusion of new products, consumers respond at different rates, depending on both the consumer's and the product's characteristics. Consumers may be innovators, early adopters, early majority, late majority, or laggards. *Innovators* are willing to try risky new ideas; *early adopters*—often community opinion leaders—accept new ideas early but carefully; the *early majority*—rarely leaders—decide deliberately to try new ideas, doing so before the average person does; the *late majority* try an innovation only after most people have adopted it; whereas *laggards* adopt an innovation only after it has become a tradition itself. Manufacturers try to bring their new products to the attention of potential early adopters, especially those who are opinion leaders.

Reviewing the Key Terms

Discussing the Concepts

1. List several factors that you could add to the model in Figure 7.1 (page 255) to make it a more complete description of consumer behaviour.

2. Canada is truly a mosaic of subcultures. Examine the four major subcultures identified in the chapter. Develop a profile of each that indicates the key characteristics that would be of most interest to marketers.

3. In designing the advertising for a bottled water product, which would you find more helpful: information about consumer demographics or consumer lifestyles? Give examples of how you would use each type of information.

4. Many marketers target opinion leaders with marketing messages. Why are opinion leaders important? How might opinion leaders influence buyer behaviour? For which products do opinion leaders appear to be most influential? For which are they least influential?

5. Abraham Maslow sought to explain why people are driven by particular needs at particular times. Which level of Maslow's hierarchy applies best to the following situations: (a) purchasing the newest, fastest personal computer; (b) purchasing food at lunch time; (c) adjusting your clothing choices to reflect the latest trends; (d) raising funds for an effort to save an endangered animal species; and, (e) purchasing a new, advanced form of water filter for your home. Explain the reasons for your choices.

6. Think about a very good or very bad experience you have had with a product. Discuss how this experience shaped your beliefs about this product. How long do you think these beliefs will last? What could change these beliefs?

7. Using the information found in Figure 7.6 (page 281), trace a recent purchase you have made. Be sure to examine each of the five stages of the buyer decision process, and detail your experiences in each stage. What could the seller have done to make your buying experience better? Did you experience any cognitive dissonance? Explain.

8. Five characteristics are especially important in influencing an innovation's rate of adoption. Indicate how each of these characteristics would affect your adoption of an electric car that travels up to 65 km per hour, has a battery storage capacity of six hours, and is intended primarily for in-town driving.

Applying the Concepts

1. SRI Consulting has created consumer VALS segments, a VALS typology designed to categorize consumers and their preferences. Companies that market on the Web or in retail can use this information to develop their appeals, strategies, and promotions. The concept is that consumers' purchases are shaped by the interplay of their psychological, physical, demographic, and material resources. Visit SRI at www.sric-bi.com and follow the links to the VALS questionnaire. Complete the survey to determine your VALS type. Answer these questions:

a. What is your VALS type? Do you agree with the assessment? Why or why not?

b. How can marketers use VALS information to serve consumers better?

c. Name five types of products or services for which VALS information would be particularly useful. Explain.

d. How could advertisers use VALS information to communicate better with consumers? Find three advertising examples from websites or current magazines that might be designed around VALS segments. Explain your reasoning.

2. When H.J. Heinz needed a boost for sagging ketchup sales, it turned to an old formula for an answer—matching consumer lifestyles with bold innovation. Heinz and competitors had for years incorrectly assumed that ketchup was for grown-ups. When the company realized that Ketchup is also for kids, Heinz discovered a substantial new avenue for growth. Heinz understood that today's kids were brought up on Nickelodeon's green slime, gummy worms, slime pops, and other gross-out products. How could Heinz tap into the market? With Blastin' Green ketchup! Although it tastes the same as traditional ketchup, in addition to the striking colour, the new version is packaged in a contoured, kid-friendly bottle complete with a nozzle for writing and drawing with ketchup. As a result, kids are taking the ketchup out of the refrigerator more often and participating in the buying process as never before. The new green ketchup initially boosted Heinz's sales by 5 percent and added 4 points to its market share. The success of Blastin' Green allowed Heinz to roll out Funky Purple and a mystery bottle from which any one of three differently coloured ketchups flows. The company is betting that when kids dress up their fries and burgers, they'll reach for red, green, or purple ketchup. Sound gross? That's just what this market segment ordered!

a. How has Heinz adapted its new products to fit kids' lifestyles? In addition to the contoured bottle, how could Heinz use packaging to enhance the product's appeal to kids? To adults?

b. How can Heinz turn the short-term sales and market share gain into a long-term advantage? What does the company need to know about lifestyles to increase sales in the future?

c. Would you buy green or purple ketchup? Why or why not? If you answered "no," construct a strategy that might change your mind. Consider the sections in the text on attitudes and beliefs as you map out your strategy.

d. Assume that Heinz has hired you to recommend the next colour for its line of ketchups. After visiting the EZ Squirt website at www.ezsquirt.com, describe how you would determine the new colour. Whom would you survey? What would you ask? How would you measure the impact of lifestyles and culture on colour preferences?

Video Short

View the video short for this chapter at **www.pearsoned.ca/kotler** and then answer the questions provided in the case description.

Company Case

The Whirlpool Duet: A Soap Opera for Kids?

What part of housework do North Americans spend the most time doing but know the least about? Now, think about this for a minute—don't blow it off. When you live away from home, what "housework" takes the biggest chunk of your time?

The answer? Laundry. North Americans spend more time each week washing and drying clothes than cleaning house, mowing lawns, or cooking. In fact, the average North American "housewife" spends seven to nine hours doing laundry each week.

There are two good reasons. We own more clothes than people in other countries (clothes are cheaper here), and we have a tendency to wash them after only one use. Unfortunately, given that we don't get our clothes very clean when we do wash them (part of the "know the least about" problem), we may *have* to wash them more often.

We don't know much about washing clothes because we tend to do it like Mom did—we haven't just studied the problem very well. In addition, there's a bewildering array of fabric types that we have to take care of, from 100 percent pure cotton to washable silk and even washable, breathable polyester. Rather than learning how to wash each of these, we adopt a sort of middle-of-the-road approach—spray some stain remover on it before throwing it in; maybe pour in some fabric softener; wash it in warm water (North Americans seem to be allergic to hot-water washing); rely on the detergent to have a lot of bleaches, colour brighteners, and whiteners; give it a cold rinse; and hope for the best.

Unfortunately, that "best," compared to clothes washed in European machines, is noticeably inferior. Why? Whereas North Americans use top-loading washing machines, Europeans use front-loading washing machines, and those front loaders do a better job of cleaning clothes. Unlike top loaders that use an agitator that beats clothes as they wash, front-loading machines tumble clothes. The result is that North American clothes get old before their time—they wear out faster.

Why do North Americans want top loaders? For one thing, they're easier to load. You don't have to stoop over to throw the clothes in or take them out. For another, they can handle larger loads. For a family of four, if you're going to wash everything after it's worn once, the capacity to wash larger loads becomes increasingly important.

Even if we had front-loading machines, we might not get it right. How many of you put in the clothes, the detergent, and extras such as bleach or fabric softener and *then* turn the machine on so that it begins to fill with water? Well, that's all wrong. You should fill the machine, then add the detergent and other concoctions—the clothes go in last.

So, North Americans wash 35 billion loads of laundry the wrong way each year—that's 1100 loads begun every second. The result is 225 kg of less-than-pristine clothing generated by each of us each year. What's more, we use 60 litres of water for each load, compared with 15 litres for a European machine. (One Ontario city projected that a household that replaced an inefficient washing-machine with a European top-loading machine would save 21 720 litres of water per year and over $100 in utilities bills.) Aha!—one statistic in our favour: The typical wash cycle in North America is 35 minutes, compared with 90 minutes in Europe. But maybe that's not good. Perhaps washing clothes more gently for longer gets them cleaner.

Given that old habits (washing clothes like Mom did) die hard, what could a North American appliance manufacturer do? Whirlpool decided to build a "global washing machine"—one that used the same "platform" or basic configuration no matter what area of the globe. Then, the basic platform could be modified for different countries and conditions. For example, the tub could be bigger in Canada for people who want to wash larger loads.

However, a global machine had to be a front loader. How did Whirlpool hope to get around North American consumers' objections? First, it put the new machine on a pedestal—that eliminated some of the stooping. Then, it put a drawer in the pedestal where cleaning supplies can be stored. To exceed customers' load-size expectations, Whirlpool gave them 0.1 cubic metres (3.7 cubic feet) of capacity, versus 0.08 cubic metres (3.0 cubic feet) in the usual North American top loader. To accommodate those with limited space, it designed the accompanying dryer to go on top of the washer (try that with a top loader).

Thus were born the new Duet washer and dryer from Whirlpool. The washer is made in Germany, where all of Whirlpool's front-loading machines are made. The Duet washer uses 68 percent less water, and along with less water, less detergent and other cleaners. It has a sanitary cycle that eliminates 99.999 percent of certain bacteria. The Duet removes more water from wet clothes because the tub spins at 900 to 1100 revolutions per minute, compared with 600 rpm in conventional top-loading machines. Extracting more water also leads to shorter drying times, which also means that the Duet dryer uses 67 percent less electricity. It has "Senseon" computerized technology that heats clothes just enough to reach the proper stage of dryness without overheating them (less wear) and it operates fast enough to dry a load of clothes in the same time that it takes to wash them. Both the washer and dryer exceed Energy Star requirements set by the U.S. Department of Energy and the Environmental Protection Agency and have won praise from Canadian provincial energy conservation boards.

How does the Duet washer actually work? Its advanced Catalyst washing technology system mixes detergent with a small amount of water and then sprays the foamy lather directly on clothes, which means there's no need for pretreatment. The tumbling action of the machine gently flexes and moves fabrics over three separate baffles that help loosen and remove soil and stains. The water-level control senses the size of the load and introduces only the water needed to clean the load.

Not only is the Duet combo energy and water conscious, it's aesthetically pleasing. The machines are white and come with your choice of two trim colours. Tidal blue is geared to the consumer who wants something that is more expensive looking; Dove Grey is for people who want a product that will blend with their existing surroundings. In a major design competition, Excellence in Design gave the Duet a best overall award for a major appliance. Their evaluative criteria were aesthetics, ergonomics/human factors, and innovative research. It's easy to understand why the Duet won the major award.

What's the catch? The price. The washer retails for $1300 to $1700, the dryer for $1000 (electric) or $1100 (gas), and the pedestal for $194. Standard agitator washer and dryers sell for about $400 and $500, respectively. Thus, the Duet duo is about three times as expensive, even without the pedestal.

Has that impacted purchase? No. Duet is actually selling at a rate double Whirlpool's original projections. Whirlpool thought that the market for the Duet would be a niche of affluent laundry-doers who would account for only 5 percent of Whirlpool's North American sales. Instead, it's reaping a surprising 10 percent of sales. Even so, any shift to front loaders will be gradual, as washing machines are expected to last 25 years. And obviously, the price would have to come down before the new design can capture mass market demand.

Why have some North Americans chosen to buy these very high-priced machines? There are many possible answers. First, there's wealth. Much of the accumulated wealth of the 1990s is still with us, even after the stock market downturn. Second, the savings rate is down, which means households are spending more than they used to. Third, baby boomers are the major market, as many of their kids are out of college and they have more disposable income to spend. Fourth, consumer aspirations have risen. No one wants to be middle class anymore—that was an aspiration for those born in the 1930s. Today, people want to be near the top and consider the middle class a starting point, not a goal. Fifth, Duet has provided a new form of entertainment for children—some of whom spend hours watching the clothes go round and round, making the Duet a kind of a "soap opera for kids."

It's also possible that North American consumers have gotten wiser about purchasing. Even though the Duet's price is higher, it does offer savings. It should use close to $150 less of water each year, plus it offers savings on electricity, detergents, bleaches, and softeners. Thus, the machines should pay for themselves in less than 15 years, maybe even 10 years. That's not

including wearing clothes longer because they don't wear out so fast. And some North Americans have gotten more quality-conscious and less price-conscious.

There's another phenomenon at work here as well. It's the emerging hourglass effect of income distribution in North America. The middle class is dividing into a lower group focused on low prices and an upscale group looking for quality. In the past, the market was pyramid-shaped with relatively few households at the top willing to pay top dollar for products. Today, however, many middle-class North Americans (feeling that wealth from the 1990s) are migrating upscale in their purchases. Sales of luxury cars, wines, jeans, jewellery, and electronics and the patronizing of high-priced specialty retailers such as Tiffany's are increasing.

How has Whirlpool marketed the Duet? Initially, TV ads and magazine ads in vehicles such as *House Beautiful* stressed energy efficiency and environmental issues. Finding that their market had an average household income of $65 000 rather than the $95 000 the company first predicted, Whirlpool pulled the original magazine and TV ads in favour of in-store promotions. Its new TV spots feature consumer testimonials stressing the product's practical appeal.

Will all this work? Are North Americans shifting to quality products for the long haul? Only time will tell. It will all have to come out in the wash.

Questions for Discussion

1. What sorts of cultural, social, and personal characteristics affect the purchase of a Duet duo?

2. In your opinion, what are the consumer motivations for buying a Duet? How has learning impacted past purchase? How will that change if they buy a Duet washer?

3. What kind of buying decision is the typical purchase of a washer and dryer? Is this different for the purchase of a Duet duo?

4. How will advertising and in-store promotions for the Duet affect the stages of the buyer decision process?

5. Think of the Duet as an innovation. Evaluate it using the product characteristics that affect the rate of adoption. What types of innovators are most likely to purchase a Duet?

6. Are Whirlpool's new marketing efforts well designed to "sell" the Duet? Are they appropriate given that the market is lower in income than Whirlpool expected?

Sources: "Dynamic Duo," *Appliance Manufacturer,* August 2001, p. 62; Paul Dodson, "Benton Harbor, Ind.–Based Whirlpool Creates New Washer, Dryer Appliances," *Knight-Ridder/Tribune Business News,* September 23, 2001; Joe Jancsurak, "Fifteen Annual EID Winners: Designing Outside the Box," *Appliance Manufacturer,* May 2002, p. 19; Emily Nelson, "Wash and Wear: In Doing Laundry, Americans Cling to Outmoded Ways—Machines, Detergents Evolve, but Clothes Still Don't Get as Clean as They Could—Shying Away from Hot Water," *Wall Street Journal,* May 16, 2002, p. A1; Gregory L. White and Shirley Leung, "Stepping Up: Middle Market Shrinks as

Americans Migrate Toward the High End—Shifting Consumer Values Create 'Hourglass' Effect; Quality Gets Easier to Sell—Six Air Bags, 22 Towels," *Wall Street Journal,* March 29, 2002, p. A1; and Regional Municipality of Waterloo, Transportation and Environmental Services, "Washing Machine Inventive Program," (memo), February 28, 2002, www.region.waterloo.on.ca/. Also see Susan James, "Collection Profiles: Washing Machines," Canada Science and Technology Museum, www.sciencetech.technomuses.ca/english/collection/wash_intro.cfm, for a history of washing machines in Canada.

CBC Video Case

Log on to your Companion Website at **www.pearsoned.ca/kotler** to view a CBC video segment and case for this chapter.

Chapter 8

Business Markets and Business Buyer Behaviour

MAGNA
Annual Report 2002

Totally Driven

After studying this chapter you should be able to

1. define the business market and explain how business markets differ from consumer markets

2. identify the major factors that influence business buyer behaviour

3. list and define the steps in the business buying decision process

4. compare the institutional and government markets and explain how they make their buying decisions

Looking Ahead: Previewing the Concepts

In the previous chapter, you studied *final consumer* buying behaviour and factors that influence it. In this chapter, we'll do the same for *business customers*—those that buy goods and services for use in producing their own products and services or for resale to others.

Before moving on, let's look first at Magna International Inc., the Canadian firm that is a leading global supplier of technologically advanced automotive systems. In some ways, selling automotive components is like selling household appliances to final consumers. In other ways, however, it's very, very different. For example, think about who might be involved in the purchase decision about the thousands of parts and components that annually go into the manufacture of cars, trucks, and mini-vans. Also, think about the factors that might influence each person's buying behaviour. As you'll see, such buying decisions can be pretty complex.

How would you feel if your client list showed only five main customers? Pretty good, if serving those customers translated into $13 billion in sales. Even better if you knew that those sales increased by 18 percent between 2001 and 2002. The company in question is Aurora, Ontario-based Magna International Inc. Magna is a leading global supplier of technologically advanced automotive systems, components, and complete modules. This global giant employs approximately 72 000 people at 202 manufacturing divisions and 45 product development and engineering centres through North and South America, Mexico, Europe, and Asia.

Despite its size, Magna is a relatively young company. It was founded by Frank Stronach in 1957 when he opened a one-man tool and die shop called Multimatic. His first-year sales amounted to only $13 000. However, in 1960, the firm landed a contract with General Motors for sun visor brackets. Being able to supply the giant auto firm with reliable cost-effective parts, even small ones, was the start of something big. In the 1970s, the company changed its name to Magna International Inc., undertook a major product diversification program, and organized its divisions into product groups. It diversified into aerospace and defence operations, only to divest these operations in the early 1980s so that it could concentrate on its automotive business.

Today, Magna (www.magnaint.com) is one of the most diversified automotive suppliers in the world. It doesn't sell to the public, but does provide automotive systems to original equipment manufacturers (OEMs). Its top customer is DaimlerChrysler, which accounts for 29 percent of Magna's business. Next is General Motors, a firm that generates 22 percent of Magna's sales, followed by Ford, which makes up the next 20 percent. BMW and Volkswagen round out Magna's list of major customers, respectively accounting for 6 and 5 percent of Magna's sales. However, under its category "other," Magna does sell to almost every other automotive firm in the world—firms like Honda and Toyota.

Magna owes its success to a number of factors. It has a highly motivated and loyal workforce. It prides itself on its Employee's Charter, which captures Magna's operating philosophy of fairness and concern for people. As the company notes, "In today's global market, every employee has an important role to play in making sure Magna stays competitive by making a better product for a better price and delivering them on time." Thus, Magna does a lot of internal marketing to its employees, communicating to them regularly through meetings and internal newsletters.

Social responsibility is another of Magna's differentiating factors. The company allocates a maximum of 2 percent of its pre-tax profits to support charitable and non-profit organizations in categories that include health, culture, community, education, sports, and politics.

Magna is also recognized by the world's major OEMs for its innovative technology and product design, as well as its total vehicle program management. In fact, Magna's product and process development expertise is legendary. For example, in 1989, Magna co-designed the built-in child safety seat, which was recognized by the Smithsonian Institute as one of the great innovations of the 1980s. In the mid-1990s, it developed a groundbreaking systems integrator contract to manage the complete interior and exterior systems integration of a vehicle. It also created hydroforming technology, a unique manufacturing process that utilizes water pressure to bend and form metal. In 1999 Magna knew it had arrived among the world's most respected firms when *Forbes* magazine named it the world's top auto parts company. In 2000, Magna added total vehicle engineering to its portfolio of offerings. Today the company is recognized as one of the world's leading suppliers of niche vehicle production, assembly, and concept development.

The automotive industry in general, and the automotive parts sub-sector in particular, are highly competitive. The parts industry is consolidating, and as tier-one suppliers become bigger and bigger, they are performing more research and are assuming more control over the building of car interiors. Magna's sales have been increasing because each year it has been contributing a higher proportion of what goes into making up the contents of a vehicle.

Magna is successful only if its customers are successful. Magna's revenues depend on how many cars the auto manufacturers build and sell. Auto sales were sluggish throughout much of 2003, but as the economy improves, North American automakers predict that they will boost vehicle production to 4.2 million cars, trucks, minivans, and sport-utility vehicles (an increase from earlier projections of 4 million vehicles). This trend should give Magna a further boost.

When economic times are tough, Magna's large customers look for cost savings and a competitive edge wherever possible. Thus, Magna's sales and customer service teams must not only sell high-quality, innovative, cost-effective products that are delivered precisely when they are needed, it must also help its customers find solutions to their engineering, design, supply, and inventory challenges. When marketing, Magna cannot just appeal to the needs of one type of person. It must deal with a vast array of decision makers and product users—everyone from

automotive design engineers and professional purchasing managers to people working on the car manufacturers' lines and loading docks.

To understand its clients' needs and help them meet their challenges, Magna must build strong relationships. As one analyst notes when describing Magna, "Building and keeping good relationships—it's what will separate a good company from a great one." Relationships are two-way streets that can benefit both partners, especially if they collaborate on a number of efforts.

Consider the story of how Magna came to the new Powerway technology, which it adopted as part of its ebusiness initiatives. Magna learned of Powerway through DaimlerChrysler, which was nudging some of its suppliers to use the system for certain collaboration functions. Magna didn't resent this little push. Instead, the company saw it as a way to work better with DaimlerChrysler. Says Ted Wozniak, Magna's CIO, "We didn't come at this the way a lot of suppliers do. We came at it with a partnership process." Furthermore, by listening to the customer and quickly responding to DaimlerChrysler's needs and new way of doing business, Magna got a jump on its competitors. Not only did the Powerway technology save Magna both time and money, it helped it consolidate a key relationship. Savings came through the elimination of a pile of paperwork and personal visits between Magna's plants and those of DaimlerChrysler.

Moving early to form tight electronic relationships with its key customers was another important strategy for Magna. It is estimated that by 2005, Canada's automotive supply chain will sell $91 billion online.

While parts manufacturers like Magna have traditionally marketed solely to automakers, there are new marketing moves afoot in the auto industry. More and more automotive component suppliers are planning to take their brands directly to consumers. "There's a huge movement from the auto suppliers toward consumer branding," says one source at J.D. Power and Associates in Detroit. "With the auto industry in the throes of consolidation, suppliers are peddling their wares to fewer manufacturers. The suppliers that thrive will be those that can offer original equipment manufacturers added value at no extra cost. One way to do this, of course, is to create a recognizable brand that consumers value and trust." Tire manufacturers have long understood this formula. Firms like Michelin and Goodyear know that having their branded tires on vehicles adds to end customer's sense of value. In a similar fashion, Bose has branded its vehicle sound systems.

Business-to-business firms have traditionally ignored branding. However, many are now seeing the power of brands. Just look at what BASF, the German-based chemical did. It launched a major television campaign in North America, anchored by the tag line, "We don't make a lot of the products you buy—we make a lot of the products you buy better." While consumers would never directly buy a

BASF product, they are more willing to buy a manufacturer's product that incorporates BASF—thanks to the fact that by associating BASF with quality and reliability, the company's brand positioning has made it stand out from other suppliers.

This trend indicates that if Magna can show that end customers are asking for Magna interiors by name, then the supplier will be in a stronger bargaining position with its customers. But to build its brand, Magna will have to undertake some new marketing initiatives. Says one car manufacturer, "From an OEM perspective, there needs to be either additional marketing or merchandising that makes the supplier's product add value to our product.... If Magna came to us with something, we'd have to look at it and ask, 'Well, what's the value to us of your name—does it mean anything to consumers?'"

As Richard Cooper, an analyst with J.D. Power and Associates in Toronto, notes, "The issue right now is that most of these suppliers are not particularly well-known to consumers. We've got a way to go before a Magna interior becomes a selling point for consumers." There is no doubt Magna will rise to this challenge, as it has to others throughout its history.[1]

In one way or another, most large companies sell to other organizations. Many companies, such as Alcan Aluminium, Bombardier, NOVA Corp., 3M Canada, Nortel Networks, DuPont, and Caterpillar, sell *most* of their products to other businesses. Even large consumer products companies, which make products used by final consumers, must first sell their products to other businesses. For example, Kraft Canada (www.kraftcanada.com) makes many familiar consumer products— Post cereals, Kraft Dinner, Jell-O, Kraft peanut butter, and others. But to sell these products to consumers, Kraft Canada must first sell them to the wholesalers and retailers that serve the consumer market.

Business buyer behaviour
The buying behaviour of the organizations that buy goods and services for use in the production of other products and services or for the purpose of reselling or renting them to others at a profit.

Business buyer behaviour refers to the buying behaviour of the organizations that buy goods and services for use in the production of other products and services that are sold, rented, or supplied to others. It also includes the behaviour of retailing and wholesaling firms that acquire goods for the purpose of reselling or renting them to others at a profit. In the **business buying process**, business buyers determine which products and services their organizations need to purchase, and then find, evaluate, and choose among alternative suppliers and brands. Companies that sell to other business organizations must do their best to understand business markets and business buyer behaviour.

Business buying process
The decision process by which business buyers determine which products and services their organizations need to purchase, and then find, evaluate, and choose among alternative brands and suppliers.

Business Markets

The business market is *huge*. In fact, business markets involve far more dollars and items than do consumer markets. Consider the size of just one industry sector, the Canadian Information and Communications Technologies (ICT) sector. It contributed $58.1 billion to Canada's GDP in 2001 alone—representing 6.2 percent of the total economy and accounting for almost 600 000 jobs.[2] While some of the revenues result from sales to end consumers, most are generated by sales between companies. For example, when firms make investments in new technologies, such as customer relationship management technologies, more than 200 different hardware and software vendors, integrators, and consultants may be involved.

Another way to understand why the business market is so large is to think about the large number of business transactions involved in producing and selling a single set of Goodyear tires. Various suppliers sell Goodyear the rubber, steel, and manufacturing equipment that it needs to produce the tires. Goodyear then sells the finished tires to original equipment manufacturers (like GM or Ford), and wholesale distributors who sell them to retailers, who in turn sell them to consumers. Thus, many sets of *business* purchases were made for only one set of *consumer* purchases.

Characteristics of Business Markets

In some ways, business markets are similar to consumer markets. Both involve people who assume buying roles and make purchase decisions to satisfy needs. However, business markets differ in many ways from consumer markets. The main differences, shown in Table 8.1 and discussed below, are in *market structure and demand,* the *nature of the buying unit,* and the *types of decisions and the decision process* involved.

Market Structure and Demand

The business marketer typically deals with *far fewer but far larger buyers* than the consumer marketer does. For example, when Goodyear sells replacement tires to final consumers, its potential market includes the owners of the millions of cars currently in use in Canada and the United States. But Goodyear's fate in the business market depends on getting orders from one of only a few large automakers. Even in large business markets, a few buyers typically account for most of the purchasing.

Business markets are also more *geographically concentrated.* About 58 percent of all Canadian businesses are located in Ontario and Quebec, concentrated in the metropolitan areas between Windsor and Quebec City (an area which also accounts for about one-third of Canada's population). Thirty-five percent of Canada's businesses are in the Western provinces; 6 percent are located in the Atlantic provinces. The provinces of Ontario and Quebec are home to the country's auto industry, while Canada's high-tech firms are clustered in Ottawa, Montreal, and Toronto. The petroleum industry calls Calgary and Edmonton home. New Brunswick attracts the telemarketing industry and is the location of many companies' call centres. Most agricultural output comes from a relatively few provinces.[3]

Derived demand
Business demand that ultimately comes from (derives from) the demand for consumer goods.

Further, business demand is **derived demand**—it ultimately derives from the demand for consumer goods. General Motors Canada (www.gmcanada.com) buys steel because consumers buy cars. If consumer demand for cars drops, so will the demand for steel and all the other products used to make cars. Therefore, business marketers sometimes promote their products directly to final consumers to increase business demand.

Table 8.1   Characteristics of Business Markets

Marketing Structure and Demand

- Business markets contain fewer but larger buyers.
- Business customers are more geographically concentrated.
- Business buyer demand is derived from final consumer demand.
- Demand in many business markets is more inelastic—not affected as much in the short run by price changes.
- Demand in business markets fluctuates more, and more quickly.

Nature of the Buying Unit

- Business purchases involve more buyers.
- Business buying involves a more professional purchasing effort.

Types of Decisions and the Decision Process

- Business buyers usually face more complex buying decisions.
- The business buying process is more formalized.
- Business buyers and sellers work more closely together and build close long-term relationships.

For example, Intel's long-running "Intel Inside" advertising campaign sells personal computer buyers on the virtue of Intel microprocessors. The increased demand for Intel chips boosts demand for the PCs containing them, and both Intel and its business partners win. Similarly, DuPont promotes Teflon directly to final consumers as a key ingredient in many products—from non-stick cookware to stain-repellent, wrinkle-free clothing. You see Teflon Fabric Protector hangtags on clothing lines such as Levi's Dockers, Donna Karan's menswear, and Ralph Lauren denim.[4] By making Teflon familiar and attractive to final buyers, DuPont also makes the products containing it more attractive.

Many business markets have *inelastic demand;* that is, total demand for many business products is not affected much by price changes, especially in the short run. A drop in the price of leather will not cause shoe manufacturers to buy much more leather unless it results in lower shoe prices that, in turn, will increase consumer demand for shoes.

Finally, business markets have more *fluctuating demand*. The demand for many business goods and services tends to change more—and more quickly—than the demand for consumer goods and services does. A small percentage increase in consumer demand can cause large increases in business demand. Sometimes a rise of only 10 percent in consumer demand can cause as much as a 200 percent rise in business demand during the next period.

Nature of the Buying Unit

Compared with consumer purchases, a business purchase usually involves *more buyers* and a *more professional purchasing effort*. Often, business buying is done by trained purchasing agents who spend their working lives learning how to buy better. The more complex the purchase, the more likely that several people will participate in the decision-making process. Buying committees composed of technical experts and top management are common in the buying of major goods. As one observer notes, "It's a scary thought: Your customers may know more about your company and products than you do…. Companies are putting their best and brightest people on procurement patrol."[5] Therefore, business marketers must have well-trained salespeople to deal with well-trained buyers.

Derived demand: Intel's long-running "Intel Inside" logo advertising campaign boosts demand for Intel chips and for the PCs containing them. Now, most computer markets feature a logo like this one in their ads.

Types of Decisions and the Decision Process

Business buyers usually face *more complex* buying decisions than do consumer buyers. Purchases often involve large sums of money, complex technical and economic considerations, and interactions among many people at many levels of the buyer's organization. Because the purchases are more complex, business buyers may take longer to make their decisions. The business buying process tends to be *more formalized* than the consumer buying process. Large business purchases usually call for detailed product specifications, written purchase orders, careful supplier searches, and formal approval.

Finally, in the business buying process, buyer and seller are often much *more dependent* on each other. Consumer marketers are usually at a distance from their customers. In contrast, B2B marketers may roll up their sleeves and work closely with their customers during all stages of the buying process—from helping customers define problems, to finding solutions, to supporting after-sale operation. They often customize their offerings to individual customer needs.

In the short run, sales go to suppliers who meet buyers' immediate product and service needs. However, business marketers also must build close *long-run* partnerships with customers. In recent years, relationships between customers and suppliers have been changing from downright adversarial to close and chummy. For example, Caterpillar no longer calls its buyers "purchasing agents"—they are managers of "purchasing and supplier development." Says one purchasing expert, "You no longer treat your supplier as a 'supplier' but as an extension of your business." Consider this example:

> Motoman, a leading supplier of industry robotic systems, and Stillwater Technologies, a contract tooling and machinery company and a key supplier to Motoman, are tightly integrated. Not only do they occupy office and manufacturing space in the same facility, they also link their telephone and computer systems and share a common lobby, conference room, and employee cafeteria. Philip Morrison, chairman and CEO of Motoman, says it's like "a joint venture without the paperwork." Short delivery distances are just one benefit of the unusual partnership. Also key is the fact that employees of both companies have ready access to each other and can share ideas on improving quality and reducing costs. This close relationship has also opened the door to new opportunities. Both companies had been doing work for Honda Motor Company, and Honda suggested that the two work together on systems projects. The symbiotic relationship makes the two bigger and better than they could be individually.[6]

In the long run, business marketers keep a customer's sales by meeting current needs *and* by partnering with customers to help them solve their problems. This is true for marketers in small as well as large businesses. For example, small industrial detergent maker ChemStation does more than simply supply its customers with cleaning chemicals. It works closely with them to custom-design total solutions to their unique cleaning problems. "Our customers...oftentimes think of us as more of a partner than a supplier," says the company's newsletter (see Real Marketing 8.1).[7]

A Model of Business Buyer Behaviour

At the most basic level, marketers want to know how business buyers will respond to various marketing stimuli. Figure 8.1 on page 304 shows a model of business buyer behaviour. In this model, marketing and other stimuli affect the buying organization and produce certain buyer responses. As with consumer buying, the marketing stimuli for business buying consist of the four *P*s: product, price, place, and promotion. Other stimuli include major forces in the environment: economic, technological, political, cultural, and competitive. These stimuli enter the organization

8.1 ChemStation: More of a Partner than a Supplier

ChemStation sells industrial cleaning chemicals to a wide range of business customers, ranging from car washes to airlines. Whether a customer is washing down a fleet or a factory, a store or a restaurant, a distillery or port, this small market nicher comes up with the right cleaning solution every time. The company's motto: "Our system is your solution!"

ChemStation will tackle just about any customer cleaning problem. It supplies thousands of products in hundreds of industries. The company has created customized cleaning solutions for all kinds of surfaces: floors, walls, ceilings, machinery, parts, vehicles, and even windows. It has brewed special formulas for cleaning hands, feathers, mufflers, flutes, perfume vats, cosmetic eye makeup containers, yacht-making moulds, concrete trucks, ocean-going trawlers, and about anything else you can imagine.

ChemStation does more than simply supply its customers with cleaning chemicals. "Our customers...think of us as more of a partner than a supplier."

But for most customers, ChemStation is much more than just a cleaning-chemicals *supplier*. Instead, it makes itself a partner in helping customers solve their special cleaning problems. ChemStation starts by learning all it can about customers and their industries. The company's people subscribe to customers' trade journals, attend their industry conferences and trade shows, and even join their trade associations. However, the real partnering takes place at the individual customer level.

What cleans a car won't work to clean an airplane or equipment in a mineshaft. So ChemStation works closely with each individual customer to concoct a soap formula specially designed for that customer. Salespeople collect information about the specific customer's cleaning needs and enter it into a customer database called the Tank Management System (TMS). Next, a company chemist develops a special "detergent recipe" for the customer. The recipe is fed into a computer-controlled machine, which mixes up a batch of the special brew. ChemStation delivers the custom-made mixture to a tank installed at the customer's site. It then maintains the tank by monitoring usage and automatically refilling the tank when supplies run low.

Working closely with an individual customer creates a lasting relationship that helps ChemStation to lock out the competition. No one—not even the customer—knows what goes into each formula, making it hard for a customer to jump to competitors. "We tell customers it's a secret," says founder and CEO George Homan. "We're not as protective about our formulas as Coca-Cola, but we're close." Moreover, maintaining the ChemStation tank at the customer's business creates regular customer contact. This regular contact helps ChemStation to detect and smooth out any wrinkles in the customer relationship.

Put it all together and the term *supplier* doesn't really fit ChemStation. Instead, the company is like an extension of each customer's own business. When a customer comes up with a seemingly impossible cleaning challenge, ChemStation is quick to respond, "Yeah, we do that!" As noted in the a recent issue of

Insights, ChemStation's customer newsletter, "Our customers...oftentimes think of us as more of a partner than a supplier."

Sources: Sarah Schafer, "Have It Your Way," *Inc.,* November 18, 1997; "Keeping Up with Your Industry," *Insights,* February 2000, p. 1; "Common Bond?" *Insights,* February 2001, p. 1; "BJ's Knows...Our System Is Their Solution," *Insights,* March 2002, p. 1; and information from the ChemStation website, www.chemstation.com (accessed July 2002).

and are turned into buyer responses: product or service choice; supplier choice; order quantities; and delivery, service, and payment terms. In order to design good marketing mix strategies, the marketer must understand what happens within the organization to turn stimuli into purchase responses.

Within the organization, buying activity consists of two major parts: the buying centre, comprising all the people involved in the buying decision, and the buying decision process. The model shows that the buying centre and the buying decision process are influenced by internal organizational, interpersonal, and individual factors as well as by external environmental factors.

Business Buyer Behaviour

The model in Figure 8.1 suggests four questions about business buyer behaviour: What buying decisions do business buyers make? Who participates in the buying process? What are the major influences on buyers? How do business buyers make their buying decisions?

Major Types of Buying Situations

There are three major types of buying situations.[8] At one extreme is the *straight rebuy,* which is a fairly routine decision. At the other extreme is the *new task,* which may call for thorough research. In the middle is the *modified rebuy,* which requires some research.

Straight rebuy
A business buying situation in which the buyer routinely reorders something without any modifications.

In a **straight rebuy**, the buyer reorders something without any modifications. It is usually handled on a routine basis by the purchasing department. Based on past buying satisfaction, the buyer simply chooses from the various suppliers on its list. "In" suppliers try to maintain product and service quality. They often propose automatic reordering systems so that the purchasing agent will save reordering time. "Out" suppliers try to offer something new or exploit dissatisfaction so that the buyer will consider them.

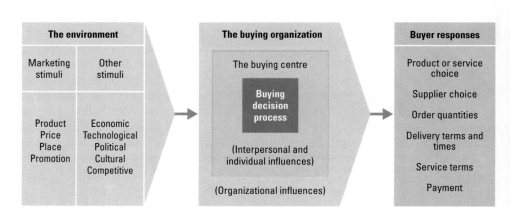

Figure 8.1 Model of business buyer behaviour

Modified rebuy
A business buying situation in which the buyer wants to modify product specifications, prices, terms, or suppliers.

New task
A business buying situation in which the buyer purchases a product or service for the first time.

In a **modified rebuy**, the buyer wants to modify product specifications, prices, terms, or suppliers. The modified rebuy usually involves more decision participants than the straight rebuy. "In" suppliers may become nervous and feel pressured to put their best foot forward to protect an account. "Out" suppliers may view the modified rebuy situation as an opportunity to make a better offer and gain new business.

A company buying a product or service for the first time faces a **new task** situation. In such cases, the greater the cost or risk, the larger the number of decision participants and the greater their efforts to collect information will be. The new task situation is the marketer's greatest opportunity and challenge. The marketer not only tries to reach as many key buying influences as possible, but also provides help and information.

The buyer makes the fewest decisions in the straight rebuy and the most in the new task decision. In the new task situation, the buyer must decide on product specifications, suppliers, price limits, payment terms, order quantities, delivery times, and service terms. The order of these decisions varies with the situation, and different decision participants influence each choice.

Many business buyers prefer to buy a packaged solution to a problem from a single seller. Instead of buying and putting together all the components, the buyer may ask sellers to supply the components *and* assemble the package or system. The sale often goes to the firm that provides the most complete system meeting the customer's needs. Thus, **systems selling** is often a key business marketing strategy for winning and holding accounts.

Systems selling
Buying a packaged solution to a problem from a single seller, thus avoiding all the separate decisions involved in a complex buying situation.

Sellers increasingly have recognized that buyers like this method and have adopted systems selling as a marketing tool. Systems selling is a two-step process. First, the supplier sells a group of interlocking products. For example, the supplier sells not only glue, but also applicators and dryers. Second, the supplier sells a system of production, inventory control, distribution, and other services to meet the buyer's need for a smooth-running operation.

Systems selling is a key business marketing strategy for winning and holding accounts. The contract often goes to the firm that provides the most complete solution to customers' problems. For example, the Indonesian government requested bids to build a cement factory near Jakarta. A North American firm's proposal included choosing the site, designing the cement factory, hiring the construction crews, assembling the materials and equipment, and turning the finished factory over to the Indonesian government. A Japanese firm's proposal included all of these services, plus hiring and training workers to run the factory, exporting the cement through their trading companies, and using the cement to build some needed roads and new office buildings in Jakarta. Although the Japanese firm's proposal cost more, it won the contract. Clearly, the Japanese viewed the problem not as just building a cement factory (the narrow view of systems selling) but of running it in a way that would contribute to the country's economy. They took the broadest view of the customer's needs. This is true systems selling.[9]

Participants in the Business Buying Process

Who does the buying of the trillions of dollars worth of goods and services needed by business organizations? The decision-making unit of a buying organization is called its **buying centre**: all of the individuals and units that participate in the business decision-making process. The buying centre includes all members of the organization who play a role in the purchase decision process. This group includes the actual users of the product or service, those who make the buying decision, those who influence the buying decision, those who do the actual buying, and those who control buying information.

Buying centre
All the individuals and units that participate in the business buying decision process.

The buying centre includes all members of the organization who play any of five roles in the purchase decision process.[10]

Users
Members of the organization who will use the product or service; users often initiate the buying proposal and help define product specifications.

Influencers
People in an organization's buying centre who affect the buying decision; they often help define specifications and provide information for evaluating alternatives.

Buyers
People who make the actual purchase.

Deciders
People in the organization's buying centre who have formal or informal power to select or approve the final suppliers.

Gatekeepers
People in the organization's buying centre who control the flow of information to others.

- **Users** are members of the organization who will use the product or service. In many cases, users initiate the buying proposal and help define product specifications.
- **Influencers** often help define specifications and provide information for evaluating alternatives. Technical personnel are particularly important influencers.
- **Buyers** have formal authority to select the supplier and arrange terms of purchase. Buyers may help shape product specifications, but their major role is in selecting vendors and in negotiating. In more complex purchases, buyers may include high-level officers participating in the negotiations.
- **Deciders** have formal or informal power to select or approve the final suppliers. In routine buying, the buyers are often the deciders, or at least the approvers.
- **Gatekeepers** control the flow of information to others. For example, purchasing agents often have authority to prevent salespersons from seeing users or deciders. Other gatekeepers include technical personnel and even personal secretaries.

The buying centre is not a fixed and formally identified unit within the buying organization. It is a set of buying roles assumed by different people for different purchases. Within the organization, the size and makeup of the buying centre will vary for different products and for different buying situations. For some routine purchases, one person—such as a purchasing agent—may assume all the buying centre roles and serve as the only person involved in the buying decision. For more complex purchases, the buying centre may include 20 or 30 people from different levels and departments in the organization.

The buying centre concept presents a major marketing challenge. The business marketer must learn who participates in the decision, each participant's relative influence, and what evaluation criteria each decision participant uses. For example, Cardinal Health (www.cardinal.com), the large health-care products and services company, sells disposable surgical gowns to hospitals. It identifies the hospital personnel involved in this buying decision as the vice-president of purchasing, the operating room administrator, and the surgeons. Each participant plays a different role. The vice-president of purchasing analyzes whether the hospital should buy disposable gowns or reusable gowns. If analysis favours disposable gowns, then the

Buying centre: Cardinal Health deals with a wide range of buying influences, from purchasing executives and hospital administrators to the surgeons who actually use its products.

operating room administrator compares competing products and prices and makes a choice. This administrator considers the gown's absorbency, antiseptic quality, design, and cost, and typically buys the brand that meets requirements at the lowest cost. Finally, surgeons affect the decision later by reporting their satisfaction or dissatisfaction with the brand.

The buying centre usually includes some obvious participants who are involved formally in the buying decision. For example, the decision to buy a corporate jet will probably involve the company's CEO, chief pilot, a purchasing agent, some legal staff, a member of top management, and others formally charged with the buying decision. It may also involve less obvious, informal participants, some of whom may actually make or strongly affect the buying decision. Sometimes, even the people in the buying centre are unaware of all the buying participants. In the opening Magna example, the decision about which auto component to buy could actually be made by a corporate board member who has a passion for a particular brand of automobile and a certain type of interior. This board member may work behind the scenes to sway the decision. Many business buying decisions result from the complex interactions of ever-changing buying centre participants.

Major Influences on Business Buyers

Business buyers are subject to many influences when they make their buying decisions. Some marketers assume that the major influences are economic. They think buyers will favour the supplier who offers the lowest price, or the best product, or the most service. They concentrate on offering strong economic benefits to buyers. However, business buyers actually respond to both economic and personal factors. Far from being cold, calculating, and impersonal, business buyers are human and social as well. They react to both reason and emotion.

Today, most business-to-business marketers recognize that emotion plays an important role in business buying decisions. For example, you might expect that an advertisement promoting large trucks to corporate truck fleet buyers would stress objective technical, performance, and economic factors such as fuel usage. However, a recent ad for Volvo heavy-duty trucks shows two drivers arm wrestling and claims, "It solves all your fleet problems. Except who gets to drive." It turns out

Emotions play an important role in business buying: This Volvo truck ad mentions objective factors, such as efficiency and ease of maintenance. But it stresses more emotional factors such as the raw beauty of the truck and its comfort and roominess, features that make "drivers a lot more possessive."

INTRODUCING THE VOLVO 660. IT SOLVES ALL YOUR FLEET PROBLEMS. EXCEPT WHO GETS TO DRIVE.

that, in the face of industry-wide driver shortages, the type of truck a fleet provides can help a firm attract qualified drivers. The Volvo ad stresses the raw beauty of the truck and its comfort and roominess, features that make it more appealing to drivers. The ad concludes that Volvo trucks are "built to make fleets more profitable and drivers a lot more possessive."

When suppliers' offers are similar, business buyers have little basis for strictly rational choice. Because they can meet organizational goals with any supplier, buyers can allow personal factors to play a larger role in their decisions. However, when competing products differ greatly, business buyers are more accountable for their choice and tend to pay more attention to economic factors. Figure 8.2 lists various groups of influences on business buyers—environmental, organizational, interpersonal, and individual.[11]

Environmental Factors

Business buyers are influenced heavily by factors in the current and expected *economic environment*, such as the level of primary demand, the economic outlook, and the cost of money. As economic uncertainty rises, business buyers cut back on new investments and attempt to reduce their inventories.

An increasingly important environmental factor is shortages in key materials. Many companies now are more willing to buy and hold larger inventories of scarce materials to ensure adequate supply. Business buyers are also affected by technological, political, and competitive developments in the environment. Culture and customs can strongly influence business buyer reactions to the marketer's behaviour and strategies, especially in the international marketing environment (see Real Marketing 8.2). The business marketer must consider these factors, determine how they will affect the buyer, and try to turn these challenges into opportunities.

Organizational Factors

Each buying organization has its own objectives, policies, procedures, structure, and systems, and the business marketer must understand these factors as well. Questions such as these arise: How many people are involved in the buying decision? Who are they? What are their evaluative criteria? What are the company's policies and limits on its buyers? Organizational size determines the answer to many of these questions. In large organizations, the buying centre is large and complex and buying is a formalized process monitored by highly trained professional buyers. In smaller firms, purchasing may be done by the person managing a particular project. They may have little training in purchasing. This is especially important in Canada, where small and medium-sized enterprises (SMEs) account for 60 percent of our economic output and 80 percent of our national employment.[12]

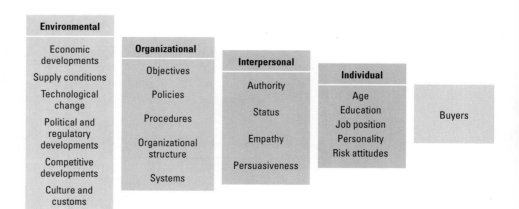

Figure 8.2 Major influences on business buying behaviour

8.2 International Marketing Manners: When in Rome, Do as the Romans Do

*P*icture this: Consolidated Amalgamation, Inc., thinks it's time that the rest of the world enjoyed the same fine products it has offered Canadian consumers for two generations. It dispatches vice-president Harry E. Slicksmile to Europe, Africa, and Asia to explore the territory. Mr. Slicksmile stops first in London, where he makes short work of some bankers—he rings them up on the phone. He handles Parisians with similar ease. After securing a table at La Tour d'Argent, he greets his luncheon guest, the director of an industrial engineering firm, with the words, "Just call me Harry, Jacques."

EGYPT
Be patient.

ITALY
What exactly do you mean?

GREECE
That's just perfect.

Never underestimate the importance of local knowledge.

To truly understand a country and its culture, you have to be part of it. That's why, at HSBC, all our offices around the world are staffed by local people. In fact, you'll find we've got local people in more countries than any other bank. It's their insight that allows us to recognize financial opportunities invisible to outsiders.

But those opportunities don't benefit just our local customers. Innovations and ideas are shared throughout the HSBC network, so that everyone who banks with us can benefit.

Think of it as local knowledge that just happens to span the globe.

HSBC
The world's local bank

Issued by HSBC Bank USA

This HSBC ad recognizes the difficulties of doing business globally and understanding international customers, needs, and customs.

In Germany, Mr. Slicksmile is a powerhouse. Whisking through a lavish, state-of-the-art marketing presentation, complete with flip charts and audio-visuals, he shows 'em that this prairie boy *knows* how to make a buck. Heading on to Milan, Harry strikes up a conversation with the Japanese businessman sitting next to him on the plane. He flips his card onto his neighbour's tray and, when the two say goodbye, shakes hands warmly and clasps the man's right arm. Later, for his appointment with the owner of an Italian packaging-design firm, our hero wears his comfy corduroy sport coat, khaki pants, and deck shoes. Everybody knows Italians are zany and laid back.

Mr. Slicksmile next swings through Saudi Arabia, where he coolly presents a potential client with a multi-million dollar proposal in a classy pigskin binder. His final stop is Beijing, China, where he talks business over lunch with a group of Chinese executives. After completing the meal, he drops his chopsticks into his bowl of rice and presents each guest with an elegant Tiffany's clock as a reminder of his visit.

A great tour, sure to generate a pile of orders, right? Wrong. Six months later, Consolidated Amalgamation has nothing to show for the trip but a pile of bills. Abroad, they weren't wild about Harry.

This hypothetical case has been exaggerated for emphasis. Businesspeople are seldom such dolts. But experts say success in international business has much to do with knowing the territory and its people. By learning English and extending themselves in other ways, the world's business leaders have met North Americans more than halfway. In contrast, North Americans too often do little except assume that others will march to their music. "We want things to be just like they are at home when we travel. Fast. Convenient. Easy. So we demand that others change," says one world trade expert. "I think more business would be done if we tried harder."

Poor Harry tried, all right, but in all the wrong ways. The British do not, as a rule, make deals over the phone as much as North Americans do. It's not so much a "cultural" difference as a difference in approach. The French neither like instant familiarity—

questions about family, church, or alma mater—nor refer to strangers by their first names. "That poor fellow, Jacques, probably wouldn't show anything, but he'd recoil. He'd not be pleased," explains an expert on French business practices. "It's considered poor taste," he continues. "Even after months of business dealings, I'd wait for him or her to make the invitation [to use first names].... You are always right, in Europe, to say 'Mister' or 'Madam.'"

Harry's flashy presentation would likely have been a flop with the Germans, who dislike overstatement and ostentation. According to one German expert, however, German businesspeople have become accustomed to dealing with North Americans. Although differences in body language and customs remain, the past 20 years have softened them. "I hugged an American woman at a business meeting last night," he said. "That would be normal in France, but [older] Germans still have difficulty [with the custom]." He says that calling secretaries by their first names would still be considered rude: "They have a right to be called by the surname. You'd certainly ask—and get—permission first." In Germany, people address each other formally and correctly—someone with two doctorates (which is fairly common) must be referred to as "Herr Doktor Doktor."

When Harry Slicksmile grabbed his new Japanese acquaintance by the arm, the executive probably considered him disrespectful and presumptuous. Japan, like many Asian countries, is a "no-contact culture" in which even shaking hands is a strange experience. Harry made matters worse by tossing his business card. The Japanese revere the business card as an extension of self and as an indicator of rank. They do not *hand* it to people, they *present* it—with both hands. In addition, the Japanese are sticklers about rank. Unlike North Americans, they don't heap praise on subordinates in a room; they will praise only the highest-ranking official present.

Hapless Harry also goofed when he assumed that Italians are like Hollywood's stereotypes of them. The flair for design and style that has characterized Italian culture for centuries is embodied in the businesspeople of Milan and Rome. They dress beautifully and admire flair, but they blanch at garishness or impropriety in others' attire.

To the Saudi Arabians, the pigskin binder would have been considered vile. An American salesman who really did present such a binder was unceremoniously tossed out and his company was blacklisted from working with Saudi businesses. In China, Harry's casually dropping his chopsticks could have been misinterpreted as an act of aggression. Stabbing chopsticks into a bowl of rice and leaving them signifies death to the Chinese. The clocks Harry offered as gifts might have confirmed such dark intentions. To "give a clock" in Chinese sounds the same as "seeing someone off to his end."

Thus, to compete successfully in global markets, or even to deal effectively with international firms in their home markets, North American companies must help their managers to understand the needs, customs, and cultures of international business buyers. The old advice is still good advice: When in Rome, do as the Romans do.

Sources: Adapted from Susan Harte, "When in Rome, You Should Learn to Do What the Romans Do," *Atlanta Journal-Constitution,* January 22, 1990, pp. D1, D6. Additional examples from Terri Morrison, Wayne A. Conway, and Joseph J. Douress, *Dun & Bradstreet's Guide to Doing Business Around the World* (Upper Saddle River, N.J.: Prentice Hall, 2000); Craig S. Smith, "Beware of Green Hats in China and Other Cross-Cultural Faux Pas," *New York Times,* April 30, 2002, p. C11; and James K. Sebenius, "The Hidden Challenge of Cross-Border Negotiations," *Harvard Business Review,* March 2002, pp. 76–85.

Interpersonal Factors

The buying centre usually includes many participants who influence each other, so *interpersonal factors* also influence the business buying process. However, it is often difficult to assess such interpersonal factors and group dynamics. As one writer notes, "Managers do not wear tags that say 'decision maker' or 'unimportant person.' The powerful are often invisible, at least to vendor representatives."[13] Nor does the buying centre participant with the highest rank always have the most influence. Participants may have influence in the buying decision because they control rewards and punishments, are well liked, have special expertise, or have a special relationship with other important participants. Interpersonal factors are often very subtle. Whenever possible, business marketers must try to understand these factors and design strategies that take them into account. While many people think that only rational messages appeal to today's sophisticated purchasers, Ceridian Canada has discovered that powerful brand messages with an emotional element also help to win over business clients:

Ceridian Canada Ltd. (www.ceridian.ca), headquartered in Winnipeg, Manitoba, provides payroll management and related services to large and small business across Canada. It is the country's leading payroll services provider, with offices from coast to coast. It serves 38 500 businesses, paying more than 2.4 million Canadians. In 2002, Ceridian launched a new multifaceted campaign based on the platform "the freedom to succeed." The advertisements were full of images associated with success and freedom, but they also provided information on cost-savings and employee satisfaction. "This brand strategy allows Ceridian to communicate the benefits of their services at an emotional level," said the president of Ceridian's advertising agency.[14]

Individual Factors

Each participant in the business buying decision process brings in personal motives, perceptions, and preferences. These individual factors are affected by such personal characteristics as age, income, education, professional identification, personality, and attitudes toward risk. Also, buyers have different buying styles. Some may be technical types who make in-depth analyses of competitive proposals before choosing a supplier. Other buyers may be intuitive negotiators who are adept at pitting sellers against one another for the best deal.

The Business Buying Process

Figure 8.3 lists the eight stages of the business buying process.[15] Buyers who face a new task buying situation usually go through all stages of the buying process. Buyers making modified or straight rebuys may skip some stages. We shall examine these steps for the typical new task buying situation.

Problem recognition
The first stage of the business buying process in which someone in the company recognizes a problem or need that can be met by acquiring a good or a service.

Problem Recognition

The buying process begins when someone in the company recognizes a problem or need that can be met by acquiring a specific good or service. **Problem recognition** can result from internal or external stimuli. Internally, the company may decide to launch a new product that requires new production equipment and materials. Or a

Ceridian Canada's "freedom to succeed" campaign has hit home with its business clients on both an emotional and a rational level.

Success to me is having the freedom to be strategic

CERIDIAN
the freedom to succeed

Canada's most successful companies rely on Ceridian's payroll and HR solutions as part of their formula for success. Whatever your type of business or unique requirements, Ceridian can manage your payroll and human resources with flexible solutions tailored to meet your needs. Call us today for a free needs analysis at 1-877-CERIDIAN (237-4342). Or visit our website at www.ceridian.ca.

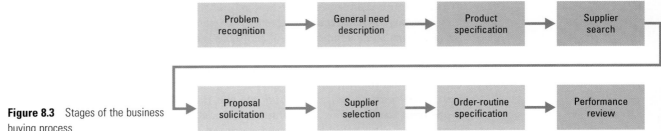

Figure 8.3 Stages of the business buying process

machine may break down and need new parts. Perhaps a purchasing manager is unhappy with a current supplier's product quality, service, or prices. Externally, the buyer may get some new ideas at a trade show, see an ad, or receive a call from a salesperson who offers a product that is better or less expensive. In fact, in their advertising, business marketers often alert customers to potential problems, and then show how their products provide solutions.

General Need Description

General need description
The stage in the business buying process in which the company describes the general characteristics and quantity of a needed item.

Having recognized a need, the buyer next prepares a **general need description** that describes the characteristics and quantity of the needed item. For standard items, this process presents few problems. For complex items, however, the buyer may have to work with others—engineers, users, consultants—to define the item. The team may want to rank the importance of reliability, durability, price, and other attributes desired in the item. In this phase, the alert business marketer can help the buyers define their needs and provide information about the value of different product characteristics.

Product Specification

Product specification
The stage of the business buying process in which the buying organization decides on and specifies the best technical product characteristics for a needed item.

The buying organization then develops the item's technical **product specifications**, often with the help of a value analysis engineering team. **Value analysis** is an approach to cost reduction in which components are carefully studied to determine if they can be redesigned, standardized, or made by less costly methods of production. The team decides on the best product characteristics and specifies them accordingly. Sellers, too, can use value analysis as a tool to help secure a new account. By showing buyers a better way to make an object, outside sellers can turn straight rebuy situations into new task situations that give them a chance to obtain new business.

Value analysis
An approach to cost reduction in which components are studied carefully to determine if they can be redesigned, standardized, or made by less costly methods of production.

Supplier Search

Supplier search
The stage of the business buying process in which the buyer tries to find the best vendors.

The buyer now conducts a **supplier search** to find the best vendors. The buyer can compile a small list of qualified suppliers by reviewing trade directories, doing a computer search, or phoning other companies for recommendations. Today, more and more companies are turning to the Internet to find suppliers. For marketers, this has levelled the playing field—the Internet gives smaller suppliers many of the same advantages as larger competitors.

These days, many companies are viewing supplier search more as *supplier development*. These companies want to develop a system of supplier-partners that can help them bring more value to their customers. For example, Wal-Mart has set up a Supplier Development Department that seeks out qualified suppliers and helps them through the complex Wal-Mart buying process. It offers a Supplier Proposal Guide and maintains a website offering advice to suppliers wishing to do business with Wal-Mart (www.walmartstores.com/wmstore/wmstores/Mainsupplier.jsp).

The newer the buying task, and the more complex and costly the item, the greater the amount of time the buyer will spend searching for suppliers. The supplier's task is to get listed in major directories and build a good reputation in the marketplace. Salespeople should watch for companies in the process of searching for suppliers and make certain that their firm is considered.

Proposal Solicitation

Proposal solicitation
The stage of the business buying process in which the buyer invites qualified suppliers to submit proposals.

In the **proposal solicitation** stage of the business buying process, the buyer invites qualified suppliers to submit proposals. In response, some suppliers will send only a catalogue or a salesperson. However, when the item is complex or expensive, the buyer will usually require detailed written proposals or formal presentations from each potential supplier.

Business marketers must be skilled in researching, writing, and presenting proposals in response to buyer proposal solicitations. Proposals should be marketing documents, not just technical documents. Presentations should inspire confidence and should make the marketer's company stand out from the competition.

Supplier Selection

Supplier selection
The stage of the business buying process in which the buyer reviews proposals and selects a supplier or suppliers.

The members of the buying centre now review the proposals and select a supplier or suppliers. During **supplier selection,** the buying centre often draws up a list of the desired supplier attributes and their relative importance. In one survey, purchasing executives listed the following attributes as most important in influencing the

Supplier development: Wal-Mart's Supplier Development Department offers a Supplier Proposal Guide and maintains a website offering advice to suppliers wishing to do business with Wal-Mart.

relationship between supplier and customer: quality products and services, on-time delivery, ethical corporate behaviour, honest communication, and competitive prices. Other important factors include repair and servicing capabilities, technical aid and advice, geographic location, performance history, and reputation. The members of the buying centre will rate suppliers against these attributes and identify the best suppliers.

Buyers may attempt to negotiate with preferred suppliers for better prices and terms before making the final selections. In the end, they may select a single supplier or a few suppliers. Many buyers prefer multiple sources of supplies to avoid being totally dependent on one supplier and to allow comparisons of prices and performance of several suppliers over time.

Order-Routine Specification

Order-routine specification
The stage of the business buying process in which the buyer writes the final order with the chosen supplier(s), listing the technical specifications, quantity needed, expected time of delivery, return policies, and warranties.

The buyer now prepares an **order-routine specification**. It includes the final order with the chosen supplier or suppliers and lists items such as technical specifications, quantity needed, expected time of delivery, return policies, and warranties. In the case of maintenance, repair, and operating items, buyers may use *blanket contracts* rather than periodic purchase orders. A blanket contract creates a long-term relationship in which the supplier promises to resupply the buyer as needed at agreed prices for a set period. A blanket order eliminates the expensive process of renegotiating a purchase each time stock is required. It also allows buyers to write more but smaller purchase orders, resulting in lower inventory levels and carrying costs.

Blanket contracting leads to more single-source buying and to buying more items from that source. This practice locks the supplier in tighter with the buyer and makes it difficult for other suppliers to break in unless the buyer becomes dissatisfied with prices or service.

Performance Review

Performance review
The stage of the business buying process in which the buyer rates its satisfaction with suppliers, deciding whether to continue, modify, or drop the arrangement.

In this stage, the buyer reviews supplier performance. The buyer may contact users and ask them to rate their satisfaction. The **performance review** may lead the buyer to continue, modify, or end the arrangement. The seller's job is to monitor the same factors used by the buyer to ensure that it is giving the buyer expected satisfaction.

We have described the stages that typically would occur in a new-task buying situation. The eight-stage model provides a simple view of the business buying decision process. The actual process is usually much more complex. In the modified rebuy or straight rebuy situation, some of these stages would be compressed or bypassed. Each organization buys in its own way, and each buying situation has unique requirements. Different buying centre participants may be involved at different stages of the process. Although certain buying process steps usually do occur, buyers do not always follow them in the same order, and they may add other steps. Often, buyers will repeat certain stages of the process. Finally, a customer relationship might involve many different types of purchases ongoing at a given time, all in different stages of the buying process. The seller must manage the total customer relationship, not just individual purchases.

Business Buying on the Internet

During the past few years, incredible advances in information technology have changed the face of the business-to-business marketing process. Online purchasing, often called *eprocurement*, is growing rapidly. Online business trade in Canada will reach $272 billion by 2005, representing 18 percent of all B2B transactions. On a provincial basis, Ontario and Quebec will emerge as online leaders, accounting for 71 percent of all of Canada's B2B trade. They will be followed by Alberta and

Online purchasing—or *eprocurement:* Public trading exchanges, like the auto industry's Covisint exchange, offer "a faster, more efficient way to communicate, collaborate, buy, sell, trade, and exchange information—business to business." The exchange handled more than $50 billion in auto-parts orders in 2002.

British Columbia. Since Ontario is second only to Michigan in North American automotive manufacturing, it is not surprising that much of its online trade is in this sector. By 2005 it is predicted that $69 billion of motor vehicle trade will shift online in Ontario alone. Twenty-nine percent of Quebec's total online B2B trade will flow through its computing and electronics supply chains. Alberta's online petrochemical trade will hit $23 billion by 2005, while British Columbia's electronics and automotive firms will account for 45 percent of its online B2B trade. While only 16 percent of Canadian companies have a clear B2B strategy, "they will increasingly recognize the benefits of the Net and come to depend on it to plan, source, distribute, and sell product over the next five years," says James Sharp, a Toronto-based analyst for Forrester Research.[16]

In addition to their own webpages on the Internet, companies are establishing extranets that link a company's communications and data with its regular suppliers and distributors. Much online purchasing also takes place on public and private online trading exchanges, or through *reverse auctions* in which companies put their purchasing requests online and invite suppliers to bid for the business. Such "cyberpurchasing" gives buyers access to new suppliers, lowers purchasing costs, and hastens order processing and delivery. In turn, business marketers can connect with customers online to share marketing information, sell products and services, provide customer support services, and maintain ongoing customer relationships.

So far, most of the products bought online are MRO materials—maintenance, repair, and operations. The actual dollar amount spent on these MRO materials pales in comparison to the amount spent for items like airplane parts, computer systems, and steel tubing. Yet MRO materials make up 80 percent of all business orders, and the transaction costs for order processing are high. Thus, companies have much to gain by streamlining the MRO buying process on the Web. Business Depot (www.staples.ca), which operates Staples and Bureau en Gros stores across Canada, is using the Net in a bid to become a one-stop online shop for the growing small business market in Canada.[17] And National Semiconductor has automated almost all of the company's 3500 monthly requisitions to buy materials ranging from the sterile booties worn in its fabrication plants to state-of-the-art software.

General Electric, one of the world's biggest purchasers, plans to be buying *all* of its general operating and industrial supplies online within the next two years. Five years ago, GE set up its Global eXchange Services network, a central website through which all GE business units could make their purchases. The site was so successful that it was spun off as an independent company in 2002. Global eXchange Services (www.gxs.com/) continues to operate the GE Global Supplier Network, creating a vast electronic cyberbuying clearinghouse.

Business-to-business eprocurement yields many benefits.[18] First, it shaves transaction costs and results in more efficient purchasing for both buyers and suppliers. A Web-powered purchasing program eliminates the paperwork associated with traditional requisition and ordering procedures. On average, companies can trim the costs of purchased goods alone by 15 to 20 percent. For example, Owens Corning estimates that eprocurement has shaved 10 percent off its annual purchasing bill of $4.4 billion.

Eprocurement also reduces order-processing costs. "The first advantage is clearly the lower prices (about 20 percent) that we are paying," says Hewlett-Packard's vice president of supply-chain services. "But we are now also 20 to 25 percent more efficient." Through online purchasing, Texas Instruments has trimmed its cost of processing a purchase order from $103 to $32. And 3M slashed the price of processing an order from $155 to under $50, while also cutting its error rate dramatically. A more efficient centralized purchasing platform also saves time and money. One key motivation for GE's massive move to online purchasing has been a desire to get rid of overlapping purchasing systems across its many divisions.

Eprocurement reduces the time between order and delivery. Time savings are particularly dramatic for companies with many overseas suppliers. Adaptec, a leading supplier of computer storage, used an extranet to tie all of its Taiwanese chip suppliers together in a kind of virtual family. Now messages from Adaptec flow in seconds from its headquarters to its Asian partners, and Adaptec has reduced the time between the order and delivery of its chips from as long as 16 weeks to just 55 days—the same turnaround time for companies that build their own chips.

Finally, beyond the cost and time savings, eprocurement frees purchasing people to focus on more-strategic issues. For many purchasing professionals, going online means reducing drudgery and paperwork and spending more time managing inventory and working creatively with suppliers. "That is the key," says an HP executive. "You can now focus people on value-added activities. Procurement professionals can now find different sources and work with suppliers to reduce costs and to develop new products."

The rapidly expanding use of epurchasing, however, also presents some problems. For example, at the same time that the Web makes it possible for suppliers and customers to share business data and even collaborate on product design, it can also erode decades-old customer-supplier relationships. Many firms are using the Web to search for better suppliers. Japan Airlines (JAL) has used the Internet to post orders for in-flight materials such as plastic cups. On its website it posted drawings and specifications that will attract proposals from any firm that comes across the site, rather than from just the usual Japanese suppliers. (In April 2000 JAL's procurement operations were transferred to JALUX Inc., which coordinates procurement for JAL

and the JAL Group: www.jalux.com/english/.)

Epurchasing can also create potential security disasters. More than 80 percent of companies say security is the leading barrier to expanding electronic links with customers and partners. Although email and home banking transactions can be protected through basic encryption, the secure environment that businesses need to carry out confidential interactions is still lacking. Companies are spending millions for research on defensive strategies to keep hackers at bay. Cisco Systems, for example, specifies the types of routers, firewalls, and security procedures that its partners must use to safeguard extranet connections. In fact, the company goes even further—it sends its own security engineers to examine a partner's defences and holds the partner liable for any security breach that originates from its computer.

Institutional and Government Markets

So far, our discussion of organizational buying has focused largely on the buying behaviour of business buyers. Much of this discussion also applies to the buying practices of institutional and government organizations. However, these two non-business markets have additional characteristics and needs, which we now address.

Institutional Markets

Institutional market
Schools, hospitals, nursing homes, prisons, and other institutions that provide goods and services to people in their care.

The **institutional market** consists of schools, hospitals, nursing homes, prisons, and other institutions that provide goods and services to people in their care. Institutions differ from one another in their sponsors and in their objectives. For example, Shouldice Hospital (www.shouldice.com), a facility based in Thornhill, Ontario, that specializes in hernia repairs, is run for profit, whereas most other hospitals in Canada are operated on a not-for-profit basis.

Many institutional markets are characterized by low budgets and captive patrons. For example, hospital patients have little choice but to eat whatever food the hospital supplies. A hospital purchasing agent must decide on the quality of food to buy for patients. Because the food is provided as part of a total service package, the buying objective is not profit. Nor is strict cost minimization the goal—patients receiving poor-quality food will complain to others and damage the hospital's reputation. Thus, the hospital purchasing agent must search for institutional food vendors whose quality meets or exceeds a certain minimum standard and whose prices are low.

Many marketers set up separate divisions to meet the special characteristics and needs of institutional buyers. For example, Heinz produces, packages, and prices its ketchup and other products differently to better serve the requirements of hospitals, universities, and other institutional markets.

Government Markets

Government market
Governmental units—federal, provincial, and municipal—that purchase or rent goods and services for carrying out the main functions of government.

The **government market** offers large opportunities for many companies. Federal, provincial, and municipal governments contain buying units. The Department of Public Works and Government Services Canada helps to centralize the buying of commonly used items in the civilian section (for example, office furniture and equipment, vehicles, fuels) and in standardizing buying procedures for the other agencies. Federal military buying is carried out by the Department of National Defence.

Government buying and business buying are similar in many ways. But there are also differences that must be understood by companies that wish to sell products and services to governments. To succeed in the government market, sellers must locate key decision makers, identify the factors that affect buyer behaviour, and understand the buying decision process.

Government organizations typically require suppliers to submit bids, and normally they award the contract to the lowest bidder. In some cases, the government unit will make allowance for the supplier's superior quality or reputation for completing contracts on time. Governments will also buy on a negotiated contract basis, primarily in the case of complex projects involving major R&D costs and risks, and in cases where little competition exists. There are sometimes extra benefits associated with supplying government departments. In an effort to improve the competitiveness of Canadian businesses, products purchased by the government are evaluated for the potential to be marketed worldwide. For example, rations developed for the military by Magic Pan are now marketed to global institutions.

Government organizations tend to favour domestic over foreign suppliers. For example, a major complaint of multinationals operating in Europe is that each country shows favouritism toward its nationals, despite superior offers made by foreign firms. The European Economic Commission is gradually removing this bias. Despite the governmental bias toward buying from domestic firms, some Canadian companies have been highly successful marketing their products to foreign governments. Take the case of Forensic Technology (www.fti-ibis.com):

Montreal-based Forensic Technology has become a global leader in marketing state-of-the-art technology to law enforcement organizations around the world. It secured a large contract with the U.S. Department of Alcohol, Tobacco, Firearms, and Explosives (ATF), beating out a U.S. competitor. Its Integrated Ballistics Identification System (IBIS®) allows law enforcement organizations to identify weapons used in crimes. Although the company was only born in 1992, its innovative technology is now employed in thirty countries and territories around the world. Agencies using IBIS include thirty-three federal, state, provincial, and local law enforcement agencies, including the South African Police Service's ballistic identification network and the New York City Police Department. Its performance has been so outstanding that the firm has won a number of awards, including being one of the recipients of the 2002 "Canada's 50 Best Managed Companies" award and the Ernst & Young 2002 Quebec Entrepreneur of the Year Award.[19]

Like consumer and business buyers, government buyers are affected by environmental, organizational, interpersonal, and individual factors. One unique aspect of government buying is that it is carefully watched by outside publics, from Parliament to various private groups interested in how the government spends taxpayers' money. Because their spending decisions are subject to public review, government organizations require considerable paperwork from suppliers, who often complain about excessive paperwork, bureaucracy, regulations, decision-making delays, and frequent shifts in procurement personnel. Given all the red tape, why would any firm want to do business with the government? Here's the answer given by a consultant who has helped numerous clients obtain government contracts:

Breakthrough technology that helps law enforcement agencies crack gun-related crimes has enabled Forensic Technology to sell to governments around the world.

Helping to ensure a better quality of life today and **for the future.**

At Forensic Technology we work around the clock to help create safer communities by producing high-tech solutions that national security & law enforcement agencies around the world depend on for removing violent criminals from our streets.

An ISO 9001 Certified Company.

www.forensictechnologyinc.com

Canada Toll free: +1 888 984.4247

When I hear that question, I tell the story of the businessman who buys a hardware store after moving to a small town. He asks his new employees who the biggest hardware customer in town is. He is surprised to learn that the customer isn't doing business with his store. When the owner asks why not, his employees say the customer is difficult to do business with and requires that a lot of forms be filled out. I point out that the same customer is probably very wealthy, doesn't bounce his cheques, and usually does repeat business when satisfied. That's the type of customer the federal government can be.[20]

Most governments provide would-be suppliers with detailed guides describing how to sell to the government. The federal government issues a weekly bulletin, *Government Business Opportunities,* to alert prospective suppliers to the government's plans to purchase products or services. Federal and provincial governments offer guides to help business firms understand their purchasing policies.[21]

Federal, provincial, and municipal governments are now posting information online to help businesses better understand their purchasing processes and supplier selection criteria. On the federal government website Contracts Canada (http://contractscanada.gc.ca), for example, you can find a wealth of information with only a click of the mouse on the "How we buy" or "What we buy" buttons. You can also access information about how to become a registered government supplier, as well as a list of current contract opportunities. The Canadian Business Service Centre (www.cbsc.org) is another site the government established to help Canadian businesses. This site is a gold mine of information on a variety of topics such as training, importing, and taxation. It features online workshops for small businesses as well as a comprehensive database of government services and programs.

If anyone knows how to market to government clients, it is Bombardier. It has more than 50 years of experience serving the military in both Canada and the United States (www.bombardier.com):

Bombardier has twice been voted the most respected company in Canada. While the company may once have been better known for recreational products such as Ski-Doos and Sea-Doos, it now makes rail transportation and aerospace equipment that it markets to governments and private firms around the world. In fact, Bombardier earns more than 90 percent of its revenues from customers in 60 markets outside Canada. It has sold aircraft to China and transportation systems to Romania. It provides state-of-the art rail cars to Deutsche Bahn AG, and in 2003 alone it received orders for 298 additional double-deck cars valued at $633 million. Through its affiliation with Canadair, Bombardier helps the

Dell Computer provides special websites for government buyers.

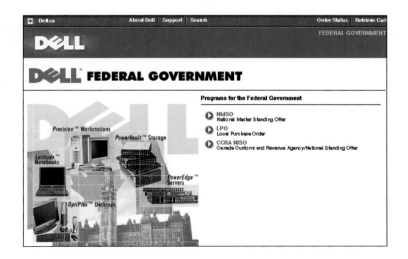

armed forces of many countries maintain, repair, and overhaul their aircraft and public transportation equipment. Since government clients are very sensitive to cost, Bombardier locates facilities near its clients' operations. This not only increases responsiveness and flexibility, it also ensures cost-effective service delivery while respecting the tight security requirements of its military clients.[22]

Many companies that sell to the government have not been marketing-oriented for a number of reasons. Total government spending is determined by elected officials rather than by any marketing effort to develop this market. Government buying has emphasized price, making suppliers invest their effort in technology to bring down costs. When the product's characteristics are specified carefully, product differentiation is not a marketing factor. Nor do advertising or personal selling matter much in winning bids on an open-bid basis.

As provincial governments downsize and move toward privatization, there are growing opportunities for businesses. Firms ranging from professional engineering firms to cleaning contractors are bidding to take over functions that government employees formerly performed. Many companies, such as Bombardier, SNC-Lavalin, Eastman Kodak, Goodyear, and Computing Devices Canada (CDC), have people who specialize in marketing to governments both nationally and internationally.

Looking Back: Reviewing the Concepts

Business markets and consumer markets are alike in some key ways. For example, both include people in buying roles who make purchase decisions to satisfy needs. But business markets also differ in many ways from consumer markets. For one thing, the business market is *enormous,* far larger than the consumer market. Within Canada alone, the business market includes more than one million organizations that annually purchase billions of dollars worth of goods and services.

1. Define the business market and explain how business markets differ from consumer markets.

Business buyer behaviour refers to the buying behaviour of the organizations that buy goods and services for use in the production of other products and services that are sold, rented, or supplied to others. It also includes the behaviour of retailing and wholesaling firms that acquire goods for the purpose of reselling or renting them to others at a profit. Compared with consumer markets, business markets usually have fewer, larger buyers who are more geographically concentrated. Business demand is *derived,* largely *inelastic,* and more *fluctuating.* More buyers are usually involved in the business buying decision, and business buyers are better trained and more professional than are consumer buyers. In general, business purchasing decisions are more complex, and the buying process is more formal than consumer buying.

2. Identify the major factors that influence business buyer behaviour.

Business buyers make decisions that vary with the three types of buying situations: *straight rebuys, modified rebuys,* and *new tasks.* The buying centre, which can consist of many different persons playing many different roles, is the decision-making unit of a buying organization. The business marketer needs to know the following: Who are the major participants? In what decisions do they exercise influence? What is their relative degree of influence? What evaluation criteria does each decision participant use? The business marketer also needs to understand the major environmental, interpersonal, and individual influences on the buying process.

3. List and define the steps in the business buying decision process.

The business buying decision process itself can be quite involved, with eight basic stages: (1) *problem recognition*—someone in the company recognizes a problem or need that can be met by acquiring a product or a service; (2) *general need description*—the company determines the general characteristics and quantity of the needed item; (3) *product specification*—the buying organization decides on and specifies the best technical product characteristics for the needed item; (4) *supplier search*—the buyer seeks the best vendors; (5) *proposal solicitation*—the buyer invites qualified suppliers to submit proposals; (6) *supplier selection*—the buyer reviews proposals and selects a supplier or suppliers; (7) *order-routine specification*—the buyer writes the final order with the chosen supplier(s), listing the technical specifications, quantity needed, expected time of delivery, return policies, and warranties; (8) *performance review*—the buyer rates its satisfaction with suppliers, deciding whether to continue, modify, or cancel the relationship.

4. Compare the institutional and government markets and explain how they make their buying decisions.

The *institutional market* consists of schools, hospitals, prisons, and other institutions that provide goods and services to people in their care. These markets are characterized by low budgets and captive patrons. The *government market*, which is vast, consists of government units—federal, provincial, and municipal—that purchase or rent goods and services for carrying out the main functions of government. Government buyers purchase products and services for defence, education, public welfare, and other public needs. Government buying practices are highly specialized and specified, with open bidding or negotiated contracts characterizing most of the buying. Government buyers operate under the watchful eye of Parliament and many private watchdog groups. Therefore, they tend to require more forms and signatures, and to respond more slowly and deliberately when placing orders.

Reviewing the Key Terms

Business buyer behaviour 299	Government market 317	Product specification 312
Business buying process 299	Influencers 306	Proposal solicitation 313
Buyers 306	Institutional market 317	Straight rebuy 304
Buying centre 305	Modified rebuy 305	Supplier search 312
Deciders 306	New task 305	Supplier selection 313
Derived demand 300	Order-routine specification 314	Systems selling 305
Gatekeepers 306	Performance review 314	Users 306
General need description 312	Problem recognition 311	Value analysis 312

Discussing the Concepts

1. Although business markets are similar in many ways to consumers markets, significant differences exist. What similarities and difference might Staples (www.staples.ca) or Office Depot (www.officedepot.ca) encounter in selling to the business market versus the consumer market the following products: (a) a personal computer, (b) paper for a printer or photocopier, (c) a desk chair, and (d) paper clips?

2. Review Table 8.1 (page 300) and create an example that illustrates the types of decisions facing business buyers and the decision process they use.

3. Compare Figure 7.1 (in the previous chapter on page 255) with Figure 8.1 (page 304). What similarities and differences do you find in inputs and outputs of these two buying models? Comment on them.

4. Which of the major types of buying situations is represented by each of the following: (a) Dell's purchase of the latest Intel chip to increase its PCs' processing speed, (b) IBM's purchase of batteries for its line of portable computers, and (c) Hewlett-Packard's purchase of speaker wire for its standard mini-speakers that accompany all of its PCs.

5. Systems selling is a key business marketing strategy for winning and holding accounts. Why?

6. Your company sells standard telephone handsets. You have just been assigned the task of winning the sales account at your former undergraduate university. Although your contacts at the university should make the sale easier, the university relies on a buying centre for all major purchases. Considering the roles and needs of the members of a buying centre at the university, design a plan for winning the sales account.

7. List and briefly describe the eight stages in the business buying process. Create an example that demonstrates how a business buyer might move through this process.

8. Business buying on the Internet has increased dramatically in the past few years. Why? What are the benefits of eprocurement? What are the drawbacks? Give an example of a product that is likely to be offered at a reverse auction.

Applying the Concepts

1. Many companies use outside suppliers to produce raw materials or parts instead of producing these components themselves. In the extreme, companies like Dell Computer own no production facilities and have suppliers make everything to order. This type of company has been nicknamed a "virtual corporation."

    a. Do you think that buyers and suppliers are likely to be more cooperative or more adversarial in this type of corporate structure?

    b. List the advantages and disadvantages of this sort of supplier relationship for both the buyer and the supplier.

    c. Explain how the supplier search process might work in the Dell "virtual corporation" example.

    d. Go to the Dell website at www.dell.com and review the information on the company. What can you determine about the "outside" parts that are contained in a Dell computer—for example, the processor, monitor, or CPU itself? Do buyers know which components are original Dell parts and which are not? Would this be of concern to potential buyers?

    e. Since Dell purchases outside parts for its computers, what do you think would be the most important considerations in supplier selection? Explain.

2. Performance review is one of the most critical stages in a business buying process. Perhaps nowhere is this more important than in the highly competitive aircraft manufacturing business. Whether the planes are large or small, once a purchase is made the buyer enters a long-term relationship with the manufacturer for service and parts requirements. Boeing is working to expand its supplier base. Historically, Boeing has produced parts internally or outsourced domestically. Today, Boeing gets product designs from Moscow, tail sections from central China, aircraft doors from Poland, and fuselage-insulation blankets from Mexico. Although this global outsourcing offers tremendous savings, it can also result in significant problems when not well managed.

    a. What complications can occur in the performance review process for foreign suppliers?

    b. What problems could Boeing face as it expands its global outsourcing?

    c. Besides potential cost advantages, why would Boeing consider global outsourcing?

    d. JAL, the huge Japanese airline, represents a substantial account for any aircraft manufacturer. What relationships should Boeing build to secure a long-term contract with JAL? Considering the Japanese affinity for high-class quality control, what role could performance review play in winning the JAL account?

Video Short

View the video short for this chapter at **www.pearsoned.ca/kotler** and then answer the questions provided in the case description.

Company Case

Emerson Process Management: Accelerating on the Internet

If you were selling automation products for manufacturing plants, the 1970s were a wonderful time—sales were booming. By 2000, however, the market had changed. Sales had slowed and purchasers were beginning to think of automation products as commodities. So many buyers were using fewer suppliers.

That was the situation that the Fisher-Rosemount division of Emerson Electric faced. How could it attract the interest and attention of industrial purchasers for services that helped buyers optimize their plants and processes? Such decisions are made infrequently and can involve big money, ranging from $25 000 to $25 000 000. How could Fisher-Rosemount demonstrate in an engaging and dynamic way the benefits of reworking processes in customers' existing plants? How could the company *show* what its services could accomplish?

Fisher-Rosemount tackled this situation by first repositioning its services. By looking at the relevant purchase processes from the customer's point of view, it realized that customers were not looking for individual products that they had to assemble themselves, *if* they had the needed in-house expertise. Instead, they were looking for complete *solutions*. Competitors—especially software vendors—had already realized this. Seeking to capitalize on their own expertise, the competitors had assembled product portfolios that included everything from PC-based process control solutions to supply chain management solutions. However, although Fisher-Rosemount's repositioning strategy was similar to that of other industry suppliers, the company had the advantage of being part of a much larger organization.

Emerson Electric was founded in 1890 in St. Louis, Missouri, to manufacture reliable electric motors. By 1892, it was selling North America's first electric fans, still one of its major lines. Over the years, however, Emerson Electric has benefited from stable management and consistent growth in its product and service lines. Today, it has over 60 divisions selling a variety of products from fans to process solutions, from refrigeration and air-conditioning technologies to tools for do-it-yourselfers and professionals, from plastics joining and cleaning compounds to world-class engineering and consulting services. The year 2002 was a tough one for the company. Despite its 43-year history of increased earnings, revenues equalled $20 billion,

down almost 11 percent from the previous year. Emerson regards this is a temporary setback and an exception to its enviable record. Emerson continues to stress increased growth—particularly in global markets—and innovation.

One way Emerson stays ahead of the competition is through heavy use of the Internet. It has over 115 ebusiness projects under way. In 2000, it transacted 10 percent of its sales (that's over $2 billion) online, and 70 percent of its 60-plus divisions had Web projects up and running.

The Internet provides a good channel for selling technical products. A survey of industrial users of the Internet indicated that much of the industry (85 percent) has access to the Internet, and that engineers are among early adopters and frequent users of the Net. They use the Internet primarily to gather information, but given the lack of relevant information found there, they spend only up to three hours a week on the Net. Therefore, it appears that supplier companies can best increase the value of the Internet in selling their services by providing more detailed information about products and services.

The folks at Fisher-Rosemount must have seen this report, because they chose to develop an information-packed site called PlantWeb (http://plantweb. emersonprocess.com). The home page of this website provides visitors with information on PlantWeb. Right away, visitors learn how they can understand today's technologies better, access information more quickly, reduce costs, and increase revenues. They can do this by taking advantage of PlantWeb University, which provides short business courses on how to improve plant profitability, and engineering courses in which they can explore leading automation technologies. The page also provides short "testimonial-descriptions" of companies that have recently used PlantWeb to improve their operations. Visitors who want more information than that provided by the short testimonials can call up longer case studies for information. PlantWeb News provides recent examples of new users of PlantWeb services and gives a chronological listing for the last five years of successful applications of its services.

What is most interesting, engaging, and unusual about this website is a feature called TestDrive PlantWeb. In the test drive, visitors can *see* how much

PlantWeb architecture can reduce capital expenditures compared with traditional DCS (Distributed Control Systems) architecture. What does that mean? Assume that you are a manager of a pulp and paper plant. Visit the website, go to the TestDrivePlantWeb page (www.testdriveplantweb.com), and click on the link of your industry. Click on Pulp & Paper, then select and continue the test drive, and you'll get a diagram showing all the processes in the pulp and paper industry, from waste treatment through papermaking, recovery, bleaching, and pulping. By using the various buttons, such as Customize Areas and Design Cost Assumptions, you can input data for your plant. All the while, the site provides an estimate of how much you can save using process management from Fisher-Rosemount. In addition to a summary of savings, you'll receive information detailing how you would achieve those savings. Can't you just imagine engineers inputting various data to see how much they could save? In fact, the site has proven very effective in attracting new customers. No doubt that's why TestDrivePlantWeb has won several awards.

What is PlantWeb? According to the website, it's a revolutionary field-based architecture that changes the economics of process automation. TestDrivePlantWeb allows you to build your own virtual plant to evaluate the economics of process automation. It employs an easy-to-use, drag-and-drop interface that allows users to customize models by adding or deleting process areas, units, or devices or by adjusting variables such as labour rates and average wire run. The effects are shown immediately in the summary. Specific benefits of retrofitting your old plant with automation from Fisher-Rosemount include reduced process variability, increased plant availability, reduced capital and engineering costs, reduced operations and maintenance costs, and streamlined regulatory compliance.

In 2001, as part of its corporate repositioning strategy, Emerson Electric renamed the Fisher-Rosemount division, calling it the Emerson Process Management division. The goal was to enhance the overall corporate brand and to provide insight into the division's services. The repositioning also involved the integration of Fisher-Rosemount with other services in Emerson Electric, such as Emerson Performance Solutions, in order to provide complete solutions to purchasers.

Emerson Process Management does not rely only on the Internet to sell its services. To promote PlantWeb, it hired 50 sales reps (dubbed "Plant Web Champs") and trained them on Internet technology. To support

their efforts, it used print advertising and direct marketing to reach prospects that it calls "technical evangelists." The print ads used brilliant colours and images that contrasted old and new technology—for example, a weather vane and a weather satellite. These ads stood out amid the wordy competitor ads surrounding them. Emerson also used the TestDrivePlantweb site to collect names of prospects and their affiliations. It then sent direct mail to higher-level executives in each organization. The idea was to intrigue the "technical evangelist's" supervisor, who was more likely to be involved in the purchase decision. Perhaps they would meet in the hallway, and the technical evangelist, who was excited from taking a "test drive" on PlantWeb, would exchange information with the supervisor who had questions about costs.

Such simple hallway conversations can be the beginning of a process that takes months to complete. During that time, Emerson sends prospects promotional materials and invitations to seminars to keep their interest from flagging. If all of those marketing efforts are not enough, PlantWeb has a guarantee that the purchaser will reduce total installed cost using PlantWeb automation solutions as compared with traditional DCS architectures.

Does this work? You decide. In the first 18 months that TestDrivePlantWeb was up, Emerson identified 65 000 unique visitors to the site, and that translated into 850 installations of the PlantWeb product.

Questions for Discussion

1. What type of purchase decision is involved in buying solutions to a company's process systems from Emerson Process Management (Fisher-Rosemount)?

2. Who might participate in the buying process? How can the PlantWeb site and the associated marketing campaign impact each of the buying-decision participants?

3. How can the PlantWeb site and the associated marketing campaign affect each stage in the business buying process?

4. What purpose do the testimonials, case studies, and PlantWeb guarantee serve?

5. Is promotion and selling on the Internet a wise decision for Emerson Process Management? Why or why not? What are the advantages of using the Internet compared with using only personal selling and advertising? The disadvantages?

6. In your opinion, is Emerson wise to reposition itself by branding all of its divisions with the Emerson name? Why would this be beneficial in selling to business markets? How might it be a disadvantage?

Sources: "Briefly Noted," *Mechanical Engineering,* May 1999, p. 24; David Lewis, "Emerson's Web Rollouts to Keep Earnings Rolling Too," *Internet Week,* November 13, 2000, p. 1181; Kevin Parker, "Fisher-Rosemount Out, Solutions Selling In," *Manufacturing Systems,* June 2001, p. 121; Weld Royal, "Web Marketing's New Wave," *Industry Week,* November 6, 2000, pp. 29–32; George Short, "Information Engineering," *Plant Engineering,* June 1999, p. 541; and information, including the 2002 Annual Report, from the Emerson and PlantWeb websites, www.gotoemerson.com/ and http://plantweb.emersonprocess.com/ (accessed July 2002).

CBC Video Case

Log on to your Companion Website at **www.pearsoned.ca/kotler** to view a CBC video segment and case for this chapter.

Chapter 9

Segmentation, Targeting, and Positioning: Building the Right Relationships with the Right Customers

After studying this chapter you should be able to

1. define the three steps of target marketing: market segmentation, market targeting, and market positioning

2. list and discuss the bases for segmenting consumer and business markets

3. explain how companies identify attractive market segments and choose a market coverage strategy

4. explain how companies position their products for maximum competitive advantage in the marketplace

Looking Ahead: Previewing the Concepts

So far, you've learned what marketing is and about the complex environments in which marketing operates. With that as background, you're now ready to delve more deeply into marketing strategy and tactics. This chapter looks further into key marketing strategy decisions—how to divide up markets into meaningful customer groups (market segmentation), choose which customer groups to serve (target marketing), and create marketing offers that best serve targeted customers (positioning). Then, the chapters that follow explore in depth the tactical marketing tools—the 4*P*s—by which marketers bring these strategies to life.

As an opening example of segmentation, targeting, and position at work, let's look first at Procter & Gamble, one of the world's premier consumer goods companies. Some 99 percent of all North American households use at least one of P&G's more than 250 brands, and the typical household regularly buys and uses from one to two *dozen* P&G brands. How many P&G products can you name? Why does this superb marketer compete with itself on supermarket shelves by marketing seven different brands of laundry detergent? The P&G story provides a great example of how smart marketers use segmentation, targeting, and positioning.

*P*rocter & Gamble (P&G) began operations in Canada in 1915. Today it employs over 650 people at its Canadian headquarters in Toronto. It also operates manufacturing facilities in Belleville and Brockville, has a Distribution Centre in Hamilton, Ontario, and runs regional sales offices in Halifax, Montreal, and Calgary. P&G Canada is one of the top profit contributors in the P&G World—a global organization that markets more than 250 products to more than five billion consumers in 130 countries.

Tim Penner, the Canadian president, aims to make Procter & Gamble the fastest growing consumer goods company in Canada, and to make Canada the fastest growing country in which P&G operates worldwide. He believes there are five factors that will ensure this growth. First,

P&G is innovative, as evidenced by the many new products it brings to market (such as Febreze and the Swiffer). Then there are its innovative marketing campaigns and its innovative selling strategies. Next, P&G prides itself on being externally competitive while working collaboratively internally. P&G encourages the personal growth and development of all of its employees. Finally, Penner notes the firm's reputation for integrity: "Our employees, when faced with tough choices, are simply asked to 'do the right thing.'" In fact, EthicScan, Canada's foremost ethics consultancy, ranks P&G as Number 1 in its industry for Corporate Social Responsibility.

Let's take a look at some of P&G's many brands. It sells seven brands of laundry detergent in North America (Tide,

Cheer, Bold, Gain, Era, Dreft, and Ivory Snow). It also sells six brands of hand soap (Ivory, Safeguard, Camay, Olay, Zest, and Old Spice); eight brands of shampoo (Pantene, Head & Shoulders, Herbal Essences, Aussie, Infusium, Pert, Physique, and Vidal Sassoon); four brands of dishwashing detergent (Dawn, Ivory, Joy, and Cascade); three brands each of tissues and towels (Charmin, Bounty, Puffs), and deodorant (Secret, Sure, and Old Spice); and two brands each of fabric softener (Downy and Bounce), cosmetics (Cover Girl and Max Factor), skin-care potions (Olay and Noxema), and disposable diapers (Pampers and Luvs). Moreover, P&G has many additional brands in each category for different international markets. For example, it sells 16 different laundry product brands in Latin America and 19 in Europe, the Middle East, and Africa. (See Procter & Gamble's website at www.pg.com for a full view of the company's impressive line-up of familiar brands.)

These P&G brands compete with one another on the same supermarket shelves. But why would P&G introduce several brands in one category instead of concentrating its resources on a single leading brand? The answer lies in the fact that different people want different *mixes of benefits* from the products they buy. Take laundry detergents as an example. People use laundry detergents to get their clothes clean. But they also want other things from their detergents—such as economy, bleaching power, fabric softening, fresh smell, strength or mildness, and lots of suds or only a few. We all want *some* of every one of these benefits from our detergent, but we may have different *priorities* for each benefit. To some people, cleaning and bleaching power are most important; to others, fabric softening matters most; still others want a mild, fresh-scented detergent. Thus, there are groups—or segments—of laundry detergent buyers, and each segment seeks a special combination of benefits.

Procter & Gamble has identified at least seven important laundry detergent segments, along with numerous subsegments, and has developed a different brand designed to meet the special needs of each. The seven brands are positioned for different segments as follows:

- *Tide* provides "fabric cleaning and care at its best." It's the all-purpose family detergent that is "tough on greasy stains."
- *Cheer* is the "colour expert." It helps protect against fading, colour transfer, and fabric wear, with or without bleach. *Cheer Free* is "dermatologist tested...contains no irritating perfume or dye."
- *Bold* is the detergent with built-in fabric softener and pill/fuzz removal.
- *Gain,* originally P&G's "enzyme" detergent, was repositioned as the detergent that gives you clean, fresh-smelling clothes. It "cleans and freshens like sunshine. Great cleaning power and a smell that stays clean."

- *Era* is "the power tool for stain removal and pretreating." It contains advanced enzymes to fight a family's tough stains and help get the whole wash clean. *Era Max* has three types of active enzymes to help fight many stains that active families encounter.
- *Ivory Snow* is "Ninety-nine and forty-four one hundredths percent pure." It provides "mild cleansing benefits for a pure and simple clean."
- *Dreft* also "helps remove tough baby stains...for a clean you can trust." It's "pediatrician recommended and the first choice of mothers." It "doesn't remove the flame resistance of children's sleepwear."

Within each segment, Procter & Gamble has identified even *narrower* niches. For example, you can buy regular Tide (in powder or liquid form) or any of several formulations:

- *Tide with Bleach* helps to "keep your whites white and your colours bright." Available in regular or "mountain spring" scents.
- *Tide Liquid with Bleach Alternative* uses active enzymes in pretreating and washing to break down and remove the toughest stains while whitening whites.
- *Tide High Efficiency* "unlocks the cleaning power of high-efficiency top-loading machines"—it prevents oversudsing.
- *Tide Clean Breeze* gives the fresh scent of laundry line-dried in a clean breeze.
- *Tide Mountain Spring* lets you "bring the fresh clean scent of the great outdoors inside—the scent of crisp mountain air and fresh wildflowers."
- *Tide Free* "provides all the stain removal benefits without any dyes or perfumes."
- *Tide Rapid Action Tablets* are portable and powerful. It's Tide "all concentrated into a little blue and white tablet that fits into your pocket."

By segmenting the market and having several detergent brands, Procter & Gamble has an attractive offering for consumers in all important preference groups. As a result, P&G has traditionally cleaned up in the $5.2 billion North American laundry detergent market. Tide, by itself, captures a whopping 38 percent market share. All P&G brands combined take a 57 percent share of the market—three times that of nearest rival Unilever and much more than any single brand could obtain by itself. P&G will have to stay on its toes, however. Marketers of private-label brands, such as President's Choice (marketed by Loblaws), threaten to make inroads into the brand franchise. The popularity of private labels has been increasing in Canada due to their lower prices and competitive quality. In 2001, private labels accounted for nearly 9 percent of sales of household cleaning products.[1]

Companies today recognize that they cannot appeal to all buyers in the marketplace, or at least not to all buyers in the same way. Buyers are too numerous, too widely scattered, and too varied in their needs and buying practices. Moreover, the companies themselves vary widely in their abilities to serve different segments of the market. Rather than try to compete in an entire market, sometimes against superior competitors, each company must identify the parts of the market that it can serve best and most profitably.

Thus, most companies are being more choosy about the customers with whom they wish to build relationships. Most have moved away from mass marketing toward *market segmentation and targeting*—identifying market segments, selecting one or more of them, and developing products and marketing programs tailored to each. Instead of scattering their marketing efforts (the "shotgun" approach), firms are focusing on the buyers who have greater interest in the values they create best (the "rifle" approach).

Companies have not always practised market segmentation and targeting. For most of the past century, major consumer products companies held fast to *mass marketing*—mass-producing, mass-distributing, and mass-promoting the same product in about the same way to all consumers. Henry Ford typified this marketing strategy when he offered the Model T Ford "in any colour—as long as it is black." Similarly, Coca-Cola at one time produced only one drink for the whole market, hoping it would appeal to everyone.

These companies argued that mass marketing creates the largest potential market, which leads to the lowest costs. This, in turn, can translate into either lower prices or higher margins. However, many factors now make mass marketing more difficult. For example, the world's mass markets have slowly splintered into a profusion of smaller segments—the baby boomers here, the Gen-Xers there; here the Chinese segment, there the French Canadian segment; here working women, there single parents; here eastern Canada, there the West. Today, marketers find it very hard to create a single product or program that appeals to all of these diverse groups.

The proliferation of distribution channels and advertising media has also made it difficult to practise "one-size-fits-all" marketing. Today's consumers can shop at megamalls, superstores, or specialty shops, and through mail catalogues, by telephone, or from online retailers. They are bombarded with messages in media ranging from old standards such as television, radio, magazines, newspapers, and telephone to newcomers such as Web ads, faxes, and emails. No wonder some have claimed that mass marketing is dying. Not surprisingly, many companies are retreating from mass marketing and turning to segmented marketing.

Figure 9.1 shows the three major steps in target marketing. The first is **market segmentation**—dividing a market into distinct groups of buyers with different needs, characteristics, or behaviours who might require separate products or marketing mixes. The company identifies different ways to segment the market and develops profiles of the resulting market segments. The second step is **target marketing**—evaluating each market segment's attractiveness and selecting one or more of the market segments to serve. The third step is **market positioning**—setting the competitive positioning for the product and creating a detailed marketing mix. We discuss each of these steps in turn.

Market segmentation
Dividing a market into distinct groups with distinct needs, characteristics, or behaviours who might require separate products or marketing mixes.

Target marketing
The process of evaluating each market segment's attractiveness and selecting one or more segments to serve.

Market positioning
Arranging for a product to occupy a clear, distinctive, and desirable place relative to competing products in the minds of target consumers.

Figure 9.1 Steps in market segmentation, targeting, and positioning

Market Segmentation

Markets consist of buyers, and buyers differ in one or more ways. They may differ in their wants, resources, locations, buying attitudes, and buying practices. Through market segmentation, companies divide large, heterogeneous markets into smaller segments that can be reached more efficiently with products and services that match their unique needs. In this section, we discuss four important segmentation topics: segmenting consumer markets, segmenting business markets, segmenting international markets, and requirements for effective segmentation.

Segmenting Consumer Markets

There is no single way to segment a market. A marketer has to try different segmentation variables, alone and in combination, to find the best way to view the market structure. Table 9.1 outlines the major variables that might be used in segmenting consumer markets. Here we look at the major *geographic*, *demographic*, *psychographic*, and *behavioural variables*.

Table 9.1   Major Segmentation Variables for Consumer Markets

Variable	Typical Breakdown
Geographic	
World region or country	North America, Western Europe, Middle East, Pacific Rim, China, India, Canada, Mexico
Region	Maritimes, Quebec, Ontario, Prairies, British Columbia, Northern Territories
City size	under 5000; 5000–20 000; 20 000–50 000; 50 000–100 000; 100 000–250 000; 250 000–500 000; 500 000–1 000 000; 1 000 000–4 000 000; 4 000 000 and over
Density	Urban, suburban, rural
Climate	Northern, Southern, Coastal, Prairie, Mountain
Demographic	
Age	under 6, 6–11, 12–19, 20–34, 35–49, 50–64, 65+
Gender	male, female
Family size	1–2, 3–4, 5+
Family life cycle	young, single; young, married, no children; young, married, youngest child under 6; young, married, youngest child 6 or over; older, married, with children; older, married, no children under 18; older, single; same-sex partners; unmarried partners, no children; unmarried partners, with children; other
Income	under $10 000; $10 000–15 000; $15 000–20 000; $20 000–30 000; $30 000–50 000; $50 000–75 000; $75 000 and over
Occupation	professional and technical; managers, officials, and proprietors; clerical, sales; craftspeople, foremen; operatives; farmers; retired; students; homemakers; unemployed
Education	grade school or less; some high school; high school graduate; college; some university; university graduate; post-graduate
Religion	Catholic, Protestant, Jewish, Muslim, Hindu, other
Ethnic origin	British, French, German, Scandinavian, Italian, Latin American, Native Canadian, Middle Eastern, East Indian, Japanese, Chinese, African Canadian
Generation	Baby boomer, Generation X, Generation Y
Psychographic	
Social class	Lower lowers, upper lowers, working class, middle class, upper middles, lower uppers, upper uppers
Lifestyle	achievers, believers, strivers
Personality	compulsive, gregarious, authoritarian, ambitious
Behavioural	
Occasions	Regular occasion, special occasion
Benefits	Sought quality, service, economy
User status	Non-user, ex-user, potential user, first-time user, regular user
Usage rate	Light user, medium user, heavy user
Loyalty status	None, medium, strong, absolute
Readiness state	Unaware, aware, informed, interested, desirous, intending to buy
Attitude toward product	Enthusiastic, positive, negative, hostile

Geographic Segmentation

Geographic segmentation
Dividing a market into different geographical units such as nations, provinces, regions, counties, cities, or neighbourhoods.

Geographic segmentation calls for dividing the market into different geographical units such as nations, regions, provinces, counties, cities, or neighbourhoods. A company may decide to operate in one or a few geographical areas, or to operate in all areas but pay attention to geographical differences in needs and wants.

Many companies are localizing their products, advertising, promotion, and sales efforts to fit the needs of individual regions, cities, and even neighbourhoods. For example, Parker Brothers offers localized versions of its popular Monopoly game for several major cities, including Chicago, New York, San Francisco, St. Louis, and Las Vegas. The Las Vegas version features a black board with The Strip rather than Boardwalk, hotel casinos, red Vegas dice, and custom pewter tokens including blackjack cards, a wedding chapel, and a roulette wheel.[2]

When it was recently announced that Vancouver will host the 2010 Winter Olympics and Paralympics, brand strategists rushed to link their products with the Vancouver victory. They created ads that were distinctly Canadian but also had a West Coast flavour. The Olympic logo is one of the world's best known brands, so regional marketing can also have international impact. As Jacquie Ryan, senior manager of sponsorship marketing for RBC Financial, notes, "The Olympic Games is the biggest marketing platform this country has seen." Coca-Cola, another long-time Olympic sponsor, also began a regional initiative selling commemorative cans in Vancouver. The Coca-Cola Classic can sported a maple leaf and the message "Congratulations Vancouver." According to Jenny Dickson, acting Coke marketing director in the coastal region, "It's all about creating the emotional connection between Coca-Cola, the Olympics, and the tradition of shared moments....We want to celebrate Vancouver's passion for the Olympics and the success of the bid."[3]

Other companies use geographic segmentation as they seek to cultivate as-yet-untapped geographic territory. For example, many large companies are fleeing the fiercely competitive major cities to set up shop in smaller towns. Sheraton Four-

The RBC Financial Group, an Olympic Sponsor since 1947, combined a regional theme with their national brand to create a powerful ad that celebrated Vancouver's winning bid for the Olympics.

The Games start in 2010. The celebrations start now.

You earned your victory, Vancouver. Congratulations. Bringing the Winter Olympic Games back to Canada took a lot of hard work and we're proud to have been on the team. For our part, we will continue to celebrate the spirit behind Canada's Olympic dreams. We've been doing it since 1947 and we plan to keep doing it.

RBC Financial Group

Supporting Olympic dreams since 1947

Points hotels have opened a chain of smaller-format hotels in places like Kingston, Ontario, that are too small for its standard-size, more upscale hotels.

In contrast, other retailers are developing new store concepts that will give them access to higher-density urban areas. For example, Home Depot is introducing neighbourhood stores that look a lot like its traditional stores but at about two-thirds the size. It is placing these stores in high-density markets where full-size stores are impractical. Similarly, Wal-Mart is testing Neighbourhood Market grocery stores to complement its supercentres.[4]

Demographic Segmentation

Demographic segmentation means dividing the market into groups based on such demographic variables as age, gender, family size, family life cycle, income, occupation, education, religion, race, and nationality. Demographic factors are the most popular bases for segmenting customer groups. One reason is that consumer needs, wants, and usage rates often vary closely with demographic variables. Another is that demographic variables are easier to measure than most other types of variables. Even when marketers first define market segments using other bases, such as personality or behaviour, they must know their demographic characteristics to assess the size of the target market and to reach it efficiently.

Age and Life Cycle Stage   Consumer needs and wants change with age. Some companies use **age and life cycle segmentation**, offering different products or using different marketing approaches for different age and life cycle groups. For example, McDonald's targets different age groups—from children and teens to adults and seniors—with different ads and media. Its ads to teens feature dance-beat music, adventure, and fast-paced cutting from scene to scene; ads to seniors are softer and more sentimental. Procter & Gamble boldly targets its Oil of Olay ProVital moisturizing creams and lotions at women over 50 years of age—it helps to improve the elasticity and revitalize the appearance of "maturing skin."[5] And Gap has branched out to target people at different life stages. In addition to its standard line of clothing, the retailer now offers Baby Gap, Gap Kids, and Gap Maternity. Here's another example:

> In several of its stores around the country, clothing retailer Eddie Bauer places large, high-definition video screens in its storefront windows to draw in customers who might otherwise walk on by. The screens allow stores to customize in-store advertising to target different generational segments, depending on the time of day. For example, a store might post images featuring older models during the morning hours when retirees frequently shop, then change the posters to reflect the younger shopping crowd of the evening. In one initial nine-month test, sales at one location rose 56 percent from the previous nine months.[6]

Marketers must be careful to guard against stereotypes when using age and life-cycle segmentation. Although you might find some 70-year-olds in wheelchairs, others play tennis. Similarly, whereas some 40-year-old couples are sending their children off to college, others are just beginning new families. Thus, age is often a poor predictor of a person's life cycle, health, work or family status, needs, and buying power. Companies marketing to mature consumers usually employ positive images and appeals. For example, ads for Olay ProVital feature attractive older spokeswomen and uplifting messages. "Many women 50 and older have told us that as they age, they feel more confidant, wiser, and freer than ever before," observes Olay's marketing director. "These women are redefining beauty."[7]

Gender   Understanding differences in what men and women buy and the way they shop provides marketers with important insights. Thus, **gender segmentation** has long been used in clothing, cosmetics, and magazines. For example, Procter & Gamble was among the first with Secret, a brand specially formulated for a woman's

Margin definitions

Demographic segmentation
Dividing the market into groups based on such demographic variables as age, gender, family size, family life cycle, income, occupation, education, religion, race, and nationality.

Age and life-cycle segmentation
Dividing a market into different age and life-cycle groups.

Gender segmentation
Dividing a market into different groups based on gender.

Video screens in some Eddie Bauer storefront windows allow stores to customize in-store advertising to target different generational segments, depending on the time of day.

chemistry, packaged and advertised to reinforce the female image. Since women make 70 percent of shopping decisions, big-box home chains like Rona are courting them with trendy "paint cafés" and luxurious display kitchens. Owens-Corning consciously aimed a major advertising campaign for home insulation at women after its study on women's role in home improvement showed that two-thirds were involved in materials installation, with 13 percent doing it themselves. Half the women surveyed compared themselves to Bob Vila rather than Martha Stewart.[8]

 Similar thinking was behind Home Depot Canada's new strategy. It recently teamed up with Grocery Gateway (www.grocerygateway.com), a consumer-direct online service, to offer customers in Greater Toronto and Southern Ontario home delivery of hundreds of home improvement and household items. Home Depot entered the partnership in order to expose its products to a different kind of shopper—people who might not venture into a superstore for a screwdriver or roll of tape. Currently, most Home Depot shoppers are male and are shopping to complete a renovation project, while most Grocery Gateway customers are female and are shopping for consumables and products that are used on an ongoing basis. The partnership will enable cross-selling to these different segments.[9]

If any company knows how to market to women, it's Toronto-based Harlequin, a name synonymous with romance:

> Harlequin is Canada's largest and most global publisher, issuing more than 1000 new book titles each and every year. It sells about 200 million books annually to 131 international markets in 25 languages. Canada accounts for only 3 percent of its sales; 47 percent go to the United States and Mexico, and the rest are sold in its global markets. The average Harlequin reader is most often a married 40-something. What's astounding is Harlequin's ability to appeal to women in different age groups around the world. Harlequin's success is based partly on its ability to build a brand that resonates with readers worldwide. It also uses imaginative distribution like its direct-to-home subscribers program.
>
> It is Harlequin's insight into the tastes of different segments of female readers that really powers its expanding product line. For example, its newest line,

Insight into the life themes of different-aged female readers has been the powerhouse behind Harlequin's incredible international marketing efforts.

Red Dress Ink, is aimed at the 20- or 30-something single woman. Inspired by the Bridget Jones-esque "chick lit" phenomenon, the line is all about dating, first jobs, and the trials and tribulations of careers. The books are priced at about $16, compared to the standard Harlequin titles that run at about $5 (roughly the same price as a magazine). Donna Hayes, the CEO, describes the new strategy: "We wanted to reinvent the company this year. There's huge growth in women's fiction and we want to move from being a publisher of series romance paperbacks into women's fiction in all formats. We already own 80 percent of the series romance market in the U.S., but our share of the women's fiction market beyond romance, like suspense, thrillers and mysteries, is only 7 percent. That's a whole other ball game."[10]

The automobile industry knows women buy nearly half of all new cars sold and influence 80 percent of all new car purchasing decisions. Thus, women have become a valued target market for the auto companies. "Selling to women should be no different than selling to men," notes one analyst. "But there are subtleties that make a difference." Women have different frames and greater safety concerns. To address these issues, automakers are designing cars with hoods and trunks that are easier to open, seats that are easier to adjust, and seat belts that fit women better. They've also increased their safety focus, emphasizing such features as air bags and remote door locks.

A growing number of websites as well as television stations also target women. For example, Oxygen Media runs a website "designed for women by women" (www.oxygen.com). It appeals to 18- to 34-year-old women with fresh and hip information, features, and exchanges on a wide variety of topics—from health and fitness, money and work, and style and home to relationships and self-discovery.[11] The W Network offers Canadian women television programming tailored to their interests and issues (www.wnetwork.com).

While understanding individual gender-based shopping behaviour is important, insight into the behaviour of couples who shop together may be even more powerful. "Even traditional male bastions, like Canadian Tire, are now dominated by couples," says Diane Brisebois, president of the Retail Council of Canada. "Especially when it's a big-ticket item, you will often see the couple together making that decision." People behave differently when they shop together than when they shop alone. IKEA's research, for example, found that six out of ten couples argue while shopping at its stores. To strengthen relationships and smooth the shopping experience, it brought in counsellors one Valentine's Day to take couples through conflict-resolution exercises. In other words, the fact that shopping can make or break a relationship—and that a relationship can make or break shopping expeditions—is one that retailers are paying attention to. Glasgow's Braehead Mall offers women a "shopping boyfriend," a guy who "takes a girl around, helps her pick her outfits, stands outside the change rooms—does all the things men don't like about shopping.[12]

Gender-based segmentation must be used carefully, avoiding stereotypes. Men's shopping attitudes, for example, have changed. As one consumer behaviour expert notes, "For many younger men, the mall was the first place they became themselves." In the "gender-bender" world that is evolving, retailers need to rethink the needs of shoppers. "Part of what we're looking at is, are there shopping aids which are perceived as either less 'female' or more 'unisex' or more 'masculine'? Can we get beyond the Little Red Riding Hood basket you find at Shopper's Drug Mart?" Men seem to prefer pulling grocery carts rather than pushing them, pram-style, and this expert envisions a shopping cart with the "practicality and style of a Corvette."[13]

Income segmentation

Dividing a market into different income groups.

Income   **Income segmentation** has long been used by the marketers of such products and services as automobiles, boats, clothing, cosmetics, and travel. Many companies target affluent consumers with luxury goods and convenience services. For example, Holt Renfrew specializes in serving fashion-conscious, affluent buyers. To entice them to purchase, it offers them personal shoppers and concierge services. And Neiman Marcus (www.neimanmarcus.com), an upscale U.S. retailer that mails its catalogues to wealthy Canadian consumers, pitches everything from expensive jewellery, fine fashions, and exotic furs to glazed Australian apricots priced at $25 a pound. To cater to its best customers, Neiman Marcus created its InCircle Rewards program. Members, who must spend $3900 a year using their Neiman Marcus credit cards to be eligible, earn one point for each dollar spent. They then cash in points for anything from a snakeskin-patterned Nokia phone cover (10 000 points) to a photo shoot with celebrity photographer Annie Liebowitz (1 million points). InCircle members have an average household income of $741 833 and an average net worth of over $3 million.[14]

However, not all companies that use income segmentation target the affluent. Many firms also serve low-income consumers. In 2002, the average per capita income in Canada was $28 678. However, 10.3 percent of Canada's population and 15.5 percent of our children live in poverty. Compare the Canadian percentage of those living in poverty to rates in the United States (17.0 percent), Mexico (21.9 percent), and Finland (4.9 percent, the lowest poverty rate of OECD countries). In Canada, the poverty line for a family of four is $19 662. Poverty is based on relative expenditures. Those living in poverty spend 55 percent or more of their income on food, shelter, and clothing.[15]

Income segmentation: To thank its very best customers, Neiman Marcus created the InCircle Rewards Program. In 2002, its upscale members were offered fabulous incentives. For five million points, they could indulge themselves and 15 friends in the vacation of a lifetime—a six-night Virtuosa-designed itinerary across Europe aboard an Intrav Boeing jet.

Greyhound Lines, with its inexpensive nationwide bus network, is one firm that targets lower-income consumers. Almost half of its revenues come from people with annual incomes under $22 000. Many retailers also target this group, including chains such as Silver Dollar, Dollarama, A Buck or Two, and Family Dollar stores.

Sales at these stores grew by 12.6 percent in 2002 alone, compared with the 6 percent growth rate average for other types of retailers. Better merchandising and the direct sourcing of merchandise from overseas manufacturers has enabled these retailers to keep their prices low and have enabled them to expand their franchises rapidly. Dollarama and Buck or Two, the two largest chains, each had over 300 outlets in 2003. These stores are no longer just attracting the budget conscious. Upscale shoppers are now frequenting their aisles, a fact not missed by competitive retailers such as Wal-Mart and Loblaws that are experimenting with dollar aisles in their stores.[16]

Psychographic Segmentation

Psychographic segmentation
Dividing a market into different groups based on lifestyle or personality characteristics.

Psychographic segmentation divides buyers into groups based on lifestyle or personality characteristics. People in the same demographic group can have very different psychographic makeups. For example, a recent Nova Scotia study of food preferences identified seven lifestyle segments: environmentally concerned, well organized, community oriented, economy minded, adventurous, weight conscious, and wellness oriented.[17]

In Chapter 7, we discussed how the products people buy reflect their *lifestyles*. As a result, marketers often segment their markets by consumer lifestyles. For example, Toronto-based Modrobes Saldebus Lounge Clothing Inc. was born to target the casual student lifestyle. Modrobes' comfortable, easy-care clothing has been a hit among the 16- to 25-year-old crowd. The firm began with a single product—something every student needed—exam pants! Today, Modrobes sells a full line of clothing through 350 stores, including Athletes World as well as their own retail stores.[18]

One forward-looking grocery store found that segmenting its self-service meat products by lifestyle had a big payoff:

> Walk by the refrigerated self-service meat cases of most grocery stores and you'll usually find the offering grouped by type of meat—pork in one case, lamb in another, and chicken in a third. However, [one entrepreneurial supermarket] decided to experiment and offer groupings of different meats by lifestyle. For instance, the store had a section called "Meals in Minutes." There was another section called "Cookin' Lite" and one called "I Like to Cook," while still another, filled with prepared products like hot dogs and ready-made hamburger patties, was called "Kids Love This Stuff." By focusing on lifestyle needs and not on protein categories, this test store encouraged habitual beef and pork buyers to consider lamb and veal as well. As a result, the five-metre service case has seen a substantial improvement in both sales and profits.[19]

Marketers also have used personality to segment markets. For example, the marketing campaign for Honda's Helix and Elite motor scooters *appears* to target hip and trendy 22-year-olds. But it is *actually* aimed at a much broader personality group. One ad, for example, shows a delighted child bouncing up and down on his bed while the announcer says, "You've been trying to get there all your life." The ad reminds viewers of the euphoric feelings they got when they broke away from authority and did things their parents told them not to do. It suggests that they can feel that way again by riding a Honda scooter. Thus, Honda is appealing to the rebellious, independent kid in all of us. As Honda notes on its webpage, "Fresh air, freedom, and flair—on a Honda scooter, every day is independence day! When it comes to cool, this scooter is off the charts!" In fact, more than half of Honda's scooter sales are to young professionals and older buyers—15 percent are purchased by the over-50 group. Aging baby boomers, now thrill-seeking middle-agers, caused a 26 percent jump in scooter sales in 2002.[20]

Behavioural Segmentation

Behavioural segmentation divides buyers into groups based on their knowledge, attitudes, uses, or responses to a product. Many marketers believe that behaviour variables are the best starting point for building market segments.

Occasions   Buyers can be grouped according to occasions when they get the idea to buy, actually make their purchase, or use the purchased item. **Occasion segmentation** can help firms build up product usage. For example, orange juice is most often consumed at breakfast, but orange growers have promoted drinking orange juice as a cool and refreshing drink at other times of the day. Some holidays, such as Mother's Day and Father's Day, were originally promoted partly to increase the sale of candy, flowers, cards, and other gifts. And many marketers prepare special offers and ads for holiday occasions. For example, Altoids offers a special "Love Tin" for a "curiously strong valentine." Canada's electronics retailer RadioShack featured electronic gift certificates to increase sales during the holiday season.[21] Some marketers don't want to be limited to special occasion use. Butterball, for example, advertises "Happy Thanksgrilling" during the summer to increase the demand for turkeys on non-Thanksgiving occasions.

Kodak, Konica, Fuji, and other camera makers use occasion segmentation in designing and marketing their single-use cameras. By mixing lenses, film speeds, and

Behavioural segmentation
Dividing a market into groups based on consumer knowledge, attitude, use, or response to a product.

Occasion segmentation
Dividing a market into groups according to occasions when buyers get the idea to buy, actually make their purchase, or use the purchased item.

Occasion segmentation: Altoids created a special "Love Tin"—a "curiously strong valentine."

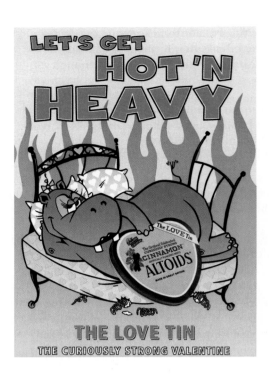

accessories, they have developed special disposable cameras for about any picture-taking occasion:

> Standing on the edge of the Grand Canyon? Try Konica's Panoramic, which features a 17 mm lens that takes in nearly 100 degrees horizontally. Going rafting, skiing, or snorkelling? You need Kodak's Max Sport, a rugged camera that can be used underwater to 4.25 metres. It has big knobs and buttons that let you use it with gloves. Want some pictures of the baby? Kodak offers a model equipped with a short focal-length lens and fast film requiring less light for parents who would like to take snapshots of their darlings without the disturbing flash. In one Japanese catalogue aimed at young women, Kodak sells a package of five pastel-coloured cameras, including a version with a fish-eye lens to create a rosy, romantic glow. To make certain that the right cameras are available in the right places, Kodak is rolling out climate-controlled, Internet-connected vending machines in as many as 10 000 locations, including zoos, stadiums, parks, hotels, and resorts.[22]

Benefit segmentation

Dividing a market into groups according to the different benefits that consumers seek from the product.

Benefits Sought   A powerful form of segmentation is to group buyers according to the *benefits* they seek from the product. **Benefit segmentation** requires finding the major benefits people look for in the product class, the kinds of people who look for each benefit, and the major brands that deliver each benefit. For example, our chapter-opening example pointed out that Procter & Gamble has identified several different laundry detergent segments. Each segment seeks a unique combination of benefits, from cleaning and bleaching to economy, fabric softening, fresh smell, strength or mildness, and lots of suds or only a few.

The Champion athletic wear division of Sara Lee Corporation segments its markets according to benefits that different consumers seek from their activewear. For example, "fit and polish" consumers seek a balance between function and style—they exercise for results but want to look good doing it. "Serious sports competitors" exercise heavily and live in and love their activewear—they seek performance and function. By contrast, "value-seeking moms" have low sports interest and low activewear involvement—they buy for the family and seek durability and value.

In this Australian ad, Colgate Fluoriguard uses benefit segmentation to appeal to families.

Thus, each segment seeks a different mix of benefits. Champion must target the benefit segment or segments that it can serve best and most profitably using appeals that match each segment's benefit preferences.

User Status   Markets can be segmented into groups of non-users, ex-users, potential users, first-time users, and regular users of a product or service. For example, after a series of tainted blood scandals, Canadians became wary of giving or receiving blood. Currently, only 3.5 percent of eligible Canadians donate blood out of a potential donor pool of 13 million Canadians. The Canadian Blood Services used advertising to help meet this challenge. Using the slogan, "Blood: it's in you to give," it halted the ten-year decline in blood donations. Since launching the campaign, the amount of blood shipped to hospitals has grown by 15 percent and 70 000 Canadians became new blood donors.[23]

Usage Rate   Markets can also be segmented into light, medium, and heavy product users. Heavy users are often a small percentage of the market, but account for a high percentage of total consumption. Marketers usually prefer to attract one heavy user to their product or service rather than several light users. A study of branded ice cream buyers showed that heavy users make up only 18 percent of all buyers—but consume 55 percent of all the ice cream sold.

Similarly, in the fast-food industry, heavy users make up only 20 percent of patrons but eat up about 60 percent of all the food served. A single heavy user, typically a single male who doesn't know how to cook, might spend as much as $60 in a day at fast-food restaurants and visit them more than 20 times a month. Heavy users "come more often, they spend more money, and that's what makes the cash registers ring," says a Burger King marketing executive.[24]

Despite the importance of heavy users, light users can also represent important targets:

Danone International Brands Canada Inc., makers of Lea & Perrins® Worcestershire Sauce, knew that most people were light users of their product. People used Lea & Perrins only occasionally—usually to make Bloody Caesars. Few consumers were aware of the product's versatility, thereby limiting the brand's sales growth. While the firm could have tried to attract new users to the category, it believed a better route was to target the current light users with exciting ideas on how to use the product to enliven everyday meals. The resulting ad campaign featured recipes designed to fit within the lives of busy consumers. Dishes were easy to remember and simple to prepare. The ads also communicated Lea & Perrins Worcestershire Sauce's primary point of difference—its exotic ingredients. Not only did the program significantly increase sales, it opened up additional channels of communication. Consumers started calling Lea & Perrins' toll-free number to request advertised recipe books featuring new uses for the product.[25]

Loyalty Status   A market can also be segmented by consumer loyalty. Consumers can be loyal to brands (Tide), stores (The Bay), and companies (Ford). Buyers can be divided into groups according to their degree of loyalty. Some consumers are completely loyal—they buy one brand all the time. Others are somewhat loyal—they are loyal to two or three brands of a given product or favour one brand while sometimes buying others. Still other buyers show no loyalty to any brand. They either want something different each time they buy or they buy whatever is on sale.

A company can learn a lot by analyzing loyalty patterns in its market. It should start by studying its own loyal customers. For example, to better understand the needs and behaviour of its core soft drink consumers, Pepsi observed them in places where its products are consumed—in homes, in stores, in movie theatres, at sporting events, and at the beach. "We learned that there's a surprising amount of loyalty and passion for Pepsi's products," says Pepsi's director of consumer insights. "One fellow had four or five cases of Pepsi in his basement and he felt he was low on Pepsi

Lea & Perrins's award-winning campaign targeted light users with ideas to enliven everyday meals while also promoting the brand's high-quality ingredients.

and had to go replenish." The company used these and other study findings to pinpoint the Pepsi target market and develop marketing appeals.[26]

Understanding and improving customer loyalty are at the heart of customer relationship management programs. Companies as diverse as RBC Royal Bank, Sears, RadioShack, and Nortel are using a combination of technology and data analysis to better understand what drives customer loyalty. By studying its less loyal buyers, a company can detect which brands are most competitive with its own. If many Pepsi buyers also buy Coke, Pepsi can attempt to improve its positioning against Coke, possibly by using direct-comparison advertising. By looking at customers who are shifting away from its brand, the company can learn about its marketing weaknesses. As for non-loyals, the company may attract them by putting its brand on sale.

Using Multiple Segmentation Bases

Marketers rarely limit their segmentation analysis to one or a few variables. Rather, they are increasingly using multiple segmentation bases in an effort to identify smaller, better-defined target groups. Thus, a bank may not only identify a group of wealthy retired adults, but within that group distinguish several segments depending on their current income, assets, savings and risk preferences, and lifestyles. Companies often begin by using one segmentation base, then expand by using other bases.

One good example of multivariable segmentation is "geodemographic" segmentation. Several business information services have arisen to help marketing planners link Canadian and U.S. Census data with lifestyle patterns to better segment their markets down to neighbourhoods, and even city blocks. Leading systems include PRIZM by Claritas, Inc., and Compusearch's Psyte neighbourhood classification system. IRI Canada, a market information company, offers results from its retail-purchase checkout tracking systems to Canadian marketers. The data allow marketers to follow the purchase patterns of each store's trading area and overlay this information with geodemographic census data. Firms can then link census data with lifestyle and purchase patterns to develop estimates of market potential at the level of postal codes or neighbourhoods.

Canadian marketers know it is often essential to combine income with information on regional differences. A Print Measurement Bureau (www.pmb.ca) study revealed that regional differences act as powerful determinants of Canadians' behaviour and choices. When one looks at the narrow segment of affluent consumers, one finds not only that the concentration of this group varies by region, but also by buying and lifestyle habits. Affluent consumers living in Quebec, for example, have significantly different preferences from affluent consumers living in other provinces. High-income French Canadians read more magazines and live in more moderately priced housing. They shop at specialty clothing stores more often and spend more on clothing and cosmetics. They are also more likely to bike, golf, swim, or ski than other affluent Canadians, who prefer to jog, garden, or visit health clubs. Although Quebec's affluent consumers don't travel as much as other high-income Canadians, they prefer Latin American destinations when they do travel. Thus, it can be seen that geodemographic segmentation provides a powerful tool for refining demand estimates, selecting target markets, and shaping promotion messages.

Segmenting Business Markets

Consumer and business marketers use many of the same variables to segment their markets. Business buyers can be segmented geographically or by benefits sought, user status, usage rate, and loyalty status. Yet, as Table 9.2 shows, business marketers can also use some additional variables, such as customer *operating characteristics,*

Table 9.2 Major Segmentation Variables for Business Markets

Demographics

Industry: Which industries that buy this product should we focus on?

Company size: What size companies should we focus on?

Location: What geographical areas should we focus on?

Operating Variables

Technology: What customer technologies should we focus on?

User/non-user status: Should we focus on heavy, medium, or light users or non-users?

Customer capabilities: Should we focus on customers needing many services or few services?

Purchasing Approaches

Purchasing function organization: Should we focus on companies with highly centralized or decentralized purchasing organizations?

Power structure: Should we focus on companies that are engineering dominated, finance dominated, or marketing dominated?

Nature of existing relationships: Should we focus on companies with which we already have strong relationships or go after the most desirable companies?

General purchase policies: Should we focus on companies that prefer leasing? Service contracts? Systems purchases? Sealed bidding?

Purchasing criteria: Should we focus on companies that are seeking quality? Service? Price?

Situational Factors

Urgency: Should we focus on companies that need quick delivery or service?

Specific application: Should we focus on certain applications of our product rather than all applications?

Size of order: Should we focus on large or small orders?

Personal Characteristics

Buyer–seller similarity: Should we focus on companies whose people and values are similar to ours?

Attitudes toward risk: Should we focus on risk-taking or risk-avoiding customers?

Loyalty: Should we focus on companies that show high loyalty to their suppliers?

Sources: Adapted from Thomas V. Bonoma and Benson P. Shapiro, *Segmenting the Industrial Market,* Lexington, MA: Lexington Books, 1983. Also see John Berrigan and Carl Finkbeiner, *Segmentation Marketing: New Methods for Capturing Business,* New York: Harper-Business, 1992.

purchasing approaches, situational factors, and *personal characteristics.* The table lists major questions that business marketers should ask to determine which customers they want to serve.

By pursuing segments instead of the whole market, companies have a much better opportunity to deliver value to consumers and to receive maximum rewards for close attention to consumer needs. Thus, Hewlett-Packard's Computer Systems Division targets specific industries that promise the best growth prospects, such as telecommunications and financial services. Its "red team" sales force specializes in developing and serving these major customers in these targeted industries.[27] Within the chosen industry, a company can further segment by *customer size* or *geographic location.* For example, Hewlett-Packard's "blue team" telemarkets to smaller accounts and to those that don't fit neatly into the strategically targeted industries on which HP focuses.

A company can also set up separate systems for dealing with larger or multiple-location customers. For example, Cisco Systems Canada divides the marketplace into eleven groups, ranging from health care to transportation to retailing. Steelcase, a major producer of office furniture, segments its customers into ten industries, including banking, insurance, and electronics. Next, company salespeople work with independent Steelcase dealers to handle smaller, local, or regional customers in each segment. But many national multiple-location customers, such as Exxon or IBM,

Cisco Systems Canada is using demographic segmentation when it targets the medical community with this ad.

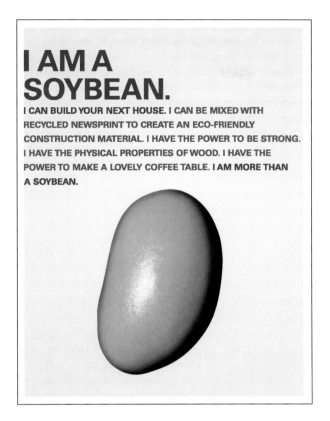

I AM A SOYBEAN.

I CAN BUILD YOUR NEXT HOUSE. I CAN BE MIXED WITH RECYCLED NEWSPRINT TO CREATE AN ECO-FRIENDLY CONSTRUCTION MATERIAL. I HAVE THE POWER TO BE STRONG. I HAVE THE PHYSICAL PROPERTIES OF WOOD. I HAVE THE POWER TO MAKE A LOVELY COFFEE TABLE. I AM MORE THAN A SOYBEAN.

have special needs that may go beyond the scope of individual dealers. So Steelcase uses national accounts managers to help its dealer networks handle these accounts.

Within a target industry and customer size, the company can segment by purchase approaches and criteria. As in consumer segmentation, many marketers believe that buying behaviour and benefits provide the best basis for segmenting business markets.[28]

Segmenting International Markets

Few companies have either the resources or the will to operate in all, or even most, countries. Although some large companies, such as Coca-Cola and Sony, sell products in more than 200 countries, most international firms focus on a smaller set. Operating in many countries presents new challenges. Different countries, even those that are close together, can vary greatly in their economic, cultural, and political makeup. Thus, just as they do within their domestic markets, international firms need to group their world markets into segments with distinct buying needs and behaviours.

Companies can segment international markets using one or a combination of variables. They can segment by *geographic location*, grouping countries by regions such as Western Europe, the Pacific Rim, the Middle East, or Africa.

Geographic segmentation assumes that nations close to one another will have many common traits and behaviours. Although this is often the case, there are many exceptions. For example, although the United States and Canada have much in common, overlooking differences between the two countries can be dangerous. Furthermore, both differ culturally and economically from Mexico. Even within a region, consumers can differ widely. For example, many marketers think that all Central and South American countries, with their 400 million inhabitants, are the same. However, the Dominican Republic is no more like Brazil than Italy is like

Sweden. Many Latin Americans don't speak Spanish, including 140 million Portuguese-speaking Brazilians and the millions in other countries who speak a variety of Indian dialects.

World markets can be segmented on the basis of *economic factors*. For example, countries can be grouped by population income levels or by their overall level of economic development. Some countries, such as the United States, Britain, France, Germany, Japan, Canada, Italy, and Russia, have established, highly industrialized economies. Other countries have newly industrialized or developing economies (China, India, Singapore, Taiwan, Korea, Brazil, Mexico). Still others are less developed. Some analysts state that there are 172 less developed countries (LDCs) in the world. These include Afghanistan, Algeria, Bangladesh, Barbados, the Republic of the Congo, El Salvador, Madagascar, Sierra Leone, and Zimbabwe.[29] A company's economic structure shapes its population's product and service needs and, thus, the marketing opportunities it offers.

Countries can be segmented by *political and legal factors,* such as the type and stability of government, receptivity to foreign firms, monetary regulations, and the amount of bureaucracy. Such factors can play a crucial role in a company's choice of which countries to enter and how. *Cultural factors* also can be used, grouping markets according to common languages, religions, values and attitudes, customs, and behavioural patterns.

Segmenting international markets on the basis of geographic, economic, political, cultural, and other factors assumes that segments should consist of clusters of countries. However, many companies use a different approach, called **intermarket segmentation**. Using this approach, they form segments of consumers who have similar needs and buying behaviour, even though they are located in different countries. For example, Mercedes-Benz targets the world's well-to-do, regardless of their country. MTV targets the world's teenagers. One study of more than 6500 teenagers from 26 countries showed that teens around the world live surprisingly parallel lives. "A group of teenagers chosen randomly from around the world will share many tastes," notes one expert. Says another, "From Rio to Rochester, teens can be found enmeshed in much the same regimen:...drinking Coke,...dining on Big Macs, and surfin' the Net on their computers."[30] The world's teens have a lot in common: they study, shop, and sleep. They are exposed to many of the same major issues: love, crime, homelessness, ecology, and working parents. In many ways, they have more in common with each other than with their parents. MTV bridges the gap

Intermarket segmentation
Forming segments of consumers who have similar needs and buying behaviour even though they are located in different countries.

Intermarket segmentation: Teens show surprising similarity no matter where in the world they live. For instance, these two teens could live almost anywhere. Thus, many companies target teenagers with worldwide marketing campaigns.

between cultures, appealing to what teens around the world have in common. Sony, Reebok, Nike, Swatch, and Benetton are just a few of many firms that actively target global teens.[31]

Requirements for Effective Segmentation

Clearly, there are many ways to segment a market, but not all segmentations are effective. For example, buyers of table salt could be divided into blond and brunette customers. But hair colour obviously does not affect the purchase of salt. Furthermore, if all salt buyers bought the same amount of salt each month, believed all salt is the same, and wanted to pay the same price, the company would not benefit from segmenting this market.

To be useful, market segments must be:

- *Measurable*. The size, purchasing power, and profiles of the segments can be measured. Certain segmentation variables are difficult to measure. For example, there are around four million left-handed people in Canada—which is 15 percent of the population. Yet few products are targeted toward this left-handed segment. The major problem may be that the segment is hard to identify and measure. There are no data on the demographics of lefties, and Statistics Canada does not keep track of left-handedness in its surveys. Private data companies keep reams of statistics on other demographic segments, but not on left-handers.
- *Accessible*. The market segments can be effectively reached and served. Suppose a fragrance company finds that heavy users of its brand are single men and women who stay out late and socialize a lot. Unless this group lives or shops at certain places and is exposed to certain media, its members will be difficult to reach.
- *Substantial*. The market segments are large or profitable enough to serve. A segment should be the largest possible homogeneous group worth pursuing with a tailored marketing program. It would not pay, for example, for an automobile manufacturer to develop cars for people who are under 1.25 metres tall.
- *Actionable*. Effective programs can be designed for attracting and serving the segments. For example, although one small airline identified seven market segments, its staff was too small to develop separate marketing programs for each segment.

Market Targeting

Market segmentation reveals the firm's market segment opportunities. The firm now has to evaluate the various segments and decide how many and which ones to target. We now look at how companies evaluate and select target segments.

Evaluating Market Segments

In evaluating different market segments, a firm must look at three factors: segment size and growth, segment structural attractiveness, and company objectives and resources. The company must first collect and analyze data on current segment sales, growth rates, and expected profitability for various segments. It will be interested in segments that have the right size and growth characteristics. (See "Measuring and Forecasting Demand" on the Companion Website at www.pearsoned.com/Kotler.) But "right size and growth" is a relative matter. The largest, fastest-growing segments are not always the most attractive ones for every company. Smaller companies may find that they lack the skills and resources needed to serve the larger segments. Or they may find these segments too competitive. Such companies may select segments that are smaller and less attractive, in an absolute sense, but that are potentially more profitable for them.

The company also needs to examine several major structural factors that affect long-run segment attractiveness.[32] For example, a segment is less attractive if it already contains many strong and aggressive *competitors*. The existence of many actual or potential *substitute products* may limit prices and the profits that can be earned in a segment. The relative *power of buyers* also affects segment attractiveness. Buyers with strong bargaining power relative to sellers will try to force prices down, demand more services, and set competitors against one another—all at the expense of seller profitability. Finally, a segment may be less attractive if it contains *powerful suppliers* who can control prices or reduce the quality or quantity of ordered goods and services.

Even if a segment has the right size and growth and is structurally attractive, the company must consider its own objectives and resources in relation to that segment. Some attractive segments could be dismissed quickly because they do not mesh with the company's long-run objectives. The company must then decide whether it possesses the skills and resources needed to succeed in that segment. If the company lacks the strengths needed to compete successfully in a segment and cannot readily obtain them, it should not enter the segment. Even if the company possesses the *required* strengths, it needs to employ skills and resources *superior* to those of the competition to win in a market segment. The company should enter only segments where it can offer superior value and gain advantages over competitors.

Selecting Target Market Segments

After evaluating different segments, the company must decide which and how many segments to serve. A **target market** consists of a set of buyers who share common needs or characteristics that the company decides to serve.

Target market
A set of buyers sharing common needs or characteristics that the company decides to serve.

Because buyers have unique needs and wants, a seller could potentially view each buyer as a separate target market. Ideally, then, a seller might design a separate marketing program for each buyer. However, although some companies do attempt to serve buyers individually, most face larger numbers of smaller buyers and do not find individual targeting worthwhile. Instead, they look for broader segments of buyers. More generally, target marketing can be carried out at several different levels. Figure 9.2 shows that companies can target very broadly (undifferentiated marketing), very narrowly (micromarketing), or somewhere in between (differentiated or concentrated marketing).

Undifferentiated Marketing

Undifferentiated (mass) marketing
A market-coverage strategy in which a firm decides to ignore market segment differences and go after the whole market with one offer.

Using an **undifferentiated** (or **mass**) **marketing** strategy, a firm might decide to ignore market segment differences and target the whole market with one offer. This mass-marketing strategy focuses on what is *common* in the needs of consumers rather than on what is *different*. The company designs a product and a marketing program that will appeal to the largest number of buyers. It relies on mass distribution and mass

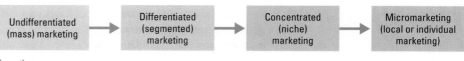

Figure 9.2 Target marketing strategies

Targeting broadly   Targeting narrowly

advertising, and it aims to give the product a superior image in people's minds. As noted earlier in this chapter, most modern marketers have strong doubts about this strategy. Difficulties arise in developing a product or brand that will satisfy all consumers. Moreover, mass marketers often have trouble competing with more focused firms that do a better job of satisfying the needs of specific segments and niches.

Differentiated Marketing

Differentiated (segmented) marketing

A market coverage strategy in which a firm targets several market segments and designs separate offers for each.

Using a **differentiated** (or **segmented**) **marketing** strategy, a firm decides to target several market segments and designs separate offers for each. General Motors tries to produce a car for every "purse, purpose, and personality." Nike offers athletic shoes for a dozen or more sports. Weston Foods appeals to the needs of different shopper segments with its No Frills discount stores, Loblaws SuperCentres, and Price Club Warehouse stores. Cadbury Chocolate Canada (www.cadbury. chocolate.ca) changed the way chocolate bars were marketed by targeting its Mr. Big candy bars to teenagers, its Crispy Crunch bars to young adults, and its Time Out bars to harried businesspeople. And American Express Canada offers not only its traditional green cards but also an Air Miles Gold card, a Costco Platinum Cash Rebate Card, and for a $99 annual fee, a Tiger Woods credit card that provides the additional benefits of a green fee pass, complimentary issues of *ScoreGolf* magazine, and discounts at Golf Town stores.

By offering product and marketing variations, these companies hope for higher sales and a stronger position within each market segment. Developing a stronger position within several segments creates more total sales than undifferentiated marketing across all segments. Procter & Gamble gets more total market share with seven brands of laundry detergent than it could with only one. And American Express's combined brands give it a much greater market share than any single brand could.

But differentiated marketing also increases the costs of doing business. A firm usually finds it more expensive to produce, say, 10 units of 10 different products than 100 units of one product. Developing separate marketing plans for the separate segments requires extra marketing research, forecasting, sales analysis, promotion planning, and channel management. And trying to reach different market segments with different advertising increases promotion costs. Thus, the company must weigh increased sales against increased costs when deciding on a differentiated marketing strategy.

Concentrated Marketing

Concentrated (niche) marketing

A market coverage strategy in which a firm goes after a large share of one or a few submarkets.

The third market coverage strategy, **concentrated** (or **niche**) **marketing**, is especially appealing when company resources are limited. Instead of pursuing a small share of a large market, the firm pursues a large share of one or a few submarkets. For example, Oshkosh Truck is the world's largest producer of airport rescue trucks and front-loading concrete mixers. Tetra sells 80 percent of the world's tropical fish food. Steiner Optical captures 80 percent of the world's military binoculars market. And Clearly Canadian concentrates on a narrow segment of the soft-drink market.

Whereas segments are fairly large and normally attract several competitors, niches are smaller and may attract only one or a few competitors. Through concentrated marketing, the firm achieves a strong market position because of its greater knowledge of consumer needs in the niches it serves and the special reputation it acquires. It can market more *effectively* by fine-tuning its products, prices, and programs to the needs of carefully defined segments. It can also market more *efficiently*, targeting its products or services, channels, and communications programs toward only consumers that it can serve best and most profitably.

Niching offers smaller companies an opportunity to compete by focusing their limited resources on serving niches that may be unimportant to or overlooked by

Niche marketing: Tiny Vans Inc. specializes in making thick-soled, slip-on sneakers for skateboarders that can absorb the shock of a five-foot leap on wheels.

larger competitors. For example, tiny Vans Inc. specializes in making thick-soled, slip-on sneakers for skateboarders that can absorb the shock of a five-foot leap on wheels. Although it captures only a point or two of market share in the overall athletic shoe market, Vans's small but intensely loyal customer base has made the company more profitable than many of its larger competitors.[33]

Many companies start as nichers to get a foothold against larger, more resourceful competitors, then grow into broader competitors. For example, WestJet began operations in 1996 with 220 employees and three aircraft. Its aim was to provide low-cost air service to select western Canadian cities: Vancouver, Kelowna, Calgary, Edmonton, and Winnipeg. Today, it is the second most profitable carrier in North America (only trailing Southwest Airlines) and it is listed among Canada's most respected companies. Wal-Mart, which got its start by bringing everyday low prices to small towns and rural areas, is now the world's largest company.

Today, the low cost of setting up shop on the Internet makes it even more profitable to serve seemingly minuscule niches. Small businesses, in particular, are realizing riches from serving small niches on the Web. Here is a "Webpreneur" who achieved astonishing results:

> Whereas Internet giants like Amazon.com have yet to even realize a consistent profit, Steve Warrington is earning a six-figure income online selling ostriches—and every product derived from them—online (www.ostrichesonline.com). Launched for next to nothing on the Web in 1996, Ostriches On Line now boasts that it sends newsletters to 29 000 subscribers and sells 17 500 ostrich products to more than 12 000 satisfied clients in more than 100 countries. The site tells visitors everything they ever wanted to know about ostriches and much, much more—it supplies ostrich facts, ostrich pictures, an ostrich farm index, and a huge ostrich database and reference index. Visitors to the site can buy ostrich meat, feathers, leather jackets, videos, eggshells, and skin care products derived from ostrich body oil.[34]

Concentrated marketing can be highly profitable. At the same time, it involves higher-than-normal risks. Companies that rely on one or a few segments for all of their business will suffer greatly if the segment turns sour. Or larger competitors may decide to enter the same segment. For example, California Cooler's early success in the wine cooler segment attracted many large competitors, causing the original owners to sell to a larger company that had more marketing resources. For these reasons, many companies prefer to diversify in several market segments.

Micromarketing

Differentiated and concentrated marketers tailor their offers and marketing programs to meet the needs of various market segments and niches. At the same time, however, they do not customize their offers to each individual customer. **Micromarketing** is the practice of tailoring products and marketing programs to suit the tastes of specific individuals and locations. Micromarketing includes *local marketing* and *individual marketing*.

Local Marketing   **Local marketing** involves tailoring brands and promotions to the needs and wants of local customer groups—cities, neighbourhoods, and even specific stores. Retailers such as Sears and Wal-Mart routinely customize each store's merchandise and promotions to match its specific clientele. Kraft helps supermarket chains identify the specific cheese assortments and shelf positioning that will optimize cheese sales in low-income, middle-income, and high-income stores and in different ethnic communities. When McDonald's Restaurants of Canada rolled out its Lighter Choices Menu in 2002, it also found that local understanding was important. It knew people were looking for healthier food alternatives. However, focus group research conducted in Vancouver, Calgary, Edmonton, London, Toronto, Montreal, and eastern Canada, and in-store intercept interviews undertaken after customers had sampled the new products, revealed striking local differences. For instance, the West Coast emerged as the most "green" region—consumers wanted balance in their lives. Albertans demonstrated a desire for more red meat, and people living in Quebec had attitudes toward health that were remarkably different from those held by the rest of the country. While Quebecers valued health, they weren't prepared to give up as much to achieve a healthier lifestyle.[35]

Local marketing has some drawbacks. It can drive up manufacturing and marketing costs by reducing economies of scale. It can also create logistics problems as companies try to meet the varied requirements of different regional and local markets. Further, a brand's overall image might be diluted if the product and message vary too much in different localities. Still, as companies face increasingly fragmented markets, and as new supporting technologies develop, the advantages of local marketing often outweigh the drawbacks. Local marketing helps a company to market more effectively in the face of pronounced regional and local differences in demographics and lifestyles. It also meets the needs of the company's first-line customers—retailers—who prefer more fine-tuned product assortments for their neighbourhoods.

Individual Marketing   In the extreme, micromarketing becomes **individual marketing**—tailoring products and marketing programs to the needs and preferences of individual customers. Individual marketing has also been labelled *one-to-one marketing, customized marketing,* and *markets-of-one marketing.*[36]

The widespread use of mass marketing has obscured the fact that for centuries consumers were served as individuals: The tailor custom-made the suit, the cobbler designed shoes for the individual, the cabinetmaker made furniture to order. Today, however, new technologies are permitting many companies to return to customized marketing. More-powerful computers, detailed databases, robotic production and flexible manufacturing, and immediate and interactive communication media such as email, fax, and the Internet—all have combined to foster "mass customization." *Mass customization* is the process through which firms interact one-to-one with masses of customers to create customer-unique value by designing products and services tailor-made to individual needs (see Real Marketing 9.1).

Micromarketing
The practice of tailoring products and marketing programs to the needs and wants of specific individuals and local customer groups—includes *local marketing* and *individual marketing*.

Local marketing
Tailoring brands and promotions to the needs and wants of local customer groups—cities, neighbourhoods, and even specific stores.

Individual marketing
Tailoring products and marketing programs to the needs and preferences of individual customers—also labelled "markets-of-one marketing," "customized marketing," and "one-to-one marketing."

REAL MARKETING

9.1   Markets of One: Anything You Can Digitize, You Can Customize

*M*any companies are now using technology to tailor their products to individual customers. Dell creates custom-configured computers, Reflect.com formulates customized beauty products, Ford lets buyers "build a vehicle" from a palette of options, and Golf to Fit crafts custom clubs based on consumer measurements and preferences.

Imagine walking into a booth that bathes your body in patterns of white light and, in a matter of seconds, captures your exact three-dimensional form. The digitized data are then imprinted on a credit card, which you then use to order customized clothing. No, this isn't a scene from the next *Star Wars* sequel; it's a peek ahead at how you will be able to buy clothing in the not-so-distant future. A consortium of over 100 apparel companies, including Levi-Strauss, has banded together to develop body scanning technology in the hope of making mass customization the norm.

In 1994, Levi's began making measure-to-fit women's jeans under its in-store Personal Pair program. Consumer response was so positive that Levi's developed an expanded in-store customization concept

Mass customization: Levi's Original Spin lets you create your own Levi jeans from scratch or modify a pair of authentic Levi jeans. Its website tells how it works and directs consumers to nearby retail locations.

called Original Spin, which works a lot like the futuristic sizing scenario described above. Original Spin lets buyers create their own jeans from scratch or modify an existing pair. Customers—both men and women—enter a booth in which a 3-D Body Scanner creates personalized measurements against a backdrop of strobe lights and space-age music. Using the Original Spin terminals, customers can then choose from a range of cuts and styles that represent hundreds of different pairs of jeans available for purchase. Whereas a fully stocked Levi's store carries 130 pairs of ready-to-wear jeans for a given waist and inseam, with Original Spin the number jumps to 750.

Now while customized marketing might work for jeans, can a packaged-goods firm be on the forefront of one-to-one marketing, you might ask? Certainly if you are Kraft Canada, one of the country's leaders in utilizing tailored permission-based marketing and customer information to glean insights and find solutions to consumers' meal problems. Consumers buy Kraft products like Shake 'n Bake and Philadelphia cream cheese because they feel closer to a company that has offered them no-fuss help in the kitchen. Many who have picked up the phone and talked to someone at Kraft comment that Kraft listens and "gets me." In other words, Kraft has developed relationships with consumers the likes of which have never before been experienced in the packaged-goods industry. Kraft has been so successful that in 2002 *Marketing Magazine* named it to its annual top-ten list of "Marketers that Mattered."

Before Kraft could build relationships and market one-to-one, it had to work hard to better understand the dilemmas busy working families face each and every day in preparing school lunches, family meals, and special occasion dinners. Kraft came to see itself as more than a provider of food products. Today, providing "food solutions" is at the heart of its strategy. *Family. Food. Simple.* These are three words that capture Kraft's strategy. Kraft tailors its offerings and provides help through a number of venues. Over 900 000 Canadians received targeted mailings—its *What's Cooking* magazine in English Canada and its *Qu'est-ce-qui mijote* in French Canada, as well as through bi-weekly opt-in emails. These mailings are customized to the needs of various groups (singles, parents with young children, people planning seasonal activities for Halloween, etc.). Permission-based emails are sent to help consumers with special needs find what they are looking for. If you have young children, for example, you'll receive an email message that alerts you to recipes that delight kids on a specific page of the magazine. Thousands also click on Kraft's website (www. kraftcanada.com) to find recipes, tips, and food guides. Hundreds call its 1-800 chef line and rush to enrol in popular classes offered at the Kraft Kitchens Cooking School. Even more tune into its new *Food in the Fast Lane* show on the Food Network. All find the help they seek, whether it is advice to help them shop more efficiently, prepare meals on the run with simple ingredients, or impress guests with that special dinner.

Here are just a few examples of consumer and business-to-business marketers that customize their products:

Mattel. Since 1998, girls have been able to log on to the "My Design" page of the Barbie website (www.barbie.com) and create their very own "friend of Barbie" doll. They choose the doll's skin tone, eye colour, hairdo and hair colour, clothes, accessories, and name. They even fill out a questionnaire detailing their doll's likes and dislikes. When Barbie's Special Friend arrives in the mail, the girls find the doll's name on the packaging along with a computer-generated paragraph about her personality.

Nike ID. This Nike website (www.NikeID.com) lets customers design their own athletic shoes online. The site leads buyers through a set of questions about their preferences for shoe style, base and accent colours, shoe construction, and even personalized IDs of up to 16 characters to be printed on the sole of each shoe. When the customers submit the final design, Nike transmits the order to a specially equipped plant in China or Korea, where the information is fed into a production line that pumps out the customized shoes. Customers pay only an extra $13 for this service. The Nike ID website was designed by Calgary's Critical Mass. In recognition of their innovative work, Critical Mass won a Cyber Grand Prix at the International Advertising Festival in Cannes, France.

TELUS. Canada's second-largest telecommunication company sees one-to-one marketing as a core strategy for targeting small to medium-sized businesses. TELUS knows that other Canadian telephone companies can offer products and services to these businesses. To make itself stand out from the crowd, TELUS focuses on customer service and tailors solutions to meet small firms' unique communication needs.

Oshkosh Truck. Oshkosh Truck specializes in making fire, garbage, cement, and military trucks. Oshkosh is small—a tenth the size of larger rivals—and the truck industry is slumping. Yet Oshkosh has doubled its sales and increased its earnings fivefold over the past five years. What's the secret to Oshkosh's success? Mass customization—its ability to personalize its products and services to the needs of individual customers. For example, when firefighters order a truck from Oshkosh, it's an event. They travel to the plant to watch the vehicle, which may cost as much as $1 million, take shape. Says the president of Oshkosh's firefighting unit, Pierce Manufacturing, "Buying a fire truck is a very personal thing."

Two trends are behind the growth in one-to-one marketing. First, today's consumers have very high expectations—they expect products and services that meet their individual needs. Yet, it would be prohibitively expensive or downright impossible to meet these individual demands if it weren't for another trend: rapid advances in new technologies. Data warehouses allow companies to store trillions of bytes of customer information. Computer-controlled factory equipment and industrial robots can now quickly readjust assembly lines. Bar code scanners make it possible to track parts and products. Most important of all, the Internet ties it all together and makes it easy for a company to interact with customers, learn about their preferences, and respond. Indeed, the Internet appears to be the ultimate one-to-one medium.

Unlike mass production, which eliminates the need for human interaction, mass customization has made relationships with customers more important than ever. For instance, when Levi's sells made-to-order jeans, the company not only captures consumer data in digitized form but also becomes the customer's "jeans adviser." And Mattel is building a database of information on all the customers of My Design dolls so it can start long-term, one-to-one relationships with each customer.

Just as mass production was the marketing principle of the last century, mass customization is becoming the marketing principle for the twenty-first century. The world appears to be coming full circle—from the good old days when customers were treated as individuals, to mass marketing when nobody knew your name, and back again. As Joseph Pine, author of *Mass Customization,* concludes, "Anything you can digitize, you can customize."

Sources: Peggy Cunningham interview with Gannon Jones, Customer Relationship Manager, Kraft Canada, May 5, 2002; Samson Okalov, "Packaged Goods Go Direct," *Strategy,* June 2, 2003, p. D1; Bernadette Johnson, "Kraft Connects the CRM Dots: Packaged Goods Kingpin Nears Completion of Long-Term DM Strategy," *Strategy,* January 28, 2002; "Nine More Marketers That Mattered," *Marketing Magazine,* February 11, 2002, www.marketingmag.ca; Lesley Young, "One Bite at a Time," *Marketing Magazine,* November 5, 2001, www.marketingmag.ca; "Critical Mass takes Cyber Lion," *Marketing Magazine,* June 24, 2001, www.marketingmag.ca; Eve Lazarus, "The Telus target," *Marketing Magazine,* May 22, 2000, www.marketingmag.ca; Erick Schonfeld, "The Customized, Digitized, Have-It-Your-Way Economy," *Fortune,* September 28, 1998, pp. 115–124; Ronald Alsop, "A Special Report on Trends in Industry and Finance," *Wall Street Journal,* April 29, 1999, p. A1; James H. Gilmore and B. Joseph Pine, *Markets of One: Creating Customer-Unique Value Through Mass Customization* (Boston: Harvard Business School Press, 2001); Diane Brady, "Customizing for the Masses," *Business Week,* March 20, 2000, pp. 130B–130F; Mark Tatge, "Red Bodies, Black Ink," *Forbes,* September 18, 2000, p. 114; Paul Zipkin, "The Limits of Mass Customization," *MIT Sloan Management Review,* Spring 2001; and information accessed online at www.us.levi.com, www.Barbie.com, www.NikeID.com, www.chemstation.com, and www.oshkoshtruck.com (July 2002).

The Ritz-Carlton Hotel Company is one firm that creates custom-designed experiences for its delighted guests:

> Check into any Ritz-Carlton hotel around the world, and you'll be amazed at how well the hotel's employees anticipate your slightest need. Without ever asking, they seem to know that you want a non-smoking room with a king-size bed, a non-allergenic pillow, and breakfast with decaffeinated coffee in your room. How does Ritz-Carlton work this magic? The hotel employs a system that combines information technology and flexible operations to customize the hotel experience. At the heart of the system is a huge customer database, which contains information gathered through the observations of hotel employees. Each day, hotel staffers—from those at the front desk to those in maintenance and housekeeping—discreetly record the unique habits, likes, and dislikes of each guest on small "guest preference pads." These observations are then transferred to a corporate-wide "guest preference database." Every morning, a "guest historian" at each hotel reviews the files of all new arrivals who have previously stayed at a Ritz-Carlton and prepares a list of suggested extra touches that might delight each guest. Guests have responded strongly to such markets-of-one service. Since inaugurating the guest-history system in 1992, Ritz-Carlton has boosted guest retention by 23 percent. An amazing 95 percent of departing guests report that their stay has been a truly memorable experience.

Business-to-business marketers are also finding new ways to customize their offerings. For example, IBM Canada positions itself as the Internet solutions provider, whether that means providing technologies for distribution and customer relationship management or supply chain management and security. It tailors its solutions to organization's specific needs. For instance, IBM Canada used a solution called Advance Scout so the Toronto Raptors could have statistical breakdowns and analysis of opposing teams' signature moves. Using its Web Hosting product, IBM enabled Winnipeg-based Ceridian, a payroll services company, to securely handle highly confidential payroll information. Unlike its U.S. parent, the challenge for IBM Canada was to convince a market made up mostly of modestly sized businesses that IBM wasn't too large or arrogant to customize its services to meet the needs of smaller customers.[37]

The move toward individual marketing mirrors the trend in consumer *self-marketing.* Increasingly, individual customers are taking more responsibility for determining which products and brands to buy. Consider two business buyers with two different purchasing styles. The first sees several salespeople, each trying to persuade him to buy his or her product. The second sees no salespeople but rather logs on to the Internet. She searches for information on available products; interacts electronically with various suppliers, users, and product analysts; and then makes

B2B customization: IBM Canada's Advance Scout was developed as a solution for the Toronto Raptors, who needed statistical breakdowns and analysis of opposing teams' signature moves.

up her own mind about the best offer. The second purchasing agent has taken more responsibility for the buying process, and the marketer has had less influence over her buying decision.

As the trend toward more interactive dialogue and less advertising monologue continues, self-marketing will grow in importance. As more buyers look up consumer reports, join Internet product discussion forums, and place orders via phone or online, marketers will have to influence the buying process in new ways. Many companies now practise *customerization*.[38] They combine operationally driven mass customization with customized marketing to empower consumers to design products and services to their own preferences. They involve customers more in all phases of the product development and buying processes, increasing opportunities for buyers to practise self-marketing.

Choosing a Target Marketing Strategy

Companies need to consider many factors when choosing a target marketing strategy. Which strategy is best depends on *company resources*. When the firm's resources are limited, concentrated marketing makes the most sense. The best strategy also depends on the degree of *product variability*. Undifferentiated marketing is more suited for uniform products such as grapefruit or steel. Products that can vary in design, such as cameras and automobiles, are more suited to differentiation or concentration.

The *product's life-cycle stage* also must be considered. When a firm introduces a new product, it may be practical to launch only one version, and undifferentiated marketing or concentrated marketing begins to make the most sense. In the mature stage of the product life cycle, however, differentiated marketing begins to make more sense. Another factor is *market variability*. If most buyers have the same tastes, buy the same amounts, and react the same way to marketing efforts, undifferentiated marketing is appropriate. Finally, *competitors' marketing strategies* are important: When competitors use differentiated or concentrated marketing, undifferentiated marketing can be suicidal. Conversely, when competitors use undifferentiated marketing, a firm can gain an advantage by using differentiated or concentrated marketing.

Socially Responsible Target Marketing

Smart targeting helps companies to be more efficient and effective by focusing on the segments that they can satisfy best and most profitably. Targeting also benefits consumers—companies reach specific groups of consumers with offers carefully tailored to satisfy their needs. However, target marketing sometimes generates controversy and concern. Issues usually involve the targeting of vulnerable or disadvantaged consumers with controversial or potentially harmful products.

For example, over the years, the cereal industry has been heavily criticized for its marketing efforts directed toward children. Critics worry that premium offers and high-powered advertising appeals presented through the mouths of lovable animated characters will overwhelm children's defences. The marketers of toys and other children's products have been similarly battered, often with good justification.

Other problems arise when the marketing of adult products spills over into the kid segment—intentionally or unintentionally. For example, regulators and citizen action groups have accused tobacco companies of targeting underage smokers.[39] Some critics have even called for a complete ban on advertising to children. To encourage responsible advertising to children, the Canadian Association of Broadcasters and Advertising Standards Canada have partnered to develop the Broadcast Code for Advertising to Children, which is designed to complement the general principles for ethical advertising outlined in the Canadian Code of Advertising Standards. This supplementary code was developed in recognition of the special needs of child audiences (see www.adstandards.com/en/Clearance/childrencode.asp). The code includes such stipulations as advertisements cannot directly urge children to pressure their parents to buy products and it forbids the use of well-known puppets, persons, or characters (including cartoon characters) as product endorsers. While the code has improved children's advertising on those television and radio stations licensed by the Canadian Radio-television and Telecommunications Commission (CRTC), it has not stopped the spillover advertising from the United States, where 75 percent of the advertisements seen by Canadian children originate.

Fast-food and packaged-goods marketers have also generated much controversy in recent years by their attempts to target vulnerable consumers. For example, McDonald's and other chains have drawn criticism for pitching their high-fat, salt-laden fare to low-income people. The meteoric growth of the Internet and other carefully targeted direct media has raised fresh concerns about potential targeting abuses. The Internet allows increasing refinement of audiences and, in turn, more precise targeting. This might help makers of questionable products or deceptive advertisers to more readily victimize the most vulnerable audiences. As one expert observes, "In theory, an audience member could have tailor-made deceptive messages sent directly to his or her computer screen."[40]

Not all attempts to target children, minorities, or other special segments draw such criticism. In fact, most provide benefits to targeted consumers. Take a recent case:

A large pharmaceutical company was concerned that some parents still lack confidence in vaccinations and refuse to have their children vaccinated. The company, therefore, needed to better understand parent attitudes and beliefs around vaccines to help those on the front lines—health-care providers—

address any questions and concerns parents might have. With the help of research firm Ipsos Reid, it identified four groups of parents that had different attitudes, levels of knowledge, and acceptance of vaccination for their children:

- "Vaccine Believers"—this group (representing 33 percent of parents) was convinced of the value of vaccination.
- "Cautious" parents (23 percent), complied with their health provider's advice and recommendations, but can become quite emotional about and intimately involved in their child's care.
- "Relaxed" parents (34 percent) brought less emotion to the process, but harboured some skepticism about vaccines.
- "Unconvinced" parents—the last and smallest group (10 percent)—were distrustful of vaccinations and vaccination policy.

Knowing there were four segments wasn't enough, however. The firm had to help health-care providers recognize the groups and act to address the relevant concerns. To address this challenge, a simple test based on six questions was developed that a health-care provider could administer in a waiting room. It allowed the health-care provider to differentiate among the parent groups, and then promptly address specific concerns about vaccinations.[41]

Another example is Colgate, a company that makes a large selection of toothbrushes and toothpaste flavours and packages for children—from Colgate Barbie Sparkling Bubble Fruit toothpaste to Colgate Pokémon and Disney *Monsters, Inc.* character toothbrushes. Such products help make tooth-brushing more fun and get children to brush longer and more often.

More and more marketers are tailoring their offerings to the more than 1 million people in Canada of Chinese ancestry (3.5 percent of the Canadian population). Bell ExpressVu, for example, increased its Chinese subscriber base by 50 percent after a five-week Chinese language TV, print, and radio campaign that offered "TV on your terms," and a discount to those making the switch from basic cable.[42]

Nacara Cosmetiques markets cosmetics for "ethnic women who have a thirst for the exotic." The line is specially formulated to complement the darker skin tones of African women and dark-skinned women of Latin American, Indian, and Caribbean origins.

Thus, in market targeting, the issue is not really *who* is targeted but rather *how* and for *what*. Controversies arise when marketers attempt to profit at the expense of targeted segments—when they unfairly target vulnerable segments or target them with questionable products or tactics. Socially responsible marketing calls for segmentation and targeting that serve not just the interests of the company but also the interests of those targeted.

Most target marketing benefits both the marketer and the consumer. Nacara Cosmetiques markets cosmetics for "ethnic women who have a thirst for the exotic." Colgate targets children with special flavours, shapes, and packages that help make tooth-brushing more fun and get children to brush more often.

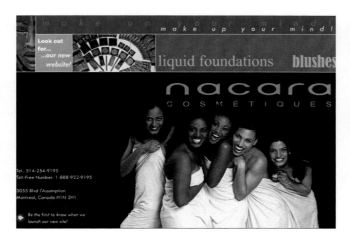

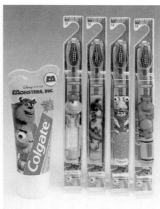

Positioning for Competitive Advantage

Product position

The way the product is defined by consumers on important attributes—the place the product occupies in consumers' minds relative to competing products.

Beyond deciding which segments of the market it will target, the company must decide what positions it wants to occupy in those segments. A **product's position** is the way the product is *defined by consumers* on important attributes—the place the product occupies in consumers' minds relative to competing products. Positioning involves implanting the brand's unique benefits and differentiation in customers' minds. In other words, it involves creating a mental map for the consumer. Tide is positioned as a powerful, all-purpose family detergent; Ivory Snow is positioned as the gentle detergent for fine washables and baby clothes. In the automobile market, the Toyota Echo and Ford Focus are positioned on economy, Mercedes and Cadillac on luxury, and Porsche and BMW on performance. Volvo positions powerfully on safety. At Subway restaurants, you "Eat Fresh." At Olive Garden restaurants, "When You're Here, You're Family."

Consumers are overloaded with information about products and services. They cannot re-evaluate products every time they make a buying decision. To simplify the buying process, consumers organize products, services, and companies and "position" them in their minds. A product's position is the complex set of perceptions, impressions, and feelings that consumers hold for the product compared with competing products.

Consumers position products with or without the help of marketers. But marketers do not want to leave their products' positions to chance. They must *plan* positions that will give their products the greatest advantage in selected target markets, and they must design marketing mixes to create these planned positions. Mark Smith, a Canadian positioning consultant, provides companies with a set of tools to help them improve their position strategies (see Real Marketing 9.2).

Choosing a Positioning Strategy

Some firms find it easy to choose their positioning strategy. For example, a firm well known for quality in certain segments will go for this position in a new segment if there are enough buyers seeking quality. But in many cases, two or more firms will go after the same position. Then, each will have to find other ways to set itself apart. Each firm must differentiate its offer by building a unique bundle of competitive advantages that appeal to a substantial group within the segment.

The positioning task consists of three steps: identifying a set of possible competitive advantages on which to build a position, choosing the right competitive advantages, and selecting an overall positioning strategy. The company must then effectively communicate and deliver the chosen position to the market.

Identifying Possible Competitive Advantages

Competitive advantage

An advantage over competitors gained by offering consumers greater value, either through lower prices or by providing more benefits that justify higher prices.

The key to winning and keeping customers is to understand their needs better than competitors do and to deliver more value. To the extent that a company can position itself as providing superior value, it gains **competitive advantage**. But solid positions cannot be built on empty promises. If a company positions its product as *offering* the best quality and service, it must then *deliver* the promised quality and service. Thus, positioning begins with actually *differentiating* the company's marketing offer so it will give consumers more value than competitors' offers do.

To find points of differentiation, marketers must think through the customer's entire experience with the company's product or service. An alert company can find ways to differentiate itself at every point where it comes in contact with customers.[43]

9.2 Hourglass1998 Positioning Method

What Is Positioning?

Concepts. Positioning is a battle of concepts. The objective is to find and attach a brand representing a product to a high-ranking concept in the consumer's mind. In today's crowded and confusing marketplace, absolutely nothing is better than owning a word in the consumer's mind.

Positioning concepts for toothpaste include: cavity fighter = *Crest;* tarter and gum disease fighter = *Colgate;* fresh breath = *CloseUp;* white teeth = *Pearl Drop.* Companies battle over the best concepts on which to position their products. However, there are rules to the positioning game and many pitfalls. Mistakes at this level directly affect market share and new product development. Successful strategic positioning requires a clear understanding of all 3*C*s of marketing—company, consumer, and competition. Basically, positioning is a strategy game of "capture the concept."

The Problem

Confusion. Today's consumers are bombarded with choice—25 181 new products in 1998; supermarkets with 40 000 SKUs; 150 TV channels; 1000+ ads viewed per day. How do you break though the clutter?

Hourglass1998™ Positioning Chart

Strategy Tool. The Hourglass1998 Positioning Chart is a strategic planning tool that helps marketers clearly visualize all 3*C*s of marketing. It pinches the traditional marketing process, creating a focal point for all marketing activities (Exhibit A). A perfect hourglass shape is formed when the entire marketing mix mirrors the target market's expectations. Ideally, a brand image transfers into the consumer's mind, becoming the brand's reputation. The method was developed and refined over several years by Mark E. Smith as he assisted hundreds of companies in defining their positioning strategy. In 1998, the detailed charting system (not shown) was able to accurately plot over 100 checkpoints and combine over 52 marketing theories, all on a one-page template.

What Is the Main Benefit?

Simplicity. The Hourglass1998 Positioning Chart is a simple tool that helps strategists define, refine, align, and differentiate their products' positioning strategy. It helps marketers visualize and convey important marketing principles such as positioning, focus, differentiation, niche marketing, segmentation, targeting, gap analysis, relativity, repositioning, flanking, opposites, polarity, category killers, brand management, control, ranking, force, division, product management, USP, 4*P*s, depth, brand equity, sacrifice, fragmentation, leadership, choice modelling, consistency, knowledge networks, family branding, 4*D*s, alignment, mirroring, bait-and-switch, line-extensions, transference, brand building, and conversion. It is a quick, simple, and effective way to understand the perceptual battlefield. Every strategist needs a map.

Exhibit A

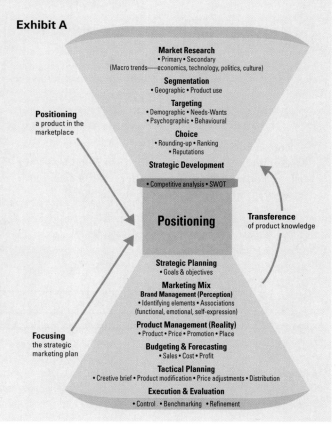

Exhibit B

1. Alignment and repositioning:

Marketing executives can accurately test the alignment of the brand or product mix. *Eatons'* brand *image* became severely misaligned with its "conservative" *reputation* when it tried to reposition itself as a "hip" fashion store for young people.

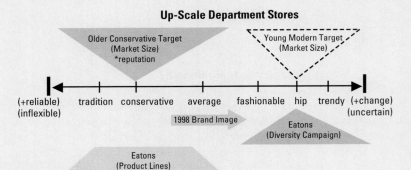

Up-Scale Department Stores

2. Brand building and comparison:

Marketing executives can compare the components of each brand mix in competing products. As the brand identities of the two coffee shops fill out, the differences are very apparent. *Tim Hortons* dominates by being *consistently* fast, fresh, and friendly.

Coffee Shops

3. Focus: Category killer

Marketing executives can clearly plan category killers. *Home Depot, Future Shop, Chapters,* and *Toys "R" Us* are using *"concentration of force"* to rip out a category from the generalist department stores; the *strong* (deep and narrow) versus the *weak* (broad and shallow).

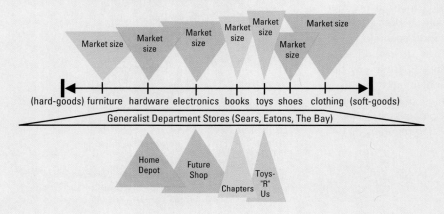

Different from Other Methods?

Big Picture. The Hourglass1998 Positioning Chart is unique because it puts a position into context relative to the customer, company, and competition. Seeing the "big picture" makes strategic planning easier.

Exact Formulas

Focus. The precise formula for exact positioning can be derived. An example would be, "What is the common denominator between Harvard, Rolex, Rolls-Royce, Glen Abby Golf Course, and Rosedale?" Prestige is the main positioning attribute. It is a formula made up of three sub-attributes: Prestige = Quality + Price + Exclusivity.

Description of the Method

The chart starts with a line on which product attributes are ranked and plotted according to the laws and principles of marketing. The upper half of the hourglass represents the uncontrollable target markets. The bottom half represents various controllable competing products. Each product strives to be first to build a reputation on a high-ranking attribute. Exhibit B shows a few of the many positioning strategies and manoeuvres that can be illustrated using the chart.

Source: Mark E. Smith, positioning consultant and professor specializing in positioning theory in post-graduate marketing management & international marketing at Humber College, Toronto; www.hourglass1998.com.

In what specific ways can a company differentiate its offer from those of competitors? A company or market offer can be differentiated along the lines of *product, service, people,* or *image.*

Product differentiation takes place along a continuum. At one extreme we find products that allow little variation: chicken, steel, aspirin. Yet even here, some meaningful differentiation is possible. For example, Perdue claims that its branded chickens are better—fresher and more tender—and gets a 10 percent price premium based on this differentiation. At the other extreme are products that can be highly differentiated, such as automobiles, clothing, and furniture. Such products can be differentiated on features, performance, or style and design. Thus, Volvo provides new and better safety features; Maytag is known for the reliability of its appliances; Bose positions its speakers on their striking design characteristics; Air Canada's fleet of Airbus 340 jets offers passengers wider seating. Similarly, companies can differentiate their products on such attributes as *consistency, durability, reliability,* or *repairability.*

Beyond differentiating its physical product, a firm can also differentiate itself by the amount and quality of service it offers customers. Some companies gain *services differentiation* through speedy, convenient, or careful *delivery.* For example, CIBC partnered with Loblaws to form President's Choice Banking, opening branches in Loblaws supermarkets to provide location convenience along with Saturday, Sunday, and weekday-evening hours. And by providing vast selections, ease of search, and fast delivery, both Chapters.Indigo.ca and Amazon.ca have won over many Canadian book buyers who had previously shopped in traditional stores.

Installation can also differentiate one company from another, as can *repair* services. Many an automobile buyer will gladly pay a little more and travel a little farther to buy a car from a dealer that provides top-notch repair service. Some companies differentiate their offers by providing *customer training* services or *consulting services*—data, information systems, and advising services that buyers need. McKesson Corporation, a major drug wholesaler, consults with its 12 000 independent pharmacists to help them set up accounting, inventory, and computer ordering systems. By helping its customers compete better, McKesson gains greater customer loyalty and sales.

Firms that practise *channel differentiation* gain competitive advantage through the way they design their channel's coverage, expertise, and performance. The entry of virtual bank ING Direct (www.ingdirect.ca) shook up Canada's financial services industry with its online channel strategy and promises of higher interest rates on savings and more convenient banking. Caterpillar's success in the construction-

Porsche positions powerfully on performance and the freedom it generates: "The engine launches you forward with its distinctive growl. Any memory of life on a leash evaporates in the wind rushing overhead. It's time to run free."

©2000 Porsche Cars North America, Inc. Porsche recommends seat belt usage and observance of all traffic laws at all times. Specifications for comparison only.

Boxster S, sunflower field, Route 55, CO.

What a dog feels when the leash breaks.

Instant freedom, courtesy of the Boxster S. The 250 horsepower boxer engine launches you forward with its distinctive growl. Any memory of life on a leash evaporates in the wind rushing overhead. It's time to run free. Contact us at 1-800-PORSCHE or porsche.com.

PORSCHE

equipment industry is based on superior channels. Its dealers worldwide are renowned for their first-rate service. Dell Computer and Avon distinguish themselves by their high-quality direct channels. And Iams pet food achieved success by going against tradition, distributing its products only through veterinarians and pet stores.

Companies can gain a strong competitive advantage through *people differentiation*—hiring and training better people than their competitors do. Thus, Disney people are known to be friendly and upbeat. IBM offers people who make sure that the solution customers want is the solution they get: "People Who Get It. People Who Get It Done." Toronto's Four Seasons Hotel is famous for its people and the service it provides to business travellers. For example, Four Seasons employees consider it all in a day's work to fly to New York to return luggage or business papers left behind by distracted business travellers. The hotel concierge does everything in her power to make guests feel welcome and comfortable, including renting a chartered plane to get a first-time father home for a premature delivery or sodding a balcony to make a guest's dog feel more at home.[44]

Even when competing offers look the same, buyers may perceive a difference based on company or brand image differentiation. A company or brand image should convey the product's distinctive benefits and positioning. Developing a

Both firms and professional organizations like CMA Canada often use their great people to differentiate themselves.

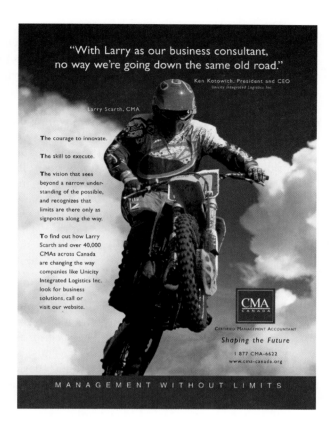

strong and distinctive image calls for creativity and hard work. A company cannot implant an image in the public's mind overnight using only a few advertisements. If Ritz-Carlton means quality, this image must be supported by everything the company says and does.

Symbols—such as the McDonald's golden arches, the Prudential rock, the Nike swoosh, the Intel Inside logo, or the Pillsbury doughboy—can provide strong company or brand recognition and image differentiation. Companies design signs and logos that provide instant recognition. They associate themselves with objects or characters that symbolize quality or other attributes. The company might build a brand around some famous person, as Nike did with its Air Jordan basketball shoes and Tiger Woods golfing products. Some companies even become associated with colours, such as IBM (blue), Campbell (red and white), or UPS (brown). The chosen symbols, characters, and other image elements must be communicated through advertising that conveys the company or brand personality.

Choosing the Right Competitive Advantages

Suppose a company is fortunate enough to discover several potential competitive advantages. It must choose the ones on which to build its positioning strategy. It must decide *how many* differences to promote and *which ones*.

How Many Differences to Promote?   Many marketers think that companies should aggressively promote only one benefit to the target market. Ad man Rosser Reeves said a company should develop a *unique selling proposition (USP)* for each brand and stick to it. Each brand should choose an attribute and tout itself as "number one" on that attribute. Buyers tend to remember number one better, especially in an over-communicated society. Thus, Crest toothpaste consistently promotes its anti-cavity protection, and Volvo promotes safety. A company that hammers away at one of these positions and consistently delivers on it probably will become best known and remembered for it.

Other marketers think that companies should position themselves on more than one differentiating factor. This may be necessary if two or more firms are claiming to be best on the same attribute. Today, in a time when the mass market is fragmenting into many small segments, companies are trying to broaden their positioning strategies to appeal to more segments. For example, Unilever introduced the first three-in-one bar soap—Lever 2000—offering cleansing, deodorizing, *and* moisturizing benefits. Clearly, many buyers want all three benefits. In a recent innovative campaign, Toronto's Gardiner Museum of Ceramic Art used a 12-foot by 15-foot vinyl inflatable teapot and an ad showing the Red Devil teapot (complete with graphically placed spout) to convey its new position as a bold, colourful, spirited, and energetic place to visit. This is a change in direction, says one museum spokesperson, who noted the need to differentiate the museum from the Royal Ontario Museum (ROM), located right across the road. "The great advantage is that the ROM has chosen to be stately and big. The idea was to look at what this larger institution was doing, and look at what our small institution was capable of." The new positioning strategy has helped the museum increase its funding and membership base.[45]

In general, a company needs to avoid three major positioning errors. The first is *underpositioning*—failing ever to really position the company at all. Some companies discover that buyers have only a vague idea of the company or that they do not know anything special about it. The second error is *overpositioning*—giving buyers too narrow a picture of the company. Thus, a consumer might think that the Steuben glass company makes only fine art glass costing $1400 and up, when in fact it makes affordable fine glass starting at around $70.

Finally, companies must avoid *confused positioning*—leaving buyers with a confused image of a company. For example, over the past two decades, Burger King has fielded a dozen separate advertising campaigns, with themes ranging from "Herb the nerd doesn't eat here" to "Sometimes you've got to break the rules," "BK

The Gardiner Museum of Ceramic Art successfully repositioned itself with the help of this provocative and attention-grabbing ad.

Tee Vee," "Got the Urge?" and "Have It Your Way." This barrage of positioning statements has left consumers confused and Burger King with poor sales and profits. Similarly, Zellers has not fared well against more strongly positioned competitors:

> Zellers has faced a continuous identity crisis as it struggles to ward off arch-rival Wal-Mart. Wal-Mart positions itself forcefully as offering "Always low prices. Always!" Since Zellers couldn't win against its arch rival with its traditional promise that "the lowest price is the law," it first repositioned itself as the place "where young families shop." Next, it used a co-branding strategy hoping to get fashion cachet from its house brands: Martha Stewart, Gloria Vanderbilt, Cherokee, Truly, and Delta Burke. Another about-face suggested Zellers was the place for "Everyday home fashions." It next went back to its roots and used more price-promotional advertising and its Club Z loyalty program. In 2002, Zellers senior-vice-president David Strickland recognized the company was facing a positioning crisis. "There is no question we were looking for more consistency in terms of voice." Research revealed that Zellers was being judged based on its past history. However, although Zellers has revamped its stores, many people who had abandoned Zellers didn't know about the store renovations or improved assortments. Thus, the newest positioning effort is focused on two truths: that Zellers is focused on a single customer, which is moms, and that it strives for continuous improvement. Its new motto, "Zellers: better and better," is an expression of its commitment to the customer.[46]

Which Differences to Promote?   Not all brand differences are meaningful or worthwhile. Not every difference makes a good differentiator. Each difference has the potential to create company costs as well as customer benefits. Therefore, the company must carefully select the ways in which it will distinguish itself from competitors. A difference is worth establishing to the extent that it satisfies the following criteria:

- *Important:* The difference delivers a highly valued benefit to target buyers.
- *Distinctive:* Competitors do not offer the difference, or the company can offer it in a more distinctive way.
- *Superior:* The difference is superior to other ways that customers might obtain the same benefit.
- *Communicable:* The difference is communicable and visible to buyers.
- *Pre-emptive:* Competitors cannot easily copy the difference.
- *Affordable:* Buyers can afford to pay for the difference.
- *Profitable:* The company can introduce the difference profitably.

Many companies have introduced differentiations that failed one or more of these tests. The Westin Stamford hotel in Singapore advertised that it was the world's tallest hotel, a distinction that was not important to many tourists—in fact, it turned many off. Polaroid's Polavision, which produced instantly developed home movies, bombed too. Although Polavision was distinctive and even pre-emptive, it was inferior to another way of capturing motion, namely, camcorders. When Pepsi introduced clear Crystal Pepsi some years ago, customers were unimpressed. Although the new drink was distinctive, consumers didn't see "clarity" as an important benefit in a soft drink. Thus, choosing competitive advantages upon which to position a product or service can be difficult, yet such choices may be crucial to success.

Selecting an Overall Positioning Strategy

Consumers typically choose products and services that give them the greatest value. Therefore, marketers want to position their brands on the key benefits that they

Value proposition
The full positioning of a brand—the full mix of benefits upon which the brand is positioned.

offer relative to competing brands. The full positioning of a brand is called the brand's **value proposition**—the full mix of benefits upon which the brand is positioned. It is the answer to the customer's question "Why should I buy your brand?" Volvo's value proposition hinges on safety but also includes reliability, roominess, and styling, all for a price that is higher than average but seems fair for this mix of benefits.

Figure 9.3 shows possible value propositions upon which a company might position its products. In the figure, the five blue cells represent winning value propositions—positioning that gives the company competitive advantage. The orange cells, however, represent losing value propositions. The centre yellow cell represents at best a marginal proposition. In the following sections, we discuss the five winning value propositions companies can use to position their products: more for more, more for the same, the same for less, less for much less, and more for less.[47]

More for More   "More for more" positioning involves providing the most upscale product or service and charging a higher price to cover the higher costs. Ritz-Carlton hotels, Mont Blanc writing instruments, Mercedes-Benz automobiles—each claims superior quality, craftsmanship, durability, performance, or style, and charges a price to match. Not only is the marketing offer high in quality, it also offers prestige to the buyer. It symbolizes status and a lofty lifestyle. Often, the price difference exceeds the actual increment in quality.

Sellers offering "only the best" can be found in every product and service category, from hotels, restaurants, food, and fashion to cars and kitchen appliances. Consumers are sometimes surprised, even delighted, when a new competitor enters a category with an unusually high-priced brand. Starbucks coffee entered as a very expensive brand in a largely commodity category; Häagen-Dazs came in as a premium ice cream brand at a price never before charged.

In general, companies should be on the lookout for opportunities to introduce a "much-more-for-much-more" brand in any underdeveloped product or service category. Yet "more for more" brands can be vulnerable. They often invite imitators who claim the same quality but at a lower price. Luxury goods that sell well during good times may be at risk during economic downturns when buyers become more cautious in their spending.

More for the Same   Companies can attack a competitor's more-for-more positioning by introducing a brand offering comparable quality but at a lower price. For example, Toyota introduced its Lexus line (www.lexuscanada.com) with a "more-for-the-same" value proposition. Its headline read: "Perhaps the first time in history that trading a $100 000 car for a $54 000 car could be considered trading up." It communicated the high quality of its new Lexus through rave reviews in car

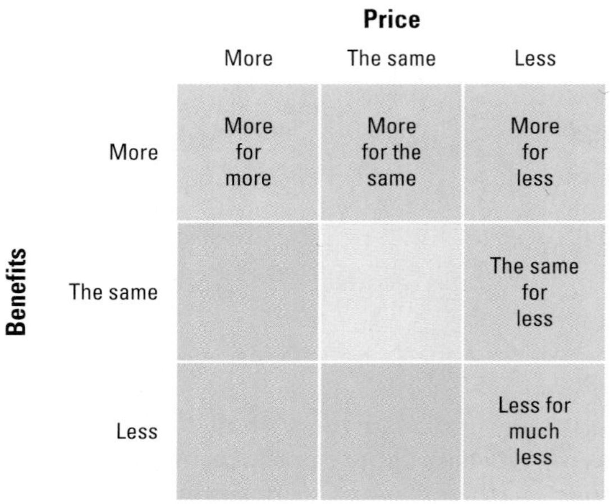

Price

	More	The same	Less
More	More for more	More for the same	More for less
The same			The same for less
Less			Less for much less

Benefits

Figure 9.3   Possible value propositions

"Much more for much more" value proposition: Häagen-Dazs offers its super-premium ice cream at a price never before charged.

magazines, through a widely distributed videotape showing side-by-side comparisons of Lexus and Mercedes automobiles, and through surveys showing that Lexus dealers were providing customers with better sales and service experiences than were Mercedes dealerships. Many Mercedes owners switched to Lexus, and the Lexus repurchase rate has been 60 percent, twice the industry average.

The Same for Less   Offering "the same for less" can be a powerful value proposition—everyone likes a good deal. For example, Amazon sells the same book titles as its bricks-and-mortar competitors but at lower prices, and Dell Computer offers equivalent quality at a better "price for performance." Discount stores such as Wal-Mart and "category killers" such as Winners, Business Depot, Costco, Best Buy, Circuit City, and Sportmart also use this positioning. They don't claim to offer different or better products. Instead, they offer many of the same brands as department stores and specialty stores but at deep discounts based on superior purchasing power and lower-cost operations.

Other companies develop imitative but lower-priced brands in an effort to lure customers away from the market leader. For example, AMD makes less expensive versions of Intel's market-leading microprocessor chips. Many personal computer companies make "IBM clones" and claim to offer the same performance at lower prices.

Less for Much Less   A market almost always exists for products that offer less and therefore cost less. Few people need, want, or can afford "the very best" in everything they buy. In many cases, consumers will gladly settle for less than optimal performance or give up some of the bells and whistles in exchange for a lower price. For example, many travellers seeking lodgings prefer not to pay for what they consider unnecessary extras, such as a pool, attached restaurant, or mints on the pillow. Motel chains such as Motel 6 and Holiday Inn Express suspend some of these amenities and charge less accordingly. Canada's discount airlines—WestJet, Jetsgo, Jazz, Zip, and Tango—eliminate costly extra services to compete on price against Air Canada, the country's full-service carrier. Air Canada has been feeling the heat, and is starting to charge passengers for movie snacks and meals to improve its revenues.

"Less-for-much-less" positioning involves meeting consumers' lower performance or quality requirements at a much lower price. For example, Family Dollar and Dollar General stores offer more affordable goods at very low prices. Sam's Club and Costco warehouse stores offer less merchandise selection and consistency, and much lower levels of service; as a result, they charge rock-bottom prices.

More for Less Of course, the winning value proposition would be to offer "more for less." Many companies claim to do this. For example, Dell Computer claims to have better products *and* lower prices for a given level of performance. Procter & Gamble claims that its laundry detergents provide the best cleaning *and* everyday low prices. In the short run, some companies can actually achieve such lofty positions. For example, when it first opened for business, Home Depot had arguably the best product selection and service *and* the lowest prices compared with local hardware stores and other home improvement chains.

Yet in the long run, companies will find it very difficult to sustain such best-of-both positioning. Offering more usually costs more, making it difficult to deliver on the "for less" promise. Companies that try to deliver both may lose out to more focused competitors. For example, facing determined competition from Lowe's stores, Home Depot must now decide whether it wants to compete primarily on superior service or on lower prices.

All said, each brand must adopt a positioning strategy designed to serve the needs and wants of its target markets. "More for more" will draw one target market, "less for much less" will draw another, and so on. Thus, in any market, there is usually room for many different companies, each successfully occupying different positions.

The important thing is that each company develop its own winning positioning strategy, one that makes it special to its target consumers. Offering only "the same for the same" provides no competitive advantage, leaving the firm in the middle of the pack. Companies offering one of the three losing value propositions—"the same for more," "less for more," and "less for the same"—will inevitably fail. Here, customers soon realize that they've been underserved, tell others, and abandon the brand.

Developing a Positioning Statement

Positioning statement

A statement that summarizes company or brand positioning—it takes this form: *To (target segment and need) our (brand) is (concept) that (point-of-difference).*

Company and brand positioning should be summed up in a **positioning statement**. The statement should follow this form: *To (target segment and need) our (brand) is (concept) that (point-of-difference).*[48] For example: "To *busy professionals who need to stay organized, Palm Pilot* is *an electronic organizer* that *allows you to back up files on your PC more easily and reliably than competitive products.*" Sometimes a positioning statement is more detailed:

> To young, active soft-drink consumers who have little time for sleep, Mountain Dew is the soft drink that gives you more energy than any other brand because it has the highest level of caffeine. With Mountain Dew, you can stay alert and keep going even when you haven't been able to get a good night's sleep.[49]

Note that the positioning first states the product's membership in a category (Mountain Dew is a soft drink) and then shows its point of difference from other members of the category (has more caffeine). Placing a brand in a specific category suggests similarities that it might share with other products in the category. But the case for the brand's superiority is made on its points of difference. Sometimes marketers put a brand in a surprisingly different category before indicating the points of difference:

DiGiorno's is a frozen pizza whose crust rises when the pizza is heated. Instead of putting it in the frozen pizza category, the marketers positioned it in the delivered pizza category. Their ad shows party guests asking which pizza delivery service the host used. But he says, "It's not delivery, its DiGiorno!" This helped highlight DiGiorno's fresh quality and superior taste over the normal frozen pizza.

Communicating and Delivering the Chosen Position

Once it has chosen a position, the company must take steps to deliver and communicate the desired position to target consumers. All the company's marketing mix efforts must support the positioning strategy. Positioning the company calls for concrete action, not just talk. If the company decides to build a position on better quality and service, it must first *deliver* that position. Designing the marketing mix—product, price, place, and promotion—essentially involves working out the tactical details of the positioning strategy. Thus, a firm that seizes on a more-for-more position knows that it must produce high-quality products, charge a high price, distribute through high-quality dealers, and advertise in high-quality media. It must hire and train more service people, find retailers who have a good reputation for service, and develop sales and advertising messages that broadcast its superior service. This is the only way to build a consistent and believable high-quality, high-service position.

Companies often find it easier to develop a good positioning strategy than to implement it. Establishing a position or changing one usually takes a long time. In contrast, positions that have taken years to build can quickly be lost. Once a company has built the desired position, it must take care to maintain the position through consistent performance and communication. It must closely monitor and adapt the position over time to match changes in consumer needs and competitors' strategies. However, the company should avoid abrupt changes that might confuse consumers. Instead, a product's position should evolve gradually as it adapts to the ever-changing marketing environment.

Looking Back: Reviewing the Concepts

Marketers know that they cannot appeal to all buyers in their markets, or at least not to all buyers in the same way. Buyers are too numerous, too widely scattered, and too varied in their needs and buying practices. Therefore, most companies are moving away from mass marketing. Instead, they practise *target marketing*— identifying market segments, selecting one or more of them, and developing products and marketing mixes tailored to each. In this way, sellers can develop the right product for each target market and adjust their prices, distribution channels, and advertising to reach the target market efficiently.

1. **Define the three steps of target marketing: market segmentation, market targeting, and market positioning.**

   Market segmentation is the act of dividing a market into distinct groups of buyers with different needs, characteristics, or behaviours, who might require separate products or marketing mixes. Once the groups have been identified, *target marketing* evaluates each market segment's attractiveness and suggests one or more segments to enter. *Market positioning* consists of setting the competitive positioning for the product and creating a detailed marketing mix.

2. **List and discuss the major bases for segmenting consumer and business markets.**

   There is no single way to segment a market. Therefore, the marketer tries different variables to see which give the best segmentation opportunities. For consumer marketing, the major segmentation variables are geographic, demographic, psychographic, and behavioural. In *geographic segmentation,* the market is divided into different geographical units such as nations, provinces, regions, counties, cities, or neighbourhoods. In *demographic segmentation,* the market is divided into groups based on demographic variables, including age, gender, family size, family life cycle, income, occupation, education, religion, race, and nationality. In *psychographic segmentation,* the market is divided into different groups based on lifestyle or personality characteristics. In *behavioural segmentation,* the market is divided into groups based on consumers' knowledge, attitudes, uses, or responses to a product.

   Business marketers use many of the same variables to segment their markets. But business markets can also be segmented by business consumer *demographics* (industry, company size), *operating characteristics, purchasing approaches,* and *personal characteristics.* The effectiveness of segmentation analysis depends on finding segments that are *measurable, accessible, substantial,* and *actionable.*

3. **Explain how companies identify attractive market segments and choose a market coverage strategy.**

   To target the best market segments, the company first evaluates each segment's size and growth characteristics, structural attractiveness, and compatibility with company resources and objectives. It then chooses one of four market coverage strategies—ranging from very broad to very narrow targeting. The seller can ignore segment differences and target broadly using *undifferentiated (or mass) marketing.* This involves mass-producing, mass-distributing, and mass-promoting about the same product in about the same way to all consumers. Or the seller can adopt *differentiated marketing*—developing different market offers for several segments. *Concentrated (or niche) marketing* involves focusing on only one or a few market segments. Finally, *micromarketing* is the practice of tailoring products and marketing programs to suit the tastes of specific individuals and locations. Micromarketing includes *local marketing* and *individual marketing.* Which targeting strategy is best depends on company resources, product variability, product life-cycle stage, market variability, and competitors' marketing strategies.

4. **Explain how companies position their products for maximum competitive advantage in the marketplace.**

   Once a company has decided which segments to enter, it must decide on its *market positioning* strategy—on which positions to occupy in its chosen segments. The positioning task consists of three steps: identifying a set of possible competitive advantages upon which to build a position, choosing the right competitive advantages, and selecting an overall positioning strategy. The brand's full positioning is called its *value proposition*—the full mix of benefits upon which the brand is positioned. In general, companies can choose from one of five winning value propositions upon which to position their products: more for more, more for the same, the same for less, less for much less, or more for less. Company and brand positioning are summarized in a positioning statement that states the target segment and need, positioning concept, and specific points of difference. The company must then effectively communicate and deliver the chosen position to the market.

Reviewing the Key Terms

Discussing the Concepts

1. Figure 9.1 (page 329) shows three steps in target marketing. Briefly discuss each step.

2. Assume that you are the marketing manager for a cosmetics company that has just developed a new line of male cosmetics. The cosmetics are invisible on the skin, reduce aging lines significantly, and provide some protection from the sun. Using the major segmentation variables found in Table 9.1 (page 330), construct a brief profile of three market segments that you suspect might be interested in this new product line. Explain your profiling procedure.

3. One approach in segmenting international markets is called intermarket segmentation. Explain this approach and illustrate it with an example.

4. Need help with your financial planning? Intuit's Quicken (financial planning software) and TurboTax (income-tax preparation software) have secured the company's success in the rapidly growing financial planning and services market. Assuming that the company would like to expand, which of the target marketing strategies shown in Figure 9.2 (page 346) would you suggest? Explain how the strategy helps Intuit overcome competitive challenges from other software makers, such as Microsoft.

5. Sleeman is one of several microbreweries attacking the established brewers' domestic beers. What is micromarketing, and how might microbreweries use it to take on larger competitors? How might Sleeman use local or individual marketing to advance its products?

6. Socially responsible marketing calls for segmentation and targeting that serve not just the interests of the company but also the interests of those targeted. Do these goals conflict with one another? Provide an example of a company that you believe takes a socially responsible approach to segmentation and targeting. Explain your reasoning.

7. A company or market offer can be differentiated along several lines. Find advertisements for several competitors in a particular industry. Using the advertisements, demonstrate how the companies differentiate themselves with respect to products, services, prices, and image. Which company seems to be more successful in the differentiation attempt? Explain.

8. McDonald's has long been an innovator in the fast-food field. To avoid the flat growth that has recently plagued the fast-food industry, McDonald's plans to experiment with waiter-service diners, McDonuts, Internet access for patrons, Spam breakfast platters, and a Town Centre concept where adults can enjoy karaoke while kids go to Playland. Use Figure 9.3 (page 364) to discuss what value propositions McDonald's would be addressing with these innovations.

Applying the Concepts

1. In 1969, Nissan Motor launched the Datsun 240Z, and for nearly two decades the Z-series ruled the sports car world in North America. The early Zs were stylish Jaguar look-alikes with a budget price tag for the cost-conscious car buyer interested in a sleek sports car. The car's tremendous success inspired competitors to enter the market. Eventually, the sports car market became saturated, and Z sales declined. Today, Nissan is again vying for a piece of the budget sports car market with the introduction of the Nissan 350Z, and buyers are taking notice. The 350Z combines the spirit and power of the original model with twenty-first-century styling and technology. There is little question that the 350Z will turn a few heads, but will it generate the same response as its predecessor? Nissan is betting that the answer is yes.

   a. Assume you are the marketing director for the Nissan 350Z. Follow the steps in Figure 9.1 (page 329) and construct a brief segmentation plan for introducing the car into the Canadian market. For additional product information, visit www.nissandriven.com.

   b. What segmentation, targeting, and positioning strategies would you recommend? Explain.

   c. What competitive advantage would you stress in your marketing campaign? Explain.

   d. What value proposition should be stressed? Why?

2. Have you used a SpinBrush to clean your teeth? If not, you're just the person Procter & Gamble's Crest SpinBrush is seeking. The SpinBrush is a battery-powered toothbrush that is taking the electric toothbrush market by storm. The product is fun, creatively styled (there's even a race car version), great at cleaning your teeth and gums, and is attractively priced. Most innovative products begin with a premium pricing strategy. SpinBrush used the opposite approach to secure maximum market penetration and avoid knockoff competitors. The company even skipped the traditional heavy prelaunch advertising campaign in order to keep the product's price down. Instead, it relied on creative packaging that allowed customers to self-demonstrate the product in the store. The SpinBrush's special "Try Me" feature rocketed sales to 10 million units in its introductory year. Procter & Gamble followed the successful launch by expanding into 35 countries. Competitors have arrived, but they may be too late to take the spin off of SpinBrush's success.

   a. For more information on the Crest SpinBrush, visit the Procter & Gamble website at www.pg.com. Consider the information shown in Table 9.1 (page 330). Which psychographic and behavioural segmentation variables might have been used by SpinBrush to define its initial market segments? Explain.

   b. How could Procter & Gamble encourage consumers of traditional toothbrushes to use SpinBrush? What challenges might P&G marketers face? Explain.

   c. What competitive advantage(s) does SpinBrush have?

   d. As indicated in the text, not all brand differences are meaningful. Review the product's features on the Proctor & Gamble website and explain which characteristics give SpinBrush an advantage over traditional toothbrushes.

Video Short

View the video short for this chapter at **www.pearsoned.ca/kotler** and then answer the questions provided in the case description.

Company Case

GM: Downsizing the Hummer

A Little Military History

Quickly. What is a "High Mobility Multi-Purpose Wheeled Vehicle"? Well, if you've kept up with Arnold Schwarzenegger films or studied the 1991 Gulf War, you may have recognized the formal military description of what soldiers describe using the acronym "Humvee." If you don't really know what a Humvee is, just stand by—General Motors is going to tell you.

This story starts in 1979, when AM General, a specialty vehicle manufacturer, earned a contract from the U.S. Army to design the Humvee. The Army wanted a new vehicle to replace the Jeep, the ever-present multipurpose vehicle that had transported generations of soldiers. The Army believed it needed a more modern, up-to-date vehicle to meet the needs of the modern soldier. AM General produced the big, boxy Humvee, which laboured in relative obscurity until the Gulf War in 1991. In that war, the United States and its allies mounted a military operation against Iraq, which had just invaded Kuwait. Television coverage of the military buildup in advance of the short war and live broadcasts of the war itself introduced the public to the workhorse Humvee.

In 1992, AM General, responding to the Humvee's notoriety, decided to introduce the first *civilian* version of the Humvee—the Hummer. Weighing in at 3220 kg, the Hummer featured a huge, 6.5-litre V-8, turbo-diesel engine that produced 195 horsepower and propelled the Hummer from 0 to 95 km per hour in a snail-like 18 seconds. But the Hummer's purpose was not speed. AM General designed it, like its military parent, to take people off the beaten path—way off. The Hummer could plough through water to a depth of 75 cm and climb almost vertical, rocky surfaces. It even had a central tire inflation system that allowed the driver to inflate or deflate the vehicle's tires while on the move.

The advertising tag line dubbed the Hummer "The world's most serious 4 × 4," and ad copy played up the vehicle's off-road capabilities and its military heritage. AM General targeted serious, elite road warriors who were willing to pay more than $130 000 to have the toughest vehicle in the carpool. These were people who also wanted to tell the world that they had been successful. To help buyers learn how to handle the Hummer in extreme off-road situations, AM General even offered a Hummer Driving Academy, where drivers learned to handle 56 cm vertical walls, high water, 40 percent side slopes, and 60 percent inclines.

GM's Market Research

In 1998, GM was conducting market research using a concept vehicle that it described as rugged and militaristic. When the vehicle bore the GMC brand name (GM's truck division), the company found that consumers had a lukewarm reaction. However, when GM put the Hummer name on the vehicle, researchers found that it had the highest and most widespread appeal of any vehicle GM had *ever* tested. Armed with this insight, GM turned to AM General, which had just abandoned acquisition discussions with Ford Motor Company. In December 1999, GM signed an agreement with AM General giving GM rights to the Hummer brand. AM General also signed a seven-year contract to produce the Hummer H2 sport utility vehicle for GM.

Based on its research, GM believed that the Hummer H2, a smaller version of the Hummer, would appeal to rugged individualists and wealthy baby boomers who wanted the ability to go off-road and to "successful achievers," thirty- and forty-something wealthy consumers who had jobs in investment banking, and the like. GM believed that it could introduce the H2 in the luxury SUV market and compete successfully with brands such as the Lincoln Navigator or GM's own Cadillac Escalade. The company charted production plans that called for AM General to build a new $260 million manufacturing facility in Indiana and for GM to launch the H2 in July 2002 at a base sticker price of about US$64 000. It predicted that it could sell 19 000 H2s in 2002 (the 2003 model year) and then ramp up production to sell 40 000 units per year thereafter—a number that would make the H2 the largest seller in the luxury SUV market. Further, GM planned to introduce the H3, a still smaller and more affordable version of the Hummer in 2005. It believed it could sell 80 000 units of the H3 per year. These numbers compared with annual sales of only about 800 Hummers.

Softening Up the Market

During 2000, GM and AM General did not advertise the Hummer, but they mapped out a campaign for the year leading up to the H2's 2002 introduction that would raise awareness of the Hummer brand and serve as a bridge to the introduction. GM hired marketing firm Modernista to develop the estimated $4 million campaign. Modernista found that the Hummer had about a 50 percent awareness level among buyers of full-size SUVs, mainly due to its appearance in movies. AM General had been spending less than $1.3 million a year on advertising and promotion. Further, 13 to 20 percent of these buyers had considered the Hummer.

In mid-2001, GM launched the Modernista campaign using the tag line "Hummer. Like nothing else." Placements in the *Wall Street Journal, Barron's, Spin, Business Week, Cigar Aficionado,* and *Esquire* used four different headlines:

"How did my soul get way out here?"
"What good is the world at your fingertips if
    you never actually touch it?"
"You can get fresh air lots of places, but this is
    the really good stuff."
"Out here you're nobody. Perfect."

Following each headline was the same copy: "Sometimes you find yourself in the middle of nowhere. And sometimes in the middle of nowhere you find yourself. The legendary H1." One agency official said the ads used journalistic-type photography to make them more believable and to play down the he-man imagery. "Authenticity is probably the most important word when it comes to branding," the official argued. Whereas previous Hummer ads had featured the tough SUV ploughing through snow and streams, the new ads featured the Hummer with gorgeous Chilean vistas. The new ads, the agency suggested, were as much about the people who buy Hummers as they were about the vehicle. Hummer owners often believed they got a bum rap as show-offs, the representative suggested, but he argued that the new ads would show the buyer's other side.

The Launch

Right on schedule in July 2002, GM introduced the 2003 Hummer 2 SUT (Sport Utility Truck). GM and AM General designed and built the H2 in just 16 months, much more quickly than the three-to-four-year time normally required. GM built the H2 on GM's GMT 800 truck platform, and it shared a number of parts with other GM models. The H2 was about the same size as the Chevy Tahoe, about 13 cm narrower than the Hummer and about 315 kg lighter. However, it was about 635 kg heavier than other SUVs. It had a 316-horsepower

engine that slurped a litre of gasoline every 5 km. It also featured a nine-speaker Bose stereo system. Buyers could upgrade the base model with a $3355 luxury package that added heated leather front seats and a six-disc CD changer or with a $2880 Adventure package that added air suspension, brush guards, and crossbars for the roof rack.

GM had about 150 dealers who would initially offer the H2. The dealers had to agree to build a special showroom and a test track.

For promotion, GM stayed with the Modernista firm. Late in the summer of 2002, TV ads broke on shows such as *CSI: Miami* and featured a well-dressed woman behind the H2's steering wheel. The Modernista representative indicated that the message was that the H2 is not about blowing things up. Twenty-four print ads showed the H2 not in action but sitting still. Modernista believed that people knew the H2 would be tough—it wanted people to see that the H2 looked good.

The On-Road Test

GM targeted buyers with an average age of 42 and annual household incomes above $165 000 versus H1 owners' averages of about 50 years old and household incomes above $260 000. The questions were, could GM position the H2 to appeal to its target market, and was that market large enough to ensure that GM could reach its sales and profitability targets?

One writer who had driven the H2 found it to be comfortable and surprisingly smooth on the highway. However, he criticized the interior and the lack of storage space. He noted that the H2 seated just six people versus eight or nine for other large SUVs.

Analysts argued that GM was pursuing a risky strategy. Would its having borrowed parts from other GM models to keep costs down and speed the time to market damage the H2's image? Would GM be able to justify the H2's high price when it had so much in common with other SUVs that cost thousands less? Would consumers really spend so much for an off-the-road vehicle that, studies showed, only 10 percent of image-conscious buyers would actually take off road? Finally, could GM make the Hummer 2 stand out in an increasingly crowded market? (See Exhibit 1.)

Arnold Schwarzenegger appeared in an H2 promotional video, suggesting, "Don't call it the baby Hummer, you'll make it angry." Will the Hummer H2 be a hum-dinger and make GM happy, or will it get stuck in the rocky luxury SUV market?

Exhibit 1   Hummer H2's Existing or Coming Competition

Model/ Manufacturer	Base Price (Can $)
BMW X5 4.6is	$87 147
Mercedes G500	$95 385
Cadillac Escalade EXT	$65 205
Land Rover Range Rover	$91 252
Lincoln Navigator	$63 588
Porsche Cayenne	$58 666–$97 777
Volvo XC 90	$42 629–$58 665
Cadillac SRX	$52 143–$65 184
Infiniti FX 45	$52 143–$65 184

Source: Gregory B. White and Joseph L. White, "Automakers Take One-Up-Manship to New Level with New Extreme SUVs," *Wall Street Journal,* July 19, 2002, p. W1.

Questions for Discussion

1. How has GM used the major segmentation variables for consumer markets in segmenting the SUV market?

2. What target-market decisions has GM made in selecting targets for the Hummer H2? How are those decisions different from AM General's target for the original Hummer?

3. How has GM attempted to position the H2?

4. Why do you think some consumers will pay $52 000 or more for an off-road vehicle that 90 percent of them will never take off-road?

5. What segmentation, targeting, and positioning recommendations would you make to GM for the H2?

6. What other marketing recommendations would you make?

Sources: Melanie Well, "Muscle Car," *Forbes,* July 22, 2002, p. 181; David Welch, "More Sport, Less Utility," *Business Week,* July 8, 2002, p. 110; John O'Dell, "GM Sets Price for Hummer H2 SUV," *Los Angeles Times,* May 29, 2002, www.latimes.com; Trevor Jensen, "GM Tones Down Macho in New Ads for Hummer," *Adweek Midwest Edition,* August 6, 2001, p. 5; Jean Halliday, "Of Hummers and Zen," *Advertising Age,* August 6, 2001, p. 29; Gregory L. White, "GM's New Baby Hummer Shares Its Toys with Chevy," *Wall Street Journal,* April 10, 2001, p. B1; and Rick Kranz, "H2 Baby Hummer Won't Be Far from Concept, GM Says," *Automotive News,* November 20, 2000, p. 6.

CBC Video Case

  Log on to your Companion Website at **www.pearsoned.ca/kotler** to view a CBC video segment and case for this chapter.

Case Pilot

Log on to your Companion Website at **www.pearsoned.ca/kotler** to access the case project provided for this part of the text. Take the Case Pilot Challenge!

Chapter 10

Product, Services, and Branding Strategies

After studying this chapter you should be able to

1. define *product* and the major classifications of products and services

2. describe the decisions companies make regarding their individual products and services, product lines, and product mixes

3. discuss branding strategy—the decisions companies make in building and managing their brands

4. identify the four characteristics that affect the marketing of a service and the additional marketing considerations that services require

5. discuss two additional product issues: socially responsible product decisions and international product and services marketing

Looking Ahead: Previewing the Concepts

Now that you've had a good look at marketing strategy, we'll take a deeper look at the marketing mix—the tactical tools that marketers use to implement their strategies. In this and the next chapter, we'll study how companies develop and manage products and brands. Then, in the chapters that follow, we'll look at pricing, distribution, and marketing communication tools. The product is usually the first and most basic marketing consideration. How well firms manage their individual brands and their overall product and service offerings has a major impact on their success in the marketplace. We'll start with a seemingly simple question: What *is* a product? As it turns out, however, the answer is not so simple.

To start things off, think about cosmetics marketing. Remember that seemingly simple question—what is a product? The following cosmetics industry example shows why there is no easy answer. What, really, *are* cosmetics? Cosmetics makers like Aveda know that when a woman buys cosmetics, she buys much, much more than scented ingredients in fancy bottles.

Each year, cosmetics companies sell billions of dollars' worth of potions, lotions, and fragrances to consumers around the world. In one sense, these products are no more than careful mixtures of oils and chemicals that have nice scents and soothing properties. But the cosmetics companies know that they sell much more than just mixtures of ingredients—they sell the promise of what these concoctions will do for the people who use them.

Of course, in the cosmetics business, like anywhere else, quality and performance contribute to success or failure. For example, perfume marketers agree, "No smell, no sell." However, $180-an-ounce perfume may cost no more than $10 to produce. Thus, to perfume consumers, many things beyond the scent and a few dollars' worth of ingredients add to a perfume's allure. Fragrance names such as Obsession, Passion, Gossip, Wildheart, Opium, Joy, White Linen, Youth Dew, Eternity, and Love suggest that the perfumes will do something more than just make you smell better.

The growth in the use of cosmetic products has been accompanied by a growth in related services. For example, more and more Canadians are breaking away from the stress of ubiquitous cell phones, email, pagers, and a barrage of work with trips to the spa. According to PricewaterhouseCoopers's "2002 Spa Industry Study," there are now 1300 spas countrywide. Consumers no longer view going to these services as "pampering," but more as a necessity, and also that consumers' limited free time means they have less time to spend at the spa. Patrick Corbett, president of Calgary-based Spa Canada, notes that the growth in spas "is fuelled by consumers' desire to continue to look younger and feel younger."

The increased popularity of spas hasn't gone unnoticed by health-and-beauty marketers. While some are marketing products to spas themselves, others are responding with their own accessible and less expensive options to deliver a Zen-like experience in the comfort of one's own home. Procter & Gamble has been promoting its Olay Daily Facials for a couple of years as being able to deliver a salon-style facial at home, using the tag-line "You feel like you've had a little bit of a facial every day." Body Shop has jumped on-board with its Bajik Spa collections. Toronto-based Estée Lauder Canada recently launched its new Idealist Micro-D Deep Thermal Refinisher, the latest in its Idealist line of skin-care products, that is sold at retail for $60 and is touted as being an alternative to costly and time-consuming spa treatments. Judi Barr, manager of global communications, says the association with spas helps to foster the brand's position as an innovator in skin care. She says that up to 20 000 people visit the Estée spa in Toronto yearly, and adds, "Many customers are introduced to the brand through our spas." Montreal-based Lise Watier introduced its Spa line of products in 2002 with names like Soufflé body cream and Flambé-Glacé Stress Relief Patches. Lise Watier emphasizes the pleasurable, playful aspects of its products, which come in vibrant green packaging and have an energizing citrus scent.

Think spas and cosmetics are just for women? Not today! Tanning powders, concealers, mascaras, and beard and brow tints are just some of the new items hitting the market. Although men don't want to be seen as vain, they are lining up at male-only salons for waxes and facials. Cosmetics companies are now creating separate lines designed for men and are being very careful to market their products as "masculine." M·A·C Cosmetics, for example, has packaged its products as gender neutral, resulting in a steady increase of male customers. Father's Day 2003 saw cosmetics counters of mainstream department stores laden with men's newly launched grooming products. Biotherm, Clarins, Clinique, and Estée Lauder offered "fatigue fighting" creams, eye gels, and self-tanners. Male lines swelled to more than twenty products where just a few years ago there were three.

What *is* the promise of cosmetics and spa services? The following account suggests the extent to which cosmetics take on meaning far beyond their physical makeup:

> Last week I bathed in purple water (*I Trust* bubble bath, made by Philosophy) and powdered up with pink powder (*Rebirth,* by 5S, "to renew the spirit and recharge the soul"). My moisturizer was *Bliss* (Chakra VII by Aveda, for "the joyful enlightenment and soaring of the spirit"); my nail polish was *Spiritual* (by Tony and Tina, "to aid connection with the higher self"). My teeth

> were clean, my heart was open—however, my bathroom was so crowded with bottles and brochures, the latest tools and totems from the human potential movement, that I could hardly find my third eye. Still, my "Hope in a Jar" package (from Philosophy) pretty well summed it up: "Where there is hope there can be faith. Where there is faith miracles can occur."

> 5S, a new sprout of the Japanese cosmetics company Shiseido, offers a regimen that plays, the company says, on the "fundamental and mythical significance of 5" (Five Pillars of Islam, Five Classics of Confucianism, and so on), and which is organized into emotional rather than physical categories. At the 5S store in SoHo, you don't buy things for dry skin, you buy things that are "energizing" or "nurturing" or "adoring." The company also believes in colour therapy. Hence, *Rebirth,* products tinted "nouveau pink" (the colour of bubble gum). A customer can achieve rebirth with 5S pink soap, pink powder, and pink toner.

> Here are products that are not intended to make you look better, but to make you act better, feel better, and be a better person. You don't need a month's visit to India to find your higher self; you need only buy this bubble bath, that lipstick, this night cream. The beauty business's old come-on (trap your man!) has been swept away in favour of a new pitch. I don't have wrinkles anymore. I've got a chakra blockage.

> Of course, who knew about chakras before Aveda? In 1989, the plant-based, eco-friendly cosmetics company Aveda trademarked Chakras I through VII to use as titles for moisturizers and scents. Chakra products were perhaps a little ahead of their time back then. However, the purchase of Aveda [a while] ago by the Estée Lauder Companies, the General Motors of the cosmetics world, suggests that the pendulum of history has finally caught up. "Aveda isn't a marketing idea," says Jeanette Wagner, the vice chairman of Estée Lauder. "It is a passionately held belief. From my point of view, the appeal is first the spirituality, and then the products."

All this might sound like only so much marketing hype, but the underlying point is legitimate. The success of such brands affirms that products really are more than just the physical entities.

When people buy cosmetics, they really buy much, much more than just oils, chemicals, and fragrances. The cosmetic's image, its promises and positioning, its ingredients, its name and package, the company that makes it, the stores that sell it—all become a part of the total cosmetic product. When Aveda, Philosophy, and 5S sell cosmetics, they sell more than just tangible goods. They sell lifestyle, self-expression, exclusivity, and spirituality; achievement, success, and status; romance, passion, and fantasy; memories, hopes, and dreams.[1]

Clearly, as the cosmetics example demonstrates, products can be more than just a physical entity. Thus, this chapter begins with a deceptively simple question: *What is a product?* After answering this question, we look at ways to classify products in consumer and business markets. Then we discuss the important decisions that marketers make regarding individual products, product lines, and product mixes. Next, we look into the critically important issue of how marketers build and manage brands. Finally, we examine the characteristics and marketing requirements of a special form of product—services.

What Is a Product?

Product

Anything that can be offered to a market for attention, acquisition, use, or consumption that might satisfy a want or need.

Service

Any activity or benefit that one party can offer to another that is essentially intangible and does not result in the ownership of anything.

A Sony DVD player, a Supercuts haircut, a Céline Dion concert, a Jasper vacation, a GMC truck, H&R Block tax preparation services, and advice from a lawyer—all are products. We define a **product** as anything that can be offered to a market for attention, acquisition, use, or consumption and that might satisfy a want or need. Products include more than just tangible goods. Broadly defined, products include physical objects, services, persons, places, organizations, ideas, or mixes of these entities. Thus, throughout this text, we use the term *product* broadly to include any or all of these entities.

Because of their importance in the world economy, we give special attention to services. **Services** are a form of product that consist of activities, benefits, or satisfactions offered for sale that are essentially intangible and do not result in the ownership of anything. Examples are banking, hotel accommodation, tax preparation, and home repair services. We shall look at services more closely later in this chapter.

Products, Services, and Experiences

Products are a key element in the *market offering*. Marketing-mix planning begins with formulating an offering that brings value to target customers and satisfies their needs. This offering becomes the basis upon which the company builds profitable relationships with customers.

A company's market offering often includes both tangible goods and services. Each component can be a minor or a major part of the total offer. At one extreme, the offer may consist of a *pure tangible good,* such as soap, toothpaste, or salt—no services accompany the product. At the other extreme are *pure services,* for which the offer consists primarily of a service. Examples include a doctor's exam or financial services. Between these two extremes, however, many goods-and-services combinations are possible.

Today, as products and services become more commoditized, many companies are moving to a new level in creating value for their customers. To differentiate their offers, they are developing and delivering total customer *experiences.* Whereas products are tangible and services are intangible, experiences are memorable. Whereas products and services are external, experiences are personal and take place in the minds of individual consumers. Companies that market experiences realize that customers are really buying much more than just products and services. They are buying what those offers will do for them (see Real Marketing 10.1).[2]

Core product

The problem-solving services or core benefits that consumers are really buying when they obtain a product.

Levels of Product

Product planners need to think about products and services on three levels (see Figure 10.1 on page 380). Each level adds more customer value. The most basic level is the **core product**, which addresses the question: *What is the buyer really buying?*

REAL MARKETING

10.1 Beyond Products and Services: Welcome to the Experience Economy

In their book *The Experience Economy,* Joseph Pine and James Gilmore argue that, as products and services become less differentiated, companies are moving to a new level in creating value for customers. Beyond simply making products and delivering services, companies are staging, marketing, and delivering memorable experiences. Consider the evolution of the birthday cake:

Sony's Metreon markets an "interactive entertainment experience."

[In an] *agrarian* economy, mothers made birthday cakes from scratch, mixing farm commodities (flour, sugar, butter, and eggs) that together cost mere dimes. As the *goods-based* industrial economy advanced, moms paid a dollar or two to Betty Crocker for premixed ingredients. Later, when the *service* economy took hold, busy parents ordered cakes from the bakery or grocery store, which, at $10 or $15, cost ten times as much as the packaged ingredients. Now,...time-starved parents neither make the birthday cake nor even throw the party. Instead, they spend $100 or more to "outsource" the entire event to Chuck E. Cheese's, The Mining Company, McDonald's, the Discovery Zone, the Rainforest Café, or some other business that stages a memorable event for the kids—and often throws in the cake for free. Welcome to the emerging *experience* economy.... From now on, leading-edge companies—whether they sell to consumers or businesses—will find that the next competitive battleground lies in staging experiences.

Experiences are sometimes confused with services, but experiences are as distinct from services as services are distinct from goods. Whereas products and services are external, experiences exist only in the mind of the individual. They are rich with emotional, physical, intellectual, or spiritual sensations created within the consumer. According to Pine and Gilmore:

An experience occurs when a company intentionally uses services as the stage, and goods as props, to engage individual customers in a way that creates a memorable event.... To appreciate the difference between services and experiences, recall the episode of the old television show *Taxi* in which Iggy, a usually atrocious (but fun-loving) cab driver, decided to become the best taxi driver in the world. He served sandwiches and drinks, conducted tours of the city, and even sang Frank Sinatra tunes. By engaging passengers in a way that turned an ordinary cab ride into a memorable event, Iggy created something else entirely—a distinct economic offering. The experience of riding in his cab was more valuable to his customers than the service of being transported by the cab—and in the TV show, at least, Iggy's customers happily responded by giving bigger tips. By asking to go around the block again, one patron even paid more for poorer service just to prolong his enjoyment. The service Iggy provided—taxi transportation—was simply the stage for the experience that he was really selling.

Experiences have always been important in the entertainment industry—Disney has long manufactured memories through its movies and theme parks. Today, however, all kinds of firms are recasting their traditional goods and services to create experiences. For example, restaurants create value well beyond the food they serve. Starbucks patrons are paying for more than just coffee. "Customers at Starbucks are paying for staged experiences," comments one analyst. "The company treats patrons to poetry on its wallpaper and tabletops, jaunty apron-clad performers behind the espresso machine, and an interior ambience that's both cozy and slick, marked by earth tones, brushed steel, and retro music (also for sale). Few people leave without feeling a little more affluent, sophisticated, or jazzed."

Many retailers also stage experiences. Niketown stores create "shoppertainment" by offering interactive displays, engaging activities, and promotional events in a stimulating shopping environment. Newer Loblaws stores have the visual appeal of small town markets. In their upstairs cafés, shoppers can enjoy a cup of coffee while listening to a live string quartet one day, a country and western band the next. Toronto-based Playdium Entertainment's 29 Canadian locations bill themselves as "entertainment centres." While some might call them hyped-up video arcades, Playdium's goal is to make game playing a rich and engaging experience, not just an addictive pastime. Much of the distinction between arcade and "entertainment centre" comes down to the way in which the experience is packaged, according to Playdium's design consultants: "We wanted to create an immersive environment." Walking into a Playdium centre is a visual experience. Graphic displays serve to heighten the energy and excitement of the place while working to guide visitors from one zone—for example, Speed, Sports, Music, Kids—to the next. "The fun of the game should start long before people start playing," the design team notes.

Similarly, in San Francisco, Sony of America developed Metreon, an "interactive entertainment experience," where visitors can shop, eat, drink, play, or simply soak up the experiences (check it out at www.metreon.com). The huge Metreon complex features 17 theatres, including a Sony-IMAX theatre, eight restaurants, and several interactive attractions, such as "Where the Wild Things Are" (an interactive playspace inspired by Maurice Sendak's popular children's book) and Moebius's Airtight Garage (an adventure zone featuring original interactive games based on the work of French graphic novelist Jean Giraud). Visitors can also experience any of nine interactive stores, including the flagship Discovery Channel Store: Destination San Francisco (featuring interactive educational exhibits inspired by programming from the Discovery Channel, TLC, and Animal Planet cable networks), Sony Style (a high-touch boutique of Sony products), and microsoftSF (where shoppers can play with the latest computer software and hardware). In all, Metreon offers a dazzling experience that far transcends the goods and services assortment it contains.

The experience economy goes beyond the entertainment and retailing businesses. All companies stage experiences whenever they engage customers in a personal, memorable way:

> In the travel business, former British Airways chairman Sir Colin Marshall has noted that the "commodity mindset" is to "think that a business is merely performing a function—in our case, transporting people from point A to point B on time and at the lowest possible price." What British Airways does, according to Sir Colin, is "to go beyond the function and compete on the basis of providing an experience." The company uses its base service (the travel itself) as the stage for a distinctive en route experience—one that attempts to transform air travel into a respite from the traveller's normally frenetic life.

Business-to-business marketers also stage experiences for their customers. For example, one computer installation and repair company has found a way to turn its otherwise humdrum service into a memorable encounter. Calling itself the Geek Squad, it sends "special agents" dressed in white shirts with thin black ties and pocket protectors, carrying badges, and driving old cars.

Thus, as we move into the twenty-first century, marketers seeking new ways to bring value to customers must look beyond the goods and services they make and sell. They must find ways to turn their offers into total customer experiences. As the experience economy grows, Pine and Gilmore caution, it "threatens to render irrelevant those who relegate themselves to the diminishing world of goods and services."

Sources: Excerpts and quotes from "Welcome to the Experience Economy," *Harvard Business Review,* July–August 1998, pp. 97–105; Wade Roush, "Now Playing: Your Business," *Technology Review,* May–June 1999, p. 96; Wendy Cuthbert, "Playdium Creates Order from Chaos," *Strategy,* March 13, 2000, p. 24; and Sony's Metreon website, www.metreon.com, (accessed August 2002). Also see B. Joseph Pine and James H. Gilmore, *The Experience Economy* (New York: Free Press, 1999); Scott Mac Stravic, "Make Impressions Last: Focus on Value," *Marketing News,* October 23, 2000, pp. 44–45; and Stephen E. DeLong, "The Experience Economy," *Upside,* November 2001, p. 28.

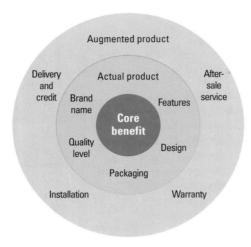

Figure 10.1 Three levels of product

When designing products, marketers must first define the core, problem-solving benefits that consumers seek when they buy a product. A woman buying lipstick buys more than lip colour. Charles Revson of Revlon recognized this early: "In the factory, we make cosmetics; in the store, we sell hope." London Life sells more than insurance and investment products—they sell financial freedom.

At the second level, product planners must turn the core benefit into an **actual product**. They need to develop product and service features, design, a quality level, a brand name, and packaging. For example, a Sony camcorder is an actual product. Its name, parts, styling, features, packaging, and other attributes have all been combined carefully to deliver the core benefit—a convenient, high-quality way to capture important moments.

Actual product

A product's parts, quality level, features, design, brand name, packaging, and other attributes that combine to deliver core product benefits.

Core, actual, and augmented product: Consumers perceive this Sony camcorder as a complex bundle of tangible and intangible features and services that deliver a core benefit—a convenient, high-quality way to capture important moments.

Augmented product

Additional consumer services and benefits built around the core benefit and actual product.

Finally, the product planner must build an **augmented product** around the core benefit and actual product by offering additional consumer services and benefits. Sony must offer more than just a camcorder. It must provide consumers with a complete solution to their picture-taking needs. Thus, when consumers buy a Sony camcorder, Sony and its dealers also might give buyers a warranty on parts and workmanship, instructions on how to use the camcorder, quick repair services when needed, and a toll-free telephone number to call if they have problems or questions.

Consumers tend to see products as complex bundles of benefits that satisfy their needs. When developing products, marketers first must identify the *core* consumer needs the product will satisfy. They must then design the *actual* product and find ways to *augment* it to create the bundle of benefits that will provide the most satisfying customer experience.

Product and Service Classifications

Products and services fall into two broad classes based on the types of consumers that use them—*consumer products* and *industrial products*. Broadly defined, products also include other marketable entities such as experiences, organizations, persons, places, and ideas.

Consumer Products

Consumer product

Product bought by final consumer for personal consumption.

Consumer products are those bought by final consumers for personal consumption. Marketers usually classify these goods further based on *how consumers go about buying them*. Consumer products include *convenience products, shopping products, specialty products*, and *unsought products*. Since these products differ in the ways consumers buy them, they differ in how they are marketed (see Table 10.1).

Convenience product

Consumer product that the customer usually buys frequently, immediately, and with a minimum of comparison and buying effort.

Convenience products are consumer products and services that the customer usually buys frequently, immediately, and with a minimum of comparison and buying effort. Examples include soap, candy, newspapers, and fast food. Convenience products are usually low priced, and marketers place them in many locations to

Table 10.1 Marketing Considerations for Consumer Products

Marketing Considerations	Type of Consumer Product			
	Convenience	**Shopping**	**Specialty**	**Unsought**
Customer buying behaviour	Frequent purchase, little planning, little comparison or shopping effort, low customer involvement	Less frequent purchase, much planning and shopping effort, comparison of brands on suitability, price, quality, design	Strong brand preference and loyalty, special purchase effort, little comparison of brands, low price sensitivity	Little product awareness, knowledge (or if aware, little or even negative interest)
Price	Low price	Higher price	High price	Varies
Place	Widespread distribution in convenient locations	Selective distribution in fewer outlets	Exclusive distribution in only one or a few outlets per market area	Varies
Promotion	Mass promotion by the producer	Advertising and personal selling by both producer and resellers	More carefully targeted promotion by both producer and resellers	Aggressive advertising and personal selling by producer and resellers
Examples	Toothpaste, magazines, laundry detergent	Major appliances, televisions, furniture, clothing	Luxury goods, such as Rolex watches or fine crystal	Life insurance, dental services

Mad River® did a masterful job connecting this convenience product to the lives of the target market.

Shopping product
Consumer good that the customer, in the process of selection and purchase, characteristically compares on such bases as suitability, quality, price, and design.

Specialty product
Consumer product with unique characteristics or brand identification for which a significant group of buyers is willing to make a special purchase effort.

Unsought products
Consumer products and services that the consumer either does not know about or knows about but does not normally think of buying.

Industrial product
Product bought by individuals and organizations for further processing or for use in conducting a business.

make them readily available when customers need them. Selling convenience products doesn't have to be bland or boring. Ads for Mad River® beverages (owned by the Coca-Cola Company) helped boost sales among Canadian outdoor enthusiasts.

Shopping products are less frequently purchased consumer products and services that customers compare carefully on suitability, quality, price, and design. When buying shopping products, consumers spend much time and effort in gathering information and making comparisons. Examples include furniture, clothing, used cars, major appliances, hotel and airlines services, vacations, and restaurant meals. Shopping product marketers usually distribute their products through fewer outlets but provide deeper sales support to help consumers in their comparisons.

Specialty products are consumer products and services with unique characteristics or brand identification for which a significant group of buyers is willing to make a special purchase effort. Examples include specific brands and types of cars, high-priced photographic equipment, designer clothes, and the services of legal or investment specialists. A Lamborghini automobile, for example, is a specialty product because buyers are usually willing to travel great distances to buy one. Buyers normally do not compare specialty products. They invest only the time needed to reach dealers carrying the wanted products.

Unsought products are consumer products and services that the consumer either does not know about or knows about but does not normally think of buying. Most major innovations are unsought until the consumer becomes aware of them through advertising. Classic examples of known but unsought products are life insurance, funeral plans, and blood donations. By their very nature, unsought products require a lot of advertising, personal selling, and other marketing efforts.

Industrial Products

Industrial products are those products and services purchased for further processing or for use in conducting a business. Thus, the distinction between a consumer product and an industrial product is based on the *purpose* for which the product is bought. If a consumer buys a lawn mower for use around home, the lawn mower is a consumer product. If the same consumer buys the same lawn mower for use in a landscaping business, the lawn mower is an industrial product.

The three groups of industrial products include materials and parts, capital items, and supplies and services. *Materials and parts* include raw materials and manufactured materials and parts. Raw materials consist of farm products (wheat, cotton, livestock, fruits, vegetables) and natural products (fish, lumber, crude petroleum, iron ore). Manufactured materials and parts consist of component materials (iron, yarn, cement, wires) and component parts (small motors, tires, castings). Most manufactured materials and parts are sold directly to industrial users. Price and service are the major marketing factors; branding and advertising tend to be less important.

Capital items are industrial products that aid in the buyer's production or operations, including installations and accessory equipment. Installations consist of major purchases such as buildings (factories, offices) and fixed equipment (generators, drill presses, large computer systems, elevators). Accessory equipment includes portable factory equipment and tools (hand tools, lift trucks) and office equipment (computers, fax machines, desks). They have a shorter life than installations and simply aid in the production process.

The final group of business products is *supplies and services*. Supplies include operating supplies (lubricants, coal, computer paper, pencils) and repair and maintenance items (paint, nails, brooms). Supplies are the convenience products of the industrial field because they usually are purchased with a minimum of effort or comparison. Business services include maintenance and repair services (window cleaning, computer repair) and business advisory services (legal, management consulting, advertising).

Organizations, Persons, Places, and Ideas

In addition to tangible products and services, in recent years marketers have broadened the concept of a product to include other "marketable offerings"—organizations, persons, places, and ideas.

Organizations often carry out activities to "sell" the organization itself. *Organization marketing* consists of activities undertaken to create, maintain, or change the attitudes and behaviour of target consumers toward an organization. Both for-profit and non-profit organizations practise organization marketing. Business firms sponsor public relations or corporate advertising campaigns to polish their images. *Corporate image advertising* is a major tool companies use to market themselves to various publics. For example, Lucent puts out ads with the tag-line "We make the things that make communications work." Domtar puts employees in its ads to create a "face" for the corporation and build better relationships, noting, "Paper needs people." And General Electric "brings good things to life." Similarly, non-profit organizations, such as churches, universities, charities, museums, and performing arts groups, market their organizations to raise funds and attract members or patrons.

People can also be thought of as products. *Person marketing* consists of activities undertaken to create, maintain, or change attitudes or behaviour toward particular people. All kinds of people and organizations practise person marketing. Prime ministers and provincial premiers skilfully market themselves, their parties, and their platforms to get needed votes and program support. Entertainers and sports figures use marketing to promote their careers and improve their impact and incomes. Professionals such as opera singers, dentists, lawyers, accountants, and architects market themselves to build their reputations and increase business. Businesses, charities, sports teams, fine arts groups, religious groups, and other organizations also use person marketing. Creating or associating with well-known personalities often helps these organizations achieve their goals better. That's why more than a dozen different companies combined—including Nike, Target, Buick, American Express, Disney, and Titleist—pay more than $65 million a year to link themselves with golf superstar Tiger Woods. And that's why DaimlerChrysler is paying Céline Dion tens of millions of dollars to give its products a classier image.[3]

Place marketing involves activities undertaken to create, maintain, or change attitudes or behaviour toward particular places. Cities, provinces, regions, and even entire nations compete to attract tourists, new residents, conventions, and company offices and factories. Travel Canada, Canada's multilingual tourism site, can be found at www.travelcanada.ca/travelcanada/app. It challenges Canadians and prospective tourists from around the world to "Discover our True Nature." Newfoundland describes itself as the place where "land, water and sky embrace like old friends…the edge of North America [that] holds an adventure as big as the sky." The Irish Development Agency has attracted more than 1200 companies to locate their plants in Ireland. At the same time, the Irish Tourist Board has built a flourishing tourism business by advertising "…a different life: friendly, beautiful, relaxing." And the Irish Export Board has created attractive markets for Irish exports.[4]

Ideas also can be marketed. In one sense, all marketing is the marketing of an idea, whether it is the general idea of brushing your teeth or the specific idea that Crest provides the most effective decay prevention. Here, however, we narrow our focus to the marketing of *social ideas*. This area has been called **social marketing**, defined by the Social Marketing Institute as the use of commercial marketing concepts and tools in programs designed to influence individuals' behaviour to improve their well-being and that of society.[5] Such programs include public health campaigns to reduce smoking, alcoholism, drug abuse, and overeating. Other social marketing efforts include environmental campaigns to promote wilderness protection, clean air, and conservation. Still others address issues such as family planning, human rights, and racial equality.

 The Canadian Landmine Foundation (www.canadianlandmine.org) used a TV campaign and event marketing titled the "Night of a Thousand Dinners." During the annual one-night event, individuals host dinner parties to raise funds for the Adopt-a-Minefield program. This Canadian-led initiative is now used in more than 30 countries. The Ad Council of America has developed dozens of social advertising campaigns, including classics such as "Only You Can Prevent Forest Fires," "Friends Don't Let Friends Drive Drunk," "Say No to Drugs," and "A Mind Is a Terrible Thing to Waste" (www.adcouncil.org). Toronto-based Covenant House, Canada's largest youth shelter, brought home the message that many kids are homeless with an award-winning poster campaign (www.covenanthouse.on.ca). But social marketing involves much more than just advertising. The Social Marketing Institute encourages the use of a broad range of marketing. tools. "Social marketing goes well beyond the promotional 'P' of the marketing mix to include every other element to achieve its social change objectives," says the SMI's executive director.[6]

Social marketing

The design, implementation, and control of programs seeking to increase the acceptability of a social idea, cause, or practice within targeted groups.

Product and Service Decisions

Marketers make product and service decisions at three levels: individual product and service decisions, product line decisions, and product mix decisions. We discuss each in turn.

Individual Product and Service Decisions

Figure 10.2 shows the important decisions in the development and marketing of individual products. We shall focus on decisions about *product and service attributes, branding, packaging, labelling,* and *product support services.*

Covenant House, Canada's largest youth shelter, won awards for its hard-hitting campaign that brought attention to the problem of homeless youth.

NOT ALL KIDS WANT THE SAME THING FOR CHRISTMAS.

COVENANT HOUSE 1-800-HELP-308

Product and Service Attributes

Developing a product or service involves defining the benefits that the product will offer. These benefits are communicated and delivered by such product attributes as *quality*, *features*, and *style and design*.

Product quality

The ability of a product to perform its functions; it includes the product's overall durability, reliability, precision, ease of operation and repair, and other valued attributes.

Product Quality **Product quality** is one of the marketer's major positioning tools. Quality has a direct impact on product or service performance; thus, it is closely linked to customer value and satisfaction. In the narrowest sense, quality can be defined as "freedom from defects." But most customer-centred companies go beyond this narrow definition. Instead, they define quality in terms of customer satisfaction. Siemens, for example, defines quality this way: "Quality is when our customers come back and our products don't."[7] These customer-focused definitions suggest that quality begins with customer needs and ends with customer satisfaction.

Total quality management (TQM) is an approach in which all the company's people are involved in constantly improving the quality of products, services, and business processes. During the past two decades, companies large and small have credited TQM with greatly improving their market shares and profits. Recently, however, the total quality management movement has drawn criticism. Too many companies viewed TQM as a magic cure-all and created token total quality programs that applied quality principles only superficially. Still others became obsessed with narrowly defined TQM principles and lost sight of broader concerns for customer value and satisfaction. As a result, many such programs failed, causing a backlash against TQM.

Figure 10.2 Individual product and service decisions

Product and service attributes → Branding → Packaging → Labelling → Product support services

When applied in the context of creating customer satisfaction, however, total quality principles remain a requirement for success. Although many firms don't use the TQM label anymore, for most top companies customer-driven quality has become a way of doing business. Today, companies are taking a "return on quality" approach, viewing quality as an investment and holding quality efforts accountable for bottom-line results.[8]

Product quality has two dimensions—level and consistency. In developing a product, the marketer must first choose a *quality level* that will support the product's position in the target market. Here, product quality means *performance quality*—the ability of a product to perform its functions. For example, a Rolls Royce provides higher performance quality than a Chevrolet: It has a smoother ride, handles better, and lasts longer. Companies rarely try to offer the highest-possible performance quality level—few customers want or can afford the high levels of quality offered in products such as a Rolls-Royce automobile, a Sub-Zero refrigerator, or a Rolex watch. Instead, companies choose a quality level that matches target market needs and the quality levels of competing products.

Beyond quality level, high quality also can mean high levels of quality *consistency*. Here, product quality means *conformance quality*—freedom from defects and *consistency* in delivering a targeted level of performance. All companies should strive for high levels of conformance quality. In this sense, a Chevrolet can have just as much quality as a Rolls Royce. Although a Chevy doesn't perform as well as a Rolls, it can consistently deliver the quality that customers pay for and expect.

Many companies today have turned customer-driven quality into a potent strategic weapon. They create customer satisfaction and value by consistently and profitably meeting customers' needs and preferences for quality. In fact, quality has now become a competitive necessity—in the twenty-first century, only companies with the best quality will thrive.

Product Features   A product can be offered with varying features. A "stripped-down" model, one without any extras, is the starting point. The company can create higher-level models by adding more features. Features are a competitive tool for differentiating the company's product from competitors' products. Being the first producer to introduce a needed and valued new feature is one of the most effective ways to compete.

How can a company identify new features and decide which ones to add to its product? The company should periodically survey buyers who have used the product and ask these questions: How do you like the product? Which specific features of the product do you like most? Which features could we add to improve the product? The answers provide the company with a rich list of feature ideas. The company can then assess each feature's *value* to customers versus its *cost* to the company. Features that customers value little in relation to costs should be dropped; those that customers value highly in relation to costs should be added.

Product Style and Design   Another way to add customer value is through distinctive *product style and design*. Design is a larger concept than style. *Style* simply describes the appearance of a product. Styles can be eye-catching or yawn-inspiring. A sensational style and pleasing aesthetics may grab attention, but they do not necessarily make the product *perform* better. Unlike style, *design* is more than skin deep—it goes to the very heart of a product. Good design contributes to a product's usefulness as well as to its looks.

Good style and design can attract attention, improve product performance, cut production costs, and give the product a strong competitive advantage in the target market. Here are two examples:

Who said that computers have to be beige and boxy? Apple's iMac is anything but. The first iMac—which featured a sleek, egg-shaped monitor and hard drive, all in one unit, in a futuristic translucent turquoise casing—redefined the

Product design: The design of the dramatic iMac helped re-establish Apple as a legitimate contender in the PC industry. The innovative Discover 2GO card is a gotta-have-it accessory for people who want to dash off to the gym, the mall, or a restaurant with nothing more than their keys and a credit card.

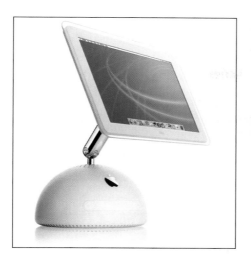

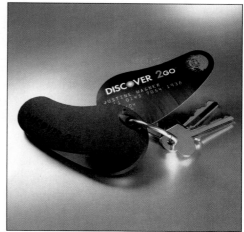

look and feel of the personal computer. There was no clunky tower or desktop hard drive to clutter up your office area. Featuring one-button Internet access, this machine was designed specifically for cruising the Internet (that's what the "i" in "iMac" stands for). The dramatic iMac won raves for design and lured buyers in droves. Within a year, it had sold more than a million units, marking Apple's re-emergence in the personal computer industry. Four years later, Apple did it again with a stunning new iMac design—a clean, futuristic machine featuring a flat-panel display that seems to float in the air. Within only three months, Apple-lovers had snapped up nearly one-quarter million of these eye-pleasing yet functional machines.[9]

You turn the flat, kidney-shaped plastic gadget over in your hands, puzzling over what it does. Then you realize that a sliver of red plastic pivots out of the black case like a pocket-knife blade. You recognize a familiar strand of embossed numbers, a magnetic stripe, and a signature bar. It's a credit card! To be precise, it's a Discover 2GO card, complete with a key chain, belt clip, and protective case. In consumer terms, the Discover 2GO card is a gotta-have-it accessory for people who want to dash off to the gym, the mall, or a restaurant with nothing more than their keys and a credit card. In industry terms, it's a big design innovation in a business that has rarely thought much outside the two-by-three-inch box. The new design has drawn praise from card marketing experts. "This is slick. It's different, which is good. And it's functional," says one consultant. "It's the card you'll use when you have your keys in your hand."[10]

Branding

Perhaps the most distinctive skill of professional marketers is their ability to create, maintain, protect, and enhance brands for their products and services. A **brand** is a name, term, sign, symbol, or design, or a combination of these, that identifies the maker or seller of a product or service. Canada's *Report on Business* magazine conducted an international poll in 2000 to determine what were the greatest logos of all time. Want to guess the winners? The Michelin Man took the number one spot, and the London underground logo followed as number two. In third place was a non-profit logo, the Red Cross. The Nike swoosh, a symbol designed to convey speed and movement, grabbed fourth place, while the Volkswagen logo, the icon for the "people's car," drove into fifth spot. Canadian brand logos were among the top 50: the Esso logo was given twenty-eighth place and CN's logo took thirty-eighth spot.[11]

Brand
A name, term, sign, symbol, or design, or a combination of these, intended to identify the goods or services of one seller or group of sellers and to differentiate them from those of competitors.

Branding has become so strong that hardly anything goes unbranded, even fruits and vegetables.

Consumers view a brand as an important part of a product, and branding can add value to a product. For example, most consumers would perceive a bottle of White Linen perfume as a high-quality, expensive product. But the same perfume in an unmarked bottle would likely be viewed as lower in quality, even if the fragrance were identical.

Branding has become so important that today hardly anything goes unbranded. Salt is packaged in branded containers; common nuts and bolts are packaged with a distributor's label, and automobile parts—spark plugs, tires, filters—bear brand names that differ from those of the automakers. Even fruits and vegetables are branded—Sunkist oranges, Dole pineapples, Chiquita bananas, Fresh Express salad greens, and Perdue chickens.

Branding helps buyers in many ways. Brand names help consumers identify products that might benefit them. Brands also tell the buyer something about product quality. Buyers who always buy the same brand know that they will get the same features, benefits, and quality each time they buy. Branding also gives the seller several advantages. The brand name becomes the basis on which a whole story can be built about a product's special qualities. The seller's brand name and trademark provide legal protection for unique product features that otherwise might be copied by competitors. And branding helps the seller to segment markets. For example, General Mills can offer Cheerios, Wheaties, Total, Lucky Charms, and many other cereal brands, not just one general product for all consumers.

Building and managing brands is perhaps the marketer's most important task. We will discuss branding strategy in more detail later in the chapter.

Packaging

Packaging
The activities of designing and producing the container or wrapper for a product.

Packaging involves designing and producing the container or wrapper for a product. The package includes the product's primary container (the tube holding Colgate toothpaste). It may also include a secondary package that is thrown away when the product is about to be used (the cardboard box containing the toothpaste). Finally, it can include the shipping package necessary to store, identify, and ship the product (a corrugated box carrying six dozen tubes of Colgate toothpaste). Labelling—printed information appearing on or with the package—is also part of packaging.

Traditionally, the primary function of the package was to contain and protect the product. In recent times, however, numerous factors have made packaging an important marketing tool. Increased competition and clutter on retail store shelves mean that packages must perform many sales tasks—from attracting attention, to describing the product, to making the sale.

Companies are realizing the power of good packaging to create instant consumer recognition of the company or brand. For example, in an average supermarket that stocks 15 000 to 17 000 items, the typical shopper passes by some 300 items per minute, and more than 60 percent of all purchases are made on impulse. In this highly competitive environment, the package may be the seller's last chance to influence buyers. It becomes a "five-second commercial." The Campbell Soup Company estimates that the average shopper sees its familiar red and white can 76 times a year, creating the equivalent of $30 million worth of advertising.[12]

Innovative packaging can give a company an advantage over competitors. In contrast, poorly designed packages can cause headaches for consumers and lost sales for the company (see Real Marketing 10.2). For example, Planters LifeSavers Company attempted to use innovative packaging to create an association between fresh-roasted peanuts and fresh-roasted coffee. It packaged its Fresh Roast Salted Peanuts in vacuum-packed "Brik-Pacs" similar to those used for ground coffee. Unfortunately, the coffee-like packaging worked too well: consumers mistook the peanuts for a new brand of flavoured coffee and ran them through supermarket coffee-grinding machines, creating a gooey mess, disappointed customers, and lots of irate store managers.[13]

Developing a good package for a new product requires making many decisions. First, the company must establish the *packaging concept,* which states what the package should *be* or *do* for the product. Should it mainly offer product protection, introduce a new dispensing method, suggest certain qualities about the product or the company, or do something else? Decisions then must be made on specific elements of the package, such as size, shape, materials, colour, text, and brand mark.

In recent years, product safety has also become a major packaging concern. We have all learned to deal with hard-to-open "childproof" packages. After the rash of product tampering scares in the 1980s, most drug producers and food makers are now putting their products in tamper-resistant packages. In making packaging decisions, the company must also heed environmental concerns. Fortunately, many companies have gone "green" by reducing their packaging and using environmentally responsible materials. For example, SC Johnson repackaged Agree Plus shampoo in a stand-up pouch using 80 percent less plastic. P&G eliminated outer cartons from its Secret and Sure deodorants, saving 1.5 million kilograms of paperboard per year.

Labelling

Labels may range from simple tags attached to products to complex graphics that are part of the package. They perform several functions. At the very least, the label *identifies* the product or brand, such as the name *Sunkist* stamped on oranges. The label may also *describe* several things about the product—who made it, where it was made, when it was made, its contents, how it is to be used, and how to use it safely. Finally, the label may *promote* the product with attractive graphics.

There has been a long history of legal and ethical concerns about labels. Labels have the potential to mislead customers, fail to describe important ingredients, and fail to include needed safety warnings. Labelling regulations depend on the type of product being sold. Canada's *Consumer Packaging and Labelling Act,* which covers many non-food products, was passed to protect consumers from labelling or packaging that is false or misleading. The *Weights and Measures Act* deals with the units of measurement on labels. The Government of Canada's "Consumer Packaging and Labelling" page (see www.strategis.ic.gc.ca) details the requirements for the principal display panel of prepackaged, non-food consumer products.

10.2 Those Frustrating, Not-So-Easy-to-Open Packages

*S*ome things, it seems, will never change. This classic letter from an angry consumer to Robert D. Stuart, then chairman of Quaker Oats, beautifully expresses the utter frustration all of us have experienced in dealing with so-called easy-to-open packages.

Dear Mr. Stuart:

I am an 86-year-old widow in fairly good health. (You may think of this as advanced age, but for me, that description pertains to the years ahead. Nevertheless, if you decide to reply to this letter I wouldn't dawdle, actuarial tables being what they are.)

As I said, my health is fairly good. Feeble and elderly, as one understands these terms, I am not. My two Doberman pinschers and I take a brisk three-mile walk every day. They are two strong and energetic animals, and it takes a bit of doing to keep "brisk" closer to a stroll than a mad dash. But I manage because as yet I don't lack the strength. You will shortly see why this fact is relevant.

I am writing to call your attention to the cruel, deceptive, and utterly [false] copy on your Aunt Jemima buttermilk complete pancake and waffle mix. The words on your package read, "to open—press here and pull back."

Mr. Stuart, though I push and press and groan and strive and writhe and curse and sweat and jab and push, poke and ram...whew!—I have never once been able to do what the package instructs—to "press here and pull back" the [blankety-blank]. It can't be done! Talk about failing strength! Have you ever tried and succeeded?

My late husband was a gun collector who among other lethal weapons kept a Thompson machine gun in a locked cabinet. It was a good thing that the cabinet was locked. Oh, the number of times I was tempted to give your package a few short bursts.

The lock and a sense of ladylike delicacy kept me from pursuing that vengeful fantasy. Instead, I keep a small cleaver in my pantry for those occasions when I need to open a package of your delicious Aunt Jemima pancakes.

For many years, that whacking away with my cleaver served a dual purpose. Not only to open the [blankety-blank] package but also to vent my fury at your sadists who wilfully and maliciously did design that torture apparatus that passes for a package.

Sometimes just for the [blank] of it I let myself get carried away. I don't stop after I've lopped off the top. I whack away until the package is utterly destroyed in an outburst of rage, frustration, and vindictiveness. I wind up with a floorful of your delicious Aunt Jemima pancake mix. But that's a small price to pay for blessed release. (Anyway, the pinschers lap up the mess.)

So many ingenious, considerate (even compassionate) innovations in package closures have been designed since Aunt Jemima first donned her red bandana. Wouldn't you consider the introduction of a more humane package to replace the example of marketing malevolence to which you resolutely cling? Don't you care, Mr. Stuart?

I'm really writing this to be helpful and in that spirit I am sending a copy to Mr. Tucker, president of Container Corp. I'm sure their clever young designers could be of immeasurable help to you in this matter. At least I feel it's worth a try.

Really, Mr. Stuart, I hope you will not regard me as just another cranky old biddy. I am The Public, the source of your fortunes.

Ms. Roberta Pavloff
Malvern, PA

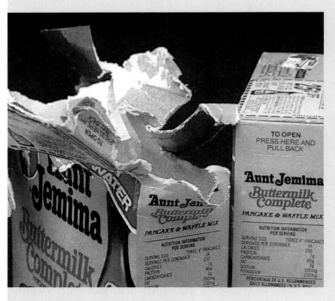

An easy-to-open package?

Source: This letter was reprinted in "Some Designs Should Just Be Torn Asunder," *Advertising Age*, January 17, 1983, p. M54.

Innovative labelling can help to promote a product.

Consumer advocates have long lobbied for additional legislation that would require more informative food labelling and the efforts have finally met with success. Starting in January 2003, Canadians saw a lot more information on food packaging labels as a result of new government legislation. It became mandatory for food labels to display *Nutrition Facts*, a table that lists calories and 13 key nutrients. Specifically labels must list the amount of fat, saturated and *trans* fats, cholesterol, sodium, carbohydrate, fibre, sugars, protein, vitamins A and C, calcium, and iron in a specified amount of food. "Nutritional information is essential to helping Canadians make informed choices for healthy living," Health Minister Anne McLellan noted. "The *Nutrition Facts* table will allow Canadians to compare products more easily, assess the nutritional value of more foods and better manage special diets." Labels also must be in an easy-to-read, standardized format.[14]

Product Support Services

Customer service is another element of product strategy. A company's offer to the marketplace usually includes some support services, which can be a minor or a major part of the total offering. Later in the chapter we discuss services as products in themselves. Here, we discuss services that augment actual products.

A company's first step is to survey customers periodically to assess the value of current services and to obtain ideas for new ones. For example, Cadillac holds regular focus group interviews with owners and carefully watches complaints that come into its dealerships. From this careful monitoring, Cadillac has learned that buyers are very upset by repairs that are not done correctly the first time.

Once the company has assessed the value of various support services to customers, it must assess the costs of providing these services. It can then develop a package of services that will both delight customers and yield profits to the company. Based on its consumer interviews, Cadillac set up a system directly linking each dealership with a group of 10 engineers who can help mechanics with difficult repairs. Such actions helped Cadillac jump, in one year, from fourteenth to seventh in independent rankings of service.[15]

Many companies are now using the Internet and other modern technologies to provide support services that were not possible before. Using the Web, 24-hour telephone help lines, self-service kiosks, and other digital technologies, these companies are now empowering consumers to tailor their own service and support experiences. Pratt & Whitney Canada, the world's leading producer of engines for corporate jets, commuter aircraft, and helicopters, uses its website to provide information on engine maintenance. Transportation companies like Air Canada and Via Rail provide support services for their frequent users and members of their loyalty programs. Members can book tickets, check the status of their frequent flyer accounts, and take advantage of special member fares.

Product Line Decisions

Product line

A group of products that are closely related because they function in a similar manner, are sold to the same customer groups, are marketed through the same types of outlets, or fall within given price ranges.

Beyond decisions about individual products, product strategy also calls for building a product line. A **product line** is a group of products that are closely related because they function in a similar manner, are sold to the same customer groups, are marketed through the same types of outlets, or fall within given price ranges. For example, Nike produces several lines of athletic shoes, Nortel produces several lines of telecommunication products, Nokia produces several lines of telecommunication products, and Charles Schwab produces several lines of financial services.

The major product line decision involves *product line length*—the number of items in the product line. The line is too short if the manager can increase profits by adding items; the line is too long if the manager can increase profits by dropping items. The company should manage its product lines carefully. Product lines tend to lengthen over time, and most companies eventually prune unnecessary or unprofitable items or services from their lines to increase overall profitability. Product line length is influenced by company objectives and resources. For example, one objective might be to allow for upselling. Thus BMW wants to move customers up from its 3-series models to 5- and 7-series models. Another objective might be to allow cross-selling: Hewlett-Packard sells printers as well as cartridges. Still another objective might be to protect against economic swings: Gap runs several clothing-store chains (Gap, Old Navy, Banana Republic) covering different price points.

A company can lengthen its product line in two ways: by *product line stretching* or by *product line filling*. *Product line stretching* occurs when a company lengthens its product line beyond its current range. The company can stretch its line downward, upward, or both ways.

Companies located at the upper end of the market can stretch their lines *downward*. A company may stretch downward to plug a market hole that otherwise would attract a new competitor or to respond to a competitor's attack on the upper end. Or it may add low-end products because it finds faster growth taking place in the low-end segments. DaimlerChrysler stretched its Mercedes line downward for all these reasons. Facing a slow-growth luxury car market and attacks by Japanese automakers on its high-end positioning, it successfully introduced its Mercedes C-Class cars. These models sell at less than $40 000 without harming the firm's ability to sell other Mercedes for $130 000 or more (www.mercedes-benz.com). Similarly, Rolex launched its Rolex Tudor watch retailing for about $1750, compared with a Rolex Submariner, usually priced at $5000.[16]

Companies at the lower end of the market can stretch their product lines *upward*. Sometimes, companies stretch upward in order to add prestige to their current products. Or they may be attracted by a faster growth rate or higher margins at the higher end. For example, each of the leading Japanese auto companies introduced an upmarket automobile: Toyota launched Lexus, Nissan launched Infiniti, and Honda launched Acura. They used entirely new names rather than their own names.

Companies in the middle range of the market may decide to stretch their lines in *both directions*. Marriott (www.marriott.com) did this with its hotel product line. Along with regular Marriott hotels, it added the Renaissance Hotels line to serve the upper end of the market and the TownePlace Suites line to serve the moderate and lower ends. Each branded hotel line is aimed at a different target market. Renaissance aims to attract and please top executives; Marriott, upper and middle

managers; Courtyard, salespeople and other "road warriors"; and Fairfield Inn, vacationers and business travellers on a tight travel budget. ExecuStay by Marriott provides temporary housing for those relocating or away on long-term assignments of 30 days or longer. Marriott's Residence Inn provides a relaxed, residential atmosphere—a home away from home for people who travel for a living. Marriott TownePlace Suites provide a comfortable atmosphere at a moderate price for extended-stay travellers.[17] The major risk with this strategy is that some travellers will trade down after finding that the lower-price hotels in the Marriott chain give them pretty much everything they want. However, Marriott would rather capture its customers who move downward than lose them to competitors.

An alternative to product line stretching is *product line filling*—adding more items within the present range of the line. There are several reasons for product line filling: reaching for extra profits, satisfying dealers, using excess capacity, being the leading full-line company, and plugging holes to keep out competitors. Sony filled its Walkman line by adding solar-powered and waterproof Walkmans, an ultralight model that attaches to a sweatband for exercisers, the MiniDisc Walkman, the CD Walkman, and the Memory Stick Walkman, which enables users to download tracks straight from the Net. However, line filling is overdone if it results in cannibalization and customer confusion. The company should ensure that new items are noticeably different from existing ones.

Product Mix Decisions

Product mix (product assortment)

The set of all product lines and items that a particular seller offers for sale.

An organization with several product lines has a product mix. A **product mix** (or **product assortment**) is the set of all product lines and items that a particular seller offers for sale. Avon's product mix consists of four major product lines: beauty products, wellness products, jewellery and accessories, and "inspirational" products (gifts, books, music, and home accents). Each product line consists of several sublines. For example, the beauty line breaks down into makeup, skin care, bath and beauty, fragrance, and outdoor protection products. Each line and subline has many individual items. Altogether, Avon's product mix includes 1300 items. In contrast, a typical Kmart stocks 15 000 items, 3M markets more than 60 000 products, and General Electric manufactures as many as 250 000 items.

A company's product mix has four important dimensions: width, length, depth, and consistency. Product mix *width* refers to the number of different product lines the company carries. Procter & Gamble markets a fairly wide product mix consisting of 250 brands organized into many product lines. These lines include fabric and home care, baby care, feminine care, beauty care, health care, and food and beverage products. Product mix *length* refers to the total number of items the company carries within its product lines. P&G typically carries many brands within each line. For example, it sells seven laundry detergents, six hand soaps, five shampoos, and four dishwashing detergents.

Product line *depth* refers to the number of versions offered of each product in the line. Thus, P&G's Crest toothpaste comes in 13 varieties, ranging from Crest Multicare, Crest Cavity Protection, and Crest Tartar Protection to Crest Sensitivity Protection, Crest Dual Action Whitening, Crest Whitening Plus Scope, Kid's Cavity Protection, and Crest Baking Soda & Peroxide Whitening formulations.[18] (Talk about niche marketing! Remember our Chapter 8 discussion?)

Table 10.2 illustrates these concepts with selected Procter & Gamble consumer products. The *width* of P&G's product mix refers to the number of different product lines the company carries. The table shows a product mix width of six lines. (In fact, P&G produces many more lines, including mouthwashes, paper products, disposable diapers, health-care products, and cosmetics.) The *length* of P&G's product mix refers to the total number of items the company carries. While P&G has over 300 brands, the table shows only 60 of these. We can also compute the average length of a line at P&G by dividing the total length (here 60) by the number of lines

Table 10.2 Product Mix Width and Product Line Length for Selected Procter & Gamble Products

	Fabric Care	Household Care	Deodorants	Personal Cleansing	Prestige Fragrances	Hair Care
Product Mix Width →						
	Tide Original Powder	Mr. Clean	Old Spice Deodorant	Camay	Hugo Boss	Head & Shoulders
	Ultra Tide Powder	Mr. Clean Top Job	Old Spice Red Zone	Ivory	Giorgio	Pantene Shampoo
	Liquid Tide	Mr. Clean Wipe-Ups	Secret	Ivory Moisture Care	Helmet Lang	Pantene Hair Spray
	Deep Clean Liquid Tide	Febreze	Sure	Zest	Herve Leger	Pert Plus
	Powder Ultra Tide with Bleach	Cascade		Olay Beauty Bar		Vidal Sassoon Shampoo
	Liquid Tide Mountain Spring	Cascade Rinse Aid		Coast		Vidal Sassoon Conditioner
	Gain Fresh Scent	Fit Fruit & Vegetable Wash		Olay Moisturizing Body Wash		Vidal Sassoon Styling Gel
	Tide Rapid Action Tablets	Dawn Dishwashing Liquid		Olay Cleanser		Physique Daily Defense
	Safeguard Conditioner	Febreze Clean Wash				
	Bounce	Ivory Dishwashing Liquid				
	Bounce Fresh Scent	Bold				
	Bounce Gentle Breeze	Joy Dishwashing Liquid				
	Bounce Free	Bold 3				
	Downy	Comet				
	Downy Premium Care	Cheer				
	Dryel	Spic & Span				
	Oxydol	Ivory Snow				
		Swiffer				

Product Line Length (vertical axis label on left)

(here 6). In the table, the average P&G product line consists of 10 brands. The *depth* of P&G's product mix refers to the number of versions offered of each product in the line. Thus, if Tide comes in three forms (powder, liquid, and tablets) and three formulations (regular, with bleach, scented), Tide has a depth of nine. By counting the number of versions within each brand, we can calculate the average depth of P&G's product mix.

Finally, the *consistency* of the product mix refers to how closely related the various product lines are in end use, production requirements, distribution channels, or in some other way. P&G's product lines are consistent insofar as they are consumer products. The lines are less consistent insofar as they perform different functions for buyers.

These product mix dimensions provide the handles for defining the company's product strategy. The company can increase its business in four ways. It can add new product lines, thus widening its product mix. In this way, its new lines build on the company's reputation in its other lines. The company can lengthen its existing product lines to become a more full-line company. Or it can add more product versions of each product and thus deepen its product mix. Finally, the company can pursue more product line consistency—or less—depending on whether it wants to have a strong reputation in a single field or in several fields.

Branding Strategy: Building Strong Brands

Some analysts see brands as *the* major enduring asset of a company, outlasting the company's specific products and facilities. John Stewart, co-founder of Quaker Oats, once said, "If this business were split up, I would give you the land and bricks and mortar, and I would keep the brands and trademarks, and I would fare better than you." The CEO of McDonald's agrees:

> A McDonald's board member who worked at Coca-Cola once talked to us about the value of our brand. He said if every asset we own, every building, and every piece of equipment were destroyed in a terrible natural disaster, we would be able to borrow all the money to replace it very quickly because of the value of our brand. And he's right. The brand is more valuable than the totality of all these assets.

In 2003, *Reader's Digest Canada* announced the results of its national survey identifying Canada's most trusted brands. Respondents were asked to name the brand they most trusted in 35 product categories and were also asked to rate the brand's level of quality, innovation, customer service, advertising, and value for money. Says Mr. Thomas, *Reader's Digest* spokesperson, "While quality and value are the entry points for a brand to earn consumer trust, strong customer service can tip the scale, especially for retailers and hard goods manufacturers." In some categories one brand is a clear winner—in fact, if a brand received a trust score more than three times that of the nearest competitor, it is designated a "platinum" winner. Included on the platinum list are Robin Hood (flour), Campbell's (soup), Becel (margarine), and Kellogg's (breakfast cereal). Other winners included Black & Decker (small kitchen appliances), Home Depot (do-it-yourself stores) VISA (credit cards), Sears and Wal-Mart (major retailers), Dell and IBM (personal computers).

Thus, brands are powerful assets that must be carefully developed and managed. In this section, we examine the key strategies for building and managing brands.[19]

Brand Equity

Brands are more than just names and symbols. Brands represent consumers' perceptions and feelings about a product and its performance—everything that the

A strong brand is a valuable asset. How many familiar brands and brand symbols can you find in this picture?

product or service *means* to consumers. As one branding expert suggests, "Ultimately, brands reside in the minds of consumers."[20] Thus, the real value of a strong brand is its power to capture consumer preference and loyalty.

Brands vary in the amount of power and value they have in the marketplace. A powerful brand has high *brand equity*. **Brand equity** is the positive differential effect that knowing the brand name has on customer response to the product or service. A measure of a brand's equity is the extent to which customers are willing to pay more for the brand. One study found that 72 percent of customers would pay a 20 percent premium for their brand of choice relative to the closest competing brand; 40 percent said they would pay a 50 percent premium. Tide and Heinz lovers are willing to pay a 100 percent premium.[21] Loyal Coke drinkers will pay a 50 percent premium and Volvo users a 40 percent premium.

A brand with strong brand equity is a valuable asset. *Brand valuation* is the process of estimating the total financial value of a brand. Measuring such value is difficult. Measuring the actual equity of a brand name is difficult. However, according to one estimate, the brand equity of Coca-Cola is $US69 billion, Microsoft is $US65 billion, and IBM is $US53 billion. Other brands rating among the world's most valuable include General Electric, Nokia, Intel, Disney, Ford, McDonald's, AT&T, and Harlequin (see Real Marketing 10.3).[22] "Brand equity has emerged over the past few years as a key strategic asset," observes a brand consultant. "CEOs in many industries now see their brands as a source of control and a way to build stronger relationships with customers."[23]

High brand equity provides a company with many competitive advantages. A powerful brand enjoys a high level of consumer brand awareness and loyalty. Because consumers expect stores to carry the brand, the company has more leverage in bargaining with resellers. Because the brand name carries high credibility, the company can more easily launch line and brand extensions, as when Coca-Cola leveraged its well-known brand to introduce Diet Coke or when Procter & Gamble introduced Ivory dishwashing detergent. Above all, a powerful brand offers the company some defence against fierce price competition.

Brand equity
The positive differential effect that knowing the brand name has on customer response to the product or service.

10.3 Harlequin: One of the World's Most Powerful Brand Names

If you were asked to name the world's most powerful brand names, Coca-Cola, Toyota, McDonald's, Sony, Disney, Kodak, or BMW would probably spring to mind. But it may surprise you to learn that one of the leading world brands is a homegrown Canadian product—Harlequin romance novels. With annual revenues for 2002 in excess of $618 million, Harlequin contributes about 40 percent of the operating revenues of its parent, Torstar Corp., publisher of the *Toronto Star*, and it remains phenomenally profitable. It makes 15 percent on every book it sells (three to four times the industry average), and in 2002 it sold over 146 million books worldwide.

The firm had humble beginnings. Founded in Winnipeg in 1949 by Richard Bonnycastle, Harlequin began by reprinting books sold in the United Kingdom or the United States. Harlequin's advance is another story of a woman being the power behind the throne. Bonnycastle's wife Mary first noticed how popular romances were with readers, and she suggested that the firm specialize in the genre. This, combined with another marketing insight, led to much of Harlequin's success. Rather than distributing its products in book-

Harlequin uses its strong brand equity to effectively market its products on the Web.

stores, Harlequin placed them where women shopped, in supermarkets and drugstores. The rest is history. The firm enjoyed growth rates in excess of 25 percent throughout the 1970s. However, many analysts thought that the women's movement of the 1980s would spell disaster for the company. How wrong they were! Harlequin has been labelled a company with products written for women, by women.

While many people have made fun of the romance genre, Harlequin attributes much of its success to having a high-quality marketing program. Quality begins with the product. The product, its books, is much higher in quality than most literary critics care to admit, Harlequin believes. They are written according to well-researched, carefully designed plot lines by over 1300 authors. Product quality is followed up with superb production capabilities and topped off by top-notch advertising.

Harlequin conducts meticulous market research to understand the demographics and attitudes of the market. Its North American readers are mainly women whose average age is 39. They are well educated, with over half having some university education. They are employed and have household incomes of about $35 000. Story setting is important to them. While Texas is the most popular location for romance, readers do not like stories set in Washington, DC, or circus venues. Most of all, readers want happy endings. High-quality research has enabled Harlequin to target the segment of heavy users. While most Canadians buy only six books a year, Harlequin's romance readers spend $30 a *month* on books.

You might not consider packaging to be an important aspect of marketing when it comes to selling paperbacks, but it is another of Harlequin's secrets of success. In Harlequin's case, the package is the book's cover. Careful research is again conducted to help Harlequin's 100 to 125-plus illustrators create the right cover to attract readers who may be searching through stores that carry hundreds of titles.

Another key to Harlequin's success is high repeat sales rates. This is where strong brand equity helps.

Readers know what to expect from Harlequin. This consumer confidence has made acceptance of the 64 new titles Harlequin introduces every month in its core series almost a certainty. Brand equity also lowers Harlequin's costs of advertising and promotion since its loyal readers are highly familiar with the brand and all that it stands for.

Harlequin's success is not confined to the North American market. In 2002 Harlequin sold books in 27 languages in 94 international markets, with overseas sales accounting for over 35 percent of its revenues. It keeps costs low by following its standardized marketing strategy. Harlequin also attributes its success to formulating alliances with overseas partners that help the firm establish a distribution system, gain access to the television and print media essential to build demand, and handle the repatriation of book royalties (that is, ensure that Harlequin receives the profits generated by overseas book sales).

In its continual quest to find new ways to serve the romance novel reader, Harlequin Enterprises was one of the first movers when it came to marketing online. In 1996 it launched www.romance.net, which by 2000 had evolved into eHarlequin.com. The mission of eHarlequin.com is to provide "romance lovers with a safe and engaging place to escape the day-to-day pressures of a busy lifestyle. On the site, visitors can interact with like-minded romance readers in addition to purchasing romance novels with ease and comfort."

One Harlequin executive noted that the website is "really a way of taking that intimacy we have with the customer to a level that you could not get off-line.... We [can] understand more about the customer and her preferences, be able to communicate directly with her and her with us, and be able to take all that information and develop a really rich profile with the customer and then target offers to her that are specific to what her needs and desires and wants are." Not an organization to avoid hyperbole, eHarlequin.com calls itself "the ultimate destination for romantic escape on the Internet."

So the next time you think about powerful brands, think about Harlequin, a firm that has found success through branding and superior product management in an industry plagued by high failure rates.

Sources: Andrea Zoe Aster, "How Harlequin Woos Women," *Marketing Magazine,* March 31, 2003, www.marketingmag.ca/; Jim Milliot, "Harlequin Has Record Year," *Publisher's Weekly,* March 17, 2003, http://publishersweekly.reviewsnews.com/; Ryan Starr, "True Love Pays: Harlequin's Rebranding Is Paying Off," *Canadian Business,* November 11, 2002, www.canadianbusiness.com/; Suzanne Wintrob, "Web Strategists Set Their Sites on Women," *Globe and Mail,* May 25, 2001, www.globeandmail.com/; Torstar website, "Book Publishing: Harlequin Book Publishing," www.torstar.com/; Romance Writers of America, "Romance Novels: Industry Statistics," August 26, 2002, www.rwanational.org/statistics.stm#reader; Kevin Brown, "The Top 200 Mega-Brands," *Advertising Age,* May 2, 1994, p. 33; and Gina Mallet, "The Greatest Romance on Earth," *Canadian Business,* August 1993, pp. 19–23. See also Paul Grescoe, *The Merchants of Venus: Inside Harlequin and the Empire of Romance* (Vancouver: Raincoast Books, 1996).

Therefore, the fundamental asset underlying brand equity is *customer equity*—the value of the customer relationships that the brand creates. A powerful brand is important, but what it really represents is a set of loyal customers. Thus, the proper focus of marketing is building customer equity, with brand management serving as a major marketing tool.[24]

Building Strong Brands

Branding poses challenging decisions to the marketer. Figure 10.3 shows that the major brand strategy decisions involve brand positioning, brand name selection, brand sponsorship, and brand development.

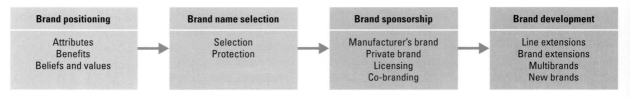

Figure 10.3 Major brand strategy decisions

Brand Positioning

Marketers need to position their brands clearly in target customers' minds. They can position brands at any of three levels.[25] At the lowest level, they can position the brand on *product attributes*. Thus, marketers of Dove soap can talk about the product's attribute of one-quarter cleansing cream. However, attributes are the least desirable level for brand positioning. Competitors can easily copy attributes. More important, customers are not interested in attributes as such; they are interested in what the attributes will do for them.

A brand can be better positioned by associating its name with a desirable *benefit*. Thus, Dove marketers can go beyond the brand's cleansing cream attribute and talk about the resulting benefit of softer skin. Some successful brands positioned on benefits are Volvo (safety), Hallmark (caring), Harley-Davidson (adventure), FedEx (guaranteed overnight delivery), Nike (performance), and Lexus (quality).

The strongest brands go beyond attribute or benefit positioning. They are positioned on strong *beliefs and values*. These brands pack an emotional wallop. Thus, Dove's marketers can talk not just about cleansing cream attributes and softer skin benefits, but about how these will make you more attractive. Brand expert Marc Gobé argues that successful brands must engage customers on a deeper level, touching a universal emotion.[26] His brand design agency, which has worked on such brands as Starbucks, Victoria's Secret, Godiva, Versace, and Lancôme, relies less on a product's tangible attributes and more on creating surprise, passion, and excitement surrounding a brand.

When positioning a brand, the marketer should establish a mission for the brand and a vision of what the brand must be and do. A brand is the company's promise to deliver a specific set of features, benefits, services, and experiences consistently to the buyers. It can be thought of as a contract to the customer regarding how the product or service will deliver value and satisfaction. The brand contract must be simple and honest. Motel 6, for example, offers clean rooms, low prices, and good service but does not promise expensive furniture or large bathrooms. In contrast, Ritz-Carlton offers luxurious rooms and a truly memorable experience but does not promise low prices.

Brand Name Selection

A good name can add greatly to a product's success. However, finding the best brand name is a difficult task. It begins with a careful review of the product and its benefits, the target market, and proposed marketing strategies. Desirable qualities for a brand name include the following:

1. It should suggest something about the product's benefits and qualities. Examples: Beautyrest, Craftsman, Sunkist, Spic & Span, Snuggles, Merrie Maids, OFF! Bug spray.

2. It should be easy to pronounce, recognize, and remember. Short names help. Examples: Tide, Crest, Puffs. But longer ones are sometimes effective. Examples: "Love My Carpet" carpet cleaner, "I Can't Believe It's Not Butter" margarine, President's Choice "Too Good To Be True" products.

3. The brand name should be distinctive. Examples: Taurus, Kodak, Oracle.

4. It should be extendable: Amazon.com began as an online bookseller but chose a name that would allow expansion into other categories.

5. The name should translate easily into foreign languages. Before spending $130 million to change its name to Exxon, Standard Oil of New Jersey tested the name in 54 languages in more than 150 foreign markets. It found that another choice—the name Enco—referred to a stalled engine when pronounced in Japanese.

6. It should be capable of registration and legal protection. A brand name cannot be registered if it infringes on existing brand names. Also, brand names that are

merely descriptive or suggestive may be unprotectable. For example, Labatt registered the name "Ice" for its new beer and invested millions in establishing the name with consumers. But the courts later ruled that the term Ice is generic and that Labatt could not use the Ice name exclusively.

Once chosen, the brand name must be protected. Many firms try to build a brand name that will eventually become identified with the product category. Brand names such as Kleenex, Levi's, Jell-O, Scotch Tape, Formica, Ziploc, and Fiberglas have succeeded in this way. However, their very success may threaten the company's rights to the name. Many originally protected brand names—such as cellophane, nylon, kerosene, linoleum, yo-yo, trampoline, escalator, thermos, and shredded wheat—are now names that any seller can use.

Brand Sponsorship

A manufacturer has four sponsorship options. The product may be launched as a *manufacturer's brand* (or *national brand*), as when Kellogg and IBM sell their output under their own brand names. Or the manufacturer may sell to resellers who give it a *private brand* (also called *store brand* or *distributor brand*). Although most manufacturers create their own brands, others market *licensed brands*. Finally, two companies can *co-brand* a product.

Private brand (store brand)
A brand created and owned by a reseller of a product or service.

Manufacturers' Brands versus Private Brands   Manufacturers' brands have long dominated the retail scene. In recent times, however, an increasing number of retailers and wholesalers have created their own **private brands** (or **store brands**). For example, Sears has created several names—Kenmore appliances, Diehard batteries, Craftsman tools, Weatherbeater paints—that buyers look for and demand. Canadian Tire's private-label tires are as well known as the manufacturers' brands of Goodyear and Bridgestone. Wal-Mart offers Sam's Choice beverages and food products, Spring Valley nutritional products, Ol' Roy dog food (named for Sam Walton's Irish setter), and White Cloud brand toilet tissue, diapers, detergent, and fabric softener to compete against major national brands. Private brands can be hard to establish and costly to stock and promote. However, they yield higher profit margins for the reseller. They also give resellers exclusive products that cannot be bought from competitors, resulting in greater store traffic and loyalty.

In the so-called *battle of the brands* between manufacturers and private brands, retailers have many advantages. They control what products they stock, where they go on the shelf, and which ones they will feature in local circulars. Retailers price their store brands lower than comparable manufacturers' brands, thereby appealing to budget-conscious shoppers, especially in difficult economic times. And most shoppers believe that store brands are often made by one of the larger manufacturers anyway.

Most retailers also charge manufacturers **slotting fees**—payments demanded by retailers before they will accept new products and find "slots" for them on the shelves. Store brands have the advantage of not having to pay these fees, which have to be paid by all other food manufacturers. Vancouver coffee roaster and marketer of fair-trade coffee Roy Hardy is one person who has a bitter taste in his mouth as a result of these fees. He couldn't afford to get his product on store shelves because of such payments. While one supermarket was willing to take his coffee on a trial basis, they demanded that Hardy provide 40 pounds (18 kg) of free coffee per store as an incentive for providing shelf space. Hardy just couldn't afford even this version of a slotting fee.

Like Hardy, many claim that slotting fees favour large manufacturers and effectively shut out the small players. Slotting fees can range from a few hundred dollars to $25 000 per item or up to $3 million per supermarket chain. Canadian grocery manufacturers face demands for slotting fees ranging from "pay-to-play," staying fees ("pay-to-stay"), and failure fees. In other words, stores can charge a company for access to shelf space, to keep their place on the shelf, or to remove a dud product. Because ownership of Canada's grocery stores rests in the hands of a few companies, Canada's Competition Bureau has been studying the issue.[27]

As store brands continue to improve in quality and as consumers' gain confidence in their store chains, store brands are posing a strong challenge to manufacturers' brands. Consider the case of Loblaws:

> Loblaw's President's Choice Decadent Chocolate Chip Cookies brand is now the leading cookie brand in Canada. Its private-label President's Choice cola racks up 50 percent of Loblaws' canned cola sales. Based on this success, the private-label powerhouse has expanded into a wide range of food categories. For example, it now offers more than 2500 items under the President's Choice label, ranging from frozen desserts to prepared foods, boxed meats, and paper. In a partnership with CIBC, Loblaws extended its brand into financial services under the brand name President's Choice Financial. The brand has become so popular that Loblaws now licenses it to retailers across the United States and eight other countries where Loblaws has no stores of its own. President's Choice Decadent Chocolate Chip Cookies are now sold by Jewel Food Stores in Chicago, where they are the number-one seller, beating out even Nabisco's Chips Ahoy brand. The company also offers a website where consumers can purchase its branded products directly (www.presidentschoice.ca).[28]

Private-label products control almost a quarter of the Canadian grocery market and the drug store market. In some categories, private-label sales are even higher. For example, in the paper and wrap category, private-label goods account for 45.7 percent of the market. They control 36 percent of the frozen food marketplace and almost 29 percent of the pet product market.[29] To fend off private brands, leading brand marketers will have to invest in R&D to bring out new brands, new features, and continuous quality improvements. They must design strong advertising programs to maintain high awareness and preference. They must find ways to "partner" with major distributors in a search for distribution economies and improved joint performance.

Licensing   Most manufacturers take years and spend millions to create their own brand names. However, some companies license names or symbols created by other manufacturers, names of well-known celebrities, and characters from popular movies and books. For a fee, any of these can provide an instant and proven brand name.

Store brands: Loblaw's President's Choice brand has become so popular that the company now licenses it to retailers across the United States and in eight other countries where Loblaws has no stores of its own.

Apparel and accessories sellers pay large royalties to adorn their products—from blouses to ties, and linens to luggage—with the names or initials of such fashion innovators as Alfred Sung, Calvin Klein, Tommy Hilfiger, Gucci, or Armani. Sellers of children's products attach an almost endless list of character names to clothing, toys, school supplies, linens, dolls, lunch boxes, cereals, and other items. Licensed character names range from classics such as *Sesame Street*, Disney, Peanuts, Winnie the Pooh, the Muppets, Scooby Doo, and Dr. Seuss characters to the more recent Teletubbies, Pokémon, Powerpuff Girls, Rugrats, and Harry Potter characters. Maple Leaf Consumer Foods successfully paired its Top Dogs brand with *The Hulk* to target kids nine to fourteen, knowing that the character also had nostalgic appeal to parents. Almost half of all retail toy sales come from products based on television shows and movies such as *Scooby Doo, The Rugrats Movie, The Lion King, Star Trek, Star Wars, Spider-Man*, or *Men in Black*.[30]

Name and character licensing has grown rapidly in recent years. Annual retail sales of licensed products in the United States and Canada have grown from only $5.2 billion in 1977 to $70 billion in 1987 and more than $90 billion today. Licensing can be a highly profitable business for many companies. For example, Warner Brothers has turned *Looney Tunes* characters into one of the world's most sought-after licences. More than 225 licensees generate $5 billion in annual retail sales of products sporting Bugs Bunny, Daffy Duck, Foghorn Leghorn, or one of more than a hundred other *Looney Tunes* characters. Warner Brothers has yet to tap the full potential of many of its secondary characters. The Tazmanian Devil, for example, initially appeared in only five cartoons. But through cross-licensing agreements with organizations such as Harley-Davidson and the NFL, Taz has become something of a pop icon—as this Canadian example shows:

In a real marketing coup, Quebec City-based Biscuits Leclerc licensed the whirling cartoon dervish for its Le P'tit Bonjour (Sweet Mornings) cereal. Biscuits Leclerc (www.leclerc.ca), an independent packaged goods manufacturer largely unknown outside of the Quebec market, knew from the outset that if Le P'tit Bonjour were to stand any chance against the powerhouse brands of Kellogg, General Mills, or Post, it needed instant notoriety and it was Taz who accomplished this task. While a number of private-label cereal brands have

Maple Leaf Consumer Foods successfully promoted its Top Dogs brand by licensing *The Hulk* for its in-store promotion.

appeared on supermarket shelves in recent years, Biscuits Leclerc is the first independent Canadian manufacturer to launch a brand of its own into this country's $862 million breakfast cereal market since 1934, when Canadian consumers were introduced to Weetabix.[31]

The fastest-growing licensing category is corporate brand licensing, as more for-profit and non-profit organizations license their names to generate additional revenues and brand recognition. Coca-Cola, for example, has some 320 licensees in 57 countries producing more than 10 000 products, ranging from baby clothes and boxer shorts to earrings, a Coca-Cola Barbie doll, and even a fishing lure shaped like a tiny Coke can. Last year, licensees sold more than $1.3 billion worth of licensed Coca-Cola products.[32]

Co-branding

The practice of using the established brand names of two different companies on the same product.

Co-Branding Although companies have been **co-branding** products for many years, there has been a recent resurgence in co-branded products. Co-branding occurs when two established brand names of different companies are used on the same product. For example, Nabisco joined forces with Pillsbury to create Pillsbury Oreo Bars baking mix, and Kellogg joined with ConAgra to co-brand Healthy Choice from Kellogg's cereals. Ford and Eddie Bauer co-branded a sport utility vehicle—the Ford Explorer, Eddie Bauer edition. Mattel teamed with Coca-Cola to market Soda Fountain Sweetheart Barbie. In its advertising IBM Canada features companies and organizations it has helped become ebusinesses. Canada Post runs an ad that features Intrawest's CEO to reinforce its claims about the power of using direct marketing. In most co-branding situations, one company licenses another company's well-known brand to use with its own. Co-branding has also become an important tool as Internet marketers work to increase the credibility of their sites. Many online marketers partner with such well-known brands as Visa, MasterCard and E-Trust to give online consumers a greater sense of trust in their offerings.[33]

Co-branding offers many advantages. Because each brand dominates in a different category, the combined brands create broader consumer appeal and greater brand equity. Co-branding also allows companies to enter new markets with minimal risk or investment. For example, by licensing its Healthy Choice brand to Kellogg, ConAgra entered the breakfast segment with a solid product that was backed by Kellogg's substantial marketing support. In return, Kellogg could leverage the brand awareness of the Healthy Choice name in cereal.

Co-branding also has its limitations. Such relationships usually involve complex legal contracts and licences. Co-branding partners must carefully coordinate their advertising, sales promotion, and other marketing efforts. Finally, when co-branding, each partner must trust the other will take good care of its brand. For example, consider the marriage between Kmart and the Martha Stewart housewares brand. When Kmart declared bankruptcy, it cast a shadow on the Martha Stewart brand. In turn, when Martha Stewart was charged with unethical financial dealings, it created negative associations for Kmart. As one Nabisco manager puts it, "Giving away your brand is a lot like giving away your child—you want to make sure everything is perfect."[34]

Brand Development

A company has four choices of brand development strategy (see Figure 10.4). It can introduce *line extensions* (existing brand names extended to new forms, sizes, and flavours of an existing product category); *brand extensions* (existing brand names extended to new product categories); *multibrands* (new brand names introduced in the same product category; or *new brands* (new brand names in new product categories).

Line extension

Using a successful brand name to introduce additional items in a given product category under the same brand name, such as new flavours, forms, colours, added ingredients, or package sizes.

Line Extensions Line extensions occur when a company introduces additional items in a given product category under the same brand name, such as new flavours, forms, colours, ingredients, or package sizes. Danone recently introduced several

Product Category

	Existing	New
Brand Name Existing	Line extension	Brand extension
New	Multibrands	New brands

Figure 10.4 Brand development strategies

line extensions, including seven new yogurt flavours, a fat-free yogurt, and a large, economy-size yogurt. The vast majority of new product activity consists of line extensions.

A company might introduce line extensions as a low-cost, low-risk way to introduce new products to meet consumer desires for variety, to utilize excess capacity, or simply to command more shelf space from resellers. However, line extensions involve some risks. An overextended brand name might lose its specific meaning, or heavily extended brands can cause consumer confusion or frustration. For example, a consumer buying cereal at the local supermarket will be confronted by more than 150 brands, including up to 30 different brands, flavours, and sizes of oatmeal alone. By itself, Quaker offers its original Quaker Oats, several flavours of Quaker instant oatmeal, and several dry cereals such as Oatmeal Squares, Toasted Oatmeal, and Toasted Oatmeal-Honey Nut.

Another risk is that sales of an extension may come at the expense of other items in the line. For example, although Fig Newton's cousins Cranberry Newtons, Blueberry Newtons, and Apple Newtons are all doing well for Kraft, the original Fig Newton brand now seems like just another flavour. A line extension works best when it takes sales away from competing brands, not when it "cannibalizes" the company's other items.

Brand extension

Using a successful brand name to launch a new or modified product in a new category.

Brand Extensions   A **brand extension** involves the use of a successful brand name to launch new or modified products in a new category. Mattel has extended its enduring Barbie Doll brand into new categories ranging from Barbie home furnishings, Barbie cosmetics, and Barbie electronics to Barbie books, Barbie sporting goods, and even a Barbie band—Beyond Pink. Honda uses its company name to cover different products such as its automobiles, motorcycles, snowblowers, lawn mowers, marine engines, and snowmobiles. This allows Honda to advertise that it can fit "six Hondas in a two-car garage." Swiss Army brand sunglasses, Disney Cruise Lines, Cosmopolitan low-fat dairy products, Century 21 Home Improvements, and Brinks home security systems—all are brand extensions.

A brand extension gives a new product instant recognition and faster acceptance. It also saves the high advertising costs usually required to build a new brand name. At the same time, a brand extension strategy involves some risk. Brand extensions such as Bic pantyhose, Heinz pet food, LifeSavers gum, and Clorox laundry detergent met early deaths. The extension may confuse the image of the main brand. In June 2000, Canadian business press headlines proclaimed, "The beaver has landed!" in recognition of one of the most unusual brand extensions ever announced. Fashion icon Roots Canada announced that it was going to partner with Skyservice Airlines to launch Roots Air, a new airline aimed at the business traveller. It wasn't long, however, before it was discovered that beavers can't fly and the brand extension crash landed.[35]

If a brand extension fails, it may harm consumer attitudes toward the other products carrying the same brand name. Further, a brand name may not be appropriate to a particular new product, even if it is well made and satisfying—would you consider buying Texaco milk or Alpo chili? A brand name may lose its special positioning in the consumer's mind through overuse. Companies that are tempted to transfer a brand name must research how well the brand's associations fit the new product.[36]

Multibrands   Companies often introduce additional brands in the same category. Thus, P&G markets many different brands in each of its product categories. *Multibranding* offers a way to establish different features and appeal to different buying motives. It also allows a company to lock up more reseller "shelf space." Or the company may want to protect its major brand by setting up *flanker* or *fighter brands*. Seiko uses different brand names for its higher-priced watches (Seiko Lasalle) and lower-priced watches (Pulsar) to protect the flanks of its mainstream Seiko brand.

A major drawback of multibranding is that each brand may obtain only a small market share, and none may be very profitable. The company may end up spreading its resources over many brands instead of building a few brands to a highly profitable level. These companies should reduce the number of brands it sells in a given category and set up tighter screening procedures for new brands.

New Brands   A company may create a new brand name when it enters a new product category for which none of the company's current brand names are appropriate. For example, Toyota created the Lexus brand to differentiate its luxury car from the established Toyota line. Japan's Matsushita uses separate names for its different families of products: Technics, Panasonic, National, and Quasar. Or, a company may believe that the power of its existing brand name is waning and a new brand name is needed.

As with multibranding, offering too many new brands can result in a company spreading its resources too thin. And in some industries, such as consumer packaged goods, consumers and retailers have become concerned that there are already too many brands with too few differences between them. Thus, Procter & Gamble, Frito-Lay, and other large consumer product marketers are now pursuing *megabrand* strategies—weeding out weaker brands and focusing their marketing dollars on brands that can achieve the number-one or number-two market share positions in their categories.

Managing Brands

Companies must carefully manage their brands. First, the brand's positioning must be continuously communicated to consumers. Major brand marketers often spend huge amounts on advertising to create brand awareness and to build preference and loyalty. For example, General Motors spends nearly $1 billion annually to promote its Chevrolet brands. McDonald's spends more than US$860 million.[37]

Such advertising campaigns can help to create name recognition, brand knowledge, and maybe even some brand preference. However, the fact is that brands are not maintained by advertising but by the *brand experience*. Today, customers come to know a brand through a wide range of contacts and touch points. These include advertising, but also personal experience with the brand, word of mouth, personal interactions with company people, telephone interactions, company webpages, and many others. Any of these experiences can have a positive or negative impact on brand perceptions and feelings. The company must put as much care into managing these touch points as it does into producing its ads.

The brand's positioning will not take hold fully unless everyone in the company lives the brand. Therefore the company needs to train its people to be customer-centred. Even better, the company should build pride in its employees regarding their products and services so that their enthusiasm will spill over to customers. Companies such as Mountain Equipment Co-op, Lexus, Dell, and Harley-Davidson have succeeded in turning all of their employees into enthusiastic brand builders. Companies can carry on internal brand building to help employees to understand, desire, and deliver on the brand promise.[38] Many companies go even further by training and encouraging their distributors and dealers to serve their customers well.

All of this suggests that managing a company's brand assets can no longer be left only to brand managers. Brand managers do not have enough power or scope to do all the things necessary to build and enhance their brands. Moreover, brand managers often pursue short-term results, whereas managing brands as assets calls for a longer-term strategy. Thus, some companies are now setting up brand asset management teams to manage their major brands. Canada Dry and Colgate-Palmolive have appointed *brand equity managers* to maintain and protect their brands' images, associations, and quality, and to prevent short-term actions by overeager brand managers from hurting the brand. Similarly, Hewlett-Packard has appointed a senior executive in charge of the customer experience in each of its two divisions, consumer and B2B. Their job is to track, measure, and improve the customer experience with H-P products. They report directly to the presidents of their respective divisions.

Finally, companies need to periodically audit their brands' strengths and weaknesses.[39] They should ask: Does our brand excel at delivering benefits that consumers truly value? Is the brand properly positioned? Do all of our consumer touch points support the brand's positioning? Do the brand's managers understand what the brand means to consumers? Does the brand receive proper, sustained support?

The brand audit may turn up brands that need to be repositioned because of changing customer preferences or new competitors. Some cases may call for completely *rebranding* a product, service, or company. The Clarica brand was born, for example, when Mutual Life of Canada became a public company and its business model transformed. The new name was chosen to portray the power of clear dialogue in making personal financial choices. The recent wave of corporate mergers, acquisitions, and divestures has set off a flurry of corporate rebranding campaigns. These are never simple exercises:

> When Fraser Valley Credit Union and Edelweiss Credit Union merged to become Fraser Valley Edelweiss Credit Union, it sought the help of the agency Grapheme/Koo, a subsidiary of Cossette Communications. Rebranding isn't a simple task. Grapheme/Koo knew it had to stick close to the history and capabilities of the two new partners and reflect the credit union's corporate pillars of hi-touch service excellence combined with hi-tech banking products. Grapheme/Koo first did an organizational audit and brand analysis. A positioning strategy was then developed followed by name generation and the development of a visual identity. The name *Prospera* was finally arrived at as a means of projecting prosperity and growth. The job didn't stop there. Employee enthusiasm and pride in the brand had to be generated and this was accomplished through an internal marketing effort using an upbeat campaign theme— "Say yes to prosperity." Presentations were made to all employees and a handbook entitled *Your Part in Prosperity* was developed for each employee. Ambassadors for the new brand also were sent to each branch. To communicate the new brand to the membership of the two credit unions, direct mail was used. The effort was deemed a great success and the new brand rolled out to rave reviews.[40]

However, building a new image and re-educating customers can be a huge undertaking. When Verizon Corporation was created by the merger of Bell Atlantic and GTE, the cost of the brand overhaul included tens of millions of dollars just for a special four-week advertising campaign to announce the new name, followed by considerable ongoing advertising expenses. And that was only the beginning. The company had to repaint its fleet of 70 000 trucks along with its garages and service centres. The campaign also required relabelling 250 000 pay phones, redesigning 91 million customer billing statements, and producing videos and other in-house employee educational materials.[41]

Services Marketing

Services have grown dramatically in recent years. Service industries account for 68 percent of Canada's GDP, almost three-quarters of employment in the country, and nearly 90 percent of new job creation. Moreover, the service sector continues to grow faster than other sectors of the economy. Services are growing even faster in the world economy, making up a quarter of the value of all international trade.[42]

Service industries vary greatly. *Governments* offer services through courts, employment services, hospitals, loan agencies, military services, police and fire departments, postal service, regulatory agencies, and schools. *Private non-profit organizations* offer services through museums, charities, churches, universities and colleges, foundations, and hospitals. A large number of *business organizations* offer services—airlines, banks, hotels, insurance companies, consulting firms, medical and law practices, entertainment companies, real estate firms, advertising and research agencies, and retailers.

The Nature and Characteristics of a Service

A company must consider four special characteristics of services when designing marketing programs: *intangibility, inseparability, variability,* and *perishability* (see Figure 10.5).

Service intangibility means that services cannot be seen, tasted, felt, heard, or smelled before they are bought. For example, people undergoing cosmetic surgery cannot see the result before the purchase. Airline passengers have nothing but a ticket and the promise that they and their luggage will arrive safely at the intended destination, hopefully at the same time.

To reduce uncertainty, buyers look for "signals" of service quality. They draw conclusions about quality from the place, people, price, equipment, and communication material that they can see. Therefore, the service provider's task is to make the service tangible in one or more ways. Whereas product marketers try to add intangibles to their tangible offers, service marketers try to add tangibles to their intangible offers.

Physical goods are produced, then stored, later sold, and still later consumed. In contrast, services are first sold, then produced and consumed at the same time. **Service inseparability** means that services cannot be separated from their providers,

Service intangibility
A major characteristic of services—they cannot be seen, tasted, felt, heard, or smelled before they are bought.

Service inseparability
A major characteristic of services—they are produced and consumed at the same time and cannot be separated from their providers, whether the providers are people or machines.

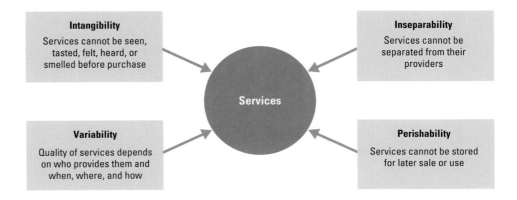

Figure 10.5 Four service characteristics

whether the providers are people or machines. If a service employee provides the employee service, then the employee is a part of the service. Because the customer is also present as the service is produced, *provider–customer interaction* is a special feature of service marketing. Both the provider and the customer affect the service outcome. Gerry Moore, director of the CN customer support centre, explains, "We're counting on our customers to help us move forward together.... They work with us to provide accurate, timely information, such as bills of lading and short-term production forecasts."[43]

Service variability

A major characteristic of services—their quality may vary greatly, depending on who provides them and when, where, and how they are provided.

Service variability means that the quality of services depends on who provides them as well as when, where, and how they are provided. For example, some hotels, such as the Westin or Marriott, have reputations for providing better service than others. Still, within a given Marriott hotel, one registration desk employee may be cheerful and efficient, whereas another standing just a metre away may be unpleasant and slow. Even the quality of a single Marriott employee's service varies according to his or her energy and frame of mind at the time of each customer encounter.

Service perishability

A major characteristic of services—they cannot be stored for later sale or use.

Service perishability means that services cannot be stored for later sale or use. Some dentists charge patients for missed appointments because the service value existed only at that point and disappeared when the patient did not show up. The perishability of services is not a problem when demand is steady. However, when demand fluctuates, service firms often have problems. For example, because of rush-hour demand, public transportation companies have to own much more equipment than they would if demand were even throughout the day. Thus, service firms often design strategies for producing a better match between demand and supply. Hotels and resorts charge lower prices in the off-season to attract more guests. And restaurants hire part-time employees to serve during peak periods.

Marketing Strategies for Service Firms

Just like manufacturing businesses, good service firms use marketing to position themselves strongly in chosen target markets. Southwest Airlines and WestJet position themselves as no-frills, short-haul airlines charging very low fares. A&W Foods of Canada positions itself as combining fast food with friendly service. The Westin Hotel chain positions itself to offer excellence, yet allows each hotel to retain its individual personality—for example, the Winnipeg Westin positions itself as "the finest hotel in our marketplace," with the goal of "exceeding all of our customers' expectations by delivering exceptional and caring service." WestJet positions itself to compete against Air Canada. Modelling itself on the American innovator Southwest Airlines, WestJet offers deep-discounted fares combined with no-frills service: no meals and no printed tickets.[44] These and other service firms establish their positions through traditional marketing mix activities.

However, because services differ from tangible products, they often require additional marketing approaches. In a product business, products are fairly standardized and can sit on shelves waiting for customers. But in a service business, the customer and front-line service employee *interact* to create the service. Thus, service providers must work to interact effectively with customers to create superior value during service encounters. Effective interaction, in turn, depends on the skills of front-line service employees, and on the service production and support processes backing these employees.

Service-profit chain

The chain that links service firm profits with employee and customer satisfaction.

The Service-Profit Chain

Successful service companies focus their attention on both their employees and customers. They understand the **service-profit chain**, which links service firm profits with employee and customer satisfaction. This chain consists of five links:[45]

- *Internal service quality:* superior employee selection and training, a quality work environment, and strong support for those dealing with customers, which results in...
- *Satisfied and productive service employees:* more satisfied, loyal, and hard-working employees, which results in...
- *Greater service value:* more effective and efficient customer value creation and service delivery, which results in...
- *Satisfied and loyal customers:* satisfied customers who remain loyal, repeat purchase, and refer other customers, which results in...
- *Healthy service profits and growth:* superior service firm performance.

Therefore, reaching service profits and growth goals begins with taking care of those who take care of customers (see Real Marketing 10.4).

Thus, service marketing requires more than just traditional external marketing using the four *P*s. Figure 10.6 shows that service marketing also requires both *internal marketing* and *interactive marketing*. **Internal marketing** means that the service firm must effectively train and motivate its customer-contact employees and all the supporting service people to work as a *team* to provide customer satisfaction. Marketers must get everyone in the organization to be customer-centred. In fact, internal marketing must *precede* external marketing. Ritz-Carlton orients its employees carefully, instils in them a sense of pride, and motivates them by recognizing and rewarding outstanding service deeds.

Interactive marketing means that perceived service quality depends heavily on the quality of the buyer-seller interaction during the service encounter. In product marketing, product quality often depends little on how the product is obtained. But in service marketing, service quality depends on both the service deliverer and the quality of the delivery. Service marketers, therefore, have to master interactive marketing skills. Thus, Ritz-Carlton selects only "people who care about people" and instructs them carefully in the fine art of interacting with customers to satisfy their every need.

In today's marketplace, companies must know how to deliver interactions that are not only "high-touch" but also "high-tech." For example, customers can log on to the Charles Schwab website and access account information, investment research, real-time quotes, after-hours trading, and the Schwab learning centre. They can also participate in live online events and chat online with customer service representatives. Customers seeking more-personal interactions can contact service reps by phone or visit a local Schwab branch office. Thus, Schwab has mastered interactive marketing at all three levels—calls, clicks, *and* visits.[46]

As competition and costs increase and as productivity and quality decrease, more service marketing sophistication is needed. Service companies face three major marketing tasks: They want to increase their *competitive differentiation, service quality,* and *productivity.*

Internal marketing

Marketing by a service firm to train and effectively motivate its customer-contact employees and all the supporting service people to work as a team to provide customer satisfaction.

Interactive marketing

Marketing by a service firm that recognizes that perceived service quality depends heavily on the quality of the buyer-seller interaction during the service encounter.

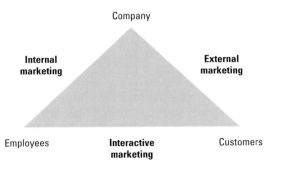

Figure 10.6 Three types of marketing in service industries

REAL MARKETING

10.4 Ritz-Carlton: Taking Care of Those Who Take Care of Customers

itz-Carlton, a chain of luxury hotels renowned for outstanding service, caters to the top 5 percent of corporate and leisure travellers. The company's Credo sets lofty customer service goals: "The Ritz-Carlton Hotel is a place where the genuine care and comfort of our guests is our highest mission. We pledge to provide the finest personal service and facilities for our guests who will always enjoy a warm, relaxed yet refined ambience. The Ritz-Carlton experience enlivens the senses, instils well-being, and fulfills even the unexpressed wishes and needs of our guests." The company's webpage concludes, "Here a calm settles over you. The world, so recently at your door, is now at your feet."

The Credo is more than just words on paper—Ritz-Carlton delivers on its promises. In surveys of departing guests, some 95 percent report that they've had a truly memorable experience. In fact, at Ritz-Carlton, exceptional service encounters have become almost commonplace. Take the experiences of Nancy and Harvey Heffner:

"The hotel is elegant and beautiful," Mrs. Heffner said, "but more important is the beauty expressed by the staff. They can't do enough to please you." When the couple's son became sick last year in Naples, the hotel staff brought him hot tea with honey at all hours of the night,

she said. And when Mr. Heffner had to fly home on business for a day and his return flight was delayed, a driver for the hotel waited in the lobby most of the night.

Such personal, high-quality service has also made the Ritz-Carlton a favourite among conventioneers. "They not only treat us like kings when we hold our top-level meetings in their hotels, but we just never get any complaints," comments one convention planner. "Perhaps the biggest challenge a planner faces when recommending The Ritz-Carlton at Half Moon Bay to the boss, board, and attendees is convincing them that meeting there truly is work," says another. "The...first-rate catering and service-oriented convention services staff [and] the Ritz-Carlton's ambiance and beauty—the elegant, Grand Dame-style lodge, nestled on a bluff between two championship golf courses overlooking the Pacific Ocean—makes a day's work there seem anything but."

The Ritz-Carlton was the first hotel company to win the Malcolm Baldrige National Quality Award, and the company has received virtually every major award that the hospitality industry bestows. Not surprisingly, service quality has resulted in high customer retention: Over 90 percent of Ritz-Carlton customers return. Despite its hefty room rates, the chain enjoys a 70 percent occupancy rate, almost nine points above the industry average.

Most of the responsibility for keeping guests satisfied falls to Ritz-Carlton's customer-contact employees. Thus, the hotel chain takes great care in selecting its personnel. "We want only people who care about people," notes the company's vice-president of quality. Once selected, employees are given intensive training in the art of coddling customers. New employees attend a two-day orientation, in which top management drums into them the "20 Ritz-Carlton Basics." Basic number one: "The Credo will be known, owned, and energized by all employees."

THE RITZ-CARLTON®

CREDO

The Ritz-Carlton Hotel is a place where the genuine care and comfort of our guests is our highest mission.

We pledge to provide the finest personal service and facilities for our guests who will always enjoy a warm, relaxed yet refined ambience.

The Ritz-Carlton experience enlivens the senses, instils well-being, and fulfills even the unexpressed wishes and needs of our guests.

THREE STEPS OF SERVICE

1
A warm and sincere greeting. Use the guest name, if and when possible.

2
Anticipation and compliance with guest needs.

3
Fond farewell. Give them a warm good-bye and use their name, if and when possible.

THE EMPLOYEE PROMISE

At The Ritz-Carlton, our Ladies and Gentlemen are the most important resource in our service commitment to our guests.

By applying the principles of trust, honesty, respect, integrity and commitment, we nurture and maximize talent to the benefit of each individual and the company.

The Ritz-Carlton fosters a work environment where diversity is valued, quality of life is enhanced, individual aspirations are fulfilled, and The Ritz-Carlton mystique is strengthened.

"We Are Ladies and Gentlemen Serving Ladies and Gentlemen"

The Credo and Employee Promise: Ritz-Carlton knows that to take care of customers, you must first take care of those who take care of customers.

Employees are taught to do everything they can so they never lose a guest. "There's no negotiating at Ritz-Carlton when it comes to solving customer problems," says the quality executive. Staff learn that *anyone* who receives a customer complaint *owns* that complaint until it's resolved (Ritz-Carlton Basic number eight). They are trained to drop whatever they're doing to help a customer—no matter what they're doing or what their department. Ritz-Carlton employees are empowered to handle problems on the spot, without consulting higher-ups. Each employee can spend up to $3000 to redress a guest grievance, and each is allowed to break from his or her routine for as long as needed to make a guest happy. "We master customer satisfaction at the individual level," adds the executive. "This is our most sensitive listening post...our early warning system." Thus, while competitors are still reading guest comment cards to learn about customer problems, Ritz-Carlton has already resolved them.

Ritz-Carlton instils a sense of pride in its employees. "You serve," they are told, "but you are not servants." The company motto states, "We are ladies and gentlemen serving ladies and gentlemen." Employees understand their role in Ritz-Carlton's success. "We might not be able to afford a hotel like this," says employee Tammy Patton, "but we can make it so people who can afford it will want to keep coming here." And so they do. When it comes to customer satisfaction, no detail is too small.

Ritz-Carlton recognizes and rewards employees who perform feats of outstanding service. Under its 5-Star Awards program, outstanding performers are nominated by peers and managers, and winners receive plaques at dinners celebrating their achievements. For on-the-spot recognition, managers award Gold Standard Coupons, redeemable for items in the gift shop and free weekend stays at the hotel. Ritz-Carlton further rewards and motivates its employees with such events as Super Sports Day, an employee talent show, luncheons celebrating employee anniversaries, a family picnic, and special themes in employee dining rooms. As a result, Ritz-Carlton's employees appear to be just as satisfied as its customers. Employee turnover is less than 30 percent a year, compared with 45 percent at other luxury hotels.

Ritz-Carlton's success is based on a simple philosophy: To take care of customers, you must first take care of those who take care of customers. Satisfied employees deliver high service value, which then creates satisfied customers. Satisfied customers, in turn, create sales and profits for the company.

Sources: Quotes and other information from Edwin McDowell, "Ritz-Carlton's Keys to Good Service," *New York Times,* March 31, 1993, p. D1; Howard Schlossberg, "Measuring Customer Satisfaction Is Easy to Do—Until You Try," *Marketing News,* April 26, 1993, pp. 5, 8; Ginger Conlon, "True Romance," *Sales & Marketing Management,* May 1996, pp. 85–90; "The Ritz-Carlton, Half Moon Bay," *Successful Meetings,* November 2001, p. 40; and the Ritz-Carlton website, www.ritzcarlton.com (accessed August 2002). Also see Patricia Sheehan, "Back to Bed: Selling the Perfect Night's Sleep," *Lodging Hospitality,* March 15, 2001, pp. 22–24; and Nicole Harris, "Can't Sleep? Try the Eye Gel in the Minibar—Hotels Roll Out Products to Help Tired Travelers Snooze," *Wall Street Journal,* June 20, 2002, p. D1.

Managing Service Differentiation   In these days of intense price competition, service marketers often complain about the difficulty of differentiating their services from those of competitors. To the extent that customers view the services of different providers as similar, they care less about the provider than the price.

The solution to price competition is to develop a differentiated offer, delivery, and image. The *offer* can include *innovative features* that set one company's offer apart from competitors' offers. Some hotels offer car rental, banking, and business centre services in their lobbies. Airlines introduced such innovations as in-flight movies, advance seating, air-to-ground telephone service, and frequent-flyer reward programs to differentiate their offers. British Airways even offers international travellers beds and private "demi-cabins," hot showers, and cooked-to-order breakfasts.

Service companies can differentiate their service *delivery* by having more able and reliable customer-contact people, by developing a superior physical environment in which the service product is delivered, or by designing a superior delivery process. For example, many banks offer their customers Internet banking as a better way to deliver banking services than having to drive, park, and wait in line.

Finally, service companies can differentiate their *images* through symbols and branding. Royal Bank's stylized "Leo the Lion" (although you have to look hard to see it) symbolizes strength and power—desirable qualities of a large bank. Other well-known service symbols include Canadian National Railway's CN symbol, Air

Service differentiation: British Airways differentiates its offer by providing first-class world travellers private "demi-cabins" and other amenities.

Canada's maple leaf, TD Canada Trust's green armchair, and Bell Canada's swirl and stylized face symbol.

Managing Service Quality   One of the major ways a service firm can differentiate itself is by delivering consistently higher quality than its competitors do. Like manufacturers before them, most service industries have now joined the customer-driven quality movement. And like product marketers, service providers need to identify the expectations of target customers concerning service quality. Unfortunately, service quality is harder to define and judge than is product quality. For instance, it is harder to get agreement on the quality of a haircut than on the quality of a hair dryer. Customer retention is perhaps the best measure of quality—a service firm's ability to hang on to its customers depends on how consistently it delivers value to them.[47]

Top service companies are customer obsessed and set high service quality standards. They do not settle for merely good service; they aim for 100 percent defect-free service. A 98 percent performance standard may sound good, but using this standard, ten words would be misspelled on each printed page, 400 000 prescriptions would be misfilled daily in the United States, and drinking water would be unsafe eight days a year.[48] Top service firms also *watch service performance closely*, both their own and that of competitors. They communicate their concerns about service quality to employees and provide performance feedback.

Unlike product manufacturers who can adjust their machinery and inputs until everything is perfect, service quality always will vary since quality depends on the interactions between employees and customers. As hard as they try, even the best companies will have an occasional late delivery, burned steak, or grumpy employee. Hence good *service recovery* programs can turn angry customers into loyal ones. In fact, good recovery can win more customer purchasing and loyalty than if things had gone well in the first place. Therefore, companies should take steps not only to provide good service every time but also to recover from service mistakes when they do occur.[49]

The first step is to *empower* front-line service employees—to give them the authority, responsibility, and incentives they need to recognize, care about, and tend to customer needs. At Marriott, for example, employees at all levels are given the authority to do whatever it takes to solve guests' problems on the spot while ferreting out the cause of those problems. At the CN customer support centre, representatives are expected to take total ownership for their customers' requests: everything from daily car orders to billing issues. The centre combines high-tech with a human element. Toll-free numbers allow customers to access the centre. As soon as a call comes in, the customer's profile appears on the service representative's computer screen. Customers deal with the same service rep each time they call, providing a sense of continuity. The state-of-the-art communication lets customers save money by giving them information on empty rail cars available throughout the system.[50]

Managing Service Productivity   With their costs rising rapidly, service firms are under great pressure to increase service productivity. They can do so in several ways. The service providers can train current employees better or hire new ones who will work harder or more skilfully. Or they can increase the quantity of their service by giving up some quality. The provider can "industrialize the service" by adding equipment and standardizing production, as in McDonald's assembly-line approach to fast-food retailing. Finally, the service provider can harness the power of technology. Although we often think of technology's power to save time and costs in manufacturing companies, it also has great—and often untapped—potential to make service workers more productive. Consumers can visit the Tourism Whistler website (www.myWHISTLER.com), for instance, and find the answers to a wide range of questions. Not only can they find out the hours of operation and current snow conditions, but they can also book their vacation online and access a comprehensive Whistler business directory.

However, companies must avoid pushing productivity so hard that doing so reduces quality. Attempts to industrialize a service or to cut costs can make a service company more efficient in the short run. But they can also reduce its longer-run ability to innovate, maintain service quality, or respond to consumer needs and desires. In short, they can take the "service" out of service.

Whistler Mountain enhances its customer service through use of its webpage.

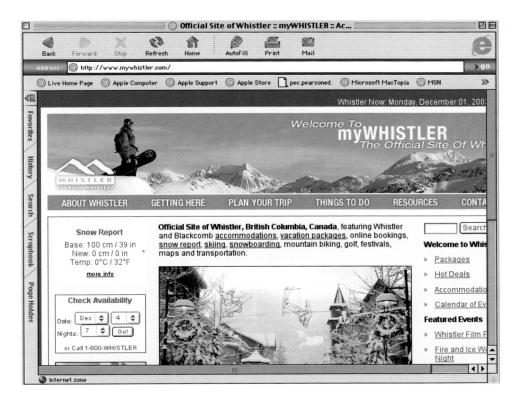

Additional Product Considerations

Here, we discuss two additional product policy considerations: social responsibility in product decisions and issues of international product and service marketing.

Product Decisions and Social Responsibility

Product decisions have attracted much public attention. Marketers should carefully consider public policy issues and regulations concerning acquiring or dropping products, patent protection, product quality and safety, and product warranties.

Canadian manufacturers must navigate a complex web of government departments and legislation when considering their product policies. Agriculture Canada, the Canadian Food Inspection Agency, and the Consumer Products Division of Health Canada, for example, govern food and product safety. The Competition Bureau regulates many aspects of the marketing of products. The *Competition Act*'s provisions cover pricing and advertising, not just the maintenance of a competitive marketplace. When considering a merger that would give a firm access to new products, a company has to be aware that the government may invoke the *Competition Act* if it thinks the merger would lessen competition. Companies dropping products must be aware that they have legal obligations, written or implied, to their suppliers, dealers, and customers who have a stake in the discontinued product. Companies must also obey patent laws when developing new products. A company cannot make its product illegally similar to another company's established product. Firms may also have to be aware of legislation controlled by Environment Canada and the Department of Transport.

Federal statutes cover product safety (except electrical equipment), competition, labelling, and weights and measures. The *Hazardous Products Act*, for example, controls the marketing of dangerous or potentially dangerous consumer and industrial products; the *Food and Drugs Act* covers safety of cosmetics as well as food and drugs. Both acts can be found on the Canadian Department of Justice website (http://canada.justice.gc.ca).[51] Provincial statutes deal with such matters as conditions of sale, guarantees, and licensing, as well as unfair business practices.

Consumers who have been injured by a defectively designed product can sue the manufacturer or dealer. The number of product liability suits have been increasing, and settlements often run in the millions of dollars. This, in turn, has resulted in huge increases in the cost of product liability insurance premiums. Some companies pass these higher rates along to consumers by raising prices. Others are forced to discontinue high-risk product lines.

International Product and Service Marketing

International product and service marketers face special challenges. First, they must figure out what products and services to introduce and in which countries. Then, they must decide how much to standardize or adapt their products and services for world markets.

On the one hand, companies would like to standardize their offerings. Standardization helps to develop a consistent worldwide image. It also lowers manufacturing costs and eliminates duplication of research and development, advertising, and product design efforts. On the other hand, consumers around the world differ in their cultures, attitudes, and buying behaviours. And markets vary in their economic conditions, competition, legal requirements, and physical environments. Companies usually must respond to these differences by adapting their product and service offerings. Something as simple as an electrical outlet can create big product problems:

Those who have travelled across Europe know the frustration of electrical plugs, different voltages, and other annoyances of international travel.... Philips, the electrical appliance manufacturer, has to produce twelve kinds of irons to serve just its European market. The problem is that Europe does not have a universal [electrical] standard. The ends of irons bristle with different plugs for different countries. Some have three prongs, others two; prongs protrude straight or angled, round or rectangular, fat, thin, and sometimes sheathed. There are circular plug faces, squares, pentagons, and hexagons. Some are perforated and some are notched. One French plug has a niche like a keyhole.[52]

Packaging also presents challenges for international marketers. Packaging issues can be subtle. For example, names, labels, and colours may not translate easily from one country to another. A firm using yellow flowers in its logo might fare well in Canada or the United States but meet with disaster in Mexico, where a yellow flower symbolizes death or disrespect. Similarly, although Nature's Gift might be an appealing name for gourmet mushrooms in North America, it would be deadly in Germany, where *gift* means poison. Packaging may also have to be tailored to meet the physical characteristics of consumers in various parts of the world. For instance, soft drinks are sold in smaller cans in Japan to better fit the smaller Japanese hand. Thus, although product and package standardization can produce benefits, companies usually must adapt their offerings to the unique needs of specific international markets.

Service marketers also face special challenges when going global. Some service industries have a long history of international operations. For example, the commercial banking industry was one of the first to grow internationally. Banks had to provide global services to meet the foreign exchange and credit needs of their home-country clients wanting to sell overseas. In recent years, many banks have become truly global operations: Germany's Deutsche Bank, for example, serves more than 12 million customers in 70 countries. For its clients around the world who wish to grow globally, Deutsche Bank can raise money not only in Frankfurt but also in Zurich, London, Paris, and Tokyo.[53]

Cossette Communications is Canada's largest advertising agency and among the top 30 in the world. It serves a number of international clients, including McDonald's Restaurants of Canada.

c'est ça que j'm

Professional and business service industries—such as accounting, engineering, management consulting, and advertising—have only recently globalized. The international growth of these firms followed the globalization of the manufacturing companies they serve. For example, as their client companies began to use global marketing and advertising strategies, advertising agencies and other marketing service firms responded by globalizing their own operations. Cossette Communications, the largest advertising agency in Canada, is among the top 15 agencies in North America and the top 30 in the world. It serves major clients as diverse as McDonald's, General Motors Canada, Coca-Cola, Bell, and BMO Financial Group. Cossette's main offices are in Montreal, Toronto, and New York, and the company employs approximately 1300 people.[54]

Retailers are among the latest service businesses to go global. As their home markets become saturated with stores, retailers such as Wal-Mart, Toys "R" Us, Office Depot, Saks Fifth Avenue, and Disney are expanding into faster-growing markets abroad. For example, every year since 1995, Wal-Mart has entered a new country; its international division's sales grew 40 percent in 2002, skyrocketing to more than $41.6 billion. Japanese retailer Yaohan now operates the largest shopping centre in Asia, the 21-storey Nextage Shanghai Tower in China, and Carrefour of France is the leading retailer in Brazil and Argentina. Asian shoppers now buy North American products in Dutch-owned Makro stores, now Southeast Asia's biggest store group, with sales in that region of more than $2.6 billion.[55]

Service companies wanting to operate in other countries are not always welcomed with open arms. Whereas manufacturers usually face straightforward tariff, quota, or currency restrictions when attempting to sell their products in another country, service providers are likely to face more subtle barriers. In some cases, rules and regulations affecting international service firms reflect the host country's traditions. In others, they appear to protect the country's own fledgling service industries from large global competitors with greater resources. In still other cases, however, the restrictions seem to have little purpose other than to make entry difficult for foreign service firms.

Despite these difficulties, the trend toward growth of global service companies continues, especially in banking, airlines, telecommunication, and professional services. Today service firms are no longer simply following their manufacturing customers; they are taking the lead in international expansion.

Retailers are among the latest service businesses to go global. Here Malaysian shoppers buy North American products in a Dutch-owned Makro store in Kuala Lumpur.

Looking Back: Reviewing the Concepts

A product is more than a set of tangible features. Each product or service offered to customers can be viewed on three levels. The *core product* consists of the core problem-solving benefits that consumers seek when they buy a product. The *actual product* exists around the core and includes the quality level, features, design, brand name, and packaging. The *augmented product* is the actual product plus the various services and benefits offered with it, such as warranty, free delivery, installation, and maintenance.

1. **Define *product* and the major classifications of products and services.**

   Broadly defined, a *product* is anything that can be offered to a market for attention, acquisition, use, or consumption that might satisfy a want or need. Products include physical objects, but also services, persons, places, organizations, ideas, or mixes of these entities. *Services* are products that consist of activities, benefits, or satisfactions offered for sale that are essentially intangible, such as banking, hotel accommodation, tax preparation, and home repair services.

   Products and services fall into two broad classes based on the types of consumers that use them. *Consumer products*—those bought by final consumers—are usually classified according to consumer shopping habits (convenience products, shopping products, specialty products, and unsought products). *Industrial products,* purchased for further processing or use in conducting a business, include materials and parts, capital items, and supplies and services. Other marketable entities, such as organizations, persons, places, and ideas, can also be thought of as products.

2. **Describe the decisions companies make regarding their individual products and services, product lines, and product mixes.**

   Individual product decisions involve product and service attributes, branding, packaging, labelling, and product support services. *Product and service attribute* decisions involve product quality, features, and style and design. *Branding* decisions include selecting a brand name and developing a brand strategy. *Packaging* provides many key benefits, such as protection, economy, convenience, and promotion. Package decisions often include designing *labels,* which identify, describe, and possibly promote the product. Companies also develop *product support services* that enhance customer service and satisfaction and safeguard against competitors.

   Most companies produce a product line rather than a single product. A *product line* is a group of products that are related in function, customer-purchase needs, or distribution channels. *Product line stretching* involves extending a line downward, upward, or in both directions to occupy a gap that might otherwise be filled by a competitor. In contrast, *product line filling* involves adding items within the present range of the line. The set of product lines and items offered to customers by a particular seller make up the *product mix.* The mix can be described by four dimensions: width, length, depth, and consistency. These dimensions are the tools for developing the company's product strategy.

3. **Discuss branding strategy—the decisions companies make in building and managing their brands.**

   Some analysts see brands as *the* major enduring asset of a company. Brands are more than just names and symbols—they embody everything that the product or service *means* to consumers. *Brand equity* is the positive differential effect that knowing the brand name has on customer response to the product or service. A brand with strong brand equity is a very valuable asset.

   In building brands, companies need to make decisions about brand positioning, brand name selection, brand sponsorship, and brand development. The most powerful *brand positioning* builds around strong consumer beliefs and values. *Brand name selection* involves finding the best brand name based on a careful review of product benefits, the target market, and proposed marketing strategies. A manufacturer has four *brand sponsorship* options: It can launch a *manufacturer's brand* (or national brand), sell to resellers who use a *private brand,* market *licensed brands,* or join forces with another company to *co-brand* a product. A company also has four choices when it comes to developing brands. It can introduce *line extensions, brand extensions, multibrands,* or *new brands* (new brand names in new product categories).

Companies must build and manage their brands carefully. The brand's positioning must be continuously communicated to consumers. Advertising can help, although brands are not maintained by advertising but by the *brand experience*. Customers come to know a brand through a wide range of contacts and touch points. The company must put as much care into managing these touch points as it does into producing its ads. Thus, managing a company's brand assets can no longer be left only to brand managers. Some companies are now setting up brand asset management teams to manage their major brands. Finally, companies must periodically audit their brands' strengths and weaknesses. In some cases, brands may need to be repositioned because of changing customer preferences or new competitors.

Other cases may call for completely *rebranding* a product, service, or company.

4. Identify the four characteristics that affect the marketing of a service and the additional marketing considerations that services require.

Services are characterized by four key characteristics. They are *intangible*, *inseparable*, *variable*, and *perishable*. Each characteristic poses problems and marketing requirements. Marketers work to find ways to make the service more tangible, to increase the productivity of

providers who are inseparable from their products, to standardize the quality in the face of variability, and to improve demand movements and supply capacities in the face of service perishability.

Good service companies focus attention on *both* customers and employees. They understand the *service-profit chain* that links service firm profits with employee and customer satisfaction. Service marketing strategy calls for not only external marketing but also *internal marketing* to motivate employees and *interactive marketing* to create service delivery skills among service providers. To succeed, service marketers must create *competitive differentiation*, offer high *service quality*, and find ways to increase *service productivity*.

5. Discuss two additional product issues: socially responsible product decisions and international product and service marketing.

Marketers must consider two additional product issues. The first is *social responsibility*. This includes public policy issues and regulations involving acquiring or dropping products, patent protection, product quality and safety, and product warranties. The second involves the special challenges facing international product and service marketers. International marketers must decide how much to standardize or adapt their offerings for world markets.

Reviewing the Key Terms

Actual product   380
Augmented product   381
Brand   387
Brand equity   396
Brand extension   404
Co-branding   403
Consumer product   381
Convenience product   381
Core product   377
Industrial product   382

Interactive marketing   409
Internal marketing   409
Line extension   403
Packaging   388
Private brand (store brand)   400
Product   377
Product line   392
Product mix (product
assortment)   393
Product quality   385

Service   377
Service inseparability   407
Service intangibility   407
Service perishability   408
Service-profit chain   408
Service variability   408
Shopping product   382
Social marketing   384
Specialty product   382
Unsought products   382

Discussing the Concepts

1. What are the primary differences between products and services? Give illustrations of the differences that you identify. Provide an example of a hybrid offer.

2. List and explain the core, actual, and augmented products for educational experiences that universities offer. How are these products different, if at all, from those offered by junior colleges? Which of these products could be easily moved online? How would such a move affect the educational institution's marketing efforts?

3. List and summarize the characteristics of the four types of consumer products. Provide an example of each.

4. How does an industrial product differ from a consumer product? List and summarize the characteristics of the three major groups of industrial products identified in the text.

5. The text identifies social marketing as the use of commercial marketing concepts and tools in programs designed to influence individuals' behaviour in a way that improves their well-being and that of society. Consider a recent social marketing effort, such as Mothers Against Drunk Driving. Identify its intended target market, list the primary objectives of the campaign, suggest how effectiveness could be measured, and document the overall impact of the campaign. Critique the campaign and comment on what you would do to improve the effort.

6. For many years there was one type of Coca-Cola, one type of Tide, and two types of Crest (mint and regular). Now we find Coke in seven or more varieties; Tide in Ultra, Liquid, and Unscented versions; and Crest Gel with sparkles for kids. List some of the issues these brand extensions raise for manufacturers, retailers, and consumers. Is more always better? How does co-branding affect brand extensions? Suggest a co-branding opportunity that you believe makes sense from a marketing perspective.

7. Explain the types of product line stretching and their benefits. Give an example of each. What is product line filling? Why would a marketing manager choose product line filling over product line stretching?

8. Illustrate how a movie theatre can deal with the intangibility, inseparability, variability, and perishability of the services it provides. Give specific examples to illustrate your thoughts. How could the movie theatre use internal and interactive marketing to enhance its service-profit chain?

Applying the Concepts

1. The core product in the automobile industry is transportation. The major problem-solving benefit is getting from one place to another quickly and safely. However, most automobile manufacturers differentiate their products with additional service benefits. The service approaches are almost as varied as are the automobile manufacturers themselves. Examine the websites for Ford (www.ford.ca), General Motors (www.gmcanada.com), Chrysler (www.daimlerchrysler.ca), Honda (www.honda.ca), Lexus (www.lexuscanada.com), Mercedes-Benz (www.mercedes-benz.ca), and Toyota (www.toyota.ca). Look beyond the automobiles themselves and closely examine the manufacturers' services and service options.

   a. What primary services do the various automobile manufacturers offer? Prepare a grid that compares each company with the others.

   b. What services do the different companies appear to offer in common? What services do they use to differentiate themselves from one another?

   c. Do any of the sites suggest that a company understands the service-profit chain? Explain.

   d. Do any of the auto companies use interactive marketing with respect to the service component? Explain.

   e. Visit the Saturn website at www.saturncanada.com. Does anything make this company different from those you have already visited? What seems to be the company's focus and differential advantage? Suggest ways in which Saturn could use its service component to compete more effectively against its competitors.

   f. What role does the Internet play in the product/service strategies of the companies in question 1?

2. Which company has the world's strongest brand? Is brand strength determined by sales volume, a global presence, innovation, reputation, amount of advertising, success on the Internet, positive public relations, stock value, or all of the these things? Marketing managers know that strong brand equity is the key to entering new markets and successfully penetrating old ones. Strong brands can command premium prices. Brand image also shapes corporate strategy, advertising campaigns, and overall marketing effort. Alliances

are made and broken based on brand reputation and confidence. In contrast, loss of confidence in a brand can affect not only the companies involved but also all of the brand's distributors, service providers, and secondary publics. As a result, many consider a strong brand a company's most important asset. So, what is the world's strongest brand? According to recent studies, the Coca-Cola brand tops the list, followed by Microsoft, IBM, and GE. Why do these brands garner so much respect?

a. What makes a strong brand? How would you go about measuring brand equity?

b. What makes Coca-Cola the number one brand in the world? What characteristics differentiate the company and brand from its competitors?

c. With its ongoing legal difficulties, how can Microsoft be considered a strong global brand? Does its international dominance help it overcome public relations and legal problems? Explain.

d. Examine the websites for Coca-Cola (www.cocacola.com), Microsoft (www.microsoft.com), IBM (www.ibm.com), and GE (www.ge.com) for indications of brand strength. Based on your answers to question "a" above, construct a grid that evaluates each of these brands based on the characteristics you listed. Examine the information in your grid. Which company is superior based on your evaluation?

Video Short

View the video short for this chapter at **www.pearsoned.ca/kotler** and then answer the questions provided in the case description.

Company Case
Starbucks: Brewing a Worldwide Experience

Grounded in History

In 1971, entrepreneurs Jerry Baldwin, Gordon Bowker, and Zev Siegl launched the first Starbucks in Seattle's Pike Place Market. At that time, a bitter price war had thrown the American coffee market into turmoil. Trying to maintain profit margins, producers of the major coffee brands had begun using cheaper beans, resulting in what many consumers believed was a dramatic decline in coffee quality.

The Starbucks entrepreneurs brewed the idea of opening a retail store dedicated to selling only the finest coffee-brewing equipment to brew only the highest-quality, whole-bean coffee. They believed that such a store could satisfy the few coffee enthusiasts who had to order coffee from Europe and convert other coffee drinkers to the gourmet coffee experience. To differentiate its coffee from the bland, dishwater-like store brands, Starbucks scoured the globe for arabica beans grown above 3000 metres in altitude by a carefully selected group of growers in countries like Sumatra, Kenya, Ethiopia, and Costa Rica. The company focused on arabica beans, rather than the cheaper robusta beans, because consumers could brew the arabica beans at higher temperatures, thus producing a richer coffee flavour.

Despite early success, Starbucks remained a small-time Seattle operation until the company hired Howard Schultz as its marketing director in 1982. In 1983, Schultz, while travelling in Italy, visited a coffeehouse and realized that Starbucks's future was not in retailing coffee beans and equipment but in serving freshly brewed coffee by the cup in its own coffeehouses. Schultz saw that the coffeehouse strategy would allow Starbucks to differentiate itself from other vendors of beans and equipment that were springing up. Further, although more people were developing tastes for gourmet coffee, many people did not have the time or equipment to brew specialty coffees properly. By brewing the coffee in its coffeehouses, Starbucks could use the proper equipment and well-trained employees to produce the best possible coffee in an environment that enhanced the coffee-drinking experience. And, offering the coffee by the cup made the experience convenient for the busy Seattle businesspeople who were Starbucks's prime customers.

In 1987, Schultz became president of Starbucks and began to reshape its image as a prelude to rapid growth. He updated the company's logo from an earthen brown colour to green. He worked to shape Starbucks's coffeehouses to be a blend of Italian elegance and American informality. He carefully designed the store to "enhance the quality of everything the customers see, touch, hear, smell, or taste." He wanted the store to be a "personal treat" for the customers, providing a refreshing break in their day or a place to relax at night. To achieve this goal, Schultz and his managers invested in employee training and a strong employee benefit program so that they could attract and retain skilled employees who would enhance the customer's experience.

By the late 1990s, Schultz's strategy was paying off handsomely. In 1993, the American coffee market had been worth about US$13.5 billion, with specialty coffees, like those Starbucks sold, accounting for only about US$1 billion. By 1999, the U.S. coffee market had mushroomed to over US$18 billion, with specialty coffees capturing US$7.5 billion. In 1996 alone, Starbucks added a store a day and almost matched that by adding 325 in 1997. By the end of 1997, it had added 30 000 employees. Since Schultz joined the company, it was hiring 500 employees a week. Sales had almost doubled from US$700 million in just 1996 to over US$1.3 billion by 1998. A typical Starbucks customer visited his or her favourite store 18 times a month!

Crossing Cultures

Despite Starbucks's success in the U.S. market, Schultz and his team realized that American consumers accounted for only 20 percent of the world coffee market. If Starbucks were going to achieve its goals, it had to venture into foreign markets and prove that a really good cup of coffee was a true global product. Starbucks entered Canada in 1987, opening its first shop in Vancouver. The similarity of cultures and tastes made rapid expansion possible. By 2002, Starbucks operated 270 Canadian outlets.

The company first ventured into Japan and Singapore in 1996. In Japan, the company went against

the Japanese love of cigarettes and refused to allow smoking in its coffeehouses, as it does in all its markets, arguing that the smoke would overwhelm the coffee aroma. Contrary to some predictions, Japanese women loved the smoke-free stores, and Japanese men followed suit. By early 2000, Starbucks had more than 200 stores in Japan and was profitable two years ahead of schedule.

Then, in 1998, the company looked to Europe. It purchased the Seattle Coffee Company from Scott and Ally Svenson, U.S. expatriates who started the Starbucks look-alike in 1990, when they moved to London and couldn't find a good cup of coffee. By 1998, Seattle Coffee had 56 coffee stores in Britain and had begun to make coffee drinking an important part of the British social scene. Whereas England had earned the reputation as a nation of tea drinkers that offered only terrible coffee, by 1998 the country's annual coffee consumption actually topped tea consumption. The Svensons sold the chain to Starbucks for US$84 million and stayed to work with the company to help it become a springboard into the European market.

On to the Continent

The major unanswered question was how Starbucks would do when it entered continental Europe, where it would encounter established coffee cultures, anti-American sentiment at times, and, above all, 121 000 existing espresso bars in Italy—the ultimate challenge.

In early 2001, Schultz decided to take the plunge into continental Europe by opening a coffeehouse in Zurich, Switzerland—the first of 650 stores the company said it would open in six neighbouring countries by 2003. Schultz knew that continental Europe would be a big challenge, as American coffee had a long-standing bad reputation. He chose Switzerland to develop about 11 stores, seeing the country as a good test market because it mixed French, German, and Italian cultures.

To enter Switzerland, Starbucks followed a strategy it had developed for other international markets. Many of the new stores would be 50–50 partnerships with local business partners who shared its values and wanted to grow aggressively. Partnering allowed Starbucks to utilize the partners' local knowledge and to leverage its capital to expand more rapidly. Before going into a country, Starbucks conducted extensive focus groups and quantitative market research. It would vary its food offerings to meet local tastes, but it would not alter its coffee, like its caramel macchiato. Peter Maslen, president of Starbucks Coffee International, noted, "We want to elicit the same emotional response all over the world." To learn the Starbucks way, new managers spent twelve weeks in Seattle learning the barista's art and customer service.

Then, in late 2001, Starbucks took its boldest European step to date by opening its first coffeehouse in Vienna, Austria—a stronghold where 1900 coffee shops catered to persnickety customers, who sometimes visited four times a day to smoke, drink coffee from china cups, and linger while black-jacketed waiters served them. Austria already had one coffeehouse for every 530 people, and the average citizen drank 1000 cups of coffee a year. Starbucks offered its standard paper cups for to-go orders and counter service. Further, it maintained its no-smoking policy, even as critics noted that 40 percent of Europeans and 60 percent of Italians smoke—about half of Starbucks's potential market. Although it offered some "required" apple strudel and some cakes with poppy seeds, its food fare consisted basically of American-style sweets. The head of Starbucks's Austrian joint venture noted, "We don't want to sell coffee; we want to sell a relaxed 15 minutes."

As of mid-2002, the Austrian experiment was going well. Starbucks had four stores in Vienna serving a mixture of well-to-do tourists and locals in their thirties who spent about $5 per visit, about the same as in other shops. Its total global chain numbered 5405 stores, with 1153 of those stores located outside the United States.

In 2002, the company would also enter the Spanish and German markets as it continued its caffeine-laden assault on Europe in preparation for completing the global circle by entering Italy, where Howard Schultz first had his vision for a global frappuccino, and Greece, the site of the 2004 Olympics.

Due to its global expansion, Starbucks Coffee Company is the leading retailer, roaster, and brand of specialty coffee in the world. In addition to its retail locations in North America, Europe, the Middle East, and the Pacific Rim, Starbucks sells coffee and tea products through its specialty operations, including its online store at Starbucks.com. Starbucks has its own branded packaged goods including the bottled frappuccino coffee drink, a line of super-premium ice creams, and Hear Music, a line of compact discs.

Questions For Discussion

1. What is the core product that Starbucks offers? What are the actual and augmented levels of that product?

2. How would you classify the Starbucks product using the marketing considerations for a consumer product outlined in the chapter? What individual product decisions has Starbucks made?

3. How has Starbucks dealt with issues of brand equity, customer equity, and brand positioning?

4. Is Starbucks a product or a service? How are the concepts of service marketing important to Starbucks?

5. How has Starbucks dealt with the issues it faces in international marketing?

6. What marketing recommendations would you make to Starbucks as it continues its international expansion?

Sources: Starbucks Corporation, "Starbucks Licensed to Sell Fair Trade Certified Coffee in Canada Through Agreement with TransFair Canada" (press release), May 17, 2002, www.businesswire.com/webbox/bw.051702/221370273.htm; Cora Daniels, "The 2003 Fortune 500: Mr. Coffee", *Fortune,* March 30, 2003, www.fortune.com/fortune/fortune500/articles/0,15114,438809,00.html; Steven Erlanger, "An American Coffeehouse (or 4) in Vienna, *New York Times,* June 1, 2002, www.nytimes.com; Alwyn Scott, "Starbucks Wins Fans in Europe," *Knight-Ridder/Tribune Business News,* May 19, 2002, item 02139001; Hans Greimel, "Starbucks' Final Frontier Is Winning European Palates," *Detroit News,* March 9, 2001; Mark Pendergrast, "The Starbucks Experience Going Global," *Tea and Coffee Trade Online* 176 (2), February/March, 2002; "Abuzz; Coffee-shop Chains; American Coffee Chains Invade Europe," *The Economist,* May 19, 2001, article A74692901; Dori Jones Yang, "An American (Coffee) in Paris—and Rome," *U.S. News and World Report,* February 19, 2001, p. 47; Steve Ernst, "Starbucks Europe, Asia Next," *Puget Sound Business Journal,* June 2, 2000, p. 33; and Chloe Beacham, "Is That to Go?" *The European,* May 11, 1998, p. 25.

Chapter 11

New-Product Development and Product Life-Cycle Strategies

After studying this chapter you should be able to

1. explain how companies find and develop new-product ideas

2. list and define the steps in the new-product development process

3. describe the stages of the product life cycle

4. describe how marketing strategies change during the product's life cycle

Looking Ahead: Previewing the Concepts

In the previous chapter, you learned about decisions that marketers make in managing individual brands and entire product mixes. In this chapter, we'll look into two additional product topics: developing new products and managing products through their life cycles. New products are the lifeblood of an organization. However, new-product development is risky, and many new products fail. So, the first part of this chapter lays out a process for finding and growing successful new products. Once introduced, marketers want their products to enjoy a long and happy life. In the second part of the chapter, you'll see that every product passes through several life-cycle stages and that each stage poses new challenges requiring different marketing strategies and tactics.

For openers, consider Microsoft. The chances are good that you use several Microsoft products and services. Microsoft's Windows software owns a mind-boggling 97 percent share of the PC operating-system market, and its Office software captures a 90 percent share! However, this $32.5 billion company doesn't rest on past performance. As you'll see, it owes much of this success to a passion for innovation, abundant new-product development, and its quest for the "Next Big Thing."

No matter what brand of computer you're using or what you're doing on it, you're almost certain to be using some type of Microsoft product or service. In the world of computer and Internet software and technology, Microsoft dominates.

Microsoft's Windows operating system captures an astonishing 97 percent share of the PC market and a better than 40 percent share in the business server market. Microsoft Office, the company's largest moneymaker, grabs 90 percent of all office applications suite sales. Microsoft's Hotmail is the world's most used free mail service, hosting more than 100 million accounts, and its instant messaging service has nearly 30 million users. In June 2003, Bell Canada and Microsoft Corporation entered a strategic alliance co-branding their Sympatico.ca and MSN.ca portals to offer Canadians improved Internet services. The part-nership will enable delivery of a unique package of powerful and easy-to-use services, including MSN's recently launched premium services MSN® 8, along with Bell's uniquely Canadian perspective.

These and other successful products and services have made Microsoft incredibly profitable. During its first 27 years, the software giant has racked up more than $65 billion in profits. An investment of $3600 in 100 shares of Microsoft stock made back when the company went public would by now have mushroomed into 14 400 shares worth more than a cool $1.3 million. All this has made Microsoft co-founder Bill Gates the world's richest man, worth over $60 billion.

A happy ending to a rags-to-riches fairy tale? Not quite. In Microsoft's fast-changing high-tech world, nothing lasts forever—or even for long. Beyond maintaining its core products and businesses, Microsoft knows that its future depends on its ability to conquer new markets with innovative new products.

Microsoft hasn't always been viewed as an innovator. In fact, it has long been regarded as a "big fat copycat." Gates bought the original MS/DOS operating system software upon which he built the company's initial success from a rival programmer for $65 000. Later, Microsoft was accused of copying the user-friendly Macintosh "look and feel." More recently, the company was accused of copying Netscape's Internet browser. It wasn't innovation that made Microsoft, critics claim, but rather its brute-force use of its PC operating-system monopoly to crush competitors and muscle into markets. But no more. The technology giant is now innovating at a breakneck pace.

Thanks to its Windows and Office monopolies, and to Microsoft's legendary cash horde of more than $46 billion, the company has plenty of resources to pump into new products and technologies. In 2003 alone, it spent over $5.2 billion on R&D, more than competitors America Online, Sun Microsystems, and Oracle combined. Along with the cash, Microsoft has a strong, visionary leader in its efforts to innovate—no less than Bill Gates himself. Three years ago, Gates turned the CEO-ship of the company over to longtime number two, Steve Ballmer, and named himself "Chief Software Architect." He now spends most of his time and considerable talents happily attending to the details of Microsoft's new-product and technology development.

At the heart of Gates's innovation strategy is the Internet. "Gates sees a day when Microsoft software will... be at nearly every point a consumer or corporation touches the Web,...easily connecting people to the Internet wherever they happen to be," says *Business Week* analyst Jay Greene. In this new world, any software application on your computer—or on your cell phone, handheld device, or home electronics device—will tap directly into Internet services that help you manage your work and your life. To prepare for such "anytime, anywhere" computing, Microsoft will transform itself from a software company into an Internet service company. As a part of its Web services, Microsoft will one day rent out the latest versions of its software programs via the Net. "Once that happens," says Greene, "Microsoft hopes to deliver software like a steady flow of electricity, collecting monthly or annual usage fees that will give it a lush, predictable revenue stream."

This vision drives a major new Microsoft innovation initiative—dubbed ".Net My Services."

.Net My Services is the first of Microsoft's "personal Web services" strategy to upgrade the Internet to be more versatile and interactive. Its initial service, called Passport, provides an online repository for all sorts of personal information and privileges that you can tap into from any computer with a Web browser: contacts, credit card accounts, calendar, file space for documents,...an electronic ID card, and more. It will give you access to your important information from anywhere and also simplify online transactions such as purchasing merchandise or airline tickets. Because Passport knows you already, no matter which Web merchant you deal with, it promises to let you transact your business with far fewer clicks and much tighter security and privacy.

Passport members can subscribe to other .Net My Services services, including everything from notifying them of specific events to automatically updating their calendars when they purchase tickets or make an appointment online.

Within this broad strategic framework, Microsoft is now unleashing its biggest-ever new-products assault. "We've never had a year with this many new products," crows Gates. Here are just a few of the new products and technologies that Microsoft has recently launched or will soon introduce (as described in recent *Business Week* and *Fortune* accounts):

- *Dot.Net Services:* technology that lets unrelated websites talk with one another and with PC programs. One click can trigger a cascade of actions without the user having to open new programs or visit new websites.

- *Stinger:* Microsoft's latest software for cell phones. It will incorporate the functions of a PDA-address book, calendar, audio and video capabilities, and Internet connectivity to give access to .Net My Services services, mail, and Web browsing.

- *Natural-language processing:* software that will let computers respond to questions or commands in everyday language, not just computerese or a long series of mouse clicks. Combine that with speech recognition—another area in which Microsoft researchers are plugging away—and one day you'll be able to talk to your computer the same way you do to another person.

- *Face mapping:* using a digital camera to scan a PC user's head into a 3D image. Software then adds a full range of emotions. The point? Microsoft thinks that gamers will want to use their own images in role-playing games.

- *Information agents:* software agents that help you sort the deluge of electronic information. One day, an agent will study what types of messages you read first and know your schedule. Then it will sort mail and voice mail, interrupting you with only key messages.

- *Small business technologies:* customer-relationship, human resources, and supply-chain software for small and medium-size businesses. Microsoft also offers bCentral, a website and commerce hosting service. For a monthly fee, it will host a website and provide mail services, as well as a shopping-cart set-up for commerce transactions, credit card clearing, and customer management.

- *The digital home:* next-generation technologies aimed at making the PC the electronic hub of the twenty-first-century digital home. The new technologies will route music, movies, TV programming, mail, and news between the Web and PCs, TV set-top boxes, gadgets, and wall-size viewing screens, and sound systems that would make the neighbours call the cops. "Everything in the home will be connected," predicts Gates. And if he gets his way, most of the gizmos will use Microsoft software. Sales from Microsoft's consumer group will account for 18 percent of Microsoft's total business in 2003. The first major Microsoft connected-home product will be a gizmo code-named Mira. It's a flat-panel monitor that detaches from its stand and continues to connect wirelessly to the PC from anywhere in the house. With a stylus tapping icons or scrawling letters on a touch screen, Mom can check mail from the kitchen, the kids can chat with online buddies from the couch while watching MTV, and Dad can shop at Amazon.com from the back porch.

So, far from resting on its remarkable past successes, Microsoft is on a quest to discover tomorrow's exciting new technologies. "Even while its latest products are waiting on the launchpad, it continues to pour money into R&D in search of the Next Big Thing," comments Greene. Gates is jazzed about the future. "He gets wound up like a kid over stuff like creating a computer that watches your actions with a small video camera and determines if you're too busy to be interrupted with a phone call or mail," says Greene. An excited Gates shares the simple but enduring principle that guides innovation at Microsoft: "The whole idea of valuing the user's time, that's the Holy Grail," he says.[1]

A company has to be good at developing and managing new products. Every product seems to go through a life cycle—it is born, goes through several phases, and eventually dies, as newer products come along that better serve consumer needs. This product life cycle presents two major challenges. First, because all products eventually decline, the firm must be good at developing new products to replace aging ones (the problem of *new-product development*). Second, the firm must be good at adapting its marketing strategies in the face of changing tastes, technologies, and competition, as products pass through life-cycle stages (the problem of *product life-cycle strategies*). We first look at the problem of finding and developing new products and then at the problem of managing them successfully over their life cycles.

New-Product Development Strategy

New-product development
The development of original products, product improvements, product modifications, and new brands through the firm's own R&D efforts.

Given the rapid changes in consumer tastes, technology, and competition, companies must develop a steady stream of new products and services. A firm can obtain new products in two ways. One is through *acquisition*—by buying a whole company, a patent, or a licence to produce someone else's product. The other is through **new-product development** in the company's own research and development (R&D) department. By *new products*, we mean original products, product improvements, product modifications, and new brands that the firm develops through its own research and development efforts. In this chapter, we concentrate on new-product development.

New products have been the lifeblood of many firms, and Canadians have had a long history as inventors in this process. McIntosh apples, Pablum, frozen fish, and instant mashed potatoes are food products that all originated in Canada. Canadians are responsible for developing such sports and leisure activities as basketball, five-pin bowling, table hockey, and Trivial Pursuit. Many of these inventions spawned entire industries. Consider these other Canadian achievements:

- The modern communications industry was born with the invention of the telephone (Alexander Graham Bell).

- Reginald Fessenden, born near Sherbrooke, Quebec, was known as the father of radio after he invented amplitude modulation (AM) radio and transmitted his first broadcast in 1900.
- Another Canadian, Charles Fenerty, with his ability to make paper from wood pulp, founded that industry.
- Modern air travel was made possible by another Canadian, Wallace Rupert Turnbull, who developed the variable-pitch propeller.
- Dr. Cluny McPherson, of St. John's, Newfoundland, invented the gas mask used to save the lives of many allied soldiers in the First World War.
- A quintessentially Canadian tool, the snowblower was invented in 1925 by Quebec resident Arthur Sicard.
- Olivia Poole invented the Jolly Jumper, the internationally popular baby seat, in the 1950s.
- Steve Pacjack of Vancouver invented the beer case with a tuck-in handle that helps you lug your beer home.
- Three Canadian Olympic sailors—Bruce Kirby, Hans Fogh, and Ian Bruce—designed the world-class Laser sailboat in 1970.
- Wendy Murphy, a medical research technician, developed the Weevac 6—so named because it can carry six wee babies. Her idea was born when she realized, during the devastation of the 1985 Mexico City earthquake, that no apparatus existed to evacuate young children.
- Dr. Dennis Colonello designed the Abdomenizer in 1986 while practising as a chiropractor in northern Ontario. Before you laugh, note that he has rung up more than $100 million in sales!
- Dr. Frank Gunston, of Brandon, Manitoba, may have been one of the most philanthropic inventors. After developing and building a total knee-joint replacement, he decided not to patent his invention. This made it freely available to manufacturers and allowed patients needing the joint to benefit quickly from the technology and walk without pain. He received the prestigious Manning Principal Award in 1989 for his efforts.

To learn more about inventions and inventors, explore the About.com inventors' website (http://inventors.about.com/science/inventors/library/weekly).

Innovation can be very risky. RCA lost $800 million on its SelectaVision videodisc player; and Texas Instruments lost a staggering $920 million before withdrawing from the home computer business. General Mills spent $122 million to launch Wahoos!, a crispy corn chips snack, in 2002; however, the product achieved less than $26 million in sales. Even these amounts pale in comparison to the failure of the $6.5 billion Iridium global satellite-based wireless telephone system. Other costly product failures from sophisticated companies include Eagle Snacks (Anheuser-Busch), Pepsi Clear, Zap Mail electronic mail (FedEx), Polavision instant movies (Polaroid), Premier "smokeless" cigarettes (R.J. Reynolds), Clorox detergent (Clorox Company), and Arch Deluxe sandwiches (McDonald's).[2]

New products continue to fail at a disturbing rate. One study estimated that new consumer packaged goods (consisting mostly of line extensions) fail at a rate of 80 percent. Another study suggested that of the staggering 25 000 new consumer food, beverage, beauty, and health-care products to hit the market each year, only 40 percent will be around five years later. Moreover, failure rates for new industrial products may be as high as 30 percent. Still another estimates new-product failures to be as high as 95 percent.[3]

Why do so many new products fail? There are several reasons. Although an idea may be good, the market size may have been overestimated. Perhaps the actual product was not designed as well as it should have been. Or maybe it was incorrectly positioned in the market, priced too high, or advertised poorly. A high-level executive might push a favourite idea despite poor marketing research findings. Sometimes the costs of product development are higher than expected, and sometimes competitors fight back harder than expected.

Because so many new products fail, companies are anxious to learn how to improve their odds of new-product success. One way is to identify successful new products and determine what they have in common. Another is to study new-product failures to see what lessons can be learned (see Real Marketing 11.1). In all, to create successful new products, a company must understand its consumers, markets, and competitors, and develop products that deliver superior value to customers.

So companies face a problem—they must develop new products, but the odds weigh heavily against success. The solution lies in strong new-product planning and in setting up a systematic *new-product development process* for finding and growing new products. Figure 11.1 shows the eight major stages in this process.

Idea Generation

New-product development starts with **idea generation**—the systematic search for new-product ideas. A company usually has to generate many ideas to find a few good ones. According to one well-known management consultant, "For every 1000 ideas, only 100 will have enough commercial promise to merit a small-scale experiment, only 10 of those will warrant substantial financial commitment, and of those, only a couple will turn out to be unqualified successes." His conclusion? "If you want to find a few ideas with the power to enthral customers, foil competitors, and thrill investors, you must first generate hundreds and potentially thousands of unconventional strategic ideas."[4]

Major sources of new-product ideas include internal sources and external sources such as customers, competitors, distributors and suppliers, and others.

Internal Idea Sources

Using *internal sources*, the company can find new ideas through formal research and development. It can pick the brains of its scientists, engineers, manufacturing personnel, and salespeople. Some companies have developed successful "intrapreneurial" programs that encourage employees to think up and develop new-product ideas. For example, 3M's well-known "15 percent rule" allows employees to spend 15 percent of their time "bootlegging"—working on projects of personal interest whether or not those projects directly benefit the company. The spectacularly successful Post-it Notes evolved out of this program. Similarly, Texas Instruments' IDEA

Idea generation
The systematic search for new-product ideas.

Figure 11.1 Major stages in new-product development

REAL MARKETING

11.1 New-Product Failures: What Were They Thinking?

*S*trolling the aisles at Robert McMath's New Product Showcase and Learning Center or browsing the company's website is like finding yourself in some nightmare version of a supermarket. There's Gerber food for adults (puréed sweet-and-sour pork and chicken Madeira), Hot Scoop microwaveable ice cream sundaes, Ben-Gay aspirin, Premier smokeless cigarettes, and Miller Clear Beer. How about Avert Virucidal Tissues, Dr. Care Aerosol Toothpaste, Richard Simmons Dijon Vinaigrette Salad Spray, Look of Buttermilk shampoo, or garlic cake in a jar, parsnip chips, and aerosol mustard? Most of the 80 000 products on display were abject flops. Behind each of them are squandered dollars and hopes, but McMath, the genial curator of this product graveyard, believes that even failure—or perhaps especially failure—offers valuable lessons.

The New Product Showcase and Learning Center (now residing as part of the NewProductWorks consulting organization in Ann Arbor Michigan) is a place where product developers pay hundreds of dollars an hour to visit and learn from others' mistakes. McMath's unusual showcase represents $5.2 billion in product

The New Product Showcase and Learning Center is like finding yourself in some nightmare version of a supermarket. Each product failure represents squandered dollars and hopes.

investment. From it, he has distilled dozens of lessons for an industry that, by its own admission, has a very short memory. McMath "draws large audiences and commands a hefty speaking fee by decrying the convoluted thought processes of marketers, package designers, and consumer-opinion pundits who brought these and thousands of other duds-in-the-making to market," comments one analyst. "He gets laughs when he asks, 'What were they thinking?'" For those who can't make the trip to the centre or pay a steep consulting fee, McMath has now put his unique insights into a book by that same name, *What Were They Thinking?* Here are a few of the marketing lessons McMath offers:

- *Offer real value:* Many classic flops failed to deliver what customers really wanted. New Coke flopped when Coca-Cola failed to see the real value of the Coke brand to customers—tradition as well as taste. Ford pitched its Edsel as revolutionary; consumers saw it as merely revolting. And consumers quickly snuffed out R.J. Reynolds's Premier smokeless cigarettes. It seemed like a good idea at the time—who could argue against a healthier, non-polluting cigarette? But Premier didn't deliver what smokers really wanted—smoke. "It took them a while to figure out that smokers actually like the smoke part of smoking," McMath notes. "The only people who loved the product were non-smokers, and they somehow aren't the market RJR was trying to reach." Looking back, what was RJR thinking?

- *Cherish thy brand!:* The value of a brand is its good name, which it earns over time. People become loyal to it. They trust it to deliver a consistent set of attributes. Don't squander this trust by attaching your good name to something totally out of character. Louis Sherry No Sugar Added Gorgonzola Cheese Dressing was everything that Louis Sherry, known for its rich candies and ice cream, shouldn't be: sugarless, cheese, and salad dressing. Similarly, when you hear the name Ben-Gay, you immediately think of the way that Ben-Gay cream sears and stimulates your skin. Can you imagine swallowing Ben-Gay aspirin? Or how would you feel about quaffing a can of Exxon fruit punch or Kodak quencher? Cracker Jack cereal, Smucker's premium ketchup, and Fruit of the Loom laundry detergent were other misbegotten attempts to stretch a good name. What were they thinking?

• *Be different:* Me-too marketing is the number one killer of new products. Most such attempts fail. The ones that succeed usually require resources and persistence beyond the capabilities of most marketers. Pepsi-Cola led a very precarious existence for decades before establishing itself as the major competitor to Coca-Cola. More to the point, though, Pepsi is one of the few survivors among dozens of other brands that have challenged Coke for more than a century. Ever hear of Toca-Cola? Coco-Cola? Yum-Yum cola? French Wine of Cola? How about King-Cola, "the royal drink"? More recently, Afri Cola failed to attract African American soda drinkers and Cajun Cola pretty well flopped in the land of gumbo. All things being equal, an established product has a distinct advantage over any new product that is not notably different.

• *But don't be too different:* Some products are notably different from the products, services, or experiences that consumers normally purchase. *Too* different. They fail because consumers don't relate to them. You can tell that some innovative products are doomed as soon as you hear their names: Toaster Eggs. Cucumber antiperspirant spray. Health-Sea sea sausage. Look of Buttermilk shampoo. Dr. Care Aerosol Toothpaste (many

parents questioned the wisdom of arming their kids with something like this!). Other innovative ideas have been victims of a brand's past success. For example, Nabisco's Oreo Little Fudgies, a confectionery product with a chocolate coating meant to compete with candy, sounds like a natural. But for many years Nabisco has encouraged people to pull apart Oreo cookies and lick out the filling. And it's very messy to open an Oreo with a chocolate coating. What *was* Nabisco thinking?

• *Accentuate the positive:* Don't be fooled by the success of all the Dummies or Idiot's guides. People usually don't buy products that remind them of their shortcomings. Gillette's For Oily Hair Only shampoo wavered because people did not want to confess that they had greasy hair. People will use products that discreetly say "for oily hair" or "for sensitive skin" in small print on containers that are otherwise identical to the regular product. But they don't want to be hit over the head with reminders that they are overweight, have bad breath, sweat too much, or are elderly. Nor do they wish to advertise their faults and foibles to other people by carrying such products in their grocery carts. Really, what were they thinking?

Sources: Quotes from Gary Slack, "Innovations and Idiocities," *Beverage World,* November 15, 1998, p. 122; and Cliff Edwards, "Where Have All the Edsels Gone?" *Greensboro News Record,* May 24, 1999, p. B6. Bulleted points based on information found in Robert M. McMath and Thom Forbes, *What Were They Thinking? Money-Saving, Time-Saving, Face-Saving Marketing Lessons You Can Learn from Products That Flopped* (New York: Times Business, 1999), various pages; Melissa Master, "Spectacular Failures," *Across the Board,* March–April 2001, p. 24; and the NewProductWorks website, www.newproductworks.com/ (accessed July 2002).

program provides funds for employees who pursue their own ideas. Among the successful new products to come out of the IDEA program was TI's Speak 'n' Spell, the first children's toy to contain a microchip. Many other speaking toys followed, ultimately generating several hundred million dollars for TI.[5]

External Idea Sources

Good new-product ideas result from watching and listening to *customers*. The company can analyze customer questions and complaints to find new products that better solve consumer problems. Company engineers or salespeople can meet with and work alongside customers to get suggestions.

Heinz did just that when its researchers approached children, who consume more than half of the ketchup sold, to find out what would make ketchup more appealing to them. "When we asked them what would make the product more fun,"

When Heinz asked kids what would make the product more fun, they said, "Change the colour!" So, Heinz developed and launched EZ Squirt, now in a variety of colours targeted at kids. The EZ Squirt bottle's special nozzle also emits a thin ketchup stream, so tykes can autograph their burgers.

 says a Heinz spokesperson, "changing the colour was among the top responses." So, Heinz developed and launched EZ Squirt, green ketchup that comes in a soft, squeezable bottle targeted at kids. The new product was a smash hit, so Heinz followed up with an entire rainbow of EZ Squirt colours, including Funky Purple, Passion Pink, Awesome Orange, and Totally Teal. The EZ Squirt bottle's special nozzle also emits a thin ketchup stream, "so tykes can autograph their burgers (or squirt someone across the table, though Heinz neglects to mention that)."[6]

Kellogg Canada (www.kelloggs.ca) sought some consumer insights with the launch of its Jacks Pack initiative in 2000. In a bid to forge better connections with the youth market, Kellogg turned the future of its Apple Jacks cereal brand over to a panel of 21 youngsters aged 15 and under. The Jacks Pack "brand management team" influenced all key marketing decisions for the cereal, including new package designs and advertising campaigns. Mark Childs, vice-president of marketing for Kellogg, says, "When you think about it, it's such a simple idea—to have a kids' brand managed by kids, as opposed to a bunch of suits." Too much kid-targeted marketing these days amounts to one-way communication. "What this idea does is bring back the concept of two-way communication and feedback," Childs says.[7]

Consumers often create new products and uses on their own, and companies can benefit by finding these products and putting them on the market. For example, Avon capitalized on new uses discovered by consumers for its Skin-So-Soft bath oil and moisturizer. For years, customers have been spreading the word that Skin-So-Soft bath oil is also a terrific bug repellent. Whereas some consumers were content simply to bathe in water scented with the fragrant oil, others carried it in their backpacks to mosquito-infested campsites or kept a bottle on the deck of their beach houses. Now, Avon offers a complete line of Skin-So-Soft Bug Guard products, including Bug Guard Mosquito Repellent Moisturizing Towelettes and Bug Guard Plus, a combination moisturizer, insect repellent, and sunscreen.[8]

Finally, some companies even give customers the tools and resources to design their own products:

Many companies have abandoned their efforts to figure out exactly what products their customers want. Instead, they have equipped customers with tools that let them design their own products. The user-friendly tools employ new

technologies like computer simulation and rapid prototyping to make product development faster and less expensive. For example, Bush Boake Allen (BBA), a global supplier of specialty flavours to companies like Nestlé, provides a tool kit that enables its customers to develop their own flavours, which BBA then manufactures. Similarly, GE Plastics gives customers access to company data sheets, engineering expertise, simulation software, and other Web-based tools for designing better plastic products. Companies like LSI Logic and VLSI Technology provide customers with do-it-yourself tools that let them design their own specialized chips and customized integrated circuits. Using customers as innovators has become a hot new way to create value.[9]

Companies must be careful not to rely too heavily on customer input when developing new products. For some products, especially highly technical ones, customers may not know what they need. In such cases, "customers should not be trusted to come up with solutions; they aren't expert or informed enough for that part of the innovation process," says the head of an innovation management consultancy. "That's what your R&D team is for. Rather, customers should be asked only for outcomes—that is, what they want a product or service to *do* for them."[10]

Competitors are another good source of new-product ideas. Companies can watch competitors' ads and other communications for clues about their new products. Or they can buy competing new products, take them apart to see how they work, analyze their sales, and decide whether they should introduce a new product of their own.

Distributors and suppliers can also contribute many good new-product ideas. Resellers are close to the market and can pass along information about consumer problems and new-product possibilities. Suppliers can tell the company about new concepts, techniques, and materials that can be used to develop new products. Other idea sources include trade magazines, shows, and seminars; government agencies; new-product consultants; advertising agencies; marketing research firms; university and commercial laboratories; and inventors.

The search for new-product ideas should be systematic rather than haphazard. Otherwise, few new ideas will surface, and many good ideas will sputter in and die. Top management can avoid these problems by installing an idea management system that directs the flow of new ideas to a central point where they can be collected, reviewed, and evaluated. In setting up such a system, the company can do any or all of the following:[11]

- Appoint a respected senior person to be the company's idea manager.
- Create a multidisciplinary idea management committee of people from R&D, engineering, purchasing, operations, finance, and sales and marketing to meet regularly and evaluate proposed new product and service ideas.
- Set up a toll-free number or website for anyone who wants to send a new idea to the idea manager.
- Encourage all company stakeholders—employees, suppliers, distributors, dealers—to send their ideas to the idea manager.
- Set up formal recognition programs to reward those who contribute the best new ideas.

The idea-manager approach yields two favourable outcomes. First, it helps create an innovation-oriented company culture. It shows that top management supports, encourages, and rewards innovation. Second, it yields a larger number of ideas, among which will be found some especially good ones. As the system matures, ideas will flow more freely. No longer will good ideas wither for the lack of a sounding board or a senior product advocate.

Idea Screening

Idea screening

Screening new-product ideas to identify good ideas and drop poor ones as soon as possible.

The purpose of idea generation is to create a large number of ideas. The purpose of the succeeding stages is to *reduce* that number. The first idea-reducing stage is **idea screening**, which helps spot good ideas and drop poor ones as soon as possible. Product development costs rise greatly in later stages, so the company wants to proceed only with the product ideas that will turn into profitable products. As one marketing executive suggests, "Three executives sitting in a room can get 40 good ideas ricocheting off the wall in minutes. The challenge is getting a steady stream of good ideas out of the labs and creativity campfires, through marketing and manufacturing and all the way to consumers."[12]

Many companies require their executives to write up new-product ideas on a standard form that can be reviewed by a new-product committee. The write-up describes the product, the target market, and the competition. It makes some rough estimates of market size, product price, development time and costs, manufacturing costs, and rate of return. The committee then evaluates the idea against a set of general criteria. At Kao Company, the large Japanese consumer products company, the committee asks such questions as: Is the product truly useful to consumers and society? Is it good for our particular company? Does it mesh well with the company's objectives and strategies? Do we have the people, skills, and resources to make it succeed? Does it deliver more value to customers than competing products? Is it easy to advertise and distribute? Many companies have well-designed systems for rating and screening new-product ideas.

Concept Development and Testing

Product concept

A detailed version of the new-product idea stated in meaningful consumer terms.

An attractive idea must be developed into a **product concept**. It is important to distinguish between a product idea, a product concept, and a product image. A *product idea* is an idea for a possible product that the company can see itself offering to the market. A *product concept* is a detailed version of the idea stated in meaningful consumer terms. A *product image* is the way consumers perceive an actual or potential product.

Concept Development

DaimlerChrysler is getting ready to commercialize its experimental fuel-cell-powered electric car. This car's non-polluting fuel-cell system runs directly on methanol, which delivers hydrogen to the fuel cell with only water as a by-product. It is highly fuel efficient (75 percent more efficient than gasoline engines) and gives the new car an environmental advantage over standard internal combustion engine cars or even today's superefficient gasoline-electric hybrid cars. DaimlerChrysler is currently road-testing its NECAR 5 (New Electric Car) subcompact prototype and plans to deliver the first fuel-cell cars to customers in 2004. Based on the tiny Mercedes A-Class, the car accelerates quickly, reaches speeds of 144 kilometres per hour, and has a 448-kilometre driving range, giving it a huge edge over battery-powered electric cars that travel only about 128 kilometres before needing three to twelve hours of recharging.[13]

DaimlerChrysler's task is to develop this new product into alternative product concepts, find out how attractive each concept is to customers, and choose the best one. It might create the following product concepts for the fuel-cell electric car:

Concept 1   A moderately priced subcompact designed as a second family car to be used around town. The car is ideal for running errands and visiting friends.

Concept 2   A medium-cost sporty compact appealing to young people.

Concept 3   An inexpensive subcompact "green" car appealing to environmentally conscious people who want practical transportation and low pollution.

Concept 4   A high-end SUV appealing to those who love the space SUVs provide but lament the poor gas mileage.

Concept Testing

Concept testing calls for testing new-product concepts with a group of target consumers. The concepts may be presented to consumers symbolically or physically. Here, in words, is Concept 3:

> An efficient, fun-to-drive, fuel-cell-powered subcompact car that seats four. This methanol-powered wonder provides practical and reliable transportation with virtually no pollution. It goes up to 130 km per hour and, unlike battery-powered electric cars, never needs recharging. It's priced, fully equipped, at $26 000.

Concept testing
Testing new-product concepts with a group of target consumers to find out if the concepts have strong consumer appeal.

DaimlerChrysler's task is to develop its fuel-cell-powered car into alternative product concepts, find out how attractive each concept is to customers, and choose the best one.

For some concept tests, a word or picture description might be sufficient. However, a more concrete and physical presentation of the concept will increase the reliability of the concept test. Today, some marketers are finding innovative ways to make product concepts more real to concept test subjects. For example, some are using virtual reality to test product concepts. Virtual reality programs use computers and sensory devices (such as gloves or goggles) to simulate reality. A designer of kitchen cabinets can use a virtual reality program to help a customer "see" how his or her kitchen would look and work if remodelled with the company's products. Although virtual reality is still in its infancy, its applications are increasing daily.[14]

After being exposed to the concept, consumers then may be asked to react to it by answering the questions in Table 11.1. The answers will help the company decide which concept has the strongest appeal. For example, the last question asks about the consumer's intention to buy. Suppose 10 percent of the consumers said they "definitely" would buy and another 5 percent said "probably." The company could project these figures to the full population in this target group to estimate sales volume. Even then, the estimate is uncertain because people do not always carry out their stated intentions.

Many firms routinely test new-product concepts with consumers before attempting to turn them into actual new products. Every month, Richard Saunders Inc.'s Acu-POLL research system tests 35 new-product concepts in person on 100 nationally representative grocery-store shoppers, rating them as "Pure Gold" or "Fool's Gold" concepts. In past polls, Nabisco's Oreo Chocolate Cones concept received a rare A1 rating, meaning that consumers think it is an outstanding concept that they would try and buy. Glad Ovenware, Reach Whitening Tape dental floss, and Lender's Bake at Home Bagels were also big hits.

Other product concepts didn't fare so well. Nubrush anti-bacterial toothbrush spray disinfectant, from Applied Microdontics, received an F. Consumers found Nubrush to be overpriced, and most don't think they have a problem with "infected" toothbrushes. Nor did consumers think much of Excedrin Tension Headache Cooling Pads or Moist Mates premoistened toilet tissues. Another concept that fared poorly was Chef Williams 5 Minute Marinade, which comes with a syringe customers use to inject the marinade into meats. "I can't see that on grocery shelves," comments an Acu-Poll executive. Some consumers might find the thought of injecting something into meat a bit repulsive, and "it's just so politically incorrect to have this syringe on there."[15]

Marketing Strategy Development

Marketing strategy development
Designing an initial marketing strategy for a new product based on the product concept.

Suppose DaimlerChrysler finds that Concept 3 for the fuel-cell-powered car tests best. The next step is **marketing strategy development**—designing an initial marketing strategy for introducing this car to the market.

Table 11.1   Questions for Electric Car Concept Test

1. Do you understand the concept of a fuel-cell-powered electric car?
2. Do you believe the claims about the car's performance?
3. What are the major benefits of the fuel-cell-powered electric car compared with a conventional car?
4. What are its advantages compared with a battery-powered electric car?
5. What improvements in the car's features would you suggest?
6. For what uses would you prefer a fuel-cell-powered electric car to a conventional car?
7. What would be a reasonable price to charge for the car?
8. Who would be involved in your decision to buy such a car? Who would drive it?
9. Would you buy such a car? (Definitely, probably, probably not, definitely not)

The *marketing strategy statement* consists of three parts. The first part describes the target market, the planned product positioning, and the sales, market share, and profit goals for the first few years. Thus:

> The target market is younger, well-educated, moderate- to high-income individuals, couples, or small families seeking practical, environmentally responsible transportation. The car will be positioned as more economical to operate, more fun to drive, less polluting than today's internal combustion engine or hybrid cars, and less restricting than battery-powered electric cars, which must be recharged regularly. The company will aim to sell 100 000 cars in the first year, at a loss of not more than $19.5 million. In the second year, the company will aim for sales of 120 000 cars and a profit of $32.5 million.

The second part of the marketing strategy statement outlines the product's planned price, distribution, and marketing budget for the first year:

> The fuel-cell-powered electric car will be offered in three colours and will have optional air-conditioning and power-drive features. It will sell at a retail price of $26 000—with 15 percent off the list price to dealers. Dealers who sell more than 10 cars per month will receive an additional discount of 5 percent on each car sold that month. An advertising budget of $39 million will be split 50–50 between national and local advertising. Advertising will emphasize the car's fun and low emissions. During the first year, $130 000 will be spent on marketing research to find out who is buying the car and their satisfaction levels.

The third part of the marketing strategy statement describes the planned long-run sales, profit goals, and marketing mix strategy:

> DaimlerChrysler intends to capture a 3 percent long-run share of the total auto market and realize an after-tax return on investment of 15 percent. To achieve this, product quality will start high and be improved over time. Price will be raised in the second and third years if competition permits. The total advertising budget will be raised each year by about 10 percent. Marketing research will be reduced to $78 000 per year after the first year.

Business Analysis

Business analysis
A review of the sales, costs, and profit projections for a new product to determine whether these factors satisfy the company's objectives.

Once management has decided on its product concept and marketing strategy, it can evaluate the business attractiveness of the proposal. **Business analysis** involves reviewing the sales, costs, and profit projections for a new product to determine whether they satisfy the company's objectives. If they do, the product can move to the product development stage.

To estimate sales, the company should examine the sales history of similar products and survey market opinion. It should estimate minimum and maximum sales to assess the range of risk. After preparing the sales forecast, management can estimate the expected product costs and profits, including marketing, R&D, operations, accounting, and finance costs. The company then uses the sales and costs figures to analyze the new product's financial attractiveness.

Product Development

Product development
Developing the product concept into a physical product to ensure that the product idea can be turned into a workable product.

So far, for many new-product concepts the product may have existed only as a word description, a drawing, or perhaps a crude mock-up. If the product concept passes the business test, it moves into **product development**. Here, R&D or engineering develops the product concept into a physical product. The product development step, however, now calls for a large jump in investment. It will show whether the product idea can be turned into a workable product.

The R&D department will develop one or more physical versions of the product concept, with the aim of designing a prototype that will satisfy and excite consumers and that can be produced quickly and at budgeted costs. Developing a successful prototype can take days, weeks, months, or even years. Often, products undergo rigorous tests to ensure that they perform safely and effectively. These are examples of such product tests:[16]

At Shaw Industries, temps are paid $5 an hour to pace up and down five long rows of sample carpets for up to eight hours a day, logging an average of 22 km each. One regular reads three mysteries a week while pacing and shed 20 kg in two years. Shaw Industries counts walkers' steps and figures that 20 000 steps equal several years of average carpet wear.

P&G spends $195 million on 4000 to 5000 studies a year, testing everything from the ergonomics of picking up a shampoo bottle to how long women can keep their hands in sudsy water. On any given day, subjects meet in focus groups, sell their dirty laundry to researchers, put prototype diapers on their babies' bottoms, and rub mysterious creams on their faces. Last year, one elementary school raised $22 000 by having students and parents take part in P&G product tests. Students tested toothpaste, wore new sneakers, and ate brownies, while their mothers watched advertising for Tempo tissue, P&G's paper wipes packaged to fit in a car.

At Gillette, almost everyone gets involved in new-product testing. Every working day at Gillette, 200 volunteers from various departments come to work unshaven and troop to small booths with a sink and mirror. There they take instructions from technicians on the other side of a small window as to which razor, shaving cream, or aftershave to use. The volunteers evaluate razors for sharpness of blade, smoothness of glide, and ease of handling. In a nearby shower room, women perform the same ritual on their legs, underarms, and what the company delicately refers to as the "bikini area." "We bleed so you'll get a good shave at home," says one Gillette employee.

Diana Yanik, coordinator of product development at the Heinz Company of Canada, sits tensely watching eight specially trained testers enter partitioned booths where they taste three small bowls with variations of Heinz's new product, Toddler Peach Cobbler. Reaching this point took four years and

Product testing: Shaw Industries pays temps to pace up and down on sample carpets. Each averages about 22 km a day. Gillette uses employee-volunteers to test new shaving products—"We bleed so you'll get a good shave at home," says one Gillette employee.

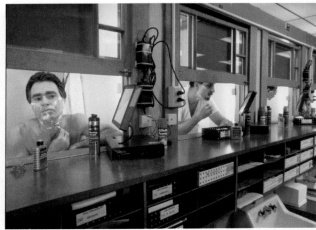

Heinz Canada's Toddler Peach Cobbler took four years to develop.

involved hundreds of decisions for Yanik, including finding a new type of peach that would withstand various processing methods. Careful testing is essential for Canada's "most health-conscious and finicky consumers"—small children who can barely hold a fork or spoon. Prototypes were tested on 900 mothers and their children. Following dozens of recipe changes, $400 000 of specialized equipment, and weeks of rigid safety testing, the product was finally ready for supermarket shelves, where it soon became a hit.

The prototype must have the required functional features and also convey the intended psychological characteristics. The fuel-cell-powered car, for example, should strike consumers as being well built and safe. Management must learn what makes consumers decide that a car is well built. For some, this means having "solid-sounding" doors. For others, it means that the car is able to withstand heavy impact in crash tests. Consumer tests are conducted in which consumers test-drive the car and rate its attributes.

Test Marketing

Test marketing
The stage of new-product development in which the product and marketing program are tested in more realistic market settings.

If the product passes functional and consumer tests, the next step is **test marketing**, the stage at which the product and marketing program are introduced into more realistic market settings. Test marketing gives the marketer experience with marketing the product before going to the expense of full introduction. It lets the company test the product and its entire marketing program—positioning strategy, advertising, distribution, pricing, branding and packaging, and budget levels.

Many global packaged goods companies are now viewing Canada as a hot test market. A slew of innovative products that have completely revolutionized their categories—Swiffer WetJet, Benylin Freezer Pops, Listerine PocketPaks, and Mr. Christie Cookie Barz—have debuted here in the last couple of years. There are

Procter & Gamble test marketed the Swiffer WetJet in Canada and Belgium before launching the product worldwide.

several reasons why Canada is an ideal test market. First, our diverse population and geographically separated markets enable marketers to isolate various consumer segments with no risk of the results being contaminated by marketing programs from other regions. Tom Vierhile, general manager at U.S.-based Marketing Intelligence Service, notes, "When companies test products, they look for markets that have relatively low-cost media and can reach a lot of people and Canada's sort of laid out that way." Moreover, when makers of new-to-the-world products like Listerine PocketPaks do a trial launch in a smaller market like Canada, they can smooth out any wrinkles that might occur while producing the product and refine their sales forecasts. PocketPaks' sleek translucent packaging and Matrix-inspired advertising—starring a female action-hero who destroys hideous aliens—made the breath-freshening strips a hit with the 15-to-30-year-old target in Canada. The product seized 18 percent of the market and the test market results helped Pfizer adjust its advertising so that it achieved a similar success rate in the United States.[17]

Janet Finlay, manager of market research for Toronto-based Cadbury Chocolate Canada, adds to the list of reasons why companies test market:[18]

- to determine the target market profile
- to assess consumer acceptability, trial, repeat purchase rate, and cycle
- to evaluate trade reception and distribution penetration
- to design effective media plans and promotions

The amount of test marketing needed varies with each new product. Test marketing costs can be high, and it takes time that may allow competitors to gain advantages. When the costs of developing and introducing the product are low, or when management is already confident about the new product, the company may do little or no test marketing. In fact, test marketing by consumer packaged-goods firms has been declining in recent years. Companies often do not test market simple line extensions or copies of successful competitor products. For example, Procter & Gamble introduced its Folger's decaffeinated coffee crystals without test marketing, and Pillsbury (www.pillsbury.com) rolled out Chewy granola bars and chocolate-covered Granola Dipps with no standard test market.

However, when introducing a new product requires a big investment, or when management is not sure of the product or marketing program, a company may do a lot of test marketing. For example, Unilever spent two years testing its highly successful Lever 2000 bar soap before introducing it internationally.[19]

Although test-marketing costs can be high, they are often small when compared with the costs of making a major mistake. For example, McDonald's made a costly mistake when it introduced its low-fat burger, the McLean Deluxe, nationally without the chain's normal and lengthy testing process. The new product failed after a big investment but lean results. And Nabisco's launch of one new product without testing had disastrous—and soggy—results. When it tried to launch a cereal based on its successful Teddy Grahams product, consumers rejected the product since it didn't stay crunchy in milk.[20]

Still, test marketing doesn't guarantee success. For example, Procter & Gamble tested its new Fit produce rinse heavily for five years and Olay cosmetics for three years. Although market tests suggested the products would be successful, P&G had to pull the plug on both shortly after their introductions.[21]

When using test marketing, consumer products companies usually choose one of three approaches—standard test markets, controlled test markets, or simulated test markets.

Standard Test Markets

Using standard test markets, the company finds a small number of representative test cities, conducts a full marketing campaign in these cities, and uses store audits, consumer and distributor surveys, and other measures to gauge product performance. The results are used to forecast national sales and profits, discover potential product problems, and fine-tune the marketing program.

Standard test markets have some drawbacks. They may be very costly and they may take a long time—some last as long as three to five years. Moreover, competitors can monitor test market results or even interfere with them by cutting their prices in test cities, increasing their promotion, or even buying up the product being tested. Finally, test markets give competitors a look at the company's new product well before it is introduced nationally. Thus, competitors may have time to develop defensive strategies, and may even beat the company's product to the market. For example, while Clorox was still test marketing its new detergent with bleach in selected markets, P&G launched Tide with Bleach nationally. Tide with Bleach quickly became the segment leader; Clorox later withdrew its detergent.

Despite these disadvantages, standard test markets are still the most widely used approach for major market testing. However, many companies today are shifting to quicker and cheaper controlled and simulated test-marketing methods.

Controlled Test Markets

Several research firms keep controlled panels of stores that have agreed to carry new products for a fee. Controlled test-marketing systems such as AC Nielsen's Scantrack and Information Resources Inc.'s (IRI) BehaviorScan track individual behaviour from the television set to the checkout counter.

In each BehaviorScan market, IRI maintains a panel of shoppers who report all of their purchases by showing an identification card at check-out in participating

IRI's BehaviorScan provides an in-market laboratory for testing new products and marketing programs under highly controlled yet real-world conditions.

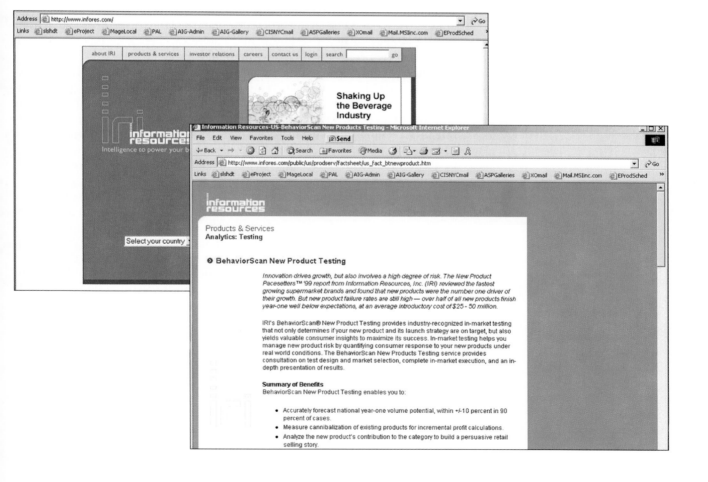

stores and by using a handheld scanner at home to record purchases at non-participating stores.[22] Within test stores, IRI controls such factors as shelf placement, price, and in-store promotions for the product being tested. IRI also measures TV viewing in each panel household and sends special commercials to panel member television sets. Direct mail promotions can also be tested.

Detailed scanner information on each consumer's purchases is fed into a central computer, where it is combined with the consumer's demographic and TV viewing information and reported daily. Thus, BehaviorScan can provide store-by-store, week-by-week reports on the sales of tested products. Such panel purchasing data enables in-depth diagnostics not possible with retail point-of-sale data alone, including repeat purchase analysis, buyer demographics, and earlier, more accurate sales forecasts after just 12 to 24 weeks in market. Most importantly, the system allows companies to evaluate their specific marketing efforts.

Controlled test markets, such as BehaviorScan, usually cost less than standard test markets. Also, because retail distribution is "forced" in the first week of the test, controlled test markets can be completed much more quickly than standard test markets. As in standard test markets, controlled test markets allow competitors to get a look at the company's new product. And some companies are concerned that the limited number of controlled test markets used by the research services may not be representative of their products' markets or target consumers. However, the research firms are experienced in projecting test market results to broader markets and can usually account for biases in the test markets used.

Simulated Test Markets

Companies can also test new products in a simulated shopping environment. The company or research firm shows ads and promotions for various products, including the new product being tested, to a sample of consumers. It gives consumers a small amount of money and invites them to a real or laboratory store where they may keep the money or use it to buy items. The researchers note how many consumers buy the new product and competing brands.

This simulation provides a measure of the trial and the commercial's effectiveness against competing commercials. The researchers then ask consumers the reasons for their purchase or non-purchase. Some weeks later, they interview the consumers by phone to determine product attitudes, usage, satisfaction, and repurchase intentions. Using sophisticated computer models, the researchers then project national sales from results of the simulated test market. Recently, some marketers have begun to use new high-tech approaches to simulate test market research, such as virtual reality and the Internet.

Firms like Canada Market Research and Gadd International Research have developed CD-ROM tools—Visionary Shopper and Simul-Shop—that recreate shopping situations in which researchers can test consumers' reactions to such factors as product positioning, store layouts, and package designs. For example, suppose a cereal marketer wants to test reactions to a new package design and store-shelf positioning. Using Visionary Shopper or Simul-Shop on a standard desktop PC, test shoppers begin their shopping spree with a screen showing the outside of a grocery store. They click to enter the virtual store and are guided to the appropriate store section. Once there, they can scan the shelf, pick up various cereal packages, rotate them, study the labels—even look around to see what is on the shelf behind them. Using the touch screen, they can "purchase" the product or return it to the shelf. About the only thing they can't do is open the box and taste the cereal. The virtual shopping trip includes full sound and video, along with a guide who directs users through the experience and answers their questions.[23]

Simulated test markets overcome some of the disadvantages of standard and controlled test markets. They usually cost much less, can be run in eight weeks or less, and keep the new product out of competitors' view. Yet, because of their small samples and simulated shopping environments, many marketers do not consider simulated test markets to be as accurate or reliable as larger, real-world tests. Still, simulated test markets are used widely, often as "pre-test" markets.

Commercialization

Commercialization
Introducing a new product into the market.

Test marketing gives management the information needed to make a final decision about whether to launch the new product. If the company goes ahead with **commercialization**—introducing the new product into the market—it will face high costs. The company may have to build or rent a manufacturing facility. And it may have to spend, in the case of a new consumer packaged good, between $13 million and $260 million for North American advertising and sales promotion in the first year.

The company launching a new product must first decide on introduction *timing*. If DaimlerChrysler's new fuel-cell electric car will eat into the sales of the company's other cars, its introduction may be delayed. If the car can be improved further, or if the economy is down, the company may wait until the following year to launch it.

Next, the company must decide *where* to launch the new product—in a single location, a region, the national market, or the international market. Few companies have the confidence, capital, and capacity to launch new products into full national or international distribution. They will develop a planned *market rollout* over time. In particular, small companies may enter attractive cities or regions one at a time. Larger companies, however, may quickly introduce new models into several regions or into the full national market.

Companies with international distribution systems may introduce new products through global rollouts. Colgate-Palmolive (www.colgate.com) used to follow a "lead-country" strategy. For example, it launched its Palmolive Optims shampoo and conditioner first in Australia, the Philippines, Hong Kong, and Mexico, then rapidly rolled it out into Europe, Asia, Latin America, and Africa. However, most international companies now introduce their new products in swift global assaults. Recently, in its fastest new-product rollout ever, Colgate introduced its Actibrush battery-powered toothbrush into 50 countries in a year, generating $115 million in sales. Such rapid worldwide expansion solidified the brand's market position before foreign competitors could react.[24]

Speeding Up New-Product Development

Sequential product development
A new-product development approach in which one company department works individually to complete its stage of the process before passing the new product along to the next department and stage.

Many companies organize their new-product development process into the orderly sequence of steps shown in Figure 11.1 (page 429), starting with idea generation and ending with commercialization. Under this **sequential product development**

Colgate introduces new products in swift global assaults, solidifying the brand's market position before foreign competitors can react.

approach, one company department works individually to complete its stage of the process before passing the new product along to the next department and stage. This orderly, step-by-step process can help bring control to complex and risky projects. But it also can be dangerously slow. In fast-changing, highly competitive markets, such slow-but-sure product development can result in product failures, lost sales and profits, and crumbling market positions. "Speed to market" and reducing new-product-development "cycle time" have become pressing concerns to companies in all industries.

To get their new products to market more quickly, many companies are adopting a faster, team-oriented approach called **simultaneous product development** (or team-based or collaborative product development). Under this approach, company departments work closely together, overlapping the steps in the product development process to save time and increase effectiveness. Instead of passing the new product from department to department, the company assembles a team of people from various departments that stays with the new product from start to finish. Such teams usually include people from the marketing, finance, design, manufacturing, and legal departments, and even supplier and customer companies.

Top management gives the product development team general strategic direction, but no clear-cut product idea or work plan. It challenges the team with stiff and seemingly contradictory goals—"turn out carefully planned and superior new products, but do it quickly"—and then gives the team whatever freedom and resources it needs to meet the challenge. In the sequential process, a bottleneck at one phase can seriously slow the entire project. In the simultaneous approach, if one functional area hits snags, it works to resolve them while the team moves on.

The Allen-Bradley Company, a maker of industrial controls, realized tremendous benefits by using simultaneous development. Under its old sequential approach, the company's marketing department handed off a new-product idea to designers, who worked in isolation to prepare concepts that they then passed along to product engineers. The engineers, also working by themselves, developed expensive prototypes and handed them off to manufacturing, which tried to find a way to build the new product. Finally, after many years and dozens of costly design compromises and delays, marketing was asked to sell the new product, which it often found to be too high-priced or sadly out of date. Now, all of Allen-Bradley's departments work together to develop new products. The results have been astonishing. For example, the company recently developed a new electrical control in just two years; under the old system, it would have taken six years.

The simultaneous approach does have some limitations. Super-fast product development can be riskier and more costly than the slower, more orderly sequential approach. Moreover, it often creates increased organizational tension and confusion. And the company must take care that rushing a product to market doesn't adversely affect its quality—the objective is not just to create products faster, but to create them *better* and faster.

Despite these drawbacks, in rapidly changing industries facing increasingly shorter product life cycles, the rewards of fast and flexible product development far exceed the risks. Companies that get new and improved products to the market faster than competitors often gain a dramatic competitive edge. They can respond more quickly to emerging consumer tastes and charge higher prices for more advanced designs. As one auto industry executive states, "What we want to do is get the new car approved, built, and in the consumer's hands in the shortest time possible.... Whoever gets there first gets all the marbles."[25]

Thus, new-product success requires more than simply thinking up a few good ideas, turning them into products, and finding customers for them. It requires a systematic approach for finding new ways to create value for target consumers, from generating and screening new-product ideas to creating and rolling out want-satisfying products to customers. More than this, successful new-product development requires a total-company commitment. At companies known for their new-product prowess—such as 3M, Gillette, and Intel—the entire culture encourages, supports, and rewards innovation (see Real Marketing 11.2).

Simultaneous (team-based) product development
An approach to developing new products in which various company departments work closely together, overlapping the steps in the product development process to save time and increase effectiveness.

REAL MARKETING

11.2 3M: A Culture for Innovation

*Y*ou see the headline in every 3M communication: "Innovation and Practical Solutions." But at 3M, innovation is more than just an advertising pitch. 3M views innovation as its path to growth and new products as its lifeblood. It markets more than 50 000 products. These products range from sandpaper, adhesives, and laser optical disks to contact lenses, heart-lung machines, and futuristic synthetic ligaments; from coatings that sleeken boat hulls to hundreds of sticky tapes—Scotch tape, masking tape, superbonding tape, acid-free photo and document tape, refastening-disposable-diaper tape, and the favourite of handyman Red Green: duct tape!

3M's goal is to derive an astonishing 30 percent of each year's sales from products introduced within the previous four years. More astonishing, it usually succeeds! Each year 3M launches more than 200 new products. And in 2002, a full third of its $20 billion in sales came from products introduced within the past four years. This legendary emphasis on innovation has consistently made 3M one of North America's most admired companies. In 2002, 3M once again earned the number one spot on *Fortune*'s list of companies most admired for innovation.

At 3M, new products don't just happen. The company works hard to create an environment that supports innovation. In 2002, it invested $1.3 billion, or 6 percent of annual sales, in research and development—almost twice as much as the average company. Its Innovation Task Force seeks out and destroys corporate bureaucracy that might interfere with new-product progress. And hired consultants help 3M find ways to make employees more inventive.

3M encourages everyone to look for new products. The company's renowned "15 percent rule" allows all employees to spend up to 15 percent of their time "bootlegging"—working on projects of personal interest. When a promising idea comes along, 3M forms a venture team made up of the researcher who developed the idea and volunteers from manufacturing, sales, marketing, and legal. The team nurtures the product and protects it from company bureaucracy. Team members stay with the product until it succeeds or fails and then return to their previous jobs. Some teams have tried three or four times before finally making a success of an idea. Each year, 3M hands out Golden Step Awards to venture teams whose new products earned more than US$2 million in U.S. sales, or US$4 million in worldwide sales, within three years of introduction.

3M knows that it must try thousands of new-product ideas to hit one big jackpot. One well-worn slogan at 3M is, "You have to kiss a lot of frogs to find a prince." "Kissing frogs" often means making mistakes, but 3M accepts blunders and dead ends as a normal part of creativity and innovation. In fact, its philosophy seems to be, "If you aren't making mistakes, you probably aren't doing anything."

As it turns out, "blunders" have turned into some of 3M's most successful products. Old-timers at 3M love to tell the story about the chemist who accidentally spilled a new chemical on her tennis shoes. Some days later, she noticed that the spots hit by the chemical had not gotten dirty. Eureka! The chemical

3M views innovation as its path to growth and new products as its lifeblood. Its entire culture encourages, supports, and rewards innovation.

eventually became Scotchgard fabric protector. They tell about the early 3M scientist who had a deathly fear of shaving with a straight razor. Instead, he invented a very fine, waterproof sandpaper that he used to sand the stubble from his face each morning. Although this invention never caught on as a shaving solution, it became one of 3M's best-selling products—wet-dry sandpaper, now used for a wide variety of commercial and industrial applications.

And then there's the one about 3M scientist Spencer Silver. Silver started out to develop a super-strong adhesive; instead he came up with one that didn't stick very well at all. He sent the apparently useless substance on to other 3M researchers to see whether they could find something to do with it. Nothing happened for several years. Then Arthur Fry, another 3M scientist, had a problem—and an idea. As a choir member in a local church, Mr. Fry was having trouble marking places in his hymnal—the little scraps of paper he used kept falling out. He tried dabbing some of Mr. Silver's weak glue on one of the scraps. It stuck nicely and later peeled off without damaging the hymnal. Thus were born 3M's Post-it Notes, a product that is now one of the top-selling office supply products in the world!

Thus, 3M could easily amend its long-running "Innovation Working for You" ad line to include "and for *3M.*" Still, there are limits. Some analysts question whether such a freewheeling, no-questions-asked creative culture is appropriate given the cost-reduction pressures of today's tougher economic times. In fact,

3M's new CEO, Jim McNerney, recently launched a "take-no-prisoners" campaign against inefficiencies. He's cutting costs and slimming down the company's workforce. He is also overhauling the 3M R&D organization and culture, one in which even 3M old-timers agree that money hasn't always been spent wisely. According to one analyst, McNerney "vows to take an organization of myriad product and research fiefdoms—which happens to be one of the most respected manufacturing concerns in the world—and hammer it into one shared corporate culture." He is carefully examining where R&D dollars are spent and setting uniform performance standards and accountability across the company.

The risk is that the changing culture and organizational restructuring might stifle 3M's hallmark creativity. "The most important thing about 3M—the single most important thing—is you get to do things your own way," says a senior 3M executive and 33-year veteran. McNerney understands the balancing act: efficiency versus hands-off R&D spending; accountability versus individual creative freedom. "My job is to add scale in a fast-moving, entrepreneurial environment," he says. "If I end up killing that entrepreneurial spirit, I will have failed."

Sources: Quotes from Rick Mullin, "Analysts Rate 3M's New Culture," *Chemical Week,* September 26, 2001, pp. 39–40; and Michael Arndt, "3M: A Lab for Growth," *Business Week,* January 21, 2002, pp. 50–51. Also see William H. Miller, "New Leader, New Era," November 2001, www.industryweek.com; "America's Most Admired Companies," *Fortune,* March 4, 2002, p. 75; and information from the 3M website, www.3m.com (July 2002).

Product Life-Cycle Strategies

After launching the new product, management wants it to enjoy a long and happy life. Although it does not expect the product to sell forever, management wants to earn a decent profit to cover all the effort and risk that went into launching it. Management is aware that each product will have a life cycle, although it cannot know the exact shape and length in advance.

Product life cycle (PLC)
The course of a product's sales and profits over its lifetime. It involves five distinct stages: product development, introduction, growth, maturity, and decline.

Figure 11.2 (on page 447) shows a typical **product life cycle (PLC)**, the course that a product's sales and profits take over its lifetime. The product life cycle has five stages:

1. *Product development* begins when the company finds and develops a new product idea. During product development, sales are zero and the company's investment costs mount.

2. *Introduction* is a period of slow sales growth as the product is being introduced in the market. Profits are non-existent in this stage because of the heavy expenses of product introduction.

3. *Growth* is a period of rapid market acceptance and increasing profits.

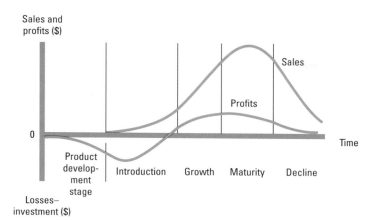

Figure 11.2 Sales and profits over the product's life from inception to demise

4. *Maturity* is a period of slowdown in sales growth because the product has achieved acceptance by most potential buyers. Profits level off or decline because of increased marketing outlays to defend the product against competition.

5. *Decline* is the period when sales fall off and profits drop.

Not all products follow this S-shaped product life cycle. Some products are introduced and die quickly; others stay in the mature stage for a long, long time. Some enter the decline stage and are then cycled back into the growth stage through strong promotion or repositioning.

Product life cycles: Companies want their products to enjoy long and happy life cycles. Hershey's Chocolate Bars have been "unchanged" since 1899.

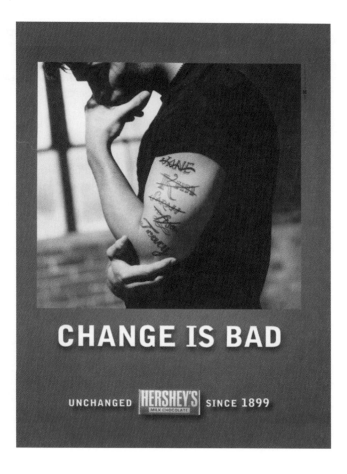

The PLC concept can describe a *product class* (gasoline-powered automobiles), a *product form* (SUVs), or a *brand* (the Ford Explorer). The PLC concept applies differently in each case. Product classes have the longest life cycles—the sales of many product classes stay in the mature stage for a long time. Product forms, in contrast, tend to have the standard PLC shape. Product forms such as "cream deodorants," the "dial telephone," and "cassette tapes" passed through a regular history of introduction, rapid growth, maturity, and decline.

A specific brand's life cycle can change quickly because of changing competitive attacks and responses. For example, although laundry soaps (product class) and powdered detergents (product form) have enjoyed fairly long life cycles, the life cycles of individual brands are much shorter. Today's leading brands of powdered laundry soap are Tide and Cheer; the leading brands 75 years ago were Fels Naptha, Octagon, and Kirkman.[26]

The PLC concept can also be applied to what are known as styles, fashions, and fads. Their special life cycles are shown in Figure 11.3. A **style** is a basic and distinctive mode of expression. For example, styles appear in homes (Victorian, ranch, modern); clothing (formal, casual); and art (realistic, surrealistic, abstract). Once a style is invented, it may last for generations, coming in and out of vogue. A style has a cycle showing several periods of renewed interest.

A **fashion** is a currently accepted or popular style in a given field. For example, the more formal "business attire" look of corporate dress of the 1980s and early 1990s has now given way to the "business casual" look of today. Fashions tend to grow slowly, remain popular for a while, then decline slowly.

Fads are fashions that enter quickly, are adopted with great zeal, peak early, and decline very fast. They last only a short time and tend to attract only a limited following. "Pet rocks" are a classic example of a fad. Upon hearing his friends complain about how expensive it was to care for their dogs, advertising copywriter Gary Dahl joked about his pet rock and was soon writing a spoof of a dog-training manual for it. Soon Dahl was selling some 1.5 million ordinary beach pebbles at four dollars a pop. Yet the fad, which broke in October 1975, had sunk like a stone by the next February. Dahl's advice to those who want to succeed with a fad: "Enjoy it while it lasts." Other examples of fads include Rubik's Cubes, lava lamps, CB radios, and scooters. Most fads do not survive for long because they normally do not satisfy a strong need or satisfy it well.[27]

The PLC concept can be applied by marketers as a useful framework for describing how products and markets work. But using the PLC concept for forecasting product performance or for developing marketing strategies presents some practical problems. For example, managers may have trouble identifying which stage of the PLC the product is in, or pinpointing when the product moves into the next stage. They may also find it hard to determine the factors that affect the product's movement through the stages. In practice, it is difficult to forecast the sales level at each PLC stage, the length of each stage, and the shape of the PLC curve.

Using the PLC concept to develop marketing strategy can also be difficult because strategy is both a cause and a result of the product's life cycle. The product's

Style
A basic and distinctive mode of expression.

Fashion
A currently accepted or popular style in a given field.

Fad
A fashion that enters quickly, is adopted with great zeal, peaks early, and declines very fast.

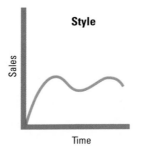
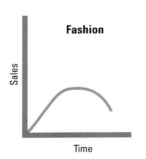
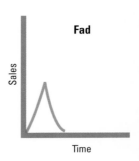

Figure 11.3 Styles, fashions, and fads

current PLC position suggests the best marketing strategies, and the resulting marketing strategies affect product performance in later life cycle stages. Yet, when used carefully, the PLC concept can help in developing good marketing strategies for different stages of the product life cycle.

We looked at the product development stage of the product life cycle in the first part of the chapter. We now look at strategies for each of the other life cycle stages.

Introduction Stage

Introduction stage
The product life-cycle stage when the new product is first distributed and made available for purchase.

The **introduction stage** starts when the new product is first launched. Introduction takes time, and sales growth is apt to be slow. Such well-known products as instant coffee, frozen orange juice, and powdered coffee creamers lingered for many years before they entered a stage of rapid growth.

In this stage, as compared with other stages, profits are negative or low because of the low sales and high distribution and promotion expenses. Much money is needed to attract distributors and build their inventories. Promotion spending is relatively high to inform consumers of the new product and get them to try it. Because the market is not generally ready for product refinements at this stage, the company and its few competitors produce basic versions of the product. These firms focus their selling on buyers who are most ready to buy.

A company, especially the *market pioneer*, must choose a launch strategy that is consistent with its intended product positioning: The initial strategy is just the first step in a grander marketing plan for the product's entire life cycle. If the pioneer chooses its launch strategy to make a "killing," it will be sacrificing long-run revenue for the sake of short-run gain. As the pioneer moves through later stages of the life cycle, it will have to continuously formulate new pricing, promotion, and other marketing strategies. It has the best chance of building and retaining market leadership if it plays its cards correctly from the start.[28]

Growth Stage

Growth stage
The product life-cycle stage in which a product's sales start climbing quickly.

If the new product satisfies the market, it will enter a **growth stage**, in which sales will start climbing quickly. The early adopters will continue to buy, and later buyers will start following their lead, especially if they hear favourable word of mouth. Attracted by the opportunities for profit, new competitors will enter the market. They will introduce new product features, and the market will expand. The increase in competitors leads to an increase in the number of distribution outlets, and sales jump just to build reseller inventories. Prices remain where they are or fall only slightly. Companies keep their promotion spending at the same or a slightly higher level. Educating the market remains a goal, but now the company must also meet the competition.

Profits increase during the growth stage, as promotion costs are spread over a large volume and as unit manufacturing costs fall. The firm uses several strategies to sustain rapid market growth as long as possible. It improves product quality and adds new product features and models. It enters new market segments and new distribution channels. It shifts some advertising from building product awareness to building product conviction and purchase, and it lowers prices at the right time to attract more buyers.

In the growth stage, the firm faces a trade-off between high market share and high current profit. By spending a lot of money on product improvement, promotion, and distribution, the company can capture a dominant position. In doing so, however, it gives up maximum current profit, which it hopes to make up in the next stage.

Just see what is happening in the sandwich category of the quick-service restaurant market:

Quizno's Sub is opening a new store in Canada every 80 hours, according to VP marketing Greg MacDonald. It has over 2000 stores in North America—200 as of late 2003 in Canada. Meanwhile, Subway and coffee-and-doughnut chain Tim Hortons each have more locations nationwide than McDonald's. These quick service restaurants are all hoping to cash in on more health-conscious consumers and are all positioning their sandwiches as freshly made. Newcomer Quizno's has targeted the food connoisseur with such gourmet offerings as the Tuscan Chicken sandwich. The Mississauga, Ontario-based chain isn't shy about touting its product quality or its trademark toasted bread to set itself apart from the pack. Its stores are painted with Italian-style terracotta colours and sophisticated, modern artwork graces its walls. Store layouts allow customers to watch their sandwiches being toasted in its see-through ovens.

To encourage people to try Quizno's upscale $5 to $10 subs, the chain sends out event teams dressed as the company's spokesperson, hockey commentator Don Cherry. The real Cherry appears in radio spots and point-of-sale materials. When Quizno's opened its two hundredth Canadian store in Toronto, Cherry manned the counter and Quizno's donated $10 000 in sales to the Rose Cherry Home, a new pediatric hospice for children with a life-limiting or life-threatening illness, named after Cherry's late wife Rose. Reaching out to the public this way, the chain has been scoring big with double-digit sales increases.[29]

Maturity Stage

Maturity stage

The product life-cycle stage in which sales growth slows or levels off.

At some point, a product's sales growth will slow down, and the product will enter a **maturity stage**. This maturity stage normally lasts longer than the previous stages, and it poses strong challenges to marketing management. Most products are in the maturity stage of the life cycle, and therefore most of marketing management deals with the mature product.

The slowdown in sales growth results in many producers with many products to sell. In turn, this overcapacity leads to greater competition. Competitors begin marking down prices, increasing their advertising and sales promotions, and increasing their R&D budgets to find better versions of the product. These steps lead to a drop in profit. Some of the weaker competitors start dropping out, and the industry eventually contains only well-established competitors.

Although many products in the mature stage appear to remain unchanged for long periods, most successful ones are actually evolving to meet changing consumer needs (see Real Marketing 11.3). Product managers should do more than simply ride along with or defend their mature products—a good offence is the best defence. They should consider modifying the market, product, and marketing mix.

In *modifying the market,* the company tries to increase the consumption of the current product. It looks for new users and market segments, as when Johnson & Johnson targeted the adult market with its baby powder and shampoo. The manager also looks for ways to increase usage among present customers. Campbell does this by offering recipes and convincing consumers that "soup is good food," while Kraft Kitchens Canada sends permission-based "What's Cooking" emails to customers, providing them with quick and simple meal ideas. Or the company may want to reposition the brand to appeal to a larger or faster-growing segment, as was the case when Mutual Life of southwestern Ontario found its name didn't accurately reflect what a modern behemoth it had become. To better convey its offerings, it chose *Clarica* as its new name. The company might also try *modifying the product*—changing such product characteristics as quality, features, or style to attract new users and to inspire more usage. It can improve the product's style and attractiveness. Thus, car manufacturers restyle their cars to attract buyers who want a new look. The makers of consumer food and household products introduce new flavours, colours, ingredients, or packages to revitalize consumer buying.

REAL MARKETING

11.3 Age-Defying Products or Just Skilful PLC Management?

*S*ome products are born and die quickly. Others, however, seem to defy the product life cycle, enduring for decades or even generations with little or no apparent change in their makeup or marketing. Look deeper, however, and you'll find that such products are far from unchanging. Rather, skilful product life cycle management keeps them fresh, relevant, and appealing to customers. Here are examples of three products that might have been only fads but instead were turned into long-term market winners with plenty of staying power.

Kraft Dinner

The Barenaked Ladies sing about it, FoodTV features a spa-inspired Kraft Dinner casserole, the *Globe and Mail* refers to it as a Canadian cultural icon, and university students, adults, and children across Canada wolf down an incredible 246 000 boxes of KD a day. Nine out of ten Canadian households buy the product and Canadians living overseas beg their friends to bring KD when they come to visit. Kraft Dinner is not only Kraft Canada's biggest business from a volume standpoint, but is also the country's number-one-selling grocery item, holding a 75 percent share of the market. Not bad for basic food that has been close to the hearts of Canadians since 1937. In fact, per capita, Canadians eat three times more Kraft dinner than their American counterparts.

Despite its Canadian success, KD's brand manager notes, "In an ever-changing market, you can't sit back and simply expect the brand to continue to be popular without trying to keep it relevant with consumers." The very popularity of the product presents its own challenges. How, you might ask, can you get Canadians to eat even more of the stuff? The biggest danger in trying to revitalize the brand is making changes that will alienate KD's core customers, just as Coke did when it introduced New Coke.

For a while, managers of the product had become too reliant on price to drive the KD business. Today, that is history. Kraft has put a lot of its market research muscle, new product development skills, and advertising savvy behind revitalizing the brand. Rather than just talking to kids, as had become its habit, Kraft Canada decided it needed to reconnect with adults. So Kraft and its agency, J. Walter Thompson, asked cultural anthropologist Grant McCracken to study the brand to uncover consumer insights about KD. This research, along with 15 000 videos of Canadians talking about why they love Kraft Dinner, revealed that everyone has their own "KD truths."

Such truths could be any of those special moments we all remember, from devouring KD at university because it was all we could afford on our tight budgets to eating it with our culinary-challenged dad while mom was away. The first TV spot based on these research insights was a hit target to young adults. Dubbed "Laundry Night," it featured a group of university-age guys filing into a laundromat, where one prepares KD in a washing machine. When another patron gives him a dirty look, he shrugs and says, "My night to cook."

Kraft has also been busy on other fronts. The famous blue and yellow box was given a face-lift, giving the lettering a 3-D look. New product versions were developed, including Easy Mac Macaroni & Cheese, a microwaveable, snack-size extension. Kraft called the launch of this product its biggest in Canada in a decade. The TV campaign used to launch the product, titled "Dog Gone Girl," won praise among viewers and critics alike. It shows a young man returning home to his apartment to find it empty but for his dog. Although not overly concerned about being abandoned by his girlfriend, he is hungry and manages to make Easy Mac in the dog's dish.

The born-again brand has even managed to score in cyberspace. The product is a feature item in many recipes on the Kraft Kitchens site. As *Marketing Magazine*'s digital critic notes, "I love this site. I have always thought of Kraft Dinner more as entertainment than food and that is the approach taken with this website. No fuzzy lifestyle shots of happy families or time-pressed yuppies, just lurid comic book pages of outrageous fun." You can visit the Internet's cheesiest site at www.kraftdinner.com.

Barbie

Talk about age-defying products. Although Mattel's Barbie is now in her mid-forties, Mattel has kept Barbie both timeless and trendy. Since her creation in 1959, Barbie has mirrored girls' dreams of what they'd like to be when they grow up. As such, Barbie has changed as girls' dreams have changed. Her aspirations have evolved from jobs such as stewardess, fashion model, and nurse to astronaut, rock singer, surgeon, and presidential candidate. These days, Barbie hardly notices her age—she's too busy being a WNBA basketball player, Olympic skater, and NASCAR race car driver.

Pursuing its mission to "engage, enchant, and empower girls," Mattel introduces new Barbie dolls every year in order to keep up with the latest definitions of achievement, glamour, romance, adventure, and nurturing. Barbie also reflects America's diverse and changing population. Mattel has produced African American Barbie dolls since 1968 and has since introduced Hispanic and Asian dolls as well. In recent years, Mattel has introduced Crystal Barbie (a gorgeous glamour doll), Puerto Rican Barbie (part of its "dolls of the world" collection), Great Shape Barbie (to tie into the fitness craze), Flight Time Barbie (a pilot), Soccer Barbie (to tie in with the recent boom in girls' soccer), and Children's Doctor Barbie (the first in the "I Can Be" Career Series Barbies). Barbie herself has received several makeovers. The most recent one gave her a wider face, her first belly button, slightly less prominent breasts, and a more athletic body.

As a result of Mattel's adept product life-cycle handling, Barbie has kept her market allure as well as her youth. Available in 150 countries, Barbie now sells at a rate of two each second worldwide and racks up sales of more than $1.9 billion a year. If you placed head to foot every doll ever sold, Barbie and her friends would circle the globe 72 times.

Crayola Crayons

Over the past century, Binney & Smith's Crayola crayons have become a household staple in more than 80 countries around the world. Few people can forget their first pack of "64s"—64 beauties neatly arranged in the familiar green and yellow flip-top box with a sharpener on the back. The aroma of a freshly opened Crayola box still drives kids into a frenzy and takes members of the older generation back to some of their fondest childhood memories.

In some ways, Crayola crayons haven't changed much since 1903, when they were sold in an eight-pack for a nickel. But a closer look reveals that Binney & Smith has made many adjustments to keep the brand out of decline. The company has added a steady stream of new colours, shapes, sizes, and packages. It has

Some products seem to defy the product life-cycle: Over the years, Crayola has lived a colourful life cycle, adding a steady stream of new colours, forms, and packages.

gradually increased the number of colours from the original eight in 1903 (red, orange, yellow, green, blue, black, brown, and violet) to 120 in 2002. Binney & Smith has also extended the Crayola brand to new markets—Crayola markers, scissors, watercolour paints, gel pens, themed stamps and stickers, and activity kits. The company has licensed the Crayola brand for use on everything from camera outfits, backpacks, and bookends to cartoon cups and mousepads. Finally, the company has added several programs and services to help strengthen its relationships with Crayola customers. Its Crayola Kids magazine and Crayola website offer features for the children along with interactive art and suggestions for parents and educators on helping develop reading skills and creativity.

Not all of Binney & Smith's life-cycle adjustments have been greeted favourably by consumers. For example, in 1990, to make room for more modern colours, it retired eight colours from the time-honoured box of 64—raw umber, lemon yellow, maize, blue grey, orange yellow, orange red, green blue, and violet blue—into the Crayola Hall of Fame. The move unleashed a groundswell of protest from loyal Crayola users, who formed such organizations as the RUMPS—the Raw Umber and Maize Preservation Society—and the National Committee to Save Lemon Yellow. Company executives were flabbergasted—"We were aware of the loyalty and nostalgia surrounding Crayola crayons," a spokesperson says, "but we didn't know we [would] hit such a nerve." The company reissued the old standards in a special collector's tin—it sold all of the 2.5 million tins made.

Thus, Crayola continues its long and colourful life cycle. Through smart product life-cycle management, Binney & Smith, now a subsidiary of Hallmark, has dominated the crayon market for almost a century. The company now makes nearly 3 billion crayons a year, enough to circle the world six times.

Sources: See Rex Murphy, "Pot PR Goes Up in Smoke," *Globe and Mail,* May 31, 2003, www.globeandmail.com; Jen Horsey, "Only in Canada You Say," Canoe website, June 29, 2000, www.canoe.ca/CNEWSCanadiana01/0629_food-cp.html; John Heinzl, "Kraft Dinner Serves Up a New Look," *Globe and Mail,* January 13, 1999, p. B30; Lara Mills, "Kraft Builds Ads around 'KD Truths,'" *Marketing Magazine,* April 26, 1999, www.marketingmag.ca; "Easy Mac simplifies Kraft Dinner," *Marketing Magazine,* September 6, 1999, www.marketingmag.ca; Michael Cavanaugh, "The digital eye," *Marketing Magazine,* March 13, 2000, www.marketingmag.ca; Kathleen Deslauriers, "Easy Mac Stirs Up Awareness," *Strategy,* March 13, 2000:18; Kraft website, http://foodtv.ca/feature/kraft/article5_2003_02_24.asp) (accessed August 2003); Alice Cuneo and Laura Petrecca, "Barbie Has to Work Harder to Help Out Sagging Mattel," *Advertising Age,* March 6, 2000, p. 4; Christopher Palmeri, "Mattel: Up the Hill Minus Jill," *Business Week,* April 9, 2001, pp. 53–54; Alexandria Peers, "Art Journal: Goodbye Dolly!" *Wall Street Journal,* January 4, 2002, p. W1; Barbie website, www.barbie.com (accessed August 2002); "Hue and Cry over Crayola May Revive Old Colors," *Wall Street Journal,* June 14, 1991, p. B1; Margaret O. Kirk, "Coloring Our Children's World Since '03," *Chicago Tribune,* October 29, 1986, sec. 5, p. 1; and "Crayola Trivia," Crayola website, www.crayola.com (accessed July 2002).

Or the company might add new features that expand the product's usefulness, safety, or convenience. For example, Sony keeps adding new styles and features to its Walkman and Discman lines, and Volvo adds new safety features to its cars. Kimberly-Clark is adding a new twist to revitalize the product life cycle of an old standby, toilet tissue:

> Almost without exception, every family knows what the paper roll next to the toilet is for, knows how to use it, and purchases it faithfully. Selling an omnipresent household item requires a vital brand that stands out at the supermarket, but how do you make toilet tissue new and exciting? Kimberly-Clark, the maker of Cottonelle and Kleenex, has the answer with an unprecedented innovation: a premoistened toilet paper called Cottonelle Rollwipes, "the breakthrough product that is changing the toilet paper category." Like baby wipes on a roll, the product is designed to complement traditional toilet tissue. "In this category, your growth has to come from significant product innovations," says a marketing director for Cottonelle. Another marketing executive agrees: "Without new products, old brands become older brands. In categories where there's basic satisfaction with the products, you still have to provide new benefits...to build brand share."[30]

Finally, the company may decide to *modify the marketing mix*—improving sales by changing one or more marketing mix elements. It can cut prices to attract new users and competitors' customers. It can launch a better advertising campaign or use aggressive sales promotions—trade deals, cents-off, premiums, and contests. The company can also move into larger market channels, using mass merchandisers, if these channels are growing. Finally, the company can offer new or improved services to buyers. Montreal-based jeweller Birks has recently used many of these tactics. It didn't use television advertising until the 2000 Christmas season. To tie the campaign to its historical symbols, Birks featured its famous blue box and the tag-line "Think inside the box." It has also trimmed its product line and now features items exclusive to Birks. Its catalogue has a younger image and it has gone online (www.birks.com), giving it a new channel to reach consumers in addition to its 38 stores. Birks, nonetheless, maintains its high standards of service and quality design, but has aimed at a younger audience with these alterations to its marketing mix.[31]

Decline Stage

The sales of most product forms and brands eventually dip. The decline may be slow, as in the case of oatmeal cereal; or rapid, as in the case of phonograph records. Sales may plunge to zero, or they may drop to a low level where they continue for many years. This is the **decline stage**.

Decline stage
The product life-cycle stage in which a product's sales decline.

Sales decline for many reasons, including technological advances, shifts in consumer tastes, and increased competition. As sales and profits decline, some firms withdraw from the market. Those remaining may prune their product offerings. They may drop smaller market segments and marginal trade channels, or they may cut the promotion budget and reduce their prices further.

Carrying a weak product can be very costly to a firm, and not just in profits. There are many hidden costs. A weak product may take up too much of management's time. It often requires frequent price and inventory adjustments. It requires advertising and sales force attention that might be better used to make "healthy" products more profitable. A product's failing reputation can cause customer concerns about the company and its other products. The biggest cost may well lie in the future. Keeping weak products delays the search for replacements, creates a lopsided product mix, hurts current profits, and weakens the company's foothold on the future.

In its maturity stage, Birks, one of Canada's oldest companies, is aiming advertising at a younger audience to broaden its appeal.

For these reasons, companies need to pay more attention to their aging products. The firm's first task is to identify those products in the decline stage by regularly reviewing sales, market shares, costs, and profit trends. Then, management must decide whether to maintain, harvest, or drop each of these declining products.

Management may decide to *maintain* its brand without change in the hope that competitors will leave the industry. For example, Procter & Gamble made good profits by remaining in the declining liquid-soap business as others withdrew. Or management may decide to reposition the brand in hopes of moving it back into the growth stage of the product life cycle. Frito-Lay did this with the classic Cracker Jack brand:

When Cracker Jack passed the 100-year-old mark, it seemed that the timeless brand was running out of time. By the time Frito-Lay acquired the classic snack-food brand from Borden Foods in 1997, sales and profits had been declining for five straight years. Frito-Lay set out to reconnect the box of candy-coated popcorn, peanuts, and a prize with a new generation of kids. "We made the popcorn bigger and fluffier with more peanuts and bigger prizes, and we put it in bags, as well as boxes," says Chris Neugent, VP Marketing for wholesome snacks for Frito-Lay. New promotional programs shared a connection with baseball and fun for kids, featuring baseball star Mark McGwire, Rawlings Sporting Goods trading cards, and Pokémon and Scooby Doo characters. The revitalized marketing pulled Cracker Jack out of decline. Sales more than doubled during the two years following the acquisition and the brand has posted double-digit increases each year since.[32]

Management may decide to *harvest* the product, which means reducing various costs (plant and equipment, maintenance, R&D, advertising, sales force) and hoping that sales hold up. If successful, harvesting will increase the company's profits in the short run. Or management may decide to *drop* the product from the line. It can sell it to another firm or simply liquidate it at salvage value. If the company plans to find a buyer, it will not want to run down the product through harvesting.

Table 11.2 summarizes the key characteristics of each stage of the product life cycle. The table also lists the marketing objectives and strategies for each stage.[33]

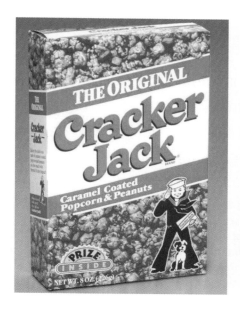

Back into the growth stage: When this timeless brand was running out of time, Frito-Lay reconnected it with a new generation of kids. Sales more than doubled during the two years following the acquisition.

Table 11.2   Summary of Product Life-Cycle Characteristics, Objectives, and Strategies

Characteristics	Introduction	Growth	Maturity	Decline
Sales	Low	Rapidly rising sales	Peak	Declining sales
Costs	High per customer	Average cost per customer	Low cost per customer	Low cost per customer
Profits	Negative	Rising profits	High profits	Declining profits
Customers	Innovators	Early adopters	Middle majority	Laggards
Competitors	Few	Growing number	Stable number beginning to decline	Declining number
Marketing Objectives				
	Create product awareness and trial	Maximize market share	Maximize profit while defending market share	Reduce expenditure and milk the brand
Strategies				
Product	Offer a basic product	Offer product extensions, service, warranty	Diversify brand and models	Phase out weak items
Price	Use cost-plus	Price to penetrate market	Price to match or best competitors	Cut price
Distribution	Build selective distribution	Build intensive distribution	Build more intensive distribution	Go selective: phase out unprofitable outlets
Advertising	Build product awareness among early adopters and dealers	Build awareness and interest in the mass market	Stress brand differences and benefits	Reduce to level needed to retain hard-core loyals
Sales Promotion	Use heavy sales promotions to entice trial	Reduce to take advantage of heavy consumer demand	Increase to encourage brand switching	Reduce to minimal level

Source: Philip Kotler and Peggy Cunningham, *Marketing Management: Analysis, Planning, Implementation, and Control,* Canadian 11th ed. (Toronto: Pearson Education Canada, 2004), p. 347.

Looking Back: Reviewing the Concepts

A company's current products face limited life spans and must be replaced by newer products. But new products can fail—the risks of innovation are as great as the rewards. The key to successful innovation lies in a total company effort, strong planning, and a systematic *new-product development* process.

1. Explain how companies find and develop new-product ideas.

Companies find and develop new-product ideas from various sources. Many new-product ideas stem from *internal and external sources.* Companies conduct formal research and development, "pick the brains" of their employees, and brainstorm at executive meetings. By conducting surveys and focus groups and analyzing *customer* questions and complaints, companies can generate new-product ideas that will meet specific consumer needs. Companies track *competitors'* offerings and inspect new products, dismantling them, analyzing their performance, and deciding whether to introduce a similar or improved product. *Distributors and suppliers* are close to the market and can pass along information about consumer problems and new-product possibilities.

2. List and define the steps in the new-product development process.

The new-product development process consists of eight sequential stages. The process starts with *idea generation.* Next comes *idea screening,* which reduces the number of ideas based on the company's own criteria. Ideas that pass the screening stage continue through *product concept development,* in which a detailed version of the new-product idea is stated in meaningful consumer terms. In the next stage, *concept testing,* new-product concepts are tested with a group of target consumers to determine whether the concepts have strong consumer appeal. Strong concepts proceed to *marketing strategy development,* in which an initial marketing strategy for the new product is developed from the product concept. In the *business analysis* stage, a review of the sales, costs, and profit projections for a new product is conducted to determine whether the new product is likely to satisfy the company's objectives. With positive results here, the ideas become more concrete through *product development* and *test marketing,* and finally the product is launched during *commercialization.*

3. Describe the stages of the product life cycle.

Each product has a *life cycle* marked by a changing set of problems and opportunities. The sales of the typical product follow an S-shaped curve composed of five stages. The cycle begins with the *product development stage* when the company finds and develops a new-product idea. The *introduction stage* is marked by slow growth and low profits as the product is distributed to the market. If successful, the product enters a *growth stage,* which offers rapid sales growth and increasing profits. Next comes a *maturity stage* when sales growth slows down and profits stabilize. Finally, the product enters a *decline stage* in which sales and profits dwindle. The company's task during this stage is to recognize the decline, and to decide whether it should maintain, harvest, or drop the product.

4. Describe how marketing strategies change during the product's life cycle.

In the *introduction stage,* the company must choose a launch strategy consistent with its intended product positioning. Much money is needed to attract distributors and build their inventories, and to inform consumers of the new product and achieve trial. In the *growth stage,* companies continue to educate potential consumers and distributors. In addition, the company works to stay ahead of the competition and sustain rapid market growth by improving product quality; adding new product features and models; entering new market segments and distribution channels; shifting some advertising from building product awareness to building product conviction and purchase; and lowering prices at the right time to attract new buyers. In the *maturity stage,* companies continue to invest in maturing products and consider modifying the market, the product, and the marketing mix. When *modifying the market,* the company attempts to increase the consumption of the current product. When *modifying the product,* the company changes some of the product's characteristics—such as quality, features, or style—to attract new users or inspire more usage. When *modifying the market mix,* the company works to improve sales by changing one or more of the marketing mix elements. Once the company recognizes that a product has entered the *decline stage,* management must decide whether to *maintain* the brand without change, hoping that competitors will drop out of the market; *harvest* the product, reducing costs and trying to maintain sales; or *drop* the product, selling it to another firm or liquidating it at salvage value.

Reviewing the Key Terms

Discussing the Concepts

1. Pick a familiar company and assume you are responsible for generating new-product ideas. How would you structure your new-product development process? What sources of new ideas would be most valuable? How would you stimulate the development of new ideas in the organization?

2. One of the challenges faced by today's new-product development manager is how to use the Internet to get innovative ideas from customers and competitors. Propose three ways to form relationships with consumers that encourage the generation of new ideas. Propose three ways to observe competitors to gain insight into their new-product ventures.

3. North America is currently undergoing a health craze that is affecting the way consumers eat. Assume you have been hired by Burger King to develop and test a new sandwich that would appeal to vegetarians. Develop three alternative product concepts for the new sandwich. Think carefully about how to test each of these concepts. What testing method(s) would you suggest? Which of your three concepts do you think has the greatest potential? Why?

4. Your company has just developed a revolutionary new skiing product. Grasskis allow the user to ski on hill slopes when there is no snow. Not only will this product allow the novice and professional to practise snow-skiing skills during summer months, Grasskis

may eventually lead to an entirely new summer sport. Construct a marketing strategy statement to present to potential investors. Construct sales forecasts based on your confidence in this new product.

5. Crayola has just developed a new product aimed at the young adult market. Tattoo Pens allow users to draw tattoos that fade in about two weeks. Initial consumer tests have been positive. However, the company would like to ensure a positive reception before beginning full commercialization. Which of the three test-marketing methods suggested in the text would be best for this new product? Support your findings.

6. Pick a soft drink, car, fashion, food product, or electronic appliance and trace the product's life cycle. Explain how you separated the stages of the product's evolution.

7. Discuss the differences between a fad, a fashion, and a style. Find a contemporary illustration for each. List three ways a fad might be extended by a creative marketing planner.

8. Which product life-cycle stage, if any, is the most important? Which stage is the riskiest? Which stage appears to hold the greatest profit potential? Which stage needs the greatest amount of "hands-on" management? Explain the thinking behind each of your answers.

Applying the Concepts

1. "Danger, Will Robinson! Danger!" might be one of the most memorable phrases ever uttered by a robot. However, today, the phrase would more likely be "Buy Me! Take Me Home!" Who will offer the first practical, affordable home robot? NASA? Intel? Sony? Lego? Did you say Lego? Yes, the same little company that developed those great plastic building blocks has now developed several models of home robots (such as the R2-D2

model from *Star Wars*) that sell for as little as $220. These Lego model kits contain Lego pieces, light and touch sensors, gears, and a minicomputer brick that forms the core of the system. The small, efficient robots already perform many hard-to-believe tasks (without complaining), and Lego is making daily upgrades. Copycat competitors have already begun a modification frenzy that will one day produce an awesome personal assistant.

a. Who might the first customers be for a Lego robot? Explain.

b. Project the product life cycle for this new product. Explain your thinking.

c. Outline a strategy for positioning this product away from the toy category and into the "personal device" category.

d. What headline would you select for a first Lego robot ad appearing in the *National Post*? In *Canadian Business*?

e. Visit www.lego.com. What other new products has Lego produced to complement its robot line? How could Lego extend the robot concept into other products?

2. What is the hottest new trend in shoes for teens? Is it Air Jordans, soccer shoes, combat boots, or retro tennis shoes? If you answered, "None of the above," you're right. Heelys are the newest fad to hit teen footwear. They may look like thick-soled sneakers, but Heelys have a hidden feature. The shoes include a detachable wheel in each heel, enabling wearers to switch from walking to skating simply by shifting their weight. Texas-based Heeling Sports, Ltd., which produces these unique shoes, has venture capitalists lined up to support the new product. Why? Because teens are lined up to buy the shoes. Heeling has kept the shoes out of mainstream stores like Target, focusing instead on skate shops, surf shops, and mall chains such as Gadzooks—stores that target teens and offer higher price margins. The response has been tremendous. Heeling expects to ship more than a million pairs this year. If the success continues, you may soon see someone on campus "heeling" to class.

a. After visiting the Heelys website at www.heelys.com, comment on the strategy devised by the company to reach its target market. What improvements in the strategy would you recommend?

b. What stage of the product life cycle is the product currently experiencing? Using the information found in Table 11.2 (page 455), comment on what the company must do to move forward to the next stage. How can Heeling Sports turn its fad into a long-term trend?

c. How has the company used the Internet to expand sales? Comment.

d. What other target markets should the company be considering? What other distribution outlets should be employed? How could the company expand into new markets and outlets but remain true to its core following?

e. As the new-product development manager for Heeling Sports, Ltd., what new product would you advise for next year's shoe market? Explain your thinking and outline a plan for developing, testing, and introducing this product.

Video Short

View the video short for this chapter at **www.pearsoned.ca/kotler** and then answer the questions provided in the case description.

Company Case

Red Bull: Waking a New Market

In the Beginning

Little did Austrian businessman Dietrich Mateschitz suspect when he visited Bankok, Thailand, in the early 1980s that his trip would launch not only a new product but also a new product category. Mateschitz, international marketing director for Blendax, a German toothpaste producer, encountered Krating Daeng, a "tonic syrup" that Red Bull Beverage Company had been marketing in Thailand for years. Mateschitz discovered that one glass of the product eliminated his jet lag.

Returning to Austria, Mateschitz began a three-year product development process that included developing the drink's image, packaging, and marketing strategy. In 1987, he obtained the marketing rights to Red Bull (the translated Thai name) from the Thai company and launched his marketing strategy.

The Product

Although marketers credit Red Bull with creating the "energy drink" category, the pursuit of drinks to enhance performance and well-being is not new. Back in 1886, some folks in Atlanta introduced a product they called "Coca-Cola" that had extracts from cola nuts and coca leaves and advertised it as an "esteemed brain tonic and intellectual beverage."

Red Bull is a lightly carbonated energy drink that comes in a slender aluminum can that holds 245 millilitres. The label indicates that it has 110 calories, 0 grams of fat, 200 milligrams of sodium, 28 grams of carbohydrates, 27 grams of sugar, and less than one gram of protein. Ingredients include sucrose, glucose, sodium citrate, taurine, glucurono-lactone, caffeine, inositol, niacinamide, calcium-pantothenate, pyridoxine HCL, vitamin B_{12}, and artificial flavours and colours, all mixed in carbonated water.

Sounds delicious, don't you think? Well, that is part of the problem. Each of an energy drink's ingredients has a specific purpose—but each also has it own taste, and in some cases, an aftertaste. It's no easy matter to blend the ingredients to get not only the correct benefits for the consumer but also something the consumer will drink voluntarily.

Energy drinks have a number of different types of ingredients. The body takes *carbohydrates* and metabolizes them into glucose (sugar). Simple sugars produce a rapid rise in blood sugar, while complex carbohydrates produce a slower rise. By combining different types of sugars, a drink can produce glycemic responses at different times.

Energy drinks sometimes include *amino acids* that are protein building blocks. Taurine, for example, is an important aid in the release of insulin and can prevent abnormal blood clotting. Because researchers have cited a deficiency of *vitamins and minerals* as being associated with a lack of energy, beverage makers often include them in energy drinks. Niacin (vitamin B_3) works with other vitamins to metabolize carbohydrates. Riboflavin (vitamin B_{12}) helps combat anemia and fatigue by helping to manufacture red blood cells.

Some drinks include *botanicals* such as gingko biloba, guarana, and ginseng. Ginkgo biloba is purported to provide mental energy and "sharpness" by stimulating blood flow to the brain. Finally, most energy drinks contain *caffeine,* an alkaloid stimulant that the body absorbs and circulates to all body tissues. Caffeine affects the central nervous system, the digestive tract, and the body's metabolism, boosting adrenaline levels to increase blood pressure and heart rate. Typical energy drinks, like Red Bull, contain about the same amount of caffeine as a cup of coffee.

Packaging is also important. Some fruity energy beverages come in glass bottles, but many energy drinks that contain light-sensitive vitamins, like B_{12}, come in slender metal cans to prevent the vitamins from breaking down.

The Marketing Strategy

Mateschitz designed an unusual marketing strategy. "We don't bring the product to the people," he argues, "we bring people to the product." Initially, when Red Bull entered the U.S. market in Santa Monica, California, it used traditional beverage distributors. But as the product gained popularity, the company began to pursue a more focused distribution strategy. Red Bull sales representatives now approach a beverage distributor and insist that he or she sell only Red Bull and no other energy drink. If the distributor will not agree, Red Bull hires young people to load the product in vans and distribute it themselves.

The company divided the United States into eight territories, with sales teams in each area responsible for developing distribution and targeted marketing plans. The local team seeks to determine where people aged 16 to 29 are hanging out and what they find interesting. First, the sales team calls on trendy clubs and bars that will offer the drink on-premise. As incentives, the team offers Red Bull coolers and other promotional items. Red Bull works with individual accounts rather than large chains because it has found that the process goes much faster due to the lack of bureaucracy. It has also found that young people in local hot spots are open to trying new things and help generate a "buzz" about Red Bull. However, the company does not endorse all the new things people try, like mixing the product with vodka or tequila, and it has a FAQ section on its website, www.redbull.com, to counter the many rumours that have developed around the product.

Second, the sales team also opens off-premise accounts such as gyms, health-food stores, and convenience stores near colleges. The product sells for about $2.00 in convenience stores. In addition, "consumer educators" roam local streets and hand out free samples. The company has encouraged students to drive around with big Red Bull cans strapped to the tops of their cars and to throw Red Bull parties focused on weird themes.

Contrary to traditional promotion practice, Red Bull starts traditional advertising only *after* it believes a local market is maturing. The company's philosophy is that media can reinforce but not introduce a brand. Thus, it builds demand even before it introduces the product at retail. Only about 19 percent of the $130 million the brand spent on promotion in 2000 was for measured media. Red Bull spends about 35 percent of sales on promotion. The company has also begun sponsoring extreme sporting events and extreme athletes.

Uncanny Results

Does all this grass-roots marketing work? Well, in 2001, Red Bull sold 1.6 billion cans in 62 countries, up 80 percent over 2000. In the United States, Red Bull entered the list of the top 10 carbonated beverage distributors with a mere 0.1 percent market share—but its case volume grew 118 percent over 2000 to 10.5 million cases. Red Bull is the number one product in Store24 and had similar results at 7-Eleven. It now captures a 70 to 90 percent share of the energy drink market.

With results like that, it did not take long for competitors to jump in. Pepsi bought South Beach Beverage Company (makers of the SoBe brand) and developed an energy drink it calls "Adrenaline Rush." Coca-Cola jumped in with KMX. Even Anheuser-Busch, of Budweiser fame, joined in with a product it calls "180" to denote that it turns your energy around 180 degrees. In early 2002, another Thai company, Otsotspa, entered the fray with its own energy drink, called "Shark."

Mateschitz does not seem concerned about competition. He knows Red Bull has a tremendous head start and strong local marketing teams. He already has plans to enter Brazil and South Africa.

However, Mateschitz does have one concern. "It makes no sense to build a company on one product,"

he argues. So far, he has put the Red Bull brand on only one other product. LunAqua is a still water that the company claims it bottles only 13 times per year, during each full moon when the moon reaches its full energy level. There is also a variety of LunAqua that contains caffeine. But Mateschitz knows that it will take more than just moon power to stay ahead of the competition in the energy drink market. You can bet he will be up all night, sipping Red Bull and developing new product ideas.

Questions for Discussion

1. Based on the information in the case, evaluate Red Bull's product development process. What process would you recommend as it considers developing new products?

2. At what stage of the product life cycle are energy drinks as a category? What does this position imply for category competitors?

3. Do you believe there is a long-term market for functional foods and beverages like energy drinks? Why or why not?

4. Using the "product-market expansion grid" presented in Chapter 2 (see Figure 2.3 on page 58), recommend specific ideas for Red Bull in the areas of market penetration, product development, and market development.

Sources: David Jago, "Global Trends: Hitting the Shelves," *Prepared Foods,* June 2002, p. 9; "Selling Energy Face Value," *The Economist,* May 11, 2002; "Sales of Red Bull Beverage in United States Grow to 10.5 Million Cases," *Knight-Ridder/Tribune Business News,* March 14, 2002, from the *Bangkok Post;* "Shark UK Launch to Challenge Red Bull's Dominance," *Marketing Magazine,* February 28, 2002, p. 6; Kenneth Hein, "A Bull's Market," *Brandweek,* May 28, 2001, p. 21; David Noonan, "Red Bull's Good Buzz," *Newsweek,* May 14, 2001, p. 39; Laura A. Brandt, "Energizing Elixirs!" *Prepared Foods,* April 2001, p. 55; Jeff Cioletti, "Boosting Beverages," *Supermarket Business,* January 15, 2001, p. 31; and the Red Bull website, www.RedBull.com (accessed July 2002).

CBC Video Case

CBC Log on to your Companion Website at **www.pearsoned.ca/kotler** to view a CBC video segment and case for this chapter.

Chapter 12

Pricing

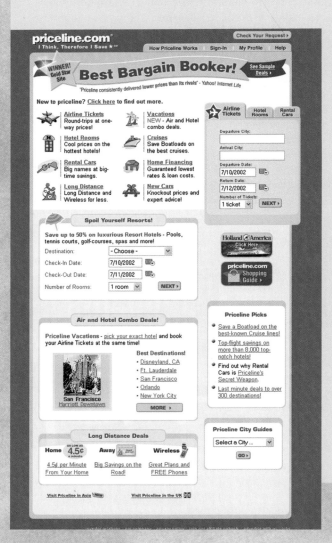

After studying this chapter you should be able to

1. identify and define the internal factors affecting a firm's pricing decisions

2. identify and define the external factors affecting pricing decisions, including the impact of consumer perceptions of price and value

3. contrast the two general approaches to setting prices

4. discuss how companies adjust their prices to take into account different types of customers and situations

5. discuss the key issues related to initiating and responding to price changes

Looking Ahead: Previewing the Concepts

In this chapter we look at a second major marketing mix tool—pricing. According to one pricing expert, pricing involves "harvesting your profit potential."[1] If effective product development, promotion, and distribution sow the seeds of business success, effective pricing is the harvest. Firms successful at creating customer value with the other marketing mix activities must still capture some of this value in the prices they earn. Yet, despite its importance, many firms do not handle pricing well. We'll consider internal and external factors that affect pricing decisions and examine three general pricing approaches. Then we'll look at pricing strategies available to marketers—new-product pricing strategies, product line pricing strategies, price adjustment strategies, and price reaction strategies.

The headlines scream: *Name your own price! Top-flight savings on more than 8000 top-notch hotels! Last-minute deals to more than 300 destinations! Save a boatload on best-known cruise lines! Big savings on long-distance calling!* Just the usual come-ons from fly-by-night operators? Too good to be true? Not at Priceline.com, at least not according to *Yahoo! Internet Life Magazine,* which recently proclaimed Priceline as the "Best Bargain Booker" on the Web. Priceline's byline: "I Think. Therefore I Save."

In 1998, founder Jay Walker launched Priceline as a radical new Internet service. It was based on an ingeniously simple concept—empower consumers to name their own prices, then dangle their offers in front of sellers and see who bites. Such transactions, he reasoned, benefited both buyers and sellers—buyers got lower prices; sellers turned excess inventory into profits. Although simple in concept, however, such "buyer-driven commerce" represented a dramatic departure from long-held pricing practices in which sellers—not buyers—set prices. Still, the idea caught on. Priceline has now grown to become the leading name-your-own-price Internet service and one of the few profitable dot-coms.

Priceline deals primarily in travel-related products—plane tickets, hotel rooms, rental cars, cruises, and vacation packages. Here's how it works—say, for a hotel room. First, you select your destination and desired dates. If it's a big city, you can scan Priceline's maps to narrow down the area in which you'd like to stay. You can also select the types of hotels you're willing to stay in—from one-star ("economy hotels that provide comfort with no frills") to five-star ("the best that money can buy"). Give Priceline the usual billing information and a credit card number—and decide how much you'd like to bid. Click on "Buy My Hotel Room," then sit back and wait for Priceline to broker the deal. Within 15 minutes, Priceline emails you with the news. If no suitable hotel is willing to accept your price, you can bid again later. If Priceline finds a taker, it immediately charges your credit card—no refunds, changes, or cancellations allowed—and lets you know where you'll be staying.

The concept of setting your own prices over the Internet has real appeal to consumers. It starts with a good value proposition—getting really low prices. Beyond that, "name-your-price is a great hook," say a Priceline marketing executive. "If you get it, it's like 'I won!'" As a result, Priceline is attracting more and more customers. Its customer base has grown to 13.5 million users, and as many as 9 million people visit the Priceline site monthly. Through strategic partnerships forged with companies such as eBay,

AOL, and LowestFare.com, over the past year Priceline has extended its online audience by 810 percent, now reaching more than 85 million unique Web users. Since it opened for business in 1998, Priceline has sold more than 12 million airline tickets, 6 million hotel room nights, and 6 million rental car days.

Despite accepting fire-sale prices, sellers also benefit from Priceline's services. It's especially attractive to those who sell products that have "time sensitivity." "If airlines or hotels don't sell seats on particular flights or rooms for certain nights, those assets become worthless," comments an analyst. "Such businesses are a natural fit for Priceline." Moreover, notes the analyst, "by requiring customers to commit to payment up front with their credit card, retailers face little risk in dumping excess inventory. It's particularly attractive in markets that have huge fixed costs from creating capacity and relatively small marginal costs, like air travel, cruise ships, and automobiles."

Priceline makes its money by buying up unsold rooms, seats, or vacation packages at heavily discounted rates, marking them up, and selling them to consumers for as much as a 12 percent return. So, on a $215 plane ticket, Priceline makes about $35, compared with the $10 gross profit made by a traditional travel agent.

Along with the successes and its recent profitability, however, Priceline has encountered some formidable obstacles. For example, not all products lend themselves to Priceline's quirky business model, and the company has met with uneven success in attempts to grow beyond travel services. Although it currently takes bids in three other categories—New Cars, Long Distance, and Home Financing (home mortgages, refinancing, and home equity loans)—selling products and services that aren't time sensitive has proven difficult. For example, efforts to expand into gasoline blew up. Priceline had no trouble lining up customers interested in buying gas over the Internet, but gas and oil companies had no incentive to dump excess inventories because gas is not a perishable good. And, as one analyst points out, "oil companies that spend millions building brands are loath to sell gasoline via a site that puts price before brand." As a result, after only eight months but millions of dollars in losses, Priceline closed its virtual gas pumps.

Moreover, not all customers are thrilled with their Priceline experiences. Forcing customers to commit to purchases before they know the details—such as which hotel or airline, flight times, and hotel locations—can leave some customers feeling cheated. One frustrated user recently summed up his Priceline experience this way: "You don't get what you think you're gonna get."

But for every disappointed customer, Priceline has hundreds or thousands of happy ones. Some 64 percent of those who now visit Priceline to name their own prices are repeat customers.

More than just changing how people pay for travel services, Priceline is perhaps the best example of how the Internet is changing today's pricing practices. "Only through the Web could you match millions of bids with millions of products, all without a fixed price," says one analyst. "In the offline world, this would be a strange market indeed," says another. Try to imagine a real-world situation in which "buyers attach money to a board, along with a note stating what they want to buy for the sum. Later, sellers come along and have a look. If they like an offer, they take the money and deliver the goods." It couldn't happen anywhere but on the Web.[2]

Companies today face a fierce and fast-changing pricing environment. The recent economic downturn has put many companies in a "pricing vise." One analyst sums it up this way: "They have virtually no pricing power. It's impossible to raise prices, and often the pressure to slash them continues unabated. The pricing pinch is affecting business across the spectrum of manufacturing and services—everything from chemicals and autos to hoteliers and phone services."[3] It seems that almost every company is slashing prices, and that is hurting their profits.

Yet cutting prices is often not the best answer. Reducing prices unnecessarily can lead to lost profits and damaging price wars. It can signal to customers that price is more important than brand. Instead, companies should "sell value, not price."[4] They should persuade customers that paying a higher price for the company's brand is justified by the greater value it delivers. Most customers will gladly pay a fair price in exchange for real value. The challenge is to find the price that will let the company make a fair profit by harvesting the customer value it creates.

In this chapter we focus on the process of setting prices. This chapter defines prices, looks at the factors marketers must consider when setting prices, and examines general pricing approaches. We look at pricing strategies for new-product pricing, product mix pricing, price adjustments for buyer and situational factors, and price changes.

What Is a Price?

All profit organizations and many non-profit organizations must set prices on their products or services. *Price* goes by many names: "You pay *rent* for your apartment, *tuition* for your education, and a *fee* to your dentist. The airline, railway, taxi, and bus companies charge you a *fare*, the local utilities call their price a *rate*, and the local bank charges you *interest* for the money you borrow."[5]

In the narrowest sense, **price** is the amount of money charged for a product or service. More broadly, price is the sum of all the values that consumers exchange for the benefits of having or using the product or service. Historically, price has been the major factor affecting buyer choice. This is still true in poorer nations, among poorer groups, and with commodity products. However, non-price factors have become more important in buyer choice behaviour in recent decades.

Throughout most of history, prices were set by negotiation between buyers and sellers. *Fixed price* policies—setting one price for all buyers—is a relatively modern idea that arose with the development of large-scale retailing at the end of the nineteenth century. Now, more than a hundred years later, the Internet promises to reverse the fixed pricing trend and take us back to an era of **dynamic pricing**—charging different prices depending on individual customers and situations (see Real Marketing 12.1).

Price is the only element in the marketing mix that produces revenue; all other elements represent costs. Price is also one of the most flexible elements of the marketing mix. Unlike product features and channel commitments, price can be changed quickly. At the same time, pricing and price competition is the number one problem facing many marketing executives. Yet many companies do not handle pricing well.

Paul Hunt, director of the Strategic Pricing Division at The Advantage Group in Toronto, notes that the average company can increase its profitability by a whopping 25 to 60 percent just by improving its pricing processes. He stresses, however, that effective pricing does not mean nickel-and-diming customers; it means practising value-based pricing. When customers perceive that they are receiving superior value, they'll be willing to pay the price to get it. Hunt's research suggests that companies with successful pricing policies follow five "best practices" with regard to their pricing strategy:[6]

- *They develop a one percent pricing mindset.* Since a 1 percent difference in price can have a dramatic impact on profit, everyone in the company must understand the importance of maintaining prices and think carefully about how even short-term discounts can affect their profitability.

- *They consistently deliver more value.* Since the most successful organizations consistently deliver more value to their customers, they are able to increase margins as a result. To deliver value, companies need insight into how their offering uniquely satisfies the customer's needs. Thus, getting close to their customers is the most critical factor in value-based pricing, since satisfied customers are profitable customers.

- *They price strategically, not opportunistically.* Paul Hunt stresses that firms should pursue price-conscious customers only if they represent the firm's core market. This is a viable strategy only for firms like Wal-Mart with a low cost structure that enables them to compete consistently on a price platform. Otherwise, the more an organization caters to price-conscious customers to boost volume, the more it puts its core business at risk by pursuing customers who don't value the product or service more than the price.

- *They know their competitors.* Their pricing strategy is driven by knowledge of their competitors' offers rather than fear.

- *They make pricing a process.* Pricing should be treated as a continual process rather than a one-time event that erodes into ad hoc or "gut-feel" pricing.

12.1 Back to the Future: Dynamic Pricing on the Web

The Internet is more than a new "marketspace"—it's actually changing the rules of commerce. Take pricing, for example. From the mostly fixed pricing policies of the nineteenth century, the Web now seems to be taking us back—into a new age of fluid pricing. "Potentially, [the Internet] could push aside sticker prices and usher in an era of dynamic pricing," says *Business Week* writer Robert Hof, "in which a wide range of goods would be priced according to what the market will bear—instantly, constantly." Here's how the Internet is changing the rules of pricing for both sellers and buyers.

Sellers Can...

- *Charge lower prices, reap higher margins.* Web buying and selling can result in drastically lower costs, allowing online merchants to charge lower prices and still make higher margins. "Thanks to their Internet connections, buyers and sellers around the world can connect at almost no cost—making instant bargaining [economically feasible]," observes Hof. Reduced inventory and distribution

The Internet is ushering in a new era of fluid pricing. mySimon is an independent site that provides product comparisons and guides and searches all merchant sites for the best prices.

costs add to the savings. For example, by selling made-to-order computers online, Dell Computer greatly reduces inventory costs and eliminates retail markups. It shares the savings with buyers in the form of the "lowest price per performance."

- *Monitor customer behaviour and tailor offers to individuals.* With the help of new technologies, Web merchants can now target special prices to specific customers. For example, Internet sellers such as Amazon.com can mine their databases to gauge a specific shopper's desires, measure his or her means, instantaneously tailor products to fit that shopper's behaviour, and price products accordingly. However, companies must be careful in how they apply dynamic pricing. When gathering information about consumers, Canadian marketers have to be careful they comply with Canada's new privacy legislation and must seek consumers' permission for their information-gathering activities. And when it recently came to light that Amazon.com had been charging different prices to different customers for the same DVDs, many customers were angry. Amazon.com claims that the pricing variations were a "pure and simple price test" and stopped the practice as soon as complaints began coming in. Despite these difficulties, Amazon.com still employs dynamic pricing by offering individualized suggestions to customers each time they log in. By doing so, it gives customers better value while also depleting unwanted inventory.

- *Change prices on the fly according to changes in demand or costs.* Just ask such online catalogue retailers as Lands' End, MEC, or Tilley. With printed catalogues, a price is a price, at least until the next catalogue is printed. Online sellers, however, can change prices for specific items on a day-by-day or even hour-by-hour basis, adjusting quickly to changing costs and merchandise movement. Many B2B marketers monitor inventories, costs, and demand at any given moment and adjust prices instantly. For example, IBM automatically adjusts prices on its servers based on customer demand and product life-cycle factors. As a result, customers will find that prices change dynamically when they visit the IBM website on any given day. Dell also uses dynamic online pricing. "If the price of memory or processors decreases, we pass those savings along to the customer almost in real time," says a Dell spokesperson.

Both Sellers and Buyers Can...

- *Negotiate prices in online auctions and exchanges.* Suddenly the centuries-old art of haggling is back in vogue. Want to sell that antique pickle jar that's been collecting dust for generations? Post it on www.eBay.com, the world's biggest online flea market. Of the dozens of Internet auction sites, eBay and Amazon.com Auctions are the largest.

Buyers Can...

- *Get instant price comparisons from thousands of vendors.* The Internet gives consumers access to reams of data about products and prices. Online comparison guides such as PriceSCAN give product and price comparisons at the click of a mouse. Other sites offer intelligent shopping agents—such as MySimon, Junglee, and Jango—that seek out products, prices, and reviews. MySimon (www.mySimon.com), for instance, takes a

buyer's criteria for a PC, camcorder, or collectible Barbie, then roots through top sellers' sites to find the best match at the best price.

- *Find and negotiate lower prices.* With market information and access come buyer power. In addition to finding the vendor with the best price, both consumers and industrial buyers armed with price information can often negotiate lower prices.

Will dynamic pricing sweep the marketing world? "Not entirely," says Hof. "It takes a lot of work to haggle—which is why fixed prices happened in the first place." However, he continues, "Pandora's e-box is now open, and pricing will never be the same. For many...products, millions of buyers figure a little haggling is a small price to pay for a sweet deal."

Sources: Quotes, extracts, and other information from Robert D. Hof, "Going, Going, Gone," *Business Week,* April 12, 1999, pp. 30–32; Hof, "The Buyer Always Wins," *Business Week,* March 22, 1999, pp. EB26–EB28; Stephen Manes, "Off-Web Dickering," *Forbes,* April 5, 1999, p. 134; Michael Vizard, Ed Scannell, and Dan Neel, "Suppliers Toy with Dynamic Pricing," *InfoWorld,* May 14, 2001, p. 28; and eBay annual reports and other information from the eBay website, www.ebay.com (accessed July 2002). Also see David Streitfeld, "On the Web, Price Tags Blur, *Washington Post,* September 27, 2000, p. A1; Walter Baker, Mike Marn, and Craig Zawada, "Price Smarter on the Net," *Harvard Business Review,* February 2001, pp. 122–127; and Ajit Kambil, H. James Wilson III, and Vipul Agrawal, "Are You Leaving Money on the Table?" *Journal of Business Strategy,* January–February 2002, pp. 40–43.

Other common mistakes made by companies with regard to pricing include pricing that is too cost oriented rather than customer-value oriented, prices that are not revised often enough to reflect market changes, pricing that does not take the rest of the marketing mix into account, and prices that are not varied enough for different products, market segments, and purchase occasions.

In this chapter, we focus on how to set prices—the factors that marketers must consider when setting prices, general pricing approaches, price adjustments for buyer and situational factors, price changes, and public policy and prices.

Factors to Consider When Setting Prices

A company's pricing decisions are affected by both internal company and external environmental factors (see Figure 12.1).[7]

Internal Factors Affecting Pricing Decisions

Internal factors affecting pricing include the company's marketing objectives, marketing mix strategy, costs, product considerations, and organizational factors.

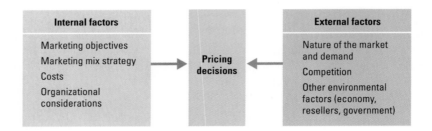

Figure 12.1 Factors affecting pricing decisions

Marketing Objectives

Before setting a price, the company must decide on its strategy for the product. If the company has selected its target market and positioning carefully, then its marketing mix strategy, including price, will be fairly straightforward. For example, when Honda and Toyota decided to develop their Acura and Lexus brands to compete with European luxury-performance cars in the higher-income segment, this required charging a high price. In contrast, Motel 6 has positioned itself as a motel that provides economical rooms for budget-minded travellers; this position requires charging a low price. Thus, pricing strategy is largely determined by decisions on market positioning.

At the same time, the company may seek additional objectives. Common objectives include *survival, current profit maximization, market share leadership,* and *product quality leadership.* Companies set *survival* as their major objective if they are troubled by too much capacity, heavy competition, or changing consumer wants. To keep a plant going, a company may set a low price, hoping to increase demand. In the long run, the firm must learn how to add value that customers will pay for or face extinction.

Many companies use *current profit maximization* as their pricing goal. They estimate what demand and costs will be at different prices and choose the price that will produce the maximum current profit, cash flow, or return on investment. Other companies want to obtain *market share leadership.* To become the market share leader, these firms set prices as low as possible. A company may decide that it wants to achieve *product quality leadership.* This normally calls for charging a high price to cover such quality and the high cost of R&D. For example, Caterpillar charges 20 percent to 30 percent more than competitors for its heavy construction equipment based on superior product and service quality. Gillette's product superiority lets it price its Mach3 razor cartridges at a 50 percent premium over its own SensorExcel and competitors' cartridges.

A company might also use price to attain other more specific objectives. It can set prices low to prevent competition from entering the market or set prices at competitors' levels to stabilize the market. It can set prices to keep the loyalty and support of resellers or to avoid government intervention. It can reduce prices temporarily to create excitement for a product or to draw more customers into a retail store. It can price one product to help the sales of other products in the company's line. Thus, pricing may play an important role in helping to accomplish the company's objectives at many levels.

Non-profit and public organizations may adopt a number of other pricing objectives. A university aims for *partial cost recovery,* knowing that it must rely on private gifts and government grants to cover the remaining costs. A non-profit theatre company may price its productions to fill the maximum number of theatre seats. A social service agency may set a *social price* geared to the varying income situations of different clients.

Marketing Mix Strategy

Price is only one of the marketing mix tools that a company uses to achieve its marketing objectives. Price decisions must be coordinated with product design,

Keeping price and marketing strategy aligned is important. Four Seasons wins customers with its high-quality service strategy. It then charges a price to match.

Target costing
Pricing that starts with an ideal selling price, then targets costs that will ensure that the price is met.

distribution, and promotion decisions to form a consistent and effective marketing program. Decisions made for other marketing mix variables can affect pricing decisions. For example, producers using many resellers who are expected to support and promote their products may have to build larger reseller margins into their prices. The decision to position the product on high performance quality means that the seller must charge a higher price to cover higher costs.

Companies often position their products on price and then tailor other marketing mix decisions on the prices they want to charge. Here, price is a crucial product positioning factor that defines the product's market, competition, and design. Many firms support such price positioning strategies with a technique called **target costing**, a potent strategic weapon. Target costing reverses the usual process of first designing a new product, determining its cost, and then asking "Can we sell it for that?" Instead, it starts with an ideal selling price based on customer considerations, then targets costs, to ensure that the price is met.

The original Swatch watch provides a good example of target costing. Rather than starting with its own costs, Swatch surveyed the market and identified an unserved segment of watch buyers who wanted "a low-cost fashion accessory that also keeps time." Swatch set out to give consumers the watch they wanted at a price they were willing to pay, and it managed the new product's costs accordingly.[8]

Other companies de-emphasize price and use other marketing mix tools to create *non-price* positions. Often, the best strategy is not to charge the lowest price, but rather to differentiate the marketing offer to make it worth a higher price. For example, for years, Johnson Controls (www.jci.com), a producer of climate-control systems for office buildings, used initial price as its primary competitive tool.

Target costing: By managing costs carefully, Swatch was able to create a watch that offered just the right blend of fashion and function at a price consumers were willing to pay.

However, research showed that customers were more concerned about the total cost of installing and maintaining a system than about its initial price:

> Repairing broken systems was expensive, time consuming, and risky. Customers had to shut down the heat or air conditioning in the whole building, disconnect a lot of wires, and face the danger of electrocution, so Johnson designed an entirely new system called Metasys. To repair the new system, customers need only pull out an old plastic module and slip in a new one—no tools required. Metasys costs more to make than the old system, and customers pay a higher initial price, but it costs less to install and maintain. Despite its higher asking price, the new Metasys system brought in more than $650 million in revenues in its first year. More than 15 000 systems are now installed around the world in markets including education, health care, hospitality, commercial office, telecommunications, government, pharmaceutical, retail, and industrial.[9]

Thus, marketers must consider the total marketing mix when setting prices. If the product is positioned on non-price factors, then decisions about quality, promotion, and distribution will strongly affect price. If price is a crucial positioning factor, then price will strongly affect decisions made about the other marketing mix elements. But even when featuring price, marketers need to remember that customers rarely buy on price alone. Instead, they seek products that give them the best value in terms of benefits received for the price paid.

Costs

Costs set the floor for the price that the company can charge for its product. The company wants to charge a price that both covers all its costs for producing, distributing, and selling the product and delivers a fair rate of return for its effort and risk. A company's costs may be an important element in its pricing strategy. Many companies—such as Southwest Airlines, Wal-Mart, and Union Carbide—work to become the "low-cost producers" in their industries. Companies with lower costs can set lower prices that result in greater sales and profits.

Fixed costs
Costs that do not vary with production or sales level.

Variable costs
Costs that vary directly with the level of production.

Total costs
The sum of the fixed and variable costs for any given level of production.

Types of Costs   A company's costs take two forms—fixed and variable. **Fixed costs** (also known as overhead) are costs that do not vary with production or sales level. For example, a company must pay each month's bills for rent, heat, interest, and executive salaries, whatever the company's output. **Variable costs** depend directly on the level of production. Each personal computer produced by Dell involves a cost of computer chips, wires, plastic, packaging, and other inputs. These costs tend to be the same for each unit produced. They are called *variable* because their total varies with the number of units produced. **Total costs** are the sum of the fixed and variable costs for any given level of production. Management wants to charge a price that will at least cover the total production costs. The company must watch its costs carefully: If it costs the company more than competitors to produce and sell a similar product, the company will have to charge a higher price or make less profit, putting it at a competitive disadvantage.

Costs at Different Levels of Production   To price wisely, management needs to know how its costs vary with different levels of production. For example, suppose Texas Instruments (TI) has built a plant to produce 1000 handheld calculators per day. Figure 12.2A shows the typical short-run average cost (SRAC) curve. It shows that the cost per calculator is high if TI's factory produces only a few per day. But as production moves up to 1000 calculators per day, average cost falls. This is because fixed costs are spread over more units, with each one bearing a smaller fixed cost. TI can try to produce more than 1000 calculators per day, but average costs will increase because the plant becomes inefficient. Workers have to wait for machines, the machines break down more often, and workers get in each other's way.

If TI believed it could sell 2000 calculators a day, it should consider building a larger plant. The plant would use more efficient machinery and work arrangements. Also, the unit cost of producing 2000 calculators per day would be lower than the unit cost of producing 1000 calculators per day, as shown in the long-run average cost (LRAC) curve (Figure 12.2B). In fact, a 3000-capacity plant would be even more efficient, according to Figure 12.2B. But a 4000 daily production plant would be less efficient because of increasing diseconomies of scale—too many workers to manage, paperwork slows things down, and so on. Figure 12.2B shows that a 3000 daily production plant is the best size to build if demand is strong enough to support this level of production.

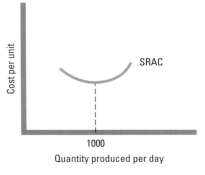

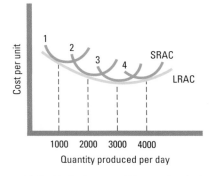

Figure 12.2   Cost per unit at different levels of production per period

A. Cost behaviour in a fixed-size plant   **B. Cost behaviour over different-size plants**

Costs as a Function of Production Experience   Suppose TI runs a plant that produces 3000 calculators per day. As TI gains experience in producing handheld calculators, it learns how to do it better. Workers learn shortcuts and become more familiar with their equipment. With practice, the work becomes better organized, and TI finds better equipment and production processes. With higher volume, TI becomes more efficient and gains economies of scale. As a result, average cost tends to fall with accumulated production experience. This is shown in Figure 12.3.[10] Thus, the average cost of producing the first 100 000 calculators is $10 per calculator. When the company has produced the first 200 000 calculators, the average cost has fallen to $9. After its accumulated production experience doubles again to 400 000, the average cost is $7. This drop in the average cost with accumulated production experience is called the **experience curve** (or the **learning curve**).

If a downward-sloping experience curve exists, this is highly significant for the company. Not only will the company's unit production cost fall, but it will also fall faster if the company makes and sells more during a given period. But the market must stand ready to buy the higher output. And to take advantage of the experience curve, TI must get a large market share early in the product's life cycle. This suggests the following pricing strategy: TI should price its calculators low; its sales will then increase, and its costs will decrease through gaining more experience, and then it can lower its prices further.

Some companies have built successful strategies around the experience curve. For example, Bausch & Lomb solidified its position in the soft contact lens market by using computerized lens design and steadily expanding its one Soflens plant. As a result, its market share climbed steadily to 65 percent. However, a single-minded focus on reducing costs and exploiting the experience curve will not always work. Experience curve pricing carries some major risks. The aggressive pricing might give the product a cheap image. The strategy also assumes that competitors are weak and not willing to fight it out by meeting the company's price cuts. Finally, while the company is building volume under one technology, a competitor may find a lower-cost technology that lets it start at lower prices than the market leader, who still operates on the old experience curve.

Product Considerations

Pricing and product line considerations are closely interrelated especially when new products are being introduced or when marketers are working with a line of related products.

New-Product Pricing   Companies bringing out a new product face the challenge of setting prices for the first time. They can choose between two strategies: *market skimming pricing* and *market penetration pricing*.

Many companies that invent new products initially set high prices to "skim" revenues layer by layer from the market. Intel is a prime user of this strategy, called

Experience curve (learning curve)

The drop in the average per-unit production cost that comes with accumulated production experience.

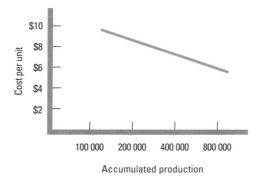

Figure 12.3 Cost per unit as a function of accumulated production: the experience curve

Getting the price right is a key consideration when firms introduce new products, like Labatt's cranberry-vodka Vbase, sold in a four-pack shaped like a battery pack. The product launched in the spring of 2003.

Market skimming pricing
Setting a high price for a new product to skim maximum revenues layer by layer from the segments willing to pay the high price; the company makes fewer but more profitable sales.

market skimming pricing. When Sony introduced the world's first high-definition television (HDTV) to the Japanese market in 1990, the high-tech sets cost $68 000. These televisions were purchased only by customers who could afford to pay a high price for the new technology. Sony rapidly reduced the price over the next several years to attract new buyers. By 1993 a 28-inch HDTV cost a Japanese buyer just over $9000. In 2001, a Japanese consumer could buy a 40-inch HDTV for about $3000, a price that many more customers could afford. HDTV sets now sell for about $3000 in North America, and "HDTV-ready" sets sell for about $1500. In this way, Sony skimmed the maximum amount of revenue from the various segments of the market.[11]

Market skimming makes sense only under certain conditions. First, the product's quality and image must support its higher price, and enough buyers must want the product at that price. Second, the costs of producing a smaller volume cannot be so high that they cancel the advantage of charging more. Finally, competitors should not be able to enter the market easily and undercut the high price.

Market penetration pricing
Setting a low price for a new product to attract a large number of buyers and a large market share.

Rather than setting a high initial price to *skim* off small but profitable market segments, some companies use **market penetration pricing.** They set a low initial price to *penetrate* the market quickly and deeply—to attract a large number of buyers quickly and win a large market share. The high sales volume results in falling costs, allowing the company to cut its price even further. For example, Dell used penetration pricing to enter the personal computer market, selling high-quality computer products through lower-cost direct channels. Its sales soared when IBM, Apple, and other competitors selling through retail stores could not match its prices. Wal-Mart, Zellers, and other discount retailers also use penetration pricing.

Product Line Pricing The strategy for setting a product's price often has to be changed when the product is part of a product mix. Pricing is difficult because the various products have related demand and costs and face different degrees of competition.

Product line pricing
Setting the price steps between various products in a product line based on cost differences between the products, customer evaluations of different features, and competitors' prices.

Companies usually develop product lines rather than single products. Toro, for example, makes many different lawn mowers, ranging from simple walk-behind versions priced at $259.95, $299.95, and $399.95, to elaborate riding mowers priced at $1000 or more. Each successive lawn mower in the line offers more features. Kodak offers not just one type of film, but an assortment including regular Kodak film, higher-priced Kodak Royal Gold film for special occasions, and still higher-priced Advantix APS film for Advanced Photo System cameras. It offers each of these brands in a variety of sizes and film speeds. In **product line pricing**, management must decide on the price steps to set between the various products in a line.

The price steps must take into account cost differences between the products in the line, customer evaluations of their different features, and competitors' prices.

In many industries, sellers use well-established *price points* for the products in their line. Thus, men's clothing stores like upscale Harry Rosen may carry men's suits at three price levels: $800, $1200, $2200. The customer probably will associate good, excellent, and exceptionally high-quality suits with the three price points. Even if the three prices are raised a little, men typically will still buy suits at their own preferred price points. The seller's task is to establish perceived quality differences that support the price differences.

Organizational Considerations

Management must decide who within the organization should set prices. Companies handle pricing in a variety of ways. In small companies, prices often are set by top management rather than by the marketing or sales departments. In large companies, pricing typically is handled by divisional or product line managers. In industrial markets, salespeople may be allowed to negotiate with customers within certain price ranges. Even so, top management sets the pricing objectives and policies, and it often approves the prices proposed by lower-level management or salespeople. In industries in which pricing is a key factor (aerospace, railway, and oil companies), companies often have a pricing department to set the best prices or help others in setting them. This department reports to the marketing department or top management. Others who have an influence on pricing include sales managers, production managers, finance managers, and accountants.

External Factors Affecting Pricing Decisions

External factors that affect pricing decisions include the nature of the market and demand, competition, and other environmental elements.

The Market and Demand

Whereas costs set the lower limit of prices, the market and demand set the upper limit. Both consumer and industrial buyers balance the price of a product or service against the benefits of owning it. Thus, before setting prices, the marketer must understand the relationship between price and demand for its product. In this section, we explain how the price–demand relationship varies for different types of markets and how buyer perceptions of price affect the pricing decision. We then discuss methods for measuring the price–demand relationship.

Pricing in Different Types of Markets   The seller's pricing freedom depends on the type of market the company operates in. Economists recognize four types of markets, each presenting a different pricing challenge because markets differ in their structure and the type of competitors present in the marketplace.

Under *pure competition*, the market consists of many buyers and sellers trading in a uniform commodity such as wheat, copper, or financial securities. No single buyer or seller has much effect on the going market price.

Roots avoids price competition by differentiating its lifestyle products through strong positioning and branding, sponsorship of major events such as the Olympics, and advertising to reduce the impact of price.

Under *monopolistic competition,* the market consists of many buyers and sellers who trade over a range of prices rather than a single market price. A range of prices occurs because sellers can differentiate their offers to buyers. Either the physical product can be varied in quality, features, or style, or the accompanying services can be varied. Buyers see differences in sellers' products and will pay different prices for them. Sellers try to develop differentiated offers for different customer segments and, in addition to price, freely use branding, advertising, and personal selling to set their offers apart. (Thus, Roots differentiates its lifestyle products from jeans to home furnishings through strong positioning and branding, through sponsorship of major events such as the Olympics, and through advertising to reduce the impact of price.) Because there are many competitors, each firm is less affected by competitors' marketing strategies than in oligopolistic markets.

Under *oligopolistic competition,* the market consists of a few sellers who are highly sensitive to each other's pricing and marketing strategies. The product can be uniform (steel, aluminum) or non-uniform (cars, computers). There are few sellers because it is difficult for new sellers to enter the market. Each seller is alert to competitors' strategies and moves. If a steel company slashes its price by 10 percent, buyers will quickly switch to this supplier. The other steelmakers must respond by lowering their prices or increasing their services. An oligopolist is never sure that it will gain anything permanent through a price cut. In contrast, if an oligopolist raises its price, its competitors might not follow this lead. The oligopolist then would have to retract its price increase or risk losing customers to competitors.

In a *pure monopoly,* the market consists of one seller. The seller may be a government monopoly (Canada Post), a private regulated monopoly (Trans Alta Utilities), or a private non-regulated monopoly (Pfizer with its patent on Viagra). Pricing is handled differently in each case. A government monopoly may set a price below cost because the product is important to buyers or it may even set the price quite high to decrease consumption. Environmentalists are encouraging governments to raise prices on electric power, for example, to encourage consumers to conserve.

In a regulated monopoly, the government permits the company to set rates that will yield a "fair return"—one that will let the company maintain and expand its operations as needed. Non-regulated monopolies are free to price at what the market will bear. However, they do not always charge the full price for a number of reasons: a desire not to attract competition, a desire to penetrate the market faster with a low price, or a fear of government regulation.

Competitors' Costs, Prices, and Offers

As the description of the different types of markets indicates, the type of competition differs. Thus, some companies use *competition-based pricing*—setting prices in line with those of their competitors. Consumers often base their judgments of a product's value on the prices that competitors charge for similar products. A consumer who is considering the purchase of a Canon camera will evaluate Canon's price and value against the prices and values of comparable products made by Nikon, Minolta, Pentax, and others. In addition, the company's pricing strategy may affect the nature of the competition it faces. If Canon follows a high-price, high-margin strategy, it may attract competition. A low-price, low-margin strategy, however, may stop competitors or drive them out of the market.

Canon needs to benchmark its costs against its competitors' costs to learn whether it is operating at a cost advantage or disadvantage. It also needs to learn the price and quality of each competitor's offer. Once Canon is aware of competitors' prices and offers, it can use them as a starting point for its own pricing. If Canon's cameras are similar to Nikon's, it will have to price close to Nikon or lose sales. If Canon's cameras are not as good as Nikon's, the firm will not be able to charge as much. If Canon's products are better than Nikon's, it can charge more. Basically, Canon will use price to position its offer relative to the competition.

Consumer Perceptions of Price and Value   In the end, the consumer will decide whether a product's price is right. Pricing decisions, like other marketing mix decisions, must be buyer oriented. When consumers buy a product, they exchange something of value (the price) to get something of value (the benefits of having or using the product). Effective, buyer-oriented pricing involves understanding how much value consumers place on the benefits they receive from the product and setting a price that fits this value.

A company often finds it hard to measure the values that customers will attach to its products. For example, calculating the cost of ingredients in a meal at a fancy restaurant is relatively easy. But assigning a value to other satisfactions such as taste, environment, relaxation, conversation, and status is very hard. And these values will vary both for different consumers and in different situations. Still, consumers will use these values to evaluate a product's price. If customers perceive that the price is greater than the product's value, they will not buy the product. If consumers perceive that the price is below the product's value, they will buy it, but the seller loses profit opportunities.

Analyzing the Price–Demand Relationship   Each price the company might charge will lead to a different level of demand. The relation between the price charged and the resulting demand level is shown in the **demand curve** in Figure 12.4. The demand curve shows the number of units the market will buy in a given time period, at different prices that might be charged. In the normal case, demand and price are inversely related: The higher the price, the lower the demand. Thus, the company would sell less if it raised its price from P_1 to P_2. Consumers with limited budgets probably will buy less of something if its price is too high.

In the case of prestige goods, the demand curve sometimes slopes upward. Consumers think that higher prices mean more quality. For example, Gibson Guitar Corporation recently toyed with the idea of lowering its prices to compete more effectively with Japanese rivals like Yamaha and Ibanez. To its surprise, Gibson

Demand curve

A curve that shows the number of units the market will buy at different possible prices in a given time period.

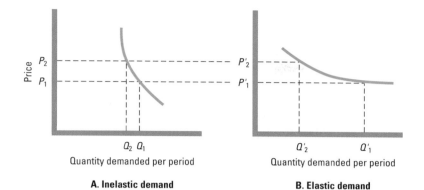

Price

P_2
P_1

Q_2 Q_1

Quantity demanded per period

A. Inelastic demand

P'_2
P'_1

Q'_2 Q'_1

Quantity demanded per period

B. Elastic demand

Figure 12.4 Demand curves

found that its instruments didn't sell as well at lower prices. "We had an inverse [price–demand relationship]," noted Gibson's chief executive officer. "The more we charged, the more product we sold." At a time when other guitar manufacturers have chosen to build their instruments more quickly, cheaply, and in greater numbers, Gibson still promises guitars that "are made one-at-a-time, by hand. No shortcuts. No substitutions." It turns out that low prices simply aren't consistent with "Gibson's century old tradition of creating investment-quality instruments that represent the highest standards of imaginative design and masterful craftsmanship."[12] Still, if the company charges too high a price, the level of demand will be lower.

Most companies try to measure their demand curves by estimating demand at different prices. The type of market makes a difference. In a monopoly, the demand curve shows the total market demand resulting from different prices. If the company faces competition, its demand at different prices depends on whether competitors' prices stay constant or change with the company's own prices.

In measuring the price–demand relationship, the market researcher must not allow other factors affecting demand to vary. For example, if Sony increased its advertising at the same time as it lowered its television prices, we would not know how much of the increased demand was due to the lower prices and how much was

The demand curve sometimes slopes upward: Gibson was surprised to learn that its high-quality instruments didn't sell as well at lower prices.

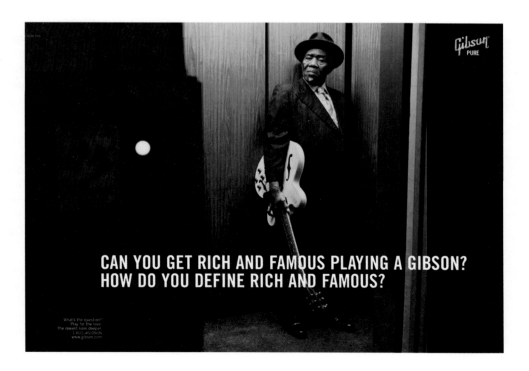

CAN YOU GET RICH AND FAMOUS PLAYING A GIBSON? HOW DO YOU DEFINE RICH AND FAMOUS?

due to the increased advertising. The same problem arises if the lower price is set over a holiday weekend—more gift giving over the holidays causes people to buy more televisions. Economists show the impact of non-price factors on demand through shifts in the demand curve rather than movements along it.

Price elasticity

A measure of the sensitivity of demand to changes in price.

Price Elasticity of Demand   Marketers also need to know **price elasticity**—how responsive demand will be to a change in price. Consider the two demand curves in Figure 12.4. In Figure 12.4A, a price increase from P_1 to P_2 leads to a relatively small drop in demand from Q_1 to Q_2. In Figure 12.4B, however, the same price increase leads to a large drop in demand from Q'_1 to Q'_2. If demand hardly changes with a small change in price, we say the demand is *inelastic*. If demand changes greatly, we say the demand is *elastic*. The price elasticity of demand is given by this formula:

$$\text{Price Elasticity of Demand} = \frac{\text{\% Change in Quantity Demanded}}{\text{\% Change in Price}}$$

Suppose demand falls by 10 percent when a seller raises its price by two percent. Price elasticity of demand is therefore –5 (the minus sign confirms the inverse relation between price and demand) and demand is elastic. If demand falls by 2 percent with a 2 percent increase in price, then elasticity is –1. In this case, the seller's total revenue stays the same: The seller sells fewer items but at a higher price that preserves the same total revenue. If demand falls by 1 percent when price is increased by 2 percent, then elasticity is –1/2 and demand is inelastic. The less elastic the demand, the more it pays for the seller to raise the price.

What determines the price elasticity of demand? Buyers are less price sensitive when the product they are buying is unique or when it is high in quality, prestige, or exclusiveness. They are also less price sensitive when substitute products are hard to find or when they cannot easily compare the quality of substitutes. Finally, buyers are less price sensitive when the total expenditure for a product is low relative to their income or when the cost is shared by another party.[13]

If demand is elastic rather than inelastic, sellers should consider lowering their price. A lower price produces more total revenue. This practice makes sense as long as the extra costs of producing and selling more do not exceed the extra revenue. At the same time, most firms want to avoid pricing that turns their products into commodities. In recent years, deregulation and the instant price comparisons afforded by the Internet and other technologies have increased consumer price sensitivity, turning products ranging from telephones and computers to new automobiles into commodities in consumers' eyes. Here's how one group of marketers responded to this pressure:

> Seven Toyota dealers in southern Manitoba developed new pricing and sales tactics designed primarily to address the concerns of the 60 percent of car buyers who surf the Web before kicking the tires. Toyota's "product advisors" point potential customers to the Access Toyota website (www.access.toyota.ca) and explain that the price shown is the "drive-away" price for the vehicle selected—not the manufacturer's suggested retail price (MSRP), but a price that provides a reasonable profit for the dealer and a fair cost for the customer who buys or leases. In other words...no haggling.[14]

Marketers need to work harder than ever to differentiate their offerings when a dozen competitors are selling virtually the same product at a comparable or lower price. More than ever, companies need to understand the price sensitivity of their customers and prospects and the trade-offs people are willing to make between price and product characteristics. In the words of marketing consultant Kevin Clancy, those who target only the price sensitive are "leaving money on the table."[15]

Other External Factors

When setting prices, the company also must consider other factors in its external environment. *Economic conditions* can have a strong impact on the firm's pricing strategies. Economic factors such as boom or recession, inflation, and interest rates influence pricing decisions because they affect both the costs of producing a product and consumer perceptions of the product's price and value. The company must also consider what impact its prices will have on other parties in its environment. How will *resellers* react to various prices? The company should set prices that give resellers a fair profit, encourage their support, and help them to sell the product effectively. The *government* is another important external influence on pricing decisions. Finally, *social concerns* may have to be considered. In setting prices, a company's short-term sales, market share, and profit goals, as well as the ability of the vulnerable to afford them, may have to be tempered by broader societal considerations.

General Pricing Approaches

The price the company charges will be somewhere between one that is too low to produce a profit and one that is too high to produce any demand. Figure 12.5 summarizes the major considerations in setting price. Product costs set a floor to the price; consumer perceptions of the product's value set the ceiling. The company must consider competitors' prices and other external and internal factors to find the best price between these two extremes.

Companies set prices by selecting from or combining two general pricing approaches: the *cost-based approach* (cost-plus pricing, break-even analysis, and target profit pricing), and the *value-based approach* (buyer-based or perceived-value pricing).

Cost-Based Pricing

Cost-plus pricing

Adding a standard markup to the cost of the product.

The simplest pricing method is **cost-plus pricing**—adding a standard markup to the cost of the product. Construction companies, for example, submit job bids by estimating the total project cost and adding a standard markup for profit. Lawyers, accountants, and other professionals typically price by adding a standard markup to their costs. Some sellers tell their customers they charge cost plus a specified markup; for example, aerospace companies price this way to the government.

To illustrate markup pricing, suppose a toaster manufacturer had the following costs and expected sales:

Variable cost	$10
Fixed cost	$300 000
Expected unit sales	50 000

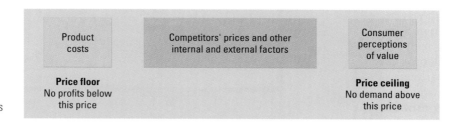

Figure 12.5 Major considerations in setting price

Product costs

Price floor
No profits below
this price

Competitors' prices and other
internal and external factors

Consumer
perceptions
of value

Price ceiling
No demand above
this price

Then the manufacturer's cost per toaster is given by:

$$\text{Unit Cost} = \text{Variable Cost} + \frac{\text{Fixed Costs}}{\text{Unit Sales}} = \$10 + \frac{\$300\ 000}{50\ 000} = \$16$$

Now suppose the manufacturer wants to earn a 20 percent markup on sales. The manufacturer's markup price is given by:[16]

$$\text{Markup Price} = \frac{\text{Unit Cost}}{1 - \text{Desired Return on Sales}} = \frac{\$16}{1 - 0.2} = \$20$$

The manufacturer would charge dealers $20 a toaster and make a profit of $4 per unit. The dealers, in turn, will mark up the toaster. If the dealers want to earn 50 percent on sales price, they will mark up the toaster to $40 ($20 + 50% of $40). This number is equivalent to a *markup on cost* of 100 percent ($20/$20).

Does using standard markups to set prices make sense? Generally, no. Any pricing method that ignores demand and competitors' prices is not likely to lead to the best price. Suppose the toaster manufacturer charged $20 but only sold 30 000 toasters instead of 50 000. Then the unit cost would have been higher since the fixed costs are spread over fewer units, and the realized percentage markup on sales would have been lower. Markup pricing only works if that price actually brings in the expected level of sales.

Still, markup pricing remains popular for many reasons. First, sellers are more certain about costs than about demand. By tying the price to cost, sellers simplify pricing—they do not have to make frequent adjustments as demand changes. Second, when all firms in the industry use this pricing method, prices tend to be similar and price competition is thus minimized. Third, many people believe that cost-plus pricing is fairer to both buyers and sellers. Sellers earn a fair return on their investment but do not take advantage of buyers when buyers' demand becomes great.

Break-Even Analysis and Target Profit Pricing

Break-even pricing (target profit pricing)

Setting price to break even on the costs of making and marketing a product; or setting price to make a target profit.

Another cost-oriented pricing approach is **break-even pricing**, or a variation called **target profit pricing**. The firm tries to determine the price at which it will break even or make the target profit it is seeking. Target pricing is used by General Motors, which prices its automobiles to achieve a 15 to 20 percent profit on its investment. This pricing method is also used by public utilities, which must make a fair return on their investment.

Target pricing uses the *break-even chart*, which shows the total cost and total revenue expected at different sales volume levels. Figure 12.6 shows a break-even

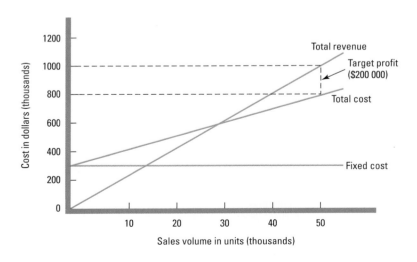

Figure 12.6 Break-even chart for determining target price

chart for our toaster manufacturer. Fixed costs are $300 000 regardless of sales volume. Variable costs are added to fixed costs to form total costs, which rise with volume. The total revenue curve starts at zero and rises with each unit sold. The slope of the total revenue curve reflects the price of $20 per unit.

The total revenue and total cost curves cross at 30 000 units. This is the *break-even volume*. At $20, the company must sell at least 30 000 units to break even; that is, for total revenue to cover total cost. Break-even volume can be calculated with this formula:

$$\text{Break-Even Volume} = \frac{\text{Fixed Cost}}{\text{Price} - \text{Variable Cost}} = \frac{\$300\ 000}{\$20 - \$10} = 30\ 000$$

If the company wants to make a target profit, it must sell more than 30 000 units at $20 each. Suppose the toaster manufacturer has invested $1 000 000 in the business and wants to set the price to earn a 20 percent return, or $200 000. In that case, it must sell at least 50 000 units at $20 each. If the company charges a higher price, it will not need to sell as many toasters to achieve its target return; but the market may not buy even this lower volume at the higher price. Much depends on the price elasticity and competitors' prices.

The manufacturer should consider different prices and estimate break-even volumes, probable demand, and profits for each. This is done in Table 12.1. The table shows that as price increases, break-even volume drops (column 2). But as price increases, demand for the toasters also falls off (column 3). At the $14 price, because the manufacturer clears only $4 per toaster ($14 less $10 in variable costs), it must sell a very high volume to break even. Even though the low price attracts many buyers, demand still falls below the high break-even point, and the manufacturer loses money. At the other extreme, with a $22 price the manufacturer clears $12 per toaster and must sell only 25 000 units to break even. But at this high price, consumers buy too few toasters, and profits are negative. The table shows that a price of $18 yields the highest profits. Note that none of the prices produce the manufacturer's target profit of $200 000. To achieve this target return, the manufacturer will have to search for ways to lower fixed or variable costs, thus lowering the break-even volume.

Value-based pricing
Setting price based on buyers' perceptions of value rather than on the seller's cost.

Value-Based Pricing

An increasing number of companies are basing their prices on the product's perceived value. **Value-based pricing** uses buyers' perceptions of value, not the seller's

---

Table 12.1   Break-Even Volume and Profits at Different Prices

(1) Price	(2) Unit Demand Needed to Break Even	(3) Expected Unit Demand at Given Price	(4) Total Revenues (1) × (3)	(5) Total Costs*	(6) Profit (4) − (5)
$14	75 000	71 000	$994 000	$1 010 000	−$16 000
16	50 000	67 000	1 072 000	970 000	102 000
18	37 500	60 000	1 080 000	900 000	180 000
20	30 000	42 000	840 000	720 000	120 000
22	25 000	23 000	506 000	530 000	− 24 000

*Assumed fixed costs of $300 000 and constant unit variable costs of $10.

Cost-based pricing

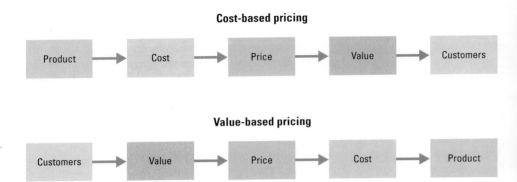

Figure 12.7 Cost-based versus value-based pricing

Source: Thomas T. Nagle and Reed K. Holden, *The Strategy and Tactics of Pricing,* 3rd ed. (Upper Saddle River, N.J.: Prentice Hall, 2002), p. 4.

cost, as the key to pricing. Value-based pricing means that the marketer cannot design a product and marketing program and then set the price. Price is considered along with the other marketing mix variables *before* the marketing program is set.

Figure 12.7 compares cost-based pricing with value-based pricing. Cost-based pricing is product driven. The company designs what it considers to be a good product, determines the costs of making the product, and sets a price that covers costs plus a target profit. Marketing must then convince buyers that the product's value at that price justifies its purchase. If the price turns out to be too high, the company must settle for lower markups or lower sales, both resulting in disappointing profits.

Value-based pricing reverses this process. The company sets its target price based on customer perceptions of the product value. The targeted value and price then drive decisions about product design and what costs can be incurred. As a result, pricing begins with analyzing consumer needs and value perceptions, and the price is set to match consumers' perceived value.

A company using value-based pricing must find out what value buyers assign to different competitive offers. Measuring perceived value, however, can be difficult. Sometimes consumers are asked how much they would pay for a basic product and for each benefit added to the offer. Or a company may conduct experiments to test the perceived value of different product offers. If the seller charges more than the buyers' perceived value, the company's sales will suffer. Many companies overprice their products, which then sell poorly. Other companies underprice products, which sell very well but produce less revenue than they would if prices were raised to the perceived value level. It's important to remember that "good value" is not the same as "low price." For example, Parker sells pens priced as high as $4500. A less expensive pen might write as well, but some consumers place great value on the intangibles they receive from a fine writing instrument.

During the past decade, marketers have noted a fundamental shift in consumer attitudes toward price and quality. Many companies have changed their pricing approaches to bring them into line with changing economic conditions and consumer price perceptions. According to Jack Welch, former CEO of General Electric, "The value decade is upon us. If you can't sell a top-quality product at the world's best price, you're going to be out of the game.... The best way to hold your customers is to constantly figure out how to give them more for less."[17]

Value pricing
Offering just the right combination of quality and good service at a fair price.

Thus, more and more marketers have adopted **value pricing** strategies—offering just the right combination of quality and good service at a fair price. In many cases, this has involved the introduction of less expensive versions of established, brand-name products. Campbell introduced its Great Starts Budget frozen-food line, Holiday Inn opened several Holiday Express budget hotels, Revlon's Charles of the Ritz created the Express Bar collection of affordable cosmetics, and fast-food restaurants such as Taco Bell and McDonald's offered "value menus." In other cases, value pricing has involved redesigning existing brands to offer more quality for a given price or the same quality for less.

Kimberly Clark makes it a virtue to shop for reasonably priced products. Its Scott towels provide value for the consumer while protecting the company from the in-roads of low-priced brands.

In many business-to-business marketing situations, the pricing challenge is to find ways to adjust the value of the company's marketing offer to escape price competition and to justify higher prices and margins. To retain pricing power—to escape price competition and to justify higher prices and margins—a firm must retain or build the value of its marketing offer. This is especially true for suppliers of commodity products, which are characterized by little differentiation and intense price competition. In such cases, many companies adopt *value-added* strategies. Rather than cutting prices to match competitors, they attach value-added services to differentiate their offers and thus support higher margins (see Real Marketing 12.2). "Even in today's economic environment, it's not about price," says a pricing expert. "It's about keeping customers loyal by providing service they can't find anywhere else."[18]

An important type of value pricing at the retail level is *everyday low pricing (EDLP)*. EDLP involves charging a constant, everyday low price with few or no temporary price discounts. In contrast, *high-low pricing* involves charging higher prices on an everyday basis, but running frequent promotions to temporarily lower prices on selected items below the EDLP level. In recent years, high-low pricing has given way to EDLP in retail settings ranging from General Motors and Chrysler car dealerships to grocery stores like Quebec's Metro chain and upscale department stores such as Nordstrom.

Retailers adopt EDLP for many reasons, the most important of which is that constant sales and promotions are costly and have eroded consumer confidence in the credibility of everyday shelf prices. Consumers also have less time and patience for such time-honoured traditions as watching for supermarket specials and clipping coupons.

12.2 Pricing Power: The Value of Value-Added

When a company finds its major competitors offering a similar product at a lower price, the natural tendency is to try to match or beat that price. While the idea of undercutting competitors' prices and watching customers flock to you is tempting, there are dangers. Successive rounds of price cutting can lead to price wars that erode the profit margins of all competitors in an industry. Or worse, discounting a product can cheapen it in the minds of customers, greatly reducing the seller's power to maintain profitable prices in the long term. "It ends up being a losing battle," notes one marketing executive. "You focus away from quality, service, prestige—the things brands are all about."

So, how can a company keep its pricing power when a competitor undercuts its price? Often, the best strategy is not to price below the competitor, but rather to price above and convince customers that the product is worth it. The company should ask, "What is the value of the product to the customer?" and then stand up for what the product is worth. In this way, the company shifts the focus from price to value.

Air Canada tried to do this with its flagship brand, but was unsuccessful because of declining service quality. To counter the erosion of its market share by the discount airlines like WestJet and Jetsgo, Air Canada introduced its own discount brands: Tango and Zip. However, an economic downturn and labour unrest furthered its woes and Air Canada is still struggling with its pricing strategy. Consumers are very frustrated with the pricing of air services overall, not just with Air Canada's offerings. They've been airing their frustration on the Internet, asking, "What if airlines sold paint?"

> *Customer:* Hi. How much is your paint?
> *Clerk:* Well, sir, that all depends on quite a lot of things.
> *Customer:* Can you give me a guess? Is there an average price?
> *Clerk:* Our lowest price is $12 a gallon, and we have 60 different prices up to $200 a gallon.
> *Customer:* What's the difference in the paint?
> *Clerk:* Oh, there isn't any difference; it's all the same paint.
> *Customer:* Well, then I'd like some of that $12 paint.
> *Clerk:* When do you intend to use the paint?
> *Customer:* I want to paint tomorrow. It's my day off.
> *Clerk:* Sir, the paint for tomorrow is the $200 paint.
> *Customer:* When would I have to paint to get the $12 paint?
> *Clerk:* You would have to start very late at night in about three weeks. But you will have to agree to start painting before Friday of that week and continue painting until at least Sunday.

But what if the company is operating in a "commodity" business, in which the products of all competitors seem pretty much alike? In such cases, the company must find ways to "decommoditize" its products—to create superior value for customers. It can do this by developing value-added features and services that differentiate its offer and justify higher prices and margins. Here are some examples of how suppliers are using value-added features and services to give them a competitive edge:

Caterpillar. Caterpillar is a master at charging premium prices for its heavy construction and mining equipment and convincing customers that its products and service justify every additional cent—or, rather, the extra tens of thousands of dollars. Caterpillar typically reaps a 20 to

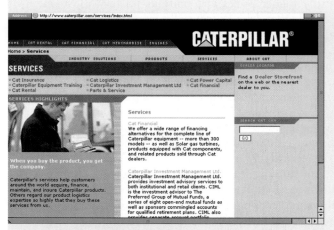

Value added: Caterpillar offers its dealers a wide range of value-added services—from guaranteed parts delivery to investment management advice and equipment training. Such added value supports a higher price.

30 percent price premium over competitors—and that can amount to an extra $235 000 or more on one of those huge yellow million-dollar dump trucks. When a large potential customer says, "I can get it for less from a competitor," rather than discounting the price, the Caterpillar dealer explains that, even at the higher price, Cat offers the best value. Caterpillar equipment is designed with modular components that can be removed and repaired quickly, minimizing machine downtime. Caterpillar dealers carry an extensive parts inventory and guarantee delivery within 48 hours anywhere in the world, again minimizing downtime. Cat's products are designed to be rebuilt, providing a "second life" that competitors cannot match. As a result, Caterpillar used-equipment prices are often 20 percent to 30 percent higher.

In all, the dealer explains, even at the higher initial price, Caterpillar equipment delivers the lowest total cost per cubic metre of earth moved, tonne of coal uncovered, or kilometre of road graded over the life of the product—guaranteed! Most customers seem to agree with Caterpillar's value proposition—the company dominates its markets, with a more than 40 percent worldwide market share.

Pioneer Hi-Bred International. A major supplier of corn seed and other agricultural products often thought of as commodities, DuPont subsidiary Pioneer Hi-Bred hardly acts like a commodity supplier. Its patented hybrid seeds yield 10 percent more corn than competitors' seeds. Beyond producing a superior product, Pioneer Hi-Bred

provides a bundle of value-added services. For example, it equips its sales representatives with notebook computers that allow them to provide farmers with customized information and advice. The rep can plug in the type of hybrid that a farmer is using, along with information about pricing, acreage, and yield characteristics, then advise the farmer on how to do a better job of farm management. The reps can also supply farmers with everything from agricultural research reports to assistance in comparison shopping.

Pioneer Hi-Bred also offers farmers crop insurance, financing, and marketing services. Backing its claim "We believe in customer success" with superior products and value-added services gives Pioneer Hi-Bred plenty of pricing power. Despite charging a significant price premium—or perhaps because of it—the company's share of the North American corn market has grown from 35 percent during the mid-1980s to its current level of 44 percent.

Sources: Jim Morgan, "Value Added: From Cliché to the Real Thing," *Purchasing,* April 3, 1997, pp. 59–61; James E. Ellis, John Jesitus, "Close Connections," *Industry Week,* October 6, 1997, pp. 28–34; James C. Anderson and James A. Narus, "Business Marketing: Understand What Customers Value," *Harvard Business Review,* November–December 1998, pp. 53–65; Tom Nagle, "How to Pull It Off," *Across the Board,* March 1999, pp. 53–56; Robert B. Tucker, "Adding Value Profitably," *American Salesman,* April 2001, pp. 17–20; Erin Stout, "Keep Them Coming Back for More," *Sales & Marketing Management,* February 2002, pp. 51–52; Pioneer website, www.pioneer.com (accessed July 2002) and Alan H. Hess, Hess Travel, "If Airlines Sold Paint," http://etntelephone.com/stories/paint.htm.

The leader of EDLP is Wal-Mart, which practically defined the concept. Except for a few sale items every month, Wal-Mart promises everyday low prices on everything it sells. To offer everyday low prices, a company must first have everyday low costs. Wal-Mart's EDLP strategy works well because its expenses are only 15 percent of sales. When Wal-Mart first entered Canada, Zellers began a price war with the American giant in an attempt to defend its well-known slogan, "The lowest price is the law!" However, Zellers soon learned that to win such a battle, lowest costs must also be the law! Since Zellers's operating costs were higher than Wal-Mart's, its profits were squeezed and the company had to abandon the fight.

Price-Adjustment Strategies

Companies usually adjust their basic prices to account for various customer differences and changing situations. Here we examine the six price-adjustment strategies summarized in Table 12.2: *discount and allowance pricing, segmented pricing, psychological pricing, promotional pricing, geographical pricing,* and *international pricing.*

Table 12.2 Price-Adjustment Strategies

Strategy	Description
Discount and allowance pricing	Reducing prices to reward customer responses such as paying early or promoting the product
Segmented pricing	Adjusting prices to allow for differences in customers, products, or locations
Psychological pricing	Adjusting prices for psychological effect
Promotional pricing	Temporarily reducing prices to increase short-run sales
Geographical pricing	Adjusting prices to account for the geographic location of customers
International pricing	Adjusting prices for international markets

Discount and Allowance Pricing

Most companies adjust their basic price to reward customers for certain responses, such as early payment of bills, volume purchases, and off-season buying. These price adjustments—called *discounts* and *allowances*—can take many forms.

Discount
A straight reduction in price on purchases during a stated period of time.

The many forms of **discounts** include a *cash discount*, a price reduction to buyers who pay their bills promptly. A typical example is "2/10, net 30," which means that, although payment is due within 30 days, the buyer can deduct 2 percent if the bill is paid within 10 days. The discount must be granted to all buyers meeting these terms. Such discounts are customary in many industries and help to improve the sellers' cash situation and reduce bad debts and credit collection costs.

A *quantity discount* is a price reduction to buyers who buy large volumes. A typical example is "$10 per unit for less than 100 units, $9 per unit for 100 or more units." Under the provisions of the *Competition Act,* quantity discounts must be offered equally to all customers and must not exceed the seller's cost savings associated with selling large quantities. These savings include lower selling, inventory, and transportation expenses. Discounts provide an incentive to the customer to buy more from one given seller, rather than from many different sources.

A *functional discount* (also called a *trade discount*) is offered by the seller to trade-channel members who perform certain functions, such as selling, storing, and record keeping. Manufacturers may offer different functional discounts to different trade channels because of the varying services they perform, but manufacturers must offer the same functional discounts within each trade channel.

A *seasonal discount* is a price reduction to buyers who buy merchandise or services out of season. For example, lawn and garden equipment manufacturers offer seasonal discounts to retailers during the fall and winter months to encourage early ordering in anticipation of the heavy spring and summer selling seasons. Hotels, motels, and airlines will offer seasonal discounts in their slower selling periods. Seasonal discounts allow the seller to keep production steady during an entire year.

Allowance
Promotional money paid by manufacturers to retailers in return for an agreement to feature the manufacturer's products in some way.

Allowances are another type of reduction from the list price. *Trade-in allowances* are price reductions given for turning in an old item when buying a new one. They are most common in the automobile industry, but are also given for other durable goods. *Promotional allowances* are payments or price reductions to reward dealers for participating in advertising and sales-support programs.

Segmented pricing
Selling a product or service at two or more prices, where the difference in prices is not based on differences in costs.

Segmented Pricing

Companies will often adjust their basic prices to allow for differences in customers, products, and locations. In **segmented pricing**, the company sells a product or service at two or more prices, even though the difference in prices is not based on differences in costs.

Segmented pricing takes several forms. Under *customer segment pricing*, different customers pay different prices for the same product or service. Museums, for example, will charge a lower admission for students and senior citizens. Under *product form pricing*, different versions of the product are priced differently, but not according to differences in their costs. For instance, Black & Decker prices its most expensive iron at $54.98, which is $12 more than the price of its next most expensive iron. The top model has a self-cleaning feature, yet this extra feature costs only a few more dollars to make.

Using *location pricing*, a company charges different prices for different locations, even though the cost of offering each location is the same. For instance, theatres vary their seat prices because of audience preferences for certain locations, and universities charge higher tuition for overseas students.

For segmented pricing to be an effective strategy, certain conditions must exist. The market must be segmentable, and the segments must show different degrees of demand. Members of the segment paying the lower price should not be able to turn around and resell the product to the segment paying the higher price. Competitors should not be able to undersell the firm in the segment being charged the higher price. Nor should the costs of segmenting and watching the market exceed the extra revenue obtained from the price difference. Of course, the segmented pricing must also be legal (see Real Marketing 12.3). Most importantly, segmented prices should reflect real differences in customers' perceived value. Otherwise, in the long run, the practice will lead to customer resentment and ill will.

Psychological Pricing

Psychological pricing
A pricing approach that considers the psychology of prices and not simply the economics; the price is used to say something about the product.

Price says something about the product. For example, many consumers use price to judge quality. A $100 bottle of perfume may contain only $3 worth of scent, but some people are willing to pay $100 because this price indicates something special.

In using **psychological pricing**, sellers consider the psychology of prices and not simply the economics. For example, consumers usually perceive higher-priced products as having higher quality. When consumers can judge the quality of a product by examining it or by calling on past experience with it, they use price less to judge quality. But when they cannot judge quality because they lack the information or skill, price becomes an important quality signal:

> Heublein produces Smirnoff, America's leading vodka brand. Some years ago, Smirnoff was attacked by another brand. Wolfschmidt, priced at one dollar less per bottle, claimed to have the same quality as Smirnoff. To hold on to market share, Heublein considered either lowering Smirnoff's price by one dollar or holding Smirnoff's price but increasing advertising and promotion expenditures. Either strategy would lead to lower profits and it seemed that Heublein faced a no-win situation.
>
> At this point, however, Heublein's marketers thought of a third strategy. They *raised* the price of Smirnoff by one dollar! Heublein then introduced a new brand, Relska, to compete with Wolfschmidt. Moreover, it introduced yet another brand, Popov, priced even *lower* than Wolfschmidt. This clever strategy positioned Smirnoff as the elite brand and Wolfschmidt as an ordinary brand, producing a large increase in Heublein's overall profits. The irony is that Heublein's three brands are pretty much the same in taste and manufacturing costs. Heublein knew that a product's price signals its quality. Using price as a signal, Heublein sells roughly the same product at three different quality positions.

Reference prices
Prices that buyers carry in their minds and refer to when they look at a given product.

Another aspect of psychological pricing is **reference prices**—prices that buyers carry in their minds and refer to when looking at a given product. They may form the reference price by noting current prices, remembering past prices, or assessing the buying situation. Sellers can influence or use these consumers' reference prices

12.3 Weblining—Segmented Pricing or Discrimination?

oncern about segmented pricing is growing as companies increasingly use their databases to build profiles of consumers. The oceans of information available on the Internet, combined with fast computers to process the data, allow companies to maintain the equivalent of profit-and-loss statements on every customer. While some customers benefit, others are forced to pay more for products and services or, even worse, may no longer be served at all.

Some banks colour code customers according to the level of profitability they represent for the bank. While customer reps are trained to treat everyone politely, the level of service customers receive and the fees they pay for that service or product depends on the coloured square that appears on the rep's computer screen when the customer's account number is entered. Greens, for example, might get better interest rates on their credit card balances. Reds may pay higher fees for such basic services.

A new term has been coined to describe this practice—*Weblining*. Weblining is the information age version of that nasty old practice of redlining, in which lenders, insurance companies, and other businesses marked whole neighbourhoods off-limits because of the perceived risk the residents represent, their low incomes, or their racial background. Redlining was damned because it was based on geographic stereotypes, not concrete evidence that specific individuals were poor credit risks. Webliners claim to have more evidence against the people they refuse to serve. Using clickstream data and transaction histories, companies can sort people into categories and, in some cases, predict how they will behave. Forrester Research estimated that in 2002, some 60 percent of companies were using the Net to "micro-segment" customers.

Nonetheless, companies' refusal to provide services or products to groups of customers, especially those who are disadvantaged, has given rise to accusations of discrimination. Firms, therefore, have to ensure that their classifications are fair and accurate. They can't be based on irrelevant, outdated, or inaccurate profiling data. Moreover, information must not be compiled without the user's knowledge. Montreal's Zero-Knowledge Systems, which markets a software program called *Freedom,* has responded to people's concerns about privacy when they surf the Net. The program enables surfers to create a pseudonym that masks their true identities when they go online, thus making their travels on the Web untraceable.

Montreal's Zero-Knowledge Systems markets software to help people protect their online privacy.

Sources: Marcia Stepanek, "Weblining: Companies Are Using Your Personal Data To Limit Your Choices—And Force You To Pay More for Products," *Businessweek* Online, April 3, 2000; and Edward Robinson, "As the Privacy Debate Rages On, a Handful Of Entrepreneurs Is Gambling on Business Models Built Around Your Online Identity," *Business 2.0,* September 12, 2000, www.business2.com/content/magazine/indepth/2000/08/22/17926.

Psychological pricing: A less expensive pen might write as well, but some consumers will pay much more for the intangibles. U.K.-based Parker Pen sells models that run from a few cents to thousands of dollars.

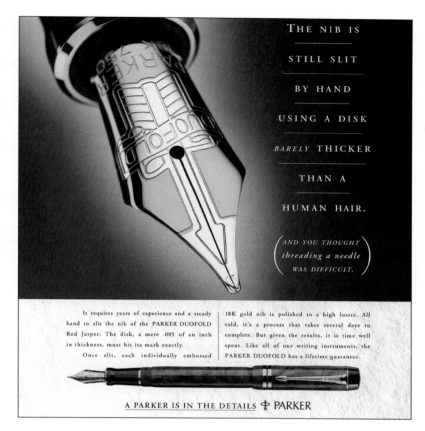

THE NIB IS STILL SLIT BY HAND USING A DISK *BARELY* THICKER THAN A HUMAN HAIR.

(*AND YOU THOUGHT threading a needle WAS DIFFICULT.*)

It requires years of experience and a steady hand to slit the nib of the PARKER DUOFOLD Red Jasper. The disk, a mere .005 of an inch in thickness, must hit its mark exactly. Once slit, each individually embossed 18K gold nib is polished to a high lustre. All told, it's a process that takes several days to complete. But given the results, it is time well spent. Like all of our writing instruments, the PARKER DUOFOLD has a lifetime guarantee.

A PARKER IS IN THE DETAILS ✦ PARKER

when setting price. For example, a company could display its product next to more expensive ones to imply that it belongs in the same class. Department stores often sell women's clothing in separate departments differentiated by price: clothing found in the more expensive department is assumed to be of better quality. Companies also can influence consumers' reference prices by stating high manufacturer's suggested prices, by indicating that the product was originally priced much higher, or by pointing to a competitor's higher price.

Even small differences in price can suggest product differences. Consider a stereo priced at $300 compared with one priced at $299.95. The actual price difference is only 5 cents, but the psychological difference can be much greater. For example, some consumers will see the $299.95 as a price in the $200 range rather than the $300 range. The $299.95 will more likely be seen as a bargain price, whereas the $300 price suggests more quality. Some psychologists argue that each digit has symbolic and visual qualities that should be considered in pricing. Thus, 8 is round and even and creates a soothing effect, whereas 7 is angular and creates a jarring effect.[19]

Promotional Pricing

Promotional pricing
Temporarily pricing products below the list price, and sometimes even below cost, to increase short-run sales.

With **promotional pricing**, companies will temporarily price their products below list price and sometimes even below cost. Promotional pricing takes several forms. Supermarkets and department stores will price a few products as *loss leaders* to attract customers to the store in the hope that they will buy other items at normal markups. For example, supermarkets often sell disposable diapers at less than cost in order to attract family buyers who make larger average purchases per trip. Sellers also use *special event pricing* in certain seasons to draw more customers. Thus, linens are promotionally priced every January to attract weary Christmas shoppers back into stores.

Promotional pricing: Companies offer promotional prices to create buying excitement and urgency.

The frequent use of promotional pricing can also lead to industry price wars. Such price wars usually play into the hands of only one or a few competitors—those with the most efficient operations. For example, until recently, the computer industry avoided price wars. Computer companies, including IBM, Hewlett-Packard, Compaq, and Gateway, showed strong profits as their new technologies were snapped up by eager consumers. When the market cooled, however, many competitors began to unload PCs at discounted prices. In response, Dell, the industry's undisputed low-cost leader, started a price war that only it could win:

> In mid-2000, Dell began a brutal price war just as the industry slipped into its worst slump ever. And Dell has no doubt it will win the battle. Its advantage is founded on its direct-selling approach and low-cost manufacturing. By taking orders straight from customers and building machines to order, Dell avoids paying retailer markups, getting stuck with unsold PCs, and keeping costly inventories. For example, at any given moment, Dell's warehouses hold just four days of stock, compared with 24 days for competitors. That gives it a gigantic edge in a market where the price of chips, drives, and other parts typically falls 1 percent a week. Moreover, Dell has mastered supply chain management. Dell requires suppliers to use sophisticated software that wires them straight into Dell's factory floor, allowing Dell's plants to replenish supplies only as needed

Market penetration: Dell used penetration pricing to enter the personal computer market, selling high-quality computer products through lower-cost direct channels.

throughout the day. That software alone saved Dell $65 million in the first six months of use.

Rapidly falling prices have left competitors with few effective weapons. IBM has responded by outsourcing its PC production and sales. And HP and Compaq merged in hopes of finding strength in numbers. However, size hasn't helped the merger overcome Dell. In 2003, less than 24 hours after Hewlett-Packard reported its personal computer division had lost money, Dell again tightened the screws on its rival by announcing even more price cuts up to 22 percent on computers, printers, and other equipment. Dell continues to increase its lead over HP and all other PC makers, setting the tone on pricing. Says Michael Dell, "When we sell these products, we make money. When our competitors sell them, they lose money."[20]

Geographical Pricing

A company also must decide how to price its products to customers located in different parts of the country or world. Should the company risk losing the business of more distant customers by charging them higher prices to cover the higher shipping costs? Or should the company charge all customers the same prices regardless of location?

Take a northern B.C.-based paper company that sells its products to customers all over Canada. The cost of freight is high and affects the companies from whom customers buy their paper. When establishing its geographical pricing policy, it is considering how to price a $100 order to three specific customers: Customer A (Vancouver), Customer B (Winnipeg), and Customer C (Halifax). One option is for the company to ask each customer to pay the shipping cost from the factory in northern B.C. to the customer's location. All three customers would pay the same factory price of $100, with Customer A paying, say, $15 for shipping; Customer B, $25; and Customer C, $50. Called **FOB-origin pricing**, this practice means that the

FOB-origin pricing
A geographical pricing strategy in which goods are placed free on board a carrier; the customer pays the freight from the factory to the destination.

goods are placed *free on board* (hence, *FOB*) a carrier. At that point the title and responsibility pass to the customer, who pays the freight from the factory to the destination. Because each customer picks up its own cost, supporters of FOB pricing feel that this is the fairest way to assess freight charges. The disadvantage, however, is that the paper company's products become higher in cost for distant customers.

Uniform-delivered pricing is the opposite of FOB pricing. Here, the company charges the same price plus freight to all customers, regardless of their location. The freight charge is set at the average freight cost. Suppose this is $45. Uniform-delivered pricing therefore results in a higher charge to the Vancouver customer (who pays $45 freight instead of $15) and a lower charge to the Halifax customer (who pays $45 instead of $50). This pricing tactic may hurt the firm's chances of winning over local buyers but improve its odds of winning distant sales. Other advantages of uniform-delivered pricing are that it is fairly easy to administer and it lets the firm advertise its price nationally.

Zone pricing falls between FOB-origin pricing and uniform-delivered pricing. The company sets up two or more zones. All customers within a given zone pay a single total price; the more distant the zone, the higher the price. For example, the company might set up a Western Zone and charge $15 freight to all customers in this zone, a Central Zone in which it charges $25, and an Eastern Zone in which it charges $50.

International Pricing

Companies that market their products internationally must decide what prices to charge in the different countries in which they operate. In some cases, a company can set a uniform worldwide price. For example, Canadair sells its jetliners at about the same price everywhere, whether in the United States, Europe, or a Third World country. However, most companies adjust their prices to reflect local market conditions and cost considerations.

The price that a company should charge in a specific country depends on many factors, including economic conditions, product and shipping costs, competitive situations, laws and regulations, and development of the wholesaling and retailing system. Consumer perceptions and preferences also may vary among countries, calling for different prices. Or the company may have different marketing objectives in

Uniform-delivered pricing
A geographical pricing strategy in which the company charges the same price plus freight to all customers, regardless of their location.

Zone pricing
A geographical pricing strategy in which the company sets up two or more zones. All customers within a zone pay the same total price; the more distant the zone, the higher the price.

Companies that market products internationally must decide what prices to charge in the different countries.

various world markets, which require changes in pricing strategy. For example, Panasonic might introduce a new product into mature markets in highly developed countries with the goal of quickly gaining mass-market share—this would call for a penetration pricing strategy. In contrast, it may enter a less developed market by targeting smaller, less price-sensitive segments—in this case, market skimming pricing makes sense. Thus, international pricing presents some special problems and complexities. We discuss international pricing issues in more detail in Chapter 18.

Price Changes

After developing their initial pricing, companies often encounter situations in which they must initiate price changes due to changes in market conditions or to respond to price changes by competitors.

Initiating Price Changes

In some cases, the company may find it desirable to initiate either a price cut or a price increase. In both cases, it must anticipate possible buyer and competitor reactions.

Initiating Price Cuts

Several situations may lead a firm to consider cutting its price. One such circumstance is excess capacity. In this case, the firm needs more business and cannot get it through increased sales effort, product improvement, or other measures. It may drop its "follow-the-leader pricing"—charging about the same price as its leading competitor—and aggressively cut prices to boost sales. Another situation leading to price changes is falling market share in the face of strong price competition. The airline, construction equipment, fast-food, and other industries facing these dual dilemmas have learned in recent years that cutting prices in an industry loaded with excess capacity may lead to price wars, as competitors try to hold on to market share. See what has happened in the Canadian auto industry:

> A recent full-page ad by DaimlerChrysler in the *Toronto Star* blared, "First time ever—0% purchase financing for up to 60 months." While these ads worked in 2002, such offers have now become the price of entry. The run on automobile showrooms has tapered off and by 2003 car sales were down 11.4 percent. While Windsor-based DaimlerChrysler Canada says it would like to move away from incentives pricing, it seems to have little choice in the face of aggressive use of incentives by competitors: "Earlier this year it was not our strategy to use incentives so aggressively," says Paul Fleet, manager, product public relations, DaimlerChrysler. "Rather, we would prefer to add content and enhance the product to increase its appeal. Our use of incentives has become increasingly aggressive in light of very aggressive use of incentives by competitors." Many analysts believe the carmakers are taking a wrong turn. "As long as automakers continue down this road, agencies are going to be stuck producing ads that have little to say about how a vehicle speaks to a buyer's aspirations. And consumers will continue to get pounded over the head with creative that has reduced cars to commodities."[21]

Initiating Price Increases

A successful price increase can greatly increase profits. For example, if the company's profit margin is 3 percent of sales, a 1 percent price increase will increase profits by 33 percent if sales volume is unaffected. A major factor in price increases is cost inflation. Rising costs squeeze profit margins and lead companies to pass cost increases along to customers. Another factor leading to price increases is overdemand. When a company cannot supply all its customers' needs, it can raise its prices, ration products to customers, or both.

Companies can increase their prices in a number of ways to keep up with rising costs. Prices can be raised almost invisibly by dropping discounts and adding higher-priced units to the line. Or prices can be pushed up openly. In passing price increases on to customers, the company must avoid being perceived as a price gouger. Companies also need to think of who will bear the brunt of increased prices. Customer memories are long, and they will eventually turn away from companies or even whole industries that they perceive as charging excessive prices.

Wherever possible, the company should consider ways to meet higher costs or demand without raising prices. For example, it can consider more cost-effective ways to produce or distribute its products. It can shrink the product instead of raising the price, as candy bar manufacturers often do. It can substitute less expensive ingredients or remove certain product features, packaging, or services. Or it can "unbundle" its products and services, removing and separately pricing elements that were formerly part of the offer. IBM, for example, now offers training and consulting as separately priced services.

Buyer Reactions to Price Changes

Whether the price is raised or lowered, the action will affect buyers, competitors, distributors, and suppliers and may interest government as well. Customers do not always interpret prices in a straightforward way. They may view a price *cut* in several ways. For example, what would you think if Joy perfume, "the costliest fragrance in the world," were to cut its price in half? You might believe that quality or status of the product has been reduced. Or you might think that the price will come down even further and that it will pay to wait and see.

Similarly, a price *increase*, which would normally lower sales, may have some positive meanings for buyers. What would you think if Joy *raised* the price of its perfume? On the one hand, you might think that the item is very "hot" and may be unobtainable unless you buy it soon. On the other hand, you might think that the company is greedy and charging what the traffic will bear.

Buyer reactions to price changes: What would you think if the price of Joy was suddenly cut in half?

Competitor Reactions to Price Changes

A firm considering a price change has to worry about the reactions of its competitors as well as those of its customers. Competitors are most likely to react when the number of firms involved is small, when the product is uniform, and when the buyers are well informed.

How can the firm anticipate the likely reactions of its competitors? If the firm faces one large competitor, and if the competitor tends to react in a set way to price changes, that reaction can easily be anticipated. But if the competitor treats each price change as a fresh challenge and reacts according to its self-interest, the company will have to figure out just what makes up the competitor's self-interest at the time.

The problem is complex because, like the customer, the competitor can interpret a company price cut in many ways. It might think the company is trying to grab a larger market share, that the company is doing poorly and trying to boost its sales, or that the company wants the whole industry to cut prices to increase total demand.

When there are several competitors, the company must guess each competitor's likely reaction. If all competitors behave alike, this amounts to analyzing only a typical competitor. In contrast, if the competitors do not behave alike—perhaps because of differences in size, market shares, or policies—then separate analyses are necessary. However, if some competitors will match the price change, there is good reason to expect that the rest will also match it.

Responding to Price Changes

Here we reverse the question and ask how a firm should respond to a price change by a competitor. The firm needs to consider several issues: Why did the competitor change the price? Was it to take more market share, to use excess capacity, to meet changing cost conditions, or to lead an industry-wide price change? Is the price change temporary or permanent? What will happen to the company's market share and profits if it does not respond? Are other companies going to respond? And what are the competitor's and other firms' responses to each possible reaction likely to be?

Besides these issues, the company must make a broader analysis. It must consider its own product's stage in the life cycle, the product's importance in the company's product mix, the intentions and resources of the competitor, and the possible consumer reactions to price changes. The company cannot always make an extended analysis of its alternatives at the time of a price change, however. The competitor may have spent much time preparing this decision, but the company may have to react within hours or days. About the only way to cut down reaction time is to plan ahead for both possible competitors' price changes and possible responses.

Public Policy and Pricing

Pricing strategies and tactics form an important element of a company's marketing mix. In setting prices, companies must carefully consider a great many internal and external factors before choosing a price that will give them the greatest competitive advantage in selected target markets. However, companies are not usually free to charge whatever prices they wish. Several laws restrict pricing practices, and a number of ethical considerations affect pricing decisions.

Legal issues surrounding pricing are outlined in Sections 34, 36, and 38 of the *Competition Act*. Canadian pricing legislation was designed with two goals in mind: to foster a competitive environment and to protect consumers. Although pricing decisions made by firms do not generally require regulatory approval, Canadian marketers should be aware of three areas of concern: price fixing, price discrimination, and deceptive pricing (also called misleading price advertising).[22]

Price Fixing

Federal legislation on price fixing states that sellers must set prices without talking to competitors. Otherwise, price collusion is suspected. Price fixing is illegal per se—that is, the government does not accept any excuses for price fixing. Even a simple conversation between competitors can have serious consequences. The legal charge under the *Competition Act* for offences of this nature is conspiracy. Six Ottawa hotels were each fined from $60 000 to $80 000 after they were convicted of colluding to fix prices offered to government employees.

Bid rigging is another indictable offence under the clauses pertaining to price fixing. A number of cases in the construction industry have resulted in heavy fines being levied when competitors have been found guilty of rigging the prices of their bids. These cases have made most executives very reluctant to discuss prices in any way with competitors. In obtaining information on competitors' pricing, they rely only on openly published materials, such as trade association surveys and competitors' catalogues.

Price Discrimination

Section 34 of the *Competition Act* seeks to ensure that sellers offer the same price terms to a given level of trade. For example, every retailer is entitled to the same price terms whether the retailer is Sears or the local bicycle shop. However, price discrimination is allowed if the seller can prove that its costs are different when selling to different retailers—for example, that it costs less per unit to sell a large volume of bicycles to Sears than to sell a few bicycles to a local dealer. In other words, quantity or volume discounts are not prohibited. However, discriminatory promotional allowances (those not offered on proportional terms to all other competing customers) are illegal. Thus, large competitors cannot negotiate special discounts, rebates, and price concessions that are not made proportionally available to smaller competitors. For example, a small customer purchasing one-third as much as a larger competitor must receive a promotional allowance equal to one-third of what the large competitor was offered.

Although functional discounts (offering a larger discount to wholesalers than to retailers) are legal in the United States, they are illegal in Canada. In Canada, retailers and wholesalers are considered competing customers who must receive proportionally equal promotional allowances. Often, Canadian marketers who work for multinational firms must explain the differences in the law to their U.S. counterparts. Canadian marketers must also keep in mind that it is illegal for a buyer to knowingly benefit from any form of price discrimination. Price differentials may be used to "match competition" in "good faith," provided the firm is trying to meet competitors at its own level of competition and the price discrimination is temporary, localized, and defensive rather than offensive.

Canadian marketers are allowed to offer price breaks for one-shot deals such as store-opening specials, anniversary specials, and stock clearance sales. However, regional price differentials that limit competition are illegal. Canadian firms cannot price products unreasonably low in one part of the country with the intent of driving out the competition.

Finally, resale price maintenance is also illegal. Canadian manufacturers can only suggest prices; it is illegal to require retailers to sell at a stipulated manufacturer's price.

Deceptive Pricing

Section 36 of the *Competition Act* covers areas where pricing and advertising practices converge. For example, firms cannot advertise a product at a low price, carry very limited stock, and then tell consumers they are out of the product so that they can entice them to switch to a higher-priced item. This "bait and switch" advertising is illegal in Canada. Firms must offer their customers "rain cheques" to avoid legal sanctions if advertised items are not stocked in sufficient quantities to cover expected demand.

Deceptive pricing occurs when a seller states prices or price savings that are not actually available to consumers. Some deceptions are difficult for consumers to discern, such as when an airline advertises a low one-way fare that is available only with the purchase of a round-trip ticket, or when a retailer sets artificially high "regular" prices, then announces "sale" prices close to its previous everyday prices.

Ethical Issues in Pricing

Compliance with the law is considered the minimum standard when judging whether pricing practices are ethical. For example, although charging inordinately high prices is not illegal, such a practice may lead to ethical concerns. Ethical criticisms have been levied when higher prices are charged for groceries in poor areas where consumers have limited access to transportation and have few choices in terms of retail outlets.

Other ethical questions centre on whether consumers can understand prices and realistically compare them. For example, consumer advocates have condemned many car-leasing contracts since the legal language used in the contracts prevents consumers from fully understanding the price they are paying for the car.

Ethical concerns about pricing also arise when consumers must negotiate prices. Often those who can least afford to pay a higher price (such as the poor, very young, elderly, or disabled) have the least ability to negotiate prices. These concerns arise when prices are not fixed. This is the case when people purchase cars, houses, professional services, or attend street markets. Many consumers are unaware that even when prices appear fixed, they may be subject to negotiation. For example, many consumers don't know that they can negotiate with their bank for more favourable terms on a consumer loan.[23]

Looking Back: Reviewing the Concepts

Price can be defined narrowly as the amount of money charged for a product or service, or more broadly as the sum of the values that consumers exchange for the benefits of having and using the product or service. Despite the increased role of non-price factors in the modern marketing process, price remains an important element in the marketing mix. It is the only element in the marketing mix that produces revenue; all other elements represent costs. Price is also one of the most flexible elements of the marketing mix. Unlike product features and channel commitments, price can be raised or lowered quickly. Even so, many companies are not good at handling pricing—pricing decisions and price competition are major problems for many marketing executives. Pricing problems often arise because prices are too cost-oriented, not revised frequently enough to reflect market changes, not consistent with the rest of the marketing mix, or not varied enough for differing products, market segments, and purchase occasions.

A company sets not a single price, but rather a *pricing structure* that covers different items in its line. This pricing structure changes over time as products move through their life cycles. The company adjusts product prices to reflect changes in costs and demand and to account for variations in buyers and situations. As the competitive environment changes, the company considers when to initiate price changes and where to respond to them.

1. Identify and define the internal factors affecting a firm's pricing decisions.

Many internal factors influence the company's pricing decisions, including the firm's *marketing objectives*, *marketing mix strategy*, *costs*, *product-related considerations*, and *organization considerations*. The pricing strategy is largely determined by the company's target market and positioning objectives. Pricing decisions affect and are affected by product design, distribution, and promotion decisions. Therefore, pricing strategies must be carefully coordinated with the other marketing mix variables when designing the marketing program.

Costs set the floor for the company's product price—the price must cover all the costs of making and selling the product, plus a fair rate of return. Common pricing objectives include survival, current profit maximization, market share leadership, and product quality leadership.

Product and pricing decisions are closely related. In pricing innovative new products, it can follow *skimming pricing* by initially setting high prices to "skim" the maximum amount of revenue from various segments of the market. Or it can use *market penetration pricing* by setting a low initial price to penetrate the market deeply and win a large market share. When dealing with a line of products versus a single item, marketing managers must decide on the price steps to set between the various products in a line.

To coordinate pricing goals and decisions, management must decide who within the organization is responsible for setting price. In large companies, some pricing authority may be delegated to lower-level managers and salespeople, but top management usually sets pricing policies and approves proposed prices. Production, finance, and accounting managers also influence pricing decisions.

2. Identify and define the external factors affecting pricing decisions, including the impact of consumer perceptions of price and value.

External factors that influence pricing decisions include the *nature of the market and demand, competitors' prices and offers,* and other factors such as the *economy,*
reseller needs, and *government regulations.* The seller's pricing freedom varies with different types of markets. Pricing is especially challenging in markets characterized by monopolistic competition or oligopoly.

Ultimately, the consumer decides whether the company has set the right price. The consumer weighs the price against the perceived values of acquiring and using the product—if the price exceeds the sum of the values, consumers will not buy the product. The more *inelastic* the demand, the higher the company can set its price. Therefore, *demand* and *consumer value perceptions* set the ceiling for prices. Consumers differ in the values they assign to different product features, and marketers often vary their pricing strategies for different price segments. When assessing the market and demand, the company estimates the demand curve, which shows the probable quantity purchased per period at alternative price levels. Consumers also compare a product's price to the prices of *competitors'* products. As a result, a company must learn the price and quality of competitors' offers and use them as a starting point for its own pricing.

3. Contrast the two general approaches to setting prices.

A company can select from one or combine two general pricing approaches: the *cost-based approach* (cost-plus pricing, break-even analysis, and target profit pricing), and the *value-based approach.* Cost-based pricing sets prices based on the seller's cost structure, while value-based pricing relies on consumer perceptions of value to drive pricing decisions.

4. Discuss how companies adjust their prices to take into account different types of customers and situations.

Pricing is a dynamic process. Companies change their pricing structure over time and adjust it to account for different customers and situations. Pricing strategies usually change as a product passes through its life cycle. Companies apply a variety of *price-adjustment strategies* to account for differences in consumer segments and situations. One is *discount and allowance pricing,* whereby the company establishes cash or quantity dis-counts, or varying types of allowances. A second strat-egy is *segmented pricing,* whereby the company sells a product at two or more prices to accommodate different customers, product forms, locations, or times. Some-times companies consider more than economics in their pricing decisions, using *psychological pricing* to better communicate a product's intended position. In *promo-tional pricing,* a company offers discounts or temporar-ily sells a product below list price as a special event, sometimes even selling below cost as a loss leader. Another approach is *geographical pricing,* whereby the company decides how to price to distant customers, choosing from such alternatives as FOB-origin pricing, uniform-delivered pricing, or zone pricing. Finally, *inter-national pricing* means that the company adjusts its price to meet different conditions and expectations in different world markets.

5. Discuss the key issues related to initiating and responding to price changes.

When a firm considers initiating a *price change,* it must consider customers' and competitors' reactions. There are different implications to *initiating price cuts* and *ini-tiating price increases.* Buyer reactions to price changes are influenced by the meaning that customers see in the price change. Competitors' reactions flow from a set reaction policy or a fresh analysis of each situation.

There are also many factors to consider in respond-ing to a competitor's price changes. The company that faces a price change initiated by a competitor must try to understand the competitor's intent as well as the likely duration and impact of the change. If a swift reaction is desirable, the firm should preplan its reactions to differ-ent possible price actions by competitors. When facing a competitor's price change, the company can sit tight, reduce its own price, raise perceived quality, improve quality and raise price, or launch a fighting brand.

Reviewing the Key Terms

Allowance   486
Break-even pricing (target profit pricing)   480
Cost-plus pricing   479
Demand curve   476
Discount   486
Dynamic pricing   465
Experience curve (learning curve)   472

Fixed costs   471
FOB-origin pricing   491
Market penetration pricing   473
Market skimming pricing   473
Price   465
Price elasticity   478
Product line pricing   474
Promotional pricing   489
Psychological pricing   487

Reference prices   487
Segmented pricing   486
Target costing   469
Total costs   471
Uniform-delivered pricing   492
Value-based pricing   481
Value pricing   482
Variable costs   471
Zone pricing   492

Discussing the Concepts

1. Explain the concept of dynamic pricing. How is dynamic pricing used on the Internet?

2. Assume you are the vice-president for financial affairs at your university or college. Like many Canadian insti-tutions, your school has suffered from government cutbacks over the last three years. Therefore, you are under tremendous pressure to increase revenue. Raising tuition fees is one option that would help accomplish your aim. However, you suspect that rais-ing tuition will anger students and lead to declining enrolments. What internal and external pricing factors should you consider before you make your decision? Explain.

3. List the typical pricing objectives, outlined in the chap-ter. Which of these objectives do you believe (a) is the most commonly used; (b) is the most difficult to achieve; (c) has the greatest potential for long-term growth of the organization; and (d) is most likely to be employed by an ecommerce company? Explain.

4. Which pricing strategy—market skimming or market penetration—does each of the following companies use? (a) McDonald's, (b) Harry Rosen (men's clothing), (c) Sony (television and other home electronics), (d) Bic Corporation (disposable pens, lighters, razors, and related products), and (e) IBM (personal computers). Are these the right strategies for each company? Explain.

5. The seller's pricing freedom varies with the type of market. Identify the four types of markets economists generally recognize and characterize the pricing chal-lenges facing each one.

6. Since becoming an assistant manager of a local Zellers, you are amazed by the number of promotional pricing techniques used by the chain. While you realize the value of promotional pricing, you also understand the problems associated with the strategy. Prepare a short report that outlines the advantages and disad-vantages of promotional pricing for Zellers.

7. As a newly appointed director of marketing for a small sports car manufacturing firm, you believe it is time to change the firm's pricing philosophy. In the past, the company used what might be described as cost-based pricing. You believe that a value-based pricing approach is superior. Write a short memo making the case for value-based pricing.

8. Assume that you have just been appointed manager of children's wear at a local department store. Formulate rules that govern (a) initiating a price cut, (b) initiating a price increase, (c) a negative reaction on the part of buyers to a price change by your company, (d) a competitor's response to your price change, and (e) your response to a competitor's price change. State the assumptions underlying your proposed rules.

Applying the Concepts

1. Wal-Mart is the king of everyday low pricing (EDLP). EDLP has allowed Wal-Mart and other value-oriented retailers to maintain steady growth even in a down economy. In fact, EDLP is overtaking high-low pricing as the pricing strategy of choice. And the spectrum of companies embracing EDLP is growing. For example, car dealerships such as Saturn and upscale department stores such as Nordstrom use EDLP to attract and keep customers. (For more details on EDLP, see www.walmart.com, www.saturn.com, and www.nordstrom.com).

   a. After reviewing material in the chapter, explain the EDLP pricing strategy. What are the advantages of the strategy? What are the disadvantages?

   b. Why is EDLP classified as a value-pricing strategy? Does EDLP make sense for every retailer? List some types of retailers that might not benefit from the strategy.

2. The computer printer industry is intensively competitive with respect to pricing. Only a few years ago, consumers were often shocked to find that a good printer could account for as much as half the cost of an entire home computer set-up. No more! Recently, such companies as Epson, Hewlett-Packard, Canon, Tektronix, and Xerox have introduced expanded lines of technologically advanced but less expensive printer models. Despite dramatic improvements in speed, quality, colour, and optional features, today's printers sell at much lower prices than their predecessors.

   a. What role does pricing play in a consumer's selection of a home printer? An office printer? A portable printer to take on business trips?

   b. What pricing strategies are Epson, Hewlett-Packard, Canon, Tektronix, Xerox, and other companies using to sell printers to the consumer and business markets? (Visit each website to get additional information.) Which companies appear to have the most effective pricing strategies? Explain.

   c. Assume that you are the marketing manager of a company introducing a new line of colour printers and seeking quick entry into the small printer market. Your products are comparable to those of primary competitors, and you have the funds necessary to compete with industry leaders. Design a pricing strategy for capturing business in the home computer, home office, and mobile office markets. What factors would be critical to your product's success? How would you combat competitive reaction to your entry?

Video Short

View the video short for this chapter at **www.pearsoned.ca/kotler** and then answer the questions provided in the case description.

Company Case

DVDs: Lieberfarbian Economics?

Here's a challenge: Let's compare prices for DVDs on the websites of Wal-Mart and HMV/Amazon.ca. What are you likely to find?

Wal-Mart: Carries a wide selection but also has a wide range of prices. The least expensive are $5.88 and include films that weren't exactly box office hits, such as *Rambo III* and *Blue Thunder*. Then there are old action films like *The Great Escape* for $10.95. For $12.74 you can buy movies such as *The Patriot,* but for just a little more ($14.87) you can get *The Lord of the Rings: The Two Towers*. Recent movies like *Chicago* ($15.98), *Bowling for Columbine* ($19.98), and *Finding Nemo* ($19.34) command higher price tags. Boxed sets of movie favourites, like the adventures of Indiana Jones, ring in at $45.48.

HMV/Amazon.ca: Carries the largest selection and widest range of prices. At the bottom of the range are DVDs for $11.99—classics such as *All That Jazz*. Recent releases vary in price. *Chicago* will cost you $24.04, *Matrix Reloaded* will set you back $26.59, *Harry Potter: The Philosopher's Stone* rings in at $27.98, and *The Lord of the Rings: The Two Towers* is at the top of the list at $31.49. You can buy the complete third season for *The Simpsons* for $45.49 or the fourth season of *Friends* for $41.24 (though the first season will only cost you $34.49). You can find the entire James Bond collection for $117.59.

Why such a wide range of assortments and prices? The answer is a tangled web of corporate pricing strategies, the speed of technological product life cycles, and consumer motivations.

The various companies involved in producing and distributing movies have different pricing objectives. Usually, production studios want to maintain prices by controlling distribution. That's why VHS tapes were usually rented out first, with purchase occurring later. The studios wanted to maximize revenue for distribution to theatres, then for rentals, and finally for home purchase. Rental companies, such as Blockbuster, found that customers sometimes made five trips to the store and still failed to rent "hot" movies, because studios allowed each rental store to stock only a few copies of the VHS tapes. To motivate studios to give them more copies of the tapes, rental companies initiated a revenue-sharing plan, giving the studios part of the rental revenue along with the purchase price paid

by firms such as Blockbuster. When VHS tapes were released for sale to the public, they initially were priced high, and then the price declined slowly to mass-market levels.

Thus, when DVDs hit the market, many in the industry expected the same pricing approach for DVDs as for VHS tapes. In the meantime, however, Blockbuster had grown to the point of capturing 40 percent of the rental market and was unwilling to give revenue sharing on DVDs. As a result, studios had to think in terms of maximizing revenue on DVD sales to retailers and final consumers.

Discount stores such as Target, Wal-Mart, and Best Buy were eager to capitalize on this opportunity. Why? Target and Wal-Mart want to offer a wide range of movies (VHS and DVD) to consumers to *prevent* them from going to electronics stores. In contrast, electronics stores such as Best Buy want a wide range of movies to attract customers who will then buy more expensive, higher-margin merchandise such as telephones or computers. By buying DVDs cheaper and reselling them at low prices, the discount stores could compete among themselves and counter the competition from rental companies such as Blockbuster.

This led to closer relations between the studios and the discounters. For example, DreamWorks produced a video for Wal-Mart in which the characters from *Shrek* did the famous Wal-Mart cheer ("Give me a W, Give me an A..."). Although originally intended to pump up Wal-Mart personnel, the video was so well received that Wal-Mart began showing it in their stores. Sales of the *Shrek* DVD skyrocketed.

Into this already hectic situation stepped Warren Lieberfarb, head of Warner Home Video. Like most large, old-line studios, Warner could use two-tiered pricing, in which it rereleased old movies from its huge inventory in DVD format at low prices while at the same time releasing recent movies at higher prices. Although ideal for large studios, such two-tiered pricing does not work well for small, newer studios such as DreamWorks that have a smaller assortment of mostly recent movies. Sensing an opportunity to gain an advantage over other studios and to outcompete Blockbuster, Lieberfarb decided to price *all* releases for the mass market. That would give Warner widespread distribution in the discount stores and, to some extent, force the smaller studios to also lower their prices. Recently dubbed "Lieberfarbian" economics, this move caused major concern among studio executives who had planned to "milk" sales of DVDs as they had with VHS tapes.

How are consumers responding to DVD technology? DVDs were introduced in 1997, and their sales increased rapidly during the next five years. By 2002, DVD player sales were expected to top those of VCRs, even though VCR prices had dropped to as low as $100 or less. In 2001, 14.1 million DVD players and 14.9 million VCRs were sold; in 2002, sales of DVD players were estimated to be 15.5 million and sales of VCRs to be 13.2 million. That meant that 35 percent of North American homes would have DVD players, while 90 percent had VCRs. Rentals of DVDs increased by more than 120 percent in 2001.

Consumers obviously appreciate the advantages of DVD—better picture quality, no rewinding, and extras such as outtakes. The only drawback is the inability to record DVDs, but companies expect to solve that problem quickly. Another problem, initially, was the higher price of DVD players, but Best Buy attacked that issue by sending out a request for a company to produce a $299 player by Christmas of 1999. Toshiba responded and prices of DVD players have been coming down ever since, increasing buyers' willingness to purchase DVDs at mass-market prices.

Why would the studios seemingly cut their own pricing throats? The answer is VOD—video on demand. The studios expect that before long, consumers will be watching movies at home on TV with all the advantages of digital technology. Digital TV is already available and VOD is already established in some communities. With VOD, consumers can watch whatever they want whenever they want to. They can fast-forward, pause, and rewind movies, and they don't have to go to stores, check availability of tapes or discs, and then store large numbers of tapes or discs at home. With the ability to record discs, consumers might even make their own DVDs at home. When VOD is successful, the studios will still be selling movies in digital format for home viewing, but Wal-Mart, Target, and Best Buy may have to find new floor-traffic builders.

But what about Blockbuster? Is it going to take all this quietly? The answer is *no.* In an effort to reduce its reliance on major studios, Blockbuster has begun to buy up independent films and even to finance the making of some movies. By mid-2002, 10 percent of all its new titles were its own movies. Although many of these are action-adventure, horror, and even R-rated movies, Blockbuster occasionally produced an "art house" film, such as *How to Kill Your Neighbor's Dog,* starring Kenneth Branagh and Robin Wright Penn. While teens stand in line at night to see "made-for-teens" Hollywood movies, parents are at Blockbuster—sometimes just looking for something interesting.

How long will it take before VOD arrives in the mass market? Will consumers continue to patronize Blockbuster in the face of VOD? Will they quickly adopt VOD or stick to DVD? The answers to these questions depend on how consumers respond, and Warren Lieberfarb is betting that lowering prices is the way to mould consumer response.

Questions for Discussion

1. What kind of pricing strategy was used for VHS tapes?

2. What are the differences in costs for old movies (from the 1940s and 1950s) and movies released to theatres within the last six months?

3. From the perspective of the studios, what external factors affect the pricing of DVDs? From the perspective the discount stores? For a rental company such as Blockbuster?

4. What kind of pricing strategies do the discount stores use for DVDs?

5. Is Lieberfarbian pricing appropriate for an oligopolistic industry such as movies? What kind of pricing strategy is it?

6. The studios expect VOD to replace both VHS tapes and DVDs. What factors might inhibit the growth of VOD? What factors will accelerate sales of VOD?

Sources: Shelly Emling, "DVD Era Dawns, but VHS Won't Be Obsolete for Years," *Greensboro News and Record,* July 15, 2002, p. F1; Bruce Orwell, Martin Peers, and Ann Zimmerman, "Disc Jockeying: DVD Gains on Tape, but Economics Have Hollywood in a Tizzy—As Format's Sales Surge, How Do You Keep Wal-Mart, Blockbuster Both Happy?—Warner's Low-Price Crusade," *Wall Street Journal,* February 5, 2002, p. A1; Martin Peers, "Blockbuster Breaks Away—Reducing Reliance on Studios, Video Chain Acquires Titles, Even Produces Its Own Films," *Wall Street Journal,* April 22, 2002, p. B1; Vito J. Racanelli, "Blockbusters?" *Barron's,* August 27, 2001, pp. 17–19; and Evan Ramstad, "As Prices Tumble, Sales of DVD Players Explode for the Holidays," *Wall Street Journal,* December 9, 1999, pp. B1–B2.

CBC Video Case

Log on to your Companion Website at **www.pearsoned.ca/kotler** to view a CBC video segment and case for this chapter.

Chapter 13

Marketing Channels and Supply Chain Management

After studying this chapter you should be able to

1. explain why companies use distribution channels and discuss the functions that these channels perform

2. discuss how channel members interact and how they organize to perform the work of the channel

3. identify the major channel alternatives open to a company

4. explain how companies select, motivate, and evaluate channel members

5. discuss the nature and importance of physical distribution

Looking Ahead: Previewing the Concepts

Firms not only create value for customers by making products or services, they also create value by delivering the right products, in the right amounts to the right places. We will now examine this third marketing-mix tool—distribution.

Firms rarely work alone in bringing value to customers. Instead, most are only a single link in a larger supply chain or distribution channel. As such, an individual firm's success depends not only on how well *it* performs but also on how well its *entire marketing channel* competes with competitors' channels. For example, BMW can make the world's best cars but still not do well if its dealers perform poorly in sales and service against the dealers of Toyota, GM, Chrysler, or Honda. BMW must choose its channel partners carefully and practise sound partner relationship management.

The first part of this chapter explores the nature of distribution channels and the marketer's channel design and management decisions. We then briefly examine physical distribution, or logistics—an area that is growing dramatically in importance and sophistication. In the next chapter, we'll look more closely at two major channel intermediaries—retailers and wholesalers.

First, we'll take a look at Caterpillar. You might think that Caterpillar's success and its ability to charge premium prices rest on the quality of the construction and mining equipment that it produces. But Caterpillar's former chairman and CEO sees things differently. The company's dominance, he claims, results from its unparalleled distribution and customer support system—from the strong and caring partnerships that it has built with independent Caterpillar dealers. Read on and see why.

For more than half a century, Caterpillar has dominated the world's markets for heavy construction and mining equipment. Its familiar yellow tractors, crawlers, loaders, bulldozers, and trucks are a common sight at any construction area. Caterpillar (www.caterpillar.com) sells more than 300 products in nearly 200 companies, generating sales of more than $26 billion annually. It captures 27 percent of the worldwide construction equipment business, more than double that of second-place Komatsu, and its share of the North American market is more than twice that of competitors Komatsu and Deere combined. In Canada, Caterpillar distributes its products through independent dealerships like Finning (Canada), located in Edmonton, Alberta. Finning is one of Caterpillar's largest dealerships and aims to be Caterpillar's best global business partner, providing unrivalled services that earn customer loyalty.

Many factors contribute to Caterpillar's enduring success—high-quality products, flexible and efficient manufacturing, a steady stream of innovative new products, and a lean organization that is responsive to customer needs. Although Caterpillar charges premium prices for its equipment, its high-quality and trouble-free operation provides greater long-term value. Yet these are not the most important reasons for Caterpillar's dominance. Instead, Caterpillar credits its focus on customers and its corps of 220 outstanding independent dealers worldwide, who do a superb job of taking care of every customer need. According to former Caterpillar CEO Donald Fites:

> After the product leaves our door, the dealers take over. They are the ones on the front line. They're the ones who live with the product for its lifetime. They're the ones customers see. Although we offer financing and insurance, they arrange those deals for customers. They're out there making sure that when a machine is delivered, it's in the condition it's supposed to be in. They're out there training a customer's operators. They service a product frequently throughout its life, carefully monitoring a machine's health and scheduling repairs to prevent costly downtime. The customer...knows that there is a [$26] billion-plus company called Caterpillar. But the dealers create the image of a company that doesn't just stand *behind* its products but *with* its products, anywhere in the world. Our dealers are the reason that our motto—Buy the Iron, Get the Company—is not an empty slogan.

Caterpillar's dealers build strong customer relationships in their communities. "Our independent dealer in Novi, Michigan, or in Bangkok, Thailand, knows so much more about the requirements of customers in those locations than a huge corporation like Caterpillar could," says Fites. Competitors often bypass their dealers and sell directly to big customers to cut costs or make more profits for themselves. However, Caterpillar wouldn't think of going around its dealers. "The knowledge of the local market and the close relations with customers that our dealers provide are worth every penny," he asserts with passion. "We'd rather cut off our right arm than sell directly to customers and bypass our dealers."

Caterpillar and its dealers work in close harmony to find better ways to bring value to customers. The entire system is linked by one worldwide computer network. For example, working at their desk computers, Caterpillar managers can check to see how many Caterpillar machines in the world are waiting for parts. Closely linked dealers play a vital role in almost every aspect of Caterpillar's operations, from product design and delivery, to product service and support financing and insurance, to market intelligence and customer feedback.

In the heavy-equipment industry, in which equipment downtime can mean big losses, Caterpillar's exceptional service gives it a huge advantage in winning and keeping customers. Consider Freeport-McMoRan, a Caterpillar customer that operates one of the world's largest copper and gold mines, 24 hours a day, 365 days a year. Located high in the mountains of Indonesia, the mine is accessible only by aerial cableway or helicopter. Freeport-McMoRan relies on more than 500 pieces of Caterpillar mining and construction equipment—worth several hundred million dollars—including loaders, tractors, and mammoth 24-ton, 2000-plus horsepower trucks. Many of these machines cost more than $1 million apiece. When equipment breaks down, Freeport-McMoRan loses money fast. Freeport-McMoRan gladly pays a premium price for machines and service it can count on. And it knows that it can count on Caterpillar and its outstanding distribution network for superb support.

The close working relationship between Caterpillar and its dealers comes down to more than just formal contracts and business agreements. The powerful partnership rests on a handful of basic principles and practices:

• *Dealer profitability.* Caterpillar's rule: "Share the gain as well as the pain." When times are good, Caterpillar shares the bounty with its dealers rather than trying to grab all the riches for itself. When times are bad, Caterpillar protects its dealers. For example, in the mid-1980s, facing a depressed global construction equipment market and cutthroat competition, Caterpillar sheltered its dealers by absorbing much of the economic damage. The company lost over $1 billion in just three years but didn't lose a single dealer. In contrast, competitors' dealers struggled and many failed. As a result, Caterpillar emerged with its distribution system intact and a stronger competitive position than ever.

• *Extraordinary dealer support.* Nowhere is this support more apparent than in the company's parts delivery system—the fastest and most reliable in the industry. Caterpillar maintains 36 distribution centres and 1500 service facilities around the world, which stock 320 000 different parts and ship 84 000 items per day every day of the year. In turn, dealers have made huge investments in inventory, warehouses, fleets of trucks, service bays, diagnostic and service equipment, and information technology. Together, Caterpillar and its dealers guarantee parts delivery within 48 hours anywhere in the world. The company ships 80 percent of parts orders immediately, and 99 percent on the same day the order is received. In contrast, it's not unusual for competitors' customers to wait four or five days for a part.

• *Communications.* Caterpillar communicates with its dealers—fully, frequently, and honestly. According to Fites, "There are no secrets between us and our dealers. We have the financial statements and key operating data of every dealer in the world.... In addition, virtually all Caterpillar and dealer employees have real-time access to continually updated databases of service information, sales trends and forecasts, customer satisfaction surveys, and other critical data.... [Moreover,] virtually everyone from the youngest design engineer to the CEO now has direct contact with somebody in our dealer organizations."

- *Dealer performance.* Caterpillar does all it can to ensure that its dealerships are run well. It closely monitors each dealership's sales, market position, service capability, financial situation, and other performance measures. It genuinely wants each dealer to succeed, and when it identifies a problem it jumps in to help. As a result, Caterpillar dealerships, many of which are family businesses, tend to be stable and profitable. The average Caterpillar dealership has remained in the hands of the same family for more than 50 years. Some actually predate the 1925 merger that created Caterpillar.

- *Personal relationships.* In addition to more formal business ties, Caterpillar forms close personal ties with its dealers in a kind of family relationship. Fites relates the following example: "When I see Chappy Chapman, a retired executive vice-president,...out on the golf course, he always asks about particular dealers or about their children, who may be running the business now. And every time I see those dealers, they inquire, 'How's Chappy?' That's the sort of relationship we have.... I consider the majority of dealers [to be] personal friends."

Thus, Caterpillar's superb distribution system serves as a major source of competitive advantage. The system is built on a firm foundation of mutual trust and shared dreams. Caterpillar and its dealers feel a deep pride in what they are accomplishing together. As Fites puts it, "There's a camaraderie among our dealers around the world that really makes it more than just a financial arrangement. They feel what they're doing is good for the world because they are part of an organization that makes, sells, and tends to the machines that make the world work."[1]

Most firms cannot bring value to customers by themselves. Instead, they must work closely with other firms in a larger value-delivery network.

Supply Chains and the Value-Delivery Network

Producing a product or service and making it available to buyers requires building relationships not just with customers, but also with key suppliers and resellers in the company's *supply chain.* This supply chain consists of upstream and downstream partners, including suppliers, intermediaries, and even intermediaries' customers.

Upstream from the manufacturer or service provider is the set of firms that supply the raw materials, components, parts, information, finances, and expertise needed to create a product or service. Marketers, however, have traditionally focused on the "downstream" side of the supply chain—on the *marketing channels* or *distribution channels* that look forward toward the customer. Marketing channel partners such as wholesalers and retailers form a vital connection between the firm and its target consumers.

Both upstream and downstream partners may also be part of other firms' supply chains. But it is the unique design of each company's supply chain that enables it to deliver superior value to customers. An individual firm's success depends not only on how well *it* performs but also on how well its entire supply chain and marketing channel competes with competitors' channels.

The term *supply chain* may be too limited—it takes a *make-and-sell* view of the business. It suggests that raw materials, productive inputs, and factory capacity should serve as the starting point for market planning. A better term would be *demand chain* because it suggests a *sense-and-respond* view of the market. Under this view, planning starts with the needs of target customers, to which the company responds by organizing resources with the goal of building profitable customer relationships.

Value-delivery network: Palm manages a whole community of suppliers, assemblers, resellers, and complementors who must work effectively together to make life easier for Palm's customers.

Value-delivery network
The network made up of the company, suppliers, distributors, and ultimately customers who "partner" with each other to improve the performance of the entire system.

Even a demand-chain view of a business may be too limited, because it takes a step-by-step linear view of purchase-production-consumption activities. With the advent of the Internet, however, companies are forming more numerous and complex relationships with other firms. For example, Ford manages numerous supply chains. It also sponsors or transacts on many B2B websites and online purchasing exchanges as needs arise. Like Ford, most large companies today are engaged in building and managing a continuously evolving *value-delivery network*.

Companies today are increasingly taking a full-value-delivery-network view of their businesses. As defined in Chapter 2, a **value-delivery network** is made up of the company, suppliers, distributors, and ultimately customers who "partner" with each other to improve the performance of the entire system. For example, Palm, the leading manufacturer of handheld devices, manages a whole community of suppliers and assemblers of semiconductor components, plastic cases, LCD displays, and accessories; of offline and online resellers; and of 45 000 complementors who have created over 5000 applications for the Palm operating systems. All of these diverse partners must work effectively together to bring superior value to Palm's customers.

This chapter focuses on marketing channels—on the downstream side of the value-delivery network. However, it is important to remember that this is only part of the full value network. To bring value to customers, companies need upstream supplier partners just as they need downstream channel partners. Increasingly, marketers are participating in and influencing their company's upstream activities as well as its downstream activities. More than marketing channel managers, they are becoming full network managers.

This chapter examines four major questions concerning channels: What is the nature of marketing channels and why are they important? How do channel firms interact and organize to do the work of the channel? What problems do companies face in designing and managing their channels? What role do physical distribution and supply chain management play in attracting and satisfying customers? In Chapter 14, we shall look at distribution channel issues from the viewpoint of retailers and wholesalers.

The Nature and Importance of Distribution Channels

Marketing channel (distribution channel)
A set of interdependent organizations involved in the process of making a product or service available for use or consumption by the consumer or business user.

Few producers sell their goods directly to the final users. Instead, most use intermediaries to bring their products to market. They try to forge a **marketing channel** (or **distribution channel**), a set of interdependent organizations involved in the process of making a product or service available for use or consumption by the consumer or business user.[2]

A company's channel decisions directly affect every other marketing decision. The company's pricing depends on whether it works with national discount chains, uses high-quality specialty stores, or sells directly to consumers via the Web. The firm's sales force and communications decisions depend on how much persuasion, training, motivation, and support its channel partners need. Whether a company develops or acquires certain new products may depend on how well those products fit the capabilities of its channel members.

FedEx's creative and imposing distribution system made it a leader in the small-package delivery industry.

Companies often pay too little attention to their distribution channels, however, sometimes with damaging results. In contrast, many companies have used imaginative distribution systems to *gain* a competitive advantage. The creative and imposing distribution system of FedEx made it a leader in the small-package delivery industry. Dell Computer revolutionized its industry by selling personal computers directly to consumers rather than through retail stores. And Charles Schwab & Company pioneered the delivery of financial services via the Internet.

Distribution channel decisions often involve long-term commitments to other firms. For example, companies such as Ford, IBM, or McDonald's can easily change their advertising, pricing, or promotion programs. They can scrap old products and introduce new ones as market tastes demand. But when they set up distribution channels through contracts with franchisees, independent dealers, or large retailers, they cannot readily replace these channels with company-owned stores or websites if conditions change. Therefore, management must design its channels carefully, with an eye on tomorrow's likely selling environment as well as today's.

How Channel Members Add Value

Why do producers give some of the selling job to channel partners? After all, doing so means giving up some control over how and to whom the products are sold. The use of intermediaries results from their greater efficiency in making goods available to target markets. Through their contacts, experience, specialization, and scale of operation, intermediaries usually offer the firm more than it can achieve on its own.

Figure 13.1 shows how using intermediaries can provide economies. Figure 13.1A shows three manufacturers, each using direct marketing to reach three customers. This system requires nine different contacts. Figure 13.1B shows the three manufacturers working through one distributor, which contacts the three customers. This system requires only six contacts. In this way, intermediaries reduce the amount of work that must be done by both producers and consumers.

From the economic system's point of view, the role of marketing intermediaries is to transform the assortments of products made by producers into the assortments wanted by consumers. Producers make narrow assortments of products in large quantities, but consumers want broad assortments of products in small quantities. In the marketing channels, intermediaries buy the large quantities from many producers and break them down into the smaller quantities and broader assortments

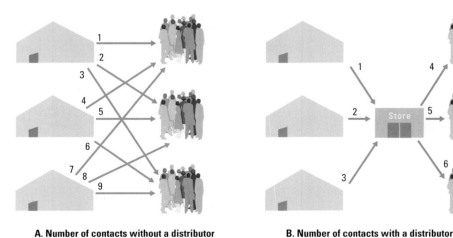

A. Number of contacts without a distributor
$M \times C = 3 \times 3 = 9$

B. Number of contacts with a distributor
$M + C = 3 + 3 = 6$

  = Manufacturer   = Customer   = Distributor

Figure 13.1 How a marketing intermediary reduces the number of channel transactions

Queen's School of Business uses state-of-the-art videoconferencing technology to deliver its top-ranked Executive MBA program and Accelerated MBA program for business graduates.

wanted by consumers. Thus, intermediaries play an important role in matching supply and demand.

The concept of distribution channels is not limited to the distribution of tangible products. Producers of services and ideas also face the problem of making their output *available* to target populations. In the private sector, retail stores, hotels, banks, and other service providers take great care to make their services conveniently available to target customers. In the public sector, service organizations and agencies develop "educational distribution systems" and "health-care delivery systems" for reaching sometimes widely spread populations. For example, the Queen's School of Business offers a two-year Executive MBA program that is delivered by videoconferencing technology to boardroom learning teams located right across Canada. The learning model has been so successful that the program was recognized by the *Financial Times* as one of the top ten programs in the world in 2003.[3]

In making products and services available to consumers, channel members add value by bridging the major time, place, and possession gaps that separate goods and services from those who would use them. Members of the marketing channel perform many key functions. Some help to complete transactions:

- *Information:* gathering and distributing marketing research and intelligence information about actors and forces in the marketing environment needed for planning and aiding exchange.
- *Promotion:* developing and spreading persuasive communications about an offer.
- *Contact:* finding and communicating with prospective buyers.
- *Matching:* shaping and fitting the offer to the buyer's needs, including such activities as manufacturing, grading, assembling, and packaging.
- *Negotiation:* reaching an agreement on price and other terms of the offer so that ownership or possession can be transferred.

Others help to fulfill the completed transactions:

- *Physical distribution:* transporting and storing goods.
- *Financing:* acquiring and using funds to cover the costs of the channel work.
- *Risk taking:* assuming the risks of carrying out the channel work.

The question is not *whether* these functions need to be performed—they must be—but rather *who* will perform them. To the extent that the manufacturer performs these functions, its costs go up and its prices have to be higher. When some of these functions are shifted to intermediaries, the producer's costs and prices may be lower, but the intermediaries must charge more to cover the costs of their work. In dividing the work of the channel, the various functions should be assigned to the channel members who can add the most value for the cost.

Number of Channel Levels

Channel level
A layer of intermediaries that performs some work in bringing the product and its ownership closer to the final buyer.

Direct marketing channel
A marketing channel that has no intermediary levels.

Companies can design their distribution channels to make products and services available to customers in different ways. Each layer of marketing intermediaries that performs some work in bringing the product and its ownership closer to the final buyer is a **channel level**. Because the producer and the final consumer both perform some work, they are part of every channel.

We use the number of intermediary levels to indicate the length of a channel. Figure 13.2A shows several consumer distribution channels of different lengths. Channel 1, called a **direct marketing channel**, has no intermediary levels; the company sells directly to consumers. Avon, Amway, and Tupperware sell their products door-to-door, through home and office sales parties, and on the Web; L.L.Bean, Mountain Equipment Co-op, and Tilley Endurables sell clothing and equipment direct through mail-order catalogues, by telephone, online, and at retail stores; and a university sells education on its campus or through distance learning.

Figure 13.2 Consumer and business marketing channels

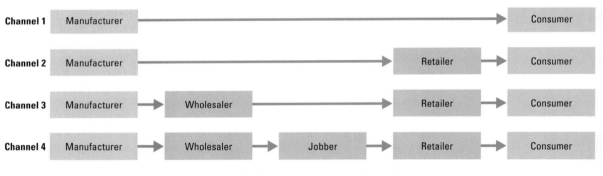

A. Consumer marketing channels

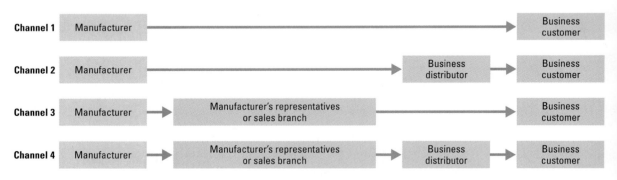

B. Business marketing channels

In a direct marketing channel, Tilley Endurables sells to Canadians and other customers around the world through its website and catalogue.

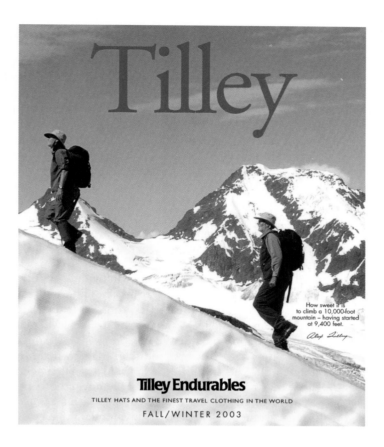

Indirect marketing channel
Channel containing one or more intermediary levels.

The remaining channels in Figure 13.2A are **indirect marketing channels**, containing one or more intermediary levels.

Figure 13.2B shows some common business distribution channels. The business marketer can use its own sales force to sell directly to business customers. Or it also can sell to various types of intermediaries, who in turn sell to business customers. Consumer and business marketing channels with even more levels are sometimes found, but less often. From the producer's point of view, a greater number of levels means less control and greater channel complexity. Moreover, all of the institutions in the channel are connected by several types of *flows*. These include the *physical flow* of products, the *flow of ownership*, the *payment flow*, the *information flow*, and the *promotion flow*. These flows can make even channels with only one or a few levels very complex.

Channel Behaviour and Organization

Distribution channels are more than simple collections of firms tied together by various flows. They are complex behavioural systems in which people and companies interact to accomplish individual, company, and channel goals. Some channel systems consist only of informal interactions among loosely organized firms; others consist of formal interactions guided by strong organizational structures. Moreover, channel systems do not stand still—new types of intermediaries surface, and whole new channel systems evolve. Here we look at channel behaviour and at how members organize to do the work of the channel.

Channel Behaviour

A marketing channel consists of firms that have banded together for their common good. Each channel member depends on the others. For example, a Ford dealer depends on Ford to design cars that meet consumer needs. In turn, Ford depends on the dealer to attract consumers, persuade them to buy Ford cars, and service cars after the sale. The Ford dealer also depends on other dealers to provide good sales and service that will uphold the reputation of Ford and its dealer body. In fact, the success of individual Ford dealers depends on how well the entire Ford distribution channel competes with the channels of other auto manufacturers.

Each channel member plays a specialized role in the channel. For example, Sony's role is to produce consumer electronics that consumers will like and to create demand through national advertising. Future Shop's role is to display these Sony products in convenient locations, to answer buyers' questions, to close sales, and to provide service. The channel is most effective when each member is assigned the tasks it can do best.

Ideally, because the success of individual channel members depends on overall channel success, all channel firms should work together smoothly. They should understand and accept their roles, coordinate their activities, and cooperate to attain overall channel goals. Cooperating to achieve overall channel goals sometimes means giving up individual company goals. Although channel members depend on one another, they often act alone in their own short-run best interests. They often disagree on who should do what and for what rewards. Such disagreements over goals, rewards, and roles generate **channel conflict.**

Channel conflict

Disagreement between marketing channel members on goals and roles—who should do what and for what rewards.

Horizontal conflict occurs between firms at the same level of the channel. For instance, some Ford dealers might complain that other dealers in their city steal sales from them by pricing too low or by selling outside their assigned territories. Or Holiday Inn franchisees might complain about other Holiday Inn operators giving poor service, overcharging guests, or hurting the overall Holiday Inn image.

Vertical conflict—conflicts between different levels of the same channel—is even more common. Take the case of the Great Canadian Bagel company:

> Theresa Slater-Smith celebrated Mother's Day, 2002, stripping the Great Canadian Bagel franchise she'd bought five years previously of everything not covered by her lease. She was taking revenge on the company, believing she would never be able to recover her original $150 000 investment—let alone the hours of labour and love she had poured into the business. Ms. Slater-Smith was not alone. High rents and sagging sales have forced more than 60 Great Canadian Bagel franchisees to close down. The original business model—large in-store bakeries pumping out fresh bagels—didn't work because the margins on bagels were too slim to support the high rents on large, full-production stores. The remaining franchisees were advised to downsize or partner with other food outlets, such as pizza parlours and cafés, to share costs and cut expenses. As Calgary franchisee Todd Bilquist noted, "There is a lot of frustration out there among franchisees. The people at head office now are going in the right direction, but there's a lot of mistrust between the franchisees and the company."[4]

H&R Block is another case in point. Franchisees complained when the parent company began using the Internet to deal directly with customers. And another recent instance took place when dealerships decided to wage war on Ford Canada:

> Car dealerships are among Canada's largest small businesses. Their dilemma: they depend on a single supplier for their inventory, and minor disputes are frequent. However, conflict reached an unprecedented level in 2000. The president of the Canadian Automobile Dealers Association lashed out at Ford Canada for its "unilateral, autocratic, and confrontational" actions that pose a "threat to

the Canadian dealer network." His comments were the result of dealer complaints about Ford Canada's new retail strategy, called Ford Retail Networks (FRN). The Networks manifested Ford's desire to limit dealer autonomy and institute more customer-friendly sales tactics.[5]

Some conflict in the channel takes the form of healthy competition. Such competition can be good for the channel—without it, the channel could become passive and non-innovative. But severe or prolonged conflict can disrupt channel effectiveness and cause lasting harm to channel relationships. Companies should manage channel conflict to keep it from getting out of hand. Here's an example:

P&G recently moved to manage channel conflict stemming from its change to multichannel distribution for Iams pet products. Traditionally, Iams had been distributed through specialized pet stores and veterinary offices. After studies showed that 70 percent of pet-food buyers never visit pet stores, P&G decided to add 25 000 grocery stores and mass retailers to its channel. To head off conflict with traditional channels, P&G's president wrote to the specialty stores and veterinarians, explaining that the new arrangements would increase brand awareness and not hurt brand equity. Although some pet stores stopped carrying Iams, most continued on, helping Iams boost sales and market share for all of its dealers.[6]

Vertical Marketing Systems

For the channel as a whole to perform well, each channel member's role must be specified and channel conflict must be managed. The channel will perform better if it includes a firm, agency, or mechanism that provides leadership and has the power to assign roles and manage conflict.

Historically, *conventional distribution channels* have lacked such leadership and power. One of the biggest channel developments in recent years has been the emergence of *vertical marketing systems* that provide channel leadership. Figure 13.3 contrasts the two types of channel arrangements.

A **conventional distribution channel** consists of one or more independent producers, wholesalers, and retailers. Each is a separate business seeking to maximize its own profits, even at the expense of the system as a whole. No channel member has much control over the other members, and no formal means exist for assigning roles and resolving channel conflict.

Conventional distribution channel

A channel consisting of one or more independent producers, wholesalers, and retailers, each a separate business seeking to maximize its own profits even at the expense of profits for the system as a whole.

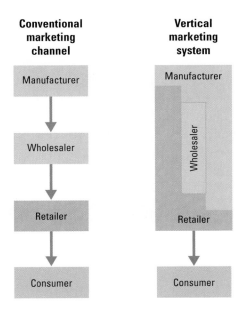

Figure 13.3 A conventional marketing channel versus a vertical marketing system

Vertical marketing system (VMS)

A distribution channel structure in which producers, wholesalers, and retailers act as a unified system. One channel member owns the others, has contracts with them, or has so much power that they all cooperate.

Franchise organization

A contractual vertical marketing system in which a channel member, called a franchiser, links several stages in the production–distribution process.

Horizontal marketing system

A channel arrangement in which two or more companies at one level join together to follow a new marketing opportunity.

In contrast, a **vertical marketing system (VMS)** consists of producers, wholesalers, and retailers acting as a unified system. One channel member owns the others, has contracts with them, or wields so much power that all members of the system cooperate. The VMS can be dominated by the producer, wholesaler, or retailer.

The **franchise organization** is the most common type of VMS. Under these contractual relationships, a channel member called a *franchiser* links several stages in the production–distribution process. Franchising has been the fastest-growing retailing form in recent years. In 2002, it was estimated that Canada had more than 75 000 franchise operations (four times more per capita than the United States). That year Canadian franchises employed more than 1 million people and rang up over $90 billion in sales. In fact, 40 percent of every dollar spent on retail items is spent at a franchise.[7] Almost every kind of business has been franchised—from motels and fast-food restaurants to dental centres and dating services, from wedding consultants and maid services to funeral homes and fitness centres.

Horizontal Marketing Systems

Another channel development is the **horizontal marketing system**, in which two or more companies at one level join together to follow a new marketing opportunity. By working together, companies can combine their capital, production capabilities, or marketing resources to accomplish more than any one company could alone.

Companies might join forces with competitors or non-competitors. They might work with each other on a temporary or permanent basis, or they may create a separate company. For example, McDonald's now places "express" versions of its restaurants in Wal-Mart stores. McDonald's benefits from Wal-Mart's considerable store traffic, while Wal-Mart keeps hungry shoppers from having to go elsewhere to eat.

Such channel arrangements also work well globally. For example, because of its excellent coverage of international markets, Nestlé jointly sells General Mills cereal brands in markets outside North America. Coca-Cola and Nestlé formed a joint venture to market ready-to-drink coffee and tea worldwide. Coke provides worldwide

Franchising is an important channel of distribution in Canada.

Horizontal marketing systems: Nestlé jointly sells General Mills cereal brands in markets outside North America.

experience in marketing and distributing beverages, and Nestlé contributes two established brand names—Nescafé and Nestea. Once major competitors, Canada's two largest wineries, T.G. Bright & Co. Ltd. and Cartier & Inniskillin Vintners Inc., formed an alliance so that they could have the economies of scale and resources necessary to export into the U.S. market and take on large American vintners such as Gallo.

Similarly, Air Canada is part of the Star Alliance (www.staralliance.com), whose partners include United Airlines, Lufthansa, SAS, and Thai Airways International. This partnership allows Air Canada to link with the routes flown by the different partners so that passengers can have seamless travel around the world.[8]

Multichannel Distribution Systems

Multichannel distribution system

A distribution system in which a single firm sets up two or more marketing channels to reach one or more customer segments.

In the past, many companies used a single channel to sell to a single market or market segment. Today, with the proliferation of customer segments and channel possibilities, many companies have adopted **multichannel distribution systems**—often called *hybrid marketing channels*. Such multichannel marketing occurs when a single firm sets up two or more marketing channels to reach one or more customer segments.

The use of multichannel systems has increased dramatically in recent years. A recent survey by Gartner Inc. of 375 retailers in North America and Europe found that 75 percent of them now have multichannel retailing strategies in place or are planning to deploy them. Among such retailers is the Hudson's Bay Co.:

> With more than 300 years of history behind it, the Canadian retailing veteran didn't see the need to rush to join the ebusiness revolution. The Bay didn't believe shoppers would shift all their buying online, as expounded by many ecommerce evangelists. Instead, it chose multichannel retailing, integrating the online store as closely as possible with its physical operations. Such integration means that customers can order goods online and have them delivered to any Bay, Zellers, or Home Outfitters store for free. Similarly, they can use the stores to return items they buy online. Taking a wait-and-see approach also allowed the Bay to learn from the mistakes of others and develop a more customer-focused online store than many of their counterparts in the United States.[9]

As a business traveler, wouldn't it be great if the airline you fly most often was linked to other major airlines that could fly you anywhere you wanted to go. Smoothly. Effortlessly. Efficiently. Wouldn't it be great if you had more access to more airport lounges. And when flying on any of these major airlines, you could earn mileage that counts toward higher status in any of their frequent flyer programs. Wouldn't it be great if you could enjoy the same high standards of service whenever and wherever you fly. That's the idea behind Star Alliance™, a network of Air Canada, Lufthansa, SAS, THAI and United Airlines. A partnership that signals a fundamental change in business travel. And these benefits are just the beginning. We will be offering even more in the months ahead. We know you have choices when you fly, and we're making sure Star Alliance is always your best choice. After all, there's no better way in the world to get around the world.

Imagine.

STAR ALLIANCE
The airline network for Earth.

Membership in a horizontal marketing system helps Air Canada market its services efficiently worldwide.

Tosia Manka, a Canadian-based analyst with the Yankee Group, says the multichannel model works better for several reasons. "Owning a brick-and-mortar store gives physical retailers an edge over pure dot-com sellers because they already hold a strong local brand, can attract customers at lower cost and can extend their existing services to complement real-world stores."[10]

Figure 13.4 shows a hybrid marketing channel. In the figure, the producer sells directly to consumer segment 1 using direct-mail catalogues, telemarketing, and the Internet, and reaches consumer segment 2 through retailers. It sells indirectly to business segment 1 through distributors and dealers, and to business segment 2 through its own sales force.

Retailers are not the only firms to use multiple channels. IBM uses multiple channels to serve dozens of segments and niches, ranging from large corporate buyers to small businesses to home office buyers. In addition to selling through its vaunted sales force, IBM also sells through a full network of distributors and value-added resellers, which sell IBM computers, systems, and services to a variety of special business segments. Final customers can buy IBM personal computers from specialty computer stores or any of several large retailers. IBM uses telemarketing to service the needs of small and medium-sized businesses. And both business and final consumers can buy online from the company's website (www.ibm.com).

Multichannel distribution systems offer many advantages to companies facing large and complex markets. With each new channel, the company expands its sales and market coverage and gains opportunities to tailor its products and services to the specific needs of diverse customer segments. But such multichannel systems are harder to control, and they generate conflict as more channels compete for

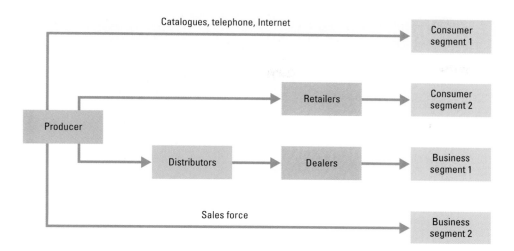

Figure 13.4 Multichannel distribution system

customers and sales. For example, when IBM began selling directly to customers through catalogues and telemarketing, many of its retail dealers cried "unfair competition" and threatened to drop the IBM line or to give it less emphasis. Many outside salespeople felt that they were being undercut by the new "inside channels."

Changing Channel Organization

Changes in technology and the rapid growth of direct and online marketing are having a profound impact on the nature and design of marketing channels. One major trend is **disintermediation**—a big term with a clear message and important consequences. Disintermediation means that more and more, product and service producers are bypassing intermediaries and going directly to final buyers, or that radically new types of channel intermediaries are emerging to displace traditional ones.

Thus, in many industries, traditional intermediaries are dropping by the wayside. Companies like Dell Computer and American Airlines are selling directly to final buyers, eliminating retailers from their marketing channels. Ecommerce merchants are growing rapidly, taking business from traditional bricks-and-mortar retailers. Consumers can buy flowers from 1-800-Flowers.com; books, videos, CDs, toys, and other goods from Chapters.Indigo.ca; household products from Wal-Mart; groceries from GroceryGateway.com; clothes from Danier Leather, Roots, Lands' End, or GAP websites; and consumer electronics from Buy.com, all without ever visiting a store.

Disintermediation presents problems and opportunities for both producers and intermediaries (see Real Marketing 13.1). To avoid being swept aside, traditional intermediaries must find new ways to add value in the supply chain. To remain competitive, product and service producers must develop new channel opportunities, such as Internet and other direct channels. However, developing these new channels often brings them into direct competition with their established channels, resulting in conflict.

To ease this problem, companies often look for ways to make going direct a plus for both the company and its channel partners. For example, to trim costs and add business, Hewlett-Packard opened three direct-sales websites—Shopping Village (for consumers), HP Commerce Center (for businesses buying from authorized resellers), and Electronic Solutions Now (for existing contract customers). However, to avoid conflicts with its established reseller channels, HP forwards all its Web orders to resellers, who complete the orders, ship the products, and get the commissions. In this way, HP gains the advantages of direct selling but also boosts business for resellers.

Disintermediation

The displacement of traditional resellers from a marketing channel by radically new types of intermediaries.

REAL MARKETING

13.1 Disintermediation: A Fancy Word but a Clear Message

*B*ayridge Travel in Kingston, Ontario, typifies the kind of business most threatened by the advent of new marketing channels, particularly the surge in Internet selling. It fears travellers like Canada's Internet guru, Jim Carroll, who notes that, "In the last two years, I've bought some $75 000 worth of airline tickets on the Internet.... By doing so directly through the websites of various airlines, I've cut travel agents out of several thousand dollars worth of commissions."

Thus, like other traditional travel agencies, Bayridge faces some scary new competitors: giant online travel supersites such as Expedia and Travelocity, which let consumers surf the Web for rock-bottom ticket prices. To make matters worse, the airlines themselves are opening websites to sell seats, not only their own but competitors' as well. For example, visitors to the United Airlines website can purchase tickets on more than 500 other airlines. These new channels give consumers more choices, but they threaten the very existence of Bayridge Travel and other traditional travel agencies.

Resellers in dozens of industries face similar situations as new channel forms threaten to make them obsolete. There's even a fancy 17-letter word to describe this phenomenon: *disintermediation*. Bob Westrope, director of the electronic markets group with KPMG in Toronto, believes it represents "a shift in

Electronic marketer ING Direct is forcing banks and credit unions to change their distribution strategies.

the structure of our economy not seen since the dawning of the industrial age."

Strictly speaking, disintermediation means the elimination of a layer of intermediaries from a marketing channel. For example, for years personal computer makers assumed that customers needed hands-on buying experience, with lots of point-of-sale inventory and hand-holding sales assistance from retailers. Then along came Dell Computer with a whole new distribution formula. By eliminating retailers, Dell eliminated many costs and inefficiencies from the traditional computer supply chain.

More broadly, disintermediation includes not just the elimination of channel levels through direct marketing but also the displacement of traditional resellers by radically new types of intermediaries. For example, the publishing industry had for decades assumed that book buyers wanted to purchase their books from small, intimate neighbourhood bookshops. Then, along came the book superstores—Chapters in Canada and Barnes & Noble in the U.S.—with their huge inventories and low prices. Disintermediation occurred as the new intermediaries rapidly displaced traditional independent booksellers. Then, most recently, online booksellers like Amazon.com emerged to threaten the category killers. Amazon.com doesn't eliminate the retail channel—it's actually a new type of retailer that increases consumers' channel choices rather than reducing them. Still, disintermediation has occurred as Amazon.com and the superstores' own websites are displacing traditional bricks-and-mortar retailers.

Disintermediation is often associated with the surge in ecommerce and online selling. In fact, the Internet is a major disintermediating force. By facilitating direct contact between buyers and sellers, the Internet is displacing channels in industries ranging from books, apparel, toys, drugs, and consumer electronics to travel, stock brokerage, and real estate services. However, disintermediation can involve almost any new form of channel competition. For example, Dell bypassed retailers through telephone and mail-order selling long before it took to the Internet.

Disintermediation works only when a new channel form succeeds in bringing greater value to consumers. Thus, if Amazon weren't giving buyers greater convenience, selection, and value, it wouldn't be able to lure customers away from traditional retailers. If Dell's direct channel weren't more efficient and effective in serving the needs of computer buyers, traditional retail channels would have little to fear. However, the huge success of these new channels suggests that they *are* bringing greater value to significant segments of consumers.

From a producer's viewpoint, although eliminating unneeded intermediaries makes sense, disintermediation can be very difficult. One analyst summarizes this way:

> You thought electronic commerce would bring nothing but good news. Here at last, you reasoned, is a way to add customers, boost market share, and cut sales costs. All manufacturers have to do is set up an electronic conduit between themselves and their customers and voilà, instant sales channel. There's just one little hitch. Those same thoughts terrify the retailers, distributors, and resellers that account for up to 90 percent of manufacturers' revenues. They fear that their role between company and customer will be rendered obsolete by the virtual marketplace. And that puts manufacturers in a bind. Either they surrender to the seductions of ecommerce and risk a mutiny from those valuable partners, or they do nothing and risk the wrath of [successful ecommerce competitors].

Thus, although bypassing channel intermediaries can help a company compete, it also may create conflict with the established channel partners that most companies count on for the bulk of their sales. Still, most producers know that when more effective channels come along, they have no choice but to change. For example, many of Canada's banks and credit unions are moving rapidly away from their bricks-and-mortar branches to electronic banking as they face new competitors, like ING Direct. Thus, despite the risks, most companies are more afraid of being late to the party than of angering their channel partners. For many businesses, the major question often is not whether to move to a new, high-growth channel but how quickly and what to do with the established channel. One answer is to join forces with channel partners so that both benefit from new channel opportunities. For example, consider Maytag:

> Appliance giant Maytag wanted to leverage its powerful brand name and great quality reputation by selling appliances on the Web. Maytag's goal was to sell to customers without forcing them to travel to a dealer, where they might be seduced by other brands. However, Maytag didn't want to damage its relationships with the thousands of dealers around the country that sell the bulk of its appliances. The solution was to help *dealers* close sales online. The company created My Maytag, a feature on its main website, by which customers could learn about and purchase Maytag products. But rather than filling the

orders directly, the company handed them off to dealers. With My Maytag, everyone wins: Online consumers get a convenient and seamless shopping experience, dealers get the sales, and Maytag avoids channel conflict and boosts its business.

What about traditional resellers? How can they avoid being "Delled" or "Amazoned"? The answer lies in continually looking for new ways to create real customer value. Many companies threatened by Internet competitors have themselves learned to leverage the Web to serve customers better. For example, Bayridge Travel now de-emphasizes airline ticket sales and specializes in a market niche—cruises. The owner plans to do what computers can't: She will get to know her customers so well that she can provide personal advice on the cruises she books. Still, she'll use a website to launch this newly reformulated travel business.

Discount brokerage Charles Schwab & Company also proves the value point. Facing a horde of price-cutting ecommerce competitors who got there first—including E*TRADE and Ameritrade—Schwab jumped into the Internet with both feet. However, instead of becoming just another no-frills Internet trading operation, Schwab has done its competitors one better. It plies customers with a wealth of financial and company information, helping them to research and manage their accounts and assuming the role of investment adviser. Schwab is even teaching courses on Web trading at some of its 300 branches. Thus, rather than dragging its feet or fighting the change, Schwab embraced the new channel as a competitive opportunity. The gamble paid off handsomely. Schwab remains North America's largest discount stockbroker and ranks number one online with a 28 percent share of the online market, twice the share of its nearest competitor E*TRADE.

Disintermediation is a big word, but the meaning is clear. Those who continually seek new ways to add real value for customers have little to fear. However, those who fall behind in adding value risk being swept aside by their customers and channel partners.

Sources: Quotes from Jim Carroll, "Futures: When Old Partners Become New Competitors," *Marketing Magazine,* November 22, 1999, www.marketingmag.ca; "Special Report: Technology and Communications Tools for Marketers: Disintermediation: No More Middleman," *Strategy,* March 1, 1999, p. 21; extracts adapted from Rochelle Garner, "Mad as Hell," *Sales & Marketing Management,* June 1999, pp. 55–61; Maricris G. Briones, "What Technology Wrought: Distribution Channel in Flux," *Marketing News,* February 1, 1999, pp. 3, 15; Barb Gomolski, "No Channel Conflict," *InfoWorld,* July 9, 2001, p. 10; and Paulette Thomas, "Case Study: Travel Agency Meets Technology's Threats," *Wall Street Journal,* May 21, 2002, p. B4. Also see Ted Kemp, "Beware the Pitfalls of Bypassing the Channel," *B to B,* February 11, 2002, pp. 1, 28; Jeff Bailey, "Enterprise: Web Sites Force Middlemen to Redefine Markets," *Wall Street Journal,* June 11, 2002, p. B4; and Everett Potter, "Helping Hand: Yes, the Internet Is Nice, but Some People Still Won't Leave Home Without Their Travel Agent," *Wall Street Journal,* June 24, 2002, p. R6.

Setting Channel Objectives

Companies state their marketing objectives in terms of targeted levels of customer service. Usually, a company can identify several segments wanting different levels of service. The company should decide which segments to serve and the best channels to use in each case. In each segment, the company wants to minimize the total channel cost of meeting customer service requirements.

The company's channel objectives are influenced by the nature of the company, its products, its marketing intermediaries, its competitors, and the environment. For example, the company's size and financial situation determine which marketing functions it can handle itself and which it must give to intermediaries. Companies selling perishable products may require more direct marketing to avoid delays and too much handling.

In some cases, a company may want to compete in or near the same outlets that carry competitors' products. In other cases, producers may avoid the channels used by competitors. Avon, for example, uses door-to-door selling rather than going head-to-head with other cosmetics makers for scarce positions in retail stores. And GEICO Direct markets auto and homeowner's insurance directly to consumers via the telephone and Web rather than through agents. Finally, environmental factors such as economic conditions and legal constraints can affect channel objectives and design. For example, in a depressed economy, producers want to distribute their goods in the most economical way, using shorter channels and dropping unneeded services that add to the final price of the goods.

Identifying Major Alternatives

When the company has defined its channel objectives, it should next identify its major channel alternatives in terms of *types* of intermediaries, *number* of intermediaries, and the *responsibilities* of each channel member.

Channel objectives: GEICO markets auto insurance via the telephone and Web for those looking to save money and do business directly with the company.

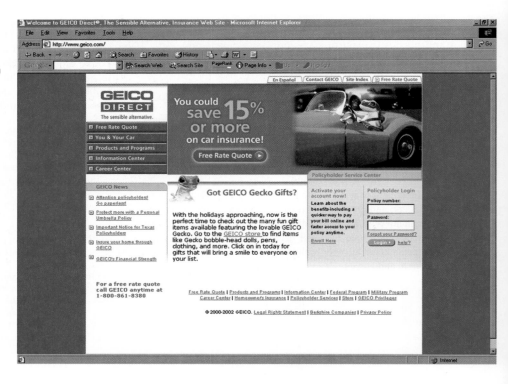

Types of Intermediaries

A firm should identify the types of channel members available to carry out its channel work. For example, suppose a manufacturer of test equipment has developed an audio device that detects poor mechanical connections in any machine with moving parts. Company executives think this product would have a market in all industries where electric, combustion, or steam engines are made or used. The company's current sales force is small, and the problem is how best to reach these different industries. The following channel alternatives may emerge from management discussion:

- *Company Sales Force.* Expand the company's direct sales force. Assign salespeople to territories and have them contact all prospects in the area or develop separate company sales forces for different industries. Or, add an inside telesales operation in which telephone salespeople handle small or midsize companies.
- *Manufacturer's Agency.* Hire manufacturer's agents—independent firms whose sales forces handle related products from many companies—in different regions or industries to sell the new test equipment.
- *Industrial Distributors.* Find distributors in the different regions or industries who will buy and carry the new line. Give them exclusive distribution, good margins, product training, and promotional support.

Sometimes it is too difficult or expensive to use a preferred channel and the company must develop another one. Sometimes new forms of distribution evolve for old products. The pharmaceutical industry in the United States, for example, has recently been challenged by a new type of intermediary—the emerging Canadian drugs-by-mail companies. After much debate, the U.S. Senate passed a bill in June 2003 that allowed U.S. pharmacists to buy prescription drugs in Canada. Drugs sell for less here and Canadian mail-order and online pharmacies saw an opportunity to undercut their American counterparts. However, given the pharmaceutical industry's opposition to Canadian imports and actions to restrict the supply of key drugs in Canada, it is difficult to say for how much longer these companies will continue to make cross-border sales.[11]

Number of Intermediaries

Companies also must determine the number of channel members to use at each level. Three strategies are available: *intensive distribution, exclusive distribution,* and *selective distribution.*

Intensive distribution
Stocking the product in as many outlets as possible.

Producers of convenience products and common raw materials typically seek **intensive distribution**—a strategy in which they stock their products in as many outlets as possible. These goods must be available where and when consumers want them. For example, toothpaste, candy, and other similar items are sold in millions of outlets to provide maximum brand exposure and consumer convenience. Kraft, Kimberly-Clark, Coca-Cola, and other consumer goods companies distribute their products in this way.

Exclusive distribution
Giving a limited number of dealers the exclusive right to distribute the company's products in their territories.

By contrast, some producers deliberately limit the number of intermediaries handling their products. The extreme form of this practice is **exclusive distribution,** in which the producer gives only a limited number of dealers the exclusive right to distribute its products in their territories. New automobiles and prestige women's clothing often enjoy exclusive distribution. For example, Bentley dealers are few and far between—even large cities may have only one dealer. By granting exclusive distribution, Bentley gains stronger distributor selling support and more control over dealer prices, promotion, credit, and services. Exclusive distribution also enhances the car's image and allows for higher markups.

Selective distribution
The use of more than one but fewer than all of the intermediaries who are willing to carry the company's products.

Between intensive and exclusive distribution lies **selective distribution**—the use of more than one but fewer than all of the intermediaries who are willing to carry a company's products. Most television, furniture, and small appliance brands are

Exclusive distribution: Luxury carmakers sell exclusively through a limited number of dealerships. Such limited distribution enhances the car's image and generates stronger dealer support.

distributed in this manner. For example, KitchenAid, Maytag, Whirlpool, and General Electric sell their major appliances through dealer networks and selected large retailers. By using selective distribution, they do not have to spread their efforts over many outlets, including many marginal ones. They can develop good working relationships with selected channel members and expect a better-than-average selling effort. Selective distribution gives producers good market coverage with more control and less cost than does intensive distribution.

Responsibilities of Channel Members

The producer and intermediaries must agree on the terms and responsibilities of each channel member. They should agree on price policies, conditions of sale, territorial rights, and specific services to be performed by each party. The producer should establish a list price and a fair set of discounts for intermediaries. It must define each channel member's territory, and it should be careful about where it places new resellers.

Mutual services and duties need to be spelled out carefully, especially in franchise and exclusive distribution channels. For example, Tim Hortons provides franchisees with promotional support, a record-keeping system, training, and general management assistance. In turn, franchisees must meet company standards for physical facilities, cooperate with new promotion programs, provide requested information, and buy specified food products.

Evaluating the Major Alternatives

Suppose a company has identified several channel alternatives and wants to select the one that will best satisfy its long-run objectives. The firm must evaluate each alternative against economic, control, and adaptive criteria.

Using *economic criteria,* a company compares the likely profitability of the channel alternatives. The company must also consider *control issues.* Using intermediaries usually means giving them some control over the marketing of the product, and some intermediaries take more control than others. Other things being equal, the company prefers to retain as much control as possible. Finally, the company must apply *adaptive criteria.* Channels often involve long-term commitments to other firms, yet the company wants to keep the channel flexible so that it can adapt to environmental changes. Thus, to be considered, a channel involving long-term commitment should be greatly superior on economic and control grounds.

Designing International Distribution Channels

International marketers face many additional complexities in designing their channels. Each country has its own unique distribution system that has evolved over time and changes very slowly. These channel systems can vary widely from country to country. Thus, global marketers usually must adapt their channel strategies to the existing structures within each country.

In some markets, the distribution system is complex and hard to penetrate, consisting of many layers and large numbers of intermediaries. Consider Japan:

> The Japanese distribution system stems from the early seventeenth century when cottage industries and a [quickly growing] urban population spawned a merchant class.... Despite Japan's economic achievements, the distribution system has remained remarkably faithful to its antique pattern.... [It] encompasses a wide range of wholesalers and other agents, brokers, and retailers, differing more in number than in function from their [North] American counterparts. There are myriad tiny retail shops. An even greater number of wholesalers supplies goods to them, layered tier upon tier, many more than most [North American] executives would think necessary. For example, soap may move through three wholesalers plus a sales company after it leaves the manufacturer before it ever reaches the retail outlet. A steak goes from rancher to consumers in a process that often involves a dozen middle agents.... The distribution network...reflects the traditionally close ties among many Japanese companies...

The Japanese distribution system has remained remarkably traditional. A profusion of tiny retail shops is supplied by an even greater number of small wholesalers.

[and places] much greater emphasis on personal relationships with users.... Although [these channels appear] inefficient and cumbersome, they seem to serve the Japanese customer well.... Lacking much storage space in their small homes, most Japanese homemakers shop several times a week and prefer convenient [and more personal] neighbourhood shops.[12]

Many Western firms have had great difficulty breaking into the closely knit, tradition-bound Japanese distribution network.

At the other extreme, distribution systems in developing countries may be scattered and inefficient, or altogether lacking. China and India are huge markets, each with populations of over 1 billion. In reality, however, these markets are much smaller than the population numbers suggest. Because of inadequate distribution systems in both countries, most companies can profitably access only a small portion of the population located in each country's most affluent cities.[13]

Thus, international marketers face a wide range of channel alternatives. Designing efficient and effective channel systems between and within various country markets poses a difficult challenge. We discuss international distribution decisions further in Chapter 18.

Channel Management Decisions

Once the company has reviewed its channel alternatives and decided on the best channel design, it must implement and manage the chosen channel. Channel management calls for selecting and motivating individual channel members and evaluating their performance over time.

Selecting Channel Members

Producers vary in their ability to attract qualified marketing intermediaries. Some producers have no trouble signing up channel members. For example, when Toyota first introduced its Lexus line in North America, it had no trouble attracting new dealers. In fact, it had to turn down many would-be resellers. In some cases, the promise of exclusive or selective distribution for a desirable product will draw plenty of applicants.

At the other extreme are producers who have to work hard to line up enough qualified intermediaries. For example, in 1986 when distributors were approached about an unknown, new game called Nintendo (www.nintendo.com), many refused to carry the product: They had recently been burned by the failure of Atari. But two Canadian distributors, Larry Wasser and Morey Chaplick, owners of Beamscope, accepted the product. Not a bad move considering that within one year after that decision, their sales went from next to nothing to $24 million![14] Similarly, when the U.S. Time Company first tried to sell its inexpensive Timex watches through regular jewellery stores, most jewellery stores refused to carry them. The company then managed to get its watches into mass-merchandise outlets. This turned out to be a wise decision because of the rapid growth of mass merchandising.

When selecting intermediaries, the company should determine what characteristics distinguish the better ones. It will want to evaluate each channel member's years in business, other lines carried, growth and profit record, cooperativeness, and reputation. If the intermediaries are sales agents, the company will want to evaluate the number and character of other lines carried, and the size and quality of the sales force. If the intermediary is a retail store that wants exclusive or selective distribution, the company will want to evaluate the store's customers, location, and future growth potential.

Managing and Motivating Channel Members

Once selected, channel members must be continuously motivated to do their best. The company must sell not only *through* the intermediaries but also *to* and *with* them. Most companies see their intermediaries as first-line customers and partners. They practise strong *partner relationship management (PRM)* to forge long-term partnerships with channel members. This creates a marketing system that meets the needs of both the company *and* its partners. (See Real Marketing 13.2.)

REAL MARKETING

13.2 Partner Relationship Management: Hewlett-Packard's No-Fly Zone

Hewlett-Packard has a long history of working *with* its channel partners, rather than *through* them or *against* them. It understands the great value that these partners add, both for HP and for customers. "Partners are core to HP's business go-to-market strategy," says Webb McKinney. "[Only by working closely] with our channel partners [can we] meet the diverse needs of our customers." Channel partners extend HP's reach far beyond its own capacity. They have a clear understanding of customers' needs and possess the resources necessary to build customer relationships and provide hands-on support. Managing channel relationships is one of the most important things HP does.

Partner relationship management: To support its channel partners and avoid conflict, HP's "hard deck" guideline clearly outlines "which accounts the channel leads and which accounts HP leads."

"Put simply, it's a partnering world," adds Kevin Gilroy, general manager for HP's channel program.

A few years back, however, HP faced a difficult decision. Given competitor Dell's incredible success at selling direct to customers, HP had to decide whether it would do the same. Not only could direct selling reduce costs and increase profits, but some customers actually prefer to deal directly with HP. Says HP CEO Carly Fiorina, "The reality is there are some customers who prefer to order through a direct distribution capability *à la* Dell, and we have to satisfy those customers." So HP really had no choice—it had to go direct. The problem? By selling direct, HP would be putting itself into direct competition with its traditional distribution channel partners. This, in turn, posed a threat to HP's prized relationships with its distributors.

Thus, HP had to find a way to both sell direct to customers *and* build support and trust among its traditional partners. To solve the problem, the company has developed a direct sales program carefully designed to avoid infringing on its partners' turf. Whereas HP's competitors were taking business from their distributors through direct sales to even the smallest customers, HP has "drawn a line in the sand," Gilroy says. Its direct sales program, sometimes referred to as the "hard deck" program, clearly limits which accounts the company will target with direct selling.

"Hard deck" refers to an aviation term that defines a boundary under which there is a "no-fly zone." For HP, it means that the company will sell direct only to potential customers that exceed a set of established specifications. To date, that includes about 1000 large accounts. Customers falling below the specifications—

those in the "no-fly zone"—are off limits to HP for direct sales. Such an arrangement allows HP to concentrate its direct sales force on the largest national and international companies that expect dedicated supplier service. At the same time, it creates a market for channel partners, below the hard deck, that is completely free from direct selling competition.

In addition to establishing the no-fly zone, HP goes out of its way to ensure that its partners find success in selling the company's products and services. When HP sales reps get leads on accounts in the no-fly zone, they pass the information along to HP distributors, who make the sale and provide service and support. In addition, HP dedicates sales and technical resources to help channel members find the best customer solutions.

The day-to-day management of relationships with more than 20 000 channel partners selling everything from computer networks to pocket calculators presents an immense challenge. Something as simple as distributing sales leads collected through various HP marketing campaigns—everything from business cards dropped in fishbowls at trade shows to requests for product information from HP's Internet site—can be a daunting task. To manage these tasks, HP set up an integrating partner relationship management (PRM) system, which links HP directly with its channel partners and helps coordinate channel-wide marketing efforts. Using a secure website, channel partners can log on at any time to obtain leads that have been generated for them. While at the website, they can also order literature and sales support materials, check product specifications, and obtain pricing information. In addition, HP communicates with channel members regularly, offering training seminars and promotional materials to support sales. In fact, many partners receive one or two emails a day offering information, resources, and support.

The PRM system not only provides strong support for channel partners, it improves their collective effectiveness and provides assessment feedback to HP. Under the old system, says an HP manager, "we would generate a mass-mailing campaign, send it off to who knows where, out it would go, and we'd hope it would work. Now we can generate a targeted campaign, see when the opportunities start coming back, and...the channel partner tells us what happened.... It's changing the way we do campaigns."

The results of HP's partner relationship marketing efforts speak for themselves. HP has won multiple awards for its support of and relationships with channel members. Most recently, HP swept almost every category it was eligible for in 2002's Channel Champions awards sponsored by *Crn*, a technology-focused trade journal. In surveys administered to determine the winners, one channel member offered that "you won't find a support network out there that's better. Overall, HP is a step above the rest." Referring to the support HP reps provide to channel partners, another distributor commented, "We treat our HP reps more like our sales managers. HP has high integrity. In a grey area, HP will always default to its partners."

Sources: Pat Curry, "Channel Changes," *Industry Week,* April 2, 2001, pp. 45–48; Hewlett-Packard, "Reinventing Partnership: Kevin Gilroy Answers Questions from the Channel," http://partner.americas.HP.com/partner/harddeck.pdf (accessed July 2002); Craig Zarley, "Making the Call," *Crn,* February 11, 2002, pp. 14–17; Joseph F. Kovar, "Channel Champions 2002: HP Software Decisive," *Crn,* March 18, 2002, p. 52; Jennifer Hagendorf Follett, "Channel Champions 2002: HP's Hard Deck Is Aces," *Crn,* March 18, 2002, p. 66; and Mike Cruz, "Channel Champions 2002: HP Takes All in Printers," *Crn,* March 18, 2002, p. 84.

In managing its channels, a company must convince distributors that they can succeed better by working together as a part of a cohesive value delivery system.[15] GE Appliances has created an alternative distribution system called CustomerNet to coordinate, support, and motivate its dealers.

GE CustomerNet gives dealers instant online access to GE Appliances' distribution and order-processing system, 24 hours a day, seven days a week. By logging on to the GE CustomerNet website, dealers can obtain product specifications, photos, feature lists, and side-by-side model comparisons for hundreds of GE appliance models. They can check on product availability and prices, place orders, and review order status. They can even create custom brochures, order point-of-purchase materials, or download "advertising slicks"—professionally prepared GE appliance ads ready for insertion in local media. GE promises next-day delivery on most appliance models, so dealers need carry only display models in their stores. This greatly reduces inventory costs, making even small dealers more price competitive. GE CustomerNet also helps dealers to sell GE appliances more easily and effectively. A dealer can put

Creating dealer satisfaction and profitability: Using GE's CustomerNet system, dealers have instant online access to GE Appliances' distribution system, 24 hours a day, 7 days a week to check on product availability and prices, place orders, and review order status. Simply put, it's an electronic one-stop shopping breakthrough that can help you sell.

a computer terminal on the showroom floor, where salespeople and customers together can use the system to dig through detailed product specifications and check availability for GE's entire line of appliances. Perhaps the biggest benefit to GE Appliances, however, is that the system builds strong bonds between the company and its dealers and motivates dealers to put more push behind the company's products.[16]

Many companies are now installing integrated high-tech partner relationship management systems to coordinate their whole-channel marketing efforts. Just as they use customer relationship management (CRM) software systems to help manage relationships with important customers, companies can now use PRM software to help recruit, train, organize, manage, motivate, and evaluate relationships with channel partners.[17]

Evaluating Channel Members

The producer must regularly check channel members' performance against standards such as sales quotas, average inventory levels, customer delivery time, treatment of damaged and lost goods, cooperation in company promotion and training programs, and services to the customer. The company should recognize and reward intermediaries who are performing well. Those who are performing poorly should be helped or, as a last resort, replaced. A company may periodically "requalify" its intermediaries and prune the weaker ones.

Finally, manufacturers need to be sensitive to their dealers. Those who treat their dealers lightly risk not only losing their support but also causing some legal problems. The next section describes various rights and duties of manufacturers and their channel members.

Public Policy and Distribution Decisions

Supply chain management, logistics, and distribution present managers with countless ethical dilemmas—everything from what types of suppliers a company should use to the types of influence strategies that are appropriate to ensure channel members comply with channel policies. Under the heading "Fulfilment Practices," the Canadian Marketing Association Code of Ethics covers some ethical issues with regard to distribution. For example, it stipulates that goods should be shipped within 30 days of the receipt of a properly completed order (or within the time limit stated in the original offer), and notes that customers have the right to cancel orders without penalty if this time frame is not respected. The American Marketing Association (AMA) code of ethics (under which Canadian marketers also operate) focuses on issues of market power in the section dealing with distribution. Ethical marketers are advised not to manipulate product availability for purposes of exploitation and not to use coercion in the marketing channel. This code puts into question practices around these issues:[18]

1. *Exclusive dealing*. Many producers and wholesalers like to develop exclusive channels for their products. When the seller allows only certain outlets to carry its products, this strategy is called *exclusive distribution*. When the seller requires that these dealers not handle competitors' products, its strategy is called *exclusive dealing*. Both parties benefit from exclusive arrangements: The seller obtains more loyal and dependable outlets, and the dealers obtain a steady source of supply and stronger seller support. But exclusive arrangements exclude other producers from selling to these dealers. They are legal as long as they do not substantially lessen competition or tend to create a monopoly and as long as both parties enter into the agreement voluntarily.

2. *Exclusive territories*. Exclusive dealing often includes exclusive territorial agreements. The producer may agree not to sell to other dealers in a given area, or the buyer may agree to sell only in its own territory. The first practice is normal under franchise systems as a way to increase dealer enthusiasm and commitment. It is also perfectly legal—a seller has no legal obligation to sell through more outlets than it wishes. The second practice, whereby the producer tries to keep a dealer from selling outside its territory, has become a major legal issue.

3. *Tying agreements*. Producers of a strong brand sometimes sell it to dealers only if the dealers will take some or all of the rest of the line—*full-line forcing*. Even though the practice isn't illegal, it causes considerable channel conflict.

4. *Dealers' rights*. Producers are free to select their dealers, but their right to terminate dealers is somewhat restricted. In general, sellers can drop dealers "for cause." But they cannot drop dealers if, for example, the dealers refuse to cooperate in a doubtful legal arrangement, such as exclusive dealing or tying agreements.

5. *Sources of supply*. As price competition increases in many industries, many firms look to overseas suppliers who can provide them with low-cost inputs. A number of ethical concerns have arisen as a result of this practice, including the loss of jobs in Canada's manufacturing sector and the use of overseas suppliers that follow questionable practices. For example, in the sporting goods market, firms have been criticized for using suppliers that pay low wages (wages far below what they pay celebrities to endorse their products) to suppliers that are reported to produce goods in *sweatshops* that use child or prison labour. Few Canadians want to think that the high-fashion apparel they wear or the sports equipment they use is made by children forced to labour instead of going to school.

    Another group of firms has come under scrutiny because of the countries within which they operate. Profits from Talisman Energy's operations in Sudan, for example, are believed by some to support the Sudanese government's civil war and the violation of the human rights of some of its citizens. Similarly, De Beers, the famous diamond miner, has been requested to ensure that it does not market "conflict diamonds," stones sold by governments that use the revenue to fund wars. While Talisman has been resistant to changing its practices, De Beers took a more proactive stance. It is working with a number of organizations, including the United Nations, to provide documentation certifying the origin of all stones and banning those coming from questionable sources from international diamond exchanges.

6. *Purchasing and shelving policies.* Coming up with winning products is a major challenge—getting goods into stores where consumers can see and purchase them is often even a bigger hurdle. Retailing in Canada is becoming increasingly concentrated, and some manufacturers believe it helps to pay a bribe to the store's representatives, or buyers, to facilitate the process. In the garment industry, these payments are known as *kickbacks, payola,* or *shmeer.* Salespeople have long worked to woo buyers with everything from lavish dinners to tickets to sporting events. However, the line has been stretched, and some buyers are treated to golf trips in Palm Beach or even cash payments. Wal-Mart Canada recently fired one of its buyers and worked with the RCMP to press charges against another who allegedly demanded money from suppliers who wanted Wal-Mart to stock their goods. To counter the practice, firms are developing strict codes of conduct for both purchasing agents and salespeople. Many codes ban giving or accepting any gifts.

Another issue related to the acquisition of shelf space that is hotly debated is the use of *slotting allowances* or *fees.* Manufacturers pay these fees to stock, display, and support new products. One study suggests that these fees represent about 16 percent of all new product introduction costs. Often negotiated in secret, they have sparked considerable controversy. Many manufacturers believe they are being held to ransom by retailers. Others contend that only large firms can afford to pay these hefty sums, thereby restricting the entry of small,

De Beers has been proactive in its efforts to avoid buying or selling "conflict diamonds."

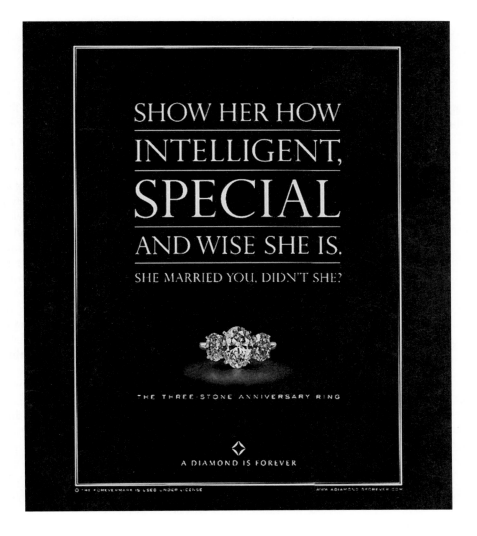

entrepreneurial firms from the marketplace. Retailers, on the other hand, claim that they are just fair compensation of the 2000 to 3000 new items they are asked to stock each year. Since many of these products will fail, the fees are compensation for taking on this risk as well as covering the costs of listing, stocking, and managing the shelf space for these products. No matter what side of the issue you sit on, you cannot deny that these fees lead to higher retail prices for consumers.

Marketing Logistics and Supply Chain Management

In today's global marketplace, selling a product is sometimes easier than getting it to customers. Companies must decide on the best way to store, handle, and move their products and services so that they are available to customers in the right assortments, at the right time, and in the right place. Physical distribution and logistics effectiveness has a major impact on both customer satisfaction and company costs. Here, we consider the *nature and importance of logistics management in the supply chain, goals of the logistics system, and major logistics functions.*

The Nature and Importance of Marketing Logistics

Marketing logistics (physical distribution)
The tasks involved in planning, implementing, and controlling the physical flow of materials, final goods, and related information from points of origin to points of consumption to meet customer requirements at a profit.

To some managers, physical distribution means only trucks and warehouses. But modern logistics is much more than this. **Marketing logistics**—also called **physical distribution**—involves planning, implementing, and controlling the physical flow of materials, final goods, and related information from points of origin to points of consumption to meet customer requirements at a profit. In short, it involves getting the right product to the right customer in the right place at the right time.

Industry Canada focuses on this area since logistics is one of the leading determinants of the cost of goods and services, and the industry plays a key role in the international competitiveness of Canadian goods and services, with a direct impact on profitability. Logistics firms' revenues exceed $50 billion and over 400 000 Canadians work directly in logistics-related industries, including transportation services, storage, postal and courier services, and business services, while another 480 000 work as in-house logisticians in manufacturing, wholesale, retail trade, and other industries.[19]

In the past, physical distribution typically started with products at the plant and low-cost solutions to get them to customers. However, today's marketers prefer customer-centred logistics thinking, which starts with the marketplace and works backwards to the factory, or even to sources of supply. Marketing logistics addresses not only *outbound distribution* (moving products from the factory to customers), but also *inbound distribution* (moving products and materials from suppliers to the factory) and *reverse distribution* (moving broken, unwanted, or excess products returned by consumers or resellers). That is, it involves entire **supply chain management**—managing upstream and downstream value-added flows of materials, final goods, and related information among suppliers, the company, resellers, and final consumers, as shown in Figure 13.5.

Supply chain management
Managing upstream and downstream value-added flows of materials, final goods, and related information among suppliers, the company, resellers, and final consumers.

Thus, the logistics manager's task is to coordinate the activities of suppliers, purchasing agents, marketers, channel members, and customers. These activities include forecasting, information systems, purchasing, production planning, order processing, inventory, warehousing, and transportation planning.

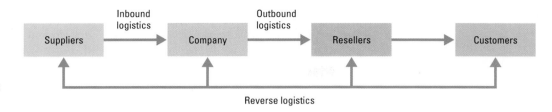

Figure 13.5 Supply chain management

Companies are placing greater emphasis on logistics for several reasons. First, companies can gain a powerful competitive advantage by using improved logistics to give customers better service or lower prices. Second, improved logistics can yield tremendous cost savings to both the company and its customers. About 15 percent of an average product's price is accounted for by shipping and transport alone. In the U.S., Ford alone has more than 450 million kg of finished vehicles, production parts, and aftermarket parts in transit at any given time, running up an annual logistics bill of around $5.2 billion. Shaving off even a small fraction of these costs can mean substantial savings.[20]

Third, the explosion in product variety has created a need for improved logistics management. In 1911, the typical A&P grocery store carried only 270 items. The shopkeeper could keep track of this inventory on about 10 pages of notebook paper. Today, the average A&P carries a bewildering stock of more than 16 700 items, and a Wal-Mart Supercenter store carries more than 100 000 products.[21] Ordering, shipping, stocking, and controlling such a variety of products presents a sizeable logistics challenge.

Finally, improvements in information technology have created opportunities for major gains in distribution efficiency. Using sophisticated supply chain management software, Web-based logistics systems, point-of-sale scanners, uniform product codes, satellite tracking, and electronic transfer of order and payment data, companies can quickly and efficiently manage the flow of goods, information, and finances through the supply chain.

Goals of the Logistics System

Some companies state their logistics objective as providing maximum customer service at the least cost. Unfortunately, no logistics system can *both* maximize customer service and minimize distribution costs. Maximum customer service implies rapid delivery, large inventories, flexible assortments, liberal returns policies, and other services—all of which raise distribution costs. In contrast, minimum distribution costs imply slower delivery, smaller inventories, and larger shipping lots—which represent a lower level of overall customer service.

The goal of marketing logistics should be to provide a *targeted* level of customer service at the least cost. A company must first research the importance of various distribution services to its customers and then set desired service levels for each segment. The objective is to maximize *profits*, not sales. Therefore, the company must weigh the benefits of providing higher levels of service against the costs. Some companies offer less service than their competitors and charge a lower price. Other companies offer more service and charge higher prices to cover higher costs.

Major Logistics Functions

Given a set of logistics objectives, the company is ready to design a logistics system that will minimize the cost of attaining them. The major logistics functions include *warehousing, inventory management,* and *transportation.*

Warehousing

Production and consumption cycles rarely match. So most companies must store their tangible goods while they wait to be sold. For example, Snapper, Toro, and other lawn-mower manufacturers run their factories all year long and store up products for the heavy spring and summer buying season. The storage function overcomes differences in needed quantities and timing, ensuring that products are available when customers are ready to buy them.

A company must decide on *how many* and *what types* of warehouses it needs, and *where* they will be located. The company might use either *storage warehouses* or *distribution centres*. Storage warehouses store goods for moderate to long periods. **Distribution centres** are designed to move goods rather than just store them. They are large and highly automated warehouses designed to receive goods from various plants and suppliers, take orders, fill them efficiently, and deliver goods to customers as quickly as possible:

> Wal-Mart's $55 million distribution centre in Cornwall, Ontario, serves its stores from Belleville, Ontario, to St. John's, Nfld. It sits on a 52-hectare site and has a 150 000 square metre parking lot for the trucks that deliver and pick up goods. Conveyor belts and sorting equipment whisk 200 000 cartons a day through the centre. Many of these goods are cross docked, meaning that they are unloaded from one trailer and then are computer routed within eight to nine minutes to another truck that takes them to their designated stores.[22]

Inventory Management

Inventory management affects customer satisfaction. Here, managers must maintain the delicate balance between carrying too little inventory and carrying too much. With too little stock, the firm may need costly emergency shipments or production. Carrying too much inventory results in higher-than-necessary inventory-carrying costs and stock obsolescence. Thus, in managing inventory, firms must balance the costs of carrying larger inventories against resulting sales and profits.

Many companies have greatly reduced their inventories and related costs through *just-in-time* logistics systems. With such systems, producers and retailers carry only small inventories of parts or merchandise, often only enough for a few days of operations. For example, Dell Computer, a master just-in-time producer, carries just five days of inventory, whereas competitors might carry 40 days or even 60.[23] New stock arrives exactly when needed, rather than being stored in inventory until being used.

Just-in-time systems require accurate forecasting along with fast, frequent, and flexible delivery, so that new supplies will be available when needed. However, these systems result in substantial savings in inventory carrying and handling costs. Marketers are always looking for new ways to make inventory management more efficient. In the not-too-distant future, handling inventory might even become fully automated:[24]

> Imagine knowing, at any time, exactly where a product—no matter how large or small—is located physically within the supply chain. Or imagine "smart shelves" that not only tell you when it's time to reorder, but also place the order automatically with your supplier. Welcome to the wonderful world of Auto-ID, an exciting new information technology application that could revolutionize distribution as we know it. MIT's Auto-ID centre is now developing "smart tag" technology, which might soon be used to embed intelligence, identity, and Internet connectivity into millions of everyday products.
>
>   Think about what that means. Physical objects would have the ability to communicate with each other and with retailers, suppliers, and consumers through the Internet. The entire global supply chain becomes a seamless network of direct, real-time supply and demand. "Smart" products could make the

Distribution centre

A large, highly automated warehouse designed to receive goods from various plants and suppliers, take orders, fill them efficiently, and deliver goods to customers as quickly as possible.

entire supply chain—which accounts for nearly 75 percent of a product's cost—intelligent and automated. Products from anywhere on Earth could be linked to the Internet, where manufacturers and retailers could access information ranging from consumer trends to theft alerts. This, in turn, would let companies effectively meet consumer demands while at the same time saving billions of dollars.

Transportation

The choice of transportation carriers affects the pricing of products, delivery performance, and condition of the goods when they arrive—all of which affect customer satisfaction. In shipping goods to its warehouses, dealers, and customers, a company can choose between five transportation modes: rail, truck, water, pipeline, and air, along with an alternative mode for digital products—the Internet. Rather than choosing a single carrier, **intermodal transportation** (combining two or more modes of transportation) is increasingly being used. For example, products manufactured in Alberta may be shipped first by rail in containers that are then loaded onto trucks for delivery in the Toronto area or are loaded onto ships in Montreal for transportation overseas.

Intermodal transportation
Combining two or more modes of transportation.

Canada has one of the most modern and highly developed transportation infrastructures in the world, as the following discussion demonstrates.[25]

Rail   Because most of Canada's population is contained in a belt that is only 300 km wide but 6400 km long, railways form the backbone of Canada's transportation system, providing the most economical method of moving containers and bulk commodities—coal, sand, minerals, farm and forest products—over great distances. Canadian railways move some 270 million tonnes of freight annually. To improve efficiency, both CP and CN have designed new equipment to handle special categories of goods and have purchased major U.S. railways to extend their services throughout the continent.

Truck   Trucks have increased their share of transportation steadily and now account for the largest portion of transportation *within* cities rather than *between*

The Canadian Pacific Railway provides rail and intermodal transportation for goods within Canada and the United States.

cities. Trucks are dependent on our more than 900 000 kilometres of public roads. Moreover, every year, there are roughly ten million truck trips across the Canada–U.S. border, with the value of goods carried totalling approximately $400 billion. This makes road transport the dominant mode of north–south transportation.

Trucks are highly flexible in their routing and time schedules. They are efficient for short hauls of high-value merchandise. Trucking firms have added many services in recent years. For example, Roadway Express (www.roadway.com) and most other major carriers now offer satellite tracking of shipments and sleeper tractors that move freight around the clock.

Water   Canada is a maritime nation with access to three oceans—the Pacific, the Atlantic, and the Arctic—and 300 commercial ports. Thus, products for both our domestic and international markets are often shipped by sea. Vancouver is Canada's largest port and the main terminal for goods being shipped to the Asia–Pacific region. The Great Lakes/St. Lawrence Seaway System is the world's longest inland waterway. The Port of Montreal is vital to the seaway operation and is Canada's leading container port. Its rail and road links allow it to serve major markets in central Canada and the U.S.

Although the cost of water transportation is very low for shipping bulky, low-value, non-perishable products such as sand, coal, grain, oil, and metallic ores, water transportation is the slowest transportation mode and may be affected by the weather.

Pipeline   Pipelines are used for shipping petroleum, natural gas, and chemicals from sources to markets. Pipeline shipment of petroleum products costs less than rail shipment but more than water shipment. Most pipelines are used by their owners to ship their own products.

Air   The importance of air transportation has grown with our international trade and with the advent of just-in-time inventory management systems. Air-freight rates are much higher than rail or truck rates, but air freight is ideal when speed is needed or distant markets have to be reached. Among the most frequently air-freighted products are perishables (fresh fish, cut flowers) and high-value, low-bulk items (technical instruments, jewellery). Companies find that air freight also reduces inventory levels, packaging costs, and the number of warehouses needed.

The Internet   The Internet carries digital products from producer to customer via satellite, cable modem, or telephone wire. Software firms, the media, music companies, and education all make use of the Internet to transport digital products. While these firms primarily use traditional transportation to distribute music, newspapers, and more, the Internet holds the potential for lower product distribution costs. One FedEx executive notes, "Planes and trucks move packages, and digital technology moves bits."[26]

In choosing a transportation mode for a product, shippers must balance many considerations: speed, dependability, availability, cost, and others. Thus, if a shipper needs speed, air and truck are the prime choices. If the goal is low cost, then water or pipeline might be best.

Looking Back: Reviewing the Concepts

Producing a product or service and making it available to buyers requires building relationships not just with customers, but also with key suppliers and resellers in the company's *supply chain.* Marketers have traditionally focused on the "downstream" side of the supply chain—on the *marketing channels,* or *distribution channels,* that look forward toward the customer.

Marketing channel decisions are among the most important decisions that management faces. A company's channel decisions directly affect every other marketing decision. Each channel system creates a different level of revenues and costs and reaches a different segment of target consumers. Management must make channel decisions carefully, incorporating today's needs with tomorrow's likely selling environment. Some companies pay too little attention to their distribution channels, but others have used imaginative distribution systems to gain competitive advantage.

1. Explain why companies use distribution channels and the functions that these channels perform.

Most producers use intermediaries to bring their products to market. They try to forge a *marketing channel*—a set of interdependent organizations involved in the process of making a product or service available for use or consumption by the consumer or business user. Through their contacts, experience, specialization, and scale of operation, intermediaries usually offer the firm more than it can achieve on its own. Distribution channels perform many key functions. Some help *complete* transactions by gathering and distributing *information* needed for planning and aiding exchange; by promotion—and spreading persuasive communications about an offer; by performing *contact* work—finding and communicating with prospective buyers; by *matching*—shaping and fitting the offer to the buyer's needs; and by entering into *negotiation* to reach an agreement on price and other terms of the offer so that ownership can be transferred. Other functions help to *fulfill* the completed transactions by offering *physical distribution*—transporting and storing goods; *financing*—acquiring and using funds to cover the costs of the channel work; and *risk taking*—assuming the risks of carrying out the channel work.

2. Discuss how channel members interact and organize to perform the work of the channel.

The channel is most effective when each member is assigned the tasks it can do best. Ideally, because the success of individual channel members depends on overall channel success, all channel firms should work together smoothly. They should understand and accept their roles, coordinate their goals and activities, and cooperate to attain overall channel goals. By cooperating, they can more effectively sense, serve, and satisfy the target market. In a large company, the formal organization structure assigns roles and provides needed leadership. But in a distribution channel composed of independent firms, leadership and power are not formally set. Traditionally, distribution channels have lacked the leadership needed to assign roles and manage conflict. In recent years, however, new types of channel organizations have appeared that provide stronger leadership and improved performance.

3. Identify the major channel alternatives open to a company.

Each firm identifies alternative ways to reach its market. Available means vary from direct selling to using one, two, three, or more intermediary *channel levels.* Marketing channels face continuous and sometimes dramatic change. Three of the most important trends are the growth of *vertical, horizontal,* and *multichannel distribution systems.* These trends affect channel cooperation, conflict, and competition. *Channel design* begins with assessing customer channel-service needs and company channel objective and constraints. The company then identifies the major channel alternatives in terms of the *types* of intermediaries, the *number* of intermediaries, and the *channel responsibilities* of each. Each channel alternative must be evaluated according to economic, control, and adaptive criteria. Channel management calls for selecting qualified intermediaries and motivating them. Individual channel members must be evaluated regularly.

4. Explain how companies select, motivate, and evaluate channel members.

Producers vary in their ability to attract qualified marketing intermediaries. Some producers have no trouble signing up channel members. Others have to work hard to line up enough qualified intermediaries. When selecting intermediaries, the company should evaluate each channel member's qualifications and select those who best fit its channel objectives. Once selected, channel members must be continuously motivated to do their best. The company must sell not only *through* the intermediaries but *to* and *with* them. It should work to forge long-term partnerships with the channel partners to create a marketing system that meets the needs of both the manufacturer *and* the partners. The company must

also regularly check channel member performance against established performance standards, rewarding intermediaries who are performing well and assisting or replacing weaker ones.

5. Discuss the nature and importance of marketing logistics.

Just as firms are giving the marketing concept increased recognition, more business firms are paying attention to *marketing logistics* (or *physical distribution*). Logistics is an area of potentially high cost savings and improved customer satisfaction. Marketing logistics addresses not only *outbound distribution* but also *inbound distribution* and *reverse distribution.* That is, it involves entire *supply chain management*—managing value-added flows between suppliers, the company, resellers, and final users. No logistics system can both maximize customer service and minimize distribution costs. Instead, the goal of logistics management is to provide a *targeted* level of service at the least cost. The major logistics functions include *warehousing, inventory management, and transportation*.

Reviewing the Key Terms

Channel conflict   514
Channel level   512
Conventional distribution
    channel   515
Direct marketing channel   512
Disintermediation   519
Distribution centre   534
Exclusive distribution   523
Franchise organization   516

Horizontal marketing systems   516
Indirect marketing channel   513
Intensive distribution   523
Intermodal transportation   535
Marketing channel (distribution
    channel)   509
Marketing logistics (physical
    distribution)   532

Multichannel distribution
    system   517
Selective distribution   523
Supply chain management   532
Value-delivery network   508
Vertical marketing system
    (VMS)   516

Discussing the Concepts

1. Explain the purpose of a company's supply chain. Why may the term "supply chain" be too limited for today's business activities? What is a value-delivery network, and how is it different from a supply chain?

2. Discuss the nature and importance of marketing channels. Define a marketing channel (distribution channel) and list its important characteristics.

3. List and briefly discuss the marketing channel functions that are involved in completing and fulfilling transactions. Which function applies most in each of the following situations? (a) A retailer puts in a rush reorder for a needed Christmas item that is in short supply. (b) An Internet marketer seeks ways to identify and contact its market. (c) A small retailer wants to

expand its order size but does not currently have funds needed to pay for the expanded order. (d) A business buyer attends a large trade show wanting to buy higher-quality products on a limited budget.

4. Describe the horizontal and vertical channel conflicts that might occur in one of the following: (a) the personal computer industry, (b) the automobile industry, (c) the music industry, or (d) the clothing industry. How would you remedy the problems you have just described?

5. What is disintermediation? Give an example other than those discussed in the chapter. What opportunities and problems does disintermediation present for traditional retailers? Explain.

6. Describe which distribution strategy—intensive, selective, or exclusive—is used for each of the following products: (a) Piaget watches, (b) Acura automobiles, (c) Snickers candy bars.

7. Analyze why franchising is such a fast-growing form of retail organization. Why do you think franchising is a more popular way of doing business in Canada than it is in the United States?

Applying the Concepts

1. You know about the Internet, but have you ever heard of an extranet? A company creates an extranet by opening part of its own internal network (or intranet) to trusted suppliers, distributors, and other selected external business partners. Via the extranet, a company can communicate quickly and efficiently with its partners, complete transactions, and share data. A supplier might analyze the customer's inventory needs. (Boeing booked $130 million in parts orders from airline customers in one year.) Partners might swap customer lists for interrelated products and services or share purchasing systems to gain savings through more efficient purchasing. (General Electric claims that $650 million of purchasing costs can be saved using an extranet.) Imagine the strategic advantages created when virtual partners communicate in seconds about shifting supply and demand situations, customer requests and opportunities, and just-in-time inventory needs. Purchase processing times can be reduced from weeks to minutes at enormous cost savings, which can then be passed along to consumers.

   - What role will extranets play in distribution decisions for retailers, wholesalers, and manufacturers?

   - Discuss the potential dangers and benefits of an extranet system. How do those benefits differ for business partners?

   - How does the extranet concept fit with outsourcing (if at all)?

   - Write a short position paper that outlines your thoughts on the advantages and disadvantages of extranets and their future in marketing commerce.

2. Although strong partnerships benefit both the supplier and the buyer, retailers often have difficulty forging strong ties with suppliers. Why? Differing marketing objectives, profit expectations, and business relationships with competitors can result in poor retailer–supplier partnerships. One organization that overcame these difficulties is Ralph Lauren's Polo brand (see

www.polo.com). To improve its customer relationship management system with retailers, Polo found new ways to bring value to the retail operation while reducing the retailer's costs. The company now offers its clients a variety of merchandise purchase options. First, retailers can purchase Polo products in the traditional way—through inventory acquisition. For retailers uninterested in carrying expensive inventory loads, Polo offers a second option—the leased department. Under this agreement, Polo leases floor space, provides its own merchandise, staffs the department with its own employees, and promotes the department in conjunction with the retailer. Though the majority of profits go to Polo, the retailer benefits from having a prestige line in its store without having the burden of inventory. Polo has found that this method not only forges a better working relationship with retailers but often results in the retailer taking over the Polo lease and operating the department on its own, creating value for both the suppliers and retailers.

   - How has Polo forged a value delivery system with retailers?

   - What are the advantages of partner relationship management? (For additional information, see Real Marketing 13.2 on page 527).

   - What conflicts between retailer and supplier might Polo avoid by using the leased department method? What conflicts might be heightened by the leasing approach?

   - Construct a short list of criteria that a retailer might use to evaluate its relationship with Polo.

   - Polo recently decided to open freestanding retail stores in selected cities. What would be the advantages and disadvantages of this strategy with respect to Polo's customer relationship management process? Do the advantages outweigh the disadvantages? Explain your reasoning.

Company Case

Staples, Inc.: Revising the Strategy

Taking Over

In January 2002, Ronald Sargent assumed the reins of office supply superstore Staples from founder Thomas Stemberg. Sargent and Staples faced many challenges. The office supply market seemed to be maturing—industry sales in 2001 actually shrank 3 percent after years of double-digit growth. Further, although Staples had significantly more stores than its two major competitors—Office Depot and OfficeMax—it trailed Office Depot in sales revenue (see Exhibit 1).

There were bright spots for Staples—whereas both Office Depot's and OfficeMax's sales had declined by 5.6 percent and 9.7 percent, respectively, in 2001, Staples's sales had inched up by 0.7 percent, and its profits had soared from just US$59.7 million in 2000 to US$265 million in 2001. Yet, analysts noted that Staples's return on net assets (RONA) was below its weighted-average cost of capital (WACC) and argued that the firm needed to improve its profitability. Sargent knew he had his work cut out for him.

Taking Stock

Sargent began by questioning one of the company's basic strategic assumptions—build a store with lots of inventory and the lowest prices in town and customers will beat a path to your door. Under this philosophy,

Staples operated 400 more stores than OfficeMax and 541 more than Office Depot. Staples's stores were typically stocked from floor to ceiling, warehouse style, with all sorts of products. Yet, Staples's sales revenue per store was well below Office Depot's.

Sargent therefore decided to slow the company's store expansion. He also closed 32 underperforming stores, the largest store closing in the company's 16-year history. And the company planned to open only 115 new stores in 2002, down from 160 in 2001. It would also open most of these new stores in existing markets rather than new market areas in order to take advantage of operating efficiencies.

Further, focus groups with Staples's target market of small-business customers indicated that those customers did not like the warehouse look. Customers wanted to be able to see across a store and to determine quickly from signage where items were located. Staples responded by experimenting with a smaller store (1858 square metres versus about 2229) with lower shelving and a more open atmosphere. This meant that it had to reduce inventory. As a result, the company removed many items that it found were not really necessary, such as child-oriented computer games and educational software. Based on customer feedback, it also stopped offering some business services, like health insurance or prepaid legal services, so that it could

Exhibit 1   Office Supply Data for Fiscal 2001

Company	Number of Stores	Sales Revenue (US$B)	Net Income (US$M)	Revenue per Store (US$M)*	Employees
Staples	1400	$10.74	$265	$5.7	53 000
Office Depot	859	$11.15	$201	$6.7	48 000
OfficeMax	1000	$ 4.64	($296)	$4.6	30 000

Revenue per store (US$) does not include revenue from Internet or catalogue sales.

Source: Westchester County Business Journal, April 1, 2002, p. 14.

focus on consumable products. Customers, it found, did not want to shop at Staples for these services.

The results with this new store format proved promising, with sales increasing by up to 10 percent with about 10 percent less inventory. Sargent noted that "we're doing the same sales volume with two printers selling for more than $100 than we did selling five printers at the different price points." As a result, Sargent decided to roll out the new format and reconfigure 280 stores in 2002 in hopes of improving both sales and inventory turnover. Staples's inventory turnover ratio was about 5.1 times as compared with Office Depot's 6.3 times.

As a second part of his strategy, Sargent turned to what the company calls its "North American Delivery" segment. This segment includes the company's Internet, catalogue, and corporate contracts operations—all of its operations that *bypass* its stores. In 2001, this segment accounted for 28 percent of sales and 40 percent of profits. Competitor Office Depot got 34 percent of its sales and 33 percent of its profits from similar operations. In a Home Furnishing Network survey of website traffic for the first four months of 2002, Office Depot had the highest number of unique website visits, over 24 million, of the top 20 retail websites, ahead of Best Buy, Wal-Mart, Target, and others. Staples's site, www.staples.com, came in seventh with just under 14 million visits, while OfficeMax finished tenth with just under 10 million visits. *Forbes* magazine named Staples's site as the "Best of the Web Pick for Entrepreneurs" for the third year in a row, based on its ability to assist smaller businesses to run as smoothly as larger organizations.

To handle its catalogue operations, Staples has a subsidiary, Quill.com. A survey ranked Quill.com as highest in terms of its online sales conversion rate of 30.3 percent versus the average site's rate of 8 percent or lower. Quill.com offered 35 percent of its products as private-label brands as compared with 7 percent for Staples. Sargent saw this as an opportunity for Staples to offer more of it own private-label brands that carried higher margins.

Although Staples had built its business by targeting small businesses, while OfficeMax had targeted household consumers, it also developed programs for businesses with more than 100 employees. Its StaplesLink program allowed companies to link their internal procurement systems with Staples's computer systems. This allowed users to place their orders directly with Staples, which then prepared the order and delivered it to the business the next day.

For both its catalogue and contract businesses, Sargent believed that Staples should beat a path to customers' doors. He ordered the doubling, to 400, of Staples's special sales force, which worked with customers to get them to order through its catalogue or its website. He also added 100 staff members to the 600-person sales force that worked exclusively with corporate and small-business accounts.

To find a way to get more small-business customers into the stores, Staples entered a test with FleetBoston Financial Corp. to opening 10 offices in select Staples stores in the U.S. Northeast. These in-store offices would have two Fleet Boston staff members who would work with business owners to open specially designed business checking accounts, get debit cards, and make small-business loan applications. The offices would not dispense cash or take deposits and would be open six or seven days a week. Fleet Boston already had more than 100 non-traditional branches, mostly in supermarkets.

Next, Sargent planned to continue Staples's international expansion. The retailer already operated 180 stores in the United Kingdom, Germany, the Netherlands, and Portugal. It planned to add 20 new stores in Europe and to expand into one more country. European operations accounted for about US$796 million of 2001's sales.

Finally, Sargent focused on customer retention. He understood that getting a customer was expensive. The company estimated that a customer doing business for three years was 4.5 times more profitable than a new customer. Staples's managers estimated that the company had a 30 percent share of their customers' office supply purchases, and they wanted to increase that share.

Taking the Challenge

Sargent knew Staples's 53 000 employees would have to execute all of these strategic moves for the company to reach its target of US$12 billion in sales and US$440 million in net income by 2003. And he knew that competition was only going to intensify. The struggling OfficeMax was trying to capture more of Staples's small-business customers. These customers were often willing to buy higher-margin items, thus leading to Staples's higher-than-average margins. In an industry with lots of stores, catalogues, and Internet sites offering similar merchandise at similar prices, maintaining a competitive advantage would not be easy. Further, Sargent worried about offering the same products and services to the same customers through multiple channels. Would this strategy generate channel conflict within the company?

Questions for Discussion

1. How are store, catalogue, and Internet-based distribution channels alike or different in terms of the channel functions they perform?

2. Do you see any potential for conflict among Staples's different channels? Why or why not?

3. Is the Staples/FleetBoston horizontal marketing effort a good idea? Why or why not?

4. What are the advantages of more intensive development of individual market areas versus the advantages of putting more stores in new markets?

5. How can Staples develop a competitive advantage in a commodity market? What marketing recommendations would you make to Staples?

Sources: "Staples, Inc.," Corporate Technology Information Services, Inc., July 3, 2002; W. Julian, "Staples, Inc.," Salomon Smith Barney, June 21, 2002; Alissa Swchmelkin, "Fleet to Open Offices in Staples," *American Banker,* July 11, 2002, p. 20; "Staples' eProcurement System Integration Available On-Line," *Office Products International,* May 2002, p. 13; Alex Philippidis, "Whither the Warehouse Look: Can Staples, OfficeMax Raise Profits by Lowering Shelves," *Westchester County Business Journal,* April 1, 2002, p. 14; "Staples Reports Strong Q4," *Office Products International,* April 2002, p. 14; Joseph Pereira, "Staples Inc. Pulls Back on Its Store-Expansion Plans, *Wall Street Journal,* March 13, 2002, p. B4; and A. H. Rubinson, "Staples," UBS Warburg, December 10, 2001.

CBC Video Case

Log on to your Companion Website at **www.pearsoned.ca/kotler** to view a CBC video segment and case for this chapter.

Chapter 14

Retailing and Wholesaling

After studying this chapter you should be able to

1. explain the roles of retailers and wholesalers in the marketing channel

2. describe the major types of retailers and give examples of each

3. identify the major types of wholesalers and give examples of each

4. explain the marketing decisions facing retailers and wholesalers

Looking Ahead: Previewing the Concepts

In the previous chapter, you learned the basics of marketing channel design and channel partner relationship management. Now, we'll look more deeply into the two major intermediary channel functions, retailing and wholesaling. You already know something about retailing—you're served every day by retailers of all shapes and sizes. However, you probably know much less about the hoard of wholesalers that work behind the scenes. In this chapter, we'll investigate the characteristics of different kinds of retailers and wholesalers, the marketing decisions they make, and trends for the future. You'll see that the retailing and wholesaling landscapes are changing rapidly to match explosive changes in markets and technology.

To start, we'll look at the Forzani Group, Canada's largest specialty sports retailer. You probably know it better as Sport Chek, Coast Mountain Sports, or Sport Mart. As Chief Executive Officer Bob Sartor says, "Our strategic focus is a simple one that is easy for all of our 11 000 corporate and franchise employees to embrace. We have a focus on being the best store in town—with a passion for exceptional merchandise, superior customer service, and extensive marketing."

When a company manages to please "hard as nails" consumers and climbs from near-bankruptcy to the top of the heap, that's extreme retailing! It was just a few years ago that many analysts were forecasting the demise of the Forzani Group Ltd. as it faced an unprecedented onslaught from American big-box sporting-goods stores. However, the Calgary-based retailer refused to roll over and play dead. Moreover, despite a brutal economic slowdown, it has been profitable for the last consecutive six years. Even more astounding may be the fact that its sales grew by over 20 percent in the 2002–2003 period, even though the sporting-goods market grew by a mere 5.4 percent!

Part of this growth is due to the firm's acquisition strategy. It acquired Coast Mountain Sports in 2000 and Sport Mart in 2001. But acquisition alone cannot explain Forzani's success. Much of it is also due to the insight, drive, and enthusiasm of owner/founder John Forzani. One analyst describes him as "the only man at the 12-mile mark in a 26-mile marathon."

John Forzani, a former lineman with the Calgary Stampeders, has always loved the sporting-goods industry and has been able to spot trends and opportunities. "The beauty of this business," he says, "is that we're in an industry that is constantly growing, and has been for the past thirty years." New technologies to improve performance and new sports such as snowboarding are constantly being born, creating the need for new, specialized equipment.

The Forzani Group Ltd. is the only national sporting-goods retailer in Canada. Unlike some of its smaller competitors, it sells a vast assortment of sports-related products, from athletic footwear to sports equipment. Its size allows it to achieve economies of scale in both purchasing and advertising. Forzani markets products using national brands as well as its own private labels, operating 376 stores under the banners Sport Chek, Sports Experts, Coast Mountain Sports, and Sport Mart. There is an online operation at www.sportchek.ca and www.sportmart.ca. The Forzani Group is also a franchisor whose operations include Sports Experts, Intersport, RnR, Econosports, and Atmosphere.

Forzani's unique, multi-banner concept allows it to tailor its mix of quality products to meet the specific needs and preferences of its broad base of consumers, no matter what price point they prefer. Expert advice, value pricing, selection, and customer service are hallmarks of the Forzani shopping experience.

By the end of 2002, the Canadian sporting goods industry accounted for $6.6 billion in sales. With over $1 billion in sales, Forzani commands 15.9 percent of this marketplace. Its competitors include department stores like Canadian Tire (9.2 percent of the market) and Sears, mass merchants like Wal-Mart (5.2 percent of industry sales), regional and independent sporting goods stores, and footwear and clothing chains.

Forzani has certainly had its ups and downs. It was founded in 1974 by John Forzani and three partners. With one Calgary store selling just two shoe brands, Adidas and Puma, their aim certainly wasn't to be top of the sports retailing heap. "The idea was to sell high-end footwear that was hard to find in Canada," Forzani remembers. The chain experienced explosive growth during the 1980s, driven by that decade's fitness boom and growing interest in professional and amateur sports. However, growth and profitability always attract competitors and soon U.S. superstores like the Sports Authority started to threaten homegrown players. Initially, their entry spelled tough times for Forzani.

Sports Authority, a Florida-based company, was extremely successful in the U.S. It attributed its success to its ability to carry extremely deep assortments of prod-

ucts—164 types of baseball bats, 500 different styles of athletic shoes, and over 20 000 apparel items. Forzani's stores were much smaller than many of their American competitors. However, as in sports, sometimes smaller, more nimble competitors win. Although the larger, standardized American stores could carry larger amounts of inventory, the flexible size and format of the Forzani stores meant they could be designed to meet the specific needs of the local marketplace. Furthermore, the smaller size of Forzani chain stores allowed the company to locate them in existing shopping malls that consumers could easily access, rather than in the fringe locations where American firms built their megastores. Finally, size and selection wasn't the deciding factor in this battle, according to Forzani. Members of the Forzani chain pride themselves on their ability to serve customers. Forzani goes out of its way to reward store personnel who give exceptional service.

Another weapon in the chain's sports bag of tricks has been its ongoing focus on keeping costs low. Again, John Forzani leads by example. He goes so far as to wedge his husky frame into economy-class seats when he travels. When Forzani managers travel in pairs, they must share rooms. Not only does this save money, it makes for effective team building, just as it does in professional sports, Forzani believes. Being able to buy in volume for the entire chain helps the firm get better deals from suppliers. Similarly, Forzani's ability to use umbrella advertising for the chain also keeps advertising costs lower than if separate ads had to be formulated for regional markets.

The key to winning has been the chain's ability to focus on its key drivers of success. It carries this thinking into the vast array of community activities it supports. Forzani only accepts sponsorship requests from sports-oriented events that promote a healthy, active lifestyle and those that give back to the community on a broad scale or have a charitable association. There is no doubt that the Forzani Group knows how to keep its eye on the ball.[1]

The Forzani Group Ltd. story provides many insights into the workings of one of Canada's most successful retailers. This chapter looks at *retailing* and *wholesaling*. In the first section we look at the nature and importance of retailing, major types of store and non-store retailers, the decisions retailers make, and the future of retailing in Canada and abroad. In the second section, we discuss these same topics as they relate to wholesalers.

Retailing
All activities involved in selling goods or services directly to final consumers for their personal, non-business use.

Retailing

What is retailing? We all know that Wal-Mart, Sears, and the Bay are retailers, but so are Avon representatives, Amazon.com, the local Holiday Inn, and a dentist seeing patients. **Retailing** includes all the activities involved in selling products or

Retailers
Businesses whose sales come primarily from retailing.

services directly to final consumers for their personal, non-business use. Many institutions—manufacturers, wholesalers, and non-profit organizations—do retailing. But most retailing is done by **retailers,** businesses whose sales come *primarily* from retailing.

Although most retailing is done in retail stores, non-store retailing has been growing much faster than has store retailing. Non-store retailing includes selling to final consumers through direct mail, catalogues, telephone, the Internet, home TV shopping shows, home and office parties, door-to-door contact, vending machines, and other direct-selling approaches. Research has shown that customers who take advantage of this wide range of channels spend ten times more than shoppers who use a single channel. Specifically, Digitrends found that one retailer's Web-only customers spent $181 per year, those buying in stores spent $291, and catalogue customers spent $438—but customers who shopped all three channels spent $1575.[2]

For ease of discussion and presentation, we've separated the different types of retailing. In this chapter, we focus on store retailing. We discuss direct marketing approaches in detail in Chapter 17.

Types of Retailers

Retailing is an important sector in the Canadian economy. The Retail Council of Canada reports that retailing accounts for 7.1 percent of employment in the country (compare this with the 9.3 percent accounted for by the manufacturing sector). In Ontario, it accounts for 12 percent of the jobs. There are 194 079 retail stores in Canada. Together, they account for almost $340 billion in operating revenues. Independent outlets account for 61 percent of total revenues, while chains make up the remaining 39 percent.[3]

Retail stores come in all shapes and sizes, and new retail types keep emerging. The most prevalent types of retail stores are described in Table 14.1 and discussed in the following sections. They can be classified in terms of several characteristics, including the *amount of service* they offer, the breadth and depth of their *product lines,* the *relative prices* they charge, and how they are *organized.*

The Canadian retail landscape has seen both consolidation and growth. For example, the number of grocery retail outlets and mass merchandisers have increased. Drug retailers, on the other hand, have closed outlets. ACNielsen Canada Homescan Panel found that Canadian consumers are shopping more frequently in mass and warehouse club channels. Dollar stores are also attracting an increased number of consumers. Grocery retailing is much more concentrated within Canada than it is in the U.S.—thus, it is not surprising that corporate grocery retailers like Loblaw Companies Limited occupy four of the top ten retailing spots. Shoppers Drug Mart similarly dominates drug retailing.[4] Table 14.2 on page 549 lists some of Canada's major retailers along with their revenues.

Amount of Service

Different products require different amounts of service, and customer service preferences vary. Retailers may offer one of three levels of service—self-service, limited service, and full service.

Self-service retailers serve customers who are willing to perform their own "locate-compare-select" process to save money. Self-service is the basis of all discount operations and typically is used by sellers of convenience goods (such as supermarkets) and nationally branded, fast-moving shopping goods (such as Future Shop and Best Buy).

Limited-service retailers, such as Sears, provide more sales assistance because they carry more shopping goods about which customers need information. Their increased operating costs result in higher prices. In *full-service retailers,* such as specialty stores like Birks and first-class department stores like Holt Renfrew,

Table 14.1   Major Store Retailer Types

Specialty Stores: Carry a narrow product line with a deep assortment, such as apparel stores, sporting-goods stores, furniture stores, florists, and bookstores. A clothing store would be a *single-line* store, a men's clothing store would be a *limited-line store,* and a men's custom-shirt store would be a *superspecialty* store. Examples: The Body Shop, Gap, The Athlete's Foot.

Department Stores: Carry several product lines—typically clothing, home furnishings, and household goods—with each line operated as a separate department managed by specialist buyers or merchandisers. Examples: The Bay, Sears.

Supermarkets: A relatively large, low-cost, low-margin, high-volume, self-service operation designed to serve the consumer's total needs for food and household products. Examples: Safeway Foods, Loblaws, Sobeys, Thrifty, Food Basics, A&P.

Convenience Stores: Relatively small stores located near residential areas, open long hours seven days a week, and carrying a limited line of high-turnover convenience products at slightly higher prices. Examples: Becker's, Mac's, Couche-Tarde, Provi-Soir, 7-Eleven.

Discount Stores: Carry standard merchandise sold at lower prices with lower margins and higher volumes. Examples: General—Zellers, Wal-Mart. Specialty—Future Shop, The Brick, Best Buy.

Off-Price Retailers: Sell merchandise bought at less-than-regular wholesale prices and sold at less than retail: often leftover goods, overruns, and irregulars obtained at reduced prices from manufacturers or other retailers. These include *factory outlets* owned and operated by manufacturers (examples: Mikasa, Liz Claiborne, Ralph Lauren); *independent off-price retailers* owned and run by entrepreneurs or by divisions of larger retail corporations (examples: Winners, Dollarama, The Silver Dollar); and *warehouse (or wholesale) clubs* selling a limited selection of brand-name groceries, appliances, clothing, and other goods at deep discounts to consumers who pay membership fees (examples: Max Club, Costco, Sam's Club, BJ's Wholesale Club).

Superstores: Very large stores traditionally aimed at meeting consumers' total needs for routinely purchased food and non-food items. Includes *category killers,* which carry a deep assortment in a particular category and have a knowledgeable staff (examples: Chapters.Indigo, Petsmart, Staples); *supercentres,* combined supermarket and discount stores (example: Wal-Mart and Loblaws supercenters); and *hypermarkets,* with up to 20 000 square metres of space combining supermarket, discount, and warehouse retailing (examples: Carrefour [France], Pyrca [Spain], Meijers [Netherlands]).

salespeople assist customers in every phase of the shopping process. Full-service stores usually carry more specialty goods for which customers like to be "waited on." They provide more services, resulting in much higher operating costs, which are passed along to customers as higher prices.

Product Line

Retailers can also be classified by the length and breadth of their product assortments. Some retailers, such as **specialty stores**, carry narrow product lines with deep assortments within those lines. Today, specialty stores are flourishing. The increasing use of market segmentation, market targeting, and product specialization has resulted in a greater need for stores that focus on specific products and segments.

In contrast, **department stores** carry a wide variety of product lines. In recent years, department stores have been squeezed between more focused and flexible specialty stores on the one hand, and more efficient, lower-priced discounters on the other. In response, many have added promotional events to meet the discount threat. Others have set up the use of store brands and single-brand "designer shops" to compete with specialty stores. Still others are trying mail-order, telephone, and Web selling. Service and outstanding product assortments remain the key differentiating factors. Department stores such as Holt Renfrew and other high-end department stores are doing well by emphasizing high-quality service.

Supermarkets are the most frequently shopped type of retail store. Today, however, they are facing slow sales growth because of slower population growth and an increase in competition from convenience stores, discount food stores, and superstores. Supermarkets also have been hit hard by the rapid growth of out-of-home eating. Thus, most supermarkets are making improvements to attract more customers. In the battle for "share of stomachs," many large supermarkets have moved

Specialty store
A retail store that carries a narrow product line with a deep assortment within that line.

Department store
A retailer that carries a wide variety of product lines—typically clothing, home furnishings, and household goods; each line is operated as a separate department managed by specialist buyers or merchandisers.

Supermarket
A large, low-cost, low-margin, high-volume, self-service store that carries a wide variety of food, laundry, and household products.

Table 14.2 Canada's Top Retailers by Category

Sector Company	2002 Revenues ($ thousands)
Food distribution	
Loblaw Companies Ltd.	$23 099 000
Sobeys Inc.	9 732 500
Westfair Foods	6 611 728
Canada Safeway	5 493 845
Metro Inc.	5 146 800
Great A&P Tea Co.	(US$)2 483 211
Alimentation Couche-Tard	2 443 952
Loeb Canada	525 869
Retailers	
Hudson's Bay Co.	7 390 733
Costco Wholesale Canada	7 318 199
Katz Group	6 600 000
Sears Canada	6 537 400
Canadian Tire Corp.	5 944 500
Zellers	4 656 274
Shoppers Drug Mart	14 030 000
Jean Coutu Group	3 586 186
Rona Inc.	2 332 119
Forzani Group	923 795
Banks	
Royal Bank of Canada	23 234 000
Bank of Nova Scotia	18 310 000
Canadian Imperial Bank of Commerce	17 055 000
Toronto-Dominion Bank	16 680 000
Bank of Montreal	16 685 000

Source: From "The Top 1000: Canada's Power Book, Revenue rankings by Industry," *Report on Business Magazine,* July 2003, pp. 132, 130, 125.

Convenience store

A small store located near a residential area that is open long hours seven days a week and carries a limited line of high-turnover convenience goods.

upscale, providing from-scratch bakeries, gourmet deli counters, and fresh seafood departments. Others are cutting costs, establishing more efficient operations, and lowering prices in order to compete more effectively with food discounters.

Convenience stores are small stores that carry a limited line of high-turnover convenience goods. These stores locate near residential areas and remain open long hours, seven days a week. When supermarkets won the right to open for business on Sundays, and drugstore chains and gas station boutiques began selling groceries and snack foods, convenience stores lost their monopoly on their key differentiating variable—*convenience*. The industry has suffered from overcapacity as its primary market of young, blue-collar men has shrunk. The result has been a huge industry shakeout.

While many of the "mom-and-pop" stores that once dominated the industry are closing, others are being opened by the huge chains. For example, even though Couche-Tard may not exactly be a household name, it is Canada's largest operator of convenience stores. Its outlets operate under the Couche-Tard name as well as such banners as Mac's, Becker's, Mike's Mart, and Daisy Mart. The chain has been growing in both size and profitability for some time, but in October 2003, it really got a boost when it purchased the U.S.-based Circle K chain. The takeover makes Couche-Tard North America's fourth largest convenience store operator, with 4630 stores.

Turning many of its convenience stores into destination outlets featuring branded products has enabled Couche-Tard to achieve superior profitability.

Le plein?

How has Couche-Tard grown so dramatically in a shrinking industry? By positioning its stores as destination outlets. Gone are the days of the dingy corner store that once sold overpriced emergency goods. Couche-Tard outlets feature a product mix carefully crafted to meet the needs of local consumers. Those in upscale areas offer such high-margin, mouth-watering, fresh-baked goods as croissants that customers can eat at in-store cafés. Those in areas frequented by male, blue-collar workers stock meat-laden sandwiches. Not only do the outlets offer a wide range of convenience items that are competitively priced, the stores feature ATMs, fax machines, photocopiers, and stamp machines. Many are combined with gas bars. Their new pay-at-the-pump technology allows drivers to check out faster.

Like their larger rivals, Couche-Tard convenience stores have started branding their own food items. Using bar-code scanners, they manage their inventory closely to avoid "dust collectors." Like many savvy marketers, Couche-Tard also knows that employee ability and satisfaction is highly correlated with customer satisfaction. Therefore, it invests heavily in employee training so that its stores can offer the service and merchandising that rival their larger competitors.[5]

Superstores are much larger than regular supermarkets and offer a large assortment of routinely purchased food products, non-food items, and services. Wal-Mart and Loblaws offer *supercentres* that emphasize cross-merchandising. Toasters are above the fresh-baked bread, kitchen gadgets are across from produce, and infant centres carry everything from baby food to clothing. SuperValu, which even calls itself "the real Canadian Superstore," has locations from Thunder Bay, Ontario, west to Vancouver, British Columbia, with stores in all of Western Canada's major cities, including Whitehorse in the Yukon. SuperValu stores carry everything from telephones and children's apparel to fresh fruit and seafood.

Recent years have seen the advent of superstores that are actually giant specialty stores, the so-called **category killers**. These "big-box" retailers are megastores that have crossed the border from the United States. They feature stores the size of airplane hangars and carry a very deep assortment of a particular line with a knowledgeable staff. Category killers are prevalent in a wide range of categories, including books, baby gear, toys, electronics, home improvement products, linens and towels, party goods, sporting goods, and even pet supplies. Home Depot Canada, Chapters, Office Depot, The Sports Authority, and Michaels Arts and Crafts are among the many recent entrants into the Canadian marketplace.

Superstore
A store almost twice the size of a regular supermarket that carries a large assortment of routinely purchased food and non-food items and offers such services as dry cleaning, post offices, photo finishing, cheque cashing, bill paying, lunch counters, car care, and pet care.

Category killer
Giant specialty store that carries a very deep assortment of a particular line and is staffed by knowledgeable employees.

Category killers: Best Buy has stores the size of airplane hangars that carry a deep assortment of consumer electronics, personal computers, entertainment software, and appliances.

Another superstore variation, the *hypermarket,* is a huge superstore perhaps as large as six football fields. Although hypermarkets have been very successful in Europe and other world markets, they have met with little success in North America.

Finally, for some businesses, the product line is actually a service. Service retailers include hotels and motels, banks, airlines, universities, movie theatres, tennis clubs, bowling alleys, restaurants, repair services, hair-care shops, and dry cleaners. Service retailers in Canada are growing faster than product retailers.

Relative Prices

Retailers can also be classified according to the prices they charge (see Table 14.1 on page 548). Most retailers charge regular prices and offer normal-quality goods and customer service. Others offer higher-quality goods and services at higher prices. The retailers that feature low prices are discount stores and "off-price" retailers.

Discount store

A retail institution that sells standard merchandise at lower prices by accepting lower margins and selling at higher volume.

Discount Stores A **discount store** sells standard merchandise at lower prices by accepting lower margins and selling at higher volume. The early discount stores cut expenses by offering few services and operating in warehouse-like facilities in low-rent, heavily travelled districts. In recent years, facing intense competition from other discounters and department stores, many discount retailers have "traded up." They have improved décor, added new lines and services, and expanded regionally and nationally, leading to higher costs and prices.

Off-price retailer

Retailer that buys at less-than-regular wholesale prices and sells at less than retail. Examples are factory outlets, independents, and warehouse clubs.

Off-Price Retailers When the major discount stores traded up, a new wave of **off-price retailers** moved in to fill the low-price, high-volume gap. Ordinary discounters buy at regular wholesale prices and accept lower margins to keep prices down. In contrast, off-price retailers buy at less-than-regular wholesale prices and charge consumers less than retail. Off-price retailers can be found in all areas, from food, clothing, and electronics to no-frills banking and discount brokerages.

There are three main types of off-price retailers: *independents, factory outlets,* and *warehouse clubs.* One of the fastest growing is the dollar store:

"Why pay $5 if you can pay $1 and get just as nice a card?" This is the kind of question more and more shoppers are answering by going to dollar stores. In the last ten years, the lowly dollar store has moved from the fringe of retailing to become one of the hottest retail trends. They've become so respectable that they are now in some better malls. Dollar stores are even setting the retailing

Dollar stores are the fastest-growing retail phenomena in Canada's retailing landscape.

agenda. Loblaw Companies Limited, Great Atlantic & Pacific Tea Co., and Wal-Mart Stores Inc. are all piloting dollar-store merchandise. "The dollar-store phenomenon is growing and consumers have accepted that," said Doug Brummer, senior vice-president of marketing at A&P Canada. "We wanted to get a piece of that action. It has certainly paid off." The numbers support this contention. In 2002, dollar stores' sales rose 12.6 percent, more than twice the 6 percent average growth rate for Canadian retailing. Stores like The Silver Dollar, Dollarama, and the franchised Buck or Two stores (Canada's largest dollar-store chain) appeal to a broader mix of consumers than ever before. Customers range from the budget-conscious to the well-heeled who shop at the stores before throwing a party or heading off to the cottage. And while the chains are building bigger and brighter stores, the real drawing power is the merchandising. Products that were unthinkable at only $1 twenty years ago are commonplace today. Product sourcing has come a long way, with the larger chains importing directly from overseas, trimming costs by cutting out the middleman. The chains are creating their own packaging and private labels. Some are adding clothing and name-brand cosmetics. And the consumers just keep flocking in to grab up better and better bargains.[6]

Organizational Approach

Although many retail stores are independently owned, an increasing number are banding together under some form of corporate or contractual organization. The major types of retail organizations—*corporate chains, voluntary chains* and *retailer cooperatives, franchise organizations,* and *merchandising conglomerates*—are described in Table 14.3.

Chain stores are two or more outlets that are commonly owned and controlled. They have many advantages over independents. Their size allows them to buy in large quantities at lower prices and gain promotional economies. They can hire specialists

Chain stores

Two or more outlets that are commonly owned and controlled, have central buying and merchandising, and sell similar lines of merchandise.

Table 14.3   Major Types of Retail Organizations

Type	Description	Examples
Corporate chains	Two or more outlets that are commonly owned and controlled, employ central buying and merchandising, and sell similar lines of merchandise. Corporate chains appear in all types of retailing, but they are strongest in department stores, variety stores, drugstores, food stores, shoe stores, and women's clothing stores.	La Senza (lingerie), Sports Experts (sports goods), Loblaws (groceries), Pottery Barn (housewares)
Voluntary chains	Wholesaler-sponsored groups of independent retailers engaged in bulk buying and common merchandising.	Independent Grocers Alliance (IGA), Western Auto, True Value Hardware
Retailer cooperatives	Groups of independent retailers that set up a central buying organization and conduct joint promotion efforts.	Calgary Group (groceries), ACE (hardware), Mountain Equipment Co-op (outdoor goods)
Franchise organizations	Contractual association between a franchiser (a manufacturer, wholesaler, or organization) and franchisees (independent businesspeople who buy the right to own and operate one or more units in the franchise system). Franchise organizations are normally based on some unique product, service, or method of doing business, or on a trade name or patent, or on goodwill that the franchiser has developed.	McDonald's, Subway, Pizza Hut, Jiffy Lube, 7-Eleven, Yogen Früz
Merchandising conglomerates	A free-form corporation that combines several diversified retailing lines and forms under central ownership, along with some integration of their distribution and management functions.	The Venator Group (owner of Foot Locker, Lady Foot Locker, Northern Reflections, Northern Traditions), Target Corporation

to deal with areas such as pricing, promotion, merchandising, inventory control, and sales forecasting.

Forty percent of Canadian retailers belong to some type of chain, making retailing more concentrated in Canada than it is in the U.S., where only 20 percent of retailers are chain members. Many U.S.-based chain stores have invaded Canada, and more are on the way. For example, Old Navy (the discount division of Gap), American Eagle Outfitters, and Skechers USA Inc. (a trendy California-based shoe store) have recently entered the Canadian market.[7] While many of these operations are welcomed by consumers, they threaten to take business away from their Canadian rivals. To fight this invasion, Canadian chains often consolidate even further.

The great success of corporate chains caused many independents to band together in contractual associations. One form is the *voluntary chain*—a wholesaler-sponsored group of independent retailers that engages in group buying and common merchandising, which we discussed in Chapter 13. Examples of this form include the Independent Grocers Alliance (IGA) and Western Auto. The other form of contractual association is the *retailer cooperative*—independent retailers that band together to set up a jointly owned, central wholesale operation and conduct joint merchandising and promotion efforts. True Value Hardware is an example of this contractual association. These organizations give independents the buying and promotion economies they need to meet the prices of corporate chains.

Franchise

A contractual association between a manufacturer, wholesaler, or service organization (a franchiser) and independent businesspeople (franchisees), who buy the right to own and operate one or more units in the franchise system.

Another form of contractual association is a **franchise**. The main difference between franchise organizations and other contractual systems (voluntary chains and retail cooperatives) is that franchise systems are normally based on some unique product or service; on a method of doing business; or on the trade name, goodwill, or patent that the franchiser has developed. Franchising has been prominent in fast foods, video stores, health and fitness centres, motels, auto rentals, hair-cutting, real estate, travel agencies, and dozens of other product and service areas. Franchising is described in detail in Real Marketing 14.1.

14.1 Franchise Fever

Once considered upstarts among independent businesses, there are now 75 809 franchised businesses operating in Canada. Collectively they generate over $100 billion in sales annually and employ 1.5 million people. Franchises account for approximately 50 percent of all service and retail sales in Canada, compared to approximately 35 percent in the United States. A new franchise opens in Canada every two hours, 365 days a year. Many franchise ideas are born right here in Canada. But now American and European franchise operators are also targeting Canada, recognizing the significant opportunities our marketplace offers.

According to Francon, Canada's sole franchise research company, Canadians have embraced franchising as a means of self-employment to a far greater extent than the population of any other country. This isn't hard to believe in a society where it's nearly impossible to stroll down a city block or drive on a suburban thoroughfare without seeing a Tim Hortons, McDonald's, Midas Muffler, Burger King, GNC, or Dollar Store. In fact, you might be forgiven for thinking every streetcorner in Canada is occupied by a Tim Hortons. In 2003, the TDL Group Ltd., which operates the franchises, had 2200 stores across Canada and employed over 55 000 people. It is also steadily growing its base of 160 locations in key markets within the United States.

Franchising is highly competitive and not without its challenges. Take Toronto-based Pet Valu Canada Inc., for example. With more than 350 stores across Ontario, Manitoba, and the northeastern United States, the franchise is facing new competition from both massive American chains such as PETsMART and a new Canadian upstart, Vancouver-based Petcetera. One Pet Valu owner notes that his staff must be as "knowledgeable and friendly as possible, because they can't offer the 15 000 to 25 000 square feet of pet merchandise that larger big-box retailers [offer]." The smaller Pet Valu stores must decide how to stock enough variety to keep customers interested and still maintain a neighbourhood approach. Pet Valu also features lines of private-label brands such as Performatrin and Feline Cuisine for customers who are on a budget, but still intend to keep their pets healthy.

Franchising is becoming an international phenomenon. While not as developed in other countries as in Canada, franchising is growing worldwide. Take McDonald's, for example: One of the best-known and most successful franchisers, it now has 30 000 stores in 120 countries, serving more than 46 million customers a day and racking up more than $40 billion in system-wide sales. More than 70 percent of McDonald's restaurants worldwide are owned and operated by franchisees. Gaining fast is Subway Sandwiches and Salads, one of the fastest-growing franchises, with more than 19 000 shops in 74 countries, including some 1700 in Canada. Franchising is even moving into new areas such as education. For example, LearnRight Corporation franchises its methods for teaching students thinking skills.

A number of Canadian franchise operations are also reaching beyond their domestic borders and trying to hook the world on the baked goods that have expanded our waistlines. Calgary-based Cinnzeo, for example, is the world's second-largest cinnamon bun franchise

Canada's Cinnzeo operates franchises in Western Canada and has ambitious plans for overseas expansion.

operation, after Atlanta-based giant Cinnabon. And their sugary empire continues to grow. It has recently opened stores in Beirut and Saudi Arabia, and forecasts further expansion into South America, Australia, Eastern Canada, and the U.S.

How does a franchising system work? The individual franchises are a tightly knit group of enterprises whose systematic operations are planned, directed, and controlled by the operation's founder, called a *franchisor*. Generally, franchises are distinguished by three characteristics:

- *The franchisor owns a trade or service mark and licenses it to franchisees in return for royalty payments.*

- *The franchisee is required to pay for the right to be part of the system.* Yet this initial fee is only a small part of the total amount that franchisees invest when they sign a franchising contract. Start-up costs include rental and lease of equipment and fixtures, and sometimes a regular licence fee. McDonald's franchisees may invest as much as $864 000 in initial start-up costs. The franchisee then pays McDonald's a service fee and a rental charge that equal 11.5 percent of the franchisee's sales volume. Subway's success is partly due to its low start-up cost of $65 000 to $100 000, which is lower than 70 percent of other franchise system start-up costs.

- *The franchisor provides its franchisees with a marketing and operations system for doing business.* McDonald's requires franchisees to attend its "Hamburger University" in Oak Brook, Illinois, for three weeks to learn how to manage the business. Franchisees must also adhere to certain procedures in buying materials.

In the best cases, franchising is mutually beneficial to both franchisor and franchisee. Franchisors can cover a new territory in little more than the time it takes the franchisee to sign a contract. They can achieve enormous purchasing power. (Consider the purchase order that Holiday Inn is likely to make for bed linens, for instance.) Franchisors also benefit from the franchisee's familiarity with local communities and conditions, and from the motivation and hard work of employees who are entrepreneurs rather than "hired hands." Similarly, franchisees benefit from buying into a proven business with a well-known and accepted brand name. And they receive ongoing support in areas ranging from marketing and advertising to site selection, staffing, and financing.

As a result of the franchise explosion in recent years, many types of franchisors are having difficulty. John Lorinc, author of *Opportunity Knocks: The Truth about Canada's Franchise Industry,* says 35 percent of all franchises fail and 80 percent may only break even. Subway, in particular, has been criticized for misleading its franchisees by telling them that it has only a 2 percent failure rate when the reality is much different. Some franchisees also believe that they've been misled by exaggerated claims of support, only to feel abandoned after the contract is signed and $100 000 is invested. Difficulties may arise due to hidden costs imposed on franchisees or the signing up of people who lack the resources to get the business off the ground. The most common complaint: franchisors focused on growth who "encroach" on existing franchisees' territory by bringing in another store. Or franchisees may object to parent-company marketing programs that may adversely affect their local operations. For instance, franchisees strongly resisted a McDonald's promotion in which the company reduced prices on Big Macs and Egg McMuffins in an effort to revive stagnant sales. Many franchisees believed that the promotion would cheapen McDonald's image and unnecessarily reduce their profit margins.

There will *always* be a conflict between the franchisors, who seek system-wide growth, and the franchisees, who want to earn a good living from their individual franchises. Some new directions that may deliver both franchisor growth and franchisee earnings are:

- *Strategic alliances, co-branding, and twinning.* The newest trend in franchising is the marriage between two independent franchises at a single location. Tim Hortons, for example, often shares facilities with Wendy's; Baskin-Robbins teams up with Dunkin Donuts; Second Cup partners with Harvey's. Since the largest costs borne by franchisees are for land and staff, forming an alliance with another franchisee to share a location makes economic sense and can draw a more broad-based market to the joint outlets.

- *Code of ethics.* Each member of the Canadian Franchise Association (www.cfa.ca) is bound by a code of ethics designed to overcome some areas of difficulty. The code stipulates these conditions: There will be a full and accurate written disclosure of all information considered material to the franchise relationship. The company selling the franchise will provide reasonable guidance, training, and supervision for franchisees. Fairness shall characterize all dealings between the franchisor and its franchisees. The franchisor shall make every effort to resolve complaints, grievances, and disputes through fair and reasonable negotiation.

- *Non-traditional site locations.* Franchises have opened in airports, sports stadiums, university campuses, hospitals, gambling casinos, theme parks, convention halls, and even riverboats.

Franchise fever is unlikely to cool down soon. Canadian franchisors like Uniglobe Travel International, Speedy Muffler King, Priority Management Systems Inc., and Manchu Wok are not only growing in Canada, they are conquering international markets as well.

Sources: BeTheBoss Canada website, www.betheboss.ca/about-franchising.htm (accessed August 2003); Jordan Heath-Rawlings,

"Pet Valu Seeks to Mark its Territory," *Globe and Mail,* August 4, 2003, pp. B1, B4; Norma Ranage, "Battle of the Buns," *Marketing Magazine,* September 2, 2002, pp. 10–11; David Stires, "Fallen Arches," *Fortune,* April 29, 2002, pp. 74–76; Anne Smith, "Landmark 16 000th Subway Restaurant Opens" (press release), March 2002, www.subway.com; "Canada: Welcome to Subway, eh!" www.subway.com/subwayroot/AroundTheWorld/Countries/canada/index.aspx; Norman D. Axelrad and Robert E. Weigand, "Franchising—A Marriage of System Members," in Sidney Levy, George Frerichs, and Howard Gordon, eds., *Marketing Managers Handbook,* 3rd ed., Chicago: Darnell, 1994:919–34; Lawrence S. Welch, "Developments in International Franchising," *Journal of Global Marketing,* 6(1–2), 1992, pp. 81–96; "Canadian Franchise Association Code of Ethics," *Globe and Mail* (advertising supplement), September 18, 1996, p. 6; Jennifer Lanthier, "How Franchises Seduce those with the Most to Lose," *Financial Post,* April 22, 1997, p. 28; Susan Noakes, "Creating Marriages of Convenience," *Financial Post,* February 14, 1997, p. 16; and Industry Canada, "Canadian Capabilities: Key facts about Canadian Franchise Expertise," strategis.ic.gc.ca/SSG/dm01301e.html; www.cfa.ca/.

Finally, *merchandising conglomerates* are corporations that combine several retailing forms under central ownership and share some distribution and management functions. The Venator Group (www.venatorgroup.com) operates a number of specialty chains including Northern Reflections, Northern Traditions, Northern Elements, and Northern Getaway, as well as Kinney Shoe Stores and Foot Locker (sports shoes). Diversified retailing, which provides superior management systems and economies that benefit all the separate retail operations, is likely to increase.

Retailer Marketing Decisions

Retailers are searching for new marketing strategies to attract and hold customers. In the past, retailers attracted customers with unique products, more or better services than their competitors offered, or credit cards. Today, national-brand manufacturers, in their drive for volume, have placed their branded goods everywhere. National brands are found not only in department stores, but also in mass-merchandise and off-price discount stores, and on the Web. As a result, stores are looking more alike.

Service differentiation between retailers has also eroded. Many department stores have trimmed their services, whereas discounters have increased theirs. Customers have become smarter and more price sensitive. They see no reason to pay more for identical brands, especially when service differences are shrinking. For all these reasons, many retailers are rethinking their marketing strategies.

As shown in Figure 14.1, retailers face major marketing decisions about their *target market* and *positioning, product assortment and services, price, promotion,* and *place.*

Target Market and Positioning Decision

Retailers first must define their target markets and decide how they will position themselves in these markets. Should the store focus on upscale, midscale, or downscale shoppers? Do target shoppers want variety, depth of assortment, convenience, or low prices? Until they define and profile their markets, retailers cannot make consistent decisions about product assortment, services, pricing, advertising, store décor, or any of the other decisions that must support their positions.

Retailer strategy	Retailer marketing mix
Target market	Product assortment and services
Retail store positioning	Price
	Promotion
	Place (location)

Figure 14.1 Retailer marketing decisions

Too many retailers fail to define their target markets and positions clearly. They try to have "something for everyone" and end up satisfying no market well. In contrast, successful retailers define their target markets well and position themselves strongly.

Even large stores such as Wal-Mart and Sears must define their major target markets to design effective marketing strategies. In fact, in recent years, thanks to strong targeting and positioning, Wal-Mart has become not just the world's largest retailer, but the world's largest *company*.

The Retail Council of Canada named Dave Ferguson, president and CEO of Wal-Mart Canada, as Distinguished Canadian Retailer of the Year in 2000, noting, "Wal-Mart Canada has become a shining star not only in the Canadian retail marketplace, but in the international Wal-Mart organization as well." Wal-Mart Canada has shaped the Canadian retailing scene by pushing other retailers to improve customer service, competitive product offerings, and supply chain management. It has also set the standard in giving back to the community, donating over $6 million to local charities and causes.

What are the secrets behind this spectacular success? Wal-Mart knows its customers and takes good care of them. As one analyst puts it, "The company gospel... is relatively simple: Be an agent for customers, find out what they want, and sell it to them for the lowest possible price." The company stays close to customers—for

Thanks to strong targeting and positioning, Wal-Mart has become not just the world's largest retailer, but the world's largest company.

example, each top Wal-Mart executive spends at least two days a week visiting stores, talking directly with customers, and getting a first-hand look at operations. Then, Wal-Mart delivers what customers want—a broad selection of carefully selected goods at unbeatable prices. But the right merchandise at the right price isn't the only key to Wal-Mart's success. Compared with other discounters, Wal-Mart also provides the kind of service that keeps customers satisfied.

Wal-Mart's success hasn't gone unnoticed at universities across North America. More and more professors use Wal-Mart Stores as an example to illustrate business concepts. Some professors hold up Wal-Mart as an example of how to do things right or to explain important concepts—one even uses Wal-Mart to illustrate ideas like "channel commander," a term for the distributor with the most power. Others turn to Wal-Mart to highlight social problems that may be overlooked in the shopping scramble—issues like the impact of goods that are made abroad and sold cheaply in North America. But the most specific lesson to emerge from Wal-Mart is its focus on controlling costs so that products can be sold for less.[8]

While many stores have closed when faced with competition from Wal-Mart, others like Canadian Tire and Zellers have survived by using improved targeting and positioning and tailored product selection.

Product Assortment and Services Decision

Retailers must decide on three major product variables: *product assortment, services mix,* and *store atmosphere.*

The retailer's *product assortment* must match target shoppers' expectations. One strategy is to offer merchandise that no other competitor carries, such as private brands or national brands on which it holds exclusives. Many of Canada's

best-performing fashion retailers—Club Monaco (www.clubmonaco.com), Roots Canada, and the Venator Group—not only stock their stores with their own brands of clothing, but also extend these brands into new lines of accessories and cosmetics products. Items such as jewellery, belts, backpacks, perfume, and toiletries are used to reinforce the store's brand image.[9] The retailer can feature blockbuster merchandising events—Ben Moss Jewellers, for example, is known throughout Western Canada for their promotions involving celebrities. Finally, the retailer can differentiate itself by offering a highly targeted product assortment—Penningtons and Cotton Ginny Plus carry goods for larger women; the It Store offers an unusual assortment of gadgets in what amounts to a toy store for adults.

The *services mix* can also help set one retailer apart from another. For example, some retailers invite customers to ask questions or consult service representatives in person or via phone or keyboard. Home Depot offers a diverse mix of services to do-it-yourselfers, from "how-to" classes to a proprietary credit card.

The *store's atmosphere* is another element in its product arsenal. Every store has a physical layout that makes moving around in it either hard or easy. Paco Underhill, a retailing consultant, captured the importance of perceived crowding in a store with his "bum-brush" theory. He suggests that the possibility of a shopper making a purchase decreases significantly every time his or her posterior is accidentally brushed by another passerby.[10]

More important, every store has a "feel": one store is cluttered, another charming, a third plush, a fourth sombre. The store must plan an atmosphere that suits the target market and moves customers to buy. For example, Mountain Equipment Co-op practises "experiential retailing": consumers can try out climbing equipment on a huge wall in the store. Many retailers add fragrances in their stores to stimulate certain moods in shoppers. London's Heathrow Airport sprays the scent of pine needles because it evokes the sense of holidays and weekend walks. Automobile dealers will spray a "leather" scent in used cars to make them smell "new." Even colour matters. Indigo's research found that while some customers like the different surroundings of the lighter-hued Indigo, others prefer the more masculine-looking Chapters.[11]

Many of today's successful new retailers, like Virgin, offer entertaining shopping experiences in addition to deep product selection.

Increasingly, retailers are turning their stores into theatres that transport customers into unusual, exciting shopping environments. The music and entertainment Virgin Megastore in downtown Vancouver is the epitome of stores combining shopping and entertainment. The 40 000-square-foot facility has a wealth of interactive features, including an in-store DJ booth, individual listening stations, booths for viewing movies, and a café where people can sip espresso. In-store performances encourage shoppers to spend more time and, of course, more money.[12]

Perhaps the most dramatic conversion of stores into theatre is the West Edmonton Mall, which bills itself as the world's largest shopping and entertainment centre. It features over 800 stores, 110 eating establishments, and seven world-class attractions, including a golf course and a water park.

All of this confirms that retail stores are much more than simply assortments of goods. They are environments to be experienced by the people who shop in them. Store atmospheres offer a powerful tool by which retailers can differentiate their stores from those of competitors.

Price Decision

A retailer's price policy is a crucial positioning factor that must be decided in relation to its target market and positioning, product and service assortment, and competition. All retailers would like to charge high markups and achieve high volume, but the two seldom go together. Most retailers seek *either* high markups on lower volume (most specialty stores) *or* low markups on higher volume (mass merchandisers and discount stores). Thus, Winnipeg-based Hanford Drewitt prices men's suits starting at $1000 and shoes at $400—it sells a low volume but makes a hefty profit on each sale. At the other extreme, Winners sells brand-name clothing at discount prices, settling for a lower margin on each sale but selling at a much higher volume.

Promotion Decision

Retailers use any or all of the promotion tools—advertising, personal selling, sales promotion, public relations, and direct marketing—to reach consumers. They advertise in newspapers, magazines, on billboards, radio, television, and the Internet.

Outdoor advertising is one means by which retailers try to reach consumers. Other media used include newspapers, magazines, radio, television, and the Internet.

Advertising may be supported by newspaper inserts and direct mail. Personal selling requires careful training of salespeople in how to greet customers, meet their needs, and handle their complaints. Sales promotions may include in-store demonstrations, displays, contests, and visiting celebrities. Public relations activities—press conferences and speeches, store openings, special events, newsletters, magazines, and public service activities—are always available to retailers. Most retailers have also set up websites, offering customers information and other features and often selling merchandise directly.

Place Decision

Retailers often point to three critical factors in retailing success: *location, location,* and *location!* It's very important that retailers select locations that are accessible to the target market in areas that are consistent with the retailer's positioning. Small retailers may have to settle for whatever locations they can find or afford. Large retailers usually employ specialists who select locations using advanced methods.

Two of the savviest location experts in recent years have been the off-price retailer TJ Maxx and toy-store giant Toys "R" Us. Both put the majority of their new locations in rapidly growing areas where the population closely matches their customer base. In an ever-intensifying war for the grocery consumer, even Canada's leading supermarket chain, Loblaws, continues to battle the franchised independent supermarkets—Foodland, Freshmart, IGA, Metro, Your Independent Grocer—for the best locations to pre-empt each other's expansion plans. The undisputed winner in the "place race" has been Wal-Mart, whose strategy of being the first mass merchandiser to locate in small and rural markets has been one of the key factors in its phenomenal success.

Most stores today cluster together to increase their customer pulling power and to give consumers the convenience of one-stop shopping.

Central business districts were the main form of retail cluster until the 1950s. Every large city and town had a central business district with department stores, specialty stores, banks, and movie theatres. When people began to move to the suburbs, these central business districts began to lose business. Downtown merchants opened branches in suburban shopping centres. However, in recent years, many cities have joined with merchants to try to revive downtown shopping areas.

The trend to move back downtown has been accelerated by big-box retailers who are scouting out alternative—often smaller—city-centre locations as they aggressively seek out new customers. They can't move into shopping malls because the rental rates are too steep—in Toronto they might pay as much as $100 a square foot (plus spiralling service fees) at an established mall such as Yorkdale, whereas a lease at a suburban power centre (their traditional location) could cost roughly $15 a square foot. At approximately $25 per square foot, downtown locations represent an attractive alternative to the less densely populated areas served by malls and power centres.

Toronto-based Home Depot Canada Inc. is an example of one retailer seeking downtown locations. Its planned downtown outlets will be about half the size of its regular 100 000-square-foot big-box format, and the stores will focus on items such as home decor and gardening rather than building materials. Staples/Business Depot is another retailer that can "do the math." It recently opened a more compact, three-storey outlet in the heart of Toronto's downtown business hub. It also opened a small shop at a central subway station in Montreal, attracting commuters it didn't reach previously. Industry watchers say the trend to non-traditional sites is picking up.[13]

A **shopping centre** is a group of retail businesses planned, developed, owned, and managed as a unit. A *regional shopping centre*, or *regional shopping mall*, the largest and most dramatic type, contains from 40 to over 200 stores. The Eaton Centre in Toronto, Place Ville Marie in Montreal, and West Edmonton Mall are regional shopping centres, featuring a mix of large department stores and many small specialty stores. They attract customers from a wide area. A *community shopping centre* contains 15 to 40 retail stores—normally a branch of a department store or variety store, a supermarket, specialty stores, professional offices, and sometimes a bank. Most shopping centres are *neighbourhood shopping centres* or strip malls that generally contain 5 to 15 stores. They are close and convenient for consumers.

Shopping centre
A retail location planned, developed, owned, and managed as a unit.

The West Edmonton Mall is the largest mall in the world. Besides containing over 800 shops and services, it features the world's largest indoor amusement park and the world's largest indoor lake.

They usually contain a supermarket, perhaps a discount store, and several service stores—dry cleaner, self-service laundry, drugstore, video rental outlet, barber or beauty shop, hardware store, or other stores.

A recent addition to the shopping centre scene is the so-called *power centre*. These huge unenclosed shopping centres consist of a long strip of retail stores, including large, freestanding anchors such as Wal-Mart, Home Depot, Best Buy, Michaels, OfficeMax, and CompUSA. Each store has its own entrance with parking directly in front for shoppers who wish to visit only one store. Power centres have increased rapidly during the past few years to challenge traditional indoor malls.

Through the past decade, on average, consumers have been going to traditional malls less often, staying a shorter period of time, and visiting fewer stores. Why are people using shopping malls less? First, with more dual-income households, people have less time to shop. "You have two workers in every family and no one has time to go to the mall for four hours anymore," observes one industry analyst. "People who used to go to the mall twenty times a year now go two or three times." While time-pressed consumers are making fewer trips, they are buying more per trip. Second, a recent survey of British Columbia shoppers revealed that 58 percent of consumers now find shopping more of a chore than they did in the past. Listed as the top three reasons for their frustration were long line-ups at checkouts, poor service, and lack of assistance in stores.[14]

Furthermore, shoppers appear to be tiring of traditional malls, which are too big, too crowded, and too much alike. Thus, the current trend is toward value-oriented outlet malls and power centres on the one hand, and smaller malls and downtown locations on the other. Many shoppers now prefer to shop at "lifestyle centres," smaller malls with upscale stores, convenient locations, and expensive atmospheres. "The idea is to combine the hominess and community of an old-time village square with the cachet of fashionable urban stores; the smell and feel of a neighbourhood park with the brute convenience of a strip centre." Add to all this the emergence of Internet shopping, and you can see why some retail analysts believe the concept of the shopping mall is beginning to look dated.[15]

The Future of Retailing

Retailers operate in a harsh and fast-changing environment that offers both threats and opportunities. For example, the industry suffers from chronic overcapacity resulting in fierce competition for customer dollars. Consumer demographics, lifestyles, and shopping patterns are changing rapidly, as are retailing technologies. To be successful, then, retailers will have to choose target segments carefully and position themselves strongly. They will have to take into account the following retailing developments as they plan and execute their competitive strategies.

New Retail Forms and Shortening Retail Life Cycles

New retail forms continue to emerge to meet new situations and consumer needs, but the life cycle of new retail forms is getting shorter. Department stores took about 100 years to reach the mature stage of the life cycle; more recent forms, such as warehouse stores, reached maturity in about 10 years. In such an environment, seemingly solid retail positions can crumble quickly.

The mantra of Canadian retailing today may have been best expressed by George Heller, chief executive officer of Hudson's Bay Co. (HBC). "Get good or get lost," he exclaimed in a recent speech. The ground is shifting under retailers and many of Canada's most familiar names—Eatons, Simpson's, Woodward's, Robinson's, Bretton's, Kmart, Woolco, and the many chains that operated under Dylex—have disappeared over the past decade. Retailers that were unable to adapt to the fierce competition from powerhouses such as Wal-Mart, Costco, and Home Depot are gone. The pressure from tough competitors has made the Bay re-evaluate some of its tactics. David Poirier, executive vice-president and chief information officer of HBC, which owns the Bay and Zellers, recently mentioned some of the dumb things the giant retailer used to do and what it is doing now to turn itself into a "retail showcase":

> In 1998, Scratch & Save and Bay Days worked so well that the company used one or the other every week of the year until it "ran out of weeks." To attract even more customers, the company then offered double Scratch & Save savings. While the price promotions drew customers to the store, they were a bust financially. To turn inventory faster, the Bay highlighted items known as "loss leaders" on the front page of its flyers and placed them at the front of stores. Loss leaders are items the stores lose money on but use to generate traffic. The combination drew customers, but the placement of items at the front door didn't tempt buyers to walk further into the stores and check out other items that were more profitable. The stores, in fact, were set up for low-return "cherry pickers" rather than for the "primary" customers who make up 25 percent of the customer base, spend 84 percent of their retail-spending dollars with the Bay, and contribute most of the profits. Today, many of the problems have been corrected. Scratch & Save has been dropped. Inventory management has improved. Both the Bay and Zellers have increased the number of branded and unique products they offer. There is a heightened emphasis on the relationship with the customer. The retailer has also expanded the HBC Rewards loyalty program to extend its Zellers Club Z to the Bay, Home Outfitters, and hbc.com. Today, HBC has a base of 11 million regular customers and Canada's biggest loyalty program. But while its better run than it was a few years ago, many analysts are unconvinced about its long-term prospects.[16]

Wheel of retailing concept
A concept of retailing that states that new types of retailers usually begin as low-margin, low-price, low-status operations but later evolve into higher-priced, higher-service operations, eventually becoming like the conventional retailers they replaced.

Retailers can no longer sit back and rely on a once-successful formula—they must keep adapting. Many retailing innovations are partially explained by the **wheel of retailing concept**.[17] According to this concept, many new types of retailing forms begin as low-margin, low-price, low-status operations. They challenge established retailers that have become "fat" by letting their costs and margins increase. The new retailers' success leads them to upgrade their facilities and offer more services. In turn, their costs increase, forcing them to increase their prices. Eventually, the new retailers become like the conventional retailers they replaced. The cycle begins again when still newer types of retailers evolve with lower costs and prices. The wheel of retailing concept seems to explain the initial success and later troubles of department stores, supermarkets, and discount stores and the recent success of off-price retailers.

Growth of Non-Store Retailing

Although most retailing still takes place the old-fashioned way, across countertops in stores, consumers now have an array of alternatives, including mail-order, television, phone, and online shopping (see Real Marketing 14.2). Some North Americans are avoiding the hassles and crowds at malls by doing more of their shopping by phone or computer. Although such retailing advances may threaten some traditional retailers, they offer exciting opportunities for others. Many store-based retailers such as Sears Canada, Canadian Tire, and Roots have now added direct retailing channels. Office-supply retailer Office Depot is now the world's biggest online retailer after Amazon.com.[18]

Despite all the talk about the Internet sounding the death knell of traditional retail operations, online shopping and retailing is still in its infancy and currently represents less than 3 percent of retail sales. While Canadians are one of the most "wired" populations in the world and declare themselves ready, willing, and able to

REAL MARKETING

14.2 Etailing: Still Alive, Well, and Growing

*M*any of us still make most of our purchases the old-fashioned way: We go to the store, find what we want, wait patiently in line to plunk down our cash or credit card, and bring home the goods. However, a growing number of retailers now provide an attractive alternative—one that lets us browse, select, order, and pay with little more effort than it takes to apply an index finger to a mouse button. They sell a rich variety of goods ranging from books, CDs, flowers, and food to stereo equipment, kitchen appliances, airplane tickets, auto parts, home mortgages, and bags of cement. One successful online retailer is tiny DeLong Farms of Nova Scotia (http://delongfarms.com). It offers fresh balsam wreaths and centre pieces. Time-pressed shoppers can order from their catalogue, online, or by phone. DeLong contacts regular customers just before the holiday season to ask if they want to duplicate their gift list from previous years. Orders are sent by mail or courier for those last-minute shoppers.

Only a few years ago, prospects for online retailing were soaring. Many experts predicted that as more and more consumers flocked to the Web, a new breed of fast-moving etailers would quickly surpass stodgy,

"old economy" store retailers. Some even saw a day when we'd be doing almost all of our shopping via the Internet. However, the dot-com meltdown of 2000 dashed these overblown expectations. Many once-brash Web sellers crashed and burned—remember eToys.com, Pets.com, Webvan.com, and Garden.com?

Although the pace has slowed, today's etailing is alive, well, and growing. With today's easier-to-use websites, improved online service, and the demise of so many early competitors, business is booming for the survivors. In fact, online buying is growing at a much brisker pace than retail buying as a whole. Leading the pack is online auction site eBay, which has been consistently profitable since its inception. Business is also booming for online travel company Travelocity, which uses the Web to sell airline tickets, hotel rooms, and discount travel packages to consumers.

Still, much of the anticipated growth in online sales will go to multichannel retailers—the marketers who can successfully merge the virtual and physical worlds. Such retailers accounted for 67 percent of total online sales last year. The true winners these days appear to be established bricks-and-mortar companies that have

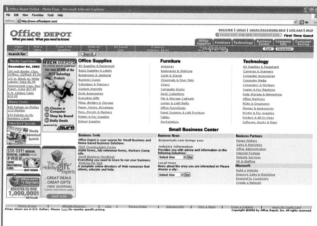

Online retailing: Today's etailing is alive, well, and growing for multi-channel players like DeLong Farms and Office Depot.

added Web selling. Examples include Sears Canada, Canadian Tire, Dell, IBM, Lands' End, L.L.Bean, Staples, and Office Depot, to name just a few.

Consider retailer Office Depot's burgeoning Web business:

Forty percent of Office Depot's major customers are using the online network to buy everything from paper clips to cherry conference-room tables. In 2002, the company's Internet sales grew 40 percent to $1.5 billion, almost 14 percent of overall sales. That makes Office Depot the biggest online retailer after Amazon.com. Better yet, Office Depot's online unit was profitable from day one. How has Office Depot succeeded online where so many dot-coms have failed? "Office Depot gets it," says an ecommerce consultant. "It used the Net to build deeper relationships with customers."

So, despite some serious setbacks and uncertainties, online retailing is anything but dead. As one analyst says about the recent successes of online retailers like Travelocity, "None of this guarantees that online travel won't crash someday like the rest of the dot-coms. But as the market takes off, these skies are looking downright friendly."

Sources: Office Depot example adapted from Charles Haddad, "Office Depot's E-Diva," *Business Week,* August 6, 2001, pp. EB22–EB24; and Meryl Davids Landau, "Sweet Revenge," *Chief Executive,* May 2002, pp. 58–62. Other information from Dennis K. Berman and Heather Green, "Cliff-Hanger Christmas," *Business Week,* October 23, 2000, pp. EB30–EB38; Molly Prior, "E-Commerce Alive and Well in the New Economy," *DSN Retailing Today,* June 4, 2001, p. 10; Wendy Zellner, "Where the Net Delivers: Travel," *Business Week,* June 11, 2001, pp. 142–144; Lewis Braham, "E-Tailers Are Clicking," *Business Week,* July 23, 2001, p. 73; Heather Green and Robert D. Hof, "Lessons of the Cyber Survivors," *Business Week,* April 22, 2002, p. 42; and Nick Wingfield, "Online Retailing Still Growing Despite Some Losses Last Year," *Wall Street Journal,* June 12, 2002, p. B4.

shop online, they often find that there are few Canadian websites on which to make their purchases. Consultancy Booz Allen Hamilton announced that, of the Group of Seven industrialized countries, Canada ranked third, behind the United States and Britain, as a "favourable environment" for ecommerce, combining an up-to-date communications infrastructure with strong political leadership. However, as high-tech consultancy IDC Canada notes, Canadian business has not yet exploited its ebusiness potential. Barely 20 percent of medium-sized enterprises are selling goods and services online.[19]

Canadian retailers have been somewhat slow in entering the etailing race for a number of reasons. First, many don't see etailing as a significant competitive threat, even though 63 percent of the dollars Canadian e-shoppers spend go to the United States. Other barriers to etailing development include lack of senior executive commitment, challenges of order fulfillment, lack of resources, and the complexity of measuring online performance.[20] However, etailing is expected to grow rapidly—Canadians have a history of being rapid adopters of new technologies, and more and more Canadian retailers are starting to enter cyberspace, using their sites to complement their store sales or provide consumers with product information.

Retail Convergence

Today's retailers are increasingly selling the same products at the same prices to the same consumers in competition with a wider variety of other retailers. For example, any consumer can buy CDs at specialty music stores, discount music stores, electronics superstores, general merchandise discount stores, video-rental outlets, and through dozens of mail-order companies and websites. You can buy books at stores ranging from independent local bookstores to discount stores such as Wal-Mart, superstores such as Chapters or Indigo, grocery stores like Loblaws, or websites such as Amazon. When it comes to brand-name appliances, department stores, discount stores, off-price retailers, electronics superstores, and a slew of websites all compete for the same customers.

This merging of consumers, products, prices, and retailers is called *retail convergence:*[21]

Retail convergence is the coming together of shoppers, goods, and prices. Customers of all income levels are shopping at the same stores, often for the same goods. Old distinctions such as discount store, specialty store, and department store are losing significance: The successful store must match a host of rivals on selection, service, and price.

Consider fashion. Once the exclusive domain of the wealthy, fashion now moves quickly from the runways of New York and Paris to retailers at all levels. Liz Claiborne sells in upscale department stores like Holt Renfrew as well as in discount outlets at the strip mall.

Such convergence means greater competition for retailers and greater difficulty in differentiating offerings. The competition between chain superstores and smaller, independently owned stores has become particularly heated. Because of their bulk-buying power and high sales volume, chains can buy at lower costs and thrive on smaller margins. The arrival of a superstore can quickly force nearby independents out of business. For example, the decision by electronics superstore Best Buy to sell CDs as loss leaders at rock-bottom prices pushed a number of specialty record store chains into bankruptcy. And Wal-Mart has been accused of destroying independents in countless small towns around the country.

Yet the news is not all bad for smaller companies. Many small, independent retailers are thriving. Independents are finding that sheer size and marketing muscle are often no match for the personal touch that small stores can provide or the specialty niches that small stores fill for a devoted customer base.

The Rise of Megaretailers

The rise of huge mass-merchandisers and specialty superstores, the formation of vertical marketing systems and buying alliances, and a rash of retail mergers and acquisitions have created a core of superpower megaretailers. Through their superior information systems and buying power, these giant retailers can offer better merchandise selections, good service, and large price savings to consumers. As a result, they grow even larger by squeezing out their smaller, weaker competitors.

The megaretailers are also shifting the balance of power between retailers and producers. A relative handful of retailers now control access to enormous numbers of consumers, giving them the upper hand in their dealings with manufacturers. For example, Wal-Mart's revenues are more than three times those of Procter & Gamble. Wal-Mart can, and often does, use this power to wring concessions from P&G and other suppliers.[22]

The Growing Importance of Retail Technology

Retail technologies are becoming critically important as competitive tools. Progressive retailers are using advanced information technology and software systems to produce better forecasts, control inventory costs, order electronically from suppliers, send email between stores, and even sell to customers within stores. They are adopting checkout scanning systems, online transaction processing, electronic funds transfer, electronic data interchange, in-store television, and improved merchandise-handling systems. Here's how technology helped to unravel a mystery:

> The managers of a newly renovated A&P in Hamilton, Ontario, were perplexed. Their scanner data revealed that the 5 percent of the store clientele who used frequent-buyer cards were purchasing less. A follow-up survey revealed that although most people liked the store's new look, they didn't like the new self-serve deli. As a result of this customer feedback, the store was remodelled again. Purchasing levels went back up, and A&P avoided making a chain-wide blunder.[23]

Perhaps the most startling advances in retailing technology concern the ways in which today's retailers are connecting with customers:[24]

In the past, life was simple. Retailers connected with their customers through stores, through their salespeople, through the brands and packages they sold, and through direct mail and advertising in the mass media. But today, life is more complex. There are dozens of new ways to attract and engage consumers.... Indeed, even if one omits the obvious—the Web—retailers are still surrounded by technical innovations that promise to redefine the way they and manufacturers interact with customers. Consider, as just a sampling, touch screen kiosks, electronic shelf labels and signs, handheld shopping assistants, smart cards, self-scanning systems, virtual reality displays, and intelligent agents. So, if we ask the question, "Will technology change the way [retailers] interface with customers in the future?" the answer has got to be *yes*.

Global Expansion of Major Retailers

Retailers with unique formats and strong brand positioning are increasingly moving into other countries. Many are expanding internationally to escape mature and saturated home markets. Over the years, several giant U.S. retailers—McDonald's, Gap, Toys "R" Us—have become globally prominent as a result of their great marketing prowess. Others, such as Wal-Mart, are rapidly establishing a global presence. Wal-Mart, which now operates more than 1200 stores in nine countries abroad, sees exciting global potential. Its international division racked up sales of more than $45.7 billion in 2002, an increase of 11 percent over the previous year. Canadian retailers are also not being left behind:

The Weston family, Canadian billionaire owners of Loblaw Companies Limited and Holt Renfrew, recently took over British luxury goods retailer Selfridges PLC for $1.6 billion. The move is designed to add even more polish and European flair to high-end fashion retailer Holt Renfrew. Industry watchers believe the acquisition will be a boost to Holt's, opening the way for it to introduce new international brands, leverage innovative presentations, and import splashy event ideas—all from Selfridges. Says Richard Blickstead, a retailing consultant, "It's going to give Holt's a window on the world that's even bigger than the one it has today." The move will also help Holt's negotiate better deals with suppliers. The Westons' international retailers don't stop here. They also own upscale Brown Thomas in Ireland and British luxury food specialist Fortnum & Mason Associated British Foods PLC.[25]

However, North American retailers are still significantly behind European and Asian retailers when it comes to global expansion. Less than 20 percent of North American retailers operate globally, while 40 percent of European retailers and 31 percent of Asian retailers use the global stage. Among foreign retailers that have gone global are France's Carrefour, Britain's Marks and Spencer, Italy's Benetton, Sweden's IKEA home furnishings stores, and Japan's Yaohan supermarkets.[26] Consider the case of French discount retailer Carrefour, the world's second-largest retailer after Wal-Mart. It has embarked on an aggressive mission to extend its role as a leading international retailer:

Carrefour now operates more than 5300 discount stores in 30 countries in Europe, Asia, and the Americas, including 657 hypermarkets. By purchasing or merging with a variety of retailers, Carrefour has accelerated its hold over the European market, where it now claims retail dominance in four leading markets: France, Spain, Belgium, and Greece—and it's the number two retailer in Italy. But one of the retailer's greatest strengths is its market position outside of France and Europe. In South America, for instance, Carrefour is the market leader in Brazil and Argentina, where it operates more than 300 stores. By comparison, Wal-Mart has only 25 units in those two countries. In China, the land of more than a billion consumers, Carrefour operates 22 hypermarkets to Wal-Mart's five supercentres and one Sam's Club. In the Pacific Rim, excluding

China, Carrefour operates 33 hypermarkets in five countries to Wal-Mart's five units in South Korea alone. In short, Carrefour is bounding ahead of Wal-Mart in most markets outside North America. The only question: Can the French titan hold its lead?[27]

See Real Marketing 14.3 for more insights about global retail trends.

Retail Stores as "Communities" or "Hangouts"

With the rise in the number of people living alone, working at home, or living in isolated and sprawling suburbs, there has been a resurgence of establishments that, regardless of the product or service they offer, also provide a place for people to meet. These places include cafés, tea shops, juice bars, bookshops, superstores, children's play spaces, brew pubs, and urban greenmarkets. This is a North America-wide phenomenon. Brew pubs such as the Kingston Brew Pub offer tastings and a place to pass the time. And today's bookstores have become part bookstore, part library, and part living room:

> Welcome to today's bookstore. The one featuring not only shelves and cash registers but also cushy chairs and coffee bars. It's where backpack-toting high school students come to do homework, where retirees thumb through the gardening books, and parents read aloud to their toddlers. If no one actually buys books, that's just fine, say bookstore owners and managers. They're offering something grander than ink and paper, anyway. They're selling comfort, relaxation, community.[28]

Bricks-and-mortar retailers are not the only ones creating community. Others have also built virtual communities on the Internet:

> Sony Computer Entertainment America (SCEA) actively builds community among its Playstation®2 customers. Its recent Playstation.com campaign created message boards where its game players could post messages to one another. The boards are incredibly active, discussing techie topics but also providing the

Today's bookstores offer something greater than just books and magazines—they're selling comfort, relaxation, and community.

14.3 Stephen Arnold: The Meaning of Retail Globalization

Stephen Arnold, a Queen's University professor renowned throughout the world for his expertise with regard to retail patronage, provided the following insights about global retail trends.

Several meanings are associated with the term "retail globalization." In one context, it refers to the decision of the international retailer to either standardize or adapt its format throughout the world. For example, U.S.-based Wal-Mart wishes to see its name on each store in every world market—a veritable McDonald's of retailing. It acquired the Woolco chain in Canada and changed the name to Wal-Mart within 10 months. Germany's Wertkauf became Wal-Mart once the store conversions were completed. This "globalization" approach contrasts with a "multinational" strategy whereby the retailer adapts to each national market. For example, Netherlands retailer Royal Ahold purchased the eastern U.S. Stop & Shop, Giant, BI-LO, and Tops food chains but maintained their original names.

A second meaning of retail globalization relates to the predicted dominance of world markets by three or four retailers pursuing growth strategies. For instance, some observers predict that Wal-Mart and France's Carrefour will soon dominate world markets for frequently purchased food and non-food merchandise. Wal-Mart is already the world's largest retailer with $287 billion at 2001 fiscal year end. Carrefour is the world's second-largest retailer with slightly less than half of Wal-Mart's volume. In contrast, Canada's largest and second-largest homegrown retailers are Loblaws and the Bay. They sold, respectively, $19.5 billion and $7.5 billion worth of goods in 1999. These much smaller national chains could either be acquired by one of the retail giants or forced out of business. They have little or no international experience to draw upon. They're not unlike members of the university downhill ski team who entered the Ontario winter games to find themselves competing against the French, Italian, and U.S. Olympic teams.

The impact of these global retailers on Canadian markets to date may predict the future. Within four years of entering Canada, Wal-Mart became this nation's largest department store. Its sales exceeded those of Zellers, Sears, and the Bay. Eatons went bankrupt and Kmart withdrew from the Canadian market. In three surveys conducted 1.5 years apart tracking the Kingston, Ontario, market, Wal-Mart's share of shoppers rose from 7 percent to 22 percent to 30 percent. This gain was at the expense of all other competitors. Similarly, Home Depot's share of shoppers in the Kingston market was 27 percent six months after the store's grand opening and 36 percent after 18 months. Cashway's share of shoppers was halved and Beaver Lumber closed its doors.

Wal-Mart has introduced its supercentre stores to Canada, adding food to its non-food offering. It uses this hypermarket format in every one of its other world markets except Canada and Puerto Rico. Predictions are that the number of stores will rise from 174 to 300 and that Canadian sales will reach $24 billion. Wal-Mart will dwarf every other Canadian retailer.

How should Canadians respond to the dominance of its retail system by an oligopoly of international retailers? In fact, they already acted and "voted" with their shopping dollars. Consumers cannot resist the

Stephen Arnold

convenient store locations, everyday low prices, wide assortments and friendly service.

The final meaning of retail globalization relates to the potential outcomes of world dominance by a small number of retail firms. One issue is whether retail globalization equates to retail homogenization and, in the long run, reduced choice and a sameness of offerings. For example, in a typical Canadian market, one will find A&P, Costco, Home Depot, Sears, and Wal-Mart, all U.S.-based retailers. A related issue concerns the transformation of the choice process by the global retailers. Is the relative importance shoppers attach to store choice attributes fixed or does the market entry of a global retailer change the manner in which consumers shop for frequently purchased products? A non-traditional view is that preferences evolve and that a new competitor can enter an existing retail market and alter consumer preferences toward the combination of attributes that the competitor represents. The new entrant is referred to as a "market spoiler," meaning that the characteristics considered ideal for this market have changed from those that favour existing competitors. Wal-Mart's propensity for changing consumer preferences for store choice attributes in its own favour was identified in studies conducted in Kingston, Atlanta, and Chicago. The importance of low prices and good service went up and the determinacy of sales and promotions fell.

Sources: S. J. Arnold and J. Fernie, "Wal-Mart in Europe: Prospects for the UK," *International Marketing Review*, 17 (4/5), 2000, pp. 433–453; S. J. Arnold, J. Handelman, and D. J. Tigert, "The Impact of a Market Spoiler on Consumer Preference Structures (or, What Happens When Wal-Mart Comes to Town)," *Journal of Retailing and Consumer Services*, 5(1), 1998, pp. 1–13; *Chain Store Age*, "World's 100 Largest Retailers," December 2000, p. 121; J. Simmons and T. Graff, *Wal-Mart Comes to Canada*, Toronto: Centre for the Study of Commercial Activity, Ryerson Polytechnic University, 1998; Neil Wrigley, "The Globalisation of Retail Capital: Themes for Economic Geography," in *Handbook of Economic Geography*, G. Clark, M. Gertler, and M. Feldman, eds., Oxford University Press, 2000, pp. 292–313.

Retailer communities: Sony Computer Entertainment America's Playstation.com website builds community among its customers. The site's message boards are incredibly active, discussing techie topics but also lifestyle issues, such as music and personal taste.

opportunity for members, fiercely competitive and opinionated, to vote on lifestyle issues, such as music and personal taste, no matter how trivial. Although SCEA is laissez-faire about the boards and does not feed them messages, the company sees the value in having its customers' adamant conversations occur directly on its site. "Our customers are our evangelists. They are a very vocal and loyal fan base," says an SCEA spokesperson. "There are things we can learn from them."[29]

Wholesaling

Wholesaling
All activities involved in selling goods and services to those buying for resale or business use.

Wholesaler
A firm engaged *primarily* in wholesaling activity.

Wholesaling includes all activities involved in selling goods and services to those buying for resale or business use. We call **wholesalers** those firms engaged *primarily* in wholesaling activity. Wholesaling is a major industry in Canada, accounting for almost $480 billion in sales. With the recent cooling off of the Canadian economy, some wholesalers, especially those selling computers and electronic products, face difficult times. Other sectors are doing well. Wholesalers of pharmaceutical products, office and professional equipment, and food products continue to flourish.[30]

Vancouver-based Group Telecom (GT), for example, is a telecommunications services wholesaler that targets Canada's 2.5 million small and medium-sized businesses. These independent business firms are price sensitive and demand a high level of service from their wholesaler. This market is one GT believes has been "underserved," so it offers customized bundles of services—all on a single bill and with one customer service number to phone.[31]

Wholesalers buy mostly from producers and sell mostly to retailers, industrial consumers, and other wholesalers. As a result, many of the largest and most important wholesalers are largely unknown to final consumers. For example, you may never have heard of Grainger, the leading wholesaler of maintenance, repair, and operating (MRO) supplies (see Real Marketing 14.4).

But why are wholesalers used at all? For example, why would a producer use wholesalers rather than selling directly to retailers or consumers? Quite simply, wholesalers are often better at performing one or more of these channel functions:

- *Selling and promoting.* Wholesalers' sales forces help manufacturers reach many small customers at a low cost. The wholesaler has more contacts and is often more trusted by the buyer than the distant manufacturer.
- *Buying and assortment building.* Wholesalers can select items and build assortments needed by their customers, thereby saving the consumers much work.
- *Bulk breaking.* Wholesalers save their customers money by buying in carload lots and breaking bulk (breaking large lots into small quantities).
- *Warehousing.* Wholesalers hold inventories, thereby reducing the inventory costs and risks of suppliers and customers.
- *Transportation.* Wholesalers can provide quicker delivery to buyers because they are closer than the producers.
- *Financing.* Wholesalers finance their customers by giving credit, and they finance their suppliers by ordering early and paying bills on time.
- *Risk bearing.* Wholesalers absorb risk by taking title and bearing the cost of theft, damage, spoilage, and obsolescence.
- *Market information.* Wholesalers give information to suppliers and customers about competitors, new products, and price developments.
- *Management services and advice.* Wholesalers often help retailers train their sales clerks, improve store layouts and displays, and set up accounting and inventory control systems.

Types of Wholesalers

Wholesalers fall into three major groups (see Table 14.4 on pages 574 and 575): *merchant wholesalers, brokers and agents,* and *manufacturers' and retailers' branches and offices.*

Merchant wholesaler
Independently owned business that takes title to the merchandise its handles.

Merchant wholesalers are the largest single group of wholesalers, accounting for about 50 percent of all wholesaling. Merchant wholesalers include two broad types: full-service wholesalers and limited-service wholesalers. *Full-service wholesalers*

14.4 Grainger: The Biggest Market Leader You've Never Heard Of?

I t's a $4.8 billion business that offers more than 500 000 products and parts to more than 1.3 million customers. Its 600 North American branches, more than 15 000 employees, and innovative website handle more than 100 000 transactions a day. Grainger's customers include businesses ranging from factories, garages, and grocers to military bases and schools. Most North American businesses are located within 20 minutes of a Grainger branch. Customers include notables such as Abbott Laboratories, General Motors, Campbell Soup, American Airlines, Mercedes-Benz, and the U.S. Postal Service. Grainger also operates one of the highest-volume B2B sites on the Web.

So, how come you've never heard of Grainger? Most likely it's because Grainger is a wholesaler. And like most wholesalers, it operates behind the scenes, selling only to other businesses. Moreover, Grainger operates in the not-so-glamorous world of maintenance, repair, and operating (MRO) supplies.

Although you may never have heard it, Grainger is by far the world's leading wholesaler of maintenance, repair, and operating supplies.

But whereas you might know little about Grainger, to its customers the company is very well known and much valued. Through its branch network, service centres, sales reps, catalogue, and website, Grainger links customers with the supplies they need to keep their facilities running smoothly—everything from lightbulbs, cleaners, and display cases to nuts and bolts, motors, valves, power tools, and test equipment. Grainger is by far the continent's largest MRO wholesaler. Notes one industry reporter, "If industrial America is an engine, Grainger is its lubricant."

Grainger serves as an important link between thousands of MRO supplies manufacturers on one side and millions of industrial and commercial customers on the other. It operates on a simple value proposition: to make it easier and less costly for customers to find and buy MRO supplies. It starts by acting as a one-stop shop for anything and everything MRO related. Most customers will tell you that Grainger sells everything—*everything*—from the ordinary to the out-of-the-ordinary. For example, it stocks thousands of lightbulbs—about every lightbulb known to mankind. If you don't believe it, go to www.grainger.com and search "lightbulbs"! As for the not-so-ordinary:

> Grainger sells 19 different models of floor-cleaning machines, has 49 catalogue pages of socket wrenches, and offers nine different sizes of hydraulic service jacks, an assortment of NFL-licensed hardhats bearing team logos, and item No. 6AV22, a $36.90 dispenser rack for two 1-gallon containers of Gatorade. According to corporate legend, Grainger is the only place that workers on the Alaskan Pipeline have been able to find repellent to cope with arctic bears during their mating season.

Beyond making it easier for customers to find the products they need, Grainger also helps them to streamline their acquisition processes. For most companies, acquiring MRO supplies is a very costly process. In fact, 40 percent of the cost of MRO supplies stems from the purchase process, including finding a supplier, negotiating the best deal, placing the order, receiving the order, and paying the invoice. Grainger constantly seeks ways to reduce the costs associated with MRO supplies acquisition, both internally and externally. Says one analyst, "Grainger will reduce your search and your process costs for items, instead of your having to order ten things from ten different companies, and you'll get one invoice. That's pretty powerful."

One company found that working with Grainger cut MRO requisition time by more than 60 percent; lead times went from days to hours. Its supply chain dropped from 12 000 suppliers to 560—significantly reducing expenses. Similarly, a large timber and paper-products company has come to appreciate the value of Grainger's selection and streamlined ordering process. It orders two-thirds of its supplies from Grainger's website at an annual acquisition cost of only $300 000. In comparison, for the remainder of its needs, this company deals with more than 1300 small distributors at an acquisition cost of $3.1 million each year—eight times the cost of dealing with Grainger for half of the volume. As a result, the company is now looking for ways to buy all of its MRO supplies from Grainger.

You might think that helping customers find what they need easily and efficiently would be enough to keep Grainger atop of the MRO mountain. But Grainger goes even further. On a broader level, it builds lasting relationships with customers by helping them find *solutions* to their overall MRO problems. Acting as consultants, Grainger sales reps help buyers with everything from improving their supply chain management to reducing inventories and streamlining warehousing operations:

> Branches...serve as the base for Grainger territory managers who provide onsite help to big facilities.... [Reps can] tour a factory or an office complex or even a hotel and suggest to its managers exactly what supplies they really need to keep the place up to snuff, right down to how many gallons of carpet cleaner they'll require each week. That's how Grainger knows, for example, that one Biltmore Hotel has 7000 lightbulbs.... "Our reps can pretty much stand outside a building and get a general feel for what kinds of products the customer needs," [says James Ryan, Grainger's executive vice president of marketing, sales, and service].

Grainger has launched a series of programs designed to add value to its commodity business. For example, through its "Click & Sell" program, Grainger uses information collected about customers, such as industry data and purchase histories, to help sales reps

find solutions for customer needs. If, for example, a customer places an order for a pump to use with caustic chemicals, the Grainger rep might also suggest gloves and safety glasses. If an item is unavailable, the database identifies alternative products to get the job done.

Grainger also offers value to customers through its links to and clout with suppliers:

> Jason Eastin is facilities operations director for JRV Management, a...company that runs community and private sports facilities in metropolitan Detroit. He relies on Grainger in part because of its clout with factory reps. When his company was opening up its newest complex, he asked Chris Clemons, a Grainger territory manager, for help figuring out the number and kinds of fixtures that would be required. Clemens summoned a rep from Rubbermaid, the household-products maker, who showed up with a laptop and a software program that churned out a reasonable supply chain within 20 minutes. Similarly, Clemens worked with a General Electric salesperson who figured out how Eastin could stretch out "relamping" his facilities to every two years, instead of annually, and cut costs significantly as well by switching to a different kind of metal-halide bulb as the primary kind of illumination for his ice arenas. "To have General Electric provide that service to me at no charge would never happen," Eastin says. "But Grainger has that buying-power structure. They open up those kinds of opportunities to me."

So now you've heard of Grainger, a wholesaler that succeeds by making life easier and more efficient for commercial and industrial buyers and sellers. Although a market leader, Grainger still captures only 4 percent of the highly fragmented U.S. market for MRO goods. That leaves a lot of room for growth. But to take advantage of the opportunities, Grainger must continue to find innovative ways to add value. "Our system makes our business partners and suppliers more efficient," says Fred Loepp, vice president of product management at Grainger, "and that benefits the entire supply chain." Says Theresa Dubiel, branch manager at Grainger's Romulus, Michigan, branch, "If we don't save [customers] time and money every time they come [to us], they won't come back."

Sources: Excerpts from Dale Buss, "The New Deal," *Sales & Marketing Management,* June 2002, pp. 25–30; and Colleen Gourley, "Redefining Distribution," *Warehousing Management,* October 2000, pp. 28–30. Also see Leslie Langnau, "B2B E-Commerce: A Look at What Works," *Material Handling Management,* February 2002, p. 42; Steve Konicki and Eileen Colkin, "Attitude Adjustment," *Informationweek,* March 25, 2002, pp. 20–22; and the Grainger website, www.grainger.com (accessed December 2002).

Table 14.4   Major Types of Wholesalers

Type	Description
Merchant wholesalers	Independently owned businesses that take title to the merchandise they handle. In different trades, they are known as *jobbers, distributors,* or *mill supply houses.* Include full-service wholesalers and limited-service wholesalers:
Full-service wholesalers	Provide a full line of services: carrying stock, maintaining a sales force, offering credit, making deliveries, and providing management assistance. There are two types:
Wholesale merchants	Sell primarily to retailers and provide a full range of services. *General-merchandise wholesalers* carry several merchandise lines, while *general-line wholesalers* carry one or two lines in greater depth. *Specialty wholesalers* specialize in carrying only part of a line. Examples include health-food wholesalers and seafood wholesalers.
Industrial distributors	Sell to manufacturers rather than to retailers. Provide several services, such as carrying stock, offering credit, and providing delivery. May carry a broad range of merchandise, a general line, or a specialty line.
Limited-service wholesalers	Offer fewer services than full-service wholesalers. Limited-service wholesalers are of several types:
Cash-and-carry wholesalers	Carry a limited line of fast-moving goods and sell to small retailers for cash. Normally do not deliver. Example: A small fish store retailer may drive to a cash-and-carry fish wholesaler, buy fish for cash, and bring the merchandise back to the store.
Truck wholesalers (or truck jobbers)	Perform primarily a selling and delivery function. Carry a limited line of semi-perishable merchandise (such as milk, bread, snack foods), which they sell for cash as they make their rounds of supermarkets, small groceries, hospitals, restaurants, factory cafeterias, and hotels.
Drop shippers	Do not carry inventory or handle the product. Upon receiving an order, they select a manufacturer, who ships the merchandise directly to the customer. The drop shipper assumes title and risk from the time the order is accepted to its delivery to the customer. They operate in such bulk industries as coal, lumber, and heavy equipment.
Rack jobbers	Serve grocery and drug retailers, mostly in non-food items. They send delivery trucks to stores, where the delivery people set up toys, paperbacks, hardware items, health and beauty aids, or other items. They price the goods, keep them fresh, set up point-of-purchase displays, and keep inventory records. Rack jobbers retain title to the goods and bill the retailers only for the goods sold to consumers.
Producers' cooperatives	Are owned by farmer members and assemble farm produce to sell in local markets. The co-op's profits are distributed to members at the end of the year. They often attempt to improve product quality and promote a co-op brand name, such as Sun Maid raisins, Sunkist oranges, or Diamond walnuts.
Mail-order wholesalers	Send catalogues to retail, industrial, and institutional customers featuring jewellery, cosmetics, specialty foods, and other small items. Maintain no outside sales force. Main customers are businesses in small outlying areas. Orders are filled and sent by mail, truck, or other transportation.
Brokers and agents	Do not take title to goods. Main function is to facilitate buying and selling, for which they earn a commission on the selling price. Generally specialize by product line or customer types.
Brokers	Chief function is bringing buyers and sellers together and assisting in negotiation. They are paid by the party who hired them, and do not carry inventory, get involved in financing, or assume risk. Examples: food brokers, real estate brokers, insurance brokers, and security brokers.
Agents	Represent either buyers or sellers on a more permanent basis than brokers do. There are several types:
Manufacturers' agents	Represent two or more manufacturers of complementary lines. A formal written agreement with each manufacturer covers pricing, territories, order handling, delivery service and warranties, and commission rates. Often used in such lines as apparel, furniture, and electrical goods. Most manufacturers' agents are small businesses, with only a few skilled salespeople as employees. They are hired by small manufacturers who cannot afford their own field sales forces, and by large manufacturers who use agents to open new territories or to cover territories that cannot support full-time salespeople.

continued

Table 14.4   Major Types of Wholesalers *(continued)*

Selling agents	Have contractual authority to sell a manufacturer's entire output. The manufacturer either is not interested in the selling function or feels unqualified. The selling agent serves as a sales department and has significant influence over prices, terms, and conditions of sale. Found in such product areas as textiles, industrial machinery and equipment, coal and coke, chemicals, and metals.
Purchasing agents	Generally have a long-term relationship with buyers and make purchases for them, often receiving, inspecting, warehousing, and shipping the merchandise to the buyers. They provide helpful market information to clients and help them obtain the best goods and prices available.
Commission merchants	Take physical possession of products and negotiate sales. Normally, they are not employed on a long-term basis. Used most often in agricultural marketing by farmers who do not want to sell their own output and do not belong to producers' cooperatives. The commission merchant takes a truckload of commodities to a central market, sells it for the best price, deducts a commission and expenses, and remits the balance to the producer.
Manufacturers' and retailers' branches and offices	Wholesaling operations conducted by sellers or buyers themselves rather than through independent wholesalers. Separate branches and offices can be dedicated to either sales or purchasing.
Sales branches and offices	Set up by manufacturers to improve inventory control, selling, and promotion. *Sales branches* carry inventory and are found in such industries as lumber and automotive equipment and parts. *Sales offices* do not carry inventory and are most prominent in dry goods and notions industries.
Purchasing offices	Perform a role similar to that of brokers or agents but are part of the buyer's organization. Many retailers set up purchasing offices in such major market centres as Montreal, Toronto, and Calgary.

Broker

A wholesaler who does not take title to goods and whose function is to bring buyers and sellers together and assist in negotiation.

Agent

A wholesaler who represents buyers or sellers on a relatively permanent basis, performs only a few functions, and does not take title to goods.

provide a full set of services, whereas the various *limited-service wholesalers* offer fewer specialized services to their suppliers and customers.

Brokers and *agents* differ from merchant wholesalers in two ways: they do not take title to goods and they perform only a few functions. Like merchant wholesalers, they generally specialize by product line or customer type. A **broker** brings buyers and sellers together and assists in negotiation. **Agents** represent buyers or sellers on a more permanent basis. *Manufacturers' agents* (also called manufacturers' representatives) are the most common type of agent wholesaler.

Merchant wholesalers: A typical Fleming Companies, Inc., wholesale food distribution centre. The average Fleming warehouse contains 500 000 square feet of floor space (with a 30-foot [9 m] ceiling), carries 16 000 different food items, and serves 150 to 200 retailers within a radius of 500 miles (805 km).

Manufacturers' sales branches and offices
Wholesaling by sellers or buyers themselves rather than through independent wholesalers.

The third major type of wholesaling is that done in **manufacturers' sales branches and offices** by sellers or buyers themselves rather than through independent wholesalers.

Wholesaler Marketing Decisions

Wholesalers now face mounting competitive pressures, more demanding customers, new technologies, and more direct-buying programs on the part of large industrial, institutional, and retail buyers. As a result, they have had to take a fresh look at the marketing strategies. As with retailers, their marketing decisions include target markets, positioning, and the marketing mix—product assortment and services, price, promotion, and place (see Figure 14.2).

Target Market and Positioning Decision

Like retailers, wholesalers must define their target markets and position themselves effectively—they cannot serve everyone. They can choose a target group by size of customer (only large retailers), type of customer (convenience food stores only), need for service (customers who need credit), or other factors. Within the target group, they can identify the more profitable customers, design stronger offers, and build better relationships with them. They can propose automatic reordering systems, set up management-training and advising systems, or even sponsor a voluntary chain. They can discourage less profitable customers by requiring larger orders or adding service charges to smaller ones.

Marketing Mix Decisions

Like retailers, wholesalers must decide on product assortment and services, price, promotion, and place. The wholesaler's "product" is the assortment of *products and services* that it offers. Wholesalers are under great pressure to carry a full line and to stock enough for immediate delivery. But this practice can damage profits. Wholesalers today are cutting down on the number of lines they carry, choosing to carry only the more profitable ones. Wholesalers also are rethinking which services count most in building strong customer relationships and which should be dropped or charged for. The key is to find the mix of services most valued by their target customers.

Price is also an important wholesaler decision. Wholesalers usually mark up the cost of goods by a standard percentage—say, 20 percent. Expenses may run 17 percent of the gross margin, leaving a profit margin of 3 percent. In grocery wholesaling, the average profit margin is often less than 2 percent. Wholesalers are trying new pricing approaches. They may cut their margin on some lines to win important new customers. They may ask a supplier for special price breaks when they can turn them into an increase in the supplier's sales.

Figure 14.2 Wholesaler marketing decisions

Although *promotion* can be critical to wholesaler success, most wholesalers are not promotion minded. Their use of trade advertising, sales promotion, personal selling, and public relations is largely scattered and unplanned. Many are behind the times in personal selling—they still see selling as a single salesperson talking to a single customer instead of as a team effort to sell, build, and service major accounts. Wholesalers also need to adopt some of the non-personal promotion techniques used by retailers. They need to develop an overall promotion strategy and to make greater use of supplier promotion materials and programs.

Finally, *place* is important—wholesalers must choose their locations, facilities, and Web locations carefully. Wholesalers typically locate in low-rent, low-tax areas and tend to invest little money in their buildings, equipment, and systems. As a result, their materials-handling and order-processing systems are often outdated. In recent years, however, large and progressive wholesalers are reacting to rising costs by investing in automated warehouses and online ordering systems. Orders are fed from the retailer's system directly into the wholesaler's computer, and the items are picked up by mechanical devices and automatically taken to a shipping platform where they are assembled. Consider the case of Winnipeg-based wholesaler, Coghlan's LTD:

> Coghlan's LTD describes itself as the number one outdoor accessory line supplier in the United States and Canada. It attributes its success to marketing better-quality products with attractive packaging, superior customer service, and huge inventories that enable it to guarantee on-time delivery to the largest retailers in Canada and the U.S. including Canadian Tire and Wal-Mart. To increase its efficiency, Coghlan's invested in an electronic data interchange (EDI) system that allows its customers to electronically submit orders, thus shortening the retailer's reorder time. It has also invested in a quick response (QR) system that allows Coghlan's to fill an order and have it on the customer's loading dock within 72 hours.[32]

Most large wholesalers use computers to carry out accounting, billing, inventory control, and forecasting. Modern wholesalers are adapting their services to the needs of target customers and finding cost-reducing methods of doing business.

Wholesaler Coghlan's LTD used a combination of technology, superior customer services, and high quality products to earn its position as the number one outdoor accessory line supplier.

Trends in Wholesaling

As the wholesaling industry moves into the twenty-first century, it faces considerable challenges. The industry remains vulnerable to one of the most enduring trends of the past decade—fierce resistance to price increases and the winnowing-out of suppliers based on cost and quality. Progressive wholesalers constantly watch for better ways to meet the changing needs of their suppliers and target customers. They recognize that, in the long run, their only reason for existence comes from adding value by increasing the efficiency and effectiveness of the entire marketing channel. To achieve this goal, they must constantly improve their services and reduce their costs.

HBPC McKesson, North America's leading wholesaler of pharmaceuticals, health and beauty care, and home health-care products, provides an example of progressive wholesaling. To survive, McKesson has to remain more cost effective than manufacturers' sales branches. Thus, the company has built efficient, automated warehouses, established direct computer links with drug manufacturers, and set up extensive online supply management and accounts-receivable systems for customers. It offers retail pharmacists a wide range of online resources, including supply management assistance, catalogue searches, real-time order tracking, and an account management system. Retailers can even use the McKesson system to maintain medical profiles on their customers. McKesson's medical-surgical supply and equipment customers receive a rich assortment of online solutions and supply management tools, including an online order-management system and real-time information on products and pricing, inventory availability, and order status. According to McKesson, it adds value in the channel by "delivering unique supply and information management solutions that reduce costs and improve quality for health care customers."[33]

The distinction between large retailers and large wholesalers continues to blur. Many retailers now operate formats such as wholesale clubs and hypermarkets that perform many wholesale functions. In return, many large wholesalers are setting up their own retailing operations. SuperValu and Fleming, both leading food wholesalers, now operate their own retailing operations. For example, SuperValu, North America's largest food wholesaling company, is also Canada's eleventh largest food retailer. Almost 45 percent of the company's $20 billion in sales comes from its Bigg's, Cub Foods, Save-A-Lot, Farm Fresh, Hornbacher's, Laneco, Metro, Scott's Foods, Shop 'n Save, and Shoppers Food Warehouse stores.[34]

Wholesalers will continue to increase the services they provide to retailers—retail pricing, cooperative advertising, marketing and management information reports, accounting services, online transactions, and others. Rising costs on the one

To improve efficiency and service, McKesson offers retail pharmacists a wide range of online resources, including supply management assistance, catalogue searches, real-time order tracking, and an account management system. Retailers can even use the McKesson system to maintain medical profiles on their customers.

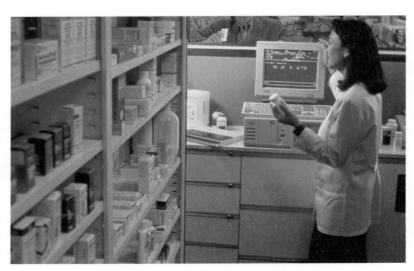

hand, and the demand for increased services on the other, will put the squeeze on wholesaler profits. Wholesalers who do not find efficient ways to deliver value to their customers will soon drop by the wayside. However, the increased use of computerized, automated systems will help wholesalers to contain the costs of ordering, shipping, and inventory holding, boosting their productivity.

Finally, facing slow growth in their domestic markets and such developments as the North American Free Trade Agreement, many large wholesalers are now going global.

Looking Back: Reviewing the Concepts

This chapter digs more deeply into the two major channel functions—retailing and wholesaling. Today's retailers face a rapidly changing environment, characterized by overcapacity, new kinds of competitors, and retail convergence. As a result, to prosper or even to survive, they must sharpen their marketing strategies. Wholesalers have also experienced recent environmental changes, most notably mounting competitive pressures. They have faced new sources of competition, more demanding customers, new technologies, and more direct-buying programs on the part of large industrial, institutional, and retail buyers.

1. Explain the roles of retailers and wholesalers in the marketing channel.

Retailing and wholesaling consist of many organizations bringing goods and services from the point of production to the point of use. *Retailing* includes all activities involved in selling goods or services directly to final consumers for their personal, non-business use. *Wholesaling* includes all the activities involved in selling goods or services to those who are buying for the purpose of resale or for business use. Wholesalers perform many functions, including selling and promoting, buying and assortment building, bulk breaking, warehousing, transporting, financing, risk bearing, supplying market information, and providing management services and advice.

2. Describe the major types of retailers and give examples of each.

Retailers can be classified as *store retailers* and *non-store retailers*. Although most goods and services are sold through stores, non-store retailing has been growing much faster than has store retailing. Store retailers can be further classified by the *amount of service* they provide (self-service, limited service, or full service); *product line* sold (specialty stores, department stores,

supermarkets, convenience stores, superstores, and service businesses); and *relative prices* (discount stores and off-price retailers). Today, many retailers are banding together in corporate and contractual *retail organizations* (corporate chains, voluntary chains and retailer cooperatives, franchise organizations, and merchandising conglomerates).

3. Identify the major types of wholesalers and give examples of each.

Wholesalers fall into three groups. First, *merchant wholesalers* take possession of the goods: They include *full-service wholesalers* (wholesale merchants, industrial distributors) and *limited-service wholesalers* (cash-and-carry wholesalers, truck wholesalers, drop shippers, rack jobbers, producers' cooperatives, and mail-order wholesalers). Second, *brokers* and *agents* do not take possession of the goods but are paid a commission for aiding buying and selling. Finally, *manufacturers' sales branches and offices* are wholesaling operations conducted by non-wholesalers to bypass the wholesalers.

4. Explain the marketing decisions facing retailers and wholesalers.

Each retailer must make decisions about its target markets, product assortment and services, price, promotion, and place. Retailers need to choose target markets carefully and position themselves strongly. Today, wholesaling is holding its own in the economy. Progressive wholesalers are adapting their services to the needs of target customers and are seeking cost-reducing methods of doing business. Facing slow growth in their domestic markets and developments such as the North American Free Trade Association, many large wholesalers are also now going global.

Reviewing the Key Terms

Agent   575

Broker   575

Category killer   550

Chain stores   552

Convenience store   549

Department store   548

Discount store   551

Franchise   553

Manufacturers' sales branches and
   offices   576

Merchant wholesaler   571

Off-price retailer   551

Retailers   547

Retailing   546

Shopping centre   561

Specialty store   548

Supermarket   548

Superstore   550

Wheel of retailing concept   563

Wholesaler   571

Wholesaling   571

Discussing the Concepts

1. Describe the similarities and differences between retailing and wholesaling. Can a company be a retailer and a wholesaler at the same time? Explain.

2. Giant superstores called category killers are an emerging trend. How is a category killer different from other types of retailers? Why has this form of retailing grown so rapidly? What types of retailers are most threatened by category killers? Why? How will online retailing affect category killers? Give an example of a category killer that has been affected by online marketing.

3. How has the growth of other types of large retailers affected the willingness of manufacturers to sell their goods at or below regular wholesale rates to off-price retailers?

4. List and characterize the major types of retail organizations. Which of these organizational forms seems to be growing in popularity? Which are declining in popularity? Why?

5. Retailers are always searching for new marketing strategies to attract and retain customers. List and briefly describe the strategies retailers use to differentiate themselves from competitors.

6. Many Canadian and U.S. retailers are significantly behind European and Asian retailers when it comes to global expansion. (a) Why is this so? (b) Which

Canadian retailers are positioned for global expansion? Explain. (c) How will online retailing affect global retail expansion? (d) Study Sweden's IKEA home furnishings stores (www.ikea.com). Why has IKEA been so successful in expanding into the North American market?

7. List and describe each of the channel functions that have been traditionally assigned to wholesalers. How will wholesalers have to change to meet the threat of increasing competition from large retailers? What type of wholesaler is best equipped to compete and evolve in the next decade? Explain.

8. Nature's Foods is a food market that will be opening soon in your local community. Nature's Foods carries only organically grown fruits and vegetables. No red meat products or products with high amounts of chemical additives or preservatives will be stocked. The store hopes to appeal to the health-conscious consumer and the vegetarian looking for an alternative to the traditional grocery store. As a specialty store, Nature's Foods has relatively few available suppliers and a limited purchasing budget. Examine the major types of wholesalers described in Table 14.4 (pages 574 and 575). Which category of wholesaler(s) should Nature's Foods pursue? Explain your reasoning.

Applying the Concepts

1. As consumers demand more and more service and customization, virtual retailing seems to have a brighter future. Through virtual retailing, a seller can come directly into your home, at your convenience, and allow you to participate in designing your own personalized product and shopping experience. This sounds great—no more ill-fitting bathing suits or greeting cards that seem like they were written for someone else, no high-pressure salespeople, no congested parking lots. At virtual retail sites, you can spend as much or as little time as you need to make up your mind. Virtual retailing has made mass customization a reality. All you have to do is point and click. Look at the following websites for more information on customizing clothing products, eyeglasses, and shoes: Interactive Custom Clothes (www.ic3d.com), Lands' End (www.landsend.com), Eyeglasses.com (www.eyeglasses.com), and Nike (www.nike.com).

a. How does virtual retailing compare with more traditional shopping formats? What are its primary advantages and disadvantages for consumers?

b. What target markets would be most interested in virtual retailing? Do the websites you just visited appear to be appealing to those segments? Explain.

c. Compare the marketing strategies of the Web retailers you just visited. Which company most appeals to you? Why?

d. Pick one of the websites and design your own product. Discuss the pros and cons of your experience. How was this experience different from buying in a retail store? Would you be willing to purchase the item you designed?

e. While some Canadian retailers like Grocery Gateway, Chapters.Indigo, and Roots have online virtual stores, others have been reluctant to take on the challenges of virtual retailing. What explains this reluctance? What advice would you give to a Canadian retailer thinking of taking the online plunge?

Video Short

View the video short for this chapter at **www.pearsoned.ca/kotler** and then answer the questions provided in the case description.

Company Case

dELiA's: Searching for the Right Way to Connect with Teens

Finding the right target market is a first step toward success; maintaining connection and community with the market comes next. Consider the case of Christopher Edgar and Steve Kahn, two college roommates who started a catalogue targeting college girls—specifically, sorority sisters. Sales were at best ho-hum until the guys realized that it was the college girls' little sisters who were actually buying the merchandise. Sensing an opportunity, in 1994 they shifted targets and aimed at the 12-to-17-year-old market with a catalogue named dELiA's. Since that decision, dELiA's has become *the* shopping place for teens.

How did dELiA's connect with teens? Initially, part of the connection was its edgy image. There were lots of fresh-faced, wide-eyed models with whipped-up hair that was sometimes green and sometimes blue. The catalogue featured styles such as wide-legged pants, clunky shoes, baby-doll dresses, ankle-length skirts, striped T-shirts, and the like—all very hip and high-spirited. Lately, however, dELiA's has softened its image. The latest look from dELiA's is called desert rose, a hippie-bohemian-gypsy look that includes drawstring peasant tops in small floral prints and jeans with lace-up trims.

As part of connecting to teens, dELiA's signed a contract with Shakira, Latin America's answer to Madonna, who was just becoming popular in the United States. Shakira appeared on the cover of the catalogue, wearing clothes she chose from dELiA's inventory. The website featured contests in which customers could win one of 500 autographed CDs, an autographed guitar, and a $500 shopping spree. It also offered a Q & A with Shakira, along with video and audio clips and editorial features. Shakira described her thing as mostly pants, boots, belts, and studs, making her an ideal hip spokesperson for the dELiA's spring 2002 look. The goal was to communicate that both were super-cool.

In another effort to connect with teens, dELiA's turned cataloguing into a two-way street. They hired high school and college girls to answer telephones, chat, answer questions, and provide shoppers with fashion tips while also finding out what was on the market's mind. Teenage girls responded by sending the cataloguers photos of themselves, letters, critiques of the clothes, suggestions for new merchandise, and tons of email. Then, specially designated employees answered all those letters and emails. The result was a major investment in relationship building with what is often a very fickle market. When selling to teens, constant communication becomes crucial to understanding what will sell.

Initially, dELiA's catalogue was passed around from hand to hand. But by the late 1990s, it had developed a stable mailing list, which has become one of dELiA's key strengths. Over the years, the company has compiled the list from telephone requests (sometimes 5000 a day). By 2002, dELiA's had a database of 13 million names that included 6 million actual buyers. To maintain the loyalty of its customers, dELiA's does not sell or share the list, and it keeps communications with customers private and confidential.

Once the catalogue was well established, Steve and Chris employed two strategies to maintain growth. In the first strategy, they moved into bricks-and-mortar retailing by acquiring TSI Soccer Corp., a soccer apparel and equipment retailer, and Screeem!, which operated 11 stores under that name and 15 under the name Jeans Country. These two purchases expanded dELiA's geographic retail coverage to include the entire East Coast. Then, in February 1999, the company opened the first of many dELiA's stores, in the Westchester Mall in White Plains, New York. By mid-2002, it had opened 54 dELiA's stores, with another 13 planned for late 2002 and 30 more in 2003.

In dELiA's stores, the merchandise assortment includes not only clothing but also cosmetics, bath products, posters, candy, novelty home accessories, and underwear. It looks like a three-dimensional version of the catalogue, with the dELiA's logo featured throughout the brightly lit store. Initially, merchandise flew off the shelves.

The second strategy took dELiA's online. It started a website, dELiA's.com, which was mostly informational and entertaining, although later it began to sell merchandise. That site was so successful that the company added other websites, such as gURL.com, aimed at teenage girls; dotdotdash.com, aimed at girls age 7 to 11; Droog.com, a site aimed at teenage boys; and contentsonline.com, which was a home furnishings site. The latter two sites were paired with their own catalogues. To manage all the sites and the connections between them, the management of dELiA's set up a subsidiary, named ITurf.

Such rapid expansion came at a high price, along with losses in every quarter in 2001. Several factors can explain this. First, direct selling and store retailing differ in operating-capital requirements. Stores are much more capital intensive than direct sales. Investments in leases, furnishings, inventory, and sales help are required up front. A catalogue with slow-selling merchandise can be quickly replaced, but a store with slow-selling merchandise suffers from sales and markdowns to move inventory. Beginning in the first quarter of 1999, the conversion of the Screeem! stores led to a $17.8 million first-quarter after-tax charge and necessitated many markdowns and additional promotions to move merchandise.

Second, Internet operations were another drain on resources. The ITurf subsidiary required building an expensive infrastructure. Unfortunately, this effort did not yield the third C of Internet operations—commerce. Internet sales were a disappointing 3 percent to 4 percent in 1999 and 2000.

As the losses continued to mount, dELiA's spun off the ITurf subsidiary in 1999, liquidated the Droog catalogue of boys' apparel in 2000, sold TSI Soccer in 2001, and sold off the assets of gURL.com. In a turnaround, it re-merged with ITurf in November of 2000.

What does this mean for dELiA's future? Clearly, the company no longer sees itself as a cataloguer. Instead, it is aiming for multi-channel mastery, like Coldwater Creek or J. Jill Group. Chairman–CEO Steve Kahn believes that dELiA's can expand to 250-plus stores if it can leverage its opportunities quickly and profitably.

Industry observers believe that moving from cataloguing to bricks-and-mortar is easier than moving from retail stores to cataloguing. Retailers can respond much more quickly to changes in trends by changing floor displays, and displays can be used along with the Web to test trends before they are put into the catalogue. Retail stores and catalogues both utilize dELiA's big database. Retailers can use the database for direct mailings promoting stores, and catalogues can be directed to teens according to their level of purchases. To keep the database growing—especially to build databases for local stores—dELiA's retailers capture customer information such as zip codes and dollar amount of sales in stores.

dELiA's faces obstacles to future success. One of these is the fickleness of its target market. Teens can turn on a retailer in an instant, and keeping up with the market is very difficult. Second, many teens don't like to order over the Internet: after they select items to purchase, they often need to get permission and a credit card number from Mom or Dad—a screening that may not always result in sales. Third, increasing postage and delivery costs coupled with mailbox glut are having a negative impact on direct selling. Fourth, there's heavy competition for any mall's floor traffic—can dELiA's brand withstand that competition?

The key to multi-channel selling is to build a unified brand across channels. dELiA's has done well at building its dELiA's website and paginating its catalogue, but it has yet to perfect the physical layout of its stores, not to mention making sure that all three retailing venues project the same image.

Questions for Discussion

1. Check out the dELiA's website (www.delias.com). Is it attractive? Is it easy to use? In your opinion, would it appeal to teens? Why?

2. Is Shakira a good spokesperson for dELiA's? Why or why not?

3. The 3Cs of Internet retailing are community, content, and commerce. Evaluate the dELiA's website on these criteria.

4. If you have a dELiA's store close by, visit it and compare it with the website and catalogue. Do they present a unified image? Why or why not?

5. What are the advantages and disadvantages of catalogues, retail stores, and the Internet? How can the advantages of one be used to overcome the disadvantages of the others?

6. In your opinion, is dELiA's likely to succeed in all three channels? Why or why not?

Sources: "ITurf IPO Lifts dELiA's Profits," *WWD,* June 10, 1999, p. 9; "DELiA's 2nd Quarter Loss Deepens," *WWD,* September 2, 1999, p. 5; "dELiA's Screeem! and Jean Country Acquisition a Done Deal," *Daily News Record,* August 3, 1998, p. 8; "Business Brief—dELiA's Corp.: Web Site Closings Are Cited as Wider Loss Is Recorded," *Wall Street Journal,* August 30, 2001; "DELiA's Sees Profitable Quarter," *WWD,* June 10, 2002, p. 12; Mark Del Franco, "dELiA's Growth Strategy, Take Two," *Catalog Age,* September 2001, pp. 5, 16; Yolanda Gault, "Marketer Drops as DELiA's Shops, but Analysts Stand by Cataloger: Marketer to Teens Makes Move to Stores," *Crain's New York Business,* June 8, 1998, p. 23; Karen Parr, "New Catalogs Target Gen Y," *WWD,* July 24, 1997, p. 12; Cynthia Redecker, "dELiA's Opens First Retail Unit," *WWD,* February 25, 1999, p. 11; and Kristin Young, "dELiA's New Diva: Shakira Signs On," *WWD,* December 21, 2001, p. 10.

CBC Video Case

Log on to your Companion Website at **www.pearsoned.ca/kotler** to view a CBC video segment and case for this chapter.

Chapter 15

Integrated Marketing Communication Strategy

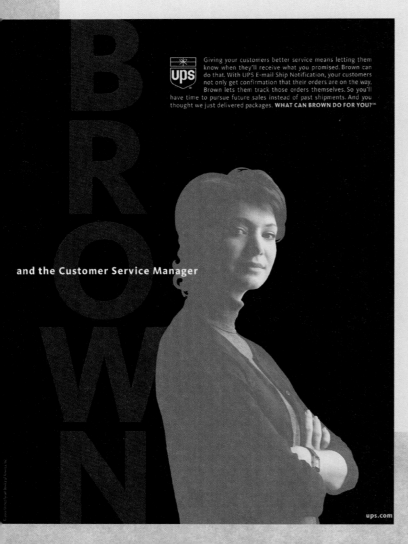

Giving your customers better service means letting them know when they'll receive what you promised. Brown can do that. With UPS E-mail Ship Notification, your customers not only get confirmation that their orders are on the way, Brown lets them track those orders themselves. So you'll have time to pursue future sales instead of past shipments. And you thought we just delivered packages. **WHAT CAN BROWN DO FOR YOU?**™

and the Customer Service Manager

ups.com

After studying this chapter you should be able to

1. name and define the five tools of the marketing communications mix

2. discuss the process and advantages of integrated marketing communications

3. outline the steps in developing effective marketing communications

4. explain the methods for setting the promotion budget and factors that affect the design of the promotion mix

Looking Ahead: Previewing the Concepts

In this and the next two chapters, we'll examine the last of the marketing mix tools—*integrated marketing communications.* Using the 4*P*s framework, this is called promotion. You'll find that promotion is not a single tool, but rather a mix of several tools. Ideally, the company will carefully coordinate these promotion elements to deliver a clear, consistent, and compelling message about the organization and its products. We'll begin by introducing you to the various promotion mix tools, the importance of integrated marketing communications, the steps in developing marketing communications, and the promotion-budgeting process. In Chapters 16 and 17, we'll visit the specific marketing communications tools.

To start, let's look at UPS. You probably know UPS as a small-package delivery company. In recent years, however, the company has grown rapidly into a corporate giant offering a broad range of supply chain management services. Its challenge: How can it communicate the "new UPS" to customers large and small while at the same time building on the rich heritage we've come to associate with the old UPS? The answer comes in the form of the question "What Can Brown Do for You?"

hen you think about UPS, you probably envision one of those familiar brown trucks with a friendly driver who hustles around your neighbourhood dropping off important parcels. And no wonder. The company's 88 000 delivery fleet (package cars, vans, tractors, and motorcycles) and 80 000 brown-clad drivers deliver more than 3.4 billion packages annually, an average of 13.6 million each day.

For most of us, seeing a brown UPS truck evokes fond memories of past packages delivered. And the drivers give UPS a friendly, local face. Stories abound of UPS delivery personnel who've gone to extremes to deliver a package or serve a customer.

In recent years, however, UPS has grown to become much more than a neighbourhood small-package delivery service. It is now a global company generating over $39.7 billion in revenue from its operations in more than 200 countries, including Canada. It is one of the most recognized and admired brands in the world. UPS offers a broad range of services to customers of all types and sizes—everything from transportation and package delivery to third-party logistics, inventory management, financing, and global customer clearance services. It serves 90 percent of the world population and 99 percent of businesses in the Fortune 1000.

While rapid growth and diversification presents many opportunities for UPS, it also presents challenges. Perhaps the greatest is communicating with all of UPS's many customers about the capabilities of UPS. The company's old communications theme—"We run the tightest ship in the shipping business"—presented UPS narrowly as a shipping company rather than an agile supply chain solutions provider. It was also myopic, focusing on the company's efficient operations rather than on what those efficiencies meant to and did for customers. UPS needed a new marketing communications campaign, one that positioned the company as an agile logistics solutions provider, while at the same time building on the rich values that customers have come to associate with UPS since its birth in 1907.

The search for a new corporate communications theme began with customers. UPS conducted focus groups and market tests with customers at every level, from residential package shippers to mail room managers to corporate CEOs—anyone and everyone who could influence the decision to use UPS. It also held interviews with UPS insiders. The question: How could UPS simplify the complicated story about its diverse portfolio of services and all of the things for which UPS stands? When they'd run the numbers on the research, UPS's marketers came up with an obvious answer: Brown! That's right, Brown. Dale Hayes, UPS vice president of brand management and customer communications, explains:

> We needed to become more aggressive in communicating to our customers without losing one of our core values...humility. We're a roll-up-your-sleeves, get-it-done kind of company; people love our drivers, they love our brown trucks, they love everything we do. We found that there was tremendous strength in the colour brown. So we built our new campaign on the idea of telling our story through the customers' eyes by talking about what brown could do for them. [The colour brown held deep meaning for UPS employees as well.] We have said for years that "we are brown" to the core, our blood runs brown.... We've been referred to for years as Big Brown.... But we had never found the voice to embrace brown publicly and to let brown speak for us.

Thus was born the "What Can Brown Do for You?" theme that now unifies UPS's communications efforts. To introduce the new theme, UPS launched its largest-ever national media campaign during the 2002 Winter Olympics. The campaign used warm, humorous ads featuring a variety of professionals discussing how UPS's broad range of services could make their jobs easier. Says John Beystehner, senior vice president of worldwide sales and marketing at UPS, "Instead of trying to convey our capabilities from *our* point of view, we are putting ourselves in the shoes of our customers and literally having them ask themselves, 'What Can Brown Do for You?'"

The corporate advertising campaign is just the tip of the UPS marketing communications effort. The ad promise has little meaning if it's not reinforced by the full mix of UPS's communications activities. "The campaign is an initial step to...help [our audiences] start thinking beyond their current perceptions of UPS, but it is just a first step," notes Beystehner. "The next step is to continue to align our organization behind the brand [promise]." Says former UPS CEO Jim Kelly, "It's important to note...that a brand can be very hollow and lifeless...if the people and the organization...are not 100 percent dedicated to [communicating and] living out the brand promise every day."

To deliver the "What Can Brown Do for You?" message every day in a more personal way, UPS is realigning its sales and marketing organization. Rather than having departments and reps that focus on one set of services, UPS is combining all of its sales, marketing, and operations units into a single team. The move will provide a single face to each customer, bringing all of Brown's capabilities to bear on providing total supply chain solutions to customers.

In addition to relying on its sales and marketing people to deliver the new message personally, UPS also communicates with customers through several websites. At www.ups.com, consumers can check shipping rates, track packages, order supplies, and schedule pickups. At www.upslogistics.com, corporate customers can learn more about UPS's business-to-business services, including supply chain management and technology solutions. Potential clients can browse through success stories of UPS's Fortune 500 customers. At www.capital.ups.com, corporate clients can establish lines of credit, apply for financing, lease equipment, and learn about UPS's insurance services.

The advertising slogan is backed by employee action at the community level as well. Global Volunteer Week (October 19–26) is part of UPS's long-standing commitment to give back to the communities in which UPS employees live and work. In Canada, more than 500 employees will volunteer over 3000 hours to various organizations—sorting and distributing food for the homeless, cleaning dog kennels for the SPCA, collecting donations for the Arthritis Society, and repairing and repainting facilities of various charitable organizations.

Communicating the new "What Can Brown Do for You" theme and giving it life will be no easy task. It will take more than just advertising and friendly drivers. UPS must communicate the new positioning at every customer touchpoint. It must integrate all of its communications—from advertising and personal contact to sales promotion, public relations, direct marketing, and its multiple websites—to deliver a seamless message about what Brown can do for its customers.[1]

Modern marketing calls for more than just developing a good product, pricing it attractively, and making it available to target customers. Companies also must *communicate* with their current and prospective customers, and what they communicate should not be left to chance. All of their communications efforts must be blended into a consistent and coordinated communications program. Just as good communication is important in building and maintaining any kind of relationship, it is a crucial element in a company's efforts to build customer relationships.

The Marketing Communications Mix

Marketing communications mix (promotion mix)
The specific mix of advertising, sales promotion, public relations, personal selling, and direct-marketing tools a company uses to pursue its advertising and marketing objectives.

Advertising
Any paid form of non-personal presentation and promotion of ideas, goods, or services by an identified sponsor.

Sales promotion
Short-term incentives to encourage purchase or sale of a product or service.

Public relations
Building good relations with the company's various publics by obtaining favourable publicity, building up a good "corporate image," and handling or heading off unfavourable rumours, stories, and events.

Personal selling
Personal presentation by the firm's sales force for the purpose of making sales and building customer relationships.

Direct marketing
Direct communications with carefully targeted individuals to both obtain an immediate response and cultivate lasting customer relationships.

A company's total **marketing communications mix**—also called its **promotion mix**—consists of the specific blend of advertising, sales promotion, public relations, personal selling, and direct-marketing tools that the company uses to pursue its advertising and marketing objectives. The five major types of promotion are:[2]

- **Advertising:** Any paid form of non-personal presentation and promotion of ideas, goods, or services by an identified sponsor.
- **Sales promotion:** Short-term incentives to encourage the purchase or sale of a product or service.
- **Public relations:** Building good relations with the company's various publics by obtaining favourable publicity, building up a good "corporate image," and handling or heading off unfavourable rumours, stories, and events.
- **Personal selling:** Personal presentation by the firm's sales force for the purpose of making sales and building customer relationships.
- **Direct marketing:** Direct communications with carefully targeted individual consumers to both obtain an immediate response and cultivate lasting customer relationships—the use of telephone, mail, fax, email, the Internet, and other tools to communicate directly with specific consumers.

Each type of promotion involves specific tools. For example, advertising includes print, broadcast, outdoor, and other forms. Sales promotion includes point-of-purchase displays, premiums, discounts, coupons, specialty advertising, and demonstrations. Public relations includes press releases and special events. Personal selling includes sales presentations, trade shows, and incentive programs. Direct marketing includes catalogues, telephone marketing, kiosks, the Internet, and more. Thanks to technological breakthroughs, marketers can now communicate through traditional media (newspapers, radio, telephone, and television), as well as through newer media forms (fax, cell phones, and computers). At the same time, communication goes beyond these specific promotion tools. The product's design, its price, the shape and colour of its package, and the stores that sell it—*all* communicate something to buyers. Thus, although the promotion mix is the company's primary communication activity, the entire marketing mix—promotion *and* product, price, and place—must be coordinated for greatest communication impact.

In this chapter, we begin by examining the rapidly changing marketing communications environment, the concept of integrated marketing communications, and the marketing communication process. Next, we discuss the factors that marketing communicators must consider in shaping an overall communications mix. Finally, we summarize the legal, ethical, and social responsibility issues in marketing communications. In Chapter 16, we look at *mass-communication tools*—advertising, sales promotion, and public relations. Chapter 17 examines the *sales force* and *direct marketing* as communication and promotion tools.

Integrated Marketing Communications

During the past several decades, companies around the world perfected the art of mass marketing—selling highly standardized products to masses of customers. In the process, they have developed effective mass-media advertising techniques to support their mass-marketing strategies. These companies routinely invested millions of dollars in the mass media, reaching tens of millions of customers with a single ad. However, as we move into the twenty-first century, marketing managers face some new marketing communications realities.

The Changing Communications Environment

Two major factors are changing the face of today's marketing communications. First, as mass markets have fragmented, marketers are shifting away from mass marketing. More and more, they are developing focused marketing programs designed to build closer relationships with customers in more narrowly defined micromarkets. Second, vast improvements in information technology are speeding the movement toward segmented marketing. Today's information technology helps marketers to keep closer track of customer needs—more information about consumers at the individual and household levels is available than ever before. New technologies also provide new communications avenues for reaching smaller customer segments with more tailored messages.

The shift from mass marketing to segmented marketing has had a dramatic impact on marketing communications. Just as mass marketing gave rise to a new generation of mass-media communications, the shift toward one-to-one marketing is spawning a new generation of more specialized and highly targeted communications efforts.

Given this new communications environment, marketers must rethink the roles of various media and promotion mix tools. Mass-media advertising has long dominated the promotion mixes of consumer product companies. However, although television, magazines, and other mass media remain very important, their dominance is now declining. *Market* fragmentation has resulted in *media* fragmentation in an explosion of more focused media that better match today's targeting strategies. Beyond these channels, advertisers are making increased use of new, highly targeted media, ranging from highly focused specialty magazines and cable television channels, to CD catalogues and Web coupon promotions, to airport kiosks and floor decals in supermarket aisles. In all, companies are doing less *broadcasting* and more *narrowcasting*.

The new media environment: The relatively few mass magazines of past decades have been replaced today by thousands of magazines targeting special-interest audiences.

More generally, advertising appears to be giving way to other elements of the promotion mix. In the glory days of mass marketing, consumer product companies spent the lion's share of their promotion budgets on mass-media advertising. Today, media advertising captures only about 26 percent of total promotion spending.[3] The rest goes to various sales promotion activities, which can be focused more effectively on individual consumer and trade segments. Marketers are using a richer variety of focused communication tools in an effort to reach their diverse target markets.

The Need for Integrated Marketing Communications

The shift from mass marketing to targeted marketing, and the corresponding use of a larger, richer mixture of communication channels and promotion tools, poses a problem for marketers. Customers don't distinguish between message sources the way marketers do. In the consumer's mind, advertising messages from different media and different promotional approaches all become part of a single message about the company. Conflicting messages from these different sources can result in confused company images and brand positions.

All too often, companies fail to integrate their various communications channels. The result is a hodgepodge of communications to consumers. Mass advertisements say one thing, a price promotion sends a different signal, a product label creates still another message, company sales literature says something altogether different, and the company's website seems out of sync with everything else.

The problem is that these communications often come from different company sources. Advertising messages are planned and implemented by the advertising department or advertising agency. Personal selling communications are developed by sales management. Other functional specialists are responsible for public relations, sales promotion, direct marketing, online sites, and other forms of marketing communications.

Recently, such functional separation has been a major problem for many companies and their Internet communications activities. Many companies first organized their new Web communications operations into separate groups or divisions, isolating them from mainstream marketing activities. However, whereas some companies have compartmentalized the new communications tools, customers won't. According to one IMC expert:

> The truth is, most [consumers] won't compartmentalize their use of the new systems. They won't say, "Hey, I'm going off to do a bit of Web surfing. Burn my TV, throw out all my radios, cancel all my magazine subscriptions and, by the way, take out my telephone and don't deliver any mail anymore." It's not that kind of world for consumers, and it shouldn't be that kind of world for marketers either.[4]

To be sure, the Internet promises exciting marketing communications potential. However, marketers trying to use the Web alone to build brands face many challenges. One limitation is that the Internet doesn't build mass brand awareness. Instead, it's like having millions of private conversations. The Web simply can't match the impact of the Super Bowl, where tens of millions of people see the same 30-second Nike or Hallmark ad at the same time. Using the Internet, it's hard to establish the universal meanings—such as "Just do it!" or "When you care enough to send the very best"—that are at the heart of brand recognition and brand value.

Thus, if treated as a special case, the Internet—or any other marketing communication tool—can be a *dis*integrating force in marketing communications. Instead, all the communication tools must be carefully integrated into the broader marketing communications mix. Today, the best bet is to wed the emotional pitch and impact of traditional brand marketing with the interactivity and real service offered online. For example, television ads for Saturn still offer the same old-fashioned humorous appeal. But now they point viewers to the company's website, which offers lots of help and very little hype. The site helps serious car buyers select a model, calculate payments, and find a retailer online.

Even marketers that can't really sell their goods via the Web are using the Internet as an effective customer communication and relationship enhancer. For example, Harpo Enterprises, the company that oversees *The Oprah Winfrey Show,* also maintains a website (www.oprah.com) that offers in-depth information on show topics, access to footage taped after the live show ends, and a sneek peek at the content of upcoming issues of *O* magazine. The website, show, and magazine are all consistently designed. Says one analyst, the "consistency in design and tone makes the brand stronger because the consumer immediately recognizes the image, which engenders emotion and brand loyalty."[5]

Integrated marketing communications (IMC)

The concept under which a company carefully integrates and coordinates its many communications channels to deliver a clear, consistent, and compelling message about the organization and its products.

In the past, no one person was responsible for thinking through the communication roles of the various promotion tools and coordinating the promotion mix. Today, however, many companies are adopting the concept of **integrated marketing communications (IMC)**. Under this concept, as illustrated in Figure 15.1, the company carefully integrates and coordinates its many communications channels to deliver a clear, consistent, and compelling message about the organization and its products.[6]

As one marketing executive puts it, "IMC builds a strong brand identity in the marketplace by tying together and reinforcing all your images and messages. IMC means that all your corporate messages, positioning and images, and identity are coordinated across all [marketing communications] venues. It means that your PR materials say the same thing as your direct mail campaign, and your advertising has the same 'look and feel' as your website."[7]

IMC calls for recognizing all contact points at which the customer may encounter the company, its products, and its brands. Each *brand contact* will deliver a message, whether good, bad, or indifferent. The company must strive to deliver a consistent and positive message at all contact points.

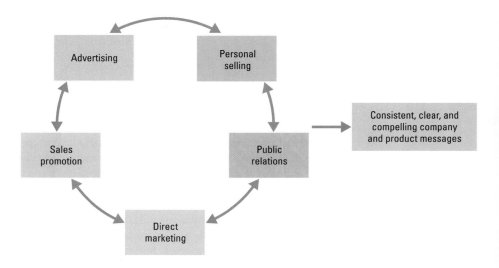

Figure 15.1 Integrated marketing communications

Today, all the marketing communication tools must be carefully integrated. For example, Saturn's television and print ads help build brand appeal while the company's website helps serious car buyers select a model, calculate payments, and find a dealer online.

To help implement integrated marketing communication, some companies appoint a marketing communications director—or *marcom manager*—who has overall responsibility for the company's communications efforts. IMC produces better communications consistency and greater sales impact. It places the responsibility in someone's hands—where none existed before—to unify the company's image as it is shaped by thousands of company activities. It leads to a total marketing communication strategy aimed at showing how the company and its products can help customers solve their problems.

A View of the Communication Process

Integrated marketing communications involves identifying the target audience and shaping a well-coordinated promotional program to elicit the desired audience response. Too often, marketing communications focus on overcoming immediate awareness, image, or preference problems in the target market. But this approach to communication is too shortsighted. Today, marketers are moving toward viewing communications as *managing the customer relationship over time*. Because customers differ, communications programs need to be developed for specific segments, niches, and even individuals. And given the new interactive communications technologies, companies must ask not only "How can we reach our customers?" but also "How can we find ways to let our customers reach us?"

Thus, the communications process should start with an audit of all the potential interactions that target customers may have with the product and company. For example, someone purchasing a new computer may talk with others, see television commercials, read articles and ads in newspapers and magazines, visit various websites, and try out computers in stores. Marketers need to assess what influence that each of these communications experiences will have at different stages of the buying process. This understanding will help marketers allocate their communication dollars more efficiently and effectively.

To communicate effectively, marketers need to understand how communication works. Communication involves the nine elements shown in Figure 15.2. Two of these elements are the major parties in a communication—the *sender* and *receiver*. Another two are the major communication tools—the *message* and the *media*. Four more are major communication functions—*encoding, decoding, response*, and *feedback*. The last element is *noise* in the system. Definitions of these elements are applied to an ad for Hewlett-Packard (HP) colour copiers:

- *Sender:* The party *sending the message* to another party—here, HP.
- *Encoding:* The process of *putting thought into symbolic form*—HP's advertising agency assembles words and illustrations into an advertisement that will convey the intended message.
- *Message:* The *set of symbols* that the sender transmits—the actual HP copier ad.
- *Media:* The *communication channels* through which the message moves from sender to receiver—in this case, the specific magazines that HP selects.
- *Decoding:* The process by which the receiver *assigns meaning to the symbols* encoded by the sender—a consumer reads the HP copier ad and interprets the words and illustrations it contains.
- *Receiver:* The party *receiving the message* sent by another party—the home office or business customer who reads the HP copier ad.
- *Response:* The *reactions of the receiver* after being exposed to the message—any of hundreds of possible responses, such as the consumer is more aware of the attributes of HP copiers, actually buys an HP copier, or does nothing.
- *Feedback:* The part of the *receiver's response communicated back to the sender*—HP research shows that consumers are struck by and remember the ad, or consumers write or call HP praising or criticizing the ad or HP's products.
- *Noise:* The *unplanned static or distortion* during the communication process, which results in the receiver's getting a different message than the one the sender sent—the consumer is distracted while reading the magazine and misses the HP ad or its key points.

Figure 15.2 Elements in the communication process

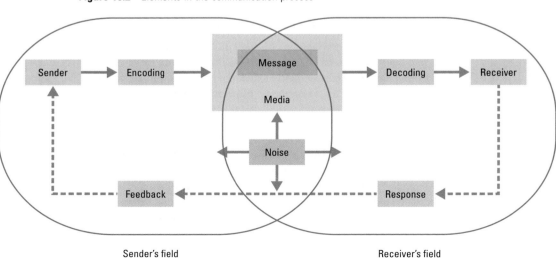

For a message to be effective, the sender's encoding process must mesh with the receiver's decoding process. Therefore, the best messages consist of words and other symbols that are familiar to the receiver. The more the sender's field of experience overlaps with that of the receiver, the more effective the message is likely to be. Marketing communicators may not always *share* their consumer's field of experience. For example, an advertising copywriter from one social stratum might create ads for consumers from another stratum—say, blue-collar workers or wealthy business owners. However, to communicate effectively, the marketing communicator must *understand* the consumer's field of experience.

This model points out several key factors in good communication. Senders need to know what audiences they wish to reach and what responses they want. They must be good at encoding messages that take into account how the target audience decodes them. They must send messages through media that reach target audiences, and they must develop feedback channels so that they can assess the audience's response to the message.

Steps in Developing Effective Communications

We now examine the steps in developing an effective integrated communications and promotion program. The marketing communicator must identify the target audience, determine the response sought, choose a message, choose the media through which to send the message, select the message source, and collect feedback. (For a close look at how one Canadian marketer has mastered the art of IMC, see Real Marketing 15.1.)

Identifying the Target Audience

A marketing communicator starts with a clear target audience in mind. The audience may be potential buyers or current users, those who make the buying decision, or those who influence it. The audience may be individuals, groups, special publics, or the general public. The target audience will affect the communicator's decisions on *what* will be said, *how* it will be said, *when* it will be said, *where* it will be said, and *who* will say it.

Determining the Desired Response

Buyer readiness stages
The stages consumers normally pass through on their way to purchase, including awareness, knowledge, liking, preference, conviction, and purchase.

Once the target audience is defined, the marketing communicator must decide what response is sought. Of course, in many cases, the final response is *purchase*. But purchase is the result of a long process of consumer decision making. The marketing communicator needs to know where the target audience now stands and to what stage it needs to be moved. The target audience may be in any of six **buyer readiness stages**, the stages that consumers typically pass through on their way to making a purchase. These stages are *awareness, knowledge, liking, preference, conviction,* and *purchase* (see Figure 15.3 on page 595).

The marketing communicator's target market may be totally unaware of the product, know only its name, or know little about it. The communicator must first build *awareness* and *knowledge*. For example, when Nissan introduced its Infiniti automobile line, it began with an extensive "teaser" advertising campaign to create name familiarity. Initial ads for the Infiniti created curiosity and awareness by showing the car's name but not the car. Later ads created knowledge by informing potential buyers of the car's high quality and many innovative features.

15.1 Alan Quarry, President of Quarry Integrated Communications

"Clients count on us to help build their business, build their brands, build their customer relationships and build their profits...and we deliver," states Alan Quarry, "head coach" of Quarry Integrated Communications, a firm based in Waterloo, Ontario, with offices in Toronto, Dallas, and Japan. The hand-lettered signs posted all around Quarry's premises capture their essence: "Our mission is to help our clients build their businesses through integrated communications." Quarry's clients—firms like Nortel Networks, Hewlett-Packard, Royal Bank, Cyanamid Crop Protection, Clarica Life, Hoffmann-la Roche, Elanco Animal Health, FedEx, Merck Frosst, and Sprint Canada—all agree that Quarry has helped them accomplish this objective.

It's hard to catch up with Alan Quarry. A person with seemingly endless energy, he not only is the president of Quarry Integrated Communications, but he also finds time to teach marketing communications to fourth-year honours business students at Wilfrid Laurier University. When he isn't teaching, travelling, working with his clients, or sharing a laugh with his family, he has his head in a book. He is a strong believer that continuous learning is the key to success in the modern economy. "As communicators, we can never stop increasing our knowledge about consumer

Alan Quarry

motivation and how effective communications work," states Quarry.

Quarry Integrated focuses on building demand for considered-purchase goods and services in the information technology, financial services, agri-business, and health-care industries. But, as Quarry notes, "Advertising doesn't work like it used to. People have grown skeptical, info-saturated, atomized in their interests, and now wired to the Internet."

"So how do you reach your customers in such a jaded marketplace?" Quarry asks. We know that advertisers can't simply deliver a snappy selling message and expect results. Increasingly, the challenge is to understand the lifestyles, attitudes, and motivations of individual customers, and find a way to reach them with a consistent, relevant message. In other words, you have to use integrated communications where integration means consistency of brand contacts. Even more importantly, Quarry notes, "Consistency means trust. Trust means better relationships with your customers."

As you may gather from the last statement, Quarry Integrated Communications is a values-led company. Three core values guide its actions: integrity, relevance, and achievement. *Integrity* means that Quarry conducts its business honestly and fairly with its clients, associates, suppliers, and the marketplace. *Relevance* means Quarry works to anticipate and identify critical success factors for clients and then exceed their expectations by delivering on its commitments in a creative, timely, and cost-effective manner. And *achievement* is when Quarry successfully builds the businesses of its clients and their brands. (Visit Quarry's website at www.quarry.com/culture/values to understand fully the importance of these guiding principles for the firm.)

In addition to being values-led, Quarry Integrated is a highly innovative firm, which broke the traditional advertising agency model in the early 1990s and developed a new model for doing business. "The structure of the traditional ad agency seemed dysfunctional and almost anti-client to me," states Alan Quarry. "All the internal politics and focus on driving mass-media spending was not the kind of organization we wanted to be. We couldn't be the type of strategic ally that our clients need to be successful in the future. We believe that mass media advertising is communications 'at' the consumer. Integrated marketing communications (IMC) is a conversation 'with' the consumer. There will be a lot less marketing in the future and a lot more 'customerizing,' as IMC guru Don Schultz has pointed out. We believe that relationship-building dialogue with the customer strengthens and can even improve products and brands."

To help make this all happen, Quarry Integrated is wired. No, not from three-martini lunches, but by ethernet hubs, Internet routers, T-1 lines, videoconferencing, and leading-edge telephony and software, which are used to improve communications between Quarry and its clients. This "technology-enhanced communications" approach is another difference between Quarry and many of its competitors. "Lots of ad agencies seem to think of buying technology as being an 'expense'...we think of acquiring the tools we use as an 'investment,'" explains Alan Quarry. "It's a mindset thing. We know that we cannot be a successful, global organization and help our clients build without being tech-savvy."

In an industry characterized by disturbingly high staff turnover rates, Quarry Integrated has had one of Canada's best track records for continuity. Many think that Quarry's high retention rate has a lot to do with the environment created at the workplace. It's an environment without corner offices—in fact, Alan Quarry, the president, does not have an assigned office at all, but instead pushes his mobile work surface around and answers to the nickname "Virtu-Al." To foster creative thinking, Quarry has idea rooms named the Eureka Room and the Kaboom Room. There's a 1950s-style diner, called Al's Diner (in honour of Albert Einstein), where the Quarry team and guests meet, work, and have access to a free supply of fruit, veggies, and other brain food. It's an environment that offers at least one view of the outside world no matter where you stand. The workplace motto—"Think like the customer, Always anticipate, And have fun!"—is posted all around.

Quarry Integrated Communications has been incredibly successful in an industry where many believe starting new communications agencies, let alone independent Canadian-owned agencies, is next to impossible. However, Quarry continues to grow. Not content to rest on its laurels, Quarry Integrated Communications has a remarkable growth objective: to be the best integrated communications organization in the galaxy! Seeing the incredible commitment and energy in this firm will convince anyone that Quarry is well on its way to accomplishing this aim.

Source: Information provided to Peggy Cunningham by Alan Quarry. Also see www.quarry.com.

Assuming target consumers *know* the product, how do they *feel* about it? Once potential buyers know about the Infiniti, Nissan's marketers wanted to move them through successively stronger stages of feelings toward the car. These stages include *liking* (feeling favourable about the Infiniti), *preference* (preferring Infiniti to other car brands), and *conviction* (believing that Infiniti is the best car for them). Infiniti marketers used a combination of the promotion mix tools to create positive feelings and conviction. Advertising extols the Infiniti's advantages over competing brands and established its "Accelerating the Future" positioning. Press releases and other public relations activities stress the car's innovative features and performance. Dealer salespeople tell buyers about options, value for the price, and after-sale service.

Finally, some members of the target market might be convinced about the product, but not quite get around to making the *purchase*. Potential Infiniti buyers might

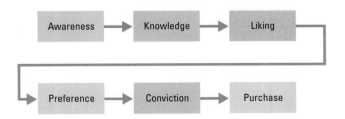

Figure 15.3 Buyer readiness stages

have decided to wait for more information or for the economy to improve. The communicator must lead these consumers to take the final step. Actions might include offering special promotional prices, rebates, or premiums. Salespeople may write to selected customers, inviting them to visit the dealership for a special showing. The Infiniti website (www.infiniti.com) allows potential buyers to virtually build their own car, explains various financing options, and invites them to visit the local dealer's showroom.

Of course, marketing communications alone cannot create positive feelings and purchases for Infiniti. The car itself must provide superior value for the customer. In fact, outstanding marketing communications can actually speed the demise of a poor product. The more quickly potential buyers learn about the poor product, the more quickly they become aware of its faults. Thus, good marketing communication calls for "good deeds followed by good words."

Designing a Message

Having defined the desired audience response, the communicator turns to developing an effective message. Ideally, the message should get *attention,* hold *interest,* arouse *desire,* and obtain *action* (a framework known as the *AIDA model*). In practice, few messages take the consumer all the way from awareness to purchase, but the AIDA framework suggests the qualities of a good message.

In putting together the message, the marketing communicator must decide what to say (*message content*) and how to say it (*message structure* and *format*).

Message Content

The communicator has to figure out an appeal or theme that will produce the desired response. There are three types of appeals: rational, emotional, and moral.

Rational appeals relate to the audience's self-interest. They show that the product will produce the desired benefits. Examples are messages showing a product's quality, economy, value, or performance. In its ads, Mercedes offers cars that are "engineered like no other car in the world," stressing engineering design, performance, and safety. Buckley's Mixture took its most recognizable quality, the bad taste of its cough syrup, and turned it into an award-winning campaign linked by the tag line, "It tastes awful. And it works."

Emotional appeals attempt to stir up either negative or positive emotions that can motivate purchase. Communicators may use such positive emotional appeals as love, pride, joy, and humour. Advocates for humorous messages claim that they attract more attention and create more liking and belief in the sponsor. These days,

Humour in advertising: These days, it seems as though almost every company is using humour in its advertising, even the scholarly American Heritage Dictionary.

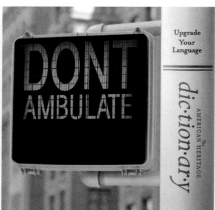

it seems as though almost every company is using humour in its advertising, from consumer product firms such as Levi-Strauss to high-tech product and service marketers such as Dell. When the new Toronto 1 TV channel launched in September 2003, it used humour to attract its narrow target audience, urban professionals aged 33 to 37. In a similar fashion, the City of Toronto used humour to make water management issues interesting in its new print and outdoor campaign. Rather than designing another dry informational campaign that directly asked consumers to disconnect downspouts to avoid overloading the sewer system during storms, the city decided to focus on the benefit for consumers: the reduced risk of leaky basements. The ad visuals, which showed furniture hanging on a clothesline, attracted immediate attention. As the creative director for the campaign noted, "It's fairly innovative and puts a fresh face on the communications."

Properly used, humour can capture attention, make people feel good, and give a brand personality. However, the advertiser must be careful when using humour. Used poorly, it can detract from comprehension, wear out its welcome fast, overshadow the product, or even irritate consumers. Take this example:

> Recent Domino's pizza ads featured a character named Bad Andy, a blue critter who looked like a cross between a monkey and a rat. Bad Andy was shown to live in the back of a Domino's Pizza store, and his voracious appetite muddled up the store's operations. Unfortunately, the attempt at humour sputtered. Despite the comic possibilities, the ads did little to highlight the quality of Domino's pizza or service, and Bad Andy's cavorting was more irritating than endearing. Bad Andy was annoying. He was obnoxious. "Bad Andy got some of the highest dislikability ratings of any spokescharacter in the history of advertising," admits a Domino's marketing executive. "Sales didn't respond." Besides, the notion of a squirrel-like animal being holed up in the back of a pizza joint was unappetizing, to say the least.[8]

Communicators can also use negative emotional appeals, such as fear, guilt, and shame, in order to get people to do things they should (brush their teeth, buy new tires), or to stop doing things they shouldn't (smoke, drink too much, eat fatty foods). One Crest ad invokes mild fear when it claims, "There are some things you just can't afford to gamble with" (cavities!). Etonic ads ask, "What would you do if you couldn't run?" and go on to note that Etonic athletic shoes are designed to avoid injuries—they're "built so you can last." A Michelin tire ad features cute babies and suggests, "Because so much is riding on your tires."

Moral appeals are directed to the audience's sense of what is "right" and "proper." They often are used to urge people to support such social causes as a cleaner environment and aid to the needy, or combat such social problems as drug abuse, discrimination, sexual harassment, and spousal abuse. The Canadian advertising industry used a moral appeal when it addressed the issue of music piracy:

> Piracy, the unauthorized copying of software and music and the use of cable signals without payment, has become endemic. For example, one study showed that over half of the Canadian population thought it was all right to copy software for personal use. Another suggested that the 20 percent drop in music sales over the past three years could be attributed largely to people's downloading of music from the Internet. Research also revealed that Canadian teens had an extremely negative view of the music industry and that many didn't care what happened to the artists. In an effort that the industry parallels to creating awareness of the negative effects of drinking and driving, the Canadian Recording Industry Association created a $700 000 public awareness campaign. It was designed to target kids aged 9 to 17 with the simple message, "You need music, music needs you: Buying music makes more music." Nova Scotia rapper Buck 65 was featured as the spokesperson.[9]

Message Structure

The communicator must also decide which of three ways to use to structure the message. The first message-structure issue is whether to draw a conclusion or leave it to the audience. Early research showed that drawing a conclusion was usually more effective. More recent research, however, suggests that in many cases the advertiser is often better off asking questions and letting buyers draw their own conclusions.

The second message-structure issue is whether to present a one-sided argument (mentioning only the product's strengths) or a two-sided argument (touting the product's strengths while also admitting its shortcomings). Buckley's Mixture built its entire business around the latter technique:[10]

> Buckley's Mixture was first developed in 1919 by pharmacist W.K. Buckley in his Toronto drugstore. W.K. was a pioneer, not only in terms of developing a highly effective product, but also because he was one of the first to recognize the power of catchy copy. He used both print and radio at a time when advertising, especially radio advertising, was a relatively new and a poorly understood phenomena. Advertising made the product a hit, despite its taste. In fact, as the years rolled on, Buckley's advertising stuck consistently with two core themes based on the product's key characteristics: its terrible taste and its tremendous efficacy. Using these two differentiating points, Buckley's produced the award-winning advertising that made Buckley's Mixture and Frank Buckley (W.K.'s son) household names in Canada. The company's simple, honest, and humorous approach to advertising and its famous tag line, "It tastes awful, and it works," attracted attention and brought in new users. Today, Buckley's Mixture is the top-selling cough syrup in Canada by volume, commanding a 10 percent share of the market. The "bad taste" campaign also solidified its position in the Caribbean, Australia, New Zealand, and the United States. If, like other Canadians, you regard Buckley's as part of your Canadian heritage,

Buckley's Mixture has won world renown by using simple and humorous two-sided advertising— "It tastes awful. And it works."

you can join other fans and view Buckley's current and historical advertising at www.buckleys.com.

Usually, a one-sided argument is more effective in sales presentations—except when audiences are highly educated, negatively disposed, or likely to hear opposing claims, or when the communicator has a negative association to overcome. In this spirit, Heinz ran the message "Heinz Ketchup is slow good" and Listerine declared that "Listerine tastes bad twice a day." In such cases, two-sided messages can enhance the advertiser's credibility and make buyers more resistant to competitor attacks.

The third message-structure issue is whether to present the strongest arguments first or last. Presenting them first gets strong attention, but may lead to an anti-climactic ending.

Message Format

The marketing communicator needs a strong *format* for the message. In a print ad, the communicator has to decide on the headline, copy, illustration, and colour. To attract attention, advertisers can use novelty and contrast, eye-catching pictures and headlines, distinctive formats, message size and position, and colour, shape, and movement. If the message will be carried over the radio, the communicator must choose words, sounds, and voices. The "sound" of an announcer promoting banking services, for example, should be different from one promoting quality furniture.

If the message is to be carried on television or in person, then all these elements plus body language have to be planned. Presenters plan their facial expressions, gestures, dress, posture, and hairstyle. If the message is carried on the product or its package, the communicator has to watch texture, scent, colour, size, and shape. For

Message format: To attract attention, advertisers can use distinctive formats, novelty, and eye-catching pictures, as in this award-winning Volkswagen ad.

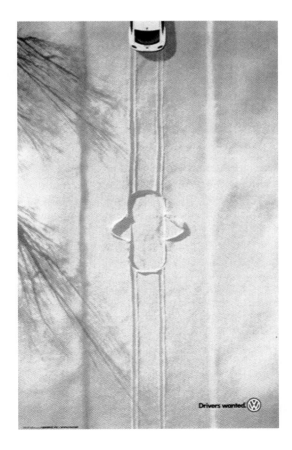

example, age and other demographics affect the way in which consumers perceive and react to colour. Consider the following:[11]

> How do you sell margarine—stodgy, wholesome margarine—to today's kids? One answer: colour. "We knew we wanted to introduce a colour product. It's been a big trend with kids since the blue M&M," says a Parkay spokesperson. So Parkay tried out margarine in blue, pink, green, and purple. "When we tested four different colours in focus groups, kids had a blast." Electric blue and shocking pink margarine emerged as clear favourites.
>
> Colour is as important to adults as it is to kids. As we get older, our eyes mature and our vision takes on a yellow cast. Colour looks less bright to older people, so they gravitate to white and other bright tones. A recent survey found 10 percent of people 55 years and older want the brightness of a white car, compared with 4 percent of 21- to 34-year-olds and 2 percent of teens. Lexus, which skews toward older buyers, makes sure that 60 percent of its cars are light in colour.

Thus, in designing effective marketing communications, marketers must consider colour and other seemingly unimportant details carefully.

Choosing Media

The communicator now must select *channels of communication*. There are two broad types of communication channels—*personal* and *non-personal*.

Personal Communication Channels

In **personal communication channels,** two or more people communicate directly with each other. They can communicate face-to-face, over the telephone, or even through an Internet "chat." Personal communication channels are effective because they allow for personal addressing and feedback.

Some personal communication channels are controlled directly by the company. For example, company salespeople contact buyers in the target market. But other personal communications about the product may reach buyers through channels not directly controlled by the company. These might include independent experts—consumer advocates, consumer buying guides, and others—making statements to target buyers. Or they may be neighbours, friends, family members, and associates talking to target buyers. This last channel, known as **word-of-mouth influence**, has considerable effect in many product areas.

Personal influence carries great weight for products that are expensive, risky, or highly visible. For example, buyers of automobiles and major appliances often go beyond mass-media sources to seek the opinions of knowledgeable people.

Companies can take several steps to put personal communication channels to work for them. For example, they can create *opinion leaders*—people whose opinions are sought by others—by supplying certain people with the product on attractive terms. **Buzz marketing** involves cultivating opinion leaders and getting them to spread information about a product or service to others in their communities (see Real Marketing 15.2 on page 602). BMW used buzz marketing to kick-start demand for its new retro-style Mini Cooper sedan:

> The Mini unit of BMW of North America is bucking car-advertising tradition by using unconventional tactics to create a buzz for its retro-looking Mini Cooper. To launch the return of the diminutive British-made sedan, "We wanted to be as different as we could because the car is so different from anything out there," says a Mini marketer. As a result, there was no national television advertising. Instead, BMW generated buzz for the Mini in less conventional ways. It achieved product placement in the 2003 movie *The Italian Job*. The car has also

Personal communication channels

Channels through which two or more people communicate directly with each other, including face to face, person to audience, over the telephone, or through the mail or email.

Word-of-mouth influence

Personal communication about a product between target buyers and neighbours, friends, family members, and associates.

Buzz marketing

Cultivating opinion leaders and getting them to spread information about a product or service to others in their communities.

been promoted on the Internet, in ads painted on city buildings, and on base-ball-type cards handed out at auto shows. To intrigue passersby, BMW put Minis on top of sport utilities and drove them around a number of cities. In addition, BMW has been selling unusual Mini-brand items—including remote-control cars, watches, and cuckoo clocks—on its website (www.mini.com). Dealers who agreed to build separate Mini showrooms have been deluged with orders. And that interest was built from the ground up through buzz marketing. Only three years ago, only 2 percent of North Americans had ever even heard of the original Mini.[12]

Non-Personal Communication Channels

Non-personal communication channels
Media that carry messages without personal contact or feedback, including major media, atmospheres, and events.

Non-personal communication channels are media that carry messages without personal contact or feedback. They include major media, atmospheres, and events. *Major media* include print media (newspapers, magazines, direct mail), broadcast media (radio, television), display media (billboards, signs, posters), and online media (online services, websites). *Atmospheres* are designed environments that create or reinforce the buyer's leanings toward buying a product. Thus, lawyers' offices and banks are designed to communicate confidence and other qualities that might be valued by their clients. *Events* are staged occurrences that communicate messages to target audiences. For example, public relations departments arrange

Labatt used non-personal communication channels for its award-winning "Know When to Draw the Line" campaign.

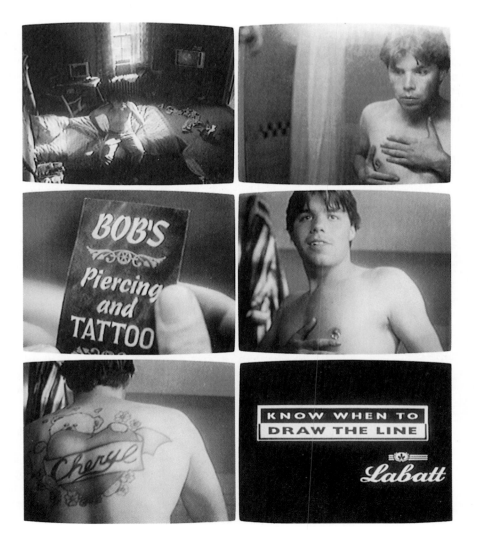

15.2 Buzz Marketing: A Powerful New Way to Spread the Word

A basketball game at Toronto's George Brown College has attracted more than just fans. Sitting in the stands is Matthew George, a "product seeder." He wants to sow the future success of a new Adidas line of athletic shoes—the $160 T-Macs. He knows that word-of-mouth sells. A recent U.S. study found that two-thirds of all consumer goods sales are now directly influenced by word-of-mouth. George looks for trendsetters—cool people who stand out in the crowd. He will give them a free product and basically turn them into walking ads. George quickly hones in a charismatic player and gives him a pair of shoes knowing he will promote the brand.

Adidas is not the only big company practising buzz marketing. When Ford, for instance, launched the Focus, it recruited trendsetters in a handful of markets, gave them each a new vehicle, and told them simply to be seen with the car. Some buzz marketers are recruiting school-aged children to push their latest video games. Others ask disk jockeys to be seen in their cars, while "mom squads" have been recruited to grill particular brands of hot dogs at barbeques. According to *Business Week*, buzz marketing has been at the heart of the success of such things as *The Blair Witch Project* and the *Harry Potter* books.

These days, buzz marketing is all the rage. Buzz marketing involves cultivating opinion leaders and getting them to spread information about a product or service to others in their communities. "In a successful buzz-marketing campaign, each carefully cultivated recipient of the brand message becomes a powerful carrier, spreading the word to yet more carriers, much as a virus rampages through a given population," says one expert. "Firms don't 'do' [buzz] marketing: It's done to you," says another. Companies of all kinds—from Procter & Gamble, Hebrew National, and Hasbro Games to Ford, Vespa, and IBM—are now using buzz marketing as a new way to connect with hard-to-reach consumers.

"Seeding" or feeding the product to trendsetters—the so-called mavens and connectors of their generation—is a powerful tool when creating buzz. It has worked especially well among youth, who mistrust all things marketing but who do react when they see a hip peer using or talking about a particular product. As Max Lenderman, a partner at Gearwerx, a youth marketing company based in Montreal, notes:

> Trend seeding relies on influencers who are obsessed with being ahead of the curve when it comes to new products and trends. Identifying and recruiting these influencers is the most arduous task. Trend seeders don't want to be an instrument of marketing; they want to be appreciated and made important by their VIP access to new products and brands.

Why the new trend? Traditional forms of advertising are losing their punch. Thus, firms are seeking new avenues to speak to consumers. York University marketing professor Alan Middleton calls buzz marketing "managed word-of-mouth." "Buzz marketing is powerful because you're dealing with networks of friendship and networks of family that exist, and that's the power," Middleton adds.

Not only is buzz marketing effective, it is cheap! It often is only one-tenth the cost of traditional marketing campaigns. It's a great way to extend brand exposure without blowing out the marketing budget. Buzz marketing's increasing popularity

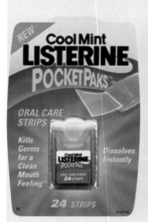
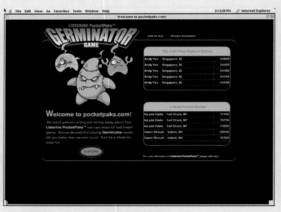

Pfizer used an elaborate array of buzz-building efforts for Listerine PocketPaks. Its "Germinator" game includes a pass-along feature that encourages players to email scores to friends to get them to play.

can also be attributed to burgeoning Internet usage. Marketers can now use the Web to reach large numbers of consumers, particularly trend leaders, quickly and easily.

Perhaps the single most important reason that marketers are employing buzz marketing is that it really works. Consider the following examples.

Lee Dungarees. In recent years, Lee had managed to re-energize the image of its stodgy Lee jeans brand among younger target consumers—mostly young males 17 to 22. But it needed to do more to convert that cooler image into sales at teen-toxic retailers like traditional department stores, its biggest outlets. So Lee came up with one of the most freewheeling and influential buzz-marketing campaigns to date. The campaign played on target consumers' weakness for video games and computers. First, Lee developed a list of 200 000 "influential" guys from a list of Web surfers. It then zapped them a trio of grainy video clips that were hilarious in their apparent stupidity. The videos appeared to be ultra-low-budget flicks meant to draw visitors to the Web game sites of amateur film-makers, such as open-shirted Curry, a 23-year-old race car driver. To the young Web surfers who received them, the clips seemed like delicious examples of the oddball digital debris that litters the Web. So not many of the recipients who eagerly forwarded the flicks to their friends would have guessed that they actually were abet-ting in a marketing campaign orchestrated by Lee.

According to Lee research, the "stupid little films" were so intriguing that, on average, recipients forwarded them to six friends apiece. Despite virtually no advertising, some 100 000 visitors stormed the fictional filmmakers' websites the week they went live, crashing the server. The marketing connection only became clear a few months later, after a TV and radio ad blitz finally revealed the three characters to be fictional antagonists developed as part of an online computer game. And that was a key to the pro-gram: to play the game at an advanced level, participants had to snag the product identification numbers—the "secret code"—off Lee items, which of course required a visit to a store. Ultimately, the effort drove thousands of kids age 17 to 22 into the stores and helped propel Lee sales upward by 20 percent.

Listerine PocketPaks. Pfizer Consumer Healthcare recently launched the $26 million TV ad portion of its mar-keting effort behind Listerine PocketPaks. But that wasn't what turned Karen Tennant into a consumer of the tiny, portable mouthwash strips that melt on your tongue. Her daughter had already heard about them from a friend. The friend had heard about them from her dad, owner of an independent pharmacy. The dad had received a case of trial-size PocketPaks he'd never ordered, along with a bill. Intrigued, he put the packs on display. They sold out almost immediately, generating a voluntary reorder.

That's just one of dozens of ways Pfizer generated buzz about Listerine PocketPaks even before the big TV push and a parallel online media effort. Pfizer used an elaborate array of buzz-building efforts, including profes-sional marketing through dentists, sampling through col-lege campus welcome packs, publicity efforts, prominent placement on retailer websites, and an online game at PocketPaks.com. The Listerine PocketPaks "Germinator" game includes a pass-along feature that's part of the buzz-marketing effort, encouraging players to email scores to friends to get them to play. Pfizer estimates that PocketPak sales will exceed $130 million in the first 12 months.

Not all companies have had such success with buzz marketing. In fact, the practice can be risky. If consumers catch on or get the wrong impression, the results can be disastrous.

Sony Pictures Entertainment generated the kind of public-ity you'd like to avoid when a couple of recent buzz strate-gies backfired. First, it turned out that Sony had fabricated quotes from a fictitious film critic praising movies such as the less-than-memorable *Vertical Limit* and *The Animal*. Soon after, two supposed moviegoers who gushed about *The Patriot* in Sony commercials were unmasked as stu-dio employees. Rather than delighting or surprising, the ham-handed efforts merely confirmed consumers' worst suspicions about marketers. "It can turn into a horrible public-relations nightmare if it turns out you're deceiving people," says one research analyst.

Buzz marketing has also been criticized on ethical grounds. Ethicists believe the practice is underhanded and manipulative. In standard advertising, consumers know that a company is promoting a product. But buzz marketing is more subtle. Consumers may not be aware they are being exposed to a product pitch when they see a friend, associate, or celebrity using a product.

Still, when done correctly, buzz marketing can gen-erate amazing results. For products that meet real needs with innovative or stylish designs, the positive word travels fast. Notes one global marketing executive, "Finding a revolutionary new way to market an estab-lished brand doesn't work unless it's grounded in the product truth.... Great marketing is simply a megaphone for the truth, and when the 'buzz' is true it delivers unconventional messages very effectively to uncon-ventional audiences."

Sources: Excerpts adapted from "Buzz Marketing," *Marketplace,* March 27, 2002; Max Lenderman, "Seed, then Sample," *Strategy,* February 24, 2003, p. 10; Gerry Khermouch and Jeff Green, "Buzz Marketing," *Business Week,* July 30, 2001, pp. 50–56; Jack Neff, "Building the Buzz for PocketPaks," *Advertising Age,* December 3, 2001, pp. 4, 42; and Micheline Maynard, "Even Cars Need to Make a Good First Impression," *New York Times,* March 8, 2002, p. F1. Also see James C. Schroer, "The Ultimate Buzz," *Marketing Management,* September–October 2001, p. 56; John Brandt, "Beware of Bad Buzz," *Chief Executive,* November 2001, p. 12; Laura Mazur, "Firms Can't 'Do' Viral Marketing: It Is Done to You," *Marketing Magazine,* June 27, 2002, p. 16; and Kathryn Shattuck, "Mouthwash Without a Bottle," *New York Times,* July 2002, p. 3.2.

press conferences, grand openings, shows and exhibits, public tours, and other events. Many Canadian companies sponsor sporting events that draw audiences that match the firm's target market. The Bank of Montreal, for example, is the lead sponsor for equestrian events held at Spruce Meadows in Calgary and at the Royal Winter Fair in Toronto. Molson Breweries holds two annual Indy races: one in Vancouver, the other in Toronto (www.molsonindy.com).

Non-personal communication affects buyers directly. In addition, using mass media often affects buyers indirectly by causing more personal communication. Communications first flow from television, magazines, and other mass media to opinion leaders and then from these opinion leaders to others. Thus, opinion leaders step between the mass media and their audiences and carry messages to people who are less exposed to media. This suggests that mass communicators should aim their messages directly at opinion leaders, letting them carry the message to others.

Selecting the Message Source

In either personal or non-personal communication, the message's impact on the target audience is affected by how the audience views the communicator. Messages delivered by highly credible sources are more persuasive. Thus, many food companies promote to doctors, dentists, and other health-care providers to motivate these professionals to recommend their products to patients. This has been an important strategy for Becel margarine, since research showed that health professionals were important influencers on their patients' dietary choices. In addition to award-winning advertising that helped the brand grow throughout the 1990s, Becel developed its Becel Heart Health Information Bureau. This "educational arm" of the brand provides health-care professionals and the public with current information on nutrition and the scientific issues affecting heart health. While maintaining its objectivity, the bureau strives to disseminate both key scientific facts about heart health and key brand messages, primarily on the Becel Canada webpage (www.becelcanada. com).[13]

Marketers also try to influence the target audience by hiring celebrity endorsers—well-known athletes, actors, and even cartoon characters—to deliver their messages. Tiger Woods speaks for Nike, Buick, and a dozen other brands. Don Cherry was hired by Molson to promote its "Bubba" mini-keg. As part of the promotion, some of Cherry's most outlandish suits have been reproduced on the party-sized containers and on cans of Molson Canadian. Canadian PGA champion golfer Mike Weir promotes the products of his sponsors—Bell, Kia, and Taylor Made. Hockey legend Wayne Gretzky is featured in ads for Ford. When Scarborough-born Paul Tracy won big at the 2003 Molson Indy, his value to his primary sponsor, Players, soared.

But companies must be careful when selecting celebrities to represent their brands. Picking the wrong spokesperson can result in embarrassment and a tarnished image. When Los Angeles Lakers' guard Kobe Bryant was charged with rape in 2003, one sponsor, hazelnut spread Nutella, cancelled its endorsement. Other sponsors (Sprite, McDonald's, Nike, and Spalding) maintained their contracts with Bryant.[14]

Collecting Feedback

After sending the message, the communicator must research its effect on the target audience. This involves asking the target audience members whether they remember the message, how many times they saw it, what points they recall, how they felt about the message, and their past and present attitudes toward the product and company. The communicator also wants to measure behaviour resulting from the message—how many people bought a product, talked to others about it, or visited the store.

Marketers hire celebrity endorsers to deliver their messages. Here, Mike Weir promotes Taylor Made golf equipment.

For example, Air Canada uses in-flight, Internet, magazine, and newspaper advertising to inform area consumers about the airline, its routes, and its fares. Suppose feedback research shows that 80 percent of all fliers in an area recall seeing the airline's ads and are aware of its flights and prices. Sixty percent of these aware fliers have flown Air Canada, but only 20 percent of those who tried it were satisfied. These results suggest that although promotion is creating *awareness*, the airline isn't giving consumers the *satisfaction* they expect. Therefore, Air Canada needs to improve its service while staying with the successful communication program. In contrast, suppose the research shows that only 40 percent of area consumers are aware of the airline, only 30 percent of those aware have tried it, but 80 percent of those who have tried it return. In this case, Air Canada needs to strengthen its promotion program to take advantage of its power to create customer satisfaction.

In other words, feedback on marketing communications may suggest changes in the promotion program or in the product offer itself.

Setting the Total Promotion Budget and Mix

We have examined the steps in planning and sending communications to a target audience. But how does the company decide on the total *promotion budget* and its division among the major promotional tools to create the *promotion mix*? We now look at these questions.

Setting the Total Promotion Budget

One of the hardest marketing decisions facing a company is how much to spend on promotion. John Wanamaker, the department-store magnate, once said: "I know that half of my advertising is wasted, but I don't know which half. I spent $2 million for advertising, and I don't know if that is half enough or twice too much." Thus, it is not surprising that industries and companies vary widely in how much they allocate to their total promotion budget and how much they spend within each category. For example, many packaged goods companies like Kraft Canada are finding that their trade spending is more effective at increasing sales than is their spending on radio, print, or television advertising. Promotion spending varies by industry. It may be 20 to 30 percent of sales in the cosmetics industry and only 2 or 3 percent in the industrial machinery industry. Within any industry, both low and high spenders can be found.[15]

How does a company decide on its promotion budget? We look at four common methods used to set the total budget for advertising: the *affordable method,* the *percentage-of-sales method,* the *competitive-parity method,* and the *objective-and-task method.*[16]

Affordable Method

Some companies use the **affordable method**: they set the promotion budget at the level they think the company can afford. Small businesses often use this method, reasoning that the company cannot spend more on advertising than it has. They start with total revenues, deduct operating expenses and capital outlays, and then devote some portion of the remaining funds to advertising.

Unfortunately, this method of setting budgets completely ignores the effects of promotion on sales. It tends to place advertising last among spending priorities, even in situations in which advertising is critical to the firm's success. It leads to an uncertain annual promotion budget, which makes long-range market planning difficult. Although the affordable method can result in overspending on advertising, it more often results in underspending.

Percentage-of-Sales Method

Other companies use the **percentage-of-sales method**, setting their promotion budget at a certain percentage of current or forecasted sales. Or they budget a percentage of the unit sales price. The percentage-of-sales method has a number of advantages. It is simple to use and helps management think about the relationship between promotion spending, selling price, and profit per unit.

Despite these claimed advantages, however, the percentage-of-sales method has little to justify it. It wrongly views sales as the *cause* of promotion rather than as the *result*. "A study in this area found good correlation between investments in advertising and the strength of the brands concerned—but it turned out to be effect and cause, not cause and effect.... The strongest brands had the highest sales and could afford the biggest investments in advertising!"[17] Thus, the percentage-of-sales budget is based on availability of funds rather than on opportunities. It may prevent the increased spending sometimes needed to turn around falling sales. Because the budget varies with year-to-year sales, long-range planning is difficult. Finally, the method does not provide any basis for choosing a *specific* percentage, except what has been done in the past or what competitors are doing.

Competitive-Parity Method

Still other companies use the **competitive-parity method**, setting their promotion budgets to match competitors' outlays. They monitor competitors' advertising or get industry promotion spending estimates from publications or trade associations, and then set their budgets based on the industry average.

Two arguments are used to support this method. First, competitors' budgets represent the collective wisdom of the industry. Second, spending what competitors spend helps prevent promotion wars. Unfortunately, neither argument is valid. There are no grounds for believing that the competition has a better idea of what a company should be spending on promotion than does the company itself. Companies differ greatly, and each has its own special promotion needs. Finally, there is no evidence that budgets based on competitive parity prevent promotion wars.

Objective-and-Task Method

Objective-and-task method
Developing the promotion budget by (1) defining specific objectives, (2) determining the tasks that must be performed to achieve these objectives, and (3) estimating the costs of performing these tasks. The sum of these costs is the proposed promotion budget.

The most logical budget-setting method is the **objective-and-task method**, whereby the company sets its promotion budget based on what it wants to accomplish with promotion. This budgeting method entails (1) defining specific promotion objectives, (2) determining the tasks needed to achieve these objectives, and (3) estimating the costs of performing these tasks. The sum of these costs is the proposed promotion budget.

The objective-and-task method forces management to spell out its assumptions about the relationship between dollars spent and promotion results. But it is also the most difficult method to use. It is often hard to determine which specific tasks will achieve specific objectives. For example, suppose Sony wants 95 percent awareness for its latest camcorder model during the six-month introductory period. What specific advertising messages and media schedules should Sony use to attain this objective? How much would these messages and media schedules cost? Sony management must consider such questions, even though they are hard to answer.

Setting the Overall Promotion Mix

The concept of integrated marketing communications suggests that the company must blend the promotion tools carefully into a coordinated *promotion mix*. But how does the company determine what mix of promotion tools it will use? Companies within the same industry differ greatly in the design of their promotion mixes. For example, Avon spends most of its promotion funds on personal selling and direct marketing, whereas Revlon spends heavily on consumer advertising, and Toronto-based M·A·C (Make-up Art Cosmetics, www.maccosmetics.com) has rocketed onto the world stage with almost no traditional advertising. Hewlett-Packard relies on advertising and promotion to retailers when marketing personal computers, whereas Dell Computer uses only direct marketing. We now look at the many factors that influence the marketer's choice of promotion tools.

The Nature of Each Promotion Tool

Each promotion tool has unique characteristics and costs. Marketers must understand these characteristics in selecting their tools.

Advertising   Advertising can reach masses of geographically dispersed buyers at a low cost per exposure, and it enables the seller to repeat a message many times. Television advertising, for example, reaches huge audiences. On an average day, 76 percent of Canadians view television at least once. This viewership may be split between Canadian English national networks (13 percent), French networks (30 percent), Canadian Global and independents (14 percent), Canadian pay and speciality channels (14 percent), U.S. conventional and superstations (7 percent), U.S. pay and speciality channels (5 percent), and others (17 percent). More than 120 to 130 million North Americans tune in to at least part of the Super Bowl, about 72 million people watched at least part of the past Academy Awards broadcast, and nearly 52 million watched the final episode of the first *Survivor* series. *Canadian Idol* drew audiences as high as 2.25 million in the summer of 2003, while the highest-rated Canadian program to date was the gold-medal men's hockey game at the 2002 Olympics, watched by more than 10 million devoted fans. "If you want to get

Promotion mix: Companies within the same industry may use different mixes. Avon relies heavily on personal selling and direct marketing; Revlon devotes significant resources to advertising.

to the mass audience," says a media services executive, "broadcast TV is where you have to be." He adds, "For anybody introducing anything who has to lasso an audience in a hurry—a new product, a new campaign, a new movie—the networks are still the biggest show in town."[18]

Beyond its reach, large-scale advertising says something positive about the seller's size, popularity, and success. Because of advertising's public nature, consumers tend to view advertised products as more legitimate. Advertising is also very expressive. It allows the company to dramatize its products through the artful use of visuals, print, sound, and colour. On one hand, advertising can be used to build a long-term image for a product (such as Coca-Cola ads). On the other hand, advertising can trigger quick sales (such as Sears' weekend sale ads).

Advertising also has shortcomings. Although it reaches many people quickly, advertising is impersonal and cannot be as persuasive as company salespeople. For the most part, advertising can carry on only a one-way communication with the audience, and the audience does not feel that it must pay attention or respond. In addition, advertising can be very costly. Although some advertising forms, such as newspaper and radio advertising, can be done on small budgets, other forms, such as network TV advertising, require very large budgets. Another challenge is audiences' resistance to advertising claims—particularly in Canada. In his book *Fire and Ice*, Michael Adams reports that more than eight out of ten Canadians are skeptical about the claims of advertisers. When asked whether they believed a widely advertised product was a good product, 17 percent of Canadians said "yes" in 2000 (versus 14 percent in 1996 and 17 percent in 1992). In contrast, 44 percent of Americans said "yes" in 2000 (versus 32 percent in 1996 and 34 percent in 1992). Adams concludes this skepticism "may explain why humour, irony, and even self-deprecation go down better than the hard sell in cynical Canada."[19]

Sales Promotion   Sales promotion includes a wide assortment of tools—including coupons, contests, cents-off deals, premiums, and others—all of which have many unique qualities. They attract consumer attention, offer strong incentives to purchase, and can be used to dramatize product offers and to boost sagging sales. Sales promotions invite and reward quick response. Whereas advertising says, "Buy our product," sales promotion says, "Buy it now." Sales promotion effects are usually short lived, however, and are not effective in building long-run brand preference.

Public Relations   Public relations is very believable: news stories, features, and events seem more real and believable to readers than ads do. Public relations also can reach many prospects who avoid salespeople and advertisements—the message gets to the buyers as "news" rather than as a sales-directed communication. And, like advertising, public relations can dramatize a company or product. Marketers tend to underuse public relations or to use it as an afterthought. Yet a well-planned public relations campaign used with other promotion mix elements can be very effective and economical.

Personal Selling Personal selling is the most effective tool at certain stages of the buying process, particularly in building up buyers' preferences, convictions, and actions. It involves personal interaction between two or more people, so each person can observe the other's needs and characteristics and make quick adjustments. Personal selling also allows all kinds of relationships to develop, ranging from a matter-of-fact selling relationship to a personal friendship. The effective salesperson keeps the customer's interests at heart to build a long-term relationship. Finally, with personal selling, the buyer usually feels a greater need to listen and respond, even if the response is a polite "no thank you."

These unique qualities come at a cost, however. A sales force requires a longer-term commitment than does advertising: Advertising can be turned on and off, but sales force size is harder to change. Personal selling is also the company's most expensive promotion tool, costing industrial companies an average of over $220 per sales call.[20] North American firms spend up to three times as much on personal selling as they do on advertising.

Direct Marketing Although there are many forms of direct marketing—telephone marketing, direct mail, online marketing, and others—they all share four distinctive characteristics. Direct marketing is *non-public:* the message is normally addressed to a specific person. Direct marketing is *immediate* and *customized:* messages can be prepared very quickly and can be tailored to appeal to specific consumers. Finally, direct marketing is *interactive:* it allows a dialogue between the marketer and consumer, and messages can be altered depending on the consumer's response. Therefore, direct marketing is well suited to highly targeted marketing efforts and to building one-on-one customer relationships.

With personal selling, the customer feels a greater need to listen and respond, even if the response is a polite "no thank you."

Promotion Mix Strategies

Push strategy

A promotion strategy that calls for using the sales force and trade promotion to push the product through channels. The producer promotes the product to wholesalers, the wholesalers promote to retailers, and the retailers promote to consumers.

Pull strategy

A promotion strategy that calls for spending a lot on advertising and consumer promotion to build up consumer demand. If the strategy is successful, consumers will ask their retailers for the product, the retailers will ask the wholesalers, and the wholesalers will ask the producers.

Marketers can choose from two basic promotion mix strategies—*push* promotion or *pull* promotion. Figure 15.4 contrasts the two strategies. The relative emphasis on the specific promotion tools differs for push and pull strategies. A **push strategy** involves "pushing" the product through distribution channels to final consumers. The producer directs its marketing activities (primarily personal selling and trade promotion) toward channel members to induce them to carry the product and to promote it to final consumers. Using a **pull strategy**, the producer directs its marketing activities (primarily advertising and consumer promotion) toward final consumers to induce them to buy the product. If the pull strategy is effective, consumers then will demand the product from channel members, who will in turn demand it from producers. Thus, under a pull strategy, consumer demand "pulls" the product through the channels.

Some small industrial goods companies use only push strategies; some direct-marketing companies use only pull. However, most large companies use some combination of both. For example, Kraft uses mass-media advertising to pull its products, and a large sales force and trade promotions to push its products through the channels. In recent years, consumer goods companies have been decreasing the pull portions of their promotion mixes in favour of more push. This has caused concern that they may be driving short-run sales at the expense of long-term brand equity (see Real Marketing 15.3 on page 611).

Companies consider many factors when developing their promotion mix strategies, including *type of product market* and the *product life-cycle stage*. For example, the importance of different promotion tools varies between consumer and business markets. B2C companies usually "pull" more, putting more of their funds into advertising, followed by sales promotion, personal selling, and then public relations. In contrast, B2B marketers tend to "push" more, putting more of their funds into personal selling, followed by sales promotion, advertising, and public relations. In general, personal selling is used more heavily with expensive and risky goods and in markets with fewer and larger sellers.

The effects of different promotion tools also vary with stages of the product life cycle. In the introduction stage, advertising and public relations are good for producing high awareness, and sales promotion is useful in promoting early trial. Personal selling must be used to get the trade to carry the product. In the growth stage, advertising and public relations continue to be powerful influences, whereas sales promotion can be reduced because fewer incentives are needed. In the mature stage, sales promotion again becomes important relative to advertising. Buyers

Figure 15.4   Push versus pull promotion strategy

REAL MARKETING

15.3 Are Consumer Goods Companies Getting Too Pushy?

Consumer packaged-goods companies such as Kraft, Procter & Gamble, Kellogg, General Mills, and Gillette grew into giants by using mostly pull promotion strategies. They used massive doses of national advertising to differentiate their products, gain market share, and build brand equity and customer loyalty. But during the past few decades, these companies have gotten more "pushy," de-emphasizing national advertising and putting more of their marketing budgets into trade and consumer sales promotions.

General trade promotions (trade allowances, displays, cooperative advertising, slotting fees) now account for 49 percent of total marketing spending by consumer product companies. Another 10 percent of the marketing budget goes to the trade in the form of "account-specific" marketing expenditures—promotional spending personalized to the local needs of a specific retail chain that backs both the brand and the retailer. The total of 59 percent represents a seven-percentage-point increase in trade spending in just the

Today's food marketers are using more and more push promotion, including consumer price promotions. But they must be careful that they don't win the battle for short-run sales at the expense of long-run brand equity.

past five years. Consumer promotions (coupons, cents-off deals, premiums) account for another 17 percent of the typical marketing budget. That leaves less than 24 percent of total marketing spending for mass-media advertising, down from 42 percent 20 years ago.

Why have these companies shifted so heavily toward push strategies? One reason is that mass-media campaigns have become more expensive and less effective in recent years. Network television costs have risen sharply while audiences have fallen off, making national advertising less cost-effective. Companies have also increased their market segmentation efforts and are now tailoring their marketing programs more narrowly, making national advertising less suitable than localized retailer promotions. And in these days of brand extensions and me-too products, companies sometimes have trouble finding meaningful product differences to feature in advertising. So they have differentiated their products through price reductions, premium offers, coupons, and other push techniques.

Another factor speeding the shift from pull to push has been the growing strength of retailers. Today's retailers are larger and have more access to product sales-and-profit information. Retail giants such as Safeway, A&P, and Wal-Mart now have the power to demand and get what they want—and what they want is more push. Whereas national advertising bypasses them on its way to the masses, push promotion benefits them directly. Consumer promotions give retailers an immediate sales boost, and cash from trade allowances and other trade promotions pads retailer profits. Thus, producers must often use push just to obtain good shelf space and advertising support from important retailers.

However, many marketers are concerned that the reckless use of push will lead to fierce price competition and a never-ending spiral of price slashing and deal making. This situation would mean lower margins, and companies would have less money to invest in the research and development, packaging, and advertising needed to improve products and maintain long-run consumer preference and loyalty.

If used improperly, push promotion can mortgage a brand's future for short-term gains. Sales promotion buys short-run reseller support and consumer sales, but advertising builds long-run brand equity and consumer preference. By robbing the media advertising budget to pay for more sales promotion, companies might win the battle for short-run earnings but lose the war for long-run brand equity, consumer loyalty, and market share. In fact, some analysts blame the shift away from advertising dollars for a recent two-decade-long drop in the percentage of consumers who buy only well-known brands.

Of special concern is the overuse of price promotions. The regular use of price as a selling tool can destroy brand equity by encouraging consumers to seek value though price rather than through the benefits of the brand. Many marketers are too quick to drive short-term sales by reducing prices rather than building long-term brand equity through advertising. In cases where price is a key part of the brand's positioning, featuring price makes sense. But for brands where price does not underlie value, "price promotions are really desperate acts by brands that have their backs against the wall," says one marketing executive. "Generally speaking, it is better to stick to your guns with price and invest in advertising to drive sales."

Jack Trout, a well-known marketing consultant, cautions that some categories tend to self-destruct by always being on sale. Discount pricing has become routine for a surprising number of companies. Furniture, automobile tires, and many other categories of goods are rarely sold at anything near list price, and

when automakers get rebate happy, the market just sits back and waits for a deal. Even Coca-Cola and Pepsi, two of the world's most popular brands, engage in regular price wars that ultimately tarnish their brand equity. Trout offers several "Commandments of Discounting," such as "Thou shalt not offer discounts because everyone else does," "Thou shalt be creative with your discounting," "Thou shalt put time limits on the deal," and "Thou shalt stop discounting as soon as you can."

Many consumer companies now are rethinking their promotion strategies and reversing the trend by shifting their promotion budgets back toward advertising. Many have realized that it's not a question of sales promotion versus advertising, or of push versus pull. Success lies in finding the best mix of the two: consistent advertising to build long-run brand value and consumer preference, and sales promotion to create short-run trade support and consumer excitement. The company needs to blend both push and pull elements into an integrated promotion program that meets immediate consumer and retailer needs as well as long-run strategic needs.

Sources: Promotion spending statistics from *2002 Trade Promotion Spending & Merchandising Industry Study,* Cannondale Associates, Wilton, Conn., 2002, p. 13. Other information from Jack Trout, "Prices: Simple Guidelines to Get Them Right," *Journal of Business Strategy,* November–December 1998, pp. 13–16; Tim Ambler, "Kicking Price Promotion Habit Is Like Getting Off Heroin—Hard," *Marketing Magazine,* May 27, 1999, p. 24; "Study: Trade Dollars Up," *Frozen Food Age,* September 2001, p. 14; and Robert Gray, "Driving Sales at Any Price," *Marketing Magazine,* April 11, 2002, pp. 24–25.

know the brands, and advertising is needed only to remind them of the product. In the decline stage, advertising is kept at a reminder level, public relations is dropped, and salespeople give the product only a little attention. Sales promotion, however, might continue to be strong.

Integrating the Promotion Mix

Having set the promotion budget and mix, the company must take steps to see that all of the promotion mix elements are smoothly integrated. Here is a checklist for integrating the firm's marketing communications.[21]

- *Analyze trends—internal and external—that can affect your company's ability to do business.* Look for areas where communications can help the most. Determine the strengths and weaknesses of each communications function. Develop a combination of promotional tactics based on these strengths and weaknesses.
- *Audit the pockets of communications spending throughout the organization.* Itemize the communications budgets and tasks and consolidate these into a single budgeting process. Reassess all communications expenditures by product, promotional tool, stage of the life cycle, and observed effect.

- *Identify all contact points for the company and its brands.* Work to ensure that communications at each point are consistent with your overall communications strategy and that your communications efforts are occurring when, where, and how your *customers* want them.

- *Team up in communications planning.* Engage all communications functions in joint planning. Include customers, suppliers, and other stakeholders at every stage of communications planning.

- *Create compatible themes, tones, and quality across all communications media.* Make sure each element carries your unique primary messages and selling points. This consistency achieves greater impact and prevents the unnecessary duplication of work across functions.

- *Create performance measures that are shared by all communications elements.* Develop systems to evaluate the combined impact of all communications activities.

- *Appoint a director responsible for the company's persuasive communications efforts.* This move encourages efficiency by centralizing planning and creating shared performance measures.

Socially Responsible Marketing Communications

In shaping its promotion mix, a company must be aware of the growing body of legal and ethical issues surrounding marketing communications. Most marketers work hard to communicate openly and honestly with consumers and resellers. Some, like the Royal Bank, Bell Canada, and Unilever Canada, use their advertising dollars to support important causes. According to the 2002 *Cone Roper Benchmark Survey,* such advertising not only helps the cause, it supports the brand:[22]

- 76 percent of respondents said they would likely buy a product associated with a cause they care about

- 66 percent said they would likely switch brands

- 62 percent would likely switch retailers to support a cause they care about

- 54 percent would pay more for a product that supported a cause they care about

KitchenAid Canada is an example of a company that understands and supports a cause important to many of its customers:

In 2002, KitchenAid Canada worked with Toronto-based Harbinger to build a partnership with the Canadian Breast Cancer Foundation (CBCF). The company made a commitment to raise funds for breast cancer research on an ongoing basis. For every limited-edition pink Stand Mixer it sells, KitchenAid Canada will donate $100 to the CBCF. But KitchenAid Canada's commitment goes beyond donating money—it has made a conscious effort to help develop ongoing grassroots support for cancer research through its KitchenAid Cook for the Cure initiative. Participants hold home parties at which guests provide donations instead of hostess gifts. By learning more about breast cancer at these gatherings, the guests become ambassadors for fund-raising and the program. Online support at www.kitchenaid-cookforthecure.ca helps hosts with party hints, including food tips from Christine Cushing of The Food Network Canada and forms for online invitations and donations. "We've created a foolproof process so that people can easily get involved," says Harbinger senior VP Jeff Weiss. As well, the program is supported through co-promotions at cooking schools, television and print advertising, and other public relations activities. "It's really changed how KitchenAid's customers perceive the brand and it's helping them to cement that relationship with their key consumer...and it's raising money and profile for breast cancer," Weiss concludes.[23]

Despite such socially responsible concerns, however, abuses may occur. Public policy makers have developed a substantial body of laws and regulations to govern advertising, personal selling, and direct marketing activities. In this section, we discuss issues regarding advertising and personal selling. Issues regarding direct marketing are addressed in Chapter 17.

Advertising and Sales Promotion

By law, companies must avoid false or deceptive advertising. Advertisers must not make false claims, such as suggesting that a product cures something when it does not. They must avoid ads that have the capacity to deceive, even though no one actually may be deceived. An automobile cannot be advertised as getting 14 kilometres per litre unless it does so under typical conditions, and a diet bread cannot be advertised as having fewer calories simply because its slices are thinner.

Sellers must avoid bait-and-switch advertising that attracts buyers under false pretences. For example, a large retailer advertised a sewing machine at $179. However, when consumers tried to buy the advertised machine, the seller downplayed its features, placed faulty machines on showroom floors, understated the machine's performance, and took other actions in an attempt to switch buyers to a more expensive machine. Such actions are both unethical and illegal.

The advertising industry in Canada is controlled both by the Canadian Radiotelevision and Telecommunications Commission (CRTC) and by voluntary industry codes administered by Advertising Standards Canada. The CRTC (www.crtc.gc.ca), which independently governs broadcast licensing, is itself governed by the *Broadcasting Act* of 1991 and the *Telecommunications Act* of 1993. The primary objective

KitchenAid Canada helps the cause of breast cancer research with its "Cook for the Cure" initiative.

of the *Broadcasting Act* is to ensure that all Canadians have access to a wide variety of high-quality Canadian programming. The main objective of the *Telecommunications Act* is to ensure that Canadians have access to reliable telephone and other telecommunication services at affordable prices.

In addition, the CRTC has the mandate to ensure that programming in the Canadian broadcasting system reflects Canadian social values, creativity, and talent, as well as the country's linguistic duality, its multicultural diversity, and the special place of Aboriginal people within Canadian society. The CRTC regulates over 5900 broadcasters, including television, cable distribution, AM and FM radio, pay and specialty television, direct-to-home satellite systems, multi-point distribution systems, subscription television, pay audio, and 61 telecommunication carriers, including major Canadian telephone companies.

The CRTC also administers several codes that have a particular impact on certain categories of advertising. For example, the Code for Broadcast Advertising of Alcoholic Beverages governs advertising of alcoholic beverages with over 7 percent alcohol.

Advertising Standards Canada (ASC), established as the Canadian Advertising Foundation in 1963, is a national industry association committed to assuring the integrity and viability of advertising through industry self-regulation. Its members include advertisers, agencies, media organizations, and suppliers to the advertising sector. ASC receives, reviews, adjudicates, and reports on complaints about advertising. Industry codes and guidelines administered by ASC include the Canadian Code of Advertising Standards, the Gender Portrayal Guidelines, Broadcast Code for Advertising to Children, the Guide to Food Labelling and Advertising, Advertising Code of Standards for Cosmetics, Toiletries & Fragrances, Guidelines for the Use of Comparative Advertising in Food Commercials, Tobacco Voluntary Packaging, and the Advertising Industry Code. Details of these codes can be found

on the ASC website at www.adstandards.com.

A company's trade promotion activities are also closely regulated. Under the *Competition Act*, sellers cannot favour certain customers through their use of trade promotions. They must make promotional allowances and services available to all resellers on proportionately equal terms.

Personal Selling

A company's salespeople must follow the rules of "fair competition." For example, salespeople may not lie to consumers or mislead them about the advantages of buying a product. To avoid bait-and-switch practices, salespeople's statements must match advertising claims.

Different rules apply to consumers who are visited by salespeople at home than to those who go to a store in search of a product. Because people called on at home may be taken by surprise and may be especially vulnerable to high-pressure selling techniques, most provincial governments have stipulated a *three-day cooling-off rule* to give special protection to customers who are not seeking products. Under this rule, customers who agree in their own homes to buy something have 72 hours in which to cancel a contract or return merchandise and get their money back, no questions asked.

Much personal selling involves business-to-business trade. In selling to businesses, salespeople may not offer bribes to purchasing agents or to others who can influence a sale. They may not obtain or use technical or trade secrets of competitors through bribery or industrial espionage. Finally, salespeople must not disparage competitors or competing products by suggesting things that are not true.[24]

Looking Back: Reviewing the Concepts

Modern marketing calls for more than just developing a good product, pricing it attractively, and making it available to target customers. Companies also must *communicate* with current and prospective customers, and what they communicate should not be left to chance. For most companies, the question is not whether to communicate, but *how much to spend* and *in what ways*.

1. Name and define the five tools of the marketing communications mix.

A company's total *marketing communications mix*—also called its *promotion mix*—consists of the specific blend of *advertising*, *sales promotion*, *public relations*, *personal selling*, and *direct marketing* tools that the company uses to pursue its advertising and marketing objectives. Advertising includes any paid form of non-personal presentation and promotion of ideas, goods, or services by an identified sponsor. Firms use sales promotion to provide short-term incentives to encourage the purchase or sale of a product or service. Public relations focuses on building good relations with the company's various publics by obtaining favourable unpaid publicity. Personal selling is any form of personal presentation by the firm's sales force for the purpose of making sales and building customer relationships. Finally, firms seeking immediate response from targeted individual customers use non-personal direct marketing tools to communicate with customers.

2. Discuss the process and advantages of integrated marketing communications.

Recent shifts in marketing strategy from mass marketing to targeted or one-on-one marketing, coupled with advances in information technology, have had a dramatic impact on marketing communications. Although still important, the mass media are giving way to a profusion of smaller, more focused media. Companies are doing less *broadcasting* and more *narrowcasting*. As marketing communicators adopt richer but more fragmented media and promotion mixes to reach their diverse markets, they risk creating a communications hodgepodge for consumers. To prevent this, companies are adopting the concept of *integrated marketing communications,* which calls for carefully integrating all sources of company communication to deliver a clear and consistent message to target markets.

To integrate its external communications effectively, the company must first integrate its internal communications activities. The company then works out the roles that the various promotional tools will play and the extent to which each will be used. It carefully coordinates the promotional activities and the timing of when major campaigns take place. Finally, to help implement its integrated marketing strategy, the company appoints a marketing communications director who has overall responsibility for the company's communications efforts.

3. Outline the steps in developing effective marketing communications.

In preparing marketing communications, the communicator's first task is to *identify the target audience* and its characteristics. Next, the communicator has to determine the *communication objectives* and define the response sought, whether it be *awareness, knowledge, liking, preference, conviction,* or *purchase*. Then a *message* should be constructed with an effective content, structure and format. *Media* must be selected, both for personal and non-personal communication. Finally, the communicator must collect *feedback* by watching how much of the market becomes aware, tries the product, and is satisfied in the process.

4. Explain the methods for setting the promotion budget and factors that affect the design of the promotion mix.

The company must decide how much to spend on promotion. The most popular approaches to making this decision are to spend what the company can afford, to use a percentage of sales, to base promotion on competitors' spending, or to base it on an analysis and costing of the communication objectives and tasks.

The company must divide the *promotion budget* among the major tools to create the *promotion mix*. Companies can pursue a *push* or a *pull* promotional strategy, or a combination of the two. The best specific blend of promotion tools depends on the type of product market, the desirability of the buyer's readiness stage, and the product life-cycle stage.

People at all levels of the organization must be aware of the many legal and ethical issues surrounding marketing communications. Companies must work hard and proactively at communicating openly, honestly, and agreeably with their customers and resellers.

Reviewing the Key Terms

Advertising 587
Affordable method 606
Buyer readiness stages 593
Buzz marketing 600
Competitive-parity method 606
Direct marketing 587
Integrated marketing
  communications (IMC) 590

Marketing communications mix
  (promotion mix) 587
Non-personal communication
  channels 601
Objective-and-task method 607
Percentage-of-sales method 606
Personal communication
  channels 600

Personal selling 587
Public relations 587
Pull strategy 610
Push strategy 610
Sales promotion 587
Word-of-mouth influence 600

Discussing the Concepts

1. A company's total marketing communications mix (promotion mix) is a blend of five major promotion tools. List and describe each of these promotion tools.

2. The shift from mass marketing to targeted marketing, and the corresponding use of a richer mixture of promotion tools and communication channels, poses problems for many marketers. Using all of the promotion mix elements suggested in the chapter, propose a plan for integrating marketing communications at one of the following: (a) your university or college, (b) Wendy's (www.wendys.com), (c) Burton Snow Boards (see www.burton.com), or (d) a local zoo, museum, theatre, or civic event. Discuss your plan in class.

3. Identify a product or service that has made effective use of a celebrity endorser. Identify another in which you think the use of a celebrity endorser was inappropriate. What criteria did you use to differentiate between a successful and unsuccessful use of a celebrity endorser?

4. The Internet promises exciting marketing communications potential. However, when mismanaged, the Internet can also serve as a disintegrating force in marketing communications. Explain. How can disintegration be avoided?

5. Using Figure 15.2 (page 592), describe the communications process for (a) a local newspaper ad for new cars,

(b) a phone call from a representative of MCI requesting service sign-up, (c) a salesperson in Sears attempting to sell you a television set, and (d) Microsoft's interactive webpage (www.microsoft.com).

6. List and briefly describe each of the six buyer-readiness stages consumers pass through on their way to making a purchase. Provide an example to illustrate how a consumer passes through these stages.

7. The marketing communicator can use one or more types of appeals or themes to produce a desired response. What are these types of appeals and when should each be used? Provide an example of each type of appeal using three different magazine ads.

8. Decide which of the promotional budget models described in the text would be most appropriate for (a) a small retail gift store, (b) an office supply company that has had a consistent sales and promotion pattern during each of the past five years, (c) a grocery store that has faced intense competition from three competitors in its immediate market area, and (d) an electronics manufacturer that is seeking to expand its market base and national appeal. Explain.

9. Marketers select from two basic promotion mix strategies: push and pull. Compare and contrast these strategies. Is it possible to balance these two strategies? Provide an example of a company that effectively employs both strategies.

Applying the Concepts

1. The manufacturers of today's highly complicated computer products face a difficult task in determining how to promote their products effectively. Consumers do not respond well to the detailed descriptions that are often needed to explain complex technological features and differences. As the personal computer and handheld computer markets continue to grow, the computer industry faces an interesting communication problem—how to tell consumers in plain terms what they need to know about new generations of products without boring them. The answer may be as close as the computer company's website. Experts predict that more and more consumers will be "surfing" for their product information and will rely less and less on traditional information sources. Examine the following websites for more information on new PC products: Sharp (www.sharpelectronics.com), IBM (www.ibm.com), Dell (www.dell.com), Casio (www.casio.com), Apple (www.apple.com), and Sony (www.sony.com).

a. How are the marketing communications at these websites different from those found in traditional advertising media? Which is more effective? Explain.

b. After reviewing each of the sites, pick a product that you might like to own (such as a laptop or handheld computer). Based solely on the information provided at the websites, which company and product most grabs your attention and purchasing interest? Critique your information-gathering experience: What information was most useful? How could the communications be improved? Would you be willing to purchase the product via the Internet? Why or why not?

2. McDonald's is one of the most powerful brands in the world. In addition to its product mix, wide distribution of restaurants, and value pricing, McDonald's has extremely effective communications with important audiences. The concept of integrated marketing communications recognizes that customers are only one group a firm wants to reach with persuasive information. In addition to targeting kids and their parents, McDonald's communicates with stockholders, potential franchisees, potential employees, and communities in which the restaurants operate.

a. Visit McDonald's online (www.mcdonalds.com) and browse the various webpages. How does McDonald's target its message to different customer groups (such as kids, senior citizens, adults, office workers, and so on) and to its publics (such as stockholders, potential franchisees, potential employees, and the community at large)? Why do you think McDonald's wants to communicate with each of the non-customer groups?

b. Although the specific messages may differ, is the overall appeal of McDonald's messages consistent to all audiences? What is the overall message you get from visiting the site? Is that message consistent with those you've seen on TV and elsewhere?

c. Assume McDonald's has hired you to review marketing communications transmitted via its website. Write a short report that critiques the site. Where does the website need improvement? What would you suggest?

Video Short

View the video short for this chapter at **www.pearsoned.ca/kotler** and then answer the questions provided in the case description.

Company Case

Procter & Gamble: Feeling the Heat

Applying Pressure

Consumer products giant Procter & Gamble has felt pressure in recent years as shareholders expressed their concerns over what they saw as the company's sometimes lacklustre performance. Shareholders and stock-market analysts pressed the company to develop new products to beef up its stable of long-term successes like Pampers, Tide, and Crest, which were competing in mature, saturated markets.

The company responded with a wave of new products. Some, like Dryel, a home dry-cleaning product, and Fit, a rinse for fruit and vegetables, failed to register with consumers. Others, however, like Crest Whitestrips, a tooth-whitening system launched in 2000, reached the company's new-product goal of $260 million in first-year sales. Such successes are not enough, however—P&G has to keep the new products coming if it is to reach its goals of 4 to 6 percent annual sales growth and double-digit earnings growth.

Pain Relief

To meet its ambitious growth goals, P&G developed a new-ventures unit, staffed with employees whose job was to develop new-product ideas and then pass them on to the appropriate business unit for development. The new-ventures unit examined the $4.3 billion pain-relief market to see if the company had any skills that it might apply to that market. It already knew much about this market due to its previous marketing of Aleve pain reliever (since sold to Bayer). Further, from its work on Pampers, Charmin, and Bounty, the company also had excellent knowledge in paper technology.

Merging these two capabilities, P&G's researchers developed the idea of the "external analgesic"—a product that consumers could use externally to provide long-lasting warmth to specific areas of the body where they experienced pain. After seven years of consumer and scientific testing, in early 2002 P&G announced that it would launch ThermaCare HeatWraps.

P&G designed ThermaCare for the temporary relief of minor muscle and joint aches and pain associated with overexertion, overuse, strains, sprains, and arthritis. Women could also use the product for temporary relief of minor menstrual cramping and associated back pain. The HeatWraps were portable, air-activated, disposable (single-use), self-heating devices that provided a continuous low-level therapeutic heat (40°C) for up to eight hours.

The HeatWrap was a small pad that resembled a very thin diaper and came in shapes designed for the lower or upper back, the neck or arm, and the abdomen. When the consumer opened the package, the HeatWrap was exposed to air. Inside the wrap were a series of oval-shaped heat discs that contained a mixture of natural heat-generating materials: iron, carbon sodium chloride, sodium thiosulfate, and water. The air penetrated a perforated film that controlled oxygen permeability. The iron in the heat discs began to oxidize, and the chemical process generated the heat. The process was basically the same one that manufacturers of hand warmers had used for years. However, P&G had found a way to use its paper technology to sustain and control the heat-generating reaction.

Doctors and pharmacists recommended that people who experienced muscle pain due to exercising should first apply ice packs for up to 20 minutes at a time, three to four times per day for one to two days, accompanied with a pain reliever, such as aspirin or aspirin-like products. Then, they recommended that the patient should use heat therapy.

P&G recommended that consumers wear the HeatWrap for at least three hours and up to eight hours, repeating the process each day for up to seven days. Users could wear the HeatWraps under their clothing and go about their normal routines. Consumers were warned that they should not use the HeatWraps with other externally applied medications like lotions or ointments due to the risk of a skin reaction.

When finished with the HeatWrap, consumers could dispose of it in the household trash, as all materials in the product were environmentally compatible.

Wrapping It Up

P&G's marketers were excited about what they saw as a breakthrough product. The company planned to price the product at about $9.00 per box at retail, producing a 25 percent profit margin for retailers, well above the margin for other pain-relief products. The package contained either two wraps in the back size or three wraps in the neck, arm, or abdomen sizes.

The company planned to concentrate on U.S. sales during the first year. It decided to allocate up to $118 million for an integrated promotional campaign to introduce ThermaCare. To design the campaign, P&G hired D'Arcy Masius Benton & Bowles, an advertising agency it had used for many years.

The agency knew that for a breakthrough product, it needed a breakthrough promotion program. After all, P&G was offering a unique product that presented consumers with many new concepts at the same time. Consumers would not be familiar with the product or how it worked. How could the advertising and promotion keep consumers from just shrugging and taking another pain pill? How could it educate consumers about what ThermaCare was, what it did, and how it was different from other pain-relief strategies? How could it help P&G make ThermaCare the next Tide?

Questions for Discussion

1. What are possible target audiences for ThermaCare? In what buyer-readiness stages will these target audiences be?

2. What issues will the advertising agency face in designing messages for the selected target audiences? What message "theme" or "headline" summarizes the positioning that you'd recommend for ThermaCare?

3. What recommendations would you make to P&G and D'Arcy to help them develop an integrated promotion strategy for ThermaCare? Be sure to deal with the issues of setting the overall promotion mix, selecting a message source, and collecting feedback.

Sources: Stuart Elliott, "Things Heat Up for P&G," *New York Times,* February 12, 2002, www.nytimes.com; "Procter and Gamble," *Drug Store News,* September 10, 2001, p. 19; Cliff Peale, "P&G Hopes ThermaCare Is a Blockbuster," *Cincinnati Enquirer,* July 22, 2001, www.cincinnati.com/; "ThermaCare Therapeutic HeatWraps," New Product Bulletin, American Pharmaceutical Association, 2001; and P&G's ThermaCare website, www.ThermaCare.com (accessed August 2002).

CBC Video Case

CBC Log on to your Companion Website at **www.pearsoned.ca/kotler** to view a CBC video segment and case for this chapter.

Chapter 16

Advertising, Sales Promotion, and Public Relations

After studying this chapter you should be able to

1. define the roles of advertising, sales promotion, and public relations in the promotion mix

2. describe the major decisions involved in developing an advertising program

3. explain how sales promotion campaigns are developed and implemented

4. explain how companies use public relations to communicate with their publics

Looking Ahead: Previewing the Concepts

Now that we've looked at overall integrated marketing communications planning, let's dig more deeply into the specific marketing communications tools. In this chapter, we'll explore the mass-communications tools—advertising, sales promotion, and public relations.

For starters, let's look closely at a highly successful campaign that you are all familiar with—the 2003 launch of *Harry Potter and the Order of the Phoenix*. The campaign integrated advertising, sales promotion, and public relations. As you read along, ask yourself just what is it that makes this such an effective campaign.

Thousands of Canadian kids were as anxious and excited as if it were Christmas Eve. But as the clock ticked close to midnight, Saturday, June 21, 2003, it wasn't Santa's sleigh they were awaiting. Instead, hundreds of thousands of books, packed in carefully sealed, unmarked boxes, had been safely shipped from Raincoast Books' Vancouver warehouse to stores across the country. Carefully guarded to preserve the secrecy of exciting plot developments, the volumes were about to be released to their eager audience. The advertising and public relations mix had cast its spell. Kids and their parents rushed to midnight sales or lined up for special store openings early Saturday morning. Others had tried online ordering for the first time and waited eagerly at home for Canada Post to deliver. *Harry Potter and the Order of the Phoenix* was about to arrive!

J.K. Rowling's Harry Potter books were already an astounding publishing phenomenon. Over 200 million copies had been sold in 200 different countries and 55 languages, making Rowling wealthier than Queen Elizabeth. Six million copies had been sold in Canada alone. For *Harry Potter and the Goblet of Fire,* the previous book in the series, Raincoast, the British author's Canadian publisher, had arranged a huge first printing of 300 000 copies—and was caught short. The book sold more than a million copies! So some looked askance when Raincoast hired Palmer Jarvis DDB Vancouver to promote the new book. Wouldn't it sell itself?

Well, it had been three years since *The Goblet of Fire*, and Rowling's first audience was getting older. Would they still be interested in the fantasy world of an English boy's adventures at a school for wizards? And could younger readers handle the challenge of such a hefty tome (768 pages, more than 100 pages longer than the preceding book)? The price, too, was proportionately higher: at $43, *The Order of the Phoenix* was $8 dollars more expensive than *The Goblet of Fire*. Then there was the fact that Rowling wouldn't be available for author tours. She had promoted *The Goblet of Fire* with a reading at Toronto's SkyDome (setting a Guinness world record for largest literary reading), but was staying home this time—she had recently given birth to her second child.

What Raincoast realized, however, was that as well as Harry's devoted fans, there was a potential audience for Rowling's new book that transcended the typical young reader. Desirée Zicko, Raincoast's marketing director, knew that a strong promotional campaign could reach "people on the margins"—the muggles (Harry-speak for unmagical mortals) who might not have felt an urgent pull to get the book but would be attracted by the energy of a creative campaign.

A modification in the package was the secret to tapping this audience. "There's a big cross-over market for Potter," said Teresa Vanderkop, Raincoast's publicity director, "but some adults don't like to be seen with a children's book." So Raincoast published 20 000 copies of a special hardcover edition that would appeal to grandparents, parents, and maturing readers who had devoured the books as children but were now teenagers and young adults. While the cover design was different, a little more sombre and subtly coloured, the content was identical to the version targeted to younger readers. Previous "adult" editions had been printed in paperback only, and Rowling's British and American publishers watched Raincoast's strategy with interest.

Another unique feature of the Canadian edition was Raincoast's decision to use Ancient Forest Friendly paper—100 percent recycled and chlorine-free, saving almost 30 000 trees and over 45 000 litres of water. This environmentally friendly decision was applauded by Rowling in a special preface to the Canadian edition. Fans emailed their praise to Raincoast's website (see www.raincoast.com/harrypotter/news.html) and public relations benefits were realized as international ecological groups urged Potter fans outside of Canada to order the Canadian edition online.

As the big day approached, Raincoast and the team at Palmer Jarvis set to work on a special advertising campaign. Radio spots were broadcast on June 19, featuring complaints from out-of-work witches who mourned that Harry's magical expertise was costing them jobs. The strategy underlying the ads was to build up excitement and presence in the two days before the book's launch.

Another tactic Palmer Jarvis used was a canny guerrilla marketing campaign. On June 20, the day before the launch, kids dressed as Harry, Ron, and Hermione swarmed train stations in Vancouver and Toronto, brandishing "tickets" for Platform 9¾. (Potter fans know that this is the mystical platform for departures to the Hogwarts school for wizards. To muggles, of course, the tickets took the form of *Phoenix* bookmarks.) Executed by Toronto-based TrojanOne, the event only cost $20 000 (about 5 percent of the promotions budget), but commuters were amused, astonished—and talking! "People were just stopping, left and right.... They would laugh and shake their heads, but they all connected with it," chortled Palmer Jarvis's Scott Keith. Meanwhile, statues across the cities—like the venerable griffins in front of Toronto's Osborne Collection of Early Children's Books—were suddenly swathed with scarves in

the yellow-and-red stripes of Gryffendor, Harry's school house at Hogwarts.

In Vancouver, Raincoast held a launch party at Vancouver's Science Centre. With tickets priced at $50, it was designed to attract adults and featured entertainment from astrologers, musicians, and stilt walkers—plus a bar. Proceeds from the event went to children's hospice Canucks Place.

The promotional magic helped drive sales across the country. Midnight parties in Indigo and other stores throughout Canada ensured spectacular business—for example, Indigo reported first-day sales of 100 000 copies, a new record, with another 100 000 copies pre-ordered online. Kidsbooks in Vancouver held a street party with prizes and balloons, magicians and wizards, and a thousand kids and muggles in costumes. Chapters stores opened at 7:00 a.m. on Saturday morning, with line-ups of 50 or more waiting for the doors to open. And Internet business boomed, attracting customers who had never bought online before (in fact, financial analysts claimed Indigo's 65 percent increase in first-quarter online sales was mostly Potter-driven, and Amazon.ca predicted sales growth in high double digits, also fuelled by Harry). Canada Post flawlessly brought off special Saturday delivery of the book to 38 cities and towns across Canada on June 21—the largest one-day delivery of an online order ever. Young readers were thrilled with the service. According to Canada Post's Rhéal Leblanc, "At one home the kids almost tried to hug the delivery driver, they were so happy to see him arrive." All in all, Raincoast's first printing of over 915 000 copies—the largest in Canadian history—was sold out in less than a week!

So did all the hoopla benefit a product so strong it seemed it could almost sell itself? Palmer Jarvis's Scott Keith thinks the brand-building effort was worth it, describing the agency's work as bringing the book "right to life on the street, and [giving] people a smile." Thanks to Raincoast's clever strategy of promoting the book to a wide range of readers and using creative campaigns, the audience for the next books in Harry's magical saga will surely continue to multiply.[1]

Companies like Raincoast Books, the Canadian publisher of the Harry Potter series, must do more than make good products—they must inform consumers about product benefits and carefully position products in consumers' minds. To do this, they must skilfully use the mass-promotion tools of *advertising*, *sales promotion*, and *public relations*. We take a closer look at each of these tools in this chapter.

Advertising
Any paid form or non-personal presentation and promotion of ideas, goods, or services by an identified sponsor.

Advertising

Advertising can be traced to the very beginnings of recorded history. Archeologists working in the countries around the Mediterranean Sea have dug up signs announcing various events and offers. The Romans painted walls to announce gladiator fights, and the Phoenicians painted pictures promoting their wares on large rocks along parade routes.

Modern advertising, however, is a far cry from these early efforts. The Canadian advertising industry accounts for about 250 000 jobs, or about 2 percent of all jobs in Canada (bigger than either the insurance or real estate agent industry and the accounting and legal services industry), while the aggregate expenditure of the Canadian advertising industry in 2000 was $16.79 billion. U.S. advertisers now run up an estimated annual advertising bill of more than US$231 billion, and worldwide ad spending approaches an estimated US$500 billion.[2]

The Canadian Marketing Association estimated that $10 billion was spent on advertising in various media in Canada in 2001. Growth in media expenditures is slowing, however. This is due to two trends in Canadian businesses: mergers that have resulted in the disappearance of some advertising budgets and decreased spending by the telecommunication sector, which believes massive new investments to educate consumers are no longer required. See Figure 16.1 for an overview of marketing clients and spending.[3]

Although advertising is used mostly by business firms, it is also used by a wide range of non-profit organizations, professionals, and social agencies that advertise their causes to various target publics. In fact, the fifteenth-largest advertising spender is a not-for-profit organization—the Canadian government. Advertising is a good way to inform and persuade, whether the purpose is to sell Coca-Cola worldwide or to get consumers in a developing nation to use birth control.

For a profile of one of Canada's most successful advertising experts, see Real Marketing 16.1.

Marketing management must make four important decisions when developing an advertising program (see Figure 16.2 on page 628): *setting advertising objectives, setting the advertising budget, developing advertising strategy (message decisions and media decisions), and evaluating advertising campaigns.*

Figure 16.1 Advertising services overview

Sources: (a) AdAge Global, cited by Industry Canada, "Advertising Services—Service Industries Overviews Series," October 2001, http://strategis.ic.gc.ca; and (b) Chris Powell, "Speciality TV Drives Spending Growth," *Marketing Magazine*, September 30, 2003, p. 4.

Setting Advertising Objectives

The first step in developing an advertising program is to set *advertising objectives*. These objectives should be based on past decisions about the target market, positioning, and marketing mix, which define the job that advertising must do in the total marketing program.

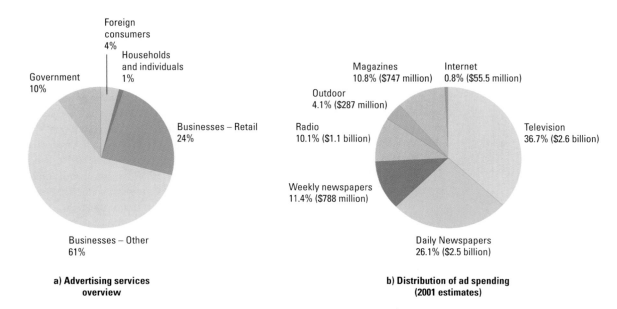

a) Advertising services overview

b) Distribution of ad spending (2001 estimates)

REAL MARKETING

16.1 Peter Elwood, Former CEO of Thomas J. Lipton Inc.

What does a former CEO of one of Canada's packaged-goods companies know about advertising, you might ask. Plenty, if that former CEO is Peter Elwood, a man who recently retired after a long career with Thomas J. Lipton Inc. and Lever Canada. These companies, both divisions of Unilever, a giant international marketer, sell such well-known brands as Lever 2000; Becel and Imperial margarines; Red Rose, Salada, and Lipton teas; Sunlight detergent; Ragu sauces; and Lipton soups.

Peter and his team created two award-winning campaigns judged the best in Canada. They also won three CASSIE (Canadian Advertising Success Stories) awards. Working with Peter were three top Canadian agencies: Ammirati Puris Lintas, Ogilvy & Mather, and MacLaren McCann.

In Peter's view, there is a great need today to develop breakthrough marketing communications. Although speaking effectively about brands and products is as old a problem as advertising itself, Peter notes that marketers have long known that over half of their advertising dollars are wasted. The critical question is: "Which half?"

In our highly competitive marketplace, consumers are exposed to more advertising messages than ever before. Peter knows only too well that marketers have

to justify every expense. But justifying advertising budgets is getting harder than ever before since the number of media outlets (including the Internet) used to carry commercial messages is growing rapidly. Moreover, Peter notes, consumers are empowered and have the technological capability to screen out many messages by using televisions that skip through advertisements. Furthermore, today's buyers are highly educated and cynical consumers. If messages are boring, uninteresting, or aren't brilliantly targeted, consumers just tune out, and those precious advertising dollars might as well have been flushed down the drain.

Some firms have reacted by just eliminating advertising. Why take the risk of using such a difficult, inefficient tool, they ask. But this isn't the solution in Peter's view. In fact, it may begin a "spiral of doom." Without advertising that builds brand positioning in the hearts and minds of consumers, firms cannot differentiate products and are forced to sell on price.

Therefore, Peter stresses, the need to develop advertising platforms that work is more important than ever. Firms need advertising that connects to consumers. However, the old ways of developing copy—determining who you are talking to, establishing the unique selling proposition, selecting effective media to convey the message—is just not good enough anymore. As a recent article in *Marketing Magazine* proclaimed, "Clients get the advertising they deserve!" Watchers of Canada's advertising industry contend that most marketers are unwilling to venture beyond the comforting den of "safe" advertising and marketing. But when it comes to taking a risk in pursuit of an innovative idea, few will reach for the brass ring. Peter Elwood is viewed as one marketer who holds that ring firmly in both hands.

Peter is adamant that there are two absolutely critical things that have to be placed front and centre in the development of effective communications. First, advertisers have to develop a deep consumer insight. Such an insight is a universal truth—not yet recognized—that is relevant to the brand. Second, they have to work as a team with their agencies, allowing all members to contribute what they do best.

Peter Elwood

What does developing this insight involve? To answer, we look to Peter's experience at Lipton. First, Peter stresses, you have to dive deep into the psyche of the consumer. You have to find out from consumers what they are thinking and saying to themselves as they use your products and services in situ. Rather than using traditional research, you need one-on-one interviews and the help of ethnographers and psychologists who observe and interpret the meanings of products in people's lives.

Take the work that Peter authorized when Lipton sought to develop a new campaign for its chicken noodle soup. Lipton had long known that kids liked their chicken noodle soup, and moms knew this, too. But why weren't they serving the soup more often? They knew it was good for their kids. If Peter had been content to use the old, simple way of advertising, he could have just instructed his agency to develop ads that would just tell moms their kids liked the soup, so go buy it. But Peter knew this just wasn't enough in today's marketplace.

Lipton's research revealed that moms did not understand their children. Moms were often afraid their kids would get bored with food. Think back. If you were like 99.9 percent of Canada's kids, you found meals boring activities that just kept you from doing other more fun things. Therefore, moms worked to serve their children lunches that would expose them to a variety of foods and nutritionally balanced meals. But what wasn't clear in their minds was that kids don't get bored doing the things they like. In fact, if they like it, they will do it over, and over, and over again. Like having the same story read every night, or watching the same movie or playing video games over and over.

Kids also like to get attention or cause a reaction. It's all part of growing up. These insights led to a series of ads including the recent "whoopee cushion" spot, the ice ad where a child repeatedly presses the ice cube maker on the fridge, and the drums ad where a repeated drum beat disturbs a father just trying to read his paper. Not only did these ads break through and speak to consumers, they drove sales.

The second route to success for great advertising, which is often given lip service in companies but is rarely followed, is taking a team approach to advertising development. To develop breakthrough campaigns, Peter stresses, you not only need the marketing strategists who want to take the brand forward, you need a team with people who can write and draw. These are the strong right-brained people. Where many companies go wrong, Peter believes, is confusing the roles of the different players. While your brand people may be intelligent and strategically insightful, they aren't the people you want writing your copy. You have to leave that to the creative people. And you will know when they have it right. The idea will be insightful, easily noticeable, and exciting. In fact, Peter notes, it may even be risky. But if that is the case, Peter recommends that is exactly what you should go with. How else will you get the communications program that will really break through?

As Peter Elwood knows, perhaps better than any other Canadian marketer, the use of consumer insight integrated into advertising in a very entertaining and appealing way can be highly effective. It put the old favourite Lipton's Chicken Noodle Soup back on Canada's lunch tables; and Canada's moms, still smiling after viewing Lipton's ads, don't feel at all guilty serving it more often.

Sources: Peggy Cunningham talked with Peter Elwood on December 1, 2000. Also see Lara Mills, "Tough Times for Heroic Marketers: Where Have All the Larger-Than-Life Leaders Gone?" *Marketing Magazine,* January 24, 2000, www.marketingmag.ca; Doug Robinson, "When Yuck Doesn't Suck: Lipton Knew Kids Liked Its Chicken Noodle Soup...the Challenge Was Convincing Their Parents," *Marketing Magazine,* March 29, 2000, www.marketingmag.ca; and "Marketing Awards: Television Campaign," *Marketing Magazine,* March 27, 2000, www.marketingmag.ca.

Advertising objective

A specific communication task to be accomplished with a specific target audience during a specific period of time.

An **advertising objective** is a specific communication *task* to be accomplished with a specific *target* audience during a specific period of *time*. Advertising objectives can be classified by primary purpose—whether the aim is to *inform, persuade,* or *remind.* Table 16.1 lists examples of each of these objectives.

Informative advertising is often used in introducing a new product category. In this case, the objective is to build primary demand. For example, producers of DVD players must first inform consumers of the image quality and convenience benefits of DVDs. *Persuasive advertising* becomes more important as competition increases. Here, the company's objective is to build selective demand. Once DVD players became established, Sony began trying to persuade consumers that *its* brand offered the best quality for their money.

The use of *comparison advertising*, a form of persuasive advertising, is becoming more common. In comparative ads, a company directly or indirectly compares

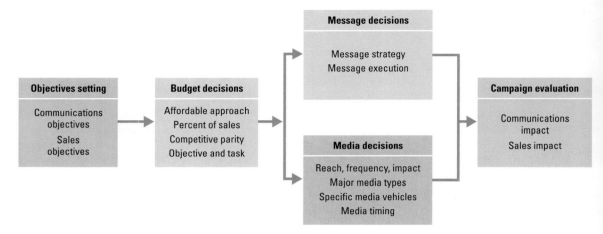

Figure 16.2 Major advertising decisions

its brand with one or more other rival brands. The classic comparison campaign was developed by Avis, which positioned itself against market leader Hertz by claiming, "We're number two, so we try harder." Other examples abound:[4]

- Progresso ran ads showing side-by-side comparisons of its soups versus Campbell's condensed soups, inviting consumers to "Enjoy a better soup...with a more adult taste."

- Volvo Canada unveiled an ad in the *Globe and Mail* for its XC90 SUV that used the tag-line, "What's the German word for envy?" The ad was a response to a BMW eight-page advertising spread that declared, "Just because you're safe, doesn't mean you have to be boring."

- TELUS took aim at Microcell's Fido in a print campaign that shows a dog tracking down a TELUS phone.

- Harvey's, the Mississauga, Ontario-based fast food chain, suggests that its burgers are better because they are served hot off the grill and custom garnished. A Harvey's TV ad depicts a hockey player going into the penalty box "hot" and

Table 16.1 Possible Advertising Objectives

Informative Advertising

Telling the market about a new product	Describing available services
Suggesting new uses for a product	Correcting false impressions
Informing the market of a price change	Reducing consumers' fears
Explaining how the product works	Building a company image

Persuasive Advertising

Building brand preference	Persuading customers to purchase now
Encouraging switching to your brand	Persuading customers to receive a sales call
Changing customers' perceptions of product attributes	

Reminder Advertising

Reminding consumers that the product may be needed in the near future	Keeping the product in customers' minds during off-seasons
Reminding consumers where to buy the product	Maintaining top-of-mind product awareness

Comparative advertising: Progresso makes side-by-side comparisons of its soup versus Campbell's, inviting consumers to "Enjoy a better soup... with a more adult taste."

Now that the kids are gone,
life just keeps getting better.

This is a time for discovery. So maybe it's time you discovered a soup with a more adult taste. One that tastes better than the condensed you served your kids. Progresso® Chicken Noodle. With tender chunks of all white meat chicken, bigger veggies, and wide curly noodles. This is your time. Enjoy a better soup.

It's time to go Progresso.

coming out cool. The use of a hockey-based theme also hints at the fact that Harvey's is the Canadian choice in a landscape dominated by U.S.-owned chains.

Firms using comparative claims must exercise caution, however. The *Competition Act* stipulates that an advertisement using competitive claims must be based on an adequate and proper test that supports it. The Canadian Code of Advertising Standards was recently tightened with regard to comparative advertising (see clause 6). It stipulates that advertisers cannot unfairly discredit, disparage, or attack competitors.[5]

Reminder advertising is important for mature products—it keeps consumers thinking about the product. In the face of the 2003 BSE scare, the Canadian Cattlemen's Association ran a campaign to assure consumers about the safety, taste, and value of Canadian beef as both a product to consume and a way to preserve Canadian jobs. Canadian grocery retailers and food chains such as McDonald's and Burger King, heavily dependent on beef products, joined in to support the effort.[6]

Setting the Advertising Budget

After determining its advertising objectives, the company next sets its *advertising budget* for each product. Four common methods for setting promotion budgets were discussed in Chapter 15. Here we discuss some specific factors that the company should consider when setting the advertising budget.

Public relations: During the 2003 "mad cow" scare, politicians joined beef producers and restaurant chains in the campaign to reassure consumers about the safety of Canadian meat.

A brand's advertising budget often depends on its *stage in the product life cycle*. For example, new products typically need large advertising budgets to build awareness and to gain consumer trial. In contrast, mature brands usually require lower budgets as a ratio to sales. *Market share* also affects the amount of advertising needed. Because building the market or taking share from competitors requires larger advertising spending than does simply maintaining current share, high-share brands usually need more advertising spending as a percentage of sales. Also, brands in a market with many competitors and high advertising clutter must be advertised more heavily to be noticed above the noise. Undifferentiated brands—those that closely resemble other brands in their product class (beer, soft drinks, laundry detergents)—may require heavy advertising to set them apart. When the product differs greatly from competitors, advertising can be used to point out the differences to consumers.

No matter what method is used, setting the advertising budget is a difficult task. How does a company know if it is spending the right amount? Some critics charge that large consumer packaged goods firms tend to spend too much on advertising while business-to-business marketers generally underspend on advertising. They claim that, on the one hand, the large consumer companies use a lot of image advertising without really knowing its effects. They overspend as a form of "insurance" against not spending enough. On the other hand, business advertisers tend to rely too heavily on their sales forces to bring in orders. They underestimate the power of company and product image in preselling to industrial customers. Thus, they do not spend enough on advertising to build customer awareness and knowledge.

Some companies such as Coca-Cola and Kraft have built sophisticated statistical models to determine the relationship between promotional spending and brand sales, and to help determine the "optimal investment" across various media. Still, because so many factors affect advertising effectiveness, some controllable and others not, measuring the results of advertising spending remains an inexact science. In most cases, managers must rely on large doses of judgment along with more quantitative analysis when setting advertising budgets.[7]

Developing Advertising Strategy

Advertising strategy consists of two major elements—creating advertising *messages* and selecting advertising *media*. Though media planning used to be viewed as secondary to the message-creation process, media fragmentation, soaring media costs, and more focused target marketing strategies have promoted the importance of the media planning function. More and more, advertisers are orchestrating a closer harmony between their messages and the media that deliver them. In some cases, an advertising campaign might start with a great message idea, followed by the choice of appropriate media. In other cases, however, a campaign might begin with a good media opportunity, followed by advertisements designed to take advantage of that opportunity. Among the more noteworthy ad campaigns based on tight media–creative partnerships is the pioneering campaign for Absolut vodka (www.absolut.com), marketed by Seagram:[8]

> For years, Seagrams Canada of Montreal has worked closely with a slew of magazines to set Absolut's media schedule. The schedule consists of up to 100 magazines, ranging from consumer and business magazines to theatre playbills. The agency's creative department is charged with creating media-specific ads. The result is a wonderful assortment of very creative ads for Absolut, tightly targeted to audiences of the media in which they appear.
>
> For example, Seagrams has long been an avid supporter of the gay community, and it wanted to develop ads specifically geared to gays and lesbians. Working closely with niche publication *Xtra!* magazine staff, it developed the concept for "Absolut Pride," "Absolut Out" (aptly featuring a closet), and "Absolut Commitment" (showcasing two grooms on a wedding cake). Brand manager Holly Wyatt believed the partnership with *Xtra!* made sense because the magazine's staff was in tune with trends in the gay and lesbian community. "Absolut Pride," in particular, received a lot of extra media coverage, including a feature on *Entertainment Tonight*. When asked why she targeted the gay and lesbian community, Wyatt noted that the market is the best representation of Absolut's target audience, regardless of sexual orientation. "They're young, sophisticated, somewhat upscale. And Absolut consumers do tend to swing towards the arts," she says. "It just makes sense for us." In all, Absolut has developed more than 500 ads for the almost two-decade-old campaign.
>
> At a time of soaring media costs and cluttered communication channels, a closer cooperation between creative and media people has paid off handsomely for Absolut. Largely as a result of its breakthrough advertising, Absolut now captures a 63 percent share of the imported vodka market in North America.

Creating the Advertising Message

No matter how high the budget, advertising can succeed only if commercials gain attention and communicate well. Good advertising messages are especially important in today's costly and cluttered advertising environment. About 99 percent of Canadian households are equipped with a television, and 76 percent of Canadians watch television at least once a day. However, the number of television channels beamed into Canadian homes has skyrocketed from two in the 1950s to over 144 commercial channels—two national English channels, two national French channels, 26 regional channels, 47 specialty networks, 43 digital specialty networks, and 9 pay TV and pay-per-view offerings. Add to this the growing number of American signals that are picked up by Canadians who, in 2002, spent 12 percent of their viewing time watching U.S. stations. Canadian media options also include 941 radio stations, 105 daily newspapers, over 1200 French and English community newspapers, and over 1600 consumer magazines. The clutter is made worse by a continuous barrage of catalogues, direct-mail and online ads, and out-of-home media.[9]

If all this advertising clutter bothers some consumers, it also causes big problems for advertisers. Take the situation facing network television advertisers in the United States. They regularly pay US$200 000 or more for 30 seconds of advertising time during a popular prime-time program, even more if it's an especially popular program such as *ER* (US$445 000 per 30-second spot), *Friends* (US$354 000 per spot), *Will & Grace* (US$320 000 per spot), or a mega-event such as the Super Bowl (more than US$2 million).[10] Then, their ads are sandwiched in with a clutter of some 60 other commercials, announcements, and network promotions per hour. In comparison, Canadian advertising is a bargain, but the reach is much lower. Thirty-second spots on national networks like CBC and CTV are often less than $80 000 and ads on specialty channels like the Discovery Channel may be as low as $5000.

Until recently, television viewers had only a few channels from which to choose and were pretty much a captive audience for advertisers. But with the growth in cable and satellite TV, VCRs, and remote-control units, today's viewers have many more options. They can avoid ads by watching commercial-free cable channels. They can "zap" commercials by pushing the fast-forward button during taped programs. With remote control, they can instantly turn off the sound during a commercial or "zip" around the channels to see what else is on. One study found that half of all television viewers switch channels when the commercial break starts. And the new wave of personal video recorders (PVRs) and personal television services—such as TiVo, ReplayTV, and Microsoft's UltimateTV—have armed viewers with an arsenal of new-age zipping and zapping weapons. A recent study of TiVo and other personal video recorder system users found that these users skip commercials 72 percent of the time, a much higher rate than for those watching live television or using VCRs.[11]

A new advertising challenge: The new wave of personal video recorders, such as TiVo, has armed viewers with an arsenal of new-age zipping and zapping weapons.

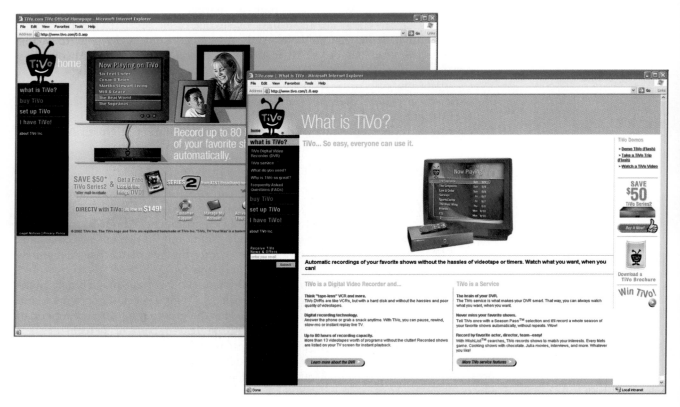

Just to gain and hold attention, advertising messages must be better planned, more imaginative, more entertaining, and more rewarding to consumers. "Today we have to entertain and not just sell, because if you try to sell directly and come off as boring or obnoxious, people are going to press the remote on you," points out one advertising executive. "When most TV viewers are armed with remote channel switchers, a commercial has to cut through the clutter and seize the viewers in one to three seconds, or they're gone," comments another.[12] Some advertisers even create intentionally controversial ads to break through the clutter and gain attention for their products (see Real Marketing 16.2).

Message Strategy   The first step in creating effective advertising messages is to decide what general message will be communicated to consumers—to plan a *message strategy*. The purpose of advertising is to get consumers to think about or react to the product or company in a certain way. People will react only if they believe that they will benefit from doing so. Thus, developing an effective message strategy begins with identifying customer *benefits* that can be used as advertising appeals. Ideally, advertising message strategy will follow directly from the company's broader positioning strategy.

Message strategy statements tend to be plain, straightforward outlines of benefits and positioning points that the advertiser wants to stress. The advertiser must develop a compelling *creative concept*—or *big idea*—that will bring the message strategy to life in a distinctive and memorable way. At this stage, simple message ideas become great ad campaigns. Usually, a copywriter and art director will team up to generate many creative concepts, hoping that one of these concepts will turn out to be the big idea. The creative concept may emerge as a visualization, a phrase, or a combination of the two.

The creative concept will guide the choice of specific appeals to be used in an advertising campaign. Advertising appeals should have three characteristics. First, they should be *meaningful,* pointing out benefits that make the product more desirable or interesting to consumers. Second, appeals must be *believable*—consumers

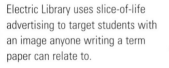

Electric Library uses slice-of-life advertising to target students with an image anyone writing a term paper can relate to.

16.2 Advertising on the Edge: You Either Hate 'Em or Love 'Em

*T*f you live in Western Canada, you were sure to have seen the outdoor campaign that drew the ire of hundreds of consumers. Huge billboards showed three nude radio announcers holding large nuts in front of their "private parts" while the ad proclaimed, "See, They're Nuts." The ads promoted Edmonton's K-Rock 97.3 FM. Steve Jones, VP programming for Dartmouth, Nova Scotia-based NewCap Broadcasting, owners of K-Rock, says he wasn't surprised people complained to the Advertising Standards Council, which ordered that the ad be taken down. He notes, however, that it made for great publicity and thus good business. "From a PR point of view, the ads did some pretty exceptional work for us. They generated a great deal of local and national newspaper and TV coverage." One reason why the campaign elicited so many complaints was its high visibility to consumers of every demographic. While the ad was aimed at the station's audience of 25- to 54-year-olds, it could be viewed by everyone, including children.

Molson ran into similar complaints with its ads that used Don Cherry as a spokesman for its Molson Canadian's "Bubba" mini kegs. Advertising Standards Canada issued a bulletin telling marketers in no uncertain terms that celebrities like Cherry, who are considered role models for minors, will not be allowed to promote alcoholic beverages, under the Canadian Radio-television and Telecommunications Commission code.

K-Rock's billboard ad and the Molson's ad are examples of a new genre of irreverent, cutting-edge advertising—commercials that intentionally create controversy, even if it means turning off some potential customers. In today's cluttered advertising environment, these ads go to extremes to get attention—you either love 'em or hate 'em. Other controversial ads abound. While flipping through your favourite magazine, you might encounter a Toyota ad targeting echo boomers with the headline "Attention nose pickers...." On the next page is a boundary-pushing ad from

SHRINKAGE MAY OCCUR
THE CURIOUSLY STRONG MINTS

CURIOUS?

WWW.TOOHOT.COM

Ads on the edge: These ads go to extremes to bust through the clutter—either you love 'em or you hate 'em.

Candies, featuring company spokesmodel Jenny McCarthy sitting on a toilet with her pants around her calves, wearing little more than her bright orange Candies shoes. Next comes an Altoids ad in which a man peers down the front of his boxer shorts: "Shrinkage may occur," proclaims the ad's headline. "The curiously strong mints." Other Altoids ads feature a woman in a seductively devilish outfit, complete with horns, and headlines such as "Hot and bothered?" "Frigid?" and "Taste like hell!"

For pure gross-out value, few ads top the "Blind Date" spot from SmartBeep, the retail paging-services provider. The spot, which generated enormous response, was part of a wacky five-part campaign that contrasted smart versus not-so-smart behaviour to promote SmartBeep's free pagers and low rates on paging services. In it, a woman climbs into the front seat of her blind date's car. While he's crossing around to the other side, thinking she is alone, she leans to one side and lets rip a frat-house blast of gas. When her date hops in the car, she hesitates then turns red with embarrassment as he introduces her to another couple in the back seat. "You guys meet? Gregg, Janice?" he asks, to which Janice in the back seat responds, "We sure did." The announcer concludes, "That was stupid.... This is smart. A beeper service for just $1.99 a month." The ad closes: "We've got chemistry here. You feel it?" says the blind-date guy. "I felt it!" says Janice from the back seat. The ad became an immediate Internet cult item.

Outpost.com ran a series of three ads that amused some consumers and outraged others. In the most widely viewed ad, a calm, deep-voiced announcer intones, "Hello, we want you to remember our name—Outpost.com. That's why we've decided to fire gerbils out of this cannon through the 'O' in Outpost." He gives a nod, and his assistant fires a nearby cannon. "*Boom!*" The cannon hurls a gerbil toward the hole. "*Splat!*" A near miss—the gerbil hits the wall, then falls to the ground and scurries away. "Cute little guy," says the announcer, smiling warmly. The ad closes with an invitation to viewers to "Send complaints to Outpost.com—the cool place to buy computer stuff online." It was all pretend, of course.

Site traffic doubled and Outpost.com signed 15 000 new customers in the two weeks after the commercials first aired, 30 000 new customers by the end of the campaign. Moreover, as a testament to its cutting-edge creativity, the campaign amassed more than

a dozen of the ad industry's highest awards and spawned many competitors. However, while the outrageous ads grabbed attention and awards, they did little to position Outpost.com or to tell people what it had to sell. Outpost.com's name was all over the place, but nobody knew why he or she should visit the site. The ads mentioned "computer stuff," laments the company's former CEO, but "the ads were so dominating that people missed that. They didn't know that we sold computers. They thought that we sold clothes or didn't sell anything. We had a lot of visitors—but no buyers."

So, it appears that to be truly cutting edge, advertising must do more than just capture attention. It must support and enhance the brand and its positioning. If used properly, cutting-edge humour can help do that, as proved by Altoids and its "Curiously Strong" campaign. In these ads, the irreverence fits the brand's "curious, strong, original" positioning. It also appeals to the tastes as well as the taste buds of Altoids' cutting-edge target consumers. As a result, in only two years, the small-budget but high-impact ad campaign has propelled Altoids past longtime strong-mint market leader Tic Tac. "Altoids is now—improbably—the boss of the mint world," says an analyst. What's the power behind this cheeky campaign? The analyst confirms that "everything links back to [the brand's] 'curiously strong' and 'original' [positioning]."

If you want to find out more about ads that offend, visit the Advertising Standards Council website at www.adstandards.com and view their annual report. It provides details about ad complaints and statistics about the complaints that were upheld.

Sources: Samson Okalow, "Now that the Ad Code Is Relaxed, How Far Should You Go?" *Strategy,* June 30, 2003, p. 2; Paul-Mark Rendon, "Cherry's Bubbas Out, Says ASC," *Marketing Magazine,* September 22, 2003, p. 3; Advertising Standards Canada, "2002 Ad Complaints Report," 2003, www.adstandards.com/en/standards/complaints_report/2002ascReportEn.pdf; Melanie Wells, "Wanted: Television Ad Complaints," *USA 1999 Complaints Report Today,* January 11, 1999, p. 4B; Dottie Enrico, "Creature Feature," *TV Guide,* January 23, 1999, p. 13; Hank Kim, "Creature Feature," *Adweek,* November 23, 1998, p. 20; Tom Kurtz, "Unsettling TV Commercials: And Now, a Gross-Out from Our Sponsor," *New York Times,* July 25, 1999, p. 7; Anne Marie Borrego, "Wild Ads Make Web Stars," *Inc.,* February 2000, p. 66; Verne Gay, "Best Use of Out-of-Home: Stargate Worldwide," *Adweek,* June 19, 2000, pp. M6–M10; Laurie J. Flynn, "As Cyberian Outpost Plunges Toward the Abyss, Two Suitors Wait Patiently to Pick Up the Pieces," *New York Times,* July 24, 2001, p. C10; and About Altoids website, www.altoids.com (accessed August 2002).

must believe that the product or service will deliver the promised benefits. Appeals should also be *distinctive*—they should tell how the product is better than the competing brands. For example, the most meaningful benefit of owning a wristwatch is that it keeps accurate time, yet few watch ads feature this benefit. Instead, based on the distinctive benefits they offer, watch advertisers might select any of a number of advertising themes. For years, Timex has been the affordable watch that "took a lickin' and kept on tickin'." In contrast, Swatch has featured style and fashion, whereas Rolex stresses luxury and status.

Message Execution   The advertiser has to turn the big idea into an actual ad execution that will capture the target market's attention and interest. The creative people must find the best style, tone, words, and format for executing the message. Any message can be presented in different *execution styles,* such as the following:

- *Slice of life.* This style shows one or more "typical" people using the product in a normal setting. For example, Electric Library shows the face of a frustrated student trying to get a term paper completed; two mothers at a picnic discuss the nutritional benefits of Jif peanut butter.

- *Lifestyle.* This style shows how a product fits in with a particular lifestyle. For example, the Ontario Milk Marketing Board shows how active Canadians get their energy. An ad for Mongoose mountain bikes shows a serious biker traversing remote and rugged but beautiful terrain and states, "There are places that are so awesome and so killer that you'd like to tell the whole world about them. But please, *don't.*"

- *Fantasy.* This style creates a fantasy around the product or its use. For instance, many ads are built around dream themes. The Gap even introduced a perfume named Dream—ads show a woman sleeping blissfully and suggest that the scent is "the stuff that clouds are made of."

- *Mood or image.* This style builds a mood or image around the product, such as beauty, love, or serenity. No claim is made about the product except through suggestion. Bermuda tourism ads create such moods.

- *Musical.* This style shows one or more people or cartoon characters singing a song about the product. One of the most famous ads in history is a Coca-Cola ad built around the song, "I'd Like to Teach the World to Sing."

- *Personality symbol.* This style creates a character that represents the product. The character might be *animated* (the Jolly Green Giant), *computer-generated* (Blockbuster's rabbit Carl and guinea pig Ray), or *real* ("Joe" from the Molson's "I Am Canadian!" campaign; Ol' Lonely, the Maytag repairman; or Morris, the 9-Lives Cat).

- *Technical expertise.* This style shows the company's expertise in making the product. Thus, Maxwell House shows one of its buyers carefully selecting the coffee beans, and Titleist explains its ability to make a better golf ball.

- *Scientific evidence.* This style presents survey or scientific evidence that the brand is better or better liked than one or more other brands. For years, Crest toothpaste has used scientific evidence to convince buyers that Crest is better than other brands at fighting cavities.

- *Testimonial evidence.* This style features a highly believable or likeable source that endorses the product. For example, Apple has run ads featuring real people who recently switched from Microsoft Windows-based PCs to Macs. And many companies use actors or sports celebrities as product endorsers.

The advertiser also must choose a *tone* for the ad. Procter & Gamble always uses a positive tone: Its ads say something very positive about its products. P&G avoids humour that might detract from the message. In contrast, many advertisers now use edgy humour to break through the commercial clutter.

Testimonials: Apple ran ads featuring real people who'd recently switched from Microsoft Windows-based PCs to Macs. "Janie Porche got her first Apple in January after she'd finally had enough of her PC's temperamental behaviour."

"My PC wasn't Plug-n-Play. It was Plug-n-Get-Mad."

The advertiser must use memorable and attention-getting *words* in the ad. For example, rather than claiming simply that "a BMW is a well-engineered automobile," BMW uses more creative and higher-impact phrasing: "The ultimate driving machine." London Life could promise prospective customers that it will help them plan for their retirement, but this would not have the impact of promising "Freedom 55."

Finally, *format* elements make a difference on an ad's impact as well as its cost. A small change in ad design can make a big difference on its effect. The *illustration* is the first thing the reader notices—it must be strong enough to draw attention. Next, the *headline* must effectively entice the right people to read the copy. Finally, the *copy*—the main block of text in the ad—must be simple but strong and convincing. Moreover, these three elements must effectively work *together*:

> Short Man by Brown's, a specialty clothing retailer for the "vertically challenged," successfully followed these lessons in a recent award-winning series of magazine ads. The goal of the campaign was to attract new customers and infuse more life, notoriety, and personality into the brand. Before launching the ads, owner Lou Brown, the consummate Short Man, had reminded agency Holmes & Lee of Toronto that, "It had goddamn well better work, or you're dead."[13]

Selecting Advertising Media

The major steps in media selection are (1) deciding on *reach, frequency,* and *impact*; (2) choosing among major *media types*; selecting specific *media vehicles*; and (3) deciding on *media timing*.

Deciding on Reach, Frequency, and Impact To select media, the advertiser must decide what reach and frequency are needed to achieve advertising objectives. *Reach* is a measure of the *percentage* of people in the target market who are exposed to the ad campaign over a given period of time. For example, the advertiser may try to reach 70 percent of the target market during the first three months of the campaign. *Frequency* is a measure of how many *times* the average person in the target market is exposed to the message. For example, the advertiser may want an average exposure frequency of three.

Ad agency Holmes & Lee took a stereotypical fashion standard and twisted it to develop arresting illustrations that made consumers laugh while looking at Short Man by Brown's in a fresh way.

The advertiser also must decide on the desired *media impact*—the *qualitative value* of a message exposure through a given medium. For example, for products that need to be demonstrated, messages on television may have more impact than messages on radio because television uses sight *and* sound. The same message in one magazine (say, *Maclean's*) may be more believable than in another (say, *The National Enquirer*). In general, the more reach, frequency, and impact the advertiser seeks, the higher the advertising budget will have to be.

Choosing among Major Media Types   The media planner must know the reach, frequency, and impact of each of the major media types. As summarized in Table 16.2, the major media types are newspapers, television, direct mail, radio, magazines, outdoor, and the Internet. Each medium has advantages and limitations.

Table 16.2   Profiles of Major Media Types

Medium	Advantages	Limitations
Newspapers	Flexibility; timeliness; good local market coverage; broad acceptability; high believability	Short life; poor reproduction quality; small pass-along audience
Television	Good mass-market coverage; low cost per exposure; combines sight, sound, and motion; appealing to the senses	High absolute costs; high clutter; fleeting exposure; less audience selectivity
Direct mail	High audience selectivity; flexibility; no ad competition within the same medium; allows personalization	Relatively high cost per exposure; "junk mail" image
Radio	Good local acceptance; high geographic and demographic selectivity; low cost	Audio only, fleeting exposure; low attention ("the half-heard" medium); fragmented audiences
Magazines	High geographic and demographic selectivity; credibility and prestige; high-quality reproduction; long life and good pass-along readership	Long ad purchase lead time; high cost; no guarantee of position
Outdoor	Flexibility; high repeat exposure; low cost; low message competition; good positional selectivity	Little audience selectivity; creative limitations
Internet	High selectivity; low cost; immediacy; interactive capabilities	Small, demographically skewed audience; relatively low impact; audience controls exposure

Media planners consider many factors when making their media choices. The *media habits of target consumers* affect media choice—advertisers look for media that reach target consumers effectively. So will the *nature of the product*—fashions are best advertised in colour magazines, and automobile performance is best demonstrated on television. Different *types of messages* may require different media. A message announcing a major sale tomorrow will require radio or newspapers; a message with a lot of technical data may require magazines, direct mailings, or an online ad and website. *Cost* is another major factor in media choice. Television is very expensive, whereas newspaper or radio advertising costs much less, but also reaches fewer consumers. The media planner considers both the total cost of using a medium and the cost per thousand exposures—the cost of reaching 1000 people using the medium.

Media impact and cost must be re-examined regularly. For a long time, television and magazines have dominated in the media mixes of national advertisers, with other media often neglected. Recently, however, as network television costs soar and audiences shrink, many advertisers are looking for new ways to reach consumers. The move toward micromarketing strategies, focused more narrowly on specific consumer groups, has also fuelled the search for new media to replace or supplement network television. As a result, advertisers are increasingly shifting larger portions of their budgets to media that cost less and target more effectively.

Three media benefiting greatly from the shift are outdoor advertising, cable television, and digital satellite television systems. Billboards have undergone a resurgence in recent years. Gone are the ugly eyesores of the past; in their place we now see cleverly designed, colourful attention grabbers. Outdoor advertising provides an excellent way to reach important local consumer segments at a fraction of the cost per exposure of other major media. Cable television and digital satellite systems are also booming. Such systems allow narrow programming formats such as all sports, all news, nutrition, arts, gardening, cooking, travel, history, and others that target select groups. Advertisers can take advantage of such "narrowcasting" to "rifle in" on special market segments rather than use the "shotgun" approach offered by network broadcasting.

Outdoor, cable, and satellite media seem to make good sense. But, increasingly, ads are popping up in far less likely places. In their efforts to find less costly and more highly targeted ways to reach consumers, advertisers have discovered a dazzling collection of "alternative media" (see Real Marketing 16.3).

Selecting Specific Media Vehicles   The media planner next chooses the best *media vehicles*—specific media within each general media type. For example, television vehicles include *This Hour Has 22 Minutes, ER, Venture, Friends,* and *Hockey Night in Canada.* Magazine vehicles include *Maclean's, Equinox,* and *Chatelaine.*

Media planners must also compute the cost per thousand persons reached by a vehicle. For example, if a full-page, four-colour advertisement in *Maclean's* costs $32 600 and *Maclean's* readership is 450 615 people, the cost of reaching each group of 1000 persons is about $60. The same advertisement in *Cottage Life* may cost only $8930 but reach only 71 321 persons—at a cost per thousand of about $125. The media planner would rank each magazine by cost per thousand and favour those magazines with the lower cost per thousand for reaching target consumers.

The media planner must consider the costs of producing ads for different media. Whereas newspaper ads can cost very little to produce, flashy television ads can cost millions. On average, U.S. advertisers pay US$332 000 to produce a single 30-second television commercial, though Nike paid a cool US$2 million to make a single ad called "The Wall."[14]

In selecting media vehicles, the media planner must balance media cost measures against several media impact factors. First, the planner must balance costs against the media vehicle's *audience quality.* For a baby lotion advertisement, for

REAL MARKETING

16.3 Advertisers Seek Alternative Media

*A*s consumers, we're used to ads on television, in magazines and newspapers, on the radio, and along the roadways. But these days, no matter where you go or what you do, you probably will run into some new form of advertising.

Tiny billboards attached to shopping carts, ads on shopping bags, and even advertising decals on supermarket floors urge you to buy Jell-O Pudding Pops or Pampers. Signs atop parking meters hawk everything from Jeeps to Minolta cameras to Recipe dog food. A city bus rolls by, fully wrapped for Trix cereal. You escape to the ballpark, only to find billboard-size video screens running Budweiser ads while a blimp with an electronic message board circles lazily overhead. How about a quiet trip in the country? Sorry—you find an enterprising farmer using his milk cows as four-legged billboards mounted with ads for Ben & Jerry's ice cream.

You pay to see a movie at your local theatre, only to learn that the movie is full of not-so-subtle promotional plugs for Pepsi, Domino's Pizza, MasterCard, Fritos, Mercedes, Ray-Ban sunglasses, Rockport shoes, or any of a dozen other products. You head home for a little TV to find your favourite sitcom full of "virtual placements" of Coca-Cola, Sony, or M&M/Mars products digitally inserted into the program.

At the local rail station, you can hop on a train pulled by a VIA locomotive painted with the KOOL-AID logo and smiling faces. Go to the airport, you're treated to the CNN Airport Network. Shortly after your plane lifts off the runway, you look out the window and spot a 500-foot-diameter crop circle carved into a farmer's field depicting Monster.com's mascot and corporate logo. As you wait to pick up your luggage, ads for Kenneth Cole baggage roll by on the luggage carousel conveyor belt.

These days, you're likely to find ads—well, anywhere. Boats cruise along public beaches flashing advertising messages for Sundown Sunscreen as sunbathers spread their towels over ads for Snapple pressed into the sand. Ad space is being sold on video

Marketers have discovered a dazzling array of "alternative media."

cases, parking-lot tickets, golf scorecards, delivery trucks, gas pumps, ATMs, and municipal garbage cans. Even church bulletins carry ads for Campbell's soup.

The following account takes a humorous look ahead at what might be in store for the future:

> Tomorrow your alarm clock will buzz at 6 a.m., as usual. Then the digital readout will morph into an ad for Burger King's breakfast special. Hungry for a Croissan'wich, you settle for a bagel that you plop into the toaster. The coils burn a Toastmaster brand onto the sides. Biting into your embossed bread, you pour a cup of coffee as the familiar green-and-white Starbucks logo forms on the side. Sipping the brew, you slide on your Nikes to go grab the newspaper. The pressure-sensitive shoes leave a temporary trail of swooshes behind them wherever you step. Walking outside, you pick up the *Globe* and gaze at your lawn, where the fertilizer you put down last month time-releases ads for Scotts Turf Builder, Toro lawn mowers, Weber grills....

Even some of the current alternative media seem a bit far-fetched, and they sometimes irritate consumers who resent it all as "ad nauseam." But for many marketers, these media can save money and provide a way to hit selected consumers where they live, shop, work, and play. For example, the average

person waits in line about 30 minutes a day. "We like to call it the captive pause [where consumers] really have nothing else to do but either look at the person in front of them or look at some engaging content as well as 15-second commercials," says an executive of an alternative-media firm,

Of course, this may leave you wondering if there are any commercial-free havens remaining for ad-weary consumers. Forget it! Even the back seat of taxis, public elevators, and stalls in public restrooms have been invaded by innovative marketers.

Sources: See Cara Beardi, "From Elevators to Gas Stations, Ads Multiplying," *Advertising Age,* November 13, 2000, pp. 40–42; Charles Pappas, "Ad Nauseam," *Advertising Age,* July 10, 2000, pp. 16–18; Beardi, "Airport Powerhouses Make Connection," *Advertising Age,* October 2, 2000, p. 8; Wayne Friedman, "Eagle-Eye Marketers Find Right Spot," *Advertising Age,* January 22, 2001, pp. S2–S3; Jean Halliday, "Mercedes Ties Car to 'Men in Black II,'" *Advertising Age,* May 27, 2002, p. 4; and Cara Griffin, "Rockport, Ray-Ban Back in Black," *Sporting Goods Business,* April 2002, p. 14; "Redrawing the TV map," *Marketing Magazine,* October 30, 1995, p. 13; Jim McElgunn, "Who's Watching What?" *Marketing Magazine,* May 29, 1995, pp. 14–15; Andrea Haman, "Boom Still on for Specialties," *Marketing Magazine,* October 30, 1995, pp. 30–31; Marina Strauss, "Is There No Hiding Place Left?" *Globe and Mail,* January 18, 1996, p. B12; and Trainscan: Canadian Railway News, June 2000, www.trainscan.com/news/scan/s0006/.

example, *New Mother* magazine would have a high-exposure value; *The Hockey News* would have a low-exposure value. Second, the planner must consider *audience attention*. Readers of *Flare*, for example, typically pay more attention to ads than do *The Economist* readers. Third, the planner must assess the vehicle's *editorial quality*—*Maclean's* and *Canadian Business* are more believable and prestigious than *The National Enquirer*.

Deciding on Media Timing   The advertiser also must decide how to schedule the advertising over the course of a year. Suppose sales of a product peak in December and drop in March. The firm can vary its advertising to follow the seasonal pattern, to oppose the seasonal pattern, or to be the same all year. Most firms do some seasonal advertising. Some do *only* seasonal advertising: For example, Hallmark advertises its greeting cards only before major holidays.

Finally, the advertiser must choose the pattern of the ads. *Continuity* means scheduling ads evenly within a given period. *Pulsing* means scheduling ads unevenly over a given time period. Thus, 52 ads could either be scheduled at one per week during the year or pulsed in several bursts. The idea is to advertise heavily for a short period to build awareness that carries over to the next advertising period. Those who favour pulsing feel that it can be used to achieve the same impact as a steady schedule, but at a much lower cost. However, some media planners believe that although pulsing achieves minimal awareness, it sacrifices depth of advertising communications.

Recent advances in technology have had a substantial impact on the media planning and buying functions. Today, for example, computer software applications called *media optimizers* allow media planners to evaluate many combinations of television programs and prices. Such software helps advertisers to make better decisions about which mix of networks, programs, and day parts will yield the highest reach per ad dollar.

Evaluating Advertising

The advertising program should regularly evaluate both the communication effects and the sales effects of advertising. Measuring the *communication effects* of an ad—*copy testing*—tells whether the ad is communicating well. Copy testing can be done before or after an ad is printed or broadcast. Before the ad is placed, the advertiser can show it to consumers, ask how they like it, and measure recall or attitude changes resulting from it. After the ad is run, the advertiser can measure how the ad affected consumer recall or product awareness, knowledge, and preference.

But what *sales* are caused by an ad that increases brand awareness by 20 percent and brand preference by 10 percent? The *sales effect* of advertising is harder to measure than the communication effect. Sales are affected by many factors besides advertising—such as product features, price, and availability.

One way to measure the sales effect of advertising is to compare past sales with past advertising expenditures. Another way is through experiments. For example, to test the effects of different advertising spending levels, Coca-Cola could vary the amount it spends on advertising in different market areas and measure the differences in the resulting sales levels. It could spend the normal amount in one market area, half the normal amount in another area, and twice the normal amount in a third area. If the three market areas are similar and all other marketing efforts in the area are the same, then differences in sales in the three cities could be related to advertising level. More complex experiments can include other variables, such as difference in the ads or media used.

Other Advertising Considerations

In developing advertising strategies and programs, the company must address two additional questions. First, how will it organize its advertising function—who will perform which advertising tasks? Second, how will it adapt its advertising strategies and programs to the complexities of international markets?

Organizing for Advertising   Different companies organize in different ways to handle advertising. In small companies, someone in the sales department may handle advertising. Large companies set up advertising departments whose job it is to set the advertising budget, work with the ad agency, and handle direct-mail advertising, dealer displays, and other advertising not done by the agency. Most large companies use outside advertising agencies because they offer several advantages.

Advertising agency
A marketing services firm that assists companies in planning, preparing, implementing, and evaluating all or portions of their advertising programs.

How does an **advertising agency** work? Advertising agencies were started in the 1800s by salespeople and brokers who worked for the media and received a commission for selling advertising space to companies. As time passed, the salespeople began to help customers prepare their ads. Eventually, they formed agencies and grew closer to the advertisers than to the media. Today's agencies employ specialists who often perform advertising tasks better than the company's own staff. Agencies also bring an outside perspective to solving the company's problems, along with a lot of experience from working with different clients and situations. Thus, today even companies with strong advertising departments use advertising agencies.

Marketing Magazine produces an annual report that ranks advertising agencies according to their revenues. For the most recent rankings, many U.S.-based agencies that have branch offices in Canada (MacLaren McCann Canada Inc., The Young & Rubicam Group of Companies, Leo Burnett, and BBDO) refused to provide financial data. Thus, the 2002 rankings leave out many large agencies. However, Cossette Communication Group, headquartered in Quebec City, remains the dominant player in the Canadian market. In 2002, the agency generated $140.4 million in revenue in Canada—a 9 percent increase over the previous year. Its international revenues were even more dramatic, topping $17.2 million, up significantly from the $3.6 million reported in 2001. Rounding out the top five are Toronto-based Maxxcom and Carlson Marketing Group Canada, Montreal's Marketel, and Toronto's Allard Johnson Communications.[15]

Having Canadian agencies with insight into our unique marketplaces is important. A recent survey revealed that 45 percent of English Canadians say they care a lot about whether the commercials they view on television are created in Canada. This percentage is even higher in Quebec, where 58 percent of the respondents stressed that they want commercials especially designed for them. Canadian viewers also believe that they can tell whether a commercial is Canadian made.[16]

Internationally, the stakes are even higher. The largest U.S. agency, McCann-Erickson Worldwide, has a worldwide annual gross income of nearly US$1.9 billion on billings (the dollar amount of advertising placed for clients) of almost US$18 billion. In recent years, many agencies have grown by gobbling up other agencies, thus creating huge agency holding companies. The largest of these agency "megagroups," WPP Group, includes several large advertising, public relations, and promotion agencies and has a combined worldwide gross income of US$8 billion on billings exceeding US$75 billion.[17]

Most large advertising agencies have the staff and resources to handle all phases of an advertising campaign for their clients, from creating a marketing plan to developing ad campaigns and preparing, placing, and evaluating ads. Agencies usually have four departments: *creative*, which develops and produces ads; *media*, which selects media and places ads; *research*, which studies audience characteristics and wants; and *business*, which handles the agency's business activities. Each account is supervised by an account executive, and people in each department are usually assigned to work on one or more accounts.

Ad agencies traditionally have been paid through commissions and fees. In the past, the agency typically received 15 percent of the media cost as a rebate. For example, suppose an agency bought $60 000 of magazine space for a client. The magazine would bill the advertising agency for $51 000 ($60 000 less 15 percent) by the magazine, and the agency would then bill the client for $60 000, keeping the $9000 commission. If the client purchased space directly from the magazine, it would have paid $60 000 because commissions are only paid to recognized advertising agencies.

However, both advertisers and agencies have become increasingly dissatisfied with the commission system. Larger advertisers complain that they pay more for the same services received by smaller ones simply because they place more advertising. Advertisers also believe that the commission system drives agencies away from low-cost media and short advertising campaigns. Another factor is vast changes in how ad agencies reach consumers, using methods that go way beyond network TV or magazine advertising.

"The commission formula tends to encourage costly media buys and has been criticized for overlooking important emerging mediums such as the Internet," says one advertising analyst. Therefore, she continues, "the 15 percent commission on media spending that...was once standard in the advertising business...is about as dead as the three-martini lunch." New agency payment methods include anything from fixed retainers or straight hourly fees for labour to incentives keyed to performance of the agencies' ad campaigns, or some combination of these.[18]

Another trend affects the advertising agency business: many agencies have sought growth by diversifying into related marketing services. These new diversified agencies offer a complete list of integrated marketing and promotion services under one roof, including advertising, sales promotion, marketing research, public relations, and direct and online marketing. Some have even added marketing consulting, television production, and sales training units in an effort to become full "marketing partners" to their clients.

However, agencies are finding that most advertisers don't want much more from them than traditional media advertising services plus direct marketing, sales promotion, and sometimes public relations. Thus, many agencies have recently limited their diversification efforts in order to focus more on traditional services. Some have even started their own "creative boutiques," smaller and more independent agencies that can develop creative campaigns for clients free of large-agency bureaucracy.

International Advertising Decisions

International advertisers face many complexities not encountered by domestic advertisers. The most basic issue concerns the degree to which global advertising should be adapted to the unique characteristics of various country markets. Some large advertisers have attempted to support their global brands with highly standardized worldwide advertising, with campaigns that work as well in Bangkok as they do in Burlington. For example, Jeep created a worldwide brand image of ruggedness and reliability. Coca-Cola's Sprite brand uses standardized appeals to target the world's youth. Gillette's ads for its Sensor Excel for Women are almost identical worldwide, with only minor adjustments to suit the local culture. Ericsson, the Swedish telecommunication giant, spent $130 million on a standardized global television campaign that featured Agent 007, James Bond, and the tag-line "make yourself heard."

DaimlerChrysler creates a worldwide brand image of ruggedness and reliability for its Jeep brand. Here, its Thai, German, and U.S. websites contain only minor adjustments in messages to suit local languages and cultures.

Standardization produces many benefits—lower advertising costs, greater global advertising coordination, and a more consistent worldwide image. But it also has drawbacks. Most importantly, it ignores the fact that country markets differ greatly in their cultures, demographics, and economic conditions. Therefore, most international advertisers "think globally but act locally." They develop global advertising *strategies* that make their worldwide advertising efforts more efficient and consistent. Then they adapt their advertising *programs* to make them more responsive to consumer needs and expectations within local markets. For example, Coca-Cola has a pool of commercials that can be used in or adapted to several international markets. Some can be used with only minor changes—such as language—in several different countries. Local and regional managers decide which commercials work best for which markets.

Global advertisers face some special problems. Advertising media costs and availability differ greatly between countries. Countries also differ in the extent to which they regulate advertising practices. Many countries have extensive systems of laws restricting how much a company can spend on advertising, the media used, the nature of advertising claims, and other aspects of the advertising program. Such restrictions often require advertisers to adapt their campaigns from country to country. Some examples:[19]

- Alcoholic products cannot be advertised or sold in Muslim countries.
- Tobacco products are subject to strict regulation in many countries—the United Kingdom, like Canada, bans all tobacco advertising, including sports sponsorships by tobacco companies.
- Regulations on advertising to children vary widely. In some countries (for example, the United States) there are no restrictions. In others (for example, Norway and Sweden) no TV ads may be directed at children under 12—and Sweden is lobbying to extend that ban to all European Union member countries. (Similarly, in Canada, Quebec forbids advertising aimed at children under 13.) To play it safe, McDonald's advertises itself as a family restaurant in countries with these restrictions.
- Comparative ads, while acceptable and even common in the U.S. and Canada, are less commonly used in the United Kingdom, unacceptable in Japan, and illegal in India and Brazil.
- China has restrictive censorship rules for TV and radio advertising. For example, the words *the best* are banned, as are ads that "violate social customs" or present women in "improper ways."
- Coca-Cola's Indian subsidiary was forced to end a promotion that offered prizes, such as a trip to Hollywood, because it violated India's established trade practices by encouraging customers to buy to "gamble."

Thus, although advertisers may develop global strategies to guide their overall advertising efforts, specific advertising programs are usually adapted to meet the requirements of local cultures, customs, media characteristics, and regulations.

Sales Promotion

Sales promotion
Short-term incentives to encourage purchase or sale of a product or service.

Advertising and personal selling often work closely with another promotion tool—sales promotion. **Sales promotion** consists of short-term incentives to encourage the purchase or sale of a product or service. Whereas advertising and personal selling offer reasons to buy a product or service, sales promotion offers reasons to buy *now*.

Examples of sales promotions are found everywhere. A free-standing insert in the Sunday newspaper contains a coupon offering 50 cents off President's Choice coffee. An email from CDNow offers $5.00 off your next CD purchase over $9.99. The end-of-the-aisle display in the local supermarket tempts impulse buyers with a wall of Coke cartons. An executive who buys a new Sony laptop computer gets a free carrying case. A family buys a new Taurus and receives a rebate cheque for $500. A hardware store chain receives a 10 percent discount on selected Black & Decker portable power tools if it agrees to advertise them in local newspapers. Sales promotion includes a variety of promotion tools designed to stimulate this earlier or stronger market response.

Rapid Growth of Sales Promotion

Sales promotion tools are used by most organizations, including manufacturers, distributors, retailers, trade associations, and non-profit institutions. They are targeted toward final buyers (*consumer promotions*), retailers and wholesalers (*trade promotions*), business customers (*business promotions*), and members of the sales force (*sales force promotions*). Today, in the average consumer packaged-goods company, sales promotion accounts for 74 percent of all marketing expenditures.[20]

Several factors have contributed to the rapid growth of sales promotion, particularly in consumer markets. Inside the company, product managers face greater pressures to increase their current sales, and promotion now is accepted more by top management as an effective sales tool. Externally, the company faces more competition, competing brands are less differentiated, competitors are using more promotions, and consumers have become more deal-oriented. Advertising efficiency has declined because of rising costs, media clutter, and legal restraints. Finally, consumers have become more deal oriented and retailers are demanding more deals from manufacturers.

The growing use of sales promotion has resulted in *promotion clutter,* similar to advertising clutter. Consumers are increasingly tuning out promotions, weakening their ability to trigger immediate purchase. Manufacturers are now searching for ways to rise above the clutter, such as offering larger coupon values or creating more dramatic point-of-purchase displays.

In developing a sales promotion program, a company must first set sales promotion objectives and then select the best tools for accomplishing these objectives.

Sales Promotion Objectives

Sales promotion objectives vary widely. Sellers may use *consumer promotions* to increase short-term sales or to help build long-term market share. Objectives for *trade promotions* include getting retailers to carry new items and more inventory, getting them to advertise the product and give it more shelf space, and getting them to buy ahead. For *sales force promotions,* objectives include getting more sales force support for current or new products or getting salespeople to sign up new accounts. Sales promotions are usually used together with advertising, personal selling, or other promotion mix tools. *Consumer promotions* must usually be advertised and can add excitement and pulling power to ads. Trade and sales force promotions support the firm's personal selling process.

In general, rather than creating only short-term sales volume or temporary brand switching, sales promotions should help to reinforce the product's position and build long-term customer relationships. Increasingly, marketers are avoiding "quick fix," price-only promotions in favour of promotions designed to build brand equity. This is what Kraft Canada has done with its website, its permission-based email newsletter, and its *What's Cooking* magazine. Included in newspapers as a free-standing insert, the magazine contains letters from consumers, cooking tips, information on maintaining a healthy diet, recipes using Kraft products, and Kraft's toll-free number, which consumers can call to get more "food made simple" ideas. Consumers look forward to receiving the magazine, and many keep it and refer to it for years to come. In such a way, marketers avoid "quick-fix," price-only promotions in favour of promotions designed to build brand equity.

Even price promotions can be designed to help build customer relationships. Examples include all of the "frequency marketing programs" and clubs that have mushroomed in recent years. For example, American Express's Custom Extras program automatically awards customers deals and discounts based on frequency of purchases at participating retailers. Norwegian Cruise Lines sponsors a loyalty program called Latitudes, a co-branding effort with Visa. Latitudes members receive exclusive deals and promotions, and up to $200 on-board credit, the services of a special person assigned to answer their questions at sea, savings on future sailings, invitations to an exclusive captain's reception, and escorted tours of the ship's bridge and galley, and *Latitudes* magazine, which contains special articles on NCL's fleet and ports. If properly designed, every sales promotion tool has the potential to build consumer relationships.

The "loyalty marketing programs" that have mushroomed in recent years are other examples of sales promotions used to solidify relationships with customers. Air Miles is one of the best known programs, but many others flourish. Shopper's Drug Market offers the Optimum card, Zellers offers its own points, and Indigo has an iREWARDS program for book and music lovers.

Major Sales Promotion Tools

Many tools are available to accomplish sales promotion objectives. Descriptions of the main consumer, trade, and business promotion tools follow.

Consumer Promotion Tools

The main *consumer promotion tools* are samples, coupons, cash refunds, price packs, premiums, advertising specialties, patronage rewards, point-of-purchase displays and demonstrations, and contests, sweepstakes, and games.

Customer relationship-building promotions: "Frequent marketing programs" and clubs have mushroomed in recent years. Lladro's Collectors Society members receive a subscription to *Expressions* magazine, a bisque plaque, free enrolment in the Lladro Museum of New York, and other relationship-building benefits.

Sample

Offer to consumers of a trial amount of a product.

Samples are offers of a trial amount of a product. Sampling is the most effective—but most expensive—way to introduce a new product. About 84 percent of consumer packaged-goods marketers use sampling as a part of their promotion strategy. For example, to launch Vanilla Coke, Coca-Cola distributed more than 1.3 million samples of the beverage. But the soft drink marketer didn't just hand out the samples. Instead, Coke staffers stopped targeted teen consumers at hangouts like malls, skate parks, concerts, and fairs, then delivered live commercials with messages like "Satisfy your curiosity, try a free Vanilla Coke." Says the president of Coca-Cola's promotion agency, "We wanted to get Vanilla Coke's target audience with a memorable live experience for the brand."[21]

Some samples are free; for others, the company charges a small amount to offset its cost. The sample might be delivered door-to-door, sent by mail, handed out in a store, attached to another product, or featured in an ad. Sometimes, samples are combined into sample packs, which can then be used to promote other products and services. Procter & Gamble has even distributed samples via the Internet:[22]

> When Procter & Gamble decided to relaunch Pert Plus shampoo, it extended its $26 million ad campaign by constructing a new website (www.pertplus.com). P&G had three objectives for the website: to create awareness for reformulated Pert Plus, get consumers to try the product, and gather data about Web users. The site's first page invited visitors to place their heads against the computer screen in a mock attempt to measure the cleanliness of their hair. After "tabulating the results," the site told visitors that they "need immediate help." The solution: "How about a free sample of new Pert Plus?" Visitors obtained the sample by filling out a short demographic form. The site offered other interesting features as well. For example, clicking "get a friend in a lather" produced a template that let a visitor send an email to a friend with an invitation to visit the site and receive a free sample.
>
> How did the sampling promotion work out? Even P&G was shocked by the turnout. Within just two months of launching the site, 170 000 people visited and 83 000 requested samples. More surprising, given that the site was only 10 pages deep, the average person visited the site 1.9 times and spent a total of 7.5 minutes on each visit.

Sampling has grown rapidly in Canada. Recent research has shown that when given a choice between a free sample and a coupon, 92 percent of consumers prefer a sample. New parents, giddy with the excitement of a new baby, soak up marketing material like sponges and are prime targets for sampling campaigns. At Starcom Worldwide in Toronto, whose clients include baby-food manufacturer H.J. Heinz Canada, VP media director Mariam Hoosen announces, "New moms are always looking for information, so sampling and direct mail are ideal ways of reaching them." Expectant mothers who sign up for baby clubs such as Mead Johnson's Baby Steps (through subscription forms available in pregnancy magazines and online) can expect to receive free samples of formula through the mail, together with information about baby nutrition. Sampling is also key for Gerber, whose products include bottles, pacifiers, and cups.[23]

Coupon

A certificate that gives buyers a saving when they purchase a specified product.

Coupons are certificates that give buyers a saving when they purchase specified products. They can stimulate sales of a mature brand or promote early trial of a new brand. A 2003 survey found that Canadians love coupons—65 percent of key grocery shoppers have used at least one coupon in the past four weeks. While coupon usage is high in all regions of the country, it is particularly popular in Quebec, where shoppers are 65 percent more likely to have used coupons within the past week than shoppers in Ontario and the West. New immigrants also quickly become accustomed to using coupons, which are rarely used outside North America and Europe. This willingness presents marketers with a great opportunity to establish brand preferences among the growing segment of new Canadians.[24]

Cash refund offer (rebate)
Offer to refund part of the purchase price of a product to consumers who send a "proof of purchase" to the manufacturer.

Price pack (cents-off deal)
Reduced price marked by the producer directly on the label or package.

Premium
Goods offered either free or at low cost as an incentive to buy a product.

Cash refund offers, or **rebates,** are like coupons except that the price reduction occurs after the purchase rather than at the retail outlet. The consumer sends a "proof of purchase" to the manufacturer, who then refunds part of the purchase price by mail. For example, Toro ran a clever pre-season promotion on some of its snowblower models, offering a rebate if the snowfall in the buyer's market area turned out to be below average. Competitors were not able to match this offer on such short notice, and the promotion was very successful.

Price packs (also called **cents-off deals**) offer consumers savings off the regular price of a product. The reduced prices are marked by the producer directly on the label or package. Price packs can be single packages sold at a reduced price (such as two for the price of one), or two related products banded together (such as a toothbrush and toothpaste). Price packs are very effective—even more so than coupons—in stimulating short-term sales.

Premiums are goods offered either free or at low cost as an incentive to buy a product, ranging from toys included with kids' products to phone cards and CDs. A premium may come inside the package (in-pack), outside the package (on-pack), or through the mail.

"Drink it. Get it" was the slogan for the Pepsi Stuff premium offer that one industry analyst called the "most successful promotion run in Canada in the last 40 years." Pepsi added value to a purchase of their product in a highly "youth-relevant" way by letting people redeem points of specially marked packages for "must-be-seen" merchandise from the Pepsi stuff catalogue. Eighty-one percent of soft-drink users were aware of the offer. The promotion increased Pepsi's market share by 7 percent. While 53 percent of the gain came from people switching brands, the remainder came because heavy Pepsi drinkers consumed more product. Although the share gains are impressive, the program also improved consumer attitude and imagery measures of Pepsi.[25]

Advertising specialty
Useful article imprinted with an advertiser's name, given as a gift to consumers.

Advertising specialties are useful articles imprinted with an advertiser's name given as gifts to consumers. Typical items are baseball caps, pens, calendars, key rings, matches, shopping bags, T-shirts, caps, nail files, coffee mugs, and mouse pads. Such items can be very effective. In a recent study, 63 percent of all consumers surveyed were either carrying or wearing an ad specialty item. More than three-quarters of those who had an item could recall the advertiser's name or message before showing the item to the interviewer.[26]

Patronage reward
Cash or other award for the regular use of a certain company's products or services.

Patronage rewards are cash or other awards offered for the regular use of a certain company's products or services. For example, hotels like the Canadian-owned Fairmont chain (operators of the Royal York in Toronto and the Banff Springs Hotel) use their Presidents' Club to reward frequent travellers with free services such as access to in-room high-speed Internet services.

Point-of-purchase (POP) promotion
Displays and demonstrations at the point of purchase or sale.

Point-of-purchase (POP) promotions include displays and demonstrations at the point of purchase or sale. An example is the five-foot-high cardboard display of Cap'n Crunch next to Cap'n Crunch cereal boxes. Unfortunately, many retailers do not like to handle the hundreds of displays, signs, and posters they receive from manufacturers each year. Manufacturers have responded by offering better POP materials, tying them in with television or print messages, and offering to set them up.

Contests, sweepstakes, games
Promotional events that give consumers the chance to win something—such as cash, trips, or goods—by luck or through extra effort.

Contests, sweepstakes, and games give consumers the chance to win something, such as cash, trips, or goods, by luck or through extra effort. A *contest* calls for consumers to submit an entry—a jingle, guess, suggestion—to be judged by a panel that will select the best entries. A *sweepstakes* calls for consumers to submit their names for a drawing. A *game* presents consumers with something—a chance to win a car or free coffee—every time they buy. Tim Hortons' celebrated "Roll up the rim to win" is Canada's most famous promotional game. A *sales contest* urges dealers or the sales force to increase their efforts, with prizes going to the top performers.

Point-of-sale couponing: Using Checkout Direct technology, marketers can dispense personalized coupons to carefully targeted buyers at the checkout counter. This avoids the waste of poorly targeted coupons delivered through FSIs (coupon pages inserted into newspapers).

Trade Promotion Tools

More sales promotion dollars are directed to retailers and wholesalers (78 percent) than to consumers. Trade promotion can persuade retailers or wholesalers to carry a brand, give it shelf space, promote it in advertising, and push it to consumers.

The Pepsi Stuff program was heralded as the most successful promotional campaign to run in Canada in 40 years.

Shelf space is so scarce these days that manufacturers often have to offer price-offs, allowances, buy-back guarantees, or free goods to retailers and wholesalers to get on the shelf and, once there, to stay on it.

Manufacturers use several trade promotion tools. Many of the tools used for consumer promotions—contests, premiums, displays—can also be used as trade promotions. Or the manufacturer may offer a straight **discount** off the list price on each case purchased during a stated period of time (also called a *price-off, off-invoice,* or *off-list*). Manufacturers also may offer an **allowance** (usually so much off per case) in return for the retailer's agreement to feature the manufacturer's products in some way. An *advertising allowance* compensates retailers for advertising the product. A *display allowance* compensates them for using special displays.

Manufacturers may offer *free goods*—extra cases of merchandise—to resellers who buy a certain quantity or who feature a certain flavour or size. They may offer *push money*—cash or gifts—to dealers or their sales force to "push" the manufacturer's goods. Manufacturers may give retailers free *specialty advertising items* that carry the company's name, such as pens, pencils, calendars, paperweights, matchbooks, and memo pads.

Business Promotion Tools

Companies spend billions of dollars each year on promotion to industrial customers. These *business promotion tools* are used to generate business leads, stimulate purchases, reward customers, and motivate salespeople. Business promotion includes many of the same tools used for consumer or trade promotions. Here, we focus on two major business promotion tools—conventions and trade shows, and sales contests.

Many companies and trade associations organize *conventions and trade shows* to promote their products. Firms selling to the industry show their products at the trade show. Worldwide, more than 4300 trade shows take place every year, drawing as many as 85 million people. The success of trade shows is revealed in the bottom lines of many Canadian companies. Recently, the 400 Canadian firms that displayed their wares at the 40 largest German trade fairs rang up more than $250 million in sales.

Vendors receive many benefits from trade shows, such as opportunities to find new sales leads, contact customers, introduce new products, meet new customers, sell more to present customers, and educate customers with publications and audio-

Discount
A straight reduction in price on purchases during a stated period of time.

Allowance
Promotional money paid by manufacturers to retailers in return for an agreement to feature the manufacturer's products in some way.

More than 4300 trade shows take place every year, drawing as many as 85 million people, giving sellers chances to introduce new products and meet new customers. At this consumer electronics trade show, 2000 exhibitors attracted more than 91 000 professional visitors.

visual materials. Trade shows also help companies reach many prospects not reached through their sales forces. About 90 percent of a trade show's visitors see a company's salespeople for the first time at the show. Business marketers may spend as much as 35 percent of their annual promotion budgets on trade shows.[27]

A *sales contest* is a contest for salespeople or dealers to motivate them to increase their sales performance over a given period. Sales contests motivate and recognize good company performers, who may receive trips, cash prizes, or other gifts. Some companies award points for performance, which the receiver can turn in for any of a variety of prizes. Sales contests work best when they are tied to measurable and achievable sales objectives, such as finding new accounts, reviving old accounts, or increasing account profitability.

Developing the Sales Promotion Program

The marketer must make several decisions to define the full sales promotion program. First the marketer must decide the *size of the incentive*. A certain minimum incentive is necessary if the promotion is to succeed; a larger incentive will produce more sales response. The marketer also must set *conditions for participation*. Incentives may be offered to everyone or only to select groups.

The marketer must decide how to *promote and distribute the promotion* program itself. A 50-cents-off coupon could be given out in a package, at the store, by mail, or in an advertisement. Each distribution method involves a different level of reach and cost. Increasingly, marketers are blending several media into a total campaign concept. The *length of the promotion* is also important. If the sales promotion period is too short, many prospects (who may not be buying during that time) will miss it. If the promotion runs too long, the deal will lose some of its "act now" force.

Evaluation is also very important, yet many companies fail to evaluate their sales promotion programs, and others evaluate them only superficially. The most common evaluation method is to compare sales before, during, and after a promotion. Suppose a company has a 6 percent market share before the promotion, which jumps to 10 percent during the promotion, falls to 5 percent right after, and rises to 7 percent later on. The promotion seems to have attracted new "triers" and stimulated more buying from current customers. After the promotion, sales fell as consumers used up their inventories. The long-run rise to 7 percent means that the company gained some new users. If the brand's share had returned to the old level, then the promotion would have changed only the *timing* of demand rather than the *total* demand.

Consumer research also would show the kinds of people who responded to the promotion and what they did after it ended. *Surveys* can provide information on how many consumers recall the promotion, what they thought of it, how many took advantage of it, and how it affected their buying. Sales promotions also can be evaluated through *experiments* that vary such factors as incentive value, length, and distribution method.

Clearly, sales promotion plays an important role in the total promotion mix. To use it well, the marketer must define the sales promotion objectives, select the best tools, design the sales promotion program, pre-test and implement the program, and evaluate the results. Moreover, sales promotion must be coordinated carefully with other promotion mix elements within the integrated marketing communications program.

Public relations
Building good relations with the company's various publics by obtaining favourable publicity, building up a good corporate image, and handling or heading off unfavourable rumours, stories, and events.

Public Relations

Another major mass promotion tool is **public relations**—building good relations with the company's various publics by obtaining favourable publicity, building up a good corporate image, and handling or heading off unfavourable rumours, stories, and events. Public relations (PR) departments may perform any or all of the following functions:[28]

- *Press relations or press agentry:* Creating and placing newsworthy information in the media to attract attention to a person, product, or service. The Canada NewsWire website (www.newswire.ca) has many examples of different firms' press releases.
- *Product publicity:* Publicizing specific products.
- *Public affairs:* Building and maintaining national or local community relations.
- *Lobbying:* Building and maintaining relations with legislators and government officials to influence legislation and regulation.
- *Investor relations:* Maintaining relationships with shareholders and others in the financial community.
- *Development:* Public relations with donors or members of non-profit organizations to gain financial or volunteer support.

Public relations is used to promote products, people, places, ideas, activities, organizations, and even nations. Marketing boards have used public relations to rebuild interest in declining commodities such as eggs, apples, milk, and potatoes. In the aftermath of the 2003 SARS crisis, the City of Toronto undertook a huge public relations and sales promotion effort to lure consumers back to the city using newspaper ads that featured offers of reduced hotel rates as well as discount prices for theatres and sporting events. Hong Kong, the epicentre of the outbreak, also faced similar devastating losses to its tourism business. It too used a public relations campaign aimed at the estimated 300 000 Chinese Canadians who visit Hong Kong every year.[29]

The City of Hong Kong used print advertising and a contest to coax Chinese Canadians back to the city after the SARS crisis.

The Role and Impact of Public Relations

Public relations can have a strong impact on public awareness at a much lower cost than advertising. The company does not pay for the space or time in the media. Rather, it pays for a staff to develop and circulate information and to manage events. If the company develops an interesting story, it may be picked up by several media, having the same effect as advertising that would cost millions of dollars. And it would have more credibility than advertising.

Public relations results can sometimes be spectacular, as the opening case describing the Canadian launch of the newest Harry Potter adventure suggests. But despite its potential strengths, public relations is often described as a marketing stepchild because of its limited and scattered use. The public relations department is usually located at corporate headquarters. Its staff is so busy dealing with various publics—shareholders, employees, legislators, city officials—that public relations programs to support product marketing objectives may be ignored. Marketing managers and public relations practitioners do not always talk the same language. Many public relations practitioners view their job as simply communicating. In contrast, marketing managers tend to be much more interested in how advertising and public relations affect sales and profits.

This situation is changing, however. Although public relations still captures only a small portion of the overall marketing budgets of most firms, PR is playing an increasingly important brand-building role. For example, when Heinz launched EZ Squirt ketchup, the value of the free media space it received based on the product's unique green colour amounted to more than three times what the company spent on traditional advertising. And when Procter & Gamble launched its highly successful Crest Whitestrips, prelaunch efforts generated $30 million in sales prior to retail availability. Of those sales, one-third were directly linked to public relations.

Good public relations can be a powerful brand-building tool. In fact, two well-known marketing consultants, Al Ries and Laura Ries, provide the following advice, which points to the potential power of public relations as a first step in building brands:[30]

Public relations involves many functions beyond product publicity, including public affairs, lobbying, and investor relations. For example, most company websites feature special sections for current and potential investors—like this one for Nike.

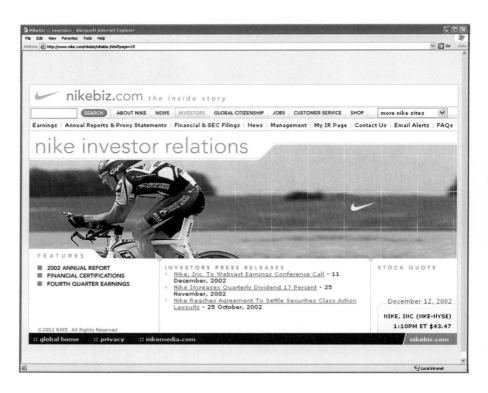

Just because a heavy dose of advertising is associated with most major brands doesn't necessarily mean that advertising built the brands in the first place. The birth of a brand is usually accomplished with [public relations], not advertising. Our general rule is [PR] first, advertising second. [Public relations] is the nail, advertising the hammer. [PR] creates the credentials that provide the credibility for advertising.... Anita Roddick built The Body Shop into a major brand with no advertising at all. Instead, she travelled the world on a relentless quest for publicity.... Until recently Starbucks Coffee Co. didn't spend a hill of beans on advertising, either. In ten years, the company spent less than $10 million on advertising, a trivial amount for a brand that delivers annual sales of $1.3 billion. Wal-Mart Stores became the world's largest retailer...with very little advertising...In the toy field, Furby, Beanie Babies, and Tickle Me Elmo became highly successful...and on the Internet, Yahoo!, Amazon.com, and Excite became powerhouse brands, [all] with virtually no advertising.

In their book *The Fall of Advertising and the Rise of PR*, Ries and Ries assert that the era of advertising is over, and that public relations is quietly becoming the most powerful marketing communications tools. Although most marketers don't go this far, the point is a good one. Advertising and public relations should work hand in hand to build and maintain brands.

Major Public Relations Tools

Public relations professionals use several tools. *News* is one of the major tools. PR professionals find or create favourable news about the company and its products or people. Sometimes news stories occur naturally, and sometimes the PR person can suggest events or activities that would create news. *Speeches* can also create product and company publicity. Increasingly, company executives must field questions from the media or give talks at trade associations or sales meetings, and these events can either build or hurt the company's image. Another common PR tool is *special events*, ranging from news conferences, press tours, grand openings, and fireworks displays to laser shows, hot-air balloon releases, multimedia presentations, star-studded spectaculars, and educational programs designed to reach and interest target publics. And recently, *mobile marketing*—travelling promotional tours that bring the brand to consumers—has emerged as an effective way to build one-to-one relationships with targeted consumers:

> These days, it seems that almost every company is putting its show on the road, with a record number of marketers launching nationwide tours. Not only are such tours relatively cheap, they offer an irresistible opportunity to build brands while attracting additional sponsorship dollars and promotional relationships with retailers and trade marketing partners. Home Depot recently brought do-it-yourself home project workshops and demonstrations to 26 NASCAR race-tracks. Court TV launched a tour that visited malls in 20 cities, challenging consumers to solve a crime by visiting six "forensic labs" and interviewing a computerized virtual witness. Mattel's Matchbox Toys launched its first-ever tour in 2002, hitting store parking lots in 25 cities over six months to celebrate Matchbox's 50th anniversary. Events included interactive games, historic displays, free gifts, and an obstacle course for kids riding battery-powered vehicles. And Krispy Kreme recently unveiled a 16-metre-long, fully functioning store on wheels at an event in Winston-Salem, North Carolina, the chain's headquarters. It takes a day to set up the shop—which sells doughnuts, coffee, and logoed merchandise—so the company is targeting planned festivals, fairs, and events. The mobile unit was scheduled to be on the road approximately 250 days during 2003, visiting cities new to the company along with more established markets.[31]

A company's website can be a good public relations tool: Butterball's site, which features turkey cooking and carving tips, received over 500 000 visits in one day during U.S. Thanksgiving week.

Public relations people also prepare *written materials* to reach and influence their target markets. These materials include annual reports, brochures, articles, and company newsletters and magazines. *Audiovisual materials,* such as films, slide-and-sound programs, and video- and audiocassettes, are being used increasingly as communication tools. *Corporate identity materials* can also help create a corporate identity that the public immediately recognizes. Logos, stationery, brochures, signs, business forms, business cards, buildings, uniforms, and company cars and trucks—all become marketing tools when they are attractive, distinctive, and memorable. Finally, companies can improve public goodwill by contributing money and time to *public service activities.*

A company's website can also be a good PR vehicle. Consumers and members of other publics can visit the site for information and entertainment. Such sites can be very popular. For example, Butterball's site, which features cooking and carving tips, received 550 000 visitors on one day during U.S. Thanksgiving week in 2002. Websites can also be ideal for handling crisis situations. For example, American Home Products quickly set up a website to distribute accurate information and advice after a model died reportedly after inhaling its Primatene Mist. The Primatene site, up less than 12 hours after the crisis broke, remains in place today (www.primatene.com). In all, notes one analyst, "Today, public relations is reshaping the Internet, and the Internet, in turn, is redefining the practice of public relations." Says another, "People look to the Net for information, not salesmanship, and that's the real opportunity for public relations."[32]

As with the other promotion tools, in considering when and how to use product public relations, management should set PR objectives, choose the PR messages and vehicles, implement the PR plan, and evaluate the results. The firm's public relations should be blended smoothly with other promotion activities within the company's overall integrated marketing communications effort.

Looking Back: Reviewing the Concepts

Companies must do more than make good products—they have to inform consumers about product benefits and carefully position products in consumers' minds. To do this, they must skilfully employ three mass-promotion tools in addition to personal selling, which targets specific buyers. These tools are *advertising, sales promotion*, and *public relations*.

1. Define the roles of advertising, sales promotion, and public relations in the promotion mix.

Advertising—the use of paid media by a seller to inform, persuade, and remind about its products or organization—is a strong promotion tool. Canadian marketers spend more than $10 billion each year on advertising, which takes many forms and has many uses. *Sales promotion* covers a variety of short-term incentive tools—coupons, premiums, contests, buying allowances—designed to stimulate final and business consumers, the trade, and the company's own sales force. In recent years, sales promotion spending has been growing faster than advertising spending. *Public relations*—gaining favourable publicity and creating a favourable company image—is the least used of the major promotion tools, although it has great potential for building consumer awareness and preference.

2. Describe the major decisions involved in developing an advertising program.

Advertising decision making involves decisions about the objectives, the budget, the message, the media, and, finally, the evaluation of results. Advertisers should set clear *objectives* as to whether the advertising is intended to inform, persuade, or remind buyers. The advertising *budget* can be based on sales, competitors' spending, or the objectives and tasks. The *message decision* calls for planning a message strategy and executing it effectively. The *media decision* involves defining reach, frequency, and impact goals; choosing major media types; selecting media vehicles; and decid-

ing on media timing. Message and media decisions must be closely coordinated for maximum campaign effectiveness. Finally, *evaluation* calls for evaluating the communication and sales effects of advertising before, during, and after the advertising is placed.

3. Explain how sales promotion campaigns are developed and implemented.

Sales promotion campaigns call for setting sales promotion objectives (in general, sales promotions should be *consumer relationship building*); selecting tools; developing and implementing the sales promotion program by using trade promotion tools (*discounts, allowances, free goods, push money*) and business promotion tools (*conventions, trade shows, sales contests*) as well as deciding on such elements as the size of the incentive, the conditions for participation, how to promote and distribute the promotion package, and the length of the promotion. After this process is completed, the company evaluates the results.

4. Explain how companies use public relations to communicate with their publics.

Companies use public relations to communicate with their publics by setting public relations objectives, choosing public relations messages and vehicles, implementing the plan, and evaluating results. To accomplish these goals, public relations professionals use several tools, including *news, speeches,* and *special events*. They also prepare *written, audiovisual,* and *corporate identity* materials and contribute money and time to *public service* activities.

Reviewing the Key Terms

Advertising   624
Advertising agency   642
Advertising objective   627
Advertising specialty   649
Allowance   651
Cash refund offer (rebate)   649

Contests, sweepstakes, games   649
Coupon   648
Discount   651
Patronage reward   649
Point-of-purchase (POP)
   promotion   649

Premium   649
Price pack (cents-off deal)   649
Public relations   652
Sales promotion   645
Sample   648

Discussing the Concepts

1. Marketing managers make four important decisions when developing an advertising program. List and briefly describe these decisions.

2. Advertising objectives can be classified by primary purpose: to inform, to persuade, or to remind. In your local newspaper, find examples of ads pursuing each of these objectives. Using Table 16.1 (page 628), discuss why your examples fit the chosen objectives.

3. Until recently, television viewers were considered a captive audience for advertisers. How has this changed? How do you think the changes in consumer television viewing habits will impact advertising? What actions should advertisers consider to regain the consumer audience?

4. Surveys show that many Canadians are skeptical of advertising claims. (a) Do you trust advertising? Explain. (b) What types of advertising do you trust the most? The least? (c) Suggest how the advertising industry could increase advertising credibility.

5. Advertisers must develop compelling creative concepts, or "big ideas," that will bring their message strategies to life in a distinctive way. The creative concept, then, will guide the choice of specific appeals to be used in an advertising campaign. Find what you perceive to be a compelling creative concept in a magazine advertisement. Identify the specific appeals being used, and comment on what you think the advertiser is trying to accomplish with the ad.

6. The chapter lists nine different execution styles that advertisers often use to meet advertising objectives. Which of these styles do you think is most commonly used? Select three styles and find an example of each. Critique each example on its content, effectiveness, and match to the selected target market.

7. A bicycle shop owner in a university town wants to target both serious cyclists and university students. Her limited annual advertising budget totals $8000. She has already constructed a website, which includes pictures of products found in the store. Review Table 16.2 (page 638) and build a media mix to help the owner target the intended audience on her limited budget.

8. Which of the sales promotion tools described in the chapter would be best for stimulating sales of the following products and services? (a) A dry cleaner that wishes to emphasize low prices on washed and pressed dress shirts; (b) Gummi Bears' new Sun Burst Orange flavour; (c) Procter & Gamble's efforts to bundle laundry detergents and fabric softeners together in a combined marketing effort, (d) an online merchant trying to engage customers in the development of a new advertising jingle, and (e) Outpost.com's effort to increase name recognition and traffic at its website.

9. The Internet is the latest public relations frontier. Web users now routinely share their experiences and problems with a company's products, service, prices, and warranties on electronic bulletin boards and chat rooms and at various websites. What kinds of special PR problems and opportunities does the Internet present to marketers? How can companies use their own websites to deal with these problems and opportunities? Find a good example of a company that uses its website as a PR tool.

Applying the Concepts

1. Beginning with a thrilling chase scene in the 1996 hit movie *The Rock,* GM's Hummer all-terrain vehicles have been all the rage among "Xtreme" drivers. The Hummer comes in two basic versions—the H1 and the H2. Both vehicles can scale a 50-centimetre vertical wall, ford 50 centimetres of water, climb a 60 percent incline, and traverse a 40 percent side slope. Despite these amazing characteristics, Hummer has a problem—it has sold itself to the "Xtreme" crowd too well. As a result, the car is no longer seen as a practical choice for the average driver. In an attempt to reposition the vehicle, Hummer is shifting the emphasis of its advertising to promote the vehicle's safety features and luxury interiors. Will the company succeed in its attempt at an image makeover?

a. Visit www.hummer.com for more information on the Hummer. Does either the H1 or the H2 appeal to you? Would either appeal to your parents?

b. Based on your visit to the company's website, how is Hummer trying to position its brand? Does the information presented on the website effectively reinforce the repositioning of the brand?

c. The environmental group the Sierra Club recently unveiled its www.hummerdinger.com website, a satirical broadside against the Hummer brand. Daniel Becker, director of the Sierra Club's global warming and energy program, damns the vehicle and its marketing, saying, "The Hummer's tagline is 'Like Nothing Else.' But it should be 'Pollutes Like

Nothing Else.'" Using popular deadpan humour to make its point, the site presents headlines like, "GM celebrates Hummer's state-of-the-art 1950s engine technology with some of today's hottest stars," adding that over-the-hill Fifties stars Fabian, Pat Boone, and Frankie Avalon have been lined up as pitchmen.

Design a magazine advertisement or materials that could be used in a public relations campaign for (i) the Sierra Club or (ii) the Hummer to appear in *Maclean's, Sports Illustrated, Canadian Business,* and *TV Guide* magazines. Construct a "rough" of an ad. Be sure to add a headline or theme line that indicates the new direction Hummer is pursuing.

2. Philip Morris the world's largest tobacco company. It's also one of the most controversial. Philip Morris is full of apparent contradictions. For example, it recently spent $130.3 million to persuade children not to smoke; it contributes $78.2 million in cash and $58.6 million in food each year to fight hunger, combat domestic violence, and support the arts. And it has paid billions of dollars to reimburse U.S. states for the costs of treating smoking-related illnesses. Even its employees have given more than $6.5 million to charities. Such numbers are impressive by any standard. So why is Philip Morris on every social crusader's hit list? The answer: the tobacco culture that engulfs the organization. For years Philip Morris operated under a siege mentality, closing itself off from the questions and criticism coming from the outside world. Recently this culture has slowly begun to change. The company is now renewing its efforts to change its image—in fact, in 2001 it announced it was changing its name to Altria Group Inc. The company's critics charge that the name change (under which Kraft Foods and other food divisions are part of Altria, while the cigarette-producing divisions do business as Philip Morris International and Philip Morris USA) is "a cynical attempt to distance itself from its tobacco roots without changing its product lines."[33] Clearly, being a responsible corporate citizen and changing the company's culture, products, and image will not be easy.

a. What public relations issues does Philip Morris/Altria Group face?

b. The Philip Morris USA and Philip Morris International websites admit that "cigarette smoking is addictive" (www.pmusa.com/health_issues/addiction.asp and www.philipmorrisinternational.com/pages/eng/smoking/fda.asp). What kind of public relations advantages does this admission create? What problems?

c. Visit the websites of companies owned by Altria (for example, Kraft Canada at www.kraftcanada.com; see www.altria.com for more). What public relations synergies do you see? What problems might these synergies create?

d. Outline a public relations program for gaining public trust and shareholder interest.

e. The use of tobacco products has been under attack in North America for many years. However, this adversarial environment does not exist in all markets. In Europe, Africa, and Asia (especially China and Japan), smoking is a popular and growing habit. Considering the social and public relations approach Philip Morris is using in the United States, outline a global public relations strategy for the company. What role do advertising, sales promotion, and the company's website play in your strategy?

Video Short

View the video short for this chapter at **www.pearsoned.ca/kotler** and then answer the questions provided in the case description.

Company Case

Pepsi: Promoting Nothing

Water Wars

Everyone's familiar with the cola wars—the epic battles between Pepsi Cola and Coca-Cola in the soft drink market. The war has featured numerous taste tests and mostly friendly, but sometimes not-so-friendly, television ads featuring Pepsi and Coke delivery-truck drivers, each trying to outdo the other.

The major problem that Pepsi and Coke face is that the cola market is mature and not growing very rapidly. Thus, to generate new sales and new customers, the companies have to look for new fronts.

In the early 1990s, the bottled-water market was just a drop in the huge North American beverage market bucket. The Evian and Perrier brands dominated the tiny niche and helped establish bottled spring water's clean, healthy image. Pepsi took an early interest in the water market. It tried several different ways to attack this market, with both spring water and sparkling water, but each failed. Then it hit on the idea of taking advantage of a built-in resource—its existing bottlers.

Pepsi's bottlers already had their own water treatment facilities to further purify the municipal tap water used in making soft drinks. All municipal tap water must be pure enough to pass constant monitoring and rigorous quarterly EPA prescribed tests. Still, cola bottlers filtered it again before using it in the production process.

Pepsi decided that it would *really* filter the tap water. It experimented with a reverse osmosis process, pushing already-filtered tap water at high pressure through fibreglass membranes to remove even the tiniest particles. Then, carbon filters removed chlorine and any other particles that might give the water any taste or smell. All this filtering removed even good particles that killed bacteria, so Pepsi had to add ozone to the water to keep bacteria from growing. The result? Aquafina—a water with no taste or odour—that Pepsi believed could compete with the spring waters already on the market. Further, Pepsi could license its bottlers to use the Aquafina name and sell them the filtration equipment. Because the process used tap water that was relatively inexpensive, Pepsi's Aquafina would also compete well on price with the spring waters.

The marketing strategy was relatively simple. Whereas Evian and the other early entrants targeted women and high-end consumers, Pepsi wanted consumers to see Aquafina as a "unisex, mainstream" water with an everyday price. When the company launched the product in 1994, it was content just to build distribution using its established system and spend very little money on promotion. Pepsi believed that soft drink advertising should be for soft drinks, not water.

Come on In—the Water's Fine

By 1999, what had been a minor trickle in the beverage market had turned into a geyser—bottled water had become the fastest-growing beverage category, and Pepsi had a big head start. Coca-Cola decided it was time to take the plunge. Like Pepsi, Coca-Cola realized its bottlers were already set up to handle a filtered-water process. Unlike Pepsi, however, rather than taking everything out of the tap water, it wanted to put something in.

Coca-Cola's researchers analyzed tap waters and bottled waters and concocted a combination of minerals they believed would give filtered tap water a fresh, clean taste. The formula included magnesium sulfate, potassium chloride, and salt. Coca-Cola guarded the new water formula just as it had the original Coke recipe. Thus, it could sell the formula to its bottlers, as it does Coke concentrate, and let them make the water.

Like Pepsi, Coca-Cola was content initially just to get its water, which it called Dasani, into distribution.

How to Promote Water

By 2001, however, the bottled-water category had over 800 competitors and had grown to $4.6 billion in sales. Analysts predicted bottled water would become the second largest beverage category by 2004. Nestlé's Perrier Group (Perrier, Poland Spring, and others) held 37.4 percent of the market, followed by Pepsi with 13.8 percent, Coca-Cola with 12 percent, Group Danone (Evian and others) with 11.8 percent, and all others with 25 percent.

Given the rapid market growth rate and all the competition, Pepsi and Coca-Cola decided they had better promote their products, just as they did their soft drinks. In 2001, Pepsi launched an $18.2 million campaign showing real people and how water was part of their lives. Coca-Cola countered with a $26 million campaign that targeted women and used the tag-line "Treat yourself well. Everyday."

Not to be outdone, Pepsi responded by more than doubling its promotion budget to $52 million in 2002. Included in the advertising was a spot featuring *Friends* star Lisa Kudrow. Lisa described how refreshing and mouth-watering Aquafina was—emphasizing that it made no promises it couldn't keep. She described Aquafina as "Pure nothing." The ads featured the tag-line "We promise nothing."

So, Pepsi and Coca-Cola had drawn new battle lines—this time for the water wars. Could Pepsi convince consumers to prefer a water that offered nothing versus Coca-Cola's water that offered something—although both products were colourless, odourless, and tasteless? Further, what would Pepsi and Coca-Cola do in response to the pressure on them to launch "aquaceuticals"—water that was *enhanced* with calcium and fluoride or perhaps even (are you ready for this?) *flavours*? What impact would such products have on Pepsi's advertising strategy?

Questions for Discussion

1. What markets should Pepsi target for Aquafina?
2. What advertising objectives should Pepsi set for Aquafina?
3. What message strategy and message execution recommendations would you make for Aquafina?
4. What advertising media recommendations would you make for Aquafina, and how would you evaluate the effectiveness of those media and your advertising?
5. What sales promotion and public relations recommendations would you make for Aquafina?
6. If Pepsi launches an "aquaceutical," should it use the Aquafina brand name?

Sources: "Non-Alcoholic Beverages: Aquafina," *Advertising Age,* May 6, 2002, p. S10; Betsy McKay, "In a Water Fight, Coke and Pepsi Try Opposite Tacks," *Wall Street Journal,* April 18, 2002, p. A1; Hillary Chura, "Dasani: Kellam Graitcer," *Advertising Age,* October 8, 2001, p. S14; Bob Garfield, "The Product Is Questionable, but Aquafina's Ads Hold Water," *Advertising Age,* July 9, 2001, p. 39; Kenneth Hein, "Coke, Pepsi Mull Jump into 'Aquaceuticals,'" *Brandweek,* June 25, 2001, p. 8; and Betsy McKay, "Coke and Pepsi Escalate Their Water Fight, *Wall Street Journal,* May 18, 2001, p. B8.

CBC Video Case

CBC Log on to your Companion Website at **www.pearsoned.ca/kotler** to view a CBC video segment and case for this chapter.

Chapter 17

Personal Selling and
Direct Marketing

After studying this chapter you should be able to

1. discuss the role of a company's salespeople in creating value for customers and building customer relationships

2. identify and explain the six major sales force management steps

3. discuss the personal selling process, distinguishing between transaction-oriented marketing and relationship marketing

4. define *direct marketing* and discuss its benefits to customers and companies

5. identify and discuss the major forms of direct marketing

Looking Ahead: Previewing the Concepts

In the previous two chapters, you learned about integrated marketing communications (IMC) and three specific elements of the marketing communications mix—advertising, sales promotion, and public relations. In this chapter, we'll learn about the final two IMC elements—personal selling and direct marketing.

Personal selling is the interpersonal arm of marketing communications in which the sales force interacts with customers and prospects to make sales and build relationships. Direct marketing consists of direct connections with carefully targeted consumers to both obtain an immediate response and cultivate lasting customer relationships. Actually, direct marketing can be viewed as more than just a communications tool. In many ways, it constitutes an overall marketing *approach*— a blend of communications and distribution channels all rolled into one. As you read on, remember that although this chapter examines personal selling and direct marketing as separate tools, they must be carefully integrated with other elements of the marketing communications mix.

We'll begin with a look at Lear Corporation's sales force. Although you may never have heard of Lear (it's not the company that makes Lear jets), the chances are good that you've spent lots of time in one or more of the car interiors that it supplies to the world's major automotive manufacturers. Before you read on, close your eyes for a moment and envision a typical salesperson. If what you see is a stereotypical glad-hander out to lighten your wallet by selling you something that you don't really need, you might be in for a surprise.

When someone says "salesperson," what image comes to mind? Perhaps it's the stereotypical "travelling salesman"—the fast-talking, ever-smiling peddler who travels his territory and foists his wares on reluctant customers.

Such stereotypes, however, are out of date. Today, most professional salespeople are well-educated, well-trained women and men who work to build long-term, value-producing relationships with their customers. They succeed not by taking customers in but by helping them out—by assessing customer needs and solving customer problems.

Consider Lear Corporation, one of the largest, fastest-growing, and most successful automotive suppliers in the world (www.lear.com). Every year, Lear produces more than $18 billion worth of automotive interiors—seat systems, instrument panels, door panels, floor and acoustic systems, overhead systems, and electronic and electrical distribution systems. Its customers include most of the world's leading automotive companies, including Ford, DaimlerChrysler, General Motors, Fiat, Toyota, Volvo, BMW, Ferrari, Rolls-Royce, and more than a dozen others. Lear operates more than 300 facilities in 33 countries around the globe, including nine in Canada. During the past few years, Lear has achieved record-breaking sales and earnings growth. Lear's sales during the past five years have more than doubled, and its "average content per car" in North America has increased more than fourfold since 1990. It currently owns about a 30 percent share of the North American interior components market.

Lear Corporation owes its success to many factors, including a strong customer orientation and a commitment to continuous improvement, teamwork, and customer value. But perhaps more than any other part of the organization, Lear's outstanding sales force makes the company's credo, "Consumer driven. Customer focused," ring true. Lear's sales force was recently given top ranking by *Sales & Marketing Management* magazine. What makes this an outstanding sales force? Lear knows that good selling these days takes much more than just a sales rep covering a territory and convincing customers to buy the product. It takes teamwork, relationship building, and doing what's best for the customer. Lear's sales force excels at these tasks.

Lear's sales depend completely on the success of its customers. If the automakers don't sell cars, Lear doesn't sell interiors. So the Lear sales force strives to create not just sales, but customer success. In fact, Lear salespeople aren't "sales reps," they're "account managers" who function more as consultants than as order getters. "Our salespeople don't really close deals," notes a senior marketing executive. "They consult and work with customers to learn exactly what's needed and when."

To more fully match up with customers' needs, Lear has diversified its product line to become a kind of "one-stop shopping" source. Until a few years ago, Lear supplied only seats; now it sells almost everything for a car's interior. Providing complete interior solutions for customers also benefits Lear. "It used to be that we'd build a partnership and then get only a limited amount of revenue from it," the executive says. "Now we can get as much as possible out of our customer relationships."

Lear is heavily customer focused, so much so that it's broken up into separate divisions dedicated to specific customers. For example, there's a Ford division and a General Motors division, and each operates as its own profit centre. Within each division, high-level "platform teams"—made up of salespeople, engineers, and program managers—work closely with their customer counterparts. These platform teams are closely supported by divisional manufacturing, finance, quality, and advanced technology groups.

Lear's limited customer base, consisting of only a few dozen customers in all, allows its sales teams to get very close to their customers. "Our teams don't call on purchasers; they're linked to customer operations at all levels," the marketer notes. "We try to put a system in place that creates continuous contact with customers." In fact, Lear often locates its sales offices in customers' plants. For example, the team that handles GM's light truck division works at GM's truck operation campus. "We can't just be there to give quotes and ask for orders," the marketing executive says. "We need to be involved with customers every step of the way—from vehicle concept through launch."

Lear's largest customers are worth billions of dollars in annual sales to the company. Maintaining profitable relationships with such large customers takes much more than a nice smile and a firm handshake. Certainly there's no place for the "smoke and mirrors" or "flimflam" sometimes mistakenly associated with personal selling. Success in such a selling environment requires careful teamwork among well-trained, dedicated sales professionals who are bent on profitably taking care of their customers.[1]

In this chapter, we examine two more marketing communications and promotion tools—*personal selling* and *direct marketing*. Both involve direct connections with customers aimed toward building customer-unique value and lasting relationships.

Personal Selling

Robert Louis Stevenson noted that "everyone lives by selling something." We are all familiar with the sales forces used by business organizations to sell products and services to customers around the world. Companies such as IBM Canada and Xerox are famous for the quality of their sales staff. Procter & Gamble, Warner-Lambert, and Wrigley's Canada all hire university graduates into sales jobs, since having highly educated, professional sales personnel is essential for building strong relationships with channel members.

But sales forces are also found in many other kinds of organizations. Canada Post uses an extensive sales force to help launch new products such as its direct-mail offerings and courier services. Universities use recruiters to attract new students. Agriculture Canada sends specialists into the field to convince farmers to use new agricultural methods and products. You will have to take on a sales role when you have to sell your knowledge and expertise to prospective employers. In the first part of this chapter, we examine the role of personal selling in the organization, sales force management decisions, and the personal selling process.

The Nature of Personal Selling

Selling is one of the oldest professions in the world. The people who do the selling go by many titles, including *salespeople, sales representatives, account executives, sales consultants, sales engineers, agents, district managers, marketing representatives,* and *account development reps,* to name just a few.

People hold many stereotypes of salespeople—including some unfavourable ones. "Salesman" may bring to mind the image of Arthur Miller's pitiable Willy Loman in *Death of a Salesman.* However, modern salespeople are a far cry from these unfortunate stereotypes. Today, most salespeople are well-trained, well-educated professionals who work to build and maintain long-term relationships listening to their customers, assessing customer needs, and organizing the company's efforts to solve customer problems. Consider Boeing, the aerospace giant competing in the rough-and-tumble worldwide commercial aircraft market (www.boeing.com). It takes more than a friendly smile and a firm handshake to sell expensive airplanes:[2]

> Selling high-tech aircraft at $90 million or more each is complex and challenging. A single big sale can easily run into the billions of dollars. Boeing salespeople head up an extensive team of company specialists—sales and service technicians, financial analysts, planners, engineers—all dedicated to finding ways to satisfy airline customer needs. The salespeople begin by becoming experts on the airlines, much like Wall Street analysts would. They find out where each airline wants to grow, when it wants to replace planes, and details of its financial situation. The team runs Boeing and competing planes through computer systems, simulating the airline's routes, cost per seat, and other factors to show that their planes are most efficient.
>
> Then the high-level negotiations begin. The selling process is nerve-rackingly slow—it can take two or three years from the first sales presentation to the day the sale is announced. Sometimes top executives from both the airline and Boeing are brought in to close the deal. After getting the order, salespeople then must stay in almost constant touch to keep track of the account's equipment needs and to make certain the customer stays satisfied. Success depends on building solid, long-term relationships with customers, based on performance

The term *salesperson* covers a wide range of positions, from the clerk selling in a retail store to the engineering salesperson who consults with client companies.

and trust. "When you buy an airplane, it is like getting married," says the head of Boeing's commercial airplane division. "It is a long-term relationship."

Salesperson
An individual acting for a company by performing one or more of these activities: prospecting, communicating, servicing, and information gathering.

The term **salesperson** covers a range of positions. At one extreme, a salesperson might be largely an *order taker,* such as the department store salesperson standing behind the counter. At the other extreme are *order getters* whose positions demand the *creative selling* of products and services, ranging from appliances, industrial equipment, and airplanes to insurance, advertising, and information technology. Here, we focus on the more creative types of selling and on the process of building and managing an effective sales force.

The Role of the Sales Force

Personal selling is the interpersonal arm of the promotion mix. Advertising consists of one-way, non-personal communication with target consumer groups. In contrast, personal selling involves two-way, personal communication between salespeople and individual customers—whether face to face, by telephone, through video or Web conferences, or by other means. Personal selling can be more effective than advertising in more complex selling situations. Salespeople can probe customers to learn more about their problems, adjust the marketing offer to fit the special needs of each customer, and then negotiate terms of sale. They can build long-term personal relationships with key decision makers.

The role of personal selling varies from company to company. Some firms have no salespeople at all—for example, companies that sell only through mail-order catalogues or companies that sell through manufacturer's representatives, sales agents, or brokers. In most firms, however, the sales force plays a major role. In companies that sell business products, such as Xerox, Cisco Systems, or DuPont, the company's salespeople work directly with customers. In consumer product companies such as Procter & Gamble and Nike that sell through intermediaries, final consumers rarely meet salespeople or even know about them. Still, the sales force plays an important behind-the-scenes role. It works with wholesalers and retailers to gain their support and to help them be more effective in selling the company's products.

The sales force serves as a critical link between a company and its customers. In many cases, salespeople serve both masters—the seller and the buyer. First, they *represent the company to customers.* They find and develop new customers and communicate information about the company's products and services. They sell products by approaching customers, presenting their products, answering objections, negotiating prices and terms, and closing sales. In addition, salespeople provide customer service and carry out market research and intelligence work.

At the same time, salespeople *represent customers to the company,* acting inside the firm as "champions" of customers' interests. Salespeople relay customer concerns about company products and actions back to those who can handle them. They learn about customer needs and work with others in the company to develop greater customer value. The old view was that salespeople should worry about sales and the company should worry about profit. The current view holds that salespeople should be concerned with more than just producing *sales*—they also must know how to produce *customer satisfaction* and *company profit.*

Sales force management
The analysis, planning, implementation, and control of sales force activities. It includes designing sales force strategy and structure, and recruiting, selecting, training, compensating, supervising, and evaluating the firm's salespeople.

Managing the Sales Force

We define **sales force management** as the analysis, planning, implementation, and control of sales force activities. It includes designing sales force strategy and structure, and recruiting, selecting, training, compensating, supervising, and evaluating the firm's salespeople. These major sales force management decisions are shown in Figure 17.1 and discussed in the following sections.

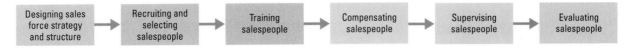

Figure 17.1   Major steps in sales force management

Designing Sales Force Strategy and Structure

Marketing managers face several sales force strategy and design questions. How should salespeople and their tasks be structured? How large should the sales force be? Should salespeople sell alone or work in teams with other people in the company? Should they sell in the field or by telephone? We address these issues below.

Sales Force Structure

A company can divide sales responsibilities along any of several lines. The decision is simple if the company sells only one product line to one industry with customers in many locations. In that case the company would use a *territorial sales force structure*. However, if the company sells many products to many types of customers, it might need a *product sales force structure*, a *customer sales force structure*, or a combination of the two.

Territorial sales force structure

A sales force organization that assigns each salesperson to an exclusive geographic territory in which that salesperson sells the company's full line.

Territorial Sales Force Structure   In the **territorial sales force structure**, each salesperson is assigned to an exclusive geographic territory and sells the company's full line of products or services to all customers in that territory. This organization clearly defines the salesperson's job and also increases the salesperson's desire to build local business relationships that, in turn, improve selling effectiveness. Finally, because each salesperson travels within a limited geographic area, travel expenses are relatively small.

A territorial sales organization often is supported by many levels of sales management positions. Campbell Soup, for example, uses a territorial structure in which each salesperson is now responsible for selling all Campbell Soup products. Starting at the bottom of the organization, *sales merchandisers* report to *sales representatives*, who report to *retail supervisors*, who report to *directors of retail sales operations*, who report to *regional sales managers*. Regional sales managers, in turn, report to *general sales managers*, who report to a *vice-president and general sales manager*.

Product sales force structure

A sales force organization under which salespeople specialize in selling only a portion of the company's products or lines.

Product Sales Force Structure   Salespeople must know their products, especially when the products are numerous and complex. This need, together with the trend toward product management, has led many companies to adopt a **product sales force structure**, in which the sales force sells along product lines. Kodak uses different sales forces for its film products than for its industrial products. The film products sales force deals with simple products that are distributed intensively, whereas the industrial products sales force deals with complex products that require technical understanding.

The product structure can lead to problems, however, if a single large customer buys many different company products. For example, Allegiance Healthcare Corporation, the large health-care products and services company, has several product divisions, each with a separate sales force. Several Allegiance salespeople might end up calling on the same hospital on the same day. This means that the salespeople travel over the same routes and wait to see the same customer's purchasing agents. These extra costs must be compared with the benefits of better product knowledge and attention to individual products.

Customer Sales Force Structure More and more companies are using a **customer sales force structure,** in which they organize the sales force along customer or industry lines. Separate sales forces may be set up for different industries, for serving current customers versus finding new ones, and for major accounts versus regular accounts.

Organizing the sales force around customers can help a company to become more customer focused and build closer relationships with important customers. For example, IBM shifted from a product-based structure to a customer-based one. Before the shift, droves of salespeople representing different IBM software, hardware, and service divisions might call on a single large client, creating confusion and frustration. Such large customers wanted a "single face," one point of contact for all of IBM's vast array of products and services. Following the restructuring, a single IBM "client executive" works with each large customer and manages a team of IBMers—product reps, systems engineers, consultants, and others—who work with the customer. The client executive becomes an expert in the customer's industry. Greg Buseman, a client executive in the distribution industry who spends most of his time working with a major consumer packaged-goods customer, describes his role this way: "I am the owner of the business relationship with the client. If the client has a problem, I'm the one who pulls together software or hardware specialists or consultants. At the customer I work most closely with, we usually have 15 to 20 projects going at once, and I have to manage them."[3] Such an intense focus on customers is widely credited for IBM's dramatic turnaround in recent years.

Complex Sales Force Structure When a company sells a wide variety of products to many types of customers over a broad geographical area, it often combines several types of sales force structures. Salespeople can be specialized by customer and territory, by product and territory, by product and customer, or by territory, product, and customer. No single structure is best for all companies and situations. Each company should select a sales force structure that best serves the needs of its customers and fits its overall marketing strategy.

Sales Force Size

Once the company has set its structure, it is ready to consider *sales force size.* Salespeople constitute one of the company's most productive—and most expensive—assets. Therefore, increasing their number will increase both sales and costs.

Many companies use some form of *workload approach* to set sales force size. Using this approach, a company first groups accounts into different classes according to size, account status, or other factors related to the amount of effort required to maintain them. It then determines the number of salespeople needed to call on each class of accounts the desired number of times. The company might think as follows: Suppose we have 1000 Type A accounts and 2000 Type B accounts. Type A accounts require 36 calls a year, and Type B accounts require 12 calls a year. In this case, the sales force's *workload*—the number of calls it must make per year—is 60 000 calls [$(1000 \times 36) + (2000 \times 12) = 36\ 000 + 24\ 000 = 60\ 000$]. Suppose our average salesperson can make 1000 calls a year. Thus, the company needs 60 salespeople (60 000 ÷ 1000).

Other Sales Force Strategy and Structure Issues

Sales management must also decide who will be involved in the selling effort and how various sales and sales-support people will work together.

Outside and Inside Sales Forces The company may have an **outside sales force** (or **field sales force**), an **inside sales force,** or both. Outside salespeople travel to call on customers. Inside salespeople conduct business from their offices via telephone or visits from prospective buyers.

Experienced telemarketers sell complex chemical products by telephone at DuPont's Customer Telecontact Center. Quips one, "I'm more effective on the phone...and you don't have to outrun dogs."

To reduce time demands on their outside sales forces, many companies have increased the size of their inside sales forces. Inside salespeople include technical support people, sales assistants, and telemarketers. *Technical support people* provide technical information and answers to customers' questions. *Sales assistants* provide clerical backup for outside salespeople. They call ahead and confirm appointments, conduct credit checks, follow up on deliveries, and answer customers' questions when outside salespeople cannot be reached. *Telemarketers* use the phone to find new leads and qualify prospects for the field sales force, or to sell and service accounts directly.

The inside sales force frees outside salespeople to spend more time selling to major accounts and finding new major prospects. Depending on the complexity of the product and customer, a telemarketer can make from 20 to 33 decision-maker contacts a day, compared with the average of four that an outside salesperson can see. And for many types of products and selling situations, *telemarketing* can be as effective as a personal call but much less expensive. Whereas the average personal sales call costs about $220, a routine industrial telemarketing call costs only about $6.50 and a complex call about $26.[4] Notes a DuPont telemarketer: "I'm more effective on the phone. [When you're in the field], if some guy's not in his office, you lose an hour. On the phone, you lose 15 seconds.... Through my phone calls, I'm in the field as much as the rep is." There are other advantages. "Customers can't throw things at you," quips the rep, "and you don't have to outrun dogs."[5]

Telemarketing can be used successfully by both large and small companies:

IBM's traditional image has long been symbolized by the salesman in the blue suit, crisp white shirt, and red tie—an imposing fellow far more comfortable in corporate Canada's plush executive suites than in the cramped quarters of some fledgling entrepreneur. Small businesses were often ignored. Now, to sell its ebusiness solutions to small businesses, IBM is boosting emphasis on its telemarketing effort. Stroll through the IBM call centre with its sea of cubicles, and a new image of the IBM salesperson emerges: men and women, many recent university grads, sporting golf shirts and khakis or—gasp!—blue jeans. They wear headsets and talk on the phone with customers they'll likely never meet in person. IBM's roughly 1200 phone reps now generate 30 percent of IBM's revenues from small and midsize businesses. The reps focus on specific industries and each calls on as many as 300 accounts. They nurture client relationships, pitch IBM solutions, and, when needed, refer customers to product and service specialists within the call centre or to resellers in their region.[6]

Climax Portable Machine Tools has proven that a small company can use telemarketing to save money and still lavish attention on buyers. Climax sales engineers, who once spent one-third of their time on the road, training distributor salespeople and accompanying them on four calls a day, now service about 30 prospects a day, following up on leads generated by ads and direct mail. Because it takes about five calls to close a sale, the sales engineers update a prospect's computer file after each contact, noting the degree of commitment, requirements, next call date, and personal comments. For example, "If anyone mentions he's going on a fishing trip, our sales engineer enters that in the computer and uses it to personalize the next phone call," says Climax's president, noting that's just one way to build good relations. Another is that the first mailing to a prospect includes the sales engineer's business card with his picture on it. Of course, it takes more than friendliness to sell $19 000 machine tools over the phone (special orders may run to $260 000), but the telemarketing approach is working well. When Climax customers were asked, "Do you see the sales engineer often enough?" the response was overwhelmingly positive. Obviously, many people didn't realize that the only contact they'd had with Climax had been on the phone.[7]

Just as telemarketing is changing the way that many companies go to market, the Internet offers explosive potential for restructuring sales forces and conducting sales operations. More and more companies are now using the Internet to support their personal selling efforts—not just for selling, but for everything from training salespeople to conducting sales meetings and servicing accounts (see Real Marketing 17.1).

Team Selling   As products become more complex, and as customers grow larger and more demanding, a single salesperson simply can't handle all of a large customer's needs. Instead, most companies now are using **team selling** to service large, complex accounts. Companies are finding that sales teams can unearth problems, solutions, and sales opportunities that no individual salesperson can. Such teams may include experts from any area or level of the selling firm—sales, marketing, technical and support services, R&D, engineering, operations, finance, and others. In team selling situations, the salesperson shifts from "soloist" to "orchestrator."

Team selling

Using teams of people from sales, marketing, engineering, finance, technical support, and even upper management to service large, complex accounts.

This Procter & Gamble "customer business development team" serves a major grocery retailer. It consists of a customer business development manager and five account executives (shown here), along with specialists from other functional areas.

17.1 Point, Click, and Sell: Welcome to the Web-Based Sales Force

There are few rules at Fisher Scientific International's sales training sessions. The chemical company's salespeople are allowed to show up for new workshops in their pyjamas. No one flinches if they stroll in at midnight for their first class, take a dozen breaks to call clients, or invite the family cat to sleep in their laps while they take an exam. Sound unorthodox? It would be if Fisher's salespeople were trained in a regular classroom. But for the past year and a half, the company has been using the Internet to teach the majority of its salespeople in the privacy of their homes, cars, hotel rooms, or wherever else they bring their laptops.

To get updates on Fisher's pricing or refresh themselves on one of the company's highly technical products, all salespeople have to do is log on to the website and select from the lengthy index. Any time of the day or night, they can get information on a new product, take an exam, or post messages for product experts—all without ever entering a corporate classroom. Welcome to the new world of the Web-based sales force.

In the past few years, sales organizations around the world have begun saving money and time by using a host of new Web approaches to train reps, hold sales

Internet selling support: Sales organizations around the world are now using the Internet to train salespeople, hold sales meetings, and even conduct live sales presentations.

meetings, and even conduct live sales presentations. "Web-based technologies are becoming really hot in sales because they save salespeople's time," says technology consultant Tim Sloane. Web-based technologies help keep reps up to speed on their company's new products and sales strategies. Fisher Scientific's reps can go online at their leisure, and whereas newer reps might spend hours online going through each session in order, more seasoned sellers might just log on for a quick refresher on a specific product before a sales call. "It allows them to manage their time better, because they're only getting training when they need it, in the doses they need it in," says John Pavlik, director of the company's training department. If salespeople are spending less time on training, Pavlik says, they're able to spend more time on what they do best—selling.

Training is only one of the ways sales organizations are using the Internet. Many companies are using the Web to make sales presentations and service accounts. For example, Digital Equipment Corporation's salespeople used to spend a great deal of time travelling to the offices of clients and prospects. But since 1997, the company (now a division of Hewlett-Packard) has been delivering sales pitches by combining teleconferences with Web presentations. For example, when Digital's account team in Calgary needed to see what their marketing manager in Toronto had prepared for a client, they just logged on to the PowerPoint presentation and uploaded it using Internet Conference Center, Web-based software. Once everyone was logged on, the marketing manager was able to take control of the browsers and lead the reps through the presentation in real time, highlighting and pointing out specific items as he went. The account reps added their comments, based on their more detailed knowledge of the client, and the revised presentation was then shown online to the client. The beauty of the whole process? It's so fast. "The use of [the Web] clearly helps shorten our sales cycle." Presentations are created and delivered in less time—sometimes weeks less than the process would take face-to-face—and salespeople are able to close deals more quickly.

Other companies are using Web-based sales presentations to find new prospects. Oracle Corporation, the $10-billion software and information technology services company, conducts online, live product seminars for prospective clients. Prospects can scan the high-tech company's website to see which seminars they might want to attend, then dial in via modem and telephone at the appropriate time (and Oracle pays for the cost of the phone call). The seminars, which usually consist of a live lecture describing the product's applications followed by a question-and-answer session, average about 125 prospective clients apiece. Once a seminar is completed, prospects are directed to another part of Oracle's website, from which they can order products. "It costs our clients nothing but time," says Oracle's manager of Internet marketing programs, "and we're reaching a much wider audience than we would if we were doing in-person seminars."

The Internet can also be a handy way to hold sales strategy meetings. Consider Cisco Systems, which provides networking solutions for the Internet. Sales meetings used to take an enormous bite out of Cisco's travel budget. Now the company saves about $1.3 million a month by conducting many of those sessions on the Web using PlaceWare virtual conference centre software. Whenever Cisco introduces a new product, it holds a Web meeting to update salespeople in groups of 100 or more on the product's marketing and sales strategy.

Usually led by the product manager or a vice-president of sales, the meetings typically begin with a 10-minute slide presentation that spells out the planned strategy. Then, salespeople spend the next 50 or so minutes asking questions via teleconference. The meeting's leader can direct attendees' browsers to competitors' websites or ask them to vote on certain issues by using the software's instant polling feature. "Our salespeople are actually meeting more online then they ever were face to face," says Mike Mitchell, Cisco's distance learning manager, adding that some

salespeople who used to meet with other reps and managers only a few times a quarter are meeting online nearly every day. "That's very empowering for the sales force, because they're able to make suggestions at every step of the way about where we're going with our sales and marketing strategies."

Thus, Web-based technologies can produce big organizational benefits for sales forces. They help conserve salespeople's valuable time, save travel dollars, and give salespeople a new vehicle for selling and servicing accounts. But the technologies also have some drawbacks. For starters, they're expensive. Setting up a Web-based system can cost up to several hundred thousand dollars. Such systems also can intimidate low-tech salespeople or clients. "You must have a culture that is comfortable using computers," says one marketing communications manager. "As simple as it is, if your salespeople or clients aren't comfortable using the Web, you're wasting your money." Also, Web tools are susceptible to server crashes and other network difficulties, not a happy event when you're in the midst of an important sales meeting or presentation.

For these reasons, some high-tech experts recommend that sales executives use Web technologies for training, sales meetings, and preliminary client sales presentations, but resort to old-fashioned, face-to-face meetings when the time draws near to close the deal. "When push comes to shove, if you've got an account worth closing, you're still going to get on that plane and see the client in person," says sales consultant Sloane. "Your client is going to want to look you in the eye before buying anything from you, and that's still one thing you just can't do online."

Sources: Portions adapted from Melinda Ligos, "Point, Click, and Sell," *Sales & Marketing Management,* May 1999, pp. 51–55. Also see Chad Kaydo, "You've Got Sales," *Sales & Marketing Management,* October 1999, pp. 29–39; Ginger Conlon, "Ride the Wave," *Sales & Marketing Management,* December 2000, pp. 67–74; and Tom Reilly, "Technology and the Salesperson," *Industrial Distribution,* January 2001, p. 88.

In many cases, the move to team selling mirrors similar changes in customers' buying organizations. According to a recent study by *Purchasing* magazine, nearly 70 percent of companies polled are using or are extremely interested in using multifunctional buying teams. Says the director of sales education at Dow Chemical, to sell effectively to such buying teams, "our sellers...have to captain selling teams. There are no more lone wolves."[8]

Some companies, including IBM Canada, Xerox, and Procter & Gamble, have used teams for a long time. P&G sales reps are organized into "customer business development (CBD) teams." Each CBD team is assigned to a major P&G customer. Teams consist of a customer business development manager, several account executives (each responsible for a specific category of P&G products), and specialists in marketing strategy, operations, information systems, logistics, and finance. This organization places the focus on serving the complete needs of each important customer.

Other companies have only recently reorganized to adopt the team concept. Cutler-Hammer, which supplies circuit breakers, motor starters, and other electrical equipment to heavy industrial manufacturers such as Ford, recently developed "pods" of salespeople that focus on a specific geographical region, industry, or market. Each pod member contributes unique expertise and knowledge about a product or service that salespeople can leverage when selling to increasingly sophisticated buying teams.[9]

Team selling does have some pitfalls. Selling teams can confuse or overwhelm customers who are used to working with only one salesperson. Salespeople who are used to having customers all to themselves may have trouble learning to work with and trust others on a team. Finally, difficulties in evaluating individual contributions to the team selling effort can create some sticky compensation issues.

Recruiting and Selecting Salespeople

At the heart of any successful sales force operation is the recruitment and selection of good salespeople. To "weed out mediocrity," Warner-Lambert Canada is one firm that hires undergraduate and graduate students to improve the skill level of those people it sends into the field. The performance difference between an average salesperson and a top salesperson can be substantial. In a typical sales force, the top 30 percent of the salespeople bring in 60 percent of the sales. Thus, careful salesperson selection can greatly increase overall sales force performance. Beyond the differences in sales performance, poor selection results in costly turnover. When a salesperson quits, the costs of finding and training a new salesperson can be very high. And a sales force with many new people is less productive.

What traits spell surefire sales success? One survey suggests that good salespeople have a lot of enthusiasm, persistence, initiative, self-confidence, and job commitment. They are committed to sales as a way of life and have a strong customer orientation. Another study suggests that good salespeople are independent and self-motivated and are excellent listeners. In contrast, other studies show that good salespeople are team players rather than loners. Still another study advises that salespeople should be a friend to the customer as well as persistent, enthusiastic, attentive, and—above all—honest. They must be internally motivated, disciplined, hard-working, and able to build strong relationships with customers.

Finally, in today's relationship-marketing environment, top salespeople are customer problem solvers and relationship builders. They have an instinctive understanding of their customers' needs. Talk to sales executives and they'll describe top performers in these terms: Empathetic. Patient. Caring. Responsive. Good listeners. Even *honest*. Top sellers can put themselves on the buyer's side of the desk and see the world through their customers' eyes. Today, customers are looking for business partners, not golf partners. "High performers don't just want to be liked, they want to add value." High-performing salespeople, he adds, are "always thinking about the big picture, where the customer's organization is going, and how they can help them get there." Concludes one top performer, "The relationship you build with your prospects and customers is more important than the close."[10]

When recruiting, companies should analyze the sales job itself and the characteristics of its most successful salespeople to identify the traits needed by a successful salesperson in their industry. Is a lot of planning and paperwork required? Does the job call for much travel? Will the salesperson face a lot of rejections? Will the salesperson be working with high-level buyers? The successful salesperson should be suited to these duties.

Recruiting Procedures

After management has decided on needed traits, it must *recruit* salespeople. The human resources department looks for applicants by getting names from current salespeople, using employment agencies, placing classified ads, and contacting university students. Another source is to attract top salespeople from other companies. Proven salespeople need less training and can be immediately productive.

Until recently, companies sometimes found it hard to sell university students on selling. Many thought that selling was a job and not a profession, that salespeople had to be deceitful to be effective, and that selling involved too much insecurity and travel. In addition, some women believed that selling was a man's career. To counter such objections, recruiters now offer high starting salaries and income growth. For example, in its *2002/2003 Sales Compensation* report, the Canadian Professional Sales Association noted that junior sales representatives can earn up to $38 000 a year (or $50 500 if they are in technical sales), while key account representatives can pull in over $69 500. Directors of sales and marketing have earnings as high as $113 200. Compensation varies considerably by city. For example, while the average compensation for a sales account manager is $55 447, in Toronto a sales account manager may earn between $52 675 and $88 993 (with the average compensation being $69 309), while in Vancouver the range is $36 703 to $58 308 (with the average compensation being $46 021).[11]

Recruiters also tout the fact that many of the presidents of large North American corporations started out in marketing and sales (Anne Mulcahy, CEO of Xerox, is one example). Recruiters also point out that more and more women are entering sales and even dominate the sales forces in some industries.

Selection Procedures

Recruiting will attract many applicants from whom the company must select the best. The selection procedures can vary from a single informal interview to lengthy testing and interviewing. Many companies give formal tests to sales applicants. Tests typically measure sales aptitude, analytical and organizational skills, personality traits, and other characteristics. Test results count heavily in such companies as IBM, Prudential, Procter & Gamble, and Gillette. Gillette claims that tests have reduced turnover by 42 percent, and that test scores have correlated well with the later performance of new salespeople. But test scores provide only one piece of information in a set that includes personal characteristics, references, past employment history, and interviewer reactions.[12]

Training Salespeople

New salespeople spend anywhere from a few weeks or months to a year or more in training. Then, most companies provide continuing sales training via seminars, sales meetings, and the Web throughout the salesperson's career. Rob Granby, vice-president of sales at Cadbury Beverages Canada, believes that ongoing training and a supportive corporate culture are essential: "If your corporate culture isn't one that nourishes and helps salespeople flourish, then no matter what you layer on in terms of bonus programs and special incentives, it won't make a difference."[13]

Although training can be expensive, it can also yield dramatic returns on the training investment. Nabisco did an extensive analysis of the return on investment of its two-day professional selling program, which teaches sales reps how to plan for and make professional presentations to their retail customers. Although it cost about $1300 to put each sales rep through the program, the training resulted in additional sales of more than $160 000 per rep and yielded almost $27 000 of additional profit per rep.[14] While some firms do their sales training in-house, others send their representatives to executive education programs or turn to the Canadian Professional Sales Association (www.cpsa.com) for help.

Many firms turn to the Canadian Professional Sales Association for help with sales training.

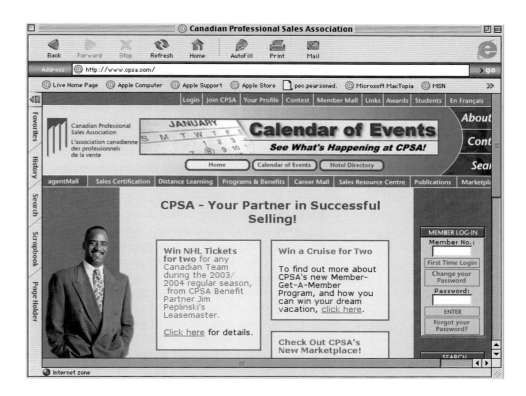

Training programs have several goals. Since salespeople need to know and identify with the company, most training programs begin in describing the company's history and objectives, its organization, its financial structure and facilities, and its chief products and markets. Salespeople also need to know the company's products, so sales trainees are shown how products are produced and how they work. They also need to know customers' and competitors' characteristics, so the training program teaches them about competitors' strategies and about different types of customers and their needs, buying motives, and buying habits. Because salespeople must know how to make effective presentations, they are trained in the principles of selling. Finally, they need to understand field procedures and responsibilities. They learn how to divide time between active and potential accounts and how to use an expense account, prepare reports, and route communications effectively.

Today, as Real Marketing 17.1 pointed out, many companies are adding Web-based training to their sales training programs. Such training may range from simple text-based product information to Internet-based sales exercises that build sales skills to sophisticated simulations that re-create the dynamics of real-life sales calls.

Compensating Salespeople

To attract salespeople, a company must have an appealing compensation plan. Compensation is made up of several elements—a fixed amount, a variable amount, expenses, and fringe benefits. The fixed amount, usually a salary, gives the salesperson some stable income. The variable amount, which may be commissions or bonuses based on sales performance, rewards the salesperson for greater effort. Sales people in Canada may earn $25 000 or more in commissions, but the median commission cheque is for approximately $6000. Expense allowances, which repay salespeople for job-related expenses, let salespeople undertake needed and desirable selling efforts. Fringe benefits, such as paid vacations, sickness or accident benefits, pensions, and life insurance, provide job security and satisfaction.[15]

Management must decide what *mix* of these compensation elements makes the most sense for each sales job. Different combinations of fixed and variable compensation give rise to four basic types of compensation plans—straight salary, straight commission, salary plus bonus, and salary plus commission. A study of sales force compensation plans showed that 70 percent of all companies surveyed use a combination of base salary and incentives. The average plan consisted of about 60 percent salary and 40 percent incentive pay.[16]

The sales force compensation plan can both motivate salespeople and direct their activities. Compensation should direct the sales force toward activities that are consistent with overall marketing objectives. Table 17.1 illustrates how a company's compensation plan should reflect its overall marketing strategy. For example, if the overall strategy is to grow rapidly and gain market share, the compensation plan might include a larger commission component coupled with new account bonuses to encourage high sales performance and new-account development. In contrast, if the marketing goal is to maximize current account profitability, the compensation plan may contain a larger base salary component, with additional incentives based on current account sales or customer satisfaction.

In fact, companies are moving away from high-commission plans that can drive salespeople to make short-term grabs for business. Notes one sales force expert: "The last thing you want is to have someone ruin a customer relationship because they're pushing too hard to close a deal." Instead, companies are designing compensation plans that reward salespeople for building customer relationships and growing the long-run value of each customer.[17] Consider the following example:

> Astra Pharma has not used a commission plan for some time. Instead, it rewards its representatives for their level of understanding of their industry, gained through company training and outside courses, and their involvement in it. And this involvement means more than a "nine-to-five" job. Reps offer evening presentations to groups that influence patients' treatment decisions, such as the Heart and Stroke Foundation and the Canadian Lung Association. They work with hospitals and drug stores to organize patient seminars.[18]

Supervising Salespeople

New salespeople need more than a territory, compensation, and training—they need *supervision*. Through supervision, the company *directs* and *motivates* the sales force to do a better job.

Table 17.1   The Relationship between Overall Marketing Strategy and Sales Force Compensation

	Strategic Goal		
	To Gain Market Share Rapidly	**To Solidify Market Leadership**	**To Maximize Profitability**
Ideal salesperson	• An independent self-starter	• A competitive problem solver	• A team player • A relationship manager
Sales focus	• Deal making • Sustained high effort	• Consultative selling	• Account penetration
Compensation role	• To capture accounts • To reward high performance	• To reward new and existing account sales	• To manage the product mix • To encourage team selling • To reward account management

Source: Adapted from Sam T. Johnson, "Sales Compensation: In Search of a Better Solution," *Compensation & Benefits Review,* November–December 1993, pp. 53–60. Copyright © 1998 American Management Association, NY, www.amanet.org. All rights reserved, used with permission.

Companies vary widely in how closely they supervise their salespeople. Many help their salespeople in identifying customer targets and setting call norms. Some may also specify how much time their sales forces should spend prospecting for new accounts and set other time-management priorities. One tool is the *annual call plan,* which shows which customers and prospects to call on in which months and which activities to carry out. Activities include taking part in trade shows, attending sales meetings, and carrying out marketing research. Another tool is *time-and-duty analysis.* In addition to time spent selling, the salesperson spends time travelling, waiting, eating, taking breaks, and doing administrative chores.

Figure 17.2 shows how salespeople spend their time. On average, actual face-to-face selling time accounts for only about 30 percent of total working time. If selling time could be raised from 30 to 40 percent, this would be a 33 percent increase in the time spent selling. Companies are always looking for ways to save time—using phones instead of travelling, simplifying record-keeping forms, finding better call and routing plans, and supplying more and better customer information.

Many firms have adopted *sales force automation systems,* computerized sales force operations for more efficient order-entry transactions, improved customer service, and better salesperson decision making. Salespeople use laptops, handheld computing devices, and Web technologies, coupled with customer-contact software and customer relationship management (CRM) software, to profile customers and prospects, analyze and forecast sales, manage accounts, schedule sales calls, enter orders, check inventories and order status, prepare sales and expense reports, process correspondence, and carry out many other activities. Sales force automation not only lowers sales force costs and improves productivity, it also improves the quality of sales management decisions. Here is an example of successful sales force automation:[19]

> Owens-Corning has put its sales force on line with FSA—its Field Sales Advantage system. FSA gives Owens-Corning salespeople a constant supply of information about their company and the people they're dealing with. Using laptop computers, each salesperson can access three types of programs. First, FSA gives them a set of *generic tools,* with everything from word processing to fax transmission to creating presentations online. Second, it provides *product information*—tech bulletins, customer specifications, pricing information, and other data that can help close a sale. Finally, it offers up a wealth of *customer information*—buying history, types of products ordered, and preferred payment terms. Before, reps stored such information in loose-leaf books, calendars, and account cards. Now, FSA makes working directly with customers easier than

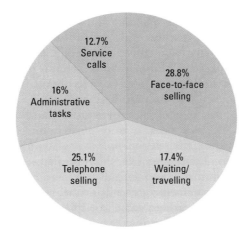

Figure 17.2 How salespeople spend their time

Source: Dartnell Corporation; *30th Sales Force Compensation Survey.* © 1999 Dartnell Corporation.

Owens-Corning's Field Sales Advantage system gives salespeople a constant supply of information about their company and the people with whom they're dealing.

ever. Salespeople can prime themselves on backgrounds of clients, call up pre-written sales letters, transmit orders and resolve customer-service issues on the spot during customer calls, and have samples, pamphlets, brochures, and other materials sent to clients with a few keystrokes. With FSA, "salespeople automatically become more empowered," says Charley Causey, regional general manager. "They become the real managers of their own business and their own territories."

Salespeople also use the Internet extensively to gather competitive information, monitor customer websites, and research industries and specific customers.

Motivating Salespeople

Beyond directing salespeople, sales managers must also motivate them. Some salespeople will do their best without any special urging from management. To them, selling may be the most fascinating job in the world. But selling can also be frustrating. Salespeople often work alone, and they must sometimes travel away from home. They may face aggressive, competing salespeople and difficult customers. They sometimes lack the authority to do what is needed to win a sale and may thus lose large orders they have worked hard to obtain. Therefore, salespeople often need special encouragement to do their best.

Management can boost sales force morale and performance through its organizational climate, sales quotas, and positive incentives. *Organizational climate* describes the feeling that salespeople have about their opportunities, value, and rewards for a good performance. Some companies treat salespeople as if they are not very important, and performance suffers accordingly. Other companies treat their salespeople as valued contributors and allow virtually unlimited opportunity for income and promotion. Not surprisingly, these companies enjoy higher sales force performance and less turnover.

Sales force incentives: Many companies offer cash, trips, or merchandise as incentives. American Express suggests that companies reward outstanding sales performers with high-tech Persona Select cards— electronically prepaid reward cards that allow recipients to purchase whatever they want most.

Sales quotas
Standards set for salespeople, stating the amount they should sell and how sales should be divided among the company's products.

Many companies motivate their salespeople by setting **sales quotas**—standards stating the amount they should sell and how sales should be divided among the company's products. Compensation is often related to how well salespeople meet their quotas. Companies also use various positive incentives to increase sales force effort. *Sales meetings* provide social occasions, breaks from routine, chances to meet and talk with "company brass," and opportunities to air feelings and to identify with a larger group. Companies like Bombardier's recreational vehicles division (makers of Ski-Doos and Sea-Doos) also sponsor *sales contests* to spur the sales force to make a selling effort above what would normally be expected.

Evaluating Salespeople

We have thus far described how management communicates what salespeople should be doing and how it motivates them to do it. This process requires good feedback. And good feedback means getting regular information from salespeople to evaluate their performance.

Management gets information about its salespeople in several ways. The most important source are *sales reports*, including weekly or monthly work plans and longer-term territory marketing plans. Salespeople also write up their completed activities on *call reports* and turn in *expense reports* for which they are partly or wholly repaid. Additional information comes from personal observation, customer surveys, and talks with other salespeople.

Using various sales force reports and other information, sales management evaluates members of the sales force. It evaluates salespeople on their ability to "plan their work and work their plan." Formal evaluation forces management to develop and communicate clear standards for judging performance. It also provides salespeople with constructive feedback and motivates them to perform well.

Selling process
The steps that the salesperson follows when selling, which include prospecting and qualifying, preapproach, approach, presentation and demonstration, handling objections, closing, and follow-up.

The Personal Selling Process

We now turn from designing and managing a sales force to the actual personal selling process. The **selling process** consists of several steps that the salesperson must master. These steps focus on the goal of getting new customers and obtaining orders from them. However, most salespeople spend much of their time maintaining existing accounts and building long-term customer *relationships*. We discuss the relationship aspect of the personal selling process in a later section.

Steps in the Selling Process

As shown in Figure 17.3, the selling process consists of seven steps: *prospecting and qualifying, preapproach, approach, presentation and demonstration, handling objections, closing,* and *follow-up*.

Prospecting and Qualifying

Prospecting
The step in the selling process in which the salesperson identifies qualified potential customers.

The first step in the selling process is **prospecting**—identifying qualified potential customers. Approaching the right potential customers is crucial to selling success. As one expert puts it, "If the sales force starts chasing anyone who is breathing and seems to have a budget, you risk accumulating a roster of expensive-to-serve, hard-to-satisfy customers who never respond to whatever value proposition you have." He continues, "The solution to this isn't rocket science. [You must] train salespeople to actively scout the right prospects. If necessary, create an incentive program to reward proper scouting."[20]

The salesperson must often approach many prospects to get just a few sales. Although the company supplies some leads, salespeople need skill in finding their own. They can ask current customers for referrals. They can build referral sources, such as suppliers, dealers, non-competing salespeople, and bankers. They can search for prospects in directories or on the Web and track down leads using the telephone and direct mail. Or they can drop in unannounced on various offices—a practice known as *cold calling*.

Salespeople need to know how to *qualify* leads—that is, how to identify the good ones and screen out the poor ones. They can qualify prospects by evaluating their financial ability, volume of business, special needs, location, and possibilities for growth.

Preapproach

Preapproach
The step in the selling process in which the salesperson learns as much as possible about a prospective customer before making a sales call.

Before calling on a prospect, the salesperson should learn as much as possible about the organization (what it needs, who is involved in the buying) and its buyers (their characteristics and buying styles). This step is known as the **preapproach**. The salesperson can consult standard industry and online sources, acquaintances, and others to learn about the company. The salesperson should set *call objectives*, which may

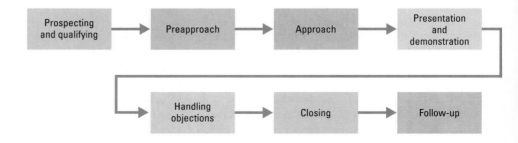

Figure 17.3   Major steps in effective selling

be to qualify the prospect, to gather information, or to make an immediate sale. Another task is to decide on the best approach, which might be a personal visit, a phone call, or a letter. The best timing should be considered carefully because many prospects are busiest at certain times. Finally, the salesperson should consider an overall sales strategy for the account.

Approach

Approach
The step in the selling process in which the salesperson meets the customer for the first time.

During the **approach** step, the salesperson should know how to meet and greet the buyer and get the relationship off to a good start. This step involves the salesperson's appearance, opening lines, and follow-up remarks. The opening lines should be positive to build goodwill from the beginning of the relationship. This opening might be followed by some key questions to learn more about the customer's needs or by showing a display or sample to attract the buyer's attention and curiosity. As in all stages of the selling process, listening to the customer is crucial.

Presentation and Demonstration

Presentation
The step in the selling process in which the salesperson tells the product "story" to the buyer, showing how the product will make or save money for the buyer.

During the **presentation** step of the selling process, the salesperson tells the "product story" to the buyer, presenting customer benefits and showing how the product solves the customer's problems. The problem-solver salesperson fits better with today's marketing concept than does a hard-sell salesperson or the glad-handing extrovert. Buyers today want solutions, not smiles; results, not razzle-dazzle. They want salespeople who listen to their concerns, understand their needs, and respond with the right products and services.

This *need-satisfaction approach* calls for good listening and problem-solving skills. "I think of myself more as a...well, psychologist," notes one experienced salesperson. "I listen to customers. I listen to their wishes and needs and problems, and I try to figure out a solution. If you're not a good listener, you're not going to get the order." Another salesperson suggests, "It's no longer enough to have a good relationship with a client. You have to understand their problems. You have to feel their pain."[21] The qualities that buyers *dislike most* in salespeople include being pushy, late, deceitful, and unprepared or disorganized. The qualities they *value most* include empathy, good listening, honesty, dependability, thoroughness, and follow-through. Great salespeople know how to sell, but more importantly they know how to listen and to build strong customer relationships.[22]

Today, advanced presentation technologies allow for full multimedia presentations to only one or a few people. Audio and videocassettes, laptop computers with presentation software, online presentation technologies, and even virtual reality presentations have replaced the flip chart, as the following example shows:

> Advanced Sterilization Products (www.sterrad.com), a Johnson & Johnson company, provides its sales force with a virtual reality presentation—the STERRAD Experience. Originally designed for use at conferences, the presentation equipment has been redesigned for sales calls and consists of a small video player with five headsets, all easily transported in an ordinary-size briefcase. Prospects don a helmet for a virtual reality tour of the inner workings of the STERRAD Sterilization System for medical devices and surgical instruments. The presentation provides more information in a more engaging way than could be done by displaying the actual machinery. For customers with less time, ASP salespeople can introduce the STERRAD system using online demonstration videos.[23]

Handling Objections

Handling objections
The step in the selling process in which the salesperson seeks out, clarifies, and overcomes customer objections to buying.

Customers almost always have objections during the presentation or when asked to place an order. The problem can be either logical or psychological, and objections are often unspoken. In **handling objections**, the salesperson should use a positive

New sales presentation technologies: Advanced Sterilization Products, a Johnson & Johnson Company, provides its sales force with a presentation in which prospects don a helmet for a virtual reality tour of the inner workings of the STERRAD Sterilization System for medical devices and surgical instruments.

approach, seek out hidden objections, ask the buyer to clarify any objections, take objections as opportunities to provide more information, and turn the objections into reasons for buying. Every salesperson needs training in the skills of handling objections.

Closing

Closing
The step in the selling process in which the salesperson asks the customer for an order.

After handling the prospect's objections, the salesperson now tries to close the sale. Some salespeople do not get around to **closing** or do not handle it well. They may lack confidence, feel guilty about asking for the order, or fail to recognize the right moment to close the sale. Salespeople should know how to recognize closing signals from the buyer, including physical actions, comments, and questions. For example, the customer might sit forward and nod approvingly or ask about prices and credit terms. Salespeople can use one of several closing techniques. They can ask for the order, review points of agreement, offer to help write up the order, ask whether the buyer wants this model or that one, or note that the buyer will lose out if the order is not placed now. The salesperson may offer the buyer special reasons to close, such as a lower price or an extra quantity at no charge.

Follow-up

Follow-up
The last step in the selling process, in which the salesperson follows up after the sale to ensure customer satisfaction and repeat business.

The last step in the selling process—**follow-up**—is necessary if the salesperson wants to ensure customer satisfaction and repeat business. Right after closing, the salesperson should complete any details on delivery time, purchase terms, and other matters. The salesperson then should schedule a follow-up call when the initial order is received to ensure that there is proper installation, instruction, and servicing. This visit would reveal any problems, assure the buyer of the salesperson's interest, and reduce any buyer concerns that might have arisen since the sale.

Personal Selling and Customer Relationship Management

The principles of personal selling just described are *transaction oriented*—their aim is to help salespeople close a specific sale with a customer. But in many cases, the company is not seeking simply a sale: it has targeted a major customer that it would like to win and keep. The company would like to show the customer that it has the capabilities to serve the customer's needs in a superior way over the long haul, in a mutually profitable *relationship*. The sales force usually plays an important role in building and managing long-term customer relationships.

Today's large customers favour suppliers who can sell and deliver a coordinated set of products and services to many locations, and who can work closely with customer teams to improve products and processes. For these customers, the first sale is only the beginning of the relationship. Unfortunately, some companies ignore these new realities. They sell their products through separate sales forces, each working independently to close sales. Their technical people may not be willing to lend time to educate a customer. Their engineering, design, and manufacturing people may have the attitude that "it's our job to make good products and the salesperson's to sell them to customers." Other companies, however, recognize that winning and keeping accounts requires more than making good products and directing the sales force to close lots of sales. It requires a carefully coordinated wholecompany effort to create value-laden, satisfying relationships with important customers.

Direct Marketing

Many of the marketing and promotion tools that we've examined in previous chapters were developed in the context of *mass marketing:* targeting broad markets with standardized messages and offers distributed through intermediaries. Today, however, with the trend toward more narrowly targeted or one-to-one marketing, many companies are adopting *direct marketing,* either as a primary marketing approach or as a supplement to other approaches. Increasingly, companies are using direct marketing to reach carefully targeted customers more efficiently and to build stronger, more personal, one-to-one relationships with them. In this section, we explore the exploding world of direct marketing.

Direct marketing
Direct communications with carefully targeted individual consumers to obtain an immediate response.

Direct marketing consists of direct communications with carefully targeted individual consumers to both obtain an immediate response and cultivate lasting customer relationships. Direct marketers communicate directly with customers, often on a one-to-one, interactive basis. Using detailed databases, they tailor their marketing offers and communications to the needs of narrowly defined segments or even individual buyers. Beyond brand and image building, they usually seek a direct, immediate, and measurable consumer response. For example, Dell Computer interacts directly with customers, by telephone or through its website, to design built-to-order systems that meet customers' individual needs. Buyers order directly from Dell, and Dell quickly and efficiently delivers the new computers to their homes or offices.

The New Direct-Marketing Model

Early direct marketers—catalogue companies, direct mailers, and telemarketers—gathered customer names and sold goods mainly through the mail and by telephone. Today, however, fired by rapid advances in database technologies and new marketing media—especially the Internet—direct marketing has undergone a dramatic transformation.

In previous chapters, we've discussed direct marketing as direct distribution—as marketing channels that contain no intermediaries. We also include direct marketing as one element of the marketing communications mix—as an approach for communicating directly with consumers. In fact, direct marketing is both of these things.

Most companies still use direct marketing as a supplementary channel or medium for marketing their goods. Thus, Lexus markets mostly through mass-media advertising and its high-quality dealer network, but also supplements these channels with direct marketing. Its direct marketing includes promotional videos and other materials mailed directly to prospective buyers and a website that provides consumers with information about various models, competitive comparisons, financing, and dealer locations. Similarly, although Zellers and the Bay conduct most of their business through bricks-and-mortar stores, their Web initiatives, launched in November 2000, allow customers great choice on how and when to shop. "The ability to be a true cross-channel retailer is crucial in today's environment, and we believe that customers really will reward retailers who offer them the most choice," says Michael LeBlanc, director of customer retention at the Hudson's Bay Company.[24]

However, for many companies today, direct marketing is more than just a supplementary channel or medium. For these companies, direct marketing—especially in its newest transformation, Internet marketing and ecommerce—constitutes a new and complete model for doing business. More than just another marketing channel or advertising medium, this new *direct model* is rapidly changing the way companies think about building relationships with customers. Whereas most companies use direct marketing and the Internet as supplemental approaches, firms employing the direct model use it as the *only* approach. Some of these companies, such as Dell Computer, Justwhiteshirts.com, Amazon.com, and eBay, began as only direct marketers. Other companies—such as Cisco Systems, Canadian Tire, IBM, and many others—are rapidly transforming themselves into direct-marketing superstars. The company that perhaps best exemplifies this new direct-marketing model is Dell Computer (see Real Marketing 17.2). Dell has built its entire approach to the marketplace around direct marketing. This direct model has proved highly successful, not just for Dell, but for the fast-growing number of other companies that employ it. Many strategists have hailed direct marketing as the marketing model of the new millennium.

Many of the marketing tools we examined in previous chapters were developed in the context of *mass marketing*—targeting broadly with standardized messages and marketing offers. Today, with the trend toward more narrowly targeted or one-to-one marketing, companies are adopting *direct marketing* as a primary marketing approach or as a supplement to other approaches. Increasingly, companies are turning to direct marketing in an effort to reach carefully targeted customers more efficiently and to build stronger, more personal, one-to-one relationships with them.

We will next examine the nature, role, and growing applications of direct marketing and its newest form—online, or Internet, marketing. We address these questions: What is direct marketing? What are its benefits to companies and their customers? How do customer databases support direct marketing? What channels do direct marketers use to reach individual prospects and customers? What marketing opportunities do online channels provide? How can companies use integrated direct marketing for competitive advantage? What public and ethical issues do direct and online marketing raise?

Benefits and Growth of Direct Marketing

Whether used as a complete business model or as a supplement to a broader integrated marketing mix, direct marketing brings many benefits to both buyers and sellers. As a result, direct marketing is growing very rapidly.

For buyers, direct marketing is convenient, easy to use, and private. From the comfort of their homes or offices, they can browse mail catalogues or company websites at any time of the day or night. Direct marketing gives buyers ready access to a wealth of products and information, at home and around the globe. Finally,

17.2 Dell: Be Direct!

When 19-year-old Michael Dell began selling personal computers from his university dorm room in 1984, competitors and industry insiders scoffed at the concept of mail-order computer marketing. PC buyers, they contended, needed the kind of advice and hand-holding that only full-service channels could provide. Yet young Michael Dell has proved the skeptics wrong. In less than two decades, he has turned his dorm-room mail-order business into a burgeoning, $40 billion computer empire.

Dell Computer is now the world's largest direct marketer of computer systems and the number one PC maker worldwide. Over the past ten years, despite the recent tech slump, Dell's sales have increased at an average rate of 40 percent, and Dell's stock has delivered a dazzling 59 percent average annual return to stockholders. Dell's stock was the number one performer of the 1990s, yielding an incredible 97 percent average annual return. In 2002, while all of Dell's competitors lost market share, Dell's share of the U.S. PC market climbed 31 percent.

The Dell Direct Model: Dell's direct-marketing approach delivers greater customer value through an unbeatable combination of product customization, low prices, fast delivery, and award-winning customer service.

Dell Canada has been fighting it out with Hewlett-Packard for the number one position in overall PC sales in Canada. As of October 2003, Dell had 20.8 percent of the total Canadian computer systems market, which includes desktop, workstation, server, and notebook sales. Not bad for a Canadian subsidiary with only 509 employees working from offices located in Halifax, Montreal, Ottawa, Toronto, and Vancouver. Lawrence Pentland, president of Dell Canada, notes, "This growth shows that Canadian businesses and consumers are embracing Dell's direct model, leading-edge technology, competitive pricing, and services and support." Direct buyers now account for nearly a third of all PC sales, and Dell's once-skeptical competitors are now scrambling to build their own direct-marketing systems. Moreover, Dell Canada has been working to solidify alliances formed with Canadian colleges and universities. Under these alliance agreements, students and employees can purchase state-of-the-art Dell branded products at prices below the standard educational price.

What's the secret to Dell's stunning success? Anyone at Dell can tell you without hesitation: It's the company's radically different business model—the *direct* model. "We have a tremendously clear business model," says Michael Dell. "There's no confusion about what the value proposition is, what the company offers, and why it's great for customers. That's a very simple thing, but it has tremendous power and appeal." An industry analyst agrees: "There's no better way to make, sell, and deliver PCs than the way Dell does it, and nobody executes that model better than Dell."

Dell's direct-marketing approach delivers greater customer value through an unbeatable combination of product customization, low prices, fast delivery, and award-winning customer service. A customer can talk by phone with a Dell representative or log on to www.dell.com on Monday morning, order a fully customized, state-of-the-art PC to suit his or her special needs, and have the machine delivered to his or her doorstep by Wednesday—all at a price that's 10 to 15 percent below competitors' prices. Dell backs its products with high-quality service and support. As a result, Dell consistently ranks among the industry leaders in product reliability and service, and its customers are routinely among the industry's most satisfied.

Dell customers receive exactly the machine they need. Michael Dell's initial idea was to serve individual buyers by allowing them to customize machines with the special features they wanted at low prices. However, this one-to-one approach also appeals strongly to corporate buyers, because Dell can easily preconfigure each computer to precise requirements. Dell routinely preloads machines with a company's own software and even undertakes such tedious tasks as pasting inventory tags on each machine so that computers can be delivered directly to an employee's desk. As a result, nearly two-thirds of Dell's sales are to large corporate, government, and educational buyers.

Direct selling results in more efficient selling and lower costs, which translate into lower prices for customers. Because Dell builds machines to order, the company carries barely any inventory, less than five days' worth by some accounts. Dealing one-to-one with customers helps the company to react immediately to shifts in demand, so Dell doesn't get stuck with PCs no one wants. Finally, by selling directly, Dell has no dealers to pay. As a result, on average, Dell's costs are 12 percent lower than those of its leading PC competitors.

Dell knows that time is money, and the company is obsessed with "speed." For example, Dell has long been a model of just-in-time manufacturing and efficient supply-chain management. Dell has also mastered the intricacies of today's lightning-fast electronic commerce. According to one account, "Dell calls it 'velocity'—squeezing time out of every step in the process—from the moment an order is taken to collecting the cash. [By selling direct, manufacturing to order, and] tapping credit cards and electronic payment, Dell converts the average sale to cash in less than 24 hours. By contrast, competitors selling through dealers might take 35 days or longer. Even mail-order rival Gateway takes 16.4 days."

Such blazing speed results in more satisfied customers and still lower costs: Customers are often delighted to find their new computers arriving within as few as 36 hours of placing an order. And because Dell doesn't order parts until an order is booked, it can take advantage of ever-falling component costs. On average, its parts are 60 days newer than those in competing machines, and hence 60 days further down the price curve. This gives Dell a 6 percent profit advantage from parts costs alone. It also gives Dell what one analyst calls a "negative cash conversion cycle." Says the analyst, "Because it keeps only five days of inventories, manages receivables to 30 days, and pushes payables out to 59 days, the Dell model will generate cash even if the company were to report no profit whatsoever."

The Internet is a perfect extension of Dell's direct marketing model. Customers who are already comfortable buying direct from Dell now have an even more powerful way to do so. Now, by simply clicking the "Buy a Dell" icon at Dell's website, customers can design and price customized computer systems electronically. Then, with a click on the "Purchase" button, they can submit an order, choosing from online payment options that include a credit card, company purchase order, or corporate lease. Dell dashes out a digital confirmation to customers within five minutes of receiving the order. After receiving confirmation, customers can check the status of the order online at any time. "The Internet," says Michael Dell, "is the ultimate direct model.... [Customers] like the immediacy, convenience, savings, and personal touches that the [Internet] experience provides. Not only are some sales done completely online, but people who call on the phone after having visited dell.ca are twice as likely to buy."

The direct-marketing pioneer now sells more than $56 million worth of computers daily from its more than 80 country-specific sites, accounting for over 50 percent of Dell's sales. Buyers range from individuals purchasing home computers to large business users buying high-end $39 000 servers. "The Internet is like a booster rocket on our sales and growth," Dell proclaims. "Our vision is to have *all* customers conduct all transactions on the Internet, globally."

As you might imagine, competitors are no longer scoffing at Michael Dell's vision of the future. In fact, competing and non-competing companies alike are studying the Dell model closely. "Somehow Dell has been able to take flexibility and speed and build it into their DNA. It's almost like drinking water," says the CEO of another Fortune 500 company, who visited recently to absorb some of the Dell magic to apply to his own company. "I'm trying to drink as much water here as I can."

It's hard to argue with success, and Dell has been very successful. By following his hunches, by the tender age of 35 he had built one of the world's hottest computer companies. In the process, he amassed a personal fortune exceeding $8 billion.

Sources: Quotes, performance statistics, and other information from Gary McWilliams, "Whirlwind on the Web," *Business Week,* April 7, 1997, pp. 132–136; "The InternetWeek Interview—Michael Dell," *InternetWeek,* April 13, 1999, p. 8; J. William Gurley, "Why Dell's World Isn't Dumb," *Fortune,* July 9, 2001, pp. 134–136; "America's 40 Richest Under 40," *Fortune,* September 17, 2001, p. 193; Andy Serwer, "Dell Does Domination," *Fortune,* January 21, 2002, pp. 71–75; Daniel Fisher, "The Best Little Factory in Texas," *Forbes,* June 10, 2002, p. 110; Dell website, www.dell.com/us/en/ gen/corporate/vision_directmodel.htm (accessed August 2002); Association of Canadian Community Colleges, "Association of Canadian Community Colleges/Dell Alliance" (news Release), August 28, 2002, www.accc.ca/english/services/Dell_ACCC_Alliance.cfm; and ICD Canada, "Canadian Market Back in the Black, According to IDC" (press release), October 30, 2003, www.idc.ca/investigate/press/pressRelease103003.html.

direct marketing is immediate and interactive—buyers can interact with sellers by phone or on the seller's website to create exactly the configuration of information, products, or services they desire, and then order them on the spot.

For sellers, direct marketing is a powerful tool for building customer relationships. Using database marketing, today's marketers can target small groups or individual consumers, tailor offers to individual needs, and promote these offers through personalized communications. Direct marketing can also be timed to reach prospects at just the right moment. Because of its one-to-one, interactive nature, the Internet is an especially potent direct-marketing tool. Direct marketing also gives sellers access to buyers that they could not reach through other channels. For example, the Internet provides access to *global* markets that might otherwise be out of reach.

Finally, direct marketing can offer sellers a low-cost, efficient alternative for reaching their markets. For example, direct marketing has grown rapidly in B2B marketing, partly in response to the ever-increasing costs of marketing through the sales force. When personal sales calls cost $220 per contact, they should be made only when necessary and to high-potential customers and prospects. Lower cost-per-contact media—such as telemarketing, direct mail, and company websites—often prove more cost-effective in reaching and selling to more prospects and customers.

As a result of these advantages to both buyers and sellers, direct marketing has become the fastest-growing form of marketing. Sales through traditional direct-marketing channels (telephone marketing, direct mail, catalogues, direct-response television, and others) have been growing rapidly. With 75 percent of Canadians (over 15 million adults) now able to access the Internet, and usage expected to reach 21.4 million by 2004, few marketers can ignore its potential. Statistics Canada reports that in 2002, 15.7 percent of the households with home Internet access used the medium to purchase goods or services. Another 26.2 percent used it for electronic banking, while 48 percent used email in 2002. Over 30 percent of Canadians access the Internet with high-speed connections. In the Conference Board of Canada's 2002 Connectedness Index, Canada ranked first among ten industrial nations for online banking, government online services, and broadband penetration. Canadian sales generated through the Internet will more than double, going from $2.3 billion in the year 2000 to $5.5 billion in 2005. While Canadian ecommerce still lags behind that in the U.S., the 2000 Canadian e-Business Roundtable meeting projected that the Canadian ebusiness sector will grow at an annual rate of 75.5 percent, with total Canadian ebusiness spending reaching $150 billion by 2004.[25]

Customer Databases and Direct Marketing

Customer database
An organized collection of comprehensive data about individual customers or prospects, including geographic, demographic, psychographic, and behavioural data.

Effective direct marketing begins with a good customer database. A **customer database** is an organized collection of comprehensive data about individual customers or prospects, including geographic, demographic, psychographic, and behavioural data. The database can be used to locate good potential customers, tailor products and services to the special needs of targeted consumers, and maintain long-term customer relationships.

Many companies confuse the customer mailing list with the customer database. A customer mailing list is simply a set of names, addresses, and telephone numbers. A customer database contains much more information. In B2B marketing, the salesperson's customer profile may contain such information as the products and services the customer has bought; past volumes and prices; key contacts (and their ages, birthdays, hobbies, and favourite foods); competitive suppliers; status of current contracts; estimated customer expenditures for the next few years; and assessments of competitive strengths and weaknesses in selling and serving the account.

In consumer marketing, the customer database may contain a customer's demographics (age, income, family members, birthdays), psychographics (activities, interests, and opinions), buying behaviour (past purchases, buying preferences), and other relevant information. Some of these databases are huge, as the following example shows:

> The Canadian Automobile Association (CAA), with its 11 geographic-based clubs, boasts 4.2 million members from almost three million Canadian households. CCA members are loyal and 92 percent annually renew their membership. The CAA is currently working to leverage this database to encourage members to buy more than mere memberships. For example, even though it has sold property, auto, travel, medical, health, dental, and life insurance since 1974, many members were unaware of these products. Furthermore, the CAA is partnering with other firms, such as Lenscrafters, who want to access the CAA database. CAA members are mailed offers from partnering firms and win in terms of being offered valuable products and services and discount prices.[26]

Armed with the information in their databases, these companies can identify small groups of customers to receive fine-tuned marketing offers and communications. Kraft Foods has amassed a list of more than 30 million users of its products who have responded to coupons or other Kraft promotions. Based on their interests, the company sends these customers tips on issues such as nutrition and exercise, as well as recipes and coupons for specific Kraft brands. FedEx uses its sophisticated database to create 100 highly targeted, customized direct-mail and telemarketing campaigns each year to its nearly 5 million customers, shipping to 212 countries. By analyzing customers carefully and reaching the right customers at the right time with the right promotions, FedEx achieves response rates of 20 to 25 percent and earns an 8-to-1 return on its direct-marketing dollars.[27]

The Royal Canadian Mint recently used a multi-pronged effort to reposition the mint and reach Canadian coin collectors:

> The Royal Canadian Mint was viewed as a stodgy institution that wasn't exactly top of mind among Canadian youth. Today, it's worked to turn its image around. It ran a contest encouraging young Canadians to design a unique coin, using a television spot to reach this target audience. For the first time, the Mint used two animated characters, a caribou and a beaver, as its spokescharacters. The ad was designed to help reposition the Mint in the minds of youth and encourage them to enter the contest. Ads ran on the Family Channel and French-language station VRAC TV. Louise de Jourdan, director of marketing at the Mint in Ottawa, says, "For the past few years, we have been shaking off our dusty image. This campaign is fun, and again part of the whole youth-oriented approach." Ten-year-old Judith Chartier of Îles-de-la Madelaine, Quebec, won the contest. The Mint then used names and addresses from its catalogue database in a direct mail campaign that publicized the coin launch to over 300 000 collectors.[28]

Companies use their databases in many ways. They can use a database to identify prospects and generate sales leads by advertising products or offers. Or they can use the database to profile customers based on previous purchasing and to decide which customers should receive particular offers. Databases can help the company to deepen customer loyalty—companies can build customers' interest and enthusiasm by remembering buyer preferences and by sending appropriate information, gifts, or other materials:

> Mars, a market leader in pet food as well as candy, maintains an exhaustive pet database. In Germany, the company has compiled the names of virtually every German family that owns a cat. It has obtained these names by contacting veterinarians, via its mypetstop.com website, and by offering the public a free booklet titled *How to Take Care of Your Cat*. People who request the booklet fill out a questionnaire, providing their cat's name, age, birthday, and other

In Germany, Mars has compiled a database containing information on virtually every German family that owns a cat. To build lasting relationships with cat owners, it sends a birthday card to each cat in Germany each year, along with samples and coupons.

information. Mars then sends a birthday card to each cat in Germany each year, along with a cat food sample and money-saving coupons for Mars brands. The result is a lasting relationship with the cat's owner.

The database can help a company make attractive offers of product replacements, upgrades, or complementary products, just when customers might be ready to act. For example, a General Electric appliance customer database contains each customer's demographic and psychographic characteristics along with an appliance-purchasing history. Using this database, GE marketers assess how long specific customers have owned their current appliances and which past customers might be ready to purchase again. They can determine which customers need a new GE range, refrigerator, clothes washer, or something else to go with other recently purchased products. Or they can identify the best past GE purchasers and send them gift certificates or other promotions to apply against their next GE purchases. A rich customer database allows GE to build profitable new business by locating good prospects, anticipating customer needs, cross-selling products and services, and rewarding loyal customers.

Like many other marketing tools, database marketing requires a special investment. Companies must invest in computer hardware, database software, analytical programs, communication links, and skilled personnel. The database system must be user-friendly and available to various marketing groups, including those in product and brand management, new-product development, advertising and promotion, direct mail, telemarketing, Web marketing, field sales, order fulfillment, and customer service. A well-managed database should lead to sales gains that will more than cover its costs.

Forms of Direct-Marketing Communications

The major forms of direct marketing—shown in Figure 17.4—include *personal selling, telephone marketing, direct-mail marketing, catalogue marketing, direct-*

Figure 17.4 Forms of direct marketing

response television marketing, kiosk marketing, and *online marketing.* We examined personal selling in depth earlier in this chapter and looked closely at online marketing in Chapter 3. Here, we examine the other direct-marketing forms.

Telephone Marketing

Telephone marketing—using the telephone to sell directly to consumers—has become the major direct-marketing communications tool. Telephone marketing now accounts for over 38 percent of all direct-marketing media expenditures and 36 percent of direct-marketing sales. We're all familiar with telemarketing directed toward consumers, but B2B marketers also use telemarketing extensively, accounting for 58 percent of all telephone marketing sales.[29]

Marketers use *outbound* telephone marketing to sell directly to consumers and businesses. *Inbound* toll-free numbers are used to receive orders from television and radio ads, direct mail, or catalogues. The use of toll-free numbers has taken off in recent years as more companies have begun using them and as current users have added new features such as toll-free fax numbers. Residential use has also grown. To accommodate this rapid growth, the original toll-free 800 code has been augmented with new toll-free area codes (888, 877, 866). After the 800 area code was established in 1967, it took almost 30 years before its 8 million numbers were used up. In contrast, 888 area code numbers, established in 1996, were used up in only two years.[30]

Properly designed and targeted telemarketing provides many benefits, including purchasing convenience and increased product and service information. However, the recent explosion in unsolicited telephone marketing has annoyed many people who object to the almost daily "junk phone calls" that pull them away from the dinner table or fill their answering machines. To help overcome this problem, "Do not call" lists are maintained by the Canadian Direct Marketing Association. As one marketing executive notes, "We want to target people who want to be targeted."

Direct-Mail Marketing

Direct-mail marketing involves sending an offer, announcement, reminder, or other item to a person at a particular address. Using highly selective mailing lists, direct marketers send out millions of mail pieces each year—letters, ads, brochures, samples, video- and audiotapes, CDs, and other "salespeople with wings." Direct mail accounts for more than 23 percent of all direct-marketing media expenditures and 31 percent of direct-marketing sales. Together, telemarketing and direct-mail marketing account for more than 60 percent of direct-marketing expenditures and 66 percent of direct-marketing sales.[31]

Direct mail is well suited to direct one-to-one communication. It permits high target market selectivity, can be personalized, is flexible, and allows easy measurement of results. Whereas the cost per thousand people reached is higher than with mass media such as television or magazines, the people who are reached are much better prospects. Direct mail has proven successful in promoting all kinds of products, from books, magazine subscriptions, and insurance to gift items, clothing, gourmet foods, and industrial products. Direct mail is also used heavily by charities, which use it to raise billions of dollars each year:

> Toronto-based Foster Parents Plan of Canada (FPP) recently began combining market and database research. By matching survey research conducted by Market Facts to its in-house database, the not-for-profit organization has been able to better understand foster parents' commitment levels. "The early indications are that it's being quite predictive of whether or not a foster parent will continue their support or leave," says one researcher. "It gives them a chance not only to look ahead and see what kind of risk they face, but also to try and take actions that will build and retain the support of a foster parent."[32]

The direct-mail industry always seeks new methods and approaches. Until recently, all mail was paper-based and handled by Canada Post, telegraphic services, or for-profit mail carriers such as Purolator, Federal Express, DHL, or Airborne Express. Recently, however, three new forms of mail delivery have become popular:

- *Fax mail*. Marketers now routinely send fax mail announcing offers, sales, and other events to prospects and customers with fax machines. Fax mail messages can be sent and received almost instantaneously. However, some prospects and customers resent receiving unsolicited fax mail, which clutters their machines and consumes their paper.

- *Email*. Many marketers now send sales announcements, offers, product information, and other messages to email addresses—sometimes to a few individuals, sometimes to large groups. As discussed in Chapter 3, today's email messages have moved far beyond the drab text-only messages of old. The new breed of email ad uses glitzy features such as animation, interactive links, streaming video, and personalized audio messages to reach out and grab attention. However, as people receive more and more email, they resent the intrusion of unrequested messages. Smart marketers are using permission-based programs, sending email ads only to those who want to receive them.

- *Voice mail*. Some marketers have set up automated programs that exclusively target voice-mail mailboxes and answering machines with prerecorded messages. These systems target homes between 10 a.m. and 4 p.m. and businesses between 7 p.m. and 9 p.m., when people are least likely to answer. If the automated dialer hears a live voice, it disconnects. Such systems thwart hang-ups by annoyed potential customers. However, they can also create substantial ill will.

These new forms deliver direct mail at incredible speeds, compared to the post office's "snail mail" pace. Yet, much like mail delivered through traditional channels, they may be resented as junk mail if sent to people who have no interest in them. For this reason, marketers must carefully identify appropriate targets so they don't waste their money and the recipients' time.

Catalogue marketing
Direct marketing through print, video, or electronic catalogues that are mailed to select customers, made available in stores, or presented online.

Catalogue Marketing

Advances in technology, along with the move toward personalized, one-to-one marketing, have resulted in dramatic changes in **catalogue marketing**. *Catalog Age*

Toronto-based N5R helps its global clients leverage their databases to build customer loyalty and run effective email direct-marketing campaigns.

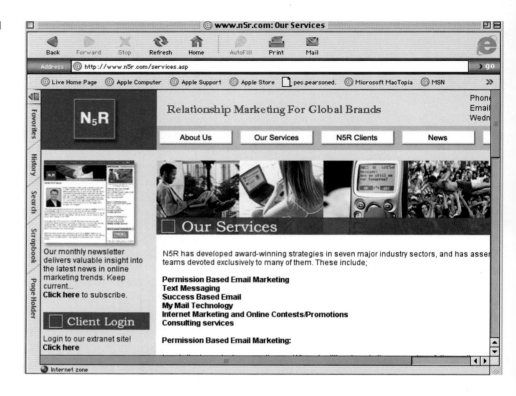

magazine used to define a *catalogue* as "a printed, bound piece of at least eight pages, selling multiple products, and offering a direct ordering mechanism." Today, only a few years later, this definition is sadly out of date. With the stampede to the Internet, more and more catalogues are going electronic. Many traditional print cataloguers have added Web-based catalogues to their marketing mixes, and a variety of new Web-only cataloguers have emerged. However, the Internet has not yet killed off printed catalogues—far from it. Web catalogues currently generate only about 13 percent of all catalogue sales. Printed catalogues remain the primary medium, and many former Web-only companies have created printed catalogues to expand their business.[33]

Catalogue marketing has grown explosively in the past 25 years. Annual catalogue sales in North America (both print and electronic) are expected to grow from a current \$90 billion to more than \$200 billion by 2006.[34] Some huge general merchandise retailers, including Sears and Canadian Tire, sell a full line of merchandise through catalogues. In recent years, the giants have been challenged by thousands of specialty catalogues that serve highly specialized market niches. According to one study, some 10 000 companies now produce 14 000 unique catalogue titles in the United States alone.[35]

Consumers can buy just about anything from a catalogue. IKEA Canada can help you furnish almost any living space with style and Harry Rosen can dress you for any occasion. Sears Canada features print and online catalogues. While some customers get Sears' print catalogue for free, others buy it on newsstands for \$6. Tilley Endurables, Mountain Equipment Co-op, and the Banana Republic Travel and Safari Clothing Company feature everything you would need to go hiking in the Sahara or the rain forest. Some larger retailers are taking on these specialty retailers with their own niche catalogues. Zellers, for example, recently launched its new *Special Delivery Baby* catalogue and online baby-gift registry, and targets "tweens" with its *Gen Z* catalogue.

Specialty department stores, such as Holt Renfrew, William Ashley China, and Neiman Marcus, use catalogues to cultivate upper-middle-class markets for high-priced, often exotic, merchandise. Several major corporations have also developed

IKEA's catalogue is a powerful selling tool that lures consumers into its stores. It is laid out as carefully as the retail outlets themselves.

or acquired catalogue divisions. Avon now issues ten women's fashion catalogues along with catalogues for children's and men's clothes. Walt Disney Company mails out over 6 million catalogues each year, featuring videos, stuffed animals, and other Disney items.

More than 90 percent of all catalogue companies now present merchandise and take orders over the Internet. For example, the successful marriage of Sears' old-style catalogue with its new-style website generated over $100 million in revenues in 2000, making it one of the most successful etail sites in Canada.[36] Sears' success is partly due to its ability to leverage the skills and infrastructure developed with its traditional catalogue. Canadian Tire and Mountain Equipment Co-op are examples of other retailers who have integrated their online and paper-based catalogues. Still others, like Nike Canada, are totally replacing their print catalogues with virtual versions:

> Every spring Nike Canada mailed catalogues to fitness instructors, offering them the latest aerobic gear at discount prices in the hope they would buy the merchandise and inspire their students to do the same. However, because only limited numbers of catalogues were produced, they were very expensive to print and distribute. CyberSight Canada, an Internet marketing services firm, offered a solution to the problem: it created a website that would serve as a virtual catalogue (www.nikeinp.ca). Members of the Instructor Network are mailed passwords to gain access to the site. Says Julia Maughan, national sports marketing co-ordinator for Nike Canada in Toronto, "Our objectives were to simplify the ordering process, reduce the cost of the catalogue, and increase the number of orders from instructors." The effort has been a huge success. Online orders exceeded those generated by the print catalogue, surpassing the company's expectations for its new digital program.[37]

Along with the benefits, Web-based catalogues present challenges. Whereas a print catalogue is intrusive and creates its own attention, Web catalogues are passive and must be marketed. "Attracting new customers is much more difficult to do with a Web catalogue," says an industry consultant. "You have to use advertising, linkage, and other means to drive traffic to it." Kevin Bartus, president of Blue*Spark, a Toronto-based Web development firm, says, "Retailers are learning an online business is not, in most cases, big enough to support a complete business offering. Retailers are turning to a tri-channel: bricks and mortar, catalogue, and Web."[38] Take the case of La Senza, the Montreal-based lingerie retailer. It first launched a website featuring a separate line of merchandise to avoid cannibalizing store sales, but finally had to relaunch the site as an arm of its existing business. To further integrate, customers can return items bought online in stores and sign up for the email club there as well. Thus, even cataloguers who are sold on the Web are not likely to abandon their print catalogues completely.

Direct-Response Television Marketing

Direct-response television marketing takes one of two major forms. The first is *direct-response advertising*. Direct marketers air commercials, often 60 or 120 seconds long, that persuasively describe a product and give customers a toll-free number for ordering. Television viewers also encounter 30-minute advertising programs, or *infomercials*, for a single product.

Some successful direct-response ads run for years and become classics. For example, Dial Media's ads for Ginsu knives ran for seven years and sold almost 3 million sets of knives, worth more than $50 million in sales. And its Armourcote cookware ads generated more than twice that much. Over the past 40 years, infomercial czar Ron Popeil's Ronco company has sold more than $1.3 billion worth of TV-marketed gadgets, including the original Veg-O-Matic, the Pocket Fisherman, Mr. Microphone, the Giant Food Dehydrator and Beef Jerky Machine, and the Showtime Rotisserie & BBQ.[39] But the current infomercial champ is a true heavyweight:

> It's three o'clock in the morning. Plagued with insomnia, you grab the remote and flip around until a grinning blonde in an apron catches your attention: "I'm going to show you something you won't believe! Juicy meals in minutes! Something else you won't believe...George Foreman!" The studio roars, and boxing's elder statesman, in a red apron, shows off his Lean Mean Fat-Reducing Grilling Machine and highlights the grease caught in the pan below. "Eew!" the audience screams. It can be yours for three easy payments of $19.95 (plus shipping and handling). Don't laugh. Such infomercials helped the Foreman grills product line notch almost $525 million in sales in 2002.[40]

For years, infomercials have been associated with somewhat questionable pitches for juicers, get-rich-quick schemes, and nifty ways to stay in shape without working very hard at it. In recent years, however, a number of large companies—GTE, Johnson & Johnson, MCA Universal, Sears, Procter & Gamble, Revlon, IBM, Cadillac, Volvo, Land Rover, Anheuser-Busch, and others—have begun using infomercials to sell their wares over the phone, refer customers to retailers, send out coupons and product information, or attract buyers to their websites. Direct-response TV commercials are usually cheaper to make and the media purchase is less costly. Moreover, results are easily measured. "Unlike branding campaigns, direct-response ads always include a 1-800 number or Web address, making it easier for marketers to gauge whether consumers are paying attention to their pitches," says an industry analyst.[41]

Home shopping channels, another form of direct-response television marketing, are television programs or entire channels dedicated to selling goods and services. Some home shopping channels, such as The Shopping Channel (tSc), broadcast 24 hours a day. The program's hosts offer bargain prices on such products as jewellery, lamps, collectible dolls, clothing, power tools, and consumer electronics—usually obtained by the home shopping channel at closeout prices.

The current infomercial champ? Direct-response TV ads helped George Foreman's Lean Mean Fat-Reducing Grilling Machines notch $525 million in sales.

 The Shopping Channel's savvy customer-centred marketers didn't take long to add the Web to their marketing mix. Long accustomed to providing consumers with the convenience of shopping at any time, day or night, in the medium of their choice, tSc launched its website in May 1999 (www.theshoppingchannel.com). The tSc website presents browsers with a full selection of products, spanning nine product categories—jewellery, health and beauty, fashions, fitness, at home, electronics, toys, crafts, and collectibles. The site has enabled the television retailer to break free of the limitations inherent in using TV, which can focus on only one product at a time. While TV did not allow shoppers to browse through the channel's full offerings, tSc's online customers can now have access to a full assortment of products at any time without having to wait for information to pop up on the TV show. The Shopping Channel's best customers, those with higher income and education, have naturally gravitated to the website, but, more importantly, the site has attracted a significant number of new customers. Moreover, the average order value is 27 percent higher than that of television-only users. View and click obviously makes a dynamic marketing option.[42]

Kiosk Marketing

Some companies place information and ordering machines—called *kiosks* (in contrast to vending machines, which dispense actual products)—in stores, airports, and other locations. Hallmark uses kiosks to help customers create personalized cards. Toyota Canada uses kiosks to target younger buyers. The Liquor Control Board of Ontario installed interactive kiosks to run advertisements for featured products and to enhance customer service. IKEA Canada allows UNICEF to set up fundraising kiosks in its stores. Queen's University's School of Business even uses kiosks to promote its three MBA programs.

Business marketers also use kiosks. Investment Canada placed a kiosk at an Atlanta trade show to introduce Canadian telecommunication and computer products to international buyers. Dow Plastics places kiosks at trade shows to collect sales leads and to provide information on its 700 products. Dow's kiosk system reads customer data from encoded registration badges and produces technical data sheets, which can be printed at the kiosk or faxed or mailed to the customer. The system has resulted in a 400-percent increase in qualified sales leads.[43]

Integrated Direct Marketing

Too often, a company's individual direct-marketing efforts are not well integrated with one another or with other elements of the marketing and promotion mixes. For example, a firm's media advertising may be handled by the advertising department working with a traditional advertising agency. Meanwhile, its direct-mail and catalogue business efforts may be handled by direct-marketing specialists, while its website is developed and operated by an outside Internet firm. Even within a direct-marketing campaign, too many companies use only a "one-shot" effort to reach and sell a prospect or a single vehicle in multiple stages to trigger purchases.

> **Integrated direct marketing**
> Direct-marketing campaigns that use multiple vehicles and multiple stages to improve response rates and profits.

A more powerful approach is **integrated direct-marketing**, which involves carefully coordinated multiple-media, multiple-stage campaigns. Such campaigns can greatly improve response. Whereas a direct-mail piece alone may generate a 2 percent response, adding a website and toll-free phone number may raise the response rate by 50 percent. Then, a well-designed outbound telemarketing effort may lift response by an additional 500 percent. Suddenly, a 2 percent response has grown to 15 percent or more by adding interactive marketing channels to a regular mailing.

More elaborate integrated direct-marketing campaigns can be used. Consider the multimedia, multistage campaign shown in Figure 17.5. Here, the paid ad creates product awareness and stimulates inquiries. The company immediately sends direct mail to those who inquire. Within a few days, the company follows up with a phone call seeking an order. Some prospects will order by phone or the company's website; others may request a face-to-face sales call. In such a campaign, the marketer seeks to improve response rates and profits by adding media and stages that contribute more to additional sales than to additional costs.

Public Policy and Ethical Issues in Direct-Marketing

Direct-marketers and their customers usually enjoy mutually rewarding relationships. Occasionally, however, a darker side emerges. The aggressive and sometimes shady tactics of a few direct marketers bother or harm consumers, casting a shadow over the entire industry. Abuses range from simple excesses that irritate consumers to instances of unfair practices or even outright deception and fraud. The direct-marketing industry also has faced growing concerns about invasion of privacy issues.

Irritation, Unfairness, Deception, and Fraud

Direct-marketing excesses sometimes annoy or offend consumers. Most of us dislike direct-response TV commercials that are too loud, too long, and too insistent. Especially bothersome are dinnertime or late-night phone calls. Beyond irritating

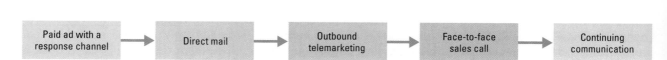

Figure 17.5   An integrated direct-marketing campaign

consumers, some direct marketers have been accused of taking unfair advantage of impulsive or less-sophisticated buyers. Television shopping shows and program-long "infomercials" seem to be the worst culprits. They feature smooth-talking hosts, elaborately staged demonstrations, claims of drastic price reductions, "while they last" time limitations, and unequalled ease of purchase to inflame buyers who have low sales resistance.

Worse yet, so-called "heat merchants" design mailers and write copy intended to mislead buyers. Even well-known direct mailers have been accused of deceiving consumers. Sweepstakes promoter Publishers Clearing House recently paid $68 million to settle accusations that its high-pressure mailings confused or misled consumers, especially the elderly, into believing that they had won prizes or would win if they bought the company's magazines.[44]

Direct-marketing fraud is not restricted by national boundaries. Consumers allegedly defrauded by a Montreal-based telemarketer will receive more than $140 000 in consumer redress under the terms of a court settlement negotiated by the U.S. Federal Trade Commission. According to the FTC, the defendants cold-called tens of thousands of American consumers in an attempt to sell them bogus identity-theft protection services and supposed advance-fee, low-interest credit cards. The order also bars the telemarketer for life from all marketing of credit-related goods or services and protection services.[45]

A few direct marketers pretend to be conducting research surveys when they are actually asking leading questions to screen or persuade consumers. Fraudulent schemes, such as investment scams or phony collections for charity, have also multiplied in recent years. Crooked direct marketers can be hard to catch. By the time buyers realize that they have been bilked, the thieves are usually somewhere else plotting new schemes.

Many consumers and businesspeople alike have had their email boxes stuffed with unsolicited commercial offers. Such so-called "spam" is costing businesses and consumers both time and money. Canadian consumers can now sign up for a free service to reduce the amount of unsolicited commercial email they receive. The Canadian Marketing Association (CMA), in cooperation with the Direct Marketing Association in the U.S. and other international direct-marketing associations, has introduced a Web-based email preference service (e-mps). Consumers who want to stop or at least reduce the spam can register at www.e-mps.org.[46] This logo is your assurance you are dealing with a member of the Canadian Marketing Association, and can be confident that they are committed to honesty and integrity in all their interactions with customers. CMA members must comply with the Association's mandatory Code of Ethics and Standards of Practice and may display the CMA member logo as a symbol of commitment to:

When you see the Canadian Marketing Association logo on a catalogue, Internet site, or piece of direct mail, you can be assured they will respect your privacy and no-call/mail instructions.

- respect and protect your privacy
- make customer service a priority
- participate in CMA's Operation Integrity, a consumer complaint resolution program
- participate in the CMA Do Not Contact Program

Invasion of Privacy

Invasion of privacy is perhaps the toughest public policy issue now confronting the direct-marketing industry. These days, it seems that almost every time consumers enter a sweepstakes, apply for a credit card, take out a magazine subscription, or order products by mail, telephone, or the Internet, their names are entered into some company's already-bulging database. Using sophisticated computer technologies, direct marketers can use these databases to "micro-target" their selling efforts.

Consumers often benefit from such database marketing—they receive more offers that are closely matched to their interests. However, many critics worry that marketers may know *too* much about consumers' lives, and that they may use this knowledge to take unfair advantage of consumers. At some point, they claim, the extensive use of databases intrudes on consumer privacy.[47]

Access to and use of information has caused much concern and debate among companies, consumers, and public policy makers. Governments around the world have been exploring the question of whether to institute privacy legislation. The first major step was taken by the European Union. In 1995, it issued a directive on the protection of personal data, which provides a framework for collecting and processing personal data.

Predictably, the U.S. and Canada have responded to the whole privacy issue differently. While the U.S. opted for industry self-regulation, Canadian governments believed more controls were needed. Until recently, Quebec was the only province with legislation dealing with the privacy of personal information, but on January 1, 2001, the *Personal Information Protection and Electronic Documents Act* came into effect. The privacy act governs all federally regulated industries and businesses that operate interprovincially. It uses a number of guiding principles to protect consumers and control how firms gather and use their personal information:

- *Consumer consent.* Knowledge and consent must be obtained from consumers before a firm can collect, use, or disclose consumers' personal information.

- *Limitations.* A firm may collect only the information appropriate for the purposes for which it is being gathered. For example, if it needs to mail you something, the firm can ask for your home mailing address, but not any additional, unnecessary information beyond what it needs to address the mailing. Furthermore, a firm may use the information only for the purpose for which it was gathered. To make additional use of the information, it must get permission from the individual. Finally, a firm may not transfer the information to a third party without the permission of the individual.

- *Accuracy.* A firm must ensure that the information it gathers is recorded accurately, and it must appoint an employee to be responsible for this. For example, to comply with this portion of the legislation, Peter Cullen was recently designated as the new corporate privacy officer at the Royal Bank of Canada.

- *Right to access.* Individuals have the right to know what information is being held about them. They can also demand that errors in their personal information be rectified and may request that their personal information be withdrawn from a firm's database.

For full details about the *Personal Information Protection and Electronic Documents Act*, visit the Privacy Commissioner of Canada website at www.privcom. gc.ca/.

Most direct marketers want the same things that consumers want: honest and well-designed marketing offers targeted only toward consumers who will appreciate and respond to them. Direct marketing is just too expensive to waste on consumers who don't want it.

Looking Back: Reviewing the Concepts

Personal selling and direct marketing are both direct tools for communicating with and persuading current and prospective customers. Selling is the interpersonal arm of the communications mix. To be successful in personal selling, a company must first build and then manage an effective sales force. Firms must also be good at direct marketing, the process of forming one-to-one connections with customers. Today, many companies are turning to direct marketing in an effort to reach carefully targeted customers more efficiently and to build stronger, more personal, one-to-one relationships with them.

1. Discuss the role of a company's salespeople in creating value for customers and building customer relationships.

Most companies use salespeople, and many companies assign them an important role in the marketing mix. For companies selling business products, the firm's salespeople work directly with customers. Often, the sales force is the customer's only direct contact with the company and therefore may be viewed by customers as representing the company itself. In contrast, for consumer product companies that sell through intermediaries, consumers usually do not meet salespeople or even know about them. The sales force works behind the scenes, dealing with wholesalers and retailers to obtain their support and helping them become effective in selling the firm's products.

As an element of the promotion mix, the sales force is very effective in achieving certain marketing objectives and carrying out such activities as prospecting, communicating, selling and servicing, and information gathering. But with companies becoming more market oriented, a market-focused sales force also works to produce both *customer satisfaction* and *company profit.* To accomplish these goals, the sales force needs skills in marketing analysis and planning in addition to the traditional selling skills.

2. Identify and explain the six major sales force management steps.

High sales force costs necessitate an effective *sales management process* consisting of six steps: *designing sales force strategy and structure, recruiting and selecting, training, compensating, supervising,* and *evaluating* salespeople.

In designing a sales force, sales management must address issues such as what type of sales force structure will work best (territorial, product, customer, or complex structure), how large the sales force should be, who will be involved in the selling effort, and how its various sales and sales support people will work together (inside or outside sales forces and team selling).

To hold down the high costs of hiring the wrong people, salespeople must be *recruited* and *selected* carefully. In recruiting salespeople, a company may look to job duties and the characteristics of its most successful salespeople to suggest the traits it wants in its salespeople and then look for applicants through recommendations of current salespeople, employment agencies, classified ads, and the Internet and by contacting college students. In the selection process, the procedure can vary from a single informal interview to lengthy testing and interviewing. After the selection process is complete, *training* programs familiarize new salespeople not only with the art of selling but also with the company's history, its products and policies, and the characteristics of its market and competitors.

The sales force *compensation* system helps to reward, motivate, and direct salespeople. In compensating salespeople, companies try to have an appealing plan, usually close to the going rate for the type of sales job and needed skills. In addition to compensation, all salespeople need *supervision,* and many need continuous encouragement because they must make many decisions and face many frustrations. Periodically, the company must *evaluate* their performance to help them do a better job. In evaluating salespeople, the company relies on getting regular information gathered through sales reports, call reports, expense reports, customer surveys, and conversations with other salespeople.

3. **Discuss the personal selling process, distinguishing between transaction-oriented marketing and relationship marketing.**

The art of selling involves a seven-step selling process: prospecting and qualifying, preapproach, approach, presentation and demonstration, handling objections, closing, and follow-up. These steps help marketers close a specific sale and as such are transaction oriented. However, a seller's dealings with customers should be guided by the larger concept of relationship marketing. The company's sales force should help to orchestrate a whole-company effort to develop profitable long-term relationships with key customers based on superior customer value and satisfaction.

4. **Define *direct marketing* and discuss its benefits to customers and companies.**

Direct marketing consists of direct connections with carefully targeted individual consumers to both obtain an immediate response and cultivate lasting customer relationships. Using detailed databases, direct marketers tailor their offers and communications to the needs of narrowly defined segments or even individual buyers.

For buyers, direct marketing is convenient, easy to use, and private. It gives them ready access to a wealth of products and information, at home and around the globe. Direct marketing is also immediate and interactive, allowing buyers to create exactly the configuration of information, products, or services they desire, and then order them on the spot. For sellers, direct marketing is a powerful tool for building customer relationships. Using database marketing, today's marketers can target small groups or individual consumers, tailor offers to individual needs, and promote these offers through personalized communications. It also offers them a low-cost, efficient alternative for reaching their markets. As a result of these advantages to both buyers and sellers, direct marketing has become the fastest growing form of marketing.

5. **Identify and discuss the major forms of direct marketing.**

The main forms of direct marketing include *personal selling, telephone marketing, direct-mail marketing, catalogue marketing, direct-response television marketing, kiosk marketing,* and *online marketing.* We discuss personal selling in the first part of this chapter and examined online marketing in detail in Chapter 3. *Telephone marketing* consists of using the telephone to sell directly to consumers. *Direct-mail marketing* consists of the company sending an offer, announcement, reminder, or other item to a person at a specific address. Recently, three new forms of mail delivery have become popular—*fax mail, email,* and *voice mail.* Some marketers rely on *catalogue marketing,* or selling through catalogues mailed to a select list of customers or made available in stores. *Direct-response television marketing* has two forms: *direct-response advertising* and *home shopping channels. Kiosks* are information and ordering machines that direct marketers place in stores, airports, and other locations. *Online marketing,* discussed in Chapter 3, involves online channels and ecommerce, which electronically link consumers with sellers.

Reviewing the Key Terms

Discussing the Concepts

1. What did Robert Louis Stevenson mean when he said that "everyone lives by selling something"? Describe the various roles the modern salesperson plays.

2. The term *salesperson* covers a wide range of positions. List and briefly describe those positions and provide an example of each. State your career ambition. How might you be involved in selling?

3. One of the most pressing issues that sales managers face is how to structure the sales force and their tasks. Evaluate the methods described in the text. For each method, provide (a) a brief description of its chief characteristics, (b) an example of how it's used, and (c) a critique of its effectiveness.

4. What is team selling, and what are its advantages and disadvantages? How would recruiting and training for a sales team differ from recruiting and training for individual selling?

5. Many people think that they do not have the attributes and abilities required for successful selling. What role does training play in helping a person develop selling skills?

6. List and briefly describe the steps in the personal selling process. Which step do you think is the most difficult for the average salesperson? Which step is the most critical to successful selling? Which step do you think is usually done most correctly? Explain each of your choices.

7. The chapter suggests that a new direct-marketing model has been created. What is direct marketing? How does it differ from other forms of marketing? How will the new direct-marketing model affect the emerging electronic marketplace?

8. List and briefly describe each of the major forms of direct marketing. Pick one of the following companies and demonstrate how it could use each form of direct marketing to sell its products and services: (a) Microsoft, (b) General Motors, or (c) the Gap.

Applying the Concepts

1. Being a stockbroker can be an exciting and challenging occupation. In years past, broker trainees received extensive training on the technical workings of the stock market and the characteristics of potential clients. One of the most difficult tasks for new brokers was finding and developing clients. This involved long and often discouraging hours of telephone "prospecting" and "cold-calling" potential clients. Today, however, things are changing. The rapid expansion of investment and information alternatives has made a broker's job more challenging. Most major investment brokerages are now online and brokers can help information-hungry investors in ways that would have been unimaginable only a few years ago. A 2002 ranking of Internet Brokers Scorecard by GomezCanada ranked them in the following order: (1) BMO InvestorLine, (2) TD Waterhouse, (3) E*TRADE, (4) Qtrade Investor, (5) ScotiaMcLeod Direct, (6) CIBC Investor's Edge, (7) Royal Bank Action Direct, (8) Merrill Lynch HSBC, (9) National Bank Invesnet, and (10) Credential Direct. Visit several of these websites.

    a. Which website is the most "user friendly"? Why? Which of the sites makes it easy to get in touch with a broker in your local area? How could a broker in your local area find out that you had been using his or her company's online service?

    b. Prepare an analysis grid that compares the above sites on sales stimulation, information services, cost, graphic design, responsiveness, security, and relationship marketing. Which site is best? Why?

    c. How have such sites changed the brokerage business? How is the selling function in the brokerage business changing?

2. Jonathan Ellermann is excited about his new job as a personal communication consultant for Nokia (www.nokia.com), the giant phone producer that captures a quarter of the global market. Rivals such as Ericsson (www.ericsson.com), Vodafone (www.vodaphone.com), Panasonic (www.panasonic.com), and Motorola (www.motorola.com) have vowed to make things much tougher for Nokia in the coming year. They have developed new designs, communications applications, and strategic alliances between hardware and software makers in an effort to lure fickle consumers away from Nokia.

    a. Ellermann is seeking to sell Nokia's latest-model personal communication device to Shell Oil's Houston branch (approximately 5000 phones). What sales strategy should Ellermann recommend to Nokia? In your answer, consider the advantages and disadvantages of Nokia's product.

    b. Would you recommend that Nokia employ individual selling or team selling? Explain.

    c. Which step of the sales process do you think will be most critical to Ellermann's success?

    d. What could Ellermann do to establish a strong relationship with local Shell representatives?

Company Case

Jefferson-Pilot Financial: Growing the Sales Force

After the Meeting

On a hot Friday afternoon in July 2002, Bob Powell and John Knowles walked across a parking lot toward Bob's car. They had just finished a two-day strategic planning meeting with other members of Jefferson-Pilot Financial's (JPF) Independent Marketing channel at the Grandover Resort and Conference Hotel just outside Greensboro, North Carolina. The group had gathered to develop the sales goals it wanted to achieve by the end of 2005, to identify strategic projects it needed to accomplish to meet those goals, and to assign responsibility for each project.

"Wow, it's going to be hot in your car," John noted. John served as vice-president for Independent Marketing and Bob was senior vice-president.

"Especially after sitting in that air-conditioned room for two days," Bob responded. "But I'm glad we're riding together. This'll give us a few minutes to talk about the sales force strategy project the group assigned us."

Jefferson-Pilot Financial

Jefferson-Pilot Corporation (JP), a holding company, was one of the U.S.'s largest shareholder-owned life insurance companies. Jefferson-Pilot's life insurance and annuity businesses, known collectively as Jefferson-Pilot Financial, included Jefferson-Pilot Life Insurance Company, Jefferson-Pilot Financial Insurance Company, and Jefferson-Pilot Life America Insurance Company. JPF offered full lines of individual and group life insurance products as well as annuity and investment products. Jefferson-Pilot Communications Company, which operated three network television stations and 17 radio stations, produced and syndicated sports programming.

In 2001, the company amassed US$3.33 billion in revenues and US$513 million in net income. JP's

insurance and investment products produced about 84 percent of its net income. JP took pride in its excellent financial ratings, having earned the highest possible financial ratings from A.M. Best, Standard and Poors, and Fitch.

Historically, the company generated its individual life insurance sales using a career sales force. The company employed managers to recruit and train life insurance agents, paying the managers commissions based on the insurance premiums their agents generated and an expense allowance to cover their overhead costs. The agents became "captive" Jefferson-Pilot employees who sold *only* JP's policies.

Like most life insurance companies, the company paid agents on a commission-only basis. The agent earned a commission of 50 percent of the *first-year* premium paid by the policyholder plus the potential for up to 20 percent more based on achieving certain annual premium sales goals. In the following years, the agent earned a much lower commission on annual renewal premiums, usually in the range of 3 percent. In addition to paying commission, the company provided the career agents with a full range of fringe benefits, such as health insurance, vacation, and sick leave. The individual agent had to pay his or her own business expenses.

A New Strategy

In 1993, JP was a conservative, well-run company. However, the board of directors wanted the company to grow more rapidly. The board brought in a new top-management team and charged the team with speeding up the company's growth. The new team immediately examined the company's sales force strategy. It concluded that although the career sales force had been a valuable asset, the company was not capable of meeting its growth goals using only a career force. It simply took too long to hire and train new agents and bring them up to the necessary productivity levels. Further, industry-wide, only about one of every seven or eight recruits actually succeeded in the insurance business.

In addition to career agents, JPF had used some independent agents all along. Independent agents worked for themselves or for independent companies. They, like captive agents, sold life insurance, but they could sell policies offered by a variety of companies. JPF decided to expand it sales force by focusing on the independent agents. It began to recruit these established, experienced independent salespeople, licensing them to sell JPF's policies and encouraging them to do so. Because the agents remained independent, JPF did not have to provide them with typical employee benefits. However, because the independent agents still had to cover these expenses, the company had to pay a higher percentage of first-year premiums, usually about 85 percent. The average first-year premium in the independent channel was about US$5000. Because there were independent agents located throughout the United States, the company was able to expand more rapidly outside of its traditional southeastern market area and have agents offering its policies nationwide.

The new focus was extremely successful, and by 1999, the independent channels had become JPF's primary distribution channel, although the company still retained its career agents. In 1999, JPF hired Bob Powell to head the Independent Marketing channel.

JPF had begun to recruit not only individual independent agents but also so-called independent marketing organizations (IMOs). An IMO was in the business of serving life insurance agents. IMOs did not produce or "manufacture" life insurance policies; they just served independent life insurance agents. Thus, the insurance company was the "manufacturer," the IMO an independent "wholesaler," and the independent agent the "retailer." The IMO represented multiple insurance companies and often had a large staff that helped agents develop customized policies to serve special customer needs.

IMOs dealt with the insurance companies, talked with underwriters and medical directors, and helped secure the needed life insurance on behalf of the agent's client. This allowed the agents to sell policies without having to worry about the massive amounts of paperwork and administrative details that someone had to perform after an agent made a sale. As a result, the IMO earned an additional fee from the insurance company on policies sold by the agents who worked through it. The insurance company was able to pay this

additional fee because the IMOs performed some functions that the insurance company would have to perform if it were supporting the agent directly.

By recruiting IMOs, JPF was able to expand its distributive capacity by bringing on more agents more rapidly than it could by having to recruit individual agents either by itself or solely through its career channel. There were also some IMOs that were "recruiting only," that is, they recruited agents but did not provide any of the administrative support for the agents.

Powell and Knowles realized that there was no way JPF could recruit and serve the thousands of IMOs in the United States from the Greensboro home office. Thus, they began to put together a field sales team. They divided the country into five multistate regions and, with the help of an executive search firm, recruited a sales vice-president (SVP) for each region.

The SVPs JPF recruited had many years of industry experience with other insurance companies, and several had held similar sales positions with other companies. The SVPs typically spent several days a week travelling to recruit new IMOs or to provide training and support for IMOs with whom JPF had a relationship. They also worked with the IMOs to resolve policy issuance or customer service problems the IMOs might have with the home office. The SVPs were relationship builders. They saw themselves as "premium gatherers" who wanted to get more "shelf space" for JPF's products with each IMO. They wanted to get the IMOs, their staff, and agents into the JPF "culture," make them comfortable doing business with JPF (versus other competitor companies the IMO also represented), and make it convenient to do so.

Like the career agents, the SVPs were JPF employees to whom it paid a small percentage of all the first-year premium dollars generated by JPF policies sold in their territory. Even though the percentage was small, because of the size of their territories, SVPs could earn a substantial income.

Because the SVPs put more "feet on the street" for JPF, and because JPF had very competitive products, policy sales had taken off in 2001. By mid-2002, the Independent Marketing channel was well ahead of its annual sales targets.

Back in the Car

"The problem we have," Bob Powell noted, "is that we are too successful. We are way ahead of 2002's targets and you know top management is going to want us to exceed what we do this year in 2003. And all of us are working as hard as we can. We can't do more by working any harder. You know that means we will have to add more SVPs."

"That's right," John Knowles observed, "but you saw in the meeting how the five SVPs reacted when we brought this up. They want to protect and keep all of their territory."

"Yes, but we all know that an SVP can't possibly cover 8 to 12 states and develop the kinds of IMO relationships we need," Bob answered. "I don't think an SVP can work with more than 30 or so IMOs. What are we going to do when an SVP gets a full client load? How do we bring on more SVPs without upsetting the apple cart?"

"Well," John said, "that brings up the additional issue of productivity. We have three salaried marketing coordinators now based in Greensboro who work with the five SVPs. However, we don't have a formal job description for them, and the SVPs are unhappy that they don't each have their own coordinator. If we add more SVPs, we will be even that much further behind in supporting their needs. And you know that in these economic times the company's reluctant to add more people, more overhead."

"I can see that some of our discussions may get as hot as this July weather," Bob said, laughing.

"When I get home," John said, "I'm going to dig out the old Kotler/Armstrong marketing textbook I had at Auburn and look back over the chapter on personal selling to see if it'll remind me of any issues we ought to be considering."

"We have a September 30 deadline for our sales force strategy proposals, so we'd better get to work," Bob concluded.

Questions for Discussion

1. What are the advantages and disadvantages of using a career sales force versus an independent sales force?

2. What are the advantages and disadvantages of commission-only compensation versus salary-only compensation?

3. What problems do you see with JPF's sales force strategy and structure decisions?

4. What recommendations would you make to JPF to help it deal with these problems?

Source: Officials at Jefferson-Pilot Financial cooperated in development of this case.

CBC Video Case

Log on to your Companion Website at **www.pearsoned.ca/kotler** to view a CBC video segment and case for this chapter.

Case Pilot

Log on to your Companion Website at **www.pearsoned.ca/kotler** to access the case project provided for this part of the text. Take the Case Pilot Challenge!

Chapter 18

The Global Marketplace

After studying this chapter you should be able to

1. discuss how the international trade system, economic, politico-legal, and cultural environments affect a company's international marketing decisions

2. describe three key approaches to entering international markets

3. explain how companies adapt their marketing mixes for international markets

4. identify the three major forms of international marketing organization

Looking Ahead: Previewing the Concepts

You've now learned the fundamentals of how companies develop competitive marketing strategies and marketing mixes to build lasting customer relationships by creating superior customer value. In this final chapter, we'll extend these fundamentals to global marketing. Although we visited this topic regularly in each previous chapter, because of its special importance we will focus exclusively on it here. As we move into the twenty-first century, advances in communication, transportation, and other technologies have made the world a much smaller place. Today, almost every firm, large or small, faces international marketing issues. In this chapter, we will examine six major decisions marketers make in going global.

Our first stop is Coca-Cola. Read on to see how finding the right balance between global standardization and local adaptation has made Coca-Cola the number one brand worldwide.

Coke got its start in an Atlanta pharmacy in 1893, where it sold for five cents a glass. From there, the company's first president, savvy businessman Asa Candler, set out to convince America that Coca-Cola really was "the pause that refreshes." He printed coupons offering complimentary first tastes of Coca-Cola and outfitted pharmacists who distributed the brand with clocks, calendars, scales, and trays bearing the now-so-familiar red-and-white Coca-Cola logo.

By 1900, Coca-Cola had already ventured into numerous countries, including Cuba, Puerto Rico, and France. By the 1920s, Coca-Cola was slapping its logo on everything from dogsleds in Canada to the walls of bullfighting arenas in Spain. During World War II, Coca-Cola built bottling plants in Europe and Asia to supply American soldiers in the field.

Strong marketing abroad fuelled Coke's popularity throughout the world. In 1971, the company ran its legendary "I'd like to buy the world a Coke" television spot, in which a crowd of children sang the song from atop a hill in Italy. More recently, Coca-Cola's increased focus on emerging markets such as China, India, and Indonesia—home to 2.4 billion people, half the world's population—has bolstered the brand's global success. Coca-Cola is now arguably the best-known and most admired brand in the world.

Coca-Cola's worldwide success results from a skilful balancing of global standardization and brand building with local adaptation. For years, the company has adhered to the mantra "Think globally, act locally." Coca-Cola spends lavishly on global Coke advertising—some $1.1 billion a year—to create a consistent overall positioning for the brand across the 200 countries it serves. In addition, Coke's taste and packaging are largely standardized around the world—the bottle of Coke you'd drink in Toronto or New York looks and tastes much the same as one you might order in Paris, Hong Kong, Moscow, Sidney, or Abu Dhabi. As one ad agency executive asserts, "There are about two products that lend themselves to global marketing—and one of them is Coca-Cola."

Although Coke's taste and positioning are fairly consistent worldwide, in other ways Coca-Cola's marketing is relentlessly local. The company carefully adapts its mix of brands and flavours, promotions, price, and distribution to local customs and preferences in each market. For example, beyond its core Coca-Cola brand, the company makes nearly 300 different beverage brands, created especially for the taste buds of local consumers. It sells a pear-flavoured drink in Turkey, a berry-flavoured Fanta for Germany, a honey-flavoured green tea in China, and a sports drink called Aquarius in Belgium and the Netherlands. Coca-Cola Bottling Company employs 5700 people across Canada, has eight production facilities and 64 sales offices located across the country and produces, sells, and distributes a full range of beverages, including Coca-Cola Classic, Diet Coke, caffeine-free Diet Coke, Sprite, Diet Sprite, Fresca, Barq's Root Beer, Barq's Cream Soda, Barq's Diet Root Beer, Fruitopia fruit beverages, Nestea iced teas, Dasani water, POWERaDE sports drinks, Minute Maid juices, and Five Alive fruit beverages.

Consistent with this local focus, within the framework of its broader global positioning, Coca-Cola adapts specific ads to individual country markets. For example, a localized Chinese New Year television ad features a dragon in a holiday parade, adorned from head to tail with red Coke cans. The spot concludes, "For many centuries, the colour red has been the colour for good luck and prosperity. Who are we to argue with ancient wisdom?" Coke's now classic "Mean Joe" Green TV ad from the United States—in which the weary football star reluctantly accepts a Coke from an admiring young fan and then tosses the awed kid his jersey in appreciation—was replicated in several different regions using the same format but substituting famous local athletes (ads in South America used Argentine soccer star Maradona; those in Asia used Thai soccer star Niat).

More recently, Coke launched local ads to support its sponsorship of the 2002 World Cup. Based on careful research on local attitudes toward the event, ads were tailored to each country's experience with the competition. An Italian ad featured a bustling Roman marketplace. An emotional Turkish TV ad shows two kids stringing red and white lightbulbs throughout Ankara, which light up the city in the team's colours. "There's even a special World Cup TV ad for the Netherlands—which scandalously failed to reach the tournament this time around," notes a global advertising analyst, "showing Dutch star Ruud Van Nistelroy quietly mowing his lawn while the drama unfolds in Japan and South Korea."

In India, Coca-Cola uses local promotions to aggressively cultivate a local image. It claimed official sponsorship for World Cup cricket, a favourite national sport, and used Indian cricket fans rather than actors to promote Coke products. Coca-Cola markets effectively in India to both retailers and imbibers. Observes one Coke watcher, "The company hosts massive gatherings of up to 15 000 retailers to showcase everything from the latest coolers and refrigerators, which Coke has for loan, to advertising displays. And its salespeople go house-to-house in their quest for new customers. In New Delhi alone, workers handed out more than 100 000 free bottles of Coke and Fanta last year."

Nothing better illustrates Coca-Cola's skill in balancing standardized global brand building with local adaptation than the explosive global growth of Sprite. Sprite's advertising uniformly targets the world's young people with the tag-line "Image is nothing. Thirst is everything. Obey your thirst." The campaign taps into the rebellious side of teenagers and their need to form individual identities. According to Sprite's director of brand marketing, "The meaning of [Sprite] and what we stand for is exactly the same globally. Teens tell us it's incredibly relevant in nearly every market we go into." However, as always, Coca-Cola tailors its message to local consumers. In China, for example, the campaign was given a softer edge: "You can't be irreverent in China, because it's not acceptable in that society. It's all about being relevant [to the specific audience]," notes the marketer. As a result of such smart targeting and powerful positioning, Sprite's worldwide sales surged 35 percent within three years of the start of the campaign, making it the world's number-four soft drink brand.

As a result of its international marketing prowess, Coca-Cola dominates the global soft drink market. More than 70 percent of the company's sales come from abroad. While it battles Pepsi for market share in North America, overseas it outsells Pepsi 2.5 to 1 and boasts four of the world's six leading soft drink brands: Coca-Cola, Diet Coke, Sprite, and Fanta.

Thus, Coca-Cola is truly an all-world brand. No matter where in the world you are, you'll find Coke "within an arm's length of desire." Yet, Coca-Cola also has a very personal meaning to consumers in different parts of the globe. Coca-Cola *is* as American as baseball and apple pie. But it's also as English as Big Ben and afternoon tea, as German as bratwurst and beer, as Japanese as sumo and sushi, and as Chinese as Ping-Pong and the Great Wall. Consumers in more than 200 countries think of Coke as *their* beverage. In Spain, Coke has been used as a mixer with wine; in Italy, Coke is served with meals in place of wine or cappuccino; in China, the beverage is served at special government occasions.

Says the company's website, "Our local strategy enables us to listen to all the voices around the world asking for beverages that span the entire spectrum of tastes and occasions. What people want in a beverage is a reflection of who they are, where they live, how they work and play, and how they relax and recharge. Whether you're a student in the United States enjoying a refreshing Coca-Cola, a woman in Italy taking a tea break, a child in Peru asking for a juice drink, or a couple in Korea buying bottled water after a run together, we're there for you.... It's a special thing to have billions of friends around the world, and we never forget it."[1]

In the past, North American companies paid little attention to international trade. If they could pick up some extra sales through exporting, that was fine. But the big market was at home, and it teemed with opportunities. The home market was also much safer. Managers did not need to learn other languages, deal with strange and changing currencies, face political and legal uncertainties, or adapt their products to different customer needs and expectations. Today, however, the situation is much different.

Global Marketing into the Twenty-First Century

The world is shrinking rapidly with the advent of faster communication, transportation, and financial flows. Products developed in one country—Gucci purses, Mont Blanc pens, McDonald's hamburgers, Japanese sushi, German BMWs—are finding enthusiastic acceptance in other countries. We would not be surprised to hear about a German businessman wearing an Italian suit and meeting an English friend at a Japanese restaurant who later returns home to drink Russian vodka and look up information about Canadian wilderness vacation spots on the Internet.

International trade is booming. Since 1969, the number of multinational corporations in the world's 14 richest countries has more than tripled, from 7000 to 24 000. Imports of goods and services now account for 24 percent of world gross domestic product worldwide, twice the level of 40 years ago. World trade now accounts for 29 percent of world GDP, a 10 percent increase from 1990.[2]

With $468.5 billion in exports of goods and services in 2002, Canada is one of the world's leading trading nations and the most export-oriented of the G7 industrialized economies. In fact, one in three jobs in Canada can be tied to trade. We export more, proportionally, than the United States or Japan. A weak global economy and a strong Canadian dollar led to recent declines in exports. In 2002, exports fell to 41.0 percent of GDP, compared to 43.1 percent in 2001. Compare these figures with those of the U.S., where international trade now accounts for a quarter of GDP. Most of Canada's exports (81.6 percent) go to the United States. Some firms, however, are broadening their trade horizons. Exports to the European Union account for approximately 6 percent of Canada's export trade, while Japan accounts for 2.5 percent.[3]

True, many companies have been carrying on international activities for decades: Bell, McCain, Bata, Nortel, Coca-Cola, IBM, Xerox, Corning, Gillette, Colgate, General Electric, Caterpillar, Ford, Kodak, 3M, Boeing, Motorola, and dozens of other North American firms have made the world their market. And in North America, such names as Sony, Toyota, Nestlé, Norelco, Mercedes, Panasonic, and Prudential have become household words. Other products and services that appear to be domestic really are produced or owned by foreign companies: Bantam books, Cadbury chocolate, Baskin-Robbins ice cream, GE and RCA televisions, Carnation milk, Pillsbury food products, Universal Studios, and Motel 6, to name just a few. "Already two-thirds of all industry either operates globally or is in the process of doing so," notes one analyst. "Michelin, the oh-so-French tire manufacturer, now makes 35 percent of its money in the United States, while Johnson & Johnson does 43 percent of its business abroad.... The scope of every manager is the world."[4]

But today global competition is intensifying. Foreign firms are expanding aggressively into new international markets, and home markets are no longer as rich in opportunity. Few industries are now safe from foreign competition. Although some companies would like to stem the tide of foreign imports through protectionism, in the long run this would only raise the cost of living and protect inefficient domestic

Many companies have made the world their market.

firms. The better way for companies to compete is to continuously improve their products at home and expand into foreign markets.

In an era of free trade, firms must learn how to enter foreign markets and increase their global competitiveness. Many Canadian companies have been successful at international marketing: Nortel, Mosaid, Corel, IMAX, Bombardier, CAE, Labatt, Moosehead, Northern Reflections, RIM, Alcan, Magna International, Barrick Gold Corp., Nova Corp., Newbridge Networks, and Atco, to name a few. Order some french fries in Thailand, Russia, Costa Rica, Tunisia, Vietnam, or Syria, and chances are you will be biting into a product manufactured by McCain International Inc. of Florenceville, New Brunswick. But you don't have to be an industry giant to venture into overseas markets:

> Cervélo Cycles Inc. (www.cervelo.com), a tiny Toronto-based company founded by two McGill engineering students, employs only 10 people. However, it was catapulted onto the world stage when Tyler Hamilton rode one of the firm's cycles to victory in one stage of the gruelling Tour de France bicycle race. The company's bikes range in price from $1600 to $6000. In addition to being distributed in Canada, they are also marketed in the United States, Australia, and Western Europe. This isn't the first victory for Cervélo. Cyclists have ridden Cervélo bikes to victory in 12 Ironman triathlons, two world time trial championships, and numerous triathlon, track, and road-racing World Cups. The owners hope the recent publicity will help it double its number of dealers in France to 50, and sell 2000 to 3000 bikes in 2004. If the team keeps winning, that may not be too difficult.[5]

Many firms are still hesitant about testing foreign waters. However, the federal government and its "Team Canada" approach, the Canadian Export Development Corp. (www.edc-see.ca), and the Department of Foreign Affairs and International Trade (www.dfait-maeci.gc.ca) are helping Canadian businesses, both large and small, make inroads in overseas markets.

Companies that delay taking steps toward internationalizing risk being shut out of growing markets in Western Europe, Eastern Europe, the Pacific Rim, and elsewhere. Firms that stay at home to play it safe might not only lose their chances to

Many small Canadian firms, such as Cervélo Cycles Inc., are successful international marketers. Cervélo hit the international spotlight with a stage win at the 2003 Tour de France.

enter other markets, but might also risk losing their home markets. Domestic companies that never thought about foreign competitors suddenly find these competitors in their own backyards. Ironically, although the need for companies to go abroad is greater than in the past, so are the risks. Companies that go global confront several major problems. High debt, inflation, and unemployment in many countries have resulted in highly unstable governments and currencies, which limits trade and exposes global firms to many risks. Governments are placing more regulations on foreign firms, such as requiring joint ownership with domestic partners, mandating the hiring of nationals, and limiting profits that can be taken from the country. Moreover, foreign governments often impose high tariffs or trade barriers to protect their own industries. Finally, corruption is an increasing problem: Officials in several countries often award business not to the best bidder but to the highest briber.

Still, companies selling in global industries have no choice but to internationalize their operations. A *global industry* is one in which the competitive positions of firms in given local or national markets are affected by their global positions. A **global firm** is one that, by operating in more than one country, gains marketing, production, R&D, and financial advantages that are not available to purely domestic competitors.

The global company sees the world as one market. It minimizes the importance of national boundaries and raises capital, obtains materials and components, and manufactures and markets its goods wherever it can do the best job. For example, Ford's "world truck" sports a cab made in Europe and a chassis built in Canada; it is assembled in Brazil and imported to the United States for sale. Otis Elevator gets its elevators' door systems from France, small-geared parts from Spain, electronics from Germany, and special motor drives from Japan, and then integrates its systems in the United States. Thus, global firms gain advantages by planning, operating, and coordinating their activities on a worldwide basis.

Global firm
A firm that, by operating in more than one country, gains R&D, production, marketing, and financial advantages that are not available to purely domestic competitors.

This does not mean that small and medium-size firms must operate in a dozen countries to succeed. These firms can practise global niching. In fact, companies marketing on the Internet may find themselves going global whether they intend it or not (see Real Marketing 18.1). But the world is becoming smaller, and every company operating in a global industry—whether large or small—must assess and establish its place in world markets.

The rapid move toward globalization means that all companies will have to answer some basic questions: What market position should we try to establish in our country, in our economic region, and globally? Who will our global competitors be, and what are their strategies and resources? Where should we produce or source our products? What strategic alliances should we form with other firms around the world?

As Figure 18.1 shows, a company faces six major decisions in international marketing. Each decision will be discussed in detail in this chapter.

Looking at the Global Marketing Environment

Tariff
A tax levied by a government against certain imported products.

Quota
A limit on the amount of goods that an importing country will accept in certain product categories.

Embargo
A ban on the import of a certain product.

Exchange controls
Government limits on the amount of its foreign exchange with other countries and on its exchange rate against other currencies.

Non-tariff trade barriers
Non-monetary barriers to foreign products, such as biases against a foreign company's bids or product standards that go against a foreign company's product features.

Before deciding whether to operate internationally, a company must thoroughly understand the international marketing environment. That environment has changed a great deal over the last two decades, creating both new opportunities and new problems. The world economy has globalized. World trade and investment have grown rapidly, with many attractive markets opening up in Western and Eastern Europe, China and the Pacific Rim, Russia, and elsewhere. There has been a growth of global brands in automobiles, food, clothing, electronics, and many other categories. The number of global companies has grown dramatically.

The International Trade System

A company looking abroad must first understand the *international trade system*. When selling to another country, the firm faces various trade restrictions. The most common is the **tariff**, which is a tax levied by a foreign government against certain imported products. The tariff may be designed either to raise revenue or to protect domestic firms. The exporter also may face a **quota**, which sets limits on the amount of goods the importing country will accept in certain product categories. The purpose of the quota is to conserve on foreign exchange and to protect local industry and employment. An **embargo**, or boycott, totally bans some kinds of imports.

Firms may face **exchange controls**, which limit the amount of foreign exchange and the exchange rate against other currencies. They also may encounter **non-tariff trade barriers**, such as biases against bids or restrictive product standards or other rules that go against North American product features:

One of the cleverest ways the Japanese have found to keep foreign manufacturers out of their domestic market is to plead "uniqueness." Japanese skin is different, the government argues, so foreign cosmetics companies must

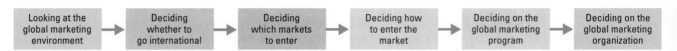

Figure 18.1 Major decisions in global marketing

REAL MARKETING

18.1 www.TheWorldIsYourOyster.com: The Ins and Outs of Global Ecommerce

The headline on McCain International Inc.'s website says it all: "One World. One Fry." It may sound like bragging, but nearly one third of all the world's french fries are produced by McCain Foods, headquartered in Florenceville, New Brunswick. To accomplish this feat, the company employs more than 18 000 employees in 55 production facilities on six continents. McCain can produce more than one million pounds of potato products every hour in its 30 potato processing plants around the world. It's not surprising, therefore, that the firm was among the winners of the 2003 Canada Export awards. McCain's uses the Web to reach both consumers and vendors. It has websites tailored specifically to the needs of certain country-markets, including the United States, the Netherlands, Poland, Scandinavia, the United Kingdom, and Germany.

Like McCain, companies large and small are now taking advantage of cyberspace's vanishing national boundaries. Major marketers doing global ecommerce range from automakers (General Motors and Toyota) to computer makers (Dell and IBM) to publishers who put their magazines online (Brunico Inc.) to direct-mail companies (L.L.Bean) to Internet superstars such as Amazon.com and Yahoo!

For some companies, global Web marketing has largely been a hit-or-miss affair. They present their website content in English for the North American market; and, if any international users stumble across it and end up buying something, so much the better. Such orders can be gravy for North American-focused marketers.

Other marketers have made a more strategic decision to dive into the global market. They're using the Web and online services to reach new customers outside their home countries, support existing customers who live abroad, source from international suppliers, and build global brand awareness. Most international companies have adapted their websites to provide country-specific content and services to their best potential international markets, often in the local language. Go to www.nike.com and Nike's home webpage first asks which site you want: North America, Europe, Asia Pacific, or Latin America. The European option lists five language choices: English, Deutsch, Français, Espagnol, and Italiano. Similarly, Dell Computer offers dozens of country-specific, local-language websites for markets, from France, Germany, China, and Japan to Belgium and Brunei. And Texas Instruments uses tailored "TI &

Marketers large and small are taking advantage of the Internet's global reach. It is one tool that winners of Canada's Export Awards like McCain's and Mega Bloks use to market their products worldwide.

Me" sites to sell and support its signal processors, logic devices, and other chips in B2B markets across Europe, Asia, and South America.

Before expanding their Web presences internationally, companies need to find the countries or regions with the largest potential online populations. The biggest growth area today is the Asia-Pacific region. By 2004, the number of Asia-Pacific Internet users is expected to swell to 188 million, thanks to declines in Internet access costs, increases in local-language content, and infrastructure improvements. In China alone, the number of Internet subscriptions is growing by 6 percent each month. Europe is another hot spot for Internet growth. Europe has typically lagged about four years behind North America but is now catching up quickly. European Internet penetration, which stood at 19 percent in 1999, reached 38 percent in 2002. By 2003, the five countries with the highest European penetration levels—Germany, France, the Netherlands, the United Kingdom, and Sweden—will have online populations totalling 60 million, up from 34 million in 1999.

Despite these encouraging global ecommerce developments in Asia and Europe, Internet marketers sometimes overstate global opportunities. Developed countries offer many choices for Internet access— Hong Kong alone has more than 240 registered Internet service providers (ISPs). However, less-developed countries in Central and South America or Africa have fewer or none at all, forcing users to make international calls to go online. As of 2000, only 6 percent of the world's population had Internet access. Even with adequate phone lines and PC penetration, high connection costs sharply restrict Internet use. In Asia, ISP subscriptions can run up to $60 a month, more than triple the average North American rate.

In addition, global marketers may run up against governmental or cultural restrictions. France, for instance, has laws against providing encrypted content. In Germany, a vendor can't accept payment via credit card until two weeks after an order has been sent. German law also prevents companies from using certain marketing techniques, such as unconditional lifetime guarantees. This affects companies with international websites, such as Lands' End, which prominently features its lifetime guarantee on its network of websites. On a wider scale, the issue of who pays taxes and duties on global ecommerce is murkier still.

Businesses need to realize that the Web does not offer complete solutions for transacting global business—and it probably never will. Most companies will always find it difficult to complete a big business-to-business deal via email. The Internet will not surmount customs red tape or local regulations regarding import or export of certain goods. The Web can't guarantee that goods will arrive in perfect condition.

What the Web can do is give companies access to markets they could never serve otherwise. The Web certainly has done that for Lands' End. The direct clothing retailer now has online stores in the United Kingdom, Ireland, France, Italy, Germany, and Japan, markets it would have great difficulty developing through its traditional catalogue channels. According to Sam Taylor, vice-president of international operations at Lands' End:

> The challenge in launching a catalogue business is customer acquisition. When you're starting out, you have to rent lists of names,...it's so expensive to print and mail those catalogues, and the conversion rate is very low. So the cost to acquire a customer is very high. Now, the Internet has changed all that. All of a sudden, we've got a French website. We do some PR, we do some limited online advertising, we get word of mouth, and the business starts to build. We're not overinvesting in upfront marketing. At some point in the future, once the business is big enough, we will launch a paper catalogue [in France], but not before the business is ready. That's one of the good things about the Internet. It has totally turned businesses upside down and changed how we do business.

However, Lands' End is landing right-side up in the international arena. The company now ships products to 185 countries, and international Web sales now contribute about 14 percent of all Lands' End's revenues.

Small companies can also market globally on the Web. Calgary's SMART Technologies Inc. was named the 2000 Exporter of the Year by the Department of Foreign Affairs and International Trade, which has given the Canada Export Awards for the past 17 years to Canadian companies that demonstrate excellence in competing internationally. SMART uses the Internet to promote sales of its Canadian-made products to over 50 countries. Visit its website, click on the "Where to buy" button, and you will find a list of SMART's international distributors. So get online and see if the world can be your oyster.

Sources: McCain Worldwide website: www.mccain.com/ McCainWorldWide/McCainOperatingCompanies (accessed November 2003); Department of Foreign Affairs and International Trade, "2003 Canada Export Awards," www.infoexport.gc.ca/ awards-prix/final-e.htm (accessed November 2003); "One In Three Europeans Will Embrace a Digital Lifestyle by 2003, According to Forrester," *Business Wire,* December 6, 2000; Brandon Mitchener, "E-Commerce: Border Crossings," *Wall Street Journal,* November 22, 1999; Janet Purdy Levaux, "Adapting Products and Services for Global E-Commerce," *World Trade,* January 2001, pp. 52–54; Carol Sliwa, "Clothing Retailer Finds Worldwide Business on the Web," *Computerworld,* April 30, 2001, p. 40; Nielsen/NetRatings website, "Nielsen/NetRatings Find China Has the World's Second Largest At-Home Internet Population," April 22, 2002, www. nielsen-netratings.com; Europemedia website, "Internet Penetration in Europe Plateaus," www.europemedia.net (accessed July 2002); and "2000 Canada Export Awards," *Canadian Business,* February 5, 2001, p. 61.

test their products in Japan before selling there. The Japanese say their stomachs are small and have room for only the *mikan*, the local tangerine, so imports of U.S. oranges are limited. Now the Japanese have come up with what may be the flakiest argument yet: Their snow is different, so ski equipment should be too.[6]

Marketers must be careful to delineate between claims that are undoubtedly trade barriers and unique needs of consumers from different cultures. While trade barriers certainly exist, certain forces *help* trade between nations. Examples include the General Agreement on Tariffs and Trade and various regional free trade agreements.

The World Trade Organization and GATT

The General Agreement on Tariffs and Trade (GATT) is a treaty designed to promote world trade by reducing tariffs and other international trade barriers. Since the treaty's inception in 1948, member nations (currently numbering 144) have met in eight rounds of GATT negotiations to reassess trade barriers and set new rules for international trade. The first seven rounds of negotiations reduced the average worldwide tariffs on manufactured goods from 45 percent to just 5 percent.

The most recently completed GATT negotiations, dubbed the Uruguay Round, dragged on for seven long years before concluding in 1993. The benefits of the Uruguay Round will be felt for many years as the accord promotes long-term global trade growth. It reduced the world's remaining merchandise tariffs by 30 percent, boosting global merchandise trade by as much as 10 percent, or $352 billion in current Canadian dollars, by 2002. The new agreement also extended GATT to cover trade in agriculture and a wide range of services, and it toughened international protection of copyrights, patents, trademarks, and other intellectual property.[7]

Beyond reducing trade barriers and setting international standards for trade, the Uruguay Round established the World Trade Organization (WTO; www.wto.org) to enforce GATT rules. One of the WTO's first major tasks was to host negotiations on the General Agreement on Trade in Services, which deals with worldwide trade in banking, securities, and insurance services. In general, the WTO acts as an umbrella organization, overseeing GATT, the General Agreement on Trade in Services, and a similar agreement governing intellectual property. In addition, the WTO mediates global disputes and imposes trade sanctions, authorities that the previous GATT organization never possessed. Top decision makers from the WTO meet once every two years to discuss matters pertaining to all WTO agreements. The most recent meetings took place in Doha, Qatar, in late 2001.

Regional Free Trade Zones

Economic community
A group of nations organized to work toward common goals in the regulation of international trade.

Certain countries have formed *free trade zones* or **economic communities**—groups of nations organized to work toward common goals in the regulation of international trade. Some of the key economic communities are discussed below.

The European Union Formed in 1957, *the European Union* (EU; http://europa.eu.int)—then called the Common Market—set out to create a single European market by reducing barriers to the free flow of products, services, finances, and labour among member countries, and developing policies on trade with non-member nations. Today, the European Union represents one of the world's single largest markets. Its current 15 member countries—Belgium, Germany, France, Italy, Luxembourg, Netherlands, Denmark, Ireland, the United Kingdom, Greece, Spain, Portugal, Austria, Finland, and Sweden—contain over 374 million consumers and account for 20 percent of the world's exports. The EU is preparing for the accession of 10 new eastern and southern European members in 2004—Cyprus, the Czech Republic, Estonia, Hungary, Latvia, Lithuania, Malta, Poland, Slovakia,

The Department of Foreign Affairs and International Trade and its trade commissioners help Canadian businesses penetrate world markets.

and Slovenia. During the next decade, as more European nations gain admission (such as current applicants Bulgaria, Romania, and Turkey), the EU could contain as many as 450 million people in 28 countries.[8]

In 2002 the EU imported $17.3 billion of goods and services from Canada—almost 5 percent of our export trade. However, we import more than twice as many goods and services from Europe than we export ($38.9 billion).[9]

European unification offers tremendous trade opportunities for North American and other non-European firms. However, it also poses threats. As a result of increased unification, European companies will grow bigger and more competitive. Perhaps an even greater concern is that lower barriers *inside* Europe will only create thicker *outside* walls. Some observers envision a "Fortress Europe" that heaps favours on firms from EU countries but hinders outsiders by imposing such obstacles as stiffer import quotas, local content requirements, and other non-tariff barriers.

Progress toward European unification has been slow—many doubt that complete unification will ever be achieved. However, on January 1, 1999, 11 of the 15 member nations took a significant step toward unification by adopting the euro as a common currency. In January 2001, Greece became the twelfth member nation to adopt the euro. Currencies of the individual countries were phased out gradually until January 1, 2002, when the euro became the only currency. Adoption of the euro will decrease much of the currency risk associated with doing business in Europe, making member countries with previously weak currencies more attractive markets. In addition, by removing currency conversion hurdles, the switch will likely increase cross-border trade and highlight differences in pricing and marketing from country to country.[10]

Even with the adoption of the euro as a standard currency, from a marketing viewpoint, creating an economic community will not create a homogeneous market. With 14 different languages and distinctive national customs, it is unlikely that the EU will ever go against 2000 years of tradition and become the "United States of

Wal-Mart and other companies are expanding rapidly in Mexico and Canada to take advantage of the many opportunities presented by NAFTA. The trade agreement establishes a single market of 360 million people in Mexico, Canada, and the United States.

Europe." Although economic and political boundaries may fall, social and cultural differences will remain, and companies marketing in Europe will face a daunting mass of local rules. Still, even if only partly successful, European unification will make a more efficient and competitive Europe a global force with which to reckon.[11]

NAFTA   In North America, the United States and Canada phased out trade barriers in 1989. In January 1994, the *North American Free Trade Agreement* (NAFTA; www.nafta-sec-alena.org) established a free trade zone among the United States, Mexico, and Canada. The agreement created a single market of 360 million people producing and consuming $8.7 trillion worth of goods and services. As it is implemented over a 15-year period, NAFTA will eliminate all trade barriers and investment restrictions among the three countries.

Thus far, the agreement has allowed trade between the countries to flourish. Each day the United States exchanges more than $1.3 billion in goods and services with Canada, its largest trading partner. Since the agreement was signed in 1993, U.S. merchandise exports to Mexico are up 170 percent, while Mexican exports to the United States grew some 241 percent. In 1998, Mexico passed Japan to become America's second-largest trading partner. Given the apparent success of NAFTA, talks are now underway to investigate establishing a Free Trade Area of the Americas (FTAA). This mammoth free trade zone would include 34 countries stretching from the Bering Strait to Cape Horn, with a population of 800 million and a combined gross domestic product of more than $14.3 trillion.[12]

APEC   Canada is also a member the *Asian-Pacific Economic Cooperation* (APEC; www.apecsec.org.sg). The 21 member economies began their association in 1989. The other APEC members are Australia, Brunei, Chile, China, Hong Kong, Indonesia, Korea, Japan, Malaysia, Mexico, New Zealand, Peru, the Philippines, Papua New Guinea, Russia, Singapore, Taiwan, Thailand, the United States, and Vietnam. As part of Canada's year of Asia Pacific, these economies met in Vancouver in 1997. The association hopes to foster free trade in a region that now accounts for 45 percent of world trade. While the more developed countries want to set a timeline for the implementation of tariff reductions, less-developed countries, such as Indonesia, Malaysia, and Thailand, have been more cautious, fearing that such actions will harm industries just in their infancy.[13]

MERCOSUR Other free trade areas are forming in Latin America and South America. For example, MERCOSUR now links six full members, including Argentina, Brazil, Paraguay, and Uruguay, and associate members Bolivia and Chile. With a population of more than 200 million and a combined economy of over $1.3 trillion a year, these countries make up the largest trading bloc after NAFTA and the EU. There is talk of a free trade agreement between the EU and MERCOSUR, and MERCOSUR's member countries are considering adopting a common currency, the merco.[14]

Although the recent trend toward free trade zones has caused great excitement and new market opportunities, it also raises some concerns. For example, many North American unions fear that NAFTA will lead to the further exodus of manufacturing jobs to Mexico, where wage rates are much lower than in Canada and the U.S. Environmentalists also worry that companies that are unwilling to play by the strict environmental protection rules will relocate in Mexico, where pollution regulation has been lax.

Each nation has unique features that must be understood. A nation's readiness for different products and services and its attractiveness as a market to foreign firms depend on its economic, politico-legal, and cultural environments.

Economic Environment

The international marketer must study each target country's economy. Two economic factors reflect the country's attractiveness as a market—the country's industrial structure and its income distribution.

The country's *industrial structure* shapes its product and service needs, income levels, and employment levels. The four types of industrial structures are:

- *Subsistence economies.* In a subsistence economy, the vast majority of people engage in simple agriculture. They consume most of their output and barter the rest for simple goods and services. They offer few market opportunities.

- *Raw-material–exporting economies.* These economies are rich in one or more natural resources but poor in other ways. Much of their revenue comes from exporting resources. Examples are Chile (tin and copper); Zaire (copper, cobalt, and coffee); and Saudi Arabia (oil). Canada's "old economy" is as a major exporter of raw materials of softwood lumber, paper, petroleum, coal, and fish. These countries are good markets for large equipment, tools and supplies, and trucks. If there are many foreign residents and a wealthy upper class, they are also a market for luxury goods. For example, the Canadian firm Crystal Fountains has received orders of about $1 million from the United Arab Emirates, where people are willing to pay $150 000 to $200 000 for fountains.

- *Industrializing economies.* In an industrializing economy, manufacturing accounts for 10 to 20 percent of the country's economy. Examples include Egypt, the Philippines, India, and Brazil. As manufacturing increases, the country needs more imports of raw textile materials, steel, and heavy machinery, and fewer imports of finished textiles, paper products, and automobiles. Industrialization typically creates a new rich class and a small but growing middle class, both demanding new types of imported goods.

- *Industrial economies.* Industrial economies are major exporters of manufactured goods and investment funds. They trade goods among themselves and also export them to other types of economies for raw materials and semi-finished goods. Canada is very dependent on trade. Over 40 percent of our gross domestic product is accounted for as exports of goods and services. For the last twenty years, to recognize the importance of such trade and showcase firms that have had huge successes abroad, the Department of Foreign Affairs and International Trade has sponsored the Canada Export Awards. As former

Trade Minister Pierre Pettigrew noted, "Exporters are the backbone of Canada's economy." The 2003 finalists alone generated export sales of $2.9 billion in 2002 and provided jobs for more than 10 000 employees. A look at the winners demonstrates that we are no longer just an exporter of natural resources and raw materials. For example, one winner, Lotek Wireless Inc. of St. John's, Newfoundland, manufactures sophisticated electronic monitoring systems to track fish and wildlife for biological and environmental information. CAE Inc. of Montreal is a world leader in aviation and marine simulators. Innova LifeSciences Corporation of Toronto manufactures innovative medical devices for the international surgical and dental markets, while Replicon Inc. of Calgary is a world leader in Web-based time-and expense-tracking products designed to increase workforce productivity. In other words, Canada's "new economy" is made up of manufacturing, service, and high-tech firms, which export a large portion of their output.[15]

The second economic factor is the country's *income distribution.* Countries with subsistence economies may consist mostly of households with very low family incomes. In contrast, industrialized nations may have low-, medium-, and high-income households. Still other countries may have only households with either very low or very high incomes. However, in many cases, poorer countries may have small but wealthy segments of upper-income consumers. Also, even in low-income and developing economies, people may find ways to buy products that are important to them:

Philosophy professor Nina Gladziuk thinks carefully before shelling out her hard-earned zlotys for Poland's dazzling array of consumer goods. But spend she certainly does. Although she earns just $715 a month from two academic jobs, Gladziuk, 41, enjoys making purchases: They are changing her lifestyle after years of deprivation under communism. In the past year, she has furnished a new apartment in a popular neighbourhood near Warsaw's Kabaty Forest, splurged on foreign-made beauty products, and spent a weekend in Paris before attending a seminar financed by her university.... Meet Central Europe's fast-rising consumer class. From white-collar workers like Gladziuk to factory workers in Budapest to hip young professionals in Prague, incomes are rising and confidence surging as a result of four years of economic growth. In the region's leading economies—the Czech Republic, Hungary, and Poland—the new class

Developing economies: In Central Europe, companies are catering to the new class of buyers with dreams of the good life and buying habits to match who are eager to snap up everything from Western consumer goods to high fashions and the latest cell phones.

of buyers is growing not only in numbers but also in sophistication.... In Hungary, ad agency Young & Rubicam labels 11 percent of the country as "aspirers," with dreams of the good life and buying habits to match. Nearly one-third of all Czechs, Hungarians, and Poles—some 17 million people—are under 30 years old, eager to snap up everything from the latest fashions to compact discs.[16]

Thus, international marketers face many challenges in understanding how the economic environment affects decisions about which global markets to enter and how.

Politico-Legal Environment

Nations differ greatly in their politico-legal environments. A company must consider at least four politico-legal factors in deciding whether to do business in a given country: attitudes toward international buying, government bureaucracy, political stability, and monetary regulations.

In their *attitudes toward international buying,* some nations are quite receptive to foreign firms, but others are quite hostile. For example, India has bothered foreign businesses with import quotas, currency restrictions, and limits on the percentage of the management team that can be non-nationals. As a result, many North American companies left India. In contrast, such neighbouring Asian countries as Singapore, Thailand, Malaysia, and the Philippines woo foreign investors and shower them with incentives and favourable operating conditions.[17]

A second factor is *government bureaucracy*—the extent to which the host government runs an efficient system for helping foreign companies: efficient customs handling, good market information, and other factors that support conducting business. North Americans are often shocked by demands for bribes to make these trade barriers disappear even though such demands are illegal and unethical. (These issues are discussed in Real Marketing 18.2.)

Political stability is another issue. Governments change hands, sometimes violently. Even without a change, a government may respond to new popular feelings. The foreign company's property may be taken, its currency holdings may be blocked, or import quotas or new duties may be set. International marketers may find it profitable to do business in an unstable country, but the unsteady situation will affect how they handle business and financial matters.

Finally, companies must consider a country's *monetary regulations*. Sellers want to take their profits in a currency of value to them. Ideally, the buyer can pay in the seller's currency or in other world currencies. Short of this, sellers may accept a blocked currency—one whose removal from the country is restricted by the buyer's government—if they can buy other goods in that country that they need themselves or can sell elsewhere for a needed currency. Besides currency limits, a changing exchange rate also creates high risks for the seller.

Countertrade
International trade involving the direct or indirect exchange of goods for other goods instead of cash. Forms include barter, compensation (buyback), and counterpurchase.

Most international trade involves cash transactions. Yet many nations have too little hard currency to pay for their purchases from other countries. They may want to pay with other items instead of cash, which has led to a growing practice called **countertrade**. Countertrade makes up an estimated 20 percent of all world trade.[18] It takes several forms. *Barter* involves the direct exchange of goods or services, as when Australian cattlemen swapped beef on the hoof for Indonesian goods including beer, palm oil, and cement. Another form is *compensation* (or *buyback*), whereby the seller sells a plant, equipment, or technology to another country and agrees to take payment in the resulting products. Thus, Goodyear provided China with materials and training for a printing plant in exchange for finished labels. *Counterpurchase* occurs when the seller receives full payment in cash but agrees to spend some portion of the money in the other country within a stated time period. For example, Pepsi sells its cola syrup to Russia for rubles and agrees to buy Russian-made Stolichnaya vodka for sale in the United States.

REAL MARKETING

18.2 The Grey Zone: International Marketing Ethics

ell-known business ethics scholar Richard De George wrote: "Business ethics is as national, international, or global as business itself, and no arbitrary geographical boundaries limit it." International business ethics is increasingly becoming front-page news, but the topic isn't a new one or even one born in modern times. For centuries, trade has brought people and cultures into direct conflict. The exploitation of numerous countries in the colonial periods of France, England, and Spain illustrate extreme cases of unethical marketing practice. Exchanges in which worthless beads were traded for gold and silver make some of the scandals presented in the modern press pale in comparison.

Marketing has long been associated with questions of ethics, both nationally and internationally. Marketing and ethics are closely aligned since the element of trust is inherent in the creation of the ongoing exchange relationships that lie at the heart of marketing. It cannot be denied that firms operating in international markets face a growing number of ethical issues. Business is increasingly global in nature: Firms operate in multiple national markets and they seek to raise capital from multiple international sources. Moreover, since foreign market growth outpaced North American

market growth, the mandate for understanding how to manage international ethical behaviour is growing.

Decisions that marketers must make while working within the context of any corporation are complex and are often fraught with conflicts of values. Such conflicts are at the heart of many ethical dilemmas even in national business enterprises. They become seemingly insurmountable problems in the arena of international businesses, where people from different cultures, political systems, economies, value systems, and ethical standards must interact. In other words, ethical concerns involve more than black-and-white decisions; they involve many shades of grey, where the values of people from one country conflict with those from another. For example, in some countries, giving and receiving gifts is customary at the close of business transactions. However, for many North American firms, acceptance of gifts, other than mere tokens of appreciation such as chocolates or flowers, is viewed as unethical or may even be illegal.

Global organizations have been formed to monitor and help improve practices in international arenas. For example, Berlin-based Transparency International and its Canadian affiliate Transparency International Canada work tirelessly to fight corruption both in Canada and abroad. Transparency International Canada was instrumental in having anti-bribery provisions written into Canadian law.

Ethical issues arise in all of the functional areas of international business and centre on such business strategy questions as market-entry decisions, bribery and gift giving, contract negotiations, human resource issues, crisis management situations, product policy, advertising practices, pricing and transfer pricing, information systems management and privacy, grey markets, environmental concerns, accounting, finance and taxation, and production. Many of these areas are of specific concern to marketers. International advertising, for example, often raises ethical concerns. While many European countries use nudity and sexual innuendo in their advertising, some North Americans find this offensive. In some countries, such as India, even showing people kissing is objectionable.

Transparency International Canada fights tirelessly against corruption both in Canada and abroad.

Offering certain products for sale in some countries has also raised ethical criticism. North American companies have been criticized for marketing harmful chemicals overseas, chemicals that are banned from use in their home markets. Avon has been criticized for selling cosmetics to people in countries where many people cannot afford enough food. Even though a product itself may not be inherently harmful, ethical criticism has been directed at companies that did not take measures to prevent harm arising to consumers who incorrectly used products (like baby formula, drugs, or pesticides) due to high rates of illiteracy and inability to understand product-use instructions. There are also ethical issues associated with packaging in international markets. In some countries, such as Germany, manufacturers must recycle all packaging. In others, due to lack of disposal facilities, packaging adds to pollution problems.

Pricing raises yet another set of ethical concerns. Sometimes, higher prices must be charged due to the increased costs of marketing overseas, but when overly high prices are levied just because a firm has a monopoly in a foreign country, ethical questions have to be asked. Ethical criticism has been levied at firms for their refusal to send female sales representatives or managers into countries with adverse gender stereotypes even though this hampers women's chances for advancement or higher earnings.

Bribery is always a thorny issue in international markets. While it is undeniable that in some countries it is viewed as a "normal" way of doing business, this is not universally the case. Marketers should be aware that in most countries, bribery is an illegal practice. And because North Americans hold the stereotypical belief that bribes are expected overseas, we often make the mistake of offering such a payment when we perceive the slightest hesitation in signing a business deal. Rather than expecting a bribe, the foreign official may just be more risk averse or want more information. The offering of a bribe, in these cases, will not only cause offence but will often terminate the relationship.

When discussing international business ethics, North Americans believe that we take the moral highroad. We've all read reports of companies being blocked from doing business in South America because of rigged bidding systems, or losing sales in China or Korea because firms cannot legally pay the bribes necessary to get the business. However, we have to be aware that some countries may have higher moral standards than we do. For example, one survey showed that fewer Japanese executives will cheat on their expense sheets than will a comparable group of North American executives. Other surveys of Canadian businesspeople have shown that most ethical problems arise not in doing business in exotic locales, but rather in dealing with our closest neighbour, the United States. While this may be due to the fact that we do more business with the U.S. than with any other country, problems such as industrial espionage, product safety concerns, sales practices, and hiring practices have been areas of growing ethical concern.

Despite the number of ethical issues marketers face, there are often few guidelines to help them come to terms with these issues. International marketers must be aware, however, that they have multiple responsibilities to the firms and their customers. They must avoid knowingly harming any of their constituents. They must sell safe products, ensure truthful advertising, and charge fair prices. As a minimum, marketers working for Canadian companies must abide by the laws of the countries in which they operate. However, being an ethical marketer often means going beyond the mere provisions of a legal system. Marketers also must consider what is right or wrong. Such considerations involve respecting the human rights of people, no matter what country they reside in. It involves avoiding the exploitation of individuals or their environment.

Many companies, such as Imperial Oil and Warner-Lambert, have developed codes of ethics to guide their employees' decisions. A 1995 survey of the CEOs of the top 500 companies in Canada revealed that 80 percent of these firms had codes of ethics. Many of these firms require that the principles outlined in the code be applied wherever the firm is operating. In other words, the rules applying to conducting business in Canada also apply to subsidiaries of the business operating overseas.

In Canada, top levels of management are responsible for setting ethics policy and ensuring its implementation throughout the firm. Leading scholars in the field of marketing ethics emphasize that planning for ethical behaviour must begin at the same time as the rest of the strategic international market planning effort. Ethics cannot be an afterthought. This type of planning includes making such decisions as which international markets to enter, since some areas are known for their inherent ethical challenges. For example, does the firm want to enter markets dominated by totalitarian and military regimes, or those known for their record of human rights violations or ongoing environmental damage? Other questions include what types of products to market. The marketing of pesticides, tobacco, liquor, and pharmaceuticals, for example, all have unique ethical questions associated with them.

In addition to having a code of ethics, a firm must actively train its employees to be more sensitive to ethical issues, especially as it sends them overseas. While fewer than 40 percent of firms offer ethics training, surveys indicate that employees want this type of training, that it has a positive effect in reducing unethical behaviour, and that it heightens ethical issue recognition and sensitivity.

In the end, although international marketing can be one of the most exciting and rewarding areas of the profession, be aware that it also presents some of the most difficult ethical problems and issues.

Source: This highlight is based on Peggy Cunningham's article "Managing Marketing Ethics in International Business: Literature Review and Directions for Future Research," published in the Proceedings of the ASAC Conference, Windsor, June 1995. Updated content was added in November 2003.

Countertrade deals can be very complex. For example, Daimler-Benz once sold 30 trucks to Romania in exchange for 150 Romanian jeeps, which it then sold to Ecuador for bananas, which were in turn sold to a German supermarket chain for German currency. Through this roundabout process, Daimler-Benz finally obtained payment in German money.[19]

Cultural Environment

Each country has its own folkways, norms, and taboos. When designing global marketing strategies, companies must understand how culture affects consumer reactions in each of its world markets. In turn, they must also understand how their strategies affect local cultures.

The Impact of Culture on Marketing Strategy

The seller must examine the way consumers in different countries think about and use certain products before planning a marketing program. There are often surprises. For example, the average French man uses almost twice as many cosmetics and beauty aids as his wife. The Germans and the French eat more packaged, branded spaghetti than do Italians. Italian children like to eat chocolate bars between slices of bread as a snack. Women in Tanzania will not give their children eggs for fear of making them bald or impotent. Companies that ignore such differences can make some very expensive and embarrassing mistakes. Here's an example:

> McDonald's and Coca-Cola managed to offend the entire Muslim world by putting the Saudi Arabian flag on their packaging. The flag's design includes a passage from the Koran (the sacred text of Islam), and Muslims feel very strongly that their Holy Writ should never be wadded up and tossed in the garbage. Nike faced a similar situation in Arab countries when Muslims objected to a stylized "Air" logo on its shoes that resembled "Allah" in Arabic script. Nike apologized for the mistake and pulled the shoes from distribution.[20]

Business norms and behaviour also vary among countries. Business executives need to be briefed on these factors before conducting business in another country. These are some examples of differing global business behaviour:[21]

- South Americans like to sit or stand very close to each other when they talk business—in fact, almost nose-to-nose. The North American business executive tends to keep backing away as the South American moves closer. Both may end up being offended.

Overlooking cultural differences can result in embarrassing mistakes. When Nike learned that this stylized "Air" logo resembled "Allah" in Arabic script, it apologized and pulled the shoes from distribution.

- Fast and tough bargaining, which works well in other parts of the world, is often inappropriate in Japan and other Asian countries. Moreover, in face-to-face communications, Japanese business executives rarely say no. Thus, North Americans tend to become impatient with having to spend time in polite conversation about the weather or other such topics before getting down to business. And they become frustrated when they don't know where they stand. However, when North Americans come to the point quickly, Japanese business executives may find this behaviour offensive.

- In France, wholesalers don't want to promote a product. They ask their retailers what they want and deliver it. If a company builds its strategy around the French wholesaler's cooperation in promotions, it is likely to fail.

- When North American executives exchange business cards, each usually gives the other's card a cursory glance and stuffs it in a pocket for later reference. In Japan, however, executives dutifully study each other's cards during a greeting, carefully noting company affiliation and rank. They show a business card the same respect they show a person. Also, they hand their card to the most important person first.

By the same token, companies that understand cultural nuances can use them to advantage when positioning products internationally. Consider the following example:

A television ad running these days in India shows a mother lapsing into a daydream: Her young daughter is in a beauty contest dressed as Snow White, dancing on a stage. Her flowing gown is an immaculate white. The garments of other contestants who dance in the background are a tad grey. Snow White, no surprise, wins the blue ribbon. The mother awakes to the laughter of her adoring family—and glances proudly at her Whirlpool White Magic washing machine.

The TV spot is the product of 14 months of research by Whirlpool into the psyche of the Indian consumer. Among other things, [Whirlpool] learned that Indian homemakers prize hygiene and purity, which they associate with white.

The trouble is, white garments often get discoloured after frequent machine washing in local water. Besides appealing to this love of purity in its ads, Whirlpool custom-designed machines that are especially good with white fabrics. Whirlpool hasn't stopped there. It uses generous incentives to get thousands of Indian retailers to stock its goods. To reach every cranny of the vast nation, it uses local contractors conversant in India's 18 languages to collect payments in cash and deliver appliances by truck, bicycles, even oxcart. Since 1996, Whirlpool's sales in India have leapt 80 percent—and were expected to hit $260 million by 2002. Whirlpool now is the leading brand in India's fast-growing market for fully automatic washing machines.[22]

Thus, understanding cultural traditions, preferences, and behaviours can help companies not only to avoid embarrassing mistakes but also to take advantage of cross-cultural opportunities.

The Impact of Marketing Strategy on Cultures

Whereas marketers worry about the impact of culture on their global marketing strategies, others may worry about the impact of marketing strategies on global cultures. For example, some critics, including Canadian writer Naomi Klein in her international bestseller *No Logo,* argue that "globalization" really means "Americanization." They worry that the more people around the world are exposed to the American culture and lifestyle in the food they eat, the stores they shop at, and television shows and movies they watch, the more they will lose their individual cultural identities.[23]

These critics contend that exposure to American values and products erodes other cultures and westernizes the world. They point out that teens in India watch MTV and ask their parents for more westernized clothes and other symbols of American pop culture and values. Grandmothers in small villas in northern Italy no longer spend each morning visiting local meat, bread, and produce markets to gather the ingredients for dinner. Instead, they now shop at Wal-Mart Supercentres. Women in Saudi Arabia see American films and question their societal roles. In China, most people never drank coffee before Starbucks entered the market. Now Chinese consumers rush to Starbucks stores "because it's a symbol of a new kind of lifestyle." Similarly, in China, where McDonald's operates 80 restaurants in Beijing alone, nearly half of all children identify the chain as a domestic brand.[24]

An American reporter writing from Japan claimed:

[It will] only be a matter of time before an Asian family [will] take cash from their corner U.S. bank, "drive off to Wal-Mart and fill the trunk of their Ford with the likes of Fritos and Snickers," then stop at the American-owned movie theatre to see the latest Disney film before returning home to check their U.S. mutual fund accounts and America Online (on their IBM computer with Microsoft software). Asians see this as no less than the U.S. "desire to bury Asian values," and they are not pleased.[25]

Recently, such concerns have led to a backlash against globalization. For example, as a symbol of Western capitalism, McDonald's has been singled out by antiglobalization protestors all over the world. For example, almost immediately after U.S. armed forces unleashed their attack on Afghanistan following the September 11, 2001, terrorist attacks, McDonald's stores in Pakistan, India, and elsewhere around the world came under attack. Local protestors burned American flags outside the restaurants and vandalized McDonald's storefronts.[26]

Some critics worry that world exposure to American culture and lifestyle will result in the "Americanization" of other cultures. Nearly half of all Chinese children identify McDonald's as a domestic brand. Chinese consumers rush to Starbucks stores "because it's a symbol of a new kind of lifestyle."

Despite the concerns, most studies reveal that, although globalization may bridge culture gaps, it does not eliminate them. Instead, the cultural exchange goes both ways:

> African consumers are more apt to be fans of Hindi musicals than MTV. And even American childhood has increasingly been shaped by Asian cultural imports. Most parents now know about the Power Rangers, Tamagotchi and Pokémon, Sega, and Nintendo. For the moment, English remains cyberspace's dominant language, and having Web access often means that Third World youth have greater exposure to American popular culture. Yet these same technologies enable Balkan students studying in the United States to hear Webcast news and music from Serbia or Bosnia.[27]

Moreover, North American companies have learned that to succeed abroad they must adapt to local cultural values and traditions rather than trying to force their own. CEO Jack Greenberg notes that McDonald's is "a decentralized entrepreneurial network of locally owned stores that is very flexible and adapts very well to local conditions. We offer an opportunity to entrepreneurs to run a local business with local people supplied by a local infrastructure." This concept is echoed on the McDonald's website and throughout its corporate culture. The company encourages franchisees to introduce menu items that reflect local tastes, including the Maharaja Mac (made of mutton) in India, the Tatsuta Burger in Japan, the McPork Burger with Thai Basil in Thailand, and the McTempeh Burger (made from fermented soybeans) in Indonesia. In fact, McDonald's restaurants in Bombay and Delhi feature a menu that is more than 75 percent locally developed.[28]

Similarly, as noted in Chapter 2, Disneyland Paris flopped at first because it failed to take local cultural values and behaviours into account. Says Euro Disney Chief Executive Jay Rasulo, "When we first launched, there was the belief that it was enough to be Disney. Now we realize that our guests need to be welcomed on the basis of their own culture and travel habits." That realization, and the changes it spawned, made Disneyland Paris the number one tourist attraction in Europe—

even more popular than the Eiffel Tower. The park now attracts more than 12 million visitors each year. And Disney recently introduced a new movie-themed park to accompany the revitalized Paris attraction. The new park blends Disney entertainment and attractions with the history and culture of European film. A show celebrating the history of animation features Disney characters speaking six different languages. Rides are narrated by foreign-born stars, including Jeremy Irons, Isabella Rossellini, and Nastassja Kinski, speaking in their native tongues. Some recent economic woes in Europe have caused attendance to decline, so Disney still has more challenges to overcome.[29]

Deciding Whether to Go International

Not all companies need to venture into international markets to survive. For example, most local businesses need to market well only in the local marketplace. Operating domestically is easier and safer. Managers need not learn another country's language and laws, deal with volatile currencies, face political and legal uncertainties, or redesign their products to suit different customer needs and expectations. However, companies that operate in global industries, where their strategic positions in specific markets are affected strongly by their overall global positions, must be able to compete on a worldwide basis if they are to succeed. Thus, a company like Nortel must organize globally if it is to gain purchasing, manufacturing, financial, and marketing advantages.

Any of several factors may draw a company into the international arena. Global competitors might attack the company's domestic market by offering better products or lower prices. The company might want to counterattack these competitors in their home markets to tie up their resources. Or it might discover foreign markets that present higher profit opportunities than the domestic market does. The company's domestic market might be stagnating or shrinking, or the company might need a larger customer base to achieve economies of scale. Or it might want to reduce its dependence on any one market to reduce its risk. Finally, the company's customers might be expanding abroad and require international servicing.

Before going abroad, the company must weigh the risks and assess its ability to operate globally. Can the company learn to understand the preferences and buyer behaviour of consumers in other countries? Can it offer competitively attractive products? Will it be able to adapt to other countries' business cultures and deal effectively with foreign nationals? Do the company's managers have the necessary international experience? Has management considered the impact of regulations and the political environments of other countries?

Because of the risks and difficulties of entering international markets, most companies do not act until some situation or event thrusts them into the global arena. Someone—a domestic exporter, a foreign importer, a foreign government—may ask the company to sell abroad. Or the company may be saddled with overcapacity and must find additional markets for its goods.

Deciding Which Markets to Enter

Before going abroad, the company must set its international *marketing objectives and policies*. It should decide what *volume* of foreign sales it wants. Most companies start small when they go abroad. Some plan to stay small, seeing international sales as a small part of their business. Other companies have bigger plans, seeing international business as equal to or even more important than their domestic business.

The company must choose *how many* countries it wants to market in. Companies must be careful not to spread themselves too thin or to expand beyond their capabilities by operating in too many countries too soon:

> Although consumer products company Amway is now breaking into markets at a furious pace, it is doing so only after decades of gradually building up its overseas presence. Known for its neighbour-to-neighbour direct-selling networks, Amway expanded into Australia in 1971, a country far away but similar to its North American market. In the 1980s, Amway expanded into 10 more countries, and the pace increased rapidly from then on. By 1994, Amway was firmly established in 60 countries, including Hungary, Poland, and the Czech Republic. Following its substantial success in Japan, China, and other Asian countries, the company entered India in 1998. Today, Amway sells its products in 90 countries and international proceeds account for over 70 percent of the company's overall revenues.[30]

Next, the company must decide on the *types* of countries to enter. A country's attractiveness depends on the product, geographical factors, income and population, political climate, and other factors. The seller may prefer certain country groups or parts of the world. In recent years, many major markets have emerged, offering both substantial opportunities and daunting challenges (see Real Marketing 18.3).

After listing possible international markets, the company must screen and rank each one. Consider this example:[31]

> Many mass marketers dream of selling to China's more than 1.3 billion people. For example, Colgate is waging a pitched battle in China, seeking control of the world's largest toothpaste market. Yet, this country of infrequent brushers

The Canadian Standards Association International can help firms with their market-entry decisions.

18.3 Emerging Markets: China and Russia

*A*s Eastern Europe and Asia reform their markets, and as the United States and Canada continue to dismantle trade barriers, North American companies are eagerly anticipating the profits that await them. Here are "snapshots" of the opportunities and challenges that marketers face in two emerging markets: China and Russia.

China: 1.3 Billion Consumers

In Guangdong province, Chinese "yuppies" walk department-store aisles to buy $125 Nike or Reebok running shoes or think nothing of spending $5 on a jar of Skippy peanut butter in the supermarket section. Although the average annual income amounts to only $470 per person, China's ever-growing pool of elite consumers still has plenty of spending money because of subsidized housing and health care and lots of savings under the mattress.

> The prevalence of wide-screen televisions, fancy stereos, and home-karaoke machines in Shanghai apartments suggests that this new upper middle class has more money than it admits to.... Among urban households, fewer than one in five households had a colour television in 1985; today the average such home has more than one. Then, 7 percent had a refrigerator; now 73 percent do. Cameras are four times more common. Among richer urban households, more than half now have a VCR, a pager, air conditioner, and shower, and nearly a third of households also own a mobile phone.

In Shenzhen, Guangdong's second-largest city, consumers have the highest disposable income in all of China—$5000 annually. With purchasing power like this, a population of 1.3 billion, and the fastest-growing economy in the world, China is encouraging companies from around the planet to set up shop there. Instead of the communist propaganda of yore, modern Chinese billboards exclaim, "Give China a chance." To further encourage foreign development, in December 2001 China joined the World Trade Organization and committed to lowering the barriers to entering the Chinese market.

Since former Prime Minister Chrétien's first highly publicized "Team Canada" trade delegation to China in 1994, Canadian exports to China have grown tremendously. The Team Canada 2001 mission to Beijing, Shanghai, and Hong Kong wrapped up 27 new business deals for Canadian enterprises totalling $5.7 billion. In 2003, another Team Canada mission for Information and Communications Technologies (including the Department of Foreign Affairs and International Trade, Industry Canada, Canada China Business Council, and the Alberta, Quebec, and Ontario provincial governments) attended the China High-Tech Fair in Shenzhen, China—one of the world's largest high-technology fairs, which attracts over 3600 exhibitors and more than 300 000 visitors. It was promoted as "an excellent showcase for innovative Canadian high-technology firms who wish to further their business interests in the large and fast-growing China market."

Yet for all its market potential, there are many hurdles to jump in entering mainland China and marketing to the Chinese. For one, China is not one market, but many, and regional governments may discriminate against certain goods. Distribution channels are undeveloped, consisting of thousands of tiny mom-and-pop stores that can afford to stock only a few bottles or packages at a time. And China's dismal infrastructure can turn a rail shipment travelling from Guanzhou to Beijing into a month-long odyssey. Smart firms, such as Kodak, try to jump these hurdles by partnering with Chinese government bodies or acquiring Chinese business partners who can help them penetrate distribution channels and hire experienced personnel.

A major concern to some North American businesses is China's distressing human rights record. Levi Strauss has turned its back on China's vast market for blue jeans because of such concerns. But other firms counter that industry can be part of the solution. "Supporting the business sector will result in economic and political freedoms for the Chinese people," says a 3M spokesperson.

Russia: Many Opportunities, Many Pitfalls

Contemporary Russia certainly looks like a nifty place for North American marketers: 150 million people; gross domestic product (GDP) growth of 7.2 percent in 2002; a young, well-educated, cultured population; a booming, younger middle class, many members of which are starting their own businesses:

> Irina Lyakhnovskaya is a go-getter. Her hometown of Samara in central Russia straddles the Volga River and is surrounded by miles of fertile grassland and the

Zhigulevskiye Mountains. Five years ago, she started a tourist company, with seed capital supplied by herself and three friends, that specializes in arranging hunting and fishing trips for visitors from Finland and Norway. She drives a Russian-made Lada that she purchased new for $4500 two years ago, and she spends weekends at a country dacha that has an apple orchard she harvests to make her own wine. Last year she took vacations in Hungary and Romania, and this year she plans to get to Britain. In a country where the average factory worker is lucky to make $195 a month, she makes as much as $650. Lyakhnovskaya, 38, embodies a major shift in Russia's economic landscape. Boosted by a resurgent national economy and by its own bootstraps, a middle class is taking root in the former land of the proletariat. Analysts estimate 12 million to 30 million Russians, some 8 percent to 20 percent of the nation's 150 million population, qualify as middle class.

On the one hand, demographics and the economy—on the rebound from the 1998 crash—are converging to make Russia one of the more attractive emerging markets on the globe. Compared with other emerging markets, its population is more literate. Moreover, it's a population that embraces technology: Television penetration is high in Russia, the number of Internet users is rising 50 percent each year, and although industries such as two-way telecommunications are in their infancy, that's changing quickly.

Still, Russia is not all sunshine and roses for North American marketers. This fast-growing market also presents rampant corruption, a widespread lack of basic business controls, a barely liquid currency, and a business culture that, while increasingly capitalist, is definitely not equivalent to Western capitalist cultures. Moreover, the newfound middle class is still fragile, fearing the prospect of a fresh national economic calamity. It's happened before. A fledgling middle class began to grow during the chaotic rein of Boris Yeltsin, only to see their fortunes wiped out by the economic crisis of 1998. "One new crisis, everything I have will be wiped out," says Lyakhnovskaya. All of this makes Russia an attractive but still tricky market in which to do business.

Russia is currently experiencing a retail invasion, especially in Moscow, where much of the country's population and wealth are concentrated. Moscow's population exceeds that of Belgium and Bulgaria combined, and Muscovites spend some US$13 billion a year shopping for food and home furnishings, a third of the country's total spending in those categories. Muscovites are now filling their shopping carts to the brim with everything from futons to Camembert at the new stores.

Food companies have done especially well in Russia. George Cohon of McDonald's Canada opened McDonald's first Russian restaurant in 1990. McDonald's now has 58 outlets there—the McDonald's in Moscow's Pushkin Square is the world's busiest. Companies in other industries are also making a push into this promising but chancy market. The world's auto companies see huge potential. By 2005, some analysts expect, Russia will become one of the world's largest automotive markets. Indeed, between 1991 and 1998, with the growth of the country's middle class, Russian auto sales skyrocketed 60 percent.

Leisure pursuits, once considered a luxury, have also trickled down to the middle class. Gold's Gym, which operates 560 gyms worldwide, opened one in Moscow in 1993 that now is one of the chain's solid performers. The Moscow facility has about 3000 members, matching the company's average worldwide. The Moscow gym looks much like one in the West, except that the signs are in Cyrillic. "If I were to show you a video of the Moscow gym, you'd think it was New York or Los Angeles," says a Gold's executive. "The women are gorgeous, and people are in good shape."

Although North American businesspeople may feel more at home in Russia now than at any time in that country's history, they still face the typical challenges of an emerging market. Beyond corruption and difficult currency, differences in culture and social habits can affect how business is done. For instance, Russians place much more value on hospitality than North Americans. "They tend to be touchy-feely; there's lots of hugging," says a Russian trade expert. Eating and drinking with business prospects is also important, although North Americans can sometimes get into trouble trying to match Russians drink for drink. (The solution? "Say up front that you can't drink for medical reasons," advises the trade expert.)

Emerging markets: Contemporary Russia—with its young, well-educated, cultured population and a booming, younger middle class—looks like a nifty place for North American marketers. However, the newfound middle class is still fragile, fearing the next national economic calamity.

The Canadian Development Corporation (CDC), a Crown corporation, has helped Canadian firms expand into the region by providing them with financial and risk management services. The Canadian International Development Agency (CIDA) runs other federal government programs designed to help firms ease their way into these markets.

Russia, a challenging market, boasts 250 Canadian companies that have thrived in the oil and gas, agricultural, housing and construction, and telecommunication markets. However, as Russia's economy struggles, Canadian exports have been falling: In 1997, Canada exported $379 million to Russia, but in 2002 (the most recent year for which data is available) exports fell to $243 million.

Sources: Portions of the Russian example adapted from Lisa Bertagnoli, "To Russia with…Reservations," *Marketing News,* April 9, 2001, pp. 1, 11. Quotes and other information in both examples from "Business: Not Quite a Billion," *The Economist,* January 2, 1999, p. 56; Paul Starobin, "Russia's Middle Class," *Business Week,* October 16, 2000, pp. 78–85; Sabrina Tavernise, "Moscow Is Getting a Taste of the Mall," *New York Times,* August 10, 2001, p. W1; Lisa Bertagnoli, "Red Square Rising," *Marketing News,* December 3, 2001, pp. 12–13; Dexter Roberts and Alysha Webb, "Motor Nation," *Business Week,* June 17, 2002, pp. 44–45; Melana Zyla, "Polish Your Connections To Prosper in Business," *Globe and Mail,* July 1, 1997, p. C13; "Central and Eastern Europe: A Market Ready To Harvest," *Canadian Business* (advertising supplement), July 1997; "Hong Kong Means Business," *Financial Post,* June 30, 1997, p. HK4; Department of Foreign Affairs and International Trade, "Team Canada 2001 Concludes with $5.7 Billion in New Deals" (news release), February 17, 2001; Industry Canada, "China High Tech Fair," October 10, 2003, http://strategis. ic.gc.ca/; and Department of Foreign Affairs and International Trade, CanadaEuropa Mundi, "Countries in *Europa:* Canada– Russia Relations," June 2003, www.dfait-maeci.gc.ca/ canadaeuropa/country_rus_c-en.asp.

offers great potential. Only 20 percent of China's rural dwellers brush daily, so Colgate and its competitors are aggressively pursuing promotional and educational programs, from massive ad campaigns to visits to local schools to sponsoring oral care research. Through such efforts, in this $457 million market dominated by local brands, Colgate has expanded its market share from 7 percent in 1995 to 35 percent today, despite competing with a state-owned brand managed by Unilever and P&G's Crest.

Colgate's decision to enter the Chinese market seems fairly straightforward: China is a huge market without established competition. Given the low rate of brushing, this already huge market can grow even larger. Yet we still can question whether market size *alone* is reason enough for selecting China. Colgate must also consider other factors. Will the Chinese government remain stable and supportive? Does China provide for the production and distribution technologies needed to produce and market Colgate's products profitably? Will Colgate be able to overcome cultural barriers and convince Chinese consumers to brush their teeth regularly? Can Colgate compete effectively with dozens of local competitors? Colgate's current success in China suggests that it could answer yes to all of these questions. Still, the company's future in China is filled with uncertainties.

Possible global markets should be ranked on several factors, including market size, market growth, cost of doing business, competitive advantage, and risk level. The goal is to determine the potential of each market, using indicators such as those shown in Table 18.1. Then the marketer must decide which ones offer the greatest long-run return on investment.

Deciding How to Enter the Market

Once a company has decided to sell in a foreign country, it must determine the best mode of entry. Its choices are *exporting, joint venturing,* and *direct investment.* Figure 18.2 shows three market entry strategies, along with the options each one offers. As the figure shows, each succeeding strategy involves more commitment and risk, but also more control and potential profits.

Table 18.1 Indicators of Market Potential

1. Demographic characteristics
Size of population
Rate of population growth
Degree of urbanization
Population density
Age structure and composition of the population

2. Geographic characteristics
Physical size of a country
Topographical characteristics
Climate conditions

3. Economic factors
GNP per capita
Income distribution
Rate of growth of GNP
Ratio of investment to GNP

4. Technological factors
Level of technological skill
Existing production technology
Existing consumption technology
Education levels

5. Sociocultural factors
Dominant values
Lifestyle patterns
Ethnic groups
Linguistic fragmentation

6. National goals and plans
Industry priorities
Infrastructure investment plans

Sources: Susan P. Douglas, C. Samuel Craig, and Warren Keegan, "Approaches to Assessing International Marketing Opportunities for Small- and Medium-Sized Businesses," *Columbia Journal of World Business,* Fall 1982, pp. 26–32. Copyright 1982, 1999, *Columbia Journal of World Business.* Reprinted with permission. Also see Pankaj Ghemawat, "Distance Still Matters," *Harvard Business Review,* September 2001, pp. 137–147.

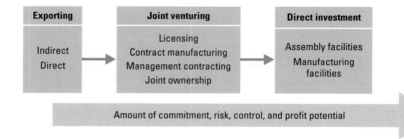

Figure 18.2 Market entry strategies

Exporting

The simplest way to enter a foreign market is through **exporting**. The company may passively export its surpluses from time to time, or it may make an active commitment to expand exports to a particular market. In either case, the company produces all of its goods in its home country. It may or may not modify them for the export market. Exporting involves the least change in the company's product lines, organization, investments, and mission.

Companies typically start with *indirect exporting*, working through independent international marketing intermediaries. Indirect exporting involves less investment because the firm does not require an overseas sales force or set of contacts. It also involves less risk. International marketing intermediaries—domestic-based export merchants or agents, cooperative organizations, and export-management companies—bring know-how and services to the relationship, so the seller normally makes fewer mistakes.

Sellers may eventually move into *direct exporting*, whereby they handle their own exports. The investment and risk are somewhat greater in this strategy, but so is the potential return. A company can conduct direct exporting in several ways. It can set up a domestic export department that carries out export activities. It can set up an overseas sales branch that handles sales, distribution, and perhaps promotion: The sales branch gives the seller more presence and program control in the foreign market and often serves as a display centre and customer service centre. The company also can send home-based salespeople abroad at certain times to find business. Finally, the company can do its exporting either through foreign-based distributors who buy and own the goods or through foreign-based agents who sell the goods on behalf of the company.

Joint Venturing

Joint venturing

Entering foreign markets by joining with domestic or foreign companies to produce or market products or services.

A second method of entering a foreign market is **joint venturing**—joining with domestic or foreign companies to produce or market products or services. Joint venturing differs from exporting in that the company joins with a partner to sell or market abroad. It differs from direct investment in that an association is formed with someone in the foreign country. There are four types of joint ventures: *licensing*, *contract manufacturing*, *management contracting*, and *joint ownership*.

Licensing

Licensing

A method of entering a foreign market in which the company enters into an agreement with a licensee in the foreign market, offering the right to use a manufacturing process, trademark, patent, trade secret, or other item of value for a fee or royalty.

Licensing is a simple way for a manufacturer to enter international marketing. The company enters into an agreement with a licensee in the foreign market. For a fee or royalty, the licensee buys the right to use the company's manufacturing process, trademark, patent, trade secret, or other item of value. The company gains entry into the market at little risk; the licensee gains production expertise for a well-known product or name without having to start from scratch.

Coca-Cola markets internationally by licensing bottlers around the world and supplying them with the syrup needed to produce the product. Molson Breweries ditched its longtime partner Anheuser Busch and licensed its beers to Coors. In Japan, Budweiser beer flows from Kirin breweries, Lady Borden ice cream is churned out at Meiji Milk Products dairies, and Marlboro cigarettes roll off production lines at Japan Tobacco, Inc. Online brokerage E*TRADE has set up E*TRADE-branded websites under licensing agreements in Canada, Australia/New Zealand, and France. And Tokyo Disneyland is owned and operated by Oriental Land Company under licence from the Walt Disney Company: The 45-year licence gives Disney licensing fees plus 10 percent of admissions and 5 percent of food and merchandise sales.[32]

Licensing has potential disadvantages, however. The firm has less control over the licensee than it would over its own production facilities. If the licensee is very successful, the firm has given up these profits, and if and when the contract ends, it may find it has created a competitor.

Contract Manufacturing

Contract manufacturing

A joint venture in which a company contracts with manufacturers in a foreign market to produce the product or provide its service.

With **contract manufacturing**, the company contracts with manufacturers in the foreign market to produce its product or provide its service. Sears used this method in opening up department stores in Mexico and Spain, where it found qualified local manufacturers to produce many of the products it sells. The drawbacks of contract manufacturing are the decreased control over the manufacturing process and the loss of potential profits on manufacturing. The benefits are the chance to start faster, with less risk, and the later opportunity either to form a partnership with or to buy out the local manufacturer.

Licensing: Tokyo Disneyland is owned and operated by the Oriental Land Co., Ltd. (a Japanese development company), under licence from the Walt Disney Company.

Management Contracting

Management contracting
A joint venture in which the domestic firm supplies the management know-how to a foreign company that supplies the capital; the domestic firm exports management services rather than products.

Under **management contracting**, the domestic firm supplies management know-how to a foreign company that supplies the capital. The domestic firm exports management services rather than products. Canada's 2000 trade mission to Russia resulted in a number of management contracts, including the $220-million deal signed between Moscow-based Aeroflot and Montreal-based engineering giant SNC-Lavalin to build a rapid transit system linking Sheremetyevo Airport with downtown Moscow.[33]

Management contracting is a low-risk method of getting into a foreign market, and it yields income from the beginning. The arrangement is even more attractive if the contracting firm has an option to buy some share in the managed company later on. The arrangement is not sensible, however, if the company can put its scarce management talent to better uses or if it can make greater profits by undertaking the whole venture. Management contracting also prevents the company from setting up its own operations for a period of time.

Joint Ownership

Joint ownership
A joint venture in which a company joins with investors in a foreign market to create a local business in which they share ownership and control.

Joint ownership ventures consist of one company joining forces with foreign investors to create a local business in which they share ownership and control. A company can buy an interest in a local firm, or the two parties can form a new business venture. Magna International, the Canadian auto parts manufacturer, acquired much of U.K. firm Marley PLC to expand its business into the European Union.[34] Joint ownership may be needed for economic or political reasons. The firm may lack the financial, physical, or managerial resources to undertake the venture alone. A foreign government may require joint ownership as a condition for entry.

KFC entered Japan through a joint ownership venture with Japanese conglomerate Mitsubishi. KFC sought a good way to enter the large but difficult Japanese fast-food market. In turn, Mitsubishi, one of Japan's largest poultry producers, understood the Japanese culture and had money to invest. Together, they helped KFC succeed in the semi-closed Japanese market.

Surprisingly, with Mitsubishi's guidance, KFC developed decidedly un-Japanese positioning for its Japanese restaurants:

While its initial reception in Japan was great, KFC still had a number of obstacles to overcome. The Japanese were uncomfortable with the idea of fast food and franchising. They saw fast food as artificial, made by mechanical means, and unhealthy. KFC Japan knew that it had to build trust in the KFC brand and flew to Kentucky to do it. There it filmed the most authentic version of Colonel Sanders's beginnings possible. To show the philosophy of KFC—the southern hospitality, old American tradition, and authentic home cooking—the agency first created the quintessential southern mother. With "My Old Kentucky Home" by Stephen Foster playing in the background, the commercial showed Colonel Sanders's mother making and feeding her grandchildren KFC chicken made with eleven secret spices. It conjured up scenes of good home cookin' from the American South, positioning KFC as wholesome, aristocratic food. In the end, the Japanese people could not get enough of this special American chicken. The campaign was hugely successful, and in less than eight years KFC expanded its presence from 400 locations to more than 1000. Most Japanese now know "My Old Kentucky Home" by heart.[35]

Joint ownership has certain drawbacks. The partners may disagree over investment, marketing, or other policies. Whereas many Canadian firms like to reinvest earnings for growth, local firms often like to take out these earnings; and whereas Canadian firms emphasize the role of marketing, local investors may rely on selling.

Direct Investment

Direct investment
Entering a foreign market by developing foreign-based assembly or manufacturing facilities.

The biggest involvement in a foreign market comes through **direct investment**—the development of foreign-based assembly or manufacturing facilities. If a company has gained experience in exporting and the foreign market is large enough, foreign production facilities offer many advantages. The firm may have lower costs in the form of cheaper labour or raw materials, foreign government investment incentives, and freight savings. The firm may improve its image in the host country because it creates jobs. Generally, a firm develops a deeper relationship with government, customers, local suppliers, and distributors, allowing it to better adapt its products to the local market. Finally, the firm keeps full control over the investment and can, therefore, develop manufacturing and marketing policies that serve its long-term international objectives.

Joint ownership: KFC entered Japan through a joint ownership venture with Japanese conglomerate Mitsubishi.

The main disadvantage of direct investment is the many risks—restricted or devalued currencies, falling markets, or government takeovers. In some cases, a firm has no choice but to accept these risks if it wants to operate in the host country:

> When Toronto-based Bata Shoes (www.bata.com) decided to return to founder Thomas Bata's Czech homeland and begin operations through the route of direct investment, the path wasn't an easy one. Negotiations with government officials to re-establish the family shoe business took years of wrangling. Legal and political hurdles represented only half the battle, as marketing manager Jeanne Milne quickly learned. She faced problems ranging from lack of customer research to redesigning window displays. She discovered that offering sales didn't work since consumers in the Czech Republic equate discounts with inferior quality. Service providers had to be trained since providing service had become a foreign concept. As one Czech employee complained, "Why should I smile at customers? They don't smile at me." Even customers had to be re-educated. When employees went to the stockroom to search for correct sizes, customers followed them, believing that shoe clerks were going elsewhere to avoid serving them. The struggle has been worth it. Bata is held up as an exemplar of one of the few truly successful privatization efforts in Eastern Europe.[36]

Deciding on the Global Marketing Program

Standardized marketing mix
An international marketing strategy for using basically the same product, advertising, distribution channels, and other elements of the marketing mix in all of the company's international markets.

Adapted marketing mix
An international marketing strategy for adjusting the marketing mix elements to each international target market, bearing more costs but hoping for a larger market share and return.

Companies that operate in one or more foreign markets must decide how much, if at all, to adapt their marketing mixes to local conditions. At one extreme, some global companies use a **standardized marketing mix**, primarily selling the same products and using the same marketing approaches worldwide. At the other extreme is an **adapted marketing mix**. In this case, the producer adjusts the marketing mix elements to each target market, bearing more costs but hoping for a larger market share and return.

The question of whether to adapt or standardize the marketing mix has been much debated in recent years. The marketing concept holds that marketing programs will be more effective if tailored to the unique needs of each targeted customer group. If this concept applies within a country, it should apply even more in international markets. Consumers in different countries have widely varied cultural backgrounds, needs and wants, spending power, product preferences, and shopping patterns. Because these differences are hard to change, most marketers adapt their products, prices, channels, and promotions to fit consumer desires in each country.

However, global standardization is not an all-or-nothing proposition but rather a matter of degree. Companies should look for more standardization to help keep down costs and prices and to build greater global brand power. But they must not replace long-run marketing thinking with short-run financial thinking. Although standardization saves money, marketers must make certain that they offer what consumers in each country want.[37]

Many possibilities exist between the extremes of standardization and complete adaptation. For example, although Whirlpool ovens, refrigerators, clothes washers, and other major appliances share the same interiors worldwide, their outer styling and features are designed to meet the preferences of consumers in different countries. Coca-Cola sells virtually the same Coca-Cola Classic beverage worldwide, positioned to have cross-cultural appeal. However, Coca-Cola is less sweet or less carbonated in certain countries. The company also sells a variety of other beverages created specifically for the taste buds of local markets and modifies its distribution channels according to local conditions.

Marketing mix adaptation: In India, McDonald's serves chicken, fish, vegetable burgers, and the Maharaja Mac—two all-mutton patties, special sauce, lettuce, cheese, pickles, onions, on a sesame-seed bun.

Similarly, McDonald's uses the same basic operating formula in its restaurants around the world but adapts its menu to local tastes. For example, it uses chili sauce instead of ketchup on its hamburgers in Mexico. In Vienna, its restaurants include "McCafes," which offer coffee blended to local tastes, and in Korea, it sells roast pork on a bun with a garlicky soy sauce. In India, where cows are considered sacred, McDonald's serves chicken, fish, vegetable burgers, and the Maharaja Mac—two all-mutton patties, special sauce, lettuce, cheese, pickles, onions on a sesame-seed bun.[38]

Some international marketers suggest that companies should "think globally but act locally." They advocate a "glocal" strategy in which the firm standardizes certain core marketing elements and localizes others. The corporate level gives strategic direction; local units focus on the individual consumer differences. They conclude: global marketing, yes; global standardization, not necessarily.

Product

Five strategies allow for adapting products and promotions to a foreign market (see Figure 18.3).[39] We first discuss the three product strategies and then turn to the two promotion strategies.

Straight product extension means marketing a product in a foreign market without any change. Top management tells its marketing people: "Take the product as is and find customers for it." The first step, however, should be to find out whether foreign consumers use that product and what form they prefer.

Straight product extension
Marketing a product in a foreign market without any change.

		Product		
		Don't change product	Adapt product	Develop new product
Promotion	Don't change promotion	1. Straight extension	3. Product adaptation	5. Product invention
	Adapt promotion	2. Communication adaptation	4. Dual adaptation	

Figure 18.3 Five international product and promotion strategies

Straight extension has been successful in some cases and disastrous in others. Kellogg cereals, Gillette razors, IBM computer services, Heineken beer, and Black & Decker tools are all sold successfully in about the same form around the world. But General Foods introduced its standard powdered Jell-O in the British market only to find that British consumers prefer a solid wafer or cake form. Likewise, Philips began to make a profit in Japan only after it reduced the size of its coffeemakers to fit into smaller Japanese kitchens and its shavers to fit smaller Japanese hands. Straight extension is tempting because it involves no additional product development costs, manufacturing changes, or new promotion. But it can be costly in the long run if products fail to satisfy foreign consumers.

Product adaptation

Adapting a product to meet local conditions or wants in foreign markets.

Product adaptation involves changing the product to meet local conditions or wants. For example, Procter & Gamble's Vidal Sassoon shampoos contain a single fragrance worldwide, but the amount of scent varies by country—less in Japan, where subtle scents are preferred, and more in Europe. General Foods blends different coffees for the British (who drink their coffee with milk), the French (who drink their coffee black), and Latin Americans (who prefer a chicory taste). Gerber serves the Japanese baby food fare that might turn the stomachs of many Western consumers— local favourites include flounder and spinach stew, cod roe spaghetti, mugwort casserole, and sardines ground up in white radish sauce. Finnish cellular phone superstar Nokia customized its 6100 series phone for every major market. Developers built in rudimentary voice recognition for Asia, where keyboards are a problem, and raised the ring volume so the phone could be heard on crowded Asian streets.

Even MTV, with its largely global programming, has retrenched along more local lines:

Pummelled by dozens of local music channels in Europe, such as Germany's Viva, Holland's The Music Factory, and Scandinavia's ZTV, MTV Europe has had to drop its pan-European programming, which featured a large amount of American and British pop along with local European favourites. In its place, the division created regional channels broadcast by four separate MTV stations—

Nokia positions its 8890 as the only phone international businesspeople need: "One phone for one world."

U.K. & Ireland, Northern Europe, Central Europe, and Southern Europe. Each of the four channels shows programs tailored to the musical tastes of its local market, along with more traditional pan-European pop selections. Within each region, MTV further subdivides its programming. For example, within the U.K., MTV offers sister stations M2 and VH-1, along with three new digital channels (MTV Extra, MTV Base, and VH-1 Classic). Says the head of MTV Europe, "We hope to offer every MTV fan something he or she will like to watch any time of the day."[40]

In some instances, products must also be adapted to local superstitions or spiritual beliefs. In Asia, the spiritual world often relates directly to sales. Hyatt Hotels' experience with the concept of *feng shui* is a good example:

> A practice widely followed in China, Hong Kong, and Singapore (and which has spread to Japan, Vietnam, Korea, and North American communities with sizeable Asian immigrant populations), *feng shui* means "wind and water." Geomancers, or practitioners of *feng shui*, will recommend the most favourable conditions for any venture, particularly the placement of office buildings and the arrangement of desks, doors, and other items within. To have good *feng shui*, a building should face the water and be flanked by mountains—but it should not block the view of the mountain spirits. The Hyatt Hotel in Singapore was designed without *feng shui* in mind and as a result it had to be redesigned to boost business. Originally the front desk was parallel to the doors and road, but this was thought to lead to wealth flowing out. Furthermore, the doors were facing northwest, which easily let undesirable spirits in. The geomancer recommended design alterations so that wealth could be retained and undesirable spirits kept out. Western businesses, from hotel chains, restaurants, and grocery retailers to Las Vegas casinos that serve many Asian visitors, are now incorporating *feng shui* principles into their facilities' designs.[41]

Product invention

Creating new products or services for foreign markets.

Product invention strategy consists of creating something new for the foreign market. This strategy can take two forms. It may mean reintroducing earlier product forms that happen to be well adapted to the needs of a given country—the National Cash Register Company reintroduced its crank-operated cash register at half the price of a modern cash register and sold large numbers in Asia, Latin America, and Spain. Or a company might create a new product to meet a need in another country. For example, an enormous need exists for low-cost, high-protein foods in less developed countries. Companies such as Maple Leaf Foods, McCain, Quaker Oats, Swift, Monsanto, and Archer Daniels Midland are researching the nutrition needs of these countries, creating new foods, and developing advertising campaigns to gain product trial and acceptance. Product invention can be costly, but the payoffs are worthwhile.

Promotion

Companies can either adopt the same promotion strategy they used in their home market or change it for each local market, a process called *communication adaptation*. If it adapts both the product and the communication, the company engages in **dual adaptation**. Consider advertising messages. Some global companies use a standardized advertising theme around the world. For example, to help communicate its global reach, IBM Global Services runs virtually identical "People Who Think. People Who Do. People Who Get It" ads in dozens of countries around the world. Of course, even in highly standardized promotion campaigns, some small changes may be required to adjust for language and minor cultural differences. Guy Laroche uses virtually the same ads for its Drakkar Noir fragrances in Europe as in Arab countries, but it subtly tones down the Arab versions to meet cultural differences in attitudes toward sensuality.

Dual adaptation

A global communication strategy of adapting both a product and its advertising message to global markets.

Some companies standardize their advertising around the world, adapting only to meet cultural differences. Guy Laroche uses similar ads in Europe (left) and Arab countries (right), but tones down the sensuality in the Arab version—the man is clothed and the woman barely touches him.

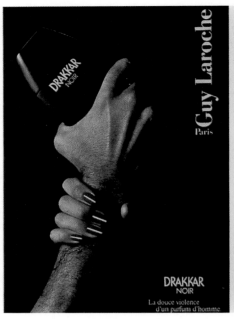

Companies must also change colours sometimes to avoid taboos in some countries. Purple is associated with death in most of Latin America, white is a mourning colour in Japan, and green is associated with jungle sickness in Malaysia. Even names must be changed. In Sweden, Helene Curtis changed the name of its Every Night Shampoo to Every Day because Swedes usually wash their hair in the morning. Kellogg had to rename Bran Buds cereal in Sweden, where the name roughly translates as "burned farmer." (See Real Marketing 18.4 for more on language blunders in international marketing.)

Communication adaptation
A global communication strategy of fully adapting advertising messages to local markets.

Other companies follow a strategy of **communication adaptation**, fully adapting their advertising messages to local markets. Kellogg ads in North America promote the taste and nutrition of Kellogg's cereals over competitors' brands. In France, where consumers drink little milk and eat little for breakfast, Kellogg's ads must convince consumers that cereals are a tasty and healthful breakfast. In India, where many consumers eat heavy, fried breakfasts, Kellogg's advertising convinces buyers to switch to a lighter, more nutritious breakfast diet. Similarly, Coca-Cola sells its low-calorie beverage as Diet Coke in North America, the United Kingdom, and the Middle and Far East but as Light elsewhere. According to Diet Coke's global brand manager, in Spanish-speaking countries Coke Light ads "position the soft drink as an object of desire, rather than as a way to feel good about yourself, as Diet Coke is positioned in the United States." This "desire positioning" plays off research showing that "Coca-Cola Light is seen in other parts of world as a vibrant brand that exudes a sexy confidence."[42]

Media also need to be adapted internationally because their availability varies from country to country. Television advertising time is very limited in Europe, for instance, ranging from four hours a day in France to none in Scandinavian countries. Advertisers must buy time months in advance and have little control over airtimes. Magazines also vary in effectiveness. For example, magazines are a major medium in Italy and a minor one in Austria. Newspapers are national in the United Kingdom but are only local in Spain.[43]

The Institute of Canadian Advertising, which represents most of Canada's major agencies, launched a 1997 marketing initiative aimed at achieving better recognition of the strong track record and worldwide capabilities of Canadian agencies. In an effort that integrated public relations, ads in trade publications, direct

REAL MARKETING

18.4 Watch Your Language!

*M*any global companies have had difficulty crossing the language barrier, with results ranging from mild embarrassment to outright failure. Seemingly innocuous brand names and advertising phrases can take on unintended meanings when translated into other languages. Careless translations can make a marketer look foolish to foreign consumers.

We've all run across examples when buying products from other countries. Here's one from a firm in Taiwan attempting to instruct children on how to install a ramp on a garage for toy cars: "Before you play with, fix waiting plate by yourself as per below diagram. But after you once fixed it, you can play with as is and no necessary to fix off again." Many North American firms are guilty of similar atrocities when marketing abroad.

The classic language blunders involve standardized brand names that do not translate well. When Coca-Cola first marketed Coke in China in the 1920s, it developed a group of Chinese characters that, when pronounced, sounded like the product name. Unfortunately, the characters actually translated to mean "bite the wax tadpole." Now, the characters on Chinese Coke bottles translate as "happiness in the mouth."

Several carmakers have had similar problems when their brand names crashed into the language barrier. Chevy's Nova translated into Spanish as *no va*—"it doesn't go." GM changed the name to Caribe and sales increased. Ford introduced its Fiera truck only to discover that the name means "ugly old woman" in Spanish. Rolls-Royce avoided the name Silver Mist in German markets, where *mist* means "manure." Sunbeam, however, entered the German market with its Mist Stick hair curling iron—and as should have been anticipated, the Germans had little use for a "manure wand." A similar fate awaited Colgate when it introduced a toothpaste in France called Cue—the name of a notorious porno magazine.

One well-intentioned firm sold its shampoo in Brazil under the name Evitol. It soon realized it was claiming to sell a "dandruff contraceptive." An American company reportedly had trouble marketing Pet milk in French-speaking areas. It seems that the word *pet* in French means, among other things, "to break wind." Hunt-Wesson introduced its Big John products in Quebec as Gros Jos before learning that it means "big breasts" in French—but this gaffe had no

apparent effect on sales! Interbrand of London, the firm that created such household names as Prozac and Acura, recently developed a brand name "hall of shame" list, which contained these and other foreign brand names you're never likely to see inside the local supermarket: Krapp toilet paper (Denmark), Crapsy Fruit cereal (France), Happy End toilet paper (Germany), Mukk yogurt (Italy), Zit lemonade (Germany), Poo curry powder (Argentina), and Pschitt lemonade (France).

Travellers often encounter well-intentioned advice from service firms that takes on meanings very different from those intended. The menu in one Swiss restaurant proudly stated, "Our wines leave you nothing to hope for." Signs in a Japanese hotel pronounced: "You are invited to take advantage of the chambermaid." At a laundry in Rome, it was: "Ladies, leave your clothes here and spend the afternoon having a good time." The brochure at a Tokyo car rental offered this sage advice: "When passenger of foot heave in sight, tootle the horn. Trumpet him melodiously at first, but if he still obstacles your passage, tootle him with vigour."

Advertising themes often lose—or gain—something in the translation. The Coors beer slogan "Get loose with Coors" in Spanish came out as "Get the runs with Coors." Coca-Cola's "Coke adds life" theme in Japanese translated into "Coke brings your ancestors back from the dead." In Chinese, the KFC slogan "finger-lickin' good" came out as "eat your fingers off." Frank Perdue's classic line, "It takes a tough man to make a tender chicken," took on added meaning in Spanish: "It takes a sexually stimulated man to make a chicken affectionate." Even when the language is the same, word usage may differ from country to country. Thus, the British ad line for Electrolux vacuum cleaners—"Nothing sucks like an Electrolux"—would capture few customers in Canada or the United States.

Sources: See David A. Ricks, "Perspectives: Translation Blunders in International Business," *Journal of Language for International Business,* 7:2, 1996, pp. 50–55; David W. Helin, "When Slogans Go Wrong," *American Demographics,* February 1992, p. 14; "But Will It Sell in Tulsa?" *Newsweek,* March 17, 1997, p. 8; "What You Didn't Learn in Marketing 101," *Sales & Marketing Management,* May 1997, p. 20; Ken Friedenreich, "The Lingua Too Franca," *World Trade,* April 1998, p. 98; Richard P. Carpenter, "What They Meant to Say Was...," *Boston Globe,* August 2, 1998, p. M6; Thomas T. Sermon, "Cutting Corners in Language Risky Business," *Marketing News,* April 23, 2001, p. 9; and Lara L Sowinski, "Ubersetzung, Traduzione, or Traduccion," *World Trade,* February 2002, pp. 48–49.

marketing, a website (www.goodmedia.com/ica), and the 126-page book *Canadian Advertising, Push the Boundaries,* the institute worked to convey the message that Canadian-produced advertising travels well beyond Canada's borders. The campaign featured work done by Canadian agencies such as a promotion for Visa ads that helped to reinforce the leadership position of the card in Canada and South America.[44]

Price

Companies also face many problems in setting their international prices. For example, how might Black & Decker price its power tools globally? It could set a uniform price all around the world, but this amount would be too high a price in poor countries and not high enough in rich ones. It could charge what consumers in each country would bear, but this strategy ignores differences in the actual costs from country to country. Finally, the company could use a standard markup of its costs everywhere, but this approach might price Black & Decker out of the market in some countries where costs are high.

Regardless of how companies go about pricing their products, their foreign prices probably will be higher than their domestic prices. A Gucci handbag may sell for $70 in Italy and $300 in Canada. Why? Gucci faces a *price escalation* problem. It must add the cost of transportation, tariffs, importer margin, wholesaler margin, and retailer margin to its factory price. Depending on these added costs, the product may have to sell for two to five times as much in another country to make the same profit. For example, a pair of Levi's jeans that sells for $40 in Canada typically fetches $82 in Tokyo and $115 in Paris. A computer that sells for $1000 in New York may cost £1,000 in the United Kingdom. A DaimlerChrysler automobile priced at $13 000 in Canada sells for more than $60 000 in South Korea. Consider this example:

> Makers of Feathercraft kayaks discovered the problem of price escalation when they marketed in Japan. Even though the kayaks cost the Japanese consumer twice as much as they do Canadian purchasers, the firm makes its lowest margins on Japanese sales. The problem results from Japan's multi-level distribution system. A kayak may have to pass through five intermediaries before reaching the consumer, and each intermediary gets a cut of the price pie.

Another problem involves setting a price for goods that a company ships to its foreign subsidiaries. If the company charges a foreign subsidiary too much, it may end up paying higher tariff duties even while paying lower income taxes in that country. If the company charges its subsidiary too little, it can be charged with *dumping.* Dumping occurs when a company either charges less than the good costs or less than it charges in its home market. Thus Harley-Davidson accused Honda and Kawasaki of dumping motorcycles on the U.S. market. The U.S. International Trade Commission agreed and responded with a special five-year tariff on Japanese heavy motorcycles, starting at 45 percent in 1983 and gradually dropping to 10 percent by 1988. Various governments are always watching for dumping abuses, and often force companies to set the price charged by other competitors for the same or similar products.[45]

Recent economic and technological forces have had an impact on global pricing. For example, in the European Union, the transition to the euro is reducing the amount of price differentiation. As consumers recognize price differentiation by country, companies are being forced to harmonize prices throughout the countries that have adopted the single currency. Companies and marketers that offer the most unique or necessary products or services will be least affected by such "price transparency":

> For Marie-Claude Lang, a 72-year-old retired Belgian postal worker, the euro is the best thing since bottled water—or French country sausage. Always on the

International pricing: Twelve European Union countries have adopted the euro as a common currency, creating "pricing transparency" and forcing companies harmonize their prices throughout Europe.

prowl for bargains, Ms. Lang is now stalking the wide aisles of an Auchan hypermarket in Roncq, France, a 15-minute drive from her Wervick home.... Ms. Lang has been coming to France every other week for years to stock up on bottled water, milk, and yogurt. But the launch of the euro...has opened her eyes to many more products that she now sees cost less across the border. Today she sees that "saucisse de campagne," is cheaper "by about five euro cents," a savings she didn't notice when she had to calculate the difference between Belgian and French francs. At Europe's borders, the euro is turning into the coupon clipper's delight. Sure, price-conscious Europeans have long crossed into foreign territory to find everything from cheaper television sets to bargain bottles of Coca-Cola. But the new transparency is making comparisons a whole lot easier.[46]

The Internet will also make global price differences more obvious. When firms sell their wares over the Internet, customers can see how much products sell for in different countries. They may even be able to order a product directly from the company location or dealer offering the lowest price. This will force companies toward more standardized international pricing.

Distribution Channels

Whole-channel view
Designing international channels that take into account all the necessary links in distributing the seller's products to final buyers, including the seller's headquarters organization, channels between nations, and channels within nations.

The international company must take a **whole-channel view** of distributing products to final consumers. Figure 18.4 shows the three major links between the seller and the final buyer. The first link, the *seller's headquarters organization*, supervises the channels and is part of the channel itself. The second link, *channels between nations*, moves the products to the borders of the foreign nations. The third link, *channels within nations*, moves the products from their foreign entry point to the final consumers. Some North American manufacturers may think their job is done once the product leaves their hands, but they would do well to pay attention to its handling within foreign countries.

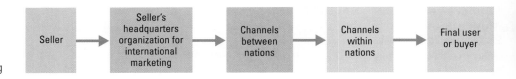

Figure 18.4 Whole-channel concept for international marketing

Channels of distribution within countries vary greatly from nation to nation. First, there are the large differences in the *numbers and types of intermediaries* serving each foreign market. For example, a Canadian company marketing in China must operate through a frustrating maze of state-controlled wholesalers and retailers. Chinese distributors often carry competitors' products and frequently refuse to share even basic sales and marketing information with their suppliers. Hustling for sales is an alien concept to Chinese distributors, who are used to selling all they can obtain. Working with or getting around this system sometimes requires substantial time and investment.

Another difference lies in the *size and character of retail units* abroad. Whereas large-scale retail chains dominate in North America, much retailing in other countries is done by many small independent retailers. In India, millions of retailers operate tiny shops or sell in open markets. Their markups are high, but the actual price is lowered through price haggling. Supermarkets could offer lower prices, but supermarkets are difficult to build and open because of many economic and cultural barriers. Incomes are low, and people who lack refrigeration prefer to shop daily for small amounts rather than weekly for large amounts. Packaging is not well developed because it would add too much to the cost. These factors have kept large-scale retailing from spreading rapidly in developing countries.

When Coke first entered China, for example, customers bicycled up to bottling plants to get their soft drinks. Many shopkeepers still don't have enough electricity to run soft drink coolers. Now, Coca-Cola has set up direct-distribution channels, investing heavily in refrigerators and trucks, and upgrading wiring so that more retailers can install coolers. Still, most of its products in China are sold through large state-owned sugar, tobacco, and wine enterprises or through former state-

A "neighbourhood committee" member sells Coke in Shanghai.

owned wholesale distributors that have now been privatized.[47] Moreover, Coke is always on the lookout for innovative distribution approaches:

> Stroll through any residential area in a Chinese city and sooner or later you'll encounter a senior citizen with a red armband, eyeing strangers suspiciously. These are the pensioners who staff the neighbourhood committees, which act as street-level watchdogs for the ruling Communist Party. In Shanghai, however, some of these socialist guardians have been signed up by the ultimate symbol of American capitalism, Coca-Cola. As part of its strategy to get the product to the customer, Coke approached fourteen neighbourhood committees...with a proposal. The head of Coke's Shanghai division outlines the deal: "We told them, 'You have some old people who aren't doing much. Why don't we stock our product in your office? Then you can sell it, earn some commission, and raise a bit of cash.'" Done. So...how are the party snoops adapting to the market? Not badly, reports the manager. "We use the neighbourhood committees as a sales force," he says. Sales aren't spectacular, but because the committees supervise housing projects with up to 200 families, they have proved to be useful vehicles for building brand awareness.[48]

Deciding on the Global Marketing Organization

Companies can manage their international marketing activities in at least three different ways. Most companies first organize an export department, then create an international division, and finally become a global organization.

A firm normally gets into international marketing by simply shipping out its goods. If its international sales expand, the company organizes an *export department* with a sales manager and a few assistants. As sales increase, the export department then can expand to include various marketing services so that it can actively pursue business. If the firm moves into joint ventures or direct investment, the export department will no longer be adequate.

Many companies become involved in several international markets and ventures. A company can export to one country, license to another, have a joint ownership venture in a third, and own a subsidiary in a fourth. Sooner or later, it will create an *international division* or subsidiary to handle all of its international activity.

International divisions can be organized in several ways. The international division's corporate staff consists of marketing, manufacturing, research, finance, planning, and personnel specialists. They plan for and provide services to various operating units, which can be organized in one of three ways. They can be *geographical organizations,* with country managers who are responsible for salespeople, sales branches, distributors, and licensees in their respective countries. Or the operating units can be *world product groups,* each responsible for worldwide sales of different product groups. Finally, operating units can be *international subsidiaries,* each responsible for its own sales and profits.

Many firms have passed beyond the international division stage and become truly *global organizations.* They stop thinking of themselves as national marketers who sell abroad and start thinking of themselves as global marketers. The top corporate management and staff plan worldwide manufacturing facilities, marketing policies, financial flows, and logistical systems. The global operating units report directly to the chief executive or executive committee of the organization, not to the head of an international division. Executives are trained in worldwide operations, not just domestic *or* international. The company recruits management from many countries, buys components and supplies where they cost the least, and invests where the expected returns are greatest.

Consider the history of Nortel Networks, Canada's premium high-tech manufacturer. In the early 1970s, it sold most of its production to another member of the BCE family, Bell Canada. By the 1980s, with its state-of-the-art digital switching technology, it was making over 50 percent of its sales to the United States, and 5 percent to other world markets. By 1994, however, 32 percent of Nortel's $8.9 billion in revenue came from global markets. Today, it does business in over 150 countries and employs over 37 000 people worldwide. After struggling during the dot-com bust in the late 1990s, with declining revenues and massive layoffs, it looks as if Nortel's fortunes are finally on the upturn again—in September 2003 it signed a $1 billion contract to upgrade the cellular network of U.S. telecom giant Verizon Wireless.[49]

In the twenty-first century, major companies must become more global if they hope to compete. As foreign companies successfully invade domestic markets, companies must move more aggressively into foreign markets. They will have to change from companies that treat their international operations as secondary concerns to companies that view the entire world as a single borderless market.

Looking Back: Reviewing the Concepts

It's time to stop and think back about the global marketing concepts you've covered in this chapter. In the past, North American companies paid little attention to international trade. If they could pick up some extra sales through exporting, that was fine. But the big market was at home, and it teemed with opportunities. Companies today can no longer afford to focus only on their domestic market, regardless of its size. Many industries are global, and firms that operate globally achieve lower costs and higher brand awareness. At the same time, *global marketing* is risky because of variable exchange rates, unstable governments, protectionist tariffs and trade barriers, and several other factors. Given the potential gains and risks of international marketing, companies need a systematic way to make their international marketing decisions.

1. **Discuss how the international trade system, economic, politico-legal, and cultural environments affect a company's international marketing decisions.**

   A company must understand the *global marketing environment*, especially the international trade system. It must assess each foreign market's *economic, politico-legal,* and *cultural characteristics*. The company must then decide whether it wants to go abroad and consider the potential risks and benefits. It must decide on the volume of international sales it wants, how many countries it wants to market in, and which specific markets it

   wants to enter. This last decision calls for weighing the probable rate of return on investment against the level of risk.

2. **Describe three key approaches to entering international markets.**

   The company must decide how to enter each chosen market—whether through *exporting, joint venturing, or direct investment*. Many companies start as exporters, move to joint ventures, and finally make a direct investment in foreign markets. In exporting, the company enters a foreign market by sending and selling products through international marketing intermediaries (indirect exporting) or the company's own department, branch, or sales representative or agent (direct exporting). When establishing a *joint venture,* a company enters foreign markets by joining with foreign companies to produce or market a product or service. In *direct investment,* the company enters a foreign market by developing foreign-based assembly or manufacturing facilities.

3. Explain how companies adapt their marketing mixes for international markets.

Companies must decide how much their products, promotion, price, and channels should be adapted for each foreign market. At one extreme, some global companies use a *standardized marketing mix* worldwide. Others use an *adapted marketing mix,* in which they adjust the marketing mix to each target market, bearing more costs but hoping for a larger market share and return.

4. Identify the three major forms of international marketing organization.

The company must develop an effective organization for international marketing. Most firms start with an *export department* and graduate to an *international division.* A few become *global organizations,* with worldwide marketing planned and managed by the top officers of the company. Global organizations view the entire world as a single, borderless market.

Reviewing the Key Terms

Adapted marketing mix   736
Communication adaptation   740
Contract manufacturing   733
Countertrade   720
Direct investment   735
Dual adaptation   739
Economic community   715
Embargo   712

Exchange controls   712
Exporting   732
Global firm   711
Joint ownership   734
Joint venturing   733
Licensing   733
Management contracting   734
Non-tariff trade barriers   712

Product adaptation   738
Product invention   739
Quota   712
Standardized marketing mix   736
Straight product extension   737
Tariff   712
Whole-channel view   743

Discussing the Concepts

1. With the advent of faster communication, transportation, and financial flows, the world is shrinking rapidly. The terms *global industry* and *global firm* are becoming more common. Define these terms and provide an example of each.

2. When exporting goods to another country, a marketer may face various trade restrictions. Discuss the effects that each of these restrictions can have on an exporter's marketing mix: (a) tariffs, (b) quotas, and (c) embargoes.

3. What is a free trade zone? What benefits and drawbacks does NAFTA present to each of its member nations? Why have trade unions been against NAFTA?

4. A country's industrial structure shapes its product and service needs, income levels, and employment levels. Briefly discuss the four major types of industrial structures.

5. Countertrade makes up an estimated 20 percent of world trade. Describe countertrade and its various forms. What are the advantages and disadvantages of countertrade in its various forms?

6. Before going abroad, a company should define its international marketing objectives, policies, and modes of entry. Assume that you are a product manager for Nike. Outline a plan for expanding your operations and marketing efforts into the nation of South Africa.

7. Once a company has decided to sell in a foreign country, it must determine the best mode of entry. Assume that you are the marketing manager for Mountain Dew and devise a plan for marketing your product in China. Pick a mode of entry, explain your marketing strategy, and comment on possible difficulties you might encounter.

8. Which type of international marketing organization would you suggest for the following companies: (a) Indigo Books and Music, (b) Ty, which intends to open a new division to sell its Beanie Babies globally, (c) a European perfume manufacturer that plans to expand into the United States, and (d) DaimlerChrysler planning to sell its full line of products in the Middle East.

Applying the Concepts

1. With the signing of the North American Free Trade Agreement (NAFTA), Canada has increased its trade with the United States and Mexico. Many towns along the U.S.–Canada border have both benefited and suffered from this trade. For example, a large distribution centre that serves Wal-Mart was built in Brockville, Ontario, a town in close proximity to the Ivey Lea bridge that joins Canada with the United States. Other towns, such as Collingwood, Ontario, have lost manufacturing jobs to Mexico, where wage rates are far lower.

   Marketers have found that moving goods and services across the border can be highly profitable and benefit the economies of all three countries. Good jobs, cheap labour, quality products, affordable products, and the spirit of cooperation are all discussed by the three countries' leaders in trade talks that occur on an increasingly frequent basis. Trade disputes still arise, however, and are a reflection of both the challenges and opportunities of free trade. For example, Canada's softwood lumber industry was hit hard when heavy duties were imposed by the United States. And there are rumblings on both sides of the Canada–U.S. border with regard to the Internet pharmacy industry that has sprung up in Manitoba to serve the U.S. marketplace.

   To learn more about the problems and challenges of the "border market," examine the following websites: (a) Department of Foreign Affairs and International Trade, "Canada and the North American Free Trade Agreement," www.dfait-maeci.gc.ca/nafta-alena/menu-en. asp, (b) the NAFTA Secretariat, www.nafta-sec-alena. org/DefaultSite/home/index_e.aspx, and (c) Economic Policy Institute Briefing Document, "NAFTA at Seven," www.epinet.org/content.cfm/briefingpapers_nafta01_ index.

   Note: Other helpful sites include the Center for International Business Education and Research—Michigan State University (http://ciber.msu.edu/); the International Trade Administration (www.ita.doc.gov); the CIA's 2003 World Fact Book (www.odci.gov/cia/ publications/factbook/index.html); the World Bank (www.worldbank.org); the World Trade Organization (www.wto.org); and Cyberatlas (www.cyberatlas. internet.com).

   a. How could a manager seeking information about trade among Canada, Mexico, and the United States use the above reference sites to find needed data?

   b. What were the most interesting facts you learned about the cross-border trade among these three countries?

   c. Place yourself in the role of a manager of a Canadian product. How could the information you discovered at the websites be converted into opportunities for market expansion for that product?

2. Nowhere is international competition more apparent than in the digital camera market. Overnight, the advent of digital cameras has changed the way many photographers view their equipment. Digital cameras offer opportunities for reproduction and Internet viewing unmatched by more traditional products. However, the market is also uncharted, chaotic, and increasingly crowded, with more than 20 manufacturers worldwide. The latest entrant is film giant Fuji (www.fujifilm.com). As the world's number two producer, Fuji now plans to meet or beat Kodak (www.kodak.com), Sony (www. sony.com), Olympus (www.olympus.com), and Konica (www.konica.com) in digital camera products. Fuji introduced its first digital cameras in its own backyard—Japan, which is also a Sony stronghold. One factor motivating the move into digital cameras was its inability to erode Kodak's worldwide share of the film market. If the wave of the future turns out to be digital, Fuji plans to ride the wave's crest for as long as it can.

   a. Analyze Fuji's strategy of entering the digital camera market. What challenges will Fuji most likely face? How can Fuji's traditional strengths in film aid its efforts in the new digital camera market?

   b. What world markets should Fuji consider after Japan? Explain.

   c. If you were the marketing manager of Fuji, what advertising strategy would you suggest for Fuji's new product venture? What distribution strategy? What role will price play in the success of the strategy?

   d. What actions will Kodak, Olympus, Konica, and Sony probably take to counter Fuji's entry?

Company Case

Wal-Mart: *The* Global Retailer

Wal-Mart is the world's largest retailer. In fact, it's the world's largest *company,* with sales in 2002 totalling nearly $287 billion. Of that total, $46.4 billion were from the fast-growing Wal-Mart International Division. Wal-Mart is growing at an incredible clip, both at home and abroad. In the early 1990s, its sales were a little less than $111 billion; it had 2200 stores and no international division. Today, it has over 3200 stores, with about 1100 of them outside the United States. Even though Wal-Mart continues to open stores in the United States, the biggest opportunity for future growth lies in international expansion.

Wal-Mart first "went abroad" to Canada when it purchased 122 Canadian Woolco stores in 1993. By mid-2002, it had 196 stores in Canada, where it was ranked the best retailer and the ninth best company for which to work. In the fall of 2003, four Sam's Clubs opened in Canada as a possible prelude to bringing Wal-Mart's mammoth supercentres to the country.

Following its move north, the retailing giant turned south into Mexico, using joint ventures and sometimes buying companies outright. Wal-Mart opened its first Mexican store in 1991. By mid-2002, it had opened 66 supercentres, 47 Sam's Clubs, 454 Superama supermarkets, 51 Suburbia Apparel outlets, 245 restaurants under the Vips division, and 110 Bodego units carrying a limited assortment of discount merchandise. In the first half of 2002, sales in Mexico totalled $6.4 billion, and the company announced plans to add 60 new stores in Mexico by the end of 2003. Obviously, Mexico has been a big success for Wal-Mart.

From Mexico, Wal-Mart moved to another Latin market, Puerto Rico. During the next 10 years, Wal-Mart opened 11 more Puerto Rican stores. In 2002 it announced that it would buy Supermercados Amigo, Puerto Rico's second-largest grocery retailer. After the

purchase, Wal-Mart would have 47 stores and an estimated $1.9 billion in Puerto Rican sales. Sensing a good market, Wal-Mart intended to invest $520 million more in Puerto Rico in the next five years.

Next, it was on to South America. In late 1995, Wal-Mart established stores in Brazil and Argentina. These have been Wal-Mart's most disappointing ventures in the western hemisphere. For one thing, the Argentinean economy is troubled; Argentina's presidency seems to be a revolving door, and inflation is spiralling upward. There's not much Wal-Mart can do about these environmental factors, but it has maintained 11 stores there in the hopes that the economic picture will eventually turn around. The picture in Brazil is a little brighter. There, Wal-Mart has 12 supercentres, 8 Sam's Clubs, and 2 small-format stores called "Todo Dia." Future investment in Brazil may follow the Todo Dia format of 45 000-square-foot stores selling general merchandise. These smaller stores enable Wal-Mart to enter crowded Brazilian neighbourhoods where they could never locate a supercentre.

From Latin America, Wal-Mart moved into Asia. Wal-Mart's first stop in Southeast Asia was Hong Kong, where it entered a joint venture with Ek Chor Distribution System Co. Ltd. to establish Value Clubs. Because Ek Chor is actually owned by C.P. Pokphand of Bangkok, Wal-Mart was then able to locate in Thailand and Indonesia. Hong Kong was also a stepping-stone to the world's most populous country, China. Wal-Mart opened its first Chinese store in 2000, operated 19 stores there by 2002, and planned to open 10 more there in 2003. It also operated 9 stores in South Korea (up from 4 in 1998), although growth potential there is not as good.

Wal-Mart has not overlooked Europe. In 1998, it bought the 21-unit Wertkauf chain in Germany, and in

1999, it snapped up the 74-unit Interspar hypermarket chain from Spar Handel. Germany looked especially attractive because it is the third-largest retail market in the world, behind the United States and Japan. From the start, however, Germany presented problems. Some of these involved real estate: strict zoning laws, scarcity of land, and high real estate prices. Another problem was well-entrenched unions, which were unlikely to allow their members to gather in the morning to respond to Wal-Mart's traditional "Give me a *W;* Give me an *A*..." motivational sessions. Another issue: retailing in Germany is dominated by a few large chains, generating intense competition. Finally, German consumers are among the most demanding in the world. Although not as price sensitive as consumers in some other countries, they are very quality conscious. This last point raises the question, Is Germany a good market for a discounter?

In fact, Germany has yet to work for Wal-Mart. By early 2002, the company was still experiencing losses across its 95 stores. In the summer of 2002, the retailer announced that it would close a store in Ingolstadt and merge two stores in Wilhelmshaven. Wal-Mart admits that it pursued too many initiatives too quickly in Germany and lost too many talented managers when the headquarters of acquired firms closed. But it will not give up on Germany and is tentatively eyeing more expansion possibilities there.

From Germany, Wal-Mart moved across the channel to the United Kingdom, where it bought the third-largest U.K. grocery chain, ASDA. Why? Margins in the U.K. are among the highest in Europe, at 5 percent to 7 percent. The expansion into the U.K. has worked brilliantly—Wal-Mart now has 260 ASDA stores, which are its International Division's largest profit contributor. ASDA sales in 2001 contributed $20 billion of the company's $46.4 billion in international sales. With such strong growth, Wal-Mart planned to add 12 more U.K. stores in 2003.

What's in store for the future? Wal-Mart recently agreed to acquire 66.7 percent of Seiyu, Japan's fourth-largest retail group. Ten years earlier, Wal-Mart had tried selling its private-label cookies in Japanese stores, and consumers had grabbed them off the shelves. But they did not repeat their purchases because the cookies were too sweet and 30 to 40 percent of them were broken. Japan, like Germany, is a land of finicky shoppers.

Having learned this lesson in Germany, Wal-Mart is moving more slowly in Japan, meticulously studying consumer habits and preferences. However, Wal-Mart will face some serious challenges. Japanese consumers differ from the typical Wal-Mart shopper in other parts of the world. They want local merchandise, look for very fresh produce and fish, and are very detail oriented and want a lot of information about products. They want name brands, buy in small quantities—just a couple of days' worth of food at one time—and want items individually wrapped.

After Japan, there's Russia. In 2002, Wal-Mart began talks with ZAO Promyshlenno-Finanovaya Kompaniya BIN, which has 31 supermarkets across Russia with forecasted sales of $222 million. Wal-Mart would acquire 75 percent of the company's stock.

In all, what has Wal-Mart learned in its international ventures? It has learned a lot about store design. For example, not all locations or markets can accommodate large supercentres. However, the Neighbourhood Market concept, first used in densely populated areas in Mexico, has been successfully transplanted elsewhere. For instance, the first Neighbourhood Market in China was in Shenzhen. It was 27 000 square feet and located underground. Customers reach it by escalators from the busy street above.

Another lesson for Wal-Mart was in global sourcing. Global sourcing at Wal-Mart is not the same as global procurement—Wal-Mart has its own definition. There, global sourcing does not mean buying things. Instead, managers in Wal-Mart's global sourcing unit focus on categories of goods or items where there is an opportunity to improve quality, lower price, or gain efficiencies on a worldwide or regional basis. First, they identify basic products that people use all over the world, and then they look for opportunities to improve supply. Next, they work with producers to improve quality or lower price. Afterwards, the improved product is made available to all managers around the world. It is the managers who make the purchase decision.

An example of successful global sourcing is Wal-Mart's success with copy paper. It first worked with a supplier to improve value to the customer through better-quality paper. As a result, sales of copy paper increased by 46 percent in the U.K., 94 percent in Germany, 38 percent in Canada, and 25 percent in the United States. In the end, Wal-Mart wound up with only one supplier of copy paper, but that isn't always the case. When global sourcing managers investigated sources of bananas, they reduced the number of suppliers to three, not just one.

Global sourcing does not always mean lost sales for some suppliers. Sometimes it can mean almost instant global sales. Take the case of OxiClean, a household cleaner. Originally sold only in the United States, it was later offered to stores elsewhere. By the end of the year, it was being sold in virtually every country where Wal-Mart operates. This is why suppliers are so keen to work with Wal-Mart. They might have to shave their costs, but the return in global sales can be enormous. What's more, Wal-Mart picks up the distribution tab.

Recently, Wal-Mart created an "in-country global sourcing champion" program. Designated in-country sourcing champions locate new items and promote them to Wal-Mart. Once that happens, Wal-Mart brings merchants from around the world to a summit meeting where they can learn about new products. The company gets the managers' buy-in and feedback so that, once they leave, they become champions of new products. In addition to ensuring that merchants are on board with new products, the summits also foster communication and the study of best practices. A recent summit featured food managers from ASDA because ASDA is a superior retailer of food. The ASDA people shared their ideas, which could then be used in other countries to enhance food retailing.

Innovative management practices, such as global sourcing and the constant sharing of ideas, have helped to make the Wal-Mart the largest worldwide retailer—and also the best.

Questions for Discussion

1. Does Wal-Mart standardize or adapt its marketing strategy around the globe? How does the global sourcing initiative support its marketing strategy?

2. Strictly defined, a global firm is one that looks at its operations from a worldwide perspective rather than from the perspective of its country of origin. In your opinion, is Wal-Mart a truly global firm?

3. In which countries has Wal-Mart done well? Can you identify any common traits across these countries that might account for Wal-Mart's success?

4. Wal-Mart has not been successful in Germany. If you were a consultant to Wal-Mart, what recommendations would you make for the retailer's German operations?

5. In your opinion, will Wal-Mart be successful in Japan and Russia? Why or why not?

6. To what countries should Wal-Mart expand next? What factors are important in making this decision? Be prepared to defend the countries that you choose.

Sources: "Mexico: Wal-Mart Mexico Earnings Rise 9 Percent," *IPR Strategic Business Information Database,* July 17, 2002; "Wal-Mart Set to Take on Russian Chain," *Grocer,* June 22, 2002, p. 16; "Wal-Mart to Buy Stakes in Japanese Chain," *Home Textiles Today,* May 27, 2002, p. 2; "Japan Company: Wal-Mart Develops a Taste for Japan," *Country ViewsWire,* May 3, 2002; "DJ: Wal-Mart January Sales," *FWN Select,* February 7, 2002; Laura Heller, "Latin Market Never Looked So Bueno," *DSN Retailing Today,* June 10, 2002, p. 1251; Laura Heller, "Southern Hemisphere Woes Persist," *DSN Retailing Today,* June 10, 2002, p. 126; Victor Homola, "Germany: Wal-Mart Closings," *New York Times,* July 11, 2002, p. 1; Mike Troy, "Global Reach Gets Broader Every Day," *DSN Retailing Today,* June 10, 2002, p. 1171; Mike Troy, "Foothold in the Orient Keeps Growing," *DSN Retailing Today,* June 10, p. 121; and Mike Troy, "Continental Divide: U.K. OK, but Germany Still Ailing," *DSN Retailing Today,* June 10, 2002, p. 118.

CBC Video Case

Log on to your Companion Website at **www.pearsoned.ca/kotler** to view a CBC video segment and case for this chapter.

Case Pilot

Log on to your Companion Website at **www.pearsoned.ca/kotler** to access the case project provided for this part of the text. Take the Case Pilot Challenge!

One aspect of marketing not discussed within the text is marketing arithmetic. The calculation of sales, costs, and certain ratios is important for many marketing decisions. This appendix describes three major areas of marketing arithmetic: the *operating statement, analytic ratios,* and *markups and markdowns.*

Operating Statement

Balance sheet
A financial statement that shows assets, liabilities, and net worth of a company at a given time.

Operating statement (profit-and-loss statement, income statement)
A financial statement that shows company sales, cost of goods sold, and expenses during a given period of time.

The operating statement and the balance sheet are the two main financial statements used by companies. The **balance sheet** shows the assets, liabilities, and net worth of a company at a given time. The **operating statement** (also called **profit-and-loss statement** or **income statement**) is the more important of the two for marketing information. It shows company sales, cost of goods sold, and expenses during a specified time period. By comparing the operating statement from one time period to the next, the firm can spot favourable or unfavourable trends and take appropriate action.

Table A.1 shows the 2003 operating statement for Dale Parsons Men's Wear, a specialty store on the Prairies. This statement is for a retailer; the operating statement for a manufacturer would be somewhat different. Specifically, the section on purchases within the "cost of goods sold" area would be replaced by "cost of goods manufactured."

The outline of the operating statement follows a logical series of steps to arrive at the firm's $25 000 net profit figure:

Net sales	$300 000
Cost of goods sold	− 175 000
Gross margin	$125 000
Expenses	− 100 000
Net profit	$ 25 000

Gross sales
The total amount that a company charges during a given period of time for merchandise.

The first part details the amount that Parsons received for the goods sold during the year. The sales figures consist of three items: *gross sales, returns and allowances,* and *net sales.* **Gross sales** is the total amount charged to customers during the year for merchandise purchased in Parsons's store. As expected, some customers returned merchandise because of damage or a change of mind. If the customer gets a full refund or full credit on another purchase, we call this a *return.* Or the customer may decide to keep the item if Parsons will reduce the price. This is called an *allowance.* By subtracting returns and allowances from gross sales, we arrive at net sales—what Parsons earned in revenue from a year of selling merchandise:

Gross sales	$ 325 000
Returns and allowances	− 25 000
Net sales	$ 300 000

The second major part of the operating statement calculates the amount of sales revenue Dale Parsons retains after paying the costs of the merchandise. We start with the inventory in the store at the beginning of the year. During the year, Parsons bought $165 000 worth of suits, slacks, shirts, ties, jeans, and other goods. Suppliers gave the store discounts totalling $15 000, so that net purchases were $150 000. Because the store is located away from regular shipping routes, Parsons had to pay

Table A.1 Operating Statement: Dale Parsons Men's Wear, Year Ending December 31, 2003

Gross sales			$325 000
Less: Sales returns and allowances			25 000
Net sales			$300 000
Cost of goods sold			
Beginning inventory, January, at cost		$ 60 000	
Gross purchases	$165 000		
Less: Purchase discounts	15 000		
Net purchases	$150 000		
Plus: Freight-in	10 000		
Net cost of delivered purchases		$160 000	
Cost of goods available for sale		$220 000	
Less: Ending inventory, December 31, at cost		$ 45 000	
Cost of goods sold			$175 000
Gross margin			$125 000
Expenses			
Selling expenses			
Sales, salaries, and commissions	$ 40 000		
Advertising	5000		
Delivery	5000		
Total selling expenses		$ 50 000	
Administrative expenses			
Office salaries	$ 20 000		
Office supplies	5000		
Miscellaneous (outside consultant)	5000		
Total administrative expenses		$ 30 000	
General expenses			
Rent	$ 10 000		
Heat, light, telephone	5 000		
Miscellaneous (insurance, depreciation)	5000		
Total general expenses		$ 20 000	
Total expenses			$100 000
Net profit			$ 25 000

an additional $10 000 to get the products delivered, giving the firm a net cost of $160 000. Adding the beginning inventory, the cost of goods available for sale amounted to $220 000. The $45 000 ending inventory of clothes in the store on December 31 is then subtracted to come up with the $175 000 **cost of goods sold**. Here again we have followed a logical series of steps to figure out the cost of goods sold:

Cost of goods sold
The net cost to the company of goods sold.

Amount Parsons started with (beginning inventory)	$ 60 000
Net amount purchased	+ 150 000
Any added costs to obtain these purchases	+ 10 000
Total cost of goods Parsons had available for sale during year	$ 220 000
Amount Parsons had left over (ending inventory)	− 45 000
Cost of goods actually sold	$ 175 000

The difference between what Parsons paid for the merchandise ($175 000) and what he sold it for ($300 000) is called the **gross margin** ($125 000).

Gross margin
The difference between net sales and cost of goods sold.

In order to show the profit Parsons "cleared" at the end of the year, we must subtract from the gross margin the *expenses* incurred while doing business. *Selling expenses* included two sales employees, local newspaper and radio advertising, and the cost of delivering merchandise to customers after alterations. Selling expenses totalled $50 000 for the year. *Administrative expenses* included the salary for an office manager, office supplies such as stationery and business cards, and miscellaneous expenses including an administrative audit conducted by an outside consultant. Administrative expenses totalled $30 000 in 2003. Finally, the general expenses of rent, utilities, insurance, and depreciation came to $20 000. Total expenses were therefore $100 000 for the year. By subtracting expenses ($100 000) from the gross margin ($125 000), we arrive at the net profit of $25 000 for Parsons during 2003.

Analytic Ratios

Operating ratios
Ratios of selected operating statement items to net sales that allow marketers to compare the firm's performance in one year with that in previous years (or with industry standards and competitors in the same year).

The operating statement provides the figures needed to compute some crucial ratios. Typically these ratios are called **operating ratios**—the ratio of selected operating statement items to net sales. They let marketers compare the firm's performance in one year to that in previous years (or with industry standards and competitors in the same year). The most commonly used operating ratios are the *gross margin percentage*, the *net profit percentage*, the *operating expense percentage*, and the *returns and allowances percentage*.

Ratio	Formula	Computation from Table A.1
Gross margin percentage	$= \dfrac{\text{gross margin}}{\text{net sales}}$	$= \dfrac{\$125,000}{\$300,000} = 42\%$
Net profit percentage	$= \dfrac{\text{net profit}}{\text{net sales}}$	$= \dfrac{\$25,000}{\$300,000} = 8\%$
Operating expense percentage	$= \dfrac{\text{total expenses}}{\text{net sales}}$	$= \dfrac{\$100,000}{\$300,000} = 33\%$
Returns and allowances percentage	$= \dfrac{\text{returns and allowances}}{\text{net sales}}$	$= \dfrac{\$25,000}{\$300,000} = 8\%$

Another useful ratio is the *stockturn rate* (also called *inventory turnover rate*). The stockturn rate is the number of times an inventory turns over or is sold during a specified time period (often one year). It may be computed on a cost, selling price, or units basis. Thus the formula can be:

$$\text{Stockturn rate} = \frac{\text{cost of goods sold}}{\text{average inventory at cost}}$$

or

$$\text{Stockturn rate} = \frac{\text{selling price of goods sold}}{\text{average selling price of inventory}}$$

or

$$\text{Stockturn rate} = \frac{\text{sales in units}}{\text{average inventory in units}}$$

We will use the first formula to calculate the stockturn rate for Dale Parsons Men's Wear:

$$\frac{\$175,000}{(\$60,000 + \$45,000) / 2} = \frac{\$175,000}{\$52,500} = 3.3$$

That is, Parsons's inventory turned over 3.3 times in 2003. Normally, the higher the stockturn rate, the higher the management efficiency and company profitability.

Return on investment (ROI)
A common measure of managerial effectiveness—the ratio of net profit to investment.

Return on investment (ROI) is frequently used to measure managerial effectiveness. It uses figures from the firm's operating statement and balance sheet. A commonly used formula for computing ROI is:

$$\text{ROI} = \frac{\text{net profit}}{\text{sales}} \times \frac{\text{sales}}{\text{investment}}$$

You may have two questions about this formula: Why use a two-step process when ROI could be computed simply as net profit divided by investment? And what exactly is "investment"?

To answer these questions, let's look at how each component of the formula can affect the ROI. Suppose Dale Parsons Men's Wear has a total investment of $150 000. Then ROI can be computed as follows:

$$\text{ROI} = \frac{\$25,000 \ (\text{net profit})}{\$300,000 \ (\text{sales})} \times \frac{\$300,000 \ (\text{sales})}{\$150,000 \ (\text{investment})}$$

$$= 8.3\% \times 2 = 16.6\%$$

Now suppose that Parsons had worked to increase his share of market. He could have had the same ROI if his sales had doubled while dollar profit and investment stayed the same (accepting a lower profit ratio to get higher turnover and market share):

$$\text{ROI} = \frac{\$25,000 \ (\text{net profit})}{\$600,000 \ (\text{sales})} \times \frac{\$600,000 \ (\text{sales})}{\$150,000 \ (\text{investment})}$$

$$= 4.16\% \times 4 = 16.6\%$$

Parsons might have increased his ROI by increasing net profit through more cost cutting and more efficient marketing:

$$\text{ROI} = \frac{\$50,000 \ (\text{net profit})}{\$300,000 \ (\text{sales})} \times \frac{\$300,000 \ (\text{sales})}{\$150,000 \ (\text{investment})}$$

$$= 16.6\% \times 2 = 33.2\%$$

Another way to increase ROI is to find some way to get the same levels of sales and profits while decreasing investment (perhaps by cutting the size of Parsons's average inventory):

$$\text{ROI} = \frac{\$25,000 \ (\text{net profit})}{\$300,000 \ (\text{sales})} \times \frac{\$300,000 \ (\text{sales})}{\$75,000 \ (\text{investment})}$$

$$= 8.3\% \times 4 = 33.2\%$$

What is "investment" in the ROI formula? *Investment* is often defined as the total assets of the firm. But many analysts now use other measures of return to assess performance. These measures include *return on net assets (RONA), return on stockholders' equity (ROE),* or *return on assets managed (ROAM).* Because investment is measured at a point in time, we usually compute ROI as the average investment between two time periods (say, January 1 and December 31 of the same year). We can also compute ROI as an "internal rate of return" by using discounted cash flow analysis (see any finance textbook for more on this technique). The objective in using any of these measures is to determine how well the company has been using its resources. As inflation, competitive pressures, and cost of capital increase, such measures become increasingly important indicators of marketing and company performance.

Markups and Markdowns

Markup
The percentage of the cost or price of a product added to cost in order to arrive at a selling price.

Markdown
A percentage reduction from the original selling price.

Retailers and wholesalers must understand the concepts of **markups** and **markdowns**. They must make a profit to stay in business, and the markup percentage affects profits. Markups and markdowns are expressed as percentages.

There are two different ways to compute markups—on *cost* or on *selling price:*

$$\text{Markup percentage on cost} = \frac{\text{dollar markup}}{\text{cost}}$$

$$\text{Markup percentage on selling price} = \frac{\text{dollar markup}}{\text{selling price}}$$

Dale Parsons must decide which formula to use. If Parsons bought shirts for $15 and wanted to mark them up $10 to a price of $25, his markup percentage on cost would be $10 ÷ $15 = 67.7%.

If Parsons based markup on selling price, the percentage would be $10 ÷ $25 = 40%. In figuring markup percentage, most retailers use the selling price rather than the cost.

Suppose Parsons knew his cost ($12) and desired markup on price (25%) for a man's tie, and wanted to compute the selling price. The formula is:

$$\text{Selling price} = \frac{\text{cost}}{1 - \text{markup}}$$

$$\text{Selling price} = \frac{\$12}{.75} = \$16$$

As a product moves through the channel of distribution, each channel member adds a markup before selling the product to the next member. This "markup chain" is shown for a suit purchased by a Parsons customer for $200:

		$ Amount	% of Selling Price
	Cost	$ 108	90%
Manufacturer	Markup	12	10
	Selling price	120	100
	Cost	120	80
Wholesaler	Markup	30	20
	Selling price	150	100
	Cost	150	75
Retailer	Markup	50	25
	Selling price	200	100

The retailer whose markup is 25 percent does not necessarily enjoy more profit than a manufacturer whose markup is 10 percent. Profit also depends on how many items with that profit margin can be sold (stockturn rate) and on operating efficiency (expenses).

Sometimes a retailer wants to convert markups based on selling price to markups based on cost, and vice versa. The formulas are:

$$\text{Markup percentage on selling price} = \frac{\text{markup percentage on cost}}{100\% + \text{markup percentage on selling cost}}$$

$$\text{Markup percentage on cost} = \frac{\text{markup percentage on selling price}}{100\% - \text{markup percentage on selling price}}$$

Suppose Parsons found that his competitor was using a markup of 30 percent based on cost and wanted to know what this would be as a percentage of selling price. The calculation would be:

$$\frac{30\%}{100\% + 30\%} = \frac{30\%}{130\%} = 23\%$$

Because Parsons was using a 25 percent markup on the selling price for suits, he felt that his markup was suitable compared with that of the competitor.

Near the end of the summer, Parsons still had an inventory of summer slacks in stock. Therefore, he decided to use a *markdown*, a reduction from the original selling price. Before the summer, he had purchased 20 pairs at $10 each, and he had since sold 10 pairs at $20 each. He marked down the other pairs to $15 and sold 5 pairs. We compute his *markdown ratio* as follows:

$$\text{Markdown percentage} = \frac{\text{dollar markdown}}{\text{total net sales in dollars}}$$

The dollar markdown is $25 (5 pairs at $5 each) and total net sales are $275 (10 pairs at $20 + 5 pairs at $15). The ratio, then, is $25 ÷ $275 = 9%.

Larger retailers usually compute markdown ratios for each department rather than for individual items. The ratios provide a measure of relative marketing performance for each department and can be calculated and compared over time. Markdown ratios can also be used to compare the performance of different buyers and salespeople in a store's various departments.

Reviewing the Key Terms

Balance sheet   A1
Cost of goods sold   A2
Gross margin   A2
Gross sales   A1
Markdown   A5
Markup   A5
Operating ratios   A3
Operating statement (or profit-and-loss statement or income statement)   A1
Return on investment (ROI)   A4

Endnotes

Chapter 1

1. All dollar amounts in this text represented Canadian dollars unless otherwise indicated.
2. VanCity, 2002 Annual Report, www.vancity.com/menuId/ 53132 (accessed June 2003); Eve Lazarus, "VanCity Makes Bold Play for Gays," *Marketing Magazine*, August 19, 2002, p. 3; Eve Lazarus, "Beyond the Gay Ghetto," *Marketing Magazine*, Oct. 14, 2002, p.8.
3. David B. Yoffie and Yusi Wang, "Wal-Mart in 2002," Harvard Business School Case #9-702-466.
4. The American Marketing Association offers this definition: "Marketing is the process of planning and executing the conception, pricing, promotion, and distributing of ideas, goods, and services to create exchanges that satisfy individual and organizational objectives."
5. Jack Neff, "Humble Try," *Advertising Age*, February 18, 2002, pp. 3, 12.
6. See Theodore Levitt's classic article, "Marketing Myopia," *Harvard Business Review,* July–August 1960, pp. 45–56. For more recent discussions, see Dhananayan Kashyap, "Marketing Myopia Revisited: A Look Through the 'Colored Glass of a Client,'" *Marketing and Research Today,* August 1996, pp. 197–201; Colin Grant, "Theodore Levitt's Marketing Myopia," *Journal of Business Ethics,* February 1999, pp. 397–406; Jeffrey M. O'Brien, "Drums in the Jungle," *MC Technology Marketing Intelligence,* March 1999, pp. 22–30; and Hershell Sarbin, "Overcoming Marketing Myopia," *Folio,* May 2000, pp. 55–56.
7. See B. Joseph Pine and James Gilmore, "Welcome to the Experience Economy," *Harvard Business Review,* July–August 1998, p. 99; Jane E. Zarem, "Experience Marketing," *Folio,* Fall 2000, pp. 28–32; and Stephen E. DeLong, "The Experience Economy," *Upside,* November 2001, p. 28.
8. Erika Rasmusson, "Marketing More than a Product," *Sales & Marketing Management,* February 2000, p. 99.
9. For more discussion on demand states, see Philip Kotler and Peggy Cunningham, *Marketing Management. Analysis, Planning, Implementation, and Control,* Canadian 11th ed. (Toronto: Pearson Education Canada, 2004), p. 7.
10. Ralph Waldo Emerson offered this advice: "If a man... makes a better mousetrap...the world will beat a path to his door." Several companies, however, have built better mousetraps yet failed. One was a laser mousetrap costing $1500. Contrary to popular assumptions, people do not automatically learn about new products, believe product claims, or willingly pay higher prices.
11. See Barry Farber and Joyce Wycoff, "Customer Service: Evolution and Revolution," *Sales & Marketing Management,* May 1991, p. 47; and Kevin Lawrence, "How to Profit from Customer Complaints," *The Canadian Manager,* Fall 2000, pp. 25, 29.
12. Philip Kotler and Peggy Cunningham, *Marketing Management. Analysis, Planning, Implementation, and Control,* Canadian 11th ed. (Toronto: Pearson Education Canada, 2004), p. 19.
13. Gary Hamel and C.K. Prahalad, "Seeing the Future First," *Fortune,* September 5, 1994, pp. 64–70; Philip Kotler, *Kotler on Marketing* (New York: Free Press, 1999), pp. 20–24; and Anthony W. Ulwick, "Turn Customer Input into Innovation," *Harvard Business Review,* January 2002, pp. 91–97.

14. Kiran Pandya, "'Healthy' Subway takes battle to fast food giants," *Mid-Day News,* December 3, 2002, http:// web.mid-day.com/news/business/2002/december/38004. htm.
15. See Erika Rasmusson, "Complaints Can Build Relationships," *Sales & Marketing Management,* September 1999, p. 89; "King Customer," *Selling Power,* October 2000, pp. 124–125; and Renee Houston Zemansky and Jeff Weiner, "Just Hang On to What You Got," *Selling Power,* March 2002, pp. 60–64.
16. Stew Leonard's Farm Fresh Foods, www.stew-leonards.com (accessed July 2002).
17. See Libby Estell, "This Call Center Accelerates Sales," *Sales Marketing Management,* February 1999, p. 72; Mark McMaster, "A Lifetime of Sales," *Sales & Marketing Management,* September 2001, p. 55; and Lauren Keller Johnson, "The Real Value of Customer Loyalty," *MIT Sloan Management Review,* Winter 2002, pp. 14–17.
18. For more on customer satisfaction, see Regina Fazio Marcuna, "Mapping the World of Customer Satisfaction," Winter 2001, pp. 16–35; and Vikas Mittal and Wagner Kamakura, "Satisfaction, Repurchase Intent, and Repurchase Behavior: Investigating the Moderating Effect of Customer Characteristics," *Journal of Marketing Research,* February 2001, pp. 131–142.
19. For more on this measure and for recent customer satisfaction scores, see Eugene W. Anderson and Claes Fornell, "Foundations of the American Customer Satisfaction Index," *Total Quality Management,* September 2000, pp. S869–S882; and Claes Fornell, "The Science of Satisfaction," *Harvard Business Review,* March 2001, pp. 120–121. Cited facts accessed at the ACSI website, www.bus.umich.edu/research/nqrc/acsi.html (July 2002).
20. Thomas O. Jones and W. Earl Sasser Jr., "Why Satisfied Customers Defect," *Harvard Business Review,* November–December 1995, pp. 88–99. Also see Thomas A. Stewart, "A Satisfied Customer Isn't Enough," *Fortune,* July 21, 1997, pp. 112–113.
21. Thomas O. Jones and W. Earl Sasser Jr., "Why Satisfied Customers Defect," *Harvard Business Review,* November–December 1995, p. 91. For other examples, see Roger Sant, "Did He Jump or Was He Pushed?" *Marketing News,* May 12, 1997, pp. 2, 2 1. Also see Denny Hatch and Ernie Schell, "Delight Your Customers," *Target Marketing,* April 2002, pp. 32–39.
22. Erin Stout, "Keep Them Coming Back for More," *Sales Marketing Management,* February 2002, pp. 51–52.
23. Larry Thomas, "Hearts and Minds: Marketing Seminar '03", Reader's Digest Canada, November 12, 2002, www.readersdigest.ca/advertising/seminar2003/index.html (accessed April 21, 2003).
24. See Roland T. Rust, Valerie A. Zeithaml, and Katherine A. Lemon, *Driving Customer Equity.* (New York: Free Press, 2000); and Roland T. Rust, Katherine A. Lemon, and Valerie A. Zeithaml, "Where Should the Next Marketing Dollar Go?" *Marketing Management,* September–October 2001, pp. 24–28.
25. This example is adapted from Roland T. Rust, Katherine A. Lemon, and Valerie A. Zeithaml, "Where Should the Next Marketing Dollar Go?" *Marketing Management,* September–October 2001, p. 25.
26. Leonard L. Berry and A. Parasuraman, *Marketing Services: Competing Through Quality* (New York: Free Press, 1991),

pp. 136–142. Also see Richard Cross and Janet Smith, *Customer Bonding. Pathways to Lasting Customer Loyalty* (Lincolnwood, Ill.: NTC Business Books, 1995); and Michelle L. Roehm, Ellen Bolman Pullins, and Harpeer A. Roehm, "Building Loyalty-Building Programs for Packaged Goods Brands," *Journal of Marketing Research,* May 2002, pp. 202–213.

27. See Mary M. Long and Leon G. Schiffman, "Consumption Values and Relationships: Segmenting the Market for Frequency Programs," *"Journal of Consumer Marketing, 2000,* p. 214+; and Naras V. Eechambadi, "Keeping Your Existing Customers Loyal," *Inter@ction Solutions,* February 2002, pp. 26–28. Examples based on information accessed online at www.swatch.com and www.hog.com (accessed September 2002).

28. Canadian E-Business Opportunities Roundtable, "Industry Leaders Say E-Business A Key Enabler Of Innovation, " March 25, 2002, http://ebusinessroundtable.ca/release_mar25.html (accessed April 21, 2003).

29. Michael J. Weiss, "Online America," *American Demographics,* March 2001, pp. 53–60; Humphrey Taylor, "Internet Penetration at 66% of Adults (137 Million) Nationwide," *The Harris Poll,* April 17, 2002; and Computer Industry Almanac Inc., "Internet Users Will Top 1 Billion in 2005" (press release), March 12, 2002, www.c-i-a.com.

30. Robert D. Hof, "The 'Click Here' Economy," *Business Week,* June 22, 1998, pp. 122–128.

31. Robert D. Hof, "Survive and Prosper," *Business Week,* May 14, 2001, p. EB60.

32. Steve Hamm, "E-Biz: Down but Hardly Out," *Business Week,* March 26, 2001, pp. 126–130; and "B2B E-Commerce Headed for Trillions," March 6, 2002, http://cyberatlas.internet.com/.

33. Philip Kotler, *Kotler on Marketing* (New York: Free Press, 1999), p. 20.

34. Thor Valdmanis, "Alliances Gain Favor over Risky Mergers," *USA Today,* February 4, 1999, p. 3B. Also see Gabor Gari, "Leveraging the Rewards of Strategic Alliances," *Journal of Business Strategy,* April 1999, pp. 40–43; Rosabeth Moss Kanter, "Why Collaborate?" *Executive Excellence,* April 1999, p. 8; and Matthew Schifrin, "Partner or Perish," *Forbes,* May 21, 2001, pp. 26–28.

35. See Ben & Jerry's full mission statement online at www.benjerry.com. For more reading on environmentalism, see Stuart L. Hart, "Beyond Greening: Strategies for a Sustainable World," *Harvard Business Review,* January–February 1997, pp. 67–76; and Peter M. Senge, Goran Carstedt, and Patrick L. Porter, "Innovating Our Way to the Next Industrial Revolution," MIT *Sloan Management Review,* Winter 2001, pp. 24–38. For more on marketing and social responsibility, see "Can Doing Good Be Good for Business?" *Fortune,* February 2, 1998, pp. 148G–148J; Sankar Sen and C. B. Bhattacharya, "Does Doing Good Always Lead to Doing Better? Consumer Reactions to Corporate Social Responsibility," *Journal of Marketing Research,* May 2001, pp. 225–243; Thea Singer, "Can Business Still Save the World?" *Inc.,* April 30, 2001, pp. 58–71; and Lois A. Mohr, Deborah J. Webb, and Katherine E. Harris, "Do Consumers Expect Companies to Be Socially Responsible? The Impact of Corporate Social Responsibility on Buying Behavior," *Journal of Consumer Affairs,* Summer 2001, pp. 45–72.

36. Patti Summerfield, "Charity Wars: No More Mr. Nice Guy: Charities Get Aggressive," *Strategy,* November 4, 2002, p. 2.

37. Mark De Wolf, "Non-profits take on private-sector marketing tactics," *Strategy*, April 12, 1999, p. D20. For other examples, and for a good review of non-profit marketing, see Philip Kotler and Alan R. Andreasen, *Strategic Marketing for Nonprofit Organizations,* 5th ed. (Upper Saddle River, NJ: Prentice Hall, 1996); Philip Kotler and Karen Fox, *Strategic Marketing for Educational Institutions (*Upper Saddle River, NJ: Prentice Hall, 1995); William P. Ryan, "The New Landscape for Nonprofits," *Harvard Business Review,* January–February 1999, pp. 127–136; Denise Nitterhouse, "Nonprofit and Social Marketing," *Nonprofit Management and Leadership,* Spring 1999, pp. 323–328.

Chapter 2

1. Robert C. Ford, Cherrill P. Heaton, and Stephen W. Brown, "Delivering Excellent Service: Lessons from the Best Firms," *California Management Review,* Fall 2001, pp. 39–56; Tim O'Brien, "North American Parks Finish 2001 on Par with Last Year," *Amusement Business,* December 24, 2001, pp. 18, 22; "Who Owns What?" *Columbia Journal Review,* posted February 19, 2002, at www.cjr.org; Geraldine Fabrikant, "Disney Profit Picture Shows Weakness, but There Are Encouraging Signs, Too," *New York Times,* April 26, 2002, p. C2; "Disney in Global Push," *BBC News,* June 8, 2001, http://news.bbc.co.uk; "Disney Opens New Paris Park," *BBC News,* March 15, 2001, http://news.bbc.co.uk; "Disney to Axe 4000 Jobs," *BBC News,* March 28, 2001, http://news.bbc.co.uk/; and information accessed online at www.Disney.go.com/corporate/ (June 2002).

2. For a more detailed discussion of corporate- and business-level strategic planning as they apply to marketing, see Philip Kotler and Peggy Cunningham, *Marketing Management: Analysis, Planning, Implementation, and Control,* Canadian 11th ed. (Toronto: Pearson Education Canada, 2004), Chapter 4.

3. For these and other examples, see Romauld A. Stone, "Mission Statements Revisited," SAM *Advanced Management Journal,* Winter 1996, pp. 31–37; Orit Gadiesh and James L. Gilbert, "Frontline Action," *Harvard Business Review,* May 2001; and eBay, "Community," www.ebay.com/community/aboutebay/community/index.html (accessed June 2002).

4. Digby Anderson, "Is This the Perfect Mission Statement?" *Across the Board,* May–June 2001, p. 16.

5. Romauld A. Stone, "Mission Statements Revisited," SAM *Advanced Management Journal,* Winter 1996, p. 33.

6. See Hummingbird's website at www.hummingbird.com/about/company.html (accessed April 24, 2003).

7. See Gilbert Fuchsberg, "'Visioning' Mission Becomes Its Own Mission," *Wall Street Journal,* January 7, 1994, B1, B3; and Sal Marino, "Where There Is No Visionary, Companies Falter," *Industry Week,* March 15, 1999, p. 20. For more on mission statements, see Barbara Bartkus, Myron Glassman, and R. Bruce McAfee, "Mission Statements: Are They Smoke and Mirrors?" *Business Horizons,* November–December 2000, pp. 23–28; George S. Day, "Define Your Business," *Executive Excellence,* February 2001, p. 12; and Gerhard Gschwandtner, "Job One: What's at the Heart of Your Brand?" *Selling Power,* April 2002, pp. 73–76.

8. See Gary Hamel, "Reinvent Your Company," *Fortune,* June 20, 2000, pp. 98–112; "Fortune 500," *Fortune,* April 16, 2001, pp. F1–F2; and "America's Most Admired: What's So Great About GE?" *Fortune,* March 4, 2002, pp. 65–67.

9. For more on strategic planning, see John A. Byrne, "Strategic Planning," *Business Week,* August 26, 1996, pp. 46–51; Pete Bogda, "Fifteen Years Later, the Return of 'Strategy,'" *Brandweek,* February 1997, p. 18; Ian Wilson, "Strategic Planning for the Millennium: Resolving the Dilemma," *Long Range Planning,* August 1998, pp. 507–513; Tom Devane, "Ten Cardinal Sins of Strategic Planning," *Executive Excellence,* October 2000, p. 15; Dave Lefkowith, "Effective Strategic Planning," *Management Quarterly,* Spring 2001, pp. 7–11; and Stan Abraham, "The Association of Strategic Planning: Strategy Is Still Management's Core Challenge," *Strategy & Leadership,* 2002, pp. 38–42.

10. Michael E. Porter, *Competitive Strategy* (New York: Free Press, 1980).

11. Michael E. Porter, *Competitive Strategy* (New York: Free Press, 1980).

12. Michael Treacy and Fred Wiersema, "Customer Intimacy and Other Value Disciplines," *Harvard Business Review,* January–February 1993, pp. 84–93; Michael Treacy and Fred Wiersema, "How Market Leaders Keep Their Edge," *Fortune,* February 6, 1995, pp. 88–98; Michael Treacy and Fred Wiersema, *The Discipline of Market Leaders: Choose Your Customers, Narrow Your Focus, Dominate Your Market* (Reading, MA: Addison-Wesley, 1997); and Fred Wiersema, *Customer Intimacy: Pick Your Partners, Shape Your Culture, Win Together* (Santa Monica, CA: Knowledge Exchange, 1998).

13. H. Igor Ansoff, "Strategies for Diversification," *Harvard Business Review,* September–October 1957, pp. 113–124. Also see Philip Kotler, *Kotler on Marketing* (New York: Free Press, 1999), pp. 46–48.

14. Business Development Bank of Canada, "You're the Brain. You're the Power. You're the Boss. Let Us Tell the World" (press release), October 21, 2002, www.bdc.ca/en/about/mediaroom/news_releases/2002/2002102115.htm (accessed April 24, 2003).

15. Leslie Brokaw, "The Secrets of Great Planning," *Inc.,* October 1992, p. 152; and Philip Kotler and Peggy Cunningham, *Marketing Management: Analysis, Planning, Implementation, and Control,* Canadian 11th ed. (Toronto: Pearson Education Canada, 2004), Chapter 3.

16. Michael E. Porter, *Competitive Advantage: Creating and Sustaining Superior Performance* (New York: Free Press, 1985); and Michel E. Porter, "What Is Strategy?" *Harvard Business Review,* November–December 1996, pp. 61–78. Also see Jim Webb and Chas Gile, "Reversing the Value Chain," *Journal of Business Strategy,* March–April 2001, pp. 13–17.

17. John C. Narver and Stanley E. Slater, "The Effect of a Market Orientation on Business Profitability," *Journal of Marketing,* October 1990, pp. 20–35. Also see Susan Foreman, "Interdepartmental Dynamics and Market Orientation," *Manager Update,* Winter 1997, pp. 10–19; and Philip Kotler, *Kotler on Marketing* (New York: Free Press, 1999), p. 20.

18. Philip Kotler, *Kotler on Marketing* (New York: Free Press, 1999), pp. 20–22.

19. David Stires, "Fallen Arches," *Fortune,* April 29, 2002, pp. 74–76.

20. Myron Magnet, "The New Golden Rule of Business," *Fortune,* February 21, 1994, pp. 60–63. For more on supply chain management and strategic alliances, see Gabor Gari, "Leveraging the Rewards of Strategic Alliances," *Journal of Business Strategy,* April 1999, pp. 40–43; Hau Lee "Survey: Chain Reaction," *The Economist,* February 2002, pp. S13–S15; and Philip Kotler and Peggy Cunningham, *Marketing Management. Analysis, Planning, Implementation, and Control,* Canadian 11th ed. (Toronto: Pearson Education Canada, 2004), p. 72.

21. The four *Ps* classification was first suggested by E. Jerome McCarthy in *Basic Marketing: A Managerial Approach* (Homewood, Ill.: Irwin, 1960). For more discussion of this classification scheme, see Walter van Waterschoot and Christophe Van den Bulte, "The 4P Classification of the Marketing Mix Revisited," *Journal of Marketing,* October 1992, pp. 83–93; Michael G. Harvey, Robert F. Lusch, and Branko Cavarkapo, "A Marketing Mix for the 21st Century," *Journal of Marketing Theory and Practice,* Fall 1996, pp. 1–15; and Don E. Schultz, "Marketers: Bid Farewell to Strategy Based on Old 4Ps," *Marketing News,* February 12, 2001, p. 7.

22. Ad Age Dataplace, www.adage.com/dataplace (accessed June 2002).

23. Robert Lauterborn, "New Marketing Litany: 4P's Passé-Words Take Over," *Advertising Age,* October 1, 1990, p. 26. Also see Philip Kotler and Peggy Cunningham, *Marketing Management: Analysis, Planning, Implementation, and Control,* Canadian 11th ed. (Toronto: Pearson Education Canada, 2004), Chapter 1.

24. See Charles H. Noble and Michael P. Mokwa, "Implementing Marketing Strategies: Developing and Testing a Managerial Theory," *Journal of Marketing,* October 1999, pp. 57–73.

25. Brian Durnaine, "Why Great Companies Last," *Business Week,* January 16, 1995, p. 129. See also James C. Collins and Jerry I. Porras, *Built to Last. Successful Habits of Visionary Companies* (New York: HarperBusiness, 1995); Rob Goffee and Gareth Jones, *The Character of a Corporation: How Your Company's Culture Can Make or Break Your Business* (New York: HarperBusiness, 1998); and Thomas A. Atchison, "What Is Corporate Culture?" *Trustee,* April 2002, p. 11.

26. Joseph Winski, "One Brand, One Manager," *Advertising Age,* August 20, 1987, p. 86. Also see Jack Neff, "P&G Redefines the Brand Manager," *Advertising Age,* October 13, 1997, pp. 1, 18; James Bell, "Brand Management for the Next Millennium," *Journal of Business Strategy,* March–April 1998, p. 7; and Kevin Lane Keller, *Strategic Brand Management,* 2nd ed. (Upper Saddle River, N.J.: Prentice Hall, 2003).

27. See Roland T. Rust, Valerie A. Zeithaml, and Katherine N. Lemon, *Driving Customer Equity: How Lifetime Customer Value Is Reshaping Corporate Strategy* (New York: Free Press, 2000); and Rust, Lemon, and Zeithaml, "Where Should the Next Marketing Dollar Go?" *Marketing Management,* September–October 2001, pp. 24–28.

28. For details, see *Management: Analysis, Planning, Implementation, and Control,* Canadian 11th ed. (Toronto: Pearson Education Canada, 2004), Chapter 22.

Chapter 3

1. "Budget Sets Up Shop in Canadian Tire Stores," *Marketing Magazine,* Marketing Daily, February 21, 2003, www.marketingmag.ca; "Canadian Tire Links Catalogue to Web," *Marketing Magazine,* Marketing Daily, March 16, 2001, www.marketingmag.ca; Canadian Tire press release, June 12, 2001, www.newswire.ca/releases/June2001/12/

c3244.html; and Canadian Tire press release, March 15, 2001, www.newswire.ca/releases/March2001/15/c3883.html.

2. See Humphrey Taylor, "Internet Penetration at 66% of Adults (137 Million) Nationwide," *The Harris Poll*, April 17, 2002; and Computer Industry Almanac Inc, "Internet Users Will Top 1 Billion in 2005" (press release), March 12, 2002, www.c-i-a.com.

3. Statistics Canada, "Electronic Commerce and Technology," *The Daily*, April 2, 2003, www.statcan.ca/Daily/English/030402/td030402.htm.

4. Robyn Greenspan, "The Web as a Way of Life," http://cyberatlas.internet.com/, May 21, 2002.

5. John A. Byrne, "Management by the Web," *Business Week*, August 28, 2000, pp. 84–96.

6. Alan Mitchell, "Internet Zoo Spawns New Business Models," *Marketing Week*, January 21, 1999, pp. 24–25. Also see Philip Kotler, *Marketing Moves: A New Approach to Profits, Growth, and Renewal* (Boston: Harvard Business School Press, 2002).

7. Statistics Canada, "Electronic commerce and technology, 2002," *The Daily*, Canada, April 2, 2003, www.statcan.ca/Daily/English/030402/td030402.htm; and Lori Enos, "Canada Poised for B2B Boom," *E-Commerce Times*, January 11, 2001.

8. Paola Hjelt, "Flying on the Web in a Turbulent Economy," *Business Week*, April 30, 2001, pp. 142–148.

9. Information accessed online at Global eXchange Services website, www.gxs.com/gxs/aboutus (June 2002).

10. See Robyn Greenspan, "The Web as a Way of Life," http://cyberatlas.internet.com/, May 21, 2002.

11. Chris Power, "The Margin in Email Marketing," *Marketing Magazine*, Marketing Daily, April 23, 2001, www.marketingmag.ca.

12. Frederick F. Reichheld and Phil Schefter, "E-Loyalty: Your Secret Weapon on the Web," *Harvard Business Review*, July–August 2000, pp. 105–113.

13. Nielsen//NetRatings, http://reports.metratings.com/ca/web/NRpublicreports.usageweekly (accessed April 26, 2003).

14. "Canadian Internet Stats Pack," No. 11, www.GDSourcing.com (October 2001).

15. "Blue Collar Occupations Moving Online," http://cyberatlas.internet.com/ (accessed April 12, 2001).

16. Statistics Canada, "E-commerce: Household Shopping on the Internet 2000," *The Daily*, October 23, 2001, www.statcan.ca/Daily/English/011023/d011023b.htm.

17. See Steve Hamm, "E-Biz: Down but Hardly Out," *Business Week*, March 26, 2001, pp. 126–130; and "B2B E-Commerce Headed for Trillions," March 6, 2002, http://cyberatlas.internet.com/.

18. Peter Loftis, "E-Commerce: Business to Business—Exchanges: Making It Work," *Wall Street Journal*, February 2002, p. R16.

19. Grant Buckler, "On-Line Exchanges Yield Healthy Hospital Savings," *Globe and Mail*, www.globeandmail.com, March 21, 2002.

20. Facts from eBay annual reports and other information accessed at eBay website, www.ebay.com (July 2002).

21. Gary M. Stern, "You Got a Complaint?" *Link-Up*, September–October 2001, p. 28; and Bob Tedeschi, "In the Current Internet Wilderness, Some Consumer Community Sites Are Hanging On, and Even Making Money," *New York Times*, January 7, 2002, p. C6.

22. Bradley Johnson, "Out-of-Sight Spending Collides with Reality," *Advertising Age*, August 7, 2000, pp. S4–S8.

23. Gary Hamel, "Is This All You Can Build with the Net? Think Bigger," *Fortune*, April 30, 2001, pp. 134–138.

24. See Ann Weintraub, "For Online Pet Stores, It's Dog-Eat-Dog," *Business Week*, March 6, 2000, pp. 78–80; "Death of a Spokespup," *Adweek*, December 11, 2000, pp. 44–46; Jacques R. Chevron, "Name Least of Pet.com's Woes," *Advertising Age*, January 22, 2001, p. 24; and Norm Alster, "Initial Offerings Take a Turn to the Traditional," *New York Times*, May 19, 2002, p. 3.4.

25. Steve Hamm, "E-Biz: Down but Hardly Out," *Business Week*, March 26, 2001, p. 127; and "Business Brief—Staples Inc.: Net Income Falls 5.2% but Its Internet Unit Posts a Pretax Profit," *Wall Street Journal*, August 22, 2001, p. B4.

26. See Chuck Martin, *Net Future* (New York: McGraw-Hill, 1999), p. 33.

27. "E-Commerce Trudges Through Current Slowdown," http://cyberatlas.internet.com/, May 22, 2001.

28. Sharon Gaudin, "The Site of No Return," *DataMation*, www.internet.com, May 28, 2002.

29. Laurie Freeman, "Why Internet Brands Take Offline Avenues," *Marketing News*, July 1999, p. 4; and Paul C. Judge, "The Name's the Thing," *Business Week*, November 15, 1999, pp. 35, 39.

30. John Deighton, "The Future of Interactive Marketing," *Harvard Business Review*, November–December 1996, p. 154.

31. Don Peppers and Martha Rogers, "Opening the Door to Consumers," *Sales & Marketing Management*, October 1998, pp. 22–29; Mike Beirne, "Marketers of the Next Generation: Silvio Bonvini," *Brandweek*, November 8, 1999, p. 64; Jack Neff, "P&G vs. Martha," *Advertising Age*, April 8, 2002, p. 24; Hassan Fattah and Pamela Paul, "Gaming Gets Serious," *American Demographics*, May 2002, pp. 38–43; and information from Candystand website, www.candystand.com (June 2002).

32. Jeffrey F. Rayport and Bernard J. Jaworski, *e-Commerce* (New York: McGraw-Hill, 2001), p. 116.

33. Lisa Bertagnoli, "Getting Satisfaction," *Marketing News*, May 7, 2001, p. 11.

34. For these and other examples, see William M. Bulkeley, "E-Commerce (A Special Report): Cover Story—Pass It On: Advertisers Discover They Have a Friend in 'Viral' Marketing," *Wall Street Journal*, January 14, 2002, p. R6.

35. Eilene Zimmerman, "Catch the Bug," *Sales & Marketing Management*, February 2001, pp. 78–82. Also see Ellen Neuborne, "Viral Marketing Alert," *Business Week*, March 19, 2001, p. EB8.

36. Rob Norton, "The Bright Future of Web Advertising," *Ecompany Now*, June 2001, pp. 50–60. Also see "Summit Participants Agree Online Poised for Growth," *Advertising Age*, April 1, 2002, p. C6.

37. Arlene Weintraub, "When E-Mail Ads Aren't Spam," *Business Week*, October 16, 2000, pp. 112–113.

38. Michael Porter, "Strategy and the Internet," *Harvard Business Review*, March 2001, pp. 63–78.

39. Timothy J. Mullaney, "Break Out the Black Ink," *Business Week*, May 13, 2002, pp. 74–76.

40. See Peter Han and Angus Maclaurin, "Do Consumers Really Care About Online Privacy?" *Marketing Management*, January–February 2002, pp. 35–38.

41. Bob Tedeschi, "Everybody Talks About Online Privacy, but Few Do Anything About It," *New York Times*, June 3, 2002, p. C6.

42. "13-Year-Old Bids over $3M for Items in eBay Auctions," *USA Today*, April 30, 1999, p. 10B.

Chapter 4

1. Information from MEC corporate website, www.mec.ca; Eve Lazarus, "MEC Facing Marketing Challenges," *Marketing Magazine*, June 19, 2000, p. 2; and Mary Lamey, "A Monument to the Environment: Focus on Recycling. Mountain Equipment is Building First 'Green' Retail Outlet in Quebec," *Montreal Gazette*, November 22, 2002, www.canada.com/montreal/. Other information from Harriot Marsh, "Has the Body Shop Lost Its Direction for Good?" *Marketing*, May 10, 2001, p. 19; Mike Hoffman, "Ben Cohen: Ben & Jerry's Homemade, Established in 1978," *Inc*, April 30, 2001, p. 68; Sarah Ellison, "Body Shop Hopes for New Image with an Omnilife Deal—Possible Takeover Could Spruce Up Brand That Has Lost Its Appeal over the Years," *Wall Street Journal*, June 8, 2001, p. B4; Sarah Ellison, "Body Shop's Two Founders to Step Aside; Sale Talks End," *Wall Street Journal*, February 13, 2002, p. A15; and Renee Volpini, "Fight Global Warming with Ice Cream, Music and Activism" (Ben & Jerry's press release), April 2, 2002, http://lib.benjerry.com/pressrel/press040202osw.html. For more on social responsibility in Canada and listing of leading Canadian firms, see the *Corporate Knights* website, www.corporateknights.ca/, and Industry Canada, http://strategis.ic.gc.ca/.
2. Imagine website, Media: Quick Facts, www.imagine.ca/content/media/quick_facts.asp?section=media (accessed July 15, 2003).
3. Suncor website, www.suncor.com/ (accessed July 15, 2003)
4. Sara Minogue, "Sustainable PR," *Strategy*, November 4, 2002, p. 17.
5. See Greg Winter, "Tobacco Producers Are Willing to Talk with Justice Department," *New York Times*, June 22, 2001, p. C1; and Gordan Fairclough, "Study Slams Philip Morris Ads Telling Teens Not to Smoke—How a Market Researcher Who Dedicated Years to Cigarette Sales Came to Create Antismoking Ads," *Wall Street Journal*, May 29, 2002, p. B1.
6. Marina Strauss, "Suzy Shier's Fake Bargains Bring $1-Million Dressing Down," *Globe and Mail*, June 14, 2003, pp. B1, B4.
7. James Heckman, "Don't Shoot the Messenger: More and More Often, Marketing Is the Regulators' Target," *Marketing News*, May 24, 1999, pp. 1, 9; "Sweepstakes Group Settles with States," *New York Times*, June 27, 2001, p. A.14; "Business Brief—Publishers Clearing House: Payment of $34 Million Set to Settle with 26 States," *Wall Street Journal*, June 27, 2001, p. B8; and "PCH Reaches $34 Million Sweepstakes Settlement with 26 States," *Direct Marketing*, September 2001, p. 6.
8. PhoneBusters, "Statistics on Phone Fraud: Canada, 2002," www.phonebusters.com/Eng/Statistics/canada_stats1_2002.html (accessed July 16, 2003).
9. John Gustavson, "The New Fraud Busters," *Marketing Magazine*, August 16, 1999, www.marketingmag.ca.
10. Theodore Levitt, "The Morality (?) of Advertising," *Harvard Business Review*, July–August 1970, pp. 84–92. For counterpoints, see James Heckman, "Don't Shoot the Messenger: More and More Often, Marketing Is the Regulators' Target," *Marketing News*, May 24, 1999, pp. 1, 9.
11. Clifton Joseph, "Fast Food," *Marketplace*, air date April 3, 2002, www.cbc.ca/consumers/market/files/food/fastfood/index.html; and "Kraft Slims Down Kids Marketing," *Marketing Magazine*, July 14/21, 2003, p. 3. See also Sandra Pesmen, "How Low Is Low? How Free Is Free?" *Advertising Age*, May 7, 1990, p. S10; and Karolyn Schuster, "The Dark Side of Nutrition," *Food Management*, June 1999, pp. 34–39.
12. David Welch, "Firestone: Is This Brand Beyond Repair?" *Business Week*, June 11, 2001, p. 48. Also see Ken Belson and Micheline Maynard, "Big Recall Behind It, Tire Maker Regains Its Footing," *New York Times*, August 10, 2002, p. 1, and CBC News, "94 000 Vehicles In Canada Affected By Ford Recall," May 30, 2001, www.cbc.ca/storyview/CBC/2001/05/24/Consumers/fordtires_010524.
13. Cliff Edwards, "Where Have All the Edsels Gone?" *Greensboro News Record*, May 24, 1999, p. B6. For a thought-provoking short case involving planned obsolescence, see James A. Heely and Roy L. Nersesian, "The Case of Planned Obsolescence," *Management Accounting*, February 1994, p. 67. Also see Joel Dryfuss, "Planned Obsolescence Is Alive and Well," *Fortune*, February 15, 1999, p. 192; and Atsuo Utaka, "Planned Obsolescence and Marketing Strategy," *Managerial and Decision Economics*, December 2000, pp. 339–344.
14. Adapted from John Markoff, "Is Planned Obsolesence Obsolete?" *New York Times*, February 17, 2002, pp. 4, 6.
15. See Judith Bell and Bonnie Maria Burlin, "In Urban Areas: Many More Still Pay More for Food," *Journal of Public Policy and Marketing*, Fall 1993, pp. 268–270; Kathryn Graddy and Diana C. Robertson, "Fairness of Pricing Decisions," *Business Ethics Quarterly*, April 1999, pp. 225–243; and Gordon Matthews, "Does Everyone Have the Right to Credit?" *USBanker*, April 2001, pp. 44–48.
16. See Brian Grow and Pallavi Gogoi, "A New Way to Squeeze the Weak?" *Business Week*, January 28, 2002, p. 92.
17. Marcia Stepanek, "Weblining," *Business Week*, April 3, 2000, pp. EB26–EB43. Also see Karin Helperin, "Wells Fargo Online Service Accused of Redlining," *Bank Systems & Technology*, September 2000, p. 19.
18. Richard W. Pollay, "The Distorted Mirror: Reflections on the Unintended Consequences of Advertising," *Journal of Marketing*, April 1986, pp. 18–36.
19. Carolyn Setlow, "Profiting from America's New Materialism," *Discount Store News*, April 17, 2000, p. 16. For interesting discussions on materialism and consumption, see Mark Rotella, Sarah F. Gould, Lynn Andriani, and Michael Scharf, "The High Price of Materialism," *Publishers Weekly*, July 1, 2002, p. 67; Lin Chiat Chang and Robert M. Arkin, "Materialism as an Attempt to Cope with Uncertainty," *Psychology & Marketing*, May 2002, pp. 389–406; John De Graaf, "The Overspent American/Luxury Fever," *Amicus Journal*, Summer 1999, pp. 41–43; and Professional Marketing Research Society, "Not Your Average Beer Drinking, Igloo-Dwelling, Hockey-Playing, 'Eh'-Sayers. Now Are We?" (press release), June 2002, www.pmrs-aprm.com/specialpr/release11.html.
20. James Twitchell, "Two Cheers for Materialism," *Wilson Quarterly*, Spring 1999, pp. 16–26. Also see Twitchell, *Lead Us into Temptation: The Triumph of American Materialism* (New York: Columbia University Press, 1999); and Twitchell, *Living It Up: Our Love Affair with Luxury* (New York: Columbia University Press, 2002).
21. Kim Clark, "Real-World-O-Nomics: How to Make Traffic Jams a Thing of the Past," *Fortune*, March 31, 1997, p. 34. Also see Marianne Jakevich, "Mixed Reviews for the HOV Lanes," *American City & County*, October 2001, pp. 640–641.
22. From an advertisement for *Fact* magazine—which does not carry advertisements.

23. Greg Winter, "Hershey Is Put on the Auction Block," *New York Times*, July 26, 2002, p. 5.

24. André Bachand, "R&D and Pharmaceuticals: Shorten Approval Process," *The Hill Times: Policy Briefings*, March17, 2003, www.thehilltimes.ca/2003/march/17/bachand/.

25. *Michael Janiga*, "Permanent Holding Pattern For Canadian Air Travellers," *Straight Goods*, undated, www.straightgoods.com/item410.asp (accessed July 17, 2003).

26. Paul Skippen and Geoff Wallace, "Both Protests And The Summit Process Depart From Genoa's Trends," *G8 Bulletin*, Volume 5, Issue 6, June 27–30, 2002, www.g7.utoronto.ca/g8bulletin/2002/bulletin6.htm. For more on the evolution of consumerism, see Paul N. Bloom and Stephen A. Greyser, "The Maturing of Consumerism," *Harvard Business Review*, November–December 1981, pp. 130–139; Robert J. Samualson, "The Aging of Ralph Nader," *Newsweek*, December 16, 1985, p. 57; Douglas A. Harbrecht, "The Second Coming of Ralph Nader," *Business Week*, March 6, 1989, p. 28; George S. Day and David A. Aaker, "A Guide to Consumerism," *Marketing Management*, Spring 1997, pp. 44–48; Benet Middleton, "Consumerism: A Pragmatic Ideology," *Consumer Policy Review*, November/December, 1998, pp. 213–217; and Penelope Green, "Consumerism and Its Malcontents," *New York Times*, December 17, 2000, p. 9.1.

27. See Consumers' Association of Canada, "Educational Publications: Be a Wise Consumer—We'll Show You How," www.consumer.ca/educationalprograms-showyouhow.htm.

28. Government of Canada news release, "Canada Shows Continued Leadership on Protecting the Ozone Layer," December 18, 2000, www.ec.gc.ca/press/001219_n_e.htm.

29. Ken MacQueen, "Ministers Declare War on Excess Packaging," *Kingston Whig-Standard*, March 22, 1990, p. 11.

30. Alan M. Robinson, "It's Easy Being Green: Environmentalism Isn't Dead," *Marketing Magazine*, October 11, 1999, www.marketingmag.ca.

31. Stuart L. Hart, "Beyond Greening: Strategies for a Sustainable World," *Harvard Business Review*, January–February 1997, pp. 66–76. Also see James L. Kolar, "Environmental Sustainability: Balancing Pollution Control with Economic Growth," *Environmental Quality Management*, Spring 1999, pp. 1–10; and Trevor Price and Doug Probert, "The Need for Environmentally Sustainable Developments," *International Need for Environmentally-Sustainable Developments*, 2002, pp. 1–22.

32. Peter M. Senge, Goran Carstedt, and Patrick L. Porter, "Innovating Our Way to the Next Industrial Revolution," *MIT Sloan Management Review*, Winter 2001, pp. 24–38.

33. Based on information from "BP Launches World's Greenest Service Station" (BP press release), April 25, 2002, accessed at www.bp.com/centres/press/media_resources/press_release/index.asp; and BP website, www.bp.com/centres/press/hornchurch/index.asp (September 2002).

34. Linda Sutherland, "Brothers Find Focus in Waste," *Globe and Mail*, January 6, 1997, p. B8.

35. Michelle Wirth Fellman, "New Product Marketer of 1997," *Marketing News*, March 30, 1998, pp. E2, E12; Mercedes M. Cardona, "Colgate Boosts Budget to Further 5-Year Plan," *Advertising Age*, May 15, 2000, p. 6; Emily Nelson, "Colgate's Net Rose 10 Percent in Period, New Products Helped Boost Sales," *Wall Street Journal*, February 2, 2001, p. B6; and Lesley Young, "Colgate Adds Motion To Brush Market," *Marketing Magazine*, April 08, 2002, www.marketingmag.ca.

36. Mountain Equipment Co-op, "Mission and Values," undated, www.mec.ca/ (accessed July 17, 2003).

37. Tim Kavander, "The Creative Eye: Canadian Hockey Association," *Marketing Magazine*, January 27, 2003, p. 16; Roy MacGregor, "Boors Under Heavy Fire in Hockey Parent Ads," *Globe and Mail*, November 28, 2003, p. A2.

38. Herman Miller website, www.HermanMiller.com (accessed October 2001). See also Jacquelyn A. Ottman, "Green Marketing: Wake Up to the Truth About Green Consuming," *In Business*, May–June 2002, p. 31.

39. Dan R. Dalton and Richard A. Cosier, "The Four Faces of Social Responsibility," *Business Horizons*, May–June 1982, pp. 19–27.

40. Joseph Webber, "3M's Big Cleanup," *Business Week*, June 5, 2000, pp. 96–98. Also see Kara Sissell, "3M Defends Timing of Scotchgard Phaseout," *Chemical Week*, April 11, 2001, p. 33; and Peck Hwee Sim, "Ausimont Targets Former Scotchgard Markets," *Chemical Week*, August 7, 2002, p. 32.

41. Barbara Crossette, "Russia and China Top Business Bribers," *New York Times*, May 17, 2002, p. A10.

42. John F. Magee and P. Ranganath Nayak, "Leaders' Perspectives on Business Ethics," *Prizm*, Arthur D. Little, Inc., Cambridge, Mass., First Quarter, 1994, pp. 65–77. Also see Turgut Guvenli and Rajib Sanyal, "Ethical Concerns in International Business: Are Some Issues More Important than Others?" *Business and Society Review*, Summer 2002, pp. 195–206.

43. John F. Magee and P. Ranganath Nayak, "Leaders' Perspectives on Business Ethics," *Prizm*, Arthur D. Little, Inc., Cambridge, Mass., First Quarter, 1994, pp. 71–72. Also see Thomas Donaldson, "Values in Tension: Ethics Away from Home," *Harvard Business Review*, September–October 1996, pp. 48–62; Patrick E. Murphy, "Character and Virtue Ethics in International Marketing: An Agenda for Managers, Researchers, and Educators," *Journal of Business Ethics*, January 1999, pp. 107–124; and Gopalkrishnan, "International Exchanges as the Basis for Conceptualizing Ethics in International Business," *Journal of Business Ethics*, February 2001, pp. 3–25.

44. See Samuel A. DiPiazza, "Ethics in Action," *Executive Excellence*, January 2002, pp. 15–16.

45. Mark Hendricks, "Ethics in Action," *Management Review*, January 1995, pp. 53–55.

46. Kenneth Labich, "The New Crisis in Business Management," *Fortune*, April 20, 1992, pp. 167–176.

47. Samuel A. DiPiazza, "Ethics in Action," *Executive Excellence*, January 2002, p. 15.

Chapter 5

1. Quotes from James R. Rosenfield, "Millennial Fever," *American Demographics*, December 1997, pp. 47–51; Keith Naughton and Bill Vlasic, "The Nostalgia Boom: Why the Old Is New Again," *Business Week*, March 23, 1998, pp. 58–64, Keith Naughton, "VW Rides a Hot Streak," *Newsweek*, May 22, 2000, pp. 48–50; Marc Peyser, "Everything Old Is...Even Older," *Newsweek*, May 6, 2002, p. 14; and Jim Kenzie, "First Drive: 2003 Volkswagen New Beetle Convertible," *Canadian Driver*, October 28, 2002, www.canadiandriver.com/articles/jk2/03nbconv.htm (accessed May 6, 2003). Also see James R. Rosenfield, "Millennial Fever Revisited," *Direct Marketing*, June 2000, pp. 44–47; "Volkswagen Is Awarded Two Best Car Picks from *Money Magazine*" (VW press release), April

4, 2001, www.vw.com; Jeff Green, "Heavy Traffic on Memory Lane," *Business Week,* January 15, 2001, p. 40; and Sholnn Freeman and Beth Demain Reigber, "The VW Bus Is Back," *Wall Street Journal,* June 12, 2002, p. D1.2.

2. Jennifer Lach, "Dateline America: May 1, 2025," *American Demographics,* May 1999, pp. 19–20. Also see Tom Weir, "Staying Stuck on the Web," *Supermarket Business,* February 15, 2001, pp. 15–16.

3. See Sarah Lorge, "The Coke Advantage," *Sales & Marketing Management,* December 1998, p. 17.

4. World POPClock, U.S. Census Bureau, www.census.gov (accessed July 2002). This website provides continuously updated projections of world and U.S. populations.

5. North South Centre website, www.nscentre.org/english/ en_news/SW2000/GEW2000-Tip%201_datas.htm (accessed June 2002).

6. Sally D. Goll, "Marketing: China's (Only) Children Get the Royal Treatment," *Wall Street Journal,* February 8, 1995, pp. B1, B3; James L. Watson, "China's Big Mac Attack," *Foreign Affairs,* May–June 2000, pp. 120–134; and Mark Dunn, "Feeding China's Little Emperors: Food, Children, and Social Change," *China Business Review,* September–October 2000, p. 32.

7. Daniel Stoffman, "Completely Predictable People," *Report on Business,* November 1990, pp. 78–84; and David Foot with Daniel Stoffman, *Boom, Bust, and Echo* (Toronto: Macfarlane Walter & Ross, 1996), pp. 18–22.

8. Dorothy Lipovenko, "Growing Old Is a Baby-Booming Business," *Globe and Mail,* April 6, 1996, pp. A1, A4; Dorothy Lipovenko, "Rich Boomers Aiming To Retire Earlier Than Parents, Poll Says," *Globe and Mail,* October 10, 1996, p. B10; and Jennifer Lach, "Dateline America: May 1, 2025," *American Demographics,* May 1999, p. 19.

9. See Joan Raymond, "The Joy of Empty Nesting," *American Demographics,* May 2000, pp. 49–54; David Rakoff, "The Be Generation," *Adweek,* March 5, 2001, pp. SR18–SR22; and Gene Koretz, "Bless the Baby Boomers," *Business Week,* June 10, 2002, p. 30.

10. CASSIE 2002 Cases, www.cassies.ca/winners/02_Pepsi.pdf (accessed May 5, 2003).

11. See Janus Dietz, "When Gen X Meets Aging Baby Boomers," *Marketing News,* May 10, 1999, p. 17; Tammy Joyner, "Gen X-ers Focus on Life Outside the Job Fulfillment," *The Secured Lender,* May–June 2000, pp. 64–68; Judi E. Loomis, "Generation X," *Rough Notes,* September 2000, pp. 52–54; Jean Chatzky, "Gen Xers Aren't Slackers After All," *Time,* April 8, 2002; Harvey Schacter, "Power Shift," *Canadian Business,* August 1995, pp. 20–30; Eric Blais, "Generation X: Targeting a tough crowd that's not easily impressed," *Marketing,* June 6, 1994, pp. 13–5; Eric Beauchesne, "Generation X not the Lost Generation: Survey," *Kingston Whig Standard,* June 15, 1997, p. 22; Leonard Zehr, "Gen-Xers Heading Home: Survey," *Globe and Mail,* February 13, 1997, p. B9

12. See Ken Gronback, "Marketing to Generation Y," *DSN Retailing Today,* July 24, 2000, p. 14.

13. Growing Up Digital website, www.growingupdigital.com/ FLecho.html (accessed October 1999). Also see Douglas Tapscott, *Growing Up Digital: The Rise of the Net Generation* (New York: McGraw-Hill, 1999); Christine Y. Chen, "Chasing the Net Generation," *Fortune,* September 4, 2000, pp. 295–298; and Pamela Paul, "Getting Inside Gen Y," *American Demographics,* September 2001, pp. 43–49.

14. See See Ken Gronback, "Marketing to Generation Y," *DSN Retailing Today,* July 24, 2000, p. 14; "Study Compares

Gen Y to Boomers," *Home Textiles Today,* September 11, 2000, p. 14; and Rebecca Gardyn, "Grandaughters of Feminism," *American Demographics,* April 2001, pp. 43–47.

15. See J. Walker Smith and Ann Clurman, *Rocking the Ages* (New York: HarperBusiness, 1998); Mercedes M. Cardona, "Hilfiger's New Apparel Lines Getting Individual Efforts," *Advertising Age,* February 8, 1999, p. 24; and Alison Stein Wellner, "Generational Divide," *American Demographics,* October 2000, pp. 53–58.

16. Erin Anderssen, "Junior's at Home and Grandma's Alone," *Globe and Mail,* October 23, 2002, p. A1; Dawn Walton, "Census Reports More Canadians Are Home Alone," *Globe and Mail,* October 23, 2002, p. A6; and Darren Yourk, "Canadian Family Portrait Changing," *Globe and Mail,* October 23, 2002, p. A6. See also Statistics Canada, "2001 Census: Marital Status, Common-Law Status, Families, Dwellings and Households," *The Daily,* October 22, 2003, www.statcan.ca/Daily/English/021022/ td021022.htm.

17. Human Resources Development Canada, Section 5.2 "Women," http://info.load-otea.hrdc-drhc.gc.ca/ workplace_equity/leep/annual/2002/2002annualrep08.shtml (accessed May 5, 2003).

18. Statistics Canada, "Population Projections for 2001, 2006, 2011, 2016, 2021 and 2026, July 1," Canadian Statistics, www.statcan.ca/english/Pgdb/demo23a.htm (accessed May 5, 2003).

19. Statistics Canada, "A Profile of the Canadian Population: Where We Live," 2001 Census Release, March 12, 2002, http://geodepot.statcan.ca/Diss/Highlights/Highlights_e.cfm; and Ross Finnie, "The Effects of Inter-Provincial Mobility on Individuals' Earnings: Panel Model Estimates for Canada," Analytical Studies Branch Research Paper Series, Report 163, Catalogue No. 11F0019MIE2001163, October 2001, http://collection.nlc-bnc.ca/100/200/301/statcan/ research_paper_analytical_11f0019-e/no163/ 11F0019MIE01163.pdf.

20. Canadian Consumer Demographics, Industry Canada, Retail Interactive, http://strategis.ic.gc.ca/SSG/ri00140e.html (accessed May 6, 2003).

21. "Who Works from Home," GDSourcing, *The Business Researcher Newsletter Archives,* Vol. 5 (3), March 22, 2002.

22. Lauri J. Flynn, "Not Just a Copy Shop Any Longer, Kinko's Pushes Its Computer Services," *New York Times,* July 6, 1998, p. D1. Also see Carol Leonetti Dannhauser, "Who's in the Home Office," *American Demographics,* June 1999, pp. 50–56; David Bouchier, "Working from Home, I Think," *New York Times,* January 20, 2002, PLI.13; and John Fetto, "You *Can* Take It with You," *American Demographics,* February 2002, pp. 10–11.

23. Statistics Canada, "Education in Canada: School Attendance and Levels of Schooling," 2001 Census Release, March 11, 2003, www12.statcan.ca/english/census01/ release/release7.cfm.

24. Statistics Canada, "Visible Minority Population, Provinces and Territories," 2001 Census Release, April 23, 2003, www.statcan.ca/english/Pgdb/demo40a.htm.

25. Canadian Media Director's Council, "Ethnic Media," *CMDC Media Digest 2003–2004,* p. 66.

26. Statistics Canada, "Families and Household Living Arrangements," 2001 Census Release, October 22, 2003, www12.statcan.ca/english/census01/release/release3.cfm.

27. Barbara Smith, "Special Feature: Gay And Lesbian Marketing: Market Becoming More Accessible," *Strategy*, September 18, 1995, p. 35.

28. For these and other examples, see Laura Koss-Feder, "Out and About," *Marketing News*, May 25, 1998, pp. 1, 20; Jennifer Gilbert, "Ad Spending Booming for Gay-Oriented Sites," *Advertising Age*, December 6, 1999, p. 58; John Fetto, "In Broad Daylight," *American Demographics*, February 2001, pp. 16, 20; Robert Sharoff, "Diversity in the Mainstream," *Marketing News*, May 21, 2001, pp. 1, 13; David Goetzl, "Showtime, MTV Gamble on Gay Net," *Advertising Age*, January 14, 2002, p. 4; and Kristi Nelson, "Canada's Gay TV Network Gets Ready for U.S.," *Electronic Media*, Chicago, May 6, 2002.

29. For these and other examples, see "Marketing to Americans with Disabilities," *Packaged Facts*, New York, 1997; Dan Frost, "The Fun Factor: Marketing Recreation to the Disabled," *American Demographics*, February 1998, pp. 54–58; Michelle Wirth Fellman, "Selling IT Goods to Disabled End-Users," *Marketing News*, March 15, 1999, pp. 1, 17; Alison Stein Wellner, "The Internet's Nest Niche," *American Demographics*, September 2000, pp. 18–19; Alan Hughes, "Taking the 'Dis' Out of Disability," *Black Enterprise*, March 2002, p. 102; and information accessed online at Volkswagen's website, www.vw.com (June 2002).

30. James W. Hughes, "Understanding the Squeezed Consumer," *American Demographics*, July 1991, pp. 44–50. For more on consumer spending trends, see Cheryl Russell, "The New Consumer Paradigm," *American Demographics*, April 1999, pp. 50–58.

31. Department of Finance Canada, "The Economy in Brief: March 2003," March 20, 2003, www.fin.gc.ca/purl/econbr-e.html.

32. Mark MacKinnon, "High-Income Neighbourhoods," *Globe and Mail*, March 1, 1999, p. B1; Mark MacKinnon, "The Lowest Incomes in Canada Are Found on Native Reserves," *Globe and Mail*, March 1, 1999, p. B2.

33. David Leonhardt, "Two-Tier Marketing," *Business Week*, March 17, 1997, pp. 82–90. Also see "MarketLooks: The U.S. Affluent Market," a research report by Packaged Facts, January 1, 2002.

34. Statistics Canada, "Average Household Expenditures, Provinces and Territories," *Canadian Statistics*, www.statcan.ca/english/Pgdb/famil16a.htm (accessed March 20, 2003).

35. For more discussion, see the "Environmentalism" section in Chapter 4. Also see Patrick Carson and Julia Moulden, *Green Is Gold* (Toronto: Harper Business Press, 1991); Michael E. Porter and Claas van der Linde, "Green *and* Competitive: Ending the Stalemate," *Harvard Business Review*, September–October 1995, pp. 120–134; Stuart L. Hart, "Beyond Greening: Strategies for a Sustainable World," *Harvard Business Review*, January–February 1997, pp. 67–76; Forest L. Reinhardt, "Bringing the Environment Down to Earth," *Harvard Business Review*, July–August 1999, pp. 149–157; "Earth in the Balance," *American Demographics*, January 2001, p. 24; and Subhabrata Bobby Banerjee, "Corporate Environmentalism: The Construct and Its Measurement," *Journal of Business Research*, March 2002, pp. 177–191.

36. "'Different' 2002 May See U.S. R&D Spending Up 3.5%," *Research Technology Management*, March–April 2002, pp. 7–8.

37. Dana Flavelle, "R&D by Canadian Firms Increases 3.3%," *Toronto Star*, June 26, 2002, www.torontostar.com.

38. "R&D Spending Up 3 Per Cent in '01," *Globe and Mail*, June 26, 2003, www.globeandmail.com. Also see the Industry Canada (www.ic.gc.ca) and NRC (www.nrc.ca) websites for descriptions of research initiatives.

39. Statistics Canada, "Multinational Firms and The Innovation Process," *The Daily*, June 27, 2000, www.statcan.ca/Daily/English/000627/td000627.htm.

40. Canadian Government, *North American Free Trade Agreement: An Overview and Description*, August 1992.

41. Also see V. Kasturi Rangan, Sohel Karim, and Sheryl K. Sandberg, "Do Better at Doing Good," *Harvard Business Review*, May–June 1996, pp. 42–54; Julie Garrett and Lisa Rochlin, "Cause Marketers Must Learn to Play by Rules," *Marketing News*, May 12, 1997, p. 4; and Sarah Lorge, "Is Cause-Related Marketing Worth It?" *Sales & Marketing Management*, June 1998, p. 72.

42. For more on Yankelovich Monitor, see http://secure.yankelovich.com/solutions/monitor/y-monitor.asp.

43. Michael Adams, *Better Happy Than Rich: Canadians, Money, and the Meaning of Life* (Toronto: Viking, 2000).

44. Ryan Bigge, "One Beer, Two Solitudes," *Marketing Magazine*, May 5, 2003, www.marketingmag.ca; Rosemary Todd, "Food for thought," *Globe and Mail*, March 12, 1988, p. D2; Maclean's/CTV Poll, "A National Mirror," *Maclean's*, January 3, 1994, pp. 12–15; "Portrait of the Quebec consumer," *Marketing*, March 22, 1993, p. 14; and "Quebec," advertising supplement to *Advertising Age*, November 22, 1993.

45. See Cyndee Miller, "Trendspotters: 'Dark Ages' Ending; So Is Cocooning," *Marketing News*, February 3, 1997, pp. 1, 16.

46. Michael Adams, *Better Happy Than Rich: Canadians, Money, and the Meaning of Life* (Toronto: Viking, 2000), p. 85.

47. Michael Adams, *Better Happy Than Rich: Canadians, Money, and the Meaning of Life* (Toronto: Viking, 2000), p. 150.

48. Agriculture and Agri Food Canada, "Organics Industry" (fact sheet), 2002, http://atn-riae.agr.ca/supply/e3313.htm.

49. Michael Valpy, "Religious Observance Continues To Decline," *Globe and Mail*, March 19, 2003, p. A18; and Clifford Krauss, "In God We Trust...Canadians Aren't So Sure," *New York Times*, www.nytimes.com, March 26, 2003.

50. Philip Kotler, *Kotler on Marketing* (New York: Free Press, 1999), p. 3.

51. See Carl p. Zeithaml and Valerie A. Zeithaml, "Environmental Management: Revising the Marketing Perspective," *Journal of Marketing*, Spring 1984, pp. 46–53.

52. Gayle MacDonald and Oliver Moore, "Shadow of SARS Is Lifted," *Globe and Mail*, May 15, 2003, p. A1.

53. Health Canada, "Canada's Seniors at a Glance," www.hc-sc.gc.ca/seniors-aines/pubs/poster/seniors/page1e.htm (accessed March 20, 2003); and Canadian Centre for Philanthropy, "Seniors Giving and Volunteering," www.givingandvolunteering.ca/factsheets.asp?fn=view&id=8257 (accessed March 20, 2003).

54. Terrence D. Burns, "Canadian 5-Pin Bowling Facts and Information," www.cvnet.net/burnstd/history.htm (accessed May 5, 2003).

Chapter 6

1. See "Coke 'Family' Sales Fly as New Coke Stumbles," *Advertising Age*, January 17, 1986, p. 1; Jack Honomichl,

"Missing Ingredients in 'New' Coke's Research," *Advertising Age,* July 22, 1985, p. 1; Leah Rickard, "Remembering New Coke," *Advertising Age,* April 17, 1995, p. 6; Rick Wise, "Why Things Go Better with Coke," *Journal of Business Strategy,* January–February 1999, pp. 15–19; "Beyond Colas and Beyond," *Beverage Industry,* March 2002, pp. 10–18; "A New Taste for Coca-Cola: Coca-Cola Launches Vanilla Coke," News Release, Toronto, May 8, 2002; and Gordon Pitts, "Coke Unit President Prizes Company's Speedier Strategy," *Globe and Mail,* September 2, 2002, p. B5.

2. Sharon Young, "Researchers Under Fire," *Strategy,* September 24, 2001, p. 19.

3. See Philip Kotler, *Kotler on Marketing* (New York: Free Press, 1999), p. 73.

4. Professional Marketing Research Society, Press Release, "Market Research Uncovers The Canadian Identity," June 2002, www.csrc.ca/CSRC/news/news200206.php.

5. Christina Le Beau, "Mountains to Mine," *American Demographics,* August 2000, pp. 40–44. Also see Joseph M. Winski, "Gentle Rain Turns into Torrent," *Advertising Age,* June 3, 1991, p. 34; David Shenk, *Data Smog: Surviving the Information Glut* (San Francisco: HarperSanFrancisco, 1997); Diane Trommer, "Information Overload—Study Finds Intranet Users Overwhelmed with Data," *Electronic Buyers' News,* April 20, 1998, p. 98; and Stewart Deck, "Data Storm Ahead," *CIO,* April 15, 2001, p. 97.

6. Alice LaPlante, "Still Drowning!" *Computer World,* March 10, 1997, pp. 69–70; and Jennifer Jones, "Looking Inside," *InfoWorld,* January 7, 2002, pp. 22–26.

7. Lesley Young, "The Auto Club Takes it Slow," *Marketing Magazine,* April 29, 2002, p. MD8.

8. Lorne Hill, "As Nimble as the Little Guys," *Marketing Magazine,* February 12, 2001, www.marketingmag.ca.

9. For these and other examples, see Stan Crock, "They Snoop to Conquer," *Business Week,* October 28, 1996, p. 172; and James Curtis, "Behind Enemy Lines," *Marketing,* May 24, 2001, pp. 28–29.

10. See Suzie Amer, "Masters of Intelligence," *Forbes,* April 5, 1999, p. 18.

11. Bruce Hager, "Dumpster Raids? That's Not Very Ladylike, Avon," *Business Week,* April 1, 1991, p. 32; and "Andy Serwer, "P&G's Covert Operation," *Fortune,* September 17, 2001, pp. 42–44.

12. "Company Sleuth Uncovers Business Info for Free," *Link-Up,* January–February 1999, pp. 1, 8.

13. James Curtis, "Behind Enemy Lines," *Marketing,* May 24, 2001, pp. 28–29.

14. For more on marketing and competitive intelligence, see David B. Montgomery and Charles Weinberg, "Toward Strategic Intelligence Systems," *Marketing Management,* Winter 1998, pp. 44–52; Morris C. Attaway Sr., "A Review of Issues Related to Gathering and Assessing Competitive Intelligence," *American Business Review,* January 1998, pp. 25–35; and Conor Vibert, "Secrets of Online Sleuthing," *Journal of Business Strategy,* May–June 2001, pp. 39–42.

15. For more on research firms that supply marketing information, see Jack Honomichl, "Honomichl 50," special section, *Marketing News,* June 10, 2002, pp. H1–H43.

16. Marina Strauss, "Sunoco Refits Its Gas Stations to Pump Milk, Pop and Profits," *Globe and Mail,* December 5, 2002, pp. B1, B8.

17. David Rider, "Confessions of a Part-Time Boozer," *Globe and Mail,* July 5, 2003, p. L10.

18. Adapted from Rebecca Piirto Heather, "Future Focus Groups," *American Demographics,* January 1994, p. 6. For more on focus groups, see Holly Edmunds, *The Focus Group Research Handbook* (Lincolnwood, Ill.: NTC Business Books, 1999); and R. Kenneth Wade, "Focus Groups' Research Role Is Shifting," *Marketing News,* March 4, 2002, p. 47.

19. Sarah Schafer, "Communications: Getting a Line on Customers," *Inc. Technology,* 1996, p. 102. Also see Alison Stein Wellner, "I've Asked You Here Because...," *Business Week,* August 14, 2000, p. F14; and Steve Jarvis, "Two Technologies Vie for Piece of Growing Focus Group Market, *Marketing News,* May 27, 2002, p. 4.

20. Adapted from examples in Gary H. Anthes, "Smile, You're on Candid Computer," *Computerworld,* December 3, 2001, p. 50.

21. Kate Maddox, "CRM to Outpace Other IT Spending," *B to B,* March 11, 2002, pp. 2, 33; and Canadian Marketing Association in partnership with Decima Research Inc., *CRM Benchmarks: Canada 2002 Edition.*

22. For this and other examples, see "What've You Done for Us Lately?" *Business Week,* September 14, 1998, pp. 142–148; Sara Sellar, "Dust Off That Data," *Sales & Marketing Management,* May 1999, pp. 71–72; Philip Kotler, *Kotler on Marketing* (New York: Free Press, 1999), p. 29; Marc L. Songini, "Fedex Expects CRM System to Deliver," *Computerworld,* November 6, 2000, p. 10; Leslie Berger, "Business Intelligence: Insights from the Data Pile," *New York Times,* January 13, 2002, p. A9; and Geoffrey James, "Profit Motive," *Selling Power,* March 2002, pp. 68–73.

23. Darrell K. Rigby, "Avoid the Four Perils of CRM," *Harvard Business Review,* February 2002, pp. 101–109.

24. Michael Krauss, "At Many Firms, Technology Obscures CRM," *Marketing News,* March 18, 2002, p. 5.

25. Robert McLuhan, "How to Reap the Benefits of CRM," *Marketing,* May 24, 2001, p. 35; Sellar, "Dust Off That Data," p. 72; and Stewart Deck, "Data Mining," *Computerworld,* March 29, 1999, p. 76. Also see Eric Almquist, Carla Heaton, and Nick Hall, "Making CRM Make Money," *Marketing Management,* May–June 2002, pp. 16–21.

26. Ravi Kalakota and Marcia Robinson, *E-Business: Roadmap for Success* (Reading, Mass: Addison-Wesley, 1999).

27. "Business Bulletin: Studying the Competition," *Wall Street Journal,* March 19, 1995, pp. A1, A5.

28. See Nancy Levenburg and Tom Dandridge, "Can't Afford Research? Try Miniresearch," *Marketing News,* March 31, 1997, p. 19; and Nancy Levenburg, "Research Resources Exist for Small Businesses," *Marketing News,* January 4, 1999, p. 19.

29. Jack Honomichl, "Honomichl Global 25," *Marketing News* (special section), August 13, 2001, pp. H1–H23; and the AC Nielsen website, www.acnielsen.com (accessed July 2002).

30. David Bosworth, "Special Report: Research: Canadian Market Research Going Global," *Strategy,* September 1, 1997, p. 27.

31. Many of the examples in this section, along with others, are found in Subhash C. Jain, *International Marketing Management,* 3rd ed. (Boston: PWS-Kent, 1990), pp. 334–339. Ken Gofton, "Going Global with Research," *Marketing,* April 15, 1999, p. 35; Naresh K. Malhotra, *Marketing Research,* 3d ed. (Upper Saddle River, N.J.: Prentice Hall, 1999), chapter 23; and Tim R. V. Davis and

Robert B. Young, "International Marketing Research," *Business Horizons,* March–April 2002, pp. 31–38.

32. Subhash C. Jain, *International Marketing Management,* 3rd ed. (Boston: PWS-Kent, 1990), p. 338. Also see Alvin C. Burns and Ronald F. Bush, *Marketing Research,* 3rd ed. (Upper Saddle River, N.J.: Prentice Hall, 2000), pp. 317–318.

33. Steve Jarvis, "Status Quo = Progress," *Marketing News,* April 29, 2002, pp. 37–38.

34. Professional Marketing Research Society, "Market Research Uncovers The Canadian Identity" (press release), June 2002, www.csrc.ca/CSRC/news/news200206.php; and Canadian Survey Research Council, "Canadian Attitudes Towards Survey Research and Issues of Privacy," October 2001, www.csrc.ca/CSRC/news/2001CSRC.pdf.

35. Canadian Survey Research Council, "Prison Call Centres Terminated" (press release), March 28, 2003, www.csrc.ca/CSRC/news/news20030328.php.

36. David Eggleston, "Canadians Condemn Doubleclick Profiling Plans," *Strategy,* March 13, 2000, p. 2; Clare Saliba, "U.S. Ends DoubleClick Privacy Probe," *E-Commerce Times,* January 23, 2001, www. ecommercetimes.com/perl/story/?id=6917; Mark McMaster, "Too Close for Comfort," *Sales & Marketing Management,* July 2001, pp. 43–48; and "DoubleClick Settles Online-Privacy Suits, Plans to Ensure Protections, Pay Legal Fees," *Wall Street Journal,* April 1, 2002, p. B8.

37. Canadian Survey Research Council, "Canadian Attitudes Towards Survey Research and Issues of Privacy," October 2001, www.csrc.ca/CSRC/news/2001CSRC.pdf.

38. See William O. Bearden, Charles S. Madden, and Kelly Uscategui, "The Pool Is Drying Up," *Marketing Research,* Spring 1998, pp. 26–33; Craig Frazier, "What Are Americans Afraid Of?" *American Demographics,* July 2001, pp. 43–49; and Steve Jarvis, "CMOR Finds Survey Refusal Rate Still Rising," *Marketing News,* February 4, 2002, p. 4.

39. Susan Vogt, "Online Privacy Laws All Over the Map," *Strategy,* September 11, 2000, p. 12.

40. John Schwartz, "Chief Privacy Officers Forge Evolving Corporate Roles," *New York Times,* February 12, 2001, p. C1. Also see Stephen F. Ambrose Jr., and Joseph W. Gelb, "Consumer Privacy Regulation and Litigation," *Business Lawyer,* May 2001, pp. 1157–1178.

41. Cynthia Crossen, "Studies Galore Support Products and Positions, but Are They Reliable?" *Wall Street Journal,* November 14, 1991, pp. A1, A9. Also see Allan J. Kimmel, "Deception in Marketing Research and Practice: An Introduction," *Psychology and Marketing,* July 2001, pp. 657–661.

42. See Professional Marketing Research Society, "PRMS Rules of Conduct and Good Practice (2001)," June 30, 2001, www.pmrs-aprm.com/What/RulesA01.html. See also Betsy Peterson, "Ethics Revisited," *Marketing Research,* Winter 1996, pp. 47–48; and O. C. Ferrell, Michael D. Hartline, and Stephen W. McDaniel, "Codes of Ethics Among Corporate Research Departments, Marketing Research Firms, and Data Subcontractors: An Examination of a Three-Communities Metaphor," *Journal of Business Ethics,* April 1998, pp. 503–516. For discussion of a framework for ethical marketing research, see Naresh K. Malhotra and Gina L. Miller, "An Integrated Model of Ethical Decisions in Marketing Research," *Journal of Business Ethics,* February 1998, pp. 263–280; and Kumar C. Rallapalli, "A Paradigm for Development and Promulgation of a Global Code of Marketing Ethics," *Journal of Business Ethics,* January 1999, pp. 125–137.

Chapter 7

1. Richard A. Melcher, "Tune-Up Time for Harley," *Business Week,* April 8, 1997, pp. 90–94; Ian P. Murphy, "Aided by Research, Harley Goes Whole Hog," *Marketing News,* December 2, 1996, pp. 16, 17; Linda Sandler, "Workspaces: Harley Shop," *Wall Street Journal,* April 21, 1999, p. B20; Robert Francis, "Leaders of the Pack," *Brandweek,* June 26, 2000, pp. 28–38; Joseph Webber, "Harley Investors May Get a Wobbly Ride," *Business Week,* February 11, 2002, p. 65; Karl Greenberg, "Harley-Davidson Hogs the Spotlight with New Ad, 100th Anniversary Bash," *Brandweek,* February 25, 2002, p. 9; Harley-Davidson website, www.Harley-Davidson.com, (accessed September 2002); Harley-Davidson Canada, "Harley-Davidson 100th Anniversary Open Road Tour Is A Treat For Every Sense: Sight, Sound And The Sense-Sational" (press release), August 27, 2002, www.harleycanada.com; and "Recommended Readings: The New Heavy Metal Thunder," *Marketing Magazine,* September 2, 2002, p. 18.

2. Statistics Canada, "Population, Provinces and Territories, 2002," www.statcan.ca/english/Pgdb/demo02.htm (accessed August 13, 2003). See also World POPClock, U.S. Census Bureau, www.census.gov, which provides continuously updated projections of the U.S. and world populations.

3. Allan R. Gregg, "Strains Across the Border," *Maclean's,* December 30, 2002, www.macleans.ca/; and "Maclean's Annual Poll," *Maclean's,* December 30, 2002, www.macleans.ca/.

4. For this and the following example, see Philip R. Cateora, *International Marketing,* 8th ed. (Homewood, Ill.: Irwin, 1993), Chapter: 4; Warren J. Keegan and Mark S. Green, *Global Marketing,* 2nd ed. (Upper Saddle River, N.J.: Prentice Hall, 2000), pp. 129–130; and Warren J. Keegan, *Global Marketing Management,* 7th ed. (Upper Saddle River, N.J.: Prentice Hall, 2002), pp. 68–69.

5. Carey Toane, "Veering Off From the Mainstream: Marketers Are Finding Divergent Ways Beyond Traditional Advertising to Reach Ethnic Consumers," *Marketing On-Line,* June 5, 2000; and Patrick Lejtenyi, "Underlying Differences: Market Researchers Must Be Diligent About Identifying Subcultures Within Ethnic Groups," *Marketing Magazine,* June 5, 2000, www.marketingmag.ca.

6. Statistics Canada, "Population by Selected Ethnic Origins, Canada (2001 Census)," modified April 28, 2003, www.statcan.ca/english/Pgdb/demo28a.htm.

7. Sara Minoque, "Chinese Explosion," *Strategy,* February 24, 2003, p. 19.

8. Cleve Lu, "Plugging the Holes," *Strategy,* September 23, 2002, p. 23; Jennifer Lynn, "Approaching Diversity," *Marketing,* July 30, 1995, p. 15; David Menzies, "TD Bank Opens a Branch in Cyberspace," *Marketing,* June 19, 1995, p. 11; James Pollock, "Opening Doors of Opportunity," *Marketing,* September 18, 1995; and Isabel Vincent, "Chasing After the Ethnic Consumer," *Globe and Mail,* September 18, 1995.

9. Loretta Lam, "Music to Ethnic Ears," *Marketing Magazine,* May 19, 2003, pp. 10–11.

10. Race Relations Advisory Council on Advertising, "The Color of Your Money," (video), 1995.

11. Gayle MacDonald, "The Gap Between Rich and Rich," *Globe and Mail,* July 5, 2003, pp. F4–5.

12. For more on social class, see Leon G. Schiffman and Leslie L. Kanuk, *Consumer Behavior*, 6th ed. (Upper Saddle River, N.J.: Prentice Hall, 1997), Chapter 13; Rebecca Piirto Heath, "The New Working Class," *American Demographics*, January 1998, pp. 51–55; and Linda P. Morton, "Segmenting Publics by Social Class," *Public Relations Quarterly*, Summer 1999, pp. 45–46.

13. Ron Szekely, "L'Oréal Generates Buzz," *Marketing Magazine*, January 7, 2002, www.marketingmag.ca.

14. See Darla Dernovsek, "Marketing to Women," *Credit Union Magazine*, October 2000, pp. 90–96; Sharon Goldman Edry, "No Longer Just Fun and Games," *American Demographics*, May 2001, pp. 36–38; Joanne Thomas Yaccato, *Reaching the Real World of Women: The 80 Per Cent Minority* (Toronto: Viking Canada, 2003); and Dana Flavelle, "'Gender Intelligence' Is Her Message," *Toronto Star*, April 9, 2003, www.torontostar.com.

15. See also Betty Liu, "Men's Playgrounds Plug Into Girl Power," *Financial Times*, December 29, 2002, www.ft.com.

16. David Leonhardt, "Hey Kids, Buy This," *Business Week*, June 30, 1997, pp. 62–67; and Jean Halliday, "Automakers Agree, Winning Youth Early Key to Future," *Advertising Age*, April 1, 2002, p. S16.

17. Tobi Elkin, "Sony Marketing Aims at Lifestyle Segments," *Advertising Age*, March 18, 2002, pp. 3, 72.

18. For a good discussion of lifestyle topics, see Michael R. Solomon, Judith L. Zaichkowsky, and Rosemary Polegato, *Consumer Behaviour*, 2nd Canadian ed. (Toronto: Pearson Education Canada, 2002), chapter 6.

19. Paul C. Judge, "Are Tech Buyers Different?" *Business Week*, January 26, 1998, pp. 64–65, 68; Josh Bernoff, Shelley Morrisette, and Kenneth Clemmer, "The Forrester Report," Forrester Research, Inc., 1998; and the Forrester website, www.forrester.com (accessed July 2001).

20. Stuart Elliot, "Sampling Tastes of a Changing Russia," *New York Times*, April 1, 1992, pp. D1, D19; and Tom Miller, "Global Segments from 'Strivers' to 'Creatives,'" *Marketing News*, July 20, 1998, p. 11. For an excellent discussion of cross-cultural lifestyle systems, see Philip Kotler, Gary Armstrong, John Saunders, and Veronica Wong, *Principles of Marketing*, 3rd European ed. (London: Prentice Hall Europe, 2001), pp. 202–204.

21. Jennifer Aaker, "Dimensions of Measuring Brand Personality," *Journal of Marketing Research*, August 1997, pp. 347–356. Also see Aaker, "The Malleable Self: The Role of Self-Expression in Persuasion," *Journal of Marketing Research*, May 1999, pp. 45–57; and Swee Hoon Ang, "Personality Influences on Consumption: Insights from the Asian Economic Crisis," *Journal of International Consumer Marketing*, 2001, pp. 5–20.

22. See Myron Magnet, "Let's Go for Growth," *Fortune*, March 7, 1994, p. 70; Aaker, "The Malleable Self," Leon G. Shiffman and Leslie Lazar Kanuk, *Consumer Behavior*, 7th ed. (Upper Saddle River, N.J.: Prentice Hall, 2000), pp. 111–118; and Swee Hoon Ang, "Personality Influences on Consumption: Insights from the Asian Economic Crisis," *Journal of International Consumer Marketing*, 2001, pp. 5–20.

23. Charles Pappas, "Ad Nauseam," *Advertising Age*, July 10, 2000, pp. 16–18.

24. David Todd, "Quebec Milk Producers Play on Emotional Ties," *Strategy*, March 1, 1999, p. 31; and Stephanie Whittaker, "Milk Grows Up," *Marketing Magazine*, August 9, 1999, www.marketingmag.ca.

25. See Henry Assael, *Consumer Behavior and Marketing Action* (Boston: Kent Publishing, 1987), Chap. 4. An earlier classification of three types of consumer buying behaviour—routine response behaviour, limited problem solving, and extensive problem solving—can be found in John A. Howard and Jagdish Sheth, *The Theory of Consumer Behavior* (New York: John Wiley, 1969), pp. 27–28. Also see John A. Howard, *Consumer Behavior in Marketing Strategy* (Upper Saddle River, N.J.: Prentice Hall, 1989).

26. For more on word-of-mouth sources, see Philip Kotler and Peggy Cunningham, *Marketing Management*, Canadian 11th ed. (Toronto: Pearson Education Canada, 2004), pp. 580–582.

27. See Leon Festinger, *A Theory of Cognitive Dissonance* (Stanford, Calif.: Stanford University Press, 1957); Leon G. Schiffman and Leslie L. Kanuk, *Consumer Behavior*, 6th ed. (Upper Saddle River, N.J.: Prentice Hall, 1997), pp. 219–220; Jeff Stone, "A Radical New Look at Cognitive Dissonance," *American Journal of Psychology*, Summer 1998, pp. 319–326; Thomas R. Schultz, Elene Leveille, and Mark R. Lepper, "Free Choice and Cognitive Dissonance Revisited: Choosing 'Lesser Evils' Versus 'Greater Goods,'" *Personality and Social Psychology Bulletin*, January 1999, pp. 40–48; Jillian C. Sweeney, Douglas Hausknecht, and Geoffrey N. Soutar, "Cognitive Dissonance After Purchase: A Multidimensional Scale," *Psychology & Marketing*, May 2000, pp. 369–385; and Patti Williams and Jennifer L. Aaker, "Can Mixed Emotions Peacefully Coexist?" March 2002, pp. 636–649.

28. See Frank Rose, "Now Quality Means Service Too," *Fortune*, April 22, 1991, pp. 97–108; Chip Walker, "Word of Mouth," *American Demographics*, July 1995, p. 40; Thomas O. Jones and W. Earl Sasser Jr., "Why Satisfied Customers Defect," *Harvard Business Review*, November–December 1995, pp. 88–99; Roger Sant, "Did He Jump or Was He Pushed?" *Marketing News*, May 12, 1997, pp. 2, 21; Vikas Mittal and Wagner Kamakura, "Satisfaction, Repurchase Intent, and Repurchase Behavior: Investigating the Moderating Effect of Customer Characteristics," *Journal of Marketing Research*, February 2001, pp. 131–142; and Denny Hatch and Ernie Schell, "Delight Your Customers," *Target Marketing*, April 2002, pp. 32–39.

29. The following discussion draws heavily from Everett M. Rogers, *Diffusion of Innovations*, 3rd ed. (New York: Free Press, 1983). Also see Hubert Gatignon and Thomas S. Robertson, "A Propositional Inventory for New Diffusion Research," *Journal of Consumer Research*, March 1985, pp. 849–867; Marnik G. Dekiple, Philip M. Parker, and Milos Sarvary, "Global Diffusion of Technological Innovations: A Coupled-Hazard Approach," *Journal of Marketing Research*, February 2000, pp. 47–59; Peter J. Danaher, Bruce G.S. Hardie, and William P. Putsis, "Marketing-Mix Variables and the Diffusion of Successive Generations of a Technological Innovation," *Journal of Marketing Research*, November 2001, pp. 501–514; and Eun-Ju Lee, Jinkook Lee, and David W. Schumann, "The Influence of Communication Source and Mode on Consumer Adoption of Technological Innovations," *Journal of Consumer Affairs*, Summer 2002, pp. 1–27.

Chapter 8

1. Magna International Corporation website, www.magnaint.com/ (accessed July 20, 2003); Sinclair Stewart, "Auto Parts Suppliers Look To Branding," *Strategy*, February 15, 1999, p. 1; Greg Keenan, "Auto Parts Maker Issues Brighter Earnings Picture for First-Quarter Results," *Globe and Mail*, February 25, 2003,

www.globeandmail.com; John Buell, "The Year of Relationships," (editorial), *Constructech*, Vol. 5, No. 3, 2003, www.constructech.com/printresources/viewarticle2.asp.

2. Government of Canada, Sector Profile, "Information and Communications Technologies Industry, Industry Innovation Profile," April 2002, www.innovationstrategy.gc.ca/cmb/innovation.nsf/SectoralE/ICTech (accessed July 20, 2003).

3. Industry Canada, Small Business Research and Policy webpage, http://strategis.ic.gc.ca/SSG/rd00254e.html#top (accessed June 8, 2003).

4. See Kate Macarthur, "Teflon Togs Get $40 Million Ad Push," *Advertising Age*, April 8, 2002, p. 3.

5. Sarah Lorge, "Purchasing Power," *Sales & Marketing Management*, June 1998, pp. 43–46.

6. This quotation and the following example are from John H. Sheridan, "An Alliance Built on Trust," *Industry Week*, March 17, 1997, pp. 66–70; and Gary S. Vasilash, "Leveraging the Supply Chain for Competitive Advantage," *Automotive Design & Production*, April 2002, pp. 50–51.

7. "Keeping Up with Your Industry," *Insights*, February 2000, p. 1, and ChemStation newsletter, www.chemstation.com (accessed July 2002).

8. Patrick J. Robinson, Charles W. Faris, and Yoram Wind, *Industrial Buying Behavior and Creative Marketing* (Boston: Allyn & Bacon, 1967). Also see Erin Anderson, Weyien Chu, and Barton Weitz, "Industrial Purchasing: An Empirical Exploration of the Buyclass Framework," *Journal of Marketing*, July 1987, pp. 71–86; and Michael D. Hutt and Thomas W. Speh, *Business Marketing Management*, 7th ed. (Upper Saddle River, N.J.: Prentice Hall, 2001), pp. 56–66.

9. See Philip Kotler and Peggy Cunningham, *Marketing Management*, Canadian 11th ed. (Toronto: Pearson Education Canada, 2004), p. 225.

10. Frederick E. Webster Jr. and Yoram Wind, *Organizational Buying Behavior* (Upper Saddle River, N.J.: Prentice Hall, 1972), pp. 78–80. Also see James C. Anderson and James A. Narus, *Business Market Management: Understanding, Creating and Delivering Value* (Upper Saddle River, N.J.: Prentice Hall, 1998), Chap. 3; and Michael D. Hutt and Thomas W. Speh, *Business Marketing Management*, 7th ed. (Upper Saddle River, N.J.: Prentice Hall, 2001), pp. 73–77.

11. Frederick E. Webster Jr. and Yoram Wind, *Organizational Buying Behavior* (Upper Saddle River, N.J.: Prentice Hall, 1972), pp. 33–37. Also see Edward G. Brierty, Robert W. Eckles, and Robert R. Reeder, *Business Marketing*, 3rd ed. (Upper Saddle River, N.J.: Prentice Hall, 1998), Chap. 3.

12. Industry Canada, "Canada Developing Strong Ebusiness Infrastructure, But Government and Industry Must Address Areas of Weakness To Maintain Global Competitiveness" (press release), May 1, 2003, www.cebi.ca/Public/Team1/Docs/ff_press.pdf.

13. Thomas V. Bonoma, "Major Sales: Who Really Does the Buying," *Harvard Business Review*, May–June 1982, p. 114. Also see Ajay Kohli, "Determinants of Influence in Organizational Buying: A Contingency Approach," *Journal of Marketing*, July 1989, pp. 50–65; and Jeffrey E. Lewin, "The Effects of Downsizing on Organizational Buying Behavior: An Empirical Investigation," *Academy of Marketing Science*, Spring 2001, pp. 151–164.

14. Ceridian Canada, "New Branding Campaign From Ceridian Canada Offers Businesses 'The Freedom To Succeed'" (news release), February 12, 2002, www.ceridian.ca/en/news/2002/february12_2002.html.

15. Patrick J. Robinson, Charles W. Faris, and Yoram Wind, *Industrial Buying Behavior and Creative Marketing* (Boston: Allyn & Bacon, 1967), p. 14.

16. Lori Enos, "Canada Poised for B2B Boom," *E-Commerce Times*, January 11, 2001, www.ecommercetimes.com/perl/story/6624.html.

17. Bernadette Johnson, "Business Depot targets SOHO sector," *Strategy*, June 19, 2000, p. D1.

18. See Verespej, "E-Procurement Explosion," pp. 25–28; Andy Reinhardt, "Extranets: Log On, Link Up, Save Big," *Business Week*, June 22, 1998, p. 134; "To Byte the Hand That Feeds," *The Economist*, January 17, 1998, pp. 61–62; Ken Brack, "Source of the Future," *Industrial Distribution*, October 1998, pp. 76–80; James Carbone, "Internet Buying on the Rise," *Purchasing*, March 25, 1999, pp. 51–56; "E-Procurement: Certain Value in Changing Times," *Fortune*, April 30, 2001, pp. S2–S3; and "Benchmark Survey: E-Procurement Adoptions Progress Slowly and Steadily," *Purchasing*, June 20, 2002, p. S8.

19. Forensic Technology Inc., press releases 2002–2003, www.fti-ibis.com/en/press.asp (accessed July 2003); Andrew Philips, "Gun Smarts," *Maclean's*, April 17, 2000, www.macleans.ca/topstories/canada/article.jsp?content=33446.

20. Paul E. Goulding, "Q&A: Making Uncle Sam Your Customer," *Financial Executive*, May–June 1998, pp. 55–57.

21. See Ottawa: Supply and Services, *Government Business Opportunities*, and *Selling to Government: A Guide to Government Procurement in Canada*.

22. Bombardier website, "Bombardier Wins $633-Million Order From Deutsche Bahn For 298 Additional Double-Deck Cars" (press release), July 6, 2003, www.bombardier.com/; Casey Mahood, "Bombardier Lands Huge Jet Order," *Globe and Mail*, March 30, 2000, pp. B1, B15; Hélèna Katz, "Hot Wheels! To Get Good Traction in the Expanding All-Terrain Market, Newcomer Bombardier Must Build Its Brand," *Marketing Magazine*, www.marketingmag.ca; Bombardier website, "Bombardier Aerospace Launches E-Business Customer Service Initiative" (news release), October 10, 2000, www.aerospace.bombardier.com.

Chapter 9

1. See Kerri Walsh, "Soaps and Detergents," *Chemical Week*, January 23, 2002, pp. 24–27; the Procter & Gamble and Tide websites, www.pg.com and www.tide.com (accessed July 2003); and Euromonitor International, "Household Cleaning Products in Canada: Executive Summary," July 2002, www.euromonitor.com/Household_Cleaning_Products_in_Canada.

2. These and other examples found in Nelson D. Schwartz, "Still Perking After All These Years," *Fortune*, May 24, 1999, pp. 203–210; and USAopoly website, www.usaopoly.com (accessed July 2002).

3. Ian Edwards, "How Can Marketers Strike Gold with Vancouver's Winter Olympics?" *Strategy*, July 14, 2003, p. 2.

4. See Bruce Hager, "Podunk Is Beckoning," *Business Week*, December 2, 1991, p. 76; David Greisling, "The Boonies Are Booming," *Business Week*, October 9, 1995, pp. 104–110; Mike Duff, "Home Depot Drops Villager's Hareware for New Concept," *DSN Retailing Today*, April 22, 2002, pp. 5, 28; and Stephanie Thompson, "Wal-Mart Tops List for New Food Lines, *Advertising Age*, April 29, 2002, pp. 4, 61.

5. Olay website, www.olay.com (accessed July 2002).

6. Carmetta Y. Coleman, "Eddie Bauer's Windows Add Electronics." *Wall Street Journal,* November 28, 2000, p. B10; and Karen M. Kroll, "Plasma Video Screens Prove Customer Hit in Eddie Bauer," *Stores,* February 2001, pp. 74–75.

7. Pat Sloan and Jack Neff, "With Aging Baby Boomers in Mind, P&G, Den-Mat Plan Launches," *Advertising Age,* April 13, 1998, pp. 3, 38.

8. Alice Z. Cuneo, "Advertisers Target Women, but Market Remains Elusive," *Advertising Age,* November 10, 1997, pp. 1, 24; and Laura Q. Hughes and Alice Z. Cuneo, "Lowes Retools Image in Push Toward Women," *Advertising Age,* February 26, 2001, pp. 3, 51.

9. "Grocery Gateway To Deliver for Home Depot," *Globe and Mail,* November 26, 2002, www.globeandmail.com.

10. Andrea Zoe Aster, "How Harlequin Woos Women," *Marketing Magazine,* March 31, 2003, pp. 8–10.

11. Michelle Orecklin, "What Women Watch," *Time,* May 13, 2002, pp. 65–66; Oxygen website, www.oxygen.com (accessed July 2002); and W Network website, www.wnetwork.com (accessed July 2003).

12. Jessica Johnson, "Walking Down the Aisle: How Shopping Tests Your Relationship," *Globe and Mail,* April 12, 2003, p. L1.

13. Jessica Johnson, "Walking Down the Aisle: How Shopping Tests Your Relationship," *Globe and Mail,* April 12, 2003, p. L1.

14. Amanda Beeler, "Heady Rewards for Loyalty," *Advertising Age,* August 14, 2000, p. S8; and Neiman Marcus website, www.neimanmarcus.com/store/sitelets/incircle/index.jhtml (accessed July 2002).

15. Canadian Centre for Cyber Citizenship, "Comparing Poverty: Canada and the World," www.mapleleafweb.com/features/general/poverty/comparison.html, and "Poverty from Coast to Coast," www.mapleleafweb.com/features/general/poverty/coast_to_coast.html (accessed July 20, 2003); and M. Förster, "Trends and Driving Factors in Income Distribution and Poverty in the OECD area," Labour Market and Social Policy Occasional Paper, No. 42, OECD, Paris, 2000.

16. Marina Strauss, "The Best Bet for Your Bottom Dollar," *Globe and Mail,* August 2, 2003, pp. B1, B5.

17. Nova Scotia Department of Agriculture and Fisheries, "1999 Nova Scotia Food Consumer Study," May 2001, www.gov.ns.ca/nsaf/marketing/research/99nsfcs.htm.

18. Modrobes website, www.modrobes.com (accessed August 18, 2003); and Astrid Van Den Broek, "Targeting Yourself," *Marketing Magazine,* August 2, 1999, p. 9.

19. "Lifestyle Marketing," *Progressive Grocer,* August 1997, pp. 107–110; and Philip Kotler and Peggy Cunningham, *Marketing Management: Analysis, Planning, Implementation, and Control,* Canadian 11th ed. (Toronto: Pearson Education Canada, 2004), pp. 296–298.

20. Laurie Freeman and Cleveland Horton, "Spree: Honda's Scooters Ride the Cutting Edge," *Advertising Age,* September 5, 1985, pp. 3, 35; "Scooter Wars," *Cycle World,* February 1998, p. 26; Jonathon Welsh, "Transport: The Summer of the Scooter: Boomers Get a New Retro Toy," *Wall Street Journal,* April 13, 2001, p. W1; and Honda's website, www.hondamotorcycle.com/scooter (accessed July 2002).

21. "RadioShack Giving E-Gifts This Holiday Season," *Adnews On-Line Daily,* 13 November 2000, www.adnews.com.

22. See Mark Maremont, "The Hottest Thing Since the Flashbulb," *Business Week,* September 7, 1992; Bruce Nussbaum, "A Camera in a Wet Suit," *Business Week,* June 2, 1997, p. 109; Dan Richards, "The Smartest Disposable Cameras," *Travel Holiday,* December 1998, p. 20; "Point and Click," *Golf Magazine,* February 1999, p. 102; and Todd Wasserman, "Kodak Rages in Favor of the Machines," *Brandweek,* February 26, 2001, p. 6.

23. British Columbia Ministry of Health, "The Need for Blood Donors" (news release), May 29, 2003, www2.news.gov.bc.ca/nrm_news_releases/2003HSER0028-000531.htm (accessed August 18, 2003); and Will Stos, "A Bloody Mess: When the Gift of Life Is Refused," *Centretown News,* February 7, 2003, www.carleton.ca/ctown/archiv/feb0703/insite1.htm.

24. See Warren Thayer, "Target Heavy Buyers!" *Frozen Food Age,* March 1998, pp. 22–24; Jennifer Ordonez, "Cash Cows: Hamburger Joints Call Them 'Heavy Users,'" *Wall Street Journal,* January 12, 2000, p. A1; and Brian Wonsink and Sea Bum Park, "Methods and Measures That Profile Heavy Users," *Journal of Advertising Research,* July–August 2000, pp. 61–72.

25. Helena Lazar, "Creating New Habits: Well-Targeted Ads Encourage Light Users To Pour on the Sauce," *Marketing Magazine,* September 20, 1999, www.marketingmag.ca.

26. Kendra Parker, "How Do You Like Your Beef?" *American Demographics,* January 2000, pp. 35–37.

27. Daniel S. Levine, "Justice Served," *Sales & Marketing Management,* May 1995, pp. 53–61.

28. For more on segmenting business markets, see John Berrigan and Carl Finkbeiner, *Segmentation Marketing: New Methods for Capturing Business* (New York: HarperBusiness, 1992); Rodney L. Griffith and Louis G. Pol, "Segmenting Industrial Markets," *Industrial Marketing Management,* no. 23, 1994, pp. 39–46; Stavros P. Kalafatis and Vicki Cheston, "Normative Models and Practical Applications of Segmentation in Business Markets," *Industrial Marketing Management,* November 1997, pp. 519–530; James C. Anderson and James A. Narus, *Business Market Management* (Upper Saddle River, N.J.: Prentice Hall, 1999), pp. 44–47; and Andy Dexter, "Egotists, Idealists, and Corporate Animals—Segmenting Business Markets, *International Journal of Marketing Research,* First Quarter 2002, pp. 31–51.

29. NationMaster.com website, "Less Developed Countries (LCDs)," www.nationmaster.com/kp/less+developed+countries (accessed August 18, 2003).

30. Cyndee Miller, "Teens Seen as the First Truly Global Consumers," *Advertising Age,* March 27, 1995, p. 9; and Warren J. Keegan, *Global Marketing Management* (Upper Saddle River, N.J.: Prentice Hall, 2002), p. 194.

31. Shawn Tully, "Teens: The Most Global Market of All," *Fortune,* May 16, 1994, pp. 90–97; "MTV Hits 100 Million in Asia," *New Media Markets,* January 28, 1999, p. 12; and Brett Pulley and Andrew Tanzer, "Sumner's Gemstone," *Forbes,* February 21, 2000, pp. 106–111. For more on international segmentation, see V. Kumar and Anish Nagpal, "Segmenting Global Markets: Look Before You Leap," *Marketing Research,* Spring 2001, pp. 8–13.

32. See Michael Porter, *Competitive Advantage* (New York: Free Press, 1985), pp. 4–8, 234–236. For more recent discussions, see Leyland Pitt, "Total E-clipse: Five New Forces for Strategy in the Digital Age," *Journal of General Management,* Summer 2001, pp. 1–15; and Stanley Slater and Eric Olson, "A Fresh Look at Industry and Market Analysis," *Business Horizons,* January–February 2002, p. 15–22.

33. Arlene Weintraub, "Chairman of the Board," *Business Week*, May 28, 2001, p. 94.

34. Paul Davidson, "Entrepreneurs Reap Riches from Net Niches," *USA Today*, April 20, 1998, p. B3; and Ostriches On Line website, www.ostrichesonline.com (accessed July 2002).

35. Astrid Van Den Broek, "The Research behind the McLaunch," *Strategy*, July 15, 2002, p. 30.

36. For a collection of articles on one-to-one marketing and mass customization, see James H. Gilmore and B. Joseph Pine, *Markets of One: Creating Customer-Unique Value Through Mass Customization* (Boston: Harvard Business School Press, 2001).

37. Chris Daniels, "Big Blue Thinks Small," *Marketing Magazine*, September 23, 2002, pp. 8–10.

38. See Jerry Wind and Arvid Rangaswamy, "Customerization: The Next Revolution in Mass Customization," *Journal of Interactive Marketing*, Winter 2001, pp. 13–32.

39. Sony A. Grier, "The Federal Trade Commission's Report on the Marketing of Violent Entertainment to Youths: Developing Policy-Tuned Research," *Journal of Public Policy and Marketing*, Spring 2001, pp. 123–132; and Greg Winter, "Tobacco Company Reneged on Youth Ads, Judge Rules," *New York Times*, June 7, 2002, p. A18.

40. Joseph Turow, "Breaking Up America: The Dark Side of Target Marketing," *American Demographics*, November 1997, pp. 51–54; and Bette Ann Stead and Jackie Gilbert, "Ethical Issues in Electronic Commerce," *Journal of Business Ethics*, November 2001, pp. 75–85.

41. Ipsos-Reid, "Case Study: When One Message Doesn't Fit All," February 2003, E-REID, www.ipsos-reid.com/html/ereid/ereid_02_07_03_cdn.htm.

42. Sara Minoque, "Chinese Explosion," *Strategy*, February 24, 2003, pp. 19, 22.

43. For interesting discussion of finding ways to differentiate marketing offers, see Ian C. MacMillan and Rita Gunther McGrath, "Discovering New Points of Differentiation," *Harvard Business Review*, July–August 1997, pp. 133–145; and Girish Punj and Junyean Moon, "Positioning Options for Achieving Brand Association: A Psychological Categorization Framework," *Journal of Business Research*, April 2002, pp. 275–283.

44. Anne Dimon, "The Concierge Can Turn Out To Be Your Friend in Need," *Globe and Mail*, February 13, 1996, p. C9; and Jeremy Ferguson, "Where Rescue Operations Are Routine," *Globe and Mail*, February 13, 1996, p. C9.

45. Lisa D'Innocenzo, "Gardiner Museum Pours on 'Bold' Campaign," *Strategy*, February 10, 2003, p. 3.

46. Lisa D'Innocenzo, "Strickland: Why Zellers Pledges To Be Better," *Strategy*, February 25, 2003, p. 1; Marina Strauss, "Zellers Returns to Pitching Prices," *Globe and Mail*, March 13, 2000, pp. B1, B3; and Fawzia Sheikh, "Zellers Plans To Expand Its Brands," *Marketing Magazine*, May 17, 1999, www.marketingmag.ca.

47. See Philip Kotler, *Kotler on Marketing* (New York: Free Press, 1999), pp. 59–63.

48. See Bobby J. Calder and Steven J. Reagan, "Brand Design," in Dawn Iacobucci, ed., *Kellogg on Marketing* (New York: John Wiley, 2001) p. 61.

49. The Palm Pilot and Mountain Dew examples are from Alice M. Tybout and Brian Sternthal, "Brand Positioning," in Dawn Iacobucci, ed., *Kellogg on Marketing* (New York: John Wiley, 2001), p. 54.

Chapter 10

1. Excerpt adapted from Penelope Green, "Spiritual Cosmetics. No Kidding," *New York Times*, January 10, 1999, p. 1. Also see Elizabeth Wellington, "The Success of Smell," *The News & Observer*, June 11, 2001, p. E1; Mary Tannen, "Cult Cosmetics," *New York Times Magazine*, Spring 2001, p. 96; Sandra Yin, "The Nose Knows," *American Demographics*, February 2002, pp. 14–15; Kristen Vinakmens, "Bringing the Spa Home," *Strategy*, August 11, 2003, p. 1; Jessica Johnson, "Just Don't Call Them the New Women," *Globe and Mail*, June 14, 2003, p. 12; and Glenn Crawford, "Boys Play Dress Up with Masculine Cosmetics," *Capital Xtra*, August 2002, www.capitalxtra.on.ca/queercapital/cx108/cx108_trends.htm.

2. See B. Joseph Pine and James H. Gilmore, *The Experience Economy* (New York: Free Press, 1999); Jane E. Zarem, "Experience Marketing," *Folio: The Magazine for Magazine Management*, Fall 2000, pp. 28–32; and Scott Mac Stravic, "Make Impressions Last: Focus on Value," *Marketing News*, October 23, 2000, pp. 44–45.

3. See Mark Hyman, "The Yin and Yang of the Tiger Effect," *Business Week*, October 16, 2000, p. 110; "Finance and Economics: A Tiger Economy," *The Economist*, April 14, 2001, p. 70; Hillary Cassidy, "Target, Tiger Swing TV Deal with TCG," *Brandweek*, December 2001, p. 11; Kate Fitzgerald, "Buick Rides the Tiger," *Advertising Age*, April 15, 2002, p. 41; and Danny Hakim, "Can Celine Dion Help Chrysler Rebound?" *New York Times*, November 5, 2002, www.nytimes.com/.

4. See Philip Kotler, Irving J. Rein, and Donald Haider, *Marketing Places: Attracting Investment, Industry, and Tourism to Cities, States, and Nations* (New York: Free Press, 1993), pp. 202, 273. Additional information from Fáilte Ireland, www.ireland.travel.ie, and IDA Ireland, www.ida.ie (accessed August 2002).

5. Social Marketing Institute website, www.social-marketing.org/aboutus.html (accessed August 2002).

6. Alan R. Andreasen, Rob Gould, and Karen Gutierrez, "Social Marketing Has a New Champion," *Marketing News*, February 7, 2000, p. 38; and Social Marketing Institute website, www.social-marketing.org (accessed August 2002).

7. Quotes and definitions from Philip Kotler, *Kotler on Marketing* (New York: Free Press, 1999), p. 17; and American Society for Quality website, www.asq.org (accessed June 2002). For more on quality, see John Dalrymple and Eileen Drew, "Quality: On the Threshold or the Brink?" *Total Quality Management*, July 2000, pp. S697–S703; and Rui Sousa and Christopher A. Voss, "Quality Management Re-Visited: A Reflective Review and Agenda for Future Research," *Journal of Operations Management*, February 2002, pp. 91–109.

8. See Roland T. Rust, Anthony J. Zahorik, and Timothy L. Keiningham, "Return on Quality (ROQ): Making Service Quality Financially Accountable," *Journal of Marketing*, April 1995, pp. 58–70; Dan Bridget, "ISO 9000 Changes the Quality Focus," *Quality*, April 2000, pp. 52–56; and Thomas J. Douglas and William Q. Judge, "Total Quality Management Implementation and Competitive Advantage," *Academy of Management Journal*, February 2001, pp. 158–169.

9. See "Hot R.I.P.: The Floppy Disk," *Rolling Stone*, August 20, 1998, p. 86; Bob Woods, "iMac Drives Apple's Q2 Results," *Computer Dealer News*, April 30, 1999, p. 39; Pui-Wing Tam, "Designing Duo Helps Shape Apple's Fortunes," *Wall Street Journal*, July 18, 2001, p. B1; Robert Dwek, "Apple Pushes Design to Core of Marketing," *Marketing Week*, January 24, 2002, p. 20; and

"John Markoff, "Apple Computer Beats Earnings Estimates in Second Quarter," *New York Times*, April 18, 2002, p. C7.

10. Adapted from information found in Mark Schwanhausser, "Thinking Outside the Wallet," *The News & Observer*, May 12, 2002, p. 12E; and "Discover on the Go," *Credit Card Management*, May 2002, p. 9. For other examples, see "Best Product Designs of the Year," *Business Week*, July 8, 2002, pp. 82–94.

11. Alice Rawsthorn, "The World's Top 50 Logos," *Report on Business Magazine*, November 2000, pp. 84–100.

12. See Joan Holleran, "Packaging Speaks Volumes," *Beverage Industry*, February 1998, p. 30; "Packaging—A Silent Salesman," *Retail World*, August 28–September 8, 2000, p. 23; and Elliot Young, "Is It Time to Upgrade Your Packaging?" *Beverage Industry*, April 2002, p. 52.

13. Robert M. McMath, "Chock Full of (Pea)nuts," *American Demographics*, April 1997, p. 60.

14. Health Canada, "Health Canada Announces New Mandatory Nutrition Labelling To Help Canadians Make Informed Choices for Healthy Eating" (news release), January 2, 2003, www.hc-sc.gc.ca/english/media/releases/2003/2003_01.htm.

15. Bro Uttal, "Companies That Serve You Best," *Fortune*, December 7, 1987, p. 116. For an excellent discussion of support services, see James C. Anderson and James A. Narus, "Capturing the Value of Supplementary Services," *Harvard Business Review*, January–February 1995, pp. 75–83.

16. Ann Marie Kerwin, "Brands Pursue Old, New Money," *Advertising Age*, June 11, 2001, pp. S1, S11.

17. Information from Marriott website, www.marriott.com (accessed August 2002).

18. Information about P&G's product lines from P&G website, www.pg.com, and Crest website, www.crest.com (accessed August 2002).

19. "McAtlas Shrugged," *Foreign Policy*, May–June 2001, pp. 26–37; and "Announcing: Canada's Most Trusted Brands," Reader's Digest Canada (press release), February 12, 2003, www.readersdigest.ca/advertising/media-february03.html.

20. See Philip Kotler and Peggy Cunningham, *Marketing Management*, Canadian 11th ed. (Toronto: Pearson Education Canada, 2004), p. 430.

21. Scott Davis, *Brand Asset Management: Driving Profitable Growth Through Your Brands* (San Francisco: Jossey-Bass, 2000); and David C. Bello and Morris. B. Holbrook, "Does an Absence of Brand Equity Generalize Across Product Classes?" *Journal of Business Research*, October 1995, p. 125.

22. Gerry Khermouch, "The Best Global Brands," *Business Week*, August 6, 2001, pp. 50–64.

23. Andrew Pierce and Eric Almquist, "Brand Building May Face a Test," *Advertising Age*, April 9, 2001, p. 22. Also see Don E. Schultz, "Mastering Brand Metrics," *Marketing Management*, May–June 2002, pp. 8–9.

24. See Roland T. Rust, Katherine N. Lemon, and Valerie A. Zeithaml, *Driving Customer Equity: How Lifetime Customer Value Is Reshaping Corporate Strategy* (New York: Free Press, 2000); Katherine N. Lemon, Roland T. Rust, and Valerie A. Zeithaml, "What Drives Customer Equity," *Marketing Management*, Spring 2001, pp. 20–25; and Rust, Lemon, and Zeithaml, "Where Should the Next Marketing Dollar Go?" *Marketing Management*, September–October 2001, pp. 24–28.

25. See Scott Davis, *Brand Asset Management: Driving Profitable Growth Through Your Brands* (San Francisco: Jossey-Bass, 2000).

26. Marc Gobé, *Emotional Branding* (New York: Allworth Press, 2001).

27. Carole Pearson, "Grocery Slotting Fees Deprive Consumers and Manufacturers of Shelf-Respect," *The Straight Goods*, March 19, 2001, www.straightgoods.com/item428.asp. See also Paul N. Bloom, Gregory T. Gundlach, and Joseph P. Cannon, "Slotting Allowances and Fees: School of Thought and the Views of Practicing Managers," *Journal of Marketing*, April 2000, pp. 92–108; and Julie Forster, "The Hidden Cost of Shelf Space," *Business Week*, April 15, 2002, p. 103.

28. Warren Thayer, "Loblaws Exec Predicts: Private Labels to Surge," *Frozen Food Age*, May 1996, p. 1; "President's Choice Continues Brisk Pace," *Frozen Food Age*, March 1998, pp. 17–18; David Dunne and Chakravarthi Narasimhan, "The New Appeal of Private Labels," *Harvard Business Review*, May–June 1999, pp. 41–52; "Marketscan," *Canadian Grocer*, February 2000; "New Private Label Alternatives Bring Changes to Supercenters, Clubs," *DSN Retailing Today*, February 5, 2001, p. 66; and information from President's Choice website, www.presidentschoice.ca (accessed July 2002).

29. Peter Berlinski, "Retailers Push Premium PL," *Private Label Magazine*, May/June 2003, www.privatelabelmag.com/pdf/may2003/canada.cfm. For more reading on store brands, see David Dunne and Chakravarthi Narasimham, "The New Appeal of Private Labels," *Harvard Business Review*, May–June 1999, pp. 41–52; Kusum L. Ailawadi, Scott Neslin, and Karen Gedenk, "Pursuing the Value-Conscious Consumer: Store Brands Versus National Promotions," *Journal of Marketing*, January 2001, pp. 71–89; and Pradeep K. Chintagunta, "Investigating Category Pricing Behavior at a Retail Chain," *Journal of Marketing Research*, May 2002, pp. 141–151.

30. See Stacy Barr, "Do You Have a Licence for That?" *Marketing Magazine*, July 28/August 4, 2003, p. P9; Doug Desjardins, "Popularized Entertainment Icons Continue to Dominate Licensing," *DSN Retailing Today*, July 9, 2001, p. 4; Emily Scardino, "Entertainment Licensing: Adding Equity Sells Apparel Programs," *DSN Retailing Today*, June 4, 2001, pp. A10–A12; Patricia Winters Lauro, "Licensing Deals Are Putting Big Brand Name into New Categories at the Supermarket," *New York Times*, June 18, 2002, p. C14; and Derek Manson, "Spidy Cents," *Money*, July 2002, p. 40.

31. See Terry Lefton, "Warner Brothers' Not Very Looney Path to Licensing Gold," *Brandweek*, February 14, 1994, pp. 36–37; Robert Scally, "Warner Builds Brand Presence, Strengthens 'Tunes' Franchise," *Discount Store News*, April 6, 1998, p. 33; "Looney Tunes Launched on East Coast," *Dairy Foods*, April 2001, p. 9; Wendy Cuthbert, "Biscuits Leclerc Scores Major Licensing Coup: Signs Deal with Warner Bros. for Right To Use Looney Tunes Characters," *Strategy*, July 5, 1999, p. 25; and "Looney Tunes Entering 696 Publix Super Markets," *Dairy Foods*, April 2002, p. 11.

32. See Laura Petrecca, "'Corporate Brands' Put Licensing in the Spotlight," *Advertising Age*, June 14, 1999, p. 1; and Bob Vavra, "The Game of the Name," *Supermarket Business*, March 15, 2001, pp. 45–46.

33. David Eggleston, "Patriot Flexes Muscles for Barbie: Canadian Computer Firm Joins with Mattel to Market Licensed PCs," *Strategy*, August 16, 1999, p. 1; Jean Gaudreau, "The Principles of Online Branding," *Strategy*, September 13, 1999, p. 29.

34. Phil Carpenter, "Some Cobranding Caveats to Obey," *Marketing News,* November 7, 1994, p. 4; Gabrielle Solomon, "Co-Branding Alliances: Arranged Marriages Made by Marketers," *Fortune,* October 12, 1998, p. 188; "Kmart Licensing Will Continue," *New York Times,* March 21, 2002, p. C5; and Daniel Kadlac, "Martha's New Ruffle," *Time,* July 1, 2002, p. 39.

35. Lisa Wright, "Rooting for a Beaver with Wings," *Toronto Star,* June 8, 2000, pp. A1, A34.

36. For more on the use of line and brand extensions and consumer attitudes toward them, see Deborah Roedder John, Barbara Loken, and Christopher Joiner, "The Negative Impact of Extensions: Can Flagship Brands Be Eroded?" *Journal of Marketing,* January 1998, pp. 19–32; Zeynep Gurrhan-Canli and Durairaj Maheswaran, "The Effects of Extensions on Brand Name Dilution and Enchancment," *Journal of Marketing,* November 1998, pp. 464–473; Vanitha Swaminathan, Richard J. Fox, and Srinivas K. Reddy, "The Impact of Brand Extension Introduction on Choice," *Journal of Marketing,* October 2001, pp. 1–15; Paul A. Bottomly and Stephen J. S. Holden, "Do We Really Know How Consumers Evaluate Brand Extensions? Empirical Generalizations Based on Secondary Analysis of Eight Studies," *Journal of Marketing Research,* November 2001, pp. 494–500; and Kalpesh Kaushik Desai and Kevin Lane Keller, "The Effect of Ingredient Branding Strategies on Host Brand Extendibility," *Journal of Marketing,* January 2002, pp. 73–93.

37. "Top 100 Megabrands by Total Measured Advertising Spending," *Advertising Age,* July 16, 2001, p. S2.

38. See Donald D. Tosti and Roger D. Stotz, "Busiling Your Brand from the Inside Out," *Marketing Management,* July–August 2001, pp. 29–33.

39. See Kevin Lane Keller, "The Brand Report Card," *Harvard Business Review,* January 2000, pp. 147–157.

40. Cossette Communication Group, "Prospera: Don't Just Bank. Prosper," (Newsroom case), April 30, 2003, www.cossette.com/.

41. Steve Jarvis, "Refocus, Rebuild, Reeducate, Refine, Rebrand," *Marketing News,* March 26, 2001, pp. 1, 11; and "Top 10 Wireless Phone Brands," *Advertising Age,* June 24, 2002, p. S-18.

42. Industry Canada, "Overview of Canada's Service Economy," March 2001, http://strategis.ic.gc.ca/pics/sc/service-eng.pdf; Ronald Henkoff, "Service Is Everybody's Business," *Fortune,* June 27, 1994, pp. 48–60; and Valerie Zeithaml and Mary Jo Bitner, *Services Marketing* (New York: McGraw-Hill, 1999), pp. 8–9

43. CN promotional brochure, undated.

44. Terry Bullick, "No-Frills Airline Takes Flight in Western Canada," *Marketing Magazine,* February 19, 1996, p. 2.

45. See James L. Heskett, Thomas O. Jones, Gary W. Loveman, W. Earl Sasser Jr., and Leonard A. Schlesinger, "Putting the Service-Profit Chain to Work," *Harvard Business Review,* March–April, 1994, pp. 164–174; and James L. Heskett, W. Earl Sasser Jr., and Leonard A. Schlesinger, *The Service Profit Chain: How Leading Companies Link Profit and Growth to Loyalty, Satisfaction, and Value* (New York: Free Press, 1997). Also see Anthony J. Rucci, Steven P. Kirn, and Richard T. Quinn, "The Employee-Customer-Profit Chain at Sears," *Harvard Business Review,* January–February 1998, pp. 83–97; and Eugene W. Anderson and Vikas Mittal, "Strengthening the Satisfaction-Profit Chain," *Journal of Service Research,* November 2000, pp. 107–120.

46. See Louise Lee, "Schwab vs. Wall Street," *Business Week,* June 3, 2002, pp. 65–71.

47. For discussions of service quality, see A. Parasuraman, Valerie A. Zeithaml, and Leonard L. Berry, "A Conceptual Model of Service Quality and Its Implications for Future Research," *Journal of Marketing,* Fall 1985, pp. 41–50; Zeithaml, Berry, and Parasuraman, "The Behavioral Consequences of Service Quality," *Journal of Marketing,* April 1996, pp. 31–46; Thomas J. Page Jr., "Difference Scores Versus Direct Effects in Service Quality Measurement," *Journal of Service Research,* February 2002, pp. 184–192; and Richard A. Spreng; James J. Jiang, Gary Klein, and Christopher L. Carr, "Measuring Information System Service Quality: SERVQUAL from the Other Side, *MIS Quarterly,* June 2002, pp. 145–166.

48. See James L. Heskett, W. Earl Sasser Jr., and Christopher W. L. Hart, *Service Breakthroughs* (New York: Free Press, 1990).

49. See Stephen S. Tax, Stephen W. Brown, and Murali Chandrashekaran, "Customer Evaluations of Service Complaint Experiences: Implications for Relationship Marketing," *Journal of Marketing,* April 1998, pp. 60–76; Stephen W. Brown, "Practicing Best-in-Class Service Recovery," *Marketing Management,* Summer 2000, pp. 8–9; and James G. Maxham III, "Service Recovery's Influence on Consumer Satisfaction, Positive Word-of-Mouth, and Purchase Intentions," *Journal of Business Research,* October 2001, p. 11; and David E. Bowen, "Internal Service Recovery: Developing a New Construct," *Measuring Business Excellence,* 2002, p. 47.

50. CN promotional brochure, undated.

51. See the *Hazardous Products Act* at http://laws.justice.gc.ca/en/H-3/index.html and the *Food and Drugs Act* at http://laws.justice.gc.ca/en/F-27/index.html.

52. See Philip Cateora, *International Marketing,* 8th ed. (Homewood, Ill.: Irwin, 1993), p. 270; and David Fairlamb, "One Currency—But 15 Economies," *Business Week,* December 31, 2001, p. 59.

53. Information from Deutsche Bank website, www.deutsche-bank.com (accessed July 2002).

54. Information from Cossette Communications website, www.cossette.com/ (accessed August 2003).

55. See Carla Rapoport, "Retailers Go Global," *Fortune,* February 20, 1995, pp. 102–108; "Top 200 Global Retailers," *Stores,* January 1998, pp. S5–S12; Jeffery Adler, "The Americanization of Global Retailing," *Discount Merchandiser,* February 1998, p. 102; Mike Troy, "The World's Largest Retailer," *Chain Store Age,* June 2001, pp. 47–49; Mike Troy, "The Super Growth Leaders—Wal-Mart: Global Dominance Puts Half Trillion in Sight," *DSN Retailing Today,* December 10, 2001, p. 17; and "Wal-Mart: International Expansion," *Home Textiles Today,* April 12, 2002, p. 84.

Chapter 11

1. Quotes, extracts, and other information from Jay Greene, "Microsoft: How It Became Stronger Than Ever," *Business Week,* June 4, 2001, pp. 74–85; Brent Schlender, "Microsoft: The Beast Is Back," *Fortune,* June 11, 2001, pp. 74–86; Robin Peek, "Microsoft Introduces.Net My Services," *Information Today,* November 2001, p. 40; Greene, "On to the Living Room," *Business Week,* January 21, 2002, pp. 68–72; Greene, "Ballmer's Microsoft," *Business Week,* June 17, 2002, pp. 66–76; Brent Schlender, "All You Need Is Love, $50 Billion, and Killer Software Code-Named Longhorn," *Fortune,* July 8, 2002,

pp. 56–68; and Microsoft Canada website, www.microsoft.com/canada/ (accessed August 2003).

2. For these and other examples, see Cliff Edwards, "Where Have All the Edsels Gone?" *Greensboro News Record,* May 24, 1999, p. B6; Simon Romero, "Once Proudly Carried, and Now Mere Carrion," *New York Times,* November 22, 2001, p. G5; and Kelly Carroll, "Satellite Telephony: Not for the Consumer," *Telephony,* March 4, 2002, p. 17. See also Lisa D'Innocenzo, "America's Testing Ground," *Strategy,* March 10, 2003, p. 1.

3. See Philip Kotler, *Kotler on Marketing* (New York: Free Press, 1999), p. 51; Martha Wirth Fellman, "Number of New Products Keeps Rising," *Marketing News,* March 29, 1999, p. 3; Eric Berggren and Thomas Nacher, "Why Good Ideas Go Bust," *Management Review,* February 2000, pp. 32–36; Eric Berggren, "Introducing New Products Can Be Hazardous to Your Company: Use the Right New-Solutions Delivery Tools," *Academy of Management Executive,* August 2001, p. 92; and Bruce Tait, "The Failure of Marketing 'Science,'" *Brandweek,* April 8, 2002, pp. 20–22.

4. Gary Hamel, "Innovation's New Math," *Fortune,* July 9, 2001, pp. 130–131.

5. See Tim Stevens, "Idea Dollars," *Industry Week,* February 16, 1998, pp. 47–49; William E. Coyne, "How 3M Innovates for Long-Term Growth," *Research Technology Management,* March–April 2001, pp. 21–24; and Michael Arndt, "3M: A Lab for Growth," *Business Week,* January 21, 2002, pp. 50–51.

6. Paul Lukas, "Marketing: The Color of Money and Ketchup," *Fortune,* September 18, 2000, p. 38; and "...And Adds a Ketchup Mystery Bottle for Kids," *Packaging Digest,* April 2002, p. 4.

7. Peter Vamos, "Kellogg Asks Kids: Cereal maker Launches Jacks Pack Initiative with Panel of Young Advisors under 15," *Strategy,* August 14, 2000, p. 1.

8. Pam Weisz, "Avon's Skin-So-Soft Bugs Out," *Brandweek,* June 6, 1994, p. 4; and Avon website, www.avon.com (accessed August 2002).

9. Stefan Thomke and Eric von Hippel, "Customers as Innovators: A New Way to Create Value," *Harvard Business Review,* April 2002, pp. 74–81.

10. Anthony W. Ulwick, "Turn Customer Input into Innovation," *Harvard Business Review,* January 2002, pp. 91–97.

11. Philip Kotler, *Kotler on Marketing* (New York: Free Press, 1999), pp. 43–44. For more on developing new-product ideas, see Andrew Hargadon and Robert I. Sutton, "Building an Innovation Factory," *Harvard Business Review,* May–June 2000, pp. 157–166.

12. Brian O'Reilly, "New Ideas, New Products," *Fortune,* March 3, 1997, pp. 61–64. Also see Michael Schrage, "Getting Beyond the Innovation Fetish," *Fortune,* November 13, 2000, pp. 225–232.

13. See John McCormick, "The Future Is Not Quite Now," *Automotive Manufacturing & Production,* August 2000, pp. 22–24; "DaimlerChrysler Unveils NECAR 5 Methanol-Powered Fuel Cell Vehicle," *Chemical Market Reporter,* November 13, 2000, p. 5; Dale Buss, "Green Cars," *American Demographics,* January 2001, pp. 57–61; Catherine Greenman, "Fuel Cells: Clean, Reliable (and Pricey) Electricity," *New York Times,* May 10, 2001, p. G8; and Stuart F. Brown, "A Wild Vision for Fuel-Cell Vehicles," *Fortune,* April 1, 2002, p. 72.

14. See Raymond R. Burke, "Virtual Reality Shopping: Breakthrough in Marketing Research," *Harvard Business Review,* March–April 1996, pp. 120–131; Mike Hoffman, "Virtual Shopping," *Inc.,* July 1998, p. 88; Christopher Ryan, "Virtual Reality in Marketing," *Direct Marketing,* April 2001, pp. 57–62; and Patrick Waurzyniak, "Going Virtual," *Manufacturing Engineering,* May 2002, pp. 77–88.

15. Adrienne Ward Fawcett, "Oreo Cones Make Top Grade in Poll," *Advertising Age,* June 14, 1993, p. 30; Becky Ebenkamp, "The New Gold Standards," *Brandweek,* April 19, 1999, p. 34; Ebencamp, "It's Like Cheers and Jeers, Only for Brands," *Brandweek,* March 19, 2001; and Ebenkamp, "The Focus Group Has Spoken," *Brandweek,* April 23, 2001, p. 24.

16. Examples adapted from those found in Faye Rice, "Secrets of Product Testing," *Fortune,* November 28, 1994, pp. 172–174; Linda Grant, "Gillette Knows Shaving—And How to Turn Out Hot New Products," *Fortune,* October 14, 1996, pp. 207–210; Emily Nelson, "Focus Groupies: P&G Keeps Cincinnati Busy with All Its Studies—While Her Sons Test Old Spice, Linda Geil Gets Swabbed," *Wall Street Journal,* January 24, 2002, p. A1; and Simone Collier, "The Littlest Gourmet," *Report on Business Magazine,* April 1997, pp. 68–74.

17. Lisa D'Innocenzo, "America's Testing Ground," *Strategy,* March 10, 2003, p. 1.

18. Chris Powell, "Sink or Swim? Test Markets Allow a Company To Evaluate Whether a New Product Will Float Before Taking the Plunge into a National Rollout," *Marketing Magazine,* October 30, 2000, www.marketingmag.ca.

19. Judann Pollack, "Baked Lays," *Advertising Age,* June 24, 1996, p. S2; and Jack Neff and Suzanne Bidlake, "P&G, Unilever Aim to Take Consumers to the Cleaners," *Advertising Age,* February 12, 2001, pp. 1, 2.

20. The McDonald's, Nabisco, and other examples can be found in Robert McMath, "To Test or Not to Test," *Advertising Age,* June 1998, p. 64; and Bret Thron, "Lessons Learned: Menu Miscues," *Nation's Restaurant News,* May 20, 2002, pp. 102–104. Also see Jerry W. Thomas, "Skipping Research a Major Error," *Marketing News,* March 4, 2002, p. 50.

21. Jack Neff, "Is Testing the Answer?" *Advertising Age,* July 9, 2001, p. 13.

22. For information on BehaviorScan, visit www.behaviorscan.com.

23. Jo Marney, "Design Testing Goes Digital," *Marketing Magazine,* March 24, 1997, www.marketingmag.ca.

24. Emily Nelson, "Colgate's Net Rose 10% in Period, New Products Helped Boost Sales," *Wall Street Journal,* February 2, 2001, p. B6.

25. For a good review of research on new-product development, see Rajesh Sethi, "New Product Quality and Product Development Teams," *Journal of Marketing,* April 2000, pp. 1–14; Rajesh Sethi, Daniel C. Smith, and C. Whan Park, "Cross-Functional Product Development Teams, Creativity, and the Innovativeness of New Consumer Products," *Journal of Marketing Research,* February 2001, pp. 73–85; Shikhar Sarin and Vijay Mahajan, "The Effect of Reward Structures on the Performance of Cross-Functional Product Development Teams," *Journal of Marketing,* April 2001, pp. 35–54; Avan R. Jassawalla and Hemant C. Sashittal, "The Role of Senior Management and Team Leaders in Building Collaborative New Product Teams," *Engineering Management Journal,* June 2001, pp. 33–39; and Joseph M. Bonner, Robert W. Ruekert, and Orville C. Walker Jr., "Upper Management Control of New

Product Development Projects and Project Performance," *Journal of Product Innovation Management,* May 2002, pp. 233–245.

26. Laurie Freeman, "Study: Leading Brands Aren't Always Enduring," *Advertising Age,* February 28, 2000, p. 26.

27. See David Stipp, "The Theory of Fads," *Fortune,* October 14, 1996, pp. 49–52; "Fads vs. Trends," *The Futurist,* March–April 2000, p. 67; Irma Zandl, "How to Separate Trends from Fads," *Brandweek,* October 23, 2000, pp. 30–33; and "Scooter Fades, as Warehouses Fill and Profits Fall," *Wall Street Journal,* June 14, 2001, p. B4.

28. For interesting discussions of how brand performance is affected by the product life-cycle stage at which the brand enters the market, see Venkatesh Shankar, Gregory S. Carpenter, and Lekshman Krishnamurthi, "The Advantages of Entry in the Growth Stage of the Product Life Cycle: An Empirical Analysis," *Journal of Marketing Research,* May 1999, pp. 269–276; William Boulding and Markus Christen, "First-Mover Disadvantage," *Harvard Business Review,* October 2001, pp. 20–21; and William T. Robinson and Sungwook Min, "Is the First to Market the First to Fail? Empirical Evidence for Industrial Goods Businesses," *Journal of Marketing Research,* February 2002, p. 120.

29. Kristen Vinakmens, "Health Trend Drives Growth in Sizzling Sandwich Category," *Strategy,* August 25, 2003, p. 2; and Quizno's Canada Corporation, "Don Cherry Toasts Quizno's Sub Sandwiches to Mark Chain's 200th Store Opening Celebration" (press release), Canada NewsWire, June 23, 2003, http://www.newswire.ca/en/releases/archive/June2003/23/c6523.html.

30. Mark McMaster, "Putting a New Spin on Old Products," *Sales & Marketing Management,* April 2001, p. 20; and Cottonelle website, www.rollwipes.com (accessed July 2002).

31. "Birks On-Air for First Time in New Campaign," *Adnews On-Line Daily,* November 30, 2000; and Birks website, www.birks.com (accessed June 23, 2003).

32. Michael Hartnett, "Cracker Jack: Chris Neugent," *Advertising Age,* June 26, 2000, p. S22.

33. For a more comprehensive discussion of marketing strategies over the course of the product life cycle, see Philip Kotler and Peggy Cunningham, *Marketing Management,* Canadian 11th ed. (Toronto: Pearson Education Canada, 2004), Chapter 11.

Chapter 12

1. Thomas T. Nagle and Reed K. Holden, *The Strategy and Tactics of Pricing,* 3rd ed. (Upper Saddle River, N.J.: Prentice Hall, 2002), p. 1.

2. Excerpts from "Business: It Was My Idea," *The Economist,* August 15, 1998, p. 54; Karl Taro Greenfeld, "Be Your Own Barcode," *Time,* July 10, 2000, pp. 96–97; Ben Rosier, "The Price Is Right," *Marketing Magazine,* February 22, 2001, p. 26; and Priceline website, www.priceline.com (accessed July 2002). See also Julia Angwin, "Priceline Founder Closes Online Bidding Site for Gas and Groceries," *Wall Street Journal,* October 6, 2000, p. B1; "Priceline.com Tops Forecast for Quarter, but Its Shares Fall," *New York Times,* February 5, 2002, p. C12; and "Priceline.com's Online 'Reach' Up 810% vs. a Year Ago" (news release), Priceline website, June 7, 2002, www.priceline.com.

3. Dean Foust, "Raising Prices Won't Fly," *Business Week,* June 3, 2002, p. 34.

4. Philip Kotler and Peggy Cunningham, *Marketing Management,* Canadian 11th ed. (Toronto: Pearson Education Canada, 2004), p. 479.

5. See David J. Schwartz, *Marketing Today: A Basic Approach,* 3rd ed. (New York: Harcourt Brace Jovanovich, 1981), pp. 270–273.

6. Paul Hunt, "Pricing for Profit," *Marketing Magazine,* April 26, 1999, www.marketingmag.ca.

7. For an excellent discussion of factors affecting pricing decisions, see Thomas T. Nagle and Reed K. Holden, *The Strategy and Tactics of Pricing,* 3rd ed. (Upper Saddle River, N.J.: Prentice Hall, 2002), Chap. 1.

8. See Timothy M. Laseter, "Supply Chain Management: The Ins and Outs of Target Costing," *Purchasing,* March 12, 1998, pp. 22–25; John K. Shank and Joseph Fisher, "Case Study: Target Costing as a Strategic Tool," *Sloan Management Review,* Fall 1999, pp. 73–82; and Melanie Wells, "On His Watch," *Forbes,* February 18, 2002, pp. 93–94.

9. Brian Dumaine, "Closing the Innovation Gap," *Fortune,* December 2, 1991, pp. 56–62; and Johnson Controls website, www.johnsoncontrols.com/Metasys (accessed July 2002).

10. Here accumulated production is drawn on a semilog scale so that equal distances represent the same percentage increase in output.

11. Philip Kotler and Peggy Cunningham, *Marketing Management,* Canadian 11th ed. (Toronto: Pearson Education Canada, 2004), p. 474; Kara Swisher, "Electronics 2001: The Essential Guide." *Wall Street Journal,* January 5, 2001; and Cliff Edwards, "HDTV: High-Anxiety Television," *Business Week,* June 10, 2002, pp. 142–146.

12. Joshua Rosenbaum, "Guitar Maker Looks for a New Key," *Wall Street Journal,* February 11, 1998, p. B1; and Gibson website, www.gibson.com (accessed July 2002).

13. See Thomas T. Nagle and Reed K. Holden, *The Strategy and Tactics of Pricing,* 3rd ed. (Upper Saddle River, N.J.: Prentice Hall, 2002), Chap. 4.

14. Judy Waytiuk, "No Haggle, No Hassle," *Marketing Magazine,* August 28, 2000, www.marketingmag.ca.

15. Kevin J. Clancy, "At What Profit Price?" *Brandweek,* June 23, 1997, pp. 24–28.

16. The arithmetic of markups and margins is discussed in Appendix 2, "Marketing Math."

17. See Philip Kotler, *Kotler on Marketing* (Upper Saddle River, N.J.: Prentice Hall, 1999), p. 54.

18. Erin Stout, "Keep Them Coming Back for More," *Sales & Marketing Management,* February 2002, pp. 51–52.

19. For more reading on reference prices and psychological pricing, see Robert M. Schindler and Patrick N. Kirby, "Patterns of Right-Most Digits Used in Advertised Prices: Implications for Nine-Ending Effects," *Journal of Consumer Research,* September 1997, pp. 192–201; Dhruv Grewal, Kent B. Monroe, Chris Janiszewski, and Donald R. Lichtenstein, "A Range Theory of Price Perception," *Journal of Consumer Research,* March 1999, pp. 353–368; Tridib Mazumdar and Purushottam Papatla, "An Investigation of Reference Price Segments," *Journal of Marketing Research,* May 2000, pp. 246–258; Indrajit Sinha and Michael Smith, "Consumers' Perceptions of Promotional Framing of Price," *Psychology & Marketing,* March 2000, pp. 257–271; and Tulin Erdem, Glenn Mayhew, and Baohong Sun, "Understanding Reference-Price Shoppers: A Within- and Across-Category Analysis,"

Journal of Marketing Research, November 2001, pp. 445–457.

20. Adapted from Andrew Park and Peter Burrows, "Dell, the Conqueror," *Business Week,* September 24, 2001, pp. 92–102. See also Andy Serwer, "Dell Does Domination," *Fortune,* January 21, 2002, pp. 70–75; Gary McWilliams, "Dell Computer's Kevin Rollins Becomes a Driving Force," *Wall Street Journal,* April 4, 2002, p. B6; and Scott Morrison, "Dell's Slap in the Face Will Test HP's Pricing Agility," *Financial Times,* August 21, 2003, www.ft.com.

21. Samson Okalow, "How Can Automakers Escape the 0% Financing Trip?" *Strategy,* August 11, 2003, p. 2.

22. See the *Competition Act,* Sections 34–38, http://laws.justice.gc.ca/en/C-34/.

23. N. Craig Smith and John A. Quelch, *Ethics in Marketing* (Boston: Irwin, 1993), pp. 389–404.

Chapter 13

1. Quotes and other information from Donald V. Fites, "Make Your Dealers Your Partners," *Harvard Business Review,* March–April 1996, pp. 84–95; DeAnn Weimer, "A New Cat on the Hot Seat," *Business Week,* March 1998, pp. 56–62; Mark Tatge, "Caterpillar Reports 26% Jump in Net Despite Weak Sales," *Wall Street Journal,* April 19, 2000, p. A8; Joseph T. Hallinan, "Caterpillar Beats Estimates, Says 2001 Will Hurt," *Wall Street Journal,* January 19, 2001, p. B6; Sandra Ward, "The Cat Comes Back," *Barron's,* February 25, 2002, pp. 21–24; and Caterpillar website, www.cat.com (accessed July 2002).

2. For definitions and a complete discussion of distribution channel topics, see Anne T. Coughlin, Erin Anderson, Louis W. Stern, and Adel El-Ansary, *Marketing Channels,* 6th ed. (Upper Saddle River, N.J.: Prentice Hall, 2001), pp. 2–3.

3. Queen's University, School of Business, "Financial Times Ranks Queen's in Global Top 10" (press release), May 19, 2003, http://business.queensu.ca/index.php.

4. John Gray, "Sour Dough," *Canadian Business,* June 23, 2003, pp. 36–41.

5. Ian Jack, "Dealers Declare War on Ford Canada," *Financial Post,* March 31, 2000, pp. C1, C5; Greg Keenan, "Ford Targets Bigger Stake in Dealerships," *Globe and Mail,* November 18, 1998, pp. B1, B16.

6. William Keenan Jr., "Sales and Marketing—(Pet) Food for Thought," *Industry Week,* March 5, 2001, www.industryweek.com/; and "P&G Plans Overhaul of Iams Brand," *Marketing Week,* May 30, 2002, p. 6.

7. See Richard C. Hoffman and John F. Preble, "Franchising into the Twenty-First Century," *Business Horizons,* November–December 1993, pp. 35–43; "Canada's Largest Franchise-Only Show Returns," *Globe and Mail* (advertising supplement), September 24, 1997, p. 1; and Industry Canada's franchising website, strategis.ic.gc.ca/SSG/dm01179e.html (accessed August 2003). See also James H. Amos Jr., "Franchising, More than Any Act of Government, Will Strengthen the Global Economy," *Franchising World,* May–June 2001, p. 8; "Answers to the 21 Most Commonly Asked Questions About Franchising," International Franchise Association website, www.franchise.org (accessed July 2002); and Canadian Franchise Directory, www.franchisedirectory.ca/ (accessed August 2003).

8. Peter Fitzpatrick, "Airlines of the World—Unite," *Financial Post,* November 22, 1997, p. 8.

9. Kevin Marron, "Multichannel Route Pays Off For Retailers," *Globe and Mail,* October 25, 2002, p. B11.

10. Kevin Marron, "Multichannel Route Pays Off For Retailers," *Globe and Mail,* October 25, 2002, p. B11.

11. Laura Meckler, "Senate Approves Drug Imports From Canada," *Associated Press,* June 20, 2003, http://204.19.134.7/News.asp; and Bernard Simon, "Canada Rebuffs U.S. on Prescription Drugs," *New York Times,* November 19, 2003, www.nytimes.com.

12. See Subhash C. Jain, *International Marketing Management,* 3rd ed. (Boston: PWS-Kent Publishing, 1990), pp. 489–491; and Warren J. Keegan, *Global Marketing Management* (Upper Saddle River, N.J.: Prentice Hall, 2002), pp. 403–404.

13. See Aruna Chandra and John K. Ryans Jr. "Why India Now?" *Marketing Management,* March–April 2002, pp. 43–45; Dana James, "Dark Clouds Should Part for International Marketers," *Marketing News,* January 7, 2002, pp. 9, 13; and Laurie Sullivan, "China Remains Tough Turf for Independent Distributors," *EBN,* July 8, 2002, p. 1.

14. Jennifer Wells, "We Can Get It for You Wholesale," *Report on Business Magazine,* March 1995, pp. 52–62.

15. For more on channel relationships, see James A. Narus and James C. Anderson, "Rethinking Distribution," *Harvard Business Review,* July–August 1996, pp. 112–120; James C. Anderson and James A. Narus, *Business Market Management* (Upper Saddle River, N.J.: Prentice Hall, 1999), pp. 276–288; Jonathon D. Hibbard, Nirmalya Kumar, and Louis W. Stern, "Examining the Impact of Destructive Acts in Marketing Channel Relationships," *Journal of Marketing Research,* February 2001, pp. 45–61; and Stavros P. Kalafatis, "Buyer–Seller Relationships Among Channels of Distribution," *Industrial Marketing Management,* April 2002, pp. 215–228.

16. Cathy Ciccolella, "GE to Offer Online Dealer Support with CustomerNet," *Twice,* April 21, 1997, p. 88; Cathy Ciccolella, "GE Online Support Wins Dealers Over," *Twice,* February 9, 1998, p. 38; Mitch Betts, "GE Appliance Park Still an IT Innovator," *Computerworld,* January 29, 2001, pp. 20–21; and "What Is GE CustomerNet?" GE website, www.geappliances.com/buildwithge/index_cnet.htm (accessed August 2002).

17. See Heather Harreld and Paul Krill, "Channel Management," *InfoWorld,* October 8, 2001, pp. 46–52; and Barbara Darrow, "Comergent Revs Up PRM, *Crn,* April 8, 2002, p. 60.

18. Marina Strauss, "Wal-Mart Supplier Was Asked for Kickbacks," *Globe and Mail,* February 2, 2000, www.globeandmail.com; P. N. Bloom, G. T. Gundlach, and J.P. Cannon, "Slotting Allowances and Fees: Schools of Thought and the Views of Practicing Managers," *Journal of Marketing,* April 2000, pp. 92–108; Andrew Stodart, "Fight for Your Rights: Marketers Are Being Far Too Passive about the Growing Concentration of Retail Power in this Country," *Marketing Magazine,* May 31, 1999, www.marketingmag.ca; and United Church of Canada, "Talisman Energy Inc. rejects shareholder proposal" (news release), March 8, 1999, www.uccan.org/news/990308a.htm.

19. Industry Canada, "Sector Competitiveness Frameworks Series: Logistics and Supply Chain Management, Highlights," http://strategis.ic.gc.ca/SSG/dm01326e.html (accessed August 2003).

20. James R. Stock, "The Seven Deadly Sins of Reverse Logistics," *Material Handling Management,* March 2001, pp. MHS5–MHS11; and Martin Piszczalksi, "Logistics: A

Difference Between Winning and Losing," *Automotive Manufacturing & Production,* May 2001, pp. 16–18.

21. Shlomo Maital, "The Last Frontier of Cost Reduction," *Across the Board,* February 1994, pp. 51–52; and "Wal-Mart to Expand Supercenters to California," *Business Journal,* May 15, 2002, http://sanjose.bizjournals.com.

22. Alex Binkley, "Wal-Mart Canada Inc.," Case Study, Tibbett & Britten Group North America, www.tbgna.com/html/sub/cs_walmart.htm (accessed August 2003).

23. J. William Gurley, "Why Dell's War Isn't Dumb," *Fortune,* July 9, 2001, pp. 134–136.

24. Bob Verdisco, "The Coming Retail Revolution," *DSN Retailing Today,* May 6, 2002, p. 12

25. Information on Canada's transportation infrastructure is taken from Industry Canada, *Canada's Transportation System,* March 13, 2003, www.tc.gc.ca/pol/en/brochure/default.htm.

26. Kay Moody, Managing Director of Strategic Planning and Intranet Development of FedEx, "Getting Down to Business on the Net at FedEx," presentation to The Information Management Forum, April 19–20, 1999 (Figure 9).

Chapter 14

1. The Forzani Group website and 2003 Annual Report, www.forzanigroup.com/ (accesssed August 2003); and Zena Olignyk, "At the Top of Its Game: Escaped from the Jaws of Defeat, Forzani Finds New Fans," *Canadian Business,* April 29, 2002, www.canadianbusiness.com/investing/article.jsp?content=45464.

2. Nathan Rudyk, "Multi-Channel Customers Spend 10 Times More," *Strategy,* November 6, 2000, p. D6.

3. Retail Council of Canada, "Retail Employment," www.retailcouncil.org/research/data/il/structure/jacobson/sld017.asp; and Statistics Canada, "Annual Retail Trade 2001," *The Daily,* April 11, 2003, www.statcan.ca/Daily/English/030411/td030411.htm.

4. Todd Hale, "Leveraging Channel Changes in Today's Market," ACNielsen website, www.acnielsen.com/pubs/ci/2001/q2/features/leveraging.htm (accessed August 2003).

5. Brian Dunn, "The King of Bread, Butts and Beer," *Marketing Magazine,* October 25, 1999, p. 23; Anita Lahey, "Cornered Stores," *Marketing Magazine,* August 4, 1997, pp. 10–11; Luis Millan, "King of the Corner Store," *Canadian Business,* September 26, 1997, pp. 101–103; and Dana Flavelle, "Quebec Retailers on a Roll in U.S.," *Toronto Star,* October 12, 2003, pp. C1, C3.

6. Marina Strauss, "The Best Bet for Your Bottom Dollar," *Globe and Mail,* August 2, 2003, p. B1.

7. Marina Strauss, "New Wave of U.S. Retailers Advance on Canada," *Globe and Mail,* January 12, 2001, p. M1.

8. Quoted material from Randy Scotland, "Wal-Mart Canada's Dave Ferguson named Distinguished Retailer of the Year" (press release), Retail Council of Canada, April 18, 2000; Constance L. Hays, "The Wal-Mart Way Becomes Topic A in Business Schools," *New York Times,* July 27, 2003, www.nytimes.com; Wal-Mart Canada press release, June 29, 2000; John Huey, "Wal-Mart: Will It Take Over the World?" *Fortune,* January 30, 1998, pp. 52–61; Carol J. Loomis, "Sam Would Be Proud," *Fortune,* April 17, 2001, pp. 131–144; and Stephanie Thompson, "Wal-Mart Tops List for New Food Lines," *Advertising Age,* April 29, 2002, pp. 4, 61. Also see Mike Troy, "The Super Growth Leaders—Wal-Mart: Global Dominance Puts Half Trillion in Sight," *DSN Retailing Today,* December 10, 2001, pp. 17–181; Cait Murphy, "Introduction: Wal-Mart

Rules," *Fortune,* April 15, 2002, pp. 94–98; and *Wal-Mart Annual Report 2002,* www.walmartstores.com (accessed July 2002).

9. Mariam Mesbah, "Special Report: Fashion Retailers Branch into Cosmetics," *Strategy,* January 20, 1997, p. 20.

10. Wendy Cuthbert, "Environment Plays Major Role in Purchase Decision: Expert," *Strategy,* September 29, 1997, p. 14.

11. Marina Strauss, "Best Buy Sees Benefit in Dual Banners," *Globe and Mail,* June 13, 2003, p. B13.

12. Erica Zlomislic, "Special Report: Store-level Marketing: Virgin's Megahit," *Strategy,* May 26, 1997, p. 24.

13. Marina Strauss, "Big-Box Retailers Think Small in Planning Latest Expansions," *Globe and Mail,* November 4, 2002, pp. B1, B7.

14. See Joanna Dale, *Consumer Attitudes towards Retail in BC,* Retail Council of Canada, September 21, 2000, www.retailcouncil.org/research/bcretail/sld026.htm; and Steven Bergsman, "Slow Times at Sherman Oaks: What's Ailing the Big Malls of America?" *Barron's,* May 17, 1999, p. 39.

15. Dean Starkman, "The Mall, Without the Haul—Lifestyle Centers Slip Quietly into Upscale Areas, Mixing Cachet and 'Curb Appeal,'" *Wall Street Journal,* July 25, 2001, p. B1.

16. Douglas Goold, "Despite Changes, the Bay Could Get Lost in the Shuffle," *Globe and Mail,* December 2, 2002, p. B7.

17. See Malcolm P. McNair and Eleanor G. May, "The Next Revolution of the Retailing Wheel," *Harvard Business Review,* September–October 1978, pp. 81–91; Stephen Brown, "The Wheel of Retailing: Past and Future," *Journal of Retailing,* Summer 1990, pp. 143–147; Stephen Brown, "Variations on a Marketing Enigma: The Wheel of Retailing Theory," *Journal of Marketing Management,* 7, no. 2, 1991, pp. 131–155; Jennifer Negley, "Retrenching, Reinventing and Remaining Relevant," *Discount Store News,* April 5, 1999, p. 11; and Don E. Schultz, "Another Turn of the Wheel," *Marketing Management,* March–April 2002, pp. 8–9.

18. Charles Haddad, "Office Depot's E-Diva," *Business Week,* August 6, 2001, pp. EB22–EB24; and Meryl Davids Landau, "Sweet Revenge," *Chief Executive,* May 2002, pp. 58–62.

19. Jack Kapica, "High-Tech Analysis a Study in Information Overload," *Globe and Mail,* December 5, 2003, p. B13.

20. IBM and the Retail Council of Canada, *E-Retail: The Race Is On,* June 1999, pp. 3–7.

21. Excerpt adapted from Alice Z. Cuneo, "What's in Store?" *Advertising Age,* February 25, 2002, pp. 1, 30–31.

22. See "The Fortune 500," *Fortune,* April 15, 2002, p. F1.

23. David Menzies, "Retail and High-Tech," *Marketing Magazine,* August 5, 1996.

24. Regina Fazio Maruca, "Retailing: Confronting the Challenges That Face Bricks-and-Mortar Stores," *Harvard Business Review,* July–August 1999, pp. 159–168. Also see Marshall L. Fisher, Ananth Raman, and Anna Sheen McClelland, "Rocket Science Retailing Is Almost Here: Are You Ready?" *Harvard Business Review,* July–August 2000, pp. 115–124.

25. Marina Strauss, "Westons Gains Posh and Spice with Selfridges," *Globe and Mail,* July 15, 2003, p. B1.

26. James Cox, "Red-Letter Day as East Meets West in the Aisles," *USA Today,* September 11, 1996, p. B1; and Wal-Mart website, "International Operations Data Sheet," July 2002, www.walmartstores.com.

27. Adapted from Tim Craig, "Carrefour: At the Intersection of Global," *DSN Retailing Today,* September 18, 2000, p. 16.

Additional information from Richard Tomlinson, "Who's Afraid of Wal-Mart?" *Fortune*, June 26, 2000, pp. 186–196; and Carrefour website, www.carrefour.com (accessed July 2002).

28. Nifong, "Beyond Browsing," p. E1. Also see Fred Brock, "Catering to the Elderly Can Pay Off," *New York Times*, February 2002, p. 3.

29. Kathleen Cholewka, "Standing Out Online: The Five Best E-Marketing Campaigns," *Sales & Marketing Management*, January 2001, pp. 51–58.

30. Statistics Canada, "Annual Wholesale trade, 2001," *The Daily*, June 24, 2003, www.statcan.ca/Daily/English/030624/td030624.htm.

31. Lara Mills, "GT Pursues 'Underserved' Telco Narket," *Marketing Magazine*, October 25, 1999.

32. Coghlan's website, www.coghlans.com/index.html (accessed August 2003).

33. "McKesson: Online Annual Report 2001," www.mckesson.com/wt/ar_2001.php (accessed August 2001); and "Supply Management Online," www.mckesson.com (accessed August 2002).

34. SuperValu website, www.supervalu.com (accessed September 2002).

Chapter 15

1. Quotes, excerpts, and other information from Dale Hayes, "It's Easy Being 'Brown,'" *NECG Edge*, May–June 2002, pp. 5–7; UPS, "UPS Legacy Of Volunteerism Goes Global"(press release), October 22, 2003, www.ups.com/content/ca/en/about/news/10_23_2003b.html; UPS, "UPS Launches Biggest, 'Brownest' Ad Campaign Ever" (press release), February 7, 2002, www.pressroom.ups.com; Roger Morton, "Small Parcel's Big 3," *Transportation & Distribution*, March 2002, pp. 71–75; John Beystehner, "Managing the Brand for Strategic Alignment," June 3, 2002, www.pressroom.ups.com; Jim Kelly, "The Living, Breathing Brand: The Human Side of Competitive Advantage," www.pressroom.ups.com (accessed July 2002); Fiona Kerr, "UPS Logistics Interview with Tim Geiken, UPS Vice President of E-Commerce Marketing," March 22, 2002, www.eyefortransport.com; and Kristin S. Krause, "One UPS Face," *Traffic World*, March 4, 2002, p. 31.

2. The first four of these definitions are adapted from Peter D. Bennett, *Dictionary of Marketing Terms* (Chicago: American Marketing Association, 1995).

3. "Promotion Practices Condensed," *Potentials*, November 1998, p. 6.

4. Don E. Schultz, "New Media, Old Problem: Keep Marcom Integrated," *Marketing News*, March 29, 1999, p. 11.

5. Fabian Robinson and Rebecca Rohan, "Developing a Brand," *Black Enterprise*, May 2002, pp. 47–48.

6. See Don E. Schultz, Stanley I. Tannenbaum, and Robert F. Lauterborn, *Integrated Marketing Communication* (Chicago: NTC, 1992), Chaps. 3 and 4. Also see James R. Ogdan, *Developing a Creative and Innovative Integrated Marketing Communications Plan* (Upper Saddle River, N.J.: Prentice Hall, 1998); and David Picton and Amanda Broderick, *Integrated Marketing Communications* (New York: Financial Times Management, 1999).

7. P. Griffith Lindell, "You Need Integrated Attitude to Develop IMC," *Marketing News*, May 26, 1997, p. 6. For more discussion of integrated marketing communications, see Stephen J. Gould, "The State of IMC Research and Applications," *Journal of Advertising Research*, September–October 2000, pp. 22–23; Don E. Schultz, "Summit Explores Where IMC, CRM Meet," *Marketing News*, March 4, 2002, p. 11; and Schultz, "Marcom Model Reverses Traditional Pattern," *Marketing News*, April 1, 2002, p. 8.

8. S. Mark McMaster, "Lessons from the Marlboro Man," *Sales and Marketing Management*, February 2002, pp. 44–46.

9. Sara Minogue, "Changing a Mind-Set: the Anti-Piracy Crusade," *Strategy*, June 30, 2003, pp. 16–17.

10. The history of Buckley's Mixture can be found online at www.buckleys.com.

11. For these and other examples, see Pamela Paul, "Color by Numbers," *American Demographics*, February 2002, pp. 31–35.

12. Adapted from Jean Halliday, "Creating Max Buzz for New BMW Mini," *Advertising Age*, June 17, 2002, p. 12.

13. Phil Connell and Peggy Cunningham, *Becel Margarine: Meeting Expectations* (case), Queen's University, January 2001.

14. Darren Rovell, "Nutella Won't Renew Its Endorsement Deal with Bryant," ESPN, http://espn.go.com/sportsbusiness/news/2003/0804/1589800.html, August 4, 2003.

15. For more on advertising spending by company and industry, see the Advertising Age Data Center at www.adage.com.

16. For more on setting promotion budgets, see J. Thomas Russell and W. Ronald Lane, *Kleppner's Advertising Procedure*, 15th ed. (Upper Saddle River, N.J.: Prentice Hall, 2002), pp. 145–149; and Kissan Joseph and Vernon J. Richardson, "Free Cash Flow, Agency Costs, and the Affordability Method of Advertising Budgeting," *Journal of Marketing*, January 2002, pp. 94–107.

17. David Allen, "Excessive Use of the Mirror," *Management Accounting*, June 1966, p. 12. Also see Laura Petrecca, "4A's Will Study Financial Return on Ad Spending," *Advertising Age*, April 7, 1997, pp. 3, 52; and Dana W. Hayman and Don E. Schultz, "How Much Should You Spend on Advertising," *Advertising Age*, April 26, 1999, p. 32.

18. Canadian Media Directors Council, *2003–04 Media Digest*, p. 13; Bill Carter, "After Super Bowl, 'Survivor' Is the Season's Top Hit on TV," *New York Times*, January 30, 2001, p. C8; Joe Flint, "Oscar Ratings Fall, but the Program Finishes on Time," *Wall Street Journal*, March 27, 2001, p. B8; Stuart Elliott, "Despite Millions of Viewers, the Super Bowl Is Not Quite So for Madison Avenue," *New York Times*, February 1, 2002, p. C2; and Jonathan Fowlie, "Idol Takes Run at TV Viewing Records," *Globe and Mail*, August 13, 2003, p. R3.

19. Michael Adams with Amy Langstaff and David Jamieson, *Fire and Ice: The United States, Canada and the Myth of Converging Values* (Toronto: Penguin Canada, 2003), p. 57.

20. Michele Marchetti, "What a Sales Call Costs," *Sales & Marketing Management*, September 2000, p. 80.

21. Based on Matthew P. Gonring, "Putting Integrated Marketing Communications to Work Today," *Public Relations Quarterly*, Fall 1994, pp. 45–48. Also see Philip Kotler, *Marketing Management*, 11th ed. (Upper Saddle River, N.J.: Prentice Hall, 2003), pp. 583–584.

22. Jim Button, "Events That Build Brands," *Marketing Magazine*, October 6/13, 2003, p. 32.

23. Michelle Warren, "Cause Commotion," *Marketing Magazine*, October 6/13, 2003, pp. 21–26; and KitchenAid Canada website, www.kitchenaid-cookforthecure.ca/ (accessed November 25, 2003).

24. For more on the legal aspects of promotion, see Russell and Lane, *Kleppner's Advertising Procedure*, Chap. 25; and Douglas J. Dalrymple, William L. Cron, and Thomas E. DeCarlo, *Sales Management*, 7th ed. (New York: Wiley, 2001), Chap. 6.

Chapter 16

1. Jim Milliot and Steven Zeitchik, "Potter Set for June 21," *Publishers Weekly*, January 20, 2003, http://publishersweekly.reviewsnews.com/; Alexandra Gill, "Harry Potter and the Goblet of Hype," *Globe and Mail*, May 31, 2003, www.globeinvestor.com/servlet/ArticleNews/story/GAM/20030531/RVRAIN; ENS Correspondents/Environment News Service, "Canadian Firm Prints Potter on Green Pages," OneWorld.net, June 19, 2003, http://us.oneworld.net/article/view/2179/1/; Steven Zeitchik, "Of Potter and Magic with Numbers," PSW Newsline, *Publishers Weekly*, June 23, 2003, http://publishersweekly.reviewsnews.com/; John Henzl, "Potter Magic for Amazon.ca," *Globe and Mail*, June 25, 2003, p. B6; Leah Hendry, "Operation Harry Potter a Big Success," *Globe and Mail*, July 10, 2003, www.globetechnology.com/archive/gam/News/20000710/UPOTTN.html; Kristen Vinakmens, "Avoiding Overkill," *Strategy*, July 28, 2003, www.strategymag.com/articles/magazine/20030728/overkill.html; Reuters, "Harry Potter Cuts Indigo Books First-Quarter Loss," *Forbes*, August 19, 2003, www.forbes.com/business/commerce/newswire/2003/08/10/rtr1061088.html; Paul-Mark Rendon, "Heard on the Streets," *Marketing Magazine*, September 15, 2003, pp. 11–12; and Raincoast Books, "Harry Potter: Frequently Asked Questions," www.raincoast.com/harrypotter/faq.html (accessed November 7, 2003).
2. Institute of Canadian Advertising, *Economic Impact Report*, 1998, www.ica-ad.com/new/sub_main.cfm. Information on U.S. and international advertising spending from Ad Age Dataplace, www.adage.com (accessed August 2002); and the International Advertising Association website, www.iaaglobal.org (accessed August 2002).
3. "Net Leads the Way in Spending," *Marketing Magazine*, September 25, 2000, www.marketingmag.ca; "2001: A Marketing Odyssey: Seven Association Leaders Predict the Challenges the Next Year May Bring," *Marketing Magazine*, December 18/25, 2000, www.marketingmag.ca; and Robert J. Coen, "Spending Spree," *Advertising Age Special Issue: The Advertising Century*, 1999, p. 126.
4. Lisa D'Innocenzo, "Is Comparative Advertising Ever Justified?" *Strategy*, March 24, 2003, p. 2.
5. Stan Sutter, "Editorial: Common Sense Evolution," *Marketing Magazine*, June 9, 2003, p. 18.
6. "Beef Up on Roasting Cuts, Industry Tells Consumers," *CBC News*, June 30, 2003, www.cbc.ca/storyview/CBC/2003/06/30/Consumers/beefindustry_030630.
7. See Andrew Ehrenberg, Neil Barnard, and John Scriven, "Justifying Our Advertising Budgets," *Marketing & Research Today*, February 1997, pp. 38–44; Dana W. Hayman and Don E. Schultz, "How Much Should You Spend on Advertising?" *Advertising Age*, April 26, 1999, p. 32; J. Thomas Russell and W. Ronald Lane, *Kleppner's Advertising Procedure*, 15th ed. (Upper Saddle River, N.J.: Prentice Hall, 2002), pp. 145–149; and Kissan Joseph and Vernon J. Richardson, "Free Cash Flow, Agency Costs, and the Affordability Method of Advertising Budgeting," *Journal of Marketing*, January 2002, pp. 94–107.
8. Information from Rosalind Stefanac, "Corporate Ads in Rainbow Colours: Big Mainstream Marketers Are Crafting Innovative Advertising Strategies in a Bid to Get Closer to Gay and Lesbian Consumers," *Marketing Magazine*, May 1, 2000, www.marketingmag.ca; Gary Levin, "'Meddling' in Creative More Welcome," *Advertising Age*, April 9, 1990, pp. S4, S8; Lynne Roberts, "New Media Choice: Absolut Vodka," *Marketing Magazine*, April 9, 1998, p. 12; Eleftheria Parpis, "TBWA: Absolut," *Adweek*, November 9, 1998, p. 172; and Absolut website, Q&A section, www.absolutvodka.com (accessed March 2000).
9. Canadian Media Directors' Council, *2003–2004 Media Digest*, pp. 13, 32, 34, 39, and 44.
10. Wayne Friedman, "TV Networks' New Reality," *Advertising Age*, September 24, 2001, pp. 1, 70; and Steven McClellan, "Super Bowl Runneth Over," *Broadcast & Cable*, June 24, 2002, p. 4.
11. Wayne Friedman, "PVR Users Skip Most Ads: Study," *Advertising Age*, July 1, 2002, pp. 4, 46.
12. Edward A. Robinson, "Frogs, Bears, and Orgasms: Think Zany if You Want to Reach Today's Consumers," *Fortune*, June 9, 1997, pp. 153–156. Also see Chuck Ross, "MBC Blasts Beyond the 15-Minute Barrier," *Advertising Age*, August 7, 2000, p. 3; and Tobi Elkin, "Courting Craftier Consumers," July 1, 2002, p. 28.
13. "Agency of the Year: Holmes & Lee, Award Winners 1999," *Strategy*, www.strategymag.com/aoy/1999/holmesandlee (accessed November 26, 2003).
14. See Ariane Herrera, "AAAA Survey Finds Three Percent Drop in Cost to Produce 30—Second TV Commercials" (news release), American Association of Advertising Agencies, December 13, 2001, www.aaaa.org.
15. Laura Medcalf, "Year of the Missing Agencies," *Marketing Magazine*, June 23, 2003, pp. 9–15.
16. Jim McElgunn, "Who Cares Where an Ad's Made?" *Marketing Magazine*, May 8, 1995, p. 20; and "Canada's Top Agencies," *Marketing*, July 24, 1995, p. 11.
17. Information on advertising agency income and billings from the Advertising Age Data Center, http://adage.com/dataplace (accessed August 2002).
18. Patricia Winters Lauro, "New Method of Agency Payments Drive a Stake Through the Heart of the Old 15% Commission," *New York Times*, April 2, 1999, p. 2. Also see Jack Neff, "P&G Hammers Last Nail into Commission Coffin," *Advertising Age*, September 20, 1999, p. 4; and John Tylee, "Nestlé Rings Death-Knell on Agency Commission," *Campaign*, October 12, 2001, p. 1.
19. See "U.K. Tobacco Ad Ban Will Include Sports Sponsorship," *AdAgeInternational*, May 1997, www.adageinternational.com; "Coca-Cola Rapped for Running Competition in India," *AdAgeInternational*, February 1997, www.adageinternational.com; Naveen Donthu, "A Cross Country Investigation of Recall of and Attitude Toward Comparative Advertising," *Journal of Advertising*, 27, June 22, 1998, p. 111; and John Shannon, "Comparative Ads Call for Prudence," *Marketing Week*, May 6, 1999, p. 32.
20. Cannondale Associates, *2002 Trade Promotion Spending and Merchandising Industry Study* (Wilton, Conn: Cannondale Associates, May 2002), p. 13.
21. Kenneth Hein, "Coke Puts New Twist on Plain Vanilla Sampler, Summer Tours," *Brandweek*, July 1, 2002, p. 35.
22. Debra Aho Williamson, "P&G's Reformulated Pert Plus Builds Consumer Relationships," *Advertising Age*, June 28, 1999, p. 52.
23. Lucy Saddleton, "Baby Money!" *Strategy*, October 6, 2003, p. 1.

24. Wayne Mouland, "Those Who Use Them, Use Them a Lot," *Marketing Magazine*, February 10, 2003, p. 29.
25. Jeff Lobb, "Stuff-ing It to Coke," *Marketing Magazine*, January 27, 1997, p. 15.
26. See "Power to the Key Ring and T-Shirt," *Sales & Marketing Management*, December 1989, p. 14; Chad Kaydo, "Your Logo Here," *Sales & Marketing Management*, April 1998, pp. 65–70; and Bill Prickett, "Promotional Products 2001 Sales—A Diverse Market" (news release), Promotional Products Association International, June 17, 2002, www.ppai.org.
27. See Richard Szathmary, "Trade Shows," *Sales & Marketing Management*, May 1992, pp. 83–84; Srinath Gopalakrishna, Gary L. Lilien, Jerome D. Williams, and Ian Sequeira, "Do Trade Shows Pay Off?" *Journal of Marketing*, July 1995, pp. 75–83; Peter Jenkins, "Making the Most of Trade Shows," *Nation's Business*, June 1999, p. 8; and Ben Chapman, "The Trade Show Must Go On," *Sales & Marketing Management*, June 2001, p. 22.
28. Adapted from Scott Cutlip, Allen Center, and Glen Broom, *Effective Public Relations*, 8th ed. (Upper Saddle River, N.J.: Prentice Hall, 1999), Chap. 1.
29. Sara Minogue, "Hong Kong Tourist Board Welcomes Chinese Canadians," *Strategy*, September 22, 2003, p. 15.
30. Al Ries and Laura Ries, "First Do Some Publicity," *Advertising Age*, February 8, 1999, p. 42. Also see Al Ries and Laura Ries, *The Fall of Advertising and the Rise of PR* (New York: HarperBusiness, 2002).
31. Portions adapted from Kate Fitzgerald, "Marketing on the Move," *Advertising Age*, March 18, 2002, p. 59; and Scott Hume, Janice Matsumoto, Allison Perlik, and Margaret Sheridan, "Krispy Kreme's Movable Feast," *Restaurants & Institutions*, June 1, 2002, p. 26.
32. See Mark Gleason, "Edelman Sees Niche in Web Public Relations," *Advertising Age*, January 20, 1997, p. 30; Michael Krauss, "Good PR Critical to Growth on the Net," *Marketing News*, January 18, 1999, p. 8; Steve Jarvis, "How the Internet Is Changing Fundamentals of Publicity," *Marketing News*, July 17, 2000, p. 6; and G. A. Markin, "Why Doesn't the Press Call?" *Public Relations Quarterly*, Spring 2002, pp. 9–10.
33. Tom Price, "Philip Morris Changes Its Name but not Its Tactics," *CorpWatch*, March 14, 2002, www.corpwatch.org/campaigns/PCD.jsp?articleid=2035.

Chapter 17

1. Quotes from Andy Cohen, "Top of the Charts: Lear Corporation," *Sales & Marketing Management*, July 1998, p. 40. Also see "Lear Corporation," *Sales & Marketing Management*, July 1999, p. 62; Fara Warner, "Lear Won't Take a Back Seat," *Fast Company*, June 2001, pp. 178–185; Judy Bocklage and Paul Welitzkin, "Lear Profit Soared in First Period, But Borg-Warner Swung to Loss, *Wall Street Journal*, April 23, 2002, p. D5; "America's 25 Best Sales Forces," *Sales & Marketing Management*, www.salesandmarketing.com (accessed July 2002); and Lear website, "This Is Lear," www.lear.com (accessed July 2002).
2. See Bill Kelley, "How to Sell Airplanes, Boeing Style," *Sales & Marketing Management*, December 9, 1985, pp. 32–34; Andy Cohen, "Boeing," *Sales & Marketing Management*, October 1997, p. 68; and Stanley Holmes, "Rumble over Tokyo," *Business Week*, April 2, 2001, pp. 80–81. Quote from Laurence Zuckerman, "Selling Airplanes with a Smile," *New York Times*, February 17, 2002, p. 3.2.
3. Geoffrey Brewer, "Love the Ones You're With," *Sales & Marketing Management*, February 1997, pp. 38–45. Also see Edward F. Moltzen and Jennifer Hagendorf, "IBM Unleashes E-Business Army," *Computer Reseller News*, January 24, 2000, pp. 3, 8.
4. Michele Marchetti, "What a Sales Call Costs," *Sales & Marketing Management*, September 2000, p. 80.
5. See Martin Everett, "Selling by Telephone," *Sales & Marketing Management*, December 1993, pp. 75–79. Also see Terry Arnold, "Telemarketing Strategy," *Target Marketing*, January 2002, pp. 47–48.
6. Geoffrey Brewer, "Lou Gerstner Has His Hands Full," *Sales & Marketing Management*, May 8, 1998, pp. 36–41; and Michelle Cioci, "Marketing to Small Businesses," *Sales & Marketing Management*, December 2000, pp. 94–100.
7. See "A Phone Is Better than a Face," *Sales & Marketing Management*, October 1987, p. 29. Also see Brett A. Boyle, "The Importance of the Industrial Inside Sales Force: A Case Study," *Industrial Marketing Management*, September 1996, pp. 339–348; Victoria Fraza, "Upgrading Inside Sales," *Industrial Distribution*, December 1997, pp. 44–49; Michele Marchetti, "Look Who's Calling," *Sales & Marketing Management*, May 1998, pp. 43–46; and Selltis, "Climax Portable Machine Tools Case Study," www.selltis.com/case_climax.html (accessed August 2002).
8. Rick Mullin, "From Lone Wolves to Team Players," *Chemical Week*, January 14, 1998, pp. 33–34; and James P. Morgan, "Cross-Functional Buying: Why Teams Are Hot," *Purchasing*, April 5, 2001, pp. 27–32.
9. Robert Hiebeler, Thomas B. Kelly, and Charles Ketteman, *Best Practices: Building Your Business with Customer-Focused Solutions* (New York: Arthur Andersen/Simon & Schuster, 1998), pp. 122–124. For more on team selling, also see Mark A. Moon and Susan Forquer Gupta, "Examining the Formation of Selling Centers: A Conceptual Framework," *Journal of Personal Selling and Sales Management*, Spring 1997, pp. 31–41; and Christian Homburg, John P. Workman Jr., and Ove Jensen, "A Configurational Perspective on Key Account Management, *Journal of Marketing*, April 2002, pp. 38–60.
10. "The Relationship You Build with Your Prospects and Customers Is More Important than the Close," *Cost Engineering*, February 2002, pp. 40–41. See also Geoffrey Brewer, "Mind Reading: What Drives Top Salespeople to Greatness?" *Sales & Marketing Management*, May 1994, pp. 82–88; Barry J. Farber, "Success Stories for Salespeople," *Sales & Marketing Management*, May 1995, pp. 30–31; Roberta Maynard, "Finding the Essence of Good Salespeople," *Nation's Business*, February 1998, p. 10; Jeanie Casison, "Closest Thing to Cloning," *Incentive*, June 1999, p. 7; Nicholas T. Miller, "Finding the Key to Sales Excellence: What Do High Performers Do?" *Commercial Lending Review*, March 2002, p. 17.
11. Anna Fredericks, "Am I Getting Paid Enough?" Workopolis website, April 2, 2003, www.workopolis.com/; and "Real-time Salary Survey Information for: Job=Account Manager Sales (Canada)," Pay Scale website, www.payscale.com/ (accessed November 9, 2003).
12. See "To Test or Not to Test," *Sales & Marketing Management*, May 1994, p. 86; Elena Harris, "Reduce Recruiting Risks," *Sales & Marketing Management*, May 2000, p. 18; and Erin Stout, "Recruiting and Hiring for Less," *Sales & Marketing Management*, May 2002, p. 61.
13. Mark De Wolf, "Special Report: Motivating the Sales Force," *Strategy*, August 18, 1997, p. 19.

14. Robert Klein, "Nabisco Sales Soar After Sales Training," *Marketing News,* January 6, 1997, p. 23. Also see Malcolm Fleschner, "Training: How to Find the Best Training Solutions for Your Sales Team," *Selling Power,* June 2001, pp. 93–97; and Christine Galea, "2002 Sales Training Survey," *Sales & Marketing Management,* July 2002, pp. 34–37.

15. "Real-time Salary Survey Information for: Job=Account Manager Sales (Canada)," PayScale website, www.payscale.com/ (accessed November 9, 2003).

16. See Christen P. Heide, "All Levels of Sales Reps Post Impressive Earnings," press release, www.dartnell.com, May 5, 1997; "Dartnell's 30th Sales Force Compensation Survey," Dartnell Corporation, August 1999; and Christine Galea, "2002 Salary Survey," *Sales & Marketing Management,* May 2002, pp. 32–36.

17. Geoffrey Brewer, "Brain Power," *Sales & Marketing Management,* May 1997, pp. 39–48; Don Peppers and Martha Rogers, "The Price of Customer Service," *Sales & Marketing Management,* April 1999, pp. 20–21; Michelle Marchetti, "Pay Changes Are on the Way," *Sales & Marketing Management,* August 2000, p. 101; and Erin Stout, "Is Your Pay Plan on Target?" *Sales & Marketing Management,* January 2002, p. 18.

18. "Editorial: New Motivational Ideas Reflect New Breed of Rep," *Strategy,* August 21, 1995, p. 14.

19. David Prater, "The Third Time's the Charm," *Sales & Marketing Management,* September 2000, pp. 101–104. For more on sales force automation (SFA), see Chris Pullig, James G. Maxham III, and Joseph F. Hair Jr., "Sales-force Automation Systems: An Exploratory Examination of Organizational Factors Associated with Effective Implementation and Sales-Force Productivity," *Journal of Business Research,* May 2002, pp. 401–415.

20. Bob Donath, "Delivering Value Starts with Proper Prospecting," *Marketing News,* November 10, 1997, p. 5. Also see "Skills Workshop: Prospecting," *Selling Power,* October 2000, pp. 54–56; and Steve Atlas, "Prospecting at Large Companies," *Selling Power,* January–February 2002, pp. 30–32.

21. David Stamps, "Training for a New Sales Game," *Training,* July 1997, pp. 46–52; and Erin Stout, "Throwing the Right Pitch," *Sales & Marketing Management,* April 2001, pp. 61–63. Also see Mary E. Shoemaker and Mark C. Johlke, "An Examination of a Crucial Selling Skill: Asking Questions," *Journal of Managerial Issues,* Spring 2002, pp. 118–131.

22. Betsey Cummings, "Do Customers Hate Salespeople?" *Sales & Marketing Management,* June 2001, pp. 44–51; and Don Chambers, "Draw Them In," *Selling Power,* March 2001, pp. 51–52.

23. "Briefcase Full of Views: Johnson & Johnson Uses Virtual Reality to Give Prospects an Inside Look at Its Products," *American Demographics,* April 1997; and Advanced Sterilization Products website, www.sterrad.com/ (accessed August 2002).

24. Bernadette Johnson, "HBC.com Aims To Give Customers Another Reason To Shop," *Strategy,* January 1, 2001, D1.

25. Canadian Marketing Association, "CMA Study Forecasts Strong Growth in Marketing Industry"(news release), December 11, 2000; Lori Enos, "Report: Canadian E-commerce Gaining Ground," *E-Commerce Times,* November 9, 2000; Statistics Canada, "Households Using the Internet from Home, Purpose of Use, 2002," Canadian Statistics (accessed November 8, 2003), www.statcan.ca/english/Pgdb/arts52a.htm; Ipsos-Reid, "The Canadian Internet Fact Page," www.ipsos-reid.com/ca/data/dsp_little_cdn_fact_book.cfm (accessed November 8, 2003); Canadian Media Directors' Council, *2003–2004 Media Digest,* p. 55; and Jack Kapica, "Canada No. 2 in Adoption of Technology, Study Says," *Globe and Mail,* August 8, 2002, www.globeandmail.com.

26. Lesley Young, "The Auto Club Takes It Slow," *Marketing Magazine,* April 29, 2002, p. MD8.

27. For these and other examples, see Jonathan Berry, "A Potent New Tool for Selling: Database Marketing," *Business Week,* September 4, 1994, pp. 56–62; Weld F. Royal, "Do Databases Really Work?" *Sales & Marketing Management,* October 1995, pp. 66–74; Daniel Hill, "Love My Brand," *Brandweek,* January 19, 1998, pp. 26–29; "FedEx Taps Into Data Warehousing," *Advertising Age's Business Marketing,* January 1999, p. 25; and Harriet Marsh, "Dig Deeper into the Database Goldmine," *Marketing,* January 11, 2001, pp. 29–30.

28. "Royal Canadian Mint Boosts Canada Day Coin," Marketing Direct Briefs, *Marketing Magazine,* August 19, 2002, p. 7.

29. *Economic Impact: U.S. Direct Marketing Today Executive Summary,* Direct Marketing Association, 2001.

30. Matthew L. Wald, "Third Area Code Is Added in the Land of the Toll-Free," *New York Times,* April 4, 1998, p. 10; and "AT&T Offers Toll-Free Number Availability Tool Online," *Direct Marketing,* May 2001, p. 24.

31. *Economic Impact: U.S. Direct Marketing Today Executive Survey,* Direct Marketing Association, 2001. Also see Cara B. Dipasquale, "Direct-Mail Sector Staying the Course," *Advertising Age,* March 11, 2002, p. 16.

32. Marlene Milczarek, "Database Diamond Mining," *Marketing Magazine,* August 13, 2001, www.marketingmag.ca.

33. "DMA Study Shows the Internet Generates 13 Percent of Catalog Sales" (press release), June 4, 2001, www.the-dma.org/cgi/disppressrelease?article=102111111.

34. "DMA Study: In Slowing Economy, Catalog Sales Growth Continues to Outpace Overall Retail Growth" (press release), June 4, 2001, www.the-dma.org/cgi/disppressrelease?article=101111111.

35. "Catalog Study Now Available," *Business Forms, Labels, and Systems,* June 20, 2001, p. 24; Richard S. Hodgson, "It's Still the Catalog Age," *Catalog Age,* June 2001, p. 156; and J.C. Penney 100th Anniversary: Rewriting the Book on Catalog Sales," *Chain Store Age,* June 2002, p. 68.

36. Scott Gardiner, "The Marketing Side of Sears," *Marketing Magazine,* December 18, 2000, www.marketingmag.ca.

37. Stephanie Whittaker, "Nike Catalogue Site Targets Instructors," *Marketing Magazine,* May 21, 2001, www.marketingmag.ca.

38. Andrea Zoe Aster, "Deciphering the New E-retail," *Marketing Magazine,* November 20, 2000, www.marketingmag.ca.

39. Ron Donoho, "One-Man Show," *Sales & Marketing Management,* June 2001, pp. 36–42.

40. Erika Brown, "Ooh! Aah!" *Forbes,* March 8, 1999, p. 56. Also see Shirley Leung, "Grill Sales Slow but Big Payouts Flow to Foreman," *Wall Street Journal,* February 2, 2001, p. B1; and Jane Bennett Clark, Robert Frick, Matt Popowksy, and Daniel Kohan, "As Seen on TV," *Kiplinger's Personal Finance,* July 2002, p. 99.

41. Suzanne Vranica, "Blue Chips Using Ads with 1-800 Numbers," *Wall Street Journal,* November 30, 2001, p. B8.

42. Shopping Channel website, www.theshoppingchannel.com (accessed November 9, 2003); Andrea Zoe Aster, "Net Merchants Luring Mall Refugees," *Marketing Magazine*, November 06, 2000, www.marketingmag.ca; and Fawzia Sheikh, "Closing the Digital Divide," *Marketing Magazine*, April 23, 2001, www.marketingmag.ca.

43. M. R. Kropko, "Card Markers Struggling with Computer Kiosks," *Marketing News*, June 3, 1996, p. 6; David Chilton, "LCBO Installs Interactive Kiosks," *Strategy*, January 24, 1997, p. 13; Wendy Cuthbert, "Cineplex gets ad kiosks," *Strategy*, March 31, 1997, p. 4; "For the Record: UNICEF Kiosks at IKEA," *Strategy*, November 24, 1997, p. 15; "Lining Up for Interactive Kiosks," *Nation's Business*, February 1998, p. 46; Warren S. Hersch, "Kiosks Poised to Be a Huge Growth Market," *Computer Reseller News*, May 18, 1998, p. 163; Catherine Yang, "No Web Site Is an Island," *Business Week*, March 22, 1999, p. EB38; "Kiosk: Disney Store," *Chain Store Age*, December 2000, p. 14A; and Larry Beck, "The Kiosk's Ship Has Come In," *DSN Retailing Today*, February 19, 2001, p. 14.

44. "Sweepstakes Groups Settles with States," *New York Times*, June 27, 2001, p. A14; and "PCH Reaches $34 Million Sweepstakes Settlement with 26 States," *Direct Marketing*, September 2001, p. 6.

45. United States, Federal Trade Commission, "Canadian Firm Charged with Telemarketing Fraud Settles FTC Complaint; Will Pay More than $111 000 in Consumer Redress" (news release), April 29, 2002, www.ftc.gov/opa/2002/04/rrconsultants.htm.

46. Royal Canadian Mounted Police, "Spam e-mail," RCMP website, www.rcmp-grc.gc.ca/scams/spam_e.htm (accessed November 9, 2003).

47. Debbie A, Connon, "The Ethics of Database Marketing," *Information Management Journal*, May–June 2002, pp. 42–44.

Chapter 18

1. Mark L. Clifford and Nicole Harris, "Coke Pours into Asia," *Business Week*, October 28, 1996, pp. 72–77; Mark Gleason, "Sprite Is Riding Global Ad Effort to No. 4 Status," *Advertising Age*, November 18, 1996, p. 30; Lauren R. Rublin, "Chipping Away," *Barron's*, June 12, 2000, pp. 31–34; Betsy McKay, "Coca-Cola Restructuring Effort Has Yet to Prove Effective," *Asian Wall Street Journal*, March 2, 2001; Hillary Chura and Richard Linnett, "Coca-Cola Readies Global Assault," *Advertising Age*, April 2, 2001, pp. 1, 34; Sean Mehegan, "Soft Drinks," *Adweek*, April 23, 2001, p. SR24; Daniel Rogers, "Coke's Local World Cup Tactics," *Marketing Magazine*, May 30, 2002, p. 15; Coca-Cola, "Our Company," www.coca-cola.com (accessed August 2002); and Coca Cola Bottle Company, "Coca-Cola Bottling to Build $150 Million Production and Sales Centre in Brampton" (news release), February 23, 2000, City of Brampton website, www.city.brampton.on.ca/economic-development/cocacola_media_package.htm/.

2. John Alden, "What in the World Drives UPS?" *International Business*, April 1998, pp. 6–7; Karen Pennar, "Two Steps Forward, One Step Back," *Business Week*, August 31, 1998, p. 116; Michelle Wirth Fellman, "A New World for Marketers," *Marketing News*, May 10, 1999, p. 13; Alan Greenspan, "International Trade: Globalization vs. Protectionism," *Vital Speeches of the Day*, April 15, 2001, pp. 386–388; and World Trade Organization, "International Trade Statistics, 2001," www.wto.org/ (accessed August 2002).

3. Trade and Economic Analysis Division, Department of Foreign Affairs and International Trade, *Fourth Annual Report of Canada's State of Trade: Trade Update*, May 2003, p. 3, www.dfait-maeci.gc.ca/eet/trade/sot_2003/SOT_2003-en.asp; Bruce Little, "Who Exports Canada's Goods to the World?" *Globe and Mail*, January 29, 2001, p. B10; Department of Foreign Affairs and International Trade, "Pettigrew Announces Finalists for 2000 Canada Export Awards" (press release), July 4, 2000; "International Trade Minister Pettigrew—Talking Trade," www.infoexport.gc.ca/; John Alden, "What in the World Drives UPS?" *International Business*, April 1998, pp. 6–7; Karen Pennar, "Two Steps Forward, One Step Back," *Business Week*, August 31, 1998, p. 116; and Michelle Wirth Fellman, "A New World For Marketers," *Marketing News*, May 10, 1999, p. 13.

4. Gail Edmondson, "See the World, Erase Its Borders," *Business Week*, August 28, 2000, pp. 113–114.

5. Sahm Adrangi, "Tiny Toronto Bike Firms Spins Success," *Globe and Mail*, July 26, 2003, pp. B1, B4.

6. "The Unique Japanese," *Fortune*, November 24, 1986, p. 8; and James D. Southwick, "Addressing Market Access Barriers in Japan Through the WTO," *Law and Policy in International Business*, Spring 2000, pp. 923–976. For more on non-tariff and other barriers, see Warren J. Keegan and Mark C. Green, *Principles of Global Marketing* (Upper Saddle River, N.J.: Prentice Hall, 2000), Chap. 8.

7. See Douglas Harbrecht and Owen Ullmann, "Finally GATT May Fly," *Business Week*, December 29, 1993, pp. 36–37; Ping Deng, "Impact of GATT Uruguay Round on Various Industries," *American Business Review*, June 1998, pp. 22–29; Helene Cooper, "U.S. Seeks a New Rounds of WTO Talks," *Wall Street Journal*, July 18, 2001, p. A12; Michael Finger, Julio J. Nogues, "The Unbalanced Uruguay Outcome: The New Areas in Future WTO Negotiations," *World Economy*, March 2002, pp. 321–340; and World Trade Organization, "WTO Annual Report, 2002," www.wto.org (accessed July 2002).

8. Information about the European Union from *Europa*, "The European Union at a Glance," http://europa.eu.int, September 7, 2003.

9. Department of Foreign Affairs and International Trade, CanadaEuropa Mundi, "European Union" (factsheet), September 2003, www.dfait-maeci.gc.ca/canadaeuropa/factsheets/Factsheet_Page54-en.html.

10. Stanley Reed, "We Have Liftoff! The Strong Launch of the Euro Is Hailed Around the World," *Business Week*, January 18, 1999, pp. 34–37; Allyson L. Stewart-Allen, "Changeover to Euro Has Hidden Expenses," *Marketing News*, July 30, 2001, p. 6; and "Finance and Economics: Up for Adoption: Central Europe and the Euro," *The Economist*, June 1, 2002, pp. 69–70.

11. For more on the European Union, see "Around Europe in 40 Years," *The Economist*, May 31, 1997, p. S4; "European Union to Begin Expansion," *New York Times*, March 30, 1998, p. A5; Joan Warner, "Mix Us Culturally? It's Impossible," *Business Week*, April 27, 1998, p. 108; and Paul J. Deveney, "World Watch," *Wall Street Journal*, May 20, 1999, p. A12.

12. Charles J. Whalen, "NAFTA's Scorecard: So Far, So Good," *Business Week*, July 9, 2001, pp. 54–56; Geri Smith, "Betting on Free Trade: Will the Americas Be One Big Market?" *Business Week*, April 23, 2001, pp. 60–62; Ernesto Zedillo, "Commentary: Free Trade Is the Best Diplomacy," *Forbes*, July 23, 2001, p. 49; and Fay Hansen,

"World Trade Update," *Business Finance*, March 2002, pp. 9–11.

13. Alan Freeman, "Leaders Aim for Free Trade at APEC Forum," *Globe and Mail*, November 12, 1994, p. B3; and "The Vancouver Summit," *Globe and Mail*, November 19, 1997, pp. D1–D4.

14. Larry Rohter, "Latin America and Europe to Talk Trade," *New York Times*, June 26, 1999, p. 2; and Bernard Malamud and Wayne A. Label, "The Merco: A Common Currency for Mercosur and Latin America," *American Business Review*, June 2002, pp. 132–139.

15. Department of Foreign Affairs and International Trade, "Pettigrew Announces Finalists for the 2003 Canada Export Awards" (news release no. 118), August 26, 2003; http://webapps.dfait-maeci.gc.ca/minpub/. For trade statistics see the Department of Foreign Affairs and International Trade website at www.dfait-maeci.gc.ca/eet/menu-en.asp.

16. David Woodruff, "Ready to Shop Until They Drop," *Business Week*, June 22, 1998, pp. 104–108. Also see John Fahy, Graham Hooley, Tony Cox, Jozsef Beracs, et al., "The Development and Impact of Marketing Capabilities in Central Europe," *Journal of International Business Studies*, First Quarter 2000, pp. 63–81; and "Card-Carrying Consumers," *Country Monitor*, July 15, 2002, p. 5.

17. Virginia Postel, "The Wealth of Nations Depends on How Open They Are to International Trade," *New York Times*, May 17, 2001, p. C2.

18. Dan West, "Countertrade," *Business Credit*, April 2001, pp. 64–67. Also see Dan West, "Countertrade," *Business Credit*, April 2002, pp. 48–51.

19. For this and other examples, see Louis Kraar, "How to Sell to Cashless Buyers," *Fortune*, November 7, 1988, pp. 147–154; Nathaniel Gilbert, "The Case for Countertrade," *Across the Board*, May 1992, pp. 43–45; Darren McDermott and S. Karen Witcher, "Bartering Gains Currency," *Wall Street Journal*, April 6, 1998, p. A10; Anne Millen Porter, "Global Economic Meltdown Boosts Barter Business," *Purchasing*, February 11, 1999, pp. 21–25; S. Jayasankaran, "Fire-Fighting," *Far Eastern Economic Review*, May 31, 2001, p. 52; and Dalia Marin and Monika Schnitzer, "The Economic Institution of International Barter," *Economic Journal*, April 2002, pp. 293–316.

20. Rebecca Piirto Heath, "Think Globally," *Marketing Tools*, October 1996, pp. 49–54; and "The Power of Writing," *National Geographic*, August 1999, pp. 128–129.

21. For other examples, see *Dun & Bradstreet's Guide to Doing Business Around the World* (Upper Saddle River, N.J.: Prentice Hall, 2000); Betsy Cummings, "Selling Around the World," *Sales & Marketing Management*, May 2001, p. 70; James K. Sebenius, "The Hidden Challenge of Cross-Border Negotiations," *Harvard Business Review*, March 2002, pp. 76–85; and Philip Kotler and Peggy Cunningham, *Marketing Management*, Canadian 11th ed. (Toronto: Pearson Education Canada, 2004), Chap. 7.

22. Pete Engardio, Manjeet Kripalani, and Alysha Webb, "Smart Globalization," *Business Week*, August 27, 2001, pp. 132–136.

23. See Naomi Klein, *No Logo: Taking Aim at the Brand Bullies* (Toronto: Knopf Canada, 2000).

24. Elisabeth Rosenthal, "Buicks, Starbucks and Fried Chicken. Still China?" *New York Times*, February 25, 2002, p. A4.

25. Walter LaFeber, *Michael Jordan and the New Global Capitalism* (New York: W. W. Norton, 1999), p. 23.

26. Paul Blustein and Ariana Eunjung Cha, "Product Protesters Face Tough Going," *The Washington Post*, April 6, 2003, p. A21.

27. Henry Jenkins, "Culture Goes Global," *Technology Review*, July–August 2001, p. 89.

28. Moises Naim, "McAtlas Shrugged," *Foreign Policy*, May–June 2001, pp. 26–37; and Suh-Kyung Yoon, "Look Who's Going Native," *Far Eastern Economic Review*, February 1, 2001, pp. 68–69.

29. Paulo Prada and Bruce Orwall, "A Certain 'Je Ne Sais Quoi' at Disney's New Park—Movie-Themed Site Near Paris Is Multilingual, Serves Wine—and Better Sausage Variety," *Wall Street Journal*, March 12, 2002, p. B1; and Dan Sabbagh, "Euro Disney in Rescue Talks," *The Times*, August 2, 2003, www.timesonline.co.uk.

30. Charles A. Coulombe, "Global Expansion: The Unstoppable Crusade," *Success*, September 1994, pp. 18–20; "Amway Hopes to Set Up Sales Network in India," *Wall Street Journal*, February 17, 1998, p. B8; Gerald S. Couzens, "Dick Devos," *Success*, November 1998, pp. 52–57; and Amway website, www.amway.com/ (accessed August 2002).

31. See "Crest, Colgate Bare Teeth in Competition for China," *Advertising Age International*, November 1996, p. I3; and Jack Neff, "Submerged," *Advertising Age*, March 4, 2002, p. 14.

32. Robert Neff, "In Japan, They're Goofy About Disney," *Business Week*, March 12, 1990, p. 64; "In Brief: ETrade Licensing Deal Gives It an Israeli Link," *American Banker*, May 11, 1998; John Engen, "Going Going Global," *USBanker*, February 2000, pp. 22S–25S; "Cowboys and Samuri: The Japanizing of Universal," *Wall Street Journal*, March 22, 2001, p. B1; Chester Dawson, "Will Toyko Embrace Another Mouse?" *Business Week*, September 10, 2001; and Bruce Orwall, "Eisner Contends Disney Is Primed for Turnaround," *Wall Street Journal*, August 9, 2002, p. B1.

33. Department of Foreign Affairs and International Trade, "Pettigrew's Trade Mission to Russia Continues To Bear Fruit: SNC-Lavalin Signs Deal with New Russian Partner" (news release no. 272), December 18, 2000, http://webapps.dfait-maeci.gc.ca/minpub/.

34. Greg Keenan, "Magna Buys U.K. Business," *Globe and Mail*, March 21, 1996, p. B1.

35. See Cynthia Kemper, "KFC Tradition Sold Japan on Chicken," *Denver Post*, June 7, 1998, p. J4; and Milford Prewitt, "Chains Look for Links Overseas," *Nation's Restaurant News*, February 18, 2002, pp. 1, 6.

36. Jason Kirby, "The Countdown Continues: 33. Bata Shoes," *Canadian Business*, September 2, 2003, pp. 69–70.

37. See Theodore Levitt, "The Globalization of Markets," *Harvard Business Review*, May–June 1983, pp. 92–102; David M. Szymanski, Sundar G. Bharadwaj, and Rajan Varadarajan, "Standardization Versus Adaptation of International Marketing Strategy: An Empirical Investigation," *Journal of Marketing*, October 1993, pp. 1–17; Ashish Banerjee, "Global Campaigns Don't Work; Multinationals Do," *Advertising Age*, April 18, 1994, p. 23; Cyndee Miller, "Chasing Global Dream," *Marketing News*, December 2, 1996, pp. 1, 2; and Jeryl Whitelock and Carole Pimblett, "The Standardization Debate in International Marketing," *Journal of Global Marketing*, 1997, p. 22.

38. See "In India, Beef-Free Mickie D," *Business Week*, April 7, 1995, p. 52; Jeff Walters, "Have Brand Will Travel," *Brandweek*, October 6, 1997, pp. 22–26; David Barboza,

"From Abroad, McDonald's Finds Value in Local Control," *New York Times*, February 12, 1999, p. 1; Nanette Byrnes, "Brands in a Bind," *Business Week,* August 28, 2000, pp. 234–238; and Suh-Kyung Yoon, "Look Who's Going Native," *Far Eastern Economic Review,* February 1, 2001, pp. 68–69.

39. For more, see Warren J. Keegan, *Global Marketing Management,* 7th ed. (Upper Saddle River, N.J.: Prentice Hall, 2002), pp. 346–351.

40. Lawrence Donegan, "Heavy Job Rotation: MTV Europe Sacks 80 Employees in the Name of 'Regionalisation,'" *The Guardian*, November 21, 1997, p. 19; "MTV Hits 100 Million in Asia," *New Media Markets,* January 28, 1999, p. 12; Brett Pulley and Andrew Tanzer, "Sumner's Gemstone," *Forbes,* February 21, 2000, pp. 106–111; Sally Beatty and Carol Hymowitz, "Boss Talk: How MTV Stays Tuned Into Teens," *Wall Street Journal,* March 21, 2000, p. B1; and Kerry Capell, "MTV's World: Mando-Pop. Mexican Hip Hop. Russian Rap. It's All Fueling the Biggest Global Channel," *Business Week,* February 18, 2002, pp. 81–84.

41. Bernd H. Schmitt and Yigang Pan, "In Asia, the Supernatural Means Sales," *New York Times,* February 19, 1995, pp. 3, 11; Sally Taylor, "Tackling the Curse of Bad Feng Shui," *Publishers Weekly,* April 27, 1998, p. 24; Michael Schrage, "Sorry About the Profits, Boss. My Feng Shui Is Off," *Fortune,* November 27, 2000, p. 306; and Barry Janoff, "East Meets West," *Progressive Grocer,* January 2001, pp. 47–49.

42. Kate MacArthur, "Coca-Cola Light Employs Local Edge," *Advertising Age,* August 21, 2000, pp. 18–19.

43. See Alicia Clegg, "One Ad One World?" *Marketing Week,* June 20, 2002, pp. 51–52.

44. "The Showcase," *Marketing Magazine,* October 20, 1997, pp. 14–19.

45. See Michael Oneal, "Harley-Davidson: Ready to Hit the Road Again," *Business Week,* July 21, 1986, p. 70; "EU Proposes Dumping Change," *East European Markets,* February 14, 1997, pp. 2–3; and Dobrin R. Kolev and Thomas J. Pruse, "Dumping and Double Crossing: The (In)effectiveness of Cost-Based Trade Policy Under Incomplete Information," *International Economic Review,* August 2002, pp. 895–918.

46. Sarah Ellison, "Revealing Price Discrepancies, the Euro Aids Bargain-Hunters," *Wall Street Journal,* January 30, 2002, p. A15.

47. See Patrick Powers, "Distribution in China: The End of the Beginning," *China Business Review,* July–August, 2001, pp. 8–12; and Drake Weisert, "Coca-Cola in China: Quenching the Thirst of a Billion," *China Business Review,* July–August 2001, pp. 52–55.

48. Richard Tomlinson, "The China Card," *Fortune,* May 25, 1998, p. 82; and Paul Mooney, "Deals on Wheels," *Far East Economic Review,* May 20, 1999, p. 53.

49. Andy Riga, "Nortel Inks $1-Billion Contract," *Montreal Gazette*, September 4, 2003, www.canada.com/montreal/.

Name Index

Subject Index

Photo Credits

Chapter 1: p. 2 Courtesy of VanCity Credit Union; p. 8 Antonio Scorza, Agence France Presse AFP; p. 15 IBM Corporation; p. 17 Used with permission of Johnson & Johnson; p. 18 Stew Leonard; p. 20 Frank LaBua, Pearson Education/PH College; p. 24 Harley Davidson; p. 26 George B. Diebold, CORBIS/Stock Market; p. 29 Courtesy of Royal Bank of Canada; p. 30 © The Procter and Gamble Company, used by permission; p. 31 © 2002 Dell Computer Corporation. All rights reserved; p. 35 Zig Advertising/Andy MacAulay, Partner; p. 36 Courtesy of William Forbes and Daniel Alter

Chapter 2: p. 48 Hillspet.com; p. 49 IBM Corporation; p. 53 General Electric; p. 58 © Federal Express; p. 59 CP/Richard Buchan; p. 63 (Both) Wal-Mart; p. 66 (Left) Bentley Motor Cars; p. 66 (Right) Toyota; p. 68 Veterinary Pet Insurance; p. 72 © Jeff Zaruba/CORBIS

Chapter 3: p. 82 Canadian Tire Corporation Limited, Dick Hemmingway; p. 102 A. Ramey, PhotoEdit; p. 87 © The Procter and Gamble Company. Used by permission; p. 89 (Both) Francisco Cruz, Getty Images Inc.; p. 93 (Top Left) David Young-Wolf; p. 93 (Top Right) Michael Newman; p. 93 (Bottom Left & Right) SuperStock Inc.; p. 95 Reprinted by permission of Sun Microsystems, Inc. Copyright © 2002 Sun Microsystems, Inc. All rights reserved; p. 97 These materials have been reproduced with the permission of eBay Inc. Copyright © eBay Inc. All rights reserved; p. 100 Getty Images Inc.-Liason; p. 105 Courtesy of McKenzie Seeds; p. 107 (Both) The Gillette Co.; p. 109 Google.com; p. 111 Office Depot; p. 114 Office of The Privacy Commission of Canada

Chapter 4: p. 122 © Ryan Creary; p. 126 AP/Lacy Atkins, CP/Andrew Vaughan; p. 128 Churchill & Klehr Photography; p. 130 Courtesy of PhoneBusters; p. 132 AP/Wide World Photos; p. 133 (Both) Enrico Ferorelli; p. 136 Susan Werner, Getty Images, Inc. – Stone; p. 138 Lester Lefkowitz/ CORBIS; p. 142 Courtesy of Packaging Association of Canada; p. 143 BP p.l.c.; p. 144 Photo courtesy of Husky Injection Molding Systems; p. 146 Works & Emergency Services Department, City of Toronto; p. 148

Courtesy of Alcan Inc.; p. 150 Hockey Canada (www.hockeycanada.ca); p. 151 Herman Miller, Inc.; p. 155 Courtesy of PricewaterhouseCoopers LLP

Chapter 5: p. 164 CP/Paul Warner; p. 169 The Terry Wild Studio, Inc.; p. 172 Printed with permission of UNFPA (United Nations Population Fund); p. 174 Caroline Von Tuempling, Superstock, Inc.; p. 175 Courtesy of PEPSI COLA CANADA LTD.; p. 177 Used with permission of Wildseed.com; p. 179 Registered trademark of Kraft Foods Holdings, Inc.; p. 181 Dan Lamont Photography; p. 182 Courtesy of Michel Laurier, Gratte Ciel; p. 184 Courtesy of the Canadian Abilities Foundation; p. 186 *Newsweek*; p. 189 McDonald's Corporation; p. 190 Joseph Van Os, Getty Images Inc. – Image Bank; p. 193 General Mills; p. 199 David McLain, Aurora & Quanta Productions

Chapter 6: p. 208 © Roger Ressmeyer/CORBIS; p. 212 Tom & Deeann McCarthy, CORBIS/Stock Market; p. 214 © 2002. USAA, all rights reserved; p. 216 Chris Volk Photography; p. 219 Courtesy of NPD Group; p. 221 The Dialog Corporation; p. 223 (Both) J.P. Moczulski Photographer; p. 224 © George D. Lepp/ CORBIS; p. 227 Focus Vision Network, Inc.; p. 229 Courtesy of itracks; p. 230 Greenfield Online, standard; p. 233 (Both) Integrated Media Systems Center; p. 236 Siebel; p. 238 Courtesy of Canada/BC Business Services Society; p. 240 Roper Starch; p. 241 Courtesy of Vanessa Vachon

Chapter 7: p. 252 AP/Wideworld Photos; p. 259 Courtesy of Bank of Montreal and Cossette Communication-Marketing; p. 261 Courtesy of Grouse Mountain Resorts Inc.; p. 262 Courtesy Toronto Symphony Orchestra; p. 263 © Rick Gomez/ Masterfile www.masterfile.com; p. 266 Trademark and copyright, Warner Bros., 2002. Used with permission of Chevrolet; p. 271 Ad copyright DaimlerChrysler Corporation; p. 273 Bachmann, PhotoEdit; p. 275 DaimlerChrysler Corporation; p. 281 Courtesy of Bell Sports; p. 285 Used with permission of 1800Flowers.com; p. 288 Used with permission of Zenith Electronic Corporation

Chapter 8: p. 296 Courtesy of Magna International; p. 301 Used with permission of Intel Corporation; p. 303 ChemStation International; p. 306

Allegiance Healthcare Corporation; p. 307 Used with permission of Volvo Trucks; p. 309 HSBC; p. 311 Ceridian Canada Ltd.; p. 313 Used with permission of Wal-Mart Stores; p. 315 Used with permission of Covisint; p. 318 Courtesy of Forensic Technology WAI Inc. Ad: Anthony Gagliardi; p. 319 © Dell Computer Corporation

Chapter 9: p. 331 Courtesy RBC Financial Group; p. 333 Ray F. Hillstrom, Jr./Courtesy Eddie Bauer; p. 334 Courtesy Harlequin Enterprises Limited; p. 336 Used with permission of Neiman Marcus; p. 338 Courtesy of Leo Burnett; p. 340 © Lea & Perrins ® is a registered trademark of Lea & Perrins Ltd. Courtesy of Lea & Perrins Ltd. and Young & Rubicam Ltd.; p. 343 The Cisco Ad Team; p. 344 (Left) Jeff Baker, Getty Images, Inc.—Hulton Archive Photos; p. 344 (Right) SW Productions, Getty Images, Inc.; p. 348 © 2001 Vans Inc. Used with permission; p. 350 Levi Strauss; p. 353 CP/Aaron Harris; p. 355 Courtesy of Nacara Cosmetics; p. 360 Used with permission of Porsche Cars North America, Inc.; p. 361 Reproduced with permission of CMA Canada; p.362 The Gardiner Museum of Ceramic Art. Marketing strategy and execution: Scott Thornley + Company (thornley@st-c.com). The Artful Teapot: 20th Century Expressions from the Kamm Collection, organized and circulated by Exhibitions International, New York. The Red Devil, Anthony Bennett; p. 365 Haagen-Dazs

Chapter 10: p. 374 Philosophy, Inc.; p. 378 (Both) Sony Corporation of America; p. 380 Sony Corporation of America; p. 382 "Mad River" trademark appears courtesy of Mad River Company, LLC; p. 385 Created pro bono by TAXI; p. 387 (Left) Apple Computer, Inc.; p. 387 (Right) Used with permission of Discover Financial Services; p. 388 James Worrell Photographs, James Worrell Photography; p. 390 Courtesy of Gary Armstrong; p. 391 Trademark by H.J. Heinz Company; p. 393 Marriott International, Inc.; p. 396 Aaron Goodman; p. 397 Courtesy Harlequin Enterprises Limited; p. 401 Loblaw Brands Limited; p. 402 © Maple Leaf Foods Inc. 2003/Universal Products; p. 410 Ritz-Carlton Hotel Company, LLC; p. 412 British Airways; p. 413 Courtesy of myWHISTLER.com/Official site of Whistler; p 415 McDonald's

Restaurants of Canada; p. 416 Munshi Ahmed Photography

Chapter 11: p. 424 Microsoft Corporation; p. 430 New Product Works; p. 432 (Left) Topham, The Image Works; p. 432 (Right) Keith Srakocic, AP/Wide World Photos; p. 433 © Kellogg Canada Inc. Used with permission of Kellogg Canada Inc. Jack's Pack is a registered trademark of Kellogg Canada Inc. in Canada; p. 435 DaimlerChrysler Corporation; p. 438 Shaw Industries, Inc.; p. 439 (Top) Heinz Canada/Smith Locke Associates Inc.; p. 439 (Bottom) Proctor & Gamble Inc.; p. 441 Used with permission of Information Resources Inc.; p. 443 Colgate-Palmolive Company; p. 445 3M Canada Company; p. 447 Courtesy of Hershey's; p. 452 Frank Siteman, Stock Boston; p. 454 Courtesy of Birks Jewelers

Chapter 12: p. 462 Courtesy of Priceline.com; p. 466 Courtesy of Cnet and MySimon.com; p. 469 Courtesy of Four Seasons Hotels; p. 470 Courtesy of Swatch Ltd.; p. 473 Echo Advertising; p. 475 Maclean's photo/Peter Gregg; p. 477 Courtesy of Gibson Guitar; p. 483 Courtesy of Kimberly Clark; p. 484 Reprinted courtesy of Caterpillar, Inc.; p. 489 Courtesy of Sanford Corp. and Parker Pens; p. 490 (Top) Tim Boyle, Getty Images Inc.—Hulton Archive Photos; p. 379 (Bottom) AP/Wide World Photos; p. 491 AP/Joe Cavaretta; p. 492 Michael Newman, PhotoEdit

Chapter 13: p. 508 Courtesy of Palm, Inc.; p. 509 © 1995–2001 FedEx. All rights reserved; p. 511 Susan Darrach, Darrach Design; p. 513 Courtesy of Tilley Endurables; p. 516 (Left) AP/Wide World Photos; p. 516 (Right) Jan Staller, TimePix; p. 517 Cereal Partners U.K.; p. 518 Courtesy of Air Canada; p. 520 CP/Kevin Frayer; p. 522 Geico; p. 524 © Dan Rubin/The Stock Shop; p. 525 Charles Gupton/Stock Boston; p. 527 Copyright 1994–2000 Hewlett-Packard Company. Reproduced with permission; p. 529 Courtesy of GE; p. 531 Courtesy of Diamond Information Center/New York; p. 535 Rick Robinson/CPR

Chapter 14: p. 544 CP/Adrian Wyldp. 550 Courtesy of A. Van Houtte; p. 551

(Left) Bonnie Kamin, PhotoEdit; p. 551 (Right) Churchill & Klehr Photography; p. 552 Great Canadian Dollar Store (1993) Ltd. Quispamsis, New Brunswick; p. 554 Courtesy of Cinnzeo/A division of Cinnaroll Bakeries Limited; p. 557 Katherine Lambert; p. 559 Courtesy of Virgin Mega Stores, Vancouver; p. 560 Ottawa Sun/Jason Ransom; p. 561 Courtesy of West Edmonton Mall; p. 564 (Left) DeLong Farms; p. 565 (Right) Courtesy of Office Depot; p. 568 Alene M. McNeill; p. 569 Courtesy of Stephen Arnold; p. 570 Courtesy © 2002 Sony Corporation Entertainment America Inc.; p. 572 W. W. Grainger, Inc.; p. 575 Fleming Companies, Inc.; p. 577 Courtesy of Coghlan's LTD; p. 578 McKesson

Chapter 15: p. 584 Courtesy of UPS; p. 588 HFM; p. 591 Courtesy of The Saturn Corporation; p. 594 Courtesy of Mr. Alan Quarry/Quarry Integrated Communications; p. 596 Courtesy of Volkswagen and Arnold Worldwide; p. 598 With permission of W.K. Buckley Ltd.; p. 599 p. 601 Courtesy of Labatt Breweries; p. 602 Listerine and Bill Aron, PhotoEdit; p. 605 CP/Paul Chaisson; p. 608 (Right) Courtesy of Revlon; p. 609 Munshi Ahmed Photography; p. 611 Michael Newman, PhotoEdit; p. 614 www.kitchenaid.ca

Chapter 16: p. 622 CP/J.P. Moczulski; p. 626 Courtesy of Mr. P. Elwood; p. 629 The Pillsbury Company; p. 630 CP/Dave Chan; p. 632 Courtesy of TiVo; p. 633 Courtesy of Electric Library Canada; p. 634 Reprinted with permission of Outpost.com Marketing; p. 637 Courtesy of Apple Computer and Janie Porche. Photography courtesy of Mark Lipson, photographer; p. 638 By permission of Peter Knight (art director) and Dan Zzimmerman (writer); p. 640 (Left) Spencer Grant, PhotoEdit; p. 640 (Middle) Michael J. Treola, AP/Wide World Photos; p. 640 (Right) CORBIS; p. 644 (All) Courtesy of the DaimlerChrysler Corporation; p. 647 Lladro Collectors Society; p. 650 (Top) Courtesy of Catalina Marketing; p. 650 (Bottom) By permission of Pepsi-Cola Canada Ltd.; p. 651 Jeff Scheid, Getty Images, Inc. Liason; p. 653 Hong Kong Tourism Board; p. 654

Courtesy of Nike; p. 656 www.butterball.com

Chapter 17: p. 662 Courtesy of Lear Corporation; p. 665 (Both) Gabe Palmer, CORBIS/Stock Market; p. 669 DuPont & Company; p. 670 Getty Images, Inc.; p. 671 Jon Feingersh/CORBIS, CORBIS; p. 675 Courtesy of Canadian Professional Sales Association; p. 678 Rob Nelson, Black Star; p. 679 American Express Incentive Services; p. 682 Courtesy of Advanced Sterilization Products, Irvine, CA; p. 685 Courtesy of Dell Computer Corporation; p. 689 Courtesy of Masterfoods and MyPetStop.com; p. 692 Courtesy of Roman Bodnarchuk; p. 693 IKEA catalogue cover 2004, Courtesy of IKEA Canada; p. 695 Salton, Inc.

Chapter 18: p. 706 © Arthur Meyerson. Courtesy of Coca Cola. "COCA COLA," the 'COCA COLA' Contour Bottle, the Red Disc icon and "ALWAYS COCA COLA" are trademarks of the Coca-Cola Company; p. 710 (Left) Courtesy of Caroline Parson; p. 710 (Middle) Jeffrey Aaronson, Network Aspen; p. 710 (Right) Pablo Bartholomew, Getty Images, Inc.—Liaison; p. 711 AP/Peter Dejong; p. 713 (Left) Courtesy McCain Foods Limited; p. 713 (Right) Courtesy of Mega Bloks; p. 716 Used by permission of Canada Department of Foreign Affairs and International Trade; p. 717 Keith Dannemiller/CORBIS SABA; p. 719 Joseph Polleross/Regina Maria Anzenberger; p. 721 Transparency International Canada; p. 724 Cary S. Wolinsky/Trillium Studios; p. 726 (Both) Michael S. Yamashita/CORBIS, CORBIS; p. 728 Courtesy of CSA International; p. 730 Peter Blakely, CORBIS/SABA Press Photos, Inc.; p. 734 © Walt Disney Attractions Japan, Ltd.; p. 735 (Left) Donald Dietz, Stock Boston; p. 735 (Right) D. Bartruff, The Image Works; p. 737 Douglas E. Curran, Agence France-Presse AFP; p. 738 Courtesy of Nokia Products Ltd.; p. 740 (Both) Courtesy of Bernard Matussiere; p. 743 Courtesy of Audio Visual Library, European Commission; p. 744 Fritz Hoffmann